Indexes:

In addition to the General Index, also use the special indexes to find the best markets for your poetry.

General Index: *Includes cross-references to all titles in book.*

Geographic Index: *Lists publications/presses by state and foreign countries.*

Subject Index: *Indexes listings by specialization, e.g., a specific form, style or theme.*

Chapbook Index: *Lists publishers of chapbooks.*

For more information on submitting your poetry for publication, read:

How to Use Poet's Market, page 3

What Poets Want to Know: 20 "Most Asked" Questions, page 6

The Business of Poetry, page 16.

1991 Poet's Market

*Judson Jerome was professor of literature at Antioch College from 1953 to 1973 and poetry editor of **Antioch Review**. He has also had an active writing career with publication of his poetry, fiction, essays and plays in magazines and books. He began writing a monthly poetry column for **Writer's Digest** in 1960. Some of those columns and his other writing about poetry have been published by Writer's Digest Books in* **The Poet and the Poem, The Poet's Handbook** *(1980) and* **On Being a Poet** *(1984). His most recent collection of poetry is* **The Village: New and Selected Poems** *(Dolphin-Moon Press, 1987), and his most recent book of prose is* **Flight from Innocence** *(The University of Arkansas Press, 1990). He became editor of the annual* **Poet's Market** *with the first edition (1986).*

"Jud" (as he prefers to be called) and Marty Jerome were married in 1948 and have four grown children. He and Marty live in Yellow Springs, Ohio, where he freelances and edits **Poet's Market** *from his home.*

1991

Poet's Market

Where & How to Publish Your Poetry

Editor: Judson Jerome

Assistant Editor: Pat Beusterien
Editorial Assistants: Lisa Carpenter
and Cathy Brookshire

Writer's
Digest
Books

Cincinnati, Ohio

If you are a poetry publisher and would like to be considered for a listing in the next edition of Poet's Market, *please request a questionnaire from* Poet's Market, *1507 Dana Ave., Cincinnati, Ohio 45207.*

Managing Editor, Market Books Department:
Constance J. Achabal

Poet's Market. *Copyright © 1990 by Writer's Digest Books. Published by F&W Publications, 1507 Dana Ave., Cincinnati, Ohio 45207. Printed and bound in the United States of America. All rights reserved. No part of this book may be reproduced in any manner whatsoever without written permission from the publisher, except by reviewers who may quote brief passages to be printed in a magazine or newspaper.*

International Standard Serial Number 0883-5470
International Standard Book Number 0-89879-423-4

Contents

The Markets

Resources

Indexes

One of my books twists the epitaph on the grave of comedian Will Rogers: "I never met a man I didn't like." I wrote, "I've never met a person who hasn't written a poem." Oh, some deny it, but I don't believe them. Writing poetry is like taking aspirin. It's what people do when they hurt. They also do it a lot when they're feeling wonderful, especially when they're in love. Kids grow up loving stories and nursery rhymes in verse, perhaps mainly because their minds delight in verbal play as their bodies do in physical play. And verse is easier to remember than prose. They make up rhymes to accompany their rope jumping and other games. And when they grow up, they break the lines of what they write in strange places. They *arrange* their words on the page. It's an immemorial device for giving words special significance, depth of feeling, sincerity, or simply calling attention to them. As in prayer. Or advertising.

The markets

And once people have used words to create art, the act somehow doesn't seem complete until their artistic creations have appeared in print. Many pay for the privilege, and I warn them in this book to beware of vanity scams that use the widespread human urge to get poems into print as a means of cleaning wallets. Some publications here (always coded **I**, for beginners, for experienced poets are not likely to be so eager) require that you subscribe or buy copies if you want to see your work in print. Apparently such publications and publishers serve a need. I have excluded those, however, that seem to me to charge poets exorbitantly to be published or use flattery to lure them. Other publishers and publications coded **I** are like friendly social clubs or pen pals. They enjoy reading and often commenting on one another's work. They try to be encouraging to beginners. They provide a helpful and harmless service in enabling poets to enter the cold waters of the literary world gradually and without threat.

Beginners are also often welcomed by publishers and publications coded **IV**, those that cater to specialized interests, or to poets in a specific area, or those who have something in common with their readers such as gender, race, sexual preference, handicaps or personal problems. Code **IV** also applies to those who have some special status, such as being alumni of a particular university, or prisoners, or habitués of the singles scene. The editors in these cases may be more interested in the subject matter of the poetry or in the background of the poet than specifically in poetic quality.

But most who take up poetry entertain, at least for a while, the desire of being recognized in the literary world, and, after suitable introduction to the field (by way of publication in a number of beginner markets), are more interested in the publications or publishers coded **II** or **III**. **II** indicates the general market to which such poets should be submitting. Many of these markets are quite prestigious, though the coding **III** is nominally the one for prestige. In practice **III** is used to *discourage* submissions. Many of the magazines and book publishers who ask for that designation really prefer to solicit a large amount of their material from poets already known to them. Sometimes these are "unknowns," but the editors may have been advised to pay special attention to poets recommended by their friends and associates. **III** doesn't mean a publisher is *more* prestigious than one coded **II**. It just means they have chosen not to be bothered with a lot of unsolicited material.

Those who *really* don't care to hear from you and me except by invitation choose the **V** coding: no unsolicited manuscripts. In practice, they may actually invite submissions from poets they don't know. Their doors aren't sealed. But I list them primarily because **Poet's**

Market is widely used as a reference book by librarians, publishers, tradespeople, and others, and I want it to be as complete as possible: to report at least *something* about these publishers, if no more than their addresses. Many have distinguished poets on their lists. Even amateurs should know of their existence.

The indexes

Though I have tried to make it, above all, a *readable* book—one that you can settle back with and peruse for enjoyment as well as edification—if **Poet's Market** is new to you (this is its sixth annual volume), you might do well to flip first to the back to familiarize yourself with the various indexes. Special indexes guide you quickly to publishers in a particular area (Geographical), or on particular topics (Subject). Another index guides you to Publishers of Chapbooks. The General Index is the place to look first for a specific listing. Also, read the introductions to the various sections of the book: Publishers of Poetry, Contests and Awards, Greeting Cards, Writing Colonies, Organizations and Publications Useful to Poets for information about these specific market categories and resources for poets.

In a new section this year, What Poets Want to Know: 20 "Most Asked" Questions, I have tried to answer the most common questions that come to my office in Yellow Springs, Ohio, or to the office of Writer's Digest Books in Cincinnati, Ohio. Wires hum between these two offices, as **Poet's Market** is a year-long operation. We are constantly updating entries, sending out new listing questionnaires and processing new market information. "Most Asked" Questions gives more detail about how we do this. That section and the one called The Business of Poetry also contain a lot of general information about the literary world—and, specifically, about how a newcomer to the market goes about becoming a part of it, down to details about preparation of manuscripts for submission.

This book is not designed to help you write better poetry. (I have other books, published by Writer's Digest Books, and a monthly poetry column in *Writer's Digest* magazine that try to teach you that.) But, you may learn much from the comments of the editors—whom I quote copiously. And as for becoming a famous poet, the oldest advice is the best: Know somebody. In the poetry world, as in business, the media and other fields, the really important deals are cut in the back rooms that neophytes don't even know exist, let alone know how to get in.

But I've done all I can here to help you get started—getting your work out, getting it read and noticed, becoming aware of what is going on in the publishing world that changes from year to year. Poetry publishers and publications are among the most ephemeral of literary phenomena. There are over 300 listings in this volume that were not in the **1990 Poet's Market**. Some of those appeared in previous years, disappeared for awhile, and have re-emerged. Others are just starting. And many of the established publishers, writers' colonies, greeting card publishers, contests and awards, and organizations and publications listed in this book have changed addresses, policies, prices or modes of operation since the last edition.

I welcome comments and criticism from users of this book. Often it is our readers who tip us off when what publishers actually do is different from what they claim or when publishers have changed their status or practices. Poetry is a community, hence is based on communication. Everyone is welcome to that community, and those who thrive in it are those who learn and use its special language. Speak up! That's what the community of poetry is all about: *every voice matters.*

Jud Jerome

How to Use Poet's Market

Before studying the listings and making your marketing plans, read these suggestions for the most productive use of all the features in **Poet's Market**. Especially note the explanations of the information given in the sample listing.

- **Start with the indexes.** We have simplified this directory by grouping all imprints or publications at one address in one listing. The General Index contains cross references to all titles in the book. Suppose you wanted to find *Nostoc Magazine*; you will find it under **N** in the General Index with a cross reference to "see **Arts End Books**" and you will be given the page number. There is also a Geographical Index that breaks down publications by state and foreign countries for those wanting to submit to a specific location. Listings coded IV are indexed by specialization in the Subject Index and if you're ready to have a chapbook of your work published, there is a Chapbook Publishers Index to consult.
- **A double dagger symbol (‡)** appears before the names of listings new to this edition.
- **Market categories:** Listing names are followed by one or more Roman numerals:
  - I. **Publishers very open to beginners' submissions.** For acceptance, some require fees, purchase of the publication or membership in an organization, but they are not, so far as I can determine, exploitative of writers, and they often encourage and advise new writers. They publish much of the material they receive and often respond with criticism and suggestions.
  - II. **The general market to which most poets familiar with literary journals and magazines should submit.** Typically they accept 10% or less of poems received and usually reject others without comment. A poet developing a list of publication credits will find many of these to be respected names in the literary world.
  - III. **Prestige markets,** typically overstocked. They do not encourage widespread submissions from poets who have not published elsewhere—although many do on occasion publish relatively new and/or little-known poets. So little chance is there of acceptance, I personally would be unlikely to submit to prestige markets, considering it probably to be a waste of my time and that of the editors.
  - IV. **Specialized publications** which encourage contributors from a geographical area, a specific age-group, specific sex or sexual orientation, specific ethnic background, or who accept poems in specific forms (such as haiku) or on specific themes. In most IV listings we also state the specialty (e.g. IV-Religious). Often a listing emphasizes a theme but is also open to other subjects; these listings are marked with two codes (e.g. I, IV-Ethnic).
  - V. **Listings which do not accept unsolicited manuscripts.** You cannot submit without specific permission to do so. If the press or magazine for some reason seems especially appropriate for you, you might query (write, with SASE). But, in general, they prefer to locate and solicit the poets whom they publish. I have included these listings because it is just as important to know where NOT to submit. Also, many are interesting publishers to know about, and this book is widely used as a reference by librarians, researchers, publishers, suppliers and others who need to have as complete a listing of publishers or poetry as possible.
- **Always include a SASE (self-addressed, stamped envelope) or, for foreign publishers, a SAE with IRCs (self-addressed envelope with International Reply Coupons purchased at the post office) when submitting, querying, or asking for a catalog, sample copy or other**

response. Be sure you have enough return postage to cover the amount of material you want returned and that the return envelope is large enough to hold such material. This information is so important that we repeat it at the bottom of many pages throughout this book rather than include it in individual listings.

● **Consult the Glossary** in the back of this book for explanations of any unfamiliar terms you might encounter while reading the listings.

● **As a guide to the information in the listings**, match the numbered phrases in this sample listing with the corresponding numbers in the explanation that follows:

> **(1) THE BLACK SCHOLAR; THE BLACK SCHOLAR PRESS (2) (IV-Ethnic)**, Box 2869, Oakland, **(3)** CA 94609, **(4)**, **(5)** founded 1969, **(6)** publisher Robert Chrisman, uses **(7) poetry "relating to/from/of the black American and other 'Third World' experience."** The **(8)** bi-monthly magazine is basically scholarly and research-oriented. They have recently published poetry by Ntozake Shange, Jayne Cortez, Andrew Salkey, and D. L. Smith. **(9)** As a sample the editor selected these lines from "Tata on the Death of Don Pablo" by Nancy Morejan:
>
> > *your set mouth*
> > *pausing like a great bird*
> > *over the plain, speaks:*
>
> I have not seen a copy, but the editor says it is **(10)** 64 pp., 7x10", **(11)** press run 10,000 to 9,000 subscribers of which 60% are libraries, 15% shelf sales. Single copy $5; subscription $30. **(12) Sample back issue: $6 prepaid. Send SASE for guidelines. (13) Pays 10 copies and subscription. (14) Enclose "cover letter & bio or curriculum vitae, SASE, phone number, no originals." (15) Reports in 2-3 weeks.** They also publish 1-2 books a year, average 100 pp., flat-spined. **(16) Send query letter.** For sample books, send 8½x11" SASE for catalog, average cost $10.95 including postage and handling. **(17)** "We only publish one issue every year containing poetry. Please be advised—it is against our policy to discuss submissions via telephone. Also, we get a lot of MSS, but read *every single one,* thus patience is appreciated."

(1) Names. All imprints at the same address that publish poetry are listed in the heading—in this case the magazine, *The Black Scholar*, and the imprint under which they publish books of poetry, **The Black Scholar Press**. If the publisher offers a contest or award, that is also included in the heading. The publisher (usually) decides how its listing title(s) will appear and therefore determines alphabetization.

(2) Market category. The Roman numeral indicates the market category or categories. Some publishers have more than one code number. For example (II, IV-Humor) might be used if a magazine uses all kinds of poetry, but especially wants light or humorous verse. All publishers with IV listings are cross-indexed in the Subject Index. For example, you will find this publisher listed with all others that have an ethnic focus.

(3) Postal codes. Used for all U.S. states and areas (such as District of Columbia) and Canadian provinces. For a complete list of the codes, see page 464.

(4) Phone number. Sometimes included in this space (*The Black Scholar* chose not to) for business use of this directory. A poet should not, in general, telephone publishers about submissions; it is better to have such communication in writing.

(5) Date of founding. Most entries give this date. It helps you judge the stability of the publication or publisher. Recently founded publications may be more in need of material and thus more open to submissions—but they have not yet established continuity.

(6) Contact person. Names are provided by the publisher. If no name is given, I would address the submission to "Poetry Editor." Sometimes there are specific instructions, even a separate address, for the poetry editor. Note and follow such instructions carefully.

(7) Boldface text. Indicates important information to keep in mind when submitting—the preferred themes, for example, and the specifics of actual submission policies. Quotation marks indicate the description is in the words of the editor. I often quote to enable you to sense the editor's personality and attitude.

(8) Frequency of publication. Gives you some indication of how much poetry is needed and how soon an acceptance is likely to appear.

(9) Sample lines. These are brief excerpts representative of the quality of the poetry published, quoted whenever editors supply them or allow me to select them. If possible, the excerpts are somewhat self-contained in form and meaning. Samples are indented and italicized to make them easy to spot.

(10) Format. I ask all publishers to send me samples of their publications, but not all do so. When I have a copy I tell more about how it looks than is given here—whether it is flat-spined or saddle-stapled (see the Glossary for definitions of special terms), what kind of graphics and cover it has, and other details. I give as much information about the appearance of the publication as possible because poets, especially, like to imagine in what form their work will appear and the quality of the printing and binding.

(11) Circulation figures. Usually indicate the total of subscriptions (individual and library) plus off-the-shelf sales and free distribution.

(12) Sample copy, guidelines. Almost all editors advise you to read sample publications before submitting—and to obtain guidelines if they are available. If ordering a sample copy from England or other countries in the U.K., send a draft for sterling (from your bank) in payment, since U.K. banks charge a commission, sometimes in excess of the amount of the check, to exchange U.S. funds.

(13) Payment. Most small presses pay only in copies. If they pay cash, that information would be in the listing. A few (all in category I) do not even pay a copy; the poet has to buy the magazine (or book) to see the work in print.

(14) Submission requirements. Publishers state their individual requirements (see page 9 for a sample cover letter), and these may differ for a magazine and press within the same listing (see **16**). Most magazines object to simultaneous submissions (poems sent to more than one publisher at the same time) and previously published poems. Unless the listing says otherwise, assume that simultaneous submissions and previously published poems are *not* acceptable.

(15) Reporting time. The length of time a publisher needs to respond to your submission is approximate and can fluctuate greatly. If you have had no response within the reporting time plus a week or so, it is appropriate to query politely (with SASE) whether the manuscript is still under consideration. If a second or third query, spaced a few weeks apart, gets no response, it is appropriate to notify the editor that you are submitting the manuscript elsewhere. Always, of course, keep copies of manuscripts submitted. Sometimes you will be unable to get them returned.

(16) Query letter. Publishers often require a query letter rather than a manuscript as a first contact. The query letter is written to a publisher to elicit interest in a manuscript (see page 10 for a sample book query letter) or to determine whether the publisher is interested in receiving submissions.

(17) Editorial comments. I ask editors whether they would like to make any general comments about poetry, trends or their publishing plans, or offer advice for poets (especially beginners) and quote them—sometimes at length.

These special features of **Poet's Market** will help you select the best publishers for your poetry and submit it properly. Also read the introductions to the Publishers of Poetry, Contests and Awards and Greeting Cards sections for additional information on those markets.

— *What Poets Want to Know: 20 "Most Asked" Questions*

by Judson Jerome

At the **Poet's Market** office in Cincinnati, and at my office (in my home) in Yellow Springs, Ohio, questions pour in every day from poets who use this book. Pat Beusterien at the Cincinnati office and I value highly hearing from our readers. Along with their questions, they often bring us up to date on information about publishers. Sometimes they suggest new listings to us. And their reports on their experiences with various publishers, contests, organizations or other resources help us sort out those that are reputable from those that aren't. There are more sharks in the waters where poets swim than endanger writers of prose. We appreciate hearing about operations that seem to be exploitative of writers just as we do about helpful and responsive editors.

I'll try to answer here, and also in the prefaces to individual sections, in How to Use Poet's Market, and in The Business of Poetry, the most common of all the questions we receive.

About the listings...

1. Were do we get information for the listings?

My assistant here in Yellow Springs, Cathy Brookshire, spends a lot of her time with her nose in literary magazines. Some job, eh? Well, it's not all pleasure. She reads ads, news notes, market lists, even letters to the editors that mention new presses, publications, contests or other resources. She checks the files on her computer to see whether we have the listing at all, and, if so, whether the information matches ours. If she finds a publisher or resource that isn't in our file, Cathy sends them a listing questionnaire for **Poet's Market**. When a questionnaire is filled out and returned, I write the listing based on the information given in the questionnaire. Listings are free; they are not advertisements and we edit out what seems to us merely promotional material the editors may include.

2. How can we be sure that what we print is accurate?

We can't be 100% sure, but we do everything we can to verify what we publish. I examine sample publications to see whether they match the descriptions provided by the editors. Each year we send out verification forms for each listing and do not include the listing unless that form has been approved either by mail or telephone. Each year we suggest that, in addition to advising us of changes in policy, deadline, address, etc., editors also update their listings by giving us names of poets recently published and sample lines of poems. I send important changes monthly to *Writer's Digest*, along with brief summaries of new listings. The Poetry Markets section of *WD* contains these updates of **Poet's Market**.

3. Why are some publishers and magazines not listed?

Maybe we haven't found out about them, but chances are we have written them for information and they have not responded, or if they have previously appeared in **Poet's Market**, they have not returned their verification forms. For further information see the list of

Other Poetry Publishers at the end of the publishers' section. Along with the names there, you will find a brief explanation of why there is no listing in this edition. We also have in our files the names of many more publishers and magazines that have not responded to our mailings. (Some we have excluded because they seem exploitative of writers or are vanity operations — "publishers" who essentially publish anything you will pay to have them print.) If you want to submit to publishers and magazines not listed in **Poet's Market** most of their addresses can be found in **Writer's Market** (Writer's Digest Books), **Literary Market Place** (Bowker), **The International Directory of Little Magazines and Small Presses** (Dustbooks) and **Directory of Publications** (Gale) available in most libraries. Write a brief letter (enclosing SASE) to the publishers or magazines to determine if they are interested in receiving poetry submissions. Many specialized and trade magazines, such as **Leatherneck** or **Western Cowboy** or **American Fitness**, may use a few poems per year of special interest to their readers, but they prefer not to open their publications to poets in general because they don't want to deal with a flood of submissions. But if you let us know about a magazine or publisher that you think should be listed, we'll send a questionnaire to them for a future listing.

4. Are there any shortcuts that will make finding a market quicker and easier?

Sure! Use the various indexes in the back of the book to find specialized publications and publishers or those in a specific geographic area. I've tried to make **Poet's Market** an interesting, readable book, a way of giving you a guided tour through the contemporary literary world. I hope it is good reading, especially when you're not sure what you are looking for. When I use the book myself, I often resort to these shortcuts. For example, I just got off the phone after telling a poet about **Byline Magazine** and **Writer's Journal** — but offhand I could remember the name of neither one. I knew **Writer's Journal** was in Minnesota, so I found the name in the geographical list. And I knew that **Byline** used only poetry about writing, so I found it in the Subject Index under "Themes," that is, writing on specific subjects. Also, I would recommend using the market categories, e.g., if you're a beginning poet, read the listings coded (**I**) and then submit your work to the appropriate ones. (See How to Use **Poet's Market** for the complete explanation of market categories.)

5. Do you recommend the publishers you list?

There are as many different kinds of publishers as there are different kinds of poets, and I would have no idea which ones to recommend to poets whom I don't know. I try to be as objective as possible and to let the editors speak for themselves. Sometimes I think what they say reveals ignorance, insensitivity or bad taste, but some of my readers may find the same words appealing. There are a lot of clues scattered through the book to help you decide where to submit your poetry. When editors are asked to list some of the better-named poets their magazine or press has recently published, and they list only obscure poets, that tips me off not to send my work there. If the sample lines quoted look like nonsense to me, or seem deadly as poetry, I would decide I wouldn't want my work to appear there. But you may figure, "If they'll take that surely *I* can get in!" I give a lot of attention to a magazine's format, too, because there are so few other rewards in having one's poems published. I like mine to at least appear in a quality publication. But that might not matter to you. Also, if a publication charges several dollars for what is obviously a few pages of photocopied newsletter, I would figure the publisher didn't have the best interest of poets at heart, but you may think otherwise. Sometimes I permit myself to slip into the listing an evaluative adjective or two, but, remember, these listings have been verified by the publishers, and they would not be likely to approve of something that seemed to denigrate them. So I try to stick to the facts and let you judge.

6. How do I know whether publishers are being fair when they charge me a fee to read my work or require me to buy something?

There is no easy way to distinguish. Most reputable magazines do not require a purchase or a subscription and most people in the field regard those who *do* as running a questionable operation. Most magazines pay at least one copy, and the norm is two, for each poem or group of poems accepted. Most book publishers will respond to a query and a small sample of poems without charge. On the other hand, *any* editor of a magazine appreciates your purchase of a sample copy or subscription, and these may influence the judgment of some of the smaller publications who are desperate to increase circulation. The practice of charging a reading fee for full-length book considerations has in recent years become widespread, even among highly esteemed publishers. Some, including several university presses, consider book manuscripts only in competitions with entry reading fees. I insist on classifying as **I** or **IV-Subscribers** magazines requiring a purchase or subscription or those that do not pay even one free copy. They may serve some purpose for beginners, but few experienced poets would consider letting their work be used under those circumstances. Of book or chapbook publishers charging reading fees for competitions, I have the greatest respect for those who promise to send every entrant a copy of the winning book or chapbook. That may be a way of squeezing out a bit of paid circulation, but at least they offer something in return for the fee besides reading, and it seems to me not an unreasonable way for a small press to be able to afford to offer the competition.

7. Is it better to query first, or just submit? How about query letters? Is there a recommended form?

For magazines a query is almost never necessary. The exceptions are the magazines that devote special issues to specific themes. You have to know what they are before you can reasonably submit, and these are almost never decided early enough to be included in **Poet's Market**. Some magazine editors request a cover letter with submissions, but unless one is requested, it also is not necessary. An envelope containing poems and a SASE is obviously intended as a submission. But for those who want to use cover letters see the sample in this section.

Many book publishers prefer queries. That doesn't necessarily mean they won't consider a complete manuscript if they receive it. Hardly any editor rejects a manuscript simply because it doesn't follow the "rules." But it is more economical for you and time-saving for editors if you send a sample and query letter with a brief statement of biographical background and previous publications, and that is the most common expectation and practice. See the sample cover-query letter for book (or chapbook) consideration. The last paragraph of the query letter would be especially relevant to a small press. Often publishing arrangements with presses that do not have national distribution are cooperative ventures involving the poet in promotion, and sometimes even in the production and financing of books.

8. Can I submit queries or manuscripts simultaneously to more than one publisher?

So far as I know it is customary to *query* more than one publisher at a time regarding book or chapbook publication. That's the implication of a query. You are asking editors whether they want the opportunity to consider your manuscript, and there is no harm in asking several that question at the same time. On the other hand, some publishers express an objection to *simultaneous submissions*. They don't want to give their time to considering a manuscript only to find out that it has been accepted elsewhere. Most agents submit a book

SAMPLE COVER LETTER

321 Howard Drive
Benton AZ 12345
(602)111-3456

January 10, 1991

Linda Martin
Poetry Editor
Cloud Quarterly
123 Four St.
Capital, ME 45678

Dear Ms. Martin: (<u>use</u> Dear Poetry Editor <u>if no name is</u> <u>given in listing</u>)

Enclosed are my poems "After the Storm," "Spring Rain" and "Autumn Night" for your consideration. My poetry has recently appeared in <u>Nimbus</u>, <u>Seasons</u> and <u>Equator Monthly</u>.

I grew up in the Southwest and am now employed by the U.S. Forestry Service. My poetry has been greatly influenced by my work in the outdoors and in the conservation of our natural resources.

In your most recent (Spring) issue I especially enjoyed Rita Wilson's "Mountain Climber" and Robert Carson's "Cylcone." It would be an honor to see my poetry in your pages.

Sincerely,

Christopher Smith

Christopher Smith

SAMPLE QUERY LETTER
(for book or chapbook submission)

456 Campbell Drive
Bay Island NY 45678
(200)122-3345

January 15, 1991

Lawrence Marshall
Poetry Editor
Coastal Press
Merrymount, CA 12345

Dear Mr. Marshall: (use Dear Poetry Editor if no name is given
in listing)

Enclosed is my manuscript End of the Forest, 32 pages, which
I hope you will consider for chapbook publication. Some of
these poems have appeared in Verdant Magazine, Lemon Tree
and Nature Quarterly. I have previously had one book collection, Trees and Sky, and one chapbook, Green Meadows, both
published by Moore Press.

I was attracted to Coastal Press by the fact that you have published books I admire, such as Penny Ander's Web of Doubt
and Arnold Parker's Winding Way, both of them handsome
examples of the art of printing as well as spellbinding in content. You seem to respect poets able to work with the confines
of form, and I believe I am such a poet.

I would be able to help you promote sales by supplying you
with a list of the subscribers to Nature Land Magazine, where
my articles and poetry have frequently appeared, and through
my freelance writing connections with local newspaper people
and arts groups. I would actively assist sales by soliciting reviews and poetry readings, and help in any other way I could
to make my book a financial success.

Sincerely,

Janice Cook

Janice Cook

manuscript to several publishers at once as a matter of course, and, if one takes it, they notify the others to see whether they can elicit a competitive bid. Given the slow rate of return of manuscripts from many publishers, poets and other writers are increasingly submitting simultaneously to several. Most editors like to be told if that is what you are doing, and you should immediately notify all those to whom you have submitted a manuscript if it is taken.

These practices are much more strictly followed in regard to prose, especially nonfiction, than in regard to poetry. Nonfiction content may have a timeliness that is important to editors, and they are much more likely to object if they are not offered exclusive rights to consider a manuscript, even if only for a limited period such as three weeks. But because poetry generally requires a smaller space commitment and does not have currency and news value, editors may take longer in making decisions about it and be less concerned if it is simultaneously being considered elsewhere.

9. What is the difference between the way solicited and unsolicited manuscripts are handled?

Many editors of literary journals and presses solicit work from well-known poets as a way of increasing the prestige of their publications. Ironically, lesser known poets benefit from this practice, because it is to their advantage to be published in a highly-respected publication or by a respected press which has gained its reputation by publishing known names. These publishers aren't closed to lesser-known names, necessarily, but having solicited work, they have some obligation to publish what they receive. However, it often appears that poets with national reputations have emptied their bottom drawers in response to solicitations. This may mean that the best work of lesser-known poets is in somewhat unfair competition for space with relatively poor work from big names, with the advantage going to the names. On the other hand, most editors, even of major markets, take genuine pride and pleasure in discovering new voices. Few completely disregard unsolicited submissions, though they may take longer in reaching a decision about them and may find they don't have the space at any given time to accommodate even work they like.

Mass circulation magazines and top-ranking book publishers often have readers to weed out the unsolicited manuscripts of poorest quality and to decide which manuscripts should be passed on to the editors. Small press editors are likely to read everything they receive (at least in part, as John Ciardi used to point out when he confessed that he didn't read all the way through most of the poems submitted to him as poetry editor of *Saturday Review*. "You don't have to hear a whole concert to know whether a fellow can play.") Solicited manuscripts go directly to the editors who solicited them and so bypass the readers.

If editors ask for a manuscript, they are not likely to reject it with a form, but most unsolicited manuscripts are rejected with impersonal forms. Most editors say they haven't time for a personal response to everything they receive. And if there is no SASE (self-addressed stamped envelope) or SAE with International Reply Coupons (for submissions between nations: self-addressed envelope with postage coupons purchased at the post office), they may not respond at all.

Finding the right market

10. Can Poet's Market editors recommend a publisher or magazine for my work?

See question 5. **Poet's Market** is not quite as objective a reference work as **Literary Market Place**, for example (which gives only names and addresses), but you should think of **Poet's Market** chiefly as a source of information, not judgment. You know your needs and aspirations, and it is up to you to key these to the available markets for your poetry with the help of the listings and indexes in **Poet's Market**.

11. Where should I start—with contests, magazines, or books?

Magazines. Even the best contests are to some degree lotteries, often indicative of the luck-of-the draw (Who is judging? How is his digestion that day?) and most confer little literary prestige and their prizes are likely to be small. You have to rack up a record of good magazine publications before your work is even likely to be considered for book publication (and contest winnings are not a substitute).

12. To which magazines should I submit?

Let's start with this question: which interests you more—what your poem is saying or the art of poetry? If your answer is the first, you will find it much easier to get your work published and much harder to gain status as a poet. If you are new to marketing, start not only with those magazines coded **I** (for beginners), but with those marked **IV** (specialized) and those in your area (see the Geographical Index). The editors of specialized markets are more likely to be interested in what you are writing *about* than your poetic expertise. Local publications are likely to pay more attention to their immediate audience. It is always a good idea to order sample copies of magazines (or look at them at newsstands or, in the case of small literary magazines, in libraries) to which you hope to submit, and to show some familiarity with the publication when you send in your work. If guidelines are offered, you should see these *before* submitting. The thousands of poets who submit inappropriately are the bane of our business, causing editors everywhere to become very impatient with unsolicited submissions and closing many of the best markets even to those who go about submitting with good professional judgment.

13. How do I go about getting a book published?

Put it out of your mind until you have accumulated a substantial number (I would say no less than twenty) of acceptances by magazines in the **II** and **III** categories. Most book publishers expect you to query with perhaps a half-dozen sample poems and a good record of magazine publications. They will probably want to include in the book your better magazine publications. Even at that point it is extremely difficult to interest a major publisher in your work. Connections help. A good place to start is with publishers in your area. See the Geographical Index in the back. Show your willingness to address yourself to the problem of promotion of your book. It helps to know as much about the work of a small press as possible before submitting a manuscript to it, so you may want to buy a sample or samples of their books and study these before submitting. As with magazine publishers, be scrupulous in avoiding inappropriate submissions.

14. Should I get an agent?

No. Forget it. The reputable agents will not handle poetry unless it is for celebrity clients such as Jimmy Stewart or those, such as novelists with national reputations, whose names are likely to sell their poetry (sometimes regardless of its quality). Any others who say they are willing to look at your poetry are likely to want money up front to evaluate it. I have known poets who paid more than a hundred dollars to a well-known book agent for an evaluation only to be told that their book has little market value. You know that going in: you don't have to pay someone to tell you. Be realistic. A reputable agent makes his living (and maintains an office) on a percentage of book royalties and advances (usually 10-15%). When there are any royalties or advances for books of poetry (and there usually are not), they are so small that they do not make the sale worth an agent's time.

15. How does Poet's Market respond to complaints about publishers they list?

These letters are always forwarded to me personally. I send a copy of the complaint letter to the publishers and ask for their explanation. I ask them to rectify the situation if the complaint is accurate, and to let me know what action they have taken. Then I send a copy of my correspondence to the publisher to the writer with a note thanking him for helping us keep informed about conditions in the market. We are very grateful for your active efforts to help us keep abreast. If I have unresolved or many complaints about a particular publisher, I drop that listing from future editions.

Business and etiquette

16. What should I do when I don't get a reply to my query or manuscript within the reporting time given in Poet's Market?

At best, reporting times are estimates, and many publishers, especially new ones, are overly optimistic about how soon they can report and whether or not they will be able to comment on submissions. Nonetheless, it is perfectly proper for you to query politely (always with SASE) if you have waited 3-4 weeks *beyond* their estimated reporting time and had no response. If you get no response to the query within a reasonable time (a couple of weeks), you might write them again to say that you are withdrawing your submission and will be submitting the work elsewhere. In that case, they may throw away the manuscript and you can bid farewell to the SASE you sent with it, but there is no need to let a poem be grounded eternally when there are so many other available markets.

But it is wise to remember that, especially with small press publications, there are inescapable delays. Many of these publications have only an editor/publisher, working without pay and without a staff. They can get sick, or move, or have a family emergency, or have other reasons to get behind. One highly respected quarterly that had accepted my work still had not appeared months after the announced date of publication. When I inquired I discovered that the editor had a volunteer putting the magazine on disk. The volunteer quit and refused to turn the disk over to the editor. Another editor had a student assistant who dropped out of school and left the magazine's manuscripts in a state of total disarray. On the other hand, quite a few people who start up magazines or presses live lifestyles that may well confuse carelessness and indifference with creativity and unconventionality. If you want to deal only with conventional professional practices, I suggest you write nonfiction or go into business, though you may be disappointed in those areas, too. It helps one live a mellow life to maintain a firm check on one's self-righteousness.

17. Should I telephone my queries?

Personally, I am often annoyed by telephone calls from strangers. My office, like that of most small press publishers, is in my home, and a call is likely to be an intrusion on my family and personal life. There are few occasions when a call is better than a letter (with SASE, whenever you expect a response). For one thing, you should keep a written record of your dealings with publishers and a copy of a letter makes this record precise. For another, you never know what the ring of your telephone is interrupting in someone's home or office. Telephone numbers are included in some listings (with the publisher's permission) in **Poet's Market** primarily for business purposes. They help us follow up quickly when verification forms are not returned on time, for example. And some publishers do not mind calls (especially those large enough to maintain offices; a call may be cheaper and more convenient for them to handle than a written response), and some small press publishers even welcome personal contact by phone. But my advice is not to take chances on calling unless you have reason to believe your call will be welcome or some emergency warrants it.

18. What rights does a magazine or book publisher acquire over my poetry?

Normally a paying market buys first North American serial rights, meaning they have the right to publish for the first time only in the United States and Canada. That leaves you free to sell the reprint rights to another publication. Some magazines buy all rights and pay for the privilege, but this rarely applies to poetry. It is a matter of politeness, as well as legality when all rights have been purchased, to request permission from the magazine or publisher who first published your poem when you want to reprint it in another magazine or in a book. Permission is usually given automatically and without cost to the writer: the editor writes a letter assigning rights back to the author, then you can transfer those rights to whomever you please. Book publishers ordinarily take out a copyright in the name of the author (if it is a collection of work by an individual; if it's an anthology, the same procedures apply as are used in copyrighted magazines). But if you have signed a book contract, which authorizes only the publisher to reprint your work, and you want to use the poetry elsewhere, you must request permission from the publisher, which is almost always granted as a courtesy.

However, practices in regard to copyright for poetry are much looser in practice (though not in law) than those for other kinds of writing. But many little magazines (and even chapbooks) are not copyrighted by their editors. There is so little likelihood of someone "stealing" a poem (and so little to be gained or lost if they do), it hardly seems worth worrying about. (And a small press magazine or publisher might decide not to bother with your work at all if you insist on too punctilious an approach to these matters.)

It's a different matter, however, when you are dealing with plagiarism. Jean Burden, poetry editor of *Yankee*, reports that she has caught instances of plagiarism several times and may have let others slip by without ever discovering them. But there's a good chance that those who submit the poetry of others under their own names, and have it accepted and published in a magazine with the circulation of *Yankee*, will be caught. I find it hard to imagine what satisfaction they get out of passing someone else's work off as their own (payment, even at *Yankee*, is not large enough to be tempting financially), but there are all kinds of kooks out there.

19. How should I respond to abusive letters of rejection or other unprofessional conduct on the part of editors?

The literary world is full of zany people on both sides of the editorial desk. Probably every small press editor can tell you tales of outrageous letters of denunciation from poets and other writers, often after a record of the abusers having submitted without SASE or submitting messy or illegible manuscripts or other annoying practices. And many poets have encountered incivility in editors. They are usually very ignorant people, whether editors or writers, who engage in uncivil behavior, and their behavior will soon reap its just reward. Most of the time I would recommend ignoring such conduct. Just don't deal with that person anymore. Send your work elsewhere. There is little chance that you can personally clean the Augean stables of the literary subculture. But we appreciate hearing about these cases at **Poet's Market** and we dutifully record complaints and act on them when they multiply. Word gets around the network of writers and publishers, too. Many of us who have been editors exchange knowing nods (through the mail or otherwise) when the names of certain poets and writers are mentioned, and writers, in workshops and personal correspondence, pass on such information and experiences, too. To a great extent, the literary world is a small community, riven by gossip and fashion and sustained by mutual support.

Join it in good spirit, and, knowing the world, be more sad than outraged that not all its members do the same.

20. When can I start calling myself a poet?

Why, you have my authorization to do so today. But what does that mean? You are a poet at the time you are writing poetry. The next moment you may be a busy mother or engaged citizen or engineer. This has nothing to do with publication. Think of an actor who spends perhaps 10% of his life acting and much of the rest of the time scrounging up a new role for next season. Writing poetry and publishing poetry are entirely different concerns. You have to be schizoid to stick with it. One part of my brain writes poems for the love of it. It is connected to my heart and expects no reward for writing other than the joy and fulfillment of artistic creation and communication as it writes letters and carries on conversations with poet friends. A second part is a clerk, mechanically sending out manuscripts, receiving rejections and acceptances, keeping records, watching for opportunities, exploiting associations, playing the game. A third part, not on speaking terms with either the poet or the clerk, earns a living to support the prodigal habit of indulging in poetry as some indulge in gambling at the track or scuba-diving in the tropics. **Poet's Market** is intended to help the functions of that second part of the brain. You will soon discover that many magazines and books of poetry are filled with poetry that doesn't seem nearly as good as yours. That happens to all of us. Sometimes we are merely blind to our own defects or to the achievements of others, but it is also true that in the literary world quality does not necessarily rise to the top, especially without assistance. So tell your clerk to get busy and use **Poet's Market** intelligently. Meanwhile, the poet in you can be devoted to artistic excellence and purity of heart.

The Business of Poetry

by Judson Jerome

Though I won't say writing poetry is easy, I will warn you that writing it is a lot easier than selling it, or even getting it published in a nonpaying market. And publication itself is a lot easier than getting people to read it—people, that is, other than your friends and relations.

But by using **Poet's Market** judiciously and following the advice given in What Poets Want to Know: 20 "Most Asked" Questions and in this article, getting your poetry published can be easier.

Fitting in

The popular conception of the creative person dies hard: that an artistic sensibility necessarily resides in one who is a nonconformist, an irrepressible individual who can't be bothered with the manners that the word *professional* implies. True, great poetry, like all great art, has a powerful component of revolution built into it. We poets may want to overthrow convention. But, to do that, we have to be heard, and that requires recognizing and complying with certain formalities. It is what our poetry contains that conveys the force of strong individual vision and often unsettling thought. We shouldn't confuse that with the relatively trivial concerns of outward behavior. Though we all start as amateurs, we must, from the start of our careers, be aware of how seasoned professionals go about their business and make an effort to fit in.

Writing poetry is the fun part. Finding a publisher for it is tough—like slogging the streets in response to want ads. At any given time I have about 30 manuscripts in circulation, and nearly every day one or several come back to me just like yours come back to you, with rejection slips and no comment. We all get impatient with the need to be sure the manuscript looks fresh before we send it out again, to keep records telling us where it has gone and when it was returned, and to find still another possible publisher and get it back into the mail. But there is no other way to build up a list of publications and establish our names as recognized poets.

Keeping records

Having a number of manuscripts in circulation at one time is the best hedge against the anguish of waiting like a wallflower for invitations that never seem to come. Typically editors like to see packets of some 3-5 poems at a time. But if you have a dozen such packets out there in the marketplace, it is easy to get confused. I keep several record files. One lists each poem I have sent out, and, after it, the names of the magazines that have seen it and rejected it (with an indication if there was a comment from the editor). Another file is by magazines—an alphabetical index telling me what poems I have sent to each. I put the dates of submission and return in this file so that I have a running account of how long I can expect each magazine to hold material before returning it. Since I have articles and stories out also, these require still other files, though I put both prose and poetry titles in what I call my "magazine file." I also have several book manuscripts in circulation—both of poetry and of prose—and these require still another record.

Such records may be kept in a 3×5 card file or in a notebook. Luckily, all this is made much simpler for me by my computer. I think of my records as card files (as the computer record replaces 3×5 index cards I used to use). Since I have little reason to print out my record files (I keep those on my hard disk backed up on floppies), I follow each item with a hard return (Control-Enter, which makes a double line of hyphens across the screen, a forced page-break). That makes it easy to see where each record ends. And the Find function takes me quickly to the one I want. When I am adding a new "card," it is easy to insert it in its alphabetical position. I have reviewed a few software programs specifically for writers, designed to help you keep all this straight, and some database or "notebook" programs can be adapted to this purpose. But I haven't found one I like as well as the method I have designed myself, within my word-processing program, and you, too, can probably devise a way of keeping records that is precisely tailored to your particular needs and business habits.

I almost always send "simultaneous submissions." That is, I send out packets of the same poems to more than one potential publisher at a time. Some editors, you will notice from their listings, object strenuously to this practice, and others don't mind. But the whole process of sending out manuscripts and waiting for returns from small presses is so slow and tedious, more and more writers are submitting simultaneously, and I believe that in time most editors will come to expect that.

Minding our manners

Again and again editors tell me they take poor proofreading, dim printing or other varieties of manuscript carelessness as evidence that the poet doesn't care about his or her work—and can't, therefore, expect an editor to care. A crisp, easily readable, correct manuscript is a sign of respect for the work and for the editor.

Also, remember editors are individuals. I was quite surprised, as I gathered material for this book, to discover that some editors actually like cover letters, and some are even offended when none is enclosed. In my experience most editors felt exactly the opposite. But I also found editors who like chatty letters which give some sense of the poet's personality; some editors write long chatty letters back. For specific advice and models for cover letters as well as book queries, see the section titled What Poets Want to Know: 20 "Most Asked" Questions, question seven. That section also contains advice about telephone calls, or rather, advises you, in general, *not* to phone editors about poetry submissions.

Preparing your manuscript

Unless editors instruct you otherwise, these are standard procedures:
● Manuscripts should be typed or word-processed on white 8½x11″ paper—not erasable bond, not *italic* or other abnormal type style. Be sure the type is clean and dark. When editors say "no dot-matrix," they object to poor quality dot-matrix. If you have a modern printer, with characters that look like those on a typewriter, and "correspondence quality" (double-strike) printing, they probably will consider it.
● Name and address should be at the upper right of the first page of each poem. Your name, at least, should be at the upper right of each page if the poem is longer than 1 page.
● No more than 1 poem per page. Exception: some editors will accept more than 1 haiku per page. It is rarely wise to send a single poem or more than 10 pages of poetry at one time.
● Title should be centered on the page, several spaces down from your name and address. Do *not* use ALL CAPS either for the title or the poem. Set the left margin so that poem will be approximately centered on the page. Drop down a few lines and type the poem.
● Usually single-space the poem, double space between stanzas. If the poem is short, it is acceptable to double-space for a more balanced appearance on the page.
● Unless you say otherwise in your cover letter, the editor will assume the submitted poems are your original work; they have not been previously published and are not being simultaneously submitted elsewhere. In general, those are the kinds of submissions most editors will consider.

• Proofread carefully. Most editors are outraged by spelling, grammatical, and punctuation errors. If you are employing unconventional usages deliberately, that should be clear from the context of the poem. Many editors object to corrections in handwriting on typed copy. Make sure the poem is *exactly* the way you want to see it in print.

• Unless you are sending more than 10 pages, use a #10 business envelope (4¼ × 9½″) both for mailing and for SASE (self-addressed, stamped envelope for return of your manuscript). Fold both the manuscript and SASE into thirds for insertion. If you are submitting to another country, use an SAE (self-addressed envelope) and IRC's (International Reply Coupons—purchased at the post office) sufficient to cover the cost of return (1 IRC = 1 ounce surface mail). Some poets send U.S. dollar bills instead of IRCs—acceptable to most foreign editors. An alternative practice is to enclose 2 IRCs for an airmail reply and request the editor to let you know the decision but throw the rejected manuscripts away. Recently the U.S. Postal Service announced their nationwide stamps-by-phone system, operating 24 hours every day, whereby customers can buy stamps using major credit cards. To order, call 1-800-782-6724. If not accessible from your location, call 816-455-4880, 8 a.m.-5 p.m. CST. Canadians can use their VISA card to order U.S. stamps for their SASEs to the U.S. instead of using the more expensive IRCs; however there is a $5 service charge for foreign orders.

• For most editors, a cover letter is not required. If you use one, it should be *brief*— giving your most important recent publications or acceptances and perhaps a line or two of biography. Do *not* explain what you are trying to do in your poems or discuss their merits.

Copyrighting your work

You *can* write the Copyright Office, Library of Congress, Washington, D.C. 20559 and get the forms to copyright your poems for a small fee, if you wish. Then you can mark each poem with ©_____ (filling in the year and your name). But it's unneccessary, and I don't advise it. No one is going to steal your poem. (You should be so lucky!) Besides, in my opinion, a copyright notice on your manuscript also looks amateurish. Most little magazines are copyrighted when printed, which covers your poem. You can use the poem elsewhere, as in a book, unless you gave the editor, in writing, more than first rights for his copyrighted magazine. If that's the case, you should write the editor for permission to use the poem, or to have the copyright assigned to you, a request that will be granted automatically (and without cost) by almost all publishers. Book publishers ordinarily take out a copyright in the name of the author (if it is a collection of work by an individual; if it's an anthology, the same procedures apply as are used in copyrighted magazines). But if you have signed a book contract, which authorizes only the publisher to reprint your work, and you want to use the poetry elsewhere, you must request permission from the publisher, which is almost always granted as a courtesy.

Being patient. . .

Once your precious packet is in the mail, you learn to wait. When the editor has indicated the length of time you may expect to wait before getting a response, I include that in the listing. But this information is very much a guess—and sometimes a hope—on the editor's part. If I have not had a response from an editor, I may query—with SASE, or sometimes a stamped, self-addressed postcard—asking whether my manuscript is still under consideration. If I get no response within a couple of weeks, I may query again. And if I get no response from a second query, I write to say I am submitting my manuscript elsewhere and that the editor should discard the manuscript on hand. Then I don't send material to that publisher again.

But much of a poet's time is spent in waiting. There is a great deal of excitement when one finishes a poem—a moment that feels like pure triumph. There may be another such moment when one reads the poem to a friend—or the friend reads it. Months or even years later there is another ripple of excitement—when the poem is accepted somewhere for publication. And it may be months or even years after that when the third ripple comes with the arrival of your contributor's copy with your poem in it. Sometimes there's even a check. (Most publishers of poetry, other than the very big, mass-circulation magazines, pay upon publication, not upon acceptance.) Occasionally—but very rarely—there are further ripples when someone reports actually having read the poem. Maybe that person even tells you he or she liked it! But for the most part publishing a poem is like dropping a leaf in a well and listening for the splash. That's one more reason you should not be bothering with all this unless you truly love the writing process itself, unless you can get your primary gratification from your engagement with language and art and put external rewards out of your mind.

Anthologies

Beyond magazine publication there are basically two forms in which our works are immortalized—anthologies and individual collections. The term anthology used to mean a selection of works by a number of writers chosen by an editor. Individuals do not submit work to such an anthology, except by invitation. And it is an honor to be asked. Inclusion in these anthologies is the principal way that a poet becomes established as one of the major poets. This is the type of anthology you find in bookstores, the type used in college courses.

Increasingly, though, another kind of anthology is proliferating—the *vanity anthology*. I refuse to list those publishers that seem exploitative of poets—those charging exorbitant prices for the anthologies they publish, which are generally huge books with hundreds of short poems crammed in, many to the page, in small type. Usually, as a prerequisite to having a poem included, the poet must agree to buy a copy of the book. Multiply the number of poets represented by the price of the anthology, and you can guess how these businesses can afford to take out huge ads in mass-circulation magazines. The services they offer are all expensive to you—and useless, for, fairly or not, both libraries and reviewers toss such books into the trashcan without considering them, and the publicity releases these publishers send out are almost never used by newspapers. Nor do their ads sell books.

You will find, however, a number of listings in this book of publishers who, one or more times a year, bring out anthologies to which poets have submitted work. These are invariably in the (I) category because experienced poets would not be inclined to send them their work. In some cases you have to buy a copy of the anthology to be included; in others, you are encouraged to do so by the fact that you won't get a copy unless you do.

These publishers seem to offer reasonable ways for beginning poets to get a poem between book covers, if that is what you want—though usually they can put only one short poem per poet in each anthology. My advice is that you not mention these anthologies when you are listing your "credits" in a cover letter to an editor. They mark you as an amateur.

Book publication and self-publication

The more common way of getting your poems into book form is to publish a collection. Again, there are two routes. You may have a collection accepted for publication by one of the publishers listed here who will pay the printing costs, and you will be paid in some combination of copies, a stipend, or royalties. Remember that when you submit a book manuscript to such a publisher you are, in effect, asking someone—in the small presses, usually someone working at a regular job and acting as a publisher as a labor of love—to invest four or five thousand dollars in your work. To do that he or she has to have some reason to believe that, with the limited marketing means available to such publishers, enough copies can be sold to recoup that investment. If you indicate that you are aware of that fact, and willing to face it realistically, and are willing and able to help personally to promote the book and make the investment pay off, you will stand a much better chance of having your manuscript seriously considered.

The second route is self-publication. I often advise poets—especially older poets—to shortcut that long and difficult publication process and to self-publish a collection of their work. I know what an important heritage it was in my family to have a collection of my grandfather's poems around the house even before I could read. You can go to a local printer and have a chapbook or book of your poetry published anytime you want (and can afford to). That is not likely to advance your career, but it may be quite satisfying and sufficient for many. After all, career-building in poetry is a long and complex process, inevitably involving a lot of personal politics and influence and trading of favors and mutual assistance, and the rewards for the most successful are not large, either in fame or finance. If what you want is a collection of your work in print to give to friends, to pass out or sell at readings, to leave for your family, these are quite respectable motives and easily satisfied. Don't go to what are called the vanity publishers (they call themselves subsidy publishers) who advertise for manuscripts in the magazines. You can do much better, both in terms of expense and control of the product, if you go to a *printer* (not a company that calls itself a publisher). You can locate printers in the Yellow Pages of your phone directory. The advantage of a printer over a subsidy publisher is that you'll save a lot of money and have a lot more control over your book's manufacture—and you will own all the copies. For most poets an edition of a couple of hundred is sufficient. Such a collection may be treasured by your family and friends. In most cases it will not be reviewed, and you will have a hard time selling copies, but at least your work is preserved in a durable form.

A number of quite respectable small presses publish collections on what are called "cooperative" arrangements. The poet pays some or all of the printing costs and takes some of the responsibility for distribution. If they are truly respected presses, they won't do it unless they genuinely admire the poetry they are publishing and are proud to have their imprint on your book. See also the introduction to the index of Chapbook Publishers for a common way of getting poems into at least a pamphlet format.

But the books that count the most in advancement of your career are those printed at the publisher's expense, sometimes giving you an advance and a royalty contract. These are the books that get reviewed (a few of them—it is very difficult to get books of poetry reviewed). Sometimes they win awards. And such books are the most common means by which a poet establishes a national reputation.

You shouldn't even begin to think about that kind of book publication until you have a substantial number (I would say a hundred or more) of poems published in category **II** or **III** magazines. Study the collections of work of individual poets you find in the library. Read their acknowledgment pages to see where their poems first appeared. Understand the league you are trying to enter.

By the time you are ready for that you will probably be acquainted with a number of poets who have been through the process, and they can advise you about how to approach book publication. The advice and submission information in these listings will also help you. But it is never easy—and, ironically, it is often more difficult to get one's second or third or fourth book published than it was to get the first one accepted.

Do *not*, by the way, try to use a literary agent. The few agents who handle poetry will do so only for a fee. And they'll have no more luck than you will working on your own. Respected agents of other types of writing work for a percentage of the proceeds, not fees.

Cheer up

All this may sound so discouraging that you may wonder why anyone bothers with poetry at all. Well, millions of us worldwide find it worthwhile—and are actively submitting poetry all the time. It may help your morale to realize we're all in the same boat. With hundreds of my poems published in magazines and several books and anthologies, I still get rejections most of the time—and go cheerily on sending out new poems again and again. If you have a realistic view of writing and submitting poetry you can enjoy it.

The amazing thing is that so many truly do discover that dedication in themselves and persevere. Since I was a teenager I have known deep in my soul that I would go on for the rest of my life devoted to poetry, giving my life to it. And I suspect many poets feel that way. Needing to write is something of a personal characteristic, like the color of one's eyes.

Few activities are so totally absorbing and satisfying to me as wrenching words around, discovering new ones, locking words together into phrases that will stick in the mind, managing vowels and consonants so that they play off one another, making syllables ripple a little then clunk hard into place. Well *you* know, or you wouldn't be reading this.

Market conditions are constantly changing! If you're still using this book and it is 1992 or later, buy the newest edition of Poet's Market *at your favorite bookstore or order directly from Writer's Digest Books.*

Key to Symbols and Abbreviations

‡New listing
MS-manuscript; MSS-manuscripts
b/w-black and white (photo or illustration)
SASE-self-addressed, stamped envelope
SAE-self-addressed envelope
IRC-International Reply Coupon, for use on reply mail in Canada and foreign markets.

Important Market Listing Information

● Listings are based on questionnaires and verified copy. They are not advertisements *nor*
are markets reported here necessarily endorsed by the editor of this book.
● Information in the listings comes directly from the publishers and is as accurate as
possible, but publications and editors come and go, and poetry needs fluctuate between
the publication of this directory and the time you use it.
● **Poet's Market** *reserves the right to exclude any listing that does not meet its requirements.*

The Markets

_____ *Publishers of Poetry*

If you don't have a specific publisher in mind, jump into this section immediately. Flip around. Start anywhere. I have tried to put the information in these listings into a form you can sit back and read with enjoyment and can learn about all activities (including organizations, writing colonies, contests and publications useful to poets) conducted at a single address. I hope it is as fascinating and educational for you as a reader as it was for me in compiling the information.

However, **if you are looking for a specific market, don't start here!** I have to say that many times throughout this book because starting in this section might seem the most natural thing to do. But suppose you've written a poem about the Old West, and you think a likely market might be *Horizons West*. Right? Right. Only you won't find *Horizons West* in this section alphabetized under *H*. The editors requested that the listing be under the name of the publisher of the magazine, Baker Street Publications, and that's where you'll find it. You might not discover that at all unless you looked in the General Index, where *Horizons West* is cross-indexed to Baker Street.

We believe it is better to put all the information about a publisher's activities that use poetry in one place so that you can have an overview of the publisher you are dealing with. Also in this way we avoid pointless repetition of identical addresses and other information throughout the book. Your guide to where information can be found is to look first in the General Index which contains cross references to all titles in the book.

Increasingly, poetry is becoming a regional activity. There was a time when New York and Boston were the literary centers of the nation, but that is no longer true. It is easier for most people to become a part of the literary scene if they start in their home territory. Therefore the indexes to geographic location (Geographical Index) and special interests (Subject Index) will be the means to lead you quickly to publishers with whom you have most in common, either because of where you live or the kind of poetry you write and who you are—racially, sexually, politically, or otherwise.

It is not my job to evaluate these publishers for you, for I could do so only in regard to my own tastes and interests. I try to let the editors speak for themselves so you can form your own opinion of how worthy they and their publications might be for the poetry you write. Sometimes you have to read between the lines. You can learn much about publishers by what they choose not to disclose as well as by what they say. Those who have very brief listings received the same questionnaires as those who chose to be more expansive. Some were reluctant to be listed at all. They aren't much interested in having poetry submitted by any Tom, Dick or Mary who might pick up **Poet's Market**. Others refused to be listed at all, so unwilling are they to hear from you. Some dread a flood of inappropriate submissions from amateurs who abuse this book and submit indiscriminately. Use the market categories indicated by Roman numerals in each listing. (See How to Use **Poet's Market** for an explanation of what they mean.) Study the magazine or book publisher to whom you plan to submit. Buy sample copies or subscribe *before* making your first submission. Submit appropriately.

Most presses are shoestring operations and sales of samples are a big help, as studying them can be a big help to you. (Also, some publishers give preference to those who have subscribed.) Others publish poetry from their friends and from poets recommended by friends. Make friends! A reader recently wrote to tell me how surprising and pleasing that advice was for her. She had thought of publishers as big corporations and thought that ordering a single copy of one of their magazines was nothing but a bother to them. Quite the opposite is true: most of *these* publishers thrive on those single-copy sales. She discovered how easy and relatively inexpensive it is to begin participating actively in a literary community that matched her interests.

If terms and abbreviations in the listings confuse you, look at the Glossary. I have tried to make the book, as a whole, a general guide to anyone entering the field. There is a place for you, if you look. I cannot guarantee that all those who use this guide properly will find their poetry being published, but it is hard for me to imagine why they should fail. This has little to do with any abstract conception of "quality." Obviously we can't all write *great* literature. But we can all write *publishable* poetry simply because there is such a vast range of tastes to match those of almost any poet who might be writing.

All publishers require that submissions and queries and requests for guidelines, catalogs or other information be accompanied by SASEs (self-addressed, stamped envelopes) or, for those in countries other than your own, SAEs (self-addressed envelopes) and sufficient IRCs (International Reply Coupons, purchased at your post office) for reply or return of your manuscript.

Make sure you check the Other Poetry Publishers list that runs at the end of this section for the current status of publishers not included here.

ABATTOIR EDITIONS (II), Annex 22, University of Nebraska, Omaha, NE 68182, phone 402-554-2787, founded 1972, director/editor Bonnie P. O'Connell, is a "literary fine press—adjunct to a teaching laboratory (Collegiate Book Arts Press) called The Fine Arts Press, producing hand-printed, hand-bound, limited editions." They want **poetry other than song lyrics, epics, science fiction or religious poetry**. They have recently published poetry by Brenda Hillman and Sam Pereira, Ann Deagon, Bernard Copper, and, earlier, under editorship of Harry Duncan, James Merrill, Richard Wilbur, Ben Howard and Weldon Kees. As a sample they offer these lines from "Dreaming of Rio at Sixteen" by Lynn Emanuel:

> *It was always Ramon's kisses, or sometimes, or never.*
> *Even grandmother's diamond earrings burned like Brazilian*
> *noons when you and she sheeted beds and found every*
> *beautiful mother an excuse to stop work and look out.*

They publish 2-4 chapbooks (12-20 pp.) and flat-spined paperbacks and/or hardbacks (32-40 pp.) a year. **Query with 5-6 samples, bio and credits. Simultaneous submissions and photocopies OK. The editor accepts but dislikes dot-matrix. Poems should not have appeared in book form earlier. SASE with MS a must. Reports on queries in 2-3 weeks, MSS in 1-2 months. Pays 10% royalties.**

ABBEY; ABBEY CHEAPOCHAPBOOKS (II), 5360 Fallriver Row Court, Columbia, MD 21044, phone 301-730-4272, founded 1970; editor David Greisman. They want "**poetry that does for the mind what that first sip of Molson Ale does for the palate. No pornography & politics.**" They have recently published poetry by Richard Peabody, Vera Bergstrom, Margot Treitel, Harry Calhoun, Wayne Hogan, and Tom Bilicke. *Abbey*, a quarterly, aims "to be a journal but to do it so informally that one wonders about my intent." It is magazine-sized, 20-26 pp., photocopied. They publish about 150 of 1,000 poems received per year. Press run is 200. Subscription: $2. **Sample: 50¢ postpaid. Guidelines available for SASE. Pays 1-2 copies. Reports in 1 month.** *Abbey Cheapochapbooks* come out 1-2 times a year averaging 10-15 pp. **For chapbook consideration query with 4-6 samples, bio, and list of publications. Reports in 2 months. Pays 25-50 copies.** The editor says he is "definitely seeing poetry from 2 schools—the nit'n'grit school and the textured/reflective school. I much prefer the latter. One book I highly recommend for poets is 1977's *50 Contemporary Poets: The Creative Process*, edited by Alberta T. Turner."

ABORIGINAL SF (IV-Science fiction), Box 2449, Woburn, MA 01888-0849, founded 1986, editor Charles C. Ryan, is a full-color, slick magazine appearing every two months. **"Poetry should be 1-2 pp., double-spaced. Subject matter must be science fiction, science, or space-related. No long poems, no fantasy."** The magazine is 68 pp., using coated stock, with 8-16 full-color illustrations. Circulation: 30,000, mostly subscriptions. Subscriptions for "special" writer's rate: $12/6 issues, $22/12 issues, $30/ 18 issues." **Sample: $3.50 postpaid. Pays $20 per poem and 2 copies. Reports in 2-8 weeks, has no backlog. Poems should be double-spaced. No simultaneous submissions. Good photocopies, dot-matrix OK. Send SASE for guidelines.**

ABOVE THE BRIDGE MAGAZINE (IV-Regional, humor), SR 550, Box 189C, Marquette, MI 49855, founded 1985, editor Jacqueline Miller, is a quarterly magazine, circulation 1,500, for Upper Peninsula readers. They buy about 20 poems/year—**free verse, light verse and traditional. "No abstractions such as Life, Love, etc. Be specific, preferably specific about the Upper Peninsula of Michigan—humor is our first choice.** *Above the Bridge* is magazine-sized, 48 pp., saddle-stapled, typeset with glossy cover, using b/w graphics and local ads. As a sample the editor selected the opening stanza of "April Storm" by Mary B. Knapp:

> *placid, gray*
> *lukewarm day*
> *abruptly metamorphic*
> *horizon blackness, breezy air . . .*

Submit maximum of 3 poems, 20 lines each. Considers simultaneous submissions. Pays $5. Sample $3 postpaid. Send SASE for guidelines.

ABRAXAS MAGAZINE; GHOST PONY PRESS (III), 2518 Gregory St., Madison, WI 53711, phone 608-238-0175, *Abraxas* founded 1968, Ghost Pony Press in 1980, by editor/publisher Ingrid Swanberg, who says "Ghost Pony Press is a small press publisher of poetry books; *Abraxas* is a literary journal (irregular) publishing contemporary poetry criticism and reviews of small press books. *Do not confuse these separate presses!*" She wants to see **"contemporary lyric and narrative, some experimental." Does not want to see "political posing; academic regurgitations."** They have recently published poetry by Andrei Condrescu, Ivan Argüelles, Denise Levertov, Laura Boss and Charles Bukowski. As a sample I selected the opening stanza of "Gauguin" by T. L. Kryss:

> *Baby kangaroos*
> *bounce like yellow lightning*
> *and under the volcano*
> *pear-breasted maidens*
> *hang colorforms of laundry*

The magazine is 80 pp., flat-spined, 6×9", litho offset, with original art on its matte card cover, using "unusual graphics in text, original art and collages, concrete poetry, exchange ads only, letters from contributors, essays." It appears "irregularly, 4-9 month intervals." They receive about 1,800 pp. of submissions per year, accept 2% of unsolicited material. Press run 600, 300 subscriptions of which 150 are libraries. **Sample: $3 postpaid. Send SASE for guidelines. Pays 1 copy plus 40% discount on additional copies. "Suggest no more than 5 poems per submission." No simultaneous submissions or previously published poems. Reports in 3 weeks to 5 months. Up to a year between acceptance and publication. To submit to Ghost Pony Press, inquire with SASE plus 5-10 poems and cover letter. Photocopy, dot-matrix, previously published material OK for book publication by Ghost Pony Press, which reports on queries in 4 weeks to 3 months, MSS in 3 months. Payment varies per project. Send SASE for catalog to buy samples. Editor sometimes comments briefly on rejections.**

ABSCOND: EXPERIMENTAL AUDIO DIRECTIONS; ARTIFACT COLLECTIVE TEXTS; ANOMALY (Audio Magazine) (IV-Form), 2251 Helton Dr. #N7, Florence, AL 35630, phone 205-760-0415, founded 1986, "front man" Jake Berry. "*Abscond* is the overall name for anything we publish: poetry, fiction, collages, graphics—all **experimental**, in a variety of formats, from postcards and magazines to broadsheets. *Experimental Audio Directions* is the tape label for spoken/sound poetry and other audio explorations. **The key words are *experiment* and *explore*. Poetry that breaks new ground for the poet personally, that comes from the commitment to a vision. Also graphic poetry. Poetry using devices other than straight linear narrative, that makes use of things otherwise considered nonsensical or absurd. No sentimental pablum please, no puritanical or purely superficial religious versifying, no**

weepy, confessional poetry—there are plenty of other magazines for that." They have recently published poetry by Jack Foley, Chris Winkler, Malok, Richard Kostelanetz, Ivan Argüelles, and John M. Bennett. As a sample the editor selected these lines by Mike Miskowski:

> *blendering on reverb dice, my feet. corner inta that plasterer or,*
> *couch the sprinkling mechanism greenwise a sunsetter. circuit*
> *clippings. thermostat though ink in.*

ACT and *Anomaly* (formerly *Artifact Collective Audio*) appear irregularly: "something appears 2 to 4 times a year." The issue of *ACT* I have seen is 20 pp. digest-sized, saddle-stapled, photoreduced typescript, with matte card cover. They use about 10 of 150 submissions received a year. Press run is 100-200. **Sample $4 postpaid. "All checks or money orders should be made out to Jake Berry, not the name of the mag and not to *Abscond*."** They pay 1 copy. "Of course poems submitted for the tape mag should be on tape and include an SASE for its return." No simultaneous submissions. They use some previously published work. They publish chapbooks by invitation only, pay 15-20 copies. Editor sometimes comments on rejections. He says, "We publish as much as we can as often as we can, attempting to expand the area of poetic, visionary concentration. Going to the mailbox to find it full of work that ignores conventional limitations and is highly involved with creating new things, bringing new insights, is what makes us happy. It makes no difference if the material is marketable or not. If you're trying to get rich or famous or both don't send it to us. Overambition creates thin, superficial art."

ACTA VICTORIANA (I, II), 150 Charles St.,W., Toronto, ON M5S 1K9 Canada, appears twice a year. The magazine reaches the University of Toronto community as well as students of other universities. For poetry, one of its editors (who change yearly), Emma Thom, says they are **"wide open. No homophobic, sexist or racist content. No novels or epics please. No bad poetry."** They have published poetry by Irving Layton, Al Purdy, and John Riebetenz. As a sample she selected these lines from "Emblem" by Douglas Brown:

> *A figure for our lives is a dying elm*
> *In a green field. The library has a book*
> *With the ordinary charges, such as the oak*
> *But let this stand for our regretful realm.*

AV is magazine-sized, printed on glossy stock and they publish about 25 of 150 poems received from university students as well as other writers. Press run is 1,600. Subscription: $9. **Sample: $5 postpaid. Pays 1 copy. Submit "one poem per page without name or address; SASE and small bio accompanying."** Simultaneous submissions OK, and previously published poems "sometimes." She adds, "READ your work carefully. It's a real pity to see an otherwise good poem be trashed by a sloppy line at the end. We accept any form of poetry but only print that which has been carefully edited—it shows a respect for the English language which every writer should have. We will publish 'unknowns' but not big on responding with helpful hints."

ACUMEN MAGAZINE; EMBER PRESS (I, II), 6, The Mount, Higher Furzeham, Brixham, S. Devon TQ5 8QY England, phone 08045/51098, press founded 1971. *Acumen* founded 1984, poetry editor Patricia Oxley, is a "small press publisher of a general literary magazine with emphasis on good poetry." They want **"well-crafted, high quality, imaginative poems showing a sense of form. No experimental verse of an obscene type."** They have published poetry by Dannie Abse, Kathleen Raine, Ken Smith, Elizabeth Jennings, Roy Fuller, and Boris Pasternak. As a sample Mrs. Oxley selected these lines from "Spring Night" by William Oxley:

> *Spring night, night without suffering,*
> *Black mottled with stars.*
> *Peace's infinite clinging*

Acumen appears in April and October of each year, digest-sized, 100 pp. flat-spined, professionally printed with illustrations and ads. Of about 2,000 poems received they accept about 80. Press run is 500 for 250 subscriptions (12 libraries). $10 per issue, $25 subscription. **Sample: $10 postpaid. Pays "by negotiation" and one copy.** Simultaneous submissions OK, no previously published poems. **Reports in one month.** Patricia Oxley advises, "Read as many literary and poetry magazines as possible, as well as books of poetry both past and present."

ADARA (IV-Science Fiction); NOT YOUR AVERAGE ZINE (I), 905 Wild Circle, Clarkston, GA 30021, phone 404-659-1410, editor Elizabeth Shaw. *Adara*, founded 1986, is a magazine of fiction and poetry pertaining to Dr. Who, appearing twice a year. *Not Your Average Zine*, is a publication (founded 1987)

‡The double dagger before a listing indicates that the listing is new in this edition. New markets are often the most receptive to submissions.

"for people whose thoughts, ideas and experiences won't fit on a bumper sticker," using articles, reviews, short fiction and poetry, **welcoming work from beginners.** *Adara* wants poetry of **"up to 2 pages, single-spaced, any format, dealing with the universe of Doctor Who — as it was, is, might be, or seemed to be. Decision — point reflections are the most common."** The editor **does not want** " 'Mary Sue' romantic slush about the poet's desire to corner the Doctor! My main criterion for judging a poem is, 'Would I show this to Aunt Lucy? Would she turn pale and call for her salts?' Too much modern poetry is either obscure or obscene. Many of my multinational readers are quite young (13-19) and don't appreciate the abstract ... and their parents don't appreciate the obscene."** As a sample of the kind of poetry she likes, the editor selected these lines from "The Search for Diamonds Continues" by John Grey:

> *In the desert, the centuries should have*
> *made diamonds, glittering diadems scattered*
> *through the snow-faced yucca.*

The purpose of *Adara* is "to explore the personal relationships aboard the Tardis, from a friendship perspective." I have not seen either magazine, but she describes *Adara* as magazine-sized, 100 pages, typeset on a laser jet printer, with professional artwork and cover, using "swap" ads. There are about 50 subscribers. It sells for $8 per issue, **postpaid sample $8.** *NYAZ* is 8½ × 11, subscription $10 for 4 issues. **Sample copy $1. Send SASE for guidelines. Contributors receive one copy. Reports by return mail.** "I retype onto IBM/PC/AT — any readable format okay, but diskette on WANG PC, IBM Displaywriter 3 (3.10) or Word Perfect (5.0) welcomed ecstatically." Editor comments "always — I am also a writer and try to be constructive." For *NYAZ,* she says "typewritten work is preferred, but legibly handwritten material will be accepted. Remember, we're not submitting this zine for the Nobel Prize in Literature, so please contribute, whether or not you consider yourself 'a writer' or a perfect speller and/or grammarian, even if you're *positive* nobody could possibly be interested in what you have to say."**

ADASTRA PRESS (II), 101 Strong St., Easthampton, MA 01027, 413-527-3324, founded 1980 by Gary Metras, who says, "I publish poetry because I love poetry. I produce the books on antique equipment using antique methods because I own the equipment and because it's cheaper — I don't pay myself a salary — it's a hobby — it's **a love affair with poetry and printing of fine editions.** I literally sweat making these books and I want the manuscript to show me the author also sweated." All his books and chapbooks are **limited editions, handset, letterpress,** printed with handsewn signatures. "Chances of acceptance are slim. About 1 in 200 submissions is accepted, which means I only take 1 or 2 unsolicited mss a year." The chapbooks are in square-spine paper wrappers, cloth editions also handcrafted. He wants **"no rhyme, no religious. Poetry is communication first, although it is art. Long poems and thematic groups are nice for chapbooks. No subjects are tabu, but topics should be drawn from real life experiences. I include accurate dreams as real life."** Poets published include Judith Neeld, W.D. Ehrhart, Joseph Langland, and David Chorlton. Here are some lines from the poem, "Mill Town," in the chapbook, **The Ballad of Harmonica George & Other Poems,** by David Raffeld:

> *Every day a little more life beaten.*
> *Sons of creosote, daughters of wool and dye,*
> *children of the raw fiber,*
> *fathers of chain saw and pick up,*
> *grandfathers of marble, your names*
> *are dust to the lungs of this town.*

1-4 such chapbooks are brought out each year. Author is paid in copies, usually 10% of the print run. **"I only read chapbook manuscripts in the month of February, picking one or two for the following year. Queries, with a sample of 3-5 poems from a chapbook manuscript, are read throughout the year and if I like what I see in the sample, I'll ask you to submit the MS in February. Do not submit or query about full-length collections. I will only be accepting chapbook manuscripts of 12-18 double-spaced pages. Any longer collections would be a special invitation to a poet. If you want to see a typical handcrafted Adastra chapbook, send $5 and I'll mail a current title.** If you'd like a fuller look at what, how and why I do what I do, send check for $11.50 ($10 plus $1.50 postage and handling) and I'll mail a copy of **The Adastra Reader: Being the Collected Chapbooks in Facsimile with Author Notes, Bibliography and Comments on Hand Bookmaking,** published in 1987. This is a 247-page anthology covering Adastra publishing from 1979-1986."

ALWAYS submit MSS or queries with a stamped, self-addressed envelope (SASE) within your country or International Reply Coupons (IRCs) purchased from the post office for other countries.

ADRIFT (II, IV-Ethnic), 4D, 239 East 5th St., New York, NY 10003, founded 1980, editor Thomas McGonigle, who says, "The **orientation of magazine is Irish, Irish-American. I expect reader-writer knows and goes beyond Yeats, Kavanagh, Joyce, O'Brien." The literary magazine is open to all kinds of submissions, but does not want to see "junk." Simultaneous submissions OK.** Poets recently published include James Liddy, Thomas McCarthy, Francis Stuart, and Gilbert Sorrentino. As a sample, the editor selected this poem, "Mussel" by Beatrice Smedley:

> *eating with*
> *friend his other*
> *pleasure now*
> *more limpid*

Adrift appears twice a year and has a circulation of 1,000 with 200 subscriptions, 50 of which go to libraries. Price per issue is $4, subscription $8. **Sample: $5 postpaid. Magazine pays, rate varies; contributors receive 1 copy.** Magazine-sized, 32 pp., offset on heavy stock, cover matte card, saddle-stapled.

‡**THE ADROIT EXPRESSION (V,I)**, Box 73, Courtney, PA 15029, phone 412-379-8019, founded 1986, editor/publisher Xavier F. Aguilar, appears 3 times a year, and is **"open to all types of poetry, including erotica that is well written." They are currently overstocked and not accepting poetry submissions.** They have recently published poetry by Arthur Knight, Eda Howink, and Kathleen Clark. As a sample the editor selected the poem "Memory" by Bernard Hewitt:

> *laughing eyes*
> *linger vividly.*
> *she skipped down the hill,*
> *shining transparently.*

I have not seen an issue, but the editor describes it as magazine-sized, 3-5 pp., circulation 75. **Sample, postpaid: $4.** They sponsor an annual poetry competition "entry fee required; awards prizes (sometimes cash)." The editor says, "In publishing poetry—I try to exhibit the unique reality that we too often take for granted and acquaint as mediocre."

‡**ADVOCACY PRESS (IV-Children)**, P.O. Box 236, Santa Barbara, CA 93102, founded 1983, director of operations Kathy Araujo, publishes children's books using **"equity materials only, in 2 series: (1) an event in the life of a little-known woman of history that had significant impact (see Berta Benz and the Motorwagen** by Mindy Bingham); (2) self-esteem, self-sufficiency concept-story (see **Minou** by Bingham). **Must have rhythm and rhyme."** They have published **Father Gander** featuring nursery rhymes that are non-sexist and non-violent, such as in this sample:

> *Peter, Peter, pumpkin eater,*
> *Had a wife and wished to keep her.*
> *Treated her with fair respect,*
> *She stayed with him and hugged his neck.*

That book is available hardback for $16.45 postpaid. Their books average 32 pp. **Query with description of concept and sample. Simultaneous submissions and previously published poems OK. SASE required for reply. "Please do not submit manuscripts that do not meet our subject requirements."**

THE ADVOCATE (I), 301A Rolling Hills Park, Prattsville, NY 12468, Phone 518-299-3103, editor Remington Wright, founded 1987, is an advertiser-supported tabloid appearing bimonthly, 12,000 copies distributed free. They want **"nearly any kind of poetry, any length, but not religious or porno-graphic. Poetry ought to speak to people and not be so oblique as to have meaning only to the poet. If I had to be there to understand the poem, don't send it."** As a sample here are the opening lines from "Lighthouse" by Andria Parry Witman:

> *Wintry clouds billow over the old abandoned lighthouse.*
> *White weathered tower,*
> *Its paint blisters from the season's blows.*

Sample: $1.50 postpaid. Pays 3 copies. Reports in 6-8 weeks; publishes accepted material an average of 4-6 months after acceptance. No simultaneous submissions. Editor "often" comments on rejections. Accepts about 25% of poems received. Offers occasional contests.

AEGINA PRESS, INC.; UNIVERSITY EDITIONS (I, II), 59 Oak Lane, Spring Valley, Huntington WV 25704, founded 1983, publisher Ira Herman, is **primarily subsidy for poetry,** strongly committed to publishing new or established poets. Publishes subsidy titles under the University Editions imprint. Aegina has published non-subsidized poetry as well. Authors of books accepted on a non-subsidized basis receive a 15% royalty. "We try to provide a way for talented poets to have their collections published, which otherwise might go unpublished because of commercial, bottom-line considerations. Aegina Press will publish quality poetry that the large publishers will not handle because it is not commercially viable. We believe it is unfair that a poet has to have a 'name' or a following in order to have a book of poems accepted by a publisher. Poetry is the purest form of literary art, and it should be made available to those who appreciate it." Poets recently published include David Manzo and Dean Jarboe. The editor selected these sample lines from David Manzo's "The Gift":

> *You were an anchor*
> *To my balloon-like sensibilities;*
> *A mooring when I drifted sailless*
> *In disquietude and fear . . .*

 "**Most poetry books we accept are subsidized by the author (or an institution).** In return, the author receives all sales proceeds from the book, and any unsold copies left from the print run belong to the author. Minimum print run is 500 copies. We can do larger runs as well. Our marketing program includes submission to distributors, agents, other publishers, and bookstores and libraries." **Manuscripts should be typed and no shorter than 40 pages. There is no upper length limit. Simultaneous and photocopied submissions OK. Reporting time is 30 days for full manuscripts, 7-10 days for queries.** They publish perfect-bound (flat-spined) paperbacks with glossy covers. **Sample books are available for $5 each plus $1.50 postage and handling.**

AERIAL (II), Box 25642, Washington, DC, 20007, phone 202-333-1544, founded 1984, editor Rod Smith; editorial assistants Gretchen Johnson and Wayne Kline, a once- or twice-yearly publication. Issue #4 was a special issue on Douglas Messerli. They have recently published work by Carla Harryman, Eric Wirth, Charles Bernstein, Harrison Fisher, and Tina Darragh. The editor chose this sample from "My Ovaries Don't Have Enough Room" by Bruce Andrews:

> *perform to be unlike meaning*

The magazine is 6×9", offset, varies 60-180 pp. Circulation is 1,000. Single copy price is $6. **Sample available for $6 postpaid. Poets should submit 1-10 pages. Reporting time is 1 week-2 months and time to publication is 3-12 months.** Also looking for critical/political/philosophical writing.

AESTHETIC RAPTURE; THE 5 SENSES PRESS, PHILOSOPHICAL CORRESPONDENCE SOCIETY (I, IV-Themes), 5430 Churchward St., San Diego, CA 92114, phone 619-264-7525, founded 1988, poetry editor Francesco Sanfilippo, appears every 1-2 months using **"anything having to do with philosophy, and anything commenting upon the human condition. Maximum length 3 pp. Nothing sentimental, religious, trivial, repetitious, or common, unless it contains a philosophical message."** They have recently published poetry by Chris Brockman, Steve Jackson, Laura Magdalany, Darin Zimpel, and Pamella Neely. As a sample the editor selected these lines from "An Eye for an Eye" by himself:

> *but remember to watch out for those fools who play word games*
> *they're on lethal drugs called anxiety and fear*
> *afraid to escape and taste reality*
> *too inhibited to accept*
> *that the meaning of life is just*
> *pleasure.*

I have not seen the publication, but the editor describes it as 5-10 pp., magazine-sized, photocopied, with no artwork, graphics, or ads. "Instead, quotes and questions fill space between poems." Their press run is "less than 100" with about that many subscriptions of which 3 are libraries. Subscription: $10. **Sample: $1 postpaid. Pays copies and occasionally subscriptions. "I would definitely like cover letters explaining philosophies, the poets, and related material. Photos are desired, but optional. I report in less than two months with a personal letter including criticism.** I am not too busy to make friends with readers and contributors. For this purpose exists the Philosophical Correspondence Society, which is a direct and informal line of communication between you and I. The Chess Group has been aborted, and I no longer accept short stories. My personal philosophy entails fragments of and variations on hedonism, empiricism, materialism, nihilism, existentialism, relativism, and psychological egoism. I have deep interest in the ties between philosophy and linguistics, anthropology, neurology, and psychology. If you would like to submit relevant poetry and/or discuss philosophical issues, this is the editor to contact." **Simultaneous submissions are accepted.**

‡AETHLON: THE JOURNAL OF SPORT LITERATURE (IV-Sports), East Tennessee State University, Johnson City, TN 37614-0002, founded 1983, general editor, Don Johnson, Professor of English, ETSU, poetry editor Robert W. Hamblin, Professor of English, Southeast Missouri State University,

Market categories: (I) Beginning; (II) General; (III) Prestige; (IV) Specialized; (V) Closed.

Cape Girardeau, MO 63701. (Submit poetry to this address.) *Aethlon* publishes a variety of sport-related literature, including scholarly articles, fiction, poetry, personal essays, and reviews; 6-10 poems per issue; two issues annually, fall and spring. **Subject matter must be sports-related; no restrictions regarding form, length, style or purpose. They do not want to see "doggerel, cliché-ridden, or oversentimental" poems.** Some poets recently published are Neal Bowers, Joseph Duemer, Robert Fink, Jan Mordenski, H.R. Stonebeck, Jim Thomas, Stephen Tudor, and Don Welch. As a sample, the editor selected the following lines by Hillel Schwartz:

> Ground is all there
> is as you feel yourself grow old,
> and your small flights from it,
> a foot or two at the most,
> this jogging a consolation
> for the rest of the running,

The magazine is digest-sized, offset printed, flat-spined, with illustrations and some ads, 200 pp. per issue. Circulation is 1,000 of which 750 are subscriptions, 250 to libraries. Price per issue is $12.50; subscription is included with membership ($30) in the Sport Literature Association. **Sample $12.50 postpaid. Contributors receive 10 offprints and a copy of the issue in which their poem appears. Submissions are reported on in 6-8 weeks and the backlog time is 6-12 months; "only typed MSS with SASE considered." Will accept simultaneous submissions.**

AFRICA WORLD PRESS (IV-Ethnic), Box 1892, Trenton, NJ 08607, founded 1979, editor Kassahun Checole, publishes poetry by Africans, African-Americans, Caribbean and Latin Americans. Two poetry publications by Africa World Press are: **Under A Soprano Sky**, by Sonia Sanchez and **From the Pyramid to the Projects** by Askia Muhammad Toure, winner of an American Book Award for 1989. **Authors receive 7½% royalty; number of copies negotiable. Considers simultaneous submissions. Send SASE for catalog.**

AFRO-HISPANIC REVIEW (IV-Ethnic), Romance Languages, #143 Arts & Sciences, University of Missouri, Columbia, MO 65211, founded 1982, uses some **poetry related to Afro-Hispanic life and issues.** Appears 3 times a year. **Pays 5 copies.**

AGADA (IV-Ethnic, translations), 2020 Essex St., Berkeley, CA 94703, phone 415-848-0965, founded 1981, editor-in-chief Reuven Goldfarb, "**is a Jewish literary magazine replete with illustrative graphic art, which is published semiannually." They want "quality work with Jewish subject matter or sensibility. Send SASE for guidelines. We welcome original lyric or narrative work, translations of Scriptural or other Hebrew, Yiddish, or Ladino poetry** — or from any language which has successfully incorporated at least some aspects of the Jewish experience. Form doesn't matter as long as the **forms are used well — with some awareness of what masters of that technique have achieved. Don't like: inappropriate line breaks; poems that degenerate into prose — that break rhythm — that never really take off; loading excessive meaning on key words which are often placed on a line of their own; verse that is preponderantly didactic; clichés. Admire: fresh ways of looking at familiar material; original use of language and metaphor; fusing various levels of meaning allusively; real humor; tenderness." They have published poetry by Arlene Maass. and Paul Raboff. The editor selected these sample lines by Ben-Zion Niditch from "Haifa":

> What holds me here
> an unshaven man
> once a refugee of night
> now returned to this port
> thinking of his illuminated life
> by the beach blue white.

The $7 \times 10''$ professionally-printed, saddle-stapled magazine has a circulation of 1,000, 250 subscriptions of which about 35-40 are libraries. Each issue uses about 14 pp. of poetry. They receive over 200 submissions per year, use "a couple of dozen," have as much as a 6-month backlog. **Sample: $7.50 for current issue, $6.50 for back issue. Subscription: $14/2 copies. Submissions acknowledged. Submit up to 6 poems, typed, double-spaced. Photocopy OK. Contributor guidelines available. Include SASE and return postcard. Advise if submitted elsewhere or if it has been published elsewhere.** "No objection to republishing if there is no serious overlap in audience." Likewise, a commitment to request credit being given to *Agada* if it should be published again **is appreciated. Reports within 3-4 months. Payment in copies. The editor advises, "Learn from**

Use the General Index to find the page number of a specific publication or publisher.

the greats, pay attention to small details in daily life, play with words, listen deeply."

AGASSIZ REVIEW (II), (formerly *Streamlines*), 207 Lind Hall, 207 Church St. SE, Minneapolis, MN 55455, founded 1979, poetry editor changes annually, is an annual using **"all types of poetry."** *Agassiz Review* is magazine-sized, 40 pp., saddle-stapled, professionally printed, with matte card cover. Of "45 manuscript packets received we accept 10-12 poems." **"MSS should be no longer than 3,000 words, typed and double-spaced; include page number and abbreviated title at top of each page. Name only on cover letter, along with title of submission, short bio, and phone number. Include SASE."** Reports in 6 months.

AGENDA EDITIONS; AGENDA (II), 5 Cranbourne Ct., Albert Bridge Rd., London, England SW11 4PE, founded 1959, poetry editors William Cookson and Peter Dale. *Agenda* is a $7 \times 5''$, 80 pp. (of which half are devoted to poetry), quarterly (1 double, 2 single issues per year), circulation 1,500-3,000, 1,500 subscriptions of which 450 are libraries. They receive some 2,000 submissions per year, use 40, have a 5-month backlog. **Pays £10 per page for poetry. Sample: £4 ($8) postpaid.** "We seek poetry of 'more than usual emotion, more than usual order' (Coleridge). We publish special issues on particular authors such as T. S. Eliot, Ezra Pound, David Jones, Stanley Burnshaw, Thomas Hardy, etc." Some of the poets who have appeared in *Agenda* are Peter Dale, Geoffrey Hill, Seamus Heaney, C. H. Sisson, Patricia McCarthy and W. S. Milne. The editors selected these sample lines (poet unidentified):

> *How will you want the snowy impermanence of ash,*
> *your dust, like grass-seed, flighted over heathland,*
> *drifting in spinneys where the boughs clash,*
> *with matted needles laying waste beneath them.*

Reports in 1 month. Pays. To submit book MS, no query necessary, "as little as possible" in cover letter. SAE and IRC coupon for return. Reports within a month. Payment in copies. The editors say poets "should write only if there is an intense desire to express something. They should not worry about fashion."

AGNI (II), Boston University, 236 Bay State Rd., Boston, MA 02215, phone 617-353-5389, founded 1972, editor Askold Melnyczuk, wants "wonderful poetry." They have recently published poetry by Seamus Heaney, Edwin Honig, Derek Walcott, Tony Harrison, Ai, William Harmon, and Rita Dove. As a sample I selected the first of 16 stanzas of "In The Gap" by Glyn Maxwell:

> *The road is dark and wet and red.*
> *I never went. I never was.*
> *It was an insult, what you said*
> *and you shall bleed for it, because*
> *I am the stranger up ahead.*

Agni is 300+ pp, flat-spined, digest-sized, typeset, with glossy card cover with art, appearing twice a year. They take "1 out of 1,000" poems received. Their press run is 2,000 with 500 subscriptions. Subscription: $12. **Sample: $7 postpaid. Pays $8-10 per page, maximum $50, plus 3 copies. Submit 3-5 poems. They will consider simultaneous submissions but not previously published poems. Reports in 1-4 months.**

AGOG PUBLICATIONS; AGOG; AGOG AGO GO (I, IV-Humor), 116 Eswyn Rd., Tooting, London, SW17 8TN Great Britain, phone 01-682-0745, founded 1988, editor Edward Leonardo Jewasinski. Both *Agog* and *Agog ago go* appear 4 times a year, the first as a magazine, the second as a P.C. (IBM compatible) computer disk (also available for the BBC microcomputer). They want **"humor, short and concise, accessible. Anything of a humorous nature will be given special consideration. We prefer poets to provide original artwork with their poems whenever possible.** *Agog* is often handtinted! *Agog ago go* now has CGA monochrome graphics, we welcome artwork, visual poetry and small art/poetry programmes animations, articles on disk (360k)." As a sample the editor selected these lines from "Poxy Poets" by Neil K. Henderson:

> *Poxy poets, take your hearts*
> *Your flowers and your Cupid's darts*
> *Your sighing arts and fretful farts*
> *And shove them up your nether parts*

Agog press run is 1,000 with 50 subscriptions. Subscription: $18. **Sample: $5 postpaid** (*Agog ago go* $15, $50 for 4 editions). **"We welcome submissions for** *Agog* **or** *Agog ago go* **on disk in the following formats (text only): PC 360K and 720K, Amiga, ST and Apple Mac." Pays 1 copy and at discretion of editor. Reports** *same day.* Editor sometimes comments on rejections, or for $5 fee, "explain that you want detailed assessment, just ask." Agog Publications publishes about 8 chapbooks per year, 50 pp. The editor says, "Poets must be industrious and persistent. *Agog ago* *go* will bring literature to your computer. *Agog* will be the premier poetry magazine in the English language within five years."

AG-PILOT INTERNATIONAL MAGAZINE (IV-Nature/rural/ecology, humor), 405 Main St., Mt. Vernon, WA 98273, phone 206-336-9737, editor Tom Wood, "is intended to be a fun-to-read, technical, as well as humorous and serious publication for the ag pilot and operator." It appears monthly, 48-64 pp., circulation 7,600. Interested in **agri-aviation (crop dusting) related poetry only." Buys 1 per issue, pays $10-50.**

AHSAHTA PRESS (IV-Regional), 1910 University Dr., Boise, ID 83725, phone 208-385-1246, founded 1975. This is a project of Boise State University to publish **contemporary poetry of the American West.** But, say editors Tom Trusky, Orv Burmaster and Dale Boyer, "**Spare us paens to the pommel, Jesus in the sagebrush, haiku about the Eiffel Tower, 'nice' or 'sweet' poems.**" The work should "**draw on the cultures, history, ecologies of the American West.**" They publish collections (60 pp.) of individual poets in handsome flat-spined paperbacks with plain matte covers, with an appreciative introduction, about 3 per year. Occasionally they bring out an anthology on cassette of their authors. And they have published an anthology (94 pp.) Women Poets of the West, with an introduction by Ann Stanford. Some of their poets are Susan Deal, Leo Romero, David Baker, Richard Speakes, Philip St. Clair, Judson Crews. Here are some lines from Marnie Walsh's "Dakota Winter," in the collection **A Taste of the Knife**:

> it is where the long-fingered
> hand of winter
> clangs down a crystal lid
> to the sound of snow

You may submit only during their January-March reading period each year—a sample of 15 of your poems with SASE. They will report in about 2 months. Multiple and simultaneous submissions, photocopy, dot-matrix OK. If they like the sample, they'll ask for a book MS. If it is accepted, **you get 25 copies of the 1st and 2nd printings and a 25% royalty commencing with the 3rd.** They seldom comment on the samples, frequently on the MSS. Send SASE for their catalog and order a few books, if you don't find them in your library. "Old advice but true: read what we publish before submitting. **75% of the submissions we receive should never have been sent to us. Save stamps, spirit, and sweat.**" See also listing for *Cold Drill.*

AILERON PRESS; AILERON: A LITERARY JOURNAL; VOWEL MOVEMENT (II), P.O. Box 891, Austin, TX 78767-0891, founded 1980, editors Edwin Buffaloe and Cynthia Farar. *Aileron* is a periodical (at least once a year, sometimes twice) consisting **of poetry and occasional short fiction,** with some art. **The editors are looking for "poetry that moves us, that makes us want to read it again and again. We are especially keen on innovative uses of language—the unexpected word and the unusual cadence. We would like to see more poetic craft displayed, and, though not inimical to rhymed work, feel that few contemporary poets handle rhyme well.**" The editor selected these lines by Elkion Tumbalé as an example of what he likes:

> Blue cup modal gorges
> Lurk frondly on
> Orchid Zontal
> Obsidian felines

Recent poets published there include Anselm Hollo, Simon Perchik, Hal J. Daniel III, and Tomaz Salamun. It's a digest-sized format, saddle-stapled, typeset (in small type), b/w original line art up to 8 × 10, stiff cover with art. Circulation is 350, with 25 subscriptions. **Sample $3.50 postpaid,** subscription $12 for 4 issues. Each issue contains 40-60 pages of poetry garnered from 400-600 submissions each year of which 60-100 are used, 6 month backlog. **All formats acceptable; must have name & address on each page; payment is 1 copy; no limitations on form, length or subject matter; guidelines available for SASE. Reporting time: 6 weeks.** *Vowel Movement,* "a 'pataphysical journal,' is published occasionally as a special issue of *Aileron.* It contains **avantgarde humor, satire, and work that is outrageous or experimental in nature.**"

AIM MAGAZINE (I, IV-Social issues, ethnic), 7308 S. Eberhart Ave., Chicago, IL 60619, phone 312-874-6184, founded 1974, poetry editor Henry Blakely, is a magazine-sized quarterly, circulation 10,000, glossy cover, "**dedicated to racial harmony and peace.**" They use 3-4 poems ("poetry with social significance mainly") in each issue, **paying $3/poem. They ask for 32 lines average length, but most poems in the sample issues I have seen were much shorter, and some were by children.** They have recently published poems by Loretta A. Hawkins, J. Douglas Studer, Wayne Dowdy, and Maria De-Guzman. The editor selected the third stanza of "Afrique Unique" by Loretta A. Hawkins:

> In all of history, have yet I read
> where man's not been allowed to

mourn his dead
where truth has in a heavy blanket hid
where God has seen yet not a word has said.
They have 3,000 subscriptions of which 15 are libraries. Subscription: $8; per issue: $2. **Sample: $3 postpaid. They receive only about 30 submissions per year of which they use half. Photocopy, simultaneous submissions OK, no dot-matrix. Reports in 3-6 weeks.** The editor's advice: "Read the work of published poets."

AIREINGS (II, IV-Women), 24, Brudenell Rd., Leeds, West Yorkshire LS6 1BD, UK, phone 0532-785893, founded 1980, editor Jean Barker. "Poems acceptable from all over the world. **Primarily like women's work** as we are a Women's Co-op running the mag and like to redress the balance a bit, but we are **happy to receive work by men also. Poetry on all subjects. We do draw a line on sexist/racist stuff, but we like a broad spectrum of work as long as it is not too long, as we only run to 40 pp.**" They have recently published poetry by Geoffrey Holloway, Janet Faraday and Pauline Kirk. As a sample the editor selected these lines (poet unidentified):
Fat bees buzzed through drowsy afternoons
While 'planes duelled above,
gleaming like armoured knights in sunlight.
We sat in gardens cheering them on.
The magazine appears twice a year, "illustrated by our own artist. No ads yet, but we may have to later, if we are under extreme financial pressure." They publish about 5% of the poetry received. *Aireings* is digest-sized, 40 pp., saddle-stapled, photocopied from typescript with matte b/w card cover. They print 300-350 copies for 100 subscriptions (10 libraries) and shelf sales. It costs £1. per copy, which includes UK postage (overseas £3.50). **Pays 2 copies. "Work should be typed if possible—just legible if not."** Simultaneous submissions and previously published (if **not in the North of England) OK. Reports "after our editorials in January and July."**

AJAX POETRY LETTER (I), % Edward McCloud, P.O. Box 444, Jacksonville, FL 32201, phone 904-389-9886, founded 1988, editor Edward Ansel McCloud, is a monthly 11 × 17″ (folds to a 4-p signature) publication **using poetry of up to 40 lines and 40 characters wide. "I want it alive, concise, and moving; looking for fresh styles. No ill-conceived, boring, contrived, poor craft, poor thought. I want submissions from the heart according to the true spirit of poetry. No bending for me or anyone."** *APL* has recently published poetry by Herman Clark, Ana Pine, Ruth E. Cunliffe, and Donald Clark. As a sample the editor selected these lines from "Uninvited Sleeper" by Amigo:
I slept as never before, thistledown on a breeze, nothing
between me and the white cheek of the moon
but my dreams and they danced softer than beams among pulses of perfect stars.
He will consider previously published poems. Pays 1 copy.

ALABAMA LITERARY REVIEW (II), English Dept., Troy State University, Troy, AL 36082, phone 205-566-3000, ext. 3286, poetry editor Ed Hicks, a biannual, **wants poetry that is "imagistic—but in motion. Will look at anything."** They have published poetry by Larry McLeod, Coleman Barks, Leo Luke Marcello, George Ellenbogen, Roald Hoffman, Wayne Hogan, Elizabeth Dodd, and James Ashbrook Perkins. I selected these sample lines, by Paul Grant from "Getaway":
Mr. Piano man in the dark
listening to his hands
wanting words to hang in air
The beautifully printed 100 pp., 6 × 9″ magazine, matte cover with art, b/w art and some colored pages inside, receives 300 submissions per year, uses 30, has a 2 month backlog. **Will consider simultaneous submissions. Sample: $4 postpaid. Query not necessary. Reports in 1-2 months. Pays copies. Sometimes comments on rejections.**

ALASKA QUARTERLY REVIEW (II), Department of English, University of Alaska at Anchorage, 3221 Providence Dr., Anchorage, AK 99508, phone 907-786-1750. Started in 1981, Ronald Spatz and J. Liszka, executive editors; Thomas Sexton, poetry editor. "A journal devoted to contemporary literary art. **We publish both traditional and experimental fiction, poetry, essays and criticism on contemporary writing, literature and philosophy of literature."** They publish two double-issues a year, **each using about 25 pp. of poetry.** They have a circulation of 1,000; 200 subscribers, of which 25 are libraries, $4 an issue, $8 per subscription, **$4 for a sample (postpaid).** They receive up to 2,000 submissions each year, of which they take about 50. **Pay depends on funding. They take up to 4 months to report, and there is usually no comment on MSS. No query. Manuscripts are not read during May, June, July and the first half of August.**

ALBATROSS; THE ANABIOSIS PRESS (II, IV-Nature), 125 Horton Ave., Englewood, FL 34223, founded 1985, editors Richard Smyth and Richard Brobst. *Albatross* appears in the spring and fall, 32-44 pp., **"We consider the albatross to be a metaphor for an environment that must survive. This is not to say that we publish only environmental or nature poetry, but that we are biased toward such subject matters. We publish mostly free verse 200 lines/poem maximum, and we prefer a narrative style, but again, this is not necessary. We do not want trite rhyming poetry which doesn't convey a deeply felt experience in a mature expression with words."** They have recently published poetry by A.McA. Miller, Lenny Dellarocca, Walter Griffin, Duane Locke and Eileen Eliot. As a sample, the editors selected these lines by Stephen Meats:

> On the prairie,
> fences are coming down, highways are blowing away,
> road cuts are filling in. Elk, grizzly, buffalo, and
> wolf materialize out of the sod.

The magazine is 5½ × 8½" offset from typescript with matte card cover, some b/w drawings, and, in addition to the poetry, has an interview with a poet in each issue. Circulation 500, 75 subscriptions of which 10 are to libraries. Many complimentary copies are sent out to bookstores, poets and libraries. Subscription: $5/2 issues. **Sample $3 postpaid. Send SASE for guidelines. Pays 2 copies. Reports in 2-3 months, has 6-12 month backlog. "Poems should be typed single-spaced, with name and address in left corner and length in lines in right corner. Photocopies are accepted, but we do not appreciate simultaneous submissions."** Also holds a chapbook contest. **Submit 16-20 pp. poetry, any theme, any style, between September 1 and December 31. Include name, address, and phone number on the page. Charge $5 reading fee (check payable to *Albatross*). Winner receives $50 and 25 copies of his/her published chapbook. All entering receive one issue of *Albatross* and a free copy of the winning chapbook.** Comments? "We expect a poet to read as much contemporary poetry as possible."

THE ALCHEMIST (II), Box 123, Lasalle, Quebec, Canada H8R 3T7, founded 1974, poetry editor Marco Fraticelli, is a 100 pp., small digest-sized, flat-spined, handsomely printed and illustrated with b/w drawings, irregularly-issued literary journal, using mostly poetry. **No restrictions on form, style or content, (though in the issue I examined, #8, there is a section of haiku and a useful catalog of haiku markets. Considers simultaneous submissions.** They have a print-run of 500, 200 subscriptions, of which 30 are libraries, and they send out some 200 complimentary copies. Subscription $12 for 4 issues, $3 per issue. They have a 6 month backlog. **Sample: $2 postpaid. Reports in 1 month. Payment: 2 copies.** I selected these sample lines, the opening of "Dreams" by A. D. Winans:

> the dreams will not leave me alone
> they come and go through my skull
> opening the memory bank
> like an overfilled suitcase

‡ALCHEMY PRESS; FRAGMENTS (II, IV-Spiritual, political, ethnic, fantasy/horror), 1789 McDonald Ave., Brooklyn, NY 11230, phone 718-339-0184, founded 1985, editor/publisher Fred Calero, who says, **"I am interested in poetry that shakes conventional thought. A poetry that illuminates the soul and rattles the spirit. I am also interested in work that deals with the problems of good and evil. Also anything that is simple yet profound. I want honest poetry. There is so much poetry today that is contrived, and I just don't have the energy to read it all."** They have recently published poetry by Richard Kostelanetz, Jim Feast, and Eve Teitelbaum. As a sample the editor selected these lines from his own "Rage":

> There is a place where a dark flower blooms in the blackness of his mind
> Full of rage and savagery, he follows his destiny, a poetry too dark to comprehend.
> Like blue jays picking at the bones, in the dampness of her shallow grave.

Fragments is a quarterly. I have not seen an issue, but the editor describes it as digest-sized, saddle-stapled, photocopied. Press run: 1,000 for 400 subscriptions of which 20 are libraries. "I receive about 1,500 poems yearly and use about 15%." Subscription: $12. **Sample, postpaid: $4. Send SASE for guidelines. Pays 25 copies. "Five poems at a time is fine. The poet's name and address should appear on each and every poem." Simultaneous submissions and previously published poems OK. "The backload is tremendous,"** but the editor usually responds in 2 months. **For chapbook publication send 10 sample poems, cover letter, bio, and other publications. Pays 50 copies. Sample chapbook: $5.** Editor comments on submissions "at times, if a poem seems to need a little more work, I may offer suggestions." He says, "Read, read, read. Be familiar with the great poets of various cultures. Look for work that has survived the test of time. Never limit yourself, like so many poets do, to just reading their contemporary writers. Never limit yourself to just poetry when reading. Be awake to the world around you and thrive."

‡ALGILMORE (I), 125 N. Main St., Galena, IL 61036, phone 815-777-9688, founded 1968 as Studio Five, thought-merchant Jay Son, conducts new age sessions and publishes video tapes, cassettes, and flyers, **paying no less than $10 per use for "higher thoughts—New Age—no restriction on style, length, subject, good teaching thoughts. Longhand acceptable, spelling mistakes OK. Charity important. No jokes, militant, smut. I am more interested in the message than in 'better-known poets.'"** Allow 30 days for report. As a sample the editor selected these lines:

> *We loved their arts*
> *and*
> *Took their lands.*

ALIVE NOW!; POCKETS; WEAVINGS (IV-Religious, children); THE UPPER ROOM (V), 1908 Grand Ave., Box 189, Nashville, TN 37202, phone 615-340-7200. This publishing company brings out about 20 books a year and four magazines: *The Upper Room, alive now!, Pockets* and *Weavings.* Of these, two use freelance poetry. *Pockets, Devotional Magazine for Children*, which comes out 11 times a year, circulation 68,000-70,000, is for children 6-12, "offers stories, activities, prayers, poems—all **geared to giving children a better understanding of themselves as children of God. Some of the material is not overtly religious but deals with situations, special seasons and holidays, ecological concerns from a Christian perspective."** It uses 3-4 pp. of poetry per issue. **Sample: $1.70 plus 85¢ postage. Ordinarily 24 line limit on poetry. Pays $25-50. Send SASE for themes and guidelines.** The other magazine which uses poetry is *alive now!*, a bimonthly, circulation 75,000, for a general Christian audience interested in reflection and meditation. **Sample and guidelines free. They buy 30 poems a year, avant-garde and free verse. Submit 5 poems, 10-45 lines. Pays $10-25.** *The Upper Room* magazine does not accept poetry.

ALLARDYCE, BARNETT PUBLISHERS; POETICA (V), Barnett Publishers, 14 Mount St., Lewes BN7 1HL, England, founded 1982, editorial director Anthony Barnett. Allardyce, Barnett publishes important substantial collections by current English language poets; "our financial situation does not currently allow for an extension of this programme into other areas. **We cannot at this time encourage unsolicited manuscripts."** Some of the better-known poets they have published are J. H. Prynne, Andrew Crozier, Douglas Oliver, and Veronica Forrest-Thomson. The press usually publishes simultaneous cloth and paper editions, currently less than 1 per year, with an average page count of 320, digest-sized. In the U.S., their books can be obtained through Small Press Distribution in Berkeley, CA. Also publishes the occasional review *Poetica*, founded 1989.

ALLEGHENY PRESS (II), Box 220, Elgin, PA 16413, founded 1967, poetry editor Bonnie Henderson, publishes **poetry books.** The editor selected these sample lines:

> *You ride to me upon a different horse*
> *Special riding tricks, lofty circus stunts*
> *Come mount the steed, together we shall fly*
> *Dark silhouettes of love against the sky.*

They have published 4 books of poetry, 2 anthologies, and 4 chapbooks since 1967. **Query with 2 samples. Cover letter should tell how many pages are estimated for the proposed book. Replies to queries in 2 weeks, to submissions (if invited) in 2 weeks. Simultaneous submissions, photocopy OK, no dot-matrix. Publishes on 10% royalty contract plus 2 copies. Editor sometimes comments on rejections, but "We don't like people to send MS to us expecting** *AP to improve their skills."* **Sample book $2, chapbook $1.** She comments, "Poetry has never paid its way in our publishing program. We still plan to publish meritorious (as suits the fancy of our editors) poetry even though it represents a financial loss, not to mention time and effort of our make-up and editorial staff. We do not like poets who write poetry but do not read other's poetry or buy books of poetry." They occasionally publish anthologies of previously published poetry.

ALLEGHENY REVIEW (I, IV-Students), Box 32, Allegheny College, Meadville, PA 16335, founded 1983, editors Nancy Williams and Erik Schuckers. "Each year *Allegheny Review* compiles and publishes a review of the nation's best **undergraduate literature.** It is entirely composed of and by college undergraduates and is nationally distributed both as a review and as a classroom text, particularly suited to creative writing courses. We will print **poetry of appreciable literary merit on any topic, submitted by college undergraduates. No limitations except excessive length (2-3 pp.)** as we wish to represent as many authors as possible, although exceptions are made in areas of great quality and interest." They have published poetry by Eric Sanborn, Cheryl Connor, Rick Alley, and Kristi Coulter and selected these lines by Eric Schwerer (Allegheny College) as a sample:

> *I drop to the ground*
> *and make a melting slushy angel in the snow*
> *coming up heavy with water*
>
> *She rolls her eyes*

> *I remind her too much of potato soup*
> *and other clumsy memories*

The *Review* appears in a 6×9", flat-spined, professionally-printed format, b/w photo on glossy card cover. **Submissions should be accompanied by a letter "telling the college poet is attending, year of graduation, any background, goals and philosophies that the author feels are pertinent to the work submitted." Reports 1-2 months following deadline. Submit 3 to 5 poems, typed, photocopy, dot-matrix OK. Sample: $3.50 and 11 × 18" SASE. Poem judged best in the collection earns $50-75 honorarium.** "Ezra Pound gave the best advice: 'Make it new.' We're seeing far too much imitation; there's already been a Sylvia Plath, a Galway Kinnell. Don't be afraid to try new things. Be innovative. Also, traditional forms are coming 'back in style,' or so we hear. Experiment with them; write a villanelle, a sestina, or a sonnet. And when you submit, please take enough pride in your work to do so professionally. Handwritten or poorly-typed and proofed submissions definitely convey an impression, a negative one."

ALLY PRESS CENTER (V), 524 Orleans St., St. Paul, MN 55107, founded 1973, owner Paul Feroe, **publishes and distributes work by Robert Bly, including chapbooks and cassette tapes. Two to three times a year a complete catalog is mailed out along with information about Bly's reading and workshop schedule. The press is not accepting unsolicited mss at this time. Book catalog is free on request.**

ALMS HOUSE PRESS (I), 130 Madison Ave., 6th Fl., New York, NY 10016, founded 1985, poetry editors Lorraine De Gennaro and Alana Sherman, **holds an annual poetry competition with $6 entry fee (contestants receive a copy of a chapbook). "We have no preferences with regard to style as long as the poetry is high caliber. We like to see previous publication in the small press, but we are open to new writers. We look for variety and excellence and are open to new and experimental forms as well as traditional forms. Any topics as long as the poems are not whiny or too depressing, pornographic or religious."** They have recently published chapbooks by Martin Anderson and Harry Waitzman. As a sample they selected these lines by Evelyn Sharenov:

> *Standing complacent and half-asleep*
> *In her yard, caressed by skewed wild flowers*
> *Unfashionable and pregnant, she grins for the camera*
> *Sun streams into her hair*
> *Down her shoulders, out her fingers*

Submit 16-24 pp. chapbook including all front matter, title page and table of contents, between March 1 and May 31. Name, address and phone number should apear on title page only. Winner receives 50 copies. Send SASE for current rules. Sample copy: $4 postpaid. They offer a critical and editorial service for $25.

ALOHA, THE MAGAZINE OF HAWAII AND THE PACIFIC (IV-Regional), Suite 309, 49 S. Hotel St., Honolulu, HI 96813, editor Cheryl Chee Tsutsumi, is a bimonthly (every 2 months) "consumer magazine with Hawaii and Pacific focus," Circulation 65,000. **"Not interested in lengthy poetry. Poems should be limited to 100 words or less. Subject should be focused on Hawaii."** Poems are matched to color photos, so it is "difficult to say" how long it will be between acceptance and publication. As a sample the editor selected these lines from "Beautiful Hawaii," by Ann Pape:

> *The valley whispers to its gentle people*
> *who revere beauty and harvest.*
> *It cradles them.*

ALOHA is magazine-sized, 80 pp., flat-spined, elegantly printed on glossy stock with many full-color pages, glossy card cover in color. They publish 6 of more than 50 poems received per year. **Sample: $2.95 postpaid. Send SASE for guidelines. Pays $25 plus 1 copy (and up to 10 at discount). MS should be double-spaced, typed, name, address and phone number on all MSS. Reports within 60 days.**

ALPHA BEAT SOUP (I, IV-Form/Style), 68 Winter Ave., Scarborough, ON M1K 4M3 Canada, founded 1987, poetry editor David Christy, appears twice a year **emulating the Beat literary tradition.** *Alpha Beat Soup* is a literary journal in the spirit of the '50s and '60s. Christy says that **25% of each issue is devoted to little known or previously unpublished poets.** They have recently published works by Joy Walsh, Pradip Choudhuri, Joan Reid, Erling Friis-Baastad, Jack Micheline, Janine Pommy Vega, and Diane Wakoski. As a sample the editor selected these lines by Peter Bakowski:

> *art goes wherever the "no entry" signs plead,*
> *plays happily in the universe of a vacant lot.*
> *art dances the arabesque with old steamships and streetcars*

ABS is 7×8½", 50-75 pp., photocopied from IBM laser printer, card cover offset, graphics included. They will use 50% of most poetry received. Press run is 300 for 115 subscriptions (11 of them libraries). Subscription: $5. Single copy: $3. **Sample: $5 (includes first-class postage). Pays**

Close-up
Gwendolyn Brooks
Poet

The Chicago Picasso, 1986
Set,
seasoned,
sardonic still,
I continue royal among you.
I astonish you still.
You never knew what I am.
Mostly
you almost supposed I almost Belong; that I
have a Chicago Beauty, that I
have a booming Beauty.

I tell you that although royal
I am a mongrel opera strange in the street
I am radical, rhymeless—
   but warranted!

Surely I shall remain.

(From **The Near-Johannesburg Boy and Other Poems**, The David Company, 1986)

Gwendolyn Brooks is Black. The Pulitzer Prize-winning poet is proud of that, and through her chosen medium, she strives to make other Blacks proud too. Her career, spanning almost half a century, has always been devoted to detailing Black experiences. In that capacity, her message has stayed the same, but her style of writing that message has not.

Brooks says she started putting rhymes together as early as age seven, and the encouragement and support she received from her parents contributed to her hobby being more than just a passing fancy. "They thought anything I wrote was perfection."

Her first book, **A Street in Bronzeville**, debuted in 1945. It was followed by **Annie Allen**, for which she received the 1950 Pulitzer prize. These works demonstrate the controlled, traditional European forms she used in the first half of her career. But that style of writing, along with her outlook on life, changed in 1967 when, in the midst of the Civil Rights movement, she attended a Black writers conference at Nashville's Fisk University. "I went to that conference and found some young Black poets who felt the old way of expressing yourself when it came to race matters was faulty. I was favoring a kind of pleading, begging sound, and these young poets would have none of that." As a result of that visit, she consciously made the effort to transform her poetry to make it count for Blacks. It became freer, more direct, and more accessible to a listening audience concerned about problems in the Black community.

Brooks describes Black poetry as being "written by Blacks, about Blacks, to Blacks," though she does not purposely limit herself to only Black poetry. "If I get excited about something, hear something, or believe something, and it stirs me, I go to the table with no concern about who I'm writing for. However, I do have many things to say to Blacks. A poem such as 'To Those of My Sisters Who Kept Their Naturals' (a tribute to Black women who resist the temptations of hair straighteners and skin bleaches) could only be [directly] addressed to my own women folk." However, she concedes the poem also disperses a universal message, being that people must accept and be proud of their origins.

Many familiar with Brooks' poetry feel she has not received from the white literary community the respect due to her. Brooks disagrees. "It was not a jury of Blacks that gave me a Pulitzer prize in 1950. So much has been made of this business that I have not had my due. I believe I've had a lot of attention," she says, citing her string of awards and honorary degrees.

Currently she is working on several projects, including a sequel to her 1972 autobiography **Report from Part One**; a book entitled **Children Coming Home**, which depicts adolescent trials and tribulations; and **Old**, a project sparked by Brooks' realization she has passed middle age. **Old** ponders the "pluses and minuses of being old. I want to have fun exploring them."

Beginning poets need to watch out for and avoid clichés, says Brooks. "Surely [an expression such as] 'the wind howls' has been used enough. I've always claimed that if they listen and put that personal ear to the wind, they'll hear something besides howling. This is where the personal touch comes in." Her remedy for such triteness or imitation rests within the art of revision. "I believe in revising everything you write. By that I mean go over every line. No matter how much I admire Adrienne Rich, Sylvia Plath, Sterling Brown or Langston Hughes, I don't want to sound like any of them. I want my work to be mine."

Brooks also recommends conferences and workshops for poets whose development is still in the early growth stages, saying she thinks they are helpful, but adds, "there comes a time when you've been at it a long time and you don't feel the need to ask your neighbor, 'how does that line sound to you?' I think by the time you've written steadily for a long time, your own ear ought to be reliable.

"I do admire subtlety [in a poem] and feel it has its uses. A little mystery is fascinating," says Brooks, "but too much is irritating. I don't believe a poet should venture into obscurity. That's most annoying to most of the people in the world, except for that little group of poets that are practicing it—they *love* each other."

All in all, Brooks insists a poet must write from the soul to be truly successful, saying those who write solely for publication or money possess the wrong motives. "I would hope poets would have more in mind than literary success. Their main concern should be in writing exactly what they feel, what they're thinking. Get it down on paper. That's the most important thing. And then success will or will not come."

Despite all of her commercial success, it is not that, but the love of the art that keeps her going. "Even if [when I started] I had known I would never have a single line published, I still would have gone right on writing."

—Lisa Carpenter

---

2 copies. **Simultaneous submissions and previously published poems OK. Editor comments on rejections "only on request."** He says, *"ABS* is a very free-spirited journal publishing in the tradition of journals once published in the '50s and '60s. Beat and modern literature."

ALPHABOX PRESS (V), 41, Mapesbury Rd., London, NW2 4HJ, England, founded 1971, is a small press publishing small editions, about 2 chapbooks a year averaging 20 pp. **Publications include simply produced experimental and visual poetry. "No submissions wanted."**

ALTA NAPA PRESS; GONDWANA BOOKS (IV-Form), 1969 Mora Ave., Calistoga, CA 94515, founded 1976, FAX 707-226-7708, publishes various kinds of books, but the imprint **Gondwana Books is for epic poetry only.** A number of the books in their catalog (available for $9 \times 12''$ SASE and $1) are by the editor, Carl T. Endemann. He **publishes other authors on a "co-operative basis,"** which means partial or full subsidy but gives no details of how that works. Write directly for information, and when you do **send three poems, and your covering letter might include biographical background, personal or aesthetic philosophy, poetic goals and principles, and the hour, date and place of your birth.** He says "No, I am not a fortune teller!" but he is apparently interested in **astrology and reincarnation.** He says he wants poetry which is **"clear, clean, concise/rhythm, reason and 'rammar/rare rational**

rhymes" on any subject of universal appeal; spiritual OK, but effusions of personal frustrations no. No trite drivel. Sex yes, Porno no, no spectator sports. Recently published Erme Burton Hand (2 books of poetry for children and juniors) and Carl Heinz Kurz (2 poetry translations from German). Here are some lines from the editor's poem "Dream Girl, Sweet Girl, Cream Girl":

> *Here comes my delightful spouse*
> *Singing dancing through the house*

He publishes 3-4 chapbooks (30-148 pp.) and 3-4 flat-spined paperbacks (50-240 pp.) per year. Advice: "Join a *good* creative writing class now for three years and read *Writer's Digest* in depth. Poetry is not a commercial endeavor, but it can eventually pay for itself — mainly give you the feeling of having done something *worthwhile* which *no* money can buy. He offers **criticism for $1.30 per page of MS.**

ALTERNATIVE FICTION & POETRY (IV-Form/Style), 7783 Kensington Lane, Hanover Park, IL 60103, founded 1986, editor/publisher Philip Athans, publishes experimental/avant-garde literature. He wants to see "**wildly experimental form and content. No religion, sci-fi or other fantasy. No racism, sexism.**" He has recently published poetry by Charles Bukowski, Jello Biafra, Bob Z, and Roque Dalton. *Alternative Fiction & Poetry* is magazine-sized, 64 pp., offset, perfect bound, with b/w graphics, two-color cardstock cover. He receives approx. 250 submissions per month and accepts approx. 15. Subscription: $10. **Sample $3. Pays 2 copies. Submit no more than six poems at one time, regardless of length. Query if over 40 lines. Reports in 1-6 months, 1-4 months between acceptance and publication. No response without SASE. No cover letter needed.** No chapbooks or audio/video cassettes.

‡**ALTERNATIVE PRESS MAGAZINE (I,II)**, Box 205, Hatboro, PA 19040, founded 1989, editor Bob Lennon, appears quarterly using "**experimental, philosophical poetry; open to most subjects or style as long as it's in good taste. Nothing pornographic, traditional, religious, no worn-out love poems.**" They have recently published poetry by Lawrence T. Kirsch. As a sample the editor selected these lines from "The Iconoclast" by Glenn Bykowski:

> *The temples and mausoleums he desecrates at will*
> *Unscathed by objectors seething with hate*
> *He slams and he smashes their paraphernalia of gloom*
> *He laughs at their lovely naivete*

"*Alternative Press* **will attempt to print most poems submitted unlike other magazines that print trash and reject most poems. Responds on submissions within 2-3 weeks, no backlog. Simultaneous submissions and previously published poems OK.**" It is photocopied from photoreduced typescript, digest-sized, 15-40 pp. with matte card cover, saddle-stapled. Press run 100-200. Subscription: $6 for 4 issues. **Sample, postpaid: $2. Pays 1-5 copies and "occasionally small sums." Editor comments on submissions "sometimes."** He says, "We like to publish new poets, but they should read at least one copy to see what the magazine is about. We are trying to expand our size and output, so the need for more poems is great."

ALURA (II), P.O. Box 44, Novinger MO 63559, phone 816-488-5216, founded 1975, poetry editor Ruth Lamb, is a poetry quarterly whose "aim is to reach the general public with understandable poetry." Its format is 51 pp., saddle-stapled, with colored matte cover illustrated (as are many inside pages) with b/w amateur drawings. The magazine is typeset with small, dark type. They use "**well-written poetry in all styles but not 'typewriter gymnastics' nor uninterpretable symbolism. Poems must communicate. Prefer poems of not more than 48 lines and spaces. All subject-matter in good taste. Do not waste reader's time with obscure meanings.**" They have recently published poetry by Martha Forstrom, Laura Sanders, Fontaine Falkoff, C. David Hay, Charles B. Dickson, Charles Roach and Gerald Burke. The editor selected an excerpt from "Harbinger" by Edward B. Kovar:

> *The breath of winter frosts the chastened sun*
> *And hones the hardened air to chiseled points;*
> *Lethargic insects crawl that once had run,*
> *An aging army with arthritic joints.*

They have a circulation of 325, with 93 subscriptions of which 5 are libraries, receive 1,500-2,000 submissions per year and use about 350. **Sample: $3. Subscription: $10. "Submissions should be folded and sent in a regular business envelope. We accept simultaneous submissions and previously published poems** *if* **poets have retained all rights. Poets published in** *Alura* **do retain all rights. Prefer no more than 5-6 poems at a time. Photocopies OK. Because of our filing system, we would appreciate receiving poems in a regular business envelope with poet's last name** *first* **in the upper left corner of envelope and** *large enough* **to be read in a file. Return address stickers are too small to read in a file drawer. Please use a dark ribbon!"** Poems should be typed single-spaced with the poet's name, address and phone number directly under each poem. They report in 6 months, pay 2 copies. **"We appreciate loose stamps (4) to help with postage."** The editors comment, "We accept both rhymed and unrhymed poetry as long as it is well-written and the meaning clear. We applaud the return of traditional poetry. We think poetry has decreased in popularity the last few decades because much of the poetry written has been unintelligible, shocking and far-out. We will accept no poetry with obscenities and expletives. Due to the diversity of religions, we accept no religious poetry."

‡**THE AMARANTH REVIEW; WINDOW PUBLICATIONS (II)**, P.O. Box 56235, Phoenix, AZ 85079, founded 1989, editor Dana L. Yost. "Window Publications is a small-press publisher of poetry, fiction and non-fiction. *The Amaranth Review* is a literary journal (twice a year) that exists as a forum for contemporary thought. All questions have answers, and we believe that literature provides a sound vehicle for the exploration of alternatives. **In poetry, quality, while subjective, is our main concern— no preferred form, length, subject-matter or style. We publish what we like and prefer to place few if any restrictions on those who contribute—I would rather wade through dozens of poems that I don't like rather than take the chance of discouraging someone and possibly missing that 'one' poem every editor is waiting for. Prefer no pornography—however, that too is a subjective term.**" They have recently published poetry by Rod Farmer, John Grey, Nina Silver, Angela Patten, Mindy Kronenberg, and Craig Van Riper. As a sample the editor selected these lines from "Mystical Moments of Grace" by Brent Short:

> *Malice is a black pointy-eared dog.*
> *The strange beauty and tragic loneliness of life,*
> *the thousand anxieties and agonies of our age,*
> *God trapped within.*

Amaranth is magazine-sized, 60+ pp., offset professional printing in small type, 80# matte cover stock. "We average around 100 submissions per month; in our last issue we published 32 poems." Press run: 1,500 for 230 subscriptions of which 2 are libraries, 230 shelf sales. Subscription: $10. **Sample, postpaid: $5.50. Send SASE for guidelines. Pays 2 copies plus 40% discount on extras plus free subscription. Simultaneous submissions OK. Reports in 4 weeks. For books or chapbook publication query with 5-10 sample poems, bio, and publications. Pays 10-15% royalties. Editor comments on submissions "usually only when requested to do so." Sponsors poetry and fiction contests. Send SASE for guidelines.** The editor says, "The advice I would give a beginning poet would be to write from the heart, to write honest poetry that means something to you— find out what you really care about and then tap into the power of those feelings. And never quit—I don't care how many times you are rejected or how many people laugh when you tell them you're a poet—if you are a poet you have no choice but to write, and quitting is never an option. There are hundreds of small magazines publishing poetry today, and with enough perseverance and some careful market analysis (treat your **Poet's Market** like a bible) you will see your work in print."

‡**AMATEUR WRITERS JOURNAL; FOUR SEASONS POETRY CLUB (I)**, 3457 Monroe St., Bellaire, OH 43906, founded 1967, editor/publisher Rosalind Gill. Though **you have to buy a copy to see your work in print,** *AWJ* "accepts all types of articles, essays, short stories, and **poetry of any theme. No avantgarde or pornographic material accepted. Prefer material of seasonal nature to be submitted in the season prevalent at the time. Length up to 40 regular lines (no longer than 10 words per line). Rhymed or unrhymed. Also accept haiku, limericks and all types of short poems. Do not want to see pornographic—pertaining to raw sex. Considers simultaneous submissions.** They have recently published poetry by Sylvia Martin, Edna Janes Kayser, William Dauenhauer, and Mr. Jan Brevet. As a sample the editor selected this poem, "Autumn," poet unidentified:

> *Goldenrod and bittersweet of Autumn*
> *Are shivering in a lacy cloak of frost,*
> *The bright red leaves of Sumac and the dogwood*
> *Soon to cruel, barren Winter will be lost.*

AWJ is a bimonthly (6 times per year), with 38 pp., magazine-sized, photocopied from typescript, side-stapled with colored paper cover, circulation 500+, subscription $7.50/year. **Sample: $1.25 postpaid. Send SASE for guidelines. Reports "upon publication." Backlog varies, but seasonal poetry is published immediately. "More than one per page. Single-spaced, camera-ready if writer has a typewriter available. Photocopy OK.** Certificates of merit are given for "best of issue." The editor advises: "Always adhere to editor's guidelines; send seasonal poems in correct season; write or print legibly if you can't send typed material."

AMAZING STORIES (IV-Science fiction), Box 111, Lake Geneva, WI 53147, founded 1926, editor Patrick L. Price, "is the world's first and oldest science fiction magazine, a bimonthly primarily devoted to fiction," but **uses a small amount of poetry. "Must have science fictional or fantastic content, clearly expressed. Any form or style is OK as long as it's not obscure. In poetry, as in any other type of writing, say what you mean. Poems should not exceed 30 lines.**" They have recently published poetry by Ruth Berman, Bruce Boston, Mike Curry, Robert Frazier, Elissa Makohn, Frederik Phol, and Jonathan V.

Ambergris   No. 5

Autumn 1989

Alison Dignan's cover illustration for Ambergris #5 depicts the clock tower of the U.S. Playing Card Company in Norwood, Ohio. The city was the subject of this issue's special section. "Ambergris publishes poetry works by North American writers, but gives special consideration to works with Midwestern (particularly Ohio) themes," says editor Mark Kissling.

Post. The issue I examined had 7 poems. The following sample is from "Nuclear Winter" by Mike Curry.

> *And the acid ice thickens in permanent sheets*
> *Across frozen rivers, impassible streets,*
> *And inundates farm lands and kills off the crops*
> *And empties the factories and closes the shops.*

The digest-sized, flat-spined magazine, newsprint with glossy cover with art, has a circulation of 13,000 including 3,000 subscribers, receives "several hundred" submissions per year, of which they use 50. **Sample: $2.50 postpaid. Submit double-spaced, typed (photocopy OK, not dot-matrix). Submit a minimum of 3 poems at a time, and be sure to include SASE, or submissions will be discarded. No query. Reports in 4 weeks, pays $1/line.**

AMBERGRIS (II), P.O. Box 29919, Cincinnati, OH 45229, founded 1986, member Council of Literary Magazines and Presses, editor Mark Kissling, appears twice a year using **"poems of everyday experience, psychological penetration. No fantasy, pornographic, or strictly adolescent poetry."** They have recently published poetry by Rick Stansberger, Susan Grimm, Richard Hague, and Norman Finkelstein. As a sample the editor selected these lines from "After the Green Man" by Brian Stapleton:

> *Lights from distant porches*
> *shine in rough constellations.*
> *Their pale coronas illuminate*
> *A logic within the tangled branches.*

Ambergris is digest-sized, 90 pp. perfect bound, typeset in dark type with matte card b/w cover, using b/w photos. They accept 25 out of 500 poems received per year. Press run is 500 for 75 subscriptions (5 of them libraries), 150 shelf sales. **Sample $3 postpaid. Send SASE for guidelines. Pays 2 copies. No simultaneous submissions. Reports in 2 months. Submit maximum of 5 poems with 3-sentence biographical sketch. No fee.** Mark Kissling says, "As with many magazines, our format for poetry is most clear when the writer can see what we've published before. Take a look at *Ambergris* before sending material. It's the best way to send appropriate poetry."

AMELIA; CICADA; SPSM&H; THE AMELIA AWARDS (II, IV-Form), 329 "E" St., Bakersfield, CA 93304, phone 805-323-4064. *Amelia*, founded 1983, Frederick A. Raborg, Jr. poetry editor, is a quarterly magazine that publishes chapbooks as well. Central to its operations are a series of contests, most with entry fees, spaced evenly throughout the year, awarding more than $3,500 annually, but they publish many poets who have not entered the contests as well. Among poets published are Pattiann Rogers, Stuart Freibert, John Millett, David Ray, Larry Rubin, Charles Bukowski, Maxine Kumin, Charles Edward Eaton, and Shuntaro Tanikawa. These sample lines are by Michael Lassell:

The hairs on my greying chest
cast a lengthening shade,
pluck my father's name
from the hollow corridor where
my grandfather grows
into a legend, his
hair as steel as age.

They are "**receptive to all forms to 100 lines. We do not want to see the patently-religious or overtly-political. Erotica is fine; pornography, no.**" The digest-sized, flat-spined magazine is offset on high-quality paper and usually features an original four-color cover; its circulation is about 1,250, with 522 subscriptions, of which 28 are libraries. **Sample: $7.95 postpaid. Submit 3-5 poems, photocopies OK, dot-matrix acceptable but discouraged, no simultaneous submissions except for entries to the annual Amelia Chapbook Award. Reports in 2-12 weeks, the latter if under serious consideration.** Pays $2-25 per poem plus 2 copies. "Almost always I try to comment." This magazine represents one of the most ambitious and promising ventures in publishing poetry I know of. The editor comments, "*Amelia* is not afraid of strong themes, but we do look for professional, polished work even in handwritten submissions. Poets should have something to say about matters other than the moon. We like to see strong **traditional pieces as well as the contemporary and experimental. And neatness *does* count.**" Subscriptions to *Amelia* are $25 per year. *Cicada,* is a quarterly magazine that publishes **haikus, senryu and other Japanese forms,** plus essays on the form—techniques and history—as well as fiction which in some way incorporates haiku or Japanese poetry in its plot, and reviews of books pertaining to Japan and its poetry or collections of haiku. Among poets published are Roger Ishii, H.F. Noyes, Knute Skinner, Katherine Machan Aal, Ryah Tumarkin Goodman, and Ryokufu Ishizaki. These sample lines are by Irene K. Wilson:

Sipping the thin tea
made from young green leaves'
tranquility

They are receptive to experimental forms as well as the traditional, and "**appreciate ironic wit when very good. Try to avoid still-life as haiku; strive for the *whole* of an emotion, whether minuscule or panoramic. Erotica is fine; the Japanese are great lovers of the erotic.**" The magazine is offset on high quality paper, with a circulation of 600, with 432 subscriptions of which 26 are libraries. **Subscription: $14/year. Sample: $4.50 postpaid. Submit 3-10 haiku or poems, photocopies OK, dot-matrix acceptable but discouraged, no simultaneous submissions. Reports in 2 weeks. No payment, except three "best of issue" poets each receive $10 on publication plus copy.** "I try to make some comment on returned poems always." *SPSM&H* is a quarterly magazine that publishes **only sonnets, sonnet sequences,** essays on the form—both technique and history—as well as romantic or Gothic fiction which, in some way, incorporates the form, and reviews of sonnet collections or collections containing a substantial number of sonnets. Among poets published are Margaret Ryan, Harold Witt, Sharon E. Martin, Rhina P. Espaillat and Robert Wolfkill. Fred Raborg selected these sample lines from my "On the Young Man's Perfection":

What if she, like a cranky child, knocks all
stacked blocks into a random distribution,
allows empires to rise so they may fall,
and cancels with an R our evolution?

They are "**receptive to experimental forms as well as the traditional, and appreciate wit when very good.** Perhaps it may help to know the editor's favorite Shakespearean sonnet is #29, and he feels John Updike clarified the limits of experimentation with the form in his "Love Sonnet" from **Midpoint. Erotica is fine; pornography, no.**" The magazine is offset on high quality paper, with a circulation of 600, for 432 subscribers and 26 libraries. **Subscription: $14/year. Sample: $4.50 postpaid. Submit 3-5 poems, photocopies OK, dot-matrix acceptable but discouraged, no simultaneous submissions. Reports in 2 weeks. No payment, except two "best of issue" poets each receive $14 on publication plus copy.** "I always try to comment on returns." *Amelia* offers the widest range of prize contests of any magazine I know of. All winning poems are published in *Amelia* and each winner also receives two contributor copies. The following annual contests have various entry fees: The Amelia Awards (six prizes of $200, $100, $50 plus three honorable mentions of $10 each); The Anna B. Janzen Prize for Romantic Poetry ($100, annual deadline January 2); The Bernice Jennings Traditional Poetry Award ($100, annual deadline January 2); The Georgie Starbuck Galbraith Light/Humorous Verse Prizes (six awards of $100, $50, $25 plus three honorable mentions of $5 each, annual deadline March 1); The Charles William Duke Longpoem Award ($100, annual deadline April 1); The Lucille Sandberg Haiku Awards (six awards of $100, $50, $25 plus three honorable mentions of $5 each, annual deadline April 1); The Grace Hines Narrative Poetry Award ($100, annual deadline May 1); The Amelia Chapbook Award ($250, book publication, 50 copies and 7½% royalty, annual deadline July 1); The Johanna B. Bourgoyne Poetry Prizes (six awards of $100, $50, $25, plus three honorable mentions of $5 each), The Douglas Manning Smith Epic/Heroic Poetry Prize ($100, annual deadline August 1); The Hildegarde Janzen Prize for Oriental Forms of Poetry (six awards of $50, $30, $20 and three honorable mentions of $5 each, annual deadline September 1); The Eugene Smith Prize For Sonnets (six awards of $140, $50, $25 and three honorable mentions of $5 each); The A&C Limerick Prizes (six awards of $50, $30, $20 and three honorable mentions of $5 each); The Montegue Wade Lyric Poetry Prize ($100, annual deadline November 1). Submit to Box 2385, Bakersfield, CA 93303 or 329 "E" Street, Bakersfield, CA 93304, phone 805-323-4064.

AMERICA; FOLEY POETRY CONTEST (II), 106 W. 56th St., New York, NY 10019, phone 212-581-4640, founded 1909, poetry editor Patrick Samway, S. J., is a weekly journal of opinion published by the Jesuits of North America. They primarily publish articles on religious, social, political and cultural themes. **They are "looking for imaginative poetry of all kinds. We have no restrictions on form or subject-matter, though we prefer to receive poems of 35 lines or less."** They have recently published poetry by Howard Nemerov, Fred Chappell, William Heyen, and Eve Shelnutt. *America* is magazine-sized, 24 pp., professionally printed on thin stock with thin paper cover, circulation 35,000. Subscription: $28. **Sample: $1 postpaid. Pays $1.40/line plus 2 copies. Send SASE for excellent guidelines. Reports in 2 weeks. Editor comments "if asked to do so."** The annual Foley Poetry Contest offers a prize of $500, usually in late winter. Send SASE for rules. The editor says, "*America* is committed to publishing quality poetry as it has done for the past 80 years. We would encourage beginning and established poets to submit their poems to us."

AMERICAN ASSOCIATION OF HAIKUISTS NEWSLETTER; RED PAGODA; WALPURGIS NIGHT (IV-Form, horror), 125 Taylor St., Jackson, TN 38301, phone 901-427-7714. *RP* was founded in 1982, *AAH* and its newsletter in 1983, and *WN* in 1988, editor Lewis Sanders. *AAHN* and *RP* are both haiku publications. You may join the American Association of Haikuists for $3 and receive the newsletter, 10 or fewer pages on white paper of photocopied typescript stapled at the corner (1-2 a year). *Walpurgis Night* is a horror magazine. *RP* is a journal that will consider "**haiku, modern and traditional. Renga, tanka, heibun, senyru, linked poems**, articles and book reviews on books and subjects dealing with haiku." The editor says, "I try to publish 4 times a year, but sometimes run late." They have recently published haiku by Alexis Rotella, John J. Soldo and Elizabeth Lamb. As a sample the editor offers this haiku by Kiri:

> Fall out from Russia —
> may wind
> moans in the chimney

The Red Pagoda is digest-sized, 52 pp., saddle-stapled, photocopied from various typescripts on bond paper with red paper cover. Subscription (4 issues) is $12 in the U.S. mailed first class; $14 outside the U.S. mailed airmail; and $12 outside the U.S. mailed surface mail. Libraries receive a 10% discount on subscriptions. Checks should be made out to Henry L. Sanders. **You must buy a copy to see your work in print (price is $3/copy), but poets do not have to subscribe or purchase a copy to be published. Editor sometimes comments on rejections.** *WN*, the newest of the publications, will appear intermittently using: "**gothic horror/modern horror/erotic vampire poetry not more than 2 pp. in length (1-page poems preferred). Nothing obscene or pornographic.**" As a sample I chose this stanza of "The Hanging at Four" by R. Schmitz III:

> Seconds slowly sail away
>   Down streams of muddied time.
> Will they bring me to the light of day,
> Or cast me in the Old One's way,
>   and end this pantomime?

WN is newsletter format on colored paper. **Sample: $3 prepaid. Pays 1 copy. "Poets who are accepted do not have to purchase a copy to be published, but if they do I will give an extra copy. If this proves too costly, I will have to revert to simply charging per copy." Reports in 3 weeks. Editor comments on rejections "often."**

AMERICAN ATHEIST PRESS; GUSTAV BROUKAL PRESS; AMERICAN ATHEIST (IV-Political, themes), 7215 Cameron Rd., Austin, TX 78752, phone 512-458-1244, founded 1958, editor R. Murray-O'Hair, publishes the monthly magazine **with 30,000 circulation**, *American Atheist* and, under various

ALWAYS submit MSS or queries with a stamped, self-addressed envelope (SASE) within your country or International Reply Coupons (IRCs) purchased from the post office for other countries.

imprints some dozen books a year reflecting "concerns of Atheists, such as separation of state and church, civil liberties, and atheist news." **Poetry is used primarily in the poetry section of the magazine. It must have "a particular slant to atheism, dealing with subjects such as the atheist lifestyle. Anticlerical poems and puns are more than liable to be rejected. Any form or style is acceptable. Preferred length is under 40 lines."** Poets they have published include Salvatore Galioto and Angeline Bennett. The editor chose these lines by Angeline Bennett from "Lowercasing the Fear Words":

> *Old certitudes die hard . . .*
> *but die they have, and now*
> *inspiration is left clear and clean*
> *for those uncluttered minds who find*
> *that God is just another god.*

Of their 17,000 subscriptions, 1,000 are libraries. The magazine-sized format is professionally printed, with art and photos, glossy, color cover; subscription, $25, single copy price $2.95, **sample: free.** They receive over 20-30 poetry submissions per week, use about 36 a year. **Submit typed, double-spaced (photocopy, dot-matrix, simultaneous submissions OK). Time-dependent poems (such as winter) should be submitted 4 months in advance. Reports within 10-12 weeks. Pays "first-timers" 10 copies or 6 month subscription or $12 credit voucher for AAP products. Thereafter, $15/poem plus 10 copies. Guidelines available for SASE, but a label is preferred to an envelope.** They do not normally publish poetry in book form but will consider them. ("We no longer do subsidy books.") **Sometimes comments on rejected MSS.**

AMERICAN DANE (IV-Ethnic), 3717 Harney St., Omaha, NE 68131, phone 402-341-5049, founded 1916, editor Pamela K. Dorau, is the monthly magazine of the Danish Brotherhood in America, circulation 10,000, which uses **poetry with a Danish ethnic flavor. Sample: $1.50 postpaid. Send SASE for guidelines. Buys 1-3 poems a year. Pays $35 maximum plus 3 copies. Reports in 2 weeks, up to 12 month backlog. Simultaneous submission OK.** The magazine is 20-28 pp., magazine-sized. Subscription: $6.

‡AMERICAN KNIGHT (I), Rt. 1, Box 274, South Haven MN 55382. founded 1989, editor Nancy Morin, is a quarterly publishing **poetry by those who contribute poetry or subscribe. "Open-minded acceptance; we prefer poetry with reflective insight and that which encourages the reader to release the limitations of physical and emotional perception. Nothing trite, 'mushy-love' rhymes."** These sample lines are the editor's:

> *Whether to be mild and subtle or*
> *to be wild and coddled*
> *I turn to your wisdom of grace sitting still on your shores*
> *absorbing your soft brilliant sword of power*
> *which leaves me lambent in the wake*
> *of your wined maze of delicacy.*

The editor says, "To make a living in America today is quite a rare thing. *AK* has been developed for poets and poetry. It is here to give those who love the excitement of seeing their work in print and knowing that their poetry is being read by others, a chance to reach and enhance a broader audience. **Let it all out when you write, then do it. That is poetry. Everyone has a good chance of being printed here; we try to print something from everyone. This is a nonprofit quarterly written by the writers who contribute poetry or prose. Cost per issue: $2 plus 50¢ loose stamps. First issue free to contributors of poetry for asking and 50¢ loose postage.** Donations are greatly appreciated however, and can be made to Nancy Morin." The editor describes it as 11 × 17″ folded at center, printed on 20# or heavier paper, typed, with art on cover, more than 6 pp. Each issue has a featured poet. **Sample, postpaid: $2. Send SASE for guidelines. Pays "at least 1" copy. Deadlines February 20, March 23, August 23, November 20. Send up to 5 poems. Do not staple.**

AMERICAN POETRY REVIEW; WORLD POETRY, INC.; JEROME J. SHESTACK PRIZES (III), 1704 Walnut St., Philadelphia, PA 19103, founded 1972, is probably the **most widely circulated (24,000 copies bimonthly) and best-known periodical devoted to poetry in the world.** Poetry editors are Stephen Berg, David Bonanno and Arthur Vogelsang, and they have **published most of the leading poets writing in English and many translations.** The poets include Gerald Stern, Brenda Hillman, John Ashbery, Norman Dubie, Marvin Bell, Galway Kinnell, James Dickey, Lucille Clifton, and Tess Gallagher. As a sample, I selected some lines of my own published there, from "Encounters Of Kind," a poem based on a journal entry by Anton van Leeuwenhoek of Delft:

> *The ladder down into the well appears*
> *to have infinite and ever-smaller rungs.*
> *Look up into the dark sky where it reaches*
> *and hear the wind stirred by those alien tongues.*

15,000 subscriptions, of which 1,000 are libraries, tabloid format. **Sample and price per issue: $2.50.** They receive about 4,000 submissions per year, use 200, **pay $1.25 per line, 12 weeks to report, 1-3 year backlog, no simultaneous submissions**. The magazine is also a major resource for opinion, reviews, theory, news and ads pertaining to poetry. The Jerome J. Shestack Prizes of $1,000, $500 and $250 are awarded by the editors each year for the best poems, in their judgment, published in *APR*.

THE AMERICAN SCHOLAR (III), 1811 Q St. NW, Washington, DC 20009, phone 202-265-3808, founded 1932, associate editor Sandra Costich, is an academic quarterly which **uses about 5 poems per issue, pays $50 each.** Two-month response time. They have published poets such as Robert Pack, Alan Shapiro and Gregory Djanikian. **"We would like to see poetry that develops an image, a thought or event, without the use of a single cliché or contrived archaism. The most hackneyed subject matter is self-conscious love; the most tired verse is iambic pentameter with rhyming endings. The usual length of our poems is 30 lines. From 1-4 poems may be submitted at one time;** *no more* **for a careful reading."** Study before submitting (**sample: $5.50, guidelines available for SASE**).

AMERICAN SQUAREDANCE MAGAZINE (IV-Themes), 216 William St., Huron, OH 44839, phone 419-433-2188, founded 1945, co-editor Catherine Burdick, **"deals with all phases of square dancing internationally. Poems must relate to square dance."** The monthly magazine is 100-112 pp., digest-sized, saddle-stapled with a colored card cover, and is 50-55% ads, circulation to 22,000 subscribers. They accept about 6 of 25 poems received per year. Per issue: $1.25. Subscription $12 for 1 year, $22 for 2 years. **Sample back issue free. Send SASE for guidelines. They pay $10-25 per poem, depending on length, and 1 copy (unless more are requested). No simultaneous submissions or previously published poetry. Reports in 2 weeks, usually publishes within 6 months, though seasonal poems may be held longer.**

AMERICAN STUDIES PRESS, INC.; MARILU BOOKS; HERLAND BOOKS (II, IV-Women, themes), 13511 Palmwood Lane, Tampa, FL 33624, founded 1977 publishes under a variety of imprints: **ASP Books, Rattlesnake Books,** and **Harvest Books,** but poetry primarily as **Marilu Books** which includes **HERLAND** (poems by women about women and WOMAN). These are generally low-budget, offset, flat-spined books of 35-70 pp. with simple art, but some good poetry. Editor-in-chief Don Harkness says he wants **"poetry with a central (and American) theme** — possibilities are wide." He has recently published work by Normajean MacLeod, Chick Wallace, Hans Juergensen and Rochelle Lynn Holt, and offers these lines by Ruth Moon Kempher from "At Evelyn Thorne's Crescent City" in **The Lust Songs and Travel Diary of Sylvia Savage:**

> *Here she weaves sibyl syllables*
> *spiderwise. A webbing of waterdrops*
> *flowers out from the sprinkler, leaking*
> *knowledge everywhere*

Send SASE for a free catalog; books cost from $3-7. **Submit query (with SASE) before sending any samples or manuscripts;** *ASP* **is very limited in publishing books of poetry. Reports in 1-2 months, pays 10% royalties after printing expenses are met plus 10 copies. Poets have earned from $6 to $250 on their books.** Don Harkness advises, "(1) Poetry began in rhythm, meter and rhyme; the current pathological avoidance of same has begun to pall. (2) I generally find, in poems which I reject out of hand, an excessive solipsism and unreconstructed prose. All books of poetry must have central theme."

AMERICAN TOLKIEN SOCIETY; MINAS TIRITH EVENING STAR; W.W. PUBLICATIONS (IV-Themes), Box 373, Highland, MI 48031-0373, phone 313-887-4703, founded 1967, editor Philip W. Helms. There are special poetry issues. Membership in the ATS is open to all, regardless of country or residence, and entitles one to receive the journal. Dues are $5 per annum to addresses in U.S. and $10 elsewhere. Their magazines and chapbooks use **poetry of fantasy about Middle-Earth and Tolkien.** They have recently published poetry by Thomas M. Egan, Anne Etkin, Nancy Pope, and Martha Benedict. *Minas Tirith Evening Star* is magazine-sized, offset from typescript with cartoon-like b/w graphics. **Pays contributor's copies.** The editor selected a sample by Joe Christopher:

> *The hobbits have fallen in this fallen world,*
> *Who once in burrows lived with round doors burled,*
> *but now must make their livings as they can:*
> *with one a baker, and one an artisan*
> *and one a bagpipe player with notes that skirled . . .*

They have a press run of 400 for 350 subscribers of which 10% are libraries. Per issue: $3.50. Subscription: $5. **Sample: $1.50 postpaid. Send SASE for guidelines. Prefer photocopies. Simultaneous submissions OK and previously published poems "maybe." Reports in 2 weeks. Editor sometimes comments on rejections.** Under imprint of W.W. Publications they publish collections of poetry 50-100 pp. **For book or chapbook consideration, submit sample poems. Published 2 chapbooks per year.** They sometimes sponsor contests.

THE AMERICAN VOICE (II), 332 W. Broadway, Louisville, KY 40202, phone 502-562-0045, founded 1985, editor Frederick Smock, is a literary quarterly — one of the best markets I've seen — publishing North and South American writers. They prefer **free verse, avant-garde.** They have recently published poetry by Linda Pastan, Wendell Berry, Odysseus Elytis, Cheryl Clarke, Marge Piercy, and Ernesto Cardenal. As a sample I selected one stanza of a long poem, "Mother's Day at the Air Force Museum," by George Ella Lyon:

> My son loves the machine guns.
> He looks through a sight,
> he strafes the still air.
> At home, his Lego men
> die smiling.

TAV is elegantly printed, flat-spined, 140+ pp. of high-quality stock with card matte cover printed in silver, circulation 2,000 with 800 subscriptions of which 100 are libraries. Subscriptions: $12/year. **Sample: $5 postpaid. Pays $150/poem and 2 copies. (They pay $75 to translator of a poem.) Reports in 6 weeks, has a 3 month backlog. No simultaneous submissions; photocopy and dot-matrix OK. Occasionally comments on rejections.**

AMERICAS REVIEW; AMERICAS REVIEW POETRY COMPETITION (II, IV-Political), Box 7681, Berkeley, CA 94707, founded 1985, editor Gerald Gray, a "literary annual with **emphasis on political content of the poetry** and prose we publish. **Only limit is subject-matter; it is almost always political in some general sense (though a few items of poetry are not). We do print, for instance, the love poetry of political figures.** We deliberately publish little-known or obscure poets, but we have included works by Nicholis Guillen, Otto Rene Castillo, Julia Vinograd, Dorianne Laux, Sergio Ramirez, Claribel Algeria, and (probably) Gary Snyder." As a sample Gerald Gray selected these lines by Gioconda Belli:

> That's why I sit down to brandish these poems;
> to build against wind and tide
> a small space of happiness
> having faith that all this will not end —

I have not seen the annual, but the editors describe it as 6 × 9″, flat-spined, about 75 pp., offset, using b/w graphics. It has a press run of 1,000 for 50 subscriptions (10 of them libraries) and the rest are for shelf sales. Per issue: $4 ($6 to libraries). **Sample: $3 postpaid. Pays $10 per author, plus 1 copy. Editor "sometimes" comments on rejections.** Their annual contest has a reading fee of $4 for up to five poems. They award three prizes of $100 each for published, unpublished, or translated poetry. The contest runs September 1-November 30. They note, "Our poetry and fiction is usually, but not exclusively, political in nature. All poems submitted will be considered for publication. Poems other than the winners chosen for publication will be paid in cash at our usual rate. Winners and other accepted will appear in the annual issue."

THE AMICUS JOURNAL (V, IV-Nature), 40 W. 20th St., New York, NY 10011, phone 212-727-2700, poetry editor Brian Swann, is the **journal of the Natural Resources Defense Council, a quarterly with a circulation of about 60,000, which pays $25/poem. Brian Swann says the poetry is "nature based, but *not* 'nature poetry.' " They will not be accepting submissions in 1991 "because our cup runneth over with poetry."** They have used poems by some of the best known poets in the country, including David Wagoner, Gary Snyder, David Ignatow, Marvin Bell and William Stafford. As a sample, I selected the opening stanza of Mary Oliver's "Starfish":

> In the sea rocks,
> in the stone pockets
> under the tide's lip
> in water dense as blindness

The Amicus Journal is finely-printed, saddle-stapled, on high quality paper with glossy cover, using much art, photography and cartoons. **Free sample for SASE.**

‡ANALECTA (IV-Students), Liberal Arts Council, FAC 19, University of Texas, Austin, TX 78712, phone 512-471-6563, founded 1974, editor Paula Bilstein, is an annual of literary works and photography by **college/university U.S. and Canadian students and graduate students chosen in an annual contest**, a 200 pp. magazine, glossy plates for interior artwork in both color and b/w, 7 × 12″, flat-spined, soft cover. **"No restrictions on type; limited to 7 poems/submission.** Our purpose is to provide a forum for excellent student writing. **We prefer the work not to have been previously published."** Of about 700 submissions received, they publish about 40. Press run 700 for 600 subscriptions, 100 shelf sales. **Sample, postpaid: $4. Send SASE for guidelines. Prizes in each category. Pays 1 copy and $65**

for poetry. Entries should be typed with no names "on the actual work." As a sample, the editor selected this excerpt from "Losses" by Laura Long:

> *Embers glowed in circles of stone, dew*
> *dropped through silvered foliage, dreams*
> *flared and dissolved by morning.*

‡AND; CORE; AND PRINT (IV-Form, themes), 421 Park St., Oxford, PA 19363, founded 1990, editor Robert A. Nagler, all use **computer-related poetry, either in form of submission or content.** All are "biannual journals of experimental literature and the magnetic media. *And* appears in 2 modes, first a poetry-on-computer-diskette exchange, second a poetry-on-audio-tape exchange. **Both are open to beginners.** *And* (first mode) requires submissions on a 5¼" single- or doubled-sided diskette running under Apple DOS 3.3 or PRODOS. Submissions may be in the form of text files or (preferably) a BASIC program. Neither should exceed 30 sectors in length. For second mode, submission should be on a C-90 audio tape. Performance time should not exceed 5 minutes. *Core* likewise appears in 2 modes: computer diskette and audio tape. However *Core* is a journal of *advanced* literature and the magnetic media. Submissions may be made regardless of the poet's status. If rejected by *Core*, the poet may be offered publication in *And*. Some entries in *Core* are invited. *And Print* is a print journal/ newsletter emphasizing the creative use of word processors and desk-top publishing. Submissions should be 'camera-ready' on 8.5 × 11" paper in black and white as they will be reproduced *exactly* as received. Subscriptions are not presently available and donations are not solicited." **Submit to *And* and *Core* (first mode)** on 5¼" disk with suitable cardboard envelope for return. For the second mode of these publications submit **"on C-90 cassette with a suitable (padded if possible) SASE. *And Print* accepted poets will be notified by *their* SASE and advised of the postage required to send the full edition. Preferences: poems that exploit the special qualities of the computer (i.e.: animation, random- ized elements), audio-taping (i.e.: mixing, overdubbing) and desk top publishing (graphic/text font mixes) in the making of poetry."** As a sample the editor selected his own poem, "Mr. America:"

> *Spotlighted, the flayed men twitch, grimace. No one turns aside.*

["A print version of a poem that uses various computer techniques."] **"Submissions processed came day. No backlog at present. Editor is sole judge. Computers and poetry? Let's do it!"**

THE AND REVIEW; MID-OHIO CHAPBOOK PRIZE (II), 10485 Iams Rd., Plain City, OH 43064, founded 1987, appears twice a year. **They are "open to all forms and styles, but prefer shorter, imagistic poems. No self-indulgent first attempts."** They have recently published poetry by William Stafford, Diane Glancy and William Heyen. As a sample the editors selected these lines from "River's Mind" by Gordon Grigsby:

> *Beneath layers of silt, leaves turning to silt,*
> *in bedrock limestone*
> *the ghosts of brachipods*
> *swim motionlessly forever*

Their press run is 500 with 200 subscriptions of which 10 are libraries. The magazine consists of "all poetry with one or two reviews of new books of poetry. We also feature in each issue an author reviewing his/her own book." It is digest-sized, professionally printed with a matte card cover, using b/w photos and ink drawings. No ads. **They receive 4,000 poems annually and publish 50-55. Subscription: $5. Sample: $3 postpaid. Pays 1 copy. Reports in 1 month.** Guidelines available for SASE. The Mid-Ohio Chapbook Prize is awarded annually to the best chapbook of 15-20 pages received between April and June. The winning manuscript is published in a special supplement within the magazine. The author receives 50 separately bound copies. A $10 reading fee is required for entry and includes a 1 year subscription to *The And Review*. Editor sometimes comments on rejections. The editors pass on Marvin Bell's advice, "Making the simple complicated is commonplace; making the complicated simple, awesomely simple, that's creativity."

ANDROGYNE BOOKS; ANDROGYNE (IV-Themes), 930 Shields, San Francisco, CA 94132, founded 1971, poetry editor, Ken Weichel. *Androgyne* is a literary journal (an issue about every 18 months) **on specific themes, such as alchemy, erotic fantasy, auto/biographical writing, Surrealism/Dada. Will not be accepting MSS until the first of 1991.** "The best guidelines for submission is a sample copy." Graphics, especially collage, welcome. They have recently published poetry by Laura Beausoleil, Ivan Argüelles, Geoffrey Cook, Alice Polesky, Ronald Sauer, Tonay D'Arpino, and Toby Kaplan. As a sample, the editor selected these lines by Michael Koch:

> *We translate it 'sperm of a nightingale'*
> *then settle for 'candle drippings'*
> *Obsure slang for cliques of angels.*

Besides publishing the literary journal, Androgyne Books also publishes chapbooks. **Unsolicited book length mss are not encouraged. Please query first. Simultaneous submissions OK, reports** in 1 month, payment 2 copies and a subscription. Sample copy and a catalogue: $4.

ANERCA (I, IV-Form), 3989 Arbutus St., Vancouver, BC V6J 4I2 Canada, phone 604-732-1648, founded 1986, editors Wreford Miller, Kedrick P.A. James, and Adeena Karasick, is a "quarterly magazine of poetry and poetics. **Our bias is toward non-traditional 'open' poetry, avant garde poetry, and language-motivated poetry. As long as it shows innovation and good craftsmanship as a stylistic feature, we have no other prejudices. We do not want to see the unskillful use of archaisms, we do not enjoy confessional poetry, and we dislike excessive rhyme or strict meter. We are now inviting critical essays on language — post structural poetics, where all art meets."** They have recently published poetry by Bill Bissett, Michael McClure, Gerry Gilbert, Opal L. Nations, Jerome Rothenberg and Karen MacCormack. The editors selected these sample lines by bp Nichol, from **The Martyrology**, Book 5:

> spun out the puns fabric of the word
> i mine the language for the heard world
> seen scenes unfurled by such activity

At present *Anerca* is between 20-30 pages in length. The editors describe it as offset, printed with graphics, and is side-stapled. Circulation 450, sent throughout North America and Europe. Subscription: $15 for 5 issues. **Sample $3 postpaid. Send SASE for guidelines. (Please use international reply coupons!) Pays 2 copies. Editors comment on rejected MSS.** Kedrick James advises, "Listen inside — more ear, less sentiment, more language, less poet."

‡ANGEL SUN (II), Box 8288, Flushing, NY 11352, founded 1989, editor Ms. M.K., prints books of poetry. **"I am especially interested in lyrical, sensual, surreal work that is at once clear and visionary. It must be 'finished' but not sterile. No excessively 'formal' or academic work."** As a sample the editor selected these lines from **Idealism and Early Wish-Fulfillment** by Richard Pérez Séves:

> Her hair
> as warm as sunlight
> Her lips
> were as soft as sleep.

That book is digest-sized, 114 pp., flat-spined, photocopied from typescript with glossy card cover, $5. **"Before submitting a MS all poets are advised to purchase a sample copy. Purchase price of the sample book is refundable if returned in good condition within five days."** Pays royalties 10-20% plus $500 honorarium and 100 copies. **"MSS that are under consideration are kept for some time (up to eight months) before I will begin the actual financial estimations. I must first *like* the work."** The editor adds, "I think that an artist should be open to all influences, cultural or technological. Study the great poets: Blake, Whitman, Keats, Shakespeare. Absorb the history of poetic tradition. Understand that there is much more that is left to be said and that you (yes, *you*) are the one who should say it. *Trust your intuition.* The greatest artists have always been those who trusted their intuition. Believe in the power of the imagination, the breeding ground of hope. Then remind yourself that you must persist. Spend your time *creating* art, not theorizing. Allow yourself to fail, but don't wallow in disappointment. You are given only so much time on this earth: remind yourself of that and make use of your life. Take responsibility for your talent."

‡ANHINGA PRESS; ANHINGA PRIZE; CYNTHIA CAHN MEMORIAL PRIZE (II), Box 10595, Tallahassee, FL 30302, phone 904-575-5592, founded 1972, poetry editors Julie Weiler and Van Brock, publishes **"books, chapbooks and anthologies of poetry. We also offer the Anhinga Prize for poetry — $500 and publication — for a book-length manuscript each year. We want to see contemporary poetry which respects language. We're inclined toward poetry that is not obscure, that can be understood by any literate audience."** Considers simultaneous submissions. They have recently published poetry by Shery Rind, Yvonne Sapia, Judith Kitchen, Ricardo PaulLlosa, Robert J. Levy, Michael Mott, Rick Lott and Will Wells, Gary Corseri, Julianne Seeman, and Nick Bozanic. The editors chose this sample poetry from "Son, Skating":

> I am only a red car, a voice,
> a yes or a no. His skates are more
> than wings; he slips into
> the envelope of his body, tall
> and silent, no more mine
> than he ever was.

Send SASE for rules (submissions accepted in January) of the Anhinga Prize for poetry, which requires an entry fee, for which all contestants receive a copy of the winning book. The contest has been judged by such distinguished poets as William Stafford, Louis Simpson, Henry Taylor, Hayden Carruth and Denise Levertov. A sample chapbook will be mailed for $3. Send a "business size" SASE for catalog and contest information. **"We do not read manuscripts except those entered in our competition."** Cynthia Cahn Memorial Prize (II) for the best single poem previously unpublished submitted during October. Entry fee $3 per poem, $5 for 2 poems, $10 for 5 poems (5 poem limit). Send SASE for further guidelines, responses, name of winner.

ANIMA: THE JOURNAL OF HUMAN EXPERIENCE (II, IV-Women, feminist), 1053 Wilson Ave., Chambersburg, PA 17201, founded 1973, "celebrates the wholistic vision that emerges from thoughtful and imaginative encounters with the differences between woman and man, East and West, yin and yang—*anima* and *animus*. **Written largely by and about women** who are pondering new experiences of themselves and our world, this equinoctial journal welcomes contributions, verbal and visual, from the known and unknown." Poetry editors John Lindberg and Harry Buck say, "We publish very few poems, but they are carefully selected. **We are not interested in simply private experiences. Poetry must communicate. Advise all would-be poets to study the kinds of things we do publish. No restrictions on length, form, or such matters.**" As a sample I chose the first stanza of Kay Ryan's "Why Animals Dance":

> *Because of their clickety hoofs*
> *Because of their scritchety claws*
> *Because of their crackety beaks*
> *Because they don't have any boots*

There are 5-10 pages of poetry in each semiannual issue of the elegantly-printed and illustrated 8½" square, glossy-covered magazine, circulation 750, for 700 subscriptions of which 150 are libraries. Price per issue: $5.95. **Sample: $5.95. Slow reporting—sometimes 3-6 months, payment: offprints with covers.**

ANJOU (V), P.O. Box 322 Sta. P., Toronto, Ontario M5S 2S8 Canada, founded 1980, edited by Richard Lush and Roger Greenwald, publishes broadsides of poetry. **"We do not wish to receive submissions because we publish only by solicitation."**

ANSUDA PUBLICATIONS; THE PUB (II), Box 158JA, Harris, IA 51345, founded 1978, "is a small press operation, publishing independently of outside influences, such as grants, donations, awards, etc. Our operating capital comes from magazine and book sales only. Their magazine *The Pub* uses some poetry, and we also publish separate chapbooks of individual poets. We **prefer poems with a social slant and originality—we do** *not* **want love poems, personal poems that can only be understood by the poet, or anything from the haiku family of poem styles. No limits on length, though very short poems lack the depth we seek—no limits on form or style, but rhyme and meter must make sense. Too many poets write senseless rhymes using the first words to pop into their heads. As a result, we prefer blank and free verse.**" They have recently published Real Faucher, Virgil Chabre, D. Roger Martin, Miriam A. Cohen and Barbara Colleen Best. They offer no sample because "most of our poems are at least 25-30 lines long and every line complements all other lines, so it is hard to pick out only four lines to illustrate." *The Pub*, which appears irregularly (1-3 times a year) is a low-budget publication, digest-sized, mimeographed on inexpensive paper, making it possible to print 80 or more pages and sell copies for **$2.50 (the price of a sample).** Its minimum print-run is 350 for 130 subscriptions, of which 7 are libraries. Each issue has 8-12 pages of poetry, but **"we would publish more if we had it; our readers would like more poetry."** Everything accepted goes into the next issue, so there is no backlog; **reports immediately to 1 month, payment 2 copies, guidelines available for SASE. They also publish 1-2 chapbooks (24-28 pp.) per year. For these, query with 3-6 sample poems.** "We need cover letters so we know it's for a book MS query, but you should only include information *relevant* to the book (education, experience, etc.). We are *not* interested in past credits, who you studied under, etc. Names mean nothing to us and we have found that small press is so large that big names in one circle are unknown in another circle. In fact, **we get better material from the unknowns who have nothing to brag about (usually)." Replies to queries immediately, reports in 1-2 months on submissions, no dot-matrix, simultaneous submissions only if clearly indicated. Payment: royalties plus 5 copies.** They will also subsidy publish if poet pays 100% of costs, picks own press name (Ansuda does not appear on subsidy publications), and handles distribution. Prices on request. Daniel Betz adds, "About all I have left to say is to tell the beginner to keep sending his work out. It won't get published in a desk drawer. There are so many little mags out there that eventually you'll find homes for your poems. Yes, some poets get published on their first few tries, but I've made first acceptances to some who have been submitting for 5 to 10 years with no luck, until their poem and my mag just seemed to click. It just takes time and lots of patience."

ANTHOLOGY OF MAGAZINE VERSE & YEARBOOK OF AMERICAN POETRY (III, IV-Anthology), % Monitor Book Company, P.O. Box 9078, Palm Springs, CA 92263, phone 619-323-2270, founded 1950, editor Alan F. Pater. The annual **Anthology** is a selection of the **best poems published in American magazines during the year and is also a basic reference work for poets.** Alan F. Pater says, "We want poetry that is 'readable' and in any poetic form; we also want translations. **All material must first have appeared in magazines.** Any subject matter will be considered; we also would like to see some rhyme and meter, preferably sonnets." They have recently published poetry by Margaret Atwood, Richard Eberhart, Stanley Kunitz, Stephen Spender, William Stafford, Robert Penn Warren, Richard Wilbur, Robert Bly, Maxine Kunin and John Updike. Indeed, the anthology is a good annual guide to the best poets actively publishing in any given year. For the most part selections are made by the editor from magazines, but some poets are solicited for their work which has been in magazines in a given year. The current edition is: **Anthology of Magazine Verse & Yearbook of American Poetry-1989**.

ANTIETAM REVIEW (IV-Regional), Washington County Arts Council, Bryan Center, 4th Floor, 82 W. Washington St., Hagerstown, MD 21740, an annual founded 1981, poetry editor Ann B. Knox, looks for well-crafted literary quality poems. We discourage inspirational verse, haiku, doggerel, **uses poets only from the states of Maryland, Pennsylvania, Virginia, West Virginia, Delaware and District of Columbia. Needs 10 poems per issue, up to 30 lines each, pays $20/poem, depending on funding**. Poets they have published include Grace Cavalieri, David McKain, and Philip Jason. The editor chose this sample by Hilary Tham called "Lint Filter":

> *Monday is not her washday*
> *Tuedsay is,*
> *Monday, bending again and again,*
> *She gathers the weekend blooms—*

They have a press run of 1,000, 8½x11″ saddle-stapled, **sample: $3 postpaid.**

THE ANTIGONISH REVIEW (II), St. Francis Xavier University, Antigonish, Nova Scotia, Canada B2G 1C0, phone 902-867-3962, FAX 902-867-5153, founded 1970, poetry editor Peter Sanger. This high-quality quarterly "tries to produce the kind of literary and visual mosaic that the modern sensibility requires or would respond to." They want poetry **not over "80 lines, i.e., 2 pp.; subject-matter can be anything, the style is traditional, modern or post-modern limited by typographic resources. Purpose is not an issue."** No "erotica, scatalogical verse, excessive propaganda toward a certain subject." They have recently published poetry by Milton Acorn, Andy Wainwright, Janice Kulyk-Keefer, M. Travis Lane, Douglas Lochhead, Lorna Crozier, Irving Layton, Peter Dale, Roger Finch, W.J. Keith and W.S. Milne. As a sample the editor selected these lines by Lloyd Abbey:

> *not jigs but threnodies:*
> *ancestral sounds,*
> *the thud of flame,*
> *collapsing bone,*
> *cold wind*
> *across chimneys*

TAR is flat-spined 6×9″, 150 pp. with glossy card cover, offset printing, using "in-house graphics and cover art, no ads." They accept about 10% of some 2,500 submissions per year. Press run is 1,100 for 800 subscriptions. Subscription: $16. **Sample: $3 postpaid. Pays 2 copies. No simultaneous submissions or previously published poems. Editor "sometimes" comments on rejections**. The editor advises, "The time for free verse form is exhausting itself as a technical possibility. **We are sympathetic to poets working with strong rhythmic patterns**. Poets will have to return to the traditional devices of rhythm, rhyme and manipulation of line length. Many more poets would and could be published if more of them were also readers of the full range of poetry in English, old and new. We are *not* responsible for return of submissions sent with improper postage. **Must include self-addressed stamped envelope (SASE) or International Reply Coupons (IRC) if outside Canada."**

THE ANTIOCH REVIEW (III), Box 148, Yellow Springs, OH 45387, founded 1941, "is an independent quarterly of critical and creative thought . . . **For 45 years, now, creative authors, poets and thinkers have found a friendly reception . . . regardless of formal reputation**." Poetry editor: David St. John. "We get far more poetry than we can possibly accept, and the competition is keen. Here, where form and content are so inseparable and reaction is so personal, it is difficult to state requirements or limitations. Studying recent issues of *The Review* should be helpful. No '**light' or inspirational verse**." Recently published poets: Molly Peacock, Joyce Carol Oates, Debra Nystrom, Karen Fish, Michael Collier, and Andrew Hudgins. I selected these sample lines from Craig Raine's "Inca":

> *And the swans display*
> *their dripping beaks for us,*
> *but your lips are parted:*
> *to kiss, or to speak.*

Circulation is primarily to their 4,000 subscribers, of which half are libraries. They receive about 3,000 submissions per year, publish 12-16 pages of poetry in each issue, have about a 6 month backlog. Subscription: $20. **Sample: $5. Pays $10/published page plus 2 copies, general guidelines for contributors available for SASE, reports in 4-6 weeks.**

Close-up

Ann Knox
Editor
Antietam Review

Photo by Benita Keller

The Crone Remembers Her Husband
Two crows hunt the meadow, they move
in small starts, one halts, feet
wide, the other hunched, opens its beak
ready for the quick strike, the head's
toss. No sign passes between them,
but together they turn, unfold ragged wings
and skim over the sumacs, close as fighter planes.

As in much of Ann Knox's poetry I love, I find it is the silences in that poem that nudge me to understanding. She is always tight, concrete and clear, and always means a lot more than she says.

By the time Ann turned to writing she had raised five children, taught for 12 years in elementary and junior high schools and spent much of her life overseas. Her husand was in the Foreign Service. They lived in Moscow under Stalin, in Austria during the Occupation, in England, and in Pakistan, with stints in Washington between. Her teaching career began with a third-grade class in Karachi, where, without experience or training, she says, she "had to wing it." When they returned to the States she went to Catholic University (her BA had been from Vassar) "to learn how kids learn." She taught for nine years after that before focusing on writing.

"A teaching colleague startled me into writing," she says. He commented, "You know, you're a poet." She asked what he meant. "You think in images," he said. A few weeks later she showed him a poem written on the strength of his statement, and he said, "Wow!"

And she was on her way. She discovered that I lived over the mountain from her cabin and at the time I was offering tutorial sessions and poetry workshops at Downhill Farm, and so we became acquainted. I was impressed by both her poetry and fiction. She says, "I enrolled in the Goddard (later the Warren Wilson) MFA program and never went back to teaching school. My first fiction teacher, Ray Carver, made me see that writing was a way to know my life on another level, and he taught me to love the craft."

She says that "poetry is how I clarify experience, and teaching writing is a means of sharpening my understanding of the craft." She teaches at the Writer's Center (see listing under Organizations Useful to Poets) and at writers' workshops, such as the one offered annually at Antioch College in Yellow Springs, Ohio (where I also often teach). "Students come," she says, "because they want to write better. It's hugely satisfying to work with them. You can't teach the impulse for poetry, but you can teach craft. You can pass on love for the language, for the sound of words, for the power of the right image. Learning craft is a matter of 'getting it,' the student suddenly sees how a linebreak works to press the poem forward, how adverbs undercut a simple statement, how short, tough Anglo-Saxon words carry a coiled power."

Antietam Review, which she edits, is published by the Washington County Arts Council. It started as a showcase for local Maryland writers, but, as Ann says, "it rapidly widened its focus to include Virginia, West Virginia, Pennsylvania, Delaware, and the District of Columbia. The editors felt writers deserve more than a free copy of the magazine and established a policy to pay writers for work we publish. We carry work of both emerging and established writers and take particular pride in first-time published writers.

"We have high standards and of the poems we receive, the two major weaknesses are poor crafting and a lack of something revealed. As a child I learned woodworking from a New England carpenter who taught the essence of the craft was to love the wood, to know its grain, density and nature, to respect the tools, and to honor the work itself. I carry the same respect to writing and am troubled by sloppy craft. As for the content of poems, we see too often the 'so what?' poem, one without tension or press against the current, without something to say."

Ann spends her time between an isolated cabin that "looks onto the first folds of the Appalachians" and her apartment in Washington DC. "The shift from city to country, from writing to editing to teaching, creates a kind of balance. The most difficult part is claiming time to write. I try to put in at least three hours a day, but it takes discipline to push off the diversions that nibble at the edges of my attention."

As I read "The Crone Remembers Her Husband," I thought of how it has been over the years working with her, without a sign between us, yet "close as fighter planes."

—Judson Jerome

APALACHEE QUARTERLY; APALACHEE PRESS (II, IV-Themes), Box 20106, Tallahassee, FL 32316, founded 1971, editors Barbara Hamby, Pamela Ball, Claudia Johnson, Bruce Boehrer, and Paul McCall, want **"no formal verse."** They have published poetry by David Kirby, Peter Meinke and Jim Hall. There are 55-95 pp. of poetry in each issue, circulation 500, with 250 subscriptions of which 50 are libraries, a 1-3 month backlog. "Every year we do an issue on a special topic. Past issues include a Dental, Revenge and Cocktail Party issues copies." Subscription: $15. **Sample: $5 postpaid. Submit clear copies of up to 5 poems, name and address on each, no dot-matrix; photocopied, simultaneous submissions OK. Payment 2 copies. Guidelines available for SASE. Sometimes comments on rejections. We don't read during the summer (June 1-August 31).**

APPALACHIAN HERITAGE (IV-Regional), Hutchins Library, Berea College, Berea KY 40404, phone 606-986-9341, ext. 5260, FAX 606-986-9494, founded 1972, editor Sidney Saylor Farr, a literary quarterly with Southern Appalachian emphasis. The journal publishes several poems in each issue, and the editor wants to see **"poems about people, places, the human condition, etc., with Southern Appalachian settings. No style restrictions but poems should have a maximum of 25 lines, prefer 10-15 lines."** She does not want **"blood and gore, hell-fire and damnation, or biased poetry about race or religion."** She has recently published poetry by Jim Wayne Miller, Louise McNeill and Bettie Sellers. As a sample, she selected the following lines by James Still:

> *They have come down astride their bony nags*
> *In the gaunt hours when the lean young day*
> *Walks the grey ridge, and coal light flags*
> *Smooth-bodied poplars piercing a hollow sky.*

The flat-spined magazine is $7 \times 9\frac{1}{2}''$, professionally printed on white stock with b/w line drawings and photos, glossy white card cover with four-color illustration. **Sample copy: $4. Contributors should type poems one to a page, simultaneous submissions are OK, and MSS are reported on in 2-4 weeks. Pay is 3 copies.**

APPLEZABA PRESS (II), Box 4134, Long Beach, CA 90804, founded 1977, poetry editor D. H. Lloyd, is "dedicated to printing and distributing poetry to as wide an audience as we can." They publish both chapbooks and flat-spined collections of individual poets and occasional anthologies, about 3 titles per year. **"As a rule we like 'accessible' poetry, some experimental. We do not want to see traditional."** They have recently published poetry by Leo Mailman, Gerald Locklin, John Yamrus, Toby Lurie and Nichola Manning. These sample lines are from Lyn Lifshin's "Parachute Madonna":

> *either quite manic or depressive*
> *either up and flying or down*
> *with a huge crash.*

No query. Submit book MS with brief cover letter mentioning other publications and bio. Reports in 3 months. Simultaneous submissions, photocopy OK, dot-matrix accepted but not preferred. Pays 8-12% royalties and 10 author's copies. Send SASE for catalog to order samples. The samples I have seen are digest-sized, flat-spined paperbacks with glossy covers, sometimes with cartoon art, attractively printed.

‡APROPOS; THYME CONTEST (I, IV-Subscribers), RD 4, Ashley Manor, Easton, PA 18042, founded 1989, editors Nancy C. Lansing and Ashley C. Anders, appears 6/year, and **publishes all poetry submitted by subscribers (subscription: $25/year) except that judged by the editor to be pornographic or in poor taste. Each issue awards prizes of $50, $25, and $10, as judged by readers (no entry fee). "Poems will not be returned; please retain copies. Maximum length 46 lines. One submission per publication."** Sample: $3 postpaid. Simultaneous submissions and previously published poems OK. It is a newsletter format, 8½×11" stapled at the corner. As a sample, I selected one stanza of a poem by the editor:

> My life is full of mysteries,
>   each day—a new surprise;
> I savor every rainbow,
>   then I thank God for my eyes.

Thyme Contest is sponsored twice a year, deadlines August 31 and February 28, $1/poem entry fee, **open to all, not only subscribers.** Prizes of $50, $25, $10 and "possibly more depending upon number of entries received, limit 4-46 lines. Submit 2 copies, one without name/address for judging.

‡ARARAT (IV-Ethnic), 585 Saddle River Rd., Saddle Brook, NJ 07662. Editor-in-Chief: Leo Hamalian. 80% freelance written. **Emphasizes Armenian life and culture for Americans of Armenian descent and Armenian immigrants. They do not want to see traditional, sentimental love poetry.** "Most are well-educated; some are Old World." Quarterly magazine. Circ. 2,400. Pays on publication. Publishes MS an average of 1 year after acceptance. Buys first North American serial rights and second (reprint) rights to material originally published elsewhere. **Submit seasonal/holiday material at least 3 months in advance.** Photocopied and previously published submissions OK. Computer printout submissions acceptable. Reports in 6 weeks. Sample copy $3 plus 4 first class stamps. **Any verse that is Armenian in theme. Buys 6 per issue. Pays $10.**

‡ARCHAE: A PALAEO-REVIEW OF THE ARTS (I, II); RAPA NUI JOURNAL (V), 10 Troilus, Old Bridge, NJ 08857-2724, founded 1971 senior editor/publisher Alan Davis-Drake. *Archae* is a quarterly using in each issue "5-7 poems/song/chants/invocations/legends/myths, any length. **Poetry should be well grounded in the traditional yet express the unaffected voice of universal experience in contemporary language and form. We do not wish to see overly self-conscious poetry, with the private 'I' as its primary focus. Poetry should have cross-cultural appeal and at the same time accurately examine/ share one's own time and place. A sense of place is very important. We are as interested in contemporary 'Western' poetry in all forms as we are in other cultures.** We strongly encourage critical reviews of world poetry. Proof sheets are provided to all writers for approval before publication. Line drawings with an anthropological twist will be considered, including renderings of archaeological sites, artifacts, etc." As a sample the editor selected these lines from a contemporary Manova'a (South Pacific) chant:

> Last night the island bird spoke its heart to me:
>   "Our Father Atua Atoa has been dead for a thousand years,
>   But his children still fly across the crazy ocean."
> This morning I fly north to the great city of Paris.
> I bring Atua Atoa's seed with me—good for a thousand more years.

It appears twice a year, 7×8½", 50 pp. "laserprinted and linotronics." Press run 500 for 300 subscribers of which 7 are libraries. **Sample, postpaid: $6 U.S. funds only. Send SASE for guidelines. Pays 2 copies.** Their editorial board of 4 members often comments on rejections. **Reports in 2-4 weeks.** The editors of *Archae* also edit the quarterly *Rapa Nui Journal*, an international journal of anthropological/archaeological studies and current events occurring on Easter Island and throughout the South Pacific. **It rarely accepts poetry.**"*Archae* grew out of the anthropological experience of seeing 'primitive' cultures misunderstood as 'noble.' On the contrary, most cultures are essentially in the same boat: mismanagement, rivalry and a lack of forward vision of the future. Each issue will aim towards concentrating on a select group of 'poets' from around the world, rather than on publishing single poems by a long list of individual writers. Anthropologists with recent ethnographic collections of chants/songs/invocations/legends/myths/etc. are encouraged to contact *Archae*. *Archae* is the combined form from the Greek 'ancient, primitive' and 'beginning.' "

THE ARCHER (II), 2285 Rogers Lane, Salem, OR 97304, founded 1951 as a publication of Camas Press, 1986 as a publication of Pro Poets of Salem, editor Winifred Layton, is a semiannual of poetry using **"nothing over 30 lines. Any subject, any form except limerick and parody. Free verse preferred unless rhyme is professional."** They don't want to see **"bad taste (obscene), sci-fi, religious, political" poetry.** They have recently published poetry by Jay Giammarino and Ruth Wildes Schuler. As a sample the editors selected these lines from Sandy Fink's "The Heron":

> *Still, shallow water —*
> *A sun-kissed heron drinking*
> *its own reflection.*

The magazine is digest-sized, photocopied from typescript, with matte card cover, 68 pp., using 90-100 poems/issue, press run of 200. **Sample: $2 postpaid, $4 if issue since 1988 desired; the $2 is for the old quarterly. "Must be typewritten on full 8 × 11" sheet, 1 poem to page." Reports in 2 weeks-3 months, with 3-13 months between acceptance and publication. Simultaneous submissions, previously published poems OK. Pay in contributor's copy.** There is a semiannual prize of $15 for best sonnet, annual prize of $15 for humor, annual $15 for five lines or under. "We are receiving too many mss with no identification on each page. Many write a letter and think the address on that is sufficient. The editor tosses out the letter after reading it, only to her dismay finds no ID on the poems. Since several do this, it is impossible to tell which SASE to fill."

ARETE: FORUM FOR THOUGHT (III), 405 W. Washington St. #418, San Diego, CA 92103, phone 619-237-0074, founded 1987, poetry editor Dana Plank, is a high-quality, oversized, comprehensive magazine appearing every other month, using poetry and fiction. **"We prefer well-developed, imagistic poetry of any genre or form — from traditional to modern. Though shorter poems are preferred, length is open and content may range from light to serious."** They have recently published poetry by Philip Levine, Robert Creeley and Sandra McPherson. Their press run is 25,000 with 5,000 subscriptions. The editor describes it as a "comprehensive forum of ideas. We present both conservative and liberal viewpoints. We include social and political commentary, review of the arts, music, fiction, and poetry." The elegant magazine has 88 large pages, professionally printed, using quality advertising and b/w and color photos and graphics, They accept less than 2% of poetry received. **Sample: $3.50 postpaid. Guidelines available for SASE. Pays $75-200 + per poem. No more than 5 poems per submission. No previously published poems or simultaneous submissions. Reports in 2-8 weeks. Editors rarely comment on submissions.** "We prefer our potential poets be familiar with the magazine."

‡ARGONAUT (I, IV-Science Fiction/Fantasy), P.O. Box 4201, Austin, TX 78765, founded 1972, editor/publisher Michael Ambrose, is an **"annual magazine anthology of weird fantasy/science fiction and poetry, illustrated." They want "speculative, weird, fantastic poetry with vivid imagery or theme, up to 50 lines. Prefer traditional forms. Nothing ultramodernistic, non-fantastic."** They have recently published poetry by Sardonyx, J.R. Ericson, Robert R. Medcalf, Jr., and Joey Froehlich. I have not seen an issue, but the editor describes it as 48 pp. digest-sized, typeset. They accept 5-8 of 100-200 poems received. Press run: 300 for 50 subscriptions of which 3 are libraries. Subscription: $5/2 issues. **Sample, postpaid: $3. Send SASE for guidelines. Pays 2 copies. Submit no more than 5 poems at a time. Reports in 4-8 weeks. Editor comments on submissions "occasionally."** He says, "Too much of what I see is either trite, limited in scope or language, and/or inappropriate for the theme of *Argonaut*. Poets should know what the particular market to which they submit is looking for and not simply shotgun their submissions."

‡ARIEL, A REVIEW OF INTERNATIONAL ENGLISH LITERATURE (III), English Dept., University of Calgary, Calgary, Alberta, Canada T2N 1N4, phone 403-220-4657, founded 1970, is a "critical, scholarly quarterly with about 5-8 pp. of poetry in each issue," circulation 825, subscriptions of which 650 are libraries. As a sample, I selected these lines from "Ecstasy!" by Fritz Hamilton:

> *being the*
> *Jackson Pollock of*
> *poetry I*
>
> *dance over the paper in*
> *the street with*
> *my pen poised to*
>
> *pour my words of*
> *poetry onto*
> *the world &*

Ariel is professionally printed, flat-spined, 100 + pp., digest-sized, with glossy card cover. Subscription: $18 institutions; $12 individuals. They receive about 300 freelance submissions of poetry per year, use 20-30. **Sample: $5 postpaid. Prefer 4-8 poems. No long poems. No simultaneous submissions. Reports in 4-6 weeks. Pays 10 offprints plus 1 copy. Editor comments on rejections, "only occasionally and not by request."**

‡**ARIZONA WOMEN'S VOICE (I, IV-Women)**, 5515 N. 7th St. #5-173, Phoenix, AZ 85014, phone 602-279-1457, founded 1985, managing editor Christy Compton, who says. "Our newspaper publishes a Poetry Corner which runs ½-¾ page. We are totally volunteer staffed. We encourage writers and poets to submit to us to gain experience and networking contacts. **We need short pieces—no more than 15-20 lines—submit typed and double-spaced. Subject matter is anything speaking to the issues, concerns, and achievements of women. We accept from both female and male authors.**" They have recently published poetry by Melissa L. Brody and Joyce Salfingere. As a sample the editor selected these lines (poet unidentified):

> *I don't want another chance*
> *At loving someone new*
> *If another voice should speak my name*
> *I'd only think of you.*

Sample, postpaid: $2. Pays copies "upon request." Reports in 4 weeks. I have not seen a copy, but their publicity says they have over 46,000 readers, average age 37.2, average income $36,000, 89% attended college, 61% professional.

‡**ARJUNA LIBRARY PRESS; JOURNAL OF REGIONAL CRITICISM (I, II)**, 1025 Garner St., Space 18, Colorado Springs, CO 80905, library founded 1963, press founded 1979, editor Joseph A. Uphoff, Jr. "The Arjuna Library Press is avant garde, designed to endure the transient quarters and marginal funding of the literary phenomenon (as a tradition) while presenting a context for the development of current mathematical ideas in regard to theories of art and literature; photocopy printing allows for very limited editions and irregular format. Quality is maintained as an artistic materialist practice." He wants to see **"surrealist prose poetry, dreamlike, short and long works, not obscene, profane (will criticize but not publish), unpolished work."** He has recently published work by Tom Norton, Mike Axtel and Randall Brock. As an example the editor selected these lines from "Until the Routine Shave," by Timothy Lamarre of the People's Republic of China:

> *Yesterday evening he had fried peanuts in a wok*
> *on the stove . . . He dabbed the vacuum cleaner brush*
> *in the darkened oil and applied some to the ball*
> *joint of his left leg, worked it in moving the*
> *joint back and forth . . .*

JRC is published on loose photocopied pages of collage, writing, and criticism, appearing irregularly in an irregular format. Press run: 1 copy each. **Pays "notification." Previously published poems and simultaneous submissions OK. "I like ingenuity, legibility, convenience, polish. I expect some sympathy for mathematical, convenience, polish. I expect some sympathy for mathematical, logical, and philosophical exposition and criticism. These arguments remain our central ambition."** Arjuna Library Press publishes 6-12 chapbooks/year, averaging 50 pp. **To submit to the press send complete MS, cover letter including bio, publications, "any information the author feels is of value." The press pays royalties "by agreement, if we ever make a profit" and copies. Send 50¢ for sample.** The editor says, "The nature of absurdity is both comic and serious. When we dismiss the comic nature as being applicable only to humor and discuss the serious even tragic nature of autonomic absurdity we have realized that the true potential of the irrational is ironic. This is the metaphor upon which the spirits have based the horror of their criticism. This horror has been sublimated by a dry wit in the sense of humor of some authors and rhetoricians, a challenge which the imagination meets not as libel but as discernment. It is nevertheless true that such irony can be indulged in out of context becoming slander; that has not been our goal. Our goal is self defense!"

THE ARK (V, IV-Translations), 35 Highland Ave., Cambridge, MA 02139, phone 617-547-0852, founded 1970 (as BLEB), poetry editor Geoffrey Gardner, publishes books of poetry. **"We are unable to take on new projects at this time."** They have published poetry by David Budbill, John Haines, Joseph Bruchac, Elsa Gidlow, W. S. Merwin, Eliot Weinberger, Kathy Acker, George Woodcock, Kathleen Raine, Marge Piercy and Linda Hogan. The editor selected these lines by Kenneth Rexroth (a translation from the Sanskrit) as a sample:

> *You think this is a time of Shiva's waking*
> *You are wrong*
> *You are Shiva*
> *But you dream*

THE UNIVERSITY OF ARKANSAS PRESS; ARKANSAS POETRY AWARD (III), Fayetteville, AR 72701, founded 1980, acquisitions editor James Twiggs, publishes flat-spined paperbacks and hardback collections of individual poets. Miller Williams, director of the press, says, **"We are not interested in poetry that says, 'Guess what I mean' or 'Look what I know.' "** They have published poetry by Dan Masterson,

Leon Stokesbury, George Garrett and John Ciardi. As a sample, I selected the opening stanza of "Navy Town Spring" by Debra Bruce:

> *A big-bellied bouncer bangs*
> *the door open wide and leans*
> *on it and lights up the sun.*

That's from her book **Sudden Hunger**, digest-sized, 66 pp., flat-spined, elegantly printed on eggshell stock with glossy 2-color card cover. **Query with 5-10 sample poems. Replies to query in 2 weeks, to submissions in 2-4 weeks. No replies without SASE. MS should be double-spaced with 1½″ margins. Clean photocopy OK. No dot-matrix unless letter quality. Discs compatible with IBM welcome. Pays: 10% royalty contract plus 10 author's copies.** Send SASE for catalog to buy samples. The Arkansas Poetry Award competition is open to any original MS by a living American poet whose work has not been previously published or accepted for publication in book form. Chapbooks, self-published books, and books produced with the author's subsidy are not considered previously published books. No translations. Submit 50-80 pp., not more than one poem/page, counting title page in page count. An acknowledgments page listing poems previously published should accompany MS. Author's name should appear on the title page only. $10 reading fee. Postmark no later than May 1. Publication the following spring.

ARNAZELLA (II), Bellevue Community College, 3000 Landerholm Circle, SE, Bellevue, WA 98007-6484, phone 206-641-2341, established 1979, advisor Roger George, is a literary annual, published in spring, using **well-crafted poetry, no "jingles, greeting card" poetry.** They have recently published poetry by William Stafford, Judith Skillman and Coleen McElroy. I have not seen this student publication (which uses work from off campus), but the editor describes it as 75 pp., 6×8″, offset, using photos and drawings. Of 150-200 poems received per year they use about 30. Press run 500 for 3 subscriptions, one of which is a library. **Sample: $5 postpaid. Send SASE for guidelines and submission form, pays 1 copy. Submit up to 4 poems. Deadline is usually at beginning of February. Reports in 1-4 months.**

ARROWOOD BOOKS, INC. (II), Box 2100, Corvallis, OR 97339, phone 503-753-9539, founded 1985, editor Lex Runciman, is a "small-press publisher of quality literary works." He publishes sewn paperbacks and hardcover books, always on acid-free papers, 1-2 per year, 60-80 pp. **Query first. Simultaneous submissions, photocopies, poems previously published in magazines all OK. Reports to queries in 3 weeks, on MSS in 2 months. Pays royalties and advance.** I have not seen a sample. If you want one, he offers a 10% writer's discount (limit 1 copy). He advises, "Write well, and work hard to separate the act of writing from the fear of publishing (or not)."

ARS POETICA PRESS NEWSLETTER; POETRY WEST (II), 1200 E. Ocean Blvd. #64, Long Beach CA 90802, phone 213-495-0925 (founded 1987 the first issue of *Poetry West* will be 1990 or spring 1991). Publisher John Brander publishes "poetry anthologies, fiction, a literary quarterly, videotapes and cassettes. The operation would also assist self-publishers to produce quality books. This part of the operation would be commercial but would not operate as a vanity press." At the time of responding John Brander had not fully determined the policies of Ars Poetica Press and the forthcoming literary journals. I suggest you write with SASE for an updating.

ART TIMES: CULTURAL AND CREATIVE JOURNAL (II), Box 730, Mount Marion, NY 12456, phone 914-246-6944, editor Raymond J. Steiner, a monthly tabloid newspaper devoted to the arts that publishes some poetry and fiction. The editor wants to see **"traditional and contemporary poetry with high literary quality."** He does not want to see "poorly written, pointless prose in stanza format." The most well-known poet he has published recently is Helen Wolfert. As a sample, he selected the following lines by Anne Mins:

> *Your finical ear, my friend*
> *Neat file of images, pile of esoteric words*
> *Compendium of rhymes, blend of assonance,*
> *Your pyrotechnic metric, Spare me, spare me.*

Art Times focuses on cultural and creative articles and essays. The paper is 16-20 pp., on newsprint, with reproductions of art work, some photos, advertisement-supported. Frequency is monthly and circulation is 15,000, of which 5,000 are by request and subscriptions; most distribution is free through galleries, theatres, etc. They receive 700-1,000 poems per month, use only 40-50 a year. Subscription is $15/year. **Sample: $1 postage cost. Guidelines available for SASE. They have a 2-year backlog. Pay is 6 free copies plus one year complimentary subscription. Submissions are reported on in 6 months. There is a 20-line limit for poetry. Simultaneous submissions OK. Typed MSS should be submitted to the editor. Criticism of MSS is provided "at times but rarely."**

‡ARTCRIMES (I), Box 14457, Cleveland, OH 44114, phone 216-575-9943, founded 1986, publisher/editor Steven B. Smith, "is a limited edition collaborative collection of international art and words; the magazine has a liberal, anti-authority, pro-thought bias." He wants poetry of **"all types, from Zen to blank verse, nothing simplistic and mindless."** They have recently published poetry by Russell Atkins, M.J. Arcangelini, John Bennett, John Byrum, and Amy Sparks. As a sample the editor selected these lines from his own poetry:

> *yet dark ripples still unstill light*
> *small deaths linger lightly on sheets*
> *no longer washed nor nightly scented*
> *with reason wrinkled, or raw*

The magazine appears in various formats, from 52-100 pp., photocopied from typescript, appearing 3-4 times a year, using about half of 200 poems received. Press run 300-400. **Sample, postpaid: $5. Pays 1 copy. Simultaneous submissions and previously published poems OK. Reports in 1-4 months.**

ARTE PUBLICO PRESS; THE AMERICAS REVIEW (IV-Ethnic), University of Houston, Houston TX 77204-2090, founded 1972, poetry editor Julian Olivares, publisher Nicolas Kanellos. (Note: *The Americas Review* is also the name of another magazine with a political focus published in Berkeley CA.) The press publishes 20 books of fiction and 2 of poetry by U.S. **Hispanic writers** per year. They have recently published books by Gary Soto, Alberto Rios, and Sandra Cisneros. *The Americas Review* is a triquarterly of fiction and poetry. I have not seen it, but the publisher says it is digest-sized, 120-200 pp., flat-spined, circulation 3,000; 2,100 subscribers (of which 40% are libraries). **Pays a varying amount plus 5 copies. Reports in 4 months. No simultaneous submissions. For book publication, publish first in the magazine. They pay a $500 advance and 25 copies for book publication. There is an annual award for the best poetry published in the magazine.**

ARTFUL DODGE (II, IV-Translations), Dept. of English, College of Wooster, Wooster, OH 44691, founded 1979, poetry editor Daniel Bourne, is an annual literary magazine that "takes a strong interest in poets who are continually testing what they can get away with successfully in regard to subject, perspective, language, etc., but who also show mastery of current American poetic techniques—Its varied textures and its achievement in the illumination of the particular. What all this boils down to is that we require high (and preferably innovative) craftsmanship as well as a vision that goes beyond *one's own* storm windows, grandmothers, or sexual fantasies—to paraphrase Hayden Carruth. **Poems can be on any subject, of any length, from any perspective, in any voice, but we don't want anything that does not connect with both the human and the aesthetic. Thus, we don't want cute, rococo surrealism, someone's warmed-up, left-over notion of an avant-garde that existed 10-100 years ago, or any last bastions of rhymed verse in the civilized world.** On the other hand, we are interested in poems that utilize stylistic persuasions both old and new to good effect. We are not afraid of poems which try to deal with large social, political, historical, and even philosophical questions—especially if the poem emerges from one's own life experience and is not the result of armchair pontificating. We often offer encouragement to writers whose work we find promising, but *Artful Dodge* **is more a journal for the already emerging writer than for the beginner looking for an easy place to publish. We also have a sustained commitment to translation, especially from Polish and other East European literatures,** and we feel the interchange between the American and foreign works on our pages is of great interest to our readers. We also feature interviews with such outstanding literary figures as Jorge Luis Borges, W. S. Merwin, James Laughlin, Czeslaw Milosz, Nathalie Sarauté, Stanislaw Baranczak, Omar Pound, Gwendolyn Brooks, John Giorno, Stuart Dybek, Edward Hirsch and William Matthews. Recent and forthcoming poets include Naomi Shihab Nye, Walter McDonald, Stuart Friebert, Nicholas Kolumban, William Stafford, Len Roberts, Karl Krolow (German), Tomasz Jastrun (Polish), Mahmud Darwish (Palestinian), Tibor Zalan (Hungarian) and Joseph Salemi's faithfully erotic versions of Martial. The editor selected these sample lines from "How to Eat in the House of Death" by Katharyn Machan Aal:

> *Absolutely, ignore the faces peering*
> *in through darkened windows. If—*
> *well, no need to warn you.*
> *They are hungry too.*

There are about 40 pp. of poetry in each issue, circulation 750, 100 subscriptions of which 30 are libraries. They receive at least 2,000 poems per year, use 20-30, and the backlog is 1-12 months between acceptance and publication. **Sample: $5.75 for recent issues, $3 for others. "No simultaneous submissions but typed photocopies of any technological persuasion are OK. Please limit submissions to 6 poems. Long poems may be of any length, but send only one at a time. We encourage translations, but we ask as well for original text and statement from translator that he/she has copyright clearance and permission of author." Reports from immediately to four months. Pays 2 copies, plus, currently, $5 honorarium because of grants from Ohio Arts**

Council. The digest-sized, perfect-bound format is professionally printed, glossy cover, with art, ads.

ARTS END BOOKS; NOSTOC MAGAZINE (II), Box 162, Newton, MA 02168, founded 1978, poetry editor Marshall Brooks. "**We publish good contemporary writing. Our interests are broad and so are our tastes.** People considering sending work to us should examine a copy of our magazine and/or our catalog; check your library for the former, send us a SASE for the latter." Their publications are distinguished by excellent presswork and art in a variety of formats: postcard series, posters, pamphlets, flat-spined paperbacks and hardbacks. As a sample Brooks chose Rogue Dalton's "The Captain" (translated by Sesshu Foster):

> The captain in his hammock the captain
> asleep under the chirping of the night
> the guitar hanging against the wall
> his pistol set aside his bottle
> awaiting like a rendezvous with love
> the captain the captain
> —he should know—
> under the same darkness as his prey.

The magazine appears irregularly in printruns of 300-500, about 30 pp. of poetry in each, 100 subscriptions of which half are libraries. **Sample: $2.50 postpaid.** They receive a few hundred submissions per year, use 25-30; "**modest payment plus contributor's copies." A cover letter is a very good idea for any kind of submission;** we receive *very* few good, intelligent cover letters; what to include? That's up to the writer, whatever he/she feels important in terms of the work, in terms of establishing a meeting." **Tries to report within a few weeks, discourages simultaneous submissions, frequently comments on rejected MSS.** Brooks says, "We try to respond warmly to writers interested in making genuine contact with us and our audience."

‡ARUNDEL PRESS; MERCER & AITCHISON (III), 11349 Santa Monica Bl., Los Angeles, CA 90025, phone 213-477-1640, founded 1984, managing editor Phillip Bevis, speaking for Arundel Press, "publishes only major texts (as we see them) in limited editions printed letterpress. **We will consider only established authors.** Most work is illustrated with original graphics. Mercer & Aitchison publishes definitive editions of major (as we see them) works of poetry, literature & literary criticism." They publish about 6 hardbacks/year. Phillip Bevis recommends to beginning poets the Mercer & Aitchison publication, Clayton Eshleman's **Novices: A Study of Poetic Apprenticeship** (paperback, $12.95). He says, "The only thing worth adding to what is said there is that there are only a handful of poets in America (at the most) making a living *as* poets. The majority of even the most prominent must teach or work in other fields to support their poetic endeavors. Poetry must be something you do because you want to—not for the money."

THE ASHLAND POETRY PRESS (II, IV-Anthologies, Themes), Ashland College, Ashland, OH 44805, founded 1969, editor Robert McGovern, publishes anthologies on specific themes and occasional collections. He has recently published collections by Harold Witt, Alberta Turner, and Richard Snyder. As a sample he selected lines from "Journey" by Hollis Summers:

> Unless bored stands as another word
> For wise, they were not wise, only bored,
> And rich. Only the bored and rich wander.
> Wise men linger and produce at home.

That poem appears in Summers' book **After the Twelve Days.** "Watch publications such as *Poets & Writers* for calls for MSS, but don't submit otherwise." On collections, poet gets 10% royalty; **anthologies, poets are paid stipulated price when sufficient copies are sold. Write for book and price list. "We do not read unsolicited MSS; anthology readings take quite a bit of time."** Considers simultaneous submissions.

‡ASYLUM (II, IV-Form, translations), P.O. Box 6203, Santa Maria, CA 93456, founded 1985, editor Greg Boyd, is "a literary quarterly with emphasis on short fiction, **the prose poem, and poetry. No restrictions on form, subject-matter, style or purpose, though we are especially receptive to prose poems.**" They have recently published poetry by Thomas Wiloch, Philip Dacey, Edouard Roditi, and Tom Whalen. As a sample, I selected this poem, "Stain," by Pierre Jean Jouve, translated from the French by Eric Basso:

> I saw a thick stain of green oil
> Drained from an engine and on
> The hot sidewalk in that sleazy district
> I thought long, long of my mother's blood.

Asylum is digest-sized, 40-60 pp. professionally printed with matte card cover. They accept about

Volume 5, Number 4

ASYLUM

WALT PHILLIPS

Editor Greg Boyd says this cover of Asylum "seems to represent, in its loosely-drawn, near cartoon simplicity, the spontaneity, openness of form and experimental qualities inherent in the writing that typically appears in the magazine." Illustrator Walt Phillips is "well-known to readers of little magazines for his drawings and short, humorous poems."

10% of submissions. Print run 500 for 130 subscriptions of which 10 are libraries. Subscription: $10. **Sample, postpaid: $3. Pays 3 copies. Put name and address on each page. Reports in 2 weeks-3 months.**

ATALANTIK (IV-Ethnic, Foreign language), 7630 Deercreek Drive, Worthington, OH 43085, phone 614-885-0550, founded 1979, editor Prabhat K. Dutta, is a "literary quarterly **mainly in Bengali** and containing short stories, poems, essays, sketches, book reviews, interviews, cultural information, science articles, cinema/theater news, children's pages, serialized novels, etc., **with occasional English writings (non-religious, non-political.)**" They have published "all major poets of West Bengal, India (Sunil Ganguli, Shakti Chattopadhyay, Niren Chakrabarti, Arun Mitra, Alok Sarkar, Pabitra Mukhopadhyay, Bijay Dutta, and Tanushree Bhattacharya as well as of Bangladesh (Shamsur Rahaman, Rafique Azad, Nirmalendu Gun, etc.)" As a sample the editor selected four lines from "Monsoon in Calcutta" by Bibhas De:

> *In June again, may be in June*
> *When with the sweat and filth and the milling horde*
> *And the streetcars and buses listing under the load*
> *The day stands once again at a scorching noon*

"*Atalantik*, the first Bengali literary magazine in USA, was started to keep Bengali language alive to Bengalees in USA. Number of pages differ widely and average out to 60. Original printing by electric press in Calcutta, India; USA printing is by offset or photocopy and the number varies according to order; artwork both on the cover and inside the magazine." It is magazine-sized, flat-spined, with b/w matte card cover. The annual subscription is $20. Some copies are distributed free. **Sample: $6 postpaid. Send SASE for guidelines. Pays 1-2 copies. Simultaneous submissions and previously published poems OK. Reports in 1 month.** "We are actively and seriously considering publishing books under 'Atalantik Publications.' **For book consideration submit sample poems, cover letter with bio and publications. Simultaneous submissions, photocopies, dot-matrix OK. Pays** "25 copies usually, may vary." Editor sometimes comments on rejections. He adds, "Poetry comes from pain and feelings, from loss and sufferings, from death and frustration, but eventually poetry rejoins all separations." The operations of a smaller version of *Atalantik* are managed by Keshab Dutta, from 36B, Bakul Bagan Road, Calcutta-700025, India (phone 75-1620) for distribution in India.

THE ATLANTIC (III), 745 Boylston St., Boston, MA 02116, phone 617-536-9500, founded 1857, poetry editor Peter Davison, publishes 1-5 poems monthly in the magazine. **Some of the most distinguished poetry in American literature** has been published by this magazine, including recent work by William Matthews, Mary Oliver, Stanley Kunitz, Richard Shelton, Rodney Jones, May Swenson and W.S.

Merwin. The magazine has a circulation of 500,000, of which 5,800 are libraries (**sample: $3 postpaid**). They receive some 75,000 poems per year, of which they use 35-40 and have a backlog of 6-12 months. **Submit 3-5 poems, no dot-matrix, no simultaneous submissions, payment about $3/line**. Peter Davison says he wants "to see poetry of the highest order; we do *not* want to see workshop rejects. **Watch out for workshop uniformity. Beware of the present indicative. Be yourself.**"

‡**ATTICUS REVIEW/PRESS (II, IV-Form)**, 720 Heber Ave., Calexico, CA 92231, founded 1981, poetry editor H. Polkinhorn, is a "small-press publisher of cut-up and experimental and visual/verbal work," publishing the magazine, *Atticus Review*, chapbooks and flat-spined editions, wanting "**open form, open subject-matter, experimental.**" They do not want to see traditional forms. As a sample I selected this stanza from "Serpent Rock" by Karl Kempton:

> *Atop any formation*
> *never again*
> *will I watch*
> *a young jackrabbit*
> *fifteen minutes*
> *chase*
> *a five foot rattler*

Atticus Review is magazine-sized, clipped on one side, illustrations by the author, glossy card cover, $7 (plus $1 "transportation"). *AR* appears 3 times a year, but the editor describes it as having a similar format. They receive about 500 poems per year, 25-50 accepted. **Sample: $4 postpaid. Pays 2 copies. Simultaneous submissions, previously published OK. Reports in 4-6 weeks. They publish 1 chapbook a year. Submit samples. Chapbook publication pays 10% of run.**

‡**AUGURIES (IV-Science fiction)**, 48 Anglessy Rd., Alverstoke, Gosport, Hants, England, phone 581220, founded 1983, editor Nik Morton, is a quarterly using **science fiction and fantasy poetry, "any length, any style, good imagery.**" They have recently published poetry by J.F. Haines, Garry Legg, J.V. Stewart, Steve Sneyd, Dave W. Hughes and John Light. As a sample the editor selected these lines from "Intergalactic Fool" by Larry Blazek:

> *In a spaceborne hind*
> *before a starry wind*
> *a dreamer set asail*
> *on a beam of light...*

The digest-sized quarterly is lithographed from photoreduced typescript on bond paper, thin glossy card cover with b/w art, 52 pp., saddle-stapled. They take about 40% of 50 poems received per year. Press run 250 for 50 subscriptions, about 50 shelf sales. Price per issue: $3; subscription: $10. **Sample back issue $3 postpaid. Pays 1 copy. No simultaneous submissions. Previously published poems "not usually" used. Reports in 5 weeks. Editor comments on rejections "if possible.**" He says, "My choice of poetry is very subjective, may even appear arbitrary: if it appeals to me, I will accept (perhaps offering advice where necessary before acceptance)."

AURA LITERARY/ARTS MAGAZINE (II), Box 76, University of Alabama at Birmingham, Birmingham, AL 35294, phone 205-934-3216, founded 1974, editors Adam Pierce and Stefanie Truelove, a semiannual magazine that publishes "fiction and art though majority of acceptances are poetry—90-100 per year. **Length—open, style open, subject matter open. We are looking for quality poetry. Both first-time and often published poets are published here.** *Aura* has recently published work by Lyn Lifshin, Adrian C. Louis, and William Miller. As a sample the editors selected these lines by Robert Anderson:

> *I saw a movie once,*
> *They put a saint inside*
> *a bell and rang it.*
> *Poetry is like that.*

The 6x9" magazine has 90-120 pp., perfect bound, printed on white matte with b/w photos, lithography, and line art. Circulation is 500, of which 40-50 are subscriptions; other sales are to students and Birmingham residents. Price per issue is $2.50, subscription $6. **Sample available for $2.50 postpaid, guidelines for SASE. Pay is 2 copies. Writers should submit "3-5 poems, with SASE, no simultaneous submissions, will take photocopies or even neatly hand written.**" Reporting time is 2-3 months. The editors say, "Quality is our quantity. If it's good we will find a place for it, if not this issue, the next."

‡**AURORA POETRY LETTER (I)**, 2 Jasmine Court, Millsbrae, CA 94030, founded 1989, editor Dawn Zapletal, is a quarterly publication using "**all forms—prefer 16 lines or less, all subjects in good taste, no profanity, pornography or overtly religious. Beauty of language especially welcome. No greeting**

card verse, political and/or totally inaccessible poetry." As a sample of poetry she likes the editor selected "Don't Stop" by Pat Everitt:

> So the trees cry out as Orpheus strides by,
> musically inclined.
> So the sailor pleads a Siren's encore,
> steering his erstwhile ship
> upon such lovely rocks.

The example I have seen is photocopied from typescript, both sides of the page. It is 3-10 sheets corner-stapled, with simple b/w drawings, with a featured poet in each issue. The editor says that submissions are "read same day (by me)." No backlog, at present. **Reports in 1 week. Time to publication 3 months maximum. She always provides comments on submissions and suggests other markets.** For her first issue she received 27 poems, accepted 8, made 24 copies of the first issue, and had 4 subscribers. **Sample, postpaid, for 2 first-class stamps. Subscription: 10 first-class stamps. Send SASE for guidelines. Pays 1 copy.** The editor says, "For me, poetry is the written essence of universal truth and beauty." She advises, "Love poetry, read poetry, write poetry and keep on submitting."

AWEDE PRESS (II), Box 376, Windsor, VT 05089, phone 802-484-5169, founded 1975, editor, Brita Bergland. **Awede** is a small press that publishes letterpress books, sewn with drawn-on covers, graphically produced. The editor wants **"contemporary, 'language' poetry with a strong visual interest."** They have recently published poetry by Charles Bernstein, James Sherry, Rosemarie Waldrop and Hannah Weiner. The editor selected these sample lines by Charles Bunstein:

> No priority other than the vanished
> Imagination of some other
> Time—inlets of dilapidated
> Incredulity harbored
> On the deleterious Bus to Air Landing

Awede publishes two poetry chapbooks per year, 32 pp., 6 × 9″, flat-spined. **Freelance submissions are accepted, but author should query first. Queries are answered in 2 weeks, MSS reported on in 4-5 months, simultaneous submissions are acceptable, as are photocopied MSS. Pay is in author's copies, 10% of run.** No subsidy publishing, book catalog free on request, with SASE a must. Sample books available at list price of $4-8.

‡AXE; MATTHEW BUGGEY ANNUAL AWARD (I), 421 Park St., Oxford, PA 19363, founded 1990, editor Ms. P.I. Nagler. *Axe* requires **$1/poem reading fee. "Accepted contributors must pay postage/handling for that issue (85¢ postage, 15¢ envelope, word-processing supplies).** We hope to do away with this postage-needed condition as a subscriber base is established." It appears twice a year using **"lean and mean poetry. The right poem for *Axe* hits hard, cuts deep. Nothing inspirational, greeting card, calendar, SPCA verse, 'feel-good' save-the-earth-whales-redwoods."** As a sample the editor selected these lines from "Stillbirth" by Robert Nagler:

> The nurse presents the dead infant to the mother and father.
> (Recent medical research mandates this.)
>
> They move the child's hand and note the fingernails are fully formed. They cry like children
> themselves: united, a while, in grief.

It is digest-sized, 30-40 pp., "photoreproduced from word processed copy, card covers, very few graphics, saddle-stapled." **Sample: $2 postpaid (available 1991). Guidelines for SASE.** The Matthew Buggey Annual Award of $50 is for the best poem published in *Axe* that year.

AXE FACTORY REVIEW (II), Box 11186, Philadelphia, PA 19136, phone 215-331-7389, founded 1984, poetry editor Joseph Farley. First issue, March 1986. They started with the annual magazine and hope to publish chapbooks and full-sized collections in the future as **Axe Factory Publications**. Their first issue included poetry by Charles Bukowski, Etheridge Knight, Arthur Knight, William Stafford, J.B. Goodenough, and Stephen Dunn. Sample lines by Greg Geleta from "Benito Mussolini is Alive and Well":

> Benito Mussolini is alive and well
> and selling used cars in Memphis, Tennessee.
> I once saw a photograph of him and his mistress
> strung by their necks in Milan.
> Evidently he was holding his breath . . .

"We publish what we like—open to any school/style. As editors, we want to 'enjoy' our magazine. We want our readers to feel the same way." They use 50% poetry, approximately 32 pp. per issue, a printrun of 500. **Reports in 2-5 weeks, pays in copies. Regarding possible chapbook publication, query with 5-10 samples and cover letter conveying "personality as well as back-**

ground info (publications, bio, personal aesthetics/philosophies, etc.)" They comment "when so moved and have time to do so."

AXIS (IV-Themes, specialized, spiritual), P.O. Box 1134, Huntington, NY 11743-0656, founded 1988 as *Sun/Father Journal*, editor Jeff Zeth, appears twice a year using "poetry from a uniquely male/ecological/religious perspective; free verse, blank verse, or traditional rhymed forms. Under 30 lines best, but will consider longer poems that are well-crafted. Poems inspired by men's relationships and by Jungian, shamanic, hermetic, occult and Native American traditions. No poems that have nothing to do with men as a gender; poems that are overly secular and delight in titillation and *trivial* eroticism." They have recently published poetry by Steve Langan. As samples the editor selected these lines by Clyde Glandon:

> . . . the pine cone has its father's darkness
> inside its sharp scales
> where the pine cone is crafty
> crafty enough to show its gold

and these lines by Wolf Knight:

> Then stand you ready to take my greeting
> when brother welcomes brother—
> I sound the Bell!

It is magazine-sized, 28 pp., desktop published, saddle-stitched with matte card cover. Subscription: $7 for 2 issues; single copy $3.75. **They will consider previously published poems. Reports in 4-6 weeks, "generally." Publication is approximately 1 year from date of acceptance. Pays 2 copies. "Often will include writer's guidelines."** The editor says their mentors include both contemporary and historical figures, such as William Morris, St. Francis, Robert Bly and Joseph Campbell. The editor's advice is, "Look for a voice that speaks freely and that is proud of who and whose you are. Don't make apologies."

‡THE BABY CONNECTION NEWS JOURNAL (IV-Themes), Drawer 13320, San Antonio, TX 78213-3320, phone Tues-Fri 10-3 CST 512-342-4632, founded 1986, Ms. Gina G. Morris, C.I.D.I./editor, is "a monthly news journal **to support, educate, move and inspire new and expectant parents** in their role of rearing babies and pre-schoolers 0-5 years of age. Parenting is such a tough job—our publication strives to reward and motivate positive and nurturing parenting skills." They use **"poetry only on the subjects of mothering, fathering, birthing, pregnancy, child rearing, the power, the love, the passion and momentum, fertility. Humor a big plus. No Eastern mysticism, anything too far left or right. Ours is a straight and narrow journal, and I will not alienate my readers with weird poetry. Poets, be real; basic humanity is massively appealing."** They have recently published poetry by Chanel Falovolito and Marcia Lietzke. As a sample the editor selected these lines from "The Child's Sight" by Hy Sobiloff:

> The child is a little inspector when it crawls
> It touches and tastes the earth
> Rolls and stumbles toward the object
> Zigzags like a sail. . . .

The tabloid-sized newsprint publication is 8 pp. **"We would like to receive and publish all poetry that specifically pertains to our publishing needs."** Press run: 30,000 for 1,700 subscriptions of which 10% are libraries. Subscription: $18. **Sample, postpaid: $3 for 2 different issues.** For #3 you get 2 issues and "writer's kit" giving guidelines, submission form, and pre-routed return envelope. Pays 5 copies. "We encourage a reduced rate subscription of $9 for 6 months so we can be assured the poet knows our context and cares enough to follow us for a term. However, there is no obligation. We encourage all caring persons." Simultaneous submissions and previously published poems OK. Reports "immediately" if possible. Editor comments on submis-

---

ALWAYS submit MSS or queries with a stamped, self-addressed envelope (SASE) within your country or International Reply Coupons (IRCs) purchased from the post office for other countries.

sions "**if poet requests feedback.**" They also publish 5-8 chapbooks and flat-spined paperbacks/ year averaging 16-72 pp. **For book or chapbook publication, submit 3-4 samples, bio ("a very personable bio — about the real poet, not accomplishments"), publications. Pays 6 copies and honorarium averaging $25.** They are open to subsidy arrangements for "small books of poetry specifically dealing with family, birthing, and parenting, and we will advertise it free of charge in our newspaper and in our Baby's Mart catalog." Query for details of arrangements. The editor says, "Our Parent Center is very interested in collections of family and birthing poetry to inspire positive parenting. Be part of American-realized family values and give us basic, *almost* abrasive, blatant perspectives on womanhood, fathering, fertility, and the joy of bringing a new life into this world."

THE BAD HENRY REVIEW; 44 Press (II), Box 150045, Van Brunt Station, Brooklyn, NY 11215-0001, founded 1981, poetry editors Evelyn Horowitz, Michael Malinowitz and Mary du Passage. They have recently published poetry by John Ashbery, Gilbert Sorrentino, Stephen Sandy and William Mathews. Press run is 500-1,000 for 200 subscriptions of which 15 are for libraries; 200-300 for shelf sales. *The Bad Henry Review* is an annual publishing quality poetry, 64 pp., digest-sized. **Sample: $4. Per issue $5; subscription $9/2 issues. Pays 2 copies. Submit no more than 5 poems, include SASE. No simultaneous submissions. No previously published poems unless advised. Rarely comments on rejected MSS.** The editor comments, "We've done one issue of long poems and we're considering doing an issue on translations." 44 Press publishes about 1 book of poetry per year.

BAKER STREET PUBLICATIONS; THE HAUNTED JOURNAL; THE VAMPIRE JOURNAL; THE COLLINSPORT RECORD; NOCTURNAL NEWS; BAKER STREET GAZETTE; HORIZONS BEYOND; HORIZONS WEST; DEEP SOUTH JOURNAL; POISON PEN WRITERS' NEWS; THE LOVECRAFT REVIEW; THE POE JOURNAL; THE SALEM JOURNAL; REV. TRASK ANTHOLOGY; MOVIE MEMORIES; SLEUTH JOURNAL (I, IV-horror, science fiction, fantasy, themes, romance), Box 994, Metairie, LA 70004, phone 504-733-9138, founded 1983, poetry editors Sharida Rizzuto, Thomas Schellenberger, Sidney J. Dragon. All of these magazines, chapbooks, perfect-bound paperbacks, and newsletters use poetry. "**No strict requirements on form, length or style. Must be suitable for horror, mystery, science fiction, fantasy, romance, western, or literary. Nothing pornographic or punk.**" They have recently published poetry by Wayne Allen Sallee and John B. Rosenman, Brenda Corbett, Elizabeth Stinson, Lyn Lifshin, Daisy Takacs and Billy Wolfenbarger. As a sample, the editor selected the poem "Starving" by Dwight Humphries, which appeared in *The Haunted Journal*:

> There is eternal hunger
> In my frayed soul;
> My heart a fenris wolf
> Beneath my ribs that
> Starves for all things.

The editor says, "Most zines are 60-120 pp., and digest-size; newsletters are magazine-sized and 6-12 pp., chapbooks and paperbacks vary. All publications include artwork and graphics inside and on covers. All have ads in the back. Most of them contain photos." Their press run is "under 10,000." **Send SASE for guidelines. Sample copies are $3-5. Pays "mainly in copies but fees negotiable." Submissions are "preferably typewritten. Author should include a bio sheet." Simultaneous submissions OK, as are previously published poems that are "very good and haven't been published in over 3 years." Reports in 2-4 weeks. For book publications send 3-5 sample poems, bio. Simultaneous submissions, photocopies, dot matrix, all OK. Responds to queries in 1-3 weeks, to MSS in 4-6 weeks. Pays 50% royalties after printing and advertising costs are covered. Publishes 2-4 chapbooks per year. Same submission requirements as for other publications.** Sharida Rizzuto advises, "Just be yourself; don't try to imitate anyone else. Respect helpful criticism."

THE BANK STREET PRESS; THE PORT AUTHORITY POETRY REVIEW (V), 24 Bank Street, New York, NY 10014, phone 212-255-0692, founded 1985, poetry editor Mary Bertschmann. A small group of poets meet at the Bank Street home of Mary Bertschmann and publish their poetry annually in a series of flat-spined paperbacks called *The Port Authority Poetry Review*. The first of these was devoted to experiments in bad poetry. The third, which I have seen, is inspired by Shakespeare. The fifth volume, published in October, 1988 is a collection of romantic poetry and feature contributions from four of the poets of The Port Authority Poetry League. The sample poetry given is from "Poet at Work" (Vol. VI, May, 1990) by Mary York Sampson:

> Snow is swirling, whirling to please,
> Kissing the pigeons, tickling March trees,
> Teasing the iron girder and cement grid,
> Light as a breath, man's harshness to rid,
> How can I not feel true ecstasy . . . .

With this heavenly effort to make poetry?
Sample $7 including postage and handling. Please make check payable to Mary Bertschmann.

‡BAPTIST SUNDAY SCHOOL BOARD; BROADMAN PRESS; LIVING WITH PRESCHOOLERS; LIVING WITH CHILDREN; LIVING WITH TEENAGERS; HOME LIFE (IV-Religious); MATURE LIVING (IV-Religious, senior citizen), 127 Ninth Ave. N., Nashville, TN 37234, the publishing agency for Southern Baptists. "We publish magazines, monthlies, quarterlies, books, filmstrips, films, church supplies, etc., for Southern Baptist churches." Books of poetry are published under the Broadman Press imprint. **Query with samples.** For most of their publications they want **"inspirational and/or religious poetry. No 'word pictures'. We want poetry with a message to inspire, uplift, motivate, amuse. No longer than 24 lines,"** typed, double-spaced, no simultaneous submissions. Reports within 60 days, rate of pay figured on number of lines submitted. The biggest of the monthlies is *Home Life*, which began in 1947. Circulation 750,000; 20,000 subscriptions—a magazine-sized 60+ pp., saddle-stapled slick magazine, illustrated (no ads). Its poetry editors, Charlie Warren and Mary Paschall Darby, say they want **"religious poetry; treating marriage, family life, and life in general from a Christian perspective. We rarely publish anything of more than 25 lines."** Sample: $1 to authors with SASE! Submit no more than 6 poems at a time. "Prefer original, but photocopy and dot-matrix acceptable. Query unnecessary." Send SASE for guidelines. Reports in 6-8 weeks, pays $15-24. *Mature Living: A Christian Magazine for Senior Adults*, founded in 1977, is a monthly mass circulation (330,000) magazine providing **"leisure reading for senior adults. All material used is compatible with a Christian life-style."** The poetry they use is of Christian content, inspirational, about "nature/God," rhymed, 8-24 lines. Assistant editor Judy Pregel says, **"We dislike free-verse or poems where a word is dragged in just to piece out a meter."** Apparently you do not have to be a senior citizen to submit. The editor selected "Coloring Book" by Marion Schoeberlein:

> *Spring is a new greed meadow—*
> *A murmuring brook*
> *Spring is God filling in*
> *A coloring book!*

Mature Living is magazine-sized, 52 pp., saddle-stapled, using large print on pulp stock, glossy paper cover, with color and b/w art. They "receive hundreds" of poems per year, use about 125-150. Most of their distribution is through churches who buy the magazine in bulk for their senior adult members. **For sample, send 9x12" self-addressed envelope and 85¢ postage. Pays $5-25. Reports in 6-8 weeks,** but there might be a 3 year delay before publication.

‡THE BASSETTOWN REVIEW (II), 312 Van Buren Ave., West Brownsville, PA 15417, phone 412-785-7931, founded 1988, poetry editors Fred Lapisardi and George Swaney, is a literary annual. **"We want to see Whitman, Dickinson, Larkin, Yeats—but we know the chances are slim. I guess we want to see anyone; it's so lonely without poems to read. No pseudo-confessional junk about a loved one boffing your brains out, nature crap about a sunset we've all seen a zillion times, Popean heroics dedicated to your good friend Harvey Keitel, baloney about birthing a baby and flushing it down the toilet and now you're born again, open form imitation Olson psychosis, assistant professor-penned quasi-Derrida-inspired Heideggerian Paradoxes. Otherwise anything."** They have published poetry by Roger Bower, Michael Wurster, and Arthur Winfield Knight. As a sample the editor selected these lines from "Letting Go" by Fred Lapisardi:

> *Crystal needles of frozen stream flash*
> *as we glide past a sudden hillside falls;*
> *a field glazed with frost flutters past—*
> *an unwashed sheet wrinkled across an empty bed.*

It is magazine-sized, 36 pp. saddle-stapled with paper cover, professionally printed. Press run 1,500 for 30 subscribers of which 2 are libraries, 100+ shelf sales. **Sample, postpaid: $1.75. Reports in 3 months. Pays 3 copies.** The editor adds, "Donald Hall said it best: 'Be as good as George Herbert; take as long as you wish.'"

‡WILLIAM L. BAUHAN, PUBLISHER (V, IV-Regional), P.O. Box 443, Old County Road, Dublin, NH 03444, phone 603-563-8020, founded 1966, editor William L. Bauhan, publishes poetry and art, especially New England regional books. **They currently accept no unsolicited poetry.** They have published books of poetry by Henry Chapin and Dorothy Richards.

‡BAY AREA POETS COALITION (BAPC); POETALK (I), 1527 Virginia St., Berkeley, CA 94703, phone 415-845-8409, founded 1974, poetry editor Maggi H. Meyer. Coalition sends monthly poetry letter, *Poetalk* to over 400 people. They publish annual anthology (11th—164 pp., out in 1990), giving one page to each member of BAPC who has had work published in *Poetalk* during the prior year. *Poetalk* publishes 50-60 poets each issue. BAPC has 190 members, 80 subscribers, but *Poetalk* is open to all. **Predictable rhyme only if clever vocabulary. Each poem 3×4" maximum.** One poem from each new

submitter will usually be printed. Typewritten, single-spaced OK. Editor fits as many poems as she can on 3 legal size pages. Send 4 poems each 6 months only. You'll get a copy of *Poetalk* in which your work appears. Write (with SASE) for 2 month's free copies. Membership: $12 for 12 months *Poetalk*, copy of anthology, and other privileges if you live in the Bay Area. The editor chose these sample lines by M.P.A. Sheaffer:

> *Echoes of laughter*
> *Play among branches and leaves*
> *Then, swirling among*
> *The rushes in a still pond,*
> *Open the tightest lily.*

BAPC holds monthly readings, contests, etc.; has mailing list open to local members; a PA system members may use for a small fee. People from 27 states other than California and 8 countries have contributed to *Poetalk* or entered their 10 annual contests. Simultaneous and previously published work OK. All subject matter should be in good taste. Response time 2 weeks-4 months.

BAY WINDOWS (IV-Gay/lesbian), 1523 Washington St., Boston, MA 02118, FAX 617-266-5973, founded 1983, poetry editors Rudy Kikel and Patricia A. Roth. *Bay Windows* is a weekly gay and lesbian newspaper published for the New England community, regularly using "short poems of interest to lesbians and gay men. Poetry that is 'experiential' seems to have a good chance with us, but we don't want poetry that just 'tells it like it is.' Our readership doesn't read poetry all the time. A primary consideration is giving *pleasure*. We'll overlook the poem's (and the poet's) tendency not to be informed by the latest poetic theory, if it *does* this: pleases. Pleases, in particular, by articulating common gay or lesbian experience, and by doing that with some attention to form. I've found that a lot of our choices were made because of a strong image strand. Humor is *always* welcome — and hard to provide with craft. Obliquity, obscurity? Probably not for us. We won't presume on our audience." They have recently published poetry by Judith Barrington, Paul Monette, Jacqueline Lapidus, Steven Riel and Terri L. Jewell. As a sample, Rudy Kikel picked these lines from "Icarus Flies Air France" by Lawrence Kinsman:

> *My hands tremble at the thought of you,*
> *eating miniature Coq au Vin, reading a book,*
> *chatting with a male model who will ask for your*
> *phone number, nothing beneath you but currents of*
> *treacherous air. Oh, my Icarus, why can't we sail to*
> *La Havre on the Mauretania as the Vanderbilts and the*
> *Carnegies did?*

"We try to run four poems (two by lesbians, two by gay men) each month, print-run 13,000, 700 subscriptions of which 15 are libraries. Subscription: $35; per issue: 50¢. They receive about 1,000 submissions per year, use 1 in 20, have a 3 month backlog. **Sample: $1 postpaid. Poems by gay males should be sent care of Rudy Kikel, *Bay Windows*, at the address above; by lesbians, care of Patricia A. Roth % Schwartz, 11 Belmont Ave., Somerville, MA 02143. "3-5 poems, 5-25 lines are ideal." Reports in 4 weeks, pays copies. Editors "often" comment on rejections.**

BEAR TRIBE PUBLISHING; WILDFIRE MAGAZINE (IV-Nature, themes, ethnic), Box 9167, Spokane, WA 99209, phone 509-326-6561, founded 1965 (the magazine's former name, *Many Smokes Earth Awareness Magazine*), poetry editor Elisabeth Robertson. The magazine uses **short poetry on topics appropriate to the magazine, such as earth awareness, self-sufficiency, sacred places, native people, etc. Press run is 10,000 for 6,000 subscriptions of which 5% are libraries, 3,500 shelf sales. Subscription $12.50. Sample: $4 postpaid. Send SASE for guidelines and brochure.** They have published poetry by Gary Snyder, W. D. Ehrhart, P. J. Brown and Evelyn Eaton. The quarterly devotes 1-2 pp. to poetry each issue. They want a "positive and constructive viewpoint, no hip or offensive language." Poets published receive 1 year subscription. The Press publishes books that incorporate Native American poems and songs, but no collections by individuals. They comment on rejections, "especially on good poetry."

‡BEAT SCENE MAGAZINE (IV-Form), 27 Court Leet, Binley Woods, Coventry, England CV3 2JQ, phone 0203-543604, founded 1983, editor Kevin Ring, is a "news/information/review magazine based around American Beat Generation writers: Kerouac, Burroughs and modern USA-linked writers/

‡The double dagger before a listing indicates that the listing is new in this edition. New markets are often the most receptive to submissions.

artists/films, etc., i.e., Kathy Acker, Jim Carroll, Jack Micheline" and uses **poetry appropriate to that purpose "free form, based on living in USA." They don't want "totally introspective, elusive poetry, poems with classical basis."** They have recently published poetry by Jack Micheline and Jack Kerouac. I have not seen the publication, but the editor says it appears 6 times a year in "standard magazine size with glossy covers, using cover art and planning to include photos." They receive about 5 poems a week, use about 2 poems an issue. Press run 600 for 200 subscriptions of which 5 are libraries, 250 shelf sales. Subscription: $26. **Sample, postpaid: $7. Pays 1 copy. Contributors are expected to buy a copy or copies of the magazine or their other publications. No previously published poems or simultaneous submissions.** They also publish 3 chapbooks a year averaging 30 pp. **To submit for chapbook publication query with bio and publications. Pays 20-40% royalties. Editor comments on submissions "always."** He says, "The publishing of poetry in the UK is shoddy. America leaves us standing. Class still has a grip on poetry in this country. The old school tie attitude still prevails. Result: ancient poetry that doesn't relate to now. For beginners: be persistent."

‡THE BELLADONNA (IV-Psychic/occult, spirituality/inspirational), P.O. Box 935, Simpsonville, SC 29681, founded 1988, editor Elizabeth H. Finnell, co-editor Susan Seel, appears annually with **"unusual, New Age poems that tell stories. No greeting card verse."** As a sample Elizabeth Finnell selected these lines from "The Sun and Moon are Baby Buggies" by Nancy Berg:

> *My baby feels the tides come in*
> *he shares a secret with the sand*
> *he knows he is the ocean's kin*
> *waves rise and fall inside his hand*

Belladonna is 30-40 pages, limited editions 50 to 100 per run. "Very unique, strong attitude." **No formal guidelines—"magical attitude-slant." Pays 1 copy. Reporting time 4-12 weeks. "Need writers not afraid to be different."**

‡THE BELLEVUE PRESS (II), 60 Schubert St., Binghamton, NY 13905, phone 607-729-0819, founded 1973 by Gil and Deborah H. Williams. "Publishing art, photography and poetry post-cards; signed letter-press poetry broadsides, and small and large letter-press books of poetry and art." Their presswork is elegant. **They are looking for "original work which reflects current or future trends in style, not work which simply rehashes styles of the past!"** They have recently published poetry by Stephen Sandy, Barbara Unger, L. Fixel, Carole Stone and Edouard Roditi. These sample lines are from a postcard, Richard F. Fleck's "Springtime at John Burroughs' Woodchuck Lodge":

> *Yellow glimmerings illume*
> *entire eastern sky—*
> *then bright burning*
> *Chinese lantern rises*
> *through white blossoms*
> *of shadwood and chess apple*

Their average production of books is two 30 pp. chapbooks per year. **Query with about 5 samples and "a one-page mini-bio listing some publications (preferably book or anthology appearances) and recent accomplishments." MS should be "as the poet intends the book to appear." Photocopy OK. Replies to query in 2-3 weeks, to MS in 6 weeks. Payment: 10% of press run.** Gil Williams **comments** "when I'm asked to, or sometimes when I have extra (?) time. But everyone in America has a poetry manuscript these days! Yet for every order we actually get at the Press, we must receive 10 letters from hopeful poets seeking publication! Poets had better start *buying* books and using our postcards or there will be *no* Bellevue Press! As I write, I sit surrounded with some 4,500 poetry books I have *bought!*"

BELLFLOWER PRESS (II, IV-Themes, children), Box 24749 Dept. WD, Cleveland, OH 44124-0749, founded 1974 (new management as of 1988), poetry editor/owner Louise Wazbinski, **publishes poetry 50% of the time on a subsidized basis.** She wants rhymed poetry **"that is helpful to someone emotionally, spiritually, or physically, e.g., breathing techniques or other ways to help cope, or bad foods we consume too much of (sugar); also, children's and humorous poetry."** They have recently published poetry by A.L. Lazarus, from whose poem, "Local Habitation," in his collection **Some Light**, I selected these sample lines:

> *Breathe deep breathe shallow, breathe systole*
> *diastole, like gasping fish we're hooked upon*
> *catastrophe. In breathless haste, in mal*
> *de mer, pull what we will from Anywhere,*
> *this ineluctable elixir is all*
> *that's there; and here it is, this island air.*

Reports in 2-4 weeks on queries, 6-8 weeks on MSS. "Contract depends upon subvention by author, usually 50%. Often the author will subsidize a small percentage and receive books as

payment. **In other cases, there is no subsidy and the author receives a royalty based on the specific arrangements made at the time of agreement."**

BELLOWING ARK PRESS; BELLOWING ARK (II), Box 45637, Seattle, WA 98145, phone 206-545-8302, founded 1984, editor Robert R. Ward. *Bellowing Ark* is a bi-monthly literary tabloid that **"publishes only poetry which demonstrates in some way the proposition that existence has meaning, or, to put it another way, that life is worth living. We have no strictures as to length, form or style; only that the work we publish is to our judgment life-affirming."** They do not want **"academic poetry, in any of its manifold forms."** Poets recently published include Natalie Reciputi, John Elrod, Ray Mizer, and Mark Allan Johnson. As a sample the editor selected "Contemplation on the 20th Anniversary of the Moonshot; July 20, 1989," by Bethany Reid:

> *Above these dim, suburban lights*
>
> *The Universe unfolds, whole,*
> *Its precious molecular structures*
> *Recycling, recombining, invisible*
> *Wheels of science. And the spirit also,*
>
> *Rising unnoticed perhaps*
> *Like the moon over sleeping children*

The paper is tabloid-sized, 24 pp. printed on electrobright stock with b/w photos and line drawings. Circulation is 1,000, of which 200+ are subscriptions and 600+ are sold on newsstands. Price is $2/issue, subscription is $12/year. **Sample: $2 postpaid. Pay is 2 copies. The editors say, "absolutely *no* simultaneous submissions, prefer not to see dot-matrix or photocopy." They reply to submissions in 2-6 weeks and publish within the next 1 or 2 issues. Occasionally they will criticize a MS if it seems to "display potential to become the kind of work we want."** Bellowing Ark Press publishes collections of poetry by invitation only.

BELL'S LETTERS POET(I), Box 2187, Gulfport, MS 39505, founded 1956 as *Writer's Almanac*, 1958 as *Thunderhead for Writers*, 1966 as *Bell's Letters*, publisher and editor Jim Bell, is a quarterly which you must buy ($3 per issue, $12 subscription) to be included. The editor says "most fall in love with its family-like ties," and judging by the many letters from readers, I would judge that to be the case. Though there is no payment for poetry accepted, many patrons send awards of $5 or $10 to the poets whose work they especially like. Subscription "guarantees them a byline each issue." Poems are "12-16 lines in good taste." They have recently published poetry by Dolores Malaschak, Karen Schuff, Margie Zimmerman and Alice Lile. As a sample the editor chose these lines by Ethel Pittman:

> *A lone cardinal*
> *Sheltered in snow covered birch—*
> *Garnet in white gold.*

It is digest-sized, 72 pp., offset from typescript on plain bond paper (including cover). **Sample $3 postpaid. Send SASE for guidelines. MS may be typed or even hand-written. No simultaneous submissions. Previously published poems OK "if cleared with prior publisher." Reports in 10 days. Acceptance of poems by subscribers go immediately into the next issue.** "Our publication dates fall quarterly on the spring and autumn equinox and winter and summer solstice. Deadline for poetry submissions is 30 days prior to publication." "50 BL Classics" is a competition in each issue. Readers are asked to vote on their favorite poems, and the winners are announced in the next issue, along with awards sent them by patrons.

THE BELOIT POETRY JOURNAL (II), Box 154, RFD 2, Ellsworth, ME 04605, phone 207-667-5598, founded 1950, editor Marion K. Stocking, a well-known, long-standing quarterly of quality poetry and reviews. **"We publish the best poems we receive, without bias as to length, school, subject, or form.** It is our hope to discover the growing tip of poetry and to introduce new poets alongside established writers. We publish occasional chapbooks on special themes to diversify our offerings." They want **"fresh, imaginative poetry, with a distinctive voice. We tend to prefer poems that make the reader share an experience rather than just read about it, and these we keep for up to 3 months,** circulating them among our readers, and continuing to winnow out the best. At the quarterly meetings of the Editorial Board we read aloud all the surviving poems and put together an issue of the best we have." They have recently published Bruce Cutler, Hillel Schwartz, Lola Haskins, Albert Goldbarth, and Susan Tichy. The editor chose this sample from "The Dissolution of Memory" by James Sullivan:

> *A picture of a boy with dirt on his face appears*
> *Against a page, blocks out a paragraph. Try to remember.*
>
> *Now try to read again. A picture of a boy,*
> *A picture of a woman leading a boy toward a station wagon:*

> *Begin again. "The dissolution of memory over time . . ."*
> *A station wagon distant in the next yard, by a lake.*

Submit any time, without query, any legible form, *"No simultaneous submissions."* (If you send photocopies or carbons, include a note saying the poems are not being submitted elsewhere.) "Any length of MS, but most poets send what will go in a business envelope for one stamp. Don't send your life work." Payment: 3 copies. It's an attractively printed digest-sized, 40 pp. format, with tasteful art on the card covers. Sample copy: $2, includes guidelines, or SASE for guidelines alone. They have a circulation of 1,200 with 575 subscriptions, of which 325 are libraries. No backlog: "We clear the desk at each issue."

‡BENNETT & KITCHEL (IV-Form), P.O. Box 4422, East Lansing, MI 48826, phone 517-355-1707, founded 1989, editor William Whallon, publishes 3-4 hardbacks/year of "poetry of form and meaning. Short pieces with perhaps one or two longer ones. Any subject. No free verse or haiku." As a sample of poetry he likes the editor selected these lines by Lord Alfred Douglas:

> *And from the great*
> *Gates of the East,*
> *With a clang and a brazen blare,*
> *Forth from the rosy wine and the feast*
> *Comes the god with the flame-flaked hair.*

In 1990 Bennett & Kitchel published a volume of verse for The Society for Creative Anachronism. Sample, postpaid: $6. Reports in 2 weeks. Terms "variable, negotiable." Simultaneous submissions and previously published poems OK if copyright is clear. Minimum volume for a book "might be 750 lines." If a book is accepted, publication within 9 months. Editor comments on submissions "seldom." He advises, "Read 'Writing a Narrative in Poetry,' *Writer's Digest,* August, 1988."

BERKELEY POETRY REVIEW (II), 700 Eshleman Hall, University of California, Berkeley, CA 94720, founded 1973, poetry editors Natacia Apostoles and Jonathan Brennan, is an annual review "which publishes poems and translations of local as well as national and international interest. We are open to any form or length which knows how to express itself through that form." They have recently published poetry by Federico Garcia Lorca, Thom Gunn, August Kleinzahler, Robert Hass and John Tranter. I have not seen an issue, but the editors describe it as a flat-spined paperback, averaging 150 pp., circulation 500. Subscription: $10/year. For book publication submit 5 sample poems with bio. Include SASE; allow 2-6 months for reply. Simultaneous submissions, photocopies, dot-matrix, previously published poems (if not copyrighted) all OK, pays 1 copy. 1987 issue featured an interview with Heather McHugh.

‡BERKELEY POETS COOPERATIVE (WORKSHOP & PRESS) (II), Box 459, Berkeley, CA 94701, founded 1969, poetry editor Charles Entrekin (plus rotating staff), is "a nonprofit organization which offers writers the opportunity to explore, develop and publish their works. Our primary goals are to maintain a free workshop open to writers, and to publish outstanding collections of poetry and fiction by individual writers." The *New York Times* has called it "the oldest and most successful poetry cooperative in the country." Chapbooks recently published by J.D. Woolery and Robert Frazier. Charles Entrekin says he prefers "modern imagist—open to all kinds, but we publish very little rhyme." These sample lines are by Bruce Hawkins:

> *The sandtormented stingray lies*
> *up near the logline,*
> *a smouldering necktie,*
> *a suffering piece of geometry.*

They publish one 48 pp. chapbook by an individual each year, for which the poet receives 50% of the profit and 20 copies. You can order a sample book for $3. Criticism sometimes provided on rejected MSS. Poets elsewhere might consider BPWP as a model for forming similar organizations.

‡THE BERKELEY REVIEW OF BOOKS (I), 1731 10th St. Apt. A, Berkeley, CA 94710, founded 1988, editor Harold David Moe, appears 3 times a year, using "experimental" poetry. They don't want to see "99.9% of what's written today." They have recently published poetry by Lisa Chang, Nanos Valaoritis, David Meltzer, and Dale Jensen. As a sample the editor selected these lines (poet unidentified):

> *Anklestocking photographs*
> *miming charades*
> *oppossuming diamonds*
> *rites, energy, aura into light*

> *deepbleep big truth*
> *it's the letter carriers' tooth fairy.*

I have not seen an issue, but the editor describes it as magazine-sized, flat-spined, with a press run of 1,000. Subscription: $7. **Sample, postpaid: $5. Pays "1 copy at discount price." Editor comments on submissions "often."** He says, "Most so-called poets are rebels without vision or warmth—timid craftsmen of the academy who wouldn't know a poem if it muff-dived their birth. Yet, the *only* objective criterion for poetry is, 'Is it legible?' The rest is personal considerations. Any poetry sent to us will be reviewed."

‡**BEYOND (IV-Science fiction/fantasy)**, P.O. Box 136, New York, NY 10024, founded 1985, editor Shirley Winston, a quarterly magazine of **science fiction and fantasy**. For poetry, the editor wants **"anything short of a major epic"** on those themes. **She does not often use anything longer than 120 lines.** *Beyond* **does not print material in the horror genre.** She has recently published poetry by Dan Crawford and Genevieve Stephens, from whose "Under a Lunar Canopy" she chose the following lines as a sample:

> *Under a lunar canopy*
> *One day*
> *Will there be*
> *A house?*
> *A yard?*
> *A child at play?*

The magazine-sized *Beyond* is 54 pp., saddle-stapled, offset from letter-quality word processor printout, with b/w drawings to illustrate the pieces and a b/w drawing on the cover. Circulation is 200. Price per issue is $5, subscription $17/year. **Sample available for $5 postpaid. Pay is 3¢/ line plus 1 copy. Submissions "must be legible (dot-matrix is OK if dark enough)." Reporting time is 3 months. The editor "always" provides criticism on rejected MSS.**

THE BIG MOUSE (IV-Humor), 81 Castlerigg Dr., Burnley, Lancashire U.K. BB12 8AT, founded 1984, poetry editor Andrew Savage (Sir), wants **"each issue to contain short poems that are inanely funny beyond belief. Must include at least one rude limerick and one poem written specifically to be shouted out as loud as humanly possible. No very long works."** They have recently published poetry by Ann Keith, Alex Warner, King Kong Smith, Lovely Ivos, and Betty J. Silconas. As a sample the editor selected these lines by Brenda Williamson:

> *The summer day started out just right*
> *All sunny & warm & cheesy bright*
> *until the split*
> *from where he sit*
> *& the moon came out of the pants too tight.*

The format consists of one sheet folded into tall quarters. It appears "so irregularly it's unbelievable." Accepts about 20% of poetry received. Their press run is 1,000, and it is distributed free. **Sample for 3 International Reply Coupons (IRCs). Pays 15 copies. Considers simultaneous submissions and previously published poems that have not appeared in the U.K.**

BILINGUAL REVIEW PRESS; BILINGUAL REVIEW/REVISTA BILINGÜE (IV-Ethnic, bilingual), Hispanic Research Center, Arizona State University, Tempe, AZ 85287, phone 602-965-3867, journal founded 1974, press in 1976. Managing editor Karen Van Hooft says they are "a small-press publisher of U.S. Hispanic creative literature and of a journal containing poetry and short fiction in addition to scholarship." The journal contains some poetry in each issue; they also publish flat-spined paperback collections of poetry. **"We publish poetry by and/or about U.S. Hispanics and U.S. Hispanic themes. We do not publish translations in our journal, or literature about the experiences of Anglo Americans in Latin America. We have published a couple of poetry volumes in bilingual format (Spanish/English) of important Mexican poets."** They have recently published poetry by Elías Miguel Múnoz, Marjorie Agosín, Martín Espada and Demetria Martínez. I have not seen the journal, which appears 3 times a year, but the editor says it is $7 \times 10''$, 96 pp. flat-spined, offset, with 2-color cover. They use less than 10% of hundreds of submissions received each year. Press run is 1,000 for 850+ subscriptions. Subscriptions are $16 for individuals, $26 for institutions. **Sample: $6 individuals/$9 institutions postpaid. Pays 2 copies. Submit "2 copies, including ribbon original if possible, with loose stamps for return postage. For book submissions, send 4-5 sample poems, bio, publications." Pays $100 advance, 10% royalties, and 10 copies.**

BIRD WATCHER'S DIGEST (IV-Nature), Box 110, Marietta, OH 45750, founded 1978, editor Mary Beacom Bowers, is a specialized but promising market for **poems of "true literary merit"** in which birds figure in some way, at least by allusion. 2-3 poems are used in each bimonthly issue and earn $10/poem. Some poets who have appeared there recently include Susan Rea, Nancy G. Westerfield,

Lois Barkett, and William D. Barney. I liked these lines from David Hopes' "The Kingdom of the Birds," describing cranes:

> *pointed upward, flight a repose*
> *between two agonies, striving and beating*
> *as though together all might lift*
> *the swamp up rung by rung into the sky.*

"Preferred: no more than 20 lines, 40 spaces, no more than 3 poems at a time, no queries." Sample copy postpaid: $3. Reports in 2 months. They have up to a year's backlog and use 12-20 of the approximately 500 poems received each year.

BIRMINGHAM POETRY REVIEW (II, IV-Translations), English Department, University of Alabama at Birmingham, Birmingham, AL 35294, phone 205-934-8573, founded 1988, editor Robert Collins, associate editor Randy Blythe. Appears twice a year using poetry of **"any style, form, length, or subject. We are biased toward exploring the cutting edge of contemporary poetry. Style is secondary to the energy, the *fire* the poem possesses. We don't want poetry with cliché-bound, worn-out language."** Recently published poetry by Ivan Argüelles, Jay Blumenthal, Steven Ford Brown, Elton Glaser, Naomi Clark and Peter Wild. They describe their magazine as 50 pp, 6×9″, offset, with b/w cover. Their press run is 500 with 75 subscriptions. Subscription: $3. **Sample: $2 postpaid. Guidelines available for SASE. Pays 2 copies and one-year subscription. Submit 3-5 poems, "no more."** No simultaneous submissions, and previously published poems only if they are translations. **Reports in 1-3 months. Editor sometimes comments on rejections.** He says, "Advice to beginners: Read as much good contemporary poetry, national and international, as you can get your hands on. Then be persistent in finding your own voice."

‡BISHOP PUBLISHING CO. (IV-Themes), 2131 Trimble Way, Sacramento, CA 95825, professor Roland Dickison, is a "small press publisher of **folklore in paperbacks, including contemporary** and out-of-print." They want to see **"American folk poetry, either current or historical. No modern free verse. Folk poetry is usually anonymous."**

BITS PRESS, (III, IV-Humor), English Dept., Case Western Reserve University, Cleveland, OH 44106, phone 216-795-2810 (press founded 1974), poetry editors Robert Wallace, C. M. Seidler, Bonnie Jacobson and Nicholas Ranson. Robert Wallace says, **"Bits Press is devoted to poetry. We publish books and chapbooks (and sometimes limited editions) by young as well as well-known poets. Our main attention at present is given to light verse and funny poems."** The chapbooks are distinguished by elegant but inexpensive format. They have published chapbooks by David R. Slavitt, George Starbuck and Margaret Lally. These sample lines are from Howard Nemerov's "Po Biz":

> *It's been a long time coming,*
> *But after the Cavalier Poets*
> *We've finally got the pedestrian ones,*
> *Coming in on little flat feet.*

The few chapbooks they publish are mostly solicited. Send $2 for a sample or two of the chapbooks; payment to poet in copies (10%+ of run). Wallace sometimes offers criticism with rejections.

BITTERROOT; WM. KUSHNER AWARD; HEERSHE DAVID BADONNEH AWARD (II, IV-Translations), Box 489, Spring Glen, NY 12483, founded 1962, poetry editor Menke Katz, tries "to inspire and discover talented, promising poets. We **discourage stereotyped forms that imitate fixed patterns and encourage all poets who seek their own identity through original poetry."** They are looking for **"rich imagery which leaves an individual mark. Up to 50 lines, unless we consider it an unusual, inspiring poem. We are more interested in *how* the poet writes than what he says, though; this is important. Translations."** Among poets they have recently published are John Tagliabue, Thomas Kretz and Robert Chute. "We don't necessarily look for famous names but for new talent, which we hope will take a place in American poetry one day." As a sample he chose these lines by Rita G. Conroy:

> *I cannot recall your face*
> *though sad rooms*
> *hold a trace of your scent*
> *a hollow lingers*
> *in the chair where you sat*

The 72 pp., digest-sized, flat-spined magazine appears 3 times a year, has a circulation of 850, 50 of which are libraries and colleges. **Sample: $4 postpaid. Subscription: $10 per year. Submit 3-4 poems, typed legibly, double-spaced, with name, address and zip code on each page with SASE. Clear photocopies OK, no simultaneous submissions. Payment: 1 copy. Reports within 6 weeks. Send SASE for guidelines.** Rules for William Kushner Award ($60 first prize, $40 second,

$25 third) and Heershe David Badonneh Award ($100 first prize, $60 second, $40 third) contests: poems up to 40 lines (no more than 3 poems to each contest), any subject, any form, any level, no fee. Please do not send SASE for contest entries, as we do not return them. Winners are published in **Bitterroot**. December 31 deadline. They are hoping for a grant to begin paying contributors. Menke Katz advises, "Poets must place poetry in the center of their lives — to beware of clichés, to find their own path, close to earth or fantastic. Just as every face is different, so must every poet be himself in reality as well as in dreams. Great poets throughout the ages taught us that genuine poetry cannot be pinned down to the past or the future. The poetry of poor poets was and always will have the quality of tin. The work of the poets was and will forever have the quality of gold."

BKMK PRESS (II), University of Missouri-Kansas City, 109 Scofield Hall, 5100 Rockhill Rd., Kansas City, MO 64110-2499, founded 1971, editor Dan Jaffe, publishes 5-6 poetry collections per year, **pays in copies and permission fees. Query with sample poems and bio.** Recently published poets include Harry Martinson, George Gurley, Joan Yeagley, Peter Simpson, Alfred Kisubi, and John Knoepsle. The editor selected these sample lines by Jo McDougall, "After the Quarrel" from the book **The Women in the Next Booth**:

> My car follows yours,
> down the mountain road
> scattering crows and gravel.
> our backs to one another

BLACK AMERICAN LITERATURE FORUM (IV-Ethnic), Dept. of English, Indiana State University, Terre Haute, IN 47809, founded 1967 (as *Negro American Literature Forum*), poetry editors Sterling Plumpp, Thadious M. Davis, and Pinkie Gordon Lane, is a "magazine primarily devoted to the analysis of Afro-American literature, **although one issue per year focuses on poetry by black Americans.** No specifications as to form, length, style, subject matter or purpose. They have recently published poems by Amiri Baraka, Gwendolyn Brooks, Leon Forrest, Jan Carew, Clarence Major, Dudley Randall and Owen Dodson. As a sample I selected the opening lines of "on the line (with 11 million unemployed 9/3/82)" by Mel Donalson:

> and still they wait
> no less in need than the generation before
> their names altered to percentage rates
> their faces mere decimal points along economic indicators

Forum is $6 \times 9''$, 128 pp. with photo on the cover. Individual subscriptions: $19 USA, $24 foreign. They receive about 500 submissions per year, use 50. **Sample: $7.50 postpaid. Submit maximum of 6 poems to editor Joe Weixlmann. Pays in copies. Reports in 2-3 months. Send SASE for guidelines. The editors sometimes comment on rejections.**

BLACK BEAR PUBLICATIONS; BLACK BEAR REVIEW; POETS ELEVEN . . . AUDIBLE (II, IV-Political, social), 1916 Lincoln St., Croydon, PA 19021, phone 215-788-3543, founded 1984, poetry and art editor Ave Jeanne, review and audio editor Ron Zettlemoyer. *Black Bear Review* is a semi-annual international literary and fine arts magazine that also publishes chapbooks and holds an annual poetry competition. Poets published in *BBR* are John M. Bennett, Harry Calhoun, ivan argüelles, John Elsberg, and Todd Moore. *Poets Eleven . . . Audible* has released poetry on tape by A. D. Winans, Tony Moffeit, Kevin Zepper and Mike Maggio. As a sample from *BBR*, the editors selected the poem from "Girl In a Coffin, Photograph, San Salvador, 1979," by John Ekholm:

> This tree is trying hard to be
> a poem.
> I pass her everyday, she claims
> to be an artist, a magician,
> she has many tricks up her sleeve,
> hollow arms and many crotches . . .
> Her womb is filled with squirrels.
> Unable to bear children, she has
> rocked generations of birds.

Circulation of *BBR* is 500, of which 300 are subscriptions; 15 libraries. Price: $4/issue; subscription $8. Catalog is available for SASE. Book catalog is free for SASE. The magazine is perfect bound, digest-sized, 64 pp., offset from typed copy on white stock, with line drawings, collages and woodcuts. The editors explain that *Poets Eleven . . . Audible* was started for accommodation of longer poems for the reader to take part in poetry as a listener; **the author may submit up to 10 minutes of original poetry. SASE for return of your tape; sample copies available for $4 postpaid. Contributor's payment is in copies and royalties.** "We like well crafted poetry that

1989

BLACK BEAR REVIEW

Black Bear Review *prints poetry under the theme of "social concern." According to art and poetry editor Ava Jeanne, Lisette Lugo's cover art "depicts the essence of our poetry by portraying both the submission of humans within the environment and their innate struggle to have a unique voice. Lugo's style and strength are characteristic of the feeling we wish to integrate in the balance of poetry and art."*

mirrors real life — void of camouflage, energetic poetry, avant-garde, free verse and haiku which relate to the world today. We seldom publish the beginner, but will assist when time allows. No traditional poetry is used. The underlying theme of *BBR* is social and political, but the review is interested also in environmental, war/peace, ecological, and minorities themes." Submissions are reported on in 2 weeks, publication is in 6-12 months, any number of poems may be submitted, one to a page, photocopies are OK but they prefer not to read dot-matrix. They publish two chapbooks per year. Chapbook series requires a reading fee of $5, samples and cover letter. For book publication, they would prefer that "*BBR* has published the poet and is familiar with his/her work, but we will read anyone who thinks they have something to say." Queries are answered in 2 weeks, MSS in 4; simultaneous submissions are not considered. Sample of *BBR*: $4 postpaid; back copies when available are $3 postpaid. Guidelines available for SASE. "We appreciate a friendly/brief cover letter. Tell us about the poet; omit degrees or any other pretentious dribble. All submissions are handled with objectivity and quite often rejected material is directed to another market. If you've not been published before — mention it. We are always interested in aiding those who support small press. We frequently suggest poets keep up with **Poet's Market** and read the listings and reviews in issues of *Black Bear*. We are partial to vets, prisoners, and winos. If you don't fit into any of those categories — just send your best stuff. Our yearly poetry competition offers cash awards to poets." Annual deadline is November 1. Guidelines are available for a SASE.

BLACK BUZZARD PRESS; BLACK BUZZARD REVIEW; VISIONS — INTERNATIONAL, THE WORLD JOURNAL; THE BLACK BUZZARD ILLUSTRATED POETRY CHAPBOOK SERIES, (II, IV-Translations), 1110 Seton Lane, Falls Church, VA 22046, founded 1979, poetry editor Bradley R. Strahan, associate editor Shirley G. Sullivan. "We are an independent nonsubsidized press dedicated to publishing fine accessible poetry and translation (particularly from lesser known languages such as Armenian, Gaelic, Urdu, Vietnamese, etc. . . .) accompanied by original illustrations of high quality in an attractive format. We want to see work that is carefully crafted and exciting work that transfigures everyday experience or gives us a taste of something totally new; in all styles except concrete and typographical 'poems.' Nothing purely sentimental. No self-indulgent breast beating. No sadism, sexism or bigotry. No unemotional pap. No copies of Robert Service or the like. Usually under 100 lines but will consider longer." They have published Ted Hughes, Marilyn Hacker, James Dickey, Allen Ginsberg and Marge Piercy; and though he protests that "no 4 lines can possibly do even minimal justice to our taste or interest!" Bradley Strahan offers this 4 line poem *Landscape* by Katherine Smith Manceron:

> The wind coalesces. Suddenly, you have a name and a home.
> This is your childhood.
> Look closer. If you don't know, ask yourself

Who Loved this Light? This canvas filled with boats, rivers, refusals.

Visions, a digest-sized, saddle-stapled magazine finely printed on high-quality paper, appears 3 times a year, uses 56 pages of poetry in each issue. Circulation 750 with 300 subscriptions of which 50 are libraries, **sample: $3.50 postpaid. Current issue: $4.** They receive well over a thousand submissions each year and use 130, have a 3-18 month backlog. *Black Buzzard Review* is a "more or less annual informal journal, dedicated mostly to North American poets and entirely to original English-language poems. We are *letting it all hang out* here, unlike the approach of our prestigious international journal *Visions*, and taking a more wide-open stance on what we accept (including the slightly outrageous)." **Sample of *BBR*: $2.50 + $1 postage. Current issue issue $3.50 + $1 postage.** It is magazine-sized, 36pp., side-stapled, with matte card cover. **"Poems must be readable (not faded, light photocopy or smudged) and *not* handwritten. We resent having to pay postage due, so use adequate postage! No more than 8 pages, please." Reports in 3 days—3 weeks, pays in copies or $5-10 "if we get a grant.** *Visions* is international in both scope and content, publishing poets from all over the world and having readers in 48+ US states, Canada and 24 other foreign countries." **To submit for the chapbook series, send samples (5-10 poems) and a *brief* cover letter "pertinent to artistic accomplishments." Reports in 3 days—3 weeks, pays in copies, usually provides criticism. Send $4 for sample chapbook.** Bradley Strahan adds that in *Visions* "We often publish helpful advice about 'getting published' and the art and craft of poetry and interesting notes about poets and the world of poetry on our editorial page."

‡**BLACK FLY REVIEW (II)**, University of Maine, Fort Kent, ME 04743, phone 207-834-3162, ext. 118, founded 1980, editors Roland Burns and Wendy Kindred. **"We want poetry with strong, sensory images that evoke a sense of experience, place, person; poetry that generates ideas; no overtly philosophical poetry, bad poetry."** They have recently published poetry by Walter McDonald, John Tagliabue, Terry Plunkett, and Constance Hunting. As a sample the editors selected these lines (poet unidentified):

> We listen to hail waste itself
> on hardscrabble shale and cactus,
> rain rushing in gullies to the crookbed.
> Cramped in a cave
> we share with snakes and scorpions

The annual is digest-sized, 56 pp., using woodcuts and prints by Wendy Kindred, professionally printed in small type on tinted, heavy stock with matte card cover with art. They accept 40-50 of 500-600 submissions per year. Press run of 700-1,000 for 50 subscriptions of which 30 are libraries, and 500 shelf sales. **Sample: $2 postpaid. Send SASE for guidelines. Pays 5 copies. No simultaneous submissions or previously published poems. Reports in 6 months.** Roland Burns advises, "The publishing situation for poets is good and getting better. There are more good poets writing in America than at any other time. The essence of poetry is the image that provides sensory focus and that generates a sense of experience, place, persons, emotions, ideas."

BLACK HORSE; BLACK HORSE PRESS (I, II, IV-Gay/Lesbian), 1206 E. Pike, Seattle, WA 98122, founded 1989, editor Lawrence Michael Dickson, is a literary biannual, first issue June, 1989, **"open to most topics, styles, gay, lesbian poetry reflecting human life. No haiku. No untitled poetry."** The editor says there is "too much prose on the market, and little of today's poetry will last in five years. I prefer reading 'real' voice and not imitation of older writers. Send me what you want to say, not what I want to hear." **Send SASE for guidelines. Pays $25 award for best poetry.**

‡**BLACK MOUNTAIN REVIEW; LORIEN HOUSE (IV-Themes)**, P.O. Box 1112, Black Mountain, NC 28711-1112, phone 704-669-6211, founded 1969. editor David A. Wilson, is a small press publishing many books under the Lorien House imprint (poetry on a subsidy basis) and the annual *Black Mountain Review*. They want **poetry with "quality form/construction—a full thought, specifically fitting the theme, 16-80 lines. No blatant sex, violence,horror."** As a sample, I selected these lines from "A Walk with my Father" by Sal St. John Buttaci, in *BMR #5* on "The Human Spirit":

> Hemmed in and hurried along by
> treadmilling pedestrians,
> I soloed across the madness of that street,
> fear, a gagging in my throat;
> tears in my eyes blurred the winter colors
> of coats that brushed against me.

BMR is digest-sized, saddle-stapled, 44 pp. with matte card cover, photocopied from typescript. The issue I saw was printed in blue ink. Press run "about 300" of which they sell about 200. They accept 1-5 poems of about 200 received per year. **Sample, postpaid: $3.75. Send SASE for guidelines. Pays 2 copies plus small quarterly royalties as copies are sold. Previously published** poetry OK. Reports in a few days. Query regarding subsidized book publication. Editor comments on submissions "occasionally," and he offers "full analysis and marketing help" for $1/ typed page of poetry. He says, "I receive tons of general poetry that prove to be of no use to me. Take the theme idea, *do research*, come up with a way to express the theme need, and write a well-constructed, meaningful poem — any style — which carries the thought well."

BLACK RIVER REVIEW; STONE ROLLER PRESS (II, IV-Translations), 855 Mildred Ave., Lorain, OH 44052, phone 216-244-9654, founded 1985, poetry editor Michael Waldecki, editorial contact Kaye Coller, is a literary annual using "**contemporary poetry, any style, form and subject matter, 50 line maximum (usually), poetry with innovation, craftsmanship and a sense of excitement and/or depth of emotion.** Do *not* **want Helen Steiner Rice, greeting card verse, poetry that mistakes stilted, false or formulaic diction for intense expression of feeling.**" They have recently published poetry by Aisha Eshe, Diane Kendig, Richard Kostelanetz, Simon Perchik, Timothy Russell, Laurel Speer and William Stafford. The editor selected these lines "Anorexics at Summer Camp" by Deborah S. Glaefke:

> *We share the Auschwitz diet plan:*
> *the musselmanner, the dancing*
> *skeletons. At dawn, precisely then,*
> *you jog five wobbled miles:*
> *gray bones wrapped in parchment,*
> *tight. You are all spider-colored*
> *hair and empty shorts that flap*
> *at your sharp pelvis, wings.*

The magazine-sized annual is photocopied from typescript on quality stock, saddle-stapled with matte card cover with art, about 60 pp., using ads, circulation 300 (sold in college bookstore). **Sample: $3 (backcopy); $3.50 (current issue); $6 (two copies of any issue) postpaid. Pays 1 copy. Submit between January and May 1, limit of 10, photocopy OK, no simultaneous submissions. Will consider previously published if acknowledged. They conduct contests with cash prizes, $1 entry fee. Send SASE for rules. Editor may comment on submissions**, not on contest entries. Kaye Coller comments, "We want strong poems that show a depth of vision beyond the commonplace. We don't care if a poet is well-known or not, but we don't publish amateurs. An amateur is not necessarily a new poet, but one who doesn't believe in revision, tends to be preachy, writes sentimental slush, tells the reader what to think and/or concludes the poem with an explanation in case the reader didn't get the point. If we think we can use one or more of a poet's poems, we keep them until the final choices are made in June; otherwise, we send them back as soon as possible. Follow the MS mechanics in **Poet's Market.We are also looking for poems written in Spanish. If selected, they will be published with English translation by either the poet or one of our staff.**"

THE BLACK SCHOLAR; THE BLACK SCHOLAR PRESS (IV-Ethnic), Box 2869, Oakland, CA 94609, founded 1969, publisher Robert Chrisman, uses poetry "**relating to/from/of the black American and other 'Third World' experience.**" The bi-monthly magazine is basically scholarly and research-oriented. They have published poetry by Ntozake Shange, Jayne Cortez, Andrew Salkey, and D. L. Smith. As a sample the editor selected these lines from "Tata on the Death of Don Pablo" by Nancy Morejan:

> *your set mouth*
> *pausing like a great bird*
> *over the plain, speaks:*

I have not seen a copy, but the editor says it is 64 pp., 7 × 10″, press run 9,000 to 10,000 subscribers of which 60% are libraries, 15% shelf sales. Single copy $5; subscription $30. **Sample back issue: $6 prepaid. Send SASE for guidelines. Pays 10 copies and subscription. Enclose "letter & bio or curriculum vita, SASE, phone number, no originals.**" They also publish 1-2 books a year, average 100 pp., flat-spined. **Send query letter.** For sample books, send 8½ × 11″ SASE for catalog, average cost $10.95 including postage and handling. "We only publish one issue every year containing poetry. Please be advised — it is against our policy to discuss submissions via telephone. Also, we get a lot of MSS, but read *every single one*, thus patience is appreciated."

‡BLACK SPARROW PRESS (III), 24 Tenth St., Santa Rosa, CA 95401, phone 707-579-4011, founded 1966, assistant to the publisher Julie Curtiss Voss, publishes poetry, fiction, literary criticism, and bibliography in flat-spined paperbacks, hardcovers and deluxe/limited editions (hardback). "We do not publish chapbooks. Our books are 150 pp. or longer." They have recently published poetry by Charles Bukowski, Tom Clark, Wanda Coleman, Robert Kelly, Diane Wakoski, John Weiners and John Yau. As a sample the editor selected these lines by Charles Bukowski:

> *It's not the large things that send a man to the madhouse . . .*
> *No, It's the continuing of small tragedies*
> *that send a man to the madhouse . . .*

> *Not the death of his love*
> *but the shoelace that snaps*
> *with no time left . . .*

Reports in 60 days. Pays 10% minimum royalties plus author's copies.

BLACK TIE PRESS (II), P.O. Box 440004-0004, Houston, TX 77244, phone 713-789-5119, founding 1986, publisher and editor Peter Gravis, is **"looking for distinct voices (not academic), poets previously without national recognition. Wants to hear from people who don't** *teach* **poetry. No limitations vis-a-vis form, length, subject matter, style, etc. Poetry must reflect an awareness of contemporary poetics, material must be imaginative, innovative, at risk, excellent use of imagery. Read** *American Poetry Review, Associated Writing Programs Newsletter, Poetry,* **and** *Poets & Writers.* **No conventional or 'traditional' rhyme; no nature or heavy-handed narrative.** Recently published poets: Harry Burns, Laura Ryder, Guy R. Beining, Juan, Delgado, Toni Ortner, Larry O. Dean and S.K. Duff. From the Black Tie Press publication **American Poetry Confronts the 1990's** by Donald Rawley, the editor selected these sample lines:

> *The orchid is the sister*
> *of the moon.*
> *She is a soft clap*
> *Of manicured hands*
> *She is the opening . .*

He plans to publish 6 books this year. **"We are not a magazine. We do not publish chapbooks. We are not seeking unsolicited manuscripts because we already know of worthy material and have poets in mind we want to publish. We do read and consider unsolicited material. We strongly suggest you buy one of our books first. Submit complete ms; 35-60 poems, along with a bio. No reply without SASE. We like to respond by return mail, and do (rarely), but due to the quantity of work we receive it sometimes requires several months to get it out and back. We read all submitted material. Please do not submit or query if you are not a serious reader of contemporary poetics and if you do not regularly purchase poetry books." Sample copies: $10 plus $1.50 postage.** Peter Gravis advises, "Beginning poets: Read. Read. Read. Study poetics from the Greeks through today. Learn other languages. Attend readings, workshops. Take courses — but mainly read and write. Don't write for anyone other than yourself — your audience will find you. Take risks. Immerse yourself in poetry. Take it seriously; be aware of theatre, opera, music, painting and all other forms of art. Know history. Be familiar with history, history of the arts, and particularly be aware of the development of poetry since Whitman."

THE BLACK WARRIOR REVIEW (II), Box 2936, Tuscaloosa, AL 35486-2936, phone 205-348-4518, founded 1974. Poets whose work has recently appeared in the *Black Warrior Review* include Richard Jackson, Judith Berke, Jorie Graham, Jill Gonet, Mary Ruefle, Mark Rubin and William Trowbridge. **Address submissions to the Poetry Editor. Submit 3-6 poems, simultaneous (say so) and photocopied submissions OK, awards one $500 prize annually, payment $5-10 per printed page; two contributor's copies. Reports in 1-3 months.** It is a 6 × 9″ semiannual of 144 pages, circulation 1,800. **Sample: $4 postpaid. Send SASE for guidelines.** The editor chose this sample from "Black Fish Blues" by Beckian Fritz Goldberg:

> *. . . I've got a view and a neighbor with a drainpipe*
> *running off his roof. I've got a feel for the plumbing*
> *broken in those shadows. I've got May light*
> *coming in strong on all stations and branches*
>
> *knocking their shadows flat on the blocks of the fence.*
> *I've got a whole cluster of black fish bobbing*
> *in the top block. Fish that touch you quick*
> *constellations below the water . . .*

"We solicit a nationally-known poet for the chapbook. For the remainder of the issue, we solicit a few poets, but the bulk of the material is chosen from unsolicited submissions. Many of our poets have substantial publication credits, but our decision is based simply on the quality of the work submitted."

BLANK (IV-Regional), P.O. Box 60824, Oklahoma City, OK 73146, is an occasional (4 times a year) publication, circulation 500-1,200, using **poetry by present or former residents of Oklahoma.** "Most issues are single page, 11 × 17″ folded, newsletter format. **Considers simultaneous submissions.**

BLIND ALLEYS (II); SEVENTH SON PRESS (V), Box 13224, Baltimore, MD 21203, founded 1981, *Blind Alleys* founded 1982 by Michael S. Weaver, editors Michael S. Weaver, Glenford H. Cummings, Charles Lynch, and Aissatou Mijiza. *BA* appears twice a year, digest-sized, 78 pp., saddle-stapled, professionally printed on thin stock, matte card cover, circulation 500. **Sample $5 postpaid. Submit about 5 poems in a batch, none longer than 100 lines. Pays 2 copies.** They have published poetry by Lucille Clifton, Arthur Winfield Knight, Kimiko Hahn, Peter Harris and Ethelbert Miller. As a sample I selected the first stanza of "Fells Point" by James Taylor:

> *First step. Land fall. A site*
> *in near future of a colonial black painter,*
> *shipwrights and quick to please prostitutes.*
> *Some towns are born old and born hookers.*

The Press publishes broadsides but is not at present accepting unsolicited book MSS.

BLIND BEGGAR PRESS; LAMPLIGHT EDITIONS; NEW RAIN (IV-Ethnic, anthology, children), Box 437, Williamsbridge Station, Bronx, NY 10467, founded 1976, literary editor Gary Johnston publishes work **"relevant to Black and Third World people, especially women."** New Rain is an annual anthology of such work. Lamplight Editions is a subsidiary which publishes "educational materials such as children's books, manuals, greeting cards with educational material in them, etc." They want to see **"quality work that shows a concern for the human condition and the condition of the world — arts for people sake."** They have recently published work by Judy D. Simmons, A.H. Reynolds, Mariah Britton, Kurt Lampkins, Rashidah Ismaili, Jose L. Garza and Carletta Wilson. As a sample I chose the first four lines of Jayne Cortez's "Big Fine Woman From Ruleville":

> *How to weave your web of medicinal flesh into words*
> *cut the sutures to your circumcised name*
> *make your deformed leg into a symbol of resistance*
> *Big fine woman from Ruleville*

New Rain is a digest-sized saddle-stapled, 60 pp. chapbook, finely printed, with simple art, card covers. **Sample: $4 postpaid.** They also publish about 3 collections of poetry by individuals per year, 60 pp., flat-spined paperback, glossy, color cover, good printing on good paper. **Sample: $5.95. For either the anthology or book publication, first send sample of 5-10 poems with cover letter including your biographical background, philosophy and poetic principles. Considers simultaneous submissions. They reply to queries in 3-4 weeks, submissions in 2-3 months, pay in copies (the number depending on the print run).** Willing to work out individual terms for subsidy publication. Catalog available for SASE.

‡BLUE BUILDINGS (II), Department of English, Drake University, Des Moines IA 50311, phone 515-277-4298, founded 1978, managing editor Guillaume Williams; editors Tom Urban and Ruth Doty, appears twice a year. **"Bias is toward long poems, experimental work heavy on images, or surreal works. No philosophical, educational, or sentimental work."** They have recently published poetry by Richard Shelton, Marge Piercy, Gary Finke and Peter Wild. As a sample the editor selected these lines from "Quai de la Madeleine — A Pavane" (poet unidentified):

> *in August you burst from her womb*
> *the Sanskrit wheel abraded by the Fimb-*
> *rias violet light opening its Tomb*
>
> *I walked the stars*
> *searching for Harlequin bugs a lamb's ear*
> *Love lies bleeding to throw on your grave*

Blue Buildings is magazine-sized, 66 pp. flat-spined, professionally printed on quality stock with matte card cover. Press run 700-1,000. They accept about 10% of 500 submissions per issue. Subscription: $12 (2 issues). **Sample, postpaid: $4. Pays 2 copies, sometimes cash when funds available. Send SASE for guidelines.** The editor says, "Submit, submit, submit. One editor's remarks do not reflect the views of all publishers."

‡BLUE LIGHT RED LIGHT (II), 496A Hudson St., Suite F-42, New York, NY 10014, phone 201-432-3245, founded 1988, editors Alma Rodriquez and Joy Parker, appears 2-3 times a year using **"the finest works of new and established writers, fusing mainstream writing, magic realism and surrealism together with speculative fiction.** As an interdisciplinary periodical we seek not to isolate these genres but to discover the points of contact between them and mainstream writing itself. As contemporary life becomes fragmented, the search for meaning, for personal myths, becomes all the more intense. We want to participate in this search for meaning." They ask of submissions **"Does this piece have magic? Please, no cyberpunk, or nihilist's declarations that there is no meaning."** They have recently published poetry by Susan Osberg, Juan Julian Caicedo, Steven Doloff, Janet Holbrook, Peter Beck, Joan Harvey, and Z. As a sample the editor selected "Concerto for Astronauts" by Wahn Yoon. Here are the opening lines of this 7-page poem:

> *What could I give you,*
> *black panther sky,*

that you haven't already
swallowed and transformed?

It comes in a 6×9″ flat-spined format with glossy cover, 176 pp. Press run: 2,000. Subscription: $15/3 issues. **Sample, postpaid: $5.50. Pays small honorarium plus 5 copies. Submit only 3-4 poems at a time. Simultaneous submissions and previously published poems OK.**

BLUE LIGHT REVIEW (II), Box 1621, Pueblo, CO 81002, founded 1983 (magazine), poetry editor Paul Dilsaver. The *Review* is a semiannual literary magazine, circulation 200, which uses about 30 pp. of poetry in each issue: inexpensively printed (offset from various varieties of typescript) in a digest-sized saddle-stapled format. **Sample: $4. Reports in 6 months. Pays 1 copy.** I selected these sample lines, the opening stanza of "November Morning" by Victoria McCabe:

Someone is walking behind,
walking very deliberately behind,
as if he had a mission
he walks, whoever he is, behind.

BLUE UNICORN, A TRIQUARTERLY OF POETRY; BLUE UNICORN POETRY CONTEST (II, IV-Translations), 22 Avon Rd., Kensington, CA 94707, phone 415-526-8439, founded 1977, poetry editors Ruth G. Iodice, Harold Witt, and Daniel J. Langton, wants **"well-crafted poetry of all kinds, in form or free verse, as well as expert translations on any subject matter. We shun the trite or inane, the soft-centered, the contrived poem. Shorter poems have more chance with us because of limited space."** Some poets they have published recently are James Applewhite, Kim Cushman, Charles Edward Eaton, Patrick Worth Gray, Joan LaBombard, James Schevill, John Tagliabue, and Gail White. These sample lines are from "S Is for Sonnet" by Elizabeth Michel:

Sand whispers sibilants on soles, a storm shakes
Them from sycamores, and the sea
Shouts them out on shoals. And your mouth makes
S's its own way: slurping soup noisily
It sucks them in, from sky and star and space
It spills a song of cosmos on the doily's lace.

The magazine is **"distinguished by its fastidious editing, both with regard to contents and format."** It is 56 pp., narrow digest-sized, saddle-stapled, finely printed, with some art, **sample: $4 postpaid.** They receive over 35,000 submissions a year, use about 200, have a year's backlog. **Submit 3-5 poems on normal typing pages, original or clear photocopy or clear, readable dot-matrix, no simultaneous submissions or previously published poems. Reports in 1-3 months, payment one copy, guidelines available for SASE.** They sponsor an annual contest with small entry fee to help support the magazine, with prizes of $100, $75 and $50, distinguished poets as judges, publication of 3 top poems and 6 honorable mentions in the magazine. Entry fee: $3 for first poem, $2 for others to a maximum of 5. Write for current guidelines. **Criticism occasionally offered.** "We would advise beginning poets to read and study poetry—both poets of the past and of the present; concentrate on technique; and **discipline yourself by learning forms before trying to do without them.** When your poem is crafted and ready for publication, study your markets and then send whatever of your work seems to be compatible with the magazine you are submitting to."

BLUELINE (IV-Regional), English Dept., Potsdam College, Potsdam NY 13676, founded 1979, editor-in-chief Anthony Tyler, and an editorial board, "is an annual literary magazine dedicated to prose and **poetry about the Adirondacks and other regions similar in geography and spirit." They want "clear, concrete poetry pertinent to the countryside and its people. It must go beyond mere description, however. We prefer a realistic to a romantic view. We do not want to see sentimental or extremely experimental poetry."** Usually 44 lines or fewer, though "occasionally we publish longer poems" on **"nature in general, Adirondack Mountains in particular. Form may vary, can be traditional or contemporary."** They have recently published poetry by Phillip Booth, George Drew, Eric Ormsby, L. M. Rosenberg, John Unterecker, Lloyd Van Brunt, Laurence Josephs, Maurice Kenny and Nancy L. Nielsen. As a sample they offer these lines from "Eagle Lake" by Noelle Oxenhandler:

Sometimes the lines fall this way,
the canoe's narrowness
filling my mind, and my arms
sending their weight through the water.

It's a handsomely printed, 112 pp., 6×9″ magazine with 40-45 pp. of poetry in each issue, circulation 700. **Sample copies: $6 on request.** They have a 3-11 month backlog. **Submit August 1-December 1, no more than 5 poems with short bio. No simultaneous submissions. Photocopy, dot-matrix OK if neat and legible. Reports in 2-10 weeks. Pays copies. Guidelines available for**

SASE. **Occasionally comments on rejections.** "We are interested in both beginning and established poets whose poems evoke universal themes in nature and show human interaction with the natural world. We look for **thoughtful craftsmanship rather than stylistic trickery.**

BOA EDITIONS, LTD. (III), 92 Park Ave., Brockport, NY 14420, phone 716-637-3844, founded 1976, poetry editor A. Poulin, Jr., **generally does not accept unsolicited MSS.** They have published some of the major American poets, such as W. D. Snodgrass, John Logan, Isabella Gardner, and Richard Wilbur, and they publish introductions by major poets of those less well-known. For example, Gerald Stern wrote the foreword for Li-Young Lee's **Rose.** The editor selected from that book "Eating Together" as a sample poem:

> In the steamer is the trout
> seasoned with slivers of ginger,
> two sprigs of green onion, and sesame oil.
> We shall eat it with rice for lunch,
> brothers, sisters, my mother who will
> taste the sweetest meat of the head,
> holding it between her fingers
> deftly, the way my father did
> weeks ago. Then he lay down
> to sleep like a snow-covered road
> winding through pines older than him,
> without any travelers, and lonely for no one.

Query with samples. Pays outright grants or royalties.

BOGG PUBLICATIONS; BOGG (II), 422 N. Cleveland St., Arlington, VA 22201, founded 1968, poetry editors: John Elsberg (USA); George Cairncross (UK: 31 Belle Vue St., Filey, N. Yorkshire YO 14 9HU, England); and Sheila Martindale (Canada: Suite 104, 121 Avenue Rd., Toronto ON M5R 2G3). "We publish *Bogg* magazine and occasional free-for-postage pamphlets. The magazine uses a great deal of poetry in each issue (with several featured poets) — "**poetry in all styles, with a healthy leavening of shorts (under 10 lines). Our emphasis on good work per se, and Anglo-American cross-fertilization.**" This is one of the liveliest small press magazines published today. It started in England, and in 1975 began including a supplement of American work; it now is published in the US and mixes US, Canadian and UK work with reviews of small press publications on both sides of the Atlantic. It's thick (64 pp.), typeset, saddle-stitched, in a 6×9″ format that leaves enough white space to let each poem stand and breathe alone. They have published work by Ann Menebroker, Steve Richmond, Peter Meinke, Rochelle Ratner, Jon Silkin, Gerald Dorset, Robert Peters, Harold Witt, Ron Androla, Charles Plymell, Steve Sneyd, Tina Fulker, Andy Darlington, and offer these lines from "Exorcism" by Winona Baker (Canada) as a sample:

> Get out of my room
> Get out of my bed
> Get out of my body
> Get out of my poems.

All styles, all subject matter. "Some have even found the magazine's sense of play offensive. Overt religious and political poems have to have strong poetical merits — statement alone is not sufficient. Prefer typewritten manuscripts, with author's name and address on each sheet. Photocopy OK. We will reprint previously published material, but with a credit line to a previous publisher." No simultaneous submissions. Prefers to see 6 poems. About 40 pp. of poetry per issue, print run of 750, 400 subscriptions of which 20 are libraries, **sample $3 postpaid.** Subscription: $10, for 3 issues. They receive over 7,000 poems per year and use 100-150. "We try to accept only for next 2 issues. SASE required or material discarded (no exceptions)." **Reports in 1 week, pays 2 copies, guidelines available for SASE.** Their occasional pamphlets and chapbooks are by invitation only, the author receiving 25% of the print run, and you can get **chapbook samples free for SASE.** Better make it at least 2 ounces worth of postage. John Elsberg advises, "Become familiar with a magazine before submitting to it. Always enclose SASE. Long lists of previous credits irritate me, as if I should be influenced by them in my own judgment of the material submitted. Short notes about how the writer has heard about, or what he finds interesting in *Bogg*, I read with some interest."

BONE AND FLESH (II), Box 349, Concord, NH 03302-0349, founded 1988, co-editors Lester Hirsh, Frederick Moe, Bob Shannahan, *Bone & Flesh* appears twice yearly with the *Annual* and *Aside* issues. They want "**quality calibre work from seasoned writers with a literary slant. All forms: prose poems, short fiction, haiku, essays, art work, are welcome. Themes may vary but should focus on the substance of our lives or the link with other lives and times. We do not want to see anything that is overtly religious, banal, trite, or conventional. Submissions are accepted September-February only.**" They have recently published works by Jean Battlo, Joel Oppenheimer, Alan Catlin, Chelsea Adams, David Brooks, and Bayla Winters. As a sample, the editors selected these lines by Bob Shannahan:

> Our lives in both
> bone and flesh
> like a boy's footprint
> caught for centuries
> under the ash of Pompeii
> here and gone

The *Annual* issue is magazine sized, 75-100 pages. The *Aside* is digest-sized, 32 pp. Press run may vary from 200 to 300 or more, according to issue. **Payment is in contributor's copies. Reporting time and or correspondence averages 6 to 8 weeks. "We sometimes hold work for final consideration." Submit no more than 6 poems at a time.** Editors attempt to comment on rejections and provide suggestions when appropriate. Guidelines available for SASE. Sample copies: $5, postpaid.

BOREALIS PRESS; TECUMSEH PRESS LTD.; JOURNAL OF CANADIAN POETRY (V, IV-Regional), 9 Ashburn Dr., Ottawa, Canada K2E 6N4, founded 1972. Borealis and Tecumseh are imprints for books, including **collections of poetry, by Canadian writers only, and they are presently not considering unsolicited submissions.** Send SASE (or IRC's) for catalog to buy samples. Poets published recently include John Ferns, Giorgio Di Cicco, and Russell Thornton. These sample lines are by Russell Thornton:

> My longing brought me a far distance
> to your kisses, flying slowly for my mouth like melting birds,
> to your braided river hair and faun-brown skin
> and your eyes, lighting like hazel flames of candles.

The annual *Journal* publishes reviews and criticism, not poetry. **Sample: $6.95 postpaid.**

‡BOSTON LITERARY REVIEW (BLUR) (II), Box 357, W. Somerville, MA 02144, phone 617-625-6087, founded 1984, editor Gloria Mindock-Duehr, appears twice a year using **"work with a strong voice and individual style; experimental work welcome. Submit 5-10 poems."** They have recently published poetry by Stuart Friebert, David Ray, Eric Pankey and Richard Kostelanetz. I have not seen an issue, but the editor describes it as "24 pp., 4 × 12", offset, no ads." They publish about 40 of 2,500 poems received per year. Press run: 200 for 20 subscriptions of which 5 are libraries. Subscription: $6/year. **Sample, postpaid: $4. Pays 2 copies. Reports in 1-2 months.** Editor comments on submissions "sometimes."

BOSTON REVIEW (II), 33 Harrison Ave., Boston, MA 02111, editor Margaret Roth, founded 1975, a bimonthly arts and culture magazine, uses about a **half-page of poetry per issue, or 10 poems a year**, for which they receive about 700 submissions. Circulation 10,000 nationally including subscriptions and newsstand sales. **Sample: $4 postpaid.** They have a 4-8 month backlog. **Submit any time, no more than 6 poems, photocopy OK, simultaneous submissions discouraged; reports in 2 months "if you include SASE," pay varies.** The editor advises, "To save the time of all those involved, poets should be sure to send only *appropriate* poems to particular magazines. This means that a poet should not submit to a magazine that he/she has not read. Poets should also avoid lengthy cover letters and allow the poems to speak for themselves."

BOTTOMFISH (II), De Anza College, Creative Writing Program, 21250 Stevens Creek Blvd., Cupertino CA 95014, editor Robert Scott. This college-produced magazine appears annually. The spring 1990 issue *Bottomfish Eleven* contains poems by Walter Griffin, Edward Kleinschmidt, Janice Dabney, and Jared Smith. Poetry sample is from "Penny Loaves and Sea-Gulls," by William Meyer:

> You remember, on the verge of sleep,
> on the prow of the ferry,
> the larger-than-life glossy eyes,
> and
> (larger than death)
> the failing in your arm before
> the toss.

Bottomfish is 7 × 8¼", well-printed on heavy stock with tasteful b/w graphics, 60 pp. perfect bound. Circulation is 500, free to libraries, schools, etc., but **$3.50/copy to individual requests. "Before submitting, writers are strongly urged to purchase a sample copy; subject matter is at the writer's discretion, as long as the poem is skillfully and professionally crafted." Reporting time is 2-6 months, depending on backlog. Pay is 2 copies.** The editor says, "Spare us the pat, generic greeting-card phrases. We want sharp, sensory images that carry a strong theme."

BOULEVARD (II), % editor Richard Burgin, 2400 Chestnut St. #3301, Philadelphia, PA 19103, phone 215-561-1723, founded 1985, appears 3 times a year. **"We've published everything from John Ashbery to Howard Moss to a wide variety of styles from new or lesser known poets. We're eclectic. Do not want to see poetry that is uninspired, formulaic, self-conscious, unoriginal, insipid."** They have published poetry by Amy Clampitt, Kenneth Koch, Molly Peacock, Jorie Graham, and Marvin Bell. As a sample editor Richard Burgin selected these lines from "Buying a Dress" by James Lasdun:

> *Thirty a day and enough gin to float*
> *A goldfish, Guinness sluicing down her throat*
> *The barman's spaniel, one damp eye a-cock*
> *Wiggling his nose like a toe in a sock*

Boulevard is 150+ pp, flat-spined, professionally printed, with glossy card cover. Their press run is 2,500 with 600 subscriptions of which 100 are libraries. Subscription: $10. **Sample: $6 postpaid. Pays $25-250 per poem, depending on length, plus 2 copies. "Prefer name and number on each page with SASE. Encourage cover letters but don't require them. Will consider simultaneous submissions but not previously published poems."** Editor sometimes comments on rejections. Richard Burgin says, "We believe the grants we have won from the National Endowment for the Arts etc., as well as the anthologies which continue to recognize us, have rewarded our commitment. My advice to poets: 'Write from your heart as well as your head.' "

BOX DOG PRESS; FEMINIST BASEBALL; AVANT-GARDE WORLD (I), Box 9609, Seattle, WA 98109, founded 1983, editor Craig Joyce, publishes "chapbooks, flatsheets, fanzines" and wants **poetry, "experimental, innovative, good work in any genre/style"** but not **"metaphysical, racist, sexist, ultrapretentious."** They have published poetry by Cholah Ciccone. I have not seen a copy of *Feminist Baseball,* but the editor describes its purpose as to "destroy art and literature, worship cool 10-year-old girls," and says it's 40 pp. magazine-sized, appearing 2-3 times a year, and that it uses ¾ of the 10 submissions it receives a year, press run 200 for 17 subscriptions. Per issue: $1. **Sample: $2 postpaid. Pays 1-2 copies. Simultaneous submissions, previously published poems OK. For chapbook consideration send sample poems. Charges $2 reading fee.** Jeff Smith's advice is Ezra Pound's: "Do your work. Don't listen to anyone's advice."

BOX 749 MAGAZINE; THE PRINTABLE ARTS SOCIETY INC. (II), 411 W. 22nd St., New York, NY 10011, phone 212-989-0519, founded 1972, editor-in-chief David Ferguson. *Box 749* is an annual using **"fiction and poetry of every length and any theme;** satire, belles-lettres, plays, music, and any artwork reproducible by photo-offset. **We have no particular stylistic or ideological bias.** *Box 749* is directed to people of diverse backgrounds, education, income and age—an audience not necessarily above or underground. Such an audience is consistent with our belief that literature (plus art and music) is accessible to and even desired by a larger and more varied portion of our society than has generally been acknowledged." I have not seen it, but the editor describes it as 96 pp., magazine-sized. It has a circulation of 2,000 with 300 subscriptions of which 20 are libraries, other copies sold in the street by the editor. Per issue: $2.50. **Sample: $3.50 postpaid. Guidelines available for SASE. Pays 2-5 copies. Prefers letter-quality printing. Reports in up to 3 months or longer, depending on length. Publishes MS an average of 1 year after acceptance.** The editor says, "MSS are rejected because of lack of imagination for character, not well-written, or not about anything that is worth sharing with the general public."

BRADFORD POETRY QUARTERLY (I), 9 Woodvale Way, Bradford, West Yorkshire BD7 2SJ England, phone 0274-575993, founded 1983, editor Clare Chapman, is a small-press quarterly using **poetry with "no restrictions at all. Prefer to print reasonably short poems, but happy to accept some longer work. Anything good is gratefully received."** She doesn't want **"the trite, the dull."** As a sample the editors selected these lines by Michael Levene:

> *Above our heads, Queen Mary stared; stern, stony,*
> *the hydrochloric gaze of an Indian chief*
> *A rumour went. She won the war, you know,*
> *she looked at Adolph Hitler and he died*

The quarterly is digest-sized, 8 pp. "Prontoprinted" from photoreduced typescript with Clare Chapman's own drawings as illustrations. She accepts about 10% of "hundreds" of submissions. She has about 30 subscriptions. **Sample: £1.70. Pays 1 copy. Simultaneous submissions and previously published submissions OK. Editor sometimes comments on rejections.** She says, "I think this is a happy era for poets. There are many outlets for them. I receive many worthwhile MSS from poets in the US and Britain. Publishing poetry is not easy, but more people read it and see these 'little' magazines than the editors realize. The best advice I can give poets is to read the masters of the craft and find contemporary poetry that they can admire."

BRAVO: THE POET'S MAGAZINE; JOHN EDWIN COWEN, LTD. (II), 1081 Trafalgar St., Teaneck, NJ 07666, founded 1979, poetry editor José Garcia Villa, managing editor John Cowen. *Bravo*, a 6×9″ literary journal, appears irregularly, circulation 500, 350 subscriptions of which 50 are libraries, using about 50 pp. of poetry in each issue. "*Bravo* **believes that poetry must have formal excellence; poetry must be lyrical; poetry is not prose. We want lyrical poems, not prose poems. We do not want formless poetry. Models: Cummings, Moore, Donne, Wylie, Schwartz, Thomas, Hopkins. Experimental lyrics are possibilities; crafted poems that are clean, economical.**" They have recently published poetry by Mort Malkin, Gloria Potter, Nick Joaquin, Larry Francia, Virginia Moreno, and Cirilo F. Bautista. The editor selected these sample lines from "Gift From Manila":

> *and I must,*
> *too, give—and learn*
> *the beauteous secret*
> *how suddenly*
> *each gift passes*
> *words/non-words*

They receive about 100 freelance submissions per year of which they use "few." **Sample: $3.50 less 20%. Read a sample before submitting. Reports in 3 weeks. Pays 2 copies. Prefers MS typed, double-spaced. Photocopies OK, dot-matrix "not preferred."** Inquire about buying samples. "Please read our magazine before sending manuscripts."

BREAKTHROUGH!; AARDVARK ENTERPRISES (I, IV-Membership/subscription), 204 Millbank Dr. SW, Calgary, Alberta T2Y 2H9 Canada, phone 403-256-4639, founded 1982, poetry editor J. Alvin Speers. *Breakthrough!* is a general interest quarterly with 9 page "Poetry Corner." Aardvark publishes chapbooks on subsidy arrangements. **Breakthrough!**'s editor says, "**Prefer rhyme—no porn. Any length.**" They have recently published poetry by Ellen Sandry, Edna Janes Kayser, Muriel Kovinow, and W. Ray Lundy. As a sample the editor selected these lines, from "Shared Legacy" by J. Alvin Speers:

> *We miss them, but they are part of us,*
> *Though they crossed the great divide,*
> *Leaving us just the memories*
> *Of times with them by our side;*
> *To live a life that lets no one down*
> *Who trusts in our love and care*
> *Is the least we can do with the legacy*
> *That they passed this way to share.*

The editor says *Breakthrough!* is "dedicated to life improvement, starting with primary resources—the individual" and describes it as "52 pp., 8½×5½", digest-sized, plus ad inserts periodically. Good quality photocopy, color paper cover, using b/w illustrations." They receive about 100 poems a month, use approximately 20%. Press run is "over 100 and growing nicely." Price per issue is $4, subscription $15. **Sample: $4 postpaid. Send SASE for guidelines. Pays "small cash award to best 3 items per issue, chosen by readers' votes. Subscribers only submissions." Simultaneous submissions, previously published poems OK. Replies "prompt! Usually by return mail."** For subsidized chapbook publication query with 3-5 samples, bio, previous publications. "We publish for hire—quoting price with full particulars. We do not market these except by special arrangement. Prefer poet does that. We strongly recommend seeing our books first. Same goes for submitting to *Breakthrough!*; best to see magazine first." Send SASE for catalog to buy book samples. Contest information for SASE. The editor advises, "Be professional and considerate. Our files bulge with abandoned manuscripts—we respond by return mail and never hear from authors again. Treat editors as you would like to be treated."

‡**BREITENBUSH BOOKS, INC. (III)**, Box 82157, Portland, OR 97282, founded 1977, managing editor Tom Booth, publishes 2-3 flat-spined paperbacks/cloth editions per year, 64-150 pp., 6×9″. They have published books by Mary Barnard, Naomi Shihab Nye and Peter Sears. **Query with 7-9 poems, bio, publications. Pays royalties, advance and author's copies. Send $1 or stamps for postage for catalog.**

‡**THE BRIDGE: A JOURNAL OF FICTION AND POETRY (II)**, 14050 Vernon St., Oak Park, MI 48237, founded 1990, editor Jack Zucker, appears twice a year using "**exciting, realistic, expressionist, romantic, not pious, trite, simplistic, poetry with little rational coherence.**" They have recently published poetry by James Reiss and Judith McCombs. It is digest-sized, 100 pp., flat-spined, press run 400. Subscription: $5. **Sample, postpaid: $3. Pays $3 plus 2 copies. Editor comments on submission "often."** An editorial board of 3 considers MSS; decision made by editor and 1 special editor.

BROKEN STREETS (I, IV-Religious, children), 57 Morningside Dr. E., Bristol, CT 06010, founded 1981, poetry editor Ron Grossman, is a "**Christian-centered outreach ministry to poets. Chapbooks are sent free to encourage poets.**" The digest-sized magazine, photocopied typescript, 40-50 pp., card covers, appears 4-5 times a year—100 copies, **$3.50, for a sample.** The editor wants **"Christian-centered, city poetry, feelings, etc., usually 5-15 lines, haiku, no more than 5 poems at a time, not necessary to query, but helpful." Reports in 1 week. Uses about 150 of the 200 poems submitted per year—by children, old people, etc. No pay but copies.** He has published recently B. Z. Niditch, Bettye K. Wray, Ruth Wilder Schuller. I selected this poem by Crystall Carman, age 10, as a sample:

> *The sea runs against the shore*
> *while thunder roars beyond the distant sunset*
> *and God smiles at his creations*
> *while the thunder drifts away*

‡**BROOKLYN REVIEW (II)**, Dept. of English, Brooklyn College, Brooklyn, NY 11210, founded 1974, editors change each year, address Poetry Editor, is a flat-spined, 80 pp., digest-sized annual, indexed by the Index of American Periodical Verse, professionally printed, with glossy, color cover and art. They have published such poets as John Ashbery, Elaine Equi, Amy Gerstler, Jana Harris, Joan Larkin, Eileen Myles, Alice Notley, Honor Moore, Ron Padgett, David Trinidad. They offer these sample lines by James Schuyler:

> *Showered, shaved, splashed*
> *(Ajaccio Vilets) I*
> *at first light*
> *on Synday morning go*

They have a circulation of 500. **Sample: $5 postpaid, pays in copies. Reporting time 6 weeks to 6 months.**

BRUNSWICK PUBLISHING COMPANY (I), Rt. 1, Box 1A1, Lawrenceville, VA 23868, founded 1978, poetry editor Walter J. Raymond, is a **partial subsidy publisher. Query with 3-5 samples. Response in 2 weeks if postage enclosed with SASE. If invited, submit double-spaced, typed MS (photocopy, dot-matrix OK). Reports in 3-4 weeks, reading fee only if you request written evaluation. Poet pays 80% of cost, gets same percentage of profits for market-tester edition of 500, advertised by leaflets mailed to reviewers, libraries, book buyers and book stores.** The samples I saw were flat-spined, matte-covered, 54 pp. paperbacks. **Send SASE for "Statement of Philosophy and Purpose," which explains terms, and catalog to order samples.** I quote from that Statement: "We publish books because that is what we like to do. Every new book published is like a new baby, an object of joy! We do not attempt to unduly influence the reading public as to the value of our publications, but we simply let the readers decide that themselves. We refrain from the artificial beefing up of values that are not there. . . . We are not competitors in the publishing world, but offer what we believe is a needed service. We strongly believe that in an open society every person who has something of value to say and wants to say it should have the chance and opportunity to do so."

BRUSSELS SPROUT (IV-Form), Box 1551, Mercer Island, WA 98040, phone 206-232-3239, founded 1980 by Alexis Rotella, revived by poetry editor Francine Porad in 1988. This magazine of **haiku, senryu and art** appears each January, May, and September. **They want "any format (1-4 lines); subject matter open; seeking work that captures the haiku moment in a fresh way."** It has recently published poetry by Vincent Tripi, Anne McKay, George Swede, H.F. Noyes, and Marlene Mountain. As a sample the editor selected this haiku by A. Araghetti:

> *falcon held spell bound*
> *falling falling*
> *the red glove*

The magazine is digest-sized, professionally printed, 40 pp. saddle-stapled with matte b/w card cover featuring an artist each issue. **Sample: $5 postpaid. Guidelines available for SASE. No payment, other than 3 $10 Editor's Choice Awards each issue. Submit only original work, 4-12 poems (can be on one sheet), name and address on each sheet. No simultaneous submissions or previously published poems. Reports in 3 weeks. Editor sometimes comments on rejections.** The editor advises, "If you want to see your work in print, take the risk. Send it out. The difference between a published writer and an unpublished one is the U.S. mail system."

BUFFALO SPREE MAGAZINE (II), 4511 Harlem Rd., Buffalo, NY 14226, founded 1967, poetry editor Janet Goldenberg, is the quarterly regional magazine of western New York. It has a controlled circulation (21,000) in the Buffalo area, mostly distributed free (with 3,000 subscriptions, of which 25 are libraries). Its glossy pages feature general interest articles about local culture, plus book reviews, fiction and poetry contributed nationally. It receives about 300 poetry submissions per year and uses about 25, which have ranged from work by Robert Hass and Carl Dennis to first publications by younger poets. As an example, the editor chose 5 lines of Martha Bosworth's "Alien in Spring":

> *I am a tall pale animal in boots*

> *trampling forget-me-nots and scaring birds*
> *from the lemon tree: with my long-handled claw*
> *I pull down lemons — tear-shaped, dimpled, round,*
> *bouncing they vanish into vines and weeds.*

They use 5-7 poems per issue, **paying $20 for each; these are selected 3-6 months prior to publication; sample copy, $3.75 postpaid. Considers simultaneous submissions, "but we must be advised that poems have been or are being submitted elsewhere."**

BYLINE MAGAZINE (IV-Themes), P.O. Box 130596, Edmond, OK 73013, founded 1981, editor Marcia Preston, is a **magazine for the encouragement of writers and poets, using 9-12 poems per issue about writers or writing, paying $5-10 per poem.** They have 2,500 subscriptions (a figure rapidly growing), receive 3,000 submissions per year, of which they use 144. These sample lines are from "On Receiving a Native Carving From Africa" by John D. Engle, Jr.:

> *Thank you for the African poem,*
> *carved from ebony*
> *by ebony hands.*
> *Seeing and touching*
> *this tangible song*
> *of silent harmony*
> *awakens subtle senses*
> *too long aslumber.*

Byline is professionally printed, magazine-sized, with illustrations, art, cartoons and ads. **Sample: $3 postpaid. No more than 4 poems per submission, photocopies OK, no simultaneous submissions, reports within a month, rates $5-10, guidelines available for SASE.** Marcia Preston advises "We are happy to work with new writers, but please read a few samples to get an idea of our style."

C.A.L., CONSERVATORY OF AMERICAN LETTERS; NORTHWOODS PRESS (I,II), Box 88, Thomaston, ME 04861, phone 207-354-6550, founded 1972, C.A.L. founded 1988. C.A.L. is a nonprofit tax exempt literary/educational foundation, poetry editor Robert Olmsted. Four anthologies of poetry and prose are published each year. **There is a $1 reading fee for each submission. Reading fee goes directly to readers, not to publisher. Authors get 10% royalty on any copies where sale can be attributed to their influence.** Robert Olmsted regards his efforts as an attempt to face reality and provide a sensible royalty-contract means of publishing many books. Robert Olmsted says, **"If you are at the stage of considering book publications, have a large number of poems in print in respected magazines, perhaps previous book publication, and are confident that you have a sufficient following to insure very modest sales, send 8½ × 11″ SASE (3 oz. postage) for 'descriptions of the Northwoods Poetry Program and CAL.'** Northwoods Press is designed for the excellent *working poet* who has a following which is likely to create sales of $2,000 or more. Without at least that much of a following and at least that level of sales, no book can be published. Request 15-point poetry program." His advice is **"Poetry must be non-trite, non-didactic. It must never bounce. Rhyme, if used at all, should be subtle. One phrase should tune the ear in preparation for the next. They should flow and create an emotional response." Query with cover letter dealing with publication credits and marketing ideas. Submit "entire MS as desired for final book form." No simultaneous submissions, generally no previously published poems. Pays 10% royalties.** Bob Olmsted "rarely" comments on rejections, but he offers commentary for a fee. Query. Membership in C.A.L. is $24 a year, however, **membership is not required.** Members receive a quarterly newsletter plus 10% discount on all books and have many services available to them. C.A.L. sponsors an annual writers' conference with no tuition, only a $10 registration fee.

‡CACANADADADA REVIEW (I, IV-humor), P.O. Box 1283, Port Angeles, WA 98362, founded 1989, editor Jack Estes, appears "every 4 months, or so we hope," using poetry, short fiction, cartoons, jokes, anecdotes, interviews, book and movie reviews, recipes, letters, "index items (as in *Harper's* index but goofier), personals, **all must be iconoclastic, satiric, parodic, or just plain sophomoric. Don't want long long poems (3-4 pp.) Nothing sappy, religious, heavy."** They have recently published poetry by J. Michael Yates and Susan Musgrave. As a sample the editor selected these lines by William Slaughter:

> *Laughing man, that's his name*
> *Never had another.*
> *His mother died having him.*
> *Never had another.*

The first issue appeared in February 1990, 48 pp., 5½ × 8½″, saddle-stapled. They use about 10% of "tons of poetry" received. Press run 1,000 for 50 subscriptions of which 2 are libraries. **Subscription: $6. Sample, postpaid: $4. Send SASE for guidelines. Pays "nominal fees." Simultaneous submissions and previously published poems OK. Reports "ASAP."** Editor "seldom"

comments on rejections. He says, "I like unusual cover letters listing credits. Let poem/story stand on its own. I want *clean* poems (without rusted paper clips from dozens of submissions)."

CACHE REVIEW (II), P.O. Box 19794, Seattle, WA 98109-6794, founded 1981, poetry editor Steven Brady, "accepts **poems of any length, any style, but is highly selective.** We shoot for variety in every issue." Poets they have published recently include Andrea Hollander Budy, Jay Griswold and Gray Jacobik. These sample lines are by William Bridges:

> *All the farms have been wound*
> *and are keeping time,*
> *Keeping time.*
> *The haymow lowers its little windlass,*
> *the toy corn canters*
> *into a meadow of milk and wool.*

The magazine appears once or twice a year, 25 pp. of poetry in each, with a circulation of 250, with 50 subscriptions of which 10 are libraries. It's a magazine-sized format, laser-printed and photocopied, side-stapled (taped) spine, neat, no-nonsense appearance. **Sample: $3.50.** They use about 100 of the 1,500 submissions they receive each year. **Send 5 or more poems, any length, originals or good copies; simultaneous submissions OK. Payment: 2 copies. Comments on MSS that show promise.** Steven Brady advises, "Know your markets, be persistent, especially with editors or markets that show interest."

CADMUS EDITIONS (III), Box 687, Tiburon, CA 94920, founded 1979, editor Jeffrey Miller, publishes hardback and paperback editions of poetry: "**only that which is distinguished.**" They have recently published poetry by Federico García Lorca, Tom Clark, Bradford Morrow and Carol Tinker. These sample lines are by Ed Dorn:

> *The common duty of the poet*
> *in this era of massive disfunction*
> *& generalized onslaught upon alertness*
> *is to maintain the plant*
> *to the end that the mumbling horde*
> *bestirs its pruned tongue.*

Query first, no samples, with "an intelligent literate letter accompanied by a SASE." Answer to query in 30 days, to MS (if invited to submit) in 30-45 days. Contracts are for 5-10% royalties. Comments "occasionally but not often in that most unsolicited submissions do not warrant same."

CAESURA (II), English Dept., Auburn University, Auburn, AL 36801, founded 1984, managing editor R.T. Smith, a twice-yearly literary journal with poetry emphasis. The editor has **"no prejudices. We select the most meticulously crafted, evocative and moving poems from our submissions. No beginner work, devotional clichés, sentimentality, haiku."** He has recently published poetry by Fred Chappell, Jared Carter, David Citino and Susan Ludingson. The magazine is digest-sized, offset, 64-80 pp., with a little art and graphics. Press run 500, of which 50 are subscriptions and 10 go to libraries. **Samples $3 postpaid. Contributors receive two copies per work published and will receive payment this year due to an Alabama Arts Council grant. Writers should submit no more than 5 poems, no photocopied or dot-matrix MSS, no simultaneous submissions. "We report in February for the whole year. We occasionally offer a best-of-issue prize of $100."** The editor says, "We do not usually go for poems in the flat-delivery, me-journal style, associated with the MFA industry. We'd rather see some fireworks and subject matter outside the self."

THE CAITLIN PRESS (V), Box 35220 Station E, Vancouver, BC V6M 4G4 Canada, founded 1977, managing editor Carolyn Zonailo, **accepts no unsolicited MSS.** They publish four flat-spined paperbacks a year. **Poets they consider must have "prior periodical and/or book publications."** They pay 10% royalties in copies.

‡JOHN CALDER (PUBLISHERS) LTD.; RIVERRUN PRESS INC (V), 9-15 Neal St., London WC2H 9TU England, phone 071-497-1741, editor John Calder, a literary book publisher. On their list are Samuel Beckett, Paul Eluard, Michael Horovitz, Pier Paolo Passolini and Howard Barker. **"We do not read for the public,"** says John Calder, and he wants **no unsolicited MSS.**

CALIFORNIA STATE POETRY QUARTERLY (CQ) (II), 1200 E. Ocean Blvd., #64, Long Beach, CA 90802, phone 213-495-0925, founded 1972, editor John M. Brander, appears twice a year. The editor asks for **"contemporary themes reflective of life in the United States. Poems having geographical themes, science fiction poetry and poems using traditional forms are acceptable. Themes should be significant and imaginative. Humorous poems are welcome. Avoid sending poems written in therapy**

sessions or in poetry workshops. **No religious and love poetry, unless really excellent."** They have recently published poetry by William James Kovanda, Suzanne Lummis, Steve Kowit, Gerald Locklin, Aaron Kramer, and Wanda Coleman. As a sample the editor selected these lines by David Del Bourgo:

> *It doesn't have to be a big film*
> *with a lot of words;*
> *an innocent obsession*
> *goes often unexpressed*

The magazine is 64 pp., flat-spined, digest-sized, using artwork and graphics. They receive about 3,000 poems per year, accept about 130-200. Press run: 500-700, 250 subscriptions. Subscription $10, $4 per single copy. **Sample: $5 postpaid. Send SASE for guidelines. Pays 1 copy. Submit 6 poems at a time, name and address on each, typed. No simultaneous submissions. "Very rarely" they take previously published poetry. Reports in 1 week-4 months. 3 months between acceptance and publication.** They have an annual contest with prizes of $125, $75, $50, and 5 honorable mentions of $5; entry fee $2 per poem. **Send SASE for contest rules.** The editor advises, "Read other poets, especially those in your own geographical area. Avoid using poetry as therapy— finish therapy first, and then start writing poetry. The same applies to workshops. *Finish* your workshop courses, then start writing poetry."

CALLALOO POETRY SERIES; CALLALOO (IV-Ethnic), Johns Hopkins University Press, #275, 701 W. 40th St., Baltimore, MD 21211, phone 301-338-6987, founded 1976, editor Charles H. Rowell. Devoted to **poetry dealing with North America, Europe, Africa, Latin and Central America, South America and the Caribbean.** Their magazine and chapbooks are elegantly printed, flat-spined glossy-covered paperbacks. The magazine is published by the Johns Hopkins University Press. The poetry series is published by the University of Virginia Press. They have recently published poetry by Rita Dove, Jay Wright, Alice Walker, Yusef Komunyakaa, Aimé Césaire, Nicolás Guillén, and Michael Harper. These sample lines are by Clarence Major:

> *They've forced me to pose*
> *in the picture with them*
> *I'm the unhappy one*
> *standing next to the man*
> *with sixty smiles*
> *of summer in his smile*

The magazine is a thick quarterly with a varying amount of poetry in its nearly 200 pp., circulation 1,400, with 600 subscriptions of which half are libraries. **"We have no specifications for submitting poetry except authors should include SASE." Reports in 6 months. Payment in copies.** The *Callaloo* Poetry Series is published by the University of Virginia Press, Box 3608, University Station, University of Virginia, Charlottesville, VA 22903. **All inquiries and submissions should be directed to Charles Rowell at: Department of English, Wilson Hall, University of Virginia, Charlottesville, VA 22903.** University of Virginia sponsors the journal and the series. They publish 2-5 flat-spined paperbacks a year, 40-60 pages. **"Please inquire before submitting to chapbook series."**

CALLI'S TALES (V, IV-Themes), Box 1224, Palmetto, FL 34220, founded 1981, poetry editor Annice E. Hunt, is a **typescript quarterly newsletter "for animal-lovers of all ages,"** stapled at the corner, with a colored paper title-page, illustrated with simple art. **Currently overstocked.**

CALYX, A JOURNAL OF ART & LITERATURE BY WOMEN (IV-Women, gay/lesbian), P.O. Box B, Corvallis, OR 97339, phone 503-753-9384, founded 1976, managing editor M. Donnelly, is a journal edited by a collective editorial board, **publishes poetry, prose, art, reviews and interviews by and about women.** They want **"excellently crafted poetry that also has excellent content."** Some poets they have published recently are Olga Broumas, Marilyn Hacker, Mila D. Aguilar and Eleanor Wilner. The editor selected these sample lines from "Oedipus Drowned" by Sharon Doubiago:

> *Now in his going out I go out with him and see:*
> *In the infant's turning from the mother*
> *Lies culture's turning from the feminine*

Each issue is 7×8", handsomely printed on heavy paper, flat-spined, glossy color cover, 125-200 pp., of which 50-60 are poetry. **Sample for the single copy price, $8 plus $1 postage. "Please query with SASE for open submission dates; we are no longer open to mss submissions at all times. Send up to 6 poems with SASE and short biographical statement. We accept copies in good condition and clearly readable. If interested, we report in 2-6 months." Payment in copies. Guidelines available for SASE.** "Read the publication and be familiar with what we have published."

‡CAMELLIA (I), P.O. Box 3406, Oakland, CA 94609, editor Tomer Inbar, "is a quarterly poetry magazine available for free in the San Francisco/Oakland Bay area or by sending a 45¢ SASE. **"We publish poetry in the W.C. Williams tradition. The poetry of things, moment and sharpness. We encourage young writers and like to work with the writers who publish with us (i.e., publishing them again to widen the forum or exposure of their work). Our main goal is to get the poetry out. We do not want to see poetry where the poem is subordinate to the poet or poetry where the noise of the poetic overshadows the voice. We look for poetry that is honest and sharp and not burdened by noise."** As a sample the editor selected these lines from "If the stone is not lost" by Edward Mycue:

> *if the stone is not lost it halts into*
> *essential elements*
> *silence is a weapon as a waterfall is*
> *an ornament*

I have not seen an issue, but the editor describes it as digest-sized, 16-20 pp, desk-top published using cartoons and drawings. "We receive approximately 40-50 poems per issue and publish 9-16." Press run 500. **Sample: 45¢ SASE. Pays 1 copy. Simultaneous submissions and previously published poems OK. Reports "ASAP." Editor comments on submissions "if asked for or if I want to see more but am not satisfied with the poems sent."** He says, "We want to get the poetry out to as many people as possible, put it out and it will be read. The idea is to do it and move forward. Poetry is only really about the poem and saying it and that is tied to the tradition of the poem and pushing beyond the previous—always forward. We are a free magazine, and we are growing by a few hundred copies every issue."

CANADIAN AUTHOR & BOOKMAN; CANADIAN AUTHOR & BOOKMAN EDITOR'S POETRY PRIZE; CANADIAN AUTHORS ASSOCIATION (III), Suite 104, 121 Avenue Rd., Toronto, ON M5R 2G3, Canada, poetry editor Sheila Martindale. *Canadian Author & Bookman* is magazine-sized, 28 pp., professionally printed, with paper cover in 2 colors. It contains articles useful to writers at all levels of experience. **Sample: $4.50 postpaid. Buys 40 poems a year. Pays $15 plus one copy.** The annual Editor's Poetry Prize of $50 is awarded for the best poem published in *CA&B* in the calendar year. (See also Canadian Authors Association Literary Awards in Contest and Awards section.)

‡**CANADIAN DIMENSION: A SOCIALIST NEWS MAGAZINE (IV-Political)**, 801-44 Princess St., Winnipeg, Manitoba R3B 1K2, Canada, phone 204-957-1519, founded 1964, editorial contact Shoshana Scott, appears 8 times per year, using **"short poems on labour, women, native and other issues. Nothing more than one page."** They have recently published poetry by Tom Wayman and Milton Acorn. As a sample the editor selected these lines by Ishbel Solvason:

> *She must find a job quickly*
> *She has been told*
> *But the factory closed its doors*
> *Her English is poor*

It is 48 pp., magazine-sized, slick, professionally printed, with paper cover. Press run: 4,500-5,000 for 3,000 subscriptions of which 800 are libraries, 1,000 shelf sales. Subscription: $25 US ($21 Canadian). **Sample, postpaid: $1.50. Pays 5 copies. Simultaneous submissions OK. Reports in 1 month. Editor comments on submissions "rarely."**

CANADIAN LITERATURE (IV-Regional), 2029 West Mall, University of British Columbia, Vancouver, BC, V6T 1W5 Canada, phone 604-228-2780, founded 1959, poetry editor W. H. New, is a quarterly review which publishes **poetry by Canadian poets. "No limits on form. Less room for long poems."** They have recently published poems by Atwood, Ondaatje, Layton and Bringhurst. The following sample lines are from "The Diamond" by Anne Swannell:

> *The perfect pitches, runs completed, fouls,*
> *our batting averages recorded in the dark,*
> *these conversations joined, completed, lost:*
> *the endless innings.*
> *Repeatedly, we turn our sweaty caps peak backward,*
> *adjust the angle, look unperturbed.*

Each issue is professionally printed, large digest-sized, flat-spined, with 190+ pp., of which about 10 are poetry. It has 2,000 circulation, two-thirds of which are libraries. **Sample for the cover price: $10 Canadian.** They receive 100-300 submissions per year, of which they use 10-12. **No photocopy, round-dot-matrix, simultaneous submissions or reprints. Reports within the month, pays $10/poem plus 1 copy.**

‡**CANAL LINES (I, IV-Regional)**, 36 Brockway Pl., Brockport, NY 14420, phone 716-637-8866, founded 1987, editor Joseph Hoffman, appears 3-4 times a year. **"Subject matter and style are open, although material connected to New England/Upstate New York is preferred. Length is limited to 70 lines."**

They have recently published poetry by William Heyen, Steven Huff, and David Michael Nixon. As a sample the editor selected these lines by William Blaine Durbin:

> *When lids of night dropped over havest moons*
> *and the icy eye of winter took up watch*
> *a hungry frost ate up their golden shoots*
> *and planted in their fields a barrenness.*

Canal Lines is digest-sized, 16 pp. saddle-stapled with matte card cover, photocopied from typescript, press run 100. They accept about 40-50% of 60-70 submissions per year. **Sample, postpaid: $1.25. Pays 2 copies. "A report on any submission takes 6-7 weeks or longer."** The editor says, "Patience and determination are a must. A well-written/thought-out poem may be rejected numerous times before finally finding a 'home.' A rejection slip is *not* a statement of failure, but an ongoing process to bring a poem into the proper light.

‡**CANOE PRESS (II),** 1587 Lake Dr., Traverse City, MI 49684, phone 616-946-7680, founded 1988, publisher Brian Browning, poetry editor Joe Dionne. "We publish books of poetry, also chapbooks, broadsheets, and greeting card format with poetry featured, quality letterpress on a hand-fed Chandler and Price. We do our own sewing and binding and in every way try to produce a *work of art*. **We publish modern poetry and have no restrictions as to form whatever. We are now open for submissions. Nothing from the Rod McKuen School, however."** They have recently published poetry by Lee Upton, Jack Driscoll, Al Drake, and Barbara Drake. As a sample the editor selected these lines by Katy McConnell:

> *It's not caring that's important.*
> *It's all the things that don't count.*
> *It's all the days in the middle of a*
> *storm no one sees. It's blue wind in the night;*

They publish 3 chapbooks a year averaging 25 pp. **Pays 15-20 copies. Accepts unsolicited MSS.**

THE CAPE ROCK (II), Department of English, Southeast Missouri State University, Cape Girardeau, MO 63701, founded 1964, appears twice yearly and consists of **64 pp. of poetry and photography, with a $200 prize for the best poem in each issue and $100 for featured photography.** It's a handsomely printed, flat-spined, digest-sized magazine, **sample: $2, guidelines available for SASE. "No restrictions on subjects or forms. Our criterion for selection is the quality of the work. We prefer poems under 70 lines; no long poems or books, no sentimental, didactic, or cute poems."** They have published such poets as Stephen Dunning, Joyce Odam, Judith Phillips Neeld, Lyn Lifshin, Virginia Brady Young, Gary Pacernik and Laurel Speer. I selected these sample lines from Kevin Woster's "November Night":

> *The rough paved streets*
> *have crystalized with sudden beauty*
> *Even trash cans find*
> *an edgeless sort of grace*

Their circulation is about 500, with 200 subscribers, of whom half are libraries. They have a 2-8 month backlog and **report in 1-3 months. Do not read submissions in May, June or July. Pays 2 copies.**

THE CAPILANO REVIEW (III), 2055 Purcell Way, North Vancouver, BC V7J 3H5, Canada, phone 604-986-1712, FAX 604-984-4985, founded 1972, editor Pierre Coupey. A "literary and visual media triannual; **avant-garde, experimental, previously unpublished work." They want poetry of sustained intelligence and imagination.** *TCR* comes in a handsome digest-sized format, 150 pp., flat-spined, finely printed on ruled pages, semi-glossy stock with a glossy full-color card cover. Circulation: 1,000. **Sample: $8 prepaid. Pays an honorarium plus 2 copies. No simultaneous submissions. Reports in up to 6 months.**

‡**CAPITAL MAGAZINE (IV-Regional),** Capital Region Magazine, Inc., 4 Central Ave., Albany, NY 12210, phone 518-465-3500, editor-in-chief Dardis McNamee, is a monthly **city/regional magazine for New York's capital region.** Circ. 35,000, 20 percent freelance written. Prefers to work with published/established writers. **"Exclusively local focus." Submit seasonal/holiday material 3 months in advance. Photocopied submissions and computer printout submissions OK; prefers letter-quality. Reports in 2 months. Pays 30 days from acceptance. Publishes MS an average of 3 months after acceptance.** Sample copy for 9 × 12 SAE with $1.95; writer's guidelines for SASE. "One fiction issue per year, July; short stories, novel excerpts, poetry. Deadline February 15. For writers with a link to the region. Professional quality only; one slot for writers previously unpublished in a general circulation magazine."

CAPPER'S (I, IV-Nature, inspirational, humor), 616 Jefferson St., Topeka, KS 66607, founded 1879, poetry editor Nancy Peavler, is a biweekly tabloid (newsprint) going to **395,000 mail subscribers,** mostly small-town and farm people. Uses 6-8 poems in each issue — payment $3-6 per poem. They want short poems (4-10 lines preferred, lines of one-column width) **"relating to everyday situations, nature, inspirational, humorous."** They have recently published Helen Harrington, Emma Walker, Sheryl Nelms, Alice Mackenzie Swaim, Ralph W. Seager, and Ida Fasel. The editor selected these lines from "Correction" by R.H. Grenville:

> *"Time heals," they say*
> *to those who bear*
> *the weight of grief.*
> *Oh, I've been there!*
> *And this I know:*
> *it isn't so.*
> *It's love that heals.*
> *Time doesn't care.*

Most poems used in *Capper's* **are upbeat in tone and offer the reader a bit of humor, joy, enthusiasm, or encouragement. Short poems of this type fit our format best. Submit 4-6 poems at a time with return postage, no photocopies or simultaneous submissions. Reports within 2-3 months. Send 85¢ for sample. Not available on newsstand.**

CARAVAN PRESS; EDGAR LEE MASTERS AWARD (III), 15445 Ventura Blvd., Suite 279, Sherman Oaks, CA 91403, founded 1980, poetry editor Olivia Sinclair-Lewis, is "a small press presently publishing approximately 6-7 works per year including poetry, photojournals, calendars, novels, etc. We look for quality, freshness and that touch of genius." In poetry, **"we want to see verve, natural rhythms, discipline, impact**, etc. We are flexible but **verbosity, triteness and saccharine make us cringe."** As a sample of their publications, they sent **Litany** by Scott Sonders. It is a professionally printed, digest-sized, 100 pp., flat-spined book with 3-color glossy card cover ($9.95). The editor selected these lines from "Transformation" in that book as a sample:

> *A thin dog with one albino eye*
> *growls in sympathy for the dead*
> *or soon-to-be-dead, and sings,*
> *of metamorphosis, and slowly*
> *slowly, i feel us changing*
> *into implements of purest gold.*

In addition to Sonders they have published books by Bebe Oberon, Walter Calder, Exene Vida, Carlos Castenada, Claire Bloome and G. G. Henke. Their tastes are for poets such as Charles Bukowski, Sylvia Plath, Erica Jong, and Bob Dylan. **"We have strong liasons with the entertainment industry and like to see material that is media-oriented and au courant." Sample, postpaid: $8. Query first, with 2-3 poems and résumé. If invited to submit, send double-spaced, typed MS (photocopy, dot-matrix OK). "No manuscripts will be read without SASE."** Simultaneous **submissions OK. They reply "ASAP." They offer 20% royalty contract, 10-50 copies, advance or honorarium depending on grants or award money. "Please study what we publish before submitting."** Criticism offered on rejected MSS. (Note: Fee charged if criticism requested.) "We sponsor the Edgar Lee Masters Award: National Poetry Contest. Winners collected into 88-page, digest-sized book, approximately every two years. Established in 1981."

THE CARIBBEAN WRITER (IV-Regional), Caribbean Research Institute, University of the Virgin Islands, RR 02, P.O. Box 10,000, Kingshill, St. Croix, USVI 00850, phone 809-778-0246, founded 1987, editor Dr. Erika Smilowitz, is an annual literary magazine **with a Caribbean focus. The Caribbean must be central to the literary work or the work must reflect a Caribbean heritage, experience or perspective. Blind submissions only: name, address and title of MS should appear on a separate sheet. Title only on ms. Payment is 1 copy.** They have recently published poetry by Derek Walcott, Laurence Lieberman, Frances Sherwood, and Julia Alvarez. As a sample I selected the opening lines of "Below Blue Mountain" by Joseph Bruchac:

> *The full moon touches the crest of the peak*
> *and all is quiet at Nannytown.*
> *The conch horns of the eastern Maroons,*
> *the hands of the old man on the drum*
> *are quiet, quiet, quiet.*

The magazine is handsomely printed on heavy pebbled stock, flat-spined, 110 pp., 7×10", with glossy card cover, using advertising and b/w art by Caribbean artists. Press run is 1,000. **Sample: $7 plus $1.50 postage. Send SASE for guidelines. (Note: postage to and from the Virgin Islands is the same as within the United States.) Simultaneous submissions OK.** The annual appears in the spring.

CARING CONNECTION (IV-Theme), (formerly *Handicap News*) #342, 3060 Bridge St., Brighton, CO 80601-2724, phone 303-659-4463, founded 1984, editor-publisher Phyllis A. Burns. A 3-page (printed on both sides) newsletter, *Caring Connection* **publishes articles on caregiving experiences, tips on coping, travel items, etc. and any type, form, or style of poem except horror.** She has recently published work by Janice Airhart and Wayne Allen Sallee. The editor selected these sample lines from a poem entitled "God's Handiwork" by Janice Airhart

> *He warms himself beneath the brilliant sun*
> *Propped in his jailer-chair*
> *Dreamless eyes reflecting light*
> *Through the prisms of his soul.*

The purpose of the newsletter is to disseminate news to caregivers and others interested; it goes to associations, nonprofit organizations, caregivers, and handicapped people. Frequency is monthly, circulation 500, subscriptions 100. Ads are available for 20¢/word, no graphics. Subscription: $13.50. **No sample back issues available. Guidelines cost $2 (US currency) plus SASE. Pay in 2 free copies. The editor reports on submissions in 1 month, publishes in 10-13 months, and requests no more than 3 submissions per envelope; she will accept photocopies or simultaneous submissions.** "Content means more to me than particular style — although I would appreciate seeing something besides religious poems. Handicapped people, be creative and tell the world of your place in the world and how you see it. **We print only the work of handicapped people and caregivers. Please do** *not* **send me work unless you fall in this category. All submissions** *must* **contain a letter or note relating what the handicap is and who has it."**

CARNEGIE MELLON MAGAZINE (II, IV-Specialized/alumni), Carnegie Mellon University, Pittsburgh, PA 15213, phone 412-268-2900, editor Ann Curran, is the **alumni magazine for the university and limits selections to writers connected with the university, no payment. Direct submissions with SASE to Gerald Costanzo, poetry editor.** The issue I examined had one poem, "A Daughter," by Lee Upton (who had read her work at the Carnegie-Mellon Visiting Writers Series), from which I selected the opening stanza as a sample:

> *Water on the white blossoms,*
> *warm, almost like the touch of oil.*
> *To be ridiculous and beautiful was*
> *one task for a daughter.*

‡A CAROLINA LITERARY COMPANION (II), Box 3554, Comm. Council for the Arts, Kinston, NC 28501, founded 1985, poetry editor Patrick Bizzaro, is "a regional journal devoted to the discovery of new talent, which is published alongside writing of established talent." It appears twice a year. **"Please read a copy of the magazine. We tend to be open, but we prefer imagery, an awareness of what's out there, a new insight or perception. No clichés, greeting-card stuff, writing that shamelessly reveals that the writer is not a reader."** They have recently published poetry by R.T. Smith, Julie Fay, and Patrick Worth Gray. As a sample the editor selected these lines from "On the Surprise Discovery of My Dead Mother's Presence" by Edward Francisco:

> *Now I know that all the benevolent*
> *colors I was given to see were*
> *little more than preparation for*
> *a memory of darkness*

I have not seen an issue, but the editor describes it as digest-sized, 72 pp. saddle-stapled. They publish about 35 of 400 poems received each year. Press run 1,000 for 250 subscriptions of which half are libraries. Subscription: $8.50. **Sample, postpaid: $5. Pays 2 copies. Submit "bunches of 3-5." Editor comments on submissions "when it will do some good."** He says, "A lot of people are writing and submitting poetry despite the fact that they do not read poetry. I'm tired of reading greeting-card verse. I encourage writers to be readers as well."

CAROLINA QUARTERLY (III), Greenlaw Hall CB# 3520, University of North Carolina, Chapel Hill, NC 27599-3520, founded 1948, editor Barnesley Brown, is a small literary magazine that appears three times a year using poetry of **"all kinds, though we seek excellence always."** They have recently published poets such as Richard Kenney, Charles Simic, Michael Waters, Len Roberts and Mary Kinzie. As a sample the editor selected these lines from "Her Bread" by Stewart James:

> *But a lamp from the bathroom is shining in her*
> *wet face now. She thinks of those sucking, creaking jays*
> *that at twilight go wild somewhere in the palm trees.*

It's a professionally printed, $6 \times 9''$ flat-spined magazine, glossy cover, with 90 pp. of which about 30 are poetry, circulation 1,000, with 400 subscriptions, of which about half are libraries. They receive thousands of submissions per year, use 40-60. **Sample: $5 postpaid. Submit no more than**

2-6 poems. Use of poems over 300 lines is imp~actical. No simultaneous submissions. Submissions read *very slowly* May – September; reporting time 3 months. Pays $15/author plus 2 copies. Guidelines available for SASE. Sometimes comments on rejections.

✓ **CAROLINA WREN PRESS (IV-Women, ethnic, regional)**, Box 277, Carrboro, NC 27510, founded 1976, editor-in-chief Judy Hogan, poetry editor Marilyn Bulman, publishes **"primarily North Carolina authors; primarily people whose work I have come to know through teaching, readings, consultation; focus on women and minorities, though men and majorities also welcome."** Judy Hogan is one of the most broadly experienced editors in the small presses and offers "consultation-by-mail" at $50 for 12 pages or **"North Carolina authors can sometimes consult me free if they can come to Durham."** The consultation consists of "feedback, advice about acquiring writing skills, where to publish, support groups, classes and other community resources, and help with book-length projects." Some published poets are Jaki Shelton-Green, Li Ch'ing-Chao (in translation), Gene Fowler, T.J. Reddy and Tom Huey. The editor chose this sample from Tom Huey's "Forcehymn":

> You cannot turn from your own death, though you would like to,
> like a wrong word not needed but thought, like a wrong street
> dreamed but walked anyway. You cannot turn from a friend's death
> though you would like to. . .

Send query letter. No more than 12 pages of poetry. Report time 6 months. Pays 10% of print run in copies. Publishes 4 books per year. Request catalog to purchase samples. Some free advice: "Become good and for feedback use friends and community resources."

CAROUSEL LITERARY ARTS MAGAZINE (II, IV-regional), Rm. 217 University Center, University of Guelph, Guelph, ON N1G 2W1 Canada, founded 1983, editor Michael Carbert, is an annual using **"any type of well-written, typed poetry, mainly by Canadians (though others are accepted) as well as short stories, graphics, or short plays. We do not usually publish rhyming poetry. MSS should be well-edited before they are sent. Original, minimalist, off-beat material is encouraged."** They have recently published poetry by John B. Lee, Anne Burke, James Harrison, Mary Melfi, and W.P. Kinsella. It is flat-spined, 89 pp. Their press run is 500. They accept about 30-40 of 150 pieces received. **Sample: $3.50 postpaid. Send SASE for guidelines. Pays 1 copy. They will consider simultaneous submissions. Reports in 3-4 months. Type name and address on each page.**

CARPENTER PRESS (V, II), Box 14387, Columbus, OH 43214, founded 1973, editor Bob Fox, publishes a chapbook series and an occasional full-length collection, flat-spined. **No unsolicited MSS. Query, no samples.** They have published poetry by Steve Kowit and David Shevin. **Pays 10% royalties, 10% of press run in copies. Send SASE for catalog to purchase samples.**

‡THE CARREFOUR PRESS (V), Box 2629 Cape Town, South Africa 8000, phone 021-477280, founded 1988, managing editor Douglas Reid Skinner, is a "small press specializing in poetry, criticism, philosophy," accepting **"manuscripts by invitation only."** They have recently published poetry by Basil Du Toit, Douglas Livingstone, and Israel Ben Yosef. They publish about 6 paperbacks a year averaging 80 pp. Poets they publish **"should have an established reputation, primarily through magazines." Pays 7½-10% royalties and 20 copies.** About a third of their books are subsidized, and the poet "must assist in obtaining sponsorship."

‡CAT FANCY (IV-Themes, children), P.O. Box 6050, Mission Viejo, CA 92690, phone 714-855-8822, founded 1965, editor K.E. Segnar. *Cat Fancy* is a magazine-sized monthly that uses **poems on the subject of cats. "No more than 20 short lines; open on style and form, but a conservative approach is recommended. In our children's department we occasionally use longer, rhyming verse that tells a story about cats. No eulogies for pets that have passed away."** They have published poetry by Lola Sneyd and Edythe G. Tornow. As a sample the editor selected these lines by Lynette Combs:

> He trampolines
> from chair to chair
> and waits in ambush
> on the stair.

It has a press run of 332,755 for 252,899 subscribers, 28,056 shelf sales. Subscription: $21.97. **Sample, postpaid: $3.50. Pays $20/poem plus 2 copies. Name and address "in left-hand corner." Reports in 6 weeks. Editor sometimes comments on submissions, "especially if the MS is appealing but somehow just misses the mark for our audience."** She says, "We have an audience that very much appreciates sensitive and touching work about cats. As for advice – get input from knowledgeable sources as to the marketability of your work, and be open to learning how your work might be improved. Then send it out, and hang on. Rejection may not mean your work is bad. We are able to accept very few submissions, and the competition is fierce. Timing and luck have a lot to do with acceptance, so keep trying!"

THE CATHARTIC (II), P.O. Box 1391, Ft. Lauderdale, FL 33302, phone 305-474-7120, founded 1974, edited by Patrick M. Ellingham, "is a **small poetry magazine devoted to the unknown poet** with the understanding that most poets are unknown in America." He says, "While there is no specific type of poem I look for, **rhyme for the sake of rhyme is discouraged. Any subject matter except where material is racist or sexist in nature. Overly-long poems, over 80 lines, are not right for a small magazine normally. I would like to see some poems that take chances with both form and language.** I would like to see poems that get out of and forget about self ['I'] and look at the larger world and the people in it with an intensity that causes a reader to react or want to react to it. I am gravitating toward work that looks at the darker side of life, is intense and uses words sparingly." Recently published poets include Joy Walsh, Harry E. Knickerbocker, Paul Weinman, J.J. Snow and Sue Walker. These sample lines are from a poem by Sheila Whitehouse:

> Come to this warmth
> that pulses for your hand,
> join with my heaving breath,
> slip wide my thighs
> that welcome you

It's a modest, 28 pp. pamphlet offset printed from typescript, consisting mostly of poems, which appears twice a year. **Sample: $2 postpaid.** He receives over a thousand submissions per year, of which he uses about 60. No backlog. **Photocopy, dot-matrix, simultaneous submissions OK, submit 5-10 poems. Reports in 1 month. Uses reviews of small press books as well as some artwork and photography. Guidelines available for SASE. Contributors receive 1 copy.** He advises, "The only way for poets to know whether their work will get published or not is to submit. It is also essential to read as much poetry as possible—both old and new. Spend time with the classics as well as the new poets. Support the presses that support you—the survival of both is essential to the life of poetry."

CATS MAGAZINE (IV-Themes), Box 290037, Port Orange, FL 32029, editor Linda J. Walton, is a monthly magazine **about cats, including light verse about cats. Pays 50¢ a line. Free sample copy is available when accompanied by a 9 × 12 envelope with $1.05 postage. All submissions or requests must have SASE. Payment on publication.**

‡CCR PUBLICATIONS (II), 2745 Monterey Hwy #76, San Jose, CA 95111-3129, founded as Realities Library in 1975, as CCR Publications in 1987, editor and publisher Ric Soos. "I am going to take one book, and follow it through all stages with the author. I will not even consider a new book until the current project is finished. Please keep in mind when you contact me for projects, that I believe in Jesus Christ, and that anything I publish will be to help further the Gospel if it is for that purpose. **In poetry, I look for items that will not hinder the spread of the Gospel. In other words, the poet need not be Christian, does not need to mention Christ by name. But I will no longer be publishing for Shock Value.**" He publishes those **"who support me in some respect . . . Support is not always financial." Query with sample poems.** He has recently published books of poetry by Ruth Daigon and Ella Blanche Salmi. As a sample I selected the complete poem, "To Carol" by Don MacQueen:

> When gulls fly inland crying
> under a thin gauze sky
> it can mean storm, I told you.
>
> Now it is raining and
> you are not here to praise me.

That poem is from **Far from the Garden,** a flat-spined digest-sized book, 64 pp., professionally printed on good stock with 2-color glossy card cover, $5.

CEILIDH: AN INFORMAL GATHERING FOR STORY & SONG (II, IV-Translations), Box 6367, San Mateo, CA 94403, phone 415-591-9902, founded 1981, poetry editors Patrick S. Sullivan and Perry Oei, is interested in **"experimental, translations, long poems, and language poetry. Not interested in satire, word play or other less than literary poetry."** In recent issues they have published Patrick Smith, John Moffitt, Sarah Bliumis and translations by Joseph Salemi. These sample lines selected by the editors are from "Crotched Mountain" by William Doreski:

> how cities design themselves
> around the fluid architecture
> of the random gesture, defying
> closure, disdaining nature,
> forever about to begin.

There are 32-64 pp. per issue. Winter and summer issues are devoted to fiction; spring and fall issues each use about 36 pages of poetry. Circulation to 400 subscribers, of which 100 are libraries. **Sample: $3.50 postpaid.** They have a 2-3 month backlog. **The best time to submit is January-**

March and July-September 1. Photocopy, dot-matrix OK, but no simultaneous submissions. Reports in 6-8 weeks. Pays 2 copies. Guidelines available for SASE. The editor says, "We recommend that poets send for our guidelines and a sample copy. The best way to determine what we will publish is to see what we have published." Subscription for 4 issues is $12. Usually a contest with each issue with prizes from cash to gift certificates to poetry books. Some of their contest judges: Gerald Frassetti, James K. Bell, Michael Thornton. Occasional criticism of rejected MSS.

CELTIC DAWN; YEATS CLUB (II, IV-Translations); PREBENDAL PRESS (V), Box 30, Thame, Oxon OX9 3AD England UK, FAX 84-421-6677 (in USA: Box 402527, Miami Beach, FL 33140-0527, FAX 305-868-2011). Yeats Club founded 1986; Prebendal Press, *Celtic Dawn* founded 1988, editors Dwina Murphy-Gibb and Terence DuQuesne, who say, "If it has quality, we will consider it. We are not doctrinaire, but we like literacy. Do *not* want to see poetry that is illiterate, mannered, pretentious, fake-scholarly, etc." They have recently published poetry by Fran Landesman (from US), and Bridie Morrigan (from Ireland). As a sample I selected these lines from "Caduceus" by the editor Terence DuQuesne:

> To love each other and to serve
> The great work all my dream
> Despite the mind's old caveats
> And screams of fear

Celtic Dawn is in an elegant coated-stock format, magazine-sized, 56 pp., flat-spined, with a glossy 2-color card cover. It incorporates "The Yeats Club Review," which prints winners of their poetry competitions. Their press run is 1,000. Subscription: $34 (US), £20 (UK). **Sample: $8.50 (US) or £5 (UK) postpaid. Back numbers (issues 1-4) each $5 (US) £2.50 (UK). (US: please make checks payable to the Yeats Club Inc.).** They pay "as many copies as they request, within reason." They consider previously published poems. Editors "certainly" comment on rejections and report within 1 month. But the magazine is at present overstocked, so unsolicited contributions, unless excellent, are not encouraged. Prebendal Press published about 4 flat-spined paperbacks in 1989, paying standard royalty rates, but are not, at this writing, ready to consider MSS. The Yeats Club sponsors two open poetry competitions a year on announced themes with prizes ranging from £50 ($100) to £250 ($500) for original poems and original sculptures for poetry in translation (£2 [$2] per poem entry fee). Three of the four prizewinners in the last competition were from the American continent. For current rules and entry forms, write to Box 402527, Miami, FL 33140-0527, USA (competitors in the US and Canada) or to Box 30, Thame, Oxon OX9 3AD, UK (UK entrants and others).

UNIVERSITY OF CENTRAL FLORIDA CONTEMPORARY POETRY SERIES (II), % Dept. of English, University of Central Florida, Orlando, FL 32816, phone 407-275-2263, founded 1970, poetry editor Tom George, publishes **two 50-80 pp. hardback or paperback collections each year.** They have recently published poetry by Rebecca McClanahan Devet, Don Stap, Roald Hoffmann and Edmund Skellings. Here is a sample from Don Stap's book, **Letter at the End of Winter.** These are the first nine lines of the poem "From a Photograph":

> In your checkered dress you are smiling
> your blond hair diffused in the angelic light of a poor exposure.
> You are seven or eight,
> wearing white anklets and shoes with buckles
> standing with your hands behind your back.
> But where is the farm on Territorial Road
> and the fruit orchards of Coloma?
> Where is the black bread and blood sausage
> and where is Latvia, that dark stain on Russia's shoulder?

The only criterion is good poetry. **Reporting time, 8 weeks.**

‡**CHAKRA: A JOURNAL OF THE SPECULATIVE ARTS AND SCIENCES (I, IV-Science fiction/fantasy, spirituality)**, P.O. Box 8551 FDR Station, New York, NY 10022, founded 1988, editor Liz Camps, appears 3-4 times per year using poetry of "any length or style having to do with the occult, sci-fi/fantasy, earth worship, omnisexuality, discordia, magick, mysticism, cybershamanism — unusual but high quality works of polymorphous diversity. Prayers and ritual verse greatly encouraged." They have recently published poetry by Stephen Gill, Kenneth Lumpkin, and Michael Hathaway. As a sample the editor selected these lines from "Letter to Sarah" by Ivan Argüelles:

> that dark matter I mean your soul
> wherever it is however capable it is
> of extending itself through corporeal music
> into the bathysphere or beyond its halos . . .

Chakra has a new format I have not seen: magazine-sized, photocopied. They accept about 10% of "hundreds of poems received a year." Press run: 100-1,000 ("varying"). Subscription: $3.50. **Sample, postpaid; $1. Pays 1-2 copies.** They want MSS "typed neatly on *used* paper (encourages amateur recycling). Simultaneous submissions and previously published poems OK. Reports in "several weeks." Editor comments on submissions "seldom, but comments are extensive when merited." They had their first contest in 1990. "Send SASE for details—with request on *used* paper."

‡CHALK TALK (IV-Children), 1550 Mills Rd. RR 2, Sidney, B.C. V8L 3S1 Canada, phone 604-656-1858, founded 1987, editor Virginia Lee, is a "non-glossy magazine **written by children for children** (with parents' pages), stories, poems, drawings, published 10 months/year. **Any form or subject matter.**" As a sample I selected this poem, "Trees," By Shalan Joudry, age 10 from Toronto:

> *Trees are tall and short*
> *They make excellent tree houses and swings*
> *They keep the ground and soil down flat*
> *Children have joyful fun climbing and exploring the trees*
> *I hope the trees grow forever*

It is magazine-sized, 24 pp., newsprint. No July or August issues. Approximately 3 pp. per month are poems. Press run 3,000 for 1,500 subscribers of which 15% are libraries. Subscription: $10.95. **Sample, postpaid: $2. Send SASE for guidelines. Pays "as many copies as requested." Simultaneous submissions OK.**

CHANNELS; CURRENTS (IV-Religious, membership), 2101 Treasure Hills #344, Harlingen, TX 78550, phone 512-425-7415, founded 1974, editor Jean Hogan Dudley, a tri-annual magazine of the Christian Writer's League of America, **using the work of members.** Dues $12.50 per year. Uses about 100 poems a year, including some in *Currents*, CWLA news magazine, editor Lee Longenecker. **Pays in contributor copy, accepts photocopies, simultaneous and dot-matrix submissions, and previously published work. Sample: $4 postpaid; guidelines for SASE.** "We are looking for quality poems in any form that speak to both mind and heart. Christian emphasis includes nature, home life, social problems and aspects of the Christian faith."

CHAPMAN (IV-Ethnic); CHAPMAN PRESS (V), 80 Moray St., Blackford, Perthshire PH4 1QF Scotland, phone 031-557-2207, founded 1970, editor Joy Hendry, "provides an outlet for new work by **established Scottish writers and for new, up-and-coming writers also,** for the discussion and criticism of this work and for reflection on current trends in Scottish life and literature. But *Chapman* is not content to follow old, well-worn paths; it throws open its pages to new writers, new ideas and new approaches. In the international tradition revived by MacDiarmid, *Chapman* also **feaures the work of foreign writers and broadens the range of Scottish cultural life.**" They have recently published poetry and fiction by Alasdair Gray, Liz Lochhead, Sorley MacLean, T.S. Law, Tom Scott, and Una Flett. As a sample the editor selected this poem by Naomi Mitchison, "The Rhodesian Woman":

> *It's Us or Them she said, dry-lipped, sun-faded, Us or Them,*
> *Why, I said, why? For she scared me, she, would-be destroyer*
> *Of the tenderness that I knew, the being together,*
> *The trust warm between equals, the more than trust,*
> *The joining of hands, of worlds, the gifts of both sides.*
> *Let me be far from you, woman of my colour, not of my heart.*
> *I go to my friends*

Chapman appears 4 times a year in a 6 × 9" perfect-bound format, 104 pp., professionally printed in small type on matte stock with glossy card cover, art in 2 colors, circulation 2,000 for 900 subscriptions of which 200 are libraries. They receive "thousands" of freelance submissions of poetry per year, use about 200, **have an 8-12 month backlog. No simultaneous submissions. Sample: £2.50 (overseas). Pays £7 per page. Reports "as soon as possible." Chapman Press is not interested in unsolicited MSS.**

THE CHARITON REVIEW PRESS; THE CHARITON REVIEW (II), Northeast Missouri State University, Kirksville, MO 63501, phone 816-785-4499, founded 1975, editor Jim Barnes. *The Chariton Review* began in 1975 as a twice yearly literary magazine, and in 1978 added the activities of the Press, producing "limited editions (not chapbooks!) of **full-length collections . . . for the purpose of introducing solid, contemporary poetry to readers.** The books go free to the regular subscribers of *The Chariton Review*; others are sold to help meet printing costs." The poetry published in both books and the magazine is, according to the editor, "**open and closed forms—traditional, experimental, mainstream. We do not consider verse, only poetry in its highest sense, whatever that may be. The sentimental and the inspirational are not poetry for us.**" They have recently published poets such as Michael Spence,

Neil Myers, Ruth Good, Judy Ray, Charles Edward Eaton, Wayne Dodd and Harold Witt. These lines offered as a sample are from "Deathbed Edition" by Elton Glaser:

> And though this throat, when young, was blessed
> By crossed candles, I want
> No gospel-volume bossed in gold, no Latin chatter
> And sweet smoke invoking
> Mansions for sale in the sunlit suburbs of heaven.

There are 40-50 pages of poetry in each issue of the *Review*, a 6 × 9" flat-spined magazine of over a hundred pages, professionally printed, glossy cover with photographs, circulation about 600 with 400 subscribers of which 100 are libraries. **Sample: $2.50 postpaid.** They receive 7,000-8,000 submissions per year, of which they use 35-50, with never more than a 6-month backlog. **Submit 5-7 poems, typescript single-spaced, no carbons, dot-matrix or simultaneous submissions. Payment: $5/printed page. Contributors are expected to subscribe or buy copies. To be considered for book publication, query first — samples of magazine $2.50, of books $3 and $5. Payment for book publication: $500 with 20 or more copies. Usually no criticism is supplied.** The sample book I have seen, **The Tramp's Cup,** by David Ray, has an appearance much like the magazine and sells for $3. The prices of both the magazine and books seem remarkably low in view of the high quality of production. Jim Barnes advises poets "Submit only your *best* work."

‡**CHARNEL HOUSE (IV-Form)**, Box 281 Station S, Toronto, ON M5M 4L7, Canada, phone 416-924-5670, founded 1979, editor Crad Kilodney, is **"only interested in very bad poetry."** They publish limited editions of fiction and poetry, mostly sold on the street." I have not seen one of their publications but the editor describes them as digest-sized, saddle-stapled paperbacks. *"Bad poetry only, for a series of anthologies of bad poetry. Intended as offbeat novelty items. Any style, from semi-illiterate to pretentious avant-garde. Any subject. Preferably less than 40 lines. Nothing that shows real talent."* They have recently published poetry by Richard Truhlar, Minnie Dalton, Jon Daunt, and William McGonagall. As a sample the editor selected these lines (poet unidentified):

> Yes, this is a great nation,
> Lots of drugs but sex education.
> The streets are filled with perverts,
> And we get smog alerts.

They publish one chapbook a year, 64 pp. **Sample, postpaid: $6. Submit to the anthology only. Previously published poems and simultaneous submissions OK. Reports in 1 week. Pays 1 copy "or by arrangement."** The editor explains, "Charnel House is mainly a fiction imprint, but we are doing a series of bad poetry anthologies because no one else is doing them."

‡**CHASTITY & HOLINESS MAGAZINE; CHRISTIANIC POETIC MINISTRY; C.J.L. PRESS/ART CO.; THE POLYGLOT ARMY (IV-Religious)**, 22006 Thorncliffe P.O., Toronto, ON M4H 1N9 Canada, phone 416-423-6781, founded 1988, editor-in-chief Cecil Justin Lam, publishes "Christianic works, Christianic long poems and books by new inspirational writers. Old writers also accepted. Poetry should be **religious, Christianic, inspirational. All styles, all forms. No restriction as to poetic expressions. No limit to length. The longer is usually the more welcome; Christ and inspired poetry related, to spread the Gospel of love and truth. No Satanic or obscene poetry. No secular poetry with no fixed aim of life view. No garbage talker and poets who do not know what is happening and what they are doing with their words."** They have recently published poetry by J.M. Weston, David Castleman, and Hugh Alexander. As a sample the editor selected these lines by R.C. Teape:

> If you know
> you could do better
> at least one reason
> the other person couldn't

The magazine appears twice a year, 8½ × 7", 28 pp., photocopied from typescript, paper cover. They accept about 30% of 100 poems received a year. Press run: 200 for 50 subscriptions of which all are libraries. Subscription: $10. **Sample, postpaid: $5. Send SASE for guidelines. Pays "prayers and rewards plus 1 copy." Simultaneous submissions and previously published poems OK. Reports immediately. For book publication by C.J.L. Press submit 3 samples, bio, publications. Reports in 4 weeks. Pays 1 copy plus 20% royalties. "Awards will be granted on the basis of Christianic literary performance."** The editor says, "All living creatures, men or aliens may submit to us. The central goal of our publishing firm is to present the World and the Universe with the Holy Sacrifice and Resurrected life of Christ. Intensive Research must be carried out in ensuring all co-ordinative aspects of publishing and economics may match." He provides criticism for $100/100 pp. "Constructive comments will be used to encourage the on-going of writing ventures."

THE CHATTAHOOCHEE REVIEW (II), DeKalb, 2101 Womack Rd., Dunwoody, GA 30338, phone 404-551-3019, founded 1980, editor-in-chief Lamar York, a semiannual of poetry, short fiction, essays, reviews and interviews, published by DeKalb College. "We like to publish beginners alongside professional writers. We are open to poetry from traditional forms to avant-garde and any subject matter or length or style." They have recently published poems by Fred Chappell, Rosemary Daniell, Ed Minus, Bettie Sellers and Jessie Hill Ford. *The Review* is 6×9", professionally printed on white stock with b/w reproductions of art work, 90 pp., flat-spined, with one-color card cover. Circulation is 1,000, of which 500 are complimentary copies sent to editors and "miscellaneous VIP's." Price per issue is $4, subscription $15/year. **Sample available for $4 postpaid, guidelines for SASE. Pay is 2 copies. Writers should send 1 copy of each poem and a cover letter with bio material. Reporting time is 6 months and time to publication is 3-4 months. Queries will be answered in 1-2 weeks. No simultaneous submissions. Photocopied or dot-matrix MSS are OK but discs are not.**

CHELSEA; CHELSEA AWARD COMPETITION (III, IV-Translations), Box 5880, Grand Central Station, New York, NY 10163, founded 1958, editor Sonia Raiziss, associate editors Richard Foerster and Alfred de Palchi, assistant editor Caila Rossi, is a long-established, high-quality literary annual aiming to promote intercultural communication. "We look for intelligence and sophisticated technique in both experimental and traditional forms. Always interested in translations of contemporary poets. Length: 5-7 pp. per submission. Although our tastes are eclectic, we lean toward the cosmopolitan avant-garde. Do not want to see 'inspirational' verse, pornography, or poems that rhyme merely for the sake of rhyme."** They have recently published poetry by Lucille Clifton, Rita Dove, Jane Flanders, Reginald Gibbons and Chase Twichell. I have not seen a recent issue, but the editors describe it as "160-240 pp., flat-spined, 6×9", offset, cover art varies, occasional use of photographs, ads." Circulation: 1,300, with 600 subscriptions of which 200 are libraries. Subscription: $11. **Sample: $4 or more depending on issue. Send SASE for a brochure describing all past issues. Pays $5 per page and 2 copies. Reports immediately to 3 months. 5-7 pp. of poetry are ideal; long poems should not exceed 10 pp.; must be typed; clean photocopy OK; include brief bio; no simultaneous submissions.** "We try to comment favorably on above-average MSS; otherwise, we do not have time to provide critiques." **Guidelines for their Chelsea Award Competition, $500 for poetry, available for SASE to Box 1040, York Beach, ME 03910.** Richard Foerster, Associate Editor, comments: "Beginners should realize that a rejection often has more to do with the magazine's production schedule and special editorial plans than with the quality of the submission. They should also realize that editors of little magazines are always overworked (and almost invariably unpaid) and that it is necessary haste and not a lack of concern or compassion that makes rejections seem coldly impersonal."

THE UNIVERSITY OF CHICAGO PRESS; PHOENIX POETS (V), 5801 S. Ellis Ave., Chicago, IL 60637, series editor Robert von Hallberg. Up until the late 1960s the University of Chicago Press published a small number of poets, building a selective and distinguished list under the Phoenix imprint. This tradition gave impetus to the renewal of the **Phoenix Poets**. The series publishes poetry of all styles and persuasions, with the criteria for selection being superior quality and craftsmanship. Each volume will be published simultaneously in cloth and paper; cloth editions will have a distinctive three-piece binding. **Submissions by invitation only.** Recently published poets include Tom Sleigh, Ha Jin, Eleanor Wilner, Donald Davie and Jim Powell. The first two volumes in the renewed series were (1984) Alan Shapiro's *The Courtesy*, and David Ferry's *Strangers*. Alan Shapiro's *Happy Hour*, also in the series, received the 1987 William Carlos Williams Award from the Poetry Society of America.

CHICAGO REVIEW (III), Faculty Exchange, Box C, University of Chicago, Chicago, IL 60637, founded 1946, poetry editor Anne Myles. **"A sure hand, showing originality and precision of language, form, and tone—while avoiding the clichés of critical consensus—is the sole requirement for inclusion in** *CR*, overriding formal affiliation, regional bias, or previous history of publication. We have recently published poets as diverse as Eavan Boland, J.B. Goodenough, Kathleen Norris, Turner Cassity, Michael Donaghy, and Jim Powell; out of the 1,500 submissions we receive each year, we accept around 50." **Payment in copies. Sample: $5.50 postpaid. Response time: 3-4 months, longer in some cases.** Circulation: 2,000.

‡**CHICORY BLUE PRESS (V)**, 795 East Street N., Goshen, CT 06756, founded 1988, publisher Sondra Zeidenstein, publishes poetry but **accepts no unsolicited MSS and "am not currently accepting queries."**

CHILDREN'S BETTER HEALTH INSTITUTE; BENJAMIN FRANKLIN LITERARY AND MEDICAL SOCIETY, INC.; HUMPTY DUMPTY'S MAGAZINE; TURTLE MAGAZINE FOR PRESCHOOL KIDS; CHILDREN'S DIGEST; CHILDREN'S PLAYMATE; JACK AND JILL; CHILD LIFE; (IV-Children), 1100 Waterway Blvd., Box 567, Indianapolis, IN 46206. This publisher of magazines stressing health for children has a **variety of needs for mostly short, simple poems, for which they pay $10 minimum. Send SASE**

for guidelines. For example, *Humpty Dumpty* is for ages 4-6; *Turtle* is for preschoolers, similar emphasis, uses many stories in rhyme—talking animals, etc.; *Children's Digest* is for preteens (10-13); *Jack and Jill* is for ages 7-10. *Child Life* is for ages 9-11. *Children's Playmate* is for ages 6-8. All appear 8 times a year in a 6½ × 9" 48 pp. format, slick paper with cartoon art, very colorful. The editors advise that writers who appear regularly in their publications **study current issues carefully. Samples: 75¢ each, postpaid.**

CHINESE LITERATURE (IV-Translations), 24 Baiwanzhuang Road, Beijing, 100037 China, founded 1951, managing editor, Dong Lianghui, is a quarterly of **"translations of Chinese fiction, poetry, art, etc., for readers abroad." It does not accept foreign submissions, but chooses poetry reflecting Chinese life by such poets as Ai Qing and Lu Yuan. It has a circulation of 50,000. For samples, write to its general distributor,** China International Book Trading Corporation, P.O. Box 399, Beijing, China.

CHIRON REVIEW; CHIRON BOOKS; CHIRON REVIEW POETRY CONTEST (I, II), Rt. 2, Box 111, St. John, KS 67576, phone 316-549-3933, founded 1982 as *Kindred Spirit*, editor Michael Hathaway, assistant editor Jane Hathaway, contributing editor (poetry) Gerald Locklin, is a tabloid quarterly using photographs of featured writers. They have recently published poetry by Charles Bukowski, Lorri Jackson, Marge Piercy, and Elliot Fried. As a sample the editors selected these lines excerpted from "Let's be fair about this" by Gavin Dillard:

> God spare a few dolphins, whales, gorillas
> & forgive us the species we have already done in.
> As for this plague of humans that rages so rampantly
> out of control, God knows AIDS isn't nearly the answer.
> It doesn't even hit where we need to hit—the breeders.

Their press run is about 2,000. Each issue is 24-32 pp. and "contains dozens of poems." **Sample: $2 postpaid ($4 overseas or institutions). Send SASE for guidelines. Send 5 poems "typed or printed legibly." They will consider simultaneous submissions but not previously published poems. Pays 1 copy. Reports in 2-4 weeks. For book publication submit complete MS.** They publish 1-3 books/year, flat-spined, professionally printed, **paying 25% of press run of 100-200 copies.** Their annual poetry contest offers awards of $100 plus 1-page feature in Winter issue, $50, and 5 free subscriptions and a Chiron Press book; entry fee $4 for up to 6 poems.

THE CHRISTIAN CENTURY (II, IV-Religious, social issues), 407 S. Dearborn St., Chicago, IL 60605, founded 1884, named *The Christian Century* 1900, founded again 1908, joined by *New Christian* 1970, poetry editor Dean Peerman. This "ecumenical weekly" is a liberal, sophisticated journal of news, articles of opinion and reviews from a generally Christian point-of-view, **using approximately one poem per issue, not necessarily on religious themes but in keeping with the literate tone of the magazine.** They have recently published poems by Robert Beum, Joan Rohr Myers, Ida Fasel, Jill Baumgaertner, and J. Barrie Shepherd. As a sample the editor selected the short poem "Adam's Revenge" by James Worley:

> Condemned to be cursed by memory,
> he took four plants from paradise
> to share his fate of wanting what had been:
> the violet, made purpler by its loss;
> forsythia, forever creeping back;
> the willow drooping toward its roots;
> the ivy clinging, even as it climbed,
> to what it still remembered of un-time:
> robbed of such beauty, paradise was left
> with the same longing and the same regret.

The journal is magazine-sized, printed on quality newsprint, using b/w art, cartoons and ads, about 30 pp., saddle-stapled. **Sample: $1.25 postpaid. Submissions without SASE or IRC's will not be returned.**

THE CHRISTIAN SCIENCE MONITOR (II), 1 Norway St., Boston, MA 02115, phone 617-450-2000, founded 1908, a national daily newspaper with a weekly international edition. Poetry used regularly in The Home Forum. Pays $25 and up.

CHRISTMAS, THE ANNUAL OF CHRISTMAS LITERATURE AND ART (IV-Themes), Augsburg Fortress, Publishers, 426 S. 5th St., Box 1209, Minneapolis, MN 55440, editor Jennifer Huber, is "an annual literary magazine **focusing on the effect of the Christmas love of God on the lives of people, and how it colors and shapes traditions and celebrations,"** using poetry relevant to that theme. "No **poetry dealing with Santa Claus. Submit maximum 30 lines. Pays $35-100/poem upon acceptance."**

They use **free verse, light verse, and traditional. Submit 18 months in advance. Sample: $9.75 plus postage.** I have not seen this publication.

THE CHRISTOPHER PUBLISHING HOUSE (II), 24 Rockland St., Commerce Green, Hanover, MA 02339, FAX 617-826-5556, managing editor Nancy Lukas, says **"We will review all forms of poetry." Submit complete MS. But 50% of their publishing is on a subsidy basis based on marketability, and this is likely to include publication of poetry. "Sample copies of published works may be obtained by writing to us at the above address."**

CIMARRON REVIEW (II), 205 Morrill Hall, Oklahoma State University, Stillwater, OK 74078-0135, founded 1967, poetry editors Jack Myers, Randy Phillis and Sally Shigley, is a quarterly 96-pp. literary journal. **"Reflecting humanity in contemporary society, we seek literary examples of Man Triumphant in a technological world. We emphasize quality and style. We like clear, evocative poetry (lyric or narrative) that uses images to enhance the human situation. No obscure poetry. No sing-song verse. No quaint prairie verse. No restrictions as to subject matter, although we tend to publish more struc-tured poetry (attention to line and stanza).** Also, we are conscious of our academic readership (mostly other writers) and attempt to accept poems that everyone will admire." Among poets they have published are Robert Cooperman, James McKean, David Citino and Lynn Domina. There are 10-12 pages of poetry in each issue, circulation of 500, mostly libraries. **Submit to Deborah Bransford, managing editor, any time, 3-5 poems, name and address on each poem, typed, single- or double-spaced. Clear photocopies acceptable. No simultaneous submissions. Replies within 4-6 weeks. They pay when they have a grant to do so.** Subscription rates: $3 per issue, $12 per year ($15, Canada), $30 for 3 years ($40, Canada), plus $2.50 for all international subscriptions.

CINCINNATI POETRY REVIEW (II, IV-Regional), Dept. of English (069), University of Cincinnati, Cincinnati, OH 45221, founded 1975, editor Dallas Wiebe "attempts to set local poets in a national context. Each issue includes **a quarter to a third of work by local poets (within about 100 miles of Cincinnati)**, but most are from all over." They use **"all kinds" of poetry**, have published such poets as James Baker Hall, Judith B. Goodenough, David Citino, Colleen McElroy, Harry Humes, Keith Wahle, and Yusef Komunyakaa. The editor selected this sample from "The Big Picture" by Jeff Hillard:

> *There were no changes in the forecast*
> *he was going, regardless,*
> *There's nothing the wind can't track down.*

They try to get out two issues a year, but it's irregular — handsomely printed, flat-spined, 80 pp., digest-sized magazine, all poems, art on the glossy card cover. Circulation is about 1,000, with 92 subscriptions, 12 of which are libraries. They use about 120 of 2,000-3,000 submissions per year. **Sample: $2. Subscription: $9 for 4 issues. Typed MSS with address on each poem, photocop-ies OK. Reports in 1-3 months. Payment is 2 copies. Each issue offers a poetry contest for poems of all types. The poems judged best and second in each issue receive cash awards of $150 and $50, and they hope to increase it.**

THE CINCINNATI POETS COLLECTIVE (II), 2587 LaFeuille Ave., #42, Cincinnati OH 45211, founded 1988, editor Rebecca D. Sullivan, is an annual poetry magazine. **"Prefer that the length of the poem be such that it lends itself to the poem's content; nothing hackneyed, didactic; no greeting-card subjects or rhyme." Send SASE for guidelines. Pays 1 copy. Submit up to 5 poems at a time. They will consider simultaneous submissions but not previously published poems. Reports in 4-6 months.**

CITY LIGHT BOOKS (III), 261 Columbus Ave., San Francisco, CA 94133, phone 415-362-1901, founded 1955, publisher Lawrence Ferlinghetti, achieved prominence with the publication of Allen Ginsberg's *Howl* and other **poetry of the "beat" school.** They publish **"poetry and advance-guard writing in the libertarian tradition. Paper and cloth."** Simultaneous submissions OK, payment varies, reporting time 6 weeks.

‡THE CLASSICAL OUTLOOK (IV-Themes, translations), Classics Dept., Park Hall, University of Georgia, Athens, GA 30602, founded 1924, poetry editors Prof. David Middleton (original English verse) and Prof. Jane Phillips (translations and original Latin verse), "is an internationally circulated quarterly journal (3,700 subscriptions, of which 250 are libraries) for high school and college Latin and Classics teachers, published by the American Classical League." **They invite submissions of "origi-nal poems in English on classical themes, verse translations from Greek and Roman authors, and original Latin poems. Submissions should, as a rule, be written in traditional poetic forms and should demonstrate skill in the use of meter, diction, and rhyme if rhyme is employed. Translations should be accompanied by a photocopy of the original Greek or Latin text. Limit of 50 lines."** They have recently published work by Francis Fike and Roy Fuller. As a sample the editor selected the first two stanzas of Roy Fuller's "Somewhere in Socrates":

> Mysterious bodily changes in the night
> From powers far from understood; the force
> Of four o'clock, of just perceptible light!
>
> Socrates said: death is a dreamless sleep,
> Or the delightful prospect of questioning
> Old Homer. Though what answer from the deep-

There are 2-3 magazine-sized pages of poetry in each issue, and they use 55% of the approximately 150 submissions they receive each year. They have a 6-12 month backlog, 4 month lead time. **Submit 2 copies, double-spaced. Receipt is acknowledged by letter. Poetry is refereed by poetry editors. Reports in 3-6 months. Pays in 5 complimentary copies. Sample copies $5. Guidelines available for SASE.**

CLEANING BUSINESS MAGAZINE; WRITERS PUBLISHING SERVICE CO. (IV-Themes), 1512 Western Ave., P.O. Box 1273, Seattle, WA 98111, phone 206-622-4241, founded 1976, poetry editor William R. Griffin. *CBM* (formerly Service Business Magazine) is "a quarterly magazine **for cleaning and maintenance professionals" and uses some poetry relating to their interests. "To be considered for publication in** *Cleaning Business,* **submit poetry that relates to our specific audience—cleaning and self-employment.** He has recently published poetry by Don Wilson, Phoebe Bosche, Trudie Mercer, and Joe Keppler. I have not seen the magazine, but the editor says it is 7×8½", 100 pp., offset litho, using ads, art, and graphics. Of 50 poems received, he uses about 10. Press run is 5,000 for 3,000 subscriptions (100 of them libraries), 500 shelf sales. Subscription: $20. Per issue $5. **Sample: $3 postpaid. Send SASE and $3 for guidelines. Pays $5-10 plus 1 copy. Simultaneous submissions OK, no previously published poems.** Writers Publishing Service Co. is an imprint for subsidized publication of poetry (author's expense) and other services to writers. William Griffin suggests that "poets identify a specific market and work to build a readership that can be tapped again and again over a period of years with new books."

CLEVELAND STATE UNIVERSITY POETRY SERIES; CLEVELAND POETS SERIES; CSU POETRY CENTER PRIZE; THE GAMUT (II), Cleveland State University, Cleveland, OH 44115. The Poetry Center was founded in 1962, first publications in 1971, *The Gamut* first published in 1980. Leonard Trawick and Louis T. Milic edit *The Gamut,* whose office is 1216 Rhodes Tower, at the University; Leonard Trawick, English Department, is also one of the editors of the Poetry Center (along with Alberta Turner, Director, and David Evett). **The Poetry Center publishes the CSU Poetry Series for poets in general and the Cleveland Poets Series for Ohio poets. "Open to many kinds of form, length, subject-matter, style and purpose. Should be well-crafted, clearly of professional quality, ultimately serious (even when humorous). No light verse, devotional verse, or verse in which rhyme and meter seem to be of major importance."** They have recently published poetry by Martha Collins, Eric Trethewey, Naomi Clark and Stephen Tapscott. As a sample Leonard Trawick selected these sample lines from **At Redbones** by Thylias Moss (CSU Poetry Center, 1990):

> Whatever is in your hands goes
> into the dough, the frustration wiped
> off the brow, the desire to
> slap, the doubt of hands whose
> applause is indecisiveness
> about prayer.

Books are chosen for publication from the entries to the CSU Poetry Center Prize contest. (Write for free catalog and sampler of some 65 Poetry Center books.) Deadline March 1, entrance fee $10; which awards the winner $1,000 and publication; they publish some other entrants in the Poetry Series: 50 copies (of press run of 1,000), 10% royalty contract. The Cleveland Poets Series (for Ohio poets) offers 100 copies of a press run of 600. To submit for all series, send MS between December 1 and March 1. Reports on all submissions for the year by the end of July. MSS should be for books of 50-100 pp., pages numbered, poet's name and address on cover sheet, clearly typed. Photocopies OK, and poems may have been previously published (listed on an acknowledgement page). Send SASE for guidelines. The Center also publishes other volumes of poetry, including chapbooks (20-30 pp.), with a $5 reading fee for each submission (except for Ohio residents). *The Gamut, a Journal of Ideas and Information,* is "a general interest magazine with literary and art emphasis." Send SASE for guidelines. Leonard Trawick says they want **"poems that are more or less accessible to the educated reader, but not too simple, no trivial, greeting card, 'inspirational' poetry."** They have recently published poetry by Robert Creeley, Roy Bently, Lynn Luria-Sukenick and Jeff Gundy. The magazine has a press run of 1,500 going to 900+ subscribers of which 50 are libraries. Price per issue: $5. Subscription: $12. **Pays an average of**

$15 per page plus 2 copies. Reports within 2 months. On rejection, editor comments "on the good ones." As a sample Prof. Trawick selected these lines from "Canto 55" by Ron Ellis (*The Gamut #28* Winter, 1990):

> One of
> The A source
> said difficulties
> with the steel casing
> He takes pride were bolted
> Susan Lucci found Curtis of
> varying degrees "delicious" to
> work with together. opposition of . . . .

Professor Trawick says, "In selecting a poem perhaps the first thing we require is that the language be right. It may be complex and challenging, or it may be ostensibly simple, but if the poem doesn't work on the level of diction and syntax, it doesn't work at all for us."

‡THE CLIMBING ART (I, IV-Themes), P.O. Box 816, Alamosa, CO 81101, phone 719-589-5579, founded 1986, editor David Mazel, is a quarterly magazine **"read mainly by mountain enthusiasts who appreciate good writing about mountains and mountaineering. We are open to all forms and lengths. The only requirement is that the work be fresh, well-written, and in some way of interest to those who love the mountains. If in doubt, submit it."** As a sample the editor selected these lines by Reg Saner:

> An hour or so . . . I'll have tracked the last snowfield
> and be far down this mountain, leaving
> bootprints that believed in themselves
> to brighten . . .

It is 32 pp., magazine-sized, professionally printed on heavy stock with glossy card cover. Press run: 1,050 for 800 subscriptions of which 5 are libraries, 350 shelf sales. They use 1-4 poems per issue of 100-200 submissions received/per year. Subscription: $10. **Sample, postpaid: $2.75. Pays 3 copies and subscription. Simultaneous submissions and previously published poems OK. Reports in 2 months. Editor comments on submissions.** He says, "We'd like to publish more high-quality poetry, and we encourage all to submit."

CLOCKWATCH REVIEW (II, III), James Plath, Dept. of English, Illinois Wesleyan University, Bloomington IL 61702, phone 309-556-3352, founded 1983, James Plath is editor, and Lynn Devore, James McGowan and Pamela Muirhead are associate editors. We publish a variety of styles, leaning toward poetry which goes beyond the experience of self in an attempt to SAY something, without sounding pedantic or strained. We like a **strong, natural voice**, and lively, unusual combinations in language. **Something *fresh*, and that includes subject matter as well. It has been our experience that extremely short/long poems are hard to pull off.** Though we'll publish exceptions, we prefer to see poems that can fit on one published page (digest-sized) which runs **about 32 lines or less.**" They have recently published Peter Wild, Martha Vertreale, John Knoepfle and Rita Dove. Asked for a sample, the editors say "trying to pick only four lines seems like telling people what detail we'd like to see in a brick, when what we're more interested in is the design of the *house*." Nonetheless, they selected these sample lines from Philip Schultz's "The Horizon":

> as a boy he climbed hills beyond Minsk
> to see the sky expanding like an accordion
> of stars drifting in fiery halos, light
> rooting a thousand million flowers

The 64 pp., semiannual *CR* is printed on glossy paper with colored, glossy cover (with striking art—so that it "might serve as a coffee table book, allowing people the chance to read it bit by bit"). They use 7-10 unsolicited poems in each issue, with 1 featured poet. Circulation is 1,300, with 120 subscribers, of which 25 are libraries. They send out 200-300 complimentary copies and "The balance is wholesale distribution and single-copy sales." **Sample: $4 postpaid.** They receive 350-400 submissions per year, use 15-20. No backlog. **Prefer batches of 5-6 poems. "We are not bowled over by large lists of previous publications, but brief letters of introduction or sparse mini-vitas are read out of curiosity. One poem per page, typed, single-spacing OK, photocopy OK if indicated that it is not a simultaneous submission (which we do NOT accept). Reports in 2 weeks; 2 months if under serious consideration.** "Payment in copies, and, when possible, small cash awards or hand-made coin jewelry." They will comment "if asked, and if time permits."

‡CLOTHESPIN FEVER PRESS (IV-Lesbian), 5529 N. Figueroa, Los Angeles, CA 90042, phone 213-254-1373, founded 1985, editor Jenny Wrenn, publishes books and chapbooks on lesbian themes, including **"non-traditional free verse, contemporary forms and styles, long or short, lesbian sensibility. Subjects may vary, but they may not be heterosexual."** They have recently published poetry by Paula Gunn Allen.

CLOUD RIDGE PRESS (V), 2135 Stony Hill Rd., Boulder, CO 80303, founded 1985, editor Elaine Kohler, a "literary small press for unique works in poetry and prose." They publish letterpress and offset books in both paperback and hardcover editions. In poetry, they want **"strong images of the numinous qualities in authentic experience grounded in a landscape and its people."** The first book, published in 1985, was **Ondina: A Narrative Poem**, by John Roberts. As a sample, the editor selected the following lines:

> *Some kill, and some get killed.*
> *But who's to say what's real or not,*
> *when dreams lay open spooky life,*
> *and life comes a-swirlin at you dreamin?*

The book is 6×9¼", handsomely printed on buff stock, cloth bound in black with silver decoration and spine lettering, 131 pages. Eight hundred copies were bound in Curtis Flannel and 200 copies (of which mine is one) bound in cloth over boards, numbered and signed by the poet and artist. This letterpress edition, priced at $18/cloth and $12/paper, is not available in bookstores but only by mail from the press. The trade edition was photo-offset from the original, in both cloth and paper bindings, and is sold in bookstores. The press plans to publish 1-2 books/year. **Since they are not accepting unsolicited MSS., writers should query first. Queries will be answered in 2 weeks and MSS reported on in 1 month. Simultaneous submissions are acceptable, as are photocopied or dot-matrix MSS. Royalties are 10% plus a negotiable number of author's copies. A brochure is free on request; send #10 SASE.**

CLUBHOUSE; YOUR STORY HOUR (I, IV-Children), Box 15, Berrien Springs, MI 49103, founded 1949, poetry editor Elaine Trumbo, **pays about $12 for poems under 24 lines plus 2 contributor's copies.** The publication is printed in conjunction with the **Your Story Hour** radio program which is designed to teach the Bible and moral life to children. The magazine, *Clubhouse*, started with that title in 1982, but as *Good Deeder*, its original name, it has been published since 1950. Elaine Trumbo says, **"We do like humor or mood pieces. Don't like mushy-sweet 'Christian' poetry. We don't have space for long poems. Best—16 lines or under."** They have recently published poetry by Walter Staples, Craig Peters, Dave Morrice, O.J. Robertson and Lee Parker. As a sample the editor selected these lines by Anita Higman:

> *When you have a picnic,*
> *Don't invite the ants,*
> *'Cause they'll bring every relative*
> *From here to Paris France.*

The magazine has a circulation of 10,000, with 10,000 subscriptions of which maybe 5 are libraries. Subscription: $5, 6 issues per year. **Sample: 3 oz. postage. Writer's guidelines are available for SASE, simultaneous submissions OK. The "evaluation sheet" for returned MSS gives reasons for acceptance or rejection.**

THE CLYDE PRESS (IV-Children/teen/young adult, ethnic, political, senior citizens,), 373 Lincoln Parkway, Buffalo, NY 14216, phone 716-875-4713, 834-1254, founded 1976, poetry editor Catherine Harris Ainsworth, specializes in folklore, oral literature, ethnic tales and legends, games, calendar customs, jump rope verses, superstitions and family tales—all edited and left in the words of the informants, and all taken from collections that cover about 30 years, 1952-82. They will consider submissions of **folk poetry and songs from bona fide folk collections, "i.e. recorded from the folk or written by the folk, really sung or recited." Query with samples.** Games and Lore of Young Americans, recipient in 1985 of an award from the National Endowment for the Arts.

COACH HOUSE PRESS (II, IV-Regional), 401 (Rear) Huron St., Toronto, ON M5S 2G5 Canada, phone 416-979-7374, FAX 416-979-7006, founded 1964, poetry editors Michael Ondaatje, Christopher Dewdney and Victor Coleman, publishes "**mostly living Canadian writers of 'post-modern' poetry and fiction.**" They have printed finely-printed flat-spined paperback collections by such poets as Phyllis Webb, Michael Ondaatje, Sharon Thesen, Betsy Warland and Roy Kiyooka. They want **"no religious, confessional stuff, or traditional rhyme schemes. We lean toward experimental." Query with 10 samples. Cover letter should include bio and other publications. Double-spaced, photocopy or dot-matrix OK. Reports in 12-16 weeks. Contract is for 10% royalties, 5 copies.** Catalog sent on request, or

ALWAYS submit MSS or queries with a stamped, self-addressed envelope (SASE) within your country or International Reply Coupons (IRCs) purchased from the post office for other countries.

"Beyond Baroque Foundation and Northwestern University receive everything we do. Also, samples are on display in the Small Press Centre in N.Y.C." Carolyn Guertin publicity director, says, **"We expect poets to be familiar with the Coach House flavor and to have a few journal publication credits to their name.** You don't have to be famous, but you do have to be good. Make the effort to do a little research on us, and save yourself time and postage. No SASE, no reply . . . and Canada Post does not accept American postage."

COCHRAN'S CORNER (I, IV-Subscribers), Box 2036, Waldorf, MD 20604, phone 301-843-0485, founded 1985, poetry editor Billye Keene, is a **"family type" quarterly open to beginners, preferring poems of 20 lines or less. You have to be a subscriber to submit. "Any subject or style (except porn)."** She has recently published poetry by J. Alvin Speers, Becky Knight, and Francesco BiVone. As a sample she selected these lines from "Night of Unknown" (poet unidentified):

> *From under my door your breeze seeps confident and slow,*
> *Preparing a subtle path for your patchwork cold to creep.*

CC is a 58 pp. saddle-stapled, desk-top publishing, with matte card cover, press run of 500. Subscription: $12. **Send SASE for guidelines. Sample: $3 plus SASE. Pays 2 copies. Simultaneous submissions and previously published poems OK. Reports in average of 3 months.** Contests in March and July; $3 entry fee for 2 poems. "We provide criticism if requested at the rate of $1 per page. Write from the heart, but don't forget your readers. You must work to find the exact words that mirror your feelings, so the reader can share your feelings."

THE COE REVIEW (II), Coe College, 1220 1st Ave. NE, Cedar Rapids, IA 52402, phone 319-399-8660, founded 1972, poetry editor Matt Osing, is "an annual little literary magazine with **emphasis on the innovative and unselfconscious** poetry and fiction. We are **open to virtually any and all subject-matter."** They have recently published poetry by James Galvin and Jan Weissmiller. As a sample these lines were selected by the editor from "The Spider" by Steve Ketzer Jr.:

> *I saw him reeling web & building,*
> *And "Oh!" I thought, "It's life!"*
> *I looked up moments later,*
> *And he hung there, quite dead.*

The annual is 100-150 pp., flat-spined, digest-sized with matte card cover. "Each issue includes 4-8 reproductions of works of art, usually photographs, lithography and etched prints." Circulation is about 500. **Sample: $4 postpaid. Send SASE for guidelines. Pays 1 copy. Reports in 6-8 weeks. Accepted work appears in the next issue, published in Spring. No simultaneous submissions. Photocopy OK. Include "brief cover letter."** The editor says, "We are supportive in the endeavors of poets whose material is original and tasteful. We are eclectic in our publication choices in that variety of subject matter and style make the *Coe Review* exciting."

‡COKEFISH (I), Box 683, Long Valley, NJ 07853, phone 201-876-3824, founded 1990, editor Ana Pine, is a monthly newsletter **with an entry fee of $1/3 poems. "I want to see work that has passion behind it. From the traditional to the avant-garde, provocative to discreet, trivial to the significant. Am interested in social issues, love, relationships, and humor. No religion or rhyme for rhyme's sake."** They have recently published poetry by Sigmund Weiss, Larry Blazek, Kyle Hogg, and Kathleen Lee Mendel. As a sample the editor selected these lines from her own poem:

> *We lay like pieces of a jigsaw puzzle*
> *interlocking side by side*
> *on crisp, scented sheets*
> *our bodies damp*
> *from the heat of our love.*

The format is 20 pp., side-stapled on heavy paper with a cover printed on both sides on colored photocopy paper. Press run 50 for 30 subscribers. Subscription: $15. **Sample, postpaid: $1.75. Send SASE for guidelines. Pays 1 copy. Accepts 40% of MSS received. Note entry fee: $1/3 poems, additional $1 for additional poems. Simultaneous submissions and previously published poems OK. Reports in 1 week."** The editor advises, "Spread the word; don't let your poems sit and vegetate in a drawer."

CO-LABORER; WOMAN'S NATIONAL AUXILIARY CONVENTION (IV-Religious), Box 1088, Nashville, TN 37202, phone 615-361-1010, founded 1935, editor Lorene Miley, is a "bi-monthly publication **to give women a missionary vision and challenge. We'll consider any length or style as long as the subject is missions."** They do not want to see poetry which is not religious or not related to missions. The editor selected this sample, "Mission," written by E.A. Dixon:

> *A simple*
> *Clay conduit*
> *Lay nicked*

> *And scarred*
> *Amid the*
> *Arid expanse*
> *Of souls*
> *A sturdy grid*
> *Through which*
> *Living Water*
> *Must Flow.*

The 32 pp. magazine uses at least one poem per issue, circulation 18,000. **Sample, postpaid: $1.**

COLD-DRILL BOOKS; COLD-DRILL; POETRY IN PUBLIC PLACES (IV-Regional), Dept. of English, Boise State University, Boise, ID 83725, phone 208-385-1246, founded 1970, editor Tom Trusky, publishes **"primarily Boise State University students, faculty and staff, but will consider writings by Idahoans—or writing about Idaho by 'furriners.'"** They do some of the most creative publishing in this country today, and it is worth buying a **sample of *cold-drill* for $9** just to see what they're up to. This annual "has been selected as top undergraduate literary magazine in the US by such important acronyms as CSPA, CCLM and UCDA." It comes in a box stuffed with various pamphlets, postcards, posters, a newspaper, even 3-D comics with glasses to read them by. **No restrictions on types of poetry.** As yet they have published no poets of national note, but Tom Trusky offers these lines as a sample, from Patrick Flanagan, "Postcard From a Freshman":

> *The girls here are gorgeous, studying hard,*
> *many new friends, roommate*
> *never showers, tried to*
> *kill myself, doctor says*
> *i'm getting better*

Circulation is 400, including 100 subscribers, of which 20 are libraries. **"We read material throughout the year, notifying only those whose work we've accepted December 15-January 1st. Manuscripts should be photocopies with author's name and address on separate sheet, simultaneous submissions OK. Payment: 1 copy."** They also publish two 24 pp. chapbooks and one 75 pp. flat-spined paperback per year. **Query about book publication.** "We want to publish a literary magazine that is exciting to read. We want more readers than just our contributors and their mothers. Our format and our content have allowed us to achieve those goals, so far." I would advise discretion in regard to mothers. Poetry in Public Places is a series of 8 monthly posters per year "presenting the poets in Boise State University's creative students series and poets in BSU's Ahsahta Press poetry series. These, like all publications emanating from BSU, are elegantly done, with striking art. The posters are on coated stock. See also listing for *Ahsahta Press.*

‡COLLAGES & BRICOLAGES, THE JOURNAL OF INTERNATIONAL WRITING (I,II,IV-Translations, feminist, humor), Office of International Programs, 212 Founders Hall, University of Pennsylvania, Clarion, PA 16214, founded in 1986, editor Marie-José Fortis. *C&B* is a "small literary magazine with a strong penchant for literary, feminist, avant garde work. Strongly encourages poets and fiction writers, as well as essayists, whether English-speaking or foreign. (**Note: Writers sending their work in a foreign language must have their ms accompanied with an English translation.**) We want **strong innovative writers who have read the classics. Poems should contain powerful imagery or puns or alliterations or all of it."** *C&B* recently published Alice Brand, author of **As It Happens** and **Studies On Zone.** The editor selected sample lines from Alice Brand's "the poet does laundry":

> *I knew a secretary once*
> *older than me and with*
> *sons in college.*
> *she was proud she still*
> *bled. she made sure you knew.*

The annual is magazine-sized, 100+ pp., flat-spined, with glossy card cover. They accept 10-15% of 60-70 poetry submissions/year. Press run 400. **Sample, postpaid: $5, or $2.50/back issue. Pays 2 copies.** "It is recommended that potential contributors order a copy, so as to know what kind of work is desirable. **Enclose a personalized letter.** Be considerate to editors, as many of them work on a voluntary basis, and sacrifice much time and energy to encourage writers." Marie-José Fortis says, "It is time to stop being too plastic and too polite and too careful. The Berlin Wall is down. The East will bring to us powerful, daring literary voices, with much to tell. The American writer should follow a similar path. Too many things are left unsaid."

‡COLLEGE ENGLISH; NATIONAL COUNCIL OF TEACHERS OF ENGLISH (II), % James C. Raymond, Drawer AL, University of Alabama, Tuscaloosa, AL 35487, phone 205-348-6488, editor Dara Wier, University of Massachusetts, Amherst, MA. This journal, which goes 8/year to members of the National Council of Teachers of English (membership: $30, includes subscription to *CE*), is a scholarly journal for the English discipline, but includes poetry by such poets as James Tate, Michael Pettit, and Norman Stock. It is 100 pp., saddle-stapled, with matte card cover, 7½×9½", circulation 16,000. **Sample, postpaid: $4.50. Pays 6 copies. Reports in 4 months maximum.**

COLORADO REVIEW (II, IV-Translations, themes), Dept. of English, 359 Eddy Bldg., Colorado State University, Ft. Collins, CO 80523, phone 303-491-6428, founded 1955 as *Colorado State Review*, resurrected 1977 under "New Series" rubric, renamed *Colorado Review 1985.* Managing and poetry editor Bill Tremblay. *Colorado Review* is a journal of contemporary literature which appears twice annually; it combines short fiction, poetry, interviews with or articles about significant contemporary poets and writers, articles on literature, culture, and the arts, translations of poetry from around the world, and reviews of recent works of the literary imagination. **"We're interested in poetry that explores experience in deeply felt new ways; merely descriptive or observational language doesn't move us. Poetry that enters into and focuses on the full range of experience, weaving sharp imagery, original figures and surprising though apt insight together in compressed precise language and compelling rhythm is what triggers an acceptance here."** They have recently published poetry by Greg Kuzma, Peter Wild, and Margaret Randall. They have a circulation of 500, 150 subscriptions of which 75 are libraries. They use about 10% of the 500-1,000 submissions they receive per year. **Sample: $5 postpaid. Submit about 5 poems, typewritten or clear photocopy. Reports in 3 to 6 months. "When work is a near-miss, we will provide brief comment and encouragement."** Bill Tremblay says, "Our attitude is that we will publish the best work that comes across the editorial desk. However we sometimes do theme-issues, e.g., our issue on 'an aesthetics of open space,' and the 'post Vietnam experience.' We see poetry as a vehicle for exploring states of feeling, but we aren't interested in sentimentality (especially metaphysical)."

COLORADO-NORTH REVIEW (II), University Center, University of Northern Colorado, Greeley, CO 80639, founded 1963 as *Nova,* became *C-NR* in '70s, editor Robert Payne, is a "literature and visual art magazine. **We are extremely flexible on style, but hope that technique and content are inseparable. Rhyme is frowned upon unless it is done brilliantly. We also tend to dislike didactic work like, 'Abortion is murder,' and 'Save the bottlenose dolphins.' We publish poetry, short fiction, essays, and visual art."** It appears twice a year. Robert Payne says, **"Give me no more rhyme. Two or three contemporaries are allowed to rhyme. No one else should try it. Basically, we're looking for something that stays in our heads after we read it — long after. No socially responsible stuff, e.g., 'Drugs are real bad' or 'Jesus is my best friend.' "** They have recently published poetry by Simon Perchik, Rita Kiefer, Lyn Lifshin, and Veronica Patterson. As a sample the editor chose these lines from "Widow of the Village Maskmaker" by Mary Crow:

> My mask is an animal with a red face,
> a piece of fur between curved horns,
> the longest tongue you've ever seen,
> and two long rows of teeth that clack,
> clack, clack.

C-NR is "70 pp., flat-spined, digest-sized, heavy, glossy paper, highest quality printing, vis. arts and fiction w/poetry emphasis, ads at back of book, matte card cover." It appears every December and May. They accept about 50 of 500 manuscripts received each year. Press run is 2,500 for 59 subscriptions of which 23 are libraries. **Send SASE for guidelines. Subscription: $6. Sample: $3.50 postpaid. Pays 2 copies. They consider simultaneous submissions "reluctantly" and previously published poems "only with special arrangement." No reading during May-August. Reports in 3 months. Editor comments "on request, but briefly. When something is very close but not quite, we might point out why."**

‡COLUMBIA: A MAGAZINE OF POETRY & PROSE; EDITORS' AWARDS (II), 404 Dodge Hall, Columbia University, New York, NY 10027, phone 212-280-4391, founded 1977, is a literary annual using "quality short stories, novel excerpts, translations, interviews, nonfiction, and **poetry, usually no longer than 2 pp. Nothing juvenile, sentimental, simply descriptive."** They have recently published poetry by Henri Cole, Theresa Svoboda, Eamon Grennan, and Jimmy Santiago-Baca. It is digest-sized, approximately 180 pp., with coated cover stock. They publish about 12 poets each year from 400 submissions. Press run 1,250 for 1,000 subscriptions of which 100 are libraries, 150 shelf sales. $6/copy. **Sample, postpaid: $5. Send SASE for guidelines. Pays up to 4 copies. Submit double spaced MSS. Reports in 1-2 months. "Very brief comments at editor's discretion."** They offer annual Editors' Awards of $350 and $150 for the best poems published in each issue. To be considered for these awards enclose fee of $6 (which covers the cost of an issue) and submit before April 1.

COLUMBIA UNIVERSITY TRANSLATION CENTER; TRANSLATION; TRANSLATION CENTER AWARDS (IV-Translations), 412 Dodge, Columbia University, New York, NY 10027, phone 212-854-2305, founded 1972, director Frank MacShane. "Translation Center publishes only excerpted foreign contemporary literature in English language translations and also gives annual awards and grants to translators. *Translation* magazine uses **contemporary foreign poetry/literature in English language translations.** (Note: we do not review and do not accept translated plays.)." They have recently published translations of poetry by Anne Hébert, Bella Akmadulina, Thomas Günther, Ece Ayhan, and Richard Pietrass. *Translation* is a biannual, circulation 1,500. Subscription: $17. **Sample: $9 postpaid. Up to 10 poems may be submitted at a time, letter-quality MS. Translators must include with MS: (a) copy of original foreign language text; (b) 10-line bio of translator; (c) 10-line bio of author/ poet; (d) statement of copyright clearance. Payment is 3 copies of the magazine, 2 copies to the translator and 1 copy to the author of the original work. Send SASE for guidelines and descriptions of the various award programs they administer.** Columbia University Translation Center Awards are grants to a translator for an outstanding translation of a substantial part of a book length literary work. Awards range from $1,000-2,000 and are designed mainly to recognize excellence. Translations from any language into English are eligible, and specific awards exist for translations from the French Canadian, Dutch and Italian. All applications will automatically be considered for all awards for which they are eligible. The Center generally discourages applicants who are retranslating a work unless some very special reason exists.

COLUMBUS SINGLE SCENE (IV-Themes, humor), Box 30856, Gahanna OH 43230, founded 1985, poetry editor Jeanne Marlowe, is a monthly magazine, circulation 5,000, for Ohio singles (18 and up), **"positive, upbeat approach to single living, but we're neither yuppies nor pollyannas. Humorous treatments get priority."** Recently published poets include Lyn Lifshin and Bryan Arnold. The editor chose this sample from "Scoring" by Ronald Edward Kittell:

> *Court her*
> *rebound yr*
> *rim shots*
> *then go 4*
> *the lay*
> *up*

Sample: $2 postpaid. Considers simultaneous submissions. Submit maximum 12 poems, dealing with single living or relationships, 1-50 lines. Reporting time is 2 weeks. Pays advertising trade or copy.

COMMONWEAL (III), 15 Dutch St., New York, NY 10038, phone, 212-732-0800, poetry editor Rosemary Deen, appears every 2 weeks, circulation 20,000, is a general-interest magazine for college-educated readers by Roman Catholics. The editor selected this sample from "One is One," sonnets by Marie Ponsot:

> *Heart, you bully, you punk, I'm wrecked, I'm shocked*
> *stiff. You? you still try to rule the world — though*
> *I've got you: identified, starving, locked*
> *in a cage you will not leave alive . . .*

Sample free. Prefers serious, witty, well-written poems of up to 75 lines. They do not publish inspirational poems. Considers simultaneous submissions. Pays 50¢ a line.

‡**COMMUNICATIONS PUBLISHING GROUP; COLLEGE PREVIEW, A GUIDE FOR COLLEGE-BOUND STUDENTS; DIRECTIONS, A GUIDE TO CAREER ALTERNATIVES; JOURNEY, A SUCCESS GUIDE FOR COLLEGE AND CAREER-BOUND STUDENTS; VISIONS, A SUCCESS GUIDE FOR NATIVE AMERICAN STUDENTS; FIRST OPPORTUNITY, A GUIDE FOR VOCATIONAL TECHNICAL STUDENTS (IV-Youth, themes, ethnic)**, 3100 Broadway, 225 PennTower, Kansas City MO 64111, phone 816-756-3039, editor Georgia Clark. These five publications are 40 percent freelance written. All are designed to inform and motivate their readers in regard to college preparation, career planning, and life survival skills. All except *First Opportunity*, which is quarterly, appear in spring and fall. *College Preview* is for Black and Hispanic young adults, ages 16-21. Circ. 600,000. *Directions* is for Black and Hispanic young adults, ages 18-25. Circ. 500,000. *Journey* is for Asian-American high school and college students ages 16-25. Circ. 200,000. *Visions* is for Native American students, young adults, ages 16-25. Circ. 100,000. *First Opportunity* is for Black and Hispanic young adults, ages 16-21. Circ. 500,000. All these magazines pay on acceptance. Submit seasonal/holiday material 6 months in advance. Simultaneous, photocopied and previously published submissions OK. Computer printout submissions OK; prefers letter-quality. "Include on manuscript your name, address, phone, Social Security number." Reports in 2 months. Sample copy of any for 9 × 12″ SAE with 4 first class stamps. Writer's guidelines for #10 SASE. They use free verse. Each magazine buys 5 poems per year. Submit up to 5 poems at one time. Length: 10-25 lines. Pays $10-50/poem.

COMMUNITIES: JOURNAL OF COOPERATION (IV-Social issues), 105 Sun St., Stelle, IL 60919, phone 815-256-2252, founded 1972, managing editor Charles Betterton, is a "quarterly publication on intentional communities, cooperatives, social and global transformation," using poetry relevant to those themes. **Pays 3 copies. Previously published poems and simultaneous submissions OK. No comment on rejections.** It is magazine-sized, professionally printed on newsprint stock with 2-color glossy paper cover, 56 pp., saddle-stapled. The sample issue sent me by the editor contained no poetry (most do not), so, as a sample, I selected these lines from my own "Middle Ages," published in *Communities* some years ago:

> . . . *now in our scattered communes in*
> *the crags we keep households where kids may grow*
> *outside the law. I cannot keep those brawling*
> *nations straight. There is only one weapon*
> *against the state: indifference* . . .

‡**A COMPANION IN ZEOR (IV-Science Fiction/fantasy),** Rt. #5, Box #82, 17 Ashland Ave., Cardiff, NJ 08232, phone 609-645-6938, founded 1978, editor Karen Litman, is a "**SF, fantasy fanzine involved with the writings of Jacqueline Lichtenberg**" appearing irregularly (last issue: 1987). "**Prefer nothing obscene, usually related to the works of Jacqueline Lichtenberg. Homosexuality not acceptable unless very relevant to the piece. Prefer a 'clean' publication image.**" As a sample, I selected these lines from "Almost Home" by Jill Stone:

> *To give life, not just fight for that which dies* . . .
> *Everything is gathering, merging, intertwined.*
> *In the cold twilight, both growing blind,*
> *we have come at last to some familiar place.*
> *Beyond your shoulder is my brother's face,*
> *and I see the early snowfall in his eyes.*

It is magazine-sized, photocopied from typescript, press run 300. **Send SASE for guidelines. Pays copies.** "Always willing to work with authors or poets to help in improving their work."

‡**CONCHO RIVER REVIEW; FORT CONCHO MUSEUM PRESS (IV-Regional),** 213 E. Ave. D, San Angelo, TX 76903, phone 915-657-4441, founded 1984, editor Troy Reeves. "The Fort Concho Museum Press is a small press having published 2 major books and is entering its fourth year of publishing *Concho River Review*, a literary journal published twice a year. **Work by Texas poets or poets with a 'Texas connection'— born, lived, worked, arrested, etc., in Texas. Open form — prefer shorter poems on a subject exterior to the feelings of the poet — objective experiences, poems about real persons and places, some poems of historical interest. We rarely use poems of over 35 lines. No very subjective, fluffy, confessional, self-centered, abstract emotive pieces. Also, we have all the cowboy, tumbleweed, bluebonnet, windmill poetry we can use; no more, please!**" They have recently published poetry by Walter McDonald, William Virgil Davis, and Betsy Colquitt. As a sample the editor selected these lines by Carol C. Reposa:

> *My legs grow stiff with this much kneeling, prayers*
> *That cut through purple velvet like the claws*
> *Of ancient lions opening their jaws*
> *To Daniel, turning, pacing in their lairs.*

CRR is a 120-138 pp. flat-spined, digest-sized, with matte card cover, professionally printed. They use 35-40 of 600-800 poems received per year. Press run: 300 for about 200 subscriptions of which 10 are libraries. **Subscription: $12. Sample, postpaid: $4. Pays 1 copy. "Please submit 3-5 poems at a time. Use regular legal sized envelopes — no big brown envelopes. Please include full name and return address on outside of envelope. Type must be letter-perfect, sharp enough to be computer scanned." Reports in 1-6 weeks.** They hold an annual contest. The editor says, "We're always looking for good work — from well-known poets and from those who have never been published before."

CONDITIONED RESPONSE PRESS; CONDITIONED RESPONSE; CONDITIONED RESPONSE ANNUAL CHAPBOOK SEARCH (II), P.O. Box 3816, Ventura, CA 93006, founded 1982, poetry editor John McKinley, a small-press publisher of poetry only—magazine and occasional chapbooks. The editor says, "**I rarely publish rhyme and tend not to go with the traditional. I want to see an ingenious use of words and poetic devices around modern themes, anything that illuminates more clearly the human condition.**" He has recently published poetry by Kurt Nimmo, Michael Wilds, Belinda Subraman, John Hart, Ivan Argüelles, Nathan Whiting, John Grey, Li Min Hua, and Richard Kostelanetz. As a sample, he selected the following lines by Nell Dickinson:

> *like a corpse he passed the coffin nails to my tongue with his lips*
> *like a spinster who's learned to be handy with hardware*
> *like slamming your own coffin's screen door from the inside*
> *I've been nailing myself in the institutional bathroom shelter*
> *hammering my head off & moping & groping & playing alone.*

Conditioned Response appears bi-annually and has a circulation of 200; subscription: $4 for 2 issues. The digest-sized publication contains poetry only, no illustrations except a cover photograph. It is professionally printed on lightweight stock, 24 pp., matte card cover, saddle-stapled. **Sample: "$2 in postage or money will get several chapbooks and magazines, whatever's on hand including the current issue." Pay is 1 copy. The editor says, "Prefer 5-10 poems in one batch, typewritten, simultaneous submissions not encouraged, but who's going to know anyway, right?" Submissions are reported on in 2 weeks to 2 months and publication time is up to 1 year.** Annual chapbook search, deadline June 1. $3 fee, for which submittor receives a copy of the winning MS. Pays 25 copies. Submit 35-50 pp. minimum. "The more there is submitted, the more there is for the editor to select from. The poems can either work together as a sequence or a collection, or they may be thematically unrelated to each other. Some of the poems can be previously published in magazines. I suggest that you mail only a photocopy of your MS *without* a SASE. Returning your MS in the mail, I think, would be a waste of postage. However, I will honor all SASEs that are provided. You may include a postcard to acknowledge receipt of your MS."

CONDITIONS (IV-Women/feminism/lesbianism), P.O. Box 159046, Van Brunt Station, Brooklyn, NY 11215-9046, founded 1976, editors Cheryl Clarke, Melinda Goodman, Paula Martinac, Mariana Romo-Carmona, and Pauline Sugino, is **a feminist magazine of writing for women, with an emphasis on writing by lesbians.** They use "poetry, fiction, essays, book reviews on issues of the women's movement featuring the work of women from all backgrounds for whom relationships with women are an integral part of their lives. They want **"poetry by women in any form. The Collective is committed to publishing new writers, women of color, older women, women with disabilities, and working class women."** Recently published poetry by Joy Harjo, Jacqueline Lapidus, and Toi Derricotte. As a sample Cheryl Clarke selected these lines by Terry L. Jewell:

> *Momma sees the rushing growth*
> *of her daughter's flesh*
> *but not the scissors*
> *of her husband's fingers*
> *as a girl cries sleeplessly*
> *whispers solemn epitaphs*
> *for her own bones.*

The annual is digest-sized, flat-spined, 192 pp., professionally printed, with glossy card cover, press run 1,500 for 500 subscriptions of which 200 are libraries, 700 shelf sales. **Sample: $8.95 postpaid. Guidelines available for SASE. Pays 2 copies. They consider simultaneous submissions but not previously published poems. Reports in 8-16 weeks.**

CONFLUENCE PRESS (II, IV-Regional), Lewis Clark State College, Lewiston, ID 83501, phone 208-799-2336, founded 1975, poetry editor James R. Hepworth, is an 'independent publisher of fiction, poetry, creative non-fiction, and literary scholarship. **We are open to formal poetry as well as free verse. No rhymed doggerel, 'light verse,' 'performance poetry,' 'streetpoetry,' etc." We prefer to publish work by poets who live and work in the northwestern United States.** They have recently published poetry by Wendell Berry, John Daniel, Greg Keeler, Nancy Mairs, and Robert Wrigley. As a sample the editor selected these lines from "For the Explainers" by Wendell Berry:

> *Spell the spiel of cause and effect,*
> *Ride the long rail of fact after fact;*
> *What curled the plume in the drake's tail*
> *And put the white ring round his neck?*

They print about 3 books and 2 chapbooks a year. **Query with 6 sample poems, bio, list of publications. No simultaneous submissions. Reports in 3 weeks to queries, 2 months to MSS. Pays $100 advance and 10% royalties plus copies. Editor sometimes comments on rejections.** Send SASE for catalog to order samples.

CONFRONTATION MAGAZINE (II), English Dept., C. W. Post of Long Island University, Greenvale, NY 11548, founded 1968, poetry editor Martin Tucker, is "a semiannual literary journal with **interest in all forms.** Our only criterion is high literary merit. We think of our audience as an educated, lay group of intelligent readers. **We prefer lyric poems. Length generally should be kept to 2 pages. No sentimental verse."** They have recently published poetry by Karl Shapiro, T. Alan Broughton, David Ignatow, Philip Appleman, Jane Mayhall, and Joseph Brodsky. As a sample I selected the first stanza of David Galler's "Rotten Dreams":

> *It's no disgrace*
> *To dream you look in a mirror*
> *And see your mother's face,*
> *Or the kitchen floor.*

Basically a magazine, they do on occasion publish "book" issues or "anthologies." It's a digest-sized professionally-printed, flat-spined, 190+ pp. journal with a circulation of about 2,000. **Sample: $3 postpaid.** They receive about 1,200 submissions per year, publish 150, have a 6-12 month backlog. **Submit no more than 10 pp., clear copy (photocopy OK). "Prefer single submissions." Reports in 6-8 weeks. Pays: $5-40.**

THE CONNECTICUT POETRY REVIEW (II), Box 3783, New Haven, CT 06525, founded 1981, poetry editors J. Claire White and James William Chichetto, is a "small press that puts out an annual magazine. **We look for poetry of quality which is both genuine and original in content. No specifications except length: 10-40 lines.**" The magazine has won high praise from the literary world; they have recently published such poets as Sharon Hashimoto, Robyn Supraner, Fred Marchant, and Charles Edward Eaton. Each issue seems to feature a poet. These sample lines are by Ann Douglas:

> *The 11 o'clock light*
> *pulls the whole to a flatness*
> *like the flatness of water*
> *on which the rest of the day turns*
> *and continues.*

The flat-spined, 60 pp. large digest-sized journal is "printed letterpress by hand on a Hacker Hand Press from Monotype Bembo." Most of the 60 pp. are poetry, but they also have reviews. Circulation is 400, with 80 subscriptions of which 35 are libraries. **Sample: $3.50 postpaid.** They receive over 900 submissions a year, use about 20, have a 3 month backlog, **report in 3 months, pay $5/poem plus 1 copy.** The editors advise, "Study traditional and modern styles. Study poets of the past. Attend poetry readings. And write. Practice on your own."

‡CONVERGING PATHS (IV-Spiritual, themes), P.O. Box 63, Mt. Horeb, WI 53572, founded 1986, editor Kyril Oakwind, is a quarterly **"Pagan/Wiccan magazine focusing on traditional Wicca, using a few poems: short, fits in one column or occasionally one page, inspirational, Pagan poetry. Suggested subjects: earth, mother, God of the hunt, death and rebirth, initiation, Celtic or British myths and gods. Our prime consideration is whether it is emotionally moving to our staff. If so, it doesn't *have* to be technically perfect or have traditional form. No long, long poems or those unrelated to the Pagan theme of our magazine or bad poetry."** I have not seen an issue, but the editor describes it as magazine-sized, 32 pp., stapled. Press run 200 for 100+ subscriptions of which 1 is a library, 20-30 shelf sales. Subscription: $13. **Sample, postpaid: $4. Pays 1 copy. Reports in 1-2 months.**

‡THE COOL TRAVELER NEWSLETTER (I, IV-Themes), P.O. Box 11975, Philadelphia, PA 19145, phone 215-440-0592, founded 1988, editor Bob Moore, appears 4-6 times per year, using **"poetry that contains artistic references: painters, works, etc. and poetry about places, especially different countries, but I'll look at it all."** They have recently published poetry by Joe Farley, Addie Lee and Arthur Knight. As a sample the editor selected these lines (poet unidentified):

> *Gusting autumn winds*
> *sweep Washington Square,*
> *lift layers of fallen leaves —*
> *tawny-hued magic carpets*

It's format is long and slender, 10-25 pp., saddle-stapled, photocopied from typescript, with colored paper cover. His first year the editor received 60-70 pieces and accepted them all. Press run: 1,000 for 80-100 subscribers, ¾ of the copies go to cafes and galleries. Subscription: $10. **Sample, postpaid: $1. Pays 1 copy (more if requested). Submitting poets should, in a cover letter, "say something about themselves — a short one or two lines to be printed with their work." Reports in 2 weeks, sometimes asks for rewrites. Editor comments on submissions "often."** He says, "There are many local papers and publications that want poetry."

COOP. ANTIGRUPPO SICILIANO; TRAPANI NUOVA (II, IV-Translations), Via Argenteria, Km 4, Trapani, Sicily, Italy, 91100, phone 0923-38681, founded 1968, poetry editor Nat Scammacca, is a group of over 100 poets involved in international activities pertaining to poetry including readings, sponsored visits, and publication in the weekly cultural newspaper, *Trapani Nuova*, or in collections or anthologies. **Free samples.** Scammacca says, " **We translate and publish short poems almost every week in *Trapani Nuova* and, on occasion, in our anthologies.** We have published several thousand American poems and have included 20 American poets including Simpson, Stafford, Bly, Ferlinghetti, Corso, Ignatow, etc. We like **ironical poetry, committed poetry (anti-atomic), intelligent poetry; we do not want poetry that makes no sense, rhetorical stuff, sentimental, or poets who think each word or line is God-sent. The poem must *communicate*. We prefer short poems, but if the poem is exceptional, we want it. Short poems we can translate into Sicilian and Italian and use in our weekly in a week's time."** The editor selected a sample from his own "Lovingly":

> *Though this January morning's bitter cold the two roses I picked yesterday*
> *Have spread their petals wide to bloom, lovingly — but not my wife*

Who, with a dustpan and the broom in her hands muttered:
"Let's sweep up the trash," when I said:
    "A poem is blooming in my head."

Send poems of 4-15 lines to Nat Scammacca. Considers simultaneous submissions. "The poet must send his best poetry. If it is difficult but makes sense he can explain why he wants us to publish the poem, why he wants us to suffer. We want, otherwise, enjoyable, witty, intelligent and if possible great poetry." Apparently one gets acquainted by submitting to the weekly. If you want **to send a book MS, query first, with cover letter giving biographical background, personal or aesthetic philosophy. Payment in copies of the published book.** "They are lucky when we publish them," says the editor. The nonprofit cooperative is supported by government funds; it organizes poetry tours, radio and TV appearances and readings for some of the authors they have published. "We want other poets to be sufficiently confident in themselves so as not to ask for our opinion concerning their poetry. We prefer having the poet himself explain why he writes, for whom and why he writes as he does. We do not want to substitute our methods for his methods." (See listing for Cross-Cultural Communications.)

COPPER BEECH PRESS (II), Box 1852, English Dept., Brown University, Providence, RI 02912, phone 401-863-2393, founded 1973, poetry editor Randy Blasing, publishes **books of all kinds of poetry**, about three 48 pp., flat-spined paperbacks a year. I selected these lines by Kay Ryan as a sample:

Oh the brave and confident,
the habitual people of Egypt
who filled Heaven with Earth
by the cubit.

Free catalog. Query with 5 poems, biographical information and publications. Considers simultaneous submissions. Replies to queries in 1 month, to submissions in 3 months, payment: 10% of press run.

CORNERSTONE: THE VOICE OF THIS GENERATION (IV-Religious), Jesus People USA, 4707 N. Malden, Chicago, IL 60640, phone 312-989-2080, editor Dawn Herrin, is a mass-circulation (50,000), low-cost ($2 per copy), bimonthly **directed at youth, covering "contemporary issues in the light of Evangelical Christianity." They use avant-garde, free verse, haiku, light verse, traditional — "no limits except for epic poetry. (We've not got the room.)" Buys 10-50 poems per year, uses 1-2 pp. per issue, has a 2-3 month backlog. Submit maximum of 5 poems. Pays $25/poem. Sample: $2. Send SASE for guidelines.**

CORNFIELD REVIEW (II), Ohio State University, Marion, OH 43302-5695, phone 614-389-2361, FAX 614-389-6786, founded 1974, is an annual of poetry, art work, short fiction and personal narrative. **"We are open to all forms of high quality poetry, and we are interested in new talent."** The editor selected these lines by David Citino from "Sister Mary Appassionata Addresses the Marion County Writers' Guild" as typical of the quality they're looking for:

. . . There's no dark,
writers, you can't see into,
witnessing so ignites you, revisioning
the world until you get it right.

Everyone you care for lives forever.

CR is resuming publication after a dormant period (since 1984). It is 6 × 9", flat-spined, printed on heavy slick stock with b/w graphics, glossy cover with art, approximately 40-48 pp. Their press run is about 500. **Sample: $4.50 postpaid. Pays 3 copies. Send no more than 5 poems with brief cover letter. No simultaneous submissions or previously published poems. Reports within 2-3 months.** "Submissions should be typed or letter-quality dot-matrix, copyright reverts to contributor."

CORONA (II), Dept. of History and Philosophy, Montana State University, Bozeman, MT 59717, phone 406-994-5200, founded 1979, poetry editors Lynda and Michael Sexson, "is an interdisciplinary annual bringing together reflections from those who stand on the edges of their disciplines; those who sense that insight is located not in things but in relationships; those who have deep sense of playfulness; and those who believe that the imagination is involved in what we know." In regard to poetry they want **"no sentimental greeting cards; no slap-dash."** They have recently published poems by Richard Hugo, X. J. Kennedy, Donald Hall, Philip Dacey, Wendy Battin, William Irwin Thompson, Frederick Turner and James Dickey. Asked for a sample, they said, "See journal for examples. We are not interested in cloned poems or homogenized poets." Journal is perfect-bound, 125-140 pp., professionally printed, using about 20-25 pp. of poetry per issue, circulation 2,000. **Sample: $7 postpaid. Submit any number of pages, photocopy and dot-matrix OK, no simultaneous submissions. Reports in 1 week**

to 6 months. **Payment is "nominal" plus 2 contributor's copies.** The editors advise, "Today's poet survives only by the generous spirits of small press publishers. Read and support the publishers of contemporary artists by subscribing to the journals and magazines you admire."

‡CORONA PUBLISHING CO.; CORONA POETS (IV-Regional), 1037 S. Alamo, San Antonio, TX 78210, founded 1977, editor David Bowen, is a general trade book publisher that publishes **Texas poets only. "Shorter forms. All books in our series are 64 pp. No religious, inspirational."** They have recently published poetry by Judith McPheron and Robert Fink. They have published 6 books in the Corona Poets series and publish 1-2/year. **Sample, postpaid: $5. Pays 10% royalties on net sales plus 25 author's copies.**

COSMIC TREND (I, IV-Themes, love/romance/erotica), Box 323, Clarkson Rd., Mississauga, ON L5J 3Y2 Canada, founded 1984, poetry editor George Le Grand, publishes 3 chapbook anthologies a year of **"New Age mind-expanding material of any style, short or medium length; also: humorous, unusual, or zany entries (incl. graphics) with deeper meaning. We ignore epics, run-of-a-mill romantic and political material."** As a sample the editor selected these lines (poet unidentified):

> *Trinkets of sleepiness will shatter and blend*
> *into the solid state of the liquid crystal*
> *of the sun of love*
> *be it only half the frequency of creation*
> *time will carve*
> *into our b e i n g infinite!*

They will consider simultaneous submissions and previously published poems **"with accompanied disclosure and references." Pays 1 copy/published contribution. Send $1 for guidelines or $3 for sample publication and guidelines. Response time is usually less than 3 weeks. Editor "often" comments on rejections.** His advice is "don't give up in your gaining access to your source of being. The associated courage of expressing yourselves without compromises transcends us all in the end as one in our patterned love-learning beyond the immediate human involvements. *Cosmic Trend* wants to celebrate this courage in individuals who are ready to tune into their own creative sources, and promote poetry as a high adventure of the spirit, rather than mere intellectual posing."

COSMOPOLITAN (IV-Women), 224 W. 57th St., New York, NY 10019, founded 1886, is a monthly magazine "aimed at a female audience 18-34," part of the Hearst conglomerate, though it functions independently editorially. They want **freshly-written free verse, not more than 25 lines, either light or serious, which addresses the concerns of young women. Prefer shorter poems, use 1-4 poems each issue. "We cannot return submissions without SASE."** They have a circulation of 2,987,970. **Buy sample at newsstand. Reports in 3-5 weeks, pays $25.** "Please do not phone; query by letter if at all, though queries are unnecessary before submitting. **Poems shouldn't be too abstract. The poem should convey an image, feeling or emotion that our reader could perhaps identify with. We do publish mostly free verse, although we're also open to well-crafted rhyme poems."**

COTEAU BOOKS; THUNDER CREEK PUBLISHING CO-OP; WOOD MOUNTAIN SERIES (IV-Regional, children), 401-2206 Dewdney Ave., Regina, Saskatchewan S4R 1H3, Canada, phone 306-777-0170, founded 1975, managing editor Shelley Sopher, a "small literary press that publishes poetry, fiction, drama, anthologies, criticism, children's books — only by **Canadian writers." Poetry should be "of general interest to Canadian or American audience."** They have recently published poetry by Nancy Mattson, Kim Morrissey and Dennis Cooley. and 2 anthologies of Saskatchewan poetry. **Writers should submit 30-50 poems "and indication of whole MS", typed; simultaneous and American submissions not accepted. Letter should include publishing credits and bio and SAE with IRC if necessary. Queries will be answered in 2-3 weeks and MSS reported on in 2-4 months. Authors receive 10% royalty; 10 copies.** Their attractive catalog is free for 9 × 12" SASE or IRC and sample copies can be ordered from it. It says: "The Thunder Creek Co-op presently has two divisions — Coteau Books and Caragana Records. Membership has changed through the years in the co-op, but now stands at twelve. Each member has a strong interest in Canadian writing and culture." As a sample, the editor selected these lines from "Crows" by Catherine Buckaway:

> *A black pillar of crows*
> *rises like dusty smoke*
> *from this land.*

The imprint Wood Mountain Series is for first collections, reflecting their commitment to publishing new writers.

COTTONWOOD; COTTONWOOD PRESS (II, IV-Regional), Box J, Kansas Union, Lawrence, KS 66045, founded 1965, poetry editor Philip Wedge. **The Press "is auxiliary to *Cottonwood Magazine* and publishes material by authors in the region. Material is usually solicited.** For the magazine they are looking for "strong narrative or sensory impact, non-derivative, not 'literary,' not 'academic.' Emphasis on Midwest, but publishes the best poetry received regardless of region. Poems should be 60 lines or less, on daily experience, *perception*. They have recently published poetry by Rita Dove, Allen Ginsberg, Walter McDonald, Patricia Traxler, and Ron Schreiber. The editors selected these sample lines by Denise Low:

> Last winter I slept long nights
> pressed against my husband,
> my thigh across his belly.
> Outdoors bulbs lay below ground,
> crisp white flesh cupped
> around and around flowerlets.

The 6 × 9″, flat-spined (112 + pp.) magazine is published 3 times per year, printed from computer offset, with photos, using 20-30 pages of poetry in each issue. They have a circulation of 500-600, with 150 subscriptions of which 75 are libraries. They receive about 2,000 submissions per year, use about 60, have a maximum of 1 year backlog. Price per issue, $5, **sample: $3 postpaid. Submit up to 5 pp., dot-matrix, photocopy OK. No simultaneous submissions. Reports in 2-5 months. They sometimes provide criticism on rejected MSS. Payment: 1 copy.** The editors advise, "Read the little magazines and send to ones you like."

COUNCIL FOR INDIAN EDUCATION (IV-Ethnic, children), 517 Rimrock Rd., Billings, MT 59102, founded 1970, poetry editor Elnora Old Coyote, is a non-profit corporation publishing material (small paper-bound books) to use in schools with Indian students. They want **"poetry that will appeal to children (any age), that expresses American Indian ideas or describes Indian life, past or present — also nature and ranch life."** As a sample of poetry they like, the editor chose these lines (poet unidentified):

> Eyes on the Sunrise; Nature's Way
> Rhythm of the Redman's Great New Day
> Dance to the rhythm; chant and hum
> Never lose the Rhythm of the Raw Hide Drum.

Submit sample poems. Simultaneous submissions, photocopies, dot matrix OK. May be previously published material. Free catalog of publications sent on request. Pays for single poems in contributor's copies; 10% royalty for books of poems only. The editor says, "We publish mostly fiction, some factual, one poetry book per year. All our material is selected by an Indian Editorial Board."

‡COUNTRY JOURNAL (II), P.O. Box 8200, Harrisburg, PA 17105, phone 717-657-9555, poetry editor Donald Hall, editor Peter V. Fossel, is a bimonthly magazine featuring country living **for people who live in rural areas or who are thinking about moving there. They use free verse, light verse and traditional.** Circ. 325,000. Average issue includes 6-8 feature articles and 10 departments. They have recently published poems by Mary Oliver, Kate Barnes and Lorraine Ferra. As a sample, I selected these lines from Barbara Crooker's "Terrestial Navigation":

> We're travelling light, having cast off
> the tangled nets of our daily lives.
> Behind us, the loostrife catches fire.

Of 450-500 poems received each year they accept 20-25. Subscription: $16.95. **Sample, postpaid: $3. Simultaneous submissions, previously published poems OK. Reports in 2-3 months. Editor comments on submissions "seldom." Pays $50/poem on acceptance. Submit seasonal material 1 year in advance. Photocopied and previously published submissions OK. Computer printout submissions acceptable, prefers letter-quality; "dot-matrix submissions are acceptable if double spaced." Reports in 2-3 months.**

COUNTRY WOMAN; REIMAN PUBLICATIONS (IV-Women, humor), Box 643, Milwaukee, WI 53201, founded 1970, managing editor Kathy Pohl. *Country Woman* "is a bimonthly magazine dedicated to the lives and interests of country women. Those who are both involved in farming and ranching and those who love country life. In some ways, it is very similar to many women's general interest magazines, and yet its subject matter is closely tied in with rural living and the very unique lives of country women. **We like short (4-5 stanzas, 16-20 lines) traditional rhyming poems that reflect on a season or comment humorously or seriously on a particular rural experience. Also limericks and humorous 4-8 line filler rhymes. No experimental poetry. Poetry will not be considered unless it rhymes. Always looking for poems that focus on the seasons. We don't want rural putdowns, poems that stereotype country women, etc. All poetry must be positive and upbeat. Our poems are fairly simple, yet elegant.** They often accompany a high-quality photograph." *CW* recently published poems by Hilda Sanderson, Edith E. Cutting, and Ericka Northrop. As a sample the editor selected these lines from a poem by Betty Ekiss:

There is a feeling in the air
Born of sights and sounds,
A subtle turning of the earth
As nature makes her rounds . . .

CW, appearing 6 times a year, is magazine-sized, 68 pp., glossy paper with much color photography. Circulation to 700,000. Subscriptions, $14.98 per year, $2.50 per copy. They receive about 1,200 submissions of poetry per year, use 40-50 (unless they publish an anthology). Their backlog is 1 month to 3 years. "We're always welcoming submissions." **Sample: $2.50 postpaid. Submit maximum of 6 poems. Photocopy OK if stated not a simultaneous submission. Reports in 2-3 months. Pays $10-40 per poem plus copy.** They hold various contests for subscribers only. I examined one of their anthologies, *Cattails and Meadowlarks: Poems from the Country*, 90 + pp., saddle-stapled with high-quality color photography on the glossy card cover, poems in large, professional type with many b/w photo illustrations.

THE COUNTRYMAN (IV-Rural), Sheep St., Burford, Oxford OX8 4LH, England, phone Burford 2258, founded 1927, editor Christopher Hall, a quarterly magazine "on rural matters." The editor wants **poetry on rural themes, "available to general readership but not jingles."** It is a handsome, flat-spined, digest-sized magazine, 200 + pp., using popular articles and ads. As a sample I selected the last of six stanzas of "Hello/Goodbye" by Michael Pooley:

I want my small birds' throng, its song;
my shaded snowdrops, crocuses about the lawn.
I'm anxious for the anxious spring.

They **pay: a maximum of £15/poem. Submissions should be short. Reporting time is "within a week usually,"** and time to publication is "3 months-3 years."

‡**THE COVENTRY READER (I, II)**, P.O. Box 18418, Cleveland Heights, OH 44118, founded 1988, is a 20 pp. tabloid quarterly, circulation 10,000, using **"all types"** of poetry. They have recently published poetry by Daniel Thompson, Wendy Shaffer, and James Magner, Jr. As a sample the editor selected these lines from "Dr. Pain's Downtown Ramble Done" by Aralee Stranger

them who drive in & take out & leave
their trash behind for us to sweep up
& them who buy cheap & hike rent fix hip
& sell to any cheap son of a high bidder
who comes down the six lane pike & why not
business is good again

Subscription: $5/4 issues. **Sample, postpaid: "2 stamps." Pays 2 copies. They use about a third of submissions received. Editor comments on submissions "often."** "Northeast Ohio is our distribution area. Our staff strongly feels that each community should support its poets and writers, and that these artists deserve any recognition, respect and exposure that community can afford."

COVER MAGAZINE (II), Box 1215, Cooper Station, New York NY 10276, founded 1986, contact editor/publisher Jeff Wright, is a "broad-based arts monthly covering all the arts in every issue, a 40 pp. tabloid sold on newsstands and in select bookstores." They want **shorter poems—2-24 lines generally, favoring new romantic work. Nothing stodgy or simplistic."** They have recently published poetry by Robert Creeley and Molly Peacock. As a sample the editor chose one line:

Let all but love be now our foe.

Cover tries "to reach a cutting edge/front-line audience in touch with the creative fields." Entirely supported by ads and sales. Press run is 8,000 for 750 subscriptions (5 of them libraries), 1,000 shelf sales. Out of 250 submissions of poetry they accept 25. Subscription: $10; per issue: $1. **Sample: $2 postpaid. Pays nothing, not even a copy. Submit 4-5 poems with cover letter. Reports in 2 months. Editor often comments on rejections.**

COYDOG REVIEW (II), Box 2608, Aptos CA 95001, phone 408-761-1824, founded 1984, edited by Candida Lawrence is "a journal of poetry, short fiction, essays and graphics" appearing once a year in an elegant wide-page format, flat-spined, 100 + pp., **40 pp. of poetry per issue, sample $5 plus $1 postage. They need material. Send as many poems as you wish. Photocopy, simultaneous submissions OK.** I chose these lines as a sample, by Robert Bly:

Early in the morning the hermit wakes,
hearing the roots of the fir tree stir beneath his floor.
Someone is there. Their strength buried
in earth carries up the summer world.

Payment: 2 copies. Sometimes prize for best submission in issue. Occasional comments or suggestions for changes on rejected MSS.

CRAB CREEK REVIEW (II, IV-Translations), 4462 Whitman Ave. N., Seattle, WA 98103, phone 206-633-1090, founded 1983, editor Linda J. Clifton, appears 3 times per year, 32 pp., attractively-printed on newsprint. Their **guidelines (available for SASE) indicate that they want poetry which is "free or formal, with clear imagery, wit, voice that is interesting and energetic, accessible to the general reader rather than full of very private imagery and obscure literary allusion. Translations accepted—please accompany with copy of the work in the original language. Prefer poetry under 40 lines; occasionally use longer work, and prefer 80-120 lines there to fit our page size and layout. Payment: 2 copies. (We're working on establishing enough funding to pay in actual cash.)"** They have published poetry by Robert Bringhurst, Elizabeth Murawski, Laurel Speer, Maxine Kumin, William O'Daly translating Neruda, and William Stafford and offer as a sample these lines from "Charlotte McAllister at She-Nah-Nam" by Shannon Nelson:

> *This land's more than you can imagine—like*
> *A husband's hands, a child moving from your blood*
> *Into the air.*
> *Pinpoints of light poke through the door of hides.*
> *In the air, the smell of the fir needles giving up.*

They have about 20 pp. of poetry in each issue, circulation 350, 200 subscriptions of which 20 are libraries, receive 400-500 submissions per year from which they choose 50-60 poems, have a 1 year backlog. **Sample: $3 postpaid,** subscription $8 per year. Listed in *Index of American Periodical Verse. Member CCLM.* **Submit up to 6 pp., photocopy, dot-matrix OK, no simultaneous submissions; reports in 6-8 weeks. Sometimes comments on rejections.** "No reply if no SASE." Linda Clifton advises poets to "read a sample of the magazine, but don't try to clone what you've seen there for your submission. We appreciate poetry that responds to both the personal and the political while maintaining a crucial attention to precise use of language."

‡**CRAMPED AND WET (I)**, 1012 29th, Sioux City, IA 51104, founded 1986, editor Kidd Smiley, is a quarterly. **"I like real stuff but I want to see fun too. There's room for hard tough stuff yet I like to end up with a real warm feeling. No real conceptual self-indulgent s***."** They have recently published poetry by John McKinley, todd moore, Charles Luden, A.Q. Passmore, and Alan Catlin. As a sample the editor selected these lines from "next exit 27 miles" by George DeChant:

> *i only say this so*
> *you know why i sometimes*
> *feel like a long stretch of asphalt*
> *heading towards a stuckey's*
> *standing next to you*

C and W's size varies. It is 20-30 pp., offset printed. They accept about 10-20% of 400-500 poems per year. Press run: 150. **Sample, postpaid: $1.50. Pays 1 copy.** Editor comments on submissions "often. I usually write the poet within a couple of weeks either returning his submission or informing him of acceptance, etc.—that is if he includes a SASE." He advises, "Do what you want, feel good about yourself. The most radical attitude is the positive one. Practice self-parody like some practice self-discipline."

CRAZYQUILT QUARTERLY (II), 3341 Adams Ave., San Diego, CA 92116, founded 1986, editor Jackie Cicchetti, is a literary quarterly which has recently published poetry by Bertha Rogers, Larry D. Griffin, Virginia R. Terris, and June Owens. As a sample the editor selected these lines by Charles B. Dickson from "The Clown":

> *Their fragile bodies bent like ampersands,*
> *They hunch in nursing homes. Their eyes alight,*
> *To chuckle at his gibes, watch antic hands*
> *Pluck roses from the air for their delight.*

The magazine is digest-sized, saddle-stapled, 90 + pp., professionally printed on good stock with matte card cover, circulation 200, subscription $14.95. **Sample: $4.50 postpaid; back issue $2.50 Pays 2 copies. One poem to a page. Dot-matrix, previously published poems, and simultaneous submissions all OK. Reports in 8-10 weeks, time to publication 12-15 months.** They have an annual contest with annual prizes of $100, $50 and $25 and a $6 fee for up to 5 poems, no line limit, deadline May 31. Winning entries to be published in *Crazyquilt*. Send SASE. Poetry Chapbook Contest in even-numbered years. $10 fee; prize is $25, publication and 25 copies.

CREAM CITY REVIEW (II), Box 413, Dept. of English, University of Wisconsin at Milwaukee, Milwaukee, WI 53201, phone 414-229-4708, editor-in-chief Kit Pancoast, poetry editor Marilyn Taylor, is a nationally distributed literary magazine published twice a year by the Creative Writing Program. The editors will consider **any poem that is well-crafted and especially those poems that show an awareness of where poetry has come from and where it might be going; but they have little patience with dogma, sentimentality, sexism, or prose made to look like poetry.** They have recently published poetry by Ted

Kooser, David Ray, Amy Clampitt, George Garrett, Ann Lauterbach, Ronald Wallace, Lucien Stryk, William Stafford, Eve Shelnutt, and Robert Pack. Magazine size is 5½ × 8½", perfect bound, on 70 lb. paper, circulation 1,000, 100+ subscriptions of which 15 are libraries. **Sample: $5 postpaid. Send SASE for guidelines. Include SASE when submitting and please submit no more than 5 poems at a time. Payment varies with funding and includes 2 copies. Reports in 2 months. Simultaneous submissions OK. Editors sometimes comment on rejections.** Always looking for new talent.

CREATIVE WITH WORDS PUBLICATIONS (C.W.W.); SPOOFING; WE ARE POETS AND AUTHORS, TOO (I, IV-Children, Seniors), Box 223226, Carmel, CA 93922, phone 408-649-1682, founded 1975, poetry editor Brigitta Geltrich, **offers criticism for a fee.** It focuses "on furthering **folkloristic tall tales and such; creative writing abilities in children** (poetry, prose, language-art); creative writing in **senior citizens** (poetry and prose). The editors organize and sponsor an **annual poetry contest, offer feedback on MSS submitted to this contest,** and publish on a wide range of themes relating to human studies and the environment that influence human behaviors. **$2 reading fee per poem, includes a critical analysis.** The publications are anthologies of children's poetry, prose and language art; anthologies of senior citizen poetry and prose; and *Spoofing: an Anthology of Folkloristic Yarns and Such*, which has an announced theme for each issue. "**Want to see: folkloristic themes, poetry for and by children; poetry by senior citizens; topic (inquire). Do not want to see: too mushy; too religious; too didactic; expressing dislike for fellowmen; political; pornographic poetry.**" Latest themes are "A CWW Christmas"; "It's a Matter of Love" and "A CWW Easter." Guidelines available for SASE, catalog for 25¢. The samples I have seen of *Spoofing!* and (*We are Poets and Authors, Too!*) an anthology of poems by children are low-budget publications, photocopied from typescript, saddle-stapled, card covers with cartoon-like art. **Submit 20-line, 40 spaces wide maximum, poems geared to specific audience and subject matter.** They have published poetry by Christine Evans, Rebecca Sipper, and Danny Vu. The editor selected this sample by Alison Flint:

> Come, birds,
> Fly, fly
> And paint our world
> With happiness

"**Query with sample poems, short personal biography, other publications, poetic goals, where you read about us, for what publication and/or event you are submitting.**" Their contests have prizes of $15, $10, $5, $1, but they hope to increase them. "No conditions for publication, but CWW is dependent on author/poet support by purchase of a copy or copies of publication." The editor advises, "Trend is proficiency. Poets should research topic; know audience for whom they write; check topic for appeal to specific audience; should not write for the sake of rhyme, rather for the sake of imagery and being creative with the language. Feeling should be expressed (but no mushiness). Topic and words should be chosen carefully; brevity should be employed."

‡CREATIVITY UNLIMITED PRESS; ANNUAL CREATIVITY UNLIMITED PRESS POETRY COMPETITION (I), 30819 Casilina, Rancho Palos Verdes, CA 90274, phone 213-541-4844, founded 1989, editor Shelley Stockwell, publishes annually a collection of poetry submitted to their **contest, $4 fee for 1-5 poems; prizes of $300, $150 and $75 in addition to publication. Deadline December 31.** "**Clever spontaneous overflows of rich emotion, humor and delightful language encouraged. No inaccessible, verbose, esoteric, obscure poetry. Limit 3 pp. per poem double spaced, one side of page.**" As a sample the editor selected her own "Freeway Dilemma":

> Of all enduring questions
> A big one I can't answer;
> How come, whenever I change lanes,
> The other lane goes faster?

They also accept freelance submissions for book publication. "Poems previously published will be accepted provided writer has maintained copyright and notifies us." Editor comments on submissions "always. Keep it simple and accessible." Sample copies of their anthologies available for 40% off list.

CREEPING BENT (II), 433 W. Market St., Bethlehem, PA 18018, phone 215-691-3548, founded 1984, editor Joseph Lucia, a literary magazine that focuses on serious poetry, fiction, book reviews and essays, with very occasional chapbooks published under the same imprint. "**We publish only work that evidences a clear awareness of the current situation of poetry. We take a special interest in poems that articulate a vision of the continuities and discontinuities in the human relationship to the natural world.**" The editor does not want "**any attempt at verse that clearly indicates the writer hasn't taken a serious look at a recent collection of poetry during his or her adult life.**" He has recently published work by Turner Cassity, Charles Edward Eaton, Robert Gibb, Briget Kelly, Walter McDonald, Donald Revell, Harry Humes and Patricia Wilcox. As a sample, he chose these lines from Peter Yovu's "Once You Have a Name":

Once you have a name
for things, things begin: trees,
eucalyptus and mango like branching
magnets draw green iron out of the air;
bees drone; vines too young to strangle, spiral;
violet stems flecked with aphids like sweated milk
grow fur and here a hoopoe lifts its crest.

Creeping Bent is digest-sized, nicely printed on heavy stock with some b/w artwork, 48-64 pp., saddle-stapled with glossy white card cover printed in black and one other color. It appears at least once a year, sometimes more often. Circulation is 250, of which 175 are subscriptions, 25 go to libraries, and 25 are sold on newsstands. Price per copy is $3, subscription $6/year. **Sample available for $3 postpaid, guidelines for SASE. Pay is 2 copies plus a 1-year subscription. "Absolutely no simultaneous submissions!" Photocopied and dot-matrix MSS are OK. Reporting time is usually 2-3 weeks and time to publication is 6 months at most.** The editor says, "Before submitting to any magazine published by anyone with a serious interest in contemporary writing, make certain you understand something about the kind of work the magazine publishes. Be familiar with current styles and approaches to poetry, even if you eschew them."

‡**CRESCENT MOON (I, IV-Love/romance/erotica, occult, religious, spirituality)**, 18 Chaddesley Rd., Kidderminster, England DY10 3AD, founded 1988, editor Jeremy Robinson, publishes about 10 books and chapbooks/year on arrangements subsidized by the poet. He wants **"poetry that is passionate and authentic. Any form or length." Not "the trivial, insincere, or derivative."** They have recently published studies of Thomas Hardy, J.M.W. Turner, John Cowper Powys, Lawrence Durrell and Renaissance painting, including poetry by the editor. As a sample the editor selected the first of five stanzas from his "Aphrodite's Mirror":

Shaving one day in Aphrodite's mirror,
Using her sea-foam as ointment and the shell
For a basin, I caught sight of myself
In that speckled glass and wondered if
This love of ours was going to last beyond
A mere Rising-From-The-Sea-Attended-By-Nymphs.

The sample chapbook I have seen is the editor's **Black Angel**, 45 pp., flat-spined, photocopied from typescript, digest-sized, with matte card cover. **Sample, postpaid, in response to "written requests." Inquiries welcome. Reports on queries in 4 weeks, on MSS in 8. "I am interested in publishing collections by individual poets. Publishing fees are organized in conjunction with the author."**

CRICKET, THE MAGAZINE FOR CHILDREN (IV-Children), P.O. Box 300, Peru, IL 61354, founded 1973, publisher and editor-in-chief, Marianne Carus, is a monthly, circulation 120,000, **paying up to $3 per line for "serious, humorous, nonsense rhymes, limericks" for children. They sometimes use previously-published work.** The attractive $7 \times 9''$ magazine, 80 pp., saddle-stapled, color cover and b/w illustrations inside, receives over 1,000 submissions per month, uses 10-12, and has up to a 2 year backlog. **No query. Submit poems up to 25 lines, no restrictions on form. Sample: $2. Guidelines available for SASE. Reports in 3-4 months.** They hold poetry contests for children ages 5-9 and 10-14. Current contest themes and rules appear in each issue.

CROSS-CULTURAL COMMUNICATIONS; CROSS-CULTURAL REVIEW OF WORLD LITERATURE AND ART IN SOUND, PRINT, AND MOTION; CROSS-CULTURAL MONTHLY; CROSS-CULTURAL REVIEW CHAPBOOK ANTHOLOGY; INTERNATIONAL WRITERS SERIES (II, IV-Translations, bilingual), 239 Wynsum Ave., Merrick, NY 11566, phone 516-868-5635, FAX 516-379-1901, founded 1971, Stanley H. and Bebe Barkan. Stanley Barkan began CCC as an educational venture, a program in 27 languages at Long Island University, but soon began publishing collections of poetry translated into English from various languages—some of them (such as Estonian) quite "neglected"—in bilingual editions. During the 70s he became aware of Antigruppo (a group against groups), a movement with similar international focus in Sicily, and the two joined forces. (See Coop. Antigruppo listing; CCC is the American representative of Coop. Antigruppo.) CCR began as a series of chapbooks (6-12 a year) of collections of poetry translated from various languages and continues as the **Holocaust, Women Writers, Latin American Writers, Asian-American Writers, International Artists, Art & Poetry, Jewish, Israeli, Dutch, Turkish and Long Island** and **Brooklyn Chapbook Series**—issued simultaneously in palm-sized and regular paperback and cloth-binding and boxed editions, as well as audiocassette and videocassette. **All submissions should be preceded by a query letter with SASE; the Holocaust series is for survivors. Send SASE for guidelines. Pays 10% of print run.** In addition to publications in these series, CCC has published anthologies, translations and collections by dozens of poets from many

Close-up

Marianne Carus
General Manager and Editor-in-Chief
Cricket

Marianne Carus, general manager and editor-in-chief of *Cricket*, started the magazine for children, ages 6-12, in 1973. Her "guiding star" was *St. Nicholas* magazine, founded in 1873 by Mary Mapes Dodge, author of **Hans Brinker**. During its 64 years, **St. Nicholas** published Twain, Longfellow, Whittier, Emerson and Thoreau. The magazine always emphasized quality literature, no "editorial babble," featuring the best authors of its time. "That's exactly what I want to do," says Carus.

Her goal, she says, is to provide literature of value for children; something they can learn from. She set out to give them not only good literature, she says, "but literature from around the world so the young readers can get a feeling for the whole world." The magazine publishes many folk tales from different countries, some that were translated for the magazine. "Children who don't travel can learn about the world by reading *Cricket*," says Carus.

She receives about 300 poems a month, and they use only a couple of poems each issue. While they love to read the poems, Carus says they must be very choosy about those they accept. They can be because of the volume they receive. "We want to give readers only the very best that can be found." She says it may sometimes take a long time to publish a poem after it has been accepted because they might save it for one of their special theme issues. "But, if a poem touches us and we like the images it presents, we accept it." They don't consider long story poems for the magazine as they often fail to hold the attention of the young readers.

Carus says children are attracted to poetry for a variety of reasons. "Older children like and appreciate the lyrical poems. The younger ones like the rhythm and the musical quality of poems. That's what I think really attracts them to poetry. And also that it can be fun. Humorous poetry is so important, especially for younger children."

Surveys show that children don't want to see a great deal of poetry. Some children's magazines don't publish *any* poetry. However, Carus says you can't go strictly by surveys. "I get letters from children who mention a poem that they liked."

Cricket features two contests for children each month as the "Cricket League." The format changes between essays, poetry and drawing; they also have a photography contest once in a while. "We have poetry about four or five times a year, and I believe many of these children who send in their poetry to be published are the upcoming poets of the future. Some of them are so good, it is hard to believe," says Carus. They have to be very careful, she adds, as some children plagiarize because they can't distinguish between a poem they have heard and really like and one they have created themselves. It is always embarrassing when we use one that has won a prize for another children's magazine. We always hear about it."

Her advice for those writing poetry: "A poet should not sit down to write for the marketplace, to write for any special season. For example, we get Halloween poems just before Halloween. (We put our Halloween issue together in January.) It is not good to do that because the poetry is always forced and it always shows. Poetry is something that has to come out of your inner feelings for the moment. If it is a lyrical poem, perhaps about nature, it's like a snapshot that you take when you feel 'This is what I want to hold in mind.' Rather, you put it into words in a lyrical voice. This must be your inner voice. It should never be written to order."

—*Deborah Cinnamon*

———

countries. As a sample the editor selected the first stanza of "The Girl from Ipanêma" by Vinícius de Moraes, as translated from the Portuguese by Gregory Rabassa:

Look at her, see her, a beauty who passes, so full of grace.
See her, a girl going past here, a soft swinging pace,
A sweet side-to-side,
On her way to the sea.

That's from the title poem of **Cross-Cultural Review Chapbook 34**, published in 1982, digest-sized, 32 pp., saddle-stapled, professionally printed with matte card cover, photo of the Brazillian poet on the back—$5. **Sample $7 postpaid.** *Cross-Cultural Monthly* focuses on bilingual poetry and prose. Subscription: $36 postpaid. **Sample: $3 postpaid. Pays 1 copy.**

CROTON REVIEW (V), Box 277, Croton-on-Hudson, NY 10520, founded 1978, executive editor and founder Ruth Lisa Schechter, is published annually. 7×10″ book format, 64-80 pp., **original, unpublished poetry. "The** *Croton Review* **staff will be on editorial hiatus temporarily and will not be reading MSS until further notice. Watch literary newsletters, Poet's Market, for our future publishing schedule and editorial needs."**

CRYSTAL RAINBOW (V,I), 340 Granada Drive, Winter Park, FL 32789, editor Louise M. Turmenne, is a quarterly inspirational newsletter using **"seasonal, traditional rhyme or free verse, 24 lines maximum. Purpose to comfort, encourage, inspire our readers to improve themselves and reach out to others. No sexual situations. We are still over-stocked with acceptances for this year, but get yours ready for 1992."** Recently published poets include Ron Grossman, Hy Young, and Katherine Aker. As a sample the editor selected these lines from "Brokenness" by Emma Walker:

None but the hopeless can understand
Nerves frayed like a tattered hem
Yet all of us can understand . . .
If we search for Christ in them

The newsletter is 28 pp., 7×8½, photocopy from typescript, with illustrations and classified ads—$1.75 per issue, $7 per year. **Sample $2 plus SASE (55¢ postage). Send SASE for guidelines.** They sponsor quarterly contests with entry fees of $1-1.50 per poem, prizes from $4-8. Louise Turmenne says, "Create an emotional response within the reader. Make his/her heart leap. Emphasize relationships. Keep it brief."

CUMBERLAND POETRY REVIEW (II, IV-Translations), P.O. Box 120128, Acklen Station, Nashville, TN 37212, phone 615-373-8948, founded 1981, is a biannual with a 100+ pp., 6×9″ flat-spined format. *CPR* presents poets of diverse origins to a widespread audience. "Our aim is to support the poet's effort to keep up the language. We accept special responsibility for reminding American readers that not all excellent poems in English are being written by US citizens. We have published such poets as Laurence Lerner, Donald Davie, Emily Grosholz and Rachel Hadas." The editorial board selected these sample lines by Seamus Heaney:

When Dante snapped a twig in the bleeding wood
a voice sighed out of blood that bubbled up
like sap at the end of green sticks on a fire.

Sample: $4 postpaid. Back issues: $4. Submit poetry, translations or poetry criticism with SASE or IRC. Reports in 3 months. Circulation: 500.

THE CUMMINGTON PRESS (V, III), 1803 S. 58th St., Omaha, NE 68106, phone 402-551-2392, founded 1941, editor Harry Duncan, specializes in publishing limited first editions printed by hand in both hardbound books and sewn paperbacks. Harry Duncan says he wants the **kind of poetry "that keeps the language alive" and doesn't want "the dull kind."** He has published poetry by Ben Howard, Richard Wilbur, Jane Greer and Joe Bolton. As a sample he selected these lines from **First Song/Bankei/1653** by Stephen Berg:

nothing to see   nothing to know
before after now

call and you'll hear
it's heartbreaking silence

Query before submitting—with no sample poems, bio or previous publications. Pays 10% royalties. For samples get the computer-printed list from their distributor: Granary Books, 636 Broadway—Suite 1010, New York, NY 10012.

CUTBANK; THE RICHARD HUGO MEMORIAL POETRY AWARD (II), English Dept., University of Montana, Missoula, MT 59812, phone 406-243-6730, founded 1973, editor-in-chief David Curran, an annual publishing "the best poetry, fiction, reviews, interviews and artwork available to us." Offers 2 annual awards for best poem and piece of fiction in each double issue, The Richard Hugo Memorial Poetry Award and The A. B. Guthrie Short Fiction Award. Winners announced in spring issue. Past contributors include James Crumley, William Pitt Root, Patricia Goedicke, Jim Hall, Richard Hugo, William Stafford, Harry Humes and Rita Dove. Sample lines by Hillel Schwartz:

the miniatures are the essential us, . . .
the last condensed edition.
We have always wanted good
uncluttered copy. Here we are,
less than breviary, pruned
to the absolute.

There are about 140 pp. of poetry in each issue, which has a circulation of about 400, 180 + subscriptions of which 10-20% are libraries. **Price per issue: $9, sample: $4 postpaid. Submission guidelines for SASE. Submit 3-5 poems, single-spaced. Photocopies OK, dot-matrix discouraged, simultaneous submissions OK if informed. Reports in December (i.e., "We may hold material until final choices are made in December"). "Submit August 15-October 15. We don't read during the summer." Pays in copies.**

‡DAGGER OF THE MIND; K'YI-LIH PRODUCTIONS; BREACH ENTERPRISES (IV-Science Fiction/Fantasy/Horror), 1317 Hookridge Dr., El Paso, TX 79925, phone 915-591-0541, founded 1989, executive editor Arthur William Lloyd Breach, wants **"poetry that stirs the senses and emotions; length is open as is style. Make the words dance and sing, bring out the fire in the human soul. Show flair and fashion. No four-letter words, nothing pornographic, vulgar, blasphemous, obscene and nothing generally in bad taste."** They have recently published poetry by Jessica Amanda Salmonson. The quarterly *DOTM* is magazine-sized, saddle-stapled, with high glossy covers. They use about 50 of 100-150 poems received per year. Press run 4-5,000 with 100 subscribers. **Subscription: $8/per half year, $16/year. Sample, postpaid: $3.50. Pays $1-5/poem plus 1 copy. "Send in batches of 10. I will consider simultaneous submissions only if told in advance that they are such. Length is open as is the style. Be creative and try to reflect something about the human condition. Show me something that reflects what is going on in the world. Be sensitive but not mushy. Be intelligent not sophomoric. Don't try to carbon copy any famous poet. You lead the way—don't follow. I don't like the trend toward blood and gore and obscenity. "Reports back in 4 weeks tops."** *DOTM* is devoted to *quality* horror. The key word is quality. *DOTM* is a publication under the division of K'yi-Lih Productions whose main heading is Breach Enterprises. All publications to appear in the market will come under K'yi-Lih Productions." The editor will evaluate work for a fee, depending on length and quantity.

DAILY MEDITATION, (IV-Religious), Box 2710, San Antonio, TX 78299, editor Ruth S. Paterson, is a **nonsectarian** religious quarterly that uses **inspirational poems up to 14 lines, pays 14¢ a line. Sample: 50¢ postpaid.**

THE DALHOUSIE REVIEW (III), Sir James Dunn Bldg., Suite 314, Halifax, Nova Scotia, B3H 3J5 Canada, founded 1921, phone 902-494-2541, is **a prestige literary quarterly** with 165 + pp., per issue in a 6×9″ format, professionally printed on heavy stock with matte card cover. **Contributors receive $3 for a first poem. For each poem after (in the same issue) he or she will receive $2 per poem. They prefer poems of 40 lines or less.** Subscription: $16/year, $39/3 years, (all Canadian dollars); residents outside of Canada must add $7/year for postage. Individual copies range in cost from $5.50-25. As a sample I selected these lines for "St. Cassian of Imola, Writing Teacher, Martyr" by U.S. poet David Citino:

He ordered your writing students
to stab you with their pens.
A bad class, they were too happy
to oblige, hating you
for your stinging insistence
on the spirit and law of each letter.

JOHN DANIEL AND COMPANY, PUBLISHER; FITHIAN PRESS (II), Box 21922, Santa Barbara, CA 93121, phone 805-962-1780, founded 1980, reestablished 1985. John Daniel, a general small-press publisher, specializes in literature, both prose and poetry. Fithian Press is a subsidy imprint open to all subjects. **"Book-length MSS of any form or subject matter will be considered, but we do not want to see pornographic, libelous, illegal or sloppily written poetry."** He has recently published books by R.L. Barth, Kit Tremaine, and Thelma Shaw. As a sample John Daniel selected these lines from "Milking the Earth" by Perie Longo:

> *Children draw me a ribbon*
> *On top of the page*
> > *Look inside the pool*
> *Even you can fly on your back.*

He publishes 10 flat-spined paperbacks, averaging 64 pp., per year. **For free catalog of either imprint, send 10 sample poems and bio. Reports on queries in 2 weeks, on MSS in 8 weeks. Simultaneous submissions, photocopy, dot-matrix OK, or disks compatible with Macintosh. Pays 10-50% of net receipts royalties. Fithian Press books (50% of his publishing) are subsidized, the author paying production costs and receiving royalties of 50% of net receipts. Books and rights are the property of the author, but publisher agrees to warehouse and distribute for one year if desired.** The samples I have seen (John Daniel imprint) are handsomely printed, digest-sized, with matte card covers. John Daniel advises, "Poetry does not make money, alas. It is a labor of love for both publisher and writer. But if the love is there, the rewards are great."

DARK NERVE (I, IV-Form), 702A Moultrie St., San Francisco, CA 94110, phone 415-826-5355. *Athena Incognito*, founded 1980, merged with *Dark Nerve* 1990, editors Chris Custer and Jim Lough, appears twice a year, an **"experimental, surrealistic, dada-ist magazine dedicated to the literary movements of our obscure contemporaries. We accept submissions of any amount, but request that no single piece of writing extend beyond 6 double-spaced pages, and that they include $4 (in payment for the current issue, postage and handling). We usually report within 2 weeks to 1 month. We are partial to the works whose disturbing aesthetics manage to keep its authors out of print. Dedicated writers with a high-art conscience and a knack for conceptual, sensual imagery, and unpublished/unpopular writers are strongly encouraged to submit. Please, no metric poems, end-rhymes or poems belonging to the religions or Family Albums. We allow madness in light of the genuine. Let the Star Search begin."** They have recently published poems by Greg A. Wallace, John Taggart, Richard Kostelanetz, Lynn Lifshin, Dodie bellamy and Robert Gluck. As a sample, I chose the following lines from "Doppler Effect, Series" by Marsha Campbell:

> *Something like* uroboros,
> *or many-petaled rain, cried*
> him. *Then the woman who had*
> *something to dream, recumbent*
> *vision, saw him staring*

DN is magazine-sized, 55 pp., saddle-stapled, photocopied from typescript on mimeograph paper with glossy card cover. Circulation: 2,300+. Subscription: $6.50/year. **Sample: $4 postpaid. Pays 1 copy plus "a generous critiquing of work."**

DAYBREAK (I, IV-Form), 178 Bond Street North, Hamilton, Ontario, L8S 3W6 Canada, editor Margaret Saunders. *Daybreak* **publishes haiku and longer than haiku poems, "will consider work from beginners and established poets. But it must be good poetry."** Poets recently published include George Swede, Marianne Bluger, and C.M. Buckaway. The editor selected a sample of a haiku by C.M. Buckaway:

> *By the river's edge—*
> *here and there a duck family*
> *riding the ripples*

The magazine is digest-sized, offset printed on bond, with woodcut illustration and cover design. **Payment is 1 copy of magazine; copyright remains with author.**

‡THE DAYSPRING PRESS; NEW ANGLICAN REVIEW; NEW CATHOLIC REVIEW; DAYSPRING (I, IV-Religious), Box 135, Golden, CO 80401-0135, phone 303-279-2462, founded 1983, editor John C. Brainerd, who describes his operation as a **"little-literary and religious forum. We publish almost everything received (or find its natural market)."** They want **"short lyrics, up to 5-page narrative, trading in deep human sensibilities and problems. No purposeless, perorating, scandalous, violent, or scatological poetry."** They have recently published poetry by Aumbry Williams, Michael Davidson, and Heland James. As a sample, I selected these lines from "Pan in Pain" (poet unidentified):

> *If I should contemplate the great god Pan,*
> *He makes me sad, so little life and so much benumbed,*
> *His beauty laid upon the mind and long his hope so dimly shine.*

All magazines are in the same format: digest-sized, photocopied from typescript, about 60 pp., with paper cover. All are monthly, with an annual free issue. Press run: 980 for 130 subscriptions. Each sells for $1/issue. Subscription: $12. **Sample, postpaid: $2. Send SASE for guidelines. Pays 1 copy. For book publication send bio, sample poems. Reports in 1-4 weeks. Royalties: 50% plus a "reasonable" number of author's copies.** The editor says, "Discover—by intuition—where your heart is. Orbit very nearby."

DBQP; ALABAMA DOGSHOE MOUSTACHE; A VOICE WITHOUT SIDES; &; HIT BROADSIDES; THE SUBTLE JOURNAL OF RAW COINAGE; DBQPRESCARDS (IV-Form), 225 State St., Fahrenheit [apartment] 451, Schenectady, NY 12305, founded 1987, po. ed.t Ge(of Huth). "*dbqp* is the name of the overall press. *Alabama Dogshoe Moustache* publishes **language poetry (usually very short) & visual poetry.** It is a quarterly. *A Voice Without Sides* is an occasional magazine in very small runs (about 24 copies) and in strange formats (in jars, etc.); it uses some poetry the same as *ADM*. *&* is a series of leaflets featuring 1 poem at a time. *Hit Broadsides* is a broadside series. *The Subtle Journal of Raw Coinage* is a monthly that publishes coined words but occasionally will publish an issue of *pwoermds* (one-word poems—that is, a word coined to be a poem, as Aram Saroyan's 'eyeye') or poems written completely with neologisms. *dbqprescards* is a postcard series publishing mostly poetry. These publications are generally handmade magazines, leaflets, broadsides and objects of very small size. **I am interested only in short language poetry and visual poetry. No traditional verse or mainstream poetry.**" They have recently published poetry by John M. Bennett, Karl Kempton, and Bob Grumman. As a sample the editor selected this complete poem by David C. Kopaska-Merkel:

> Yesterday's ice
> elbow grease
> a brown pick

Their major poetry "zine" is the quarterly *Alabama Dogshoe Moustache*, which appears in various formats up to 15 pp., 8½ × 11", magazine-sized, held together with thread, staples, fasteners, or packaged inside containers. Its press run is 50-100 with 10 subscriptions. Price per issue 75¢-$2. **Sample: $1 or $2 postpaid. Catalog available for SASE. Pays "at least 2 copies." Reports within 2 weeks. Editor "always" comments on rejections.** The editor says, "Most of the poetry I reject is from people who know little about the kind of poetry I publish. I don't mind reading these submissions, but it's usually a waste of time for the submitters. There are many different types of poetry written today, and there's probably a group (or two) that any poet will fit into. If you are familiar with the work of the poets I publish, you'll have a much better idea about whether or not I'll be interested in your work."

DECISION (V,IV-Religious), 1300 Harmon Place, Minneapolis, MN 55403, phone 612-338-0500, founded 1960, is the magazine of the Billy Graham Evangelistic Association, published 11 months of the year. **Currently not accepting poetry submissions.**

‡DELAWARE VALLEY POETS, INC. (IV-Membership, anthology), Box 6203, Lawrenceville, NJ 08648, phone 609-737-0222, publications director Lois Marie Harrod. "We publish contemporary anthologies and broadsides of **poetry by invitation to submit and books or chapbooks by members who are ready to publish.**" They have recently published poetry by Maxine Kumin, Alicia Ostreicher, Theodore Weiss, Geraldine Clinton Little, David Keller, and Jana Harris. As a sample, Patricia Groth selected these lines from "Sparrow Against the Wind" by Patricia Viale Wuest:

> My grandmother
> so small against the pain
> like a sparrow tossed in the wind.
> I shiver to remember
> how cold her hands

They publish 1-3 books per year averaging 90 pages. **Members submit 6 samples, bio, publications. Reports in 6 months.** "For anthologies, poets must have some connection with the basic organization. Anthologies are paid for by DPV, Inc., and all sales go to the organization. Individual authors pay printing costs; individual editorial services and distribution are provided by DVP. All sales go to the author." Patricia Groth advises, "Poets serious about their work need to read all the poetry they can find, write poetry, attend poetry readings, and find someone to trade poetry and criticism with. If there is no workshop available, start one."

DELHI-LONDON POETRY QUARTERLY (II, IV-Themes), 50 Penywern Rd., London SW5 9SX England, phone 370-2255, founded 1977, poetry editor G. Warrier, is a literary quarterly with "emphasis on international writing, on spiritual, mystical, pilosophical, occult themes." **They want "1-2 pp. maximum, contemporary style"** and do not want "traditional, experimental." They have recently published poetry by Elizabeth Bartlett and Richard Bodien. As a sample the editor selected these lines (poet unidentified):

The **Delhi London Poetry Quarterly's** *sole purpose is to catalyze the spiritual potential in mankind, says editor Gopi Warrier. "The cover illustrates the primary concerns of mankind today as it evolves from a materialistic into a spiritual universe." The painting, which comes from Warrier's private collection, is by Indian artist G. Santosh.*

> *I tied my sword to a tree*
> *I watched it fall.*
> *I saw a silent wall shed*
>   *its edgelessness*

The magazine is beautifully printed with full-color covers, 7½×9½", 60 pp., flat-spined. There are b/w drawings throughout. It appears twice a year, press run of 5,000 for 2,000 subscriptions and 1,500 shelf sales. They accept about 10% of 500-1,000 submissions received per year. **Sample: £5. Pays £5 per poem. Previously published poems and simultaneous submissions OK. Their reports are "very late."** They sometimes sponsor contests.

DENVER QUARTERLY (II), University of Denver, Denver, CO 80208, phone 303-871-2892, founded 1965, editor Donald Revell, a quarterly literary journal that publishes fiction, poems, book reviews, and essays. **There are no restrictions on the type of poetry wanted.** They have recently published poetry by James Merrill, Linda Pastan, and William Matthews. As a sample, the editors selected the following lines from "The Inns and Outs of Irony" by William Logan:

> *All Britain this hospital between the guts*
> *and what scavenges after, vulture blood fledged*
> *with lies, light; lab where the dusty wish*
> *of culture cultures the dawn in its dish*

Denver Quarterly is 6×9", handsomely printed on buff stock, average 160 pp., flat-spined with two-color matte card cover. Circulation is 1,000, of which 600 are subscriptions (300 to libraries) and approximately 300 are sold on newsstands. Price per issue $5, subscription $15/year to individuals and $18 to institutions. **Samples of all issues after Spring 1985 are available for $5 postpaid, guidelines for SASE. Pay is 2 copies and a one-year subscription. No submissions read between May 15 and September 15 each year. Reporting time is 2-3 months.**

DEPOT PRESS (IV-Themes), Box 60072, Nashville, TN 37206, founded 1981, publishes books, **including poetry, relating to the South, Old West and Civil War.** "Our most recent title, however, is *Toreros*, the final collection of the late English lyric poet John Gawsworth (1912-1970)." Query with letter only.

DESCANT (III, IV-Regional), Box 314, Station P, Toronto, Ontario, Canada M5S 2S8, founded 1970, editor-in-chief Karen Mulhallen, calls itself **"The magazine that sings . . . a quarterly journal of the arts committed to being the finest in Canada. While our focus is primarily on Canadian writing we have published writers from around the world."** Some of the poets they have recently published are John Hollander, Peter Redgrave, Gwen MacEwen, Earle Birney and Irving Layton. As a sample, I selected the opening stanza of Lyn King's "Joyce and the Broken Window":

> *The day your hand fell to pieces*
> *and spilled itself like squeezed fruit*
> *into my fingers, I ran*
> *for towels, help, from you.*

It is an elegantly printed and illustrated flat-spined publication with colored, glossy cover, over-sized digest format, 140+ pp., heavy paper, with a circulation of 1,000 (800 subscriptions, of which 20% are libraries). **Sample: $7.50 postpaid.** They receive 1,200 freelance submissions per year, of which they use less than 10, with a 2 year backlog. **Guidelines available for SASE. Submit typed MS, unpublished work not in submission elsewhere, photocopy OK, name and address on first page and last name on each subsequent page. SASE with Canadian stamps or coupons. Reports within 4 months. They pay "approximately $50."** Karen Mulhallen says, "Best advice is to know the magazine you are submitting to. Choose your markets carefully."

‡**DESCANT: TEXAS CHRISTIAN UNIVERSITY LITERARY JOURNAL (II)**, English Dept., Texas Christian University, Fort Worth, TX 76129, 817-921-7240, founded 1956, editor Betsy Colquitt, appears twice a year. They want **"well-crafted poems of interest. No restrictions as to subject-matter or forms. We usually accept poems 40 lines or fewer but sometimes longer poems."** They have recently published poems by Walter McDonald and Lyn Lifshin. As a sample I selected the first stanza of "Worth" by Alberta Turner:

> *She does so want to be right about the way*
> *smoke rises, about what a dish pan*
> *emptied into a stream will feed,*
> *about the worth of her oath.*

It is 6×9", 92 pp. saddle-stapled, professionally printed, with matte card cover. Their press-run is 500, going to 350 subscribers. "We publish 30-40 pp. of poetry per year. We receive probably 4,000-5,000 poems annually. Per issue: $4.50; subscription: $8. **Sample: $2.50 postpaid. Pays 2 copies. Simultaneous submissions OK. Reports in 6-8 weeks, usually no more than 8 months until publication.**

DETROIT BLACK WRITERS' GUILD; WESTSIDE JOURNAL (IV-Ethnic, membership), 5601 W. Warren, Detroit, MI 48210, phone 313-897-2551, founded 1983, poetry coordinator Tom Lewis, is a "**small press publisher of books and a newsletter (poetry, fiction, how-to)."** They use Afro-American poetry. As a sample the editor selected these lines (poet unidentified):

> *Streets of city—where*
> *an old woman's purse is snatched*
> *unchaste girls sell their bodies*
> *teenage boys push not newspapers but dope.*

For book publication, poets "should consider joining our Guild and attend at least *one* of our workshops or seminars a year. Non-members may submit poetry for consideration. Can also write for free sample copy of newsletter. They publish 2 flat-spined 150 pp. paperbacks a year. **For book publication submit 3 samples and bio. No previously published poems. Pays copies. Membership: $6/year;** *Westside Journal:* **$6/year. Sample books available at 40% discount.** Their anthology, *Through Ebony Eyes*, is professionally printed, 112 pp., flat-spined with textured matte card cover, containing photos of each poet.

DEVIANCE (II, IV-Political, Spiritual, Social Issues), Box 1706, Pawtucket, RI 02862-1706, founded 1985, editor Lin R. Collette. The magazine appears three times a year, "dedicated to publishing work by persons espousing views that may differ from the 'majority.' This includes **feminist, lesbian/gay, non-religious or religious (i.e. discussions of religious issues that are not Judeo-Christian OR which may be an unorthodox view of Christianity or Judaism), political (non-Republican or Democratic, whether anarchist, socialist, etc.).** We would like to see more work focusing on politics, our personal relationships with the world, etc. We prefer that people write poetry that answers specific questions they may have or poses a situation or tells a story of sorts. Length is wide-open (no book-length, though). Study the master poets, traditional, contemporary, etc., for style. **If someone can write a good metered, rhymed poem, please send it! None of the usual nature meditations (green grass, falling rain) unless very well-done and unusual in thought; no homophobic, sexist, racist material; no gratuitous sex and violence. Please, none of the same old meditations on lovers, lost loves, etc. Unless well-done. We are getting too much of this."** They have recently published work by Trish Lehman and Patricia Slattery. As a sample, the editor selected these lines by John Grey:

> *That kind of dying is unwelcome here,*
> *No floods that sweep up half a city,*
> *just one or two heroes*
> *cuddling an American flag*
> *as they bleed our prosperity over*

> *some foreign shore . . .*

Deviance is magazine-sized, 37-50 pp., laser printed, with a taped spine, colored card cover, circulation 500 with 50 subscriptions, 250 shelf sales, $4.50 per issue, $12 for subscription of 3 issues. **Sample: $4.50 postpaid, checks payable to Lin Collette. SASE for guidelines. Pays 1 copy. Reports in 2-3 weeks. Submit maximum of 5 poems. SASE for guidelines or for replies to submissions; otherwise no reply will be sent. She comments on rejections "when appropriate; especially if it's something that might have worked for us."** She says "Publishing poetry is probably one of the more difficult avocations anyone can have. However, it's a craft as much as a hobby and it deserves to be written well. Be familiar with current and past poetry styles, but develop your own in response to them. Pick up books on writing poetry, but the most important thing is to read poetry itself, not just handbooks. Avoid clichés, and tired situations and subjects. Most of the 'new age' material we've been getting has been really awful—please be certain to write well on this subject, if you insist on doing so. Also, love poetry, if not done very well, can be really tiresome. Although *Deviance* is not specifically a women's publication and is for everyone, we'd like to see more feminist work than we've been getting."

THE DEVIL'S MILLHOPPER PRESS; THE DEVIL'S MILLHOPPER; KUDZU POETRY CONTEST (II), College of Humanities, University of South Carolina at Aiken, 171 University Parkway, Aiken, SC 29801, founded 1976, editor Stephen Gardner, publishes one magazine issue of *The Devil's Millhopper* each year and one chapbook, winner of an annual competition. **They want to see any kind of poetry, except pornography or political propaganda, up to 100 lines.** Some of the poets they have published recently are Susan Ludvigson, Ann Darr, Robert Gibb, Walt McDonald, Jared Carter, R. T. Smith, B. H. Fairchild, and Dorothy Barresi. As a sample the editor chose these lines from "Late August" by Kate Jennings:

> *The tips of the maple's leaves turn*
> *first, like sheets of paper that singe*
> *around the edges before scorching*
> *to burst up to flame: a burning bush.*

That is from the winner of their 1988 chapbook contest, **Malice,** handsomely printed 32 pp., saddle-stapled, on quality eggshell stock with matte textured card cover. The print run of *Devil's Millhopper* is 500. The annual chapbook has a print run of 600, going to 375 subscribers of which 20 are libraries. The magazine is digest-sized, 28-40 pp., saddle-stapled, printed on good stock with matte card cover and using beautiful b/w original drawings inside and on the cover. **Sample; $2.50 postpaid. Send SASE for their annual Kudzu Poetry Contest rules—prizes of $50, $100, and $150, $3 per poem entry fee, chapbook competition rules and guidelines for magazine submissions. They want name and address on every page of submissions, no simultaneous submissions. Photocopy and dot-matrix OK if it is dark, readable type. Pays copies. Reports usually in 2 months. Chapbook competition requires either $5 reading fee or $9 subscription for 2 years. Pays $50 plus 50 copies. Sometimes the editor comments on rejected MSS.** He advises, "There is no substitute for reading a lot and writing a lot or for seeking out tough criticism from others who are doing the same."

DIALOGUE: A JOURNAL OF MORMON THOUGHT (IV-Religious), University Station UMC 7805, Logan, UT 84322-7805, founded 1966, poetry editor Linda Sillitoe, "is an independent quarterly established to express Mormon culture and to examine the relevance of religion to secular life. It is edited by Latter-Day Saints who wish to bring their faith into dialogue with the larger stream of Judeo-Christian thought and with human experience as a whole and to foster artistic and scholarly achievement based on their cultural heritage. The views expressed are those of the individual authors and are not necessarily those of the Mormon Church or of the editors." **They publish 3-5 poems in each issue, "humorous and serious treatments of Mormon topics or universal themes from a Mormon perspective. Under 40 lines preferred. Must communicate with a well-educated audience but not necessarily sophisticated in poetic criticism. Free verse OK but only if carefully crafted."** They have published poetry by Emma Lou Thayne, Robert A. Rees, Marden Clark, and Linda Sillitoe. The editor selected these sample lines from "For Brother de Mik" by Dian Saderup:

> *Cupped in your papery palm the rose*
> *was like a wound, flowering.*
> *Your wife nodded when we brought it.*
> *Yes, Papa, yes is pretty . . .*

They have a circulation of 4,000-4,500 subscriptions of which 150 are libraries. The journal has

Market categories: (I) Beginning; (II) General; (III) Prestige; (IV) Specialized; (V) Closed.

an elegant 6×9″ format, 170+ pp., with color, artistically decorated cover and tasteful b/w drawings within. They receive about 70 submissions/year, use 12-16. **Sample: $7 postpaid. Submit typed MS in triplicate, 1 poem per page. Acknowledges in 10 days, reports in 2 months. Payment is 10 offprints plus one contributor's copy.**

DIALOGUE, THE MAGAZINE FOR THE VISUALLY IMPAIRED (IV-Subscription), 3100 Oak Park Ave., Berwyn, IL 60402, phone 312-749-1908, founded 1962, editor Bonnie M. Miller, "is a general interest quarterly produced on ½ speed cassette in recorded disc, braille and large-print editions." **They use 6-8 poems in each issue, want poems up to 20 lines, not avant-garde. No light verse. "Our readers prefer traditional forms of poetry, blank verse, free verse and haiku. We do not want erotic poetry that is too graphic."** The poets they publish are "all blind and visually impaired readers of *Dialogue.*" The editor selected these sample lines from "Broken Time" by Valerie Moreno:

> *Brittle feelings,*
> *sharp as bones,*
> *Crack against the pressure*
> *of silence.*

In all editions they have a circulation of 50,000, many reading through the Library of Congress. They have 6,375 subscriptions of which 4,000 are libraries. They receive about 125 poems per year, use 32-38, try to keep the backlog under 1 year. **Samples are free to the visually impaired. Enclose a note indicating nature of serious visual impairment, request guidelines and read several issues. No returns or acknowledgements without a SASE. Submissions can be in any medium (including braille and tape) except handwriting, 3 poems. They pay in copies, report within 6 weeks, usually with comment.**

JAMES DICKEY NEWSLETTER (I), DeKalb College, 2101 Womack Rd., Dunwoody, GA 30338, founded 1984, editor Joyce M. Pair, a bi-annual newsletter devoted to study of James Dickey's works/ biography and bibliography. They **"publish a few poems of** *high* **quality."** The copy I have, which is 30+ pp. of ordinary paper, neatly offset (back and front), with a card back-cover in blue, stapled top left corner, contains 1 poem, "Haft Blossom," by R.T. Smith. Its opening lines are:

> *Long-sleeping, I rose in the morning*
> *and opened the door to sunlight.*
> *Trough water woke me with sunlight,*
> *dark and the other stars having*
> *yielded their power . . .*

The newsletter is published in the fall and spring. Single copy price is $3.50, subscription to individuals $5/year; $10 to institutions. **Sample available for $3.50 postage. Contributors should follow MLA style and standard MS form, sending 1 copy, double-spaced.** The editor's advice is: "Acquire more knowledge of literary history, metaphor, symbolism, and grammar, and, to be safe, the poet should read a couple of our issues."

DICKINSON STUDIES; HIGGINSON JOURNAL; DICKINSON-HIGGINSON PRESS (II, IV-Theme), 4508 38 St., Brentwood, MD 20722, phone (after 1 PM) 301-864-8527, founded 1968, poetry editor F. L. Morey, are publications of the Dickinson-Higginson press (membership $50 individuals, $100 for libraries for 3 years). Both magazines are semiannuals, sometimes with bonus issues (e.g. in 1984 there were 9 issues instead of the minimum 4 promised to members), all distributed free to about 250 subscribers of which 125 are libraries. *Dickinson Studies* is principally for scholarship on Emily Dickinson, but uses poems about her. *Higginson Journal* **has a special poetry issue about every two years and uses a few poems in each issue — "lyric, no didactic, narrative or long dramatic; all styles welcome. No sentimental, moral; up to 50 lines in any form."** They have published poems by Roger White, Niels Kjaer, and Lyn Lifshin. As a sample, the editor chose "A Recital Featuring Some Minor Klavierstucke by Beethoven" by Michael L. Johnson:

> *The bored culturati are hunched*
> *with respectful intensity,*
> *listening for the nuances*
> *of a pianist who almost*
> *competently plays these pieces*
> *weary Ludwig wrote at the end*
> *of a long day and, if he'd thought,*
> *probably would have thrown away.*

The address of each poet is printed with the poem. The journals are both digest-sized, about 30 pp., saddle-stapled, typeset with card covers and b/w art. **Sample: $4 postpaid. Submit 3-6 poems no longer than a page each. Reports in 1-2 weeks. No payment.** F. L. Morey, a retired professor, says he receives about 20 submissions for *DS*, of which he uses 10, and 50 for *HJ*, of which he uses 20. "I am really not wishing for a deluge of poems." The Dickinson-Higginson Press also has subsidy-published several collections of poems, the poet putting up $500 and the publisher $600 for printing a flat-spined paperback on quality paper.

The DOLPHIN LOG (IV-Children, themes), 8440 Santa Monica Blvd., Los Angeles, CA 90069, phone 213-656-4422, founded 1981, editor Pamela Stacey, is a bimonthly educational publication for children offered by The Cousteau Society. "Encompasses all areas of science, history and the arts as they relate to our global water system. Philosophy of magazine is to delight, instruct and instill an environmental ethic and understanding of the interconnectedness of living organisms, including people." They want to see **"poetry related to the marine environment, ecology, natural history or any water-related subject-matter to suit the readership of 7 to 15-year-olds and which will fit the concept of our magazine. Short, witty poems, thought-provoking poems encouraged. No dark or lengthy ones (more than 20 lines)."** The editor selected these sample lines from "I Found a Tiny Starfish" by Dayle Ann Dodds:

> *I found a tiny starfish*
> *In a tidepool by the sea.*
> *I hope whoever finds him next,*
> *Will leave him there like me!*
> *And the gift I've saved for you?*
> *The best that I can give:*
> *I found a tiny starfish,*
> *And for you, I let him live.*

I have not seen the bimonthly, which the editor describes as magazine-sized, 16 pp., saddle-stapled, offset, using full-color photographs widely throughout, sometimes art, no advertising. It circulates to 100,000 members, approximately 860 library subscriptions. Membership: $10 a year. **Sample: $2.50 postpaid. Pays $10-$50 on publication and 3 copies. Reports within 6 months, up to 1 year backlog. Dot-matrix, photocopies OK. Double-spaced. First-time use preferred.** The editor advises, "Become familiar with our magazine by requesting a sample copy and our guidelines. We are committed to a particular style and concept to which we strictly adhere and review submissions consistently. We publish only a limited amount of poetry each year."

DOLPHIN-MOON PRESS; SIGNATURES (II, IV-Regional), Box 22262, Baltimore, MD 21203, founded 1973, president James Taylor, managing editor Richard Byrne, is **"a limited edition (500-1,000 copies) press which emphasizes quality work (regardless of style), often published in unusual/'radical' format."** The writer is usually allowed a strong voice in the look/feel of the final piece. "We've published magazines, anthologies, chapbooks, pamphlets, perfect-bound paperbacks, records, audio cassettes, and comic books. All styles are read and considered, but **the work should show a strong spirit and voice. Although we like the feel of 'well-crafted' work, craft for its own sake won't meet our standards either.**" They have published poetry by Gian Lombardo, John Strausbaugh, John Logan, W. D. Snodgrass, Tom O'Grady, and Nobel Laureate Jaroslav Seifert. As a sample, I selected these opening lines from James Taylor's "Fells Point," one of the poems in the Signature **Baltimore: A City in Four Poems:**

> *First step. Land fall. A site*
> *in near future of a colonial black painter,*
> *shipwrights and quick to please prostitutes.*
> *Some towns are born old and born hookers.*

The four poems in Signature collections are printed on one side of a folded 9×20" card. On the other (title side) is a beautiful sepia photo cityscape of Baltimore. The other examples they sent are similarly elegant and unusual in design. I was sufficiently impressed that I sent them my own MS: *The Village: New and Selected Poems*, $8.95 paperback, $15.95 hardcover. **Send SASE for catalog and purchase samples, or send $10 for their 'sampler' (which they guarantee to be up to $20 worth of their publications). To submit, first send sample of 6-10 pp. of poetry and a brief cover letter. Replies to query in 2-4 weeks, to submission of whole work (if invited) in 2-4 weeks. Payment in author's copies.** "Our future plans are to continue as we have since 1973, publishing the best work we can by local, up-and-coming and nationally recognized writers and publishing their work in a quality package."

THE DOMINION REVIEW (II), Old Dominion University, Bal 200, English Dept., Norfolk, VA 23529-0078, phone 804-683-3000, founded 1982, faculty advisor Wayne Ude, Creative Writing, who says, **"There are no specifications as to subject-matter, or style, but we are dedicated to the free verse tradition and will continue to support it. No poetry which has no sense of discipline toward language or which does not give a new perspective on any subject provoked by *any* motivation."** They have recently published poetry by Bob Perlongo, Paul Genega, and Grace P. Simpson. As a sample I selected these lines from "Pictures Looked at Once More" by Alberto Rios:

> *August lightning opens the afternoon sky*
> *As one might open an egg.*
> *Opens, or breaks, the same way*

Those album photographs get ripped
Then scotch taped back together.
TDR is flat-spined, 80 pp., digest-sized, professionally printed, and appears each spring. They have 300 subscriptions. **Guidelines available for SASE. No more than 5 poems per submission. No pay. They will not consider previously published poems. Reports in 3-5 months. "We would like a cover letter."**

DOOR COUNTY ALMANAK; THE DRAGONSBREATH PRESS (II, IV-Regional, themes), 10905 Bay Shore Dr., Sister Bay, WI 54234, phone 414-854-2742, press founded 1973, *DCA* founded 1982, poetry editor Fred Johnson. Dragonsbreath is a "small press producing a very small number of handmade, **limited edition books aimed at art and book collectors. He is presently not considering book MSS.** *Door County Almanak* **is a regional annual, each issue having a major theme of local interest.** The magazine has 5-10 pp. of poetry in each issue. The editor says he receives "very much" poetry and accepts "very little." I have not seen *DCA*, but the editor describes it as 300-400 pp. 6×9″, offset, flat-spined paperback using art, photos and ads, average press run 4,000. **Sample: $7.95 plus postage and handling. Send SASE for guidelines. Pays 2 copies. Simultaneous submissions and previously published poems OK.** Fred Johnson says, "Writers should be more selective of what they send out as samples. Because of lack of time for anything but the *Almanac*, I am not at this time looking for any book manuscripts."

DRAGONFLY: EAST/WEST HAIKU QUARTERLY; MIDDLEWOOD PRESS (IV-Form), Box 11236, Salt Lake City, UT 84147, phone 801-966-8034, *Dragonfly* founded 1965, Middlewood Press founded 1985, poetry editors Richard Tice and Jack Lyon. "We publish **haiku and short renku (linked verse sequences), translations of contemporary Japanese haiku,** artwork and Japanese calligraphy, explications of Japanese haiku, and articles on haiku history, criticism, and theory. We also hold **quarterly haiku and capping lines contests** with cash prizes. We are **open to beginners' work,** helping poets to understand the form and to write up to the level of the magazine. **We prefer haiku in the mainstream Japanese haiku tradition** — similar to the work of Basho, Buson, Issa, and Shiki. The well-known 5-7-5 syllable count is not too effective in English — it makes wordy haiku — but otherwise we look for 3-line poems that reflect strong qualities of time and perception, avoid figurative language or editorializing, use concrete images and pivot words, and keep the human ego from overpowering the elements in the poem. We do not want to see poetry that is not haiku or renku. We do not publish tanka or senryu. We do not want to see 3-line poems written according to Western literary theory."** They have recently published haiku by Tombo (Lorraine Ellis Harr), Sara Lee Skydell, Takada Sakuzo, Humphrey Noyes, Emily Romano, and Everett Briggs. As a sample the editors selected this haiku by Nancy Stewart Smith:

the old woman naps
beneath the sunflower—
head heavy with seed

Dragonfly is 64 pp.; saddle-stitched, digest-sized, offset, 2-color card cover, using sumie (carbon-ink brush drawings) and Japanese calligraphy, no ads. They accept about 10% of 8,000-10,000 haiku received per year. Press run: 400 for 360 subscriptions of which 30 are libraries. Subscription: $12. **Sample: $3.50 postpaid. Send SASE for free guidelines. Pays contributor copies for artwork, articles, and student haiku only. Prefer batches of 5 haiku or less, each on half of 8½×11″ paper with name and address on each half-sheet. Sequences may be longer. No simultaneous submissions or previously published poems. Reports in 4-5 months. Editors "quite often" comment on rejections.** Middlewood Press publishes collections of a poet's output over many years in the Haiku Life Works Series, **by invitation only,** pays 10% royalties. Despite the popularity of haiku, we still receive a preponderance of poetry that exhibits misconceptions about the form. *Dragonfly* **not only showcases haiku, but it also examines the form.** Richard Tice advises, "Understanding haiku theory is essential to write haiku acceptable by the dozen or more haiku magazines in the English-speaking world. I'd recommend Blyth's 4-volume work on haiku, Harold Henderson's **Introduction to Haiku**, William Higginson and Penny Harter's **The Haiku Handbook**, Cor van den Heuvel's **The Haiku Anthology**, and Donald Keene's **World within Walls** — all available from major publishers."

DRAGONGATE PRESS (V), 508 Lincoln St., Port Townsend, WA 98368, publishes poetry but **accepts no unsolicited MSS.** Catalog available.

DRAMATIKA, EPISTOLARY STUD FARM (IV-Themes, form), 429 Hope St., Tarpon Springs, FL 34689, phone 813-937-0109, founded 1968, editor and publisher John Pyros, has an **emphasis on theater and mail art.** It is a magazine that appears in various formats. **Pays 1 copy.**

‡DREAM INTERNATIONAL QUARTERLY (I, IV-Theme), Western Hemisphere editor Charles I. Jones, 121 N. Ramona St., #27, Ramona CA 92065; or Eastern Hemisphere editor Les Jones, 256 Berserker St., N. Rockhampton, Queensland 4701 Australia. Founded 1980. *DIQ* is devoted "to stimulating **interest in and research related to dreams and sleep.**" The poetry they use can be **"any form and style but must be related definitely to dreams. No restrictions except that of good taste (may be erotic if not offensive)."** Poets recently published include Gail Shafarman, Jessie Stewart Yandow, Caryl Porter and Kathleen Youmans. The editors chose this sample from "Sometimes I Sing on a String" by Takehiko Matsumoto:

> *Sometimes I sing on a string,*
> *In a deep space in the universe.*
> *I see a ship far away*
> *Away beyond the universe*
> *Sailing on the stream of time . . ..*

They have a circulation of 400 with 70 subscriptions, receive about 450 submissions per year and use 150. **Sample: $4 postpaid. Submit no more than 7 double-spaced pages, photocopy, dot-matrix OK, queries unnecessary. Pays in copies. Reports in 6 weeks. Guidelines available for SASE. Awards (subscriptions or cash) for annual best contributions. Sometimes comments on MSS.** The editors advise, "Since we're international, coax your friends in other countries to submit their dreams, in both English and their native languages . . . as a way to promote Peace in Our Galaxy."

DREAMS AND NIGHTMARES (IV-Science fiction/fantasy), 4801 Cypress Creek #1004, Tuscaloosa, AL 35405, phone 205-553-2284, founded 1986, editor David C. Kopaska-Merkel, is published quarterly. The editor says, **"I want to see intriguing poems in any form or style which are under about 60 lines (but will consider longer poems). All submissions must be either science fiction, fantasy, or horror (I prefer supernatural horror to gory horror). Nothing trite or sappy, very long poems, poems without fantastic content, excessive violence or pointless erotica. Sex and/or violence is OK if there is a good reason."** He has recently used poetry by Bruce Boston, Robert Frazier, Donna Zelzer, John Grey, Edward Mycue, Beverly J. Poston, and Ann K Schwader. As a sample he selected these lines from "The Book of Mirrors" by David Lunde:

> *You adjust your glasses*
> *and open the book*
> *of embracings*
> *to your favorite picture,*
> *but someone has marked your place*
> *with the edge of a razor.*

It has 20 pp., digest-sized, photocopied from typescript, saddle-stapled, with a colored paper cover and b/w illustrations. They accept about 60 of 600-800 poems received. Press run is 175 for 60 subscriptions. **Samples: $1 in stamps. 6 issue subscription $5. Send SASE for guidelines. Pays $2 per poem plus 1 copy. No simultaneous submissions. "Rarely" uses previously published poems. Reports in 2-6 weeks, 1-4 months.** The editor says "Speculative poetry has gained much recognition of late; most professional speculative fiction magazines publish some poetry. My advice is to actively seek information about new markets, to write a lot of poems, and to submit poems as often as necessary."

DRUID PRESS (II), 2724 Shades Crest Rd., Birmingham, AL 35216, phone 205-967-6580, founded 1981, president Anne George. "We do individual chapbooks. **We want to see concrete images, free verse, any subject-matter. No June-moon rhymes."** They have published poetry by R.T. Smith, Sue Walker, Sue Scalf, John Brugaletta, and many others. As a sample the editor selected these lines (poet unidentified):

> *South of Montgomery along the interstate*
> *redtailed hawks perch on bare trees*
> *and watch the traffic pushing through*
> *the heaviness of late fall rain*

For chapbook or book consideration query with 5 samples, bio, publications. Simultaneous submissions, photocopies, dot-matrix OK, but no previously published material. Reports in 3 weeks. Pays "Negotiable" number of author's copies. Sample books: $4 postpaid.

‡DUSTY DOG (I, II), P.O. Box 1103, Zuni, NM 87327, phone 505-782-4958, founded 1990, editor/publisher John Pierce, appears twice a year using **"accessible, humanistic poetry related to real life. Make a lasting impression, use fresh imagery. All forms and styles considered. Looking for poetry from new talent as well as established talent. Submit in batches of 3-10 poems up to 20 lines. Avoid religious and pornographic themes."** Simultaneous submissions and previously published poems OK. **Reports in 2-4 weeks.** Subscription: $8/year. Sample, postpaid: $4.25. **Pays 1 copy.** This new publication was planned to be 24 pp., digest-sized, saddle-stapled, using b/w art and photos. The editor expects to accept 10-20% of poetry received. He says, "Beginning poets should read as much contemporary poetry as they can get their hands on. Don't let rejections dicourage you. Keep writing and keep sending as many MSS as you can."

EAGLE WING PRESS (IV-Ethnic) Box 579MO, Naugatuck, CT 06770, phone 203-274-7738, founded 1981, poetry editor Ron Welburn, is an **American Indian newspaper** appearing every other month. **Poems must be on American Indian themes or written by American Indians. "Try to avoid 'typical' pieces that try to sound 'Indian.' We are looking for clear, concise, strong poetry."** They have recently published poetry by Joseph Bruchac and Ed Edmo. As a sample the editor selected lines from the poem "Just a Bundle of Twigs" by Mary Good Seeds Woman:

> *just a bundle of twigs*
> *beautiful*
> *perfect*
> *tied together with a root*
> *to keep the dream alive*

The newspaper is tabloid-sized, 28 pp., unstapled, with graphics and ads, circulation 4,700 to 3,900 subscriptions of which 120 are libraries, about 600 shelf sales. Subscriptions are $10 a year. **Sample: $2 postpaid. Pays 5 copies.**

EARTH'S DAUGHTERS: A FEMINIST ARTS PERIODICAL (IV-Women/Feminist), Box 41 Central Park Station, Buffalo, NY 14215, phone 716-837-7778, founded 1971, **submit to co-editor Bonnie Johnson, Box 143, Lockport, NY 14094.** The "literary periodical **with strong feminist emphasis**" appears 3 times a year, irregularly spaced. Its "format varies. Most issues are flat-spined, digest-sized issues of approximately 60 pp. We also publish chapbooks, magazine-sized and tabloid-sized issues. Past issues have included broadsheets, calendars, scrolls, and one which could be assembled into a box." Those I have seen are elegantly printed and illustrated on glossy stock with glossy card covers. **Poetry can be "up to 40 lines (rare exceptions for exceptional work), free form, experimental — we like unusual work. All must be strong, supportive of women in all their diversity. We like work by new writers, but expect it to be well-crafted. We want to see work of technical skill and artistic intensity. We rarely publish work in classical form, and we never publish rhyme or greeting card verse."** They have published poetry by Kathryn Daniels, Toni Mergentime Levi, Lyn Lifshin, Eileen Moeller, Joan Murray, and Susan Fantl Spivack, "and many fine 'unknown' poets, writers and artists." They publish poetry by men if it is supportive of women. As a sample the editor selected *#33/34: Lost in the Woods* "Entering the Surroundings" by Ann Fox Chandonnet:

> *Entering the surroundings*
> *one does not speak.*
> *One enters into the chickadee*
> *eating alder seeds/upside down,*
> *and into the dry crunch of snow underfoot.*

"Our purpose is to publish primarily work that otherwise might never be printed, either because it is unusual, or because the writer is not well known." Subscription: $12/3 issues for individuals; $20 for institutions. **Sample: $4 postpaid. Send SASE for guidelines. Some issues have themes, which are available for SASE after April of each year. Pays 2 copies and reduced prices on further copies. Length of reporting time is atrociously long if MSS is being seriously considered for publication, otherwise within 3 weeks. Simultaneous submissions, photocopied copies, dot-matrix OK. "Per each issue, authors are limited to a total of 150 lines of poetry, prose, or a combination of the two. Submissions in excess of these limits will be returned unread. Business-size envelope is preferred, and use sufficient postage — we do not accept mail with postage due." Editor comments "whenever we have time to do so — we want to encourage new writers."** The collective says: "Once you have submitted work, please be patient. The U.S. Mail is dependable, and we have yet to lose a manuscript. Our eight collective members have fulltime jobs, extra curricular activities and the demands of their own artistic pursuits in addition to their commitment (unpaid) to the publication of *ED* magazine. For this reason, we get impatient with writers who inquire too soon or too frequently as to the status of their work. We only hold work we are seriously considering for publications, and it can be up to a year between acceptance and publication. If you must contact us (change of address, notification that a simultaneous submission has been accepted elsewhere), be sure to state the issue theme, the title(s) of your work and enclose SASE."

EARTHWISE PUBLICATIONS/PRODUCTIONS; EARTHWISE LITERARY CALENDAR; EARTHWISE RE-VIEW (I-II), Box 680-536, Miami, FL 33168, 305-653-2875, founded 1978, poetry editors Barbara Holley and Sally Newhouse. "Earthwise Press/Publications, is engaged in a wide variety of activities for both the beginning and intermediate poet/writer/artist. We continually accept work for our **Earthwise**

Literary Calendar and **Earthwise Review**." They have published poetry by Nikki Giovanni, Robert Creeley, and Rita Dove. Barbara Holley chose these lines from "Poems Are No More Written Than Water" by J.B. Mulligan:

> *Words are only the eyes*
> *Through which you see yourself*
>
> *The poem is you*

Pays $5 per poem for *Earthwise.* **They try to report within 30-90 days.** "Write us. We try to answer promptly. Our advice to readers is Never forget SASE—never forget editors are persons, too; we need a name/address on each piece of submitted material in case any of it is separated from its source—keep submitting; your work is the 'stuff that dreams are made of.' " **Samples calendar/review $5.50.**

‡**EASTERN CARIBBEAN INSTITUTE(I, IV-Regional)**, Box 1338, Frederiksted, U.S. Virgin Islands 00841, phone 809-772-1011, founded 1982, editor S.B. Jones-Hendrickson, editoral contact Sandra Thomas; is a "small-press publisher with plans to expand," **especially interested in poetry of the Caribbean and Eastern Caribbean "but open to all subjects, style, and form."** As a sample the editor selected these lines (poet unidentified):

> *Beauty is skin deep, the sages say,*
> *and truth changes from day to day,*
> *but if truth is beauty and heaven sent,*
> *I relaxed in a beautiful apartment.*

Those last two lines rhyme in the Virgin Islands. Their books are softcover, averaging 60 pp. Sample copies available for purchase. **Submit 5 sample poems, cover letter with bio and previous publications. Simultaneous submissions and previously published poems OK. Reports in one month. Pays 50 copies.** The editor says, "In our part of the world, poetry is moving on a new level. People who are interested in regional poetry should keep an eye on the Caribbean region. There is a new focus in the Virgin Islands."

‡**ECHOES (II)**, P.O. Box 365, Wappingers Falls, NY 12590, founded 1985, editor Marcia W. Grant, "is a quarterly literary magazine that features quality prose and poetry from well-established as well as talented emerging writers. *Echoes* **has no rigid specifications as to form, length, subject-matter, style, or purpose. Excellence is the determining factor. Usual length of accepted poems is 20-40 lines, longer if exceptional. Wants to see poems whose ideas and imagery are clearly focused, well-crafted, and unusual. No sing-song rhyme, erotica, or effusive amateur efforts."** They have recently published poetry by Katherine M. Aal, Karl Elder, Gayle Elen Harvey, J.B. Goodenough, and Robert Cooperman. As a sample the editor selected these lines from "Mother and Son Reunion" by Linda Back McKay:

> *Her finger traced the familiar shape*
> *of his nail; two hands that, but for dark*
> *leaps of time's hunger, should have known*
> *each other like gloves.*

Echoes is currently magazine-sized, 44 pp., saddle-stapled, photocopied from typescript with matte card cover. (Format changes currently under consideration.) Press run 250 for about 100 subscriptions, of which 12 are libraries, some shelf sales. Subscription: $15; (libraries, $12.) **Sample, postpaid: $4.50 current issue; $3 back issue. Send SASE for guidelines. Reporting time generally 6-10 weeks. Pays 1 copy. "Five poems should be maximum submitted at one time. Contributor's notes requested." Previously published submissions OK if poet owns rights. Editor comments on submissions "rarely."** The editor says, "Poets must read good poetry to know good poetry. Familiarize yourself with our magazine before you submit."

‡**EDGE (II)**, 1933-8 Hazama-cho, Hachioji-shi, Tokyo, Japan 193, phone 0426-66-3481, founded 1988, editor Richard Evanoff, poetry editor Sherry Reniker, is an "international literary quarterly publishing poetry, fiction, features, art, and networking information. In addition, we do interviews with poets, reviews of poetry books published in Japan and abroad, poetry-related art, and publish information on readings, workshops, publications, etc., related to poetry. One of our aims is to serve as a *bridge* between Japan and overseas." They are **"looking for the play of sounds, image, energy, the grounded voice, experiments, translations; all forms are acceptable. Under 50 lines is best. No sexist or ethnic stereotypes. No hackneyed imagery about Mt. Fuji, cherry blossoms, etc., or romanticized views of Japan."** They have recently published poetry by Shuntaro Tanikawa, Kris & Tadashi Kondo, essay by Cid Corman, interviews with Allen Ginsberg and Arne Naess. As a sample the editor selected these lines by Judy Katz-Levine:

> *One day you wake up. I mean really wake up. Your eyes are*
> *moons on an ice-cold day. You are thirsty, your octopus*

> *thoughts grapple for a mirror. Your memories touch upon*
> *damp walls, send out high-pitched noises. . . .*

Edge is professionally printed on matte with glossy cover, $7 \times 10''$. Press run 600 for 300 subscriptions. Subscription: $23 overseas rate (3,000 Yen). **Sample, postpaid: $6 (500 Yen). Send SASE for guidelines.** Pays 2 copies. **"We welcome subscriptions from contributors since part of what we're trying to do is to create a sense of community for writers in English in Japan and abroad."** Contributors who don't need to have their work returned and who simply want a reply as to whether or not their work has been accepted should include a minimum of 100 Yen in postage stamps (no foreign stamps) or 2 IRCs (International Reply Coupons, purchased at the post office). They sponsor an annual poetry contest "sometimes theme-related and with various sponsors. A good selection of 4 or 5 poems should be sent as a submission. Reporting time 1-2 months. *Editor's Note*: As *Poet's Market* went to press we were notified that *Edge* ceased publication with the Autumn 1990 issue. Back issues of the magazine are available by mail order.

EDICIONES UNIVERSAL (IV-Ethnic, foreign language, regional), 3090 SW 8 St., Miami, FL 33135, phone 305-642-3234, founded 1964, general manager Marta Salvat-Golik, is a small-press subsidy publisher of **Spanish language books.** "We specialize in Cuban authors and themes." They have recently published books of poetry by Olga Rosalo and Amelia del Castillo. **Poets "must be able to purchase in advance 75% of the copies, due to the fact that poetry does not sell well." Poets receive the copies they paid for. Submit sample, bio, publications. Reports in 2 weeks.**

‡EGORAG; EGORAG PRESS (I, II, IV-Social), 4836 Ross St., Red Deer, AL T4N 5E8 Canada, founded 1989, editor Clarence Meinema, appears every-other-month using **"5-25 lines of clear poetry that explores the struggles of mankind in the world today (social issues). No nature, religion."** They have recently published poetry by Robert Stallsworthy, Melody Szabo, Macdonald Coleman, and Brian Chan. As a sample I selected the opening lines from "Doubtless" by C.A. Kamenka:

> *Entering the night doubtless*
> *our bodies follow an unseen choreographer*
> *under whose direction we dance the dance.*

It is 30 pp., saddle-stapled, digest-sized, with matte card cover. Press run 150 for 85 subscribers. Subscription: $30. **Sample, postpaid: $2.50. "Subscribers receive a small honorarium ($5); non-subscribers receive a submitter's copy." Submit MSS double-spaced.** Egorag Press published 6 chapbooks in 1990. For chapbook consideration **submit 50 pp., $10 reading fee, brief bio, publications. Pays $35 plus 10 copies.** "Authors are expected to promote their own work by readings."

EIDOS MAGAZINE: EROTIC ENTERTAINMENT FOR WOMEN, MEN & COUPLES (IV-Erotica/Women), Box 96, Boston MA 02137, founded 1982, poetry editor Brenda Loew Tatelbaum. "Our press publishes erotic literature, photography and artwork. Our purpose is to provide an alternative to women's images and male images and sexuality depicted in mainstream publications like *Playboy, Penthouse, Playgirl*, etc. We provide a forum for the discussion and examination of two highly personalized dimensions of **female sexuality: desire and satisfaction. We do not want to see angry poetry or poetry that is demeaning to either men or women. We like experimental, avant-garde material."** Poets they have recently published include Judith Arcana. *Eidos* is professionally printed, tabloid-format, with fine photography and art, **number of poems per issue varies**, print run 10,000, over 7,000 subscriptions. **Sample: $10 postpaid.** They receive hundreds of poems per year, use about 10. Backlog 6 months to a year. **1 page limit on length, format flexible, photocopy, dot-matrix, simultaneous submissions OK, reports in 4-8 weeks, payment: 1 copy, guidelines available for SASE. Only accepts sexually explicit material.** Comment or criticism provided as often as possible. Brenda Loew Tatelbaum advises, "There is so much poetry submitted for consideration that a rejection can sometimes mean a poet's timing was poor. We let poets know if the submission was appropriate for our publication and suggest they resubmit at a later date. Keep writing, keep submitting, keep a positive attitude."

THE EIGHTH MOUNTAIN PRESS; EIGHTH MOUNTAIN POETRY PRIZE (IV-Women, feminist), 624 SE 29th Ave., Portland, OR 97214, founded 1985, editor Ruth Gundle, is a "small press publisher of **feminist literary works by women.** The have recently published poetry by Judith Barrington and Irena Klepfisz. They publish 1 book of poetry per year, averaging 115 pp. **We now publish poetry *only* through the Eight Mountain Poetry Prize. Pays 8-10% royalties.** The Eighth Mountain Poetry Prize is an annual award of a $1,000 advance and publication for a book of 50-120 pp. written by a woman, no restrictions as to subject matter. Send SASE for rules. Submit during January and February. "The selection will

Use the General Index to find the page number of a specific publication or publisher.

be made anonymously. Therefore, the MS must have a cover sheet giving all pertinent information (title, name, address, phone number). No identifying information except the title should appear on any other MS page. The contest will be judged by a different feminist poet each year, whose name will be announced after the winning MS has been chosen." The 1990 contest was judged by Marilyn Hacker.

EL BARRIO (IV-Ethnic, regional); CASA DE UNIDAD (V), 1920 Scotten, Detroit, MI 48209, phone 313-843-9598, founded 1982, poetry editor Marta Lagos. They publish **poetry from Latino residents of the SW Detroit area concerning life, family, politics, repression, etc., but do not normally accept unsolicited material. Query first. "Nothing obscene. We are family oriented."** They have recently published poetry by Ana Cardona, Jose Garza, Victoria Gonzalez, Marta Lagos, Jacquelyn Sanchez, Trinidad Sanches S.F., Abel Pineiro, and Anibal Bourdon. As a sample the editor selected these lines from "from trinidad, the man" by Lolita Hernandez:

> now time and place
> has this same concept
> in one man
> with possibility
> to cross all those colors
> to show time
> that things like that
> can be done in another place

El Barrio is "to keep the Latino people of the SW Detroit area informed, to give them an opportunity to speak to the community." It appears 3-4 times a year, magazine-sized, about 28 pp., professionally printed with commissioned art on the matte card cover, using up to 3 poems per issue. Their press run is 5,000, $3 per issue, $12 for a subscription. **Sample: $3 postpaid. Send SASE for guidelines. Pays 1 copy upon request. They sometimes use previously published poems but no simultaneous submissions.** The press has published an anthology: **Detroit: La Onda Latina en Poesía** ($6). If you query about **book publication, send 3-5 copies and bio. You must be from the SW Detroit area.**

EL GATO TUERTO; EDICIONES, DE EL GATO TUERTO (IV-Ethnic, translations, bilingual), Box 210277, San Francisco, CA 94121, phone 415-752-0473, founded 1984, editor Carlota Caulfield, assistant editor Servando Gonzalez. "El Gato Tuerto Ediciones is a small press interested in **new or unpublished Spanish and Latin American poets.** *El Gato Tuerto* is a literary quarterly. We welcome work dealing **with Spanish, Latin American, and Caribbean literatures. We are especially interested in poetry by Hispanic women writers. We publish in English or Spanish. Translations must be accompanied by the originals. We are not especially interested in long poems."** They have recently published poetry by Miguel Angel Zapata, Luisa Futoransky, Soledad Fariña, Iraida Iturralde, Juana Rosa Pita, Pietro Civitareale, Gregory McNamee, H.D. Moe, Linda McFerrin, and Lourdes Gil. As a sample they selected these lines from "Electra, Clitemnestra" by Magali Alabau:

> They place a rectangle
> in the circle.
> The final witness offers Clytemnestra
> the final message from Iphigenia
> a blindfold.

El Gato Tuerto (The One-Eyed Cat) is a 10-page 8½ × 11″ gazette, circulation 1,000, $1.50/issue. Subscription: $8 individuals, $12 institutions. Some 200 copies are sent to poets in Spain, Argentina, Italy, Mexico, etc. **Sample: $2 postpaid. SASE always. Pays 2 copies. Submit double-spaced, typewritten pages, no more than 5 poems. Simultaneous submissions OK. Reports in 7-10 weeks.**

EL TECOLOTE (IV-Ethnic), Box 40037, San Francisco, CA 94140, phone 415-824-7878, founded 1970, is a "community newspaper with **subject matter primarily about Latin America.** Much cultural coverage in general, but not a lot of poetry. Monthly. They want **"short (1 page or less) poems inspired by life in U. S. Latino communities or in Latin America. Would like to see poetry that acknowledges the struggle of Latino/as who must live in a culture different from their own.** The struggle both uncovers our history and creates a positive role model for the future. Open to poetry by either sex, sexual preference, and all ages." They have recently published poetry by Manilio Argueta from El Salvador. *El Tecolote* (The Owl) is a tabloid, l6 pp., using art, graphics, and ads, press run 10,000. They accept about 1 out of 10 pages of poetry submitted. **Submit double-spaced, with name and address on each sheet. Simultaneous submissions and previously published poems OK.**

‡ELDRITCH TALES MAGAZINE OF WEIRD FANTASY; YITH PRESS (IV-Horror), 1051 Wellington Rd., Lawrence, KS 66049, editor Crispin Burnham, "a semiannual magazine of **supernatural horror,"** circulation 500. **Buys 5-10 poems on horror themes per year. Submit maximum of 3 poems 5-20 lines. Pays 10-25¢/line.**

THE ELEVENTH MUSE; POETRY WEST; POETRY WEST CONTEST (II), Box 2413, Colorado Springs, CO 80901, editors Diane Robinson and Jeremy Huffman, is published 2 times per year. *"The Eleventh Muse* welcomes quality submissions of contemporary poetry. No greeting card verse, *please."* Submit from 3-5 poems; typewritten, single-spaced. Photocopy OK. "Neatness counts. No length restrictions; however, one-page poems have a better chance of publication." No simultaneous submissions/no previously published work. Pays 1 copy. "Editors respond with personal comments, sometimes critique, within 6-8 weeks." Sample copy: $3.50 postpaid. Subscription (2 issues): $6/year. It is 30 pp. saddle-stapled, magazine-sized, photocopied from typescript, with matte card cover. Poets featured in a recent issue include Mark Cox, Gayle Elen Harvey and Jack Myers. As an example of the quality of poetry preferred, Diane Robinson selected the following lines from "A Pot of Comfort" by Anita Jepson-Gilbert:

> *The tea is patient, steeping wild chamomile*
> *in my grandmother's earthen pot.*
> *It calms the anxiousness of night*
> *the way her hand might have*

Copies of *The Eleventh Muse* are available by subscription, at bookstores in the Colorado Springs area, at poetry readings and through Poetry West memberships. Poetry West is an organization of poets which sponsors monthly poetry readings and workshops. Membership is $15/year, includes periodic newsletters and copies of *The Eleventh Muse*. A Poetry West Contest is held annually with a May 1 deadline for poems up to 40 lines. Prizes of $100, $50 and $25 are offered, plus publication in *The Eleventh Muse*.. As the contest grows, so will the prize money. Entry fee is $3/per poem for non-members. Members may enter 3 poems free. Previous judge was Victoria McCabe.

ELLIPSE (V, IV-Translations, bilingual), C.P. 10, FLSH Université de Sherbrooke, Sherbrooke Quebec, J1K 2R1, Canada, phone 819-821-7277, founded 1969, editors P. Godbout/C. Bouchara, **publishes French-English poetry in translation.** That is, on facing pages appear either poems in English and a French translation or poems in French and an English translation. **Currently they are not accepting unsolicited MSS.** They have recently published poetry by D. G. Jones, D. Livesay, A.M. Klein, and Lorna Crozier as well as R. Choquette, M. Beaulieu, S-D Garneau. As a sample, I selected the opening lines of "Winter Uplands" by Archibald Lampman:

> *The frost that sings like fire upon my cheek,*
> *The loneliness of this forsaken ground,*
> *The long white drift upon whose powdered peak*
> *I sit in the great silence as one bound;*

translated as "Des hauts plateaux d'hiver" by Joseph Bonenfant:

> *Le feu de la froidure aux joues cingle et me pique,*
> *Dans l'abandonnement de ce sol delaissé,*
> *Sur le long banc de neige à la cime poudreuse*
> *Je suis une frontière au centre du silence;*

The magazine appears twice yearly in an elegant flat-spined, $6 \times 9''$ format, professionally printed, 90+ pp. Subscription: $10. **Sample: $5 postpaid.**

EMBERS (II), Box 404, Guilford, CT 06437, phone 203-453-2328, founded 1979, poetry editors Katrina Van Tassel, Charlotte Garrett, Mark Johnson, a "poetry journal of talented new and occasional well-known poets." The editors say, "**no specifications as to length, form, or content. Interested in new poets with talent; not interested in lighter way-out verse, porn, or poetry that is non-comprehensible."** They have published poetry by Brendan Galvin, Walker MacDonald, Marilyn Waniek, and Sue Ellen Thompson. *Embers* is digest-sized, nicely printed on white stock with an occasional b/w photograph or drawing, 52 pp. flat-spined with one-color matte card cover handsomely printed in black; it appears twice a year—spring/summer and fall/winter. Price per issue is $6, subscription $11/year. **Sample available for $3 postpaid. Pay for acceptance is 2 copies. Submissions must be typed, previously unpublished, with name, address, and brief bio of poet. Deadlines: basically March 15 and October 15, but we read continuously.** Editors' advice is "Send for sample copies of any publication you are interested in. Be patient. Most editors read as quickly as they can and report likewise. If a poet sends in work at the beginning of a reading time, or long before a deadline, he/she will have to wait longer for answers. *Embers* editors are interested in the poet's voice and would like to read up to 5 submissions showing variety of subject, form, etc."

EMERALD CITY COMIX & STORIES (II), P.O. Box 95402, Seattle, WA 98145, phone 206-784-0162, founded 1985, editor Nils Osmar, is a tabloid appearing every other month, circulation 12,000, using "fantasy, SF, fiction, poetry, comics, reviews." They want "**any and all well-written poetry on any theme, no racist, misogynist."** They have recently published poetry by Laurel Speer, and Robert Bowie. As a sample the editor selected these lines by Judith Skillman:

We walk until the path
is a swath cut in the back
of the first animal: snow.
Its marble skin recedes like a claw.

The paper is 8-12 pp., newsprint. They print 15-20 of 50-60 poems received per year. The paper is distributed free, supported by ads. **Send SASE for guidelines. Pays 2 copies. They will consider simultaneous submissions and previously published poems "but we like to know where previously published." Reports in 2-3 months. Editor comments on rejections "sometimes."** They sometimes sponsor contests.

‡**THE EMSHOCK LETTER (IV-Subscribers)**, Box 411,Troy, ID 83871, phone 208-835-4902, founded 1977, editor Steve Erickson, appears 3-12 times a year with **poetry and other writings by subscribers.** It is **"a philosophical, metaphysical, sometimes poetic expression of ideas and events. It covers a wide range of subjects and represents a free-style form of expressive relation. It is a newsletter quite unlike any other."** I have not seen a copy, but the editor describes it as magazine-sized, 5-7 pp., photocopied from typescript on colored paper, subscription: $25 (as of January 1, 1991). **Pays 2 copies. "Poets [who are subscribers] should submit poetry which contains some meaning, preferably centering on a philosophic theme, and preferably 50 lines or less. Any good poetry (submitted by a subscriber) will be considered for inclusion, and will receive a personal reply by the editor, whether or not submitted material is published in** *The Emshock Letter*.**"**

‡**EN PASSANT POETRY (II)**, 4612 Sylvanus Dr., Wilmington, DE 19803, founded 1975, poetry editor James A. Costello, a poetry review, irregular, **uses about 34 pp. of poetry per issue, pays 2 copies.** They have recently published poetry by Léon-Paul Fargue, Judith Goodenough, Robert King, Mark Nepo, Celia Strome. These sample lines are by Jim Costello:

Crickets grind the corn to dust.

The couple sits fiddling
the bones of their hands
dreaming moonlight and loving
slow as the owl's pulse.

It is a flat-spined, digest-sized format with matte cover, tasteful b/w art, professional printing, circulation 300. **Sample copies $2.**

ENCOUNTER (III), 43/44 Gt. Windmill St., London WIV 7PA, England, editors Melvin J. Lasky and Anthony Hartley, poetry editor J.C. Hall, a prestige monthly (except July and December) which has published many of the major British and American poets. **Sample: $4.50 postpaid (surface mail). Submit maximum of 6 poems, 12-100 lines. Simultaneous submissions not welcome. SAE required. Pays variable fee.**

ENITHARMON PRESS (V, II, III), 40 Rushes Road, Petersfield, Hampshire, U.K., phone 0730 62753, founded 1969, poetry editor Stephen Stuart-Smith, is a publisher of fine editions of poetry and literary criticism in paperback and some hardback editions, about 12 volumes per year averaging 80 pages. **"Substantial backlog of titles to produce, so no submissions possible before 1992."** They have recently published books of poetry by John Heath-Stubbs, Phoebe Hesketh, David Gascoyne, Jeremy Hooker, Frances Horovitz, Ruth Pitter, Edwin Brock and Jeremy Reed.

ENVOI; ENVOI POETS (II, IV-Anthology), Pen Ffordd, Newport Dyfed SA42 0QT U.K., *Envoi* founded 1957, *Envoi Poets* founded 1985, editor-in-chief Anne Lewis-Smith (plus panel of 28 editors), wants **"Just good poems, technically good, not too long unless superb! No religious, political, none full of swear words."** They have recently published poetry by Bill Headdon, Teresina Malfatti, Gordon King, and Fay Chivers. As a sample this Haiku by Peggy Poole:

Gulls at the tide's edge
congregate like journalists
eager for pickings

Envoi is digest-sized, 44 pp. perfect bound, professionally litho printed with plastic covered glossy card cover, few ads, using poetry and reviews. It appears 3 times a year, print run of 900, 800 subscriptions of which 20+ are libraries. Subscription: £6 or $11.50. Single copy: £2. **Sample: £1 or $2 in bills (no checks) postpaid. Pays 2 copies. No simultaneous submissions. "6 poems is an ideal number, with name and address on each page please. If they are really good we publish. We are looking for craftsmanship as well as that extra spark which makes a good poem. Subscribing to** *Envoi* **not necessary but welcomed. No simultaneous submissions. Photocopy and dot-matrix OK. Reports to queries in 1 week, to MSS in 2-8 weeks. Each issue of the magazine has** a poetry competition with prizes of £75, £25 and £35. *"Envoi* has an editorial board of 29 poets, writers and lecturers who do a short criticism on every poem sent in by subscribers. Since the magazine was started over 30 years ago our aim has been to publish good poetry and, equally important, to help poets improve their writing and techniques. We believe that in a money oriented world the help we give is vital, assisting not only in better poetry but also in better relationships between editors and poets. Our advice to poets is when you have written a poem, put it away for 4-6 weeks, then on freshly looking at it, the faults are often clear." *Envoi Poets* is an imprint under which about 10 subsidized individual collections, 28 pp., are published each year in a format much like the magazine except that the covers are matte card. The 62nd individual collection of poetry has just been published. **For individual collections query with 6 samples, bio and credits.** *Envoi* published the first *Spring Anthology* in 1988, a hardback book containing work by over 90 modern poets. "This is a yearly feature and we welcome all enquiries accompanied by IRCs."

EPOCH; BAXTER HATHAWAY PRIZE (III), 251 Goldwin Smith, Cornell, Ithaca, NY 14853, founded 1947, has a distinguished and long record of publishing **exceptionally fine poetry** and fiction. They have published work by such poets as Ashbery, Ammons, Eshleman, Wanda Coleman, Molly Peacock, Robert Vander Molen and Alvin Aubert. The magazine appears 3 times a year in a professionally printed, $6 \times 9''$ flat-spined format with glossy b/w cover, 100+ pp., which goes to 900 subscribers. They use less than 1% of the many submissions they receive each year, have a 2-12 month backlog. **Sample: $4 postpaid. Reports in 2 months.** "We *don't read* unsolicited MSS between May 15 and September 15." **Pays $1 per line. Occasionally provides criticism on MSS.** The annual Baxter Hathaway prize of $1,000 is awarded for a long poem or, in alternate years, a novella (long poem will win in 1988 and be published in 1989). Submit between November 1 and November 30 of the year before. The editor advises, "I think it's extremely important for poets to read other poets. I think it's also very important for poets to read the magazines that they want to publish in. Directories are not enough."

EQUILIBRIUM; EAGLE PUBLISHING PRODUCTIONS (I, IV-Themes), Box 162, Golden, CO 80402, founded 1982. "**We are not responsible for any mail being received without our $3 processing fee for all submissions.** We publish everything and I mean everything **dealing with equilibrium: balance, opposites, pairs, equality, opposite and equal reactions, etc.**" They are open to "all types, lengths, and style. Very lenient!" on **themes given above.** The quarterly is striking in appearance, photocopied on pocket-edition $4\frac{1}{4}x8\frac{1}{2}''$ sheets of various colors, about 70 pp. saddle-stapled with glossy b/w paper cover, using many photos, drawings, and cartoons throughout. One page is devoted to "Poems," each with an illustration. The following sample is from "The Supposition of Opposition" by Caral Davis:

> The sun rises, just to fall.
> It's all for one and one for all.
> It rains on the rich and on the poor,
> The rich get richer and the poor get poorer.
> Winter withers summer away, only to revive
> another day.

Circulation 10,000, price per issue $4. Sample: $4 postpaid plus 5 (regular) stamps. Pays $15 and up plus 1 copy. Reports in 6 months. "We prefer to hold in files until needed." **Backlog 1-12 months. Editor sometimes comments on rejections.** He says, "We prefer for poets to keep a photocopy and send us the original for our files. They may be handwritten if you wish for your poem printed as such. It is best for the poet (even youngsters) to include art, pictures, etc., too. Letter and queries arriving at our office will become the property of our company and material may and will be published 'as-is.'"

ESSENCE (V, II, IV-Women, ethnic), 1500 Broadway, New York, NY 10036, phone 212-642-0649, founded 1970, Angela Kinamore, poetry editor, *"Essence* caters to the **needs of today's Black women. Currently not accepting poetry submissions.** *Essence* has recently published poems by Gwendolyn Brooks, Sonia Sanchez, and Lucille Clifton. The editor selected these sample lines, excerpted from the poem "Play it Again Sam" by Layding Lumumba Kaliba:

> Play it again sam, but not the way
> you played when Bogart demanded
> you rhapsody
> play it like you played it on the
> banks of the Nile
> when your name was Akhenaton and
> we were free
> Play it again sam, but this time
> from the heart
> play for our people, the ones who

gave civilization its start.
This is a mass-circulation consumer magazine, 140+ pp., slick stock with full-color art, photos and ads, with an upscale tone.

EVANGEL (IV-Religious), P.O. Box 535002, Indianapolis, IN 46253-5002, weekly since 1897, poetry editor Vera Bethel, **publishes an 8-page paper for adults. Nature and devotional poetry, 8-16 lines, "free verse or with rhyme scheme."** The circulation is 35,000; it is sold in bulk to Sunday schools. **Sample for 6x9" SASE. Pays: $5. Photocopy, simultaneous submissions OK. Reports in 1 month.** These sample lines are from "Spring Rain" by Dalene Workman Stull:

A punctured sky is leaking gentle rain
Upon the rosery, the lawn, the hay.
An iris wears a beading on its mane.
And moisture films the mushroom's fawn beret.

The editor advises, "Do not write abstractions. Use concrete words to picture concept for reader." SASE for reply or return.

THE EVANGELICAL BEACON (IV-Religious), 1515 E. 66th St., Minneapolis, MN 55423, phone 612-866-3343, is the denominational magazine of the Evangelical Free Church of America, published every third Monday. **Sample copy and guidelines: 75¢. It uses very little poetry—which must be in keeping with the aims of the magazine—"helpful to the average Christian" or "presenting reality of the Christian faith to non-Christians." Pays variable rate—$5 minimum.** "Some tie-in with the Evangelical Free Church of America is helpful but is not required."

EVENT (II, IV-Themes), Douglas College, Box 2503, New Westminster, B.C., V3L 5B2, Canada, founded 1971, editor Dale Zieroth, is "a literary magazine publishing **high-quality contemporary poetry**, short stories, and reviews. **Any good-quality work is considered.**" They have recently published Lorna Crozier, Tom Wayman, Heather Spears, Dieter Weslowski, and Elizabeth Brewster. These sample lines are from "Poetry" by Don Domanski:

is it a side street or a cat's jaw?
cerecloth or the body's flesh?
I've named it the heart's pillow
wind in a mirror   cloud-rope
lighthouse on the edge of a wound
beadwork   the mote's halo   wolf-ladder

It appears three times a year as a 6×9" flat-spined, 128+ pp., glossy-covered, finely printed paperback with a circulation of 1,000 for 700 subscriptions, of which 50 are libraries. **Sample: $5 postpaid.** They have a 6 month backlog, **report in 2-3 months, pays honorarium. Sometimes they have special thematic issues, such as: work, feminism, peace and war, coming of age. They comment on some rejections.**

‡EXISTERE(II), 120 Vanier College, 4700 Keele St., North York, ON M3J 1P3 Canada, phone 416-736-2100 ext. 7403, founded 1977, is a literary quarterly. They have published poetry by Tim Archer and Gerry Stewart. As a sample the editor selected these lines by Juni Suwa:

Laughing like crazy
are the sunflowers
the cats walk among the stalks
feeling the hairy greens

The professionally printed magazine has an unusual 9×8" format using desktop publishing on quality stock with matte card cover. Press run 500. Subscription: $8. **Sample, postpaid: $1. Send SASE for guidelines. Pays 2 copies. Reports in 2 months. MS should be "typewritten, 1 poem per page with name, address and telephone number on each page."**

‡EXIT, A JOURNAL OF THE ARTS; ROCHESTER ROUTES/CREATIVE ARTS PROJECTS (II), 232 Post Ave., Rochester, NY 14619-1313, founded 1976, editor and publisher Frank Judge, a small-press publisher of a literary review and occasional chapbooks. *Exit* publishes poetry, fiction, translations, interviews, and art work. **"We are interested primarily in quality and prefer shorter pieces.** There is no 'typical' poem; styles of acceptable material range from Bly to Wilbur, Dickey to Creeley to Merwin to concrete and 'pop'." The magazine is digest-sized, offset, 32-60 pp., with art, graphics, and ads. Circulation is 1,000, of which 50 are library subscriptions. Price per copy is $5, subscription $15/3 issues. **Sample costs $6 postpaid (back issues through 1986 out of stock). Pay is 3 copies. "We like to see a good sample of a poet's work (5-10 poems); short (1-2 pp.) preferred; photocopies, dot-matrix, disc (text files in MS/PC-DOS, Mac, Apple ProDos or 3.3) acceptable; writers should send 10 sample poems with credits and bio." Pay for chapbooks is 25 author's copies.** We publish 1 poetry book per year, digest-sized, saddle-stitched, with an average page count of 32.

EXIT 13 (I), % Tom Plante, 22 Oakwood Ct., Fanwood, NJ 07023, phone 201-889-5298, founded 1987, poetry editor Tom Plante, is a "contemporary poetry annual" using **poetry that is "short, to the point, bohemian, with a sense of geography."** They have recently published poetry by Errol Miller, Alexis Rotella, Nathan Whiting, Marijane Osborn, and Simon Perchik. As a sample the editor selected the following lines by Janet Nichols:

> *Minute black specks*
> *zig-zag around my face,*
> *trying to enter my head*
> *and dance in my brain.*
> *I escape back inside to where*
> *the larger gnats reside.*

Their press run is 300. *Exit 13*, #2, was 52 pp. **Sample: $4.50 postpaid, payable to T. Plante. Guidelines available for SASE. Pays 1 copy. They accept simultaneous submissions and previously published poems. Reports in 3 months.** The editor advises, "Write about what you know. Study geography."

EXPECTING (IV-Themes), 685 3rd Ave., New York, NY 10017, is a mass-circulation quarterly (1,200,000) for expectant mothers which **occasionally buys subject-related poetry; all forms. Length: 12-64 lines. Pays $10-30. Send SASE for guidelines.**

EXPEDITION PRESS (II, IV-Love, religious), Box A, 1312 Oakland Dr., Kalamazoo, MI 49008, publisher Bruce W. White, who publishes chapbooks of **love poems and religious poems. "I dislike violence."** He likes to see **"fresh new approaches, interesting spatial relationships, as well as quality art work. We dislike political diatribes."** Some poets he has published are J. Kline Hobbs; Jim DeWitt, Martin Cohen and C. VanAllsburg. As a sample he chose this "Haiku" by himself:

> *The sun low in the West.*
> *The warm clay courts. A*
> *moment of peace.*

Submit MS of 20-30 pp. and brief bio. Photocopy, dot-matrix, simultaneous submissions OK. MS on cassette OK. Reports in 1 month. Pays 100 copies. Bruce White provides "much" criticism on rejected MSS.

EXPLORATIONS (II), 11120 Glacier Highway, Juneau, AK 99801, editors Professor Ron Silva and Professor Art Petersen, phone 907-789-4423, founded 1980. The annual literary magazine of the University of Alaska, Southeast, *Explorations* publishes **"The best quality poetry, any form, style, or purpose. We do not want to see sentimental or religious poetry. We like traditional forms – devices and meters – used in unique ways."** Have recently published poetry by John Steele, Jonathan Russell, Charli Collins, and Joanne Townsend. The editor chose these lines from Jollie Sasseville's "To My Friend Waiting Tables at the Quicksilver Club":

> *Your smile fills your pockets*
> *with quarters and drunk men's numbers*
> *scrawled on dollar bills.*
> *You may win this waiting game*
> *but what is your prize?*
>
> *Here's a tip: Good things come*
> *to those who wait, but you could never wait.*

The publication publishes the best of the submissions received. The magazine is digest-sized, nicely printed, with front and inside back cover illustration in one color, saddle-stapled. **Pay is 2 contributors copies. Submissions are reported on in May, publication is annual, out in May. MSS should be typed with name and address on separate sheet of paper, photocopies OK, simultaneous submissions OK.** "Replies for unselected manuscripts made only to SASE." The editor says, "Poets are not sloppy with their words or their pages; they know language, form, and meter; only with their hair and dress can a poet afford to slop about thus glorified."

EXPLORER MAGAZINE; EXPLORER PUBLISHING CO. (I, IV-Inspirational, nature, love), Box 210, Notre Dame, IN 46556, phone 219-277-3465, founded 1960, editor and publisher Raymond Flory, a semi-annual magazine that contains **short inspirational, nature, and love poetry** as well as prose. The editor wants **"Poetry of all styles and types; should have an inspirational slant but not necessary. Short poems preferred – up to 16 lines. Good 'family' type poetry always needed. No real long poetry or long lines; no sexually explicit poetry or porno."** He has recently published poems by Marion Schoeberlein, Edna James Kayser, and Carrie Quick. As a sample, he chose the entire poem, "The Poet," by Jim Wyzard:

> *He puts his pen to paper,*

>*In hope that he might find,*
>*A spark of new conjecture,*
>*And a stairway to the mind.*

Explorer is digest-sized, photocopied from typed copy (some of it not too clear) on thin paper, 31 pp., cover of the same paper with title superimposed on a water-color painting, folded and saddle-stapled. Circulation is 200, subscription price $6/year. **Sample available for $3, guidelines for SASE. Pay is 1 copy. Subscribers vote for the poems or stories they like best and prizes are awarded; four prizes each issue: $25, $20, $15, and $10. Writers should submit 3-4 poems, typed or photocopied; dot-matrix OK. Material must be previously unpublished; no simultaneous submissions. Reporting time is 1 week and time to publication 1-2 years.** Explorer Publishing Company does not presently publish books except for an anthology about every 4 years; it is a paperback, digest-sized book with an average page count of 20. The editor says, "Over 90% of the poets submitting poetry to *Explorer* have not seen a copy of magazine. Order a copy first— then submit. This will save poets stamps, frustration, etc. This should hold true for whatever market a writer is aiming for!"

EXQUISITE CORPSE (II), Dept. of English, Louisiana State University, Baton Rouge, LA 70803, founded 1983, editor Andrei Codrescu (whom you can often hear in commentary segments of "All Things Considered," The National Public Radio news program). This curious and delightful monthly ($15/year), when you unfold it, is 6″ wide and 16″ long, 20 pp., saddle-stapled, professionally printed in 2 columns on quality stock. The flavor of Codrescu's comments (and some clues about your prospects in submitting there) may be judged by this note in the January/February 1986 issue: "A while ago, alarmed by the number of poems aimed at the office—a number only the currency inflation and Big Macs can hold candles to—we issued an edict against them. Still they came, and some even came live. They came in the mail and under the door. We have no poetry insurance. If we are found one day smothered under Xerox paper, who will pay for the burial? The *Corpse* wants a jazz funeral. Rejections make poets happy. Having, in many cases, made their poems out of original, primal, momentary rejections, the rejection of these rejections affirms the beings forced to such deviousness." This issue has poems by Carol Bergé, Charles Plymell, Lawrence Ferlinghetti, a very long one by Alice Notley, and many others. As a sample I selected a complete poem, "Patterns" by Wanda Phipps:

>*there are patterns aren't there?*
>*designs for waves of confusion*
>*there are plans for internal battles:*
>*we will meet for massacre*
>*at exactly 6:00 a.m. on the dot*
>*careful of land mines as we march*
>*to the breakfast table*

Payment: "Zilch/Nada." You take your chances inserting work into this wit machine.

FABER AND FABER, INC. (V), 50 Cross St., Winchester, MA 01890, phone 617-721-1427, editor Betsy Uhrig, has a distinguished list of poetry publications but is accepting **no unsolicited MS.**

FAG RAG (IV-Gay); GOOD GAY POETS PRESS (V), Box 331, Kenmore Station, Boston, MA 02215, phone 617-426-4469, founded 1970, poetry editor Freddie Greenfield, is a yearly 44 pp. saddle-stitched, circulation 5,000, **"a journal of gay male art, literature and politics" which uses poems, often sexually explicit, on gay male themes.** They have recently published poetry by Allen Ginsberg, John Wieners, Harold Norse, Maurice Kenny, Ron Schreiber, and C. Shively. There are about 10 pp. of poetry in each issue, circulation 5,000 with 500 subscriptions of which 20 are libraries. They receive about 250 submissions per year, of which they use 25. They either accept or reject all poems before going to press, so there is no backlog. **Sample: $3 postpaid.** Books of such poetry are published by Good Gay Poets Press, Box 277, Astor Station, Boston, MA 02123, but **they are not considering unsolicited MSS.**

FAMOUS LAST WORDS (II), Box 9399, Stanford, CA 94309, founded 1987, poetry editor Jon King, is a poetry magazine published twice a year, digest-sized up to 50 pp., desktop published. **Poems should not exceed 15-25 lines, although exceptions may be made for particularly interesting work. No sentimental or amateur material. Well-crafted expressions in virtually any style will be considered.** Recent contributions are B. Z. Niditch, Lyn Lifshin, Henry Rollins, Mark Salerno, Jordan Jones, and Jonathan Levant. Circulation is 400 with 100 subscriptions, 10 to libraries, many copies handed out in public spots. Subscription: $7.50, **sample available for $3.50 and SASE, guidelines $1 (checks payable to Jon King). Pays 2 copies. Reports in 1 month, backlong one issue. Submit up to 5 poems. No simultaneous submissions; photocopy, good dot-matrix, single or double space all OK. "We like a brief letter, too. Name and address on all pages."** Editor sometimes comments on rejections. He advises, "Avoid the impulse to imitate. I've seen too many demi-Bukowskis for my own comfort. I am very particular about acceptances and generally accept only about 10% of the work submitted."

This cover art, entitled "E is for Egg," is part of a continuing series. "The illustrations hearken back to early alphabet books, based on rural or rustic themes," says Jean C. Lee, the illustrator and a founding editor of Farmer's Market. She adds, "We look for [poetry] with simple, organic themes, underlaid with resounding and timeless implications."

FARMER'S MARKET; MIDWEST FARMER'S MARKET, INC. (IV-Regional), P.O. Box 1272, Galesburg, IL 61402, founded 1981, editors Jean C. Lee, John Hughes and Lisa Ress, is a biannual seeking "to provide a forum for the best of regional poetry and fiction." They want poems that are "tightly structured, with concrete imagery, specific to Midwestern themes and values, reflective of the clarity, depth and strength of Midwestern life. Not interested in highly abstract or experimental work, or light verse." They have recently published poetry by Andrea Hollander Budy, Michael McMahon, Kathleen Peirce, Joe Survant, Paul C. Hunter, and Carol Barret. As a sample, they offer these lines by James Scruton from "Drought":

> The next time words
> won't come, come walk in fields
> like these. Take in
> your hands the husks
> hollow as promises, hold beans
> like bullets on your tongue.

FM is digest-sized, 100-140 pp., perfect bound with card cover, handsomely printed with graphics and photos. Circulation 500 for 150 subscriptions, of which 15 are libraries. **Sample: $3.50 plus $1 postage and handling.** They receive about 1,500 submissions per year, of which they use 50-60, have a 6 month backlog. **Submit up to 10 pages, typed or letter-quality printout, photocopies OK, would rather not have simultaneous submissions. Reports in 6-8 weeks (summer replies take longer). Pay: 1 copy.** They comment on rejections, "only if we think the work is good."

‡FEATHER BOOKS (IV-Themes, humor), "Fair View" Old Coppice, Shrewsbury, Shropshire, SY3 0BW U.K., phone Bayston Hill 2177 (074-372-2177), founded 1967, editor Rev. John Waddington-Feather, is a small press **publishing poets recommended by friends of the editor, usually on religion or nature and humor.** Nothing "avant-garde, obscene, misspelled, badly typed and lacking any coordinating structure." As a sample, I selected the first of two stanzas of the editor's "West Coast Trail, Vancouver Island":

> This coastline bites at sky
> where eagles skewer sea for fish
> and whales gorge kelp, slow
> heaving slide of tail and fin,
> grey fan that sweeps the waves
> soft as a sigh, then disappears.

He publishes 1-2 books per year averaging 50 pp. **Submit 5 sample poems, cover letter, bio, indicating connection with editorship of Feather books. Simultaneous submissions and previously published poems OK. Pays copies.** 10% of printing costs are charged to author for editing/

publishing expenses. Author receives all copies but 20 and is expected to sell all books.

‡FEELINGS; ANDERIE POETRY PRESS; QUARTERLY EDITOR'S CHOICE AWARDS (I, IV-Subscribers), Box 390, Whitehall, PA 18052, founded 1989, owner Carole Frew, a quarterly magazine, uses "simple, understandable poems on any aspect of life, no more than 20 lines, no controversial, abortion, pornography." As a sample, I selected these sample lines from "My Little Girl" by the editor:

> You've grown so very tall.
> The tiny hand that I once held in crossing streets
> Now holds mine in unfamiliar places.
> The voice that used to question, "Why Mommy?" a hundred times a day
> Gives me explanations of new and different things.

Feelings is magazine-sized, saddle-stapled with glossy paper cover, professionally printed on lightweight paper, using "graphics appropriate to the season or subject. Subscription: $18. **Sample, postpaid: $5.50. Send SASE for guidelines. Pays $10 for 3 Editor's Choice Awards in each issue. "Space and Award priority to subscribers."**

FEELINGS; SHADY LANE PRESS; FEELINGS SCHOOL POETRY CONTEST (I, IV-Children), 30750 Shady Lane Terrace, Myakka City, FL 34251, founded 1988, editor Virginia A. Carruthers, is an annual appearing in December of each year, June 1 deadline, a **"collection of poetry and art by novice poets and artists giving them recognition and exposure." The editor prefers traditional poetry "but will accept all in good taste. Nothing vulgar, sexual, profane."** Poets recently published include Jessica Blandford, Susie Gregoire, Paula Vachon, Rebecca Blandford, and Jeff Desharnais. As a sample the editor selected the following lines by C. David Hay:

> Little man how fast you grew
> And went the way all children do—
> Into a world you've yet to know
> You needed room to stretch and grow.

She will consider simultaneous submissions and previously published poems. Limit: 6 poems per submission. Editor sometimes comments on rejections. No payment at this time. I have not seen a copy, but the editor says it is digest-sized, spiral bound, 100 pp. with color matte card cover and much artwork. They sponsor an annual school poetry contest, June 1 deadline, for children in grades 1-12, poems up to 20 lines, offering publication in the magazine. Send SASE for contest rules.

FEH! A JOURNAL OF ODIOUS POETRY (IV-Themes, humor, bilingual), P.O. Box 5806, Station B, Montreal, Quebec H3B 4T1 Canada, founded 1986, poetry editor Simeon Stylites, appears 3 times a year, using **"nasty stuff, but *good* nasty stuff; silliness and nonsense, but good silliness and nonsense; insanity; truth"; in English, but 5% is French.** They have recently published poetry by John Grey and Renato Trujillo. As a sample the editor selected these lines by Francesca Bongiorno:

> so I shall wander happily
> ignoring everything I see
> and seeing things which aren't there
> and weaving hedgehogs in my hair

It is 20 pp., 7 × 8½" with photocopied paper cover. Their press run is 200 with about 15 subscriptions, and sales through bookstores. **Sample: $1 postpaid. Guidelines available for 50¢ in *loose* stamps. Pays 1 copy. Considers simultaneous submissions and previously published poems. Reports within 4 weeks. Editor sometimes comments on rejections, if asked.** The editor says, "We run the edge between the disgusting and the sublime—some of our stuff is just people being very funny, but some of it is people telling the truth."

FELICITY (I, IV-Themes), Star Route, Box 21AA, Artemas, PA 17211, phone 814-458-3102, founded 1988, editor/publisher Kay Weems, is a monthly newsletter of poetry published by the editor of *The Bottom Line Publication* (see Publications Useful to Poets). They want **"anything in good taste. No erotica. 36 line limit. We usually write to themes."** They have recently published poetry by Angie Monnens, Betty Herrmann, Elizabeth Bernstein, and John Grey. As a sample the editor selected these lines from "Song of the Weeping Birch" by Andrea Watson:

> Deep, deep in the stillness of the winter West
> Our knot-eyes are black—watching. Bleak waiting,
> A time worn wand transforms us into wooden wardsmen
> Who whisper true to the waiting traveler: Beware!

Felicity is magazine-sized, corner-stapled, 18 pp. They take about 98% of poetry received. Press run: 200 for 150 subscriptions. Subscription: $15. **Sample: $2 postpaid. Send SASE for guidelines. They consider simultaneous submissions and previously published poems. Reports in 2 weeks or sooner. Editor sometimes comments on rejections. They list at least 10 contests in each issue.**

Cash awards vary. Kay Weems says, "We have a lot of good plans for the future of *Felicity*. Beginners should read the work of other poets, learn what and *who* their competition is. Enter contests or submit work for consideration and keep trying. Write every day. Don't let rejections get you down. I guarantee you'll see improvement in your work. It may take time, but keep at it."

‡FELLOWSHIP IN PRAYER (IV-Religious), 291 Witherspoon St., Princeton, NJ 08542, phone 609-924-6863, founded 1950, editor M. Ford-Grabowsky, is a bimonthly **"concerned with prayer, meditation, and spiritual life" using poetry "pertaining to spirituality; brief."** As a sample, I selected these lines from "Balm from the Twenty-third Psalm" by Tom Jurek:

> *The Lord is My Time Giver*
> *I Shall Not Want*
> *In Short To-Do Lists and Prioritizing He Gives Me No Repose*
> *Beside Less Caffeine and Lower Blood Pressure He leads Me*
> *He Refreshes My Soul*

It is digest-sized, professionally printed, 48 pp., saddle-stapled with glossy card cover. Press run: 20,000. They accept about 2% of submissions received. Subscription: $15. **Sample, postpaid: $3. Pays 5 copies. Double-spaced submissions. Simultaneous submissions and "sometimes" previously published poems OK. Reports in 1 month.**

FEMINIST STUDIES (IV-Women), %Women's Studies Program, College Park, MD 20742, founded 1969, poetry editor Alicia Ostriker, **"welcomes a variety of work that focuses on women's experience, on gender as a category of analysis, and that furthers feminist theory and consciousness."** They have recently published poetry by Janice Mirikitani, Paula Gunn Allen, Cherrie Moraga, Audre Lorde, Judith Small, Milana Marsenich, Lynda Schraufnagel, Valerie Fox, Diane Glancy. The editor chose these lines by Nicole Brossard:

> *She breaks the contract*
> *binding her to figuration.*
> *In the theatre of the past*
> *full of countless nostalgias,*
> *she alone, along with all women,*
> *creates the entire body*
> *of impressions*

The elegantly-printed, flat-spined, 360+ pp., paperback appears 3 times a year in an edition of 7,000, goes to 6,000 subscribers, of which 1,500 are libraries. There are **4-10 pp. of poetry in each issue. Sample: $8 postpaid. Reports in 4 months. No pay.**

FENNEL STALK (I, II), 2448 W. Freeway Lane, Phoenix, AZ 85021, phone 602-995-5338, FAX 602-864-9351, founded 1986, poetry editors Karen Bowden, Peter Bailey, and Ron Dickson. **"All forms, lengths, subject matter and styles except inspirational or sing-song rhyme or poems straining to be traditional. We select based on our response measured in spine tingles, shivers, skin temperature and neuro activity, as much as on how our lives are going when we read your work. Writers should not take rejection too seriously, although taking acceptance too seriously is probably deadlier."** They have recently published Albert Huffstickler, charlie mehrhoff, and Dick Bakken. As a sample they selected these lines by August Schaefer from "Willetta Street Summer":

> *Flutes. Tracks of dust.*
> *In the night someone hugged me.*
> *Andrew writes quickly that there are porcupines,*
> *stars, we are all running*

Their aim is "to communicate and to share." Their magazine appears twice a year, digest-sized, typeset (desktop publisher) and printed on quality stock, saddle-stapled, with a b/w card cover using b/w art, photos, graphics. Their press run is 200-300 with 30 subscriptions (3 libraries). Subscription: $8. **Sample: $4 postpaid. Make checks payable to Ron Dickson. Please include cover letter with bio, put name and address on each page. Reports in 2-4 months. Editors sometimes comment on rejections "if asked." Send SASE for information.**

THE FIDDLEHEAD (II, IV-Regional, students), Campus House, University of New Brunswick, Box 4400, Fredericton, NB E3B 5A3, Canada, founded 1945, poetry editors Robert Gibbs and Robert Hawkes. From its beginning in 1945 as a local little magazine **devoted mainly to student writers, the magazine retains an interest in poets of the Atlantic region and in young poets,** but in printing poetry from everywhere on the sole criterion of excellence, it is **open to good work of every kind, looking always for vitality, freshness and surprise.** Among the poets whose work they have published are M. Travis Lane, Gary Geddes, Genni Gunn, Harry Thurston, Yvonne Trainer, Mark Sanders, and Tom Wayman. As a sample, the editor chose a stanza from "What You're Looking For" by Karen Connelly:

> More likely, you leave in the dark
>   with a mouth still quick
>   and hungry and weasel-thin.
> You slide into the night where the ice-wind
>   wakes your skin and makes you run.

The Fiddlehead is a handsomely printed, 6 × 9" flat-spined paperback (140+ pp.) with b/w graphics, glossy colored cover, usually paintings by New Brunswick artists. Circulation is 1,000. Subscription price is $16/year (US). **Sample available for $5 (US). Pay is $10-12/printed page. They use less than 10% of submissions. Reporting time 6-8 weeks, backlog 6-12 months.**

FIELD; FIELD TRANSLATION SERIES (II, IV-Translations), Rice Hall, Oberlin College, Oberlin, OH 44074, phone 216-775-8408, founded 1969, editors Stuart Friebert and David Young, is a literary journal appearing twice a year with "emphasis on poetry, translations and essays by poets." They want the **"best possible" poetry**. They have recently published poetry by Sharon Olds, Dennis Schmitz, Sylva Fischerová, Lynne McMahon, W.S. Merwin, Linda Bierds, and Norman Dubie. A portion of "A Story" by Adrienne Rich was chosen as a sample:

> Absence is homesick. Absence wants a home
> but Absence left without a glance at Home.
> Home tried to hold in Absence's despite
> Home caved, shuddered, yet held
> without Absence's consent. Home took a walk
> in several parks, Home shivered
> in outlying boroughs, slept on strange floors,
> cried many riffs of music, many words.

The handsomely printed digest-sized journal is flat-spined, has 100 pp., rag stock with glossy card color cover, circulation 2,500, 800 library subcriptions. Subscription: $10 a year, $16 for 2 years. **Sample: $5 postpaid. Pays $20-40 per page plus 2 copies. Reports in 2 weeks, has a 3-6 month backlog.** They also publish books of translations in the Field Translation Series, averaging 150 pp., flat-spined and hardcover editions. **Query regarding translations. Pays 10-15% royalties with $400 advance and 10 author's copies.** Write for catalog to buy samples.

FIGHTING WOMAN NEWS (IV-Themes), P.O. Box 1459 Grand Central Station, New York, NY 10163, founded 1975, poetry editor Muskat Buckby, provides "a communications medium for **women in martial arts, self-defense, combative sports.**" They want **poetry "relevant to our subject matter and nothing else."** Poets they have recently published include Cher Holt-Fortin and Tzivia Gover. As a sample I selected these lines from "Karate Workout" by Susan Hansen:

> One more time
>   with speed
>   with spirit
> then it's over . . . odd
> how good you feel
>   don't want to leave

Fighting Woman News appears quarterly in a magazine-sized, saddle-stapled format, 16 pp. or more, finely printed, with graphics and b/w photos, circulation 3,500. **Sample copy $3.50 including postage, "and if you say you're a poet, we'll be sure to send a sample with poetry in it."** Only one poem in each issue, and they are overstocked—6-12 month backlog. **"If your poem *really* requires an audience of martial artists to be appreciated, then send it." Simultaneous submissions, photocopy OK. Replies "ASAP." Pays: copies.** "Because our field is so specialized, most interested women subscribe. It is not a requirement for publication, but **we seldom publish a non-subscriber.**" The editor advises, "Read first; write later." To guarantee publication of your poem(s), submit a hard core martial arts non-fiction article. Those are what we really need! Fighters who are also writers can have **priority access to our very limited poetry space by doing articles.** Please do not send any poems if you have not read any issues of *FWN.*"

‡THE FIGURES (V), 5 Castle Hill Ave., Great Barrington, MA 01230-1552, phone 413-528-2552, founded 1975, is a small press publishing poetry and fiction. As a sample I selected these lines from Ron Padgett's **The Big Something**:

> in the slow
> rotation of the sphere
> you call a star,
> a flower, a mind.

They pay 10% of press run. They currently accept no unsolicited poetry.

FINE MADNESS (II), P.O. Box 15176, Seattle, WA 98115, founded 1980, president Louis Bergsagel. *Fine Madness* is a twice-yearly magazine. They want "**contemporary poetry of any form and subject. We look for highest quality of thought, language, and imagery. We look for the mark of the individual: unique ideas and presentation; careful, humorous, sympathetic. No careless poetry, sexist poetry, greeting-card poetry, poetry that 10,000 other people could have written.**" They have recently published poetry by Paul Zimmer, Pattiann Rogers, Stuart Friebert, Andrei Codrescu, David Kirby, Naomi Shihab-Nye, William Stafford, Carol Orlock, Beth Bentley, and Barb Molloy-Olund. As a sample the editor selected these lines by Elton Glaser:

> This bullwhip and a box
> Of bowtied roses, their perfume irretrievable,
> Trailing you like a skulk of foxes,
> The odor of lost lust

Fine Madness is digest-sized, 80 pp., perfect bound, flat-spined, offset printing, 2-3 color card cover. Their press run is 800 for 100 subscriptions of which 10 are libraries. They accept about 40 of 1,000 poems received. Subscription: $9. **Sample: $4 postpaid. Guidelines available for SASE. Pays 1 copy + subscription. Submit 3-10 poems, preferably originals, not photocopy, 1 poem per page. Reports in 2-3 months.** They give 2 annual awards to editors' choice of $50 each. Coeditor Sean Bentley says, "If you don't read poetry, don't send us any."

FIREBRAND BOOKS (IV-Feminist, lesbian, ethnic), 141 The Commons, Ithaca, NY 14850, phone 607-272-0000, founded 1984, editor and publisher Nancy K. Bereano, "is a **feminist and lesbian** publishing company committed to producing quality work in multiple genres by ethnically diverse women." They publish both quality trade paperbacks and hardbacks. **Simultaneous submissions acceptable with notification. Replies to queries within 2 weeks, to MSS within one month. Pays royalties.** As a sample, I chose this stanza of a sestina, "great expectations" from the book **Living As A Lesbian** by Cheryl Clarke:

> dreaming the encounter intense as engines
> first me then you oh what a night
> of rapture and risk and dolphin
> acrobatics after years of intend-
> ing to find my lesbian sources in the window
> of longing wide open in me

The book is 94 pp., flat-spined, elegantly printed on heavy stock with a glossy color card cover, a photo of the author on the back, $7.95. Send for catalog to buy samples.

‡FIREWEED: A FEMINIST QUARTERLY (IV-Women), Box 279, Station B, Toronto, ON M5T 2W2 Canada, phone 416-323-9512, founded 1978, edited by the Fireweed Collective, is a feminist arts and political journal that "**especially welcomes contributions by women of color, working-class women, native women, lesbians, and women with disabilities.**" It is digest-sized, 100-120 pp., flat-spined, with 3-4 color-cover. Press run: 2,000. Subscription: $12 in Canada, $15 in U.S. **Sample, postpaid: $4 in Canada, $5 in U.S. Pays $20/contributor/issue plus 2 copies. Simultaneous submissions OK. Editor comments on submissions "occasionally."**

FIRST HAND (IV-Gay, subscribers), Box 1314, Teaneck, NJ 07666, phone 201-836-9177, founded 1980, poetry editor Bob Harris, is a "**homosexual erotic publication written mostly by its readers.**" The digest-sized monthly has a circulation of 70,000 with 3,000 subscribers of which 3 are libraries, and uses 1-2 pp. of poetry in each issue, for which they **pay $25 a poem.** They have published poems by Kelvin Beliele and Stephen Finch. The editor selected these sample lines from "To a Model" by Karl Tierney:

> I assure you, I mean no
> disrespect when I discover,
> beyond sex and half asleep,
> you deflate to only half the monster
> and will be that much easier
> to battle out the door at dawn.

Submit poems no longer than 1 typed page. No queries. Reports in 6 weeks. Editor Bob Harris sometimes comments on rejected MSS. They have an 18 month backlog. The editor advises, "Make sure what you're writing about is obvious to future readers. **Poems need not be explicitly sexual, but must deal overtly with gay situations and subject matter.**"

FIRST TIME; NATIONAL HASTINGS POETRY COMPETITION (I, II), Burdett Cottage, 4 Burdett Place, George Street, Old Town, Hastings, East Sussex TN34 3ED England, phone 0424-428855, founded 1981, editor Josephine Austin, who says the magazine is **open to "All kinds of poetry—our magazine goes right across the board—which is why it is one of the most popular in Great Britain."** The magazine appears twice a year; from the recent issues I have seen, I selected the following lines from "Spirit of a Loved One" by Michael Newman:

> *Then it was gone.*
> *Cars tore through the silence*
> *And the mad March Hare*
> *Bit a slice out of the moon's macaroon.*

The digest-sized magazine, 24 pp. saddle-stapled, contains several poems on each page, in a variety of small type styles, on lightweight stock, b/w photographs of editor and 1 author, glossy one-color card cover. **Sample: 50p plus postage. Pay is 1 copy. Poems submitted must not exceed 30 lines, must not have been published elsewhere, and must have name and address of poet on each. Maximum time to publication is 2 months. Poets should send 10 sample poems. The annual National Hastings Poetry Competition for poets 18 and older offers awards of £100, 50, and 25, £1/poem entry fee.** The editor advises, "Keep on 'pushing your poetry.' If one editor rejects you then study the market and decide which is the correct one for you. Try to type your own manuscripts as long hand work is difficult to read and doesn't give a professional impression. Always date your poetry — C1990 and sign it. Follow your way of writing, don't be a pale imitation of someone else — sooner or later styles change and you will either catch up or be ahead."

‡FISH DRUM (II, IV-Spiritual, regional), 626 Kathryn Ave., Santa Fe, NM 87501, founded 1988, editor Robert Winson, is a literary magazine appearing 2-4 times a year, using **"lively, modernist, lyrical poetry. No constraints beyond what strikes my eye and ear. Looking for material by Zen practitioners and NM poets especially. No unhappy, impersonal, formal verse."** They have recently published poetry by Miriam Sagan, Joy Harjo, Arthur Sze, Alice Notley, and Nathaniel Tarn. As a sample the editor selected these lines from "Poeta Nascitur" by Philip Whalen:

> *"I was happy in my dream," supposing*
> *I was quoting something, but couldn't*
> *find it in any book*
> *"Maybe you said it yourself," she said.*

FD is digest-sized, 40 pp., saddle-stapled, professionally printed, with glossy card cover. "Of sixty or so unsolicited submissions last year, accepted fewer than ten." Press run 500 for 75 subscriptions of which 10 are libraries, 400 shelf sales. Subscription: $10 for 4 issues. **Sample, postpaid: $3. Pays 2 or more copies. Contributors may purchase advance copies at $1.50 each in addition to contributor's copies. Reports in 2 months.** The editor says, "Poets should read, write, and publish. It's tremendously exciting to find a good poem in the mail. I only wish it happened more often."

FIVE FINGERS REVIEW; FIVE FINGERS PRESS (III, IV-Form, women, political, social issues, bilingual), 553 25th Ave., San Francisco, CA 94121, founded 1984, editors John High, Thoreau Lovell, Aleka Chase, Ruth Schwartz, and Malcolm Garcia, a literary bi-annual publishing "diverse, innovative writing by writers of various aesthetics who are **concerned with social issues."** Some of the better-known poets they have published are Denise Levertov, Robert Bly, C.D. Wright, Kathleen Fraser, Philip Levine, and Ron Silliman. An occasional poem is published in both English and Spanish. The editors chose a sample from "I've Forgotten Nothing" by Bella Akhmadulina, translated by John High and Katya Olmstead:

> *I've forgotten nothing-*
> *that I'm part of humanity*
> *saddens me.*

Five Fingers Review is 6 × 9", nicely printed on buff stock, 150 pp., flat-spined with one-color glossy card cover. Circulation is 1,000 copies, 25% of which go to libraries. Price per issue is $6, subscription $12/year. **Sample available for $7 postpaid. Pay is 2 copies. Reporting time is 3-6 months and time to publication is 4 months. Query for current deadlines.** Simultaneous submissions OK. Five Fingers Press also publishes a perfect-bound book series. The advice of the editors is: "Pick up a copy of the magazine. Be committed to craft and to looking at the world in fresh, surprising ways."

FLIGHTS: A LITERARY VOICE FOR THE MIAMI VALLEY (I,IV-Regional), English Dept., Sinclair Community College, 444 W. Third St., Dayton, OH 45402, phone 513-226-2590, founded 1986, editor Ed Davis, is an annual literary magazine **for Dayton and the Miami Valley area. It says on the cover "by local residents & others,"** publishing poetry, fiction, essays, photos and drawings accessible to a wide general audience. **Prefer fairly short (max. 50 lines), clear, concrete (imagaic rather than philosophical, preachy) modern (free verse and well-crafted traditional forms), unpublished, and not under consideration elsewhere, original. All themes: rural, urban, etc. No predictable rhyming, singsongy rhythms, greeting-card verse."** They have recently published poetry by Terri Meece, Jeff Gundy,

Helen Reed, and Lewis Ashman. As a sample Ed Davis selected these lines by Rick Wagner:

> *This dance is an ancestral dance that impales each dancer*
> *And the collective past is the hand that holds the dowel*
> *And we will dance like handcarved limberjacks in*
> *Rubberlegged frenzies bouncing off the throbbing earth*
> *As memory pulls us like gravity to our place.*

Flights is magazine-sized, 40 pp. saddle-stapled, computer typeset, with matte card cover with b/w photos front, back, and inside, drawings, and computer-generated art. It appears in April. They use 23 of approximately 300 poems received in a year. Press run is 600. There are about 200 shelf sales. Per issue: $2. **Sample: $1.50 postpaid. Pays 2 copies. Reports in 4 months, "sooner if obviously unacceptable." Submit 3-5 poems single-spaced with name and address on each page. Editor "quite often" comments on rejections.** He says, "All styles are welcome. Feel free to illustrate poems. **Poets from the Dayton area, or at least from Ohio, have a definite edge here, though I intend to publish the best submissions received, especially if concerns of this region are addressed."**

‡**THE FLORIDA REVIEW(II)**, Dept. of English, University of Central Florida, Orlando, FL 32816, phone 407-275-2038, founded 1972, poetry editor Russ Kesler, is a "literary biannual with emphasis on short fiction and poetry." They want **"poems filled with real things, real people and emotions, poems that might conceivably advance our knowledge of the human heart."** They have recently published poetry by Knute Skinner, Elton Glaser, and Walter McDonald. As a sample, I selected these lines from "Needlepoint" by Lisa Rhoades:

> *The draw of the yarn*
> *through the canvas rasps*
> *uneven as the breath*
> *of an old man, the*
> *murmur of a cat.*

It is 128 pp., flat-spined, professionally printed, with glossy card cover. Press run 1,000 for 400 subscriptions of which 50 are libraries. Shelf sales 50. **Sample, postpaid: $4.50. Send SASF for guidelines. Pays $15/poem plus 3 copies. Submit no more than 6. Simultaneous submissions OK. Reports in 1-3 months. Editor comments on submissions "occasionally."**

FLUME PRESS (II), 4 Casita, Chico, CA 95926, phone 916-342-1583, founded 1984, poetry editors Casey Huff and Elizabeth Renfro, publishes poetry chapbooks. **"We have few biases about form, although we appreciate control and crafting, and we tend to favor a concise, understated style, with emphasis on metaphor rather than editorial commentary." Considers simultaneous submissions.** They have recently published chapbooks by Tina Barr, Randall Freisinger, Leonard Kress, Carol Gordon, and Gayle Kaune. As a sample, the editor selected these lines from "Mother Pills" by David Graham:

> *I may also have drawn her long hair, eyes split*
> *behind bifocal lenses, but what remains*
> *is that sliver of light under my bedroom door,*
> *the voice my voice could waken, sure as rain.*

Chapbooks are chosen from an annual competition, deadline June 30. $5 entry fee. Submit 20-28 pp., including title, contents, and acknowledgments. Name and address on a separate sheet. "Flume Press editors read and respond to *every* entry. They choose the finalists and send them to the Final Judge, a nationally known poet, who selects the winner. Past judges include Frances Mayes, Madeline Defrees, David Wojahn, and Sandra Cisneros." Winner receives $100 and 25 copies. **Sample: $5 plus $1 postage and handling.**

FOLIO: A LITERARY JOURNAL (II), Dept. of Literature, Gray Hall, American University, Washington, DC 20016, phone 202-885-2973, founded 1984, editors change annually , a biannual. They have published poetry by Larry Johnson, Elisavietta Ritchie, and Donald Finkel. The editors selected these sample lines from "The Longing" by Kathrine Jason:

> *I like it here*
> *in the realm of stone*
> *and unerring geometry*
> *where a word, spoken,*
> *flies back as an answer*
> *and a wind in decline*
> *is a gargoyle's breath.*

There are 55 pp. of poetry in each 74 pp. issue, narrow digest-sized, thin flat spine, glossy cover, neatly printed from typeset. **Sample: $4.50 postpaid. Submit from August to November 1 or January to March 1, up to 6 pp., include a brief bio/contributor's note, photocopy, dot-matrix**

OK. Considers simultaneous submissions. Pays in one contributor's copy. Comments on rejection "if it came close to acceptance." They also sponsor a contest open to all contributors with a $75 prize for the best poem of the spring issue.

‡FOOLSCAP(I,II), 78 Friars Road, East Ham, London E6 1LL England, phone 01-470-7680, founded 1987, editor Judi Benson, appears in January, April, and September using poetry **"that surprises and informs with attention paid to language and voice as well as to the world around us. We are looking for a confidence, a sense of humor, and of course a vision. We are looking for a wide range of styles and opinions and most likely won't know what we want until we find it. We veer away from cliché, obvious rhyme, self-indulgence, overwriting, oversentimentalizing, lecturing, and general whittering on, not to mention that which is written in poetic line breaks but which is not poetry. We advise people to get a copy before submitting."** They have recently published poetry by Ken Smith, Nicki Jackowska, Matthew Sweeney, John Harvey, Ian Duhig, and Katherine Gallagher. As a sample the editor selected these lines from "Blues In the Woodshed" by Libby Houston:

> A knock at the door midnight and no one
> there, the click of a dumb phonecall.
> The night a brick smashed on the roughcast
> out of the sallow empty
> dark was worst. So
> nights without speech.

I have not seen an issue, but the editor describes it as 52 pp., digest-sized, camera-ready photocopying, no reductions. Black and white illustrations and sometimes half-tones. Light card cover in design of child's exercise book. No ads. No frills. They accept about 120 of 1,200 poems per year. Press run: 200 for 100-250 subscribers of which 10 are libraries, 50 shelf sales. Subscription: $12/£3. **Sample, postpaid: $4/£1.35. Pays 2 copies. Submit "not more than 6/time. Best if overseas not to have to return MSS. Include more than 1 International Postal Order as 1 = 24 pence and regular airmail is 34 pence, not to mention that which includes MS. No simultaneous submissions; previously published poems sometimes used. Editor comments on submissions** "sometimes, if we feel a poem is close but not quite there and that there is a seriousness of intent. It may seem obvious, but I would advise beginning poets to share their work with others before even considering sending to magazines (this doesn't mean Mom and Dad) and that they study the market. *Foolscap* accepts a wide range of poetry from many different geographical locations, written by a variety of people, accepting both the unknown and the well-known. We are looking for poetry which represents today's thinking and feeling, however diverse. There is an urgency in much of the work we publish, and we want the word to get out."

FOOTWORK: THE PATERSON LITERARY REVIEW; HORIZONTES; THE PATERSON POETRY PRIZE; PCC POETRY CENTER POETRY CONTEST; PASSAIC COUNTY COMMUNITY COLLEGE POETRY CENTER LIBRARY (II, IV-Bilingual/foreign language), Passaic County Community College, Cultural Affairs Dept., College Blvd., Paterson, NJ 07509. *Footwork* founded 1979, editor and director Maria Mazziotti Gillan, is an annual literary magazine using **poetry of "high quality" under 100 lines.** They have recently published poetry by William Stafford, Sonia Sanchez, Laura Boss, Marge Piercy, Kyoko Mori, and Helen Barolini. As a sample, the editor selected several lines from "Message From Your Toes" by Ruth Stone:

> How now, if you should dig him up, the bones of his left foot
> falling like dice, there would be one among them gnarled out of shape
> a ridge of calcium extruding a pattern of unutterable anguish.
> And your toes, passengers of the extreme
> clustered on your dough white body,
> say how they miss his feet, the thin elegance of his ankles.

Footwork: The Paterson Literary Review is magazine-sized, 144 pp., saddle-stapled, professionally printed with glossy card 2-color cover, using b/w art and photos, circulation 1,000 with 100 subscriptions of which 50 are libraries. **Sample: $5 postpaid. Pays 1 copy. Reports in 3 months. Send no more than 5 poems per submission.** *Horizontes*, founded in 1983, editor, José Villalongo, is an annual Spanish language literary magazine using **poetry of high quality no longer than 20 lines. Will accept English translations, but Spanish version must be included.** They have recently published poetry by Nelson Calderon, Jose Kozer, and Julio Cesar Mosches. As a sample, the editor selected these lines by the editor of *Footwork*, Maria Gillan:

> Yo he aprendido de la litanía de mi vida,
> del patrón de ordenes repetidas
> y reclusiónes.
>
> Yo he aprendido más de lo que
> quisiera saber, sueño

> con retroceder a mi inocencia,
> la vida limpia de pesadumbre y el cielo
> sin obscurecerse

Horizontes is magazine-sized 120 pp., saddle-stapled, professionally printed with full color matte cover, using b/w graphics and photos, circulation 800 with 100 subscriptions of which 20 are libraries. **Sample issue: $4 postpaid. Pays 2 copies. Reports in 3-4 months. Accepts simultaneous submissions. "On occasion we do consider published works but prefer unpublished works."** The Poetry Center of the college conducts an annual poetry contest, no fees, prizes of $250, $125 and $100, deadline April 15. Send SASE for rules. They also publish a **New Jersey Poetry Resources** book, the **PCC Poetry Contest Anthology** and the **New Jersey Poetry Calendar**. Also awards Paterson Poetry Prize of $1,000 for published books. Winner in 1989 Daniel Hoffman; judge Maxine Keemen. Deadline April 1st. Send SASE for rules. Passaic County Community College Poetry Center Library has an extensive collection of contemporary poetry and seeks small press contributions to help keep it abreast.

FOR POETS ONLY (I), P.O. Box 1382, Jackson Heights, NY 11372, founded 1985, poetry editor L.M. Walsh, **requires a $3 entry fee for each poem submitted, which may win a $10 prize (at least five promised for each issue). Others accepted are paid for with one copy of the magazine.** The issue I have has 35 pp. of poems—some with more than one to a page. Of these, 16 were awarded prizes. They have recently published poems by J. Bernier, C. Weirich, and Alice Mackenzie Swaim. As a sample I selected the first lines of one of the prize winners, "Poets Unite," by J. Mead:

> The Literary Poetry Queen
> of "For Poets Only" Magazine
> Has composed a wonderful, unique book,
> enjoy the works as you continue to look.

FPO is digest-sized, 36 pp., saddle-stapled, photocopied from typescript with glossy card cover. It appears quarterly. The editor rejects about 10% of poetry received. Press run is 200. Per copy: $3. **Sample: $3.50 postpaid. Any subject. No pornography. No comments on rejections.** The editor advises, "For beginning poets: a quote from Horst Bienek in his *The Cell.* "We are distressed but *not in despair*, distressed but *not destroyed*, persecuted but *not forsaken*, cast down but *not destroyed*."

‡THE FORMALIST (II, IV-Form, translations), 525 S. Rotherwood, Evansville, IN 47714, founded 1990, editor William Baer, appears twice a year, **"dedicated to *metrical* poetry written in the great tradition of English-language verse."** They have recently published poetry by Richard Wilbur, Elizabeth Jennings, Donald Justice, Robert Conquest, James Merrill, John Hollander, Molly Peacock, Dana Gioia, Rachel Hadas, and Elizabeth Spires. As a sample the editor chose the opening stanza from "The Amateurs of Heaven" by Howard Nemerov:

> Two lovers to a midnight meadow came
> High in the hills, to lie there hand in hand
> Like effigies and look up at the stars,
> The never-setting ones set in the North
> To circle the Pole in idiot majesty,
> And wonder what was given them to wonder.

"We are interested in metrical poetry written in the **traditional forms, including ballads, sonnets, couplets, the Greek forms, the French forms, etc. We will also consider metrical translations of major formalist non-English poets—from the Ancient Greeks to the present. We are not, however, interested in haiku (or syllabic verse of any kind) or sestinas. Although we do publish poetry which skillfully employs enjambment, we have a marked prejudice against excessive enjambment. Only rarely do we accept a poem over 2 pages, and we have no interest in any type of erotica, blasphemy, vulgarity, or racism.** Finally, like all editors, we suggest that those wishing to submit to *The Formalist* become thoroughly familiar with the journal beforehand." *The Formalist* **considers submissions between October 15 and May 15 of each year, 3-5 poems at one time. We do *not* consider simultaneous submissions, previously published work, or disk submissions. A brief cover letter is recommended** and a SASE is necessary for the return of the MSS. **Subscription: $12. Sample postpaid: $6.50. Payment 2 copies. Reports within 8 weeks.** See also the contest listing the World Order of Narrative and Formalist Poets. Contestants must subscribe to *The Formalist* to enter.

FOUR ZOAS JOURNAL OF POETRY & LETTERS; HIGH MEADOW PRESS (II), Middletown Springs, VT 05757, phone 802-235-2547, founded 1972, editor S. R. Lavin, is a literary quarterly "with emphasis on poetry which explores the human condition." **Submit 3-4 one-page poems or one long poem (3-4 pp.)** — in awe of existence but not of man-made madness — celebrating the cautions of 'ends' that result from insufficient means. No religious, 'love,' occasional poems." They have recently published poetry by G. Malanga, Jon Silkin, Lyn Lifshin, Ken Smith, George Oppen, and Alicia Ostreicher. As a sample S. R. Lavin selected these lines by Richard Elman:

> *For love we waste our lives,*
> *if that is love, or life, or waste*
> *We call this living; to be*
> *everyday there for a life*
> *like a greeting for a lonely*
> *stranger*

He describes *Four Zoas* as "a magazine with a mission, to expose evil, lies, false doctrines, misinformation." It is $7 \times 5''$, saddle-sewn, letterpress printed, using ads, photos and woodcuts, appearing 3 times a year. They accept 80-100 of some 1,000 poems received a year. Press run is 750 for 300 subscribers of which 100 are libraries, shelf sales 200. Per issue: $5; subscriptions: $20. **Sample: $5 postpaid. Pays 2 copies. Send SASE for guidelines. "Cover letter with poems helpful." Simultaneous submissions OK, and previously published poems used "occasionally." Reports in 3 weeks.** Under the imprint of High Meadow Press they publish 2-3 chapbooks per year, average 20 pp. **For chapbook consideration query with 2-3 sample poems, bio, publications. Simultaneous submissions, photocopies OK. Pays $500 (10% royalties), and 20 author's copies. Sample chapbooks: $5. Editor sometimes comments on rejections.** He adds, "Poetry is communion of consciousness, the self, and what lies beyond 'the known.' I am attracted to work which challenges assumptions of response. I adhere to Pound's 7 principles and George Oppen's objectivist formulation: 'sincerity and objectivity.' "

FOX CRY (I), University of Wisconsin Fox Valley, Midway Road, Menasha, WI 54952, phone 414-832-2600, founded 1973, editor Professor Don Hrubesky, is a literary annual using **poems up to 50 lines long, deadline February 1.** They have recently published poetry by Shirley Anders, David Graham, and Clifford Wood. Their press run is 400. **Sample: $5 postpaid. Send SASE for guidelines. Pays 1 copy. Submit maximum of 3 poems. They will consider simultaneous submissions.**

FRANK: AN INTERNATIONAL JOURNAL OF CONTEMPORARY WRITING AND ART (II, IV-Form, translations), Editor, David Applefield, B.P. 29, 94301 Vincennes Cedex France, founded 1983. *Frank* is a literary semiannual that **"encourages work of seriousness and high quality which falls often between existing genres. Looks favorably at true internationalism and stands firm against ethnocentric values. Likes translations. Publishes foreign dossier in each issue. Very eclectic."** There are no subject specifications, but the magazine **"discourages sentimentalism and easy, false surrealism. Although we're in Paris, most Paris-poems are too thin for us. Length is open."** Some poets published recently include Rita Dove, Derek Walcott, Kishwar Naheed, Duo Duo, Raymond Carver, Tomas Tranströmer, James Laughlin, Breytenbach, Michaux, Edmond Jabes, John Berger, and many lesser known poets. The journal is digest-sized, flat-spined 224 pp., offset in b/w with color cover and photos, drawings, and manuscript pages, 5 pages of ads. Circulation is 4,000, of which 2,000 are bookstore sales and subscriptions. Subscription $25 for 4 issues. **Sample: $6 postpaid airmail from Paris. Pay is $5/printed page and 2 copies. Guidelines available for SASE. Poems must be previously unpublished. Submissions are reported on in 8-10 weeks, publication is in 1-4 months. "Send only what you feel is fresh, original, and provocative in either theme or form."** The editor provides criticism on rejected MSS **"almost always, but if poet agrees to subscribe I feel more generous with my comments."** Editor organizes readings in US and Europe for *Frank* contributors. *Frank* also publishes *Paris-Anglophone*, a directory of English commercial and cultural activities in France.

FREE FOCUS; OSTENTATIOUS MIND (I, IV-Women/feminist), 224 82nd St., Brooklyn, NY 11209, phone 718-680-3899, *Free Focus* founded 1985, *Ostentatious Mind* founded 1987, poetry editor Patricia D. Coscia. *Free Focus* "is a small-press magazine which **focuses on the educated women of today** and needs stories and poems. They want **"all types except x-rated. The poems can be as long as 2 pp. or as short as 3 lines. The subject matter is of all types and the style, the same. The purpose of the magazine is to give women writers a place in literature, that women have a will to succeed and earn respect for their achievements."** As a sample Patricia D. Coscia comments, "This 4-line poem by Gretchen Busch represents the basic doubts of a woman's successfulness in writing. Is it worth all the hard work?"

> *I say I want to write, but don't*
> *Yet I could fill up a book with excuses*
> *It's fine just to say I'm awaiting a purpose*
> *But it's nothing my waiting produces.*

Ostentatious Mind "is designed to encourage the intense writer—the cutting reality. The staff deals in the truth of life: political, social and psychological. Both magazines are photocopied on $8 \times 14''$ paper, folded in the middle and stapled to make a 10 pp. (including cover) format, with simple b/w drawings on the cover and inside. *Free Focus* appears in Spring and Fall. **Sample: of** either is $2 postpaid. Send SASE for guidelines. Pays 4 copies. Poems should be "single-spaced typed on single sheets of papers. Poem submission is 3." Simultaneous submissions and previously published poems OK. Reports "as soon as possible." Comments? "Yes, very much so. It is important to the writer." They plan to sponsor contests. Patricia D. Coscia says, "I think that the poet who is unknown will never be known unless she or he sends out their poems to a publisher or gets involved in a literary magazine such as this one."

FREE LUNCH (II), P.O. Box 7647, Laguna Niguel, CA 92607-7647, founded 1988, editor Ron Offen, is a **"poetry journal interested in publishing whole spectrum of what is currently being produced by American poets. Always try to comment on submissions. Especially interested in experimental work and work by unestablished poets. Hope to provide all serious American poets with free subscription. For details on free subscription send SASE. Prefer no more than 3 poems per submission. No restriction on form, length, subject matter, style, purpose. Don't want cutsie, syrupy, sentimental, preachy religious, or agressively 'uplifting' verse. No aversion to form, rhyme."** They have recently published poetry by Neal Bowers, Lee Meitzen Grue, Frank Polite, Jim Reiss, Bill Zavatsky, and Zila Zeiger. As a sample the editor selected these lines from "My Father's Forecast" by Len Roberts:

> the chunk of oak snapped in the black stove
> as I sat with my father's face
> in my hands, his
> nights of cigarettes rising with each breath . . .

Published 3 times a year. The magazine is 32-40 pp., saddle-stapled, digest-sized, offset. Their press run is 600 with (their first year) 43 subscriptions of which 7 are libraries. Subscription $10 ($13 foreign). **Sample: $4 ($5 foreign) postpaid. Pays 1 copy plus subscription. Send SASE for guidelines. They will consider simultaneous submissions. Editor usually comments on rejections and tries to return submissions in 8 weeks.** He quotes Archibal MacLeish, " 'A poem should not mean/ But be.' Poetry is concerned primarily with language, rhythm, and sound; fashions and trends are transitory and to be eschewed; perfecting one's work is often more important than publishing it."

FREE VENICE BEACHHEAD (I, IV-Bilingual), Box 504, Venice, CA 90294, phone 213-396-0811, founded 1968, edited by the Beachhead Collective, is a monthly community tabloid, distributed free, circulation 10,000, "originally affiliated with the Peace and Freedom Party; now independent, collective community press. **We've published submitted poems from all over America — English and Spanish. It should be good, readable. Sample free for SASE."** Poems published depending on available space — shorter poems get published faster. **Would like to hear from Southern California writers.** Though the editors did not mention this, I would think from examination of one issue (which happened to contain no poetry) that poetry would stand a better chance here if it were in keeping with the tone of the paper, which is filled with articles by members of the community on political and social issues (and other things), the paper serving as an open forum: "We welcome and take responsibility for publishing contributions exactly as the contributors submit them, though the opinions expressed by the contributors are not necessarily endorsed by the Collective staff. **Accepted poems are placed in our** *accepted poetry file*. **Each month the coordinator, a job that rotates among members of the collective, selects the poem to be published in that issue. Once published, a poem is placed in the** *published poetry file*. **We do not return published poems or notify the author of date of publication."**

FRIENDS JOURNAL (II,IV-Themes), 1501 Cherry St., Philadelphia, PA 19102, phone 215-241-7277, founded 1827 as *The Friend* and 1844 as *Friends Intelligencer,* 1955 as *Friends Journal,* appears monthly, magazine-sized, circulation 9,000+. **"The Journal seeks poetry that resonates with Quakerism and Quaker concerns, such as peace and nonviolence, spiritual seeking, the sanctuary movement, the nuclear freeze."** These sample lines are from "For a Friends' Wedding" by Pulitzer Prize poet Henry S. Taylor:

> We have been schooled in silence in this place;
> whatever words I frame to wish you well
> dwindle toward the spirit in this air . . .

No multiple or simultaneous submissions. Pays 2 copies per poem. Subscription: $18 per year (12 issues).

ALWAYS submit MSS or queries with a stamped, self-addressed envelope (SASE) within your country or International Reply Coupons (IRCs) purchased from the post office for other countries.

‡**FROG GONE REVIEW (I)**, Box 46308, Mt. Clemens, MI 48046, phone 313-263-3399, founded 1988-89, editor Greg Schindler, is an annual poetry magazine. **Submit 5 poems (120-line maximum). Poetry accepted September 1 through January 15. Very seldom uses poems over 40 lines. "Economy of words and good fresh imagery wanted. No porno."** As a sample the editor selected lines from "The Waking Dragon" by Heather Renouf:

> *I awake stiff*
> *with uncountable years.*
> *Cool morning air tingles*
> *As it slips inside my yawn.*

"Submitting poets must order a copy of the magazine for $4. The five best poems are designated and awarded $10 each." Send SASE. The format is unusual. The green card cover and pages turn up like pages from a calendar. Cursive type, black ink on cream yellow-colored paper, saddle-stapled, several illustrations.

FROGMORE PAPERS; FROGMORE POETRY PRIZE (II), 42 Morehall Ave., Folkestone, Kent, England, founded 1983, poetry editor Jeremy Page, is a literary quarterly with emphasis on new poetry and short stories. **"Quality is generally the only criterion, although pressure of space means very long work (over 100 lines) is unlikely to be published."** They have recently published poetry by B.C. Leale, Geoffrey Holloway, David Phillips, Dorothy Nimmo, Margaret Browne, Elizabeth Garrett, Merryn Williams, and Ivor C. Treby. As a sample the editor selected these lines by Alan Dunnett:

> *Fissures of granite, gnarled*
> *and spangled like hunks of sugar; sky*
> *hard and bright, yet tender as*
> *a wounded membrane.*

The magazine is 22 pp. saddle-stapled with matte card cover, photocopied in photoreduced typescript. Their press run is 200 with 50 subscriptions. They accept a tenth of poetry received. Subscription: £7 ($12). **Sample: £1.50 ($4) postpaid. Pays 1 copy. Reports in 3-6 months. Considers simultaneous submissions. Editor sometimes comments on rejections.** For information about the annual Frogmore Poetry Prize write Frogmore Press, 42 Morehall Ave., Folkestone, Kent, England. The editor says, "My advice to people starting to write poetry would be: read as many recognized modern poets as you can and don't be afraid to experiment."

FROGPOND: QUARTERLY HAIKU JOURNAL; HAIKU SOCIETY OF AMERICA; HAIKU SOCIETY OF AMERICA AWARDS/CONTESTS (IV-Form, translation), % Japan Society, 333 E. 47th St., New York, NY 10017, has been publishing *Frogpond* since 1978, now edited by Elizabeth Searle Lamb, and **submissions should go directly to her** at 970 Acequia Madre, Santa Fe, NM 87501. *Frogpond* is a stapled spine quarterly of 48 pp., 5½×8½", of haiku, senryu, haiku sequences, renga, more rarely tanka, and translations of haiku. It also contains book reviews, some news of the Society, contests, awards, publications, and other editorial matter—a dignified, handsome little magazine. Poets should be familiar with modern developments in English-language haiku as well as the tradition. **Haiku should be brief, fresh, using clear images and non-poetic language. Focus should be on a moment keenly perceived. Ms. Lamb hopes contributors will be familiar with contemporary haiku and senryu as presented in** *The Haiku Handbook* (Wm. J. Higginson) and *The Haiku Anthology* (Cor van den Heuvel, Ed.). Recent contributors include Dee Evetts, LeRoy Gorman, Steve Dalachinsky, Elliot Richman, Charles Dickson, Bob Moore, Virginia Brady Young, Jane Reichhold, Charles D. Nethaway, Jr. and Cor van den Heuvel. Considerable variety is possible, as these two examples from the magazine illustrate:

> *leaden sky,*
> *a bird about to burst*
> *with song*
> L.A. Davidson © 1990

> *home late . . .*
> *she hangs her shadow*
> *on the coat rack*
> Sheldon Young © 1989

Each issue has between 25 and 35 pages of poetry. The magazine goes to some 600 subscribers, of which 15 are libraries, and reaching into over a dozen foreign countries. **Sample, postpaid—$5.** Make check payable to Haiku Society of America. They receive about 8,000 submissions per year and use about 400-450. **Accepted poems usually published within 6-12 months, reporting within 6 weeks.** They are flexible on submission format: haiku on 3×5" cards or several to a page or one to a page or half-page. Ms. Lamb prefers 5-20 at one submission, no photocopy or dot-matrix. **No simultaneous submissions.** They hope contributors will become HSA members, but it is not necessary, and all contributors receive a copy of the magazine in payment. Send

SASE for Information Sheet on the HSA. The Society also sponsors the Harold G. Henderson Haiku Award Contest, The Gerald Brady Senryu Award Contest, and gives Merit Book Awards for books in the haiku field. Two "best-of-issue" prizes are given "through a gift from the Museum of Haiku Literature, Tokyo."

FROM HERE PRESS; XTRAS; OLD PLATE PRESS (II), Box 219, Fanwood, NJ 07023, phone 201-889-7886, founded 1975, editors William J. Higginson and Penny Harter, a small-press publisher of a chapbook series called *Xtras* and flat-spined paperback anthologies and solo collections. The editors want "contemporary work; we have a particular interest in haiku, but also have done everything from haibun and renga to long poems." They do not want "5-7-5 nature poems, poorly crafted traditional verse." The *Xtras* series of books is published on a co-op basis; the author pays half the cost of production and receives half the press run. Other book contracts are individually negotiated. They have recently published poetry by Ruth Stone, Elizabeth Searle Lamb, Dee Evetts, and themselves. I have seen two sample volumes—a chapbook of haiku, **Casting Into a Cloud**, by Elizabeth Searle Lamb, and a flat-spined paperback, **Lovepoems**, by Penny Harter. As a sample, I chose the beginning lines from Harter's "Our Hair Is Happy":

> *Our hair is happy.*
>
> *You pull the brush through my hair.*
> *It crackles, lifts, curls on your wrist.*
> *My head streams into your hands.*

Lovepoems is handsomely printed on heavy beige stock with b/w drawings by Gilbert Riou, 70 pp. **"Please query with 10 pp. first."** MSS should be **"clear, typed double-spaced, no simultaneous submissions."** Queries will be answered in 1 month. Pay is usually ½ of the press run in author's copies. The press publishes 2-4 books each year, mostly digest-sized, with an average page count of 40. A catalog is free for #10 SASE; average price of books is $3. The editors say, "If you do not read 10-12 books of poetry by living authors each year, please do not consider submitting work to us."

FRONTIERS: A JOURNAL OF WOMEN STUDIES (IV-Feminist), Women Studies, Box 246, University of Colorado, Boulder, CO 80309, founded 1975, is published 3 times a year, circulation 1,000, magazine-sized format, flat spined, 80-92 pp. **Sample: $8. Uses poetry on feminist themes.** Recently published Lorna Dee Cervantes, Judith Johnson, Susanna Sturgis, Gloria Hull, and Debra Bruce. **Pays 2 copies. Reports in 3 to 5 months. No simultaneous submissions.**

FUTURIFIC MAGAZINE (IV-Themes), Foundation for Optimism, 280 Madison Ave., New York, NY 10016, phone 212-684-4913, founded 1976, publisher Balint Szent-Miklosy, is a monthly newsmagazine dealing with **current affairs and their probable outcomes. "We pride ourselves on the accuracy of our forecasting. No other limits than that the poet try to be accurate in predicting the future."** They want to see **"positive upbeat poetry glorifying humanity and human achievements."** *Futurific* is magazine-sized, 32 pp., saddle-stapled, on glossy stock, with b/w photos, art and ads, circulation 10,000. Subscription: $40. **Sample: $5 postpaid. Pays 5 copies.** The editor says, "*Futurific* is made up of the words Future-Terrific. Poets should seek out and enjoy the future if they want to see their work in *Futurific*."

G. W. REVIEW (II, IV-Translations), Marvin Center Box 20, George Washington University, Washington, DC 20052, phone 202-994-7288, founded 1980, editor Adam H. Freedman, appears 2 times a year. "The magazine is published for distribution to the University community and to the Washington, D.C. metropolitan area." It is 36-44 pp., saddle-stapled with cover photograph and b/w photos. They receive about 400 poems a year, accept 40-50. Their annual press run exceeds 3,000 with 20 subscriptions. Subscriptions: $6 for 1 year, $10 for 2 years. **Sample: $3 postpaid. Pays 2 copies per poem. They consider simultaneous submissions but not previously published poems. Reports in 1-3 months. Editor** sometimes comments on rejections when the staff likes the work but thinks it needs to be revised. The editor adds, "We do not mind writers attempting to experiment, so long as experimentation isn't used to mask lack of forethought."

GAIRM; GAIRM PUBLICATIONS (IV-Ethnic, foreign language), 29 Waterloo St., Glasgow, G2 6BZ Scotland, editor Derick Thomson, founded 1952. *Gairm* is a quarterly, circulation 2,000, which uses **poetry in Scottish Gaelic only.** It has published the work of all significant Scottish Gaelic books, and much poetry translated from European languages. An anthology of such translations, *European Poetry in Gaelic*, appeared in August 1990 (price £7.50 or $15). **All of the publications of the press are in Scottish Gaelic. Sample of *Gairm*: $2.50.**

‡GALACTIC DISCOURSE (IV-Themes, science fiction/fantasy), 1111 Dartmouth #214, Claremont, CA 91711, phone 714-621-3112, founded 1977, editor Laurie Huff, appears irregularly "when I have time, less than once per year," an anthology of fiction, poetry and art **"produced by 'Star Trek' fans**

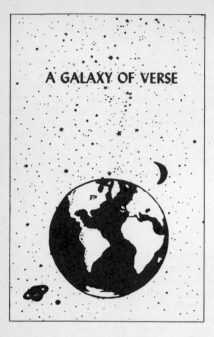

A GALAXY OF VERSE

Editor Ruth Grundy says the cover of her magazine, A Galaxy of Verse, has undergone numerous minor changes, "mainly depicting actual galactic presences such as the North Star, Big and Little Dipper and various planets rather than the indiscriminate 'dots' representing the stars in the original." Both Grundy and co-editor Linda Banks feel this cover is appropriate because of its implication of covering a wide spectrum of poets and their works.

for 'Star Trek' fans, using poetry about 'Star Trek' and its characters. Prefer structured poetry, but will look at all styles. No poorly-done satire." They have recently published poetry by Leslie Fish, Harriett Stallings, and Ellen Kobrin. The editor describes it as magazine-sized, "offset, color (silk-screen type) cover, line and half-tone art and graphics." She receives 5-10 submissions per month, uses 20-30 per issue. Press run: 1,000+. **Sample, postpaid, for SASE. Send SASE for guidelines. Pays 1 copy. Simultaneous submissions OK and previously published poems "negotiable." Editor comments on submissions "especially if requested."**

A GALAXY OF VERSE LITERARY FOUNDATION (I, IV-Membership), 10463 Sandra Lynn, Dallas, TX 75228, founded 1974, co-editors Ruth Grundy and Linda Banks, appears twice a year, and **a $12.50 membership fee guarantees each member publication of at least one poem in each issue. They want "rhymed or free form. No pornographic or unintelligible junk."** They have recently published poems by Amy Jo Schoonover, William D. Barney, Virginia Lillie, Patricia and Wilfred Johnson, Jack E. Murphy, Violette Newton, Grace Haynes Smith, and Marcella Siegel. Galaxy welcomes beginners to its cultural forum, along with its many nationally-known poets. *Galaxy* is digest-sized, saddle-stapled, photocopied from typescript with b/w card cover, 80-84 pp. **Sample copy $2.50.** *Galaxy* offers cash award contests for humor, quatrain, haiku, narrative, etc., paying $10-50. Send SASE for guidelines and contests.

THE GALILEO PRESS; GALILEO BOOK SERIES (II), 15201 Wheeler Lane, Sparks, MD 21152, founded 1981, poetry editors Julia Wendell and Jack Stephens. The imprint **Galileo Books** is used for collections of poems by individuals, 60 pp., flat-spined, hard- and paperback editions. **Query regarding book publication with publishing and biographical information. Replies to queries immediately, to submissions in 3-6 months. Considers simultaneous submissions. Payment: 10% royalties plus 25 paperback copies and 15 cloth copies. Send SASE for catalog. For sample copy, "send letter of request and we will bill you."** The editors often comment on rejections.

THE GALLEY SAIL REVIEW (II), Suite 42, 1630 University Ave., Berkeley, CA 94703, phone 415-486-0187, editor Stanley McNail. *The Galley Sail Review* was originally founded in 1958 and published until 1971 in San Francisco; second series is now based in Berkeley. Publication appears three times a year: spring, summer, and fall-winter. The editor says, "*GSR* is like many other 'littles' in that it **compensates its contributors in copies.** Since its inception it has survived without recourse to governmental or foundation grants, but is supported out of the editor's pocket and produced as a 'one-man' magazine entirely. We (editorial 'We') do not conduct contests or offer prizes, but **we endeavor to find and publish the best, most insightful and imaginative contemporary poetry extant. We do not promote any literary 'school' or ideological clique. We use both poetry and reviews."** Some recent contributors include John Oliver Simon, Serena Fusek, Gary Snyder, James Broughton, and Laurel Ann Bogen. The editor chose these lines from "The Last Walk" by Scott E. Thomas:

> Spring is here and this is our last walk
> on this familiar path, this ribbon of worn-out earth,
> a stream bed in the rainy weeks.

The Galley Sail Review is digest-sized, offset on fairly thin paper, 44 pp., saddle-stapled, with cover of the same paper. Single copy price is $3, subscription $8/3 issues; "a 6-issue minimum subscription at $15 required from institutions. Outside US and Canada add $2 for postage."

GANDHABBA; NALANDA UNIVERSITY PRESS (IV-Themes), 622 East 11th St., New York, NY 10009, phone 212-533-3893, founded 1983, editor Tom Savage, a yearly poetry magazine with **"emphasis on post-Beat, New York school and language works. Each issue is thematically oriented." The editor does not want "Academic, rhymed verse, self-indulgent, egotistical 'punk' poetry that extols violence, toughness and brutality. Also, no religious poetry, please."** He has published poems by Allen Ginsberg, Bernadette Mayer, Anne Waldman, and Jackson Mac Low. *Gandhabba* is thick (98 pp.), mimeographed on fairly rough paper, magazine-sized, with white glossy card front cover illustrated in b/w, stapled on left side. Circulation is 400, of which 50 are subscriptions, 10 go to libraries, and 100 are newsstand sales. Price per copy is $3.50, subscription $12/3 issues. **Sample available for $4 postpaid. Make all checks payable to Thomas Savage. Pay is 2 copies. Simultaneous submissions: "While I would prefer not to become the recipient of poems sent to ten or twenty magazines at the same time primarily because such poets usually have never seen my magazine, only the listing, I have no objection to prior publication or subsequent publication of work published in my magazine. In the case of previously published work, I wish only to know where it has been published." Submissions are reported on in 6-12 months and time to publication is the same.** The editor says, "My tastes are broad but my intentions for each issue are quite specific. In order to avoid time wasting and disappointment, it seems better that anyone wishing to submit to *Gandhabba* at least write to me requesting a copy and inquiring as to the theme of the next issue."

GARGOYLE; PAYCOCK PRESS (II), 4953 Desmond, Oakland, CA 94618, phone 415-658-4645, founded 1976, editor/publisher Toby Barlow, wants poetry with '90s edge, and bent irony, avoids most narrative poetry." They have recently published poetry by Rosmarie Waldrop, Ted Joans, Roy Fisher, Charles Bukowski, Elaine Equi, Heather McHugh, and James Bertolino. *Gargoyle* appears twice a year in a format that "varies all the time—from 400 pp. offset with color cover and graphics and ads to cassettes to books." Every issue I have seen has been a gorgeous flat-spined production. Circulation: 2,000 to 100 subscribers, 400 shelf sales, 200 copies for review or exchange. Subscription: $15. **Sample $7.95 postpaid. Pays 1 copy plus half-price for others. Reports in 1 month. Send 5 poems per batch, no simultaneous submissions. For book publication query with 5 sample poems, bio, previous publications. Pays 10% of press run plus 50% of sales after break-even point.**

GARM LU: A CANADIAN CELTIC ARTS JOURNAL (IV-Ethnic, foreign language), 81 St. Mary St., Toronto M5S 1J4, Canada, founded 1986, contact editor, considers **"poetry of Celtic interest, written in a Celtic language or English or French."** The magazine (which I have not seen) appears twice a year. The editor describes it as magazine-sized, typeset and copied, 50 pp., flat-spined, using pen and ink art on heavy paper. "We don't receive much poetry, but we would like 5 or 6 entries/edition." Press run of about 400 for 250 subscriptions (10 libraries), 80 shelf sales. Subscription: Canadian $6. **Sample: $3 Canadian postpaid. Pays 1 copy. Simultaneous submissions and previously published poems OK. Editor provides "limited comments" on rejections.** "There are 2 editions/year, and in one of these we hope to offer a cash award for the winning poem in our contest, but the prize will be worth about Canadian $20 only."

‡GAS: THE JOURNAL OF THE GROSS AMERICANS SOCIETY (IV-Humor, horror), P.O. Box 397, Marina, CA 93933, phone 408-384-2768, editor Jeannette M. Hopper, is a "small-press publisher of SF, horror, fiction, dark humor, cartoons, short comics, reader-interest non-fiction and satire." *Gas* is a quarterly, 32-40 pp., saddle-stapled, digest-sized magazine, computer typeset and printed with color cover; most fiction and some poetry illustrated with b/w art. Carries some classified advertising, letters of comment." "*Gas* accepts anything from limericks to epic poetry in rhymed form. Free verse acceptable if the meaning and mood are clear. 50-line limit, with vivid images and strong emotion or sensation. Much of the poetry in *Gas* is serious, intended to make the reader think about the human condition. No religious, political, or overtly pornographic (erotic is acceptable, however)." They have recently published poetry by Bruce Boston and Wayne Allen Sallee and, as a sample, offer these lines from "Symbiosis" by John Powers:

> A bed, once living;
> moving at every wheeze.
> Now to lie dormant;

> *conscious only of*
> *its death.*

Gas "appears irregularly, but schedule for submissions is approximately every 6 months. Receives about 200 poems per year, accepts 6-8 per issue." **Sample: $3.50 postpaid. Send SASE (#10) for guidelines. Pays $1 plus copy per poem. Subscription not required but "recommended, so potential contributors will know what *Gas* is about." MSS should be typed, submit batches of no more than 3 poems, 1 poem per page. No simultaneous submissions. No previously published poems.** The editors advise, "While *GAS* is made up of horror, humor, and blends of those two genres, most of the poetry published here is dark and serious. Poets have the opportunity of saying what others rarely even think about—or find too painful to think about. A poet should *discover* something in writing a poem, not merely rehash old images, emotions, and events."

GÁVEA-BROWN PUBLICATIONS; GÁVEA-BROWN: A BI-LINGUAL JOURNAL OF PORTUGUESE-AMERICAN LETTERS AND STUDIES (IV-Ethnic, bilingual), Box O, Brown University, Providence, RI 02912, phone 402-863-3042, founded 1980, editors Onésimo T. Almeida and George Monteiro, is a small-press publisher of books and a journal **relating to the Portuguese-American experience.** They publish flat-spined collections of poetry in their journal. They have recently published poetry by Jorge de Sena, João Teixeira de Medeiros and Thomas Braga. As a sample I chose the first stanza of "At the Portuguese Feast" by Nelson H. Vieira:

> *Pushing my way through the jostling crowds*
> *Where Lusitanian ancestry strikes me in every face,*
> *I celebrate my annual sensation of pride and discomfort*
> *Knowing I shall never resolve the tug-of-war that is my fate.*

Gávea-Brown is handsomely printed, 100+ pp., digest-sized, flat-spined, with a glossy colored card cover. Its "purpose is to provide a vehicle for the **creative expression of the Portuguese immigrant experience.**" It has a circulation of 450. $15 for a subscription (double issue). **Sample: $15 postpaid for a double issue, $7.50 for a pre-1982 single issue. Pays 3 copies. Reports in 3 months. Has a 1 year backlog. Submit sample poems and query regarding book publication. Photocopy, dot-matrix OK. Pays copies.** The books I have seen much resemble the journal in format.

THE GAY MEN'S PRESS; GAY VERSE (IV-Gay), P.O. Box 247, London N17 9QR, England, phone 01-365-1545, founded 1979, poetry editor Aubrey Walter. "We are the major British publishers of books of gay interest, aiming to reflect and record the extent and variety of our gay culture." **Gay Verse** is a series of poetry publications by various writers. They publish flat-spined paperbacks and want **"poetry that has something to say about the experiences of being gay in the context of wider society. No form, style, length restrictions. No egocentric coming out reflections or self-indulgent pornography."** They have recently published poetry by John Gambril Nicholson, Martin Humphries, and Steve Cranfield. As a sample the editor selected these lines (poet unidentified):

> *I'm into pain, I must be or I guess*
> *I'd stop handcuffing us in poetry*
> *Making us M's to serve love's mighty S.*
> *That's tough on you, true, tougher still on me.*

"Prefer introductory letter in advance." Send 4-8 sample poems, bio, and statement of aesthetic or poetic aims. "We actively seek new and unpublished poets with something of pertinence to say." Pays advance ("varies").

‡GAZELLE PUBLICATIONS (V, IV-Children), 5580 Stanley Dr., Auburn, CA 95603, founded 1976, editor Ted Wade, is a publisher for home schools and compatible markets including **books of verse for children. He is not currently considering unsolicited manuscripts.**

GENERATOR (IV-Form/style), 8139 Midland Rd. Mentor, OH 44060, founded 1987, poetry editor John Byrum, is a yearly magazine "devoted to the presentation of **language poetry and 'concrete' or visual poetic modes." If you don't know what these terms mean, I advise you not to submit without having seen a sample copy.** They have recently published poetry by Susan Bee, John M. Bennett, Charles Bernstein, Bruce Andrews, Tom Beckett, Stephen Ratcliffe and Ron Silliman. As a sample the editor selected these lines by Tom Beckett:

> *Sex and thought are identical—only reversed*
> *Insulated between witness and wetness*
> *one never knows what one needs*
> *Things get done in a major miniseries*
> *The world is all that takes the place*
> *of allegorical invasions*

Generator is magazine-sized, side-stapled, using b/w graphics, photocopied, with matte card cover. John Byrum says he receives work from 200 poets a year, of whom 25% are accepted. Press run is 200 copies for 20 subscriptions of which 5 are libraries. **Sample: $4.50 postpaid. Send SASE for guidelines. Pays 2 copies. "Visual works should be adaptable to 8½×11" page size. Poems should be no longer than 5 pages."** Simultaneous submissions OK, previously published poems used "occasionally." **Reports "usually 2-3 weeks."** The editor adds, "Worthwhile writers do not need advice and should not heed any but their own."

‡**GEORGIA JOURNAL (IV-Regional)**, P.O. Box 27, Athens, GA 30603-0027, poetry editor Janice Moore. The *Georgia Journal* is a quarterly magazine, circulation 5,000, covering the state of Georgia. Send SASE for guidelines. **Sample: $3. They use poetry "mostly from Southern writers but not entirely. It should be suitable for the general reader."** Publishes 20-30 poems per year. **Submit maximum of 3-4 poems, maximum length 30 lines. Pays in copies. Reports in 2-3 months.**

UNIVERSITY OF GEORGIA PRESS; CONTEMPORARY POETRY SERIES (II), Terrell Hall, University of Georgia, Athens GA 30602, phone 404-542-2830, press founded 1938, series founded 1980. Series editor Bin Ramke, publishes four collections of poetry per year, **two of which are by poets who have not had a book published,** in simultaneous hardcover and paperback edition. **"Writers should query first for guidelines and submission periods." There are no restrictions on the type of poetry submitted,** but "familiarity with our previously published books in the series may be helpful." **$10 submission fee.**

THE GEORGIA REVIEW (II), The University of Georgia, Athens, GA 30602, phone 404-542-3481, founded 1947, editor Stanley W. Lindberg, associate editor Stephen Corey. This is a distinguished, professionally printed, flat-spined quarterly, 200+ pp., 7×10", glossy card cover. They use 60-70 poems a year, less than a 10th of a percent of those received. Subscription: $12 a year. Circulation: 5,300. **Sample: $4 postpaid. No submissions accepted during June, July and August. Rarely uses translations. Submit 3-5 poems. Pays $2 per line. Reports in about 8 weeks. No simultaneous submissions.** They have recently published poetry by Gerald Stern, Lisel Mueller, Philip Booth, Seamus Heaney, Linda Pastan, Albert Goldbarth, and Charles Simic. As a sample, Stephen Corey selected the opening lines of "Horse and Tree" by Rita Dove:

> *Everybody who's anybody longs to be a tree—*
> *or ride one, hair blown to froth.*
> *That's why horses were invented, and saddles*
> *tooled with singular stars.*

‡**THE GETTYSBURG REVIEW (II)**, Gettysburg College, Gettysburg, PA 17325, phone 717-337-6770, founded 1988, editor Peter Stitt, is a multidisciplinary literary quarterly using **any poetry except that which is "badly written."** I have not seen a copy. They accept 2-3% of submissions received. Press run 3,000 for 1,500 subscriptions. **Sample, postpaid: $5. Pays $2/line.**

‡**GHOST TOWN QUARTERLY (IV-Themes)**, Box 714, Philipsburg, MT 59858, phone 406-859-3365, founded 1988, editor Donna B. McLean, is a "quarterly magazine devoted to preserving the **history surrounding ghost towns and abandoned sites** and presenting it in a manner both interesting and informative, using **poetry to provide variety and act as 'fillers.' Any form; length open, up to approximately 350 words. Pertaining to heritage, history, or the 'old West.' Can also support a photograph or historical document by the poem and have a definite value in what it says by historical content. Nothing vulgar or obscene, no modern-day crusaders, or poetry having no relation to our themes."** They have recently published poetry by Harold K. Armstrong. As a sample I selected the poem, "Wild Roses," published with a photo by the author, Garnet Stephenson:

> *'Tis summer and roses are blooming*
> *Throughout Montana and.*
> *The lovely flowers are cherished*
> *For beauty and fragrance grand.*
>
> *The old, log building does shelter,*
> *And so these beauties grow tall,*
> *Here in the golden sunshine,*
> *Against the old, log wall.*

It is magazine-sized with glossy pages, side-stapled, front and back covers in color. They use 20-30 poems/year, receive about 4 times that many. Press run: 6,000 for 650 subscriptions of which 11 are libraries, 3,800 shelf sales. Subscription: $11.50. **Sample, postpaid: $3.50. Send SASE for guidelines. Pays 5¢/word plus 1 copy. Simultaneous submissions OK, first (one time) rights preferred.**

‡GIORNO POETRY SYSTEMS RECORDS, DIAL-A-POEM POETS (V), 222 Bowery, New York, NY 10012, phone 212-925-6372, founded 1965, poetry editor John Giorno, "star of Andy Warhol's movie, *Sleep* (1963), who publishes a poetry magazine in three formats: LP record, Compact Disc, and cassette; and a videopak series. He originated Dial-A-Poem in 1968, installing it in many cities in the Unites States and Europe. He has published poetry on the "surface of ordinary objects: Matchbook Poems, T-Shirt Poems, Cigarette Package Poems, Window Curtain Poems, Flag Poems, Chocolate Bar Poems, and Silk-Screen and Lithograph Poem Prints. **No submission information provided.**

GLOBAL TAPESTRY JOURNAL; BB BOOKS (II), Spring Bank, Longsight, Copster Green, Blackburn, Lancs. BB1 9EU, U.K., founded 1963, poetry editor Dave Cunliffe. "**Experimental, avant-garde — specializing in exciting high-energy new writing. Mainly for a bohemian and counter-culture audience. Poetry in the Beat tradition. Don't want contrived, traditional, pompous and academic or pretentious mainstream.**" In addition to the magazine, *Global Tapestry Journal*, BB Books publishes chapbooks. "We want honest, uncontrived writing, strong in form and content. We don't want 'weekend hobby verse' and poetry without energy. They have recently published poetry by William James Kovanda, Billy Childish, Jim Burns, Chris Challis, and A.D. Winans. As a sample the editor selected these lines by Paul Donnelly:

> *i say we're more like clouds that*
> *print themselves on water*
> *but can't stay anywhere long*

GTJ is 9×6", 72 pp., saddle-stapled, typeset in a variety of mostly small sizes of type, rather crowded format, casual pasteup, with b/w drawings, photos, collages, display and classified ads, with a 2-color matte card cover, circulation 1,000 with 450 subscriptions of which 50 are libraries. Subscription (4 issues): $18. **Sample: $2 postpaid. Send SASE for guidelines. Considers previously published poems. Responds "soon," has an 18 month backlog. Pays 1 copy. BB Books publishes about 4 chapbooks of poetry per year. To submit for chapbook publication send 6 samples, cover letter giving publication credits. Pays 10% of press run in copies. Send SASE (with IRCs if foreign) for catalog to buy samples.** David Cunliffe comments, "UK has a limited number of magazines and small press ventures publishing poetry from unknowns. Many little mags are self-publishing cliques or small-time vanity operations. Simultaneous submissions and simultaneous publication are often resented. There is much readership crossover among the non-poet subscribers and they resent seeing the same work in many magazines over a short period. We typeset for a few UK mags and publishers and we see this in the setting jobs we do every week. Many of the editors circulate poet blacklists to help prevent this tendency from spreading."

DAVID R. GODINE, PUBLISHER (V), Horticultural Hall, 300 Massachusetts Ave., Boston, MA 02115, phone 617-536-0761, founded 1970, editor Audrey Bryant, is a "small publisher of quality fiction, poetry, non-fiction, gardening, calligraphy/typography, art and architecture, children's books, and photography. Godine has a wide scope of publishing, and is known for the quality of its production." They publish poetry in simultaneous hardcover/softcover editions. They have recently published books of poetry by Robert Pack, Roger Weingarten and Gail Mazur. As a sample the editor selected these lines by Ben Belitt, from his book **Possessions**:

> *The orange is ceremonious. Its sleep*
> *is Egyptian. Its golden umbilicus*
> *waits in pyramidal light, swath over swath, outwitting*
> *the Caesars. It cannot be ravaged by knives,*

They print 4 books per year, averaging 96 pp. The editor advises, "We are committed into 1992 and therefore cannot consider new submissions for some time to come."

GOLDEN ISIS MAGAZINE; POEM OF THE YEAR CONTEST (IV-Mystical/Occult), P.O. Box 726, Salem, MA 01970, founded 1980, editor, Gerina Dunwich. "*Golden Isis* is a mystical literary magazine of poetry, magick, pagan/Egyptian artwork, Wiccan news, occult fiction, letters, book reviews, and classified ads. **Poetry: Occult, Egyptian, cosmic, euphonic and Goddess-inspired poems, mystical haiku, and magickal chants are published. We are also interested in New Age spiritual poetry, astrological verses, and poems dealing with peace, love and ecology.** "All styles considered; under 60 lines preferred. **We do not want to see religious, pornographic, Satanic, sexist or racist material.**" Recently published poets include: Lady Jenny, Fletcher DeWolf, Vashti, and Jane Wallace Weigel. As a sample the editor chose "Ode to the Crone" by Gina Landers:

> *Queen of darkness, death and birth,*
> *Olden One with power of night,*
> *Casting magick to the Earth*
> *In shadows on a secret flight.*

The magazine is digest-sized, 25-30 pp., desktop publishing, saddle-stapled with paper cover.

International circulation is 3,600. Single copy $2.95 postpaid, subscription $10/year. **Payment: 1 free contributor's copy. Reports within 2-3 weeks. Occasionally comments on rejected material. Submit 1 poem/page, typed single-spaced, name and address on upper left corner and the number of lines on upper right corner; photocopied, previously published and simultaneous submissions OK. All rights revert back to author upon publication.** The magazine sponsors an annual "Poem of the Year" contest that offers cash prizes. Entry fee: $3/poem, deadline December 1, no limit on number of poems entered. Poems should be up to 60 lines, any form, with author's name and address on upper left corner of each page. Free guidelines and contest rules for SASE.

GOLF DIGEST (IV-Sports, humor), 5520 Park Ave., Trumbull, CT 06611, phone 203-373-7000, assistant editor Lois Hains, is a monthly magazine, circulation 1.3 million, **using light verse relating to golf, 1-2 per issue, 4-8 lines. Pays $25. Photocopy OK. Enclose SASE.**

GOOD HOUSEKEEPING (II, IV-Humor, women), Hearst Corp. 959 8th Ave., New York, NY 10019, poetry editor Andrea Krantz, circulation 6,000,000, **women's magazine, uses up to 3 poems per issue for which they pay $10 per line. Light verse and traditional. Submit up to 10 poems; maximum length: 25 lines.**" They no longer return manuscripts. "We look for poems of emotional interest to American women. Must be wholesome, clever, upbeat or poignant." **Submit short humorous verses, anecdotes and 'daffinition' to "Light Housekeeping" editor, Rosemary Leonard. Pays $25 for 2-4 lines; $50, 5-8 lines. Usually overstocked.**

GOOSE LANE EDITIONS (II, IV-Regional), 248 Brunswick St., Fredericton, NB E3B 1G9 Canada, phone 506-450-4251, FAX 506-453-0088, managing editor S. Alexander, founded 1958, a small press that publishes perfect-bound paperback collections of poetry. **"Writers should be advised that Goose Lane considers manuscripts by American poets only in exceptional circumstances, when there is an obvious Canadian connection or when the collection is of exceptional quality."** They receive approximately 400 MSS per year, 10-15 accepted. Writers recently published include Dorothy Lovesay, Alden Nowlan, Renato Trajillo, M Travishare and Douglas Lockhead. The book I have is **From the Bedside of Nightmares** by Suniti Namjoshi. As a sample, I selected the first poem in a sequence called "From Baby M. With Much Love":

> *In those early photographs you (and my father)*
> *look so very young that I'd be inclined*
> *to weep—as people do at weddings—*
> *if I weren't implicated*

The book is 6 × 9", handsomely printed on heavy buff stock, 70 pp., flat-spined with a glossy two-color card cover; its price is $6.95. Editor advises that poets write for catalog first. **"Unsolicited MSS considered. SASE essential (IRCs or Canadian postage stamps only). Reports in 8-10 weeks. Authors receive royalty of 10% of retail sale price on all copies sold. Copies available to author at 40% discount."**

‡GOSPEL PUBLISHING HOUSE; PENTECOSTAL EVANGEL; LIVE; HI-CALL; JUNIOR TRAILS (IV-Religious, children/teens), The General Council of the Assemblies of God, 1445 Boonville, Springfield MO 65802, phone 417-862-2781, FAX: 417-862-8558, editor Richard G. Champion. *Pentecostal Evangel* is a weekly magazine emphasizing **news of the Assemblies of God for members of the Assemblies and other Pentecostal and charismatic Christians,** circulation 280,000. **Religious and inspirational poetry.** "All poems submitted to us should be related to religious life. We are Protestant, evangelical, Pentecostal, and any doctrines or practices portrayed should be in harmony with the official position of our denomination (Assemblies of God)." **Free sample copy and writer's guidelines. Submit maximum 3 poems. Submit seasonal/holiday material 6 months in advance. Computer printout submissions acceptable, prefers letter-quality. Reports in 3 months. Pays 50-75¢/line on acceptance.** *Live,* editor John T. Maempa, is a weekly **for adults in Assemblies of God Sunday schools,** circulation 200,000. **Traditional free and blank verse, 12-20 lines. "Please do not send large numbers of poems at one time." Submit seasonal material 1 year in advance; do not mention Santa Claus, Halloween or Easter bunnies. Computer printout submissions acceptable. Reports within 3-6 weeks, submissions held for further consideration may require more time. Free sample copy and writer's guidelines for 7 × 10 SASE and 35¢ postage. Letters without SASE will not be answered. Pays 20¢/line on acceptance.** *Hi-Call* is a weekly magazine of Christian fiction and articles for **church-oriented teenagers, 12-17,** circulation 95,000. **Free verse, light verse and traditional, 10-30 lines. Buys 30 poems per year. Submit seasonal/holiday material 1 year in advance. Simultaneous, photocopied and previously published submissions OK if typed, double-spaced, on 8 × 11 paper. Computer printout submissions acceptable; prefers letter-quality. Reports in 6 weeks. Sample copy for 8 × 11 SAE and 2 first class stamps; writer's guidelines for SAE. Pays 25¢/line, minimum of $5 on acceptance.** *Junior Trails* is a weekly tabloid covering **religious fiction and biographical, historical and scientific articles with a spiritual emphasis for boys and girls ages 10-11,** circulation 75,000. **Free verse and light verse. Buys 6-8 poems per**

year. Submit seasonal/holiday material 1 year in advance. Simultaneous and previously published submissions OK. Computer printout submissions acceptable, prefers letter-quality. Reports in 2 months. Sample copy and writer's guidelines for 9 × 12 SAE and 2 first class stamps. Pays 20¢/line on acceptance. "We like poems showing contemporary children positively facing today's world. These poems show children who are aware of their world and who find a moral solution to their problems through the guidance of God's Word. They are not 'super children' in themselves. They are average children learning how to face life through God's help."

‡GOTTA WRITE NETWORK LITMAG; MAREN PUBLICATIONS (I,IV-Science fiction/Fantasy, membership), 612 Cobblestone Circle, Glenview, IL 60025, Founded 1988, editor/publisher Denise Fleischer, is a quarterly saddle-stapled 40-page magazine featuring "general poetry, articles and short stories. Half of the magazine is devoted to science fiction and fantasy in a section called 'Sci-Fi Fan Galleria.' **"I'm open to well-crafted, clear poetry that doesn't have to be dissected to understand its message. Poetry that leaves the reader with a special feeling. Can be of any genre. No sexually graphic material, obscenities, or lengthy poetry."** She has recently published poetry by H.R. Felgenhauer, John Grey, C.R. Riehle, Jane Andrews, Anne Simon, and C. David Hay. As a sample, the editor selected these lines from "A Fantasy—The Unicorn" by Ray DePalma:

> *Running, crushing twigs*
> *Rustling dry leaves*
> *Human voices reverberate*
> *Swallows cathedral silence of her woodland.*
> *Quick breeze cutting in and out*
> *Carrying fragrance of her presence.*

"Gotta Write Network members receive more than a quarterly magazine. In subscribing, they become part of a support group of both beginners and established poets. I offer critiques at request, will even retype a poem to point out spelling errors and suggest other appropriate markets. Members are from all walks of life: housewives, religious persons, seniors, nursing home residents. One resides in a New York prison." Press run: 100 for 38 subscribers. "I'm striving to give beginners a positive starting point and to encourage them to venture beyond rejection slips and writer's block. Publication can be a reality if you have determination and talent. There are over a thousand U.S. litmags waiting for submissions. So what are you waiting for?" Subscription: $12. **Sample, postpaid: $2.50 plus 90¢ postage.** The editor says, **"I encourage poets to purchase a sample copy before subscribing. This way they can see just how varied the information is." Pays 1 copy. Reports in "a few days. Include a cover letter and SASE. If there's an entry fee, pay it up front."** Maren Publications has published 1 chapbook, **Poetry Cafe.** She adds, "Write the way you feel the words. Don't let others mold you into an established poet's style. Poetry is about personal imagery. Write clearly or ask your family for a typewriter for Christmas. Most of all, love what you do."

GRAHAM HOUSE REVIEW (II, IV-Translations), Box 5000, Colgate University, Hamilton, NY 13346, phone 315-824-1000, ext. 262, founded 1976, poetry editors Peter Balakian and Bruce Smith, appears yearly. "We publish contemporary poetry, poetry in translation, essays, and interviews. **No preferences for styles or schools, just good poetry."** They have published poems by Seamus Heaney, Marilyn Hacker, Maxine Kumin, Michael Harper, and Carolyn Forché. As a sample the editor selected this sample from Derek Walcott's "Winter Lamps":

> *Are they earlier, these*
> *winter dark afternoons,*
> *whose lamps, like croziers*
> *ask the same questions*

GHR is digest-sized, flat-spined, 120 pp., professionally printed on heavy stock, matte color card cover with logo, using 100 pp. of poetry in each issue, circulation 500, with 300 subscriptions of which 50 are libraries. They receive about 2,000 freelance submissions of poetry per year, use 20-50. **Sample: $7.50 postpaid. No photocopies. Reports in 2 months or less, pays 2 copies.**

GRAIN; SHORT GRAIN CONTEST (II), Box 1154, Regina, Saskatchewan, Canada S4P 3B4, phone 306-757-6310, is a literary quarterly. *"Grain* strives for artistic excellence, seeks material that is accessible as well as challenging to our readers. Ideally, a *Grain* poem should be well-crafted, imaginatively stimulating, distinctly original." They have recently published poems by Maggie Helwig, Richard Stevenson and Jerry Rush. It is a digest-sized format, professionally printed using rather small, light type, with chrome-coated cover, 96 pp., circulation 1,000+, with 629 subscriptions of which 84 are libraries. Subscription: $15 (Canadian). They receive about 360 freelance submissions of poetry per year, use 40-60 poems per year. I selected as a sample the opening of "Love Words" by Janice Kulyk Keefer:

> *Your tongue in my mouth as*
> *suddenly you kiss me*

> *burns hot honey.*
> *I lie. Not honey.*
> *No such stuffed sweetness — it is*
> *no taste but the*
> *grained feel of flesh. . .*

Sample: $5 plus IRC (or 78¢ Canadian postage). They want "no poetry that has no substance." **Submit maximum of 6 poems. Photocopies OK. Prefers letter-quality to dot-matrix. Pays $30 per poem. Send SASE for guidelines.** The editor comments, "Only work of the highest literary quality is accepted. Read several back issues. Get advice from a practicing writer to make sure the work is ready to send. Then send it." *Grain* holds an annual Short Grain Contest. Entries are either prose poems (a lyric poem written as a prose paragraph or paragraphs in 500 words or less) or post-card stories. Prizes in each category, $250 first, $150 second, $100 third and honorable mentions. All winners and honorable mentions receive a certificate and regular payment for publication in *Grain*. Entries are normally accepted between January 1 and March 31.

‡**GRASSLANDS REVIEW (I)**, NT Box 13706, Denton, TX 76203, phone 817-565-2025, founded 1989, editor Laura B. Kennelly, is a magazine **"to encourage beginning writers and to give creative writing class experience in editing essays, fiction, poetry, using any type; shorter poems stand best chance."** As a sample the editor selected these lines by Holly Mulder:

> *The old will shuffle indoors,*
> *sit by lighted portraits, hide*
> *their knees under grey blankets,*
> *and clutch at quiet with prayerful hands.*

The copy I have seen is 54 pp., professionally printed, digest-sized, photocopied, saddle-stapled with soft cover. They accept 8-10 of 100 submissions received. Press run 200. **Sample, postpaid: $1. Pays 2 copies. Submit only during October and March. Reports in 6-8 weeks. Editor comments on submissions "sometimes."**

GRAYWOLF PRESS (V), Box 75006, Saint Paul, MN 55175, phone 612-222-8342, founded 1975, poetry editor Scott Walker, **does not read unsolicited MSS.** They have published poetry by Tess Gallagher, Linda Gregg, Jack Gilbert, Chris Gilbert and William Stafford. **Pays 6-10% royalties, 10 author's copies, advance negotiated.**

GREAT ELM PRESS; UPRIVER CHAPBOOK SERIES (V, IV-Nature/rural/ecology, regional), 1205 Co. Rt. 60, Rexville, NY 14877, phone 607-225-4592, founded 1984, Walt Franklin, editor/publisher. Great Elm is a small press dedicated to the writing of rural affairs, to bio-regionalism, to the universal qualities found in local life. The press produces chapbooks and anthologies in limited editions. **"We are not accepting unsolicited submissions in 1991 in order to complete other necessary projects."** The editor says, **"We hold no specifications as to form, length or style. Subject matter is often traditional, Native American, mythical or geographically informed."** They do not want **"abstract, self-involved, confessional rantings."** Some poets the press has published are Terrance Keenan, Andrea Abbott, and Ed Davis. The editor chose these sample lines from "Learning to Float in the Monocacy" by Jean Pearson:

> *I am drifting deep in a reverie of rivers.*
> *My small mouth churns with songs.*
> *All that is left of me streams*
> *with the deep, eddying Knowledge*
> *of how to go home.*

The press publishes 5-6 books/year, 24-40 pp., digest-sized, flat-spined paperbacks. T. Parkins says, "We appreciate writers with a sense of Williams' 'no ideas but in things.' Our primary interest lies in the 'bioregional,' that buzzword indicating that a given locale is more than a simple reading of humanity, but is, in fact, an intricate and interrelated realm of man, animal and plant — their histories reflected in a geographic place. In addition to books informed by places no matter the locale, we are also publishing the Upriver Chapbook Series which publishes work inspired by the upper Susquehanna River watershed." Sample publications I have seen are photo-offset from typewritten copy on buff or white stock, matte card cover with illustration, price $3.50 each.

GREAT LAKES POETRY PRESS; COASTAL CLASSIC POETRY CONTEST; MIDWEST SUMMER POETRY CONTEST; SOUTHERN CLASSIC POETRY CONTEST; POETICS (I, IV-Anthology), Box 56703, Harwood Heights, Il 60656, phone 312-631-3697, founded 1987, poetry editor Chuck Kramer, is essentially a subsidy publisher. See the listing for American Poetry Association under Contests and Awards for a discussion of a similar business. Though many feel these operations are exploitative of poets, the contests have sizable prizes — and you do not have to buy a copy of the anthology in order to win

Close-up

Dana Gioia
Poet

Photo by Jan Karp

Some nights I drove down to the beach to park
And walk along the railings of the pier.
The water down below was cold and dark,
The waves monotonous against the shore.
The darkness and the mist, the midnight sea,
The flickering lights reflected from the city—
A perfect setting for a boy like me,
The Cecil B. DeMille of my self-pity.

That stanza from Dana Gioia's "Cruising with the Beach Boys" embodies the clarity, apparent simplicity, and emotional evocation of much of his work, which, often, like this poem, has a strong narrative thrust. Poets know Gioia as one of the major practitioners of and spokespersons for the burgeoning movements known as the "new" formalism and "new" narrative.

On the other hand, the business world knows this young man (40 in December, 1990) as a key executive in one of America's major corporations. His wife, also a corporate executive, probably regards his most important function as that of family man and father of their two-year-old son.

"People always seem to ask me," he says, "how I find time to write when I have a family and a fulltime job. In some ways this strikes me as a silly question. I don't know anyone who doesn't feel he is too busy—at least anyone who isn't retired. In the 1990s everyone in America has too much to do." But, he points out, people always find time to do "the things they really feel are important."

Dana says he begins writing after all other pressing obligations are done. "I have only an hour or two each night, but I don't waste it. No matter how tired I am I sit down at my desk and get something done—even if it's only to answer a letter or correct a proof or revise a few lines in translation. On a good night I might get two paragraphs of an essay written or a few lines of a poem. I have learned to take a long-term view—a kind of mental trick, I think, to avoid despair. I know that if I get a little done each evening it will add up. The important thing is to keep working and to be self-critical. It's better to write one good line than a dozen mediocre ones."

Indeed, he believes that "there are enough bad poems in the world without adding more to the heap." Since the external rewards for poetry in money and prestige are so inconsiderable, one might as well take one's time and exercise care to write only the best.

He believes there exists an audience for first-rate serious poetry, recollecting the reaction he witnessed to Woody Allen's "Hannah and Her Sisters." Barbara Hershey, in that film, read aloud e.e. cummings' "somewhere I have never travelled," the poem that ends with "nobody, not even the rain, has such small hands." Dana says, "Out in the audience, while that poem was being read, there was an absolute hush; when it was over there was a communal sigh, an intake of breath. And I realized that these people in the audience almost never read poetry but they had a hunger for it and an ability to respond to it. What William Carlos Williams said is true: that we may not need poetry but there are people who die every day for lack of what they would find in it. That experience made me very hopeful for the future of poetry in America."

It is not uncommon for Dana's poems to go through 50-75 drafts before he considers them finished. "One struggles toward the illumination of the final poem. I try to approach revision with the same openness to inspiration with which I begin a new poem. I think that kind of slow, incremental inspiration is possible, indeed desirable for a poet."

He advises beginning poets to be patient and not to be too "hungry for quick success. Ambition is good for a writer if it is the ambition to write well, to write about important things. But if that ambition is merely a careerism that craves success by the world's standards, then it will spell doom for that poet. I think it is important to remember how late many American poets published their first books. Frost was 39. Stevens was 43. They waited until they had discovered their own voices. And their first books are still read today."

Dana waited until he was 35 to publish his first book, **Daily Horoscope**. He had already published enough poems in magazines for two full books, but he cut the number to what he regarded as the best. And the book attracted important reviews—not only positive, but negative. Intellectuals were challenged, and some quite disturbed, at Gioia's focus on the concerns of middle-class, often suburban, American readers. A number of academics and self-styled revolutionaries felt betrayed by his example of excellence for "ordinary people." Some critics also objected to his use of rhyme and meter.

"One thing I like about writing in forms," he says, "is that the meter and/or rhyme helps objectify the process of writing and revision. One can hear a bad rhyme across the room— even if the sense is OK, whereas with a free-verse poem, one sometimes leaves a merely adequate line that could be dropped or revised into something better. Working in a hard form also tends to make a poem shorter and more concentrated, whereas working in free-verse (or even blank verse) it is all too easy to run on and on and on."

His parents were working-class: his father a cab driver, his mother a telephone operator. Today his life is one of high culture as well as elegant lifestyle, as the magazine *Connoisseur* noted in an article that labeled him "The Poet in the Gray Flannel Suit." His success in dual careers of business and poetry might serve as a model for aspiring younger Americans. But included in his story is the theme of dedication to hard work. "I have never taken off any time to write in the last 13 years (except for a few vacation days here and there). I would love to have a life full of free time, but I don't think that's necessary to get good writing done. One should not blame one's life for not writing. One should only blame one's self."

—Judson Jerome

(though you might if you want a copy for yourself). Moreover, Great Lakes offers a subsidy publication plan that may interest some beginners (though you might find printers—not "publishers"—who might be more economical for self-publications). Chuck Kramer says he "conducts 3 major areas of business activity: **1) Contests.** We sponsor 6 poetry contests each year. 3 of these are Regional Contests which offer $3,000 in prize money and are open to any poet who would like to enter. We also sponsor 3 National Contests which offer another $1,125 and are open to those poets on our mailing list who receive a free subscription to our newsletter *Poetics*. The regional contests have no entry fees. **2) Anthology publication.** [The anthologies sell for $24.99 plus $3 postage and handling. They are digest sized, professionally printed in rather small type with several poems to a page, 300+ pp., flat-spined with laminated card cover. You have to buy an anthology to be included unless you are a contest prize-winner.] **3) Subsidy publishing.**" He will be glad to send you information on any of these. As a sample of poetry he likes he selected these lines by V. Grayland:

> *A signal flashed from you*
> *Another soldier in this jungle*
> *A Guerrilla on the next mountain.*
> *You took some sun with the mirror in your eye*
> *And threw it across the valley to me.*

GREAT RIVER REVIEW (II), 211 W. 7th, Winona, MN 55987, founded 1977, poetry editor Orval Lund, is published "three times every two years." They want **"high quality contemporary poetry that uses image as the basis for expression." Suggested submission: 4-6 poems."** They have recently published poetry by Jack Myers, Thom Tammaro, Margaret Hasse, Michael Dennis Browne, Pam Harrison, and Tom Hennen. *GRR* is elaborately printed, 6×8", with a featured poet per issue. They use about 50 poems per issue, receive about 500, use 5-10%. Press run of 750 goes to 300-400 subscriptions of which 30-50 are libraries, and have 200-300 newsstand or bookstore sales. Single copy: $4.50, subscription $9 for two issues. **Sample: $4.50 postpaid. Pays 2 copies. Reports on submissions in 4-10 weeks, 4-12 months between acceptance and publication. Simultaneous submissions discouraged. Editor "sometimes" comments on rejections.**

GREEN FUSE POETRY (II, IV-Political, ecology, social issues), 3365 Holland Dr., Santa Rosa, CA 95404, phone 707-544-8303, founded 1984, editor Brian Boldt, is a poetry magazine appearing twice a year. The editor wants **poetry of 60 lines or less, "political, social, environmental concerns. No religious, abstract or trivial themes, please—mostly free verse."** He has recently published poetry by Elizabeth Herron, Maureen Hurley and Elliot Richman. As a sample he selected these lines by Ralph Smith:

> The most beautiful dawn
> is still gathering prismatic pigments.
> We have not yet heard
> Earth's healing song.
> The most beautiful child
> remains unborn.

Green Fuse Poetry, is digest-sized, 44 pp., saddle-stapled, professionally printed with matte card cover with b/w drawings on cover and throughout, no ads. Of 900 poems received per year he accepts about 80. The press run is 350. **"Please no more than 3 submissions. Deadlines: January 15, July 15." Sample: $4 postpaid. Send SASE for guidelines. Pays 1 copy. Simultaneous submissions and previously published poems OK. Reports within 4 months. Editor "sometimes" comments on rejections.**

GREEN MOUNTAINS REVIEW (II), Johnson State College, Johnson, VT 05656, phone 802-635-2356, founded 1975, poetry editor Neil Shepard, appears twice a year and includes poetry (and other writing) by well-known authors and promising newcomers. They have published poetry by Denise Levertov, William Stafford, Hayden Carruth, Theodore Weiss, Roger Weingarten, and Amy Clampitt. *GMR* is digest-sized, flat-spined, 90-120 pp. Of 300 submissions they publish 30 authors. Press run is 1,000 for 200 subscriptions of which 20 are libraries. Subscription is $8/year. **Sample: $4.75 postpaid. Send SASE for guidelines. Pays 1 copy. Submit no more than 5 poems. No simultaneous submissions. Reports in 2-3 months. Editor sometimes comments on rejection slip.**

‡GREEN WORLD PRESS (V, IV-Animals, nature, ethnic), P.O. Box 417, Bethlehem, PA 18016, phone 215-691-6746, founded 1987, editor/publisher Jean Pearson, is a "small press publisher of poemcards and poetry note cards, **intends to begin publishing poetry chapbooks and possibly books by 1991, by invitation only."** She publishes **"poems on animals and nature and by primal peoples. Very well-crafted, showing knowledge of and deep regard for the natural world, no more than 14 lines, no cynical, sentimental, human-centered poems."** She has recently published poetry by Sarah Kirsch and Tommy Olofsson. As a sample the editor selected these lines by Paulus Utsi:

> The fire doesn't burn
> if you lack love
> The reindeer cannot live
> if you lose faith in him.

ALWAYS submit MSS or queries with a stamped, self-addressed envelope (SASE) within your country or International Reply Coupons (IRCs) purchased from the post office for other countries.

"At present I produce poetry postcards and notecards for non-profit organizations such as The Wildlife Information Center (Allentown, PA) and PAWS (Philadelphia). I plan to begin publishing poetry anthologies on the themes of animals and nature in 1991. Poets should understand the nature and behavior of live animals and plants before writing about them." **Sample poemcards 50¢ postpaid.**

THE GREENFIELD REVIEW PRESS (V); THE GREENFIELD REVIEW LITERARY CENTER; ITHACA HOUSE (II), P.O. Box 308, Greenfield Center, NY 12833, phone 518-584-1728, founded 1971, poetry editor Joseph Bruchac III, all from a nest of literary activity, The Greenfield Review Literary Center, which publishes a regular newsletter, has a poetry library and offers workshops and lectures in a former gas station. **Send large SASE with 2 oz. postage for a handout on "marketing tips" and sample copy of the newsletter. For book submissions query with samples.** Joe Bruchac advises, "Buy books of poetry and literary magazines. The community you support is your own. Don't be in too much of a hurry to be published." Ithaca House, an imprint acquired in 1986, has been one of the longest-going and highly respected small press publishers in the country since 1970, and will continue under Greenfield Review Press to produce a minimum of 2 titles every 2 years, editions of a minimum of 750 copies, letterpress. **Send SASE for Ithaca House guidelines. No submissions will be considered in 1990.**

GREENHOUSE REVIEW PRESS (V), 3965 Bonny Doon Rd., Santa Cruz, CA 95060, founded 1975, publishes a series of poetry chapbooks and broadsides."**No unsolicited mss will be accepted until 1991 due to backlog of titles in production.**" Send SASE for catalog to buy samples. Pays copies.

GREEN'S MAGAZINE; CLOVER PRESS (I,II), P.O. Box 3236, Regina, Saskatchewan, Canada S4P 3H1, founded 1972, editor David Green. *Green's Magazine* is a literary quarterly with a balanced diet of short fiction and poetry; Clover Press publishes chapbooks. They publish **"free/blank verse examining emotions or situations." They do not want greeting card jingles or pale imitations of the masters.** Some poets published recently are Sheila Murphy, Mary Balazs, Robert L. Tener, David Chorlton, Helene Schettler-Mason and Fritz Hamilton. As a sample I selected the poem "In Dependence" by April Rhodes:

> Against the roar
> of silence
>
> I must strain to hear
> you whisper
>
> "I'm not in love"

The magazine is digest-sized, 100 pp., with line drawings. A sample chapbook is also digest-sized, 60 pp., typeset on buff stock with line drawings, matte card cover, saddle-stapled. Circulation is 400, subscriptions $12. **Sample: $4 postpaid. Guidelines available for SASE. (International Reply Coupons for U.S. queries and/or MSS). Payment is 2 free copies. Submissions are reported on in 8 weeks, publication is usually in 3 months. The editor prefers typescript, complete originals. Freelance submissions are accepted for the magazine but not for books; query first on latter. Comments are usually provided on rejected MSS.** "Would-be contributors are urged to study the magazine first."

THE GREENSBORO REVIEW; GREENSBORO REVIEW LITERARY AWARD; AMON LINER POETRY AWARD (II), English Dept., University of North Carolina, Greensboro, NC 27412, phone 919-334-5459, founded 1966, editor Jim Clark. *TGR* appears twice yearly and has published poetry by Mary Kratt, Starkey S. Flythe, Jr., Kelly Cherry and Bobby Caudle Rogers. As a sample the editor selected these lines from "Cats Mating" by Susan O'Dell Underwood:

> Yawn of scalping sound
> arches brawling, vaults caterwauling,
> opening wide the mouth of dark,
> stretches bristling hisses of rash skirmish
> into the belly-hide of night.

The digest-sized 120+ pp. flat-spined magazine, colored matte cover, professional printing, uses about 25 pp. of poetry in each issue. Circulation 500 for 300 subscriptions of which 100 are libraries. Uses about 3% of the 1,200 submissions received each year. **Sample: $2.50 postpaid. Submissions accepted August 15-February 15 (deadlines for the 2 issues: September 15 and February 15). No simultaneous submissions, reports in 2-4 months, pays 3 copies.** They offer the Amon Liner Poetry Award and a $250 Greensboro Review Literary Award in poetry and in fiction each year.

GRIT (I), 208 W. 3rd. St., Williamsport, PA 17701, phone 717-326-1771, founded 1882, poetry editor Joanne Decker, is a weekly tabloid newspaper for a general audience of all ages in rural and small-town America. They **use traditional forms of poetry and light verse, 20 lines maximum, for which they pay $6 for 4 lines and under, 50¢ each for each additional line. Send SASE for guidelines.** These sample lines are the first stanza of James Dykes, "Across the Miles":

> *Thoughts of you go homeward winging,*
> *when I'm far away . . . alone!*
> *But my sad heart starts a singing*
> *just to hear you on the phone.*

GROUNDSWELL; HUDSON VALLEY WRITERS GUILD (I,II), P.O. Box 13013, Albany, NY 12212-3013, phone 518-449-8069, founded 1984, poetry editor Jim Flosdorf, is a literary magazine appearing twice a year. Regarding poetry, they say, **"No restrictions except quality. No sloppy, poorly crafted, sentimental work."** They have recently published poetry by Louis Hammer, Joe Bruchac, Diana Reed, Susan Shatorzek, Mark Nepo, and Paul Weinman. It is digest-sized, about 75 pp., offset. They accept 10-15% of work submitted. Press run is 500. Subscription: $12 to individual, $16 to institutions. **Sample: $6 postpaid. Pays 2 copies and "$$'s—depends on funding."** No dot-matrix. Editor sometimes comments on rejections.

GRUE MAGAZINE (IV-Horror), Box 370, New York, NY 10108, founded 1985, editor Peggy Nadramia, a horror fiction magazine "with emphasis on the experimental, offbeat, rude." The editor wants **"Poems of any length including prose-poems, with macabre imagery and themes. Not interested in Poe rip-offs, (although we'll look at rhyming poems if subject is weird enough), 'straight' vampire, ghost or werewolf poems."** She has recently published poems by Denise Dumars, Robert Frazier, Andrew Darlington, G. Sutton Breiding, Wayne Sallee, and Bruce Boston. As a sample she selected these lines from "Those Scarlet Nights in Babylon" by t. Winter-Damon:

> *"Babylon!" the clash of cymbals.*
> *Spangled chattering of tambourines.*
> *The echoing of tattoed skins.*
> *The thunderclap of thudded drums.*
> *Silk slithers across supple, perfumed*
> *curves. On flutes of bone, taunt*
> *the whispers of a thousand*
> *madmen's violet sins . . .*

The magazine is digest-sized, 96 pp., offset, with a glossy b/w cover, "sharp" graphics, and "a centerfold that is unique." It appears 3 times a year and has a circulation of 2,000, of which 500 are subscriptions and 1,000 are newsstand sales. Price per issue is $4.50, subscription $13/year. **Sample: $4.50 postpaid; guidelines are available for SASE. Poets receive 2 copies plus $5 per poem upon publication to a maximum of $5 per issue. They should submit up to 5 poems at a time, photocopied or dot-matrix MSS are OK. Submissions are reported on in 3 to 6 months and time to publication is 12 to 18 months. The editor usually provides criticism of rejected MSS.** Her advice is: "We like poems that go for the throat, with strong, visceral controlling images. We're also interested in poems that comment upon, or challenge the conventions of, the horror genre itself."

GUERNICA EDITIONS INC.; ESSENTIAL POET SERIES, PROSE SERIES, DRAMA SERIES; INTERNATIONAL WRITERS (IV-Regional, translations), Box 633 Station NDG, Montreal, Quebec, Canada H4A 3R1, founded 1978, poetry editor Antonio D'Alfonso. **"We wish to bring together the different and often divergent voices that exist in Canada. We are interested in translations. We are mostly interested right now in prose poetry and essays."** They have recently published poetry by Paol Keineg (France, USA), Roland Morisseau (Haiti), Bert Schierbeek (Holland), Nadine Ltaif (Lebanon), Dacia Maraini (Italy), Dorothy Livesay (Canada), and Claude Péloguin (Quebec). **Query with 1-2 pp. of samples. Send SASE or IRC (Canadian stamps only) for catalog to buy samples.** The editor comments, "We enjoy reading what other people are doing, to go beyond our country and study and learn to love what you originally thought little of."

GUIDELINES MAGAZINE (I, IV-Themes), Box 608, Pittsburg, MO 65724, founded in 1988, poetry editor Susan Nelene Salaki, is a market newsletter, publishing comments by editors and writers on writing and selling MSS and offering the service of distributing guidelines for the editors of various magazine and book publishers to writers who pay $2 for 5; $3/10; $4/15; $5/20. They want **"any form of poetry, maximum length 20 lines unless exceptional, relating to writing and editing."** As a sample, the editor selected this stanza from "Writing A Poem" by Ingrid Reti:

> *Writing a poem is like exploring a cave*

> *the beam of the flashlight*
> *the germ of an idea*
> *lights the opening*
> *what lies beyond is concealed*
> *requires careful, plodding steps*

They receive about 200 poems a year, 15-20 accepted. **Sample: $4 postpaid. Pays 1 copy. No simultaneous submissions or previously published works. Reports in 2-4 weeks. Submit minimum of 3 samples. Send SASE for current theme.** "Your chances of being accepted increase about 90% if your work addresses our current needs (i.e. I have selected a good poem over an excellent poem simply because the good poem lent itself to the general theme of the issue). Haiku are also accepted. All correspondence must be accompanied by an SASE."

‡**GULF STREAM MAGAZINE (II)**, English Dept. Florida International University North Miami Campus, N. Miami, FL 33181, phone 305-940-5599, founded 1989, editor Lynne Barrett, associate editors Pam Gross and Virginia Oesterle, is the biannual literary magazine associated with the creative writing program at FIU. They want **"poetry of any style and subject matter as long as it is of high literary quality."** They have recently published poetry by Gerald Costanzo, Judith Berke, Mike Carson, and Alan Peterson. As a sample, Pam Gross selected these lines from "Those People Once" by Alan Peterson:

> *They stand looking at each other from*
> *three feet away*
> *A whole galaxy could fit now in that space,*
> *though there is nothing there but maddening*
> *folding over each other so loud they*
> *block minutes*
> *a shuffling like cards, all clubs and spades can both hear*

The handsome magazine is digest-sized, flat-spined, 90+ pp. on quality stock with glossy card cover. They accept less than 10% of poetry received. Press run: 750. Subscription: $7.50. **Sample, postpaid: $4. Send SASE for guidelines. Pays 2 free subscriptions. Submit no more than 5 poems. Reports in 4-6 weeks. No simultaneous submissions. Editor comments on submissions "if we feel we can be helpful."**

GYPSY (II); VERGIN' PRESS (V,II), % Belinda Subraman, Box 370322, El Paso, TX 79937, founded 1984 (in Germany), poetry editor Belinda Subraman, publishes poetry, fiction, interviews, articles, artwork and reviews. She wants **poetry that is "striking, moving, but not sentimental, any style, any subject-matter.** They have published poetry by Charles Bukowski, James Purdy, Robert Peters, David Spicer, Al Masarik, Philip O'Conner, and Lyn Lifshin. *Gypsy* appears twice a year, with subscribers and contributors from the U.S., Canada, England, Europe, and other foreign countries. It is magazine-sized, offset, usually a hard spine, around 56-90 pages. Circulation is 800 to 300 subscriptions of which 40 are libraries, about 20 shelf sales. Subscription: $10 a year; per issue: $5. **Sample: $4 postpaid. Pays 1 copy. Reports in 1-3 months.** She publishes **2-3 chapbooks per year under the Vergin' Press imprint** but at present is not accepting unsolicited submissions for these. New writers establish themselves with her by acceptance in *Gypsy*. She **sometimes comments on rejections.** Belinda Subraman says, "This is not a place for beginners. I'm looking for the best in all genres."

HAIGHT ASHBURY LITERARY JOURNAL (II, IV-Social issues), Box 15133, San Francisco, CA 94115, phone 415-221-2017, founded 1979-1980, editors Lena Diethelm, Joanne Hotchkiss, Alice Rogoff, and Will Walker, is a newsprint tabloid that appears 1-3 times a year. They use **"all forms and lengths, subject-matter sometimes political, but open to all subjects. Poems of background — prison, minority experience — often published, as well as poems of protest and of Central America. Few rhymes.** Themes of recent issues include erotic poetry and Latin American poets. They have recently published poetry by Leslie Simon, Jack Micheline, Gary David, Bill Shields, and Eugene Ruggles. As a sample, the editors selected these lines from "Deep in the Evening" by Quill:

> *Deep in the evening*
> *when others are cold, limp creatures*
> *on damp beds, you hold the sun*
> *like a lucky stone to remind me*
> *that daybreak is only a nightmare away*

The tabloid has photos of featured poets on the cover, uses graphics, ads, 16 pp., circulation 2,000. $25 for a lifetime subscription, which includes all back issues. **Sample: $2.50 postpaid. Make checks payable to Alice Rogoff. Send SASE for guidelines. Pays 3 copies, reports in 2 months. Submit up to 6 poems or 8 pp. Photocopy OK, simultaneous OK "if we are informed.** Each issue changes its theme and emphasis. Don't be discouraged if rejected, and please submit again."

HAIKU CANADA (IV-Forms, membership), 67 Court St., Aylmer, PQ J9H 4M1 Canada, is a society of haiku poets and enthusiasts from Canada, the U.S., Japan and elsewhere. Its members share information on haiku, haiku events, societies, markets and publications. *Haiku Canada Sheets* are "an excellent way to share **haiku**," each containing about 20 haiku by one poet, a bio-bibliographical notice on the poet and a photograph. **You must be a member to submit. Pays 10 copies.** They have a large haiku library, sponsor readings, and a Haiku Canada Weekend. They publish *Haiku Canada Newsletter*, "a fact-oriented exchange of information on events, projects and publications. In addition to haiku, senryu, renga and haiku selections, it provides an annual listing of haiku magazines, as well as information on haiku markets, contests, and other societies. **Membership: $20 per year. Sample $5.**

HAIKU HEADLINES: A MONTHLY NEWSLETTER OF HAIKU AND SENRYU (IV-Form), 1347 W. 71st., Los Angeles, CA 90044, founded 1988, editor/publisher David Priebe, uses **haiku and senryu** only. They have recently published haiku by Charles B. Dickson, Matthew Louviere, Beatrice Brissman, and Catherine Buckaway. As a sample the editor selected these haiku by Rengé:

> Elusive moments
>> of communion with nature
>> the Tao of haiku

> Searching through clover
>> for a fabled lucky leaf . . .
>> finding pearls of dew

The newsletter is 4-8 pp. on a double magazine-sized folded sheet punched for a three-ring notebook, desktop publishing. They accept about 10% of submissions. Their press run is 250 with 125 subscriptions of which 3 are libraries. Subscription: $15. **Sample: $1.25 postpaid. Pays 1 copy with SASE, or free extra copy to subscribers. Haiku may be submitted with up to 10 per single page. Submissions are** "answered with proof sheets of acceptances, suggested revisions sheets, with occasional notes on originals—within 30 days."

HAIKU JOURNAL; GEPPO HAIKU JOURNAL; HAIKU JOURNAL MEMBERS' ANTHOLOGY (I, IV-Form, membership), Chabot College Valley Campus, 3033 Collier Canyon Rd., Livermore, CA 94550, phone 415-455-5300, *HJ* founded 1977 and first published by the Yuki Teipei Haiku Society, editor Jerald T. Ball. *HJ* is devoted to haiku and haiku criticism; contest winners and **"members' haiku only are published here."** *Geppo* is a mimeographed newsletter for members using **haiku, especially traditional haiku: 17 syllables with a KIGO."** I have not seen an issue, but the editor describes these as "around 60 pp., 6×9", nicely printed on heavy paper, card stock cover." Press run 300 for 100 subscriptions of which 10 are libraries. **Sample, postpaid: $4.50. Send SASE for guidelines. Simultaneous submissions and previously published poems OK. Editor comments on submissions "especially if response is requested."** They have an annual contest in the spring. Send SASE for rules.

HAIKU QUARTERLY (II,IV-Form), 542 E. Ingram, Mesa, AZ 85203, founded 1989, editor Linda S. Valentine. *Haiku Quarterly* **welcomes unpublished haiku, senryu, and haiku sequences from new and established writers.** They have published haiku by Alexis Rotella, Gary Hotham, Adele Kenny, Geraldine C. Little, Elliot Richman, Francine Porad, vincent tripi, Anthony J. Pupello, and Matthew Louvière. As a sample the editor selected this haiku by Joe Nutt:

> rain without end—
>> frogs also
>> have lost their way

Haiku Quarterly contains 32-36 pp., is professionally printed, saddle-stapled, 70 lb., with glossy 80 lb. cover, press run 250. Subscription: $16. **Sample: $4.50 postpaid. Send SASE for guidelines. No pay, but awards $5 to 4 outstanding poets in each issue. Reports in 4 weeks.** They hold periodic contests; send SASE for rules. "Capture the essense of the moment without being verbose."

HALF TONES TO JUBILEE (II), English Department, Pensacola Junior College, 1000 College Blvd., Pensacola, FL 32504, phone 904-484-1400, founded 1986, faculty editors Walter Spara, Allan Peterson. *HTTJ* is an annual literary journal featuring poetry, short fiction, art. They have recently published poetry by R.T. Smith, Sue Walker, Larry Rubin, Simon Perchik. As a sample the editors selected these lines by Peter Wild from "Smokejumper's Pants," the winner of the 1989 *HTTJ* poetry contest:

> There may be lions in the trees, thistles that
> when the sun hits them just right
> make the amateur photographer famous
> even verbena, diminutive ice cream
> that they shout at underfoot . . .

HTTJ is digest-sized, 100+ pages, perfect bound with matte card cover, professionally printed.

Their press run is 500. They receive 1,000 submissions per year, use 50-60. **Reports 2-3 months, faster when possible. Pays 1 copy.** Subscriptions $4. **Sample: $4. No previously published work, no simultaneous submissions, SASE mandatory.** *HTTJ* sponsors an annual poetry competition, $300 first prize, $200 second, two $50 third prizes, entry $2 per poem, maximum five. Send SASE for rules, deadlines.

‡**HAMMERS; DOUBLESTAR PRESS (II)**, 1718 Sherman #205, Evanston, IL 60201, founded 1989, editor Nat David, is a magazine, first issue in 1990, frequency and other details unavailable at this writing. Most of the poets in the first issue are from the Chicago area. He says he wants "**honest poetry from the depths of the poet's universe and experience, which is cognizant of our interconnectedness.**" As a sample he selected these lines from "Einstein's Daughter" by Barbara Pamp:

> *We are all daughters of Einstein*
> *our inertia grows greater*
> *the closer we get*
> *our reflections disappear*
> *from the mirror*
> *and our fathers all*
> *move away from us*
> *traveling at the speed of light.*

Editor comments on submissions "seldom." Pays 1 copy.

HANDMADE ACCENTS, THE BUYERS GUIDE TO AMERICAN ARTISANS, (IV-Themes), 488-A River Mountain Rd., Lebanon, VA 24266, editor Steve McCay, a quarterly, circulation 25,000. **Sample $3.50 postpaid.** Uses light verse and traditional which has a slant on the art world/community. **Buys 4 poems per year. Submit maximum of 3, up to 50 lines. Pays $5-10.**

HANGING LOOSE PRESS (V); HANGING LOOSE (I, IV-Teens/students), 231 Wyckoff St., Brooklyn, NY 11217, founded 1966, poetry editors Robert Hershon, Dick Lourie, Mark Pawlak and Ron Schreiber. The Press accepts no unsolicited book MSS, but welcomes work for the magazine. The magazine has published poets such as Paul Violi, Donna Brook, Kimiko Hahn, Ron Overton, Jack Anderson, and Kathleen Aguero. As a sample I selected the opening lines of "Bald" by Bill Zavatsky:

> *In the mirror it's plain to see:*
> *Soon I'll be bald, like the two faceless men*
> *Staring at each other in the word "soon."*

Hanging Loose is flat-spined, 72-96 pp., offset, typeset starting with #50, a 224 pp. 20th anniversary issue, on heavy stock with a 2-color glossy card cover. One section contains **poems by high-school-age poets.** The editor says it "**concentrates on the work of new writers.**" It comes out 3 times a year. **Sample: $4.50 postpaid. Submit 4-6 "excellent, energetic" poems, no simultaneous submissions.** "**Would-be contributors should read the magazine first.**" **Reports in 1-12 weeks. Pays.**

HANGMAN BOOKS (V), 32 May Rd., Rochester, Kent ME1 2HY England, founded 1981, director Jack Ketch, publishes literature and poetry by Billy Childish. **Accepting no unsolicited MSS.**

HANSON'S: A MAGAZINE OF LITERARY AND SOCIAL INTEREST (II), 113 Merryman Court, Annapolis, MD 21401, phone 301-626-0744, founded 1988, poetry editor Shannon Rogowski, is a biannual using "**all forms, styles, subjects, and points of view reflective of intelligence and beautifully stated.** No anti-poetry; ignorant of tradition and devoid of form and rhythm." They have recently published poetry by Walt Whitman, Lao Tsu, and William Shakespeare ("We publish one classic poem in each issue.") As a sample the editor selected "Gradual Mosaic" by Ernest Norman:

> *I'm not changing direction/ I'm changing frequency*
> *So that every word I say/ Will be like pyramid racks of*
> *oysters beneath the water.*
> *As I grow old/ The racks will be pulled.*
> *(Only the appearance of racks will be maintained*
> *The tip of the iceberg as social keel.)*
> *Though oysterless,/ I will be covered with pearls.*

It is magazine-sized, 75-100 pp., saddle-stapled with matte card cover in full color. Press run 5,000 for 3,000 subscriptions including 15 library systems. "We receive 200-300 poems per year, publish about 15-20 per year." Subscription: $8. **Sample, postpaid: $2. Send SASE for guidelines. Pays $30-40 plus 1 copy.** "Previous publication is not a prerequisite. We'd rather see honest, careful art, than a resume." Reports in 2-3 weeks. Editor comments on submissions "seldom."

HARCOURT BRACE JOVANOVICH, PUBLISHERS; HBJ CHILDREN'S BOOKS; GULLIVER BOOKS (IV-Children), 1250 Sixth Ave., San Diego, CA 92101, phone 619-699-6810, HBJ Children's Books and Gulliver Books publish hardback and trade paperback books for children. They have recently published books of children's poetry by Jane Yolen, Arnold Adoff, James Dickey, e.e. cummings, Lee Bennett Hopkins, and Carl Sandburg. **Submit complete MS. No dot-matrix. Pays favorable advance, royalty contract and copies. Send SASE for guidelines and book catalog.**

HARD ROW TO HOE; MISTY HILL PRESS (I, IV-Rural), Box 541-I, Healdsburg, CA 95448, phone 707-433-9786. *Hard Row to Hoe,* taken over from Seven Buffaloes Press in 1987, editor Joe E. Armstrong, is a "book review newsletter of literature from rural America with a section reserved for short stories (about 2,000 words) and **poetry featuring unpublished authors. The subject matter must apply to rural America including nature and environmental subjects. Poems of 30 lines or less given preference, but no arbitrary limit. No style limits. Do not want any subject matter not related to rural subjects.**" As a sample the editor selected this poem by Terri McGill:

> We thought it were a fence post,
> looked like it, with the sun goin down
> b'hind it like that. It weren't.
> It were Old Man Dew leanin gainst his hoe
> Like he's ponderin . . .
> could he finish the choppin
> or was the day dyin out
> too fast.

HRTH is magazine-sized, 12 pp. side-stapled, appearing 3 times a year, 3 pp. reserved for short stories and poetry. Press run 300, subscription $7/year. **Sample $2 postpaid. Send SASE for guidelines. Pays 3 copies. Editor comments on rejections "if I think the quality warrants."**

HARPER AND ROW (V), 10 East 53rd St., New York, NY 10022, founded 1817. Harper and Row, as you can tell from the date of founding, is an old-line, highly respected publishing house. Among the 300 titles Harper's publishes each year only 1-2 are books of poetry. **They accept no unsolicited MSS, but the questionnaire they returned does say that poets can submit 6 sample poems.** The poets they publish are, obviously, likely to be fairly well-known before Harper's publishes them; on my shelves I have, for example, volumes published by Harper and Row by William Stafford, Hayden Carruth (in the Colophon imprint), Yehuda Amichai, and Gwendolyn Brooks. All are handsomely produced. As a sample I chose the beginning lines from Gwendolyn Brooks's "Jessie Mitchell's Mother":

> Into her mother's bedroom to wash the ballooning body.
> "My mother is jelly-hearted and she has a brain of
>   jelly:
> Sweet, quiver-soft, irrelevant. Not essential.
> Only a habit would cry if she should die."

If your poetry is good enough to be published by Harper and Row, you probably don't need this directory.

‡THE HARTLAND POETRY QUARTERLY; HARTLAND PRESS (I, II, IV-Children, themes), 6429 Hartland, Fenton, MI 48430, phone 313-750-9134. Founded 1989, contact David Bock, "**prefer 24 lines or less; no style restrictions; no pornography—none—nada—nill! Looking for serious poems by Viet Nam veterans and I mean serious—don't send the one-and-only angry poem—I got that stuff coming out of my ears. Very, very open to good children's poems written only by children under 15 for a special 'coming out' part of the magazine.**" They have recently published poetry by Loriann Zimmer. As a sample the editor selected these lines (poet unidentified):

> And
> you see
> as I see,
> a rainstorm of children
> with tumbling hair
> picking buttercups in a yellow field.

‡The double dagger before a listing indicates that the listing is new in this edition. New markets are often the most receptive to submissions.

Their quarterly is digest-sized, spine-stapled, 25-30 pp. They accept about 40% of 150-200 poems received/year. Press run 150-175, with 30 subscribers of which 7 are libraries, 100 shelf sales. Subscription: $8. **Sample, postpaid: $1. Pays 2 copies. Reports in 2-4 weeks. Include bio with submission.** They publish 2 chapbooks/year of poets already published in the quarterly. Pays 20 copies. The editor says, "Write about what you have lived. Read, read, write, write — repeat cycle 'till death. Support as many small publications as you can afford."

THE HARVARD ADVOCATE (IV-Specialized/university affiliation), 21 South St., Cambridge, MA 02138, founded 1866, a quarterly literary magazine, circulation 4,000, uses **poetry, fiction, features, and art only by those affiliated with Harvard University. Sample: $5. In submitting state your exact relationship to Harvard. Pays.**

‡**HATBOX (II),** P.O. Box 336, Miller N.S.W. Australia 2168, founded 1989, editor David Zarate, is a quarterly using **"any contemporary poetry. No specifications as to form, length, subject-matter, style, etc., only that it be quality work. Nothing overly 'Romantic,' wordy."** They have recently published poetry by Dorothy Porter. As a sample the editor selected these lines from "On the Railway Near the Sea" by Chris Mansell:

> *phrases become stranded*
> *in the doppler effect*
> *sirens sing islands dance*

It is magazine-sized, 88 pp., cover using b/w art. Press run 350 for 30 subscribers. Subscription: $15 (add $8 for overseas, $10 for institutions). **Sample: $4. Pays 1 copy plus subscription. Reports in 2 months. Editor comments on submissions "often."** He says, "New poets (especially young poets) should definitely read as much poetry as they can; both from their own country and others. Also from outside their language if quality translations are available. Gives perspective."

‡**HAUNTS (IV-Science Fiction, fantasy, horror),** Nightshade Publications, Box 3342, Providence, RI 02906, phone 401-781-9438, is a "literary quarterly geared to those fans of the 'pulp' magazines of the 30s, 40s and 50s, with tales of **horror, the supernatural and the bizarre. We are trying to reach those in the 18-35 age group.**" Circulation: 1,000. **Sample: $3.50 plus $1.25 for first class delivery. Send SASE for guidelines. Photocopies OK. Uses free verse, light verse and traditional, about 12-16 poems a year. Send a maximum of 3 poems. Pays copies.**

‡**HAWAII REVIEW (I,II,IV-Form/style, erotica, translations),** % Department of English, 1733 Donaghho Rd., University of Hawaii, Honolulu, HI 96822, phone 808-948-8548, poetry editor John Gesang. "We are interested in **all sorts of poetry, from free verse to formal lyricism, rhyme and meter; heroic narrative, haiku, erotica, light verse, satire and experimentation; we're also interested in poems translated from other languages;** and while *Hawaii Review* has published poets with established reputations like lifshin, Bly, and Merwin, the absolute beginner is very welcome here as well." They have recently published poetry by lyn lifshin, Michael J. Bugeja, Edward Kleinschmidt, and Casey Finch, among others, and translations by Daniel Bourne, Carolyn Tipton, and Stuart Friebert and Andriana Varga. As a sample the editor selected the poem "Movie" by Guy Capacelatro III:

> *She walks in time with the music*
> *in my ears.*
> *Her hair is blond, etc.*
> *She stops, strikes a pose — hand on hip,*
> *hand in her hair, then walks again.*
>
> *It was the movie starring her.*

HR appears twice yearly, 160 pp., flat-spined, 6½×9½", professionally printed on heavy stock with b/w or color cover, 150 subscriptions of which 40 are libraries. Up to 500 are used by University of Hawaii students. Subscription: $12/one year; $20/two years; $5/single issue. **Sample: $5. Send SASE for guidelines. Pays $10-60 plus 2 copies. Editor sometimes comments on rejections. Reporting time: 1-3 months.** The editor says, "Good poetry shows more than psuedo-literary erudition — a good poem speaks to people not just intellectually but at the gut level."

HAYDEN'S FERRY REVIEW, (II), Matthews Center, Arizona State University, Tempe, AZ 85287-1502, phone 602-965-1243, founded 1986, managing editor Salima Keegan, is a handsome literary magazine appearing twice a year. "**No specifications other than limit in number (6) and no simultaneous submissions. We would like a brief bio for contributor's note included. Reports in 8-10 weeks. Submissions circulated to two poetry editors. Contributors receive galley proofs. Editor comments on submissions "often."**" They have recently published poetry by Dennis Schmitz, Maura Stanton, Ai, and David St. John. As a sample the editor selected these lines from "Cherish" by Ray Carver:

> *From the window I see her bend to the roses*

> *holding close to the bloom so as not to*
> *prick her fingers. With the other hand she clips, pauses*
>   *and*

HFR is 6×9", 150+ pp. flat-spined with glossy card cover. Press run 1,000 for 100 subscribers of which 30 are libraries. 500 shelf sales. They accept about 3% of 800 submissions annually. Subscription: $10. **Sample, postpaid: $6.20. Send SASE for guidelines. Pays 2 copies.**

HEART (I), Box 3097, Durango, CO 81302, phone 303-247-4107, founded 1989, editor Marcia Mulloy, is a literary tabloid appearing twice a year. They want **poetry of "any style, length, subject-matter. Preference is for clean, muscular writing, writing that has substance regardless of style. If you can make a sonnet sing the ginhouse blues and be believable, I'll probably print it. No song lyrics."** The first issue "should appear late '89," and the editor says it will be approximately 30 pp., newsprint with cover art in color, b/w art inside, ads relating to literature/art. Subscription: $18/4 issues. Per issue: $5. **Sample: $2.50 postpaid. Send SASE for guidelines. Pays 2 copies. Reports in 6-8 weeks. "Do not send only copy of MS." Editor comments on rejections "often."** The editor says that she hopes to produce a first-class journal from the outset in both appearance and contents. She hopes it will become a quarterly in its second year and "Cash payments will be made to contributors as soon as is humanly possible. I will always be willing to work with someone who is willing to engage in rewriting where necessary."

HEARTLAND JOURNAL: BY OLDER WRITERS FOR READERS OF ALL AGES (IV-Senior Citizen), published by creative artists over 60, Box 55115, Madison, WI 53705, founded 1983. Effective January 1, 1990, the *Heartland Journal* will be published by the Wisconsin Academy of Sciences, Arts, and Letters, P.O. Box 55115, Madison, WI 53705, senior editor Lenore Coberly, editor Jeri McCormick, phone outside Wisconsin, 1-800-262-6243; inside Wisconsin, 1-800-263-3020 (ask for the Academy). A quarterly in an elegant magazine-sized format on slick, heavy stock with full-color and b/w photos and art, 48 pp. saddle-stapled, **using prose and poetry by writers over 60. Sample: $5 postpaid. Submissions of articles, essays, poems, fiction, b/w photos, drawings and color slides considered 4 months to 1 year before publication. They use all types of poetry, but do not want to see "general non-specific commentaries. We accept hand-written, easy-to-read MSS. We want fresh material."** As a sample, I selected these lines from my "Darkling Plain Revisited":

> *But you were right about the need of truth*
> *between those bonded pairs who would survive.*
> *Ah love, I turn to you, may we preserve*
> *our sweet cell insulated from the hive*

Submit 5 poems at a time; pay is in copies and an annual prize. Time to publication averages 6 months.

HEAVEN BONE PRESS; HEAVEN BONE MAGAZINE (II, IV-Spiritual, nature, ecology), Box 486, Chester, NY 10918, phone 914-469-9018, founded 1986, poetry editor Steven Hirsch, publishes poetry, fiction and essays with **"an emphasis on spiritual, metaphysical, esoteric concerns. Nothing too camp or sensationalistic. Deep thought and emotion required. We crave word combinations that fire the heart with light and electric awareness. No exploitation of psychic topics. No fortune-telling or prophesy which limits or excludes the option of the self to create its own reality."** They have published poetry and fiction by Stephen-Paul Martin, Joe Richey, and Steven Fortney. As a sample I selected the opening lines of "Imitations of the Subtle Body" by David Memmott:

> *Whosoever reads the fine print of other lives*
> *Allows the itinerant self to be captured*
> *By their gravity like a new moon.*
> *I long to drop the anchors*
> *Caste my mind adrift, to let go*
> *Of little aches and pains, to rise out*
> *of my body in a slow, deliberate spiral*
> *To live among the stars . . .*

Heaven Bone is magazine-sized, saddle stapled, 48 pp. "It is Macintosh desktop published at 1240 DPI on a Linotronic 200" according to the editor, using b/w art, photos, and ads, on recycled bond stock with matte card cover. They have a press run of 500. Of 200-300 poems received they accept 20-30. Subscription: $14.95. **Sample: $4.50 postpaid. Pays 2 copies. Submit 1-10 "readable" poems. Simultaneous submissions and previously published poems OK "if notified." Reports in 1 week to 6 months, up to 6 months until publication. Editor comments on rejections occasionally.** He advises, "Take risks. Break free of any educated limitations and show the self you always wanted to. Be honest. No contrived language. Steer clear of forced end-line rhyming. Eat well. Channel the truth through you." Annual chapbook contest; send SASE for guidelines.

‡HELIKON PRESS (V), 120 W. 71st St., New York, NY 10023, founded 1972, poetry editors Robin Prising and William Leo Coakley, "tries to publish the best contemporary poetry in the tradition of English verse. We read (and listen to) poetry and ask poets to build a collection around particular poems. We print fine editions illustrated by good artists. Unfortunately we cannot encourage submissions."

HELLAS: A JOURNAL OF POETRY AND THE HUMANITIES (II, IV-Form), 304 S. Tyson Ave., Glenside, PA 19038, phone 215-884-1086, founded 1988, editor Gerald Harnett. *Hellas* is a quarterly that wants poetry of "any kind but especially poems in meter. We prize elegance and formality in verse, but specifically encourage poetry of the utmost boldness and innovation, so long as it is not willfully obscurantist; no ignorant, illiterate, meaningless free verse or political poems." They have recently accepted poetry by Mordecai Marcus, Richard Moore, Jack Butler, and Jascha Kessler. The first issue had not appeared when I wrote this, but the editor says it will be 172 pp, 6×9" flat-spined, offset, using b/w art. Their press run is to be 1,200 for first issue, 750 thereafter. Subscription: $16. **Sample: $5.50 postpaid. Send SASE for guidelines. Pays 2 copies. They will consider simultaneous submissions and previously published poems** "if they let us know, but please don't bother unless it's specifically suited to *Hellas*." Reports in a week or two on "obviously unsuitable poems, 6 weeks on more interesting submissions. Please allow up to 2 months before inquiring." Editor comments on rejections "happily if requested. If I don't understand it, I don't print it. On the other hand, we don't want obvious, easy, clichéd or sentimental verse." Their flyer says, "*Hellas* is a lively and provocative assault on a century of modernist barbarism in the arts. A unique, Miltonic wedding of *paideia* and *poesis*, engaging scholarship and original poetry, *Hellas* has become the forum of a remarkable new generation of poets, critics, and theorists committed to the renovation of the art of our time . . . Meter is especially welcome, as well as rhymed and stanzaic verse. We judge a poem by its verbal artifice and the formal harmonies of its internal order. Lines should not end arbitrarily, diction should be precise: we suggest that such principles can appear 'limiting' only to an impoverished imagination. To the contrary: we encourage any conceivable boldness and innovation, so long as it is executed with discipline and is not a masquerade for self-indulgent obscurantism. . . . We do not print poems about Nicaragua, whales, or an author's body parts. We do specifically welcome submissions from newer authors."

‡HELTER SKELTER; HETERODOX SCREAM PRESS; IMPASSIONED ARTISTS' ALLIANCE (II,IV-Science fiction/fantasy/horror), 955 La Paz Rd., Santa Barbara, CA 93108-1099, founded 1987, editor Anthony Boyd. *Helter Skelter* is an annual: "number of pages, size, cover, art and ads all vary depending on my mood, my money, and my time. The Alliance was just created and consists of writers that are featured in *HS*. Featured writers are contest winners (entry fee $1/poem, submit between August and April. Three $20 awards yearly). Submissions from first-time contributors must be through the contest. Writers previously published in *HS* may avoid contest fees. Writers who have a good grasp on their emotions will do quite well. Length: 10-50 lines is cool. Form: Some form, yes. Kind of poetry we do not want to see: the kind that says, 'publish me!' " Poets recently published include Cheryl Townsend and Albert Huffstickler. As a sample the editor selected these lines by Garrison L. Hilliard:

> So sadly do I now catch my breath
> And turn to go
> With my dreams trailing out behind me
> Like ragged streamers in the wind

"Cover letters are appreciated. Address all submissions to Anthony Boyd." **Sample, postpaid: $1. Pays 1 copy. Send SASE for guidelines.** The editor comments: "Current literary scene? I didn't think there was such a thing."

‡HEMISPHERES; PAISANO PRESS (I), Rt. 1, Box 28, Eden, WI 53019, phone 414-477-6861, founded 1989, editor Gary Scheinoha, appears twice a year using "poems up to 40 lines, open as to form, subject-matter, and style; no pornography, occult. Writers published in this magazine are pretty well open to explore their own personal hemispheres." They have recently published poetry by Peter Martin, Ken Stone, and Sigmund Weiss. As a sample the editor selected these lines from "Zero Minus Shit" by Tom Pyle:

> Death, belated echo of my birth
> You're but a moment
> Marking my return to disconception,
> I came from nothing, lived,
> Went back to nothing—

Hemispheres is a digest-sized, 20-24 pp., photocopied from photoreduced typescript, with colored paper cover. Press run (first issue) 50 copies for 2 subscriptions. Subscription: $4. **Sample, postpaid: $2. Send SASE for guidelines. Pays 1 copy. Simultaneous submissions and previously published poems OK.** The editor says, "Persist. The writers I accept are those who hang tough despite rejections and discouragement. It may be hard, but it's all part of paying your dues, and it is worth it. Just practice: write, write, and write some more. Then rewrite. Poetry may be a jewel, but it takes a lot of polishing to turn it into a gem." Paisano Press publishes **books "usually chosen from local authors as they are distributed locally." Reports in 1 month. Authors of books "usually appear in the magazine first. This is not a requirement." Pays varying number of copies.**

‡**HEN'S TEETH (V)**, (formerly Unipress), Box 689 Brookings, SD 57006, founded 1988, editor Janice H. Mikesell. As a sample of poetry she liked, she picked these lines from her poem, "My Mother's Back Yard":

> *. . . there are other memories as well, so fragile that*
> *I dare not dust them off*
> *for fear that I will break*

That poem appears in **Women Houses & Homes: an anthology of prose, poetry and photography**, $6 (plus $1 postage), a 52-page saddle-stapled book cut with a roof-line top, professionally printed with glossy card cover. She expects to publish a book every 2 years but **will not be open for submissions.** Most recent publication is **A Survivor's Manual: a book of poems**, $6 (plus $1 postage), a 52-page perfect-bound quality paperback with an arresting cover photo. Sample lines from "Closing Thoughts" are:

> *. . . the fire's in the belly now*
> *the final tyrant, time.*

HERBOOKS (V, IV-Lesbian), Box 7467, Santa Cruz, CA 95061, founded 1984, owner Irene Reti, is a small-press publisher of lesbian-feminist writing and photography, essays, poetry, short story collections, and anthologies. **They will not be accepting poetry during 1991. "We wish to achieve better balance of poetry and prose within HerBooks titles."** They want **"lesbian-feminist poetry with a strong personal voice; free verse or traditional form, 1-10 pp., written out of conviction, non-rhetorical, specific, written out of a strong sense of lesbian culture and identity." They do not want "anything racist, or pro s/m, anything vague and mushy."** They have published poetry by Lesléa Newman, Ellen Bass, and Judith Barrington. As a sample, the editor selected the poem "Geology" by D. A. Clarke:

> *They have not built the sea wall nor piled the rip rap*
> *that will keep woman from woman; it is a tide they fight*
> *that recurs, laying out our paths*
> *with a straight rule and a razor*
> *still runways crack, sidewalks buckle, and weeds*
> *push stone aside; it is a seismic activity*
> *that goes on regardless and underground:*
> *Conservations they do not hear.*

That comes from a book, **To Live with the Weeds**, which their brochure describes as 76 pp., perfect bound, $7. I have not seen samples.

HERESIES (IV-Women, themes), P.O. Box 1306, Canal St. Station, New York, NY 10013, founded 1977, editorial collective, is a "feminist publication on art and politics." **Poetry "must be by women and fit into the specific issue theme."** They have recently published poetry by Adrienne Rich, Alice Walker and Margaret Randall. As a sample I chose the opening lines of "Dance Instruction for a Young Girl" by Kimiko Hahn:

> *Stand knees slightly*
> *bent, toes in posed*
> *you watch the hawk over the river*
> *curve, until his voice, shoulders back*
> *gently overcome by Seiji's mouth*
> *against your, the white breath, and elbows*
> *close to your side . . .*

Heresies, one of the oldest and best-known feminist publications, appears 2 times a year in a 96 pp. flat-spined, magazine-sized format, offset with half-tones, 2-color glossy card cover, using non-profit, book related exchange ads. They accept about 10 out of 100 submissions. Press runs 5,000 for 3,000 subscriptions of which a fourth are libraries, 50% shelf sales. Per issue: $6.75; subscription: $23/4 issues. **Sample, back issues: $6 postpaid. Send SASE for guidelines. Pays small honorarium plus 3 copies. Simultaneous submissions OK. Reports in 6-12 months.**

‡**HERSPECTIVES (IV-women, feminism)**, Box 2047, Squamish, BC, V0N 3G0 Canada, phone 892-5723, founded 1989, editor Mary Billy, uses **"poetry that expresses women's lives in a positive experiential way—open to almost anything by, for, or about women. Nothing obscure, intellectual, wheelspinners."** As a sample the editor selected these lines by Gert Beadle:

> *When they have closed*

The windows where I fled
And gave the empty house
to fire
Will they remember how
I loved a mystery

It appears quarterly in a 20-30 pp. stapled format. Uses 4-6 poems per issue. Press run 50 for 30 subscribers of which 1 is a library. Subscription: $20. **Sample, postpaid: $3. Pays 1 copy, if funds available. Simultaneous submissions and previously published poetry OK. Editor often comments on rejections. "We are mainly interested in giving new writers exposure. I don't like poetry that is so obscure only the mentally defective can understand it."** They also use fiction and other writing. "We are about openness and ideas, about women's creative expression, wherever that may lead them."

THE HEYECK PRESS (II), 25 Patrol Ct., Woodside, CA 94062, phone 415-851-7491, founded 1976, poetry editor Robin Heyeck, is "essentially a private press, publishing very fine poetry in letterpress editions. We are able to produce only 2-3 books per year and not all of these are going to be poetry in the future. We sometimes do dual editions of paperback and fine volumes on handmade paper with special leather and marbled paper bindings." They want to see **"well crafted, well organized poetry which makes sense—poetry which shows particular sensitivity to the precise meanings of words and to their sounds."** They have published poetry by Frances Mayes, Sandra Gilbert, William Dickey, Charlotte Muse, Edward Kleinschmidt and Bernard Gershenson. Robin Heyeck selected these sample lines from Adrienne Rich's book **Sources:**

I refuse to become a seeker for cures.
Everything that has ever
helped me has come through what already
lay stored in me. Old things, diffuse, unnamed, lie strong

The sample books I have seen are, indeed, elegantly printed on heavy stock, lavish with b/w drawings. **The Summer Kitchen,** poems by Sandra Gilbert, drawings by Barbara Hazard, is a series of poems on vegetables, titles on the cover and on individual poems in red ink; and **Herbal,** poems by Honor Johnson, drawings by Wayne and Honor Johnson, is a series on herbs. **Query with 5-6 samples and cover letter stating other publications, awards and a "brief" biography. Replies to query in 3 weeks. Photocopy, dot-matrix OK. Contract is for royalties 10% of net sales.**

HIBISCUS MAGAZINE (II), P.O. Box 22248, Sacramento, CA 95822, founded 1972, editor-in-chief Margaret Wensrich, poetry editor Joyce Odam. This press formerly published *In a Nutshell*, 1975-79, and revived it under a new name (January, 1985) as a triannual, *Hibiscus Magazine*, which uses 2-4 short stories and **7-12 poems per issue. "Poetry: Traditional and modern, no line or subject limit."** They have published poetry by W. R. Moses, Carol Hamilton, Marcia L. Hurlow, Lyn Lifshin, Glynda Reynolds, Harold Witt, and James Manley. These sample lines are from "Skating At Night" by Bill Hall:

The ice is chased silver in the starlight
Half shadows skate with me
On the abandoned lake.
The night is so quiet
Every breath hangs in my wake.

Print run of 3,000. They receive about 2,000+ submissions per year, use 20-40, have a 1 year backlog. **Sample: $4 and 9×12" SASE with 3 first class stamps. Submit 1 poem per page, 4-5 poems per submission, photocopy OK. Poet's name and address on each page. Reports "can take up to six months due to backlog." Pays 1-year subscription plus 3 contributor's copies. Send SASE for guidelines.** They commission the books of poetry they publish (on a cooperative basis). Send SASE for more information and catalog. The editors advise: "Poetry is essential to the soul. The poet's place in the universe is like that of the sun: life giving. Small press magazine readers seek the sun, i.e., the poetry that is printed in small press magazines. We are pleased to be a part of that element."

‡HIGH PLAINS LITERARY REVIEW (III), 180 Adams St., Suite 250, Denver, CO 80206, phone 303-320-6827, founded 1986, editor Robert O. Greer, poetry editor Michael Rosen, appears 3/year using **"high quality poetry, fiction, essays, book reviews and interviews."** The format is 135 pp., 70 lb paper, heavy cover stock. Subscription: $20. **Sample, postpaid: $7. Pays $10/published page for poetry.**

HIGH PLAINS PRESS (IV-Regional), Box 123, Glendo, WY 82213, phone 307-735-4370, founded 1985, poetry editor Nancy Curtis, considers poetry **"specifically relating to Wyoming and the West, particularly those poems based on historical people/events. We're mainly a publisher of historical nonfiction, but do publish a book of poetry about every other year."** They have recently published poetry by Peggy Simson Curry, Robert Roripaugh, and Mary Alice Gunderson. **Reports in 2 months, publication in 18-24 months. Pays 10% of sales. Catalog available on request; sample chapbooks $5.** Publishes 1 chapbook per year.

HIGH/COO PRESS; MAYFLY; HAIKU REVIEW (IV-Subscriber, form), Rt. #1, Battle Ground, IN 47920, phone 317-567-2596, founded 1976, editor Randy Brooks. *High/Coo* is a small press publishing nothing but **haiku in English.** "We publish haiku poemcards, minichapbooks, and a bibliography of haiku publications" in addition to flat-spined paperbacks and hardbound cloth editions, and the magazine *Mayfly*, evoking emotions from contemporary experience. We are not interested in orientalism nor Japanese imitations." They publish no poetry except haiku. They have recently published haiku by Elizabeth S. Lamb, Michael Dudley, and Edward Tick. As a sample the editor selected this haiku by Ruth Yarrow:

> *Warm rain before dawn:*
> *my milk flows into her*
> *unseen*

Mayfly is a 16 pp. saddle-stapled magazine, $3 \times 5''$, professionally printed on high-quality stock, one haiku/page, with matte card cover using 2-color artwork, "ensograms" by Bill Wilson. It appears in March, August, and November. They publish "about 50" of an estimated 3,000 submissions. Subscription: $10. **Sample: $3.50 postpaid. A Macintosh computer disk of samples and haiku-related stacks is available for $1 postage and handling. Guidelines available for SASE. Pays $5/poem and no copies. "Contributors are required to be subscribers." Submit no more than 5 haiku per issue. No simultaneous submissions or previously published poems.** *High/ Coo Press* considers MSS "by invitation only." Randy Brooks says, "Publishing poetry is a joyous work of love. We publish to share those moments of insight contained in evocative haiku. We aren't in it for fame, gain or name. We publish to serve an enthusiastic readership of haiku writers. Beginners: learn to be self-selective in your submissions. Question your motives for writing and wanting to be published. Where and how do you want to be read? And don't expect freebies! Freebies are usually worth little more than their price."

HIGHLIGHTS FOR CHILDREN (IV-Children), 803 Church St., Honesdale, PA 18431, phone 717-253-1080, founded 1946, assistant editor Greg Linder, appears every month except July-August is a combined issue. Using **poetry for children aged 2-12. "Meaningful and/or fun poems accessible to children of all ages. Rarely publish a poem longer than 16 lines, most are shorter. No poetry that is unintelligible to children, poems containing sex, violence, or unmitigated pessimism."** They have recently published poetry by Nikki Giovanni, Aileen Fisher, John Ciardi, Eleanor Farjeon, Eloise Greenfield, Langston Hughes, and X. J. Kennedy. It is generally 44 pp., magazine sized, full-color throughout. They purchase 3-5 of 150 submissions per year. Press run 3.3 million for approximately 3 million subscribers. Subscription: $19.95 (one year; reduced rates for multiple years). **Sample, postpaid: free. Payment "money varies plus 2 copies. MS typed with very brief cover letter. Please indicate if a simultaneous submission." Reports "generally within 30 days."** Editor comments on submissions "occasionally, if MS has merit or author seems to have potential for our market." He says, "We are always open to submissions of poetry not previously published. However, we purchase a very limited amount of such material. We may use the verse as 'filler,' or illustrate the verse with a full-page piece of art."

HIPPO (I, II), 28834 Boniface Dr., Malibu, CA 90265, phone 213-457-7871, founded 1988, publisher/ editor Karl Heiss, appears twice a year. *"Hippo* **has two feet sunk in surreality ... the rest firmly dedicated to standing ground in the (sometimes all-too-depressing, awakening, sobering) real world. The main emphasis is fiction—also poetry, art, and essays.** *Hippo* **loves the unpretentious and lives for subtle revelations. Nothing stuffy. Words that reform language, create new understandings or meaning, and image flashes**, or very very short stories. *Hippo* also likes to try and understand people and the narrator is important sometimes to that end. They have published poetry by Lyn Lifshin, Paul Weinman, Belinda Subraman, Ronald Edward Kittell, and Dan Raphael. As a sample the editor selected these lines from "A Party for Montgomery Clift" by Susan Compo:

> *... When you crash your car*
> *in Coldwater Canyon*
> *bits of head in my lap*
> *glisten like just-exposed film ...*

It is photocopied from photoreduced typescript, 48 pp. digest-sized, saddle-stapled, with 2-color paper cover. The editor accepts about 1 of 10 poems submitted. Press run: 150 for 70 subscriptions of which 2 are libraries. Subscription: $4.50. **Sample, postpaid: $2.50. Pays 1 copy.** *"Hippo* **spends many hours in a lonely river and likes cover letters written by real people." Previously published poems may be used. Reports in up to 5 months.** The editor says *"Hippo* plans to move up to offset litho when the 200 mark is reached. Eventually color photos, cultural and environmental issues, will go hand-in-hand with the poetry published."

HIPPOPOTAMUS PRESS; OUTPOSTS POETRY QUARTERLY; OUTPOSTS ANNUAL POETRY COMPE-TITION (II, IV-Form), 22 Whitewell Rd., Frome, Somerset, BA11 4EL, England, *Outposts* founded 1943, Hippopotamus Press founded 1974, poetry editor Roland John, who explains, "*Outposts* is a general poetry magazine that welcomes all work either from the recognized or the unknown poet. **The Hippopotamus Press is specialized, with an affinity with Modernism. No Typewriter, Concrete, Surrealism.** The Press publishes 6 full collections per year." They have recently published in *OPQ* poetry by John Heath-Stubbs, Peter Dale, and Elizabeth Jennings. As a sample (though it is by no means typical, it amused me) I chose the opening quatrain of "A Reply to Keats' 'To One Who Has Been Long in City Pent' " by Shaun McCarthy:

> *To one who has been long enclosed by fields,*
> *deterred by gates wired shut and seeded land,*
> *these streets excite dulled senses — each has scanned*
> *and, dazed by choice, knows banishment repealed.*

That is from a 1984 60 pp. collection, **The Banned Man**, published in a flat-spined paperback, elegantly printed, digest-sized, with a matte card cover and pasted on matte paper flaps, selling for £3.90. *Outposts* is digest-sized, 70-100 pp. flat-spined, litho, in professionally set small type, using ads. Of 120,000 poems received he uses about 300. Press run is 3,000 for 2,800 subscriptions of which 10% are libraries, 2% of circulation through shelf sales. Subscription: $24. **Sample: $5 postpaid. Pays $8 per poem plus 1 copy. Simultaneous submissions, previously published poems OK. Reports in 2 weeks plus post time.** Hippopotamus Press publishes 6 books a year, averaging 80 pages. **For book publication query with sample poems. Simultaneous, previously published, dot-matrix, photocopies all OK. Reports in 6 weeks. Pays 10% minimum royalties plus 20 paper copies, 6 cloth. Send for book catalog to buy samples** (available in U.S. from their distributor, State Mutual Services, 521 Fifth Ave., New York, NY 10175). The magazine holds an annual poetry competition.

HIRAM POETRY REVIEW (II), P.O. Box 162, Hiram, OH 44234, founded 1967, poetry editors Hale Chatfield and Carol Donley, is a semi-annual with occasional special supplements. "**We favor new talent—and except for one issue in two years, read** *only* **unsolicited MSS.**" They are interested in "**all kinds of high quality poetry**" and have published poetry by Grace Butcher, Hale Chatfield, David Citino, Michael Finley, Jim Daniels, Peter Klappert, and Harold Witt. They offer these sample lines from "Fat People at the Amusement Park" by Rawdon Tomlinson:

> *. . .chattering as though they'd entered*
> *the kingdom, they step into the cars*
> *of the tilt-a-whirl, tilting, and take off*
> *into a scream of weightlessness.*

There are 30+ pp. of poetry in the professionally printed digest-sized saddle-stapled magazine (glossy cover with b/w photo). It has a circulation of 400, 250 subscriptions of which 150 are libraries. $4 per subscription, $2 per copy. They receive about 7,500 submissions per year, use 50, have up to a 6 month backlog. **Sample: free! No carbons, photocopies or simultaneous submissions. "Send 4-5 fresh, neat copies of your best poems." Reports in 2-4 months. Pays 2 copies plus year's subscription.**

HOB-NOB (I), 994 Nissley Rd., Lancaster, PA 17601, phone 717-898-7807, founded 1969, poetry editor Mildred K. Henderson, is a small literary semiannual with certain 'family' emphasis. About ⅓ poetry, ⅔ prose. The editor wants "**poetry up to 16-line limit, light or humorous verse, serious poetry on vital current themes, people, nature, animals, etc. Religious poetry is also acceptable. No erotica, horror, suicide, excess violence, murder, overly depressing themes, especially utter hopelessness.**" They have recently published poems by Gayle Elen Harvey, Andrew J. Grossman, and Ronald Smits. As a sample Mildred Henderson chose these lines by Sigmund Weiss:

> *Armies of daffodils rise massed for war,*
> *their spears silvered by rays of sun.*
> *Above and around horsemen ride*
> *on wings light as air.*

Hob-Nob is 64 pp. magazine-sized, saddle-stapled, offset, on 20 lb. bond and heavier cover, printed from photoreduced typescript. It offers free ads to subscribers and exchange publications. About 20 new poets are featured in each issue. Print run is 350. Subscription: $6. **Sample: $3.50 postpaid. Send SASE for guidelines. Pays 1 copy for first appearance only. After that you have to subscribe to be accepted. She reads submissions from September 1 to March 1 only; first-time contributors may submit during January and February only, 2-year wait for first-time contributors. Material received at other times will be returned unread. She prefers not to have simultaneous submissions or previously published poems. Publication is copyrighted; buys first rights only. Reports in 2 months. The editor comments on rejections "especially if I can think of a way a rejected item can be salvaged or made suitable to submit elsewhere."** The Readers

Choice contest, every issue, pays $10 for first prize, lesser amount for other place (unless special prizes are offered by readers). Awards are on the basis of votes sent in by readers. The editor advises, "Poets and would-be poets should read contemporary poetry to see what others are doing. Most of what I receive does not seem to be rhymed and metered anymore, and unless a poet is extremely skilled with rhyme and meter (few are), he will find free verse much easier to deal with. I told one poet recently that the content is vital. Say something new, or if it's not new, say it in a new way. Nobody wants to see the same old 'June-moon-spoon' stuff. Patterns can be interesting, even without formal rhyme and meter. Take an unusual viewpoint."

‡HOBO JUNGLE: A QUARTERLY JOURNAL OF NEW WRITING (I), Rucum Rd., Roxbury, CT 06783, phone 203-354-4359, founded 1987, publishers Ruth Boerger and Marc Erdrich, is a literary quarterly of new writing using poetry **"well written with no restrictions as to length or content."** They have recently published poetry by Lyn Lifshin, Davyne Verstandig, and Alvin Laster. As a sample the editor selected these lines by Deborah Lattizori:

> Come out of your skin
> Hang it on the windowless wall that widows watch
> as they
> quietly spin their web

It is professionally printed on newsprint, 64-102 pp., with textured, heavy paper cover. They accept about 25-30% of 600-800 submissions received annually. Press run: 11,000, **distributed free throughout Connecticut and parts of New York City.** ("but small contribution helps—for postage; currently offering subscriptions for $12 for anyone who would like to have the magazine mailed.") **"All submissions should be cleanly typed or photocopied, or may be submitted electronically via modem: phone 203-355-8295. Pays $10 upon publication. Reports in 10-12 weeks."** Editor comments on submissions **"always."** Marc Erdrich says, "In issue No. 6 we published more than 80 writers. As a free publication, we can easily reach a large audience. New writers, especially poets, need to hear their work read aloud."

‡HOLIDAY HOUSE, INC. (IV-Children), 40 E 49th St., New York, NY 10017, phone 212-688-0085, founded 1936, editor-in-chief Margery Cuyler, is a trade children's book house. They have published hardcover books for children by Myra Cohn Livingston. They publish 3 books a year averaging 32 pages but are interested in publishing more poetry books for ages 8-12. **Submit 5 sample poems. No simultaneous submissions or previously published poems. Photocopy and dot-matrix OK. They offer an advance and royalties. Editor rarely comments on rejections.**

THE HOLLINS CRITIC (II), Box 9538, Hollins College, VA 24020, phone 703-362-6317, founded 1964, editor John Rees Moore, publishes critical essays, poetry and book reviews, appears 5 times yearly in a 20 pp. magazine-sized format, circulation 550, **uses a few short poems in each issue, interesting in form, content or both.** They have recently published poetry by Carol Seitzer, Charles Edward Eaton, and Fritz Hamilton. The June 1989 issue contains several poems. As a sample, here are a few lines from "Tangier Repeats" by Carole Simmons Oles:

> Soon the Moroccan male
>
> will fill alleys, Lambs. Will sizzle, rise on music. Smoke.
> Like lights in a perilous harbor his cigarettes wink:
> blondes, say your prayers. The Moroccan male
> has too many mothers. His eyes are signal
>
> lights that harbor perils.

Sample: $1.50. Submit up to 5 poems, none over 35 lines. No photocopies. Reports in 6 weeks (slower in the summer). Pays $25/poem plus 5 copies.

HOLMGANGERS PRESS; KESTREL CHAPBOOK SERIES (II), 95 Carson Ct., Shelter Cove, Whitethorn, CA 95489, phone 707-986-7700, founded 1974, poetry editor Gary Elder, was "founded primarily to bring out **young or unjustly ignored 'older' poets.** We have since published as well collections of fiction, novels, history, graphic art and experimental works. We want **poetry with a sense of place, time, wonder. No confessionals, self-analysis, polemic, field-notes, grocery lists, academic playtoys."** They have recently published books by John Detro, Joan McNerney, and Ryan Cooney. Gary Elder selected these sample lines from "To Bring Spring" by George Keithley:

> Earth gives a single groan,
> that sound of the pond in winter when the
>   black flint
> of good-bye is frozen in it

They publish four Kestrel Chapbooks (28-32 pp., saddle-stapled) and two 80-pp. flat-spined paperbacks per year in elegantly printed editions, but future publishing schedule is now uncertain. Poets should **query with a sample of 5 poems. Responds to queries in 2 days, to submissions (if invited) in a month. Simultaneous submissions, photocopies OK. Authors receive 10% royalties; number of copies negotiable. Editor sometimes provides criticism on rejections.** Send SASE for catalog to buy samples. "Advice — Len Fulton said it long ago, editorializing in an early *Dust* magazine: 'young poets would do well to learn humility.' "

HENRY HOLT & COMPANY (V), 115 W 18th St., New York, NY 10011, **accepts no unsolicited poetry.**

HONEST ULSTERMAN (II, IV-Regional), 102 Elm Park Mansions, Park Walk, London, U.K. SW10 0AP, founded 1968, editors Robert Johnstone and Ruth Hooley, is a literary magazine appearing 3-4 times a year using **"technically competent poetry and prose, book reviews. Special reference to Northern Irish and Irish literature. Lively, humorous, adventurous, outspoken."** They have published poetry by Seamus Heaney, Paul Muldoon, Gavin Ewart, Craig Raine, Fleur Adcock, and Medbh McGuckian. I have not seen an issue, but the editor describes it as "75-100 pp., A-5 (digest-sized), photolithographic, phototypeset, photographs, and line drawings. Occasionally color covers." Press run: 1,000 for 300+ subscriptions. Subscription: $22. **Sample, postpaid: $5.50. Pays "a nominal fee" plus 2 copies. Editor comments on submissions "occasionally."**

HONEYBROOK PRESS (V), Box 883, Rexburg, ID 83440, phone 208-356-1456, founded 1984, poetry editor Donnell Hunter, specializes in fine printing, letterpress, handset type, of chapbooks of poetry. Donnell Hunter says, "this is more of a hobby press, so I ask some 'name' poets for MSS; but I have done some subsidized work for friends and also some poets who have seen my work." He has published books by himself, William Stafford, Marvin Bell, and Leslie Norris.

HOOSIER CHALLENGER (I, IV-Humor), 8365 Wicklow Ave., Cincinnati, OH 45236, phone 513-791-6844, founded 1956, poetry editor Claire Emerson, is a magazine for writers, one which, its editor feels, "is like a big happy family" of poets and writers. Claire Emerson says she "tries continually to **help beginners, and all other poets to improve, get published, etc. Our main purpose is to publish our writers/poets' MSS. I like all types of poetry/light verse and also use a page of humor/satire verse. I read everything received — but stress: no crude poetry. Keep everything in 'good taste.' Lengths 16-20 lines or less, and a very few exceptions of slightly longer.** I publish 250+ poets per issue." The editor selected this sample poem by Evelyn M. Letts, "Images":

> *Whirling cosmic dust*
> *Captured in the ancient stones*
> *Of noble temples*
> *Vanishes with deities*
> *Leaving traces in earthlings.*

The magazine is saddle-stapled format, offset from reduced typescript, 57 crowded pages, of which nearly half is poetry. Circulation 500. She prints about 50% of the 2,000 or more submissions she receives annually — "all I can find room for, per issue!" **Sample: $6 postpaid. Submit 4-10 poems, typed if possible ("but accept penned if it is written legibly"). No simultaneous submissions. She responds on the same day or within a couple of days and regularly supplies criticism. Send SASE for guidelines (a flyer). There are modest cash awards for poetry and prose in each issue** ("judged after all material is set up in the magazine"). Naturally, she hopes contributors will subscribe ($18 U.S., $20 foreign), but that's not necessary for acceptance. She advises poets to "read, study all the quality poetry mags you can come by; take all the criticism you are lucky enough to be offered; then, make your own judgments — but this will come only if you have exercised the above; never be satisfied with your poems — until you feel you have done the very best you are capable of doing; but keep improving. Try to 'feel' an inner inspiration to create, add originality — talent."

HOUGHTON MIFFLIN CANADA LTD. (V, IV-Children), 150 Steelcase Road West, Markham, Ontario, L3R 2J9 Canada, phone 416-475-5290, FAX 416-475-5290, founded 1977, senior editor Nicholas Stephens, is an "educational publisher — elementary and high school levels, currently developing a literature-based program for the elementary grades." **They are no longer accepting unsolicited material.**

HOUGHTON MIFFLIN CO. (V), 2 Park St., Boston, MA 02108, founded 1850, poetry editor Peter Davison. Houghton Mifflin is a high-prestige trade publisher that puts out both hardcover and paperback books, but **poetry submission is by invitation only.** They have recently issued poetry books by Ai, William Matthews, Margaret Atwood, Andrew Hudgins, and Rodney Jones. **Authors are paid 10% royalties; advance is $1,000 and up.**

HOUSEWIFE-WRITER'S FORUM (IV-Children, humor), Drawer 1518, Lafayette, CA 94549, phone 415-932-1143, founded 1988, editor/publisher Deborah Haeseler, is a magazine of "prose, poetry, information and open forum communication for and by housewives or any woman who writes while raising children of any age. **We have no specifications as to form, length, subject, style, or purpose. We publish both serious poetry and humorous. The editor's favorite poets are e.e. cummings, A.A. Milne, Ogden Nash, Judith Viorst, Phyllis McGinley, and Jack Prelutsky, if you want to get my undivided attention.** Nothing pornographic, but erudite expression is fine." As a sample she selected these lines from "Female Justice" by Carole Brost:

> *. . . this is nine months*
> *of lopsided respite,*
> *a holiday from monthly worries*
> *of blood in my shoe.*

Deborah Haeseler describes the magazine as "a small market for women who aspire to write for larger women's markets; or support each other in the quest for finding time and energy to write. It is 40 pp., desktop published, using some art, graphics and ads, appearing quarterly. Annually she publishes a collection, **Best of Housewive-Writer's Forum**, in the same general format. Press run is 1,200. **Sample: $4 postpaid. Send SASE for guidelines. Pays 1 copy plus ⅛-¼¢ and up per word. "Simultaneous submissions and previously published poems are fine." Reports in 2 months.** She holds contests in several categories, humorous and serious, with $2 per poem fee, April 15 deadline. "I'm no expert on poetry, so I keep my criticism positive. I believe anyone with an interest in writing can be published. The key is to start small, find 'little magazines' you can believe in, support them, and write about what you know. Write constantly— even a letter sharpens your writing skills. Try writing your letters as poetry, make your own greeting cards, just for fun! Never give up."

‡HOW(EVER) (IV-Women), 1171 E. Jefferson, Iowa City, IA 52245, phone 319-351-6361, founded 1983, edited by Myung Mi Kim, Meredith Stricker and guest editors, is a literary quarterly **"that encourages exchange among women poets and scholars working in the 'tentative region of the untried,' modernist/innovative directions in women's poetry.** We publish new writing with working notes alongside commentary by scholars in an explanatory vein." They have published poetry by Susan Howe, Alice Notley, Alicia Ostreicher, Barbara Guest, and Rachel Blau DuPlessis. It is magazine-sized, 16 pp., staple-bound. Press run 400-500 for 300-400 subscriptions of which 15-20% are libraries. Subscription: $10 individuals, $12 libraries. **Sample, postpaid: $3. Pays 2 copies. Previously published poems OK. Editor comments on submissions "at times."**

HOWLING DOG (II), 8419 Rhode, Utica, MI 48087, founded 1985, editor Mark Donovan, a quarterly literary journal of "letters, words, and lines." The editor likes **"found poetry, graphically interesting pieces, humorous work, avant-garde, experimental, fun and crazy. All forms. All subjects, but we tend to have a light satirical attitude towards sex and politics."** He has recently published poems by Arthur Winfield Knight, Keith Wilson, John Sinclair, Alan Catlin, and M. L. Liebler. As a sample the editor selected these lines by J. P. Doom:

> *you dropped*
> *your virtue on my foot*
> *it didn't hurt, but it was hell*
> *trying to get the stain*
> *off my new sneakers*

Howling Dog appears 2 times a year in a 64 pp. digest-sized, flat-spined format, offset, press run 500 for 80 subscriptions of which 1 is a library. They receive some 4,000 submissions per year, use maybe 150. Subscription: $20/4 issues. **Sample: $4 postpaid. Send SASE for guidelines. Pays with copies and discount. Submit 3-5 poems with name and address on each page. "We don't use much rhyme or poems under 10 lines." Simultaneous submissions OK. Previously published poems OK "but let us know." Reporting time 2-3 months, longer if we like it.** They are not presently considering book MSS. Mark Donovan says, "We desire to produce an effect similar to the howl of a dog with its foot caught in the fence. Something that may not be pleasant or permanent, yet still heard by everyone in the neighborhood until the time comes to unleash the poor beast to whatever other endeavors it may become involved in. Send your wildest pieces."

HRAFNHOH; LANGUAGE INFORMATION CENTRE (IV-Religious, form), 32 Stryd Ebeneser, Pontypridd, Wales via GB, phone 0443 492243, founded 1987, editor Joseph Biddulph, is a "small press publishing linguistic and literary works with historical, heraldic and genealogical subjects added in the irregular magazine *Hrafnhoh*. They use **"Poetry in traditional verse forms with a spiritual, Christian inspiration and purpose, with an active concern for technique and conveying a serious message in an evocative and entertaining style. No expressive free verse with iconoclastic or cynical attitude, self-indulgent, blasphemy, or indecency or verse that doesn't say anything."** They have recently published poetry by John Waddington-Feather. As a sample the editor selected these lines (poet unidentified):

> *Charles Spurgeon didn't fit a fashion's frame*
> *(Although he hangs brown-tinted on this wall) —*
> *He unexpected raised the neglected name,*
> *To which all dominations kneel and fall . . .*

I have not seen an issue, but the editor describes it as digest-sized, 12-24 pp., photocopied from typescript, illustrated with sketches and old prints. He accepts about 2 of 6-10 poems received. Press run: 100-500. **Sample, postpaid: £2.25 outside Europe. Pays "as many copies as required." Simultaneous submissions and previously published poems OK. Reports as soon as possible. Editor comments on submissions "not at any length and only if specifically requested." He offers criticism for £2 for up to 4 poems of 1-2 pp. each.** He says, "Almost all unsolicited submissions are in one form—free verse—and without substance, i.e., without a definite purpose, message, or conclusion. I am anxious to obtain verse with a strong technique and understanding of meter with some real and substantial message."

THE HUDSON REVIEW; THE BENNETT AWARD (III), 684 Park Ave., New York, NY 10021, *The Hudson Review* is a high-quality flat-spined quarterly, which **pays 50¢ a line for poetry. Reports in 6-8 weeks. Poetry is read from April 1 through September 30.** They also sponsor the Bennett Award, established in memory of Joseph Bennett, a founding editor of *HR*. Every other year $15,000 is given to honor a writer "of significant achievement, in any literary genre or genres, whose work has not received the full recognition it deserves, or who is at a critical stage in his or her career—a stage at which a substantial grant might be particularly beneficial in furthering creative development. There are no restrictions as to language or nationality. **The Bennett Award is not open to nominations, and *The Hudson Review* will not accept nominations or applications in any form."**

THE HUMAN QUEST (IV-Political), (formerly *The Churchman*), 1074 23rd Ave. N., St. Petersburg, FL 33704, editor Edna Ruth Johnson, is a "humanistic monthly dealing with society's problems, especially peace. We use practically no poetry." It is magazine-sized, appears 9 times a year, circulation 10,000, of which 1,000 go for library subscriptions. **Pays copies.**

‡HUMMINGBIRD;FIRST COAST PRESS;JOAQUIN MILLER POETRY PRIZE (I),, 428 Morrison Ave., Newport News, VA 23601, phone 804-595-1744, founded 1990, editor Ronald W. Bell, **requires a $5/poem fee for poems accepted for publication in** *Hummingbird,* their quarterly, first issue to appear January, 1991, devoted to **"foster the writer of quality traditional verse and its perpetuation."** As a sample the editor selected these lines from "Andromeda," (poet unidentified):

> *There could be mannish analogs*
> *Deep within distant Andromeda*
> *Poets, priests, strange beasts*
> *Like the rhinoceros and ape*
> *And stargazers, like you.*

New at this writing, they planned for the magazine to average 36 pp., saddle-stapled, with a colored card cover, quality printing, press run 200. Subscription: $15. **Sample, postpaid: $4. Pays 2 copies. "Poets whose work is accepted will be notified—they will be expected to submit $5 fee (check or money order) for each poem printed.** This will defray *our* costs and, what is more, help fledgling poets have a decent forum for their work—a 'beginning.' **Submit 1-3 poems typewritten, no poem more than 2 pp." Editor comments on submissions often. "Never will give high-handed criticism!" Reports within 8 weeks. No reply without SASE.** First Coast Press publishes 1 chapbook/year, the winner of the Joaquin Miller Poetry Prize, 30 pp., $5 entry fee. They want **"well-crafted verse in the vein of Robert Frost—memorable poetry. The poet who writes 'hummingbird lines,' those that resonate over a lifetime, stands the best chance for acceptance. No amateurish rhyme (though we like rhyme). No pointless free verse, rambling automatic writing that is labeled 'poetry' when it is, in fact, merely egocentric drivel. Allen Ginsberg would have zero chance with us!" Chapbook submissions for the Miller Prize should be made during January-March with $5/MS fee. Submit with cover letter, brief bio, no more than 30 pp. of poetry. "Collections must have a** *title*! **We prefer poems in the traditional mode."** The editor adds, "It is quite easy for beginning and unknown poets to become nonplussed by the 'lock' that academically based writers seem to have on many quality publishing avenues. Truthfully, some of the better writing emanates *away* from the campus scene. There are potentially great writers among the ranks of the most average, mundane professions, but they seldom have the proper forum to spur them along to accomplishment. *Hummingbird* exists to offer poets, especially thsoe who craft traditional verse, an outlet."

HURRICANE ALICE (IV-Feminist), 207 Lind Hall, 207 Church St. SE, Minneapolis, MN 55455, founded 1983, acquisitions editor Toni McNaron, a quarterly feminist review that publishes a maximum of 1-2 poems per issue; "we are not willing to read a great deal of poetry." Poems should be infused by a feminist sensibility (whether the poet is female or male) and "should have what we think of as a certain analytic snap to them." They have published poems by Alice Walker, Ellen Bass, Meridel LeSueur, Patricia Hampl, and Nellie Wong. The magazine is a "12-page folio, table of contests on cover, plenty of graphics." Circulation is 500-1,000, of which 350 are subscriptions and about 50 go to libraries. Price per issue is $1.95, subscription is $10 (or $8 low-income). **Sample available for $2 postpaid. Pay is 5-10 copies. Reporting time on submissions is 3-4 months and time to publication 3-6 months. Considers simultaneous submissions, "If we know."** The editor says, "Poets—read what one another are doing. If someone has already written your poem(s), listen to the message. Read what good poets have already written. Spare the trees—."

HUTTON PUBLICATIONS; RHYME TIME; MYSTERY TIME; WRITERS' INFO; CHRISTIAN OUTLOOK (I, IV-Theme), Box 1870, Hayden, ID 83835, poetry editor Linda Hutton. *Rhyme Time*, founded 1981, and published bimonthly beginning in 1987, consists of 3-5 sheets of typing paper, stapled at the corner, offset both sides from typescript, **"featuring rhymed poetry with some free verse and blank verse. We sponsor several contests each year, both with and without entry fees. 16 lines maximum, no avant-garde, haiku or sugary work."** She has published Betty Benoit and Sylvia Roberts. As a sample the editor selected these lines from "Unnumbered Springs" by Helen Simondet:

> *If I had never touched your mind*
> *I should not be unquiet now,*
> *And yet how else was I to find*
> *That you were not a lifeless bough?*

Sample and guidelines free for SASE (two stamps), price regularly $1.25, subscription $7.50, circulation 200, 75 subscriptions (2 libraries). She uses about half of the 300 submissions received annually, pays one free copy. *Mystery Time*, founded 1983, is an annual 44-52 pp. digest-sized chapbook, stapled-spine, containing 1-2 pages in each issue of humorous poems about mysteries and mystery writers. The editor selected these lines from "Outline" by Lura L. Bradley:

> *Be sure there's a body*
> *By page one or two;*
> *Lead down the wrong alley,*
> *Come back with a clue.*
> *Unravel the motives,*
> *Keep stirring the stew*
> *And make certain the guilty*
> *Will suffer their due.*

Circulation: 100, sample $3.50, uses 4-6 of the 12-15 submissions received. Guidelines available. Pays 25¢ per line. *Writers' Info*, founded 1984, is a monthly consisting of 3 sheets of typing paper, stapled at the corner, offset both sides from typescript. Tipsheet for the beginning freelancer. The editor has published John A. Haliburton, Barbara J. Petoskey, and Marsha Ward. This sample, "Rules For A Writer" by E.K. Alaskey:

> *A writer must have discipline,*
> *Should work at his craft each day;*
> *Then learn to take it on the chin*
> *When rejection comes his way.*

Writers' Info **"needs short poems about freelancing (fewer than 16 lines) and pays up to $10 for first rights. Payment in copies for reprint rights. A sample copy of this monthly newsletter is free for a #10 SASE with two ounces postage.** *Christian Outlook* uses **poetry to 8 lines** and 1,500-word fiction for juveniles through adults is featured and earns payment of ½¢-1¢ per word (fiction) and **25¢ per line (poetry). Previously published material is welcome and will be paid for in copies.** This sample, "Mother's Daily Prayer," is by Joan Albarella:

> *Understanding Lord, this I pray:*
> *Quiet the children, stretch the pay,*
> *Guide my steps and what I say;*
> *Give me strength for another day.*

UNIVERSITY OF ILLINOIS PRESS (V, III), 54 E. Gregory Dr., Champaign, IL 61820, phone 217-333-0950, founded 1918, poetry editor Laurence Lieberman, publishes **collections of individual poets, 65-105 pp.** Some poets they have published are Josephine Miles, Michael S. Harper, Dave Smith, Stephen Berg, Frederick Morgan, and Dennis Schmitz. **"Ordinarily open; for poetry submissions one month a year—usually October; however, we will not be open to submissions in 1990 and 1991." There is a $10 handling fee.** Laurence Lieberman (one of our best-known poets) comments: "Poets would do well to acquaint themselves with at least a few books from our list." Send SASE for poetry list.

ILLUMINATIONS PRESS; ILLUMINATIONS (IV-Subscribers), 2110 9th St., #B, Berkeley, CA 94710, phone 415-849-2102, founded 1965, poetry editor Norman Moser, an independent publisher of limited circulation books of poetry, plays, and fiction, average press run 400-800. Norman Moser says, **"I prefer visionary, mystical, and/or lyrical or nature poetry. However, I've also aired quite a lot of experimental or political poetry (or prose-poetry) in my mag** *Illuminations* **in the past and I imagine the book-series will eventually have that (eclectic) character too."** He **does not want to see "rhyming verse, light verse, religious (especially Christian) verse, blatantly propagandistic, or political tracts sans literary quality." Considers simultaneous submissions.** He has published poetry by Hadassah Haskale, Morton Felix, and himself. As a sample, he selected the following lines from "Hunting Song (Shaman Song #7)" by Gene Fowler:

> *We dance the flesh*
> > *Your skins grow shaggy*
> > *My words are fur*
> > *against the cold*
> *We dance the fur*
>
> > *You run on fours*
> > > *Run true on fours*
> > *My words are bears*
> > *with their secrets*
> *We dance the bear*

The press publishes 1-2 chapbooks/year with an average page count of 64, paperback, flat-spined some perfect-bound. The editor says, **"Usually prefer query first since so far all contributors have been taken from current subscription list or past contributors' lists." Requirements for publication? "Yes, first they must subscribe at current $40 rate. Then they'll be expected to offset some agreed-upon percent of overall costs (usually not more than 50%, sometimes less) and to help sell the book in their area, especially help with mailings and the like." Royalties are 15% (of profits).** Book catalog free for #10 SASE; book prices are $4 and $5. The editor comments, "I am extremely eclectic in my own work and in my publishing too. Yet at the same time I feel the **language should be kept to simplicity and even to lyricism wherever possible. Somewhat Beat and/or Black Mountain influenced, I'm quite fond of visionary and/or nature poetry a la Ginsberg, Snyder, Bly** *et al.*, but I strive mightily to keep myself open to new styles and am quite ashamed of the tame poetry in academic mags."

IMAGES (II), English Dept., Wright State University, Dayton, OH 45435, founded 1974, poetry editors Gary and Dorothea Pacernick, is a triannual tabloid printed on high-quality newsprint, **12 pp. of poetry of high literary quality spaciously laid out and attractively presented with b/w photo illustrations. Submit any number of poems, none over 150 lines. Photocopy OK. Reports in 4 weeks. Pays 3 copies.** They have published work by such distinguished poets as William Stafford, Marge Piercy, Harvey Shapiro, James Schevill, Edwin Honig, David Ignatow and Elizabeth Bartlett, though unknowns and newcomers are also used in each issue. I selected these sample lines by Grace Butcher:

> *Sleep is all we know of innocence anymore;*
> *we darken with daylight.*
> *Every night we are lifted by love*
> *and yearn towards the silences of stars.*

They have a circulation of 1,000. **Sample: $1 postpaid.**

IMPLOSION PRESS; IMPETUS (I, II), 4975 Comanche Trail, Stow, OH 44224, phone 216-688-5210, founded 1984, poetry editor Cheryl Townsend, publishes *Impetus*, a quarterly literary magazine, chapbooks, special issues. The editor would like to see **"strong social protest with raw emotion exuded. No topic is taboo. Material should be straight from the gut, uncensored, and real. Absolutely no nature poetry or rhyme for the sake of rhyme, oriental, or 'Kissy, kissy I love you' poems. Any length as long as it works. All subjects okay, providing it isn't too rank.** *Impetus* **is now publishing an annual erotica and all female issue. Material should reflect that theme."** They have published poetry by Charles Bukowski, Ron Androla, Todd Moore, Gerald Locklin, and Lyn Lifshin. As a sample the editor selected these lines from "And He Closes 91.43% of His Sales" by Joan McMenomey:

> *never go to bed with a man*
> *whose sheets look like graph paper*
> *when he comes inside you*
> *it will feel like a transaction*
> *he will have timed the strokes*
> *learned foreplay from a Zig Ziglar book*
> *mirror-rehearsed his pitch*
> *calculated your measurements*

into the price of the wine

The 7½×9" magazine is photocopied from typescript, saddle-stapled. Circulation about 1,000, with 300 subscriptions. Generally a 3 month backlog. **Sample: $3 postpaid; make check payable to Cheryl Townsend. The editor says, "All I ask is that they send me what best represents them, but I prefer shorter, to-the-point work." Previously published work OK if it is noted when and where. Usually reports the same day. Pays 1 copy. Send SASE for guidelines.** In her comments on rejection, the editor usually refers poets to other magazines she feels would appreciate the work more. She says, "Bear with the small press. We're working as best as we can and usually harder. We can only do so much at a time. Support the small presses!"

THE INDEPENDENT REVIEW (I), Box 113, Kingsville, MO 64061-0013, founded 1986, poetry editors Wayne Kaspar and Shirley Janner, **requires $1 reading fee per poem, all poems automatically considered as contest entries for prizes of $100, $50, $25. "Almost any type of good poetry not longer than 24 lines; we prefer concrete visual imagery, lucid understandable poems that make us think, laugh, cry, or see the world around us in a different way. No vague abstractions, literary jargon, sermons."** They have recently published poetry by Alice Mackenzie Swaim, Patricia Lawrence, and Jason Miller. As a sample they selected the last five lines of "Prison" by Susan Marie La Vallee:

I am not one
in a collection
of butterflies
though these days
press down on me like glass.

The quarterly is 8½×7", offset from typescript, 77 pp. saddle-stapled with glossy b/w card cover with photo. They use approximately 400 poems of 1,200 received each year. Press run: 250. Price per issue: $4.75. **Sample: $4. Send SASE for guidelines. No pay except prizes. Simultaneous submissions OK. Reports "within 4 weeks of contest deadline." Editor comments on rejections "if asked."** Shirley Janner advises, "Don't settle for a forced phrase or a mediocre word. Strive for excellence. Read—read good poetry, read the magazines you submit to, read the guidelines that you send for."

INDIANA REVIEW (II), 316 N. Jordan Ave., Indiana University, Bloomington, IN 47405, founded 1982, associate editor Allison Joseph, is a triquarterly of new fiction and poetry. "In general the *Review* **looks for poems with an emphasis on striking or elegant language. Any subject matter is acceptable if it is written well. We do not want to see poetry that is clichéd, amateurish or faked.** Recently published David Mura, Silivia Curbelo, and Naomi Shihab Nye. The magazine uses about 30 pp. of poetry in each issue (6×9", flat-spined, 128 pages, color matte cover, professional printing). The magazine has 600 subscriptions of which 120 are libraries. They receive about 8,000 submissions per year of which they use about 60, have a 3-4 month backlog. **Sample: $5 postpaid. Submit no more than 4-5 pp. of poetry. Photocopy, dot-matrix OK if readable. Please indicate stanza breaks on poems over 1 page. "Simultaneous submissions strongly discouraged." Pays $5 per page when available ($10 minimum per poem), plus 2 copies and remainder of year's subscription.** The editor advises, "read before sending out MSS. Read the publication, not just ours, but any you wish to submit to. And don't just recycle poems—editors can tell when a batch of poems has been shuffled across more than one desk. Keep your work neat."

‡INFINITY LIMITED: A JOURNAL FOR THE SOMEWHAT ECCENTRIC (II), P.O. Box 2713, Castro Valley, CA 94546, phone 415-581-8172, founded 1988, Editor-in-Chief Genie Lester, is a "literary quarterly dedicated to presenting emerging talent attractively illustrated. Staff artists illustrate most work, but we encourage writer-artists to submit their own illustrations. They want poetry that is **"clever, amusing, interesting, thoughtful, original, moving, not rabid, or salacious."** They have recently published poetry by Dean Baker, Paul Murphey, and Brother Camilo Chavez. I have not seen an issue, but the editor describes it as magazine-sized, "printed on 60 pound bond with parchment cover (2-3 color)" and says it appears "more or less quarterly, 4 times a year. We receive about 10 submissions per week, use about 10 poems per issue." Press run 1,000 for 150+ subscriptions. Subscription: $10. **Sample, postpaid: $2.50. Send SASE for guidelines. Pays 2 copies. Simultaneous submissions and occasionally previously published poems OK. Reports "almost immediately except during holidays. Editor comments on submissions "if writing or art shows promise."** The editor says, "We are small but growing rapidly, probably because we are willing to work with our writers and artists. We make an effort to present material attractively. The poetry we publish usually deals in an original way with concerns common to all of us."

INKSHED—POETRY AND FICTION; INKSHED PRESS (II), 387 Beverley Rd., Hull, N. Humberside HU5 ILS England, founded 1985, editorial director Anthony Smith, poetry editor Lesli Markham, is a quarterly using **"any good quality poetry, traditional or contemporary, not sexist or racist."** They have recently published poetry by Gerald Locklin, George Gott, and Shelia Murphy. As a sample the editors selected these sample lines by Sam J. Bruno:

> *Aunt Clara says she has made the news.*
> *Enclosed are the paper clippings*
> *Of her dressed as Santa Claus,*
> *Outside the Salvation Army.*
> *One clipping shows the Catholic in her*
> *Blessing the drunk with holy water.*
> *Another shows the poverty in her*
> *Lighting a match*
> *To a Sears Roebuck catalogue.*

Inkshed is digest-sized, saddle-stapled, 44 pp., printed on gloss paper from typeset. Their press run is 400 with 100 subscriptions. Subscription: $10 for 3 issues. **Sample: $3 postpaid. "Please send cash only & U.S. dollars or Sterling—dollar cheques are too expensive to exchange." Pays 1 copy. They consider simultaneous submissions and previously published poems. Reports in 1 month.** Inkshed Press publishes 1 chapbook a year averaging 30 pp., but only by invitation. Anthony Smith advises, "Please study what is being written today—note trends but don't copy— be an individual, that's what poetry is about."

INKSTONE: A MAGAZINE OF HAIKU (IV-Form), P.O. Box 67 Station H, Toronto, Ontario, M4C 5H7, Canada, founded 1982, poetry editors Keith Southward, Marshall Hryciuk and J. Louise Fletcher, "is a publication dedicated to the development of a distinctive English language haiku and to the craft of writing as it relates to haiku. Submissions reflecting these concerns are welcomed. We publish haiku and related forms, plus reviews, articles related to haiku. **Poems must be haiku or related but we use a very liberal definition of haiku.**" They have published haiku by Carol Montgomery, Alexis Rotella, Akira Kowano, and Guy Beining and this sample by Le Roy Gorman:

> *dusk*
> *cicada*
> *husk*

There are roughly 20 pp. of poetry and reviews/articles in the digest-sized format, 40 pp., offset from typescript, matte card cover, circulation 100, accepting "perhaps 10%" of the poems submitted each year, poems appear as space permits, usually in the next issue after acceptance. **Sample: $5.50 postpaid. Submit any number of poems, preferably 1 per 5½ × 8½" sheet, typewritten. Reports within 6 weeks. Pays 1 copy.** Editor "occasionally" comments on rejections.

INLET (II), Virginia Wesleyan College, Norfolk, VA 23502, phone 804-455-3238, ext. 283, founded 1971, editor Joseph Harkey, is an annual "**publishing the best poems and stories we can get, by established or unknown writers. Well-written, serious poetry—even if humorous; no sentimental stuff, no doggerel, and nothing that is indistinguishable from prose. Short (8-16 lines) in great demand; poems of 36-46 lines had better be *very* good; anything longer had better be immortal.**" They have published poetry by David Madden, Sister Mary Ann Henn, Carol Reposa, Caryl Porter, Ruth Moon Kempher, Bruce Guernsey, Brenda Nasio and Mary Balazs. 18-24 pp. of poetry are used in each 32 pp. issue, 7 × 8", pebbled matte cover with art, circulation 700, distributed free. **Sample: 75¢. MSS accepted from April 1st through March 1st; publishes in April. Photocopy OK, with name of the poet and number of lines on the first page of each poem; 7 poems or fewer, prefer 8-30 lines but will consider longer ones. Reports within 3 months,** "*usually*." **Payment in copies.** The editor advises, "Write as well as you can and present neatly typed, readable manuscripts worthy of a professional. Don't wait for one batch to come back before trying *other* magazines with new poems. No dual submissions."

‡INSIGHT PRESS (V), Box 25, Drawer 249, Ocotillo, CA 92259, founded 1983, publishers John and Merry Harris. The Harrises publish short poetry chapbook anthologies (one per year) containing the work of "**pre-selected writers (no submissions without invitation, please.)**" The work published must be "**short, non-academic poetry for the layman—clarity and lucidity a must. Prefer humorous, inspirational poetry.**" They have recently published poems by L.C. Dancer, Elizabeth Lee, Jack Adler, and Falling Blossom (Cherokee), and Merry Harris, who selected as a sample the following "4-liner" from "Roadrunner" by Ma-Lee Ridge:

> *To Mona Lisa*
> *I've seen that smile*
> *On other faces,*
> *I know your secret:*
> *You're wearing braces.*

The chapbooks are paperback, flat-spined, 40-50 pp. "We sell our chapbooks at cost and send out at least 50 of first run for promotion of our poets, who are then widely reprinted." **Sample: $3 for "Laughter: a Revelry."** Merry Harris advises, "1) one tip for beginners: Join United

Amateur Press Assn., as I did 40 years ago, to learn basics while being published. Amateur does NOT mean 'Amateurish.' AMAT = LOVE! 2) Join a local writers' co-op. 3) *Avoid those who exploit writers.* 4) As for technique, keep it simple, avoid erudite phrasing and pseudo-intellectualism." We do not publish other people's books. We publish *Merry-Go-Round, Contest Carousel,* and *Roadrunner,* literary newsletters, for UAP.

INTEGRITY INTERNATIONAL (IV-Spirituality), 4817 N. County Rd. 29, Loveland, CO 80538-9515, poetry editor Sandra M. Brown, a quarterly **"journal celebrating the heroic spirit in men and women."** Uses poetry in its WomenSpirit section, **"no longer than 45 lines, preferably shorter. Free verse is acceptable although we look for evidence of strong poetic discipline, use of imagery and metaphor, not mere proclamation. No religious or sentimental verse. Light verse is welcome if deftly handled."** As a sample the editor selected these lines from Ted Black's "Heartsease":

> Heartsease along the winter wind, wild
> Pansy of tender thought, Viola inviolate
> Sun-fronting fearless through snow caress,
> How lovely is the pattern of your prizing . . .

Integrity is magazine-sized, 16 or more pp., professionally printed with paper cover. Press run 1,500 for 600 subscriptions of which 2-3 are libraries, under 200 shelf sales. Subscription: $22. **Sample, postpaid: $2. Send SASE for guidelines. Pays 2 copies. Simultaneous submissions and previously published poems OK. Reports within 4 weeks. Editor comments on submissions** "often." Sandy Brown says, "I find most submissions I receive — ninety-nine percent plus — totally irrelevant to my needs. Also, most to all poetry is not ripe. Poets are marketing before their art is ready. I look for clarity of spiritual vision anchored to reality. Our magazine has a specific tone which is bright, tender and intelligent. I welcome like-minded contributors, but, please, study your market, study your craft, read other poets."

INTERIM (II), Department of English, University of Nevada, Las Vegas, Las Vegas, NV 89154, phone 702-739-3172, magazine, founded in Seattle, 1944-55, revived 1986. Editor A. Wilber Stevens, associate editors James Hazen, Arlen Collier, and Joseph B. McCullough. Member CCLM, New York. Indexed in **Index of American Periodical Verse**. Appears twice a year, 48 pages each issue. Professionally printed. Circulation 600. **Publishes the best poetry and short fiction it can find, no specific demands in form, new and established writers.** They have published poems by John Heath-Stubbs, William Stafford, Richard Eberhart, Diane Wakoski, Stephen Stepancher, Jim Barnes, and Anca Vlasopolos. **Pays two contributors's copies and a two-year subscription.** *Interim* acquires copyright. Poems may be reprinted elsewhere with a permission line noting publication in *Interim.* **Submit 4-6 poems, SASE, and brief biographical note. No simultaneous submissions. Decision in 60 days. Sample copy $3.** Individual subscriptions $5 one year, $8 two years, $10 three years. Institutions slightly higher.

INTERNATIONAL BLACK WRITERS; BLACK WRITER MAGAZINE (I, IV-Ethnic), Box 1030, Chicago, IL 60690, founded 1970, contact Mable Terrell executive director, poetry editor Janice Haney. *BWM* is a "literary magazine to showcase new writers and poets; educational information for writers. **Open to all types of poetry.**" The editors selected these lines as a sample:

> When, in life, a pebble
> becomes a boulder,
> Then you'll know
> that you're barefooted!

I have not seen the quarterly, but the editor describes it as magazine-sized, 30 pp., offset printing, with a glossy cover, circulation 1,000, 200 subscriptions. Subscription $19 per year. **Sample: $1.50 postpaid. Pays 10 copies. Reports in 10 days, has 1 quarter backlog. For chapbook publication (40 pp.) submit 2 sample poems and cover letter with short bio. Simultaneous submissions OK. Pays copies. For sample chapbook send SASE with bookrate postage.** They offer awards of $100, $50 and $25 for the best poems published in the magazine, and presented to winners at annual awards banquet. *IBW* is open to all writers.

INTERNATIONAL POETS OF THE HEART; THE LAY POET (IV-Membership), P.O. Box 463, Midvale, UT 84047-0463, founded 1988, poetry editor Robert E.G. Curtis. International Poets of the Heart is an organization (membership $8 year/$10 year outside U.S.) "for the mutual interaction of the ideas and ideals as concepts from the heart. Our purpose is the meaningful communication of these concepts, 'heart to heart.' " They publish a newsletter, *The Lay Poet* of "how-to and general commentary on poetry submissions on a quarterly basis. **We solicit poetry for the newsletter, and ask comments from the membership. We recognize that 'feelings' are not only 'mushy love songs,' but emotions that may range from anger to euphoria. However, for the purposes of this organization, we seek those feelings from the positive side of life's experience."** As a sample the editor selected these lines by Bob Curtis:

> *But each of us are searching deep*
> *For memories that are lasting;*
> *A friendship or acquaintance rare,*
> *Maybe, a touch in passing.*

The editor says, "We want to have **poetry submissions by members, and then we will print what we can and ask comments on those pieces."** Submissions accepted only from members. No payment. We hope to collect the best and publish a book entitled "The Best of The Best" in the future. Let the words flow from the heart, organized by the mind. Don't 'force' feeling, let feeling 'force' you to write.

INTERSTATE RELIGIOUS WRITERS ASSOCIATION (IRWA) NEWSLETTER AND WORKSHOPS (IV-Membership, religious), Box B, 419 Pearl St., Moville, IA 51039, phone 712-873-3678, founded 1981, co-editors Marvin Ceynar and Barbara Ceynar, publishes a newsletter that "gives information mostly about religious writing but also information about secular publication that religious people feel comfortable publishing in." It uses **poetry by members suitable for an ecumenical Christian readership.** As a sample Barbara Ceynar selected these lines by Carol Turner Johnston:

> *If Grandmother's bowl*
>   *could tell us*
> *through cracked and*
>   *faded clay,*
> *We'd be amazed at the*
>   *love she made*
> *in her kitchen*
>   *every day.*

IRWA Newsletter appears 6 times a year, magazine-sized 11 pp., 200 subscribers. They receive about 24 poems a year and "accept many of them." Subscription: $12. **Sample: $2.15 postpaid. Pays 2-5 copies. Simultaneous submissions and previously published poems OK. Reports immediately. Editor sometimes comments on rejections.**

INTERTEXT (III, IV-Translations), 2633 E. 17th Ave., Anchorage, AK 99508, founded 1982, poetry editor Sharon Ann Jaeger, is "devoted to producing lasting works in every sense. We specialize in poetry, translations and short works in the fine arts and literary criticism. **We are looking for work that is truly excellent — no restrictions on form, length, or style. Cannot use religious verse. Like both surrealist and realist poetry, poetry with intensity, striking insight, vivid imagery, fresh metaphor, musical use of language in both word sounds and rhythm. Must make the world — in all its dimensions — come alive."** To give a sense of her taste she says, "I admire the work of Louise Glück, William Stafford, Jim Wayne Miller, Antonio Ramos Rosa, and Rainer Maria Rilke." The editor chose these sample lines from Louis Hammer's "The Mirror Dances":

> *Because the human body is always beautiful,*
> *because there are paths through the thighs*
> *to the bones of lightning,*
>
> *because a single kiss*
> *rolls up the blood*
> *like a shade before the light*

The sample of their publishing I have seen, **17 Toutle River Haiku** by James Hanlen, is beautifully printed and illustrated with "oil and mixed media" and calligraphy: sells for $12. **Query first with 3 samples only. "Cover letter optional — the sample poems are always read first — but no form letters, please. If sample poems are promising, then the complete MS will be requested." Photocopy OK. Simultaneous queries OK. Payment: 10% royalty after costs of production, promotion, and distribution have been recovered. Send** $6 \times 9''$ **SASE for catalog to purchase sample.** No longer comments on rejected poems. No longer publishes chapbooks but only "full-length collections by poets of demonstrated achievement."

INTRO (IV-Students), AWP, Old Dominion University, Norfolk, VA 23529-0079, phone 804-683-3839, founded 1970, publications manager David Fenza. See Associated Writing Programs under Organizations Useful to Poets. **Students in college writing programs belonging to that organization may submit to this quarterly publishing student poetry, fiction and plays. They are open as to the type of poetry submitted except they do not want "non-literary, haiku, etc."** As to poets they have published, they say, "In our history, we've introduced Dara Wier, Carolyn Forché, Greg Pope, Norman Dubie and others." As a sample G. Hyman selected these lines (poet unidentified):

> *Bull-shouldered farmers,*
> *Immigrant sons,*
> *Unpile in a field of newly scraped*

> *And sown for this thumping of leather*

Circulation 9,500. **Send SASE for guidelines. "Don't submit without query."**

INVERTED-A, INC.; INVERTED-A HORN (I), 401 Forrest Hill, Grand Prairie, TX 75051, phone 214-264-0066, founded 1977, editors Amnon Katz and Aya Katz, a very small press that evolved from publishing technical manuals for other products. "Our interests center on justice, freedom, individual rights, and free enterprise." *Inverted-A Horn* is a periodical, magazine-sized, offset, usually 6 pages, which appears irregularly; circulation is 300. **Freelance submissions of poetry for *Horn* and chapbooks are accepted. They publish 1 chapbook per year. The editors do not want to see anything "modern, formless, existentialist."** As a sample, they quote the following lines by A. A. Wilson:

> *I dream betrayal and deceit,*
> *I hear the march of soldiers' feet,*
> *I see the banners in the breeze,*
> *I dream, I dream of all of these.*

Pay is one free copy and a 40% discount on further copies. Queries are reported on in 2 weeks, MSS in 2 months, simultaneous submissions are OK, as are photocopied or dot-matrix MSS. Samples: "A recent issue of the *Horn* can be had by merely sending a SASE (subject to availability)." The editor says "I strongly recommend that would-be contributors avail themselves of this opportunity to explore what we are looking for. Most of the submissions we receive do not come close."

‡IO; NORTH ATLANTIC BOOKS (V), 2800 Woolsey St., Berkeley, CA 94705, phone 415-652-5309, founded 1964, editors Richard Grossinger and Lindy Hough. *IO* appears irregularly, circulation 2,000. The editors say that in general they do "not consider unsolicited MSS. We will consider those MSS that come with clear cover letters indicating that the author has read books published by our press and is submitting with an accurate sense of what our guidelines are," and they **do not consider unsolicited poetry.**

IOTA (II), 67 Hady Crescent, Chesterfield, Derbyshire S41 0EB, Great Britain, phone +44246-276532 (UK: 0246-276532), founded 1988, poetry editor David Holliday, is a quarterly wanting **"any style and subject; no specific limitations as to length, though, obviously, the shorter a poem is, the easier it is to get it in, which means that poems over 40 lines can still get in if they seem good enough.** No concrete poetry (no facilities), or self-indulgent logorrhea." They have recently published poetry by Stanley Cook, steve sneyd, Betty Parvin, Joan Downar, Alun Rees, B.C. Leale, and Barbara Holland. As a sample the editor selected these lines by M. Munro Gibson:

> *Mellow stone bridge curves*
> *across the looking glass mere*
> *a perfect oval*

Iota is duplicated from typescript, saddle-stapled 28 pp., with colored paper cover. Their press run is 350 with 200 subscriptions of which 6 libraries. They publish about 160 of 1,000 poems received. Subscription: $5 (£3). **Sample: $1.25 (75p) postpaid "but sometimes sent free." Pays 2 copies. The editor prefers name and address on each poem, typed, "but provided it's legible, am happy to accept anything." He considers simultaneous submissions, but previously published poems "only if outstanding." Reports in 1-3 weeks. Editor usually comments on rejections, "but detailed comment only when time allows and the poem warrants it."** He says, "I am after crafted verse that says something; self-indulgent word-spinning is out. To date, most of the poetry published has been British; I am conscious of the lack of American poetry as a weakness which is in the process of being remedied. I hope, in the future, to start a series of chapbooks in the same style and format as the magazine. All editors have their blind spots; the only advice I can offer a beginning poet is to find a sympathetic editor (and you will only do that by seeing their magazines) and not to be discouraged by initial lack of success. Keep plugging!"

UNIVERSITY OF IOWA PRESS; IOWA POETRY PRIZES (III), Iowa City, IA 52242. The University of Iowa Press offers annually the Iowa Poetry Prizes **for book-length (50-120 pp.) MSS by poets who have already published at least one full-length book in editions of at least 750 copies. Two awards are given each year of $1,000 plus publication with standard royalty contract. (This competition is the only way in which this press accepts poetry). Manuscripts are received annually in February and March.** Judges are nationally prominent poets. **All writers of English are eligible, whether citizens of the United States or not. Poems from previously published books may be included only in manuscripts of selected or collected poems, submissions of which are encouraged. Simultaneous submissions OK if they are immediately notified if the book is accepted by another publisher. No reading fee is charged, but stamped, self-addressed packaging is required or MSS will not be returned.** "The Iowa Poetry Prizes have been initiated to encourage poets who are beyond the first-book stage to submit their very best work."

IOWA REVIEW (II), 308 EPB, University of Iowa, Iowa City, IA 52242, phone 319-335-0462, founded 1970, editor David Hamilton (first readers for poetry and occasional guest editors vary), appears 3 times a year in flat-spined, 170-200 pp., professionally printed format. The editor says, "We simply look for poems that at the time we read and choose, we admire. **No specifications as to form, length, style, subject-matter, or purpose.** There are around 30-40 pp. of poetry in each issue and currently we like to give several pages to a single poet." Circulation 1,200-1,300 with 1,000 subscriptions of which about half are libraries. They receive about 5,000 submissions per year, use about 100. **Sample: $5 postpaid. Their backlog is "around a year. Sometimes people hit at the right time and come out in a few months." They report in 1-4 months, pay $1 a line, 2-3 copies, and a year's subscription.** Occasional comments on rejections or suggestions on accepted poems. The editor advises, "That old advice of putting poems in a drawer for 9 years was rather nice; I'd at least like to believe the poems had endured with their author for 9 months."

‡**IOWA WOMAN (IV-Women)**, P.O. Box 680, Iowa City, IA 52244, phone 319-338-9858, founded 1976, poetry editor Sandra Witt. "We are a literary quarterly with interest in women's issues. It is a literary magazine that has received national recognition for editorial excellence. We are publishing work **by women, about women, and for women. Prefer contemporary poetry that is clear and concise. Prefer narrative and lyric. No greeting-card verse.**" They have recently published poetry by Peggy Shumaker, Lyn Lifshin, Patricia Clark, Ann Struthers, and Theresa Pappas. As a sample the editor selected these lines by Laurie Blauner:

> *the same way our dreams pass us by each year.*
> *Her only pleasure is left lying in pools*
> *of colorless light, shaped like shadows*
> *that spread over the world by the next morning.*

Iowa Woman is elegantly printed, 48 pp., magazine-sized, 4-color cover with "original cover art and illustrations." Of 2,000 poems received "I accept about 30." Press run is 4,000 for 2,000 subscriptions. **Sample: $3 postpaid. Guidelines available for SASE. Pays subscription and extra copies. No simultaneous submissions.** They hold an annual poetry contest with first place prize of $150. $6 entry fee, 3 poems, for non-subscribers. All entrants receive a copy of the issue with the winners. Deadline December 15.

IRIS: A JOURNAL ABOUT WOMEN (II, IV-Translations, women), Women's Studies, B-5 Garrett Hall, University of Virginia, Charlottesville, VA 22903, founded 1980, poetry editor Judy Longley, is a semi-annual magazine that "**focuses on issues concerning women worldwide. We also feature quality poetry, prose, and artwork — mainly by women, but will also accept work by men if it illuminates some aspect of a woman's reality. We also welcome translations. Form and length are unspecified.** The poetry staff consists of experienced poets with a diversity of tastes who are looking for new and original language in well-crafted poems." Poets who have appeared in *Iris* include Sharon Olds, Gary Snyder, Mary Oliver, Linda Hogan, Lisel Mueller, Linda Pastan, Shirley Anders, and Michael McFee. As a sample of poetry recently published, Ms. Longley selected these lines by Melanie Gause Harris:

> *At sixty men still made her blush*
> *And hope for invitations. Until yesterday*
> *When her busy heart slowed down to nothing*
> *And was no longer available.*

Iris is magazine-sized, professionally printed on heavy, glossy stock with a full-color glossy card cover, 72 pp., saddle-stapled, using graphics, photos, and cartoons. It has a circulation of 3,000, with 50 library subscriptions, 1,000 shelf sales. Per issue: $3. Subscription: $6. **Sample: $4 postpaid. Pays 2 copies. Reports in 6-8 months. "Name, address, phone number should be listed on every poem. Cover letter should include list of poems submitted." Reading year round.** "Because we are a feminist magazine, we receive a lot of poetry that tends to focus on the political experience of coming to consciousness. We are interested in *all* aspects of the reality of women's lives and because we see many poems on the same topics, freshness of imagery and style becomes even more important. Don't limit yourself to the political or to any single topic of women's reality."

IRON PRESS; IRON (II), 5 Marden Terrace, Cullercoats, North Shields, Tyne & Wear, NE30 4PD England, phone 091-2531901, founded 1973, poetry editors Peter Mortimer and David Stephenson, "publishes contemporary writing both in magazine form (*Iron*) and in individual books. Magazine concentrates on poetry, the books on prose and drama." They are "**open to many influences, but no 19th century derivatives please, or work from people who seem unaware anything has happened poetically since Wordsworth.**" Peter Mortimer says, "Writing is accepted and published because when I read it I feel the world should see it — if I don't feel that, it's no good. What's the point of poetry nobody understands except the poet?" The poets they have recently published include James Kirkup, John Latham, and Carol Rumens. As a sample the editor selected this haiku by David Cobb:

> *the gnat confides*
> *a large secret in my ear—*
> *one it told last year*

Iron is 8¼×7¾″, flat-spined, professionally printed in small type, 1-3 columns, using b/w photos and graphics, three-color glossy card cover, about 50 pp. of poetry in each issue, circulation 800, 500 subscriptions of which 30 are libraries. **Sample: $7 (bills only, no checks) postpaid, or £2. Submit a maximum of *five* poems. "Just the poems — no need for long-winded backgrounds. The poems must stand by themselves." He reports in "2 weeks maximum," pays £10 per page. He always comments on rejections "provided poets keep to our maximum of 5 poems per submission."** They do not invite poetry submissions for books, which they commission themselves. The editor advises, "don't start submitting work too soon. It will only waste your own and editors' time. Many writers turn out a few dozen poems, then rush them off before they've learnt much of the craft, never mind the art." And about his occupation as editor, this journalist, poet, playwright, and humorist says, "Small presses are crazy, often stupid, muddle-headed, anarchic, disorganized, totally illogical. I love them."

ISRAEL HORIZONS (IV-Ethnic), Suite 911, 150 Fifth Ave., New York, NY 10011, founded 1952, editor Arieh Lebowitz, a quarterly Socialist-Zionist periodical, circulation 5,000, 8½×11″, 32 pp., **uses poetry reflecting Israeli and Jewish culture and concerns.** *Israel Horizons* deals with the Israeli left and the peace camp in Israel, including but not exclusively *Mapam* and the Kibbutz Artzi Federation; Israeli culture and life and current challenges to Israeli Society; the world Jewish community and its achievements and current problems, from a Socialist-Zionist world view; and general examinations of questions confronting socialism in our day. It also contains editorial comments, regular columns on various topics, and book and film reviews. "We also print letters to the editor on occasion." They have an international readership with readers in the U.S., Israel, Canada and 22 other countries. **Sample: $3 and SASE;** subscription: $10/year.

‡ISSUE ONE, (II, IV-Humor);EON PUBLICATIONS (V), 2 Tewkesbury Dr., Grimsby, South Humberside, England DN34 4TL, founded 1983, poetry editor Ian Brocklebank, is an attractive quarterly pamphlet, professionally printed on colored card stock folded accordian-style into 5-8 letter-sized panels. A typical issue contains 8-10 short poems. The editor says he "aims to publish not only a broad mix of styles of poetry by new and established poets the world over but also strives to a consistently high standard with regard to the actual presentation of this work. **I prefer short pieces with modern themes, concise but comprehensive images. Metre etc. unimportant. Poems with a point to make. My own criterion for selection is based firmly on whether images within the poem stir something, anything else in my imagination than what seems to be the subject. No epics required. Usually nothing above 14 lines overall. Bad taste, racism, sexism are not encouraged. Humour is welcome but no limericks please!** *Issue One* will intermittently use guest editors." He has recently used poetry by KV Skene, Arnold Lipkin, Sheila E. Murphy, and Brian Daldorph. As a sample, the editor selected these lines from "Breathe" by Lisa Kucharski:

> *when I walk*
> *air trails by*
> *it forms a breeze*
> *and that is how*
> *you will recognize me*
> *if we spend our lives*
> *walking past each other*

Issue One has a circulation of about 150 for 50+ subscriptions of which 8 are libraries. He receives 300-500 submissions per edition of which he uses a maximum of 15. No backlog: "I do not hold over work but will allow re-submission." **Sample free for envelope and postage. Submit no more than 5 typed or photocopied pages "with a covering note and SASE/IRC if they require a response. Simultaneous submissions OK. General queries will be welcome with a SASE/IRC." Reports in a maximum of 2 months. Pays in single contributor's copies. Send SASE for guidelines. Prefers not to comment but "will provide observations if specifically requested." Book publication by Eon Press is by invitation only.** Ian Brocklebank says, "For someone starting out writing poetry I would advise trying out as much of your poetry on as many different magazines as you can afford. Do not become discouraged by rejection of your work. Try to keep variety in your subject matter."

‡ISSUES (IV-Religious), Box 11250, San Francisco, CA 94101, founded 1973, is an 8 pp. newsletter of Messianic Judaism distributed free, circulation 50,000, which uses some **poetry relevant to that cause. Considers simultaneous submissions. Send SASE for free sample. Pays.**

ITALICA PRESS (IV-Translations), 595 Main St., #605, New York, NY 10044, phone 212-935-4230, founded 1985, publishers Eileen Gardiner and Ronald G. Musto, is a small press publisher of **English translations of Italian works** in Smyth-sewn paperbacks, averaging 175 pp. **Query with 10 sample translations of important 20th Century Italian poets with bio, list of your publications. Simultaneous submissions, photocopies, dot-matrix OK, but material should not be "totally" previously published. Reports on queries in 3 weeks, on MSS in 3 months. Pays 7-15% royalties plus 10 author's copies. Editor sometimes comments on rejections.**

JACARANDA REVIEW (II, IV-Translations), Dept. of English, University of California at Los Angeles, Los Angeles, CA 90024, phone 213-825-4173, founded 1984, poetry editor Katherine Swiggart, is a literary journal appearing twice a year. **"We publish all kinds, from poems by poets who publish in the *New Yorker* to L.A. Beat poets, to translations from the Japanese. Subject matter and style are open. As to length, we'd be interested in a good long poem, but they seem hard to come by. No inspirational verse, etc."** They have recently published poetry by Carolyn Forché, Barry Spacks, Alfred Corn, and Phyllis Janowitz. I have not seen the magazine, but the editor describes it as digest-sized, 100-124 pp., with 2- or 4- color covers, no art inside the magazine, 4-6 ads per issue. They accept 40-50 of 750-1,000 poems received a year. Press run is 1,000 for 100 subscriptions (25 of them libraries), about 400 shelf sales. Subscription: $8. **Sample: $4 postpaid. Pays 3 copies plus 20% discount on additional copies. Simultaneous submissions OK. Reports in 4-6 weeks. Editor often comments on promising rejections.** The editor says, "We'd like to see more emotionally adventurous poetry, poetry which could but chooses not to hide behind its technical proficiency. We want poetry that matters, that changes the way people think and feel by the necessity of their vision. That's a lot to ask, but good poets deserve demanding readers."

JAM TO-DAY (II), 372 Dunstable Rd., Tyngsboro, MA 01879, founded 1973, poetry editors Don Stanford and Judith Stanford. "The editors are concerned more with quality than quantity, and so only 15 issues have appeared since the magazine began in 1973. *Jam To-Day* "is not affiliated with any institution. **Contributors are paid—not much, but something.** Money is, perhaps unavoidably, the dominant standard of value in our society, and poetry and fiction are worth at least something. At least to some people." The editors make a positive effort to be **"open to new voices. Don't send light verse. Send experimental work only if you know clearly why your work is experimental (rather than just impenetrable) and what you are trying to accomplish (other than reader bewilderment). We are biased against poems about poets and poetry, poems telling the world how awful it is (the world knows that already), and poems preaching God's love in rhyme (that doesn't mean we shun religious topics; few aspects of life are as important). We are biased in favor of work that is emotionally honest, sensitive to the English language, genuinely concerned with life's strange twistings and turnings. The best way to get a sense of what we look for is to purchase a sample copy."** To my request for names of poets recently published they responded, "Since we emphasize work by unknowns, it doesn't tell anyone much to list their names. However, occasionally we cannot control ourselves, and we solicit well-known authors for material. Those instances are abberations. *Jam To-Day* is built almost entirely from unsolicited MSS." As a sample they offer these lines from "Marge" by Brook Zelcer:

> *Marge wakes up*
> *after un eventful nights*
> *and glides noiselessly*
> *downstairs*
>
> *where she sits*
> *at her breakfast*
> *smashing puffs of cereal*
> *between her teeth like*
> *planets*

The magazine is a handsomely printed, digest-sized, flat-spined, 90+ pp., format with b/w art using 40-50 pp. of poetry in each issue, circulation 300. They receive about 720 submissions, averaging 4 poems each, per year, use 40-50. There is up to a year between acceptance and publication. **Sample: $4 postpaid. Submit no more than 4 poems. Photocopies, dot-matrix OK. Reports in 6 weeks. Pays $5 per poem (or more if it is more than 3 pages) plus 2 copies.**

ALICE JAMES BOOKS; BEATRICE HAWLEY AWARD (IV-Regional, women, ethnic), 33 Richdale Ave., Cambridge, MA 02140, phone 617-354-1408, founded 1973. "An author's collective, which publishes exclusively **poetry, with an emphasis on poetry by women; authors are exclusively from the New England Area.** We strongly encourage submissions by poets of color." Offers Beatrice Hawley Award for poets who cannot meet the work commitment due to geographical or financial restraints. They publish flat-spined paperbacks of high quality, both in production and contents, no children's poetry, and their books have won numerous awards and been very respectably reviewed. "Each poet becomes a working member of the co-op with a two-year work commitment." That is, you have to live close enough to **attend meetings and participate in the editorial and publishing process.** The editor chose these lines from "Your Skin Is A Country" by Nora Mitchell:

> *In the background her village burns.*
> *I have always hoped*
> *that after he snapped his picture, the camerman*
> *threw down his camera, folded her in his arms,*
> *and listened to her cry.*

They publish about 4 books, 72 pp., each year in editions of 1,000, paperbacks—no hardbacks. **Query first, but no need for samples: simply ask for dates of reading periods. Simultaneous submissions OK, but "we would like to know when a manuscript is being submitted elsewhere." Reports in 2-3 months. Send two copies of the MS. Payment: authors receive 100 paperback copies.**

JAPANOPHILE (IV-Ethnic), Box 223, Okemos, MI 48864, phone 517-349-1795, founded 1974, poetry editor Earl R. Snodgrass, is "a literary quarterly about Japanese culture (not just in Japan). Issues include articles, art, a short story and **poetry (haiku or other Japanese forms or any form if it deals with Japanese culture). Note: karate and ikebana in the U. S. are examples of Japanese culture.** They have published poetry by Mary Jane Sanadi, F. A. Raborg, Jr., Geraldine Daesch, Anne Marx, Egean Roggio, Catherine K. Limperis and reprints of Basho. As an example the editors selected this haiku by Michael Elsey:

> *The glass sings crystal*
> *a moist finger gently*
> *dancing on the rim.*

There are 10-15 pp. of poetry in each issue (digest-sized, about 50 pp., saddle-stapled). They have a circulation of 400 with 100 subscriptions of which 30 are libraries. They receive about 500 submissions a year, use 70, have a 1 month backlog. **Sample: $4 postpaid. Summer is the best time to submit. Photocopy OK. Reports in 6 months. Pays $1 for haiku to $15 for longer poems. Send SASE for guidelines.** They also publish books under the Japanophile imprint, but so far none have been of poetry. Query with samples and cover letter (about 2 pp.) giving publishing credits, bio.

JAZZIMINDS MAGAZINE (I), Box 237, Cold Spring Harbor, NY 11724, founded 1987, editor Jiliann Coran, appears annually, with supplemental issues, using **"uplifting poetry and fiction. Experimental. Depicting the child at heart in us adults. As Bernard Shaw would say, 'youth is wasted on the young.' We wish to see these themes. Aim high. No erotica."** They have published poetry by Albert Russo and Hugh Fox. They accept about 6-8 poems a year. Press run: 300. **Sample, postpaid: $8. No payment. Previously published poems OK. Send 2-4 poems, no photocopies. Computer OK. Editor comments on submissions "always."**

JEWISH CURRENTS (V, IV-Ethnic), Suite 601, 22 E. 17th St., New York, NY 10003, phone 212-924-5740, founded 1946, editor Morris U. Schappes, is a magazine appearing 11 times a year that uses **poetry on secular Jewish themes. "We have been forced to declare a temporary moratorium on all poetry acceptances owing to the size of our backlog of material already accepted and awaiting publication in this category."**

‡**JEWISH SPECTATOR (IV-Ethnic)**, 4391 Park Milano, Calabasas, CA 91302, phone 818-883-5141, founded 1935, poetry editor Jeff Kramer. A 64 pp., Judaic scholarly quarterly that uses **Judaically oriented poetry.** Subscribers: 1,200. **Pays "nothing." Simultaneous submissions and previously published poems are not OK.**

JOE SOAP'S CANOE (II), 30 Quilter Rd., Felixstowe, Suffolk, IP11 7JJ England, phone 0394-275569, founded 1978, poetry editor Martin Stannard, is engaged in "magazine and occasional booklet/chapbook publication; for a new poetry of optimism and despair, **caters especially to poets who are awake. I really only ever want to see good poetry, but life isn't like that. I'll promise to read whatever I'm sent. No limits, as long as it's in English."** He has recently published poetry by John Ashbery, Tom Raworth, Peter Sansom, Ian McMillan, and Lydia Tomkiw. He selected these lines by Geoff Hattersley from "Love Poem":

> *Alan hates John and Pete.*
> *Pete hates Alan and John.*
> *John hates Pete but not Alan.*
> *I hate Pete and Alan*
>
> *and John.*

joe soap's canoe appears annually, 100 pp. perfect-bound format—"it's really a paperback book." The editor describes the magazine as "quite brilliant—in fact, of all the poetry magazines published in the U.K. it's one of the 2 or 3 always worth reading. It's certainly never boring. Some people hate it. I can relate to that . . . ." Circulation 400-500, 200 subscriptions of which 32 are libraries. Subscription: £3 or $10 overseas; per copy: £1. He receives "thousands" of submissions each year, uses 60-70. **Sample $2 or £1.25. Reports within a month. Pays in copies. Photocopy, dot-matrix OK. No simultaneous submissions**. Send 9×5″ envelope with return postage for catalog to buy samples. The editor comments on rejections "only when I'm provoked." Have you any advice for poets? "No—the world is too large and poetry too various. I'm no advice agency and no tipster. Beginners should simply begin. And know when to stop."

THE JOHNS HOPKINS UNIVERSITY PRESS (V), Suite 725, 701 W. 40th St., Baltimore, MD 21211, founded 1878, Eric Halpern, Editor-in-Chief. "One of the largest American university presses, Johns Hopkins is a publisher mainly of scholarly books and journals. We do, however, publish short fiction and poetry in the series Johns Hopkins: Poetry and Fiction, edited by John Irwin on 10% royalty contracts. **Unsolicited submissions are not considered."**

JOURNAL OF NEW JERSEY POETS (IV-Regional), English Dept., County College of Morris, Randolph, NJ 07869, phone 201-328-5471, founded 1976, Editor Sander Zulauf. This biannual periodical uses poetry from **current or former residents of New Jersey. They want "serious work that is regional in origin but universal in scope." They do not want "sentimental, greeting-card verse."** Poets recently published include Kenneth Burke, Joe Salerno, and Lois Marie Harrod. As a sample, the editor selected the following lines by Dave Austin from "After the Poetry Reading":

> *Now, I am drinking wine and so is this woman.*
> *My gray crevices are widening and I say stupid things*
> *About poems and death and love and God.*
> *"Let me pick your brain," she says,*
> *and she pushes her finger in.*

Published January (spring) and June (autumn), digest-sized, offset, with an average of 64 pp. Circulation is 500, price per issue and for sample, $4. Subscriptions $5 per year. **Pay is 2 copies per published poem. There are "no limitations" on submissions; SASE required, reporting time is 2-3 months and time to publication within 1 year.**

JOURNAL OF POETRY THERAPY (IV-Themes), Human Sciences Press, 233 Spring St., New York, NY 10013-1578, phone 212-620-8000, founded 1987. **Poetry MSS should be sent to journal editor,** Dr. Nicholas Mazza, School of Social Work, Florida State University, Tallahassee, FL 32306-2024. They use **"poems that could be useful in therapeutic settings, prefer relatively short poems; no sentimental, long poems."** They have recently published peoms by Ingrid Wendt and Virginia Bagliore. The editor selected these sample lines by Karren L. Alenier:

> *Her house stands on scaly legs*
> *screening and fencing off my saviors.*
> *Its mobility reminds me*
> *a snaggled-tooth child,*
> *of my deficiencies*

"The *Journal* is devoted to the use of the poetic in health, mental health education, and other human service settings." The quarterly is 64 pp., flat-spined, digest-sized, using 3-6 pp. for poetry. They accept approximately 10% of 100 poems received. There are 500 subscriptions. Subscription: $34. **Write publisher for free sample. Pays 1 copy. Submit maximum of 3 poems, 4 copies of each with name on only 1 of them. Include a SASE. Reports in 2-3 months. Editor "occasionally" comments on rejections.**

‡**JOURNAL OF THE AMERICAN MEDICAL ASSOCIATION (JAMA) (II, IV-Themes)**, 535 N. Dearborn, Chicago, Il 60610, phone 312-280-7117, founded 1883, associate editor Charlene Breedlove, has a "Poetry and Medicine" column alternating monthly with "Literature and Medicine," and uses **poetry "in some way related to a medical experience, whether from the point-of-view of a health care worker or patient or simply an observer. No unskilled poetry."** They have recently published poetry by Diane Ackerman and Molly Peacock. As a sample the editor selected these lines from "Winter Labor" by Ronald Pies, M.D.:

> *Of winters legion children*
> *I cannot say*
> *why you were maimed;*
> *your tangled gene*
> *tells only process*
> *in its tight folds,*

>   *and claims no justice*
>   *in your pain.*

*JAMA,*magazine-sized, flat-spined, with glossy paper cover, has 360,000 subscribers of which 369 are libraries. They accept about 5% of 300 poems received per year. Subscription: $66. **Sample, postpaid: free. Pays up to 5 copies.**

THE JOURNAL: THE LITERARY MAGAZINE OF THE OHIO STATE UNIVERSITY (II), Ohio State University, Department of English, 164 W. 17th Ave., Columbus, OH 43210, founded 1973, poetry editor David Citino, appears twice yearly with reviews, essays, quality fiction and poetry. **"We're open to all forms; we tend to favor work that gives evidence of a mature and sophisticated sense of the language."** They have published poetry by David Baker, T.R. Hummer, David Ray, Miller Williams, Robert Cording, Maura Stanton, A.E. Stringer, and Carol Frost. The following sample is from the opening stanza of "The Middle Years" by Walter McDonald:

>   *Now it begins, the soft insinuation*
>   *of ferns through spark light the final*
>   *campfire flame is gone, unless we breathe*
>   *on embers shadows of pinons flare up*
>   *and fall away like ghosts. You whisper,*
>   *Will these coals live?*

The Journal is 6 × 9″ professionally printed on heavy slick stock with b/w graphics, glossy cover with art, 80-100 pp., of which about 40 in each issue are devoted to poetry, circulation 1,500. Subscription: $8; per copy: $4.50. They receive about 4,000 submissions per year, use 200, and have a 3-6 month backlog. **Sample: $4.50. Photocopy, dot-matrix OK. No restrictions on number of poems per submission. "Cover letter helpful." Reports in 2 weeks-3 months. Pays copies and an honorarium of $25-50 when funds are available. On occasion editor comments on rejections.** David Citino advises, "However else poets train or educate themselves, they must do what they can to know our language. Too much of the writing that we see indicates that poets do not in many cases develop a feel for the possibilities of language, and do not pay attention to craft. Poets should not be in a rush to publish—until they are ready."

‡**JAMES JOYCE BROADSHEET (IV-Themes)**, School of English, University of Leeds, Leeds LS2 9JT, England, founded 1980, editors Pieter Bekker, Richard Brown, and Alistair Stead, a "small-press specialist literary review, mainly book reviews connected with James Joyce; we include relevant poems in the magazine." **Poems must be short, of good quality, and connected with James Joyce. They do not want anything "long, self-indulgent."** The issue I have contains two poems, "The Ballad of Erse O. Really?" by Gavin Ewart and "Keeping Awake Over Finnegan" by Alamgir Hashmi. As a sample, the editor chose the following lines by Seamus Heaney:

>   *Then I knew him in a flash*
>   *out there on the tarmac among the cars*
>   *wintered hard and sharp as a blackthorn bush.*

The magazine is "literally a broadsheet (i.e. A2) folded into A5 [digest] sized." It is professionally printed on good paper and includes b/w line drawings and other art work. When unfolded, it is 4 pages, 11½ × 16¼″. It appears in February, June, and October and has a circulation of 700, of which 70 go to libraries; complimentary copies go to "eminent Joyceans." Subscription price is £5 (UK or Europe) or $12 (US), sent by air. **Sample available for £2 or $4. Pay is 3 copies. Writers should send 2 copies of their work. Reporting time is 1 month and time to publication 4 months. Simultaneous submissions, photocopied or dot-matrix MSS are okay.**

JUDI-ISMS; K'TUVIM: WRITINGS—A JEWISH JOURNAL OF CREATIVITY; THE LAG B'OMER LOG: AN ANTHOLOGY AND SOURCEBOOK FOR THE 33RD DAY (IV-Ethnic, themes, anthology), 27 W. Penn St., Long Beach, NY 11561, phone 516-889-7163, founded 1986, poetry editor Judith Shulamith Langer Caplan. *Judi-isms* is the overall name of the press. *Judi-isms* recently (1990) published its first chapbook, **Long Beach 11561**, featuring the poems of Shulamith Surnamer from which these lines are taken:

>   *Oh, you stiff-necked people*
>   *who still seek*
>   *the answer*
>   *from the rabbi within you.*
>   *You will yet cast all your sins*
>   *into the depths of this sea.*

Judi-isms expects to publish a chapbook of Lag B'Omer poetry and songs within the next year. *K'Tuvim* is a literary annual, theme-oriented. Initial themes are **a) Bat Mitzvah b) containers of Judaism c) grandparents d) Jewish personalities, past and present: Moses, Miriam, Bruria, and Golda. I am very free as to style and length. I do not want to see anything that would be x-**

rated, or that contained 'four-letter words.' " Pays copies. Reports within 3-6 months. Typed, photocopy, dot-matrix, simultaneous submissions, reprints all acceptable. Name and address should be on each page. Editor sometimes comments on rejections.

JUGGLER'S WORLD (IV-Themes), % Ken Letko, Department of English, BGSU, Bowling Green, OH 43403, phone 419-352-5722, founded 1982, literary editor Ken Letko, is a quarterly magazine, press run 3,500, using poems about juggling. **"Only restriction is that all content is focused on juggling."** They have recently published poems by Robert Hill Long, Barbara Goldberg, and Margo Wilding. As a sample I selected these lines from "For Benjamin Linder" by Shirley Powers:

> in a remote village in Nicaragua
> A young man watches all night
> from a nearby hillside,
> his first hydroelectric plant
> complete. At dawn he juggles for village
> children
> in celebration.

JW is magazine-sized, about 40 pp., saddle-stapled, professionally printed on glossy stock with 2-color glossy paper cover. It is circulated to more than 3,000 jugglers in more than 20 countries. They receive 50-100 poetry submission per year, use 4-8 poems per year. Subscription: $18. **Sample: "$2 or $3 depending on issue."** Pays 1 copy. They will consider previously published poems. Reports in 1-4 months. Editor sometimes comments on rejections, suggesting some revision. He advises, "Provide insights."

JUNIPER PRESS; NORTHEAST; JUNIPER BOOKS; THE WILLIAM N. JUDSON SERIES OF CONTEM-PORARY AMERICAN POETRY; HAIKU-SHORT POEM SERIES; INLAND SERIES; GIFTS OF THE PRESS (II, IV-Form), 1310 Shorewood Dr., La Crosse, WI 54601, founded 1962, poetry editors John Judson and Joanne Judson, is one of the oldest and most respected programs of publishing poetry in the country. *Northeast* is a semi-annual little magazine, digest-sized, saddle-stapled. **Most poets published in book form have first appeared in *Northeast*. Authors wishing to submit book MS *must* first send query letter and samples of work plus SASE. Any MS sent without query will be returned without being read. Reports in 2-4 months.** A subscription to *Northeast*/Juniper Press is $33 per year ($38 for institutions), which brings you 2 issues of the magazine and the Juniper books, haiku-short poem booklets, WNJ Books, and some gifts of the press, a total of about 5-8 items. (Or send SASE for catalog to order individual items. **Sample: $2.50 postpaid.**) The Juniper Books are perfect bound books of poetry by several poets; the WNJ Books are poetry books by one author; the haiku booklets are 12-40 pp. each, handsewn in wrappers; Inland Sea Series is for larger works; Gifts of the Press are usually letterpress books and cards given only to subscribers or friends of the Press. **Payment to authors is 10% of the press run of 300-1,000.** "Please read us before sending MSS. It will aid in your selection process for materials to send. If you don't like what we do, please don't submit."

‡JUST BETWEEN US; MARQUET-DUBOIS ENTERPRISES; PEOPLE'S AMATEUR POETRY COMPETI-TION; THE CHILDREN OF VERSE POETRY COMPETITION; THE EYES OF CHRISTMAS POETRY COM-PETITION (I,IV-Children, youth), Marquet-Dubois Enterprises, P.O. Box 88, Aurora, CO 80040-0088, founded 1988, editor/publisher Arthur L. DuBois, is a quarterly. You submit to their "People's Amateur Poetry Competition" with $2 fee ($100 1st prize plus other cash prizes), and all entries are considered for publication in the magazine. "Any length, style, genre, subject matter. Form open; love variety—will consider 'rap poetry.' No excessive/unnecessary violence/explicit sex/ profanity." "Children of Verse Poetry Competition": biannual (March 31, September 30 deadlines), ages 8-16, any style, length; $1/poem; royalties paid if published; parental consent required. "The Eyes of Christmas Poetry Competition": annual, entries accepted year-round, 16 lines or more, any Christmas-related theme, $3/poem. Royalties paid if published. December 1 deadline. Awards for "Children of Verse" and "Eyes of Christmas" competitions: $50 1st, $35 2nd, $25 3rd, $15 4th, $10 5th. Send SASE for guidelines. They have recently published poetry by Ruth Carol, Donald Lynskey, Doris Benson, Barbara Paul Best, Kenneth G. Geisert, Nadine Hart, J.W. Van Wyhe, and Denise Martinson. As a sample the editor selected these concluding lines from "Ravines" by Kelley Hollis, first place winner in the 2nd quarter of 1989:

> You swung me over the edge,
> And held me there laughing.
> Here, there is no stream,
> No ravine.
> I am still afraid.

JBU is digest-sized, 120+ pp., photocopied from typescript, with matte card cover. Subscription: $28/year. **Sample, postpaid: $6.25.** They use approximately 50-60% of 100-200 entries received per quarter. The editor says, **"I very rarely reject anyone's work based on my own likes/dislikes,**

Close-up

Henry Taylor
Poet

Photo by Sarah Huntington

Now I think hard for men
mangled by tractors and bulls, or crushed under trees
    that fall to ax or chainsaw in their season,
    and for myself, who for no particular reason
    so far survive, to watch the woodlot ease
        under the dark again,

        withdraw into the mist
of my unfocused eyes, into my waiting stare
    across bare trees that lift toward landscapes
    through which snakedoctors may still wheel to rest,
    then to walk home, behind the shapes
        my breath ghosts in sharp air.

(from "Taking to the Woods" in **The Flying Change**)

Henry Taylor was born in 1942 in the Virginia farm country and remembers his childhood pleasure was to saddle up a horse, wave in the direction he was going, and be back by nightfall according to his parents' rule. Many of his poems reflect that rural background he and his father and grandfather grew up in. Some of his first-person narratives "are based on things that may have happened 80 years ago."

He has published translations, a poetry textbook, chapbooks, and three books of poetry. His most recent, **The Flying Change**, won the 1986 Pulitzer Prize.

What are the benefits of winning? "You make more money. My salary increased dramatically, though I'm still doing pretty much the same work as I used to. I get asked to do a lot more readings than before.

"People want to know if you've suffered any paralysis. I appear to have, to anyone looking from way outside. When **The Flying Change** came out I decided to bear down on essays for a while, to try and finish a book I've been working on for 20 years, and only write the kinds of poems that wouldn't leave me alone. I got a couple of backlash reviews. One says the book is bland, nostalgic, wistful pastoralism and the other says it's hardnosed, willful, nasty violence."

Winning the Pulitzer "was an enormous stroke of luck. I'm grateful for it, but I know better than to—what will we say?—believe it? If you look at a list of Pulitzer prize-winning poets you'll see a lot of people you don't know anything about. So many factors have to do with this kind of thing—if the book had been published three weeks later it wouldn't have been eligible for that year and probably wouldn't have gotten the prize. Different jury, different competing titles . . ."

For a while he thought it might be too easy to get work accepted, but he says he just received two poems back from *Poetry* magazine. "It felt good."

Taylor is co-director of the M.F.A. program in Creative Writing at the American University in Washington DC and cites his own background to illustrate the benefits of such programs. He took his own M.A. at Hollins College. "It gave me a chance to work on my own poems with someone who knew a whole lot more about it than I did. There may be other ways of serving that kind of apprenticeship, but they tend to be available only to the extremely persistent or the extremely lucky.

"I understand," he allows, "some of the objections to such programs. I have a problem with constantly treating creative writing as something to be nurtured and encouraged in practically anyone. On the one hand, the Poetry-in-the Schools program demonstrates the marvelous things grade school students do when given the chance. Behaving similarly toward graduate students, I think, is a really bad idea. You can turn out someone in their late twenties who's been encouraged to 'keep writing' for a long time. Nobody, except maybe their parents, has said, 'Get out of this. You're pipe dreaming.' I think when somebody gives you a bad poem you have to tell them it's a bad poem, because not to do so is deceptive, and I think many creative writing teachers are deceptive, whether they mean to be or not."

So, before choosing a creative writing program, is the first step deciding whether one belongs in such a program? "Yes it is. If you think the degree will confer some kind of credential, don't bother. With more than 200 programs graduating between 3 and 15 students a year, there aren't creative writing teaching positions for that many people. Our program is not designed to prepare you for any specific vocation other than your own writing, which we assume you won't be able to live by—at least, at first. If ever.

"If you've decided that your writing matters enough that you want to bear down hard on it for a couple of years, then you should ask yourself what kind of guidance would be most beneficial to you. I mostly worked in my student days with teachers whose work I found sympathetic, but I learned a lot by paying attention to people like J.V. Cunningham, who once said of one of my pieces, 'This poem has a dry, muted, uncertain music that, ultimately, is forgettable.' I could disagree with it, or chew it over. Someone who would look long and hard at my work to see what the hell was the matter with it, and how it could be shaped up, was far more encouraging than someone who would just say, 'Keep writing. It's a lonely, personal art.' "

—Jim Henley

---

or for point-of-view. **I generally do use more of the works of those who demonstrate some degree of 'polish.' I put more weight on rhythm than on rhyme, though it doesn't have to be a 'toe-tapping' but I look for 'flow'**—either that of a stream leading out to sea, or that of the tides of the sea. **Would love to see more entries by** *young people, children, and more 'rap poetry,'* **though I think rap may have gotten a bad name with an emphasis on the lewd, crude, and the seamy side of language arts. I do require parental/guardian consent for under 18, for contest or publication. Will accept previously published if rights retained for publication only; may request proof of retained rights."**

K (I), 351 Dalhousie St., Brantford, ON N3S 3V9, Canada, phone 579-753-8737, founded 1985, editor G.J. McFarlane, is **"a free form exercise in terms of the turbulent technocratic social environment and the human condition thereof, appearing sporadically as funds and material allow."** I have not seen an issue, but the editor says he has a press run of 75 for 30 subscriptions. **Sample, postpaid: $4.50. Pays 1 copy.** He says, "Poetry/literature provides a balance to technological progression in a primitive, human fashion. There has been a vast relenquishment of humanity in the latter twentieth century. Poetry allows the human voice in the mire of technocratic human diminishment."

KALDRON: AN INTERNATIONAL JOURNAL OF VISUAL POETRY AND LANGUAGE ART (IV-Form), P.O. Box 7164, Halcyon, CA 93421-7164, phone 805-489-2770, editor and publisher, Karl Kempton. *Kaldron* is a "journal of visual poetry and language art interested only in works which are a true wedding of language/poetry/literature and the other arts. This is a journal which publishes works from around the world." Mr. Kempton says, **"A visual poem is a poem which takes the patterns and densities of language and molds them with other art forms, mainly the visual arts in such a way that without either element the work falls apart, that is to say the entire image is what is on the page."** The tabloid-sized, 24 pp. newspaper has no recognizable English text except the masthead, a list of contributors, short reviews, and a list of magazines with visual literature. It is impossible to quote works from the magazine without photographing them; contributors include Doris Cross, Scott Helmes, Alan Satie,

Hassan Moussady, Paula Hocks, Shoji Yoshizawa, and Giovanni Fontana. *Kaldron* appears "once or twice a year" and has a circulation of 800; single copy price $5. **Sample $5 postpaid. Contributors receive 2 to 10 copies. The only instruction for contributors is: "no image should be larger than 10¼ × 16".**" Submissions will be reported on in "one day to a month," and time to publication "varies, but contributor kept informed of any delays." Criticism will be given "if submissions are accompanied with a cover letter."** Mr. Kempton says, "Visual poetry and language art published in *Kaldron* may be considered examples of an ongoing development of an international meta-language/poetic/artistic gesturing which attempts to express what language is unable to express. Such concerns have created a strong international dialogue. The roots of this expression are ancient; the modern roots are found in movements like futurism and dadaism in the early part of this century and the more contemporary roots are found in the concrete poetry movement of the 50's and 60's, a poetry held by many to be the first true international poetic expression. Around 100 serious visual poets and language artists are at work in this country and hundreds more at work around the globe."

KALEIDOSCOPE PRESS; KALEIDOSCOPE: INTERNATIONAL MAGAZINE OF LITERATURE, FINE ARTS, AND DISABILITY (IV-Themes), 326 Locust St., Akron, OH 44302, phone 216-762-9755, founded 1979, editor Dr. Darshan C. Perusek; consulting poetry editor Christopher Hewitt. *Kaleidoscope* is based at United Cerebral Palsy and Services for the Handicapped, a nonprofit agency, and has the mission "to provide a viable national and international vehicle **for literary and artistic works dealing with the experience of disability**; stimulate ongoing literary and art programming among organizations which serve persons with disabilities; and to serve as a forum for the issues inherent to the experience of disability that popular culture and most serious art forms neglect." **Must deal with being disabled but not limited to that when artist is disabled. Photocopies with SASE. Reports in 6 months, pays up to $50 for a body of work, $100 for feature length articles. Considers simultaneous submissions. All submissions must be accompanied by an autobiographical sketch.** "Sketch should include general background information, any writing experiences, artistic achievements, a listing of previous publications (if applicable), and nature of disability. The editor says: "Poetry can be based on personal experience, though it must reach beyond the particular and must communicate vividly." They have recently published poetry by Nikki Giovanni, Vassar Miller, and Nancy Mairs. As a sample, they offer these lines by Christopher Hewitt:

> *When I am old I will be very nasty.*
> *I will lean out my attic window,*
> *My hair all cobwebs,*
> *And shout, "You're all crazy!"*

Circulation 1,500, including libraries, social service agencies, health professionals, disabled student services, literature departments, and individual subscribers. A subscription is $9 individual, $12 agency, $4.50 single. **Sample $2.** Be fresh, original, and evocative; let your images speak."

KALLIOPE, a journal of women's art (IV-Women, translations), 3939 Roosevelt Blvd., Jacksonville, FL 32205, phone 904-387-8211, founded 1978, editor Mary Sue Koeppel, a literary/visual arts journal published by Florida Community College at Jacksonville; the emphasis is on women writers and artists. The editors say, **"We like the idea of poetry as a sort of artesian well—there's one meaning that's clear on the surface and another deeper meaning that comes welling up from underneath. We'd like to see more poetry from Black, Hispanic, Native American women, and more translations. Nothing sexist, racist, conventionally sentimental."** Poets recently published include Beatrice Hawley, Marge Piercy, Kathryn Machan Aal, Judith Sornberger, and Sue Saniel Elkind. As a sample, the editors selected the following lines by Laurie Duesing:

> *Now I am rapt and looking for the still point*
> *between earth and air. I am willing*
> *to wait while the world turns red,*
> *to watch while everything comes at me.*

Kalliope calls itself "a journal of women's art," and it publishes fiction, interviews, drama, and visual art in addition to poetry. The magazine, which appears 3 times a year, is 7¼ × 8¼", handsomely printed on white stock with b/w photographs of works of art and, in the sample copy I have, a photographic (no words) essay. Average number of pages is 80. On my copy, the glossy card cover features a b/w illustration of a piece of sculpture; the magazine is flat-spined. The circulation is 1,250, of which 400-500 are subscriptions, including 50 library subscriptions, and 500 copies are sold on newsstands and bookstores. Price is $7/issue, subscription $10.50/year or $20/2 years. **Sample: $7 and guidelines can be obtained for SASE. Contributors receive 3 copies. Poems should be submitted in batches of 3-10 with bio note and phone number and address. Because all submissions are read by several members of the editing staff, response time is usually 3-4 months. Publication will be within 6 months. Criticism is provided "when time permits and the author has requested it.** Don't be discouraged by rejection slips—keep trying. We have to send back a lot of good poetry because we simply can't publish it all. Send for a sample copy, to see what appeals to us, or better yet, subscribe!"

KANSAS QUARTERLY; KANSAS ART COMMISSION AWARDS; SEATON AWARDS (II, IV-Regional, Themes), Denison Hall 122, Kansas State University, Manhattan, KS 66506, phone 913-532-6716, founded 1968 as an outgrowth of *Kansas Magazine,* poetry editors W. R. Moses and H. Schneider, is "a magazine devoted to the culture, history, art, and writing of mid-Americans, but not restricted to this area." It publishes poetry in all issues. They say, "**We are interested in all kinds of modern poetry except humorous verse, limericks, extremely light verse, or book-length MSS.**" They have published poetry by David Ray, Tom Hansen, Eugene Hollahan, Elizabeth Rees, Kathleen Spivack, David Citino, Lyn Lifshin, Robert McNamara, Roger Finch, Ronald Wallace, Mark Nepo, Peter Cooley, Denise Low, and David Kirby. As a sample the editor offers these lines from "Margaret Love" by Andrew Klavan:

> She died by fire. Lying on the couch
> and posing questions to herself,
> she slipped into a doze;
> her right arm drifted down her side;
> her fingers settled on the floor,
> the cigarette in them dropping;
> and the flames went flashing through the house
> like inspiration through the brain.

There are an average of 80 pp. of poetry in each creative issue, circulation 1,150-1,350 with 721 subscriptions of which 50% are libraries. They receive 10,000 submissions per year, use 300-400. There is at least an 18 month backlog unless a poem fits into a special number — then it may go in rapidly. **Sample: $6 postpaid ($7.50 for double number). Submit "enough poems to show variety (or a single poem if author wishes), but no books. Typed, double-spaced, photocopy OK, but no dot-matrix. No queries. We consider, reluctantly, simultaneous submissions." Reports in 1-3 months. Pays 2 copies and yearly awards of up to $200 per poet for 6-10 poets.** The *Kansas Quarterly*/Kansas Art Commission Awards are $200 (1st prize), $150 (2nd), $100 (3rd), $75 (4th), and up to 5 honorable mentions ($50). There are also similar prizes in the Seaton Awards (to native-born or resident Kansas poets). The editors **often comment on rejections, even at times suggesting revision and return.** Editors say, "Our only advice is for the poet to *know* the magazine he is sending to: consult in library or send for sample copy. Magazines need the support and their published copies should provide the best example of what the editors are looking for. We believe that we annually publish as much generally good poetry as nearly any other U.S. literary magazine — between 250 and 400 poems a year. Others will have to say how good it really is."

KARAMU (II), Dept. of English, Eastern Illinois University, Charleston, IL 61920, phone 217-581-5614, founded 1966, editor Peggy Brayfield, is an annual whose "goal is to provide a forum for the best contemporary poetry and fiction that comes our way. We especially like to print the works of new writers. **We like to see poetry that shows a good sense of what's being done with poetry currently. We like poetry that builds around real experiences, real images, and real characters and that avoids abstraction, overt philosophizing, and fuzzy pontifications. In terms of form, we prefer well-structured free verse, poetry with an inner, sub-surface structure as opposed to, let's say, the surface structure of rhymed quatrains. We have definite preferences in terms of style and form, but no such preferences in terms of length or subject matter. Purpose, however, is another thing. We don't have much interest in the openly didactic poem. If the poet wants to preach against or for some political or religious viewpoint, the preaching shouldn't be so strident that it overwhelms the poem. The poem should first be a poem.**" They have recently published poetry by Rosmarie Waldrop, Allen Ginsberg, Marianne Andrea, Janet McCann, and Rich Haydon. The editor chose these sample lines from "African Violet" by Janet McCann:

> Soft green tongues utter
> from the center, they say
> moist, they say warm. A circle
> of green voices rising, tropical
> chant here in the house of sleep.

The format is a 60 pp., 5 × 8", matte cover, handsomely printed (narrow margins), attractive b/w art. Each issue has about 20 pp. of poetry. They have a circulation of 350 with 300 subscriptions of which 15 are libraries. They receive submissions from about 200 poets each year, use 15-20 poems. Never more than a year — usually 6-7 months — between acceptance and publication. **Payment is one contributor's copy. Sample: $3; 2 recent issues $4. "Poems — in batches of no more than 5-6 — may be submitted to Peggy Brayfield at any time of the year. Photocopied work OK, although we don't much care for simultaneous submissions. Poets should not bother to query. We critique a few of the better poems. We want the poet to consider our comments and**

then submit new work. Follow the standard advice: know your market. Read contemporary poetry and the magazines you want to be published in. Be patient."

KATUAH: BIOREGIONAL JOURNAL OF THE SOUTHERN APPALACHIANS (IV-Regional), Box 638, Leicester, NC 28748, founded 1983, edited by a collective group. *Katuah* is a quarterly tabloid journal "concerned with developing a sustainable human culture in the Southern Appalachian Mountains." **The editors want to see "only regional poems or poems dealing with Appalachia and/or ecological feelings."** They have recently published poems by Jim Wayne Miller, Kay Byers, Bennie Lee Sinclair, Michael Hockaday, Scott Bird, Oliver Loveday and Patricia Shirley. The issue I have contains two poems by Stephen Knauth. As a sample, I selected the beginning lines of his "1836. In the Cherokee Overhills":

> In a pasture of the Milky Way
> where the Little Pigeon glides down over the dark
> rocks
> of Tennessee,
> a man has landed on his belly,
> drinking water from a cup made of hands,

The tabloid has 32 pp., offset on newsprint, nicely laid out with attractive b/w drawings and other illustrations, folded for mailing, not stapled. Price per copy is $1.50, subscription $10/year. Circulation is 3,500, of which 300 are subscriptions; 80% of circulation is newsstand sales. **Sample available for $2 postpaid. Pay is 10 copies. Reporting time and time to publication are both 6 months.**

THE KAU KAU KITCHEN NEWSLETTER (I, IV-Regional, themes, children), 372 Haili St., Hilo, HI 96720, phone 808-961-3984, founded 1988, editor Leilehua Yuen, comes out 6 times per year, **dealing with food, nutrition, homemaking, family health specific to Hawai'i, and uses poetry related to those themes as well as poetry by children on a children's page. No erotic poetry.** They have recently published poetry by Fumie Uratani and Lehua Pelekapu. As a sample the editor selected these lines from "Okazu" by Lehua Pelekapu:

> In a thin electric dawn
> the men line up.
>
> "Like one makizushi.
> No cut 'em too t'in!
>   E-Koji!
> Where you was,
>   yesterday?"
>
>   Koji grins

The newsletter is digest-sized, side-stapled, typeset and photocopied, using line drawings, 40+ pp. Their press run is 200 with 40 subscriptions. Subscription: $10. **Sample: $2 postpaid. Guidelines available for SASE. Buys one-time rights. Pays "copies or cash or subscription or ad space." Poem should be "typed exactly as it should appear. I won't edit poetry. If there are errors it will be tossed, unless they look like part of the poem, then I'll run it with errors."** She considers simultaneous submissions and previously published poems. "We are also interested in recipes written in poem form for publication in the newsletter and a possible cookbook/anthology." *Please* **limit submissions to those in our subject area. No "glorious God" poems, unless He's in the kitchen. No poems about Cape Cod with a palm tree. We are most likely to publish poems about food or with food/eating in them. 'Kau Kau' means 'food' or 'to eat' in Hawai'i pidgin."**

KENNEBEC: A PORTFOLIO OF MAINE WRITING (IV-Regional), University of Maine, Augusta, ME 04330, phone 207-622-7131, founded 1975, editors Carol Kontos and Terry Plunkett, is an annual tabloid of creative writing by Maine writers (whether or not currently residents) supported by the University of Maine at Augusta. 5,000 copies are distributed free as a service to the community in an effort to bring Maine writers to the attention of a wide public. **Qualified writers may submit (with a statement of their relationship to Maine) between September 15 and December 1 each year. Sample free for SASE. Pays copies.** I selected these sample lines from "North Into Love" by David Adams:

> A little on we inspect the ponds for frogs,
> guess at the names of shrubs,
> transversing a green geometry, like
> a dream through a dream.

THE KENYON REVIEW; KENYON REVIEW AWARDS FOR LITERARY EXCELLENCE (III), Kenyon College, Gambier, OH 43022, phone 614-427-3339, founded 1939, acting editor David Lynn, poetry editor David Baker, is a quarterly review of arts and letters, fiction, poetry, criticism, reviews and memoirs. It has long held a position as **one of the most distinguished of our literary journals**, regularly publishing such poets as Dave Smith, John Engles, Lawrence Lieberman, Bill Gass, Miller Williams, Don Hall, Wyatt Prunty, and Lewis Simpson. "We try to publish representative verse of the best being done—by established *and* emerging *and* new poets. No didactic or propaganda poems." The editors chose this sample, "The Swimmer" by Mary Oliver:

> *All winter the water*
> > *has crashed over*
> > > *the cold sand. Now*
> > > > *breaks over the thin*
> *branch of your body.*

The elegantly printed, flat-spined, 7 × 10″, 120 + pp. format has a circulation of 3,800 with 3,300 subscriptions of which 1,100 are libraries. They receive about 1,500-2,000 freelance submissions per year, use 15-20 (about 25 pp. of poetry in each issue), have a 1 year backlog. **Sample: $7 postpaid. Reports in 2 months, pays $15 per page for poetry and $10 per page for prose.** The Kenyon Review Awards are given annually, by distinguished outside judges, for the best contributions in poetry, fiction and the essay published in the magazine.

‡**KEY WEST REVIEW (III)**, 9 Ave. G., Key West, FL 33040, phone 305-296-1365, founded 1987, associate editor for poetry (Ms.) Marion H. Smith, appears twice a year. **"No restrictions on form or content of poetry. Nothing sentimental, amateurish, or pornographic."** They have recently published poetry by Richard Wilbur, Marge Piercy, Eleanor Ross Taylor, Richard Eberhart, James Merrill, and George Starbuck. As a sample the editor selected these lines from a poem by Judith Kazantzis called "Dusk and a Portuguese Man o' War":

> *We are in the tropics. I'm sorry to say*
> *what slews round the corner*
> *is no fun: winningly, slidingly*
> *under its indigo puff sleeve*
> *under its beacon blue eye, its arms*
> *outspread to me.*

MSS are not read during the summer. Editor comments on submissions "seldom." *KWR* is 100 + pp., digest-sized, flat-spined, professionally printed, with matte card cover. Press run: 1,000 for 250 subscribers of which 25 are libraries. 100 copies go free "to well-known authors from whom we are soliciting contributions." Subscription: $17. **Sample, postpaid: $5. Pays "token only" and 2 copies, "sometimes more."**

KINGFISHER (II), P.O. Box 9783, N. Berkeley, CA 94709, founded 1987, editors Andrea Beach, Barbara Schultz, Lorraine Hilton-Gray, and Ruthie Singer, is a "literary quarterly emphasizing short fiction. It publishes **a significant number of poems in each issue. We'll take a look at anything.** We see around 50 poems a month and accept about 4." They have recently published poetry by Mike Louth, Jack Lindemann, and Janet McCann. As a sample the editor chose these closing lines from "Hunter":

> *The legless few I trap*
> *shed syllables like snakeskin,*
> *slither away.*
> *Hollow-eyed morning*
> *I am left alone*
> *thrashing about*
> *in the torn net*
> *of my poem*

I have not seen a copy, but they say their format is 6 × 9″, flat-spined, using b/w drawings, with a 2-color cover. **Sample: $5 postpaid. Pays 2 copies. Simultaneous submissions OK and previously published poems "maybe."**

‡**KIOSK (II,IV-Themes)**, 306 Clemens Hall, SUNY, Buffalo, NY 14260, founded 1985, editors Stephanie Foote and Mark Hammer, is an annual literary magazine using **poetry of "any length, any style. Sometimes issues are devoted to particular subjects such as surrealism, so poetry will be expected to comment on/participate in surrealism for that particular issue. We want nothing that looks like, feels like a greeting card and makes us throw up the way greeting cards do."** They have recently published Bruce Holsapple, Piotr Pariej, and Fritz Bacher. As a sample the editor selected these lines by Marten Clibbens:

> *time back*

> *again refute brutal*
> *claim of labour*
> *and wit stole*

I have not seen an issue, but the editor describes it as flat-spined, digest-sized. Of 400 poems they accept 10-15. **Pays 1 copy. Free sample with SASE. Reports within 6 months.**

KITCHEN TABLE: WOMEN OF COLOR PRESS (IV-Women, ethnic), P.O. Box 908, Latham, NY 12110, phone 518-434-2057, founded 1981, is "the only publisher in North America committed to producing and distributing the **work of Third World women of all racial/cultural heritages, sexualities, and classes.**" They publish flat-spined paperback collections and anthologies. **"We want high quality poetry by women of color which encompasses a degree of consciousness of the particular issues of identity and struggle which women of color face."** The editors selected these lines from **Healing Heart, Poems 1973-1988** by Gloria T. Hull:

> *we love in circles*
> *touching round—*
> *faces in a ritual ring*
> *echoing blood and color*
> *nappy girlheads in a summer porch swing*
> *belligerent decisions to live*
> *and be ourselves.*

That book is a digest-sized, flat-spined paperback, glossy card cover, 140 pp., $8.95, with critical praise on the cover by Gwendolyn Brooks, Ntozake Shange, and Stephen E. Henderson. They publish an average of one book of poetry every other year and have published three anthologies, two of which contain poetry. All books are published simultaneously in hardback for library sales. **Submit a sample of 10 pages of poems with background information about your writing and publishing career and "a general description of the poetry collection as a whole." They reply to queries in 8 weeks, to full MS submissions (if invited) in 6 months. Simultaneous submissions OK if they are informed. MS should be typed, double-spaced. Clear photocopies OK. No dot-matrix. Payment is 7% royalties for first 10,000 copies, 8% thereafter, and 10 copies. Write for catalog to purchase samples. General comments usually given upon rejection.** The editors say, "We are particularly interested in publishing work by women of color which would generally be overlooked by other publishers, especially work by American Indian, Latina, Asian American and African American women who may be working class, lesbian, disabled or older writers."

ALFRED A. KNOPF (V), 201 E. 50th St., New York, NY 10022, poetry editor Harry Ford. Over the years Knopf has been one of the most important and distinguished publishers of poetry in the United States. **"The list is closed to new submissions at this time."**

KOLA; AFO ENTERPRISES REG'D (IV-Ethnic), C.P. 1602 Place Bonaventure, Montréal H5A 1H6 Canada, AFO Enterprises Reg'd founded 1983, Kola founded 1987, editor Dr. Horace I. Goddard. **"Poetry must reflect the black experience worldwide."** They have recently published poetry by Chezia Thompson-Cager (U.S.A.) and Ezenwa-Ohaeto (Nigeria). As a sample I selected these lines from "I Can't Go Home Again" by Shirley Small:

> *I long to reach out*
> *and touch the earth of the mother-land*
> *land that will not reach out to me:*
> *earth of my fathers washed with bloody tears.*

Kola is digest-sized, 40 pp. printed (lithographed) from typescript with matte card cover. It appears in spring, summer and fall each year and they accept 95% of the manuscripts received. Their press run is 300 with 150 subscriptions of which 4 are libraries. **Sample: $4 U.S., $3 Canada, postpaid. Pays 2 copies. Reports in 6-8 weeks. Editor sometimes comments on rejections.** AFO Enterprises Reg'd publishes paperbacks and does accept unsolicited MSS. Dr. Goddard says, "Poetry is not a saleable commodity. To be known a poet must try to read to many audiences. Try new forms and be bold with new techniques."

KORONE (IV-Women/feminist), Womanspace, 3333 Maria Linden Dr., Rockford, IL 61111, phone 815-877-0118, founded 1983, managing editor Elaine Hirschenberger, co-editors Dorothy Bock and Pat Maggio, produces one flat-spined anthology of poetry, fiction, and essays a year, 140 pp. **Manuscript must be accompanied by a $5 entry fee and a SASE. Contest: two $50 awards are given each year. "Focuses on women writers nationally. Open to all forms but shies away from archaicism; seeks women's voices that have moved beyond rage and therapy; like revisionist myth; likes to see women in a variety of roles and adventures; no hand-written, no doggerel, no ancestor worship or sentimentality."** They have recently published poetry by Sue Cowing, Olivia Diamond, and Barbara Lau. As a sample the editors selected these lines from "One Last Summer List" by Judy F. Ham:

And I shall ride my child's red scooter
Down the lakeside path, dusk wind pulling at my hair
Wearing cotton clothes, homespun blue
With lots of pockets (each tucked
with a word to make me roll
On the lawn with laughter—efficiency,
Technology—after the fireflies have gone)

The copy I have seen is digest-sized, professionally printed in small dark type on light white paper with gloss card cover. Cost: $8.25 postpaid. Their press run is 500-750. **Sample: $5 postpaid. They use about 75 of 800 submissions received a year. Guidelines available for SASE. Pays 1 copy. They consider simultaneous submissions. Reports in 1-2 months after August 1 deadline (November publication).**

KRAX; RUMP BOOKLETS (II, IV-Humor), 63 Dixon Lane, Leeds, Yorkshire, LS12 4RR England, founded 1971, poetry editors Andy Robson et al. *Krax* appears twice yearly, and they want poetry which is **"light-hearted and witty; original ideas. Undesired: anything containing the words 'nuclear' or 'Jesus.' " 2,000 words maximum. All forms and styles considered.** The editor chose these lines from "Evolution" by John Darley:

They were called Mum and Dad
my friends had ones, too,
they were older and duller
and better than you.

Krax is 6 × 8″, 48 pp. of which 30 are poetry, saddle-stapled, offset with b/w cartoons and graphics. Price per issue: £1.25 ($2.50), per subscription: £6 ($10). They receive up to 1,000 submissions per year of which they use 6%, have a 2-3 year backlog. **Sample: $1 (75p). "Submit maximum of 6 pieces. Writer's name on same sheet as poem. SASE or IRC encouraged but not vital." Reports within 10 weeks. Pays 1 copy.** *Rump Booklets* are miniature format 3x4″ 16 pp. collections. **Query with "detailed notes of projected work." Send SASE for catalog.** The editor says, "Don't send money to publishers, etc, without written proof of their existence. Keep copies of your work—all things may be lost in transit, so query if no reply. Name poets tend to shun us in favour of glossy paperbacks and hard cash, but diamonds don't come in garish packages and no one can start at the top."

‡KWIBIDI PUBLISHER; KID'S PLAYYARD; THE JOURNAL OF THE NATIONAL SOCIETY OF MINOR-ITY WRITERS AND ARTISTS; THE WRITERS' AND ARTISTS' AID (IV-Ethnic, membership, children), P.O. Box 3424, Greensboro, NC 27402-3424. Kwibidi founded 1979, *JNSMWA* 1981, *KP* 1986. Editor Dr. Doris B. Kwasikpui. Kwibidi Publisher **"needs poems, one-act plays, short stories, articles, art, jokes, book reports, research papers and how-to-do and make, for books,** *Kid's Playyard* **(a magazine for kids of all ages), and** *JNSMWA*. **Publication limited to minorities. Pay in copies. Upon acceptance, require membership in the National Society of Minority Writers and Artists ($15/year). Publishes much of the material received and often responds with suggestions. Send SASE for guidelines. Reports in about 3 weeks.** *KP* appears twice a year. As a sample of the poetry they publish I selected this poem (poet unidentified):

When snow comes down very fast
And piles upon the ground
We'll make a big snow man
A tall one and very round . . .

LA BELLA FIGURA (I,IV-Ethnic), Box 411223, San Francisco, CA 94141-1223, founded 1988, editor Rose Romano, is a quarterly using poetry **"any form, any length, about Italian-American culture and heritage or anything of special significance to Italian-Americans. Nothing insulting to I-As: no negative stereotypes, no complaining about I-A ways without affection, no spelling accents (such as tacking an** *a* **to the end of every other word), and no apologies for being I-A."** They have recently published poetry by Rina Ferrarelli, Rachel DeVries, Dan Sicoli, and Gigi Marino. As a sample the editor selected these lines from "Public School No. 18: Paterson, New Jersey" by Maria Gillan:

ALWAYS submit MSS or queries with a stamped, self-addressed envelope (SASE) within your country or International Reply Coupons (IRCs) purchased from the post office for other countries.

> Remember me, ladies,
> the silent one?
> I have found my voice
> and my rage will blow
> your house down.

La Bella Figura is 10 pp., magazine-sized, quality offset. Their press run is 200 with 100 subscriptions of which 2 are libraries. Subscription: $8. **Sample: $2 postpaid. Send SASE for guidelines. Pays 2 copies. "All potential contributors are asked to fill out a very short form to describe their Italian background and experience as an Italian-American. Part of the reason for *LBF* is to create family. Therefore, I welcome friendly, informative cover letters. I will gladly consider previously published poems. No simultaneous submissions."** The editor adds, "Few people understand our culture and, therefore, cannot appreciate poetry based on its symbols and secrets. Many I-As are simply 'writing American' or not being published. Write what you are—not what you saw in a movie by an American. I'd like to include work by all I-As—lesbians, gays, heterosexuals, and those who are half-Italian but who feel Italian very strongly, first through fourth or fifth generations."

LA NUEZ (II,IV-Foreign language), P.O. Box 1655, New York, NY 10276, phone 212-260-3130, founded 1988, poetry editor Rafael Bordao, associate editor Celeste Ewers, is a quarterly international magazine of literature and art, **published entirely in Spanish.** The focus is primarily on poetry, but essays, criticism, interviews, short fiction, and reviews of poetry books are also of interest, as well as original artwork and photography. They have recently published work by Frank Dauster, Reinaldo Arenas, Justo Jorge Padrón, Clara Janés, and José Kozer. As a sample the editor selected these lines by Amparo Amorós:

> Si la noche se acerca y vienes de muy lejos
> porque sientes la vida pesando sobre el alma
> es hora de sentarse sereno y en penumbra
> a contemplar, absorto, como queman el tiempo
> los leños del invierno.

La Nuez is magazine-sized, 30 pp. saddle-stapled and professionally printed, with glossy paper cover. Their press run is 1,000. Subscription: $12. **Sample: $3.50. No simultaneous submissions. Only unpublished work with brief biographical info and SASE. Reporting time 6-8 weeks. Payment 2 copies.**

LACTUCA (II), P.O. Box 621, Suffern, NY 10901, founded 1986, editor/publisher Mike Selender, appears 3 times a year. **"Our bias is toward work with a strong sense of place, a strong sense of experience, a quiet dignity, and an honest emotional depth. Dark and disturbing writings are preferred over safer material. No haikus, poems about writing poems, poems using the poem as an image, light poems or self-indulgent poems. First English language translations are welcome provided that the translator has obtained the approval of the author."** They have recently published poetry by Charles Bukowski, James Purdy, Joe Cardillo, Juliette Graff, Gail Schilke, Julia Nunnally Duncan, Judson Crews, and Michael Pingarron. As a sample he selected these lines from "There is a Countryside" by Herman Graff:

> There is a countryside
> of beauty and decay
> where bluebells sway in summer
> among gray, flotsam skulls.

Lactuca is digest-sized, 60 pp. saddle-stapled, laser printed or offset on 24 lb. bond with matte card cover, no ads. They receive "a few thousand poems a year of which less than 5% are accepted." Press run is 400 for 75 subscriptions. Subscription: $10/year. **Sample: $3.50 postpaid. Send SASE for guidelines. "We do not print previously published material." Pays 2-5 copies "depending on length." Reports within 3 months, "usually within one. We comment on rejections when we can. However the volume of mail we receive limits this."** He says, "The purpose of *Lactuca* is to be a small literary magazine publishing high-quality poetry, fiction and b/w drawings. Most of our circulation goes to contributors' copies and exchange copies with other literary magazines. Lactuca is not for poets expecting large circulation. Poets appearing here will find themselves in good company, appearing with that of other good writers. We've found that our acceptance rate is less than 5% for those responding to announcements in *Poets & Writers,* but significantly higher for poets who find out about *Lactuca* from other magazines."

LADIES' HOME JOURNAL (IV-Humor), 100 Park Ave., New York, NY 10017, phone 212-351-3500, founded 1883, a slick monthly, circulation 5½ million, no longer accepts serious poetry. But they do consider **light verse (1-3 stanzas) for the "Last Laughs" page. Put "Last Laughs" on the outside of the envelope. No SASE necessary because they neither return nor acknowledge submissions. If your**

poem is accepted you'll know when you get the check for $100. For a sample the editor chose the poem "How Did It Happen?" by Sara Gadeken:

They're always needing money,
My two delightful teens.
He takes his dates to restaurants.
She wears designer jeans.

He's going on a ski trip.
She's going to the prom.
There's a Springsteen concert Friday
("You're only young once, Mom!").

I don't know how it happened.
It wasn't my design.
But my children's standard of living
Is considerably higher than mine!

LAKE EFFECT (I, II, IV-Humor, regional), Box 59, Oswego, NY 13126, phone 315-342-3579, founded 1985, poetry editors Joan Loveridge-Sanbonmatsu and Carol Sue Muth, is a quarterly literary tabloid using art (graphics and b/w photographs), short fiction, non-fiction, poetry, book reviews, humor (poems and cartoons), essays and guest editorials. **"We look for imaginative, evocative, well-crafted poetry with fresh insights and images. Any style or theme, under 50 lines if possible."** As a sample, the editors selected these lines from "The Shooting of Cannons Over Rivers" by Patricia M. Smith:

So much in life we bring things up:
the digging of potatoes, the resting of crocus bulbs.
Then there are some arousals:
anger and cream

We are the resurrectors:
coal and carrots and old hatreds.

Their purpose is to "provide upstate NY State readers poetry and prose of regional interest; we also include quality work by artists from other parts of the country." The tabloid quarterly runs 24-28 pp., professionally typeset and laid-out, circulation 9,000 with 198 subscriptions of which 9 are libraries. It is distributed free to the 1,550 members and friends of the Oswego Art Guild. Subscription: $5. **Sample: $2. Send SASE for guidelines. Pays $5 per poem. Reports in 8 weeks, no backlog at present (seasonal material is held). Double-space MS. Photocopy, dot-matrix OK if legible. 2-5 poems per submission, no simultaneous submissions. "A short bio with submission is nice but not necessary." Put name, address, phone number in upper right corner.**

LAKE SHORE PUBLISHING; SOUNDINGS, (I, IV-Anthology), 373 Ramsay Rd., Deerfield, IL 60015, phone 708-945-4324, founded 1983, poetry editor Carol Spelius, is an effort "to put out decent, economical volumes of poetry." **Reading fee: $1 per page. They want poetry which is "understandable and *moving*, imaginative with a unique view, in any form. Make me laugh or cry or think. I'm not so keen on gutter language or political dogma—but I try to keep an open mind. No limitations in length."** In their first volume, they published poetry by John Dickson, Esther Kossoff, Glenna Holloway, Virginia Real Nicholas, Aimy Jo Schoonover, James W. Proctor, Ken Letco, and Alice McKenzie. The editor selected these sample lines from "Butch Bond's Funeral" by Kay Meier:

. . . His widow smug with survival and her secret
that Butch had not fathered their youngest
was deciding whether to keep
the electric fence. Before Butch,
only small animals had been stunned.

The 253 pp. anthology included over 100 poets in 1985, is a paperback, at $7.95 (add $1 mailing cost), was published in an edition of 2,000. **Soundings II** is scheduled for late 1990 or early 1991. The editor says they are selecting poetry that is "understandable and moving, humorous, imaginative or containing a unique view." It is flat-spined, photocopied from typescript, with glossy, colored card cover with art. **Pays 1 copy and half-price for additional copies. Submit any number of poems, with $1 per page reading fee, and a covering letter telling about your other publications, biographical background, personal or aesthetic philosophy, poetic goals and principles. Simultaneous submissions, photocopy, dot-matrix, all OK. Any form or length. Reports within 4 months. The editor will read chapbooks, or full length collections, with the possibility of sharing costs if** Lake Shore Publishing likes the book ($1 per page reading fee). "I split the cost if I like the book." She advises, "Keep reading classics and writing modern. Try all forms.

Pray a lot." Sample copy of anthology or random choice of full-length collections to interested poets, $4.

LANDFALL; CAXTON PRESS (IV-Regional), Box 25-088, Christchurch, New Zealand, founded 1947, poetry editor Hugh Lauder. *Landfall* is a literary quarterly of **New Zealand poetry**, prose, criticism, reviews, correspondence and interviews. *Caxton Press* publishes a poetry series of books. **They do not want to see poetry except by New Zealanders.** They have recently published poetry by Lauis Edmond, Keri Hulme, Ian Wedde, and Hone Tuwhare. As a sample I chose the first of two stanzas of "To the poet who called himself a fox among the hens" by Heather McPherson:

> *Remember Maui. He thought*
> *to snatch immortality*
> *till a fantail laughed*
> *and Hine closed her thighs.*

The handsome quarterly is digest-sized, 124+ pp., flat-spined, with full-color glossy card cover, circulation 1,800, 1,600 subscriptions of which 200 are libraries. Subscription: $44 (New Zealand dollars). **Sample: $11 (New Zealand dollars) plus postage. Pays about $40 plus 1 copy for 3-4 poems. Reports immediately. No backlog. Submit 10-12 poems, "a range." Editor always comments on rejections.** His advice: "Read poetry."

PETER LANG PUBLISHING, INC. (IV-Translation), 62 W. 45th St., New York, NY 10036, phone 212-302-6740, FAX 212-302-7574, publishes primarily scholarly monographs in the humanities and social sciences. List includes **critical editions of great poets of the past. Complete MSS preferred, 200 pages minimum, with descriptive cover letter and** *curriculum vitae.*

LANGUAGE BRIDGES QUARTERLY (I, IV-Ethnic, foreign language), Box 850792, Richardson, TX 75085, founded in 1988, editors Zofia Przebindowska-Tousty and Eva Ziem, "is a **Polish-English bilingual forum for Polish matters. One of its purposes is to introduce the English-speaking reader to Polish culture. The subject is Poland and the Polish spirit:** a picture of life in Poland, mainly after World War II, with emphasis on the new and ponderous Polish emigration problems." As a sample the editors selected these lines from "Wrak" (or Zombie—I will quote only the English) by TB (3 June 1987), translated by Karon Campbell and Eva Ziem:

> *I am a zombie.*
> *My soul*
> *is a void, hopelessly*
> *ruined, eternally pained*
> *by injustice.*

For more information send SASE.

‡LATEST JOKES NEWSLETTER (IV-Humor), Box 023304, Brooklyn, NY 11202-0066. Phone 718-855-5057, editor Robert Makinson. *LJN* is a monthly newsletter of humor for TV and radio personalities, comedians and professional speakers. Circulation 250. **Submit seasonal/holiday material 3 months in advance. Reports in 3 weeks. Sample copy $3 and 1 first class stamp. They use light verse (humorous). Submit maximum 3 poems at one time. Line length: 2-8 lines. Pays 25 cents/line.**

LATIN AMERICAN LITERARY REVIEW PRESS; LATIN AMERICAN LITERARY REVIEW (IV-Ethnic, translations, subscribers), 2300 Palmer St., Pittsburgh, PA 15218, phone 412-351-1477, poetry editor Yvette E. Miller. *Latin American Literary Review*, founded in 1972, publishes semiannually. Number of pages of poetry is variable; total circulation 1,500, subscriptions 1,000, of which 800 are libraries. $17/issue; institutional subscription $30. **Sample copy $16 postpaid; they use 25% of submitted material from Latin American poets. Send up to 10 pages, photocopies OK, reports within 3 months, no pay, contributors are expected to subscribe or buy copies.** The magazine is 150 pp., flat-spined, 6×9". Latin American Literary Review Press, founded 1977, publishes books in any Romance language and in English or English translation. Bilingual format is used for poetry. The Press publishes anthologies, flat-spined, paperbacks, and hardbacks. **Poetry is "not restricted on subject but we object to political themes. No explicit sex."** Poets recently published include Jose Emilio Pacheco, Isabel Fraire, Alejandra Pizarnik, and Violeta Parra. As a sample I selected the first stanza of "La Danza" by Marjorie Agosin, as translated by Cola Franzen:

> *As I dance submerged*
> *on the blue perch*
> *that was floating between my mother's legs*
> *and in her belly danced*
> *dark signals to announce myself.*

The press publishes 3-4 poetry chapbooks/year of about 100-160 pp., and 100 paperbacks (100-160 pp.). Freelance submissions are considered but poets should include bio and list of other publications. Replies to queries in 1 month, reports on submissions in 3 months. Photocopied MS OK. Royalties 10% of print run and 25 copies. Book catalog free on request with 9½ × 12½" envelope. Poets can request books at 10% discount. Book samples I have seen are handsome, professionally printed, with glossy card covers, flat-spined.

LATTER DAY WOMAN (IV-Religious, women, humor), Box 126, Sandy, UT 84091, is a magazine appearing every two months, circulation 40,000, which "offers inspiration and support to help today's Latter-Day Saint woman cope with her special challenges." They publish poetry as well as fiction, articles, shorts and fillers. They want poetry that is **"inspiring, insightful, with artistic fresh images. While we want some 'serious' spiritual pieces, humorous verses on homemaking, dieting, children, or any subject of general interest to women may also be accepted. Considers simultaneous submissions. Maximum length: 30 lines." Payment for poetry: $10-25. Sample: $1 plus postage.** Subscription: $8.95/ one year. "Poems should be fairly short—no epics please—and not preachy."

LAUGHING BEAR PRESS (V), Box 36159, Bear Valley Station, Denver, CO 80236, phone 303-989-5614, founded 1976, poetry editor Tom Person, is a small-press publisher of poetry books and cassette tapes of poetry. Tom Person likes **"experimental, modern poetry of any length, no lyrical, rhyme, sentimental or fantasy."** He has recently published poetry by Richard Kostelanetz and Roberta Metz Swann. As a sample, I selected the poem "No Boy Digs" by John M. Bennett:

> He was digging a hole in the yard he was
> dropping the shovel on his foot he was
> falling on the pile of dirt he was
> seeing the wires far above, a
> crow screaming as it left
>
> A Stone A Stone he shouts

That poem is on an audiocassette published by Laughing Bear Press, **No Boy**, with music by Tom Person. He publishes an average of 2 chapbooks per year, 32 pp., saddle-stapled. He **is not presently accepting submissions. Query, "always" before submitting, enclosing 4 sample poems, bio and publications. No simultaneous submissions. No dot-matrix or photocopies. Previously published material OK. Reports on queries in 4 weeks. Pays ½ the run.** For sample, send SASE for catalog or $1 for catalog and sample anthology (issue of the defunct *Laughing Bear* magazine). Comments on MSS "only if requested." Tom Person advises, "I suggest poets avoid contests and publishers that require reading fees."

LAUGHING DOG PRESS (V, IV-Regional, women, nature), 12509 S.W. Cove Rd., Vashon, WA 98070, phone 206-463-3700 or 3153, founded 1974, owner/editor Rayna Holtz, is a letterpress printer/ publisher **"of poetry, primarily by women, primarily from the Pacific Northwest"** in chapbooks in editions of 500, of which 470 are perfect-bound or hand-sewn paperbacks, 30 are handbound in cloth. They also publish poetry broadsides. The six co-owners and community volunteers share typesetting and printing. **Currently they are not accepting poetry submissions.** They are working on a book of prose poems about Nicaragua by Serena Cosgrove. As an example of what they like, they chose these lines by Melane Lohmann:

> I lean over the bark
> into the tree
> My head comes to rest
> between my arms
> on smooth bone
> I stare into shadow.

Send for their list to order samples.

‡**LAUREL REVIEW (II); GREENTOWER PRESS (V)**, Dept. of English, Northwest Missouri State University, Maryville, MO 64468, phone 816-562-1265, founded 1960, co-editors Craid Goad, William Trowbridge, and David Slater. *LR* is a literary journal appearing twice a year; **Greentower Press accepts no unsolicited MSS.** *LR* wants **"poetry of highest literary quality, nothing sentimental, religious, greeting card, workshop, spit and whistle."** They have recently published poetry by George Starbuck, Marcia Southwick, Albert Goldbarth, David Citino, and Pattiann Rogers. It is 128 pp., 6 × 9". Press run: 750 for 400 subscriptions of which 53 are libraries, 10 shelf sales. Subscription: $8/year. **Sample, postpaid: $5. Pays 2 copies plus subscription. Submit 4-6 poems/batch. Reports in 1 week-4 months.** Editor "does not usually" comment on submissions.

THE LEADING EDGE (IV-Science fiction/fantasy), 1102 JKHB, Provo, UT 84602, phone 801-378-4455, managing editor Scott R. Parkin. *The Leading Edge* is a magazine, 3 times a year. They want **"high quality poetry related to science fiction and fantasy, not to exceed 3-4 typewritten, double-spaced**

pages. No graphic sex, violence, or profanity." They have recently published poetry by Michael Collings and Thomas Easton. As a sample the editors picked these lines from "Prydwen Upon the Sea" by Doug Jole:

> *For a king we rode upon the water;*
> *undaunted we traveled the tossing teeth*
> *of white-capped green*

I have not seen the magazine, but the editors describe it as 6×9″, 112 pp., using art. They accept about 5 out of 100 poems received per year. Press run is 500, going to 100 subscriptions (10 of them libraries), and 300 shelf sales. $2.50 per issue, $7.50 for a subscription. **Sample: $2 for back issue, $2.50 for current issue postpaid. Send SASE for guidelines. Pays $5 per typeset page plus 2 copies. Submit with no name on the poem, but with a cover sheet with name, address, phone number, length of poem, title, and type of poem (science fiction, fantasy, horror, etc.). Simultaneous submissions OK, but no previously published poems. Reports in 60-90 days.** They say, "We accept traditional science fiction and fantasy poetry, but we like innovative stuff. If a poet has a good idea, go for it."

‡**THE LEDGE POETRY AND PROSE MAGAZINE (II)**, 64-65 Cooper Ave., Glendale, NY 11385, phone 718-366-5169, founded 1988, editor Timothy Monaghan, is a semiannual using poetry and prose of **"any style of poetry, from traditional to experimental, up to 3 pp. Any type or subject matter as long as it's conveyed well, but, no rhyme-scheme, religious, or limmericks."** Recent contributors are Steven Hartman, Les Bridges, Ken DiMaggio, and Margueritte. *The Ledge* is 5×7″, usually 72-80 pp. with glossy cover. They accept 15% of some 500 submissions per year. Press run is 350-425 with 56 subscribers, 275+ shelf sales. **"Submissions are reviewed by three or four writers associated with our magazine; only unanimous decisions ensure publication."** Subscription: $12 (plus $1.50 postage) for one volume (6 issues), or $6.75 (plus $1 postage) for one-half volume (3 issues). **Samples of current and back issues (#1 thru #8): $3 each (plus 50¢ postage). Pays 1 copy. Previously published poems and simultaneous submissions OK.**

‡**LEGEND: (I, IV-Fantasy)**, 1036 Hampshire Rd., Victoria, B.C., V8S 4S9, Canada, phone 604-598-2197, founded 1989, editor Janet P. Reedman, appears approximately once a year. She wants **"fantasy poetry, particularly that dealing with/based on episodes of the British TV series 'Robin of Sherwood.'** " **Length is open. No porn or dull poetry about mundane matters.** She has recently published poetry by: Cathy Buburuz, J.P. Reedman, Owen Neill, J.M. Rattray, David Cavangh, D. Linn, and Denysé Bridger. The editor selected these sample lines from "Sacrifice" (poet unidentified):

> *Red blood and dark earth a communion form,*
> *earth is England and the blood is mine,*
> *I am loth to leave when my love's lying warm,*
> *but I am sworn to be the King Divine.*

Magazine is 140+ pages, spiral-bound, photocopied from typescript, uses much b/w art. **80-90% material accepted from 2 dozen or so. "Will help with rewrites; prefer to outright rejection."** Press run: 100+. **Sample: $12 US., $14 Canadian. Payment: 4 or more poems — a copy; otherwise, a substantial discount. Typed or handwritten MSS acceptable. No previously published. Reports 1-10 weeks, usually sooner. For US submissions/inquiries: rather than IRCs please send 2 loose US stamps. Nearly always comments on rejections.**

L'EPERVIER PRESS (V), 1326 N.E. 62nd, Seattle, WA 98105, founded 1977, editor Robert McNamara, a "small press publisher of contemporary American poetry in perfect-bound and casebound books." **Currently not accepting submissions.** He has recently published books by Bruce Renner, Linda Bierds, Frederic Will, and Paul Hoover. As a sample, he chose the following lines from "The Hopper Light" by David Rigsby:

> *A slow burn. And then, even the cells*
> *whisper goodbye in a slow, vegetal loneliness.*
> *Today the stem goes to a stump, a seam*
> *along which the leaf is cloven and rains*
> *down in this vain. If the separation*
> *defines the kiss, I have seen so many*
> *falling out of love today*

The press publishes 2 poetry books each year, 6×9″ with an average page count of 64, some flat-spined paperbacks and some hardcovers. The book they sent me, **Second Sun** by Bill Tremblay, is handsomely printed on heavy buff stock, 81 pp., with glossy card cover in grey, yellow, and white; there is a b/w landscape photo on the front cover and a photo of the author on the back; the book is priced at $6.95.

‡LIBIDO: THE JOURNAL OF SEX AND SEXUALITY (I, IV-Erotic, humor), P.O. Box 146721, Chicago, IL 60614, founded 1988, editors Marianna Beck and Jack Hafferkamp, is a quarterly. "Form, length and style are open. We want poetry of any and all styles as long as it is erotic and/or erotically humorous. We make a distinction between erotica and pornography. We want wit not dirty words." They have recently published poetry by Ovid, Pietro Aretino, and Arno Karlen. As a sample the editor selected these lines (poet unidentified):

> *You'll remember, my blond and curly angel*
> *with blue-brown eyes that cradle the light,*
> *the night I laid my fingers on your hard*
> *silk thighs — thighs that wished me well . . .*

It is digest-sized, 72 pp., professionally printed, flat-spined, with 2-color matte card cover. Press run: 5,000 for 1,500 subscriptions, shelf sales of 2,500-3,000 ("it's growing quickly"). They accept about 5% of poetry received. Subscription: $20 in U.S., $30 outside. **Sample, postpaid: $6. Pays $0-25 plus 2 copies. Reports in 3 months.**

LIBRA PUBLISHERS, INC. (I), Suite 383, 3089C Clairemont Dr., San Diego, CA 92117, phone 619-581-9449, poetry editor William Kroll, publishes two professional journals, *Adolescence* and *Family Therapy* plus books, primarily in the behaviorial sciences but also some general nonfiction, fiction and poetry. "At first we published books of poetry on a standard royalty basis, paying 10% of the retail price to the authors. Although at times we were successful in selling enough copies to at least break even, we found that we could no longer afford to publish poetry on this basis. Now, unless we fall madly in love with a particular collection, **we require a subsidy.** They have published books of poetry by Martin Rosner, William Blackwell, John Travers Moore, and C. Margaret Hall, the author of these sample lines selected by the editor:

> *Writing poetry means*
> *That I can take up the brush at any minute,*
> *That I can put down the thought*
> *That was flying high.*

Prefer complete MS but accept query with 6 sample poems, publishing credits and bio. Replies to query in 2 days, to submissions (if invited) in 2-3 weeks. MS should be double-spaced. Photocopy, dot-matrix OK. Send 9x12 SASE for catalog. Sample books may be purchased on a returnable basis.

LIFTOUTS MAGAZINE; PRELUDIUM PUBLISHERS (V, IV-Translations), 1503 Washington Ave. S., Minneapolis, MN 55454, phone 612-333-0031, founded 1971, poetry editor Barry Casselman, is a "publisher of **experimental literary work and work of new writers in translation from other languages.**" **Currently accepting no unsolicited material.** *Liftouts* appears irregularly. I have not seen it, but they say it is "offset tabloid" and has a press run of "20,000."

LIGHTHOUSE (I, IV-Children), P.O. Box 1377, Auburn, WA 98071-1377, founded 1986, associate editor Lorraine Clinton, is a magazine of "timeless stories and poetry for family" appearing every other month. It has a children's section. **Uses poems up to 50 lines, "G-rated, ranging from light-hearted to inspirational."** They have recently published poetry by Dawn Zapletal, Errol Miller, David Eales, and Louise Hannah Kohr. As a sample the editor selected these lines from "Eventide" by Muriel Larsen:

> *Magenta splashed across the sky*
> *Has fallen on the tide,*
> *And mixed among the gold and blue*
> *Through twilight hour doth ride.*

I have not seen it, but the editor describes it as 56 pp., digest-sized, "professionally printed, some simple illustrations in Children's Section." Circulation is 300 for 200 subscriptions. Subscription: $7.95. **Sample: $2. Send SASE with 25¢ postage for guidelines. Pays up to $5 per poem. "Prefer typed, double-spaced, each poem on a separate sheet for evaluating purposes." Reports in 1-2 months, publication within a year.**

LILITH MAGAZINE (IV-Women, ethnic), Suite 2432, 250 W. 57th St., New York, NY 10107, phone 212-757-0818, founded in 1975, publisher Paula Gantz, "is an independent magazine with a Jewish feminist perspective" which uses **poetry by Jewish women "about the Jewish woman's experience. Generally we use short rather than long poems. Do not want to see poetry on other subjects."** They have published poetry by Irena Klepfisz, Lyn Lifshin, Yael Messinai, Sharon Neemani, Marcia Falk, and Adrienne Rich. I have not seen a copy of *Lilith*, but the editor describes it as "glossy, magazine-sized. We use colors. Page count varies. Covers are very attractive and professional-looking (one has won an award). Generous amount of art. It appears 4 times a year, circulation about 10,000, about 5,000 subscriptions." Subscription: $14 for 4 issues. **Sample: $4.50 postpaid. Send SASE for guidelines.**

Reports in 6-8 weeks. "Please send no more than 6 poems at a time; advise if it is a simultaneous." Editor "sometimes" comments on rejections. She advises: "(1) Read a copy of the publication before you submit your work. (2) Be realistic if you are a beginner. The competition is *severe*, so don't start to send out your work until you've written for a few years. (3) Short cover letters only. Copy should be neatly typed and proofread for typos and spelling errors."

‡LILLIPUT REVIEW (II, IV-Form), 4 Huddy Ave., Highlands, NJ 07732, phone 201-291-5507, founded 1989, editor Don Wentworth, is a tiny (4½×3.6″) 12 pp. magazine, appearing monthly and **using poems in any style or form no longer than 10 lines.** They also publish broadsides featuring the work of single poets. They have recently published poetry by Lyn Lifshin, Louis McKee, David Chorlton, Sheila Murphy, and Tony Moffeit. As a sample the editor selected "Fourth of July Poem" by Steven Doering:

> *countless*
> *inconspicuous*
> *hordes of illegal*
> *aliens can't be*
> *wrong*

Press run 100-150. *LR* is photocopied from typescript on colored paper, side-stapled. **Sample, postpaid: $1. Send SASE for guidelines. Pays 2 copies per poem. Submit no more than 3. Reports usually within 30 days. Editor comments on submissions** "occasionally—always at least try to establish human contact."

LIMBERLOST PRESS; THE LIMBERLOST REVIEW (II), HC 33, Box 1113, Boise, ID 83706, phone 208-344-2120, founded 1976, editor Richard Ardinger. Limberlost Press publishes poetry, fiction, and memoirs in chapbooks, flat-spined paperbacks and other formats. *Limberlost Review* appears "fairly regularly." **"We want the best work by serious writers. No restrictions on style or form."** They have recently published poetry by William Stafford, Lawrence Ferlinghetti, Charles Bukowski, Allen Ginsberg and John Clellon Holmes. I have not seen their publications, but the editor describes *LR* as digest-sized ("varies. One issue has been devoted to a series of letterpressed poem postcards.") It has a press run of 500-1,000. **Sample: $6 postpaid. Pays 2 copies** ("varies"). **No simultaneous submissions. For chapbook submission** (2-3 a year), **submit samples, bio and prior publications. Reports on queries in 1 week, on submissions in 1-2 months. Pays a varied number of author's copies. Editor sometimes comments on rejections.** "Issues often are devoted to chapbooks by poets in lieu of anthologies."

LIMESTONE: A LITERARY JOURNAL (II), Dept. of English, 1215 Patterson Office Tower, Lexington, KY 40506-0027, founded as *Fabbro* in 1979, as *Limestone* in 1986, editor Matthew J. Bond, is an annual seeking "poetry that matters, poetry that shows attention to content and form. We're interested in all poetics, but we do watch for quality of thought and a use of language that will wake up the reader and resonate in his/her mind." They have recently published poetry by Wendell Berry, Guy Davenport, Michael Cadnum, Noel M. Valis, and James Baker Hall. It is 6×9″, perfect bound, off-set. They accept 5-10 of 100-150 poems submitted annually. Press run is 500 for 30 subscriptions (20 of them libraries). **Sample: $3 postpaid. Pays 3 copies. Submit 1-10 pages. Simultaneous submissions and previously published poems OK. Reports in 3-6 months.** "If you're considering publication," the editor advises, "read as much poetry as possible. Listen carefully. Work over your poems till you're sick of them. The lack of such care shows up in many of the MSS we receive."

LIMITED EDITIONS PRESS; ART: MAG (II), #11, 2324 S. Highland Ave., Las Vegas, NV 89102, phone 702-383-8624, founded 1982, editor Peter Magliocco, an "ultra-small purveyor of 'art/mort fantasies' and sometimes gross fictions." He describes *Art: Mag* as "unusual, off-beat, even 'avant-garde' mag." He also publishes chapbooks ("art: maggies") and original limited editions of poetry. He wants to see poetry that is **"well-crafted, hopefully meaningful work of no definite formal restrictions."** He does **not want to see** "erotic fixations bordering on the pornographic, or bland academic stuff going nowhere." He has recently published poetry by John Grey, Paul Dilsaver, James Purdy, charlie mehrhoff, Mark Weber, and Steven Jacobsen. As a sample the editor selected " Straddling The Brink" by Belinda Subraman:

> *The mirror is a foreign object*
> *these days. We don't know*
> *what we're seeing.*
> *We are victims of our own making,*
> *paralyzed children,*
> *mental quadriplegics*
> *with no pity for them*
> *or else too much.*

The unusual magazine is sometimes oversized, hand crafted, many poems in handwriting, photocopied on many different kinds of paper, including a great variety of graphics (including an original oil painting in one issue I have seen), side-stapled (or bound with a plastic clasp). It appears 1-2 times a year, about 100 copies given to "friends and patron believers." **Sample: $2.50 postpaid. Send SASE for guidelines (if you're not squeamish). Pays 1 copy. Reports within 3 months.** He publishes 1-3 chapbooks per year (photocopied, stapled, 15 pp.) **For chapbooks consideration send samples with query. Pays 10 copies. Simultaneous submissions "discouraged." Photocopy OK, not dot-matrix.** Peter Magliocco, who calls himself "mag man," advises, "Poets can't editorially dictate or expect to run the show. Brilliant small press poetry is struggling against becoming an endangered species, with little exploration of the meaningful 'Word,' the guiding everyday ethic of an artist's Life. Pursue your own vision as an artist, even if it puts you at odds with others."

LINTEL (II), P.O. Box 8609, Roanoke, VA 24014, phone 703-982-2265 or 345-2886, founded 1977, poetry editor Walter James Miller, who says, "**We publish poetry and innovative fiction of types ignored by commercial presses. We consider any poetry except conventional, traditional, cliché, greeting card types, i.e., any artistic poetry.**" They have recently published poetry by Sue Saniel Elkind, Samuel Exler, and Adrienne Wolfert, and the editor selected these lines from Edmund Pennant as a sample:

> the honey in frozen hexagons,
> bees clustered darkly dormant,
> and the blizzard yet to come,
> laying down domes of stillness.

The book from which this was taken, **Mis/apprehensions and other poems**, is 80 pp. flat-spined, digest-sized, professionally printed in small bold type, glossy, color cover with art, the author's photo on the back. I notice that the author's first collection was published by Scribner's, and it is typical that poets "discovered" and then neglected by major publishers often turn to noncommercial presses for subsequent publication. Walter James Miller asks that you **query with five sample poems.** He replies to the query within a month, to the MS (if invited) in 2 months. "**We consider simultaneous submissions if so marked and if the writer agrees to notify us of acceptance elsewhere.**" MS should be typed, photocopy OK. **Pays royalties after all costs are met and 100 copies.** To see samples, send SASE for catalog and ask for "trial rate" (50%). "**We like our poets to have a good publishing record, in the literary magazines, before they begin to think of a book.**"

‡LIP SERVICE; LIP SERVICE POETRY AND PROSE SERIES CONTEST (II), P.O. Box 23231, Washington, DC 20026-3231, founded 1986, editor Robert Haynes, is a non-profit organization and publishes an annual journal of poetry. "*Lip Service* is open to new talent as well as established writers. Our criterion is excellence. **Poems should be typed and unpublished. Give us at least a month to respond; if we like a poem we tend to keep it until we can reach a final decision. At present we pay with a contributor copy, but will pay cash if we get a grant.**" Send SASE for guidelines, which offer some excellent advice for poets in general about things to avoid in poetry, such as archaic language, ellipses, hackneyed phrases and clichés, plagiarism, abstractions. **Submissions are accepted between May 15 and October 31.** *Lip Service* is digest-sized, 40-52 pp., saddle-stapled, professionally printed on bond with card cover with b/w art, **sample: $4.** The organization sponsors poetry readings and other special efforts in the Washington, D.C. area, including the Lip Service Poetry and Prose Series. Anyone living in the D.C. area and interested in reading in the contest should write with samples and must be able to appear in person. The contest awards cash prizes to the best readers in the series. Lip Service has recently published Hilary Tham, Bradford Evans, Sunil Freeman, Reuben Jackson, Mark Baechtel. As a sample of the poetry they use, the editor selected these lines from "The Fullback and the Dancer" by Edwin Ramond:

> His joy had been a headlock or towel sting
> in the damp blur of the showers
> where he could hide in the vulgar
>
> alphabet of boys hardening into men,
> who'd mastered already the harshness
> of males who can only bare their bodies.

LITERARY MARKETS (IV-Themes), 4340 Coldfall Rd., Richmond, BC V7C 1P8 Canada, or PO Drawer 1310, Point Roberts, WA 48281-1310, founded 1982, edited by Bill Marles. This very helpful bimonthly listing of new markets uses **poems up to 30 lines relating to the writing/artistic life and the writer's relation to society.** "I prefer something on the inherent conflict between the demands of a materialistic world and creative endeavor. A recently published poem about a banker and a poet, who was applying for a mortgage, tickled my fancy," says Bill Marles. As a sample I selected these lines from "A Note On Academic Verse" by David Palmer:

> *Padded lines*
> *like padded brassieres*
> *pretend to have something*
> *they don't.*

The 6 pp. newsletter is offset from typescript on 8½ × 11″ paper, stapled at the corner, circulation to 1,300 subscribers of which 25 are libraries. He uses one poem per issue. Subscription: $10 a year (six issues). **Sample: $1 postpaid. Pays a 1 year subscription. He wants "poetry that communicates well. Other writers should be able to identify with the experience being described." He prefers that poetry be "typewritten. Ideally camera-ready." He reports in 1 month, 1 month delay between acceptance and publication. Simultaneous submissions OK, and previously published poems OK if you tell him when and where it was published.**

THE LITERARY REVIEW: An International Journal of Contemporary Writing (II), Fairleigh Dickinson University, Madison, NJ 07940, phone 201-593-8564, founded 1957, editor-in-chief Walter Cummins, a quarterly, seeks **"work by new and established poets which reflects a sensitivity to literary standards and the poetic form." No specifications as to form, length, style, subject matter, or purpose.** They have published poetry by Robert Cooperman, Gary Fincke, José Bergamin, Tcmasz Jastrun, and R.S. Thomas. The editors selected these sample lines by Robert M. Chute:

> *Their savage, ragged screams*
> *are music here between*
> *jagged lines of hemlock, water maple,*
> *pine. The sun's nimbus*
> *is around them. Set wings,*
> *fantails, dried-blood brown*
> *translucent feathers shine*

The magazine is 6 × 9″, flat-spined, 128 + pp, professionally printed with glossy color cover, using 20-50 pp. of poetry in each issue, circulation 1,800, 900 subscriptions of which one-third are overseas. They receive about 1,200 submissions per year, use 100-150, have 6-12 months backlog. **Sample: $5 postpaid, request a "general issue." Submit no more than 5 poems at a time, clear typing or dot-matrix, simultaneous submissions OK, no queries. Reports in 2-3 months. Pays copies. At times the editor comments on rejections.** The editors advise, "Read a general issue of the magazine carefully before submitting."

LITERATURE AND BELIEF (II, IV-Religious), 3134 Jesse Knight Humanities Building, Brigham Young University, Provo, UT 84602, phone 801-378-2304, founded 1981, editor Jay Fox, is the "annual journal of the Center for the Study of Christian Values in Literature." **It uses poetry "with Christian-based themes"** in a handsomely published flat-spined format. They conduct an annual contest with $100 first prize for poetry. They have recently published poetry by Ted Hughes, Donnel Hunter, Leslie Norris, and William Stafford. As a sample the editor selected these lines from "Obsidian" by Dixie L. Partridge:

> *Cold, this blind glass*
> *carries more heat than topaz*
> *and ruby, more strokes*
> *from the mother-earth,*
> *and more sorrow.*

‡LITTLE RIVER PRESS (V, IV-Regional), 10 Lowell Ave., Westfield, MA 01085, phone 413-568-5598, founded 1976, editor Ronald Edwards, publishes **"limited editions of poetry collections, chapbooks and postcards of New England Poets."** They have recently published poetry by Steven Sossaman, Wanda Cook, and Frank Mello. As a sample the editor selected these lines from "The First of May" by Anne Porter:

> *All over the marshes,*
> *and in the wet meadows,*
> *wherever there is water,*
> *the companies of peepers*
> *who cannot count their members,*
> *gather with sweet shouting.*

I have not seen any of their publications. **No unsolicited poetry. Pays 60% of run.**

LIVING STREAMS (IV-Christian, membership), P.O. Box 1321, Vincennes, IN 47591, phone 812-882-4289, founded 1988, editor/founder Kevin Hrebik, a national, quarterly, "subscriber written," 76-page journal. Subscription: $15/year. They **"prefer non-controversial Christian material, especially**

good poetry, prose and fiction, also all special forms." They use 150-200 poems per year, 3-25 lines and 25-30 prose pieces, average length 1,000 words. Pays in contributor's copies. Photocopied, simultaneous, previously published and dot-matrix submissions are acceptable. Reporting time is 2-4 weeks. Sample available for $3.75 postpaid, guidelines free. Uses original art and photography; will consider submissions (nature scenes with water) for cover. The editor says, "Send 4-6 good poems, and 1 prose piece at a time. Don't write Christian 'baby' material. Assume reader is intelligent, literate and mature. Write clearly, make specific points, yet try to be original and artistic. Show off your skill."

LODESTAR BOOKS; E.P. DUTTON (IV-Children/teen, anthology), 2 Park Ave., New York, NY 07605, phone 212-725-1818, founded 1979, editorial director Virginia Buckley, is a trade publisher of juvenile and young-adult nonfiction and fiction. "A good anthology would be OK, or poetry for the very young child. No adult poetry. Although we have not published any poetry or anthologies, we are open to submissions; writers should be familiar with the juvenile market. Best place to start is in the library rather than bookstore."

‡LOLLIPOPS, THE MAGAZINE FOR EARLY CHILDHOOD EDUCATORS (IV-Themes), Good Apple, Inc., 1204 Buchanan, Box 299, Carthage, IL 62321, phone 212-357-3981, editor Jerry Aten, is a magazine published 5 times a year providing easy-to-use, hands-on practical **teaching ideas and suggestions for early childhood education. Uses light verse on themes appropriate to the focus of the magazine.** Circulation 18,000. Subscription $16.95. **Sample, postpaid: $4.50. Writer's guidelines for #10 SAE with 2 oz. postage. Submit seasonal/holiday material 6 months in advance. Computer printout submissions acceptable; prefers letter-quality. Pays "variable" rates on publication.**

‡LONDON MAGAZINE (II), 30 Thurloe Place, London SW7 England, founded 1954, poetry editor Alan Ross, is a literary and art monthly using **poetry "the best of its kind."** They accept about 150 of 2,000 poems received a year. Press run is 5,000 for 2,000 subscriptions. Subscription: £18 or $35. **Sample: £3 postpaid. Pays £20 per page. Reports "very soon."** Alan Ross says, "Quality is our only criterion."

LONDON REVIEW OF BOOKS (III), Tavistock House South, Tavistock Square, London, WC1 England, founded 1979, editor Karl Miller, is published 24 times a year, mostly reviews and essays but some stories and poems. They have published some of the most distinguished contemporary poets, such as Ted Hughes, Tony Harrison, James Fenton, Frederick Seidel, and Thom Gunn. As a sample I selected the opening stanza of "My Fuchsia" by Ruth Fainlight:

> *My fuchsia is a middle-aged woman*
> *who's had fourteen children, and though*
> *she could do it again, she's rather tired.*

The paper has a circulation of 17,000 with 14,000 subscriptions. **Considers simultaneous submissions. Sample: £2 including postage (available at some bookstores). They pay £50/poem.**

LONE STAR PUBLICATIONS OF HUMOR; LONE STAR HUMOR; THE LONE STAR COMEDY MONTHLY; LONE STAR: A COMEDY SERVICE AND NEWSLETTER (IV-Humor), Suite 103, Box 29000, San Antonio, TX 78229, founded 1981, poetry editors Lauren Barnett and Ashleigh Lynby. **"Our only interest is humor, but we're interested in every aspect of it. We use poetry in *Lone Star Humor*. Any kind of poetry as long as it's funny (and not too long). Limericks, clerihews, free verse, cheap verse, designer verse—all of this is OK. Don't want to see anything that runs more than two typed pages."** They have recently published poems by Robert N. Feinstein, Julie Eilber, Virginia Long, Lauren Barnett and Christine Sutowsky. As a sample the editors selected these lines from "Old Blue" by Neal Wilgus:

> *I've sure got to hand it to Blue:*
> *Quest's disguise Blue had quickly seen through.*
> *For Quest was six guys—all Neptunian spies,*
> *held together with some kind of glue.*

The magazine appears 2 to 3 times a year, digest-sized, 60 pp. with glossy card cover with cartoons, offset from various styles of typescript on colored paper, circulation "over 1,200." It uses 1-2 poems per issue. They receive about 800 submissions of poetry per year, use about 5% of them. **Poets should inquire before submitting material. Sample: inquire. Submit to poetry editor any time, no more than 5 poems per submission. Photocopy OK, dot-matrix no. Reports within 16 weeks. Pay: inquire. Send SASE for guidelines.** The editors comment, "Good 'serious' writers are abundant; good writers of humor are rare. Poets who feel that humorous poetry is less important or easier than 'serious' poetry should not send their material to *Lone Star*. It's not likely that their endeavors will be good enough to interest us."

LONG ISLANDER; WALT'S CORNER (II), 313 Main St., Huntington, New York 11743, phone 516-427-7000, FAX 516-427-5820, founded 1838 by Walt Whitman, poetry editor George Wallace, is a weekly newspaper, 25,000 circulation, using **unrhymed poetry up to 40 lines "grounded in personal/social matrix, no haiku, inspirational."** They have used poetry by David Ignatow, David Axelrod, and R.B. Weber. As a sample I selected the first 3 stanzas of "Love Poem-12" by Sandra Kohler:

> *A woman wakes to a midnight perfume.*
> *It is her own, transformed by sleep*
> *into something rich and strange*
> *as the words we speak dreaming,*
> *a geography of need.*

It is "48 pp. newsprint." They use 52 of about a thousand poems submitted each year. Subscription: $12 on Long Island, $17 off Long Island. **Sample: $2.50 postpaid. Simultaneous submissions OK. Pays 1 copy. Editor "normally" comments on rejections.**

LONG SHOT (II), P.O. Box 6231, Hoboken, NJ 07030, founded 1982, edited by Danny Shot, Caren Lee Michaelson, and Jack Wiler, is, they say, a "good magazine." They have published poetry by Charles Bukowski, Sean Penn, Allen Ginsberg, Marianne Faithfull, Amiri Baraka, and June Jordan. It is 120+ pp., flat-spined, professionally printed with glossy card cover using b/w photos, drawings and cartoons. It comes out twice a year, press run 1,500. They say they accept about 35 of 1,000 submissions received. **Sample: $5. Subscription $18—2 years (4 issues). Pays 2 copies. Simultaneous submissions OK. Reports in 8 weeks.**

THE LOOKOUT (IV-Themes), Seamen's Church Institute of New York and New Jersey, 50 Broadway, New York, NY 10004, phone 212-269-2710, founded 1834, poetry editor Carlyle Windley, is the "external house publication of the Institute and has been published continuously since 1909, 3 times a year, circulation 5,700. Basic purpose of the publication is to engender and sustain interest in the work of the Institute and to encourage monetary gifts in support of its philanthropic work among merchant seamen. Emphasis is on the *merchant marine*; NOT Navy, power boats, commercial or pleasure fishing, passenger vessels." It is magazine-sized, normally 20-24 pp., printed offset in two color inks. Subscription is via a minimum contribution of $5 a year to the Institute. It **"buys small amount of short verse (sea-faring related but *not* about the sea per se and the clichés about spume, spray, sparkle, etc.), paying $10."** They have published poetry by Wendy Thorne, June Owens, Irene Abel, and Kay Wissinger. The editors selected this sample poem by John E. Hall:

> *In the winter*
> *When I can . . .*
> *And the norther's high . . .*
> *I trudge to the headland*
> *and stand . . .*
> *Just to feel her shiver. . . .*

Sample free for 9 × 12″ SASE. Submit any number of poems. No photocopies. Typed originals. Reports within 2 weeks. Send SASE for guidelines.

LOOM PRESS; LOOM; BEATSCENE (II), P.O. Box 1394, Lowell, MA 01853, founded 1978, editor Paul Marion, a small-press publisher of poetry chapbooks and broadsides. The broadside series, which appears irregularly, is called *Loom* and publishes **"good contemporary poems in any form, style."** Poets recently published include Maurya Simon, George Chigas, Juan Delgado, and Eric Linder. As a sample, the editor selected the following lines from "Fifteen Years post facto" by Dana White:

> *This is not the stone quintet of Iwo Jima*
> *lunging the flag toward America's glory.*
> *This is not in the shape of a man*
> *this is not what one man rendered.*

The broadsides range from magazine-sized to 11 × 17″. They have a circulation of 100-500. Price per issue varies, but a **sample is available for $2. Pay is 10 copies. "Clear copies" are OK for submissions which will be reported on in 1 month; time to publication is 3-6 months. Writers should query first for chapbook publication, sending credits, 5 sample poems, and bio. Queries will be answered in 1 month, MSS reported on in 6 weeks. Simultaneous submissions will be considered, and photocopied or dot-matrix MSS are OK. Royalties of 10% are paid on chapbooks, plus 5% of print run. Sample chapbooks are available at $5 each. The editor comments on MSS "when time allows."** The chapbooks are saddle-stitched, 6x9″, with an average page count of 20. The editor advises, "Please support the small press publishers who are in business to support you." The editor of Loom Press is also a contributing editor for *Beat Scene*, an English magazine specializing in American literature and culture. Loom Press accepts U.S. poetry submissions for *Beat Scene*.

LOONFEATHER (I, IV-Regional, themes), Bemidji Community Arts Center, 426 Bemidji Ave., Bemidji, MN 56601, phone 218-751-4869, founded 1979, poetry editors Betty Rossi and Jeane Sliney, is a small press publisher of the literary magazine *Loonfeather* appearing 2 times a year, "primarily but not exclusively for Minnesota writers, with one theme issue per year. Prefer short poems of not over 42 lines, rhymed verse only if well done, no generalizations on worn-out topics." They have recently published poetry by Philip Dacey, Emelio De Grazia, and John Steininger. The editors selected these lines from the poem "The Cottage" by Susan Hauser:

> We want to draw water
> from the love that has gone
> before us here
>
> and to nail to new walls
> The skins of our own dreams

Loonfeather is 6×9", 48 pp., saddle-stapled, professionally printed in small type with matte card cover, using b/w art and ads. **Payment in copies (2). Submission deadlines Feb. 28 and Aug. 31 for April and October publications.** Subscriptions: $7.50 per year, single copy current issue $5 (Fall '88 through current year); back issues $2.50.

‡LOTHROP, LEE & SHEPARD BOOKS; GREENWILLOW BOOKS; MORROW JUNIOR BOOKS; MULBERRY BOOKS (IV-Children), 105 Madison Ave, New York, NY 10016, founded 1859, editor-in-chief (Lothrop, Lee & Shepard) Susan Pearson. "We accept unsolicited MSS in the following: fiction, nonfiction, poetry, picture books" **for children. Pays 5% minimum royalties.**

LOTUS PRESS INC. (V, II, IV-Ethnic), P.O. Box 21607, Detroit, MI 48221, phone 313-861-1280, FAX 313-342-9174, founded 1972, poetry editor Naomi Long Madgett. "With one exception of a textbook, we publish books of **poetry by individual authors,** although we have two anthologies and two sets of broadsides, one with a teachers' guide for use in secondary schools. We occasionally sponsor readings. **Most, but not all, of our authors are black.**" Currently, they are not accepting unsolicited MSS. Poets recently published include May Miller, Oliver LaGrone, Monifa Atungaye, Selene de Medeiros, and Naomi F. Faust. The following lines are by Beth Brown:

> Homeward, always, the end of a month
> On rails accompanied by descending fences
> Woven with the spinster hair of vines, and the stream,
> Waiting for October, under winking dogwood eyes,
> Faith of vines, opinion of vines. Where on my maps
> Does it say roads lead out of this country?

Payment is made in copies. Poets are not expected to contribute to the cost of publication. Response is usually within 6 weeks. Free catalog available upon request. "Most of the books we publish are by individual authors, usually African American, but we have also published two anthologies and are anticipating a third. **We will consider love poems by black women about black men (husbands, friends, lovers, fathers, brothers, sons) between January and June, 1991. SASE required. Not accepting unsolicited MSS except poems for this anthology.**"

LOUISIANA LITERATURE; LOUISIANA LITERATURE PRIZE FOR POETRY (II, IV-Regional), P.O. Box 792, Southeastern Louisiana University, Hammond, LA 70402, editor Tim Gautreaux, appears twice a year. They say they **"receive MSS year round. We consider creative work from anyone though we strive to showcase our state's talent. We like poetry with original language use and strong images which go beyond themselves."** They have published poems by Sue Owen, Catharine Savage Brosman, Katharyn Machan Aal, David Tillinghast, Elton Glaser, Jo McDougall and Glenn Swetmann. The editor chose these sample lines by Kathy Andre-Eames:

> You mumbled to the shed,
> shaved a desk, wrote impatiently
> slow music for a violin and bow,
> wasps droning low in the gutterpipes.

The magazine is a large (7¾×9¾") format, 92 pp., flat-spined, handsomely printed on heavy matte stock with matte card cover (using pen drawing). Subscription: $7.50 for individuals; $10 for institution. The Louisiana Literature Prize for Poetry offers a $300 award. **Guidelines for SASE.**

LOUISIANA STATE UNIVERSITY PRESS (II), Baton Rouge, LA 70893, phone 504-388-6294, founded 1935, poetry editor L.E. Phillabaum, is a highly respected publisher of collections by poets such as Lisel Mueller, Julia Randall, Fred Chappell, and Henry Taylor. The editor selected a sample from "In The Market" by Margaret Gibson:

> I thought of lillies—how they pull water

> *clear through*
> *their green channels.*
> *In them was presence,*
> *and ease of future.*

Query with 6-8 sample poems, publication credits. Replies to query in 1 month, to submission (if invited) in 3-4 months. Simultaneous submissions, photocopies OK. Royalty contract plus 10 author's copies.

THE LOUISVILLE REVIEW (II,IV-Children/Teen), 315 Bingham Humanities, University of Louisville, Louisville, KY 40232, phone 502-588-6801, founded 1976, faculty editor Sena Nasland, appears twice a year. They use any kind of poetry except translations, and they have a section of children's poetry (grades K-12). "Poetry must include permission of parent to publish if accepted. We do not publish clichéd, doggerel rhymed nor moralizing poetry. In all of our poetry we look for the striking metaphor, unusual imagery, and fresh language. We do not read in summer. "Poems are read by 3 readers; report time is 1-2 months and time to publication is 2-3 months." They have recently published poetry by Richard Jackson, Jeffry Skinner, Maura Stanton, Richard Cecil, Roger Weingarten, and Greg Pape. *TLR* is 200 pp., flat-spined, 8¾×6″. They accept about 10% of some 700 pieces received a year. Sample: $2.50 postpaid. Pays 1 copy.

LUCIDITY; BEAR HOUSE PRESS, (I), 2711 Watson, Houston, TX 77009, phone 713-869-6028, founded 1986, editor Ted O. Badger. *Lucidity* is a quarterly of poetry. You have to pay to submit—$1 per poem for "juried" selection by a panel of judges, or $2 per poem to compete for cash awards of $20, $10 and $5. Other winners paid $1 cash and in copies. In addition, the editor invites a few contributors to submit to each issue. Contributors are encouraged to subscribe or buy a copy of the magazine. The magazine is photocopied from typescript, digest-sized, saddle-stapled 56 pp. with matte card cover, press run 250, 140 subscribers. Subscription: $8. Sample: $2 postpaid. Send SASE for guidelines. The magazine is called *Lucidity* because, the editor says, "I have felt that too many publications of verse lean to the abstract in content and to the obscure in style." Ted Badger says the magazine is "open as to form. 40 line limit due to format. No restriction on subject matter except that something definitive be given to the reader. Purpose: "to give a platform to poets who can impart their ideas with clarity." He does not want "religious, nature, or vulgar poems." Recently published poets include Helen Rilling, Ana Pine, Ted Yund, and Janet Brice. As a sample of the type of verse sought, the editor offers these lines:

> *Life is the toll paid*
> *for crossing the bridge from Now*
> *to Eternity.*

Reports in 2-3 months, a 3-month delay before publication. Simultaneous submissions, previously published poems OK. Bear House Press is a subsidy arrangement by which poets can pay to have pamphlets published in the same format as *Lucidity,* prices begining at 50 copies of 32 pp. for $140. Publishes 8 chapbooks per year. A yearly chapbook competition will give the winner 50 free copies of his/her book; entry fee $10. SASE for details. The editor comments, "The only way to be published is to submit."

LUNA BISONTE PRODS; LOST AND FOUND TIMES (IV-Style), 137 Leland Ave., Columbus, OH 43214, founded 1967, poetry editor John M. Bennett, may be the zaniest phenomenon in central Ohio. John Bennett is a publisher (and practicioner) of **experimental and avant-garde writing**, sometimes sexually explicit, and art in a bewildering array of formats including the magazine, *Lost and Found Times*, post card series, posters, chapbooks, pamphlets, labels and audio cassette tapes. You can get a **sampling of Luna Bisonte Prods for $3 plus $1 postage and handling. Numerous reviewers have commented on the bizarre** *Lost and Found Times,* "reminiscent of several West Coast dada magazines"; "This exciting magazine is recommended only for the most daring souls"; "truly demented"; "Insults . . . the past 3,000 years of literature," etc. Bennett wants to see "**unusual poetry, naive poetry, surrealism, experimental, visual poetry, collaborations**—*no* poetry workshop or academic pablum." He has published poetry by I. Argüelles, G. Beining, B. Heman, R. Olson, J. Lipman, B. Porter, C. H. Ford, P. Weinman, E. N. Brookings, F. A. Nettelbeck, D. Raphael, R. Crozier, S. Sollfrey, S. Murphy, B. Heman, M. Andre, N.Vassilakis, and himself. The editor selected these lines from the poem "Maudie Mae" by Clarke A. Sany as a sample:

> *Drag your underwear on me like a tree*
> *full of the same apes*

Market categories: (I) Beginning; (II) General; (III) Prestige; (IV) Specialized; (V) Closed.

> *she looked nervously around*

The digest-sized 40 pp. magazine, photoreduced typescript and wild graphics, matte card cover with graphics, has a circulation of 350 with 60 subscriptions of which 25 are libraries. **Sample: $4 postpaid. Submit any time — preferably camera-ready (but this is not required). Reports in 1-2 days, pays copies.** Luna Bisonte also will consider book submissions: query with samples and cover letter (but "keep it brief"). Chapbook publishing usually depends on grants or other subsidies and is usually by solicitation. **Photocopy, dot-matrix OK.** He will also consider subsidy arrangements on negotiable terms.

THE LUTHERAN JOURNAL (IV-Religious), 7317 Cahill Rd., Edina, MN 55435, editor The Rev. Armin U. Deye, is a family quarterly, 32 pp., circulation 136,000, for Lutheran Church members, middle age and older. They use **poetry "related to subject matter," traditional, free verse, blank verse. Pays. Sample free for SASE. Simultaneous and photocopied submissions OK.**

‡**LYNX, A QUARTERLY JOURNAL OF RENGA (IV-Form, subscribers)**, (formerly APA-Renga), P.O. Box 169, Toutle, WA 98649, phone 206-274-6661, APA-Renga founded 1986, editor, Terri Lee Grell, one of the first APA-Renga contributors, "changed the name to *Lynx* to link an endangered species of poetry with an endangered animal, and to inspire the traditional wit of renga. The magazine, published quarterly, is **based on the ancient craft of renga, linked verse with origins in Zen and Japanese culture, publishes rengas, mostly by subscribers.** A renga is a non-narrative series of linked images as a group effort." The editor selected this sample renga (excerpt) by Tundra Wind, Eric Folsom, Jane Reichhold, and Terri Lee Grell:

> *Redwood shadows at river's edge*
> *Approaching auto's distant headlights*
> *Two white fangs of a bobcat*
> *The whimper of illuminated lovers*

Lynx also publishes essays, book reviews, articles, interviews, experimental linked forms, linked prose, art, commentaries, and "whatever encourages poets to link ideas." Published poets include Hiroaki Sato, Marlene Mountain, and Judith Skillman. *Lynx* **encourages submissions by those experienced and experimenting with collaborative forms. Subscribers participate in ongoing rengas, start trends, and otherwise determine the content. Reports in 4 weeks. Editor responds to all who submit.** Currently 100 subscribers. *Lynx* is a newsprint publication, 5½x4", 24 pp., unstapled. **Sample copy: $2 postpaid, includes guidelines. Pays copies.**

√ **THE LYRIC; LYRIC ANNUAL COLLEGE POETRY CONTEST (II, IV-Form, students)**, 307 Dunton Dr., SW, Blacksburg, VA 24060, founded 1921 ("the oldest magazine in North America in continuous publication devoted to the publication of **traditional poetry**"), poetry editor Leslie Mellichamp, uses about 50 poems each quarterly issue. "We use rhymed verse in traditional forms, for the most part, with an occasional piece of blank or free verse. 35 lines or so is usually our limit. Our themes are varied, ranging from religious ecstasy to humor to raw grief, but we feel no compulsion to shock, embitter, or confound our readers. We also avoid poems about contemporary political or social problems — grief but not grievances, as Frost put it. Frost is helpful in other ways: if yours is more than a lover's quarrel with life, we're not your best market. And most of our poems are accessible on first or second reading. Frost again: don't hide too far away. Poems must be original, unpublished, and not under consideration elsewhere." Pays 1 copy, and all contributors are eligible for quarterly and annual prizes totaling over $800. They have recently published poetry by Anne Barlow, John J. Brugaletta, R.H. Morrison, Rhina P. Espaillat, Barbara Loots, W. Gregory Stewart, Alfred Dorn, Charles Dickson, Gail White, and Tom Riley. The editor selected these sample lines by William A. Baurle:

> *Lovely, the morning in this hour shall break,*
> > *Though it be dark, the heart has hope for sight:*
> *Unburdened of its vanity, redressed,*
> > *Far out of sorrow, and far into light.*

It is digest-sized, 32 pp. format, professionally printed with varied typography, matte card cover, has a circulation of 850 with 800 subscriptions of which 290 are libraries. They receive about 5,000 submissions per year, use 200, have an average 3 month backlog. **Sample: $2 postpaid, subscription $8. Submit up to 5 poems. Photocopy, dot-matrix OK. Reports in 1 month (average). Send SASE for guidelines.** The *Lyric* also offers a poetry contest in traditional forms for fulltime undergraduate students enrolled in any American or Canadian college or university, prizes totaling $500. Send SASE for rules. Leslie Mellichamp comments, "Our *raison d'être* has been the encouragement of form, music, rhyme and accessibility in poetry. We detect a growing dissatisfaction with the modernist movement that ignores these things and a growing interest in the traditional wellsprings of the craft. Naturally, we are proud to have provided an alternative for over 70 years that helped keep the true roots of poetry alive."

M.A.F. PRESS; THIRTEEN POETRY MAGAZINE (I, IV-Form, anthology), Box 392, Portlandville, NY 13834, phone 607-286-7500, founded 1982, poetry editor Ken Stone. *Thirteen Poetry Magazine* "publishes only 13-line poetry; any theme or subject as long as in 'good' taste. We seek to publish work that touches the beauty of this life." The M.A.F. Press publishes a chapbook series, however, not reading through end of 1990—no reading fee. Chapbooks must be a total of 32 pages. They have published poetry recently by Shirley Murphy, Ida Fasel, Will Inman, Stan Proper, Irving Weiss, and Marion Cohen. As a sample the editor selected "Grossetto" by M. P. A. Sheaffer:

> I would have the memory of pines;
> But I didn't want the memory.
> I wanted to feel the pine needles in my skin,
> The salt salt against our lips

Thirteen appears quarterly in a magazine-sized 40 pp., saddle-stapled format, photocopied from typescript, matte card cover with b/w cartoon, circulation 350 for 130 subscriptions of which 20 are libraries. Ken Stone accepts about 100 of the 300 submissions he receives each year. **Sample: $2.50 postpaid. Submit 4-6 poems. Photocopies are acceptable, no reprint material. "We have even taken hand-written poems. As to queries, only if 13 lines gives the poet problems." Reports "immediately to 2 weeks." Pays 1 copy. Send SASE for guidelines. Comments on rejections "especially if requested."** The editor advises, "Send more poetry, less letters and self-promotion. Read the 'want lists' and description listings of magazines for guidelines. When in doubt request information. Read other poets in the magazines and journals to see what trends are. Also, this is a good way to find out what various publications like in the way of submissions."

MACFADDEN WOMEN'S GROUP; TRUE CONFESSIONS; TRUE ROMANCES; TRUE LOVE; TRUE STORY; SECRETS; MODERN ROMANCES (I), 233 Park Ave. S., New York, NY 10003, 212-979-4800. **Address each magazine individually; do not submit to Macfadden Women's Group.** Each of these romance magazines uses poetry—usually no more than one poem per issue. Their requirements vary, and I suggest that readers study them individually and write for guidelines. These mass-circulation magazines (available on newsstands) are obviously a very limited market, yet a possible one for beginners—especially those who like the prose contents and are tuned in to their editorial tastes.

THE MACGUFFIN (II), Schoolcraft College, 18600 Haggerty Rd., Livonia, MI 48152, phone 313-462-4400, ext. 5292, founded 1983, editor Arthur Lindenberg, who says, "*The MacGuffin* is a literary magazine which appears three times each year, in April, June and November. We publish the best poetry, fiction, non-fiction and artwork we find. We have no thematic or stylistic biases. **We look for well-crafted poetry. Long poems should not exceed 300 lines. Avoid pornography, trite and sloppy poetry."** *The MacGuffin* has recently published poetry by Louis McKee, Peter Brett, and Phillip Sterling. As a sample, the editor selected the following lines from "Year of the Snake" by Carol Morris:

> . . . Usually it coiled in the dresser drawer
> next to the silk handkerchiefs and the little net bag of lavender
> and when she took it out
> Africa held its breath
> with me on the bed
> where chenille tattooed the napes of my knees . . . .

The MacGuffin is digest-sized, professionally printed on heavy buff stock, 128 pp. with matte card cover, flat-spined, with b/w illustrations and photos. Circulation is 500, of which 51 are subscriptions and the rest are local newsstand sales, contributor copies, and distribution to college offices. Price per issue is $3.75, subscription $10. **Sample: $3 postpaid. Pay: two copies. "The editorial staff is grateful to consider unsolicited manuscripts and graphics." MSS are reported on in 8-10 weeks and the publication backlog is 6+ months. Writers should submit no more than 6 poems of no more than 300 lines; they should be typewritten, and photocopied or dot-matrix MS are OK.** "We will always comment on 'near misses.' Writing is a search, and it is a journey. Don't become sidetracked. Don't become discouraged. Keep looking. Keep traveling. Keep writing." The magazine recently sponsored a contest with a $100 first prize for Michigan poets only; they hope to be able to sponsor a national competition soon.

‡MACMILLAN OF CANADA (V), 29 Birch Ave., Toronto, M4V 1E2 Canada, phone 416-963-8830, editorial assistant Joanne Ashdown, is a "leading publisher of Canadian fiction, non-fiction, biography, and children's books. Exclusive agent for William Morrow Company, Hearst Books, Andrews & McNeel and Harraps. **They publish no unsolicited poetry or fiction MSS.**

MCPHERSON & COMPANY PUBLISHERS; TREACLE PRESS (V), Box 1126, Kingston, NY 12401-0126, founded 1974, publisher Bruce McPherson, **publishes little poetry and has "no real plans for poetry."** The only example of poetry I find in his catalog is Novalis, "Hymns to the Night," translated by Dick Higgins. He says **"Even when I'm listed for 'no unsolicited submissions' it seems I receive stuff in the**

mail; it might be appropriate to caution the overzealous not to waste time with wishful thinking." But this young publisher has developed an outstanding reputation for his finely made books of experimental literature, and if you write the "brave and often brazen" kind of material he likes ("I've always been attracted to outrageous comic invention," for instance) you should send a SASE for his catalog and see whether you might fit into his publishing plans.

THE MADISON REVIEW; FELIX POLLAK PRIZE IN POETRY; SILVER BUCKLE PRESS (II), Dept. of English, Helen C. White Hall, 600 N. Park St., Madison, WI 53706, founded 1978, poetry editor Jack Murray, wants **poems that are "serious, tough and tight. I want to arrive somewhere at the end of a poem. Spare me: love poems, God poems, light verse."** They have recently published work by Lise Goett, Lyn Lifshin, and Walter McDonald. As a sample the editor selected these lines from "These Snapshots I Have Lost" by Anya Achtenberg:

> *then the metro glides*
> *through the city and faces*
> *pass us without end on the escalator*
> *that rumbles us off*
> *hard onto our feet*
> *just as each bead on the cashier's*
> *abacus knocks hard against the one*
> *before it, releases a sound that spins off*
> *into the broken pot, hits*
> *the dying well water*
> *and pronounces the cost of our living.*

The Madison Review is published in May and December, with 30-40 pages of poetry selected from a pool of 750, use 25-45. **Sample back issue: $2.50 postpaid. Submit maximum of 5 poems. Photocopy OK. No simultaneous submissions. Usually reports in 8 weeks, may be longer in summer. Pays 1 copy. "We do appreciate a concise cover letter with submissions."** The Felix Pollak Prize in Poetry is for $500 and publication in *TMR*, for "the best group of three unpublished poems submitted by a single author." Send SASE for rules before submitting for prize. Submissions must arrive during September—winner announced December 15. "Contributors: know your market! Read before, during and after writing. Treat your poems *better* than job applications!"

THE MAGAZINE OF SPECULATIVE POETRY (IV-Science fiction), Box 564, Beloit, WI 53511, founded 1984, editors Roger Dutcher and Mark Rich, a quarterly magazine that publishes **"the best new speculative poetry. We are especially interested in narrative form, but interested in variety of styles, open to any form, length (within reason), purpose. We're looking for the best of the new poetry utilizing the ideas, imagery and approaches developed by speculative fiction and will welcome experimental techniques as well as the fresh employment of traditional forms."** They have recently published poetry by Brian Aldiss, Robert Frazier, Bruce Boston, Ron Ellis, and S.R. Compton. As a sample Roger Dutcher chose the opening lines of "In Turning's Garden" by Eileen Kernaghan:

> *these branches*
> *sprouting symmetries*
> *like petals*
> *round the hearts of flowers*

The digest-sized magazine, 20-24 pp., is offset from professional typesetting, saddle-stapled with matte card cover. They accept less than 10% of some 500 poems received per year. Press run is 200-300, going to 100 subscriptions of which 4 are libraries. Per issue: $2. Subscription: $7.50. **Sample: $1.50 postpaid. Send SASE for guidelines. Pays $1-15/poem plus 2 copies. No simultaneous submissions. Prefer double-spaced. Photocopies, dot-matrix OK ("if not old ribbon"). No previously published poems. Reports in 4-8 weeks. Editor comments on rejections "on occasion."**

THE MAGE (IV-Science fiction/Fantasy), Colgate University Student Association, Hamilton, NY 13346, founded 1984, poetry editor Sonja Gulati, a student-run journal of science and fantasy fiction, essays, poetry, and art. It publishes 4-7 poems in each issue. The editor says, **"We will consider poems of science fiction and/or fantasy themes or subjects. We do not have any categorical specifications as to form or length. We do not print erotic poetry or limericks."** They have recently published poems by Tom Rentz, Deborah A. Dessaso, Dawn Zapletal, Kathleen Jurgens, and Terry McGarry. In order to suggest quality, the editor selected these lines from "Skyship I, On the Seas" by J. L. Chambers:

> *In the Skyship we ride the cloud-swell,*
> *dark, bulging hull swinging low*
> *and snow white sails stacked up high*
> *camouflaged on the round cumulus waves.*

The Mage is 8½ × 11", professionally printed with occasional pen-and-ink illustrations, 64 pp.

saddle-stapled with white textured card cover illustrated by a b/w drawing. The magazine appears each semester (twice a year) and has a press run of 800, with subscriptions and book catalog sales plus individual sales by the staff. Price per issue is $3.50, $6/year postpaid. **Sample available for $3 postpaid. Pay is 2 copies. Submissions "only have to be readable. Desired punctuation and spacing should be clear so that we don't have to write for clarification during typesetting." Reporting time is 4-8 weeks, and accepted work is generally published in the next issue. "We** usually endeavor to make some constructive criticism on all MSS." The editor offers three pieces of advice: "1) Our needs are very specific: if your poetry does not have an element of fantasy, science fiction, or horror, it will not fit the tone of our publication. 2) Avoid the cliches which are all too common in these genres. 3) An unusual and interesting first line is much better than an unusual format (with apologies to e. e. cummings)."

MAGIC CHANGES (IV-Themes), Suite #F, 2S 424 Emerald Green Dr., Warrenville, IL 60555-9269, phone 312-393-7856, founded 1978, poetry editor John Sennett, is a literary annual in an unusual format. Photocopied from typescript on many different weights and colors of paper, magazine-sized, stapled along the long side (you read it sideways), taped flat spine, full of fantasy drawings, pages packed with poems of all varieties, fiction, photos, drawings, odds and ends—including reviews of little magazines and other small-press publications, it is **intended to make poetry (and literature) fun— and unpredictable. Each issue is on an announced theme.** There are about 100 pp. of poetry per issue, circulation 500, 28 subscriptions of which 10 are libraries. They have published poetry by Roberta Gould, A. D. Winans, Lyn Lifshin, and Dan Campion. As a sample of their poetry I selected the closing stanzas from "Time" by Sri Chinmoy:

> *O lover,*
> *You are the fulfiller of Time.*

> *O God,*
> *You are the Player of Time.*

Sample: $5 postpaid. Reports in 3-5 weeks. Submit 3-5 poems anytime. Photocopy OK. He says "no query," but I would think poets would need to know about upcoming themes. The editor sometimes comments on rejections and offers criticism for $5 per page of poetry. Pays 1 or 2 copies.

MAGNETIC NORTH (IV-Regional), Thorn Books, Timber Lane, Franconia, NH 03580, founded 1983, editor Jim McIntosh, is a **"regional quarterly for visitors to White Mountains. Poems should deal with northern New England, no more than 30 lines, easy to understand. Nature, sensing, feeling inspired by mountains, wilderness, etc. History is OK. Also the vacation experience. Rhyme—if not forced. To deepen one's appreciation of time spent in the mountains. Nothing long, obscure, obscene."** They have published poems by Barbara Crooker, Esther Leiper, Martin Robbins, and Parker Towle. As a sample the editor selected these lines by Parker Towle:

> *The sun always shone on our new home*
> *Before we moved. Clacking wipers*
> *on the U-Haul windshield scarcely cleared*
> *the blustery rain that fell that night*

It is magazine-sized, 48-56 pp., saddle-stapled, professionally printed with full-color paper cover, using many ads, some cartoons. They print 15,000 copies in the spring and winter, 24,000 in the summer and fall, for 1,000 subscriptions of which 12 are libraries, some 500 shelf sales. Subscription: $10. **Sample: $1.50 postpaid. Send SASE for writer's guidelines. Pays $25 per poem and 1 copy. Editor "sometimes" comments on rejections.** They sponsor a poetry contest. Jim McIntosh says, "Poetry should awaken an unexpected emotion. We like poems that enlarge the reader's perspective or focus the reader's vision. Our readers are not poets, they are tourists or people who simply love the mountains. They want you to enhance the experience of the mountains. This is Robert Frost country. I like muscular poems that express deep emotion with Yankee reticence—a tall order."

THE MALAHAT REVIEW; LONG POEM PRIZES (II, IV-Form), Box 1700, University of Victoria, Victoria, BC V8W 2Y2 Canada, phone 604-721-8524, founded 1967, editor Constance Rooke, is "a high quality, visually appealing literary quarterly which has earned the praise of notable literary figures throughout North America. Its purpose is to publish and promote poetry and fiction of a very high standard, both Canadian and international. **We are interested in various styles, lengths and themes. The criterion is excellence."** They have recently published poems by Angela Ball, David McFadden, Phyllis Webb, and Paulette Jiles. The editors selected these sample lines from "Winter and Then Summer" by Sharon Thesen:

> *Even now the chimes make live music*
> *with the wind and the rain—on my tongue*

a faint aftertaste of horseradish,
green salsa, Napoleon brandy, a dream
of a silky dress on a hot piano night

They use 50 pp. of poetry in each issue, have 1,800 subscriptions of which 300 are libraries. Subscription: $15. They use about 100 of 1,500 submissions received per year, have no backlog. **Sample: $7 postpaid. Submit 5-10 poems, addressed to Editor Constance Rooke. Reports within 3 months, pays $20 per poem/page plus 2 copies and reduced rates on others. Send SASE for guidelines.** The editors comment if they "feel the MS warrants some attention even though it is not accepted." The Long Poem Prizes of $300, plus publication and payment at their usual rates, entry fee $15 (which includes a year's subscription), is for a long poem or cycle 5-20 pp., (flexible minimum and maximum), deadline March 1.

‡**MALORY PRESS (IV-Horror, fantasy)**, 4998 Perkins Rd., Baton Rouge, LA 70808-3043, phone 504-766-2906, founded 1989, editor Gary W. Crawford, publishes fiction, scholarship and criticism of horror and "**horror and fantasy poetry in the tradition of Poe, Lovecraft, Clark Ashton Smith, or any modern supernatural poets, open or closed form, no length limit. No science fiction.**" They have recently published poetry by John Jones. As a sample the editor selected these lines by Richard Wolf:

I walk in shadow places
To hide from the light
I feel vampiric
To sleep bloody and stinking
Never waking until I die.

They publish 2 chapbooks per year. **Reports in 2 weeks. Pays 7-10% royalties, advance of $10, plus 3 copies. Write for catalog to buy samples.**

‡**THE MANDEVILLE PRESS (V)**, 2 Taylor's Hill, Hitchin, Hertfordshire, SG4 9AD England, founded 1974, poetry editors Peter Scupham and John Mole, publishes hand-set pamphlets of the work of individual poets, but **will not be considering new submissions through 1990.** Send SASE for catalog to buy samples.

MANHATTAN POETRY REVIEW (II, III), Box 8207, New York, NY 10150, phone 212-355-6634, founded 1981, editor Elaine Reiman-Fenton, "**publishes about half prestige market and half new and/ or little-known poets who deserve an audience, wanting carefully crafted poems in any form or style; interesting subject-matter. There are no restrictions as to length of poems although it has become the custom to avoid very long poems (more than 3 pp.); MSS should be typed, double-spaced, 5-6 pp. of poetry plus cover letter giving previous publication credits, honors, awards, teachers, etc. and SASE. New poets and unsolicited MSS are welcomed. Nothing obscene, ungrammatical, or handwritten. MSS must be ready for the typesetter in case they are accepted.**" They have published poetry by Marge Piercy, David Ignatow, Diane Wakoski, Marilyn Hacker, Judith Farr, and Robert Phillips. *MPR* appears twice a year, 52-60 pp., digest-sized, saddle-stapled, offset print, paper cover, using only poetry — no art, graphics, ads, prose or reviews. They receive about 1,500 MSS per year, accept 1-2 poems from about 10% of those submitting. Press run is 750. Subscription: $12. **Sample: $7 postpaid. Pays 1 copy. No simultaneous submissions or previously published poems. Reports in 3-4 months. Editor seldom comments on rejections.** She says, "I believe that this is an exciting period in the history of American poetry. The diversity of 'little' magazines reflects the vitality of contemporary poetry and suggests that there is a forum for virtually every type of poem. But recently many little magazines have failed for financial reasons. We need to develop a large dedicated readership, and poets must lead the way! Everyone should subscribe to and read, a selection of literary magazines — especially poets."

THE MANHATTAN REVIEW (II, IV-Translations), 440 Riverside Dr. Apt.45, New York, NY 10027, phone 212-932-1854, founded 1980, poetry editor Philip Fried, tries "**to contrast and compare American and foreign writers, and we choose foreign writers with something valuable to offer the American scene. We like to think of poetry as a powerful discipline engaged with many other fields. We want to see ambitious work. Interested in both lyric and narrative. Not interested in mawkish, sentimental poetry.** We select high-quality work from a number of different countries, including the U.S." They have recently published poetry by A. R. Ammons, Ana Blandiana, Bronisyaw Maj, Christopher Bursk, Colleen J. McElroy, D. Nurkse, Judson Jerome, and Penelope Shuttle. The editor selected these sample lines by Peter Redgrove:

The waters shall be healed the spinet declares,
And like gardens of flowers be full of fish
As the flow-er plays; and the moths

Shall carry all leprosies away on their backs,
On their scaly backs, with formal magnitude

The *MR* is "declared semiannual but more accurately an annual." The magazine has 60+ pp., digest-sized, professionally printed with glossy card cover, photos and graphics, circulation 500, 85 subscriptions of which 35 are libraries. They receive about 300 submissions per year, use few ("but I do read everything submitted carefully and with an open mind"). "I return submissions very promptly." Subscription: $8; per issue: $4. **Sample: $5.25 with 6 × 9″ envelope. Submit 3-5 pp., no photocopy, no simultaneous submissions, with short bio. Reports in 10-12 weeks. Pays copies. Sometimes comments "but don't count on it."** Philip Fried advises, "Don't be swayed by fads. Search for your own voice. Support other poets whose work you respect and enjoy. Be persistent. Keep aware of poetry being written in other countries."

MANIC D PRESS (I, II), P.O. Box 410804, San Francisco, CA 94141, founded 1984. **manic d** is interested in books/broadsides/etc. of **poetry by talented unknowns who are looking for an alternative to establishment presses. Considers simultaneous submissions. Pays copies. Send SASE for catalog to buy samples (or $5 for one of their books of their choice).**

✓ **MANKATO POETRY REVIEW (II),** Box 53, English Dept., Mankato State, Mankato, MN 56001, phone 507-389-5511, founded 1984, editor Roger Sheffer, a semi-annual magazine that is **"open to all forms of poetry. We will look at poems up to 60 lines, any subject matter."** They have recently published poems by Laurel Speer, Diane Glancy, Ron Wallace, and Phil Dacey. As a sample, the editor chose the following lines from a poem by Ron Robinson:

> *The rain paints late Monets at Hennepin and Lake;*
> *Water and glass show both through and back to,*
> *Headlights, taillights, neon: Rainbow Cafe,*

The magazine is 5 × 8″, typeset on 60 lb. paper, 30 pp. saddle-stapled with buff matte card cover printed in one color. It appears usually in May and December and has a circulation of 200. Price per issue is $2, subscription $4/year. **Sample available for $2 postpaid, guidelines for SASE. Pay is 2 copies. "Readable dot-matrix OK. Please indicate if simultaneous submission, and notify." Reporting time is about 2 months; "We accept only what we can publish in next issue."** The editor says, "We're interested in looking at longer poems—up to 60 lines, with great depth of detail relating to place (landscape, townscape)."

MANROOT BOOKS (V, IV-Gay), Box 762, Boyes Hot Springs, CA 95416, founded 1969, publisher Paul Mariah, is "America's oldest gay press." **Currently not accepting submissions.**

MARGIN (III), The Square Inch, Lower Franco St., Dunning, PH2 0SQ, Scotland, founded 1986, poetry editor Robin Magowan, managing editor Walter Perrie, is a "literary quarterly with **emphasis on adventurous, politically accurate nonfiction."** They want **intense, multi-layered poetry of "any length."** They are more "interested in poet's prose than their verse—on virtually any subject." They have recently published poetry by Myron Turner, Stephen Marquardt, and Rachel Hadas. The editor selected these lines from "Big Chair," by Ivan Argüelles:

> *of course there is a jazz a love supreme a bone-rattle in the throat*
> *pin-point of lust and fear of shadows wherever the feet of troachaic fire*
> *tread in and out as they will on such afternoons & I am fanned in newspapers*
> *and aired above the concourse of those racing for home*
> *sleeping already in the dread bone of their organized life.*

The magazine is handsomely printed, 7 × 10″, 100 pp., flat-spined, with full-color card cover, offset, litho graphics, cartoons and art-work included. Their circulation is 2,000 of which 1,500 are shelf sales. Per issue it is $5, for a subscription $20. **Sample: $6 postpaid. Pays $25 a page plus 5 copies and $40 for verse. Reports in 1-3 weeks.** Editor "rarely" comments on rejections. **"Enclose a dollar with an envelope for reply."**

‡MARK; A JOURNAL OF SCHOLARSHIP, OPINION, AND LITERATURE (II), 2801 W. Bancroft SU2514, Toledo, OH 43606, first appeared 1967-69, then resumed 1978. Editor Brenda Wyatt. "Publishes once a year a journal of fiction, poetry, photographs and sketches." *Mark* is digest-sized, 70 pp. saddle-stapled, professionally printed, with matte card cover. As a sample, I selected these sample lines from "spectral evidence" by Craig Houston:

> *pigeonholded in the back of my mind*
> *occasionally*
> *they escape to*
> *haunt the peace*
> *   intimate whispered words*

They supply no information about purchase of sample copies (the list price is $3), payment, or submission requirements, but the editor does say that they comment "very rarely."

MAROVERLAG (II, IV-Foreign language), Riedingerstr. 24, 8900 Augsburg, West Germany, phone 0821/416033, founded 1970, editor Lothar Reiserer. **Maroverlag publishes paperbacks and some hardcover books of poetry, one a year, averaging 80 pages.** The books are in German, but they have published a number of English and American poets (for example, Charles Bukowski). **Submit sample of 8-10 poems and bio. Pays 5-10% royalties.**

MARRIAGE & FAMILY (IV-Religious), St. Meinrad, IN 47577, phone 812-357-8011, a monthly magazine, circulation 30,000, **using poetry for Christian couples and parents; supports, deepens, awakens the conviction of God's presence in the communion of family life. Pays $15 on publication. Sample $1.**

THE UNIVERSITY OF MASSACHUSETTS PRESS; THE JUNIPER PRIZE (II), Mail Office, University of Massachusetts, Amherst, MA 01003, phone 413-545-2217, founded 1964. The press offers an annual competition for the Juniper Prize, in alternate years to first and subsequent books. In 1991 only "first books" will be considered: MSS by writers whose poems have appeared in literary journals and/or anthologies but have not been published, or been accepted for publication, in book form. **Submissions should be approximately 60 pp. in typescript (generally 50-60 poems). A list of poems published in literary journals and/or anthologies must accompany the MS. Such poems may be included in the MS and must be identified. Entry fee: $10. Entries must be postmarked not later than September 1.** The award is announced in April/May and publication is scheduled for winter. The amount of the prize is $1,000 and is in lieu of royalties on the first print run.

THE MASSACHUSETTS REVIEW (II), Memorial Hall, University of Massachusetts, Amherst, MA 01003, founded 1959, editors Paul Jenkins and Anne Halley. They have published poems by Andrew Salkey, Dara Weir, Paul Muldoon and Eavan Boland. The editor chose this poem "Love In the Ether" by Adélia Prado:

> There's a landscape inside me
> between noon and two p.m.
> Long-legged birds, their beaks slicing the water
> enter and don't enter this memory-place,
> a shallow lagoon with slender reeds along the shore.

I have not seen it, but the editors describe this quarterly as "off-set (some color used in art sections) 6 × 9". Of 2,500 poems received they accept about 50. Press run is 2,000 for 1,200-1,300 subscriptions (1,500 of them libraries), the rest for shelf sales. Subscription is $14 (U.S.), $20 outside U.S., $17 for libraries. **Sample: $5.25 postpaid. Send SASE for guidelines. Don't read submissions June 1 to October 1. Pays minimum of $10, or 35¢ per line plus 2 copies. No simultaneous submissions or previously published poems. Reports in 6 weeks.**

MATILDA PUBLICATIONS PRODUCTIONS, BRUNSWICK POETRY WORKSHOP (V, II), 7 Mountfield St. Brunswick, Victoria, Australia, phone 03-386-5604, founded 1974, publisher Fonda Zenofon "poet laureate," publishes nonfiction and some poetry chapbooks. **Currently not accepting poetry submissions.** "We have more than enough poems for our present needs." He will criticize MSS for a fee, but "Once a year membership fee gets you a quota of critiques and membership in the Brunswick Poetry Workshop, the first official poetry body in Australia. Sometimes we get no return postage or shortfall; we chuck out these. Send I.R.C's or US dollars; no cheques under $5, as they are not worth cashing after bank fees."

MATRIX (IV-Regional), Box 100, Ste. Anne de Bellevue, Quebec, H9X 3L4, Canada, founded 1975, is a literary appearing 3 times a year which publishes **quality poetry by Canadians without restriction as to form, length, style, subject matter or purpose.** They have published poems by Irving Layton, David Solway, Joy Kogawa, David McFadden, Carolyn Smart, and Dorothy Livesay. There are 5-8 pp. of poetry in each issue. The magazine is 8½ × 11", 80 pp., stapled, professionally printed, glossy cover with full-color art and graphics, circulation 1,000. Subscription: $15 Canadian, $20 international. They receive about 500 submissions per year, use 20-30, have a 6 month backlog. **Sample: $10 postpaid (Canadian funds). Submit 6-10 poems. Reports in 10 weeks. Pays $10-40 per poem. Editor sometimes comments on rejections. Under new editorial board.**

MATURE YEARS (IV-Senior citizen), P.O. Box 801, 201 8th Ave. South, Nashville, TN 37202, phone 615-749-6468, founded 1954, editor Donn C. Downall, is a quarterly, circulation 80,000. They use **poetry of no more than 16 lines: "fun poetry and poetry especially suited to persons in retirement or over 55 years of age."** They do not want to see "anything that pokes fun at older adults or which is too sentimental or saccharine." It is magazine-sized, 100+ pp., saddle-stapled, with full-color glossy paper cover. **Guidelines are available for writers. They pay 50¢-$1 per line, report in 2 months, a year's delay before publication.**

MAYAPPLE PRESS (V, IV-Regional, women), 5520 Briarcliff Dr., Edinboro, PA 16412, phone 814-734-3488, founded 1978, publisher/editor Judith Kerman, publishes **"women's poetry, Great Lakes regional poetry"** in chapbooks. They want **"quality contemporary poetry rooted in real experience and strongly crafted. No greeting card verse, sentimental or conventional poetry."** They have recently published chapbooks by Judith Minty and Toni Ortner-Zimmerman. They "rarely" accept freelance submissions. **Query with 5-6 samples.** "We are not likely to publish unless poet accepts a *primary* role in distribution. Reality is only poets themselves can sell unknown work." **Pays 10% of run. Publishes on "cooperative" basis.** "Generally poet agrees to purchase most of the run at 50% of cover price." Editor **"usually comments (very briefly)" on rejections.** She says, "Poets must create the audience for their work. No small press 'white knight' can make an unknown famous (or even sell more than a few books!)."

THE MAYBERRY GAZETTE; THE ANDY GRIFFITH SHOW APPRECIATION SOCIETY (IV-Themes, humor), P.O. Box 330, Clemmons, NC 27006, founded 1986, editor John Meroney, is a newsletter appearing 6 times a year using poetry about **the Andy Griffith Show TV series (CBS 1960-68). "We're looking for poetry that relates to the series or relates to an individual's involvement with the program, probably no more than 10-20 lines. Style: humorous. We really wouldn't want to see anything overly serious because it wouldn't work in the newsletter well."** As a sample the editor selected "our Official Society Pledge" by Danny Hutchins:

> *Mayberry beats everything, we all know that.*
> *Mayberry's where all the good things are at.*
> *Fair or foul weather, we all stick together.*
> *We are Mayberrians forever and ever.*

The newsletter is 4 pp., folded, professionally printed. Their press run is 7,000 with 5,000 subscriptions. Subscription: $17. **Sample: $1.50 postpaid. No simultaneous submissions or previously published poems. "Include details as to how you were influenced by the series, why you feel it was/is popular, etc." Reports in 4-6 weeks. "Please include a large SASE with all material."** Editor comments on rejections "often." They occasionally have contests announced through the newsletter.

MEANJIN QUARTERLY (II), University of Melbourne, Parkville, Victoria 3052, Australia, founded 1940, poetry editor Philip Mead, who says, **"I'm open to all kinds of new and contemporary poetry."** They have published poetry by Herbert Morris, John Tranter, Judith Rodriguez, A. D. Hope, and Edward Hirsch. As a sample I selected the first stanza of "Road Works" by Lauris Edmond:

> *In this street that has ignored so many*
> *poignant or desperate encounters*
> *I may meet my angry daughter. Will she smile,*
> *speak? Would she brush past?*

Meanjin, a quarterly, is digest-sized, 168+ pp., flat-spined, professionally printed, with color glossy card cover. They accept "a miniscule number" of about 2,500 poems by 450 poets received each year. Press run is 3,800 for 2,000 subscriptions (800 libraries — 577 local and 202 overseas). Subscription: $24. **Sample: $7.50 postpaid. "We pay the best regular rates in Australia for poetry." Reports "within a month." No more than 3-4 months between acceptance and publication.** Editor **"frequently" comments on rejections.** He says, "I am particularly interested in Australian and North American poetry."

‡THE EDWIN MELLEN PRESS (II), 240 Portage Rd., Lewiston, NY 14092, phone 716-754-2795, founded 1974, poetry editor Mrs. Patricia Schultz, is a scholarly press. "We do not have access to large chain bookstores for distribution, but depend on direct sales and independent bookstores." **They pay 2 copies, no royalties. "We require no author subsidies. However, we encourage our authors to seek grants from Councils for the Arts and other foundations because these add to the reputation of the volume." They want "original integrated work — living unity of poems, preferably unpublished poetry, encompassable in one reading."** They have recently published poetry by Toby Lurie and Robert Carter. As a sample the editor selected these lines (poet unidentified):

> *The lotus blossom calls again.*
> *Away to blue enchanted isles*
> *Where doves descend in quiet drift*
> *And sleepy men lie all about.*

Their books average 64 pp. The sample I have seen, Eleanor Snouck Hurgronje's **Quietly My Captain Waits**, is a handsome hardbound, digest-sized, flat-spined, unpaginated, on good stock. **Submit 40+ sample poems, bio, publications. "We do not print until we receive at least 75 prepaid orders. Successful marketing of poetry books depends on the author's active involvement. Authors provide us with an extensive list of names and addresses of potential readers of their book.** We send out up to 12 free review copies to journals or newspapers, the names of which may be suggested by the author. Authors may purchase more copies of their book (above the 2 free copies provided) at the same 40% discount (for quantites of 10 or more) which we allow to bookstores. An author may (but is not required to) purchase books to make up the needed 75 prepublication sales.

‡MEMORABLE MOMENTS (I, IV-Membership); BY INVITATION ONLY (V); RAIN DANCER PUBLI-CATIONS, Box 5673, Augusta, ME 04332, editors J.R. and Robin Libby. *Memorable Moments* is published 4-6 times a year, publishing poetry of "members" (or subscribers), with some space saved for non-members. Payment is "by-line only." Those who have published in *MM* may be invited to submit to *By Invitation Only*, for which payment is 2 copies. **"We want to see 4-6 of a poet's best works. We don't know what we are looking for until we read it. It is best to submit a mix of styles and lengths. Nothing foul, nothing heavy into sex."** They have recently published poetry by John Grey, Edward Francisco, John Ditsky, and Jennine Cannizo. As a sample the editor selected these opening lines from "The Ice Wall" by Bernard Hewitt:

> *It was legend that above the ice*
> *lay a land of myth.*
> *A stream of migratory travelers*
> *wound through the forested hills*
> *up from the lowlands*
> *to the base of the ice cliffs.*

"Presidential Membership is $24, $28 outside USA and includes 8 issues of *MM*, publication of 3 poems of poet's choice in upcoming issues (50 line max. per poem) along with any special issues we publish during active membership (see *By Invitation Only*). Vice-Presidential Membership is $12, $16 outside USA, and includes the next 4 issues of *MM*, publication of 1 poem of poet's choice (50 line max.), and any special issues published during active membership. All members receive 50¢ discount off issue price for those who wish to purchase copies, and members' poetry is given consideration over non-members. Sample copy: $3.50 postpaid. If accepted for publication, no purchase is required. We in courage [sic] members to submit work as often as they want – and we always keep some space open for non-members. All checks/money orders must be made out to Robin Libby." *MM* is 32-40 pp. digest-sized, photocopied from italic typescript, with matte card cover. Press run: 300 for 85 subscribers of which 7 are libraries. The editors say, "Separate yourself from the mass of poets struggling for print space. In most cases, if something different or unusual comes across my desk, I will publish it – even if I myself don't care for it. There are not enough poets out there willing to take chances with their work. I don't want to see reflections of Great poets past – I want to see what lies submerged in each poet's mind. Show me the stuff you always wanted to print – but always held back on."

MEMORY PLUS ENTERPRISES PRESS; LIFT THE COVER; WRITER'S GROUP FOR CENTRAL ILLINOIS-INDIANA (V,I), Box 225, Oakwood, IL 61858, founded 1985, chairman Karl Witsman, publishes two books of poetry per year in their Lift the Cover series. **Not accepting submissions in 1991.** They publish **"poetry with some sort of lyrical or rhythmical structure; can be free-verse; does not have to rhyme. Nothing racist. Do not like poems with lines of only one word (except the title line). Poems must make sense and have a point."** The series began with **Erindonia** by Donna Carlene ($3.50 postpaid). As a sample the editor selected these lines from "My One Love" in that collection:

> *Deep brown eyes I lose myself in,*
> *Turn this way and look at me.*
> *Let me sun myself in your dark light.*
> *Sparkle and shine,*
> *Laugh and cry, my brown eyes,*
> *Let me comfort you.*

"Would encourage participation in Writers' Group if poet lives in central Illinois or Indiana. Not required. We are still new in poetry and are very flexible."

MENNONITE PUBLISHING HOUSE; PURPOSE; STORY FRIENDS; ON THE LINE; WITH (IV-Religious, children), 616 Walnut Ave., Scottdale, PA 15683-1999, phone 412-887-8500. **Send submissions or queries directly to the editor of the specific magazine at address indicated.** The official publisher for the Mennonite Church in North America seeks also to serve a broad Christian audience. Each of the magazines listed has different specifications, and the editor of each should be queried for more exact information. *Purpose*, editor James E. Horsch, a "monthly in weekly parts," circulation 19,000, is **for adults of all ages, its focus: "action oriented, discipleship living."** It is 5⅜ × 8⅜″, with two-color printing throughout. **They buy appropriate poetry up to 12 lines.** *Purpose* uses 3-4 poems per week, receives about 2,000 per year of which they use 150, has a 10-12 week backlog. **MSS should be typewritten, double-spaced, one side of sheet only. Simultaneous submissions OK. Reports in 6-8 weeks. Pays $5-15 per poem plus 2 copies. Sample copy: free. Send SASE for guidelines.** *On the Line*, edited by

Mary C. Meyer, another "monthly in weekly parts," is **for children 10-14**, a "story paper that reinforces Christian values," circulation 10,500. It is 7x10″, saddle-stapled, with 2-color printing on the cover and inside, using art and photos. **Sample: free. Pays $5-15 per poem plus 2 copies. Poems 3-24 lines. Submit "as many as desired, but each should be typed on a separate 8 × 11½″ sheet." Simultaneous submissions, previously published poems OK. Reports in 1 month, backlog "varies."** *Story Friends*, edited by Marjorie Waybill, is for **children 4-9**, a "story paper that reinforces Christian values, also a "monthly in weekly issues, circulation 11,500, uses poems **3-12 lines, pays $5.** *With*, editor Susan E. Janzen, Box 347, Newton, KS 67114, telephone 316-238-5100, is for **"senior highs, ages 15-18,"** focusing on helping "high school youth make a commitment to Christ in the context of the church amidst the complex and conflicting values they encounter in their world," circulation 5,300, uses **poetry "dealing with youth in relation to their world."** Poems should be short (15-25 lines). No information on payment given.

‡**MERLIN BOOKS LTD. (I)**, 40 East St., Braunton, Devon EX33 2EA England, phone 0271-816430, founded 1981, editor Pam Stearn, is a subsidy publisher. **Submit complete collection for a proposal. You pay complete cost and they pay 20-25% royalties plus 12 copies.** (Suggestion: go to a *printer* and you will own *all* the books you pay to have printed.)

‡**MERLYN'S PEN: THE NATIONAL MAGAZINE OF STUDENT WRITING, GRADES 7-10 (IV-Students, young adults)**, Dept. PM, Box 1058, East Greenwich, RI 02818, founded 1985, editor R. Jim Stahl, is a quarterly using young adult writing as indicated by its title. It is magazine-sized, professionally printed, 36 pp. with glossy paper color cover. Press run: 22,000 for 20,000 subscriptions of which 5,000 are libraries. Subscription: $14.95. **Sample, postpaid: $3. Send SASE for guidelines. Pays 3 copies.** As a sample the editor selected the opening lines of "Shakespeare" by tenth grader Joanna Hearne:

> *Shakespeare, did you live in the sea?*
> *The beauty of the salty, unsmooth waves is yours,*
> > *beating roaring rhythms on the shore,*
> > *where tides have come and gone.*

‡**METAMORPHOSIS (I,II)**, % Ariel, P.O. Box 468, Gardena, CA 90248, editor/publisher Lisa Chun, appears 4-6 times a year in various formats, "but generally in a simplified book form, hand-bound, using photos, some artwork. Often does issues featuring one artist or poet." They want **well-written poems that express a very individual version of truth, very honest, very personal, writing that reaches the core and changes you. No obscene or pornographic material, no romantic slush that only touches the surface, no rhymes, nothing formal or rigid."** As a sample the editor selected these lines by Tina Phillips:

> *By the time night comes on again*
> *flat and hungry as the irreversible sky*
> *we will welcome our own, regular deaths*
> *— eyes open, swallowing them whole.*

Metamorphosis appears 4-6 times a year. "We hope to encourage those who want to overcome mediocrity and find truth in everyday life. Format changes from issue to issue, depending on content. Subscription: $20. **Sample, postpaid: $5. Pays 3 copies. "We encourage those interested in being included in our work to subscribe."** They publish 6-10 chapbooks per year. **For chapbook consideration submit samples, bio, publications. Reports in 2-4 weeks to queries, 1-2 months to MSS. Pays 5 copies.** The samples I have seen are attractive, tiny books with hand-lettered text on heavy quality stock with soft matte covers enclosed in colorful wrappers. The editor says, "Most of our work is focused on these hand-made books, some of which are sold in specialty book shops/artist's shops, and distributed to friends through the mail."

‡**METAMORPHOUS PRESS (V)**, 3249 NW 29th Ave., Portland, OR 97210, phone 503-228-4972, founded 1982, poetry editor Kelly Lee, publishes books, cassettes and video tapes on **neurolinguistic programming**, health and healing education, business and sales, women's studies, and children's books. They use **poetry only "in our subject areas which is compatible with the idea that we create our own reality and that would give individuals insight into gaining better control of their own lives."**

METRO SINGLES LIFESTYLES (I), Box 28203, Kansas City, MO 64118, phone 816-436-8424, founded 1984, editor Robert L. Huffstutter. *MSL* is a tabloid publication for women and men of all ages: single, divorced, widowed or never-married. Not a lonely hearts type of publication, but positive and upbeat. Published 6 to 9 times per year and has a circulation of 25,000 (approximately 5,000 subscribers in KC and throughout the USA), newsstand, bookstore sales and limited complimentary copies to clubs, organizations and singles groups. Interested in seeing **"free verse, lite verse, philosophical, romantic, sentimental and Frost-type poetry. All subjects considered.** They have recently published poetry by

Robert Loudin, John Grey, Laurie Kay Olson, and Dawn Zapletal. As a sample, the editor selected these lines by Earl R. Stonebridge:

> *A poem is an unopened door*
> *to an old man's closet,*
> *a quick glance through a great aunt's vanity,*
> *a passing glance at*
> *a young woman's face and then her figure.*
> *Sometimes a poem is pure lust diguised*
> *as poetry, but has been, can be*
> *and will again be*
> *a dark night in the Rockies when a*
> *couple hugs and falls asleep*
> *too tired to make love.*

Each issue features at least 12 poems by poets living throughout the USA. Poets are invited to send a photo and a brief paragraph about their goals, single status and lifestyle. This is optional and does not influence selection of poetry, but does add interest to the publication when space for this extra feature permits. **Reports in 6-8 weeks; pays from $5/poem or in subscriptions plus complimentary copies. Sample copy of current issue is $2 and mailed postpaid immediately.** Each issue about 36 pp. and printed on Webb Offset press. **MS should be typewritten, double-spaced or written in easy-to-read format. Prefer to look at original poetry. No simultaneous or previously published work.** The editor says, "We do not limit or restrict subject of poems, but insist they convey an emotion, experience, or exercise the reader's imagination."

MICHIGAN QUARTERLY REVIEW (III), 3032 Rackham Bldg., University of Michigan, Ann Arbor, MI 48109, phone 313-764-9265, founded 1962, editor-in-chief, Laurence Goldstein, is "an interdisciplinary, general interest academic journal that publishes mainly essays and reviews on subjects of cultural and literary interest." They use **all kinds of poetry except light verse. No specifications as to form, length, style, subject matter or purpose.** Poets they have recently published include Amy Clampitt, Stuart Dybek, Tess Gallagher, Robert Creeley, Marge Piercy, and Diane Wakoski. As a sample, the editors chose these lines by Robert R. Anderson:

> *How bored the stars must be*
> *by their own heavenly floorshows*
> *dragging eternities through*
> *predictable moves, dazzling*
> *the darkness, because they have to.*

The *Review* is 6×9", 160+ pp., flat-spined, professionally printed with glossy card cover, b/w photos and art, has a circulation of 2,000, 1,500 subscriptions of which half are libraries. Subscription: $13; per copy: $3.50. They receive 1,500 submissions per year, use 30, have a 1 year backlog. **Sample: $2 postpaid. They prefer typed MSS, photocopies OK. Reports in 4-6 weeks. Pays $8-12 per page.** Laurence Goldstein advises, "There is no substitute for omnivorous reading and careful study of poets past and present, as well as reading in new and old areas of knowledge. Attention to technique, especially to rhythm and patterns of imagery, is vital."

‡**MID COASTER (II)**, 2750 N. 45th St., Milwaukee, WI 53210-2429, founded 1987, editor Peter Blewett, is an annual. **"I would like good, tough poetry. No restrictions on form, length, or subject matter. Experimental, nonsensical OK. Nothing sentimental."** They have recently published poetry by Edward Field and F.D. Reeve. As a sample the editor selected these lines from "I Hear the Wife of the Governor of Wisconsin Singing" by James Liddy:

> *Over the bluff your rock-like song*
> > *passes,*
> *over soft shade me who*
> *forgets or dislikes most literature.*

Mid Coaster is magazine-sized, 36 pp. saddle-stapled, professionally printed in small type with glossy heavy paper cover. Press run: 1,000 for 50 subscribers. **Sample, postpaid: $4. Send SASE for guidelines. Pays 2 copies.** The editor quotes Owen Felltham: "Poetry should be like a coranto, short and nimble-lofty, rather than a dull lesson of a day long . . . He is something the less unwise that is unwise but in prose."

MID-AMERICAN REVIEW; JAMES WRIGHT PRIZE FOR POETRY (II, IV-Translations), Dept. of English, Bowling Green State University, Bowling Green, OH 43403, phone 419-372-2725, founded 1980, poetry editor Ken Letko, appears twice a year. **"Poetry should emanate from strong, evocative images, use fresh, interesting language, and have a consistent sense of voice. Each line must carry the poem, and an individual vision should be evident. We encourage new as well as established writers. There is**

no length limit." As a sample I selected the first stanza of Walter MacDonald's "The Truth Trees Know":

> *Mice die because their world is level.*
> *They never dream wings wait in trees*
> *above them. Whatever they fear*
> *springs on four feet over dirt,*

The review appears twice a year, 200 pp., flat-spined, offset, professional printing, using line drawings, glossy card cover. They receive a thousand MSS a year, use 60-80 poems. Press run is 1,000. Subscription: $6. Per issue: $4.50. **Samples: $3 postpaid. Send SASE for guidelines. Pays $7 per printed page plus 2 copies. They do not consider MSS June-August. Publishes chapbooks in translation.**

‡**MIDDLE EAST REPORT (IV-Regional, ethnic, themes),** Suite 119, 1500 Massachusetts Ave. NW, Washington, DC 20005, phone 202-223-3677, founded 1971, editor Joe Stork, is "a magazine on contemporary political, economic, cultural and social developments in the Middle East and North Africa and U.S. policy toward the region. We publish **poetry that addresses political or social issues of Middle Eastern peoples.**" They have recently published poetry by Dan Almagor (Israeli). The sample lines are from "It was Beirut, all over again" by Etel Adnan (Lebanese):

> *And it is Beirut all over again*
> *with water on the horizon*
> *cemeteries outcrowding hotels*
> *airplaines bringing the worst*
> *of news*
> *and infinite processions*
> *of sorrow*

It is a magazine-sized, 48 pp. saddle-stapled, professionally printed on glossy stock with glossy paper cover, 6 issues per year. Press run: 6,000. "We published 9 poems last year, all solicited." Subscription: $20. **Sample, postpaid: $4.75 domestic; $6.75 air mail overseas. Pays 3-6 copies. Simultaneous submissions and previously published poems OK. Reports in 6-8 weeks. "We key poetry to the theme of a particular issue. Could be as long as 6 months between acceptance and publication."** Editor sometimes comments on submissions.

MIDDLE EASTERN DANCER (IV-Themes, ethnic), P.O. Box 181572, Casselberry, FL 32718-1572, phone 407-831-3402, founded 1979, editor/publisher Karen Kuzsel, is a "monthly international magazine for Middle Eastern dancers and culture enthusiasts. **No specs for poetry other than sticking to the subject matter. Do not want to see anything not related to Middle Eastern dancing.**" As a sample the editor selected these lines by Martha Savage:

> *Floating in chiffon, thin silks and a belt of gold,*
> *I have a 1,000 stories with my eyes and body to be told,*
> *With outstretched arms the world I embrace,*
> *With a knowing smile of experience on my face*
> *I can create, excite, promise or tease.*
> *Or show my passion with ease.*

The monthly is magazine-sized, usually 36 pp., printed in 2-color on heavy stock with glossy paper cover, using b/w photos and graphics. They receive about 20 poems per year, accept 6-10 ("depends on room"). The press run is 2,500+. $2.50 plus $1 postage and handling per issue, $21 per year. **Sample: SASE (85¢ stamps). Pays 2 copies. Poems can be in "any form that's legible." Simultaneous submissions (if not to other Middle Eastern dance publications), previously published poems OK. Reports within 2 weeks.** Editor occasionally comments on rejections.

MIDLAND REVIEW (II, IV-Themes, women/feminism), English Dept., Morrill Hall, Oklahoma State University, Stillwater, OK 74078, phone 405-744-9474, founded 1985, poetry editor Nuala Archer, a literary annual that publishes "poetry, fiction, essays, ethnic, experimental, women's work, contemporary feminist, linguistic criticism, drama, comparative literature, interviews." Each issue seems to have a theme. The editors say, **"style and form are open." They do not want long or religious poetry."** Poets published include Amy Clampitt, William Stafford, Medbh McGuckian, and Richard Kostelanetz. As a sample, the editors chose the following lines by Robert Siegal:

> *The snow throws itself down in pity*
> *From the order of heaven where things are clear*
> *as the horizon retreating from a space shuttle*
> *or the edge of Africa, a calm and simple line.*

Midland Review is digest-sized, 100-120 pp., with photography and ads. Circulation is 500, of which 470 are subscriptions. Price per issue is $6. **Sample available for $5 postpaid. Pay is 1** copy. **Writers should submit 3-5 poems, typed MS in any form; simultaneous submissions are OK if indicated. Reporting time is 3-6 months and time to publication 6-12 months.**

MIDSTREAM: A MONTHLY JEWISH REVIEW (IV-Ethnic), 515 Park Ave., New York, NY 10022, phone 212-752-0600, editor Murray Zuckoff, is a magazine-sized, 64 pp., flat-spined national journal, circulation 10,000, appearing monthly except June/July and August/September, when it is bimonthly. It uses **short poems with Jewish themes or atmosphere.** They have published poetry by Yehuda Amichai, James Reiss, Abraham Sutzkever, and Liz Rosenberg. The editors selected these lines from "Yahrzeit" by Rodger Kamenetz as a sample:

> *She lights a candle in a jar. I put*
> *it on the mantle. The candle burns because*
> *it's the custom and our grief doesn't know*
> *where to put itself . . .*
>
> *. . . We don't believe. Despair*
> *would tell us nothing, but that's no good.*
> *We do what we can. We did what we could.*

Subscription: $18; per issue: $3. They receive about 300 submissions per year, use 5-10%. **Sample: free. No query. Reports in 1 month. Pays $25 per poem.**

MIDWEST POETRY REVIEW; RIVER CITY PUBLICATIONS (IV-Subscribers), P.O. Box 4776, Rock Island, IL 61201, founded 1980, poetry editors Tom Tilford, Grace Keller and Jilian Roth, is a "subscriber-only" quarterly, with no other support than subscriptions—that is, **only subscribers ($17 per year) may submit poetry and/or enter their contests. Subscribers may also get help and criticism on one poem per month.** "We are attempting to encourage the cause of poetry and raise the level thereof by giving aid to new poets, to poets who have lapsed in their writing, and to poets who desire a wider market, by purchasing the best of modern poetry and giving it exposure through our quarterly magazine. We want **poetry from poets who feel they have a contribution to make to the reader relating to the human condition, nature, and the environment. Serious writers only are sought. No jingly verses or limericks. No restrictions as to form, length or style. Any subject is considered, if handled with skill and taste.**" They have recently published poetry by Elizabeth Hartman, Kay Harvey, Patricia Hladikhon, Barbara Petosky, Nancy Alden, Esther Leiper, Timothy Ward, Fritz Wolf, Peter Wessel, and C. R. Mannering. The editors selected these sample lines from "North Wind" by Candice Warne:

> *Two men lean on an old Buick,*
> *passing the brown bag back and forth,*
> *pouring gold dawn morning's throat.*
> *Brothers, I wish you something to celebrate.*

The digest-sized, 52 pp., saddle-stapled magazine is professionally printed in various type styles, matte card cover, some b/w art. They have quarterly and annual contests plus varied contests in each issue, with prizes ranging from $25-500 (the latter for the annual contest), with "unbiased, non-staff judges for all competitions. Paid up subscribers enter the contests with fees. **Sample: $3 postpaid. Subscription fee of $17 must accompany first submission. No photocopies. Reports in 2 weeks. Pays $5-500 per poem. Send SASE and $1 for guidelines.** River City Publications is not currently publishing books. The editor advises, "We are interested in serious poets, whether new or published. We will help those who wish to consider serious criticism and attempt to improve themselves. We want to see the poet improve, expand and achieve fulfillment."

THE MIDWEST QUARTERLY (II), Pittsburg State University, Pittsburg, KS 66762, phone 316-235-4689, founded 1959, poetry editor Stephen Meats, "publishes articles on any subject of contemporary interest, particularly literary criticism, political science, philosophy, education, biography, sociology, and each issue contains a **section of poetry from 10-30 pages in length.** I am interested in **well-crafted, though not necessarily traditional poems that see nature and the self in bold, surrealistic images of a writer's imaginative, mystical experience of the world. 60 lines or less (occasionally longer if exceptional).**" They have recently published poetry by Amy Clampitt, Marguerite Bouvard, Jared Carter, Chris Howell, Walter McDonald, and Greg Kuzma. These are sample lines from "Yellow Woman" by Denise Low:

> *The river is a woman of yellow sand.*
> *I lie down in her, leaving a print*
> *of hips and breasts. Soft water touches inside me.*

The digest-sized, 130 pp., flat-spined, matte cover, magazine is professionally printed, has a circulation of 650, with 600 subscriptions of which 500 are libraries. They receive approximately 2,500 poems annually; publish 80. Subscription: $10; per issue: $3. "My plan is to publish all acceptances within 1 year." **Sample: $3. MSS should be typed with poet's name on each page, 10 poems or fewer. Photocopies, legible dot-matrix, OK; simultaneous submissions accepted,** but first publication in *MQ* must be guaranteed. Reports in 8 weeks, usually sooner. Pays 3 copies. Editor comments on rejections "if the poem or poems seem particularly promising." He says, "Keep writing; read as much contemporary poetry as you can lay your hands on; don't let the discouragement of rejection keep you from sending your work out to editors."

MIDWEST VILLAGES & VOICES (V,IV-Regional, membership), 3220 Tenth Ave. S., Minneapolis, MN 55407, founded 1979, is a cultural organization and small-press publisher of Midwestern poetry. They have recently published books of poetry by Ethna McKiernan, Florence Chard Dacey, Kevin FitzPatrick, Sue Doro, and Carol Connolly, whose "Divorced" was chosen as a sample:

> *I am alone, single, solitary,*
> *separated, celibate.*
> *I have borne eight children.*
> *I worry now*
> *that I will die*
> *a virgin.*

The flat-spined books are 64+ pp., professionally printed with glossy card covers, selling for $5-6. **"We encourage and support Midwestern writers and artists. Submissions by invitation only. Our next book is a collection of poetry and prose by Irene Paull."**

MILKWEED EDITIONS, (II), Box 3226, Minneapolis, MN 55403, phone 612-332-3192, founded 1979, poetry editor Emilie Buchwald. Three collections published annually. **Unsolicited MS accepted in May and October; please include return postage. Poetry titles are set through 1991.** Catalog available on request.

MINA PRESS (V), Box 854, Sebastopol, CA 95472, phone 707-829-0854, founded 1981, poetry editors Adam David Miller and Mei T. Nakano, selects MS "more for their literary merit than for their marketing value. We are overwhelmed with manuscripts for the next year."

MIND IN MOTION: A MAGAZINE OF POETRY AND SHORT PROSE (I, II), P.O. Box 1118, Apple Valley, CA 92307, phone 619-248-6512, founded 1985, a quarterly, editor Céleste Goyer wants **poetry** "15-60 lines. Explosive, provocative. Images not cliched but directly conveyant of the point of the poem. Use of free association particularly desired. We encourage free verse, keeping in mind the essential elements of rhythm and rhyme. Traditional forms are acceptable if within length restrictions. Meaning should be implicit, as in the styles of: Blake, Poe, Coleridge, Stephen Crane, Emily Dickinson, Leonard Cohen. Submit in batches of 5-6. Not interested in sentimentality, emotionalism, simplistic nature worship, explicit references."** She has recently published poetry by Robert E. Brimhall, Asher Turren, Carmen M. Pursifull and Michael Alter. As a sample she selected these lines from "Final Entry" (poet unidentified):

> *. . . Ideals reordered,*
> *Reality distorted,*
> *Abuse afforded,*
> *The future aborted—*
>
> *Consider non-vital man:*
> *From compulsive arrival*
> *Now attempting survival*
> *With no viable plan.*

MIM is 54 pp., digest-sized, saddle-stapled, photocopied from photoreduced typescript with a heavy matte cover with b/w drawing. Of approximately 2,400 poems per year she accepts about 200. Press run is 350 for 250 subscriptions. Subscription: $14. **Sample: $3.50 postpaid (overseas: $4.50, $18 per year). Send SASE for guidelines. Pays 1 copy "when financially possible." Reports in 1-6 weeks. Unpublished works only. Simultaneous submissions okay if notified. Magazine is copyrighted; all rights revert to author. Editor usually comments on rejected MSS.**

‡**MIND MATTERS REVIEW (I)**, 2040 Polk St. #234, San Francisco, CA 94109, founded 1988, editor Carrie Drake, is a **"literary quarterly with emphasis on use of science as a tool for responsible organization of information;** analysis of the role of language in conscious knowledge intelligence; social criticism particularly of metaphysics. Book reviews, poetry, short stories, art, satire." They want "short poems for fillers; will publish collections of poems by a single author if suitable to theme of a particular

Use the General Index to find the page number of a specific publication or publisher.

issue of *MMR*. Would like to see inspirational poetry; but open to satire and contemporary subjects that reflect the struggle between the 'inner voice' and external pressures. Rhythm important, but rhyme isn't." They have recently published poetry by D. Castleman, from whose "Dignity Inspires the Blessed Gift of Blushing" the editor selected these lines:

> Life's profoundest issue is not of death
> but of that disquiet we burden our souls
> by, and which is known to none else of breath:
> it's the bell that in the mind's science tolls.

MMR is magazine-sized, desktop published, includes graphics, sketches, b/w photos. Subscription: $15 U.S., $20 foreign. **Sample, postpaid: $3.50. Send SASE for guidelines. Pays 1 copy. Poets are encouraged to buy a copy before submitting. Simultaneous submissions and previously published poems OK.** The editor says, "Poetry should reflect the deeper layers of consciousness, its perceptions, observations, joys and sorrows; should reflect the independence of the individual spirit. Should not be 'trendy' or 'poetic' in a forced way."

THE MIND'S EYE, FICTION & POETRY QUARTERLY (I), Box 656, Glenview, IL 60025, founded 1986, poetry editor Gene Foreman. **Submit up to 5 poems at a time, none over 40 lines. Simultaneous and photocopied submissions OK. No previously published poems. Pays 2 copies. You do not have to subscribe to be published, but if you subscribe, your publications are automatically considered for the annual contest with prizes of $50, $25, and $10 for the best poems (and stories) published during the year.** The magazine is digest-sized, 44 pp., type photoreduced from computer composition, with light card colored cover. Subscriptions: $12 (or, for a 2-year subscription, $22.50). **Sample: $3.50.** The editor chose these lines from "In High School I Majored in Shop" by Peter Martin:

> They told us
> Assembly lines were
> Forever. That
> Assembly lines
> Never stopped.
> They showed us
> Filmstrips about
> Happy couples
> With children
> And Dad coming home
> With his lunch bucket

THE MINNESOTA REVIEW (II), English Dept., SUNY, Stony Brook, NY 11794-5350, phone 516-246-5080, founded 1960, co-editor Michael Sprinker, poetry editor Helen Cooper, appears twice a year, a literary magazine, wanting **"poetry which explores some aspect of social or political issues and/or the nature of relationships." No nature poems, and no lyric poetry without the above focus."** As a sample Michael Sprinker selected these lines from "Hotel Kitchen" by Jonathan Holden:

> Downstairs in those steel kitchens, in the loud
> bucket-brigade of orders, pots and shuttling
> of dishes hand-to-hand, you couldn't hear
> the murmurous conversation of the rich . . .

TMR is digest-sized, flat-spined 160 pp., with b/w glossy card cover and art. Circulation: 1,000, 500 subscriptions. Subscription: $8 to individuals, $16 to institutions. **Sample: $4.50 postpaid. Pays 2 copies. Reports in 2-4 months.**

‡MINOTAUR PRESS; MINOTAUR (II), Box 4904, Burlingame, CA 94011, founded 1974, editor Jim Gove. *Minotaur* is a "small press literary quarterly with emphasis on contemporary and experimental styles. Must be relevant. No rhymed and/or traditional verse." They have recently published poetry by Gerald Locklin, Steve Richmond, Lyn Lifshin, James Broughton, and Will Inman. As a sample the editor selected the first 3 lines of "Oh My Beloveds" by Paul Mariah:

> Bestruck by grief, the dirges remain
> of the lives that were, are, am
> and the aim to clarity is clair

I have not seen an issue, but the editor describes it as digest-sized, offset, "stock cover — cover graphics — sometimes use interior graphics, but rarely." They publish about 12 of 500 poems received. Press run: 400 for 300 subscriptions of which 50 are libraries. Subscription: $12. **Sample, postpaid: $3. Send SASE for guidelines. Pays 1 copy. Submit 4-8 poems. "Best of issue from subscribing contributors receives $50 cash prize. You do not need to subscribe to be published; you do need to be a subscriber to qualify for the contest."** Editor comments on submissions "if requested only." Minotaur Press publishes 2-3 chapbooks per year averaging 30 pp. **"We ask for**

MSS from regular magazine contributors." **Pays 50 copies of chapbooks.** They "rarely" subsidy publish "if quality merits and poet comes to us. Author pays; we distribute to our readership as a bonus book." The editor says, "Subscribe to the magazines that publish your work. Few poetry magazines run in the black.

MIORITA: A JOURNAL OF ROMAN STUDIES (IV-Ethnic), Department of Foreign Languages Literatures and Linguistics, University of Rochester, Rochester, NY 14627, is a scholarly annual, digest-sized, 100 pp., circulation 200, focusing on **Romanian culture and using some poetry by Romanians or on Romanian themes. Sample: $5. Pays copies.**

THE MIRACULOUS MEDAL (IV-Religious), 475 E. Chelten Ave., Philadelphia, PA 19144-5785, phone 215-848-1010, founded 1928, editor Rev. Robert P. Cawley, C.M. is a religious quarterly. **"Poetry should reflect solid Catholic doctrine and experience. Any subject matter is acceptable, provided it does not contradict the teachings of the Roman Catholic Church. Poetry must have a religious theme, preferably about the Blessed Virgin Mary."** They have recently published poetry by Gladys McKee. As a sample the editor selected these lines (poet unidentified):

> *God-Man Jesus! Is it true that You did the things I do?*
> *Did You count the stars at night,*
> *See a firefly's glowing light,*
> *Watch the wild geese winging by,*

I have not seen a copy, but the editor describes it as digest-sized, 32 pp., saddle-stapled, 2-color inside and cover, no ads. *The Miraculous Medal* magazine is no longer circulated on a subscription basis. It is used as a promotional piece and is sent to all clients of the Association. The circulation figure is now 340,000. **Sample and guidelines free for postage. Pays 50¢ and up per line payable on acceptance. Reports in 6 months-3 years, backlog is 6 months to 3 years. Poems should be a maximum of 20 lines, double-spaced. No simultaneous submissions or previously published poems. Buys first North American rights. Photocopy, dot-matrix OK.**

MIRIAM PRESS; UP AGAINST THE WALL, MOTHER (I, IV-Women, theme), 6009 Edgewood Lane, Alexandria, VA 22310, phone 703-971-2219, founded 1980, poetry editor Lee-lee Schlegel. The quarterly is **"concerned with poetry as therapy first, literary excellence second.** Our philosophy is that there are many good literary markets but few who 'help' those in trouble. They want **anything on women in crisis (we deal with the darker side here—death, rape, abuse, the frustrations of mothering/wives, etc.).** *Mother* has published poetry by Jill DiMaggio, Serena Fusek, Joan Payne Kincaid, Sally DeVall, and John Grey. Lee-lee Schlegel selected this sample poem from an untitled poem by Jadene Felina Stevens:

> *"but he loves me," she says*
> *to herself through torn lips*
> *as her blood reddens the snow,*
> *smears her cheek, her chin—*
> *drops like visual screams*
> *to shock the whitened ground.*

Each issue of the digest-sized magazine has 39-52 pp. of poetry. It has a circulation of about 500 with 400 subscriptions of which 25 are university libraries. It is inexpensively produced, offset from typescript, card covers with simple art. They receive about 6,000 submissions per year, use 800. Subscription: $12. **Sample: $3.50. Submit 4-6 poems. Simultaneous submissions, photocopies, dot-matrix OK. Usually reports the same or next week. No pay, not even a copy. Send SASE for guidelines.** "We are a friendly press open to all. We are also very poor and appreciate support. Our immediate goals include being able to pay poets in copies, eventually money. Advice: 1) study your market, 2) always send SASE, 3) please don't tell me how good your poetry is!"

‡MIRRORS; AHA BOOKS (IV-Form, subscribers), *Mirrors*, P.O. Box 1250; AHA Books, Box 767, Gualala, CA 95445, founded 1987 (out of Humidy Productions, Hamburg, Germany), editor Jane Reichhold. *Mirrors* is a **"subscriber-produced haiku magazine.** Each subscription entitles the author to the use of one 8½×11" page each quarter, or the pages may be collected. Each author is totally in control of page of choice of material, layout, artwork, copyrights, taste, quality and readability. **The author should be familiar enough with the form that he/she can publish with the top authors in this field. Beginners are not encouraged. Not poetry set into 3 lines and labeled haiku. Haiku is different and the author should know the rules—before breaking them."** They have recently published poetry by Marlene Mountain, Anne McKay, Joe Nutt, and Charles Dickson. As a sample the editor selected this haiku by Penny Crosby:

> *reflections*
> *in a quiet pool*

> *the room once white*

The magazine-sized publication is 45-50pp., perfect bound with matte card cover, appearing quarterly. Press run 200 for 130 subscriptions of which 10 are libraries, about 35 shelf sales. Subscription: $16. **Sample, postpaid: $4. Send SASE for guidelines. Pays nothing, not even copies. Submit camera-ready work with 1″ gutter for binding on plain white paper with black ink.** "Author is responsible for copyrights on artwork or quotes. Simultaneous submissions and previously published poems OK, "but most are new and experimental. Only the timid who cannot trust their own judgment use previously published poems." No report on submissions: "I reject only material that is not haiku or related. I print one day after the deadline." AHA books publishes 5 flat-spined paperbacks per year averaging 200 pp. on a subsidy basis. Readers of *Mirrors* can vote on haiku submitted to the magazine for a contest. Prize is a year's subscription to the magazine. "Poetry is the misuse of words to form a pair of spectacles in order to see the beauty within oneself through another's competence in observation. It is utterly important to be clear so no one knows you are there. This is true for editors and authors."

MISSISSIPPI REVIEW (II), University of Southern Mississippi, Southern Station, Box 5144, Hattiesburg, MS 39406-5144, phone 601-266-4321. Editor: Frederick Barthelme. Managing Editor: Rie Fortenberry. Literary publication for those interested in contemporary literature. **Does not read manuscripts in summer. Sample: $5.50. Payment in copies.**

MISSISSIPPI VALLEY REVIEW (II), English Dept., Western Illinois University, Macomb, IL 61455, phone 309-298-1514, founded 1973, poetry editor John Mann, is a literary magazine published twice a year which uses **poems of high quality, no specifications as to form, length, style, subject matter or purpose.** They have recently published poetry by Susan Fromberg Schaeffer, David Citino, A.E. Stringer, Dave Etter, Daniel J. Langton, Walter McDonald, Vince Gotera, Tony Curtis, and Catherine Sutton. The editor selected these sample lines by Daniel Bourne:

> *Her voice*
> *each syllable, tangled in the roots of my hair.*
> *She said you are a tree, leafed for summer,*
> *deaf to all the world but the rain.*

MVR uses a handsomely printed, digest-sized, flat-spined, 60+ pp. format, glossy, color cover, circulation 400. Subscription: $6; per copy $3. They have about 25 pp. of poetry in each issue, receive 1,000-2,500 submissions per year, use about 30, and have a 6-12 month backlog. **Considers simultaneous submission. Sample: $3 postpaid. Submit 5 pp. or less. Reports in 4 months. Pays 2 copies and a year's subscription. Editor comments on rejections "occasionally, particularly if we are interested in the MS. Send us poems of high quality which speak authentically from human experience."**

MISSOURI REVIEW (II), University of Missouri, 107 Tate Hall, Columbia, MO 65211, phone 314-882-4474, founded 1978, poetry editor Greg Michalson, is a quality literary journal, $6 \times 9″$, 250 pp., which appears 3 times a year, **buys 100 poems per year at $10 minimum per poem. Submit maximum of 6. No simultaneous submissions. Photocopies, dot-matrix OK. Reports in 8-10 weeks. Sample: $5.**

MR. COGITO PRESS; MR. COGITO, (II), U.C. Box 627, Pacific University, Forest Grove, OR 97116, or 3314 S.E. Brooklyn, Portland, OR 97202, founded 1973, poetry editors John M. Gogol and Robert A. Davies. *Mr. Cogito*, published 2-3 times per year, is a tall, skinny ($4\frac{1}{2} \times 11″$) magazine, 24-26 pp. of poetry. The copy I examined was printed in a variety of type styles. The editors want "**no prose put in lines. Yes: wit, heightened language, craft. Open to all schools and subjects and groups of poets.**" They have published poetry by Dian Million, Elizabeth Woody, Mark Osaki, Kevin Irie, and Tomacz Jastrum. As a sample the editors selected these lines from "The Three Kings" by Stanislaw Baranczak:

> *... as bewildered as a new-born babe,*
> *you'll open the door. There will flash*
> *the star of authority.*
> *Three men. In one of them you'll recognize ...*

They use both poems in English and translation, "preferably representing each poet with several poems." The magazine has a circulation of 400, sells for $3 a copy. Subscription for 3 issues: $6. **Sample: $3. Submit 4-5 poems. Simultaneous submissions and photocopies OK. Pays copies. Reports in 2 weeks-2 months.** Mr. Cogito Press publishes collections by poets they invite from among those who have appeared in the magazine. Send SASE for catalog to buy samples. They also conduct special theme and translation contests with prizes of $50. The editors advise, "Subscribe to a magazine that seems good. Read ours before you submit. Write, write, write."

MOBIUS (I), Lake Orion Art Center, 115 S. Anderson, Lake Orion, MI 48035, phone 313-693-4986, founded 1982 by the Orion Art Center, current editor Jean H. Herman. "We welcome beginners as well as previously published poets. We are looking for your best work even though we are not a college-based forum. **No restrictions on type of poetry (please, no pornography or obscenity). Poets may submit up to five poems, up to 80-85 lines.**" As a sample the editor selected these lines from "Consider the Cat" by A.M. Peoples:

> *She's nobody's subject and not a doormat,*
> *Has her own dignity, will, and a brain.*
> *No Tabby's enticement, no Tom's caveat*
> *Pries a pale from her fence, puts a bend in her lane.*
> *She's fond of her friends but wears her own hat.*
> *Not all need to love her, but must, she makes plain,*
> *Consider the Cat.*

"*Mobius* has been published twice a year with a press run of 500, but will be expanding due to public response. Last issue was 7×10", saddle-stapled, 40 pp., photocopied from typescript on quality stock with matte card cover." **Sample: $4 postpaid. Guidelines available for SASE. "Printed authors receive one copy free. Editor will try to comment on all rejections."**

MODERN BRIDE (IV-Love/romance), 475 Park Avenue South, New York, NY 10016, phone 212-779-1999, managing editor Mary Ann Cavlin, a slick bimonthly, occasionally buys **poetry pertaining to love and marriage. Pays $25-35 for average short poem.**

MODERN HAIKU; KAY TITUS MORMINO MEMORIAL SCHOLARSHIP (IV-Form, students), P.O. Box 1752, Madison, WI 53701, founded 1969, poetry editor Robert Spiess, "is the foremost international journal of English language haiku and criticism. We are devoted to publishing only the very best haiku being written and also publish articles on haiku and have the most complete review section of haiku books. Issues average 96-104 pages. They use **haiku only. No tanka or other forms.** The Kay Titus Mormino Memorial Scholarship of $500 is for the best haiku by a high school senior, deadline early March. Send SASE for rules. **"We publish all 'schools' of haiku, but want the haiku to elicit intuition, insight, felt-depth."** They have published haiku by Geraldine Little, Paul O. Williams, Wally Swist, and Anne McKay. The editor selected this sample (poet unidentified):

> *A single pace —*
> *and the water closes round*
> *the heron's shank*

The digest-sized magazine appears 3 times a year, printed on heavy quality stock with cover illustrations especially painted for each issue by the staff artist. There are over 200 poems in each issue, circulation 650. Subscription: $11.65; per copy: $4.25. They receive 16,000-18,000 freelance submissions per year, use 800. **Sample: $4.25 postpaid. Submit on "any size sheets, any number of haiku on a sheet; but name and address on each sheet." Reports in 2 weeks. Pays $1 per haiku (but no contributor's copy). Send SASE for guidelines. The editor "frequently" comments on rejected MSS. No simultaneous submissions.** Robert Spiess says, "In regard to haiku, Daisetz T. Szuki said it succinctly well: 'A haiku does not express ideas but puts forward images reflecting intuitions.'"

THE MOMENT (II), 22704 Ventura Blvd., #245, Woodland Hills, CA 91364, founded 1987, editors Eric Lyden and Kevin Bartnof, is "randomly published, at least 4 a year. **Our magazine has a Gonzo feel to it. We enjoy poetry with a Beat edge. Any form is fine, but keep the poetry to a page or less in length."** They have recently published poetry by Charles Bukowski, Jack Micheline, Allen Ginsberg, Sean Penn, and Dr. Timothy Leary. As a sample the editor selected these lines by Philip Bailey:

> *I accepted the assignment for the sake of The Cause*
> *Besides, I had a heavy case of Freedom Fever on my mind*
> *I thought if they could do it in Europe, why not here?*
> *Re-invent the Revolution; cut out the Partisan Politicians*
> *I was one of Jack's Kids (Kerouac and Kennedy), maybe Micheline too*
> *Traveled far stretches of The Road-Inner and Outer Space*
> *Fully equipped with Marshall McCluhan's, "New, Improved; Accelerated Brain."*
>
> *Rewriting my own wasteland . . . .*

The Moment is magazine-sized, 32 pp. saddle-stapled, photocopied from typescript on quality stock, using b/w photos and graphics. Their press run is 3,000 with 350 subscriptions. It is sold in independent book stores and at poetry readings. **Sample: $3.50 postpaid. Pays 2 copies. Reports in 4-6 weeks. They consider simultaneous submissions.** Eric Lyden advises, "Be authentic! Just let it flow and don't try to be someone you're not."

MONOCACY VALLEY REVIEW (II), P.O. Box 547, Frederick, MD 21701, founded 1985, poetry editor Mary Noel, editor William Heath, is a literary review appearing twice a year. **"Submissions should be received before October 15th and March 15th. We are unable to publish long poems; other than that**

our only criterion is excellence." They don't want "the kind that hurts the ear and unfits one to continue." As a sample I selected a complete poem, "A Song for Bernadette" by Bradley Strahan:

> Trees climb a ridge.
> The train speeds
> through a painting
> of pink and lavender.
> A great grey church
> mounts the morning light.
> Transfixed I pass Lourdes,
> kneeling at the edge
> of the Pyrenees.

MVR is magazine-sized, 16 pp. saddle-stapled. "We reject over 90% of our submissions, publish at least a dozen poems an issue." Their press run is 500 with 250 subscriptions of which 5 are libraries. Subscription: $8. **Sample: $5 postpaid. Guidelines available for SASE. Pays $10 per poem plus 2 copies.** "We judge in November and April, publish in January and June. There is no backlog. We are only publishing one issue this year, but we expect to return to two issues next year."

WILLIAM MORROW AND CO. (V), 105 Madison Ave., New York, NY 10016, phone 212-889-3050, publishes poetry on standard royalty contracts, but accepts no unsolicited MSS. **Queries with samples should be submitted through an agent.**

MOSAIC PRESS (V, IV-Regional), Box 1032, Oakville, Ontario, Canada L6J 5E9, phone 416-825-2130, founded 1974, contact poetry editor Howard Aster. Publishes some of the finest and most established authors in Canada — **but primarily Canadian authors** because they receive assistance from Canada Council and Ontario Arts Council to encourage writing in Canada. They are not accepting unsolicited MSS at this time.

MOSAIC PRESS (V), 358 Oliver Rd., Cincinnati, OH 45215, phone 513-761-5977, poetry editor Miriam Irwin. The press publishes fine hardbound small books (under 3″ tall); they want **"interesting topics beautifully written in very few words — a small collection of short poems on one subject."** The editor does not want to see haiku. She has recently published collections by Marilyn Francis; the following lines, selected by her, are from "The Tin Snips" by Robert Hoeft:

> A metal woodpecker
> jaws like sharpened sin
> harmless to lumber
> nemesis to tin.

The sample miniature book the editor sent is **Water and Windfalls,** by Marilyn Francis, illustrated by Mada Leach. It is ¾ × ⅞″, flat-spined (⅛″ thick), an elegantly printed and bound hardback, with colored endpapers and gold lettering on spine and front cover. The press publishes 1 book per year, average page count 64. **She does accept freelance submissions but the writer should query first, sending 3 or more sample poems** and **"whatever you want to tell me." She says, "We don't use pseudonyms." Simultaneous submissions are OK, as are photocopied and dot-matrix MSS,** although she doesn't like the latter. **Payment is in author's copies (5 for a whole collection or book) plus a $50 honorarium. She pays $2.50 plus 1 copy for single poems.** Criticism will be provided only if requested and **"then only if we have constructive comments. If work is accepted, be prepared to wait patiently; some of our books take 4 years to complete."** The press publishes private editions but does not call it subsidy publishing. A catalog is free for SASE, and a writer can get on the mailing list for $3. The editor advises, "Type neatly, answer letters, return phone calls, include SASE."

‡**MOTS ET IMAGES: PRESS-WORK PROJECT (I)**, 2394B Adina Dr., Atlanta, GA 30324, founded 1990, editor Mark C. Young, appears twice a year. **"Want to see brave poetry with voice and character using fresh imagery. Submit 5 samples. Prejudiced toward the more economical poem but will consider longer poems if they show promise. Do not want to see anything that tries too hard. No haiku, academic, or 'selfish' personal poetry. Nothing trite or mundane."** As a sample the editor selected "The Art of Dinner," (poet unidentified):

> I know what you ate for dinner
> There are little flecks of dried guilt
> in the corners of your mouth
> on both of your faces . . .

The editor describes it as 25-45 pp. digest-sized, professionally printed, saddle-stapled, with card cover. They accept about 10 of 600 submissions received annually. Press run 200 with 5 library subscriptions. "Most copies distributed free to other editors, publishers, and writing institutions." Subscription: $10 for 2 years. **Sample, postpaid: $2. Send SASE for guidelines. Pays 3 copies. Reports in 2-4 weeks, up to 18-month backlog. Submissions** "reviewed by a staff of three so if I personally don't like it, my two assistants could well be a poem's saving grace." **Editor often comments on rejections.** He says, "The best writers that I have seen 'do it' solely for the love of the art. Good poetry transcends the cerebral and delights the sensory. To be a good writer, one must be a good reader and an even better listener."

‡MOVING PARTS PRESS; MUTANT DRONE PRESS (V), 220 Baldwin St., Santa Cruz, CA 95060, phone 408-427-2271. *Moving Parts* founded 1977, *Mutant Drone,* 1982. Poetry editor Felicia Rice says they are a "fine arts literary publisher using letterpress printing and printmaking to produce handsome and innovative books, broadsides, and prints in limited editions." *Moving Parts* has published books of poetry by Ellen Bass, William Pitt Root, Katharine Harer, and William Everson. *Mutant Drone* "the One-&-Only-Wholly-Owned Subsidiary, is free to laugh and throw punches at the whole predicament," and has published books by Charles Bukowski and Nick Zachreson. As a sample I selected the opening lines of "On a Darkening Road" by Robert Lundquist from **before/ THE RAIN,** Moving Parts Press:

> This evening the tide is low,
> Ducks walk through bunched beds of kelp
> Looking for insects.

They **pay 10% of the edition in copies. They accept no unsolicited MSS.**

‡MUD CREEK (II); LOESS PRESS (V), Box 19417, Portland, OR 97219, phone 503-238-6329, founded 1989, editors Marty Brown and Ron Ragsdale. *Mud Creek* is a literary anthology appearing twice a year using "**writing which is a reflection of the language used — i.e. writing which is conscious of the music and rhythms of the words. Also, the content should be a strong statement by the author and not be subservient to the form or style. Our bias leans away from traditional forms, although each poem is considered on its own terms. Form should suit content and not vice versa. No poems that require footnotes, or poems addressed to famous dead people, especially famous dead writers.**" They have recently published poetry by Vern Rutsala, David Memmott, and Joseph Green. As a sample the editor selected these lines from "Consenting Adults" by Stanley Poss:

> Suddenly behind me, a warm breeze
> rattles the cottonwood by the creek
> shedding pages of poetry, discarded dreams
> catching gutters, a dry flood of fragments
> chipped from the self, destined to decay.

MC is "approx. 96 pp., 5¼×7″, high quality offset, flat-spined, graphics on cover and inside, no ads." Press run 1,000 for 50+ subscribers, 200+ shelf sales. They accept 20-40 of 300-500 poems received a year. Subscription: $10. **Sample, postpaid: $5. Send SASE for guidelines. Pays 2 copies. Previously published poems OK. Name and address on each page. Reports in 2 weeks on rejections, up to 5 months on those considered for acceptance. Editor comments on submissions** "when comments are requested, or when changes may make a MS acceptable for publication." Loess Press, which publishes 1-2 chapbooks and 1-2 paperbacks a year, averaging 75 pp., **does not consider unsolicited MSS. Pays 50% of press run. "Poets are expected to assist with the marketing and sales of their chapbooks."** The editors advise, "Do not send MSS straight from one rejection to the next potential publisher — complete with multiple crease marks, paperclip stains and address changes. If a MS is a bit travel weary, it shows, and that is not in your favor. Send clean MSS. **Never send just one poem, never more than 10.**"

MUDFISH; BOX TURTLE PRESS (I, II), 184 Franklin St., New York, NY 10013, phone 212-219-9278, founded 1983, poetry editor Jill Hoffman, art editor Vladimir Urban. *Mudfish*, published by Box Turtle Press, is a journal of poetry and art that appears once a year and is looking for **energy, intensity, and originality of voice, mastery of style, the presence of passion.**" They have recently published poetry by John Ashbery, John Ash, Gerrit Henry, Stephen Sandy, and Daisy Friedman. As a sample the editor selected these lines by Jill Hoffman:

> my joblessness mornings
> my children gone, my lost period
> a phantom mare
> while the building vacates.

The next issue will have a press run of 3,000. **Mudfish 2 is $7; Mudfish 3 $6; Mudfish 4 $8; plus $1.50 shipping and handling. These three issues are available as sample copies. Pays 2 copies. They will not consider simultaneous submissions or previously published poems. Reports from** "immediately to 3 months."

J. William Griffin, publisher of Muse, a bimonthly magazine founded in 1987, invites submissions of poetry and articles about poetry. Art director Raymond H. Coleman is responsible for creating the covers.

MUSE; THE MUSE COMPETITIONS (II), P.O. Box 45, Burlington, NC 27216-0045, phone 919-570-2918 (day), founded 1987, editor/publisher J. William Griffin, is a bimonthly for poets. **"Will consider all poetry written in English. Primary consideration will be on quality and literary merit. Generally prefer shorter poems. Rarely consider over 100 lines. Any style or form.** Recently published poets include Patricia Fargnoli, Barbara Crooker, Michael Scofield, Shannon M. Rooney, and Miriam Vermilya. As a sample, the editor selected these lines by Katharyn Machan Aal:

> *For centuries man's will has preordained*
> *monogamy, a way of being sure*
> *his chosen field awaits him, furrows pure,*
> *unplowed by others where his seed has rained*
> *But now, why not another Mother Earth?*
> *A lusty woman claiming her own birth.*

Muse is magazine-sized, 24 pp. saddle-stapled on slick paper with paper cover, using art, graphics, and ads. Subscriptions: $18. **Sample: $3.50 postpaid. Send SASE for guidelines. Pays $5 and up plus 3 copies. Reports within 90 days. "Poets should submit 3-5 poems, original, unpublished, for first rights only. Typewritten, author's name and address in upper left corner. Will consider good photocopy or dot matrix. Also considers simultaneous submissions." Editor comments "if the MS comes close to acceptance."** They sponsor The Muse Competitions (poetry) quarterly with prizes ranging from $15-300 and publication, $3/poem entry fee, deadlines February, May, August and November. They also offer an annual Calendar competition and publish a poetry calendar, paying $50 if poem is accepted, $2/poem entry fee, deadline August 31. Write for guidelines. Bill Griffin advises, "Beginning poets should learn their craft by reading quality poetry and what knowledgeable poets are writing about poetry and the craft of writing poetry. This process must be a selective process, however. Poetry is chiseled, concrete language imbued with rhythm (not necessarily metrical) working in the realm of emotion. It is not merely the sentimental outpourings of how one feels nor is poetry the vehicle for statement of ideas. To write good poetry, one should read good poetry."

MUSIC CITY SONG FESTIVAL; SOUNDMAKERS (IV-Form), Box 17899-P, Nashville, TN 37217, phone 615-834-0027, established in 1979. The Festival publishes a free annual magazine, *SoundMakers*, that "includes articles by industry pros on a variety of music-related topics, including lyric writing. The Festival also sponsors an annual contest for song lyrics (Professional, Amateur and Novice divisions) and poetry with commercial song potential (Lyric Poem). Contest also includes songwriting and vocal divisions. Prizes total over $250,000. At least 433 cash and/or merchandise winners. Past sponsors include Atari Computer, Magnavox, Peavey, Shure, Smith Corona, Tascam and Technics. Musical Categories Available: Pop/Top 40, Country, MOR/Adult Contemporary, Rock/R&B/Soul, Gospel/

Contemporary Christian and Novelty/Miscellaneous. Cash and/or merchandise awards for first through tenth place in *each* category. *SoundMakers* magazine and entry information free upon request — no obligation. Entry fee varies with level of competition. Entries must be accompanied by an official entry form. October 15 deadline. "Lyric Division entries judged on song structure, consistency, originality and commerciality. Lyric Poem Division designed for poems with commercial song potential — song structure is not one of the judging criteria." The top six Lyric Poem entries are published in the magazine. **Important Note:** "Entering the Music City Song Festival does not tie up your material in any way. You are free to continue submitting your material to other markets throughout the competition. Entering the competition or winning an award does not give the MCSF any publishing or other rights to your material." The editor advises, "Successful entries, like successful songs, follow universal themes — they express thought and emotions everyone has felt at one time or another in a fresh, new way. *Avoid clichés and abstract topics*. Individuals who write lyrics and are looking for someone to write music should contact songwriter organizations or the local chapter of the American Federation of Musicians. Reading or placing classified ads in music-related publications or association newsletters is another good way to find a collaborator. Don't pay to have your 'song poems' set to music by someone you don't know."

MUSIC WORKS (IV—Themes), 1087 Queen St. W., Toronto, Ontario M6J 1H3 Canada, phone 416-533-0192, founded 1978, editor Gayle Young, a tabloid triannual journal of contemporary music. The editor says, **"The poetry we publish usually directly relates to the musical themes we are dealing with — usually it is poetry written by the (music) composer or performers we are featuring."** Recent poets published include bpnichol, Colin Morton, and Jackson Maclow. The magazine is 48 pp., with b/w visuals, b/w photography, some illustrative graphics and scores and accompanied by 60-minute cassette. Circulation is 1,600, of which 500 are subscriptions. Price is $4/issue or $10 for the paper plus cassette. **Sample: $4 postpaid. The magazine pays Canadian contributors $20-50 per contribution plus 2-3 free copies. Considers simultaneous submissions. They report on submissions within 2 months, and there is no backlog before publication.**

‡MUTATED VIRUSES; MUTATED VIRUSES PRESS (II) 1094 W. Pratt Apt. 1E, Chicago, IL 60626, phone 312-338-1373, founded 1986, editor Angi Lowry. "We publish a little bit of everything, much of it experimental or avant-garde. We'll try on anything at least once. We produce one poetry/art magazine every other month and a series of poetry/art chapbooks. Poetry: **the more bizarre the better; we like poetry that challenges the boundaries, breaks them down. Nothing overly academic or traditional.**" They have recently published poetry by Walt Phillips, Ed Mycue, Sigmund Weiss, B.A. Niditch, Judson Crews, and Ronald Edward Kittle. As a sample the editor selected these lines by Lyn Lifshin:

> on the edge your
> voice a quilt
> of skin i sweat
> then freeze under

The magazine is digest-sized, desk-top publishing, various sized type on quality stock with avant-garde art, the number of pages varying with each issue. "I receive about 7,000 poems a year, probably more, and accept about 40%" Press run 1,500. No price indicated. **Send SASE for guidelines. Pays "as many copies as they want." Reports in 1-2 weeks. For chapbook consideration send 10 samples. Pays copies: "as many as they want."** The editor says, *M.V.* operates on a free-but-please-donate-postage-or--money-if-you-can basis. If people don't have any $$, I'll send it to them free. I like giving it away. That goes for back issues also. We believe in keeping prices as cheap as possible."

‡MY RESTLESS SOUL; ASTRAL IMAGES POETRY PUBLISHERS (I), 1415 N. Overlook Dr., Greenville, NC 27834, poetry editor Kris Phillips. *MRS* is a poetry quarterly; Astral Images publishes an annual anthology of poetry "submitted to and generally accepted in *MRS*." They also hope to publish chapbooks of contest winners in the near future. "Though our emphasis is poetry, we also publish writing tips, market updates, and some just plain good reading — sci-fi, horror, heart-grabbers — let's have a look. We like it all. **No restrictions on length, style or subject-matter as long as it is done in good taste. No aimless rambling. Let us 'see' what you are feeling. We love images. Show us the beauty in the mundane. Let us cry for the common laborer and/or feel the frustration mingled with beauty in the everyday nothings we take for granted. No tree-hugging flowers and butterflies, please! We do not publish very much rhyme. That is to say, rhyme for the *sake* of rhyme.**" They have recently published poetry by Dean Lipkind, Betty Wray, Ree Young ... "our list is small but we do have some damn good reading." As a sample the editor selected these lines (poet unidentified):

> . . . Mother too busy giving birth to nine others —
>   exactly like you
> Father too busy preachin' an' prayin' that maybe things will

> change,
>
> and they never do.

I have not seen their publications. "We probably receive about 500 submissions per year. We use about 10 poems per issue." Press run: 100 for 60 subscribers of which 4 are libraries. Subscriptions: $12. **Sample, postpaid: $3. Send SASE for guidelines. Pays 1 copy. "No hand-written submissions, please! Submit in batches of 3. Wait for a reply before submitting more material."** Reports immediately — 6 weeks "depending on backlog." Simultaneous submissions and previously published poems OK. Editor comments on submissions "only if we feel the author has exceptional potential but is not quite right for *MRS*."

NADA PRESS; BIG SCREAM (II, IV-Themes, bilingual), 2782 Dixie SW, Grandville, MI 49418, phone 616-531-1442, founded 1974, poetry editor David Cope. *Big Scream* is "a brief anthology of mostly 'unknown' poets, 1 time per year. We are promoting a **continuation of objectivist tradition begun by Williams and Reznikoff. We want objectivist-based short works; some surrealism; basically short, tight work that shows clarity of perception and care in its making. Also poems in Spanish — *not* transla-**tions." They have published poetry by Antler, James Ruggia, Richard Kostelanetz, Andy Clausen, Allen Ginsberg, John Steinbeck, Jr., Bob Rixon, and Janet Cannon. As a sample David Cope selected some lines of his own:

> an old blind black vet blows
> Camptown Races on his harp,
> stomping his one foot in time;
> another, legless, claps his hands

Big Scream is 35 pp., magazine-sized, xerograph on 60 lb. paper, side-stapled, "sent gratis to a select group of poets and editors; **sample copies $3;** subscriptions to institutions $6 per year." He has a print run of 100. He receives "several hundred (not sure)" freelance submissions per year, uses "very few." **Submit 10 pp. Simultaneous submissions OK. Reports in 1-14 days. Pays copies. No cover letter. "If poetry interests me, I will ask the proper questions of the poet."** No dot-matrix. Pays as many copies as requested within reason. Order sample chapbooks $3 each. Comments on rejections "If requested and MS warrants it." David Cope advises: "Read Pound's essay, "A Retrospect," then Reznikoff and Williams; follow through the Beats and NY School, especially Denby & Berrigan, and you have our approach to writing well in hand. I expect to be publishing *BS* regularly 10 years from now, same basic format."

NANCY'S MAGAZINE (I, IV-Theme), P.O. Box 02108, Columbus, OH 43202, founded 1983, editor Nancy Bonnell-Kangas, who describes her publication as a "variety magazine." **She wants to see "experimental, everyday life" poetry, but not "sentimental."** She has published work by Owen Hill and William Talcott. As a sample I selected this complete poem, "In the Cabin," by Danny Barbare:

> The candlelight
> Awoke a little room
> Damp and dirty

The magazine is "**often thematic,** leaning towards literary (without ever getting there)." It appears twice a year, $7 \times 8\frac{1}{2}$", 36 pp., saddle-stapled, offset from various sizes of photoreduced copy (some of it sideways, at angles, or upside down), using cartoons, b/w photos, ads, decorations, with light matte card cover, circulation 1,000, of which 200-250 are shelf sales. **Sample: $2 postpaid. Send SASE for guidelines. Pays 2 copies. Reports in 1 month.** Nancy Bonnell-Kangas advises, "Send work that helps explain why we are where we are."

THE NATION; LEONORE MARSHALL/NATION PRIZE FOR POETRY; DISCOVERY/THE NATION PRIZES (III), 72 Fifth Ave., New York, NY 10011, founded 1865, poetry editor Grace Schulman. *The Nation*'s **only requirement for poetry is "excellence,"** which can be inferred from the list of poets they have published: W.S. Merwin, Maxine Kumin, Donald Justice, James Merrill, Richard Howard, May Swenson, Sharon Olds, J. D. McClatchy, and Amy Clampitt. **Pay for poetry is 1 copy.** The magazine co-sponsors the Leonore Marshall/Nation Prize for Poetry which is an annual award of $7,500 for the outstanding book of poems published in the U.S. in each year; and the "Discovery/The Nation Prizes" ($200 each plus a reading at The Poetry Center, 1395 Lexington Ave., New York, NY 10128. Submit up to 500 lines by mid-February. Send SASE for application). The editor chose this as a sample from a poem in the *Nation*, 1939, by W.B. Yeats:

> Like a long-legged fly upon the stream
> His mind moves upon silence.

NATIONAL ENQUIRER (II, IV-Humor), Lantana, FL 33464, assistant editor Michele Cooke, is a weekly tabloid, circulation 4,550,000, which uses **short poems, most of them humorous and traditional rhyming verse. "We want poetry with a message or reflection on the human condition or everyday life.**

Avoid sending obscure or 'arty' poetry or poetry for art's sake. Also looking for philosophical and inspirational material. Occasionally uses longer poetry (up to 12 or 16 lines) of either a serious or a humorous nature. Submit seasonal/holiday material at least 3 months in advance." Send SASE with all submissions. Pays $25 after publication; original material only.

NAZARENE INTERNATIONAL HEADQUARTERS; STANDARD; WONDER TIME; LISTEN; BREAD; TEENS TODAY; HERALD OF HOLINESS (IV-Religious, children), 6401 The Paseo, Kansas City, MO 64131, phone 816-333-7000. Each of the magazines published by the Nazarenes has a separate editor, focus, and audience. *Standard*, circulation 177,000, is a weekly **inspirational "story paper" with Christian leisure reading for adults. Send SASE for free sample and guidelines. Uses a poem each week. Submit maximum of 5, maximum of 50 lines each. Pays 25¢ a line.** *Wonder Time*, poetry editors Evenlyn Beals and Robyn Ginter, a publication of the Children's Ministries Department, Church of the Nazarene, "**is committed to reinforcement of the Biblical concepts taught in the Sunday School curriculum, using poems 4-8 lines, simple, with a message, easy to read, for 1st and 2nd graders. It should not deal with much symbolism.**" The editors selected this sample poem by Sharon Briggs-Fanny:

> You're with me, Lord, when I am weak;
> I only have to pray.
> And when the evil seems so strong,
> You show me the right way.

Wonder Time is a weekly 4 pp. leaflet, magazine-sized, newsprint, circulation 37,000. **Sample free for SASE. Reports in 8-12 weeks. Pays minimum of $3 — 25¢/line, and 4 contributor's copies. Send SASE for guidelines. For** *Listen, Bread, Teens Today* and *Herald of Holiness*, write individually for guidelines and samples.

NEBO: A LITERARY JOURNAL (II), English Dept., Arkansas Tech University, Russellville, AR 72801-2222, founded 1982, poetry editor Michael Ritchie, appears in May and December. Regarding poetry they say, "**We accept all kinds, all styles, all subject matters and will publish a longer poem if it is outstanding. We are especially interested in formal poetry.**" They have published poetry by Jack Butler, Timothy Steele, Turner Cassity, Wyatt Prunty, Charles Martin, Julia Randall, Brenda Hillman. As a sample they selected the first 4 lines of "Sage Counsel" by Timothy Steele:

> If, stung to rage, you'd quell your boiling blood,
> Regard the one who happens to annoy,
> And think, The man is mortal. The thought should
> Convert your heart to pity — or to joy.

Nebo is digest-sized, 50-70 pp., professionally printed on quality matte stock with matte card cover. The press run "varies." Per issue: $3. Subscription: $5. **Sample: $1 postpaid. Pays 2 copies. "Please no onion skin or offbeat colors." Simultaneous submissions OK. Reports in 1 week-3 months. Editor comments on rejections "if the work has merit but requires revision and resubmission. We do all we can to help."**

THE NEBRASKA REVIEW; TNR AWARDS (II), ASH 212, University of Nebraska, Omaha, NE 68182-0324, phone 402-554-2771, founded 1973, co-editor Art Homer, a semi-annual literary magazine publishing fiction and poetry with occasional essays. The editor wants "**Lyric poetry from 10-200 lines, preference being for under 100 lines. Subject matter is unimportant, as long as it has some. Poets should have mastered form, meaning poems should have form, not simply 'demonstrate' it.**" He doesn't want to see "concrete, inspirational, *poesa vivsa*, didactic, merely political." He has published poetry by Laurie Blauner, David Hopes, Leslie Adrienne Miller, Richard Robbins, and Vern Rutsala. As a sample, he selected the following lines from "Matisse's Antoinette" by Peggy Shumaker:

> In the bath, she stretches full-length —
> two bruised red peonies surface.
> Because she did not love him, she allowed
> one young man to stroke the sleek slope
> of her hip, wondering what he would find
> to possess, what she had
> to parcel, what one
> needs must conserve always. How little
> it has to do with the body.

The magazine is 6 × 9", nicely printed, 60 pp. flat-spined (but the glue doesn't hold), glossy card cover with b/w illustration on green. It is a publication of the Writer's Workshop at the University of Nebraska and it was formerly called *Smackwarm*; it retains the volume and issue number of that publication. Circulation is 400, of which 260 are subscriptions and 80 go to libraries. Price per issue is $3.50, subscription $6/year. **Sample available for $2 postpaid. Pay is 2 copies and 1-year subscription. "Clean typed copy strongly preferred. Dot-matrix strongly discouraged."**

Reporting time is 3-4 months and time to publication 3-6 months. The editor says, "Your first allegiance is to the poem. Publishing will come in time, but it will always be less than you feel you deserve. Therefore, don't look to publication as a reward for writing well; it has no relationship." The TNR Awards of $300 each in poetry and fiction are published in the spring issue. Entry fee: $6 subscription. You can enter as many times as desired. Deadline November 30th.

NEGATIVE CAPABILITY; NEGATIVE CAPABILITY PRESS; EVE OF ST. AGNES COMPETITION (II), 62 Ridgelawn Rd. E, Mobile, AL 36608-2465, founded 1981, poetry editor Sue Walker. *Negative Capability* is a tri-quarterly of verse, fiction, commentary, music and art. The press publishes broadsides, chapbooks, perfect-bound paperbacks and hardbacks. They want **both contemporary and traditional poetry. "Quality has its own specifications — length and form."** They have recently published a selection of my poetry and prose, William Packard, Valentin Rasputin, Viktor Astafyev, and Leon Driskell. Sue Walker selected these lines from my poem, "A Handful of Grit":

> *Up there was where those bass did business. They*
> *would glide from their cave as from a subway, ride*
> *the invisible stream of the well and stately rise*
> *like paunchy capitalists on an elevator —*

The editor says, "Reaching irritably after a few facts will not describe *Negative Capability*. Read it to know what quality goes to form creative achievement. Shakespeare had negative capability; do you?" In its short history this journal has indeed achieved a major prominence on our literary scene. It is a flat-spined, elegantly printed, digest-sized, 150 + pp. format, glossy card color cover with art, circulation 1,000. About 60 pp. of each issue are devoted to poetry. Subscription: $12; per copy: $3.50. They receive about 1,200 freelance submissions per year, use 350. **Sample: $4 postpaid. Reports in 6-8 weeks. Pays 2 copies. Send SASE for guidelines. For book publication, query with 10-12 samples and "brief letter with major publications, significant contributions, awards. We like to know a person as well as their poem." Replies to queries in 3-4 weeks, to submissions (if invited) in 6-8 weeks. Photocopy, dot-matrix OK. Payment arranged with authors. Editor sometimes comments on rejections.** They offer an Annual Eve of St. Agnes Competition with major poets as judges.

NER/BLQ (NEW ENGLAND REVIEW/BREAD LOAF QUARTERLY), (III), Middlebury College, Middlebury, VT 05753, phone 802-388-3711, ext 5075, founded 1978, editors T.R. Hummer, Maura High, and Devon Jersild, *NER/BLQ* is a prestige literary quarterly, 6×9″, 160 + pp., flat-spined, elegant make-up and printing on heavy stock, glossy cover with art. **Pays. Reports in 6-8 weeks.** Poets published recently include Toi Derricotte, Albert Goldbarth, Norman Dubie, Philip Booth, and Carol Frost. As a sample the editors selected these lines from Chase Twichell's "The Cut":

> *I had a sorrow that misled me.*
> *Because we were childless,*
> *I had, out of some sovereign,*
> *stupid longing in my body,*
> *invented a ghost-child,*
> *a third person . . .*

NER/BLQ also sponsors an annual narrative poetry competition, first prize $500, publication of the poem, and a lifetime subscription, entry fee $2 per poem. Deadline June 1. Length: up to 400 lines. Sample: $4 postpaid. **"Poems for the competition or for regular publication in the magazine must demonstrate craft, inventiveness, and visceral appeal."**

NEW CICADA (IV-Form), 40-11 Kubo, Hobara, Fukushima, Japan 960-06, phone 0245-75-4226, founded 1984, editor Tadao Okazaki. *New Cicada* is "the first and only magazine introducing the universal definition of haiku that is applicable to all languages. Of all existing Japanese haiku magazines in English, has the longest history of publication." As a sample, he chose the following by an unidentified poet:

> *Slowly I soak*
> *my painful hands*
> *in the hillside spring*

The purpose of the magazine, which appears twice yearly in March and September, is "to raise the quality of haiku in English, and to introduce the universal definition of classical haiku." Volumes 1 through 5 of *Cicada* were published in Toronto, Canada, by Eric W. Amann, founding editor, and later by the Haiku Society of Canada. The digest-sized publication is offset from dot-matrix copy with a b/w frontispiece; one-color matte card cover, saddle-stapled. Price is $4/issue, $6 for a 1-year subscription. **Sample: $4 postpaid by US personal check or 7 international reply coupons. The editor requests a self-addressed postcard and an IRC for reports. No MSS returned. It will take up to approximately 6 months to get a report. No payment in any form is**

offered for published poems. The editor who says he "introduced the universal definition of haiku to the world for the first time" maintains that "(1) the haiku form in any language is a triplet verse of 3-4-3 beats; (2) the 3-4-3 syllable verse is the shortest, and trimeter-tetrameter-trimeter triplet in general is the longest classical haiku form in English; and (3) the Japanese haiku is recited in iambic trimeter—tetrameter—trimeter form, and is fundamentally a ballad." The editor says, "The traditional haiku is an unrhymed triplet ballad; the old definition of haiku as a form of syllabic verse is wrong. Free verse haiku must be no longer than 3 lines, preferably with subject matter of nature or man and nature."

NEW COLLAGE MAGAZINE (II), 5700 N. Tamiami Trail, Sarasota, FL 34243-2197, phone 813-359-4360, founded 1970, poetry editor A. McA. Miller. *New CollAge* provides "a forum for contemporary poets, both known and undiscovered. We are **partial to fresh slants on traditional prosodies and poetry with clear focus and clear imagery. No greeting-card verse. We prefer poems shorter than five single-spaced pages. We like a maximum of 3-5 poems per submission."** They have recently published poetry by Peter Meinke, Yvonne Sapia, Lola Haskins, J.P. White, Peter Klappert, Peter Wild, Stephen Corey, and Malcolm Glass. The editor selected these sample lines from "The Palm at the Edge of the Bay" by Daniel Bosch:

> *I would need a ship to moor here, really,*
> *if I were to earn this girth of fibrous hemp,*
> *round-waisted, tall, leaning a head*
> *into the corner a cross-breeze walls itself against . . .*

The magazine appears 3 times a year, 28-32 pp. of poetry in each issue, circulation 500 with 200 subscriptions of which 30 are libraries. They receive about 5,000 poems from freelance submissions per year, use 90. Subscription: $6; per copy: $2; **sample: $2. Photocopy OK. Simultaneous submissions not read. Reports in 6 weeks. Pays 2 copies. Editor sometimes comments on rejections.** Editor "Mac" Miller advises, "Sending a MS already marked 'copyright' is absurd and unprofessional, unless your name is Robert Lowell. MSS may be marked 'first North American Serials only,' though this is unnecessary."

THE NEW CRITERION (II), The Foundation for Cultural Review, Inc., 850 7th Ave., New York, NY 10019, poetry editor Robert Richman, is a monthly (except July and August) review of ideas and the arts, $7 \times 10''$, flat-spined, 90+ pp., which uses poetry of high literary quality. They have recently published poems by James Ulmer, Alan Shapiro, Elizabeth Spires and Herbert Morris. I selected these sample lines from "A question" by Luke Zilles:

> *The picket fence in front*
> *is a crotchety row of sticks.*
> *On the rotted sill of the window*
> *snow scrolls against the glass.*

Sample: $4 plus postage.

NEW DELTA REVIEW; THE EYSTER PRIZE (II), English Dept., Louisiana State University, Baton Rouge, LA 70803, editor Kathleen Fitzpatrick, who says, "We call ourselves a 'breakthrough magazine'; we publish work of merit by **writers who for one reason or another are still slightly outside the mainstream. Most of them are younger writers who have not yet built a reputation. We are** *wide open:* **poets who are brave enough to take chances and skilled enough not to get spattered. No minimalist, compromised workshop voice. Stay young and write poems."** They have recently published poetry by Michel DeGuy, Ava Leavell Haymon, and John Woods. *NDR* appears twice a year, $6 \times 9''$ flat-spined, 70-90 pp., typeset and printed on quality stock with full-color glossy card cover with art. Its press run is 300, with 50 subscriptions of which 10 are libraries, the rest for shelf sales. Subscription: $7. **Sample: $3.50 postpaid. Pays 2 copies (and 50% off for others). Submit "2 copies please." Photocopy OK, no dot matrix, simultaneous submissions, or previously published poems. Reports in 1-3 months. MSS not read in summer. Editor "sometimes" comments on rejections. "Often I will return a piece and ask for revision."** The Eyster Prize of $50 is awarded to the best story and best poem in each issue. Kathleen Fitzpatrick says, "The question we get asked most often is 'what sort of poetry are you looking for?' What can I say? The *good* sort. Less is still not more. The best things we see are pieces with fire in their lines by poets with the skill to put it together well. Sparks should fly from your typewriter keys."

NEW DIRECTIONS PUBLISHING CORPORATION; NEW DIRECTIONS IN PROSE AND POETRY (III, IV-Translations), 80 Eighth Ave., New York, NY 10011, founded 1936, address "Poetry Editor." New Directions is "a small publisher of 20th-Century literature with an emphasis on the experimental," publishing about 36 paperback and hardback titles each year. **"We are looking for highly unusual, literary, experimental poetry. We can't use traditional poetry, no matter how accomplished. Ninety-five percent of the time we publish poets who have built up a reputation in the literary magazines and**

journals. It is generally not financially feasible for us to take on unknown poets." They have published poetry by William Carlos Williams, Ezra Pound, Denise Levertov, Jerome Rothenberg, Robert Creeley, Michael McClure, Kenneth Rexroth, H.D., Robert Duncan, Stevie Smith, David Antin, Hayden Carruth, George Oppen, Dylan Thomas, Lawrence Ferlinghetti, Jimmy Santiago Baca, Rosmarie Waldrop, and Gary Snyder. As a sample I selected these lines from Thomas Merton's verse play, "The Tower of Babel, a Morality" in his collection, **The Strange Islands**:

> *Words have always been our best soldiers.*
> *They have defeated meaning in every engagement*
> *And have almost made an end of reality.*

Their annual anthology, **New Directions in Prose and Poetry**, is an international collection of avant-garde literature, about 190 pp., flat-spined, "trade paperbook-sized," published in cloth and paper, and they are **not looking for poetry** for the next two years—"terrible backlog." **Reports on submissions in 4 months; may be 2 years until publication. "Please send a sampling of about 10 typed, photocopied poems, preferably not a simultaneous submission." They look at all submissions but "chances are slight."** Terms for book publication "all depend." To see samples, try the library, or purchase from their catalog (available), local bookstores, or their distributor, W. W. Norton. New Directions advises, "Getting published is not easy, but the best thing to do is to work on being published in the magazines and journals, thus building up an audience. Once the poet has an audience, the publisher will be able to sell the poet's books. Avoid vanity publishers and read a lot of poetry."

NEW HOPE INTERNATIONAL (II), 20 Werneth Ave., Gee Cross, Cheshire U.K. SK14 5NL, founded 1969, editor Gerald England, is a **"magazine of poetry, fiction, literary essays, news and reviews." They also publish chapbooks. "Most types of poetry are acceptable, no limit on length. Content without form and form without content are equally unacceptable. Poems must be well-written within the form chosen but also have something to communicate in the widest sense. Don't want to see doggerel, anti-Christian work, depressive self-examinations."** They have recently published poetry by Hamish Brown, Andrew Darlington, John Ditsky, Prescott Foster, Thomas Land, Sue Moules, Colin Nixon, Teresinka Pereira, Mary Rodbeck Stanko, and John Ward. The following lines are from "Street Boys" by Ruth Wildes Schuler:

> *Hope is always for sale*
> *in the streets of Istanbul.*
> *Dreams lie layers deeper,*
> *fluttering in the wind . . .*

The digest-sized magazine, 32 pp., is lightly photocopied from computer typesetting, mimeograph paper, saddle-stapled, color paper cover, using b/w line drawings and decorations. Circulation 500 for 275 subscriptions of which 20 are libraries. $4 per issue, $20 for 6 issues including chapbooks and the *New Hope International Review Supplement* (A4 size, 28 pp. cost separately $3). **Sample: $3 postpaid. "Those who subscribe can expect much more in the way of feedback. Manuscripts read at anytime but those received in March-June or September-December can expect speedier replies." Reports in "maximum 6 months" (usually no more than 5 weeks). Pays 1 copy. Put name and address on each sheet; not more than 6 at a time; simultaneous submissions *not* encouraged. Photocopy OK, dot-matrix OK, "NLQ please!" Translations should include copy of original. For book publication, query first with 50 samples and bio. "Poets must fully participate in book marketing—buy copies at 50% discount for resale."** The editor advises, "New poets should read widely and keep their minds open to work of different styles. 'Progress is a going forward from—not towards.' "

NEW HORIZONS POETRY CLUB (II, IV-Membership), Box 5561, Chula Vista, CA 92012, phone 619-474-4715, founded 1984, poetry editor Alex Stewart. This organization offers poetry contests of various sorts for experienced writers, publishing winners in an anthology. They also offer newsletters, workshops, and critiques and publish anthologies of members' poetry. Membership (includes 4 newsletters) $10/year. Special membership (individual tuition) $25/year. **"We expect poets to know technique, to be familiar with traditional forms and to be able to conform to requirements re: category, style, length, impact, originality, imagery and craftsmanship. Nothing amateurish, trite, in poor taste or over-sentimental."** They have recently published poetry by Grace Haynes Smith, Josephine Greer, Thelma Schiller, and Judi Gerrard. Prizes in their contests "may vary from $100-$250 according to the contests. We offer other awards, prizes and trophies, and certificates for honorable mentions. 50 free anthologies and trophy for "mini-manuscript" winners. Entry fees are $5/2 poems, $10/5 poems. Alex Stewart offers criticism for $7/poem, $15/3 poems up to 25 lines. She says, "Beginning poets need to study technique before *rushing to get published! (Where* is what counts!) The current trend seems to be a healthy blend of traditional forms and comprehensible free verse." NHPC publishes 3 books annually, 2 in the NHPC Poets' Series (4 poets per book) and 1 anthology of prizewinning and selected poems from the semiannual contests. (Book list avilable on request.)

‡THE NEW LAUREL REVIEW (II, IV-Translations), 828 Lesseps St., New Orleans, LA 70117, founded 1971, editor Lee Meitzen Grue, "is an independent nonprofit literary magazine dedicated to fine art. Each issue contains poetry, translation, literary essays, short fiction reviews of small press books, and visual art." They want "**poetry with strong, accurate imagery. We have no particular preference in style. We try to be eclectic. No more than 3 poems in a submission.**" Recently published poets include Yevgeny Yetushenko, Enid Shomer, Sylvia Moss, Yusef Komunyakaa, and Martha McFerren. As a sample the editor selected these lines by Rudolph Lewis:

> *My blue creation: to tiptoe on a mind,*
> *a dry rose on the thread of a spider's web:*
> *guitar-played tales at moonlit crossroads,*
> *voted most likely to turn to dogs into men.*

The *Review* is 6×9", laser printed, 115 pp., original art on cover, accepts 30 poems of 300 MSS received. **Pays in contributor's copies.** It has a circulation of 500, subscription: $8; per copy: $8. **Sample: (back issue) $4 postpaid. Guidelines for SASE. Submit 3-5 poems with SASE "and" a short note with previous publications. Accepts simultaneous submissions. Reports on submissions in 3 months, publishes in 8-10 months.**

NEW LETTERS; NEW LETTERS POETRY PRIZE (II), University of Missouri-Kansas City, Kansas City, MO 64110, phone 816-276-1168, founded 1934 as *University Review*; became *New Letters* in 1971, managing editor Bob Stewart, editor James McKinley, "is dedicated to publishing the best short fiction, best contemporary poetry, literary articles, photography and art work by both established writers and new talents." They want "**contemporary writing of all types—free verse poetry preferred, short works are more likely to be accepted than very long ones.**" They have recently published poetry by Lyn Lifshin, Hayden Carruth, Geoff Hewitt, James B. Hall, Louis Simpson, Vassar Miller and John Tagliabue. As a sample I selected the first 2 of 9 stanzas of "Unrequited Love" by Marilyn Chin:

> *Because you stared into the black lakes of her eyes*
> *you shall drown in them.*
> *Because you tasted the persimmon on her lips*
> *you shall dig your moist grave.*

The flat-spined, professionally printed quarterly, glossy 2-color cover with art, 6×9", uses about 65 (of 120+) pp. of poetry in each issue, circulation 1,845 with 1,520 subscriptions of which about 40% are libraries. Subscription: $15; per copy: $4. They receive about 7,000 submissions per year, use less than 1%, have a 6 month backlog. **Sample: $4 postpaid. Send no more than 6 poems at once, no simultaneous submissions. "We strongly prefer original typescripts rather than photocopy or dot-matrix. We don't read between May 15 and October 15. No query needed." They report in 2-6 weeks, pay a small fee plus 2 copies. Occasionally James McKinley comments on rejections.** The New Letters Poetry Prize of $750 is given annually for a group of 3-6 poems, entry fee $10 (check payable to New Letters Literary Awards). Deadline May 15. They also publish occasional anthologies, selected and edited by McKinley.

NEW METHODS: THE JOURNAL OF ANIMAL HEALTH TECHNOLOGY (IV-Specialized/animals), P.O. Box 22605, San Francisco, CA 94122-0605, phone 415-664-3469, founded as *Methods* in 1976, poetry editor Ronald S. Lippert, AHT, is a "monthly networking service in the animal field, open forum, active in seeking new avenues of knowledge for our readers, combining animal professionals under one roof." They want poetry which is "**animal related but not cutesy**" They get few submissions, but if they received more of quality, they would publish more poetry. They publish a maximum of one poem in each monthly issue, circulation 5,600 to subscribers, of which over 73 are libraries. Price per issue, $1.50; subscription $18. **Sample: $2 each includes postage and handling; a listing of all back issues and the topics covered is available for $5. Reports in 1-2 months. Double space with one-inch margins, include dated cover letter. Everything typed. Guidelines are available for SASE. Pays complimentary copies. Comment on rejected MSS? "Always!"** Ronald Lippert advises, "Keep up with current events."

NEW MEXICO HUMANITIES REVIEW (II, IV-Regional), Humanities Dept., New Mexico Tech, Socorro, NM 87801, phone 505-835-5200, founded 1978, editors Jerry Bradley, John Rothfork, and Lou Thompson, *NMHR* is published twice a year, invites MSS "**designed for a general academic readership and those that pursue Southwestern themes or those using interdisciplinary methods.**" There are no restrictions as to type of poetry; "*NMHR* publishes first class, literary poetry," but does not want "**sentimental verse, shallow, pointlessly rhymed ideas.**" Poets published include George Garrett, Ralph Mills, Jr., Fred Chappell, Peter Wild, and Walter McDonald. As a sample the editor selected the following lines by M. L. Hester:

> *Stainless steel is the percentage sink.*
> *It will not chip, rust scratch or peel.*
> *And it shines. The beauty of light*

bouncing in the AM kills all germs democratically;
The review is digest-sized, 150 pp., printed by offset on white stock, with an embossed, one-color matte card cover, flat-spined; there are graphics and ads. Circulation is 650, of which 350 are subscriptions; other copies are sold at poetry readings, writers' workshops, etc. Price per issue is $5, subscription $10/year. *NMHR* **pays one year's subscription. Reports in 6 weeks, 6 months between acceptance and publication. No simultaneous submissions.**

NEW ORLEANS POETRY JOURNAL PRESS (II), 2131 General Pershing St., New Orleans, LA 70115, phone 504-891-3458, founded 1956, publisher/editor Maxine Cassin. **"We prefer to publish relatively new and/or little-known poets of unusual promise or those inexplicably neglected—'the real thing.' " She does not want to see "cliché or doggerel, anything incomprehensible or too derivative, or workshop exercises." Query first. She does not accept freelance submissions** for her chapbooks, which are flat-spined paperbacks. She has recently published books by Charles de Gravelles, Vassar Miller, Everett Maddox, Charles Black, and Martha McFerren. As a sample, the editor selected these lines from "Millenary" by Raeburn Miller:

The sun is an old terror.
we know it is wrong

to deduce from the eyeless denizens
of caves acquired characteristics —

Their most recent book is **Hanoi Rose** by Ralph Adamo, a professionally printed hardback. **The editor reports on queries in 2-3 months, MSS in the same time period, if solicited. Simultaneous submissions will possibly be accepted, and she has no objection to photocopied MSS. Pay is in author's copies, usually 50 to 100.** Ms. Cassin does not subsidy publish at present and does not offer grants or awards. For aspiring poets, she quotes the advice Borges received from his father: "1) Read as much as possible! 2) Write only when you *must*, and 3) Don't rush into print!" As a small press editor and publisher, she urges poets to read instructions in **Poet's Market** listings with utmost care!

NEW ORLEANS REVIEW (II,IV—Translations), Box 195, Loyola University, New Orleans, LA 70118, phone 504-865-2294, founded 1968, poetry editor John Biguenet. It is 100+ pp., flat-spined, elegantly printed with glossy card cover using a full-color painting. Circulation is 750. **Sample: $9 postpaid.** As a sample I selected these lines from "End of the Party" by James Nolan:

We spend life asking: "how much?"
and we catch "how much?"; in our parent's eyes,
in their voices, hands, how much for this,
for that, how much land, how much bread, . . .
Pays for published poems. Reports in 3 months.

NEW POETRY REVIEW (I), 709 7th St., Huntingburg, IN 47542, phone 812-683-5556, founded 1987, editor Dr. Ronald E. Sanders, is an 8 pp. monthly newsletter open to beginners, **accepting 60-70% of poetry received, "usually" responds with criticism and suggestions. "Prefer 24 lines or less. No sexually explicit, no epic poetry." Sample: $1 postpaid.** They have recently published poetry by James Bostic, Kathleen Lee Mendel, and Leona Adams. As a sample the editor selected these lines by Bobbie Taylor:

My dad only tells
Parts of war stories.
I've heard other men
do the same thing.
But I'm older now —
I've read a lot,
And I listen
Between the lines.

The newsletter is magazine-sized, desk-top published. They use over 200 of 500+ poems received a year. Press run 500-1,000 for "223 subscriptions and growing." Subscription: $8. **Sample: $1 postpaid. Pays 3-5 copies. "Subscribers receive preference but subscription is not a prerequisite for submission. Any legible form. Typed preferred, one poem to page, double-spaced, name and address in upper left hand corner, 5 poems maximum per submission" They will consider simultaneous submissions and previously published poems. Editor "always" comments on rejections.** Conducts contests with prizes of up to $100. The editor says, "We are an 'entry level' publication open to poets of all ages who seek visibility. We desire poetry which is fresh, not copycat or cliché-ridden, and guarantee publication of accepted poetry if one subscribes to *New Poetry Review*."

THE NEW POETS SERIES, INC.; CHESTNUT HILLS PRESS (II), 541 Piccadilly, Baltimore, MD 21204, phone 301-830-2863 or 828-0724, founded 1970, editors/directors Clarinda Harriss Raymond and Michael Raymond. The New Poets Series, Inc. brings out **first books by promising new poets. There is a $5 reading fee for consideration of MSS. They want "excellent, fresh, nontrendy, literate, intelligent poems. Any form (including traditional), any style. No poetry riding any one particular political, social, sexual or religous hobbyhorse."** Provides 20 copies to the author, the sales proceeds going back into the corporation to finance the next volume (usual press run: 1,000). "It has been successful in its effort to provide these new writers with a national distribution; in fact, The New Poets Series was recently named an Outstanding Small Press by the prestigious Pushcart Awards Committee, which judges some 5,000 small press publications annually." Chestnut Hills Press publishes author-subsidized books—"High quality work only, however. CHP is itself achieving a reputation for prestigious books, printing only the top 10% of MSS CHP and NPS receive." The New Poets Series also publishes an occasional anthology drawn from public reading series. They have recently published books by William Harrold, Nuala Archer, Evelyn Ritchie, Stephen Wiest, and Shelley Scott. Books by Richard Fein, Carole Lanille, and Gail Wronsky are forthcoming. Clarinda Harriss Raymond selected "Calling Canada," a complete poem by Irish writer Medbh McGuckian, as a sample:

> I talk to the darkness as if to a daughter
> Or something that once pressed from inside
> Like a street of youth. My striped notebook
> Is just a dress over my body, so I will waken
> At a touch, or for no reason at all. In it
> I learn how to cut into other people's dreams,
> How to telephone them Paris-style and how
> Like sunshine, a tenderness roughened
> Because there was so little time for snow-months
> To paint my woman's walls into sea.

Query with 10 samples, cover letter giving publication credits and bio. Reports in 6 weeks-6 months. Simultaneous submissions, photocopies OK. No dot-matrix. Editor sometimes comments briefly on rejections. MSS "are circulated to an editorial board of professional, publishing poets. NPS is very, very backlogged, but the best 10% of the MSS it receives are automatically eligible for Chestnut Hills Press consideration," a subsidy arrangement. **Send $4 for a sample volume.**

THE NEW QUARTERLY (I, II, IV-Regional), ELPP University of Waterloo, Waterloo, ON N2L 3G1 Canada, phone 519-885-1211, ext. 2837, founded 1981, managing editor Mary Merikle, is a "literary quarterly—new directions in Canadian writing." For the poetry they want, the editors have **"no preconceived conception — usually Canadian work, poetry capable of being computer typeset—4½" line length typeset lines. No greeting card verse."** They have recently published poetry by Raymond Souster, Mary di Michele, Tom Wayman, and Susan Musgrave. I have not seen *TNQ*, but the editor describes it as 120 pp., flat-spined, 6×8½", with a photograph on the cover, no graphics or art, some ads. Of 2,000 poems received per year they use 100. Press run is 600 for 300 subscriptions (10 of them libraries) and additional shelf sales. Subscription: $15 (add $2 for U.S. or overseas subscriptions). **Sample: $4 Canadian, $4 U.S. postpaid. Send SASE for guidelines. Pays $18 per poem plus 3 copies. Submit no more than 5. Reports in 3-6 months. No comments on rejections of poetry.**

THE NEW RENAISSANCE (II, IV-Translations, bilingual), 9 Heath Rd., Arlington, MA 02174, founded 1968, poetry editor James E.A. Woodbury. *the new renaissance* is "intended for the 'renaissance' person, the generalist rather than the specialist. Seeks to publish the best new writing, to offer a forum for articles of public concern, and to highlight interest in neglected writers and artists in its essay/review section. They have recently published Faiz Ahmed Faiz (Agha Shahid Ali translation), Anghel Dumbraveanu (Rob. Ward and Marcel Pop-Cornis translation), Juan Ramon Jimenez (Mary Rae translation), Joanne Speidel, Hillel Schwartz, John Wheatcroft, and Dori Appel. As a sample, the editor selected these lines from "Orkney Diptych" by Marc Hudson:

> There's the cook, my anointed killer.
> How he cringes to fulfill his office—
> yes, scullion, thou needst must break

ALWAYS submit MSS or queries with a stamped, self-addressed envelope (SASE) within your country or International Reply Coupons (IRCs) purchased from the post office for other countries.

> *this morning more than eggs*
> *in they skillet. And there's Soulfetch,*
> *my cousin's axe, in whose blue steel*
> *I see it all* sub specie aeternitatis:

tnr is flat-spined, professionally printed on heavy stock, glossy, color cover, 132-152 pp., using 16-34 pp. of poetry in each issue; usual print run 1,600, 680 subscriptions of which approximately 132 are libraries. Subscriptions: $12/3 issues per copy: $6.30 for 1988 or 1987. **They receive about 500-550 poetry submissions per year, use about 32-45, have about a 30-month backlog. "Will be reading manuscripts from January 2 through June 30, 1991." Pays $13-20, more for (occasional) longer poems, plus 1 copy. Reports in 3-6 months.** "We believe that poets should not only be readers but lovers of poetry. We're looking for 'literalists of the imagination — imaginary gardens will real toads in them.' **Our range is from traditionalist poetry to post-modern and experimental (the latter only occasionally, though). We also like the occasional 'light' poem and, of course, translations. We're especially interested in the individual voice."**

THE NEW REPUBLIC (II), 1220 19th St. NW, Washington, DC 20036, phone 202-331-7494, founded 1914, poetry editor Richard Howard. *The New Republic* is an old-line politically liberal weekly magazine that publishes occasional poetry. As a sample, I chose the following lines from "Our Days," by Gary Soto:

> *We get up to our feet, stretch, and throw practice kicks*
> *At the air, and bowing to one another,*
>
> *Begin to make bruises where the heart won't go,*
> *A hurt won't stay. I like that, the trust of bone,*
>
> *And how if I'm hit I'll step in, almost crazed,*
> *And sweep, back fist, and maybe bring him down.*

The New Republic is magazine-sized, printed on slick paper, 42 pp. saddle-stapled with 4-color cover. Subscription rate $56/year, back issues available for $3 postpaid. **I have no submission or payment information.**

NEW RIVERS PRESS; MINNESOTA VOICES PROJECT, INC. (II, IV-Regional, translation), Suite 910, 420 N. 5th St., Minneapolis, MN 55401, founded 1968, publishes collections of poetry, translations of contemporary literature, collections of short fiction, and is also involved in publishing Minnesota regional literary material. Write for free catalog, or send SASE for guidelines/inquiries. New and emerging authors living in Iowa, Minnesota, North and South Dakota and Wisconsin are eligible for the Minnesota Voices Project. Book-length manuscripts of poetry, short fiction, novellas, or familiar essays are all accepted. Send SASE for entry form. Winning authors receive a stipend of $500 plus publication by New Rivers. Second and subsequent printings of works will allow 15% royalties for author.

THE NEW WELSH REVIEW, (II, IV-Ethnic), St. David's University College, Lampeter, Dyfed, UK, phone 0570-423523, founded 1988, poetry editors Belinda Humfrey and Peter J. Foss. *TNWR* is a quarterly publishing articles, short stories and poems. They have recently published poetry by Joseph Clancy, Gillian Clarke, Lawrence Ferlinghetti, John Heath-Stubbs, Les A. Murray, Peter Porter, and Anne Stevenson. I have not seen it, but the editors describe it as 88 pp., glossy paper in three colors, laminated cover, using photographs, graphics, and ads. Their press run is 1,500. Subscription: £12. **Sample: £3.50 postpaid. Submit double-spaced. No simultaneous submissions or previously published poems. Reports in 6 weeks. Publication within 1-7 months. Editor sometimes comments on rejections.**

NEW YORK QUARTERLY (II), P.O. Box 693, Old Chelsea Station, New York, NY 10113, founded 1969, poetry editor William Packard, appears 3 times a year. They seek to publish "a cross-section of the best of contemporary American poetry" and, indeed, **have a record of publishing many of the best and most diverse of** poets, including W. D. Snodgrass, Gregory Corso, James Dickey, Charles Bukowski, Leo Connellan, Helen Adam, Macdonald Carey, Pat Farewell, and Judson Jerome. It appears in a 6 × 9″ flat-spined format, thick, elegantly printed, color glossy cover. Subscription: $15 to 305 Neville Hall, University of Maine, Orono, ME 04469. **Submit 3-5 poems. Reports within 2 weeks. Pays copies.** This magazine is sponsored by the National Poetry Foundation, listed under Organizations Useful to Poets.

THE NEW YORKER (III, IV-Translations, humor), 25 W. 43rd St., New York, NY 10036, founded 1925, poetry editor Alice Quinn, circulation 640,000, uses **poetry of the highest quality (including translations) — light verse or serious — and pays top rates. Replies in 6-8 weeks. MSS not read during the summer. Must include SASE for a reply. Price: $1.75 (available on newsstands).**

NEWSLETTER INAGO (I), Box 26244, Tucson, AZ 85726-6244, phone 602-294-7031, founded 1979, poetry editor Del Reitz, is a 4-5 pp. corner-stapled, monthly newsletter. "**Free verse preferred although other forms will be read. Rhymed poetry must be truly exceptional (nonforced) for consideration. Due to format, 'epic' and monothematic poetry will not be considered. Cause specific, political, or religious poetry stands little chance of consideration. A wide range of short poetry, showing the poet's preferably eclectic perspective is best for *NI*. No haiku, please.**" They have recently published poetry by John Brander, Cal Rollins, Jori Ranhand, Sam Silva, Mark J. Isham, Barbara Elovic, Ana Pine, Gail White, Tom O. Jones, and Salvatore Galioto. The editor says, "since editorial taste in poetry especially is such a subjective and narrow thing," a short selection cannot be chosen "with any fairness to either that taste or the poet whose material might be quoted." Below are lines from Harriet B. Shatraw's "A Late Fall Day in the Woods.":

> *Light footsteps shuffle*
> *the cornflake leaves*
> *and a grey doe statues herself*
> *in stillness*

Their press run is approximately 200 for that many subscriptions. **No price is given for the newsletter, but the editor suggests a donation of $2 an issue or $16 annually (overseas: $3 and $18). Guidelines available for SASE. Pays 4 copies. They consider simultaneous submissions and previously published poems. Reports ASAP (usually within 2 weeks). Editor sometimes comments on rejections.**

NEXT EXIT (II, IV-Regional), 92 Helen St., Kingston, Ontario K7L 4P3, Canada, founded 1980, editor Eric Folsom, a twice-yearly magazine that features poetry and reviews and focuses on Ontario and Eastern North American writers. The editor wants to see poetry that is "**lyric, narrative, meditative, concrete, explorative; any form done well,**" but nothing "**misogynist.**" He has recently published work by John Barlow and Carolyn Bond. As a sample, he chose the following lines from "Robert Ford" by A. C. Diamanti:

> *So, Robert, yes you did kill Jesse James,*
> *but, in a manner of speaking,*
> *Jesse returned the favour.*

The magazine is $5 \times 8\frac{1}{2}$" photocopied typed copy on 32 pp., saddle-stapled and folded with black lettering and illustration on cover. Circulation is 150, of which 75 are subscriptions and 10 go to libraries. Price per issue is $3, subscription $6/year. **Sample available for $3 postpaid. Pay is 1 copy plus 1-year subscription, more if requested. Submissions will be reported on in 90 days and time to publication is 6 months.**

NEXUS (II), 006 University Center, Wright State University, Dayton, OH 45435, phone 513-873-2031, founded 1967, editor Chris Rue. "*Nexus* is a student operated magazine of avant-garde and street poetry; also essays on environmental and political issues. **We're looking for truthful, direct poetry. Open to poets anywhere.** "**We look for contemporary, imagistic work as well as traditional rhyme and meter.**" Recent issues have featured themes on Japan and American West. *Nexus* appears 3 times a year—fall, winter and spring, using about 20 pp. of poetry (of 36-40) in each issue, circulation 2,000. They receive 1,000 submissions per year, use 30-50. **Send a 10x15" SASE with 5 first class stamps and $2 for first copy, $1 for each additional issue. Submit up to 6 pp. of poetry, September to May. Photocopy and simultaneous submissions OK. Send bio with submissions. Reports in 10-12 weeks except summer months. Pays 2 copies. Send SASE for guidelines. Editor sometimes comments on rejections.**

NIGHT ROSES (I), P.O. Box 393, Prospect Hts., IL 60070, phone 708-392-2435, founded 1986, poetry editor Allen T. Billy, appears 2-4 times a year. "I plan to do special poetry anthologies from time to time. We publish *Moonstone Blue*, which is a fantasy poetry anthology, but we have no set dates of publication on this series." They have recently published poems by Edna Janes Kayser, Michael Fraley, Jim Howell, Linda Bernstein, Charles Rampp, and Ida Fasel. They want "**poems about dance, bells, clocks, nature, ghost images of past or future, some haiku, romance poems, poems about flowers, roses, wildflowers, violets, etc. Do not want poems with raw language.**" As a sample the editor chose these lines by Rev. Benedict Auer:

> *A moon*
> *in full mask*
> *frosts night,*
> *one last glare*
> *before ice*
> *slick woods.*

Night Roses is 44 pp., saddle-stapled, photocopied from typescript on offset paper with tinted matte card cover, press run 200-300. Subscription: $8 for 3 issues, $3/copy. **Sample: $2.50 post-**

paid. Pays 1 copy. "Desire author's name and address on all sheets of MSS. If previously published — an acknowledgement must be provided by author with it." No simultaneous submissions; some previously published poems used. Reports in 4-10 weeks. "Material is accepted for current issue and 2 in progress. Sometimes: If I like a poem — I ask a poet if I can put it in the 'hold file' to close out a future issue."

‡**NIGHT TREE PRESS (IV-Regional)**, The Gorge Rd., RD2, P.O. Box 140G Boonville, NY 13309, founded 1985, publisher Gregg Fedchak, publishes **"poetry dealing exclusively with the Adirondacks and North Country of New York State"** in flat-spined paperbacks. Gregg Fedchak will consider **"any form, length, suitable for book format (collections acceptable, of course, of short works); subjects must deal with this region (nature, back-to-the-soil, our Native American population, poverty), any style, purpose: to show our geographical area as it really is, via the poet's eye. No pornography or near-pornography."** He has recently published **The Way to Heron Mountain** by Ed Zahniser, from which he selected these sample lines:

> *For years I thought the search for truth*
> *had changed me from the man I'd been.*
> *Now I can't remember who that was.*
> *And truth? Don't make an old fool laugh.*

The book is digest-sized, flat-spined, professionally printed in small type with b/w woodcut illustrations, glossy card cover, $5.95 (plus $1.50 postage and handling and, for New York residents, 7% sales tax). **Query with 1-5 sample poems, bio and credits. Simultaneous submissions photocopies, dot-matrix, all OK, no previously published material. Reports on queries in 2-4 weeks, on MSS in 1-2 months. Pays 10% of press run. "If I get as far as a MS"** editor will provide criticism. He says, "Poetry will be successful here only if it rings true with the real spirit of the North Country, as experienced by someone who has lived here or vacationed here for an extended period of time. All else is a waste of time."

NIGHTSUN (II), Dept. of English, Frostburg State University, Frostburg, MD 21532, founded 1981, poetry editors Douglas DeMars and Barbara Wilson, is a 64 pp., digest-sized literary annual. **They want "highest quality poetry. Subject matter open. Prefers poems not much longer than 40 lines. Not interested in the extremes of sentimental, obvious poetry on the one hand and the subjectless 'great gossamer-winged gnat' school of poetry on the other."** They have recently published poetry by William Stafford, Linda Pastan, Marge Piercy, and Diane Wakoski. They accept about 1% of poetry received. **Sample: $6.95 postpaid. Pays 1 copy. "Contributors encouraged to subscribe." Reports in 3 months.** *Nightsun* is affiliated with the annual Western Maryland Writers' Workshop.

NIMROD INTERNATIONAL JOURNAL OF CONTEMPORARY POETRY AND FICTION; RUTH G. HARDMAN AWARD: PABLO NERUDA PRIZE FOR POETRY (II), 2210 S. Main St., Tulsa, OK 74114, phone 918-584-3333, founded 1956, poetry editor Fran Ringold, "is an active 'little magazine,' part of the movement in American letters which has been essential to the development of modern literature. *Nimrod* publishes 2 issues per year: an Awards Issue featuring the prize winners of our national competition, and a thematic issue, so that in addition to bringing new, vigorous writing to the reading public, we also focus each year on the literature of an emerging nation." They want **"vigorous writing that is neither wholly of the academy nor the streets, typed MSS."** They have published poetry by Pattiann Rogers, Denise Levertov, Willis Barnstone, Alvin Greenberg, Francois Camoin, Tess Gallagher, McKeel McBride, Bronislava Volek, and Ishmael Reed. As a sample he chose these lines from "Hum-Drum Days" by Lisa Steinman:

> *It's late, and daylight ends early.*
> *Outside, everything smells of winter;*
> *the forsythia has abandoned its leaves, leans*
> *against the window, pointing in.*
> *The empty clothesline's taut.*
> *We are clearly waiting for something.*

The 6 × 9″ flat-spined, 128 + pp., journal, full-color glossy cover, professionally printed on coated stock with b/w photos and art, uses 50-60 pp. of poetry in each issue, circulation 2,000, 400 subscriptions of which 50 are libraries. Subscription: $10/year plus $1.50 inside USA; $3 outside. Per copy: $5.50. They use about 1% of the 2,000 submissions they receive each year, have a 3 month backlog. **Sample: $6.50 postpaid. Reports in 3 weeks-4 months, pays in copies.** Send business-sized SASE for guidelines and rules for the Ruth G. Hardman Award: Pablo Neruda Prize for Poetry ($1,000 and $500 prizes). Entries accepted January 1-April 1 each year $10 entry fee for which you get one copy of *Nimrod*.

NOMOS PRESS INC.; NOMOS: STUDIES IN SPONTANEOUS ORDER (IV-Political), 2870 Easy St., Ann Arbor, MI 48104, phone 708-858-7184, poetry editor Christopher Brockman, editorial contact person Carol B. Low. *Nomos* is a quarterly magazine **"dedicated to individual freedom and responsibil-**

ity." One page of each issue is devoted to poetry up to 24 lines, "although longer pieces are considered. Poetry must promote individual freedom and responsibility, skepticism toward government solutions for economic and social ills and/or celebrate the human condition. No contrived rhymes, pedestrian prose, or cryptic charades. Clarity of meaning and direct emotional appeal are paramount; form should contribute to, not detract or distract from these." They have recently published poetry by John Harllee. As a sample, the editor selected these lines by Christopher Brockman:

> *I've thought at some length and it seems to me*
> *The problem has its roots in the fact that we*
> *Have allowed ourselves to become only means*
> *To the end of someone else's bandwagon dreams.*

"Nomos' purpose is to call attention to the erosion of civil and economic rights, much of which erosion has government as its catalyst." I have not seen an issue, but the editor describes it as magazine-sized, generally 40 pp. in length, offset, matte cover occasionally printed 2-color. Ad copy, line art for cover and article illustrations are solicited. It has a circulation of 1,000 with 450 subscriptions of which 10 are libraries, 300 sent out to potential subscribers. Subscription: $15. **Sample: $4.50 postpaid. Send SASE for guidelines. Pays 3 copies. "Reviewing sample copies strongly encouraged." Reporting time varies, up to 12 months to publication. Photocopies, dot-matrix OK, name and address on each page. "SASE a must."**

‡THE NORTH; THE POETRY BUSINESS; SMITH/DOORSTOP PUBLISHING (I, II), 51 Byram Arcade, Westgate, Huddersfield HD1 1ND England, phone 0484-434-840, founded 1986, editor Peter Sansom, is a small press and magazine publisher of contemporary poetry. **"No particular restrictions on form, length, etc. But work must be contemporary, and must speak with the writer's own authentic voice. No copies of traditional poems, echoes of old voices, poems about the death of poet's grandfather, poems which describe how miserable the poet is feeling right now."** The have recently published poetry by Susan Bright, "the only U.S. poet we publish at the moment." As a sample, the editor selected these lines from "Swimming the English Channel" by Ms. Bright:

> *I did not intend to be a theater.*
> *I do not like the man in the basement who controls me.*
> *I do not want to be a house, a hotel, a car.*
> *I do not like being exposed!*

The North is "⅔ A4 format 48-52 pp. offset litho, graphics, ads, colored card cover, staple-bound." It appears 3 times/year, press run 400 for 200 subscriptions. Subscription: £5 (£10 U.S. rate). **Sample, postpaid: £20 (U.S. rate). Pays 2 copies.** Smith/Doorstop publishes 6 perfect-bound paperbacks/year. **For book consideration, submit 6 sample poems, cover letter, bio, previous publications. Responds to queries in 2 weeks, to MSS in 3 months. Pays 20 copies.** They hold an annual book (perfect-bound, laminated) competition for 16 pp. MSS; prize—joint publication with the other winner. They also publish an anthology of the runners-up. The editor says, "Read plenty of poetry, contemporary and traditional. Attend workshops, eh, and meet other writers. Keep submitting poems, even if you fail. Build up a track record in magazines before trying to a book published."

NORTH AMERICAN REVIEW (III), University of Northern Iowa, Cedar Falls, IA 50614, phone 319-273-2681, founded 1815, poetry editor Peter Cooley, is a slick magazine-sized quarterly of general interest, 72 pp. average, saddle-stapled, professionally printed with glossy full-color paper cover. In their 171st anniversary issue they had poetry by Richard Terrill, Jeannine Savard, and Katherine Soniat, from whose "That Far from Home" I selected the opening stanza (of 15) as a sample:

> *If it only depended on the young*
> *circus elephant, swaying by the river*
> *eating kudzu, or*
> *the reeling paddlewheeler*

The editor says they receive 15,000 poems a year, publish 20-30. Press run 5,200 to 2,200 subscriptions of which 1,100 are libraries, some 2,000 newsstand or bookstore sales. Single copy: $3; subscription: $11. **Sample: $2 postpaid. Send SASE for guidelines. Pays 50¢ per line and 2 copies. No simultaneous submissions or previously published poems. Reports in 1-2 months, as much as a year between acceptance and publication.**

THE NORTH CAROLINA HAIKU SOCIETY PRESS (V, IV-Form), P.O. Box 14247, Raleigh, NC 27620, phone 919-828-5551, founded 1984, editor/publisher Rebecca Rust. The press was established **"solely as a vehicle for publishing books by those authors who have received a grant from the North Carolina Haiku Society. Applicants must apply for the grant to be published. This is open to anyone."** They publish flat-spined paperbacks of, or about, haiku only. Poets recently published include Rebecca Rust. As a sample, the editor selected these lines by Lenard D. Moore:

> *the tapping*

of the coppersmith ...
snowflakes

The sample book I have seen is attractively printed on white stock with line drawings, shiny card cover with b/w art work, priced at $6.95 plus $1.50 postage and handling. **Freelance submissions are accepted in the form of application for the North Carolina Haiku Society grant. Currently the editor would rather not have any unsolicited MSS because she has a backlog. When applying for a grant, the writer should submit 30-50 haiku in any legible form. It is best to query first. Queries are answered in 1 month, MSS are reported on in 2 months.** There is no subsidy publishing. The editor says, "Please, please read *all* of the classical books of, and about, haiku and *study* writings on haiku by Blyth, Henderson, Yasuda, and Amann before attempting to submit."

NORTH DAKOTA QUARTERLY (II), Box 8237, University of North Dakota, Grand Forks, ND 58202, phone 701-777-3323, FAX 701-777-3650, founded 1910, poetry editor Jay Meek, a literary quarterly published by the University of North Dakota Press that includes material in the arts and humanities — essays, fiction, interviews, poems, and visual art. **"We want to see poetry that reflects an understanding not only of the difficulties of the craft, but of the vitality and tact that each poem calls into play."** Poets recently published include Thomas McGrath, Elton Glaser, and W.D. Snodgrass. As a sample, the editor selected lines from "Kinning Wheel" by Thomas Russell:

Father's separate portrait moved silently away,
retouching itself again and again
until this petrified civilian in matrimony's charge
became a postcard of an eroding monument.

The issue I have of *North Dakota Quarterly* is 6 × 9″, 261 pp. flat-spined, professionally designed and printed with b/w artwork on the white matte card cover and b/w photographs inside. Circulation of the journal is 700, of which 500 are subscriptions and 200 go to libraries, 100 are newsstand sales. Price per issue is $5, subscription $15/year. **Sample available for $5 postpaid. Pay is 2 copies and a year's subscription. Poems should be typed or otherwise mechanically reproduced. Reporting time is 4-6 weeks and time to publication varies.** The press does not usually publish chapbooks, but "we will consider."

‡UNIVERSITY OF NORTH TEXAS PRESS; TEXAS POET SERIES (IV-Regional), Box 13856, Denton, TX 76203, phone 817-565-2142, series editor Richard Sale, has recently published work by these Texas poets: Naomi Nye, William David, R. S. Gwynn, and Jan Seale. As a sample the editor selected these lines by Walt McDonald:

Fishing in hardscrabble, a man keeps his tackle
handy, ready to rise up and walk on water.
Rattlesnakes there are bad,
sneaking up behind and shaking like gourds
of holy rollers in tent meetings, half the congregation
*   speaking in tongues and quaking, some picking up snakes*
and writing, on fire in the spirit, ignoring
us boys outside and laughing.

Books in the series average 120-128 pp. **Query with sample poems, bio, and list of publications. Simultaneous submissions OK. Reports on queries or MSS in 8-10 weeks. Pays 10% of net sales in royalties plus 5 copies.** To buy samples, request the Texas A&M University Press catalogue, Drawer C, College Station, TX 77843.

NORTHEAST JOURNAL (II, IV-Regional), Box 217, Kingston, RI 02881, phone 401-783-2356, founded 1969, editor Tina Letcher, is a literary annual, which is **"open to conventional-experimental poetry."** They have recently published poetry by Laurel Speer and Harrison Fisher. As a sample the editor selected these lines by C. D. Wright:

The heart some bruised fruit
knocked loose by a long stick
*   aches at the stem —*
It's not forbidden to fall out of love

The purpose of *NJ* is "to encourage local (state and area) writers while remaining open to national submissions." It is a digest-sized flat-spined 100 pp. format, typeset, with glossy card cover, circulation 500, with 200 subscriptions of which 100 are libraries. **Sample: $5 postpaid. Pays 1 copy. Reports in 3-6 months.**

NORTHEASTERN UNIVERSITY PRESS; SAMUEL FRENCH MORSE POETRY PRIZE (III), Northeastern University, 360 Huntington Ave., Boston, MA 02115. The Samuel French Morse Poetry Prize, % Prof. Guy Rotella, Editor, Morse Poetry Prize, English Dept., 406 Holmes, Northeastern University, Boston, MA 02115, for book publication (MS 50-70 pp.) by Northeastern University Press and an award of

Close-up

Ron Koertge
Poet

Reading

Remember holding the book, big as a steering
wheel, memorizing the sitter's juniper breath,
pretending to be reading though the letters
were only pawprints on the snow of the page
because everything was reading—Mom & Dad
from the novel of their lives, the cat from his
small volume, the sun reading *warm*, the ground
firm.

Well, I still love it. Reading at work, imagining
the tattooed page is part of me. After sex as
stars step forward to make marching band
formations. Alone with a glass of vodka,
the books spine up all around my chair
like the tents of men who would give
their lives for me.

Little skyrockets of imagination light up poems like that one by Ron Koertge. His poems
always seem to evoke for me the poet in performance (though I have never met him or
heard him read). They are scripts—often very funny—that dance in the eyes of an audience.

Ron's first formative experiences seem to have been helping out at Koertge's Malt Shop,
which his parents ran in a small town near St. Louis. He filled water glasses and cleaned
tables from the age of eight or nine. He describes himself as skinny, with a cowlick, "a
show-off and a smart aleck (then and now). I could make people laugh or scowl. I later
discovered if I wrote things down I could broaden my audience and make them laugh, too.
Or—maybe even better—disapprove."

A bout with rheumatic fever when he was 12 caused the little extrovert to look inward.
In "Boy's Life" he describes it:

It is an odd disease that affects the heart
giving it a murmur. I couldn't go outside or play
so I lay in my bed, hands crossed on the Morning Star
quilt, and strained to hear what my heart was saying.

During this period, he says, "books replaced the dog I could not have (though they excited
me in ways a dog could not). Verbs became the things I could not do. Nouns what I was
unable to embrace or own or be. The rhythms of the prose were the music I could not
listen to."

Through Gerry Locklin, whom he knew at the University of Arizona, Ron was
introduced to the world of independent magazines. To him these little publications seemed
"wonderfully irreverent, sassy and full of life—the opposite of graduate school (in a poem
I once called it a 'cruddy little fiefdom.')" In a library he found advice from a French critic
to concentrate on the things in one's work that drew the most criticism. "I took that advice

and am still attracted to the eerie, the carnal, the easy laugh, the lyrical, the sentimental."

As a young professor at Pasadena City College (where he still teaches), he "sent poems everywhere (no magazine was too peculiar or obscure) and published books with five or six different independent presses like Jim Harrison's Sumac Press, Dennis Cooper's Little Caesar Press, Mag Press, Duck Down Press, Maelstrom and others."

W.W. Norton published his novel, **The Boogeyman**, about 1980; The University of Arkansas inaugurated their poetry series with his **Life on the Edge of the Continent**. "In the last four years, I've written novels for young adults (a form as defiant as the sonnet, by the way), published by Little, Brown."

He says, "At the risk of sounding sage — if I were, I'd win more photo finishes — I have a theory of poetry that I get to repeat to my writing workshop every semester so it always sounds new: 'I think it's good to write what you want but *very* good to write what wants to be written.' At my worst, I haul the poem out under the interrogator's bulb and badger it until it succumbs; at my best, I put my talented and indifferent hand out toward the darkness and beckon. However, I put in a lot of time at the 'poetry factory' because beckoning is more time-consuming than it sounds. Like most of us, I'm not always at my best, so I often write badly. I sound flat-headed, needy, pretentious, glib. But I only see those disguises. And the wonderful thing is that sometimes the real poem peeks out — not the pirate, ballet dancer or astronaut I imagined at all! I think poems respond to being written. Like pets, they like to be sung to and handled. Unlike pets, they're enormously protean, able and willing to change from a foolish scribble or herniated quatrain into something lovely and moving.

"I write because I can," he says, "because it's fun, and because I want to read what I'll write next. I also believe that the beauty of writing poetry isn't always on the page: that's just the residue of beauty. The real beauty is doing the work, just sitting down, taking the phone off the hook, and doing the work."

— Judson Jerome

$500, entry fee $10. Deadline of August 1 for inquiries, September 15 for single copy of MS. MS will not be returned. Open to U.S. poets who have published no more than 1 book of poetry.

NORTHERN NEW ENGLAND REVIEW (IV-Regional), Franklin Pierce College, Box 825, Rindge, NH 03451, phone 603-899-5111, ext. 420, FAX 603-899-6448, founded 1973, poetry editor Michelle Bode, is an annual using **only contributors who are from northern New England. "All forms and lengths are welcome. However, 3-4 pp. maximum is suggested."** They have recently published poetry by Lyn Lifshin, Karla Hammond, and Wesli Court. As a sample the editors selected these lines (poet unidentified):

> The ferocity of his whims,
> the atrophy of real convictions,
> his Mohawk hair,
> his glistening scalp

NNER is magazine-sized, 100 pp. flat-spined, offset from letterpress on non-coated stock with color matte card color, using graphics and 0-6 pp. of ads. They use about 20 of 800 poems submitted annually. Press run is 600 for 20 subscriptions of which 15 are libraries. About 40 shelf sales. **Sample: $3.50 postpaid. Pays 2 copies. Reports "within 2 months."**

NORTHERN PLEASURE (V), 3226 Raspberry, Erie, PA 16508, founded 1980, publisher Ron Androla, who describes his operation as a "small-press, independent publisher of true, intense, personal, avant-garde, prelapsarian, sexual, violent poetry against all otherwise moronic yawning." The magazine operates by "invitation only regarding submissions of manuscripts." Androla has recently published work by Pat Mckinnon, Cat Townsend, Zen Sutherland. *Northern Pleasure* appears irregularly, irregular photocopied pages, irregular press runs. Price per issue also irregular. **No samples or guidelines available; contributors receive 1 copy. Queries will be answered in "weeks."** Simultaneous submissions, photocopied or dot-matrix MSS are OK but no discs. In case you didn't already know, Androla informs you, "Poetry is madness!! Art is terror."

THE NORTHERN REVIEW (II, IV-Themes), Academic Achievement Center, University of Wisconsin, Stevens Point, WI 54481, phone 715-346-3568, founded 1987, managing editor Richard Behm, wants **"quality literary poetry" that appeals to an intelligent, general readership.** They have recently published poetry by Anita Skeen and Janet McCann. As a sample the editor selected these lines from "October Night" by Laurel Mills:

> *This must be what it is like*
> *when wheat stops growing.*
> *When the sky lowers itself,*
> *a grey window shade*
> *that shuts out the sun.*
> *When earth turns in*
> *and calls it a night.*

TNR, appearing spring and fall, is 8½ × 11", 48-64 pp., saddle-stapled, professionally printed on glossy stock, using b/w graphics and ads, circulation 1,000. **Sample: $4 postpaid. Send SASE for guidelines. Pays 2 copies. Reports in 4-6 weeks. No simultaneous submissions. Photocopy, dot-matrix OK. Editor sometimes comments on rejections.** He says, "We often have theme issues, and it would benefit poets interested to subscribe to our journal or to write to inquire about specific editorial needs."

THE NORTHLAND QUARTERLY; NORTHLAND QUARTERLY PUBLICATIONS, INC. (I, II, IV-Themes, regional), 51 E. 4th St. #412, Winona, MN 55987, phone 507-452-3686, founded 1987, editor Jody Wallace, is a "small-press publisher of fiction, poetry, non-fiction and scholarly publications, publishing a quarterly literary journal. Limited subsidy publishing services offered to selected authors." She wants **"poetry with commentary or insight on condition of man, contemporary relationships, man vs. nature. No religious, fantasy, or 'scenery' poetry."** They have published poetry by Norman German, John Grey, Mark Maire, and Richard Davignon. As a sample she selected these lines (poet unidentified):

> *Last night I went to bed intoxicated again. You watched*
> *"Ghandi," repressing violence.*
> *Today, I am drinking too much coffee,*
> *smoking too many cigarettes.*
> *You say you'll be late . . .*

TNQ is digest-sized, 90-128 pp, professionally printed, flat-spined. They accept 10-15% of 1,000 poems received a year. Subscription: $18. **Sample: $4 postpaid. Guidelines available for SASE. Pays 3 copies. "Contributors encouraged to buy additional copies." Submit with cover letter and bio. They consider simultaneous submissions and previously published poems. Reports in 2-4 weeks. Editor sometimes comments on rejections,** "more substantial critiques on request." Publishes 10 chapbooks a year averaging 100 pp. **For chapbook consideration either query or send MS with cover letter and bio. Reports in 6 weeks. Payment "varies with author."** Send SASE for catalog to buy samples.

‡NORTHWEST; NORTHWEST PUBLISHERS (I, II), 1011 Boren Ave., #801, Seattle, WA 98104, founded 1988, poetry editor Kay Kinghammer, is a quarterly. **"All submissions must be in good taste, under 3,500 words, and belong to the submitter."** They have recently published poetry by D. Wessell, Marilyn Fullen-Collins, Bonnie Clay, and the editor. It is magazine-sized, 36+ pp., b/w offset, professionally printed on slick stock with paper cover. Press run 3,000 for 500 subscribers of which 3 are libraries, 2,000 shelf sales. Subscription: $12. **Sample: $3.50 postpaid. Pays 2¢/word, no copies. Simultaneous submissions and previously published poems OK, provided submitter holds copyright. Editor comments on submission** "often." They plan to publish books under the imprint Northwest Publishers.

‡THE NORTHWEST GAY & LESBIAN READER (IV-Gay, lesbian), 1501 Belmont Ave., Seattle, WA 98122, phone 206-322-4609, founded 1989, editor/publisher Ron Whiteaker, is a "bi-monthly, 11 × 17" format with emphasis on book reviews, but also includes art previews and notices, articles of opinion and essays, short fiction and **poetry expressing the gay and lesbian experience. No restrictions on form or style. Light erotica is OK. Nothing sexist, racist, or 'hard-core.'** " They have recently published poetry by William Freeberg, Alan Reade, and Yvonne Eldresse. As a sample the editor selected these lines from "Next Thursday" by Erik Schutz-Macht:

> *kicking up a dustorm about gay rodeos*
> *clubs lacking enough room for boot kickers to do 'their thing'*
> *politics and cancelled events*
> *disappointments after a long drive*

They accept 90% of about 36 poems received a year. Press run: 5,000 for 2,000 subscriptions, 3,000 shelf sales. Subscription: $1.50. **Sample, postpaid: 45¢. Pays copies "by request." 1 poem per page. Reports in 6 weeks.** The editor says, " 'Coming out' as a gay or lesbian poet, whether in the work, or in the publication, has the effect of documenting the raw emotions, the feelings, the personal experiences, and the insight that the gay poet can express, and that is what is missing in politics and social rhetoric."

NORTHWEST MAGAZINE (IV-Regional), 1320 SW Broadway, Portland, OR 97201, phone 503-221-8190, poetry editor Paul Pintarich, is the Sunday magazine of the *Oregonian* newspaper. They use poems only by **poets living in the Pacific Northwest. Pays $10/poem. No restrictions or specifications as to type, etc. Length: short, no longer than 23 lines.** They have recently published poetry by Frederick Raborg, Jr. As a sample I selected the first quatrain of "Sonnet: On Sonnets" by Dana E. Scott:

> *The manufactured cadence of desire,*
> *Each measured foot true to an inner song,*
> *Recalls to mind the days when we were strong,*
> *Our life imbued with power to inspire.*

NORTHWEST REVIEW (II), 369 PLC, University of Oregon, Eugene, OR 97403, phone 503-686-3957, founded 1957, poetry editor John Witte, is "seeking excellence in whatever form we can find it" and uses **"all types" of poetry.** They have recently published poetry by Alan Dugan, Olga Broumas, William Stafford, and Richard Eberhart. The $6 \times 9''$ flat-spined magazine appears 3 times a year, uses 25-40 pp. of poetry in each issue, circulation 1,300, with 1,200 subscriptions of which half are libraries. They receive 3,500 submissions per year, use 4%, have a 0-4 month backlog. **Sample: $3 postpaid. Submit 6-8 poems clearly reproduced. No simultaneous submissions. Reports in 8-10 weeks, pays 3 copies. Send SASE for guidelines.** The editor comments **"whenever possible"** on rejections and advises, "Persist."

W. W. NORTON & COMPANY, INC. (III), 500 Fifth Ave., New York, NY 10110, phone 212-354-5500, founded 1925, poetry editor Jill Bialosky. W. W. Norton is a well known commercial trade publishing house that publishes only original work in both hardcover and paperback. They want **"quality literary poetry" but no "light or inspirational verse."** They have recently published books by Ellen Bryant Voigt, Rosanna Warren, Melissa Green, Michael Burkard, James Lasdun, Cathy Song, Sandra Gilbert, Norman Dubie, and Eugenio Montale. W. W. Norton publishes two books of poetry each year with an average page count of 64. The samples I have are flat-spined paperbacks, attractively printed (one has b/w illustrations), with two-color glossy card covers; they are priced at $6.95. **Freelance submissions are accepted, but authors should query first, sending credits and 15 sample poems plus bio. Norton will consider only poets whose work has been published in quality literary magazines. They report on queries in 2-3 weeks and MSS in 16 weeks. Simultaneous submissions will be considered if the editor is notified, and photocopied MSS are OK. Royalties are 10%, but there are no advances. Catalog is free on request. Criticism of rejected MSS is sometimes given.**

NOSTALGIA: A SENTIMENTAL STATE OF MIND (I), Box 2224, Orangeburg, SC 29116, founded 1986, poetry editor Connie Lakey Martin, appears spring and fall using **"nostalgic poetry, style open, prefer *non* rhyme, but occasional rhyme OK, relatively short poems, never longer than one page, no profanity, no ballads."** As a sample the editor selected these lines of her own:

> *Locked away, but unrestrained*
> *and limitless — little fuzzy, fragile flashbacks,*
> *figured forgotten.*
> *Forming without warning*
> *whether I am still*
> *or stirring —*

Nostalgia is digest-sized, 20 pp. saddle-stapled, offset typescript, with matte card cover. Its press run is 1,000. Subscription: $5. **Sample: $2.50 postpaid. Guidelines available for SASE.** There are contests in each issue with award of $100 and publication for outstanding poem, publication and 1-year subscription for Honorable Mentions. Entry fee $2.50 reserves future edition, covers 3 entries. Deadlines: June 30 and December 31 each year. **No simultaneous submissions or previously published poems.** Connie Martin says, "I offer criticism to most rejected poems and feature a poet each edition as 'Poet of the Season.' "

NOTEBOOK/CUADERNO: A LITERARY JOURNAL; ESOTERICA PRESS (I, IV-Ethnic, bilingual), P.O. Box 170, Barstow, CA 92312-0170, press established 1983, magazine 1985, editor Ms. Yoly Zentella. Esoterica is a small-press literary publisher. *Notebook*, a semi-annual journal. "*Notebook* reflects the ethno-cultural diversity of the Americas. **Particularly interested in Latino-American, Native American, Black, Asian and Muslim Arab American writing. Will accept Spanish. Themes based on culture, history and literature welcome. No frivolities, explicit sex, obscenities or experimentation."** Recently published poets include Aisha-Eshe, Antonia Pigno, Koryne Ortega, and Arthur W. Knight. As a sample, the editor chose these lines by Real Faucher:

> *The festival is over.*
> *Disorderly conduct*
> *on the subway,*
> *the slapping of a conga drum*
> *too loud,*
> *an illegal guanguanco*

Notebook is digest-sized, 100 pp. saddle-stapled, offset from typed copy, with b/w illustrations inside and one-color matte card cover. Circulation is 150, price per issue $6, subscription $12/ year. Guidelines available for SASE, pays 1 copy, subscriptions are required upon acceptance of work. Sample can be obtained from editor, $6. The editor wants MSS "typewritten and proofread with name and current address on top of the page. No limit in number of poems or length. Solicits unpublished work. Will not consider simultaneous submissions but will consider previously published with name of previous publisher for credit. Address all submissions with bio and SASE of appropriate size to editor." She reports on submissions in 8-12 weeks. Esoterica Press has published several chapbooks and a book of poems. She will accept MSS for chapbooks and book publication. Queries will be answered in 4 weeks and MSS accepted or rejected in 8-12 weeks; no simultaneous submissions. Original copy or photocopy OK. Pay for chapbooks is 1 copy; pay for book publication to be arranged with author. The editor says, "We are very interested in publishing and promoting underrepresented, beginning or unpublished poets."

NOTUS: NEW WRITING; MICHIGAN BROADSIDES; OTHERWIND PRESS (II, IV-Translations), 2420 Walter Dr., Ann Arbor, MI 48102, phone 313-665-0703, poetry editor Pat Smith, managing editor Marla Smith. *Notus* appears twice a year, using experimental writing and translations. No "academic writing." Each issue includes a two-sided soundsheet 33⅓ rpm of selected performance poetry. They have published poetry of Robert Creeley, Robert Kelly, Leslie Scalapino, Anselm Hollo, Clayton Eshleman, and Cid Corman. As a sample I chose the poem "Ear Shot" by Charles Bernstein:

> *Here is the spare*
> *aside the locker room*
> *where I am marooned*

Notus is magazine-sized, 96 pp. flat spined, professionally printed on heavy cream stock with glossy b/w cover with photo. No ads. Press run 500 for 50 subscriptions of which 10 are libraries. Sample $5 postpaid. Send 3-5 pieces. Pays 1 copy. Reports in 6 months. No simultaneous submissions or previously published poems. Editor "seldom" comments on rejections.

NOW AND THEN (IV-Regional, themes), Box 19180A, ETSU, Johnson City, TN 37614-0002, phone 615-929-5348, founded 1984, poetry editor Jo Carson, a regional magazine that deals with Appalachian issues and culture. The editor does not want any poetry not related to the region. Issues have themes— previous issues have focused on Appalachian veterans, working Cherokees, blacks, children, and rural life. "No haiku or sentimental, nostalgic, romantic, religious poems." They have recently published poems by Louie Crew, Jim Wayne Miller, and George Ella Lyon. As a sample the editor selected these lines from "Poem for James Collins" by Bob Henry Baber:

> *this ain't suppose to be a slavin' place*
> *tell 'em that*
> *see if they stop pattin' their hair*
> *and clicken' their pens,*
> *scream it in their ears*
> *THIS AIN'T SUPPOSE TO BE A SLAVIN' PLACE*
> *they'll say youse outa order Mister—*
> *treat youse like youse a pop machine or somethin'*

Now and Then appears three times a year, 40 pp., magazine-sized, saddle-stapled, professionally printed, with matte card cover. Its press run is 1,600-2,000 for 600 subscriptions of which 200 are libraries. Of 200 poems received they accept 6-10 an issue. Subscription: $9. **Sample: $3.50** postpaid. Guidelines available for SASE. Pays 2 copies plus subscription. Submit up to 5 poems, "include 'contributors notes.' " Reports in 3-4 months. They will consider simultaneous submissions but "not usually" previously published poems.

NRG; SKYDOG PRESS (II), 6735 SE 78th, Portland, OR 97206, founded 1975, poetry editor Dan Raphael. "Since so many presses seem closed to open-ended energized dimensional works, *NRG* was founded for the opposite purpose—to publish only those types of works. *NRG* wants works bridging the realms of order and multiplicity, starting at the far side working in. If all the pieces fit together craftily, send it elsewhere; if you feel there's something pulsing and sizzling in the poem but you can't finger what, try me. Works with a purpose are almost too closed for me. Form, length and subject matter (whether or no) don't matter, but style does—experimental, lingual, charged." He has published poetry by James Grabill, Ivan Argüelles, Stephen-Paul Martin, Janet Gray, John Bennett, Charles Bernstein, Willie Smith, and Don Webb. *NRG* is published twice a year, a tabloid (usually) "of dimensional literature and graphics" with an average of 18 pp. of poetry, 4-5 poems per page, circulation 600, 55 subscriptions of which 3 are libraries. They receive 500 freelance submissions of poetry per year, use 60. **Sample $1.50. Submit 4-6 pp., any readable format. Simultaneous submissions OK. Might help to look at sample "since strongly idiosyncratic—just excellent is not enough." Reports in less than a month, pays copies.** In order to have a book published by Skydog Press you have to be invited." Dan Raphael comments, "There're plenty of fine magazines printing many varieties of poems. *NRG* wants only ground-breaking scene-shifting avant-garde work. Not because I don't appreciate the others, but *NRG*'s writing needs the exposure."

‡NUTSHELL (I, II), 18 Pineway, Bridgnorth, Shropshire, WV15 5 DT, U.K. founded 1988, editor Jeff Phelps, is a quarterly using poetry **"all subjects considered, any length. Nothing hateful, pornographic, badly assembled."** They have recently published poetry by Ian McDonald, Tony Charles, Chris Bendon, and Patricia Pogson. As a sample the editor selected these lines from "Nutshell (for Roger & Jeff)" by Gillian Ewing:

> . . . *There's not a walnut tree in half a mile*
> *But sheer determination brought it here;*
> *Grey and effacing two soft paws picked it out*
> *From all the tendered harvest one small hoard,*
> *Piled it in triumph on the whitened leaves,*
> *Crowned the achievement with this offering.*

I have not seen an issue, but the editor describes it as "A5 size, stapled, card cover, graphics on cover only, 40-44 pp." They accept 5-10% of some 500 poems submitted per year. Press run 200 for 130 subscribers of which 7 are libraries, shelf sales 10-20. Subscription: £6. **Sample, postpaid: £2. Pays £1 or reduced rate subscription. Editor comments on submissions "always."**

OAK SQUARE (II), P.O. Box 1238, Allston, MA 02134, founded 1985, publisher Philip Borenstein, editor Anne Pluto, poetry editor Laura Haun, is a literary quarterly. They use poetry of "any length on any subject in styles ranging from contemporary free verse to the experimental." They don't want "badly written rhyming iambic pentameter but we try to be open-minded." I have not seen it, but the editor describes the magazine as $7 \times 8\frac{1}{2}$" offset. Circulation is 400. About 200 of these are for shelf sales. Subscription: $10. **Sample: $3.50 postpaid. Send SASE for guidelines. Pays 5 copies. Reports in 6-12 weeks, backlog up to a year.** They also publish photocopied chapbooks, 4-8 pp. "on a irregular basis."

OBLATES (IV-Religious, spirituality/inspirational), Missionary Association of Mary Immaculate, 15 S. 59th St., Belleville, IL 62222-9978, phone 618-233-2238, editor Jacqueline Lowery Corn, is a magazine circulating free to 500,000 benefactors, **"We use well-written, perceptive traditional verse, average-16 lines. Avoid heavy allusions. Good rhyme and/or rhythm a must. We prefer a reverent, inspirational tone, but not overly 'sectarian and scriptural' in content."** They have recently published poetry by Helen Kitchell Evans, Hilda Sanderson, Claire Puneky, and Susan Showers. As a sample the editor selected these lines by Connie Brown:

> *Dainty, diamond droplets*
> *Held fast by limb and lawn;*
> *Liquid gems He scatters*
> *Beneath the brimming dawn.*

Oblates is digest-sized, 20 pp., saddle-stapled, using color inside and on the cover. **Sample and guidelines for SASE and 55¢ postage. Six back issues—$1.25. Pays $25 plus 3 copies. Reports within 4-6 weeks. Time to publication "is usually within 1 to 2 years." Editor comments "occasionally, but always when MS 'just missed or when a writer shows promise.' " Considers simultaneous submissions.** She says, "We are a small publication very open to MSS from authors—beginners and professionals. We do, however, demand professional quality work. Poets need to study our publication, **and to send no more than one or two poems at a time. Content must be relevant to our older audience to inspire and motivate in a positive manner."**

O-BLEK (OBLIQUE) (II), Box 1242, Stockbridge, MA 01262, founded 1987, poetry editors Peter Gizzi and Connell McGrath, appears each April and November, a "journal of language arts" publishing a range of contemporary writing with an emphasis on poetry. **"We do not limit ourselves to any particular poetic; our foremost criterion is excellence. We are particularly interested in new alternative forms and styles. Poems may be of any length."** They have recently published poetry by Edmond Jabès, Barbara Guest, Michael Palmer, Charles Simic, Leslie Scalapino, Keith Waldrop, Rosemarie Waldrop,

Fanny Gowe, and Clark Coolidge. As a sample the editors selected these lines from "The Risingdale" by Michael Gizzi:

> *Men in the minds of their women*
> *Slickrock in a slot canyon. Even a morgue's got rules*
> *Cremated fore we sold 'em on the sound*
> *Musician diaphanous*

The issue of **o-blek** I have seen is digest-sized, 160-200 pp., flat-spined, professionally printed, with glossy, full-color cover. They have 150 subscriptions of which 30 are libraries. Subscription: $10. **Sample: $6 postpaid. Guidelines available for SASE. They do not consider simultaneous submissions or previously published poems. Reports in 4 months. "The editors strongly recommend that writers interested in submitting work to this journal read a copy** *before* **sending work. An average of one unsolicited manuscript is accepted per issue."**

OBSIDIAN: BLACK LITERATURE IN REVIEW (IV-Ethnic), Box 8105, North Carolina State Univ., Raleigh, NC 27695-8105, phone 919-737-3870, founded 1975, editor Gerald Barrax, appears three times a year "for the study and cultivation of creative works in English **by Black writers worldwide,** with scholarly critical studies by all writers on Black literature." They are **open as to subject-matter but want poetry (as well as fiction and drama) from Black writers only.** I have not seen an issue, but the editor describes it as 126 pp., $6 \times 9''$, press run of 700 for 500 subscriptions of which an eighth are libraries. Subscription: $10; single issue: $4. **Sample: $11 postpaid. Send SASE for guidelines. Pays 2 copies. Submit double-spaced MS on $8\frac{1}{2} \times 11''$ paper. Reports in 3-4 months.**

OFF OUR BACKS (IV-Feminist, political), 2423 18th St., NW, Washington, DC 20009, office coordinator Joanne Stato, is a **"feminist news journal with international emphasis" using "women's poetry."** It appears 11 times a year, 36 pp. tabloid size. Press run: 7,000. Subscriptions: $17. **Sample: $2 postpaid. Pays 2 copies. Simultaneous submissions OK. Reports in 6 months. They "very rarely" comment on rejections. Prefers short poetry.**

THE OHIO REVIEW (II); OHIO REVIEW BOOKS (V,II), Ellis Hall, Ohio University, Athens, OH 45701-2979, phone 614-593-1900, founded 1959, editor Wayne Dodd, attempts "to publish the best in contemporary poetry, fiction and reviews" in the *Review* and in chapbooks, flat-spined paperbacks and hardback books. They use **"all types"** of poetry and have recently published poems by William Stafford, Hayden Carruth, Deborah Boe, Joan Campbell, Gayle Roby, Campbell McGrath, and Bin Ramke, from whose work the editor selected these sample lines:

> *Not even abstraction can save us,*
> *but the abstract endures, like her body*
> *slick across the page, the woman*
> *glistening photographically*
> *like any given convert, any born-again*
> *to sex or salvation, the more furious*
> *forms of knowledge.*

The *Review* appears 3 times a year in a professionally printed, flat-spined, 140+ pp. format, matte cover with color and art, circulation 2,000, featuring about 18 poets per issue. Subscription: $12; per copy: $4.25. They receive about 3,000 freelance submissions per year, use 1% of them, and have a 6-12 month backlog. **Sample: $4.25 postpaid. Reports in 1 month. Pays $1/line for poems and $5/page for prose plus copies. Editor sometimes comments on rejections. Send SASE for guidelines. They are not at present accepting freelance submissions of book MSS. Query with publication credits, bio.**

OHIO STATE UNIVERSITY PRESS/THE JOURNAL AWARD IN POETRY (II), 180 Pressey Hall, 1070 Carmack Rd., Columbus, OH 43210-1002, poetry editor David Citino. *The Journal* (see that listing) selects for publication by Ohio State University Press for the Ohio State University Press/Journal Award **one full-length (at least 48 pp.) book MS submitted during September, typed, double-spaced, $12.50 handling fee (payable to OSU). Clear photocopies OK. Send SASE for notification of MS receipt or return of MS.** Some or all of the poems in the collection may have appeared in periodicals, chapbooks or anthologies, but must be identified. **Pays $1,000 from the Helen Hoover Santmyer fund "in addition to the usual royalties."** Each entrant receives a subscription (2 issues) to *The Journal*.

OLD HICKORY REVIEW (I), Box 1178, Jackson, TN 38302, phone 901-424-3277, founded 1969, president Edna Lackie, is a "literary semi-annual, 2 short stories and approximately 75-80 poems each issue. **No more than 24-30 lines, any form, any subject, no obscenities, no pornographic.** We publish poets from Maine to California." I have not seen it, but the editor says it is magazine-sized, about 300 press run for that many subscribers of which 15 are libraries. Subscription: $7. **Sample: $3.50 postpaid. Guidelines available for SASE. Pays 1 copy per poem.**

THE OLD RED KIMONO (I, II), P.O. Box 1864, Rome, GA 30163, phone 404-295-6312, founded 1972, poetry editors Jo Anne Starnes and Jon Hershey, a publication of the Humanities Division of Floyd College, has the "sole purpose of putting out a magazine of original, high quality poetry and fiction. **We are open to all quality poetry and are willing to consider any type of good work.**" They have recently published poetry by Walter McDonald, Peter Huggins, Kim Thomas, Dev Hathaway, John C. Morrison, and Mark R. McCulloh. The magazine is an annual, circulation 800, 7½ × 10½", 50+ pp., professionally printed on heavy stock with b/w graphics, colored matte cover with art, using approximately 40 pp. of poetry (usually several poems to the page). Sample copy $2. They receive 400-500 submissions per year, use 60-70. **Sample $2 with 9 × 12" SASE. Photocopy OK. Reports in 4-6 weeks. Pays copies. Editors sometimes comment on rejections.**

ON THE EDGE (II), 29 Concord Ave., Apt. 603, Cambridge, MA 02138, founded 1983, editor Cathryn McIntyre, who says, "**We will consider all styles and forms; prefer shorter poems (30 lines max.); will consider longer poems if subject matter appealing. Do not want to see traditional rhyme scheme.**" They have recently published poetry by Kathleen Spivack, and Marguerite Serkin. As a sample the editor selected these lines by David Schuster:

> *Past the odd lights on Central Ave.*
> *windows down*
> *playing loud —*
> *Psycho Killer, Qu'est que c'est?*
> *and you laugh*
> *I veer onto the Northway,*
> *gun the late night motor*

It appears 3-4 times a year, magazine-sized, 30-45 pp., side-stapled with card cover. Uses less than 10% of poems received. Subscription: $10/three issues. **Sample: $3.50 postpaid. Guidelines available for SASE. Prefers no simultaneous submissions, but notify them. Reports in 1-4 weeks usually, never longer than 8 weeks.** The editor says, "New writers are greatly encouraged. Past publication history has little or no effect on whether your work is accepted."

‡ONCE UPON A WORLD (IV-Science-Fiction/Fantasy), Suite 230, 816 Auto Mall Rd., Bloomington, IN 47401, founded 1988, editor Emily Alward. "**All poetry submitted should relate to science fiction or fantasy in concept and/or imagery. This does not mean it has to be 'about' space travel or dragons. None with a nihilistic outlook, extremely avant-garde style or formats.**" They have recently published poetry by Dixie Lee Highsmith, Ronald Gerard, and Dwight E. Humphries. As a sample the editor selected these lines (poet unidentified):

> *We want our men to be brave and strong*
> *but also open to the tears*
> *that sear the hurt in the mortality flask.*

I have not seen an issue, but the editor describes it as magazine-sized, 80-100 pp. with "heavy card-stock colored covers, special-bound." They accept 5-10 of 50+ submissions received. Press run 120. **Sample, postpaid: $8. Pays 1 copy.** "**We strongly recommend purchase of a copy before submitting both to give some idea of the content and tone and to help keep the magazine solvent. But this is not a requirement.**" **Reports in 2-10 weeks.** The editor says, "Our major interest is in presenting science fiction and fantasy *short* stories with well-worked-out alternate world settings and an emphasis on ideas and/or character interaction. We use poetry for fillers. Where possible we try to match a poem with an adjacent story that it somewhat resembles in subject matter or tone. We *always* attempt to indicate some reason for rejection. So far it's been through individually written messages. If volume of submissions increases drastically, we might have to go to printed forms. As the editor's major interest is fiction, she does not feel qualified to give in-depth critiques of poetry, however."

ONIONHEAD; ARTS ON THE PARK, INC. (THE LAKELAND CENTER FOR CREATIVE ARTS); WORD-ART, THE FLORIDA POETS COMPETITION; ESMÉ BRADBERRY PRIZE (II), 115 N. Kentucky Ave., Lakeland, FL 33801, phone 813-680-2787. Arts on the Park founded 1979; *Onionhead* founded 1988. *Onionhead* is a literary quarterly. "**Our focus is on provocative political, social and cultural observations and hypotheses. Controversial material is encouraged. International submissions are welcome. We have no taboos, but provocation is secondary to literary excellence. No light verse please.**" They have recently published poetry by Jessica Freeman, Arthur Knight, Lyn Lifshin, B.Z. Niditch and A.D. Winans. As a sample I selected the last of four stanzas of "Apart" by June Goodwin:

> *I mull and rock, a by-and-by evasion*
> *and possession of a yearning that satisfies and*
> *pains, ripping off the leaves, leaving*
> *boney limbs to claw across the space.*
> *Here where your absence makes love more imagined*

> *I drape myself like wings to try, as if*
> *distance, like apartheid, were only attitude.*

The magazine is digest-sized, 40-50 pp., photocopied from typescript with glossy card cover. Their press run is 250 with 60 subscriptions of which 1 is a library. Complimentary distribution to universities, reviews and libraries world-wide. They use 100 of 2,500 submissions received per year. Subscription: $8 U.S., $16 other. **Sample: $3 postpaid. Pays 1 copy. Poet's name and title of poems should appear on the upper right-hand corner of each page. Poem "should be submitted exactly as you intend it to appear if selected for publication." Editor comments on rejections "rarely."** Poems are reviewed by an Editorial Board and **submissions are reported on within two months. If accepted, poems will normally appear within one year.** WORDART, The Florida Poets Competition, established 1983, is now open to all authors. Cash awards, "including the prestigious Esmé Bradberry Prize, are announced at a reading and reception during the first part of March." $8 reading fee. For guidelines and specific dates send SASE to the sponsoring organization, Arts on the Park, Inc., at the above address.

‡ONTHEBUS; BOMBSHELTER PRESS (II, IV-Regional), 6421 ½ Orange St., Los Angeles, CA 90048, founded 1975. *Onthebus* editor Jack Grapes. Bombshelter Press poetry editors Jack Grapes and Michael Andrews. *Onthebus* uses **"contemporary mainstream poetry—no more than 6 poems (10 pp. total) at a time. No rhymed, 19th Century traditional 'verse.' "** They have recently published poetry by Charles Bukowski, Lyn Lifshin, Kate Braverman, Stephen Dobyns, Allen Ginsberg, David Mura, Richard Jones, and Ernesto Cardenal. As a sample I selected these lines that conclude "The Point of Departure" by Doraine:

> *How terrifying to have no where to go.*
> *To have only this present*
> *to unwrap.*

Simultaneous submissions and previously published poems OK, "if I am informed where poem has previously appeared and/or where poem is also being submitted. I prefer cover letters with list of poems included plus poet's bio." Onthebus is a magazine appearing 3/year, 200 pp. offset, flat-spined, with color card cover. The issue I have seen (Winter, 1989) contained a 30 pp. glossy "Portfolio" of the work of Michael Andrews with full-color illustrations. Press run 2,000 for 350 subscribers of which 20 are libraries, 700 shelf sales ("300 sold directly at readings"). Subscription: $24. **Sample: $9 postpaid. Send SASE for guidelines. Pays 1 copy. No comments on rejections. Reports in "up to 12 weeks."** Bombshelter Press publishes 4-6 flat-spined paperbacks and 5 chapbooks per year. **Query first. Primarily Los Angeles poets. "We publish very few unsolicited MSS." Reports in 3 months. Pays 50 copies.** As a sample the editors selected these lines by editor Jack Grapes from his book **Trees, Coffee and the Eyes of the Deer:**

> *VOWS:*
> *We're going to get married*
> *and have kids*
> *and live together*
> *and be bloody*

Jack Grapes advises, "Read the publication you are submitting to *first*. Send poems *neatly* typed. Sloppiness and cramped and excessively folded pages are not cute, signs of eccentric genius, but unprofessional and make my job of reading poems harder. Buy or subscribe to publications you care about or they will die."

OPEN HAND PUBLISHING INC. (V), Box 22048, Seattle, WA 98122, phone 206-323-3868, founded 1981, publisher P. Anna Johnson, is a "literary/political book publisher" bringing out flat-spined paperbacks. They have published a book by E. Ethelbert Miller, from which the editor selected these sample lines:

> *When kisses find their wings*
> *they will return to our lips to*
> *fly again.*

That's from **where are the love poems for dictators?**, a 96 pp. book printed in large type on quality cream-colored stock with glossy card 2-color cover, $7.95, offers negotiable royalty. Miller is a black poet, and many of the books published by Open Hand have a black and/or African focus. **They do not consider unsolicited MSS.**

ORBIS; RHYME INTERNATIONAL COMPETITION FOR RHYMING POETRY (II,IV-Form, translation), 199 The Long Shoot, Nuneaton, Warwickshire, CV116JQ, England, founded 1968, editor Mike Shields, considers **"all poetry so long as it's genuine in feeling and well executed of its type."** They have published poetry by Sir John Betjeman, Ray Bradbury, George Mackay Brown, Christopher Fry, Seamus Heaney, Thomas Kinsella, James Kirkup, Norman MacCaig, Naomi Mitchison, President Jose Sarney of Brazil, and R.S. Thomas, "but are just as likely to publish absolute unknowns." As a sample the editor selected the closing lines of "Stop at the Bridge" by Georgia Tiffany (Spokane, USA):

Frost crawls along the hoods of cars.
The clock tower climbs out of the fog.
Threaded across the once intimate blaze
a web of ice.
the enviable rage of spiders.

The quarterly is 6 × 8½", flat-spined, 64 pp. professionally printed with glossy card cover, circulation 1,000; 600 subscriptions of which 50 are libraries. Subscription £12 (or $24); per copy: £3 ($6). They receive "thousands" of submissions per year, use "about 5%." **Sample: $2 (or £1) postpaid. Submit typed or photocopied, 1 side only, one poem per sheet. No bio, no query. Enclose IRCs for reply, not U.S. postage. Reports in 1-2 months. Pays $10 per acceptance plus 1 free copy automatically. Each issue carries £50 in prizes paid on basis of reader votes.** The Rhyme International Competition for Rhyming Poetry has 2 categories (open, up to 50 lines, rhymed poetry; strict form class) with prizes averaging £75-300 in each class each year (at least 60% of fees received; over £1,200 paid out in 1987), entry fee £2 (or $4). Write for entry form. Deadline September 30. Adjudication takes place during a special workshop weekend in England under the supervision of a well-known poet. Editor comments on rejections "occasionally—if we think we can help. *Orbis* is completely independent and receives no grant-aid from anywhere."

ORCHISES PRESS (II), P.O. Box 20602, Alexandria, VA 22320-1602, founded 1983, poetry editor Roger Lathbury, is a small press publisher of literary and general material in flat-spined paperbacks. **"Although we will consider MS submitted, we prefer to seek out the work of poets who interest us."** Regarding the poetry he states: **"No restrictions, really; but it must be sophisticated—i.e., no religious versification, arty nonsense, etc."** He has recently published poetry by Larry Moffi and Edmund Pennant. Asked for a sample, he says, "I find this difficult, but . . ." (from Joe David Bellamy):

And the sea extends for miles, blank from above,
white and brittle, encircled by blank trees, the ice
as hard and heavy as iron, though suffused with light,
opalescent beneath the surface, then, deeper. . . .

He publishes about 2 flat-spined paperbacks of poetry a year, averaging 64 pp. **When submitting, "tell where poems have previously been published." Reports in 4 weeks. Pays 36% of money earned once Orchises recoups its initial costs.** Roger Lathbury says, "Real poets persist and endure."

ORE (II, IV-Themes), 7 The Towers, Stevenage, Hertfordshire, England SG1 1HE, founded 1955, poetry editor Eric Ratcliffe, a magazine that appears 2-3 times per year. They want poetry in **"any length or form or style, preferably romantic, idealistic, visionary, belief in after-life. No four-letter words, and that ilk. No out-and-out pessimistic poems. Many *Ore* poems reflect the ancient atmosphere of Britain and Arthurian themes and British folklore. American poets will be more likely to gain acceptance if they submit high standard poetry relative to American folklore and not social life in the States."** For example, they have published poems about Wyatt Earp, Washington crossing the Delaware, and an Indiana volunteer soldier. "The themes might be anything which *might pass into folklore*— like a great engineering feat, dam, skyscraper, etc. One advantage is that USA poets tend to change language a bit to fit in with the old times, and this cuts out a lot of college brashness about modernity which I don't want." They receive about 1,000 poems/year, accept 5%. **Sample: £1.60 or 6 IRCs. Pays 1 copy, others at ½ price. Simultaneous submissions OK.** Editor "always" comments—"no curt rejection slips." He advises: "1. Realize what your type of interest is and your educational and expression limits. 2. Read lots of poetry consistent with 1. Dwell internally on imagery, etc. 3. Write poetry when something comes in the head—don't intend to write first. 4. Put it away for a week and rewrite it."

OREGON EAST (II, IV-Regional), Hoke Center, Eastern Oregon State College, La Grande, OR 97850, founded 1950, editor changes yearly, is the "literary annual of EOSC, 50% of magazine open to off-campus professional writing. It is flat-spined, book format, typeset, with end papers, 6 × 9", approximately 80 pp., using graphics and b/w art, circulation 1,000 (300 off-campus) with 100 subscriptions of which 30-40 are libraries. Their preferences: **"Eclectic tastes in poetry with the only requirement being literary quality work for off-campus submissions. Chances of publication are better for short poems (one page) than longer ones."** No 'greeting card' verse." They have published poetry by Ling Wen Yuan, Rob Hollis Miller, Robert Hoeft, and Ron Bayes. As a sample the editor selected these lines by Lorraine Kessel, from "White Frozen Flowers":

Sisters in summer
we looked down on the blushing earth
from our tree house.
Our braids fell down our backs

ladders for climbing lovers.

Price per issue: $5. 35-year issue available for $9.95 (256 pp.) **Pays 2 copies. Deadline March 1. Notification by June. No simultaneous submissions. All submissions must be accompanied by SASE and cover letter with brief bio and phone.**

ORPHIC LUTE (II, IV-Form), 526 Paul Pl., Los Alamos, NM 87544, founded 1950, editor Patricia Doherty Hinnebusch, is $7 \times 8\frac{1}{2}''$, 40 pp. quarterly (photocopied from typescript, saddle-stapled, matte card cover) which uses **"only short forms, focusing on haiku and senryu." Prefer haiku, cinquain sequences, linked lanternes, etc. No pornography. 2-7 lines; forms only."** They have recently published haiku by H.F. Noyes, Jane Andres, and Marian Olson. The editor selected these sample lines by Matthew Louviére:

> *Moonlit beach*
> *a single wave*
> *pleats the wind*

The magazine has a circulation of 250, 200 subscriptions of which 6 are libraries. Subscription: $10; per copy: $2.50. They receive about 4,000 submissions per year, use 300, have a 2-3 month backlog. "I publish seasonal poetry in season; other poems ASAP. I work on 2 issues at a time." **Sample: $2.50 postpaid; subscription is $10/year. Submit 6-10 poems; no simultaneous submissions, no query; no unclear type or light photocopies. Reports in 8-12 weeks. Payment is one copy. Send SASE for guidelines. "Whenever asked, we critique submissions. We frequently make minor revisions a condition of acceptance."** The editor advises, "Every poem is a working poem. The poet can make improvements in successive revisions over many years. If it is worth saying, it is worth saying well."

ORTALDA & ASSOCIATES (V), 1208 Delaware St., Berkeley, CA 94702, phone 415-524-2040, FAX 415-527-3411, founded 1985, poetry editor Floyd Salas, director/editor Claire Ortalda, publishes quality flat-spined paperbacks of poetry but **is not accepting submissions at this time.** They have published poetry by Czeslaw Milosz, Robert Hass, Ishamel Reed, Gary Soto, Jack Micheline, and Carolyn Kizer. As a sample Claire Ortalda selected these lines from "He Will Bleed Me Down to Serum for his Veins" by their poetry editor Floyd Salas:

> *There is no honor among thieves*
> *He will bleed me down to serum for his veins*
> *and pop me into his arm*
> *He will sell me to the fence . . .*

The editors offer criticisms at $25 an hour. They advise: "It is your own integrity that matters. Honesty is transforming."

OSIRIS, AN INTERNATIONAL POETRY JOURNAL/UNE REVUE INTERNATIONALE (II, IV-Translations, bilingual), P.O. Box 297, Deerfield, MA 01342, founded 1972, poetry editor Andrea Moorhead, a $6 \times 9''$, saddle-stapled, 40 pp. semiannual **publishes contemporary poetry in English, French and Spanish without translations and in other languages with translation, including Polish, Danish and Italian.** They also publish graphics, interviews and photographs. They want poetry which is **"lyrical, non-narrative, multi-temporal, well crafted."** They have recently published poetry by Loss Glazier, Simon Perchik, Madeleine Gagnon (Quebec), Marin Sorescu (Rumania), Wolf Gowin (Austria), and Yann Lovelock (England). The editors selected these sample lines (poet unidentified):

> *Niagara calls and refusal is impossible*
> *water descends the night still sparkles*
> *and i have crossed the barrier of frozen blood*
> *and the trance laid on eyes unknowing*

There are 10-14 pp. of poetry in English in each issue. They have a print run of 500, send 40 subscription copies to college and university libraries, including foreign libraries. Subscription: $7; per copy: $3.50. They receive 50-75 freelance submissions per year, use 12. **Sample: $3 postpaid. Include short bio with submission. Reports in 4 weeks. Pays 5 copies.** The editor advises, "It is always best to look at a sample copy of a journal before submitting work, and when you do submit work, do it often and do not get discouraged. Try to read poetry and support other writers."

‡The double dagger before a listing indicates that the listing is new in this edition. New markets are often the most receptive to submissions.

THE OTHER SIDE MAGAZINE (II, IV-Political, religious, social issues), 1225 Dandridge St., Fredericksburg, VA 22402, phone 703-371-7416, founded 1965, poetry editor Rod Jellema, is a "magazine (published 6 times a year) concerned with social justice issues from a Christian perspective. The magazine publishes 1-2 poems per issue. We will consider no more than 4 poems at one time from the same author. Submissions should be of high quality and must speak to and/or reflect the concerns and life experiences of the magazine's readers. We look for fresh insights and creative imagery in a tight, cohesive whole. Be warned that only 0.5% of the poems reviewed are accepted. Seldom does any published poem exceed 40-50 lines. Do not want to see pious religiosity, sentimental schlock, haiku." They have recently published poetry by Eric Ormsby, Elisabeth Murawski, Nola Garrett, and Gail White; the editors selected these lines as a sample (poet unidentified):

> On our knees we see under
> the dark side of things,
> playgrounds everywhere
> wait to grind skin
> and we must rise bleeding,
> healing ourselves again.

The Other Side is magazine-sized, professionally printed on quality pulp stock, 56 pp., saddle-stapled, with full-color paper cover, circulation 13,000 to that many subscriptions. Subscription: $27. Sample: $4.50 postpaid. Send SASE for guidelines (material pertaining to poetry is quoted above). Pays $10-15 plus 4 copies and free subscription. No simultaneous submissions. Previously published poems rarely used. Editor "sometimes" comments on rejections.

OUR FAMILY (IV-Religious), Box 249, Battleford, Saskatchewan, S0M 0E0, Canada, phone 306-937-7772, FAX 306-937-7644, founded 1949, editor, Nestor Gregoire, o.m.i., is a monthly religious magazine for Roman Catholic families. "Any form is acceptable. In content we look for simplicity and vividness of imagery. The subject matter should center on the human struggle to live out one's relationship with the God of the Bible in the context of our modern world. We do not want to see science fiction poetry, metaphysical speculation poetry, or anything that demeans or belittles the spirit of human beings or degrades the image of God in him/her as it is described in the Bible." They have recently published poetry by Nadene Murphy and Arthur Stilwell. The editor selected these sample lines from "I Asked" by Jean Woodward Larson:

> I asked to be more open
> to receiving love;
> I was made more open
> in giving it.

Our Family is magazine-sized, 40 pp., glossy color paper cover, using drawings, cartoons, two-color ink, circulation 13,500 of which 48 are libraries. $1.95 per issue, subscription $15.98 Canada/$21.98 US. Sample: $2.50 postpaid. Send SASE with IRC or personal check (American postage cannot be used in Canada) for writer's guidelines. Will consider poems of 4-30 lines. Pays 75¢-$1 per line. Reports within 30 days after receipt. Simultaneous submissions OK, prefers letter-quality to dot-matrix. The editor advises, "The essence of poetry is imagery. The form is less important. Really good poets use both effectively."

OUROBOROS (V), 40 Grove Ave., Ottawa, ON K1S 3A6 Canada, founded 1982, publisher Colin Morton. They publish chapbooks, paperbacks, broadsides, postcards, posters, etc. Currently not accepting poetry submissions. They have recently published poetry by Richard Kostelanetz, Nancy Corson Carter, and John Barton. The publisher provided these sample lines by John Newlove:

> Everyone is wise. The idiot is
> a master in his idiocy and he
> knows things he cannot explain to the others.
> We're just carriers for our genes anyways.

Press runs are 200 to 500. Issues priced $1-$10. Sample: $3 postpaid. The publisher offers this general advice: "Read poetry. If you don't enjoy reading poetry, don't write it. Write only those pieces that demand to be written."

‡OUT LOUD: THE MONTHLY OF LOS ANGELES AREA POETRY EVENTS (IV-Regional), 1350 Third St. Promenade, Santa Monica, CA 90401, founded 1989, editor Carrie Etter, "is distributed at poetry venues throughout the Los Angeles area: performance spaces, theaters, bookstores, etc." and accepts poetry from poets living in Los Angeles or Orange County, up to 40 lines. No "sentimental work or work that demonstrates that the writer is not an avid reader of modern poetry." Previously published poetry OK if cover letter indicates when and where it was published. "Otherwise cover letters are not necessary." Subscription: $6/year. Format is 2 double-sided printed pages stapled at one corner, "high quality." Press run 1,500, all copies distributed free except subscriber copies. Sample, postpaid: 50¢. Pays 2 copies "unless poet requests more. Responses are within a month, but are usually immediate."

OUT MAGAZINE (I), #5-359 Davenport Rd., Toronto, ON M5R 1K5 Canada, phone 416-927-9965, founded 1986, editor Shawn Venasse, appears 4-6 times a year, using "**strong, imagistic, passionate, free verse, intelligent, challenging, aware" poetry, not that which is "nane, rhyming, sophomoric."** As a sample I selected these lines from "What We Do in Michigan" by Blake Walmsley:

> *In Michigan we sell hope*
> *in the form of instant lottery tickets.*
> *Scratch and match and lose,*
> *one dollar at a time, instantly,*
> *without the hassle of waiting for a drawing.*

Out is digest-sized, photocopied from dark type, with thin matte card cover. Their press run is 500 (increasing to 1,000). "In a slow year we receive 100 pieces and use about 20." It is distributed free. **Sample: $1 postpaid (or just postage). Pays 5-10 copies "depending on size." They prefer covering letter and bio with submissions.** The editor says, "Poems are chosen by an intuitive gut response upon first reading—if they don't leap off the page we don't publish them." Reports in 3-6 weeks. "Be original and daring—avoid clichés at all cost and know your market."

OUTERBRIDGE (II), English A323, The College of Staten Island, 715 Ocean Terrace, Staten Island, NY 10301, phone 718-390-7654, founded 1975, editor Charlotte Alexander, publishes "the most crafted, professional poetry and short fiction we can find (unsolicited except special features—to date rural, urban and Southern, promoted in standard newsletters such as *Poets & Writers, AWP, Small Press Review*), interested in newer voices. **Anti loose, amateurish, uncrafted poems showing little awareness of the long-established fundamentals of verse; also anti blatant PRO-movement writing when it sacrifices craft for protest and message. Poems usually 1-4 pp. in length."** They have recently published poetry by P. B. Newman, Cathryn Hankla, Marilyn Throne, and Candida Lawrence. The editors selected these sample lines from "Discovering Musicians" by Sharyn November:

> *They understand operations better than surgeons,*
> *how the sharpness of hair against cat-gut*
> *cuts more cleanly than a scalpel.*
> *Pasteboard and velvet cases cushion their unstrung*
> *cellos, basses, instruments whose scroll-work*
> *coils into a bass clef.*

The digest-sized flat-spined, 100+ pp. annual is about half poetry, circulation 500-600, 150 subscriptions of which 28 are libraries. They receive 500-700 submissions per year, use about 60. **Sample: $4 postpaid. Submit 3-5 poems anytime except June-July. "We dislike simultaneous submissions and if a poem accepted by us proves to have already been accepted elsewhere, a poet will be blacklisted as there are many good poets waiting in line." Reports in 2 months, pays 2 copies (and offers additional copies at half price).** The editor says, "As a poet/editor I feel magazines like *Outerbridge* provide an invaluable publication outlet for individual poets (particularly since publishing a book of poetry, respectably, is extremely difficult these days). As in all of the arts, poetry—its traditions, conventions and variations, experiments—should be studied. One current 'trend' I detect is a lot of mutual backscratching which can result in very loose, amateurish writing. Discipline!"

THE OVERLOOK PRESS; TUSK BOOKS (V), 12 West 21st St., New York, NY 10010, phone 212-675-0585, founded 1972, are trade publishers with about 8 poetry titles. They have published books of poetry by David Shapiro and Paul Auster. The editors selected these sample lines from "Mannequins" by Daniel Mark Epstein:

> *This indecent procession of the undead invades*
> *the Avenue windows, dressed to kill, sporting*
> *tomorrow's clothes and yesterday's faces.*

Tusk/Overlook Books are distributed by Viking/Penguin. **They publish on standard royalty contracts with author's copies. Query before submitting.**

‡OVERTONE PRESS; OVERTONE SERIES (II), 6927 Saybrook Ave., #2, Philadelphia, PA 19142, editor Beth Brown Preston, founded 1973. *Overtone Series* is a magazine-sized 50 pp. quarterly. **They want "the American modernistic tradition of poetry which innovates in shape, form, and sensibility. No garbage."** They have recently published poetry by Thomas Lux, and as a sample the editor selected these lines from "True Love" by Robert Penn Warren:

> *In silence the heart raves. It utters words*
> *Meaningless, that never had*
> *A meaning.*

Overtone Series is "dedicated to poetic American modernism. They receive about 100 poems per month. Press run is 4,000 for 2,500 subscriptions. Subscription: $8. **Sample: $2.50 postpaid. Send SASE for guidelines. Pays 5 copies. Simultaneous submissions and previously published poems**

OK. Reports in 3 months. For chapbook consideration (25 pp.) there is a $4 reading fee. Query with samples, bio, publications and "any pertinent information." Pays $50 and 10 copies for chapbook publication. For sample chapbook send $4. They sometimes sponsor contests. Beth Brown Preston says, "I think poets who are just beginning should gather the best materials around them and make sure they have a sense of physical or environmental organization. With this sense, one goes ahead and appeals to the gods and muses."

‡OVETA CULP HOBBY (I), 2380 Cosmos Dr., Loveland, OH 45140, founded 1987, designer/editor Melissa Baker, is an annual featuring **"visual and rhythmic poetry especially. Length—no matter, as long as it takes to express the feeling. Individual style is important and a strong secure voice. No rhymed, mainstream, dark, romantic poetry."** They have recently published poetry by Judson Crews and Stacey Solifrey. As a sample the editor selected these lines (poet unidentified):

> *nested blondes*
> *making baby*
> *slobbering*
> *dirty the rafters*

I have not seen an issue, but the editor describes it as digest-sized, approximately 20 pp., photocopied. She selects about 20 of 100 poems received. Press run 100-300. **Sample, postpaid: $3. Send SASE for guidelines. Pays 1 copy. "3-8 poems per submission would be plenty." Simultaneous submissions and previously published poems ("but hesitantly") OK. Reports within a month. "Rejected MSS receive handwritten comments/criticism."** The editor says, "Trust the brain you're given. We each have beauty in us. Make art out of your experience. Let words come, seep in, rather than wrestling them. Treat poetry delicately—the most beautifully inbred art."

OXFORD UNIVERSITY PRESS (V, III), 200 Madison Ave., New York, NY 10016, phone 212-679-7300, founded 1478, poetry editor, Jacqueline Simms (U.K.), is a large university press publishing academic, trade and college books in a wide variety of fields. Not accepting any poetry MSS. "Our list includes Conrad Aiken, Richard Eberhart, Robert Graves, Geoffrey Hill, Peter Porter, M.L. Rosenthal, Stephen Spender, Anne Stevenson, and Charles Tomlinson. These indicate our direction."

OYEZ REVIEW (II), 430 S. Michigan Ave., Chicago, IL 60605, phone 312-341-2017, founded 1965, editor Patty Magierski. An annual literary magazine published by Roosevelt University. They have published poetry by Lisel Mueller, John Jacob, and Barry Silesky. "*Oyez Review* is in its 25th year of publication and is an award-winning publication which has maintained its high level of excellence by encouraging submissions from serious writers and artists." The digest-sized review is flat-spined, about 100 pp., using b/w photography and line drawings, poetry and fiction, has glossy, color card cover. Circulation 500. It is sold at Roosevelt University events and bookstores in Chicago and throughout the nation. **Sample copies are $4. Guidelines available for SASE. Pays 3 copies. Reports in 10-12 weeks. Deadline in October or November. Published in spring.**

‡PABLO LENNIS (IV-Science fiction, fantasy), 30 N. 19th St., Lafayette, IN 47904, founded 1976, editor John Thiel, appears irregularly, is a **"science-fiction and fantasy fanzine preferring poems of an expressive cosmic consciousness or full magical approach. I want poetry that rimes and scans and I like a good rhythmic structure appropriate to the subject. Shorter poems are much preferred. I want them to exalt the mind, imagination, or perception into a consciousness of the subject. Optimism is usually preferred, and English language perfection eminently preferable. Nothing that is not science fiction or fantasy, or which contains morbid sentiments, or is perverse, or does not rime, or contains slang."** They have recently published poetry by Richard Kostelanetz, Steve Sneyd, Dan Pearl and Nathan Whiting. As a sample the editor selected these lines (poet unidentified):

> *Say there, fine fellow, have you got a light?*
> *Perish! I abhor the fall of night,*
> *When gibbering legions come to make us swoon*
> *And idly do we talk, beneath a waxen moon.*

It is magazine-sized, 30 pp. side-stapled, photocopied from typescript, with matte card cover, using fantastic ink drawings and hand-lettering. "I get maybe fifty poems a year and have been using most of them." Press run "up to 100 copies." Subscription: $10/year. **Sample, postpaid: $1. Pays 1 copy, 2 if requested. Reports "at once. I generally say something about why it was not used, if it was not. If someone else might like it, I mention an address."** The editor says, "Poetry should be respected and supported. However, trends in current poetry are toward pessimism and nililism. I like poetry that is pleasant to read and increasing of consciousness. I advise poets to attempt the positive and strive for readership appeal. They are too similar to everything else when they do not do so."

PACIFIC REVIEW (II), English and Comparative Literature, San Diego State University, San Diego, CA 93182, phone 619-594-5183, founded 1973, is a literary magazine appearing twice a year with **"no restrictions as to form or style. Length requirement is a maximum of 150 lines. We want good quality poetry—either experimental or traditional in form. No pornography or greeting-card-type work."** They have recently published poetry by Maxine Kumin, Christopher Buckley, Madeline DeFrees, David Ignatow, Daniel Halpern, Donald Finkel, Elton Glaser, and Mark Jarman. As a sample the editor selected these lines from "At Borego" by William Stafford:

> *Into the soul's own portals that thin*
> *persistent song pours. Fast-blooming*
> *desert flowers launch their brief selves.*
> *Without encouragement they stand and abide*
> *whatever comes, a gritty welcome,*
> *and then the kind scythe of the wind.*

I have not seen it, but the editor describes *PR* as 100-200 pp, 6×9″, with a glossy card cover, professionally printed. their press run is 1,000. Subscription: $12. **Sample: $4 postpaid. Send SASE for guidelines. Pays 2 copies. Reports in 3-4 months. "We do not read during the summer.** We publish in January and September."

PAINTBRUSH: A JOURNAL OF POETRY, TRANSLATIONS AND LETTERS; ISHTAR PRESS (II), Dept. of Language & Literature, Northeast Missouri S.U., Kirksville, MO 63501, founded 1974, editor Ben Bennani. *Paintbrush* is a 6×9″, 64+ pp. literary biannual, circulation 500, which uses **quality poetry. Sample: $5.** Ishtar Press publishes collections of poetry. Send SASE for catalog to buy samples.

PAINTED BRIDE QUARTERLY (II), 230 Vine St., Philadelphia, PA 19106, phone 215-925-9914, editors Louis Camp and Joanna DiPaolo, founded 1973, **"We have no specifications or restrictions. We'll look at anything."** They have recently published poetry by Robert Bly, Charles Bukowski, Al Masarik and ave jeanne. The editors selected these sample lines from a poem by Etheridge Knight:

> *Grand leaps and the girl-giggles. We*
> *are touch-tender in our fears.*
> *You break my eyes with your beauty.*
> *Oouu-ou-baby . . .I love you.*

"PBQ aims to be a leader among little magazines published by and for independent poets and writers nationally." The 80 pp. perfect-bound, digest-sized magazine uses 60+ pages of poetry per issue, receiving over a thousand submissions per year and using under 150. Neatly printed, small type. It has a circulation of 1,000; 700 subscriptions, of which 30 are libraries. $5 per copy, $16 for subscription, **sample: $5 postpaid.** *Quarterly* deadlines: ongoing. Submit no more than 6 poems, any length, typed, photocopies OK, only original, unpublished work. Payment 2 copies and 1-year subscription. "Submissions should include a *short* bio." Editors seldom comment on rejections. They have a 6-9 month backlog.

‡**PALANQUIN; PALANQUIN POETRY SERIES (II)**, 9 Kerry Place, Flanders, NJ 07836, phone 201-927-5751, founded 1989, editor Phebe Davidson. The Palanquin Poetry Series has **an issue every 2 months consisting of 3 columns of poetry showcasing a single poet, professionally printed on a folded card.** Press run: 100 for 50 subscribers. Subscription: $12.50. **Sample, postpaid: $2. Pays ½ press run.** She wants no **"sentimental, religious, clotted academic"** poetry. They have recently published poetry by Jean Hollander, Joe Weil and Patricia Celley Groth. As a sample the editor selected these lines from "Harp" by Lois Harrod:

> *This gentle plucking of all my strings now,*
> *these ferns like green fingers when*
> *I walk the road, these vines like wild serpents*
> *tongues like threads, this thrush nagging me*

"I read January-March for the following year." No previously published poems. Reports in 2 months. Annual fall chapbook contest for spring publication.

‡**PANCAKE PRESS (V)**, 163 Galewood Circle, San Francisco, CA 94131, phone 415-665-9215, founded 1974, publisher Patrick Smith, a small-press publisher of hand-bound paperbacks with sewn signatures. **"Current projects are selected. At present we can consider only solicited mss for publication. Unsolicited mss will be returned with brief comment and thanks."** The editor publishes **"poetry aware of its own language conventions, tuned to both the ear and eye, attentive to syntax, honest about its desires, clear about something, spoken or written as a member of the species."** He has recently published books by John Logan, David Ray, and Stephen Dunning. As a sample, he selected the following lines by an unidentified poet:

> *words hard as stone that can fall down*
> *a mountain and not change but we are not*

made for such a plunge spirits such as
we who breathe air and drink water thrive

on what takes shape every moment i cant
say this except in words dont keep them

The two thin chapbooks I have seen are handsomely printed on fine paper; one has b/w illustrations. Covers are either matte or glossy cards, and one is illustrated with a drawing of the author. Pancake Press publishes 2-3 chapbooks each year, with an average page count of 36, flat-spined.

PANDORA (I, IV-Science fiction/fantasy, children/teen), 2844 Grayson, Ferndale, MI 48220. Send poetry to Ruth Berman, 2809 Drew Ave. S., Minneapolis, MN 55416, founded 1978, editor Meg Mac Donald, poetry editor Ruth Berman, appears 2 times yearly, using 12-15 poems in each issue of **"science fiction, fantasy, offbeat, any form. No horror! Long poems must be of extremely high quality. Most of what we purchase is under 30 lines. No poems unrelated to the themes of our magazine."** They have recently published poetry by Sandra Lindow, Margaret Palmer Gordon-Espe, W. Gregory Stewart, and Terry McGarry. As a sample the editors selected "Still, the Challenge" by Ann K. Schwader:

Seven falling leaves . . .
on the moon, cold distant gales
Withering rootlets . . .

on Fading salt wind
a single leaf touches down
in Armstrong's footprint

It is digest-sized, 72 pp., offset, on white stock with glossy card stock cover in b/w and 1 additional color, perfect bound, using b/w graphics and ads, circulation 1,000, including some libraries, newsstand and bookstore sales. Subscription: $10 for 2 issues (U.S.); $15 for 2 issues (Canada); $20 for 2 issues. **Sample: $5 postpaid (U.S.); $7 (Canada); $10 overseas. Send SASE for guidelines. Payment per poem averages $5 and 1 copy. "Please submit no more than 6 poems at once. Simultaneous submissions OK, but discouraged. Previously published poems used "rarely." Specify previous publisher. Reports in 8 weeks. Delay to publication 6-12 months. Editor comments on rejections.** *Pandora's* **All Youth issue accepts poetry by those in grades K-12 of the current year. Send SASE for guidelines, 1990 issue $4 postpaid.** "Researching your market is probably the most valuable time you will spend as a poet. You've already spent precious time in the creation process; don't waste time and postage on blind submissions. Send for guidelines. Better yet, acquire a few issues of the magazine you are interested in submitting to. Spend some serious time scrutinizing the contents. Watch for trends, for changes in editorial tastes. Be careful not to send work that only repeats what you've seen recently. Trying to win the editor over with what you already know 'isn't quite right' is risky. When an editor can't use your work, take any comments to heart. Above all, don't be discouraged and never take rejection personally. Poetry is a very personal thing for many editors — it may not be the technical form that makes or breaks it, it may just be a gut reaction to that particular poem on that day. Take whatever clues you're given to improve your chances — or your poetry — in the future."

THE PANHANDLER (II), English Dept., University of West Florida, Pensacola, FL 32514, phone 904-474-2923, founded 1976, editors Michael Yots and Stanton Millet, appears twice a year, using **poetry "grounded in experience with strong individual 'voice' and natural language. Any subject, no 'causes.' Length to 200 lines, but prefer 30-100. No self-consciously experimental, unrestrained howling, sophomoric wailings on the human condition."** They have recently published poetry by Malcolm Glass, Lyn Lifshin, Donald Junkins, David Kirby, Joan Colby, R. T. Smith, Jim Hall and Peter Meinke. As a sample I selected the first stanza of "York, Maine" by Leo Connellan:

Through the Cutty Sark motel room 21 picture window now
the gray waves coming into York Beach like
an invasion of plows pushing snow. Tomorrow
the sun will scratch its chin and bleed along the skyline
but today everything is gray poached in a steam of fog.

The handsomely printed magazine is digest-sized, 64 pp., flat-spined, large type on heavy eggshell stock, matte card cover with art. Circulation: 500, to 100 subscriptions of which 10 are libraries and 200 complimentary copies to the English department and writing program. Subscription: $5. **Sample: $2 postpaid. Pays 2 copies. Reports in 1-2 months, 6-12 months to publication. Submit maximum of 7 poems, typewritten or letter-perfect printout. No simultaneous submissions.** The editor advises: "(1) take care with MS preparation. Sloppy MSS are difficult to evaluate fairly; (2) send only poems you believe in. Everything you write isn't publishable; send finished work." National chapbook competition each year, September 15-January 15, 24-30 pp., with $7 reading fee. Send SASE for details.

PANJANDRUM BOOKS; PANJANDRUM POETRY JOURNAL (II, IV-Translations), 5428 Hermitage Ave., North Hollywood, CA 91607, founded 1971, editor Dennis Koran, associate editor David Guss. The press publishes a distinguished list of avant-garde books. They are interested in translations (especially European) of modern poetry, surrealism, dada and experimental poetry and accept book-length MSS only with SASE; query first. The *Panjandrum Poetry Journal* is published occasionally. Submit no more than 10 poems after September 1991.

PAPER AIR MAGAZINE; SINGING HORSE PRESS (II), Box 40034, Philadelphia, PA 19106, founded 1976, editor and publisher Gil Ott, who says *"Paper Air* features poetry, interviews, essays, and letters in an attractive and well-designed format. Circulation is small and the magazine appears annually. Singing Horse Press publishes small books. Poets should read the magazine before submitting." Poets recently published include: Rosmarie Waldrop, Jackson MacLow, Charles Bernstein, Hugh Seidman, and Lyn Hejinian. *Paper Air* is magazine-sized, offset, 120 pp. flat-spined. Circulation is 800, of which 160 are subscriptions, 25 go to libraries, and 300 are sold on newsstands. Price per issue is $7. **Sample available for $5 postpaid. No simultaneous submissions. Reporting time is 1-8 weeks.** Singing Horse Press publishes 1-2 poetry chapbooks/year with an average page count of 24-48; format varies. Prices, according to their catalog, range from $2.50-4. **Writers should query before submitting.**

‡**THE PAPER BAG (I, II)**, Box 268805, Chicago, IL 60626-8805, phone 312-285-7972 (an answering service), founded 1988, editor M. Brownstein, is a quarterly using **poetry "any kind, any style. We look for strong and original imagery."** As a sample, I selected this haiku by Mikael Larsson:

> *Though snow is black*
> *With tossed-out seed, no birds come:*
> *nightfalling*

The Paper Bag is photocopied from typescript, 24 pp. digest-sized, saddle-stapled, with matte card cover. "Our circulation varies from 20-300+ and we sell out every issue." Subscription: $10/4-5 issues plus "anything else we publish." They publish about 30 of 200 poems received per issue. **Sample, postpaid: $2.50. Pays copies.** Editor comments on submissions "always." **They want a brief bio with each submission, typed MSS only, address and phone on each submission.** All checks or money orders should be made out to M. Brownstein. The editor says, "Be persistent. Because we reject one group of submissions does not mean we will reject another batch. Keep trying."

PAPER RADIO (IV-Form/style), P.O. Box 85302, Seattle, WA 98145-1302, founded 1986, poetry editors Dagmar Howard and N.S. Kvern, is a literary journal appearing 3 times a year. **"Actually what we want doesn't have a descriptive monicker because it is at the vanguard but not yet a movement. Suffice it to say, we are more in the line of descent from Wallace Stevens and the French dadaist and surrealists than from, say, W. C. Williams. Length: up to 100 lines. Style: from *ambient* to *grand mal*. Do not want to see mainstream theocratic bathos."** They have recently published poetry by Sheila E. Murphy, Bradley Goldman, Judson Crews and Stacey Sollfrey. As a sample the editor chose these lines (poet unidentified):

> *credo a face with my hands like crabbark, a face framed*
> *in terraglia permanence an Art and my knabenhaftigkeit in*
> *the new words to tinct it out like old gaunt beckettfarces*
> *like astolfo-moons like symposia weeped off my feet*

I have not seen a copy of *Paper Radio*, but the editor describes it as intended for "pointedly experimental poetry, fiction, graphics and criticism." It is digest-sized, "mixed printing (computer-generated, offset 8 or photocopy), generally ½ words and ½ graphics." They receive about 3,000 poems per year, accept 50-100. The circulation is 200+, 50+ subscriptions of which 10 are libraries. Subscription: $8. **Sample: $3 postpaid. Pays 1 copy.** "No specifications (we're anarchists) but more than 5-6 poems seems pointless or downright unstrategic (makes us feel Sisyphean)." **Simultaneous submissions OK. Reports in 1-2 months, 1-8 months delay till publication. On rejections, "we try to give some indication that a human read the work, but it depends on its quality and our workload.** Always remember Borges' comment: 'I write for myself and my friends, and to ease the passing of time.' Greed and mundane equivocation would seem, fortunately, to have no place in poetry—it's the useless utterance that is our greatest fulfillment."

PAPIER-MACHÉ PRESS (IV-Themes, women/feminism, social issues, senior citizens, anthology), 795 Via Manzana, Watsonville, CA 95076, phone 408-726-2933, FAX 408-726-1255, founded 1984, editor Sandra Martz, is a small-press publisher of anthologies, poetry and short fiction in flat-spined paperbacks. They typically **"work on specialized projects, that explore a particular aspect of**

women's experience, e.g. sports, aging, parental relationships, work, etc. Any length acceptable; primarily interested in well-written, accessible material." They have recently published poetry by Jenny Joseph, Sue Saniel Elkind, Shirley Vogler Meister, Michael Andrews, Ursula Hegi, Maude Meehan, and Elisavietta Ritchie. As a sample the editor selected these lines from "To Fish, to Remember" by Enid Shomer:

> Daddy is with me here on the pier
> at Cedar Key. The fish strung by their gills,
> the shower of water from the bait bucket
> bring him back. Night fishing
> from Biscayne Bridge. I'm six,
> chewed by mosquitoes, sticky with cocoa butter.

They publish 1-2 anthologies and 1-2 poetry collections each year. Each anthologycontains 30-40 poems; collections contain 60-80 poems. Query before submission to obtain current themes and guidelines. They report on queries in 4 weeks, on MS in 3 months. Legible photocopies and dot matrix OK. Simultaneous submissions must be identified as such. Pays 2 copies on work accepted for anthologies. Royalties and modest advances are negotiated on individual collections. Send SASE for booklist to buy samples, typically $4 to $10. *"Papier Mache's* primary objective is to publish anthologies, poetry, and short story collections by, for, and about midlife and older women. Material from socially aware men is welcome. Our strategy is to select subjects of particular importance to women, find well-written, accessible material on those themes, develop attractive, high quality book formats, and market them to an audience that might not otherwise buy books of poetry. We take particular pride in our reputation for dealing with our contributors in a caring, professional manner."

THE PARIS REVIEW; BERNARD F. CONNORS PRIZE; JOHN TRAIN HUMOR PRIZE (III, IV-Humor), 45-39 171st Pl., Flushing, NY 11358, founded 1952, poetry editor Patricia Storace. (**Submissions should go to her at 541 E. 72nd St., New York, NY 10021**). This distinguished quarterly (circulation 10,000, digest-sized, 200 pp.) has published many of the major poets writing in English. **Sample: $6.90. Study publication before submitting. Pays $35 to 24 lines, $50 to 59 lines; $75 to 99 lines; $150 thereafter.** The Bernard F. Connors prize of $1,000 is awarded annually for the best previously unpublished long poem (over 200 lines), submitted between April 1 and May 1. The John Train Humor Prize of $1,500 is awarded annually for the best previously unpublished work of humorous fiction, nonfiction or poetry submitted before March 31. **All submissions must be sent to 541 E. 72nd St., New York, NY 10021.**

PARNASSUS: POETRY IN REVIEW; POETRY IN REVIEW FOUNDATION (V, IV-Translations), Rm 804, 41 Union Square W., New York, NY 10003, phone 212-463-0889, founded 1972, poetry editor Herbert Leibowitz, provides "comprehensive and in-depth coverage of new books of poetry, including translations from foreign poetry." They have published special issues on Words & Music and Women & Poetry, and a special issue on the long poem in 1990. **"We publish poems and translations on occasion, but we solicit all poetry. Poets invited to submit are given all the space they wish; the only stipulation is that the style be non-academic."** They do consider unsolicited essays, but strongly recommend that writers study the magazine before submitting. They report on essay submissions within 8-10 weeks (response takes longer during the summer), dislike multiple submissions and dot-matrix printing, and pay $25-250 plus 2 gift subscriptions—the contributors can also take one themselves. **Editor comments on rejections—from one paragraph to 2 pages.** Subscriptions are $15/year, $29/year for libraries; they have 1,000 subscribers, of which 550 are libraries. The editor comments, "Contributors should be urged to subscribe to at least one literary magazine. There is a pervasive ignorance of the cost of putting out a magazine and no sense of responsibility for supporting a magazine. Our own plan is to publish more essays on and poems from foreign poetries."

PARNASSUS LITERARY JOURNAL (I, IV-Humor), P.O. Box 1384, Forest Park, GA 30051, founded 1975, edited by Denver Stull: "Our sole purpose is to promote poetry and to offer an outlet where poets may be heard." **One copy in payment.** This is an amiable, open magazine **emphasizing uplift.** It is photocopied from typescript, uses an occasional photo or drawing, 84 pp., saddle-stapled, low-budget production. Poets recently published include William J. Vernon, James P. Quinn, James Stratton, Diana Kwiatkowski Rubin, and Eugenia Moore. As a sample the editor selected these lines from "The Last Dance" by Dennis Grai:

> As brilliant rays of
> Sunshine dance colorfully
> From a crystal prism,
> So, too, will my soul
> Dance with the reflection
> Of Eternity . . .

Denver Stull says, **"We are open to all poets and all forms of poetry, including Oriental. Prefer**

24 lines and under but will take longer poetry if it is good. Do not see enough humor." The magazine comes out three times a year with a print run of 300 copies. Subscribers presently number 200 (5 libraries). They receive about 1,500 submissions per year, of which they use 350. Circulation includes: Japan, England, Greece, India, Korea, Germany, and Nederlands. **Reports within one week. Sample: $3.50. (regularly $4.25 per copy, $12 per subscription).** Make checks or money order payable to Denver Stull. Periodic contests with small cash prizes. **"Definitely" comments on rejected MSS.** The editor advises: "Do not be in a rush to send your work out. Study what you have written. Does it say what you want it to say? Is it understandable? Cut out excess verbiage. Be professional. Employ the basics — fresh manuscript, name and address on all copies, and do not forget the SASE."

PARTING GIFTS (II), March Street Press, 3006 Stonecutter Terrace, Greensboro NC 27405, founded 1987, poetry editor Robert Bixby. **"I want to see everything.** I'm a big fan of Jim Harrison, C. K. Williams, Amy Hempel and Janet Kauffman. If you write like them, you'll almost certainly be published. But that's pretty useless advice unless you're one of those people." He has recently published poetry by Eric Torgersen, Lyn Lifshin, Elizabeth Kerlikowske, Janet McCann, and David Shevin. As a sample I selected these lines from "Bed" by Katharyn Machan Aal:

> *A week ago I said goodbye*
> *and we pressed close in final*
> *coupling, mouth and mind and all*
> *our bodies knew to give.*

PG is digest-sized, 36 pp., photocopied, with colored matte card cover, press run 200, appearing twice a year, **send SASE for guidelines.** Subscription: $6. **Sample: $3 postpaid. Pays 2 copies. Editor "just about always" replies personally. Reports in 1-2 weeks. Submit in "groups of 3-10 with SASE and cover letter."** No previously published poems, but simultaneous submissions OK.

PARTISAN REVIEW (III, IV-Translations, themes), 236 Bay State Rd., Boston, MA 02215, phone 617-353-4260, founded 1934, editor William Phillips, is a distinguished quarterly literary journal (6 × 9″, 160 pp., flat-spined, circulation 8,200 for 6,000 subscriptions and shelf sales), using **poetry of high quality.** They have recently published poetry by Joseph Brodsky, Eavan Boland, W.S. Merwin, and C.H. Sisson. As a sample the editor chose these lines from "Daybreak" by Adam Zagajewski:

> *At daybreak, from the train window I see cities*
> *which sleep left deserted,*
> *open and defenseless like huge animals*
> *lying on their backs.*
> *Through the vast squares, only my thoughts*
> *and a cold wind are wandering . . . .*

Submit maximum of 6. Sample $5 plus $1 postage. Pays $50 and 50% discount on copies. No **simultaneous submissions. Reports in 2 months.** Editor "occasionally" comments on rejections. "Our poetry section is very small and highly selective. We are open to fresh, quality translations but submissions must include poem in original language as well as translation. We occasionally have special poetry (subject) sections.

PASQUE PETALS; SOUTH DAKOTA STATE POETRY SOCIETY, INC. (I, IV-Regional, subscribers), 909 E. 34th St., Sioux Falls, SD 57105, phone 605-338-9156, founded 1926, editor Barbara Stevens. This is the official poetry magazine for the South Dakota State Poetry Society, Inc., but it is open to non-members. **Those not residents of SD are required to subscribe when (or before) submitting. They use "all forms. 44 line limit, 50 character lines. Count titles and spaces. Lean toward SD and Midwest themes. No rough language or porno — magazine goes into SD schools and libraries."** As a sample the editor chose "Kleptomaniac" by Emma Dimit:

> *Lady-like,/ my silver Gruen/ picks up time/ as if life/*
> *is not already/ stealing away/ too fast./ Cogs rackets/*
> *click tick/ fast faster/ shop lift/ sun lit moments/*
> *of my life.*

PP appears 10 times a year (no August or November issues), digest-sized, 16-20 pp., using small b/w sketches. Circulation is 250 to member/subscribers (16 to libraries). Subscription: $15/year. **Sample: $1.50 postpaid. Send SASE for guidelines. Pays non-members only 1 copy. Reports in 3 months.** 2-3 month backlog. Submit 3 poems at a time, 1 poem (or 2 haiku) per page. Editor **"always" comments on rejections.** They sponsor one yearly contest — and sometimes smaller ones are offered by members.

PASSAGER: A JOURNAL OF REMEMBRANCE AND DISCOVERY (II, IV-Senior citizen), English Department, University of Baltimore, 1420 N. Charles St., Baltimore, MD 21201-5779, phone 301-625-3041, founded 1989, editor Kendra Kopelke. *Passager* is published quarterly and invites **"writers**

of all ages who offer vivid startling images of aging as a potent empowering experience. We also seek out older writers as we believe they are an untapped resource. No trite or sentimental verse. Have received hundreds of pieces on nursing homes, operations and death, and seek a broader, more positive vision of aging." Poets published in first issue include Josephine Jacobsen, Nina Cassian and Judson Jerome. The journal is 8 × 8", 32 pp., printed on white linen, saddle-stitched. Includes photos of writers. **Poetry, 30 line maximum; fiction and essays, 5,000 words maximum. Pays one year's subscription. Reports in 6 weeks. Simultaneous submissions acceptable if notified.**

‡**PASSAIC REVIEW (II)**, % Forstmann Library, 195 Gregory Ave., Passaic, NJ 07055, founded 1979, Richard Quatrone, poetry editor, has published **a number of our most notable poets, such as Allen Ginsberg and David Ignatow.** Here are some lines from "June 17, 1983" by Richard Quatrone:

> *These could be the lines of a dying man.*
> *Dying here in Passaic, in the fumes and poisons*
> *of modern greed and hatred, dying in the flesh*
> *of cynicism, caught within its grip with nowhere*
> *to go, with no one to listen, with only one hope*

It comes out twice a year in an offset, typescript, saddle-stapled 48 pp. digest-sized format, with occasional artwork. The editor says he wants **"direct, intelligent, courageous, imaginative, free writing."** They print a thousand copies, have 75 subscriptions (20 libraries). Each issue is $3.75, subscription $6, **sample back-issue $2.75,** have a 4-6 month backlog and **report in 4-6 months. Payment: one copy.** Rarely comments.

‡**PATH PRESS, INC. (IV-Ethnic)**, 53 W. Jackson Blvd., Suite 1040, Chicago, IL 60604, phone 312-663-0167, founded 1969, executive vice president and poetry editor Herman C. Gilbert, a small publisher of books and poetry primarily **"by, for, and about Black Americans and Third World people." The press is open to all types of poetic forms except "poor quality." Submissions should be typewritten in manuscript format. Writers should send sample poems, credits, and bio.** The books are "hardback and quality paperbacks."

PEACE AND FREEDOM (I), 17 Farrow Rd., Whaplode Drove, Spalding, Lincs. PE12 OTS England, phone 0406-330242, editor Paul Rance, founded 1985, is a "small-press publisher of poetry, music, art, short stories and general features, tapes," and also is a distributor. *Peace and Freedom* is a magazine appearing 4 times a year. **"We are looking for poetry particularly from U.S. poets who are new to writing, and women. The poetry we publish is anti-war, of environmental slant, poems reflecting pop culture, love poetry; erotic, but not obscene, poetry, spiritual, humanitarian poetry. With or without rhyme/metre.** Recently published poetry by Peter Gibbs, Hayley Tagg, Jo Ersser, Sara Burlace, Andy Savage and Andy Bruce. These sample lines are by John Passerello:

> *The voice is heard*
> *across many lands and*
> *by one too many*
> *the Motherland.*

Peace and Freedom has a card cover, multi-colour pages, normally 50 pages. "Pen pal ads included, and a correspondence section for poets is planned. 50% of submissions accepted. Poetry is judged on merit, but non-subscribers may have to wait longer for their work to appear than subscribers." **Sample: U.S. $2; 75 p and SAE UK. "Sample copies can only be purchased from the above address, and various mail-order distributors too numerous to mention. Advisable to buy a sample copy first.** Banks charge the equivalent of $5 to cash foreign cheques in the U.K., so advisable to send either I.M.O. or bills, preferably by registered post. We're not too impressed by poems sent without an accompanying note or letter. We like the personal touch." Subscription U.S. $8, U.K. £4 for 4 issues. **Payment 1 copy. Simultaneous submissions and previously published poems OK. "Replies to submissions normally under a month, without IRC/SAE indefinite."**

PEACEMAKING FOR CHILDREN (IV-Children, social issues, themes), 2437 N. Grant Blvd., Milwaukee, WI 53210, phone 414-445-9736, founded 1983, editor Jacqueline Haessly, is a magazine appearing 5 times a year, covering **peace education themes** *for* children. Circulation: 10,000 and growing "includes schools, libraries, churches, families on 6 continents. We are a peace education center. The magazine is highly specialized in this field. **Writers must have a sensitivity to interdependence of justice and peace issues, a commitment to non-violence, and an ability to write for children's level of comprehension." Sample: $2 prepaid. Send SASE for guidelines.** All issues have a single-focus theme such as the environment, handicapped, "all the ways we are family, space exploration vs. exploitation, understanding racism, our Latin friends." They do not want "Bible-related" poetry. **Poems 5-20 lines. No avant-garde. Pays 2 copies.**

‡**PEACOCK BOOKS; PEACOCK POSTCARD SERIES (I)**, College Square, Cuttack, Orissa, India 753003, founded 1988, editor Bibhu Padhi, **requires poets "to purchase at least 100 paperbound copies of their books at a 30% discount on list price which varies between US $10 and $15/UK 5.95 to 9.95 pounds (depending on the size of the book). We are a non-profit small press and receive no grants. The poets themselves, we assume, would be our first buyers. We pay 10% of print run in lieu of royalties. Full-length volumes of poetry and poem-postcards; sometimes chapbooks. All our books will be set, printed, and bound by hand, using high-quality paper — both hardback and hand-bound paperbacks. Collections of miscellaneous poems; poem sequences; long-poems. We are particularly interested in poems that are emotionally mature and genuine, that have something to say — poems that forcefully address problems and do not merely state them. Serious poetry only. No pornographic verse; no gay verse; no experiment for its own sake; nothing, in fact, that is less than first-rate; and of course no mush romantic lyrics. No children's verse."** He has recently published on postcards poetry by Naomi Shihab Nye and Robert Richman. As a sample the editor selected these lines from a postcard of William Stafford's "Starting the Day":

> Day waits, then imperceptibly has come.
> Yesterday, gone, fades, is brown,
> gray, pale, extinct, then never was.
> Time starts again, rises, becomes
> now, the steam above your cup.

"At this time, **we are on the lookout for 2-3 good, 56-80 page (typed, double-spaced) collections from writers who haven't had a book published yet, but who have had at least some magazine publication."** Recently published **Magic Places** (Margaret Cok). Forthcoming titles: **Planet Requiem** (Cliff Forshaw) and **diary of an American heart** (Thomas J.L. Bronsberg-Adas). In the postcard series: Roger Elkin. Titles available for **Writer's Market** and **Poet's Market** readers for $6 in paperback, $9 hardbound (list prices: $10 and $15). Poemcards are available for $3 for a set of 10. **Responds to queries in 2 weeks, MSS 4 weeks. "We expect potential authors to have had some magazine-publishing experience."**

PEARL; PEARL CHAPBOOK CONTEST (II), 3030 E. Second St., Long Beach, CA 90803, phone 213-434-4523 or 714-848-0891, founded 1974, folded after 3 issues, resurrected in 1987, poetry editors Joan Jobe Smith, Marilyn Johnson, and Barbara Hauk, is a literary magazine appearing twice a year. **"We are interested in accessible, humanistic poetry that communicates and is related to real life. Humor and wit are welcome, along with the ironic and serious. No taboos stylistically or subject-wise. Prefer poems up to 35 lines, with lines no longer than 10 words. We don't want to see sentimental, obscure, predictable, abstract, or cliché-ridden poetry. Our purpose is to provide a forum for lively, readable poetry that reflects a wide variety of contemporary voices, viewpoints, and experiences — that speaks to *real* people about *real* life in direct, living language, profane or sublime."** They have recently published poetry by Gerald Locklin, Laurel Speer, Fred Voss, Mary Morris, Ralph Angel, Diane Glancy, Frank Gaspar, and Dorianne Laux. As a sample they selected these lines from "Confessional-*Berkeley*, 1952" by Catherine Lynn:

> . . . on the lam from my grandmother's house
> in search of excitement and lust
> I knew I had found it
> when you offered to massage my feet.

Pearl is digest-sized, 64 pp., saddle-stapled, professionally printed (offset from camera-ready copy). Their press run is 500 with 70 subscriptions of which 7 are libraries. Subscription: $7 per year. **Sample: $4 postpaid. Guidelines available for SASE. Pays 2 copies. "Handwritten submissions and unreadable dot-matrix print-outs are not acceptable. Cover letters appreciated." Reports in 6-8 weeks. No simultaneous submissions or previously published poems.** Each issue contains the work of 25-30 different poets and a special 10-15 page section that showcases the work of a single poet. "We now sponsor an annual chapbook contest, judged by one of our more well-known contributors. Winner receives publication, $100, and 50 copies, with an introduction by the final judge. (To date, judges have been Gerald Locklin and Laurel Speer). Entries accepted during the months of May and June. There is a $10 entry fee, which includes a copy of the winning chapbook." Send SASE for complete rules and guidelines. "Advice for beginning poets? Just write from your own experience, using images that are as concrete and sensory as possible. Keep these images fresh and objective, and always listen to the music. . . ."

PEGASUS (II), 525 Ave. B., Boulder City, NV 89005, founded 1986, editor M. E. Hildebrand, is a poetry quarterly. **Submit 3-5 poems, 3-40 lines. "All forms and styles are considered. In sharing your experience, make a lasting impression by using fresh imagery,"** but avoid **"religious, political, pornographic themes."** They have recently published poetry by Vivian Trollope-Cagle and Stan Moseley. As a sample I selected the opening lines of "Desert Song" by Elizabeth Perry:

> Like the red-gold phoenix

> *dawn rises out of blackness*
> *to slip a violet shawl*
> *across dark, barren shoulders.*

Pegasus has 32 pp., digest-sized, saddle-stapled, inexpensively produced—offset from typescript, colored paper cover, subscription $12.50, circulation 200. **Sample: $3 plus postage. Send SASE for guidelines. Reports in 2-3 weeks. Previously published poems OK.**

THE PEGASUS REVIEW (I, II, IV-Themes), P.O. Box 134, Flanders, NJ 07836, founded 1980, is a 14 page (counting cover) pamphlet entirely in calligraphy, illustrated on high-quality paper, some color overlays. Poetry editor Art Bounds says, "This magazine is a bimonthly, **based on specific themes. Poetry not more than 24 lines, the shorter the better;** fiction (short story); essays and cartoons. **Brevity is the key. If theme can be approached differently that will create interest. Open to all types of writing but do not obscure the thought behind the piece.**" The have recently published Nan Sherman, t.k. splake and Charles van Heck. The editor selected these lines as a sample from "All the Words" by Ana Pine:

> *time has its*
> *way*
> *of making us*
> *forget*
> *why we are*
> *together.*

Sample: $2. Subscription: $7. **Query to find out themes for the year. Most replies prompt.** 156 copies are printed for 132 subscriptions, of which 3 are libraries. **Reports within a month, often with a personal response. Payment: 2 copies.** Occasional book awards, of interest to writers. The editor advises, "Constantly read, the old as well as the new. Write on a daily basis. The discipline is important. Study your markets and market your work diligently. Refer to *Writer's Digest* and other sources for information, ideas, markets. This could be the year you can do it!"

PELICAN PUBLISHING COMPANY (IV-Children), Box 189, Gretna, LA 70054, phone 504-368-1175, founded 1926, editor Nina Kooij, is a "moderate-sized publisher of cookbooks, travel guides, regional books and inspirational/motivational books," which accepts **poetry for "hardcover children's books** *only*, preferably with a Southern focus. However, our needs for this are very limited; we do fewer than 5 juvenile titles per year, and most of these are prose, not poetry." No dot-matrix, no simultaneous submissions; clear photocopies OK. Query with credits and bio. Reports on queries in 3 months, on MSS in 3 months. Pays royalties.** These are 32 pp. large-format (magazine-sized) books with illustrations. Two of their popular series are prose books about Gaston the Green-Nosed Alligator by James Rice and Clovis Crawfish by Mary Alice Fontenot. They have a variety of books based on "The Night Before Christmas" adapted to regional settings such as Cajun, prairie, and Texas. Typically their books sell for $11.95. **Write for catalog to buy samples.**

PEMBROKE MAGAZINE (II), Box 60, Pembroke State University, Pembroke, NC 28372, founded 1969 by Norman Macleod, edited by Shelby Stephenson, a heavy (252+pp., 6×9″), flat-spined, quality literary annual, has published Fred Chappell, Stephen Sandy, Charles Edward Eaton, M.H. Abrams and Betty Adcock. Here is one of A.R. Ammons' poems "Cold Rheum":

> *You can't*
> *tell what's*
>
> *snot from*
> *what's not*

Print run: 500, subscriptions: 125, of which 100 are libraries. **Sample: $5 postpaid**, the single copy price, **reports within 3 months, payment in copies, sometimes comments on rejections.** Stephenson advises, "Publication will come if you write. Writing is all."

PENNINE PLATFORM (II), Ingmanthorpe Hall Farm Cottage, Wetherby, W. Yorkshire, England LS22 5EQ, phone 0937-64674, founded 1973, poetry editor Brian Merrikin Hill, appears 3 times a year. The editor wants **any kind of poetry but concrete ("lack of facilities for reproduction"). No specifications of length, but poems of less than 40 lines have a better chance. "All styles**—effort is to find things good of their kind. **Preference for religious or socio-political awareness of an acute, not conventional kind.**" They have recently published poetry by Elizabeth Bartlett, Anna Adams, John Ward, Stanley Cook, Judith Kazantzis, John Latham and John Sewell. The editor selected these sample lines by Martyn Lowery, from a poem on his father's death:

> *While all I ever seem to say*
> *and not in any grand or gesticulating way*
> *concerns the peacetime pity of it all. So much is missed*

behind these barricades where we build
a myth and fly a flag as best we may;
where we live and where word by word are killed.

The 6×8", 48 pp. journal is photocopied from typescript, saddle-stapled, with matte card cover with graphics, circulation 400, 300 subscriptions of which 16 are libraries. Subscription £3.60 for 3 issues (£6 abroad; £16 if not in sterling); per copy: £1. They receive about 300 submissions per year, use about 30, have about a 6-month backlog. **Sample: £1 postpaid. Submit 1-6 poems, typed or photocopied. Reports in about a month. No pay. Editor occasionally comments on rejections.** Brian Hill comments, "It is time to avoid the paradigm-magazine-poem and reject establishments—ancient, modern or allegedly contemporary. Small magazines and presses often publish superior material to the commercial hyped publishers."

PENNSYLVANIA ENGLISH (II), Indiana University, Indiana, PA 15701, founded 1988 (first issue in March, 1989), contact poetry editor, is "a journal sponsored by the Pennsylvania College English Association." They want poetry of **"any length, any style."** It is magazine-sized, saddle-stapled, and appears twice a year, press run 300. Subscription: $10, which includes membership in PCEA. **Pays 2 copies. Submit 4-5 typed poems. They consider simultaneous submissions but not previously published poems. Reports in 1 month.**

‡THE PENNSYLVANIA REVIEW (II), English Dept., 526 CL, University of Pittsburgh, Pittsburgh, PA 15260, phone 412-624-0026, founded 1985, editor Deborah Pursifull. This ambitious new journal was described by *Choice* as "a fine small literary magazine." **There are no restrictions on subject matter, style, or length, although they do not want to see "light verse or greeting card verse."** Some poets recently published are Nance Van Winckel, Eric Pankey, Maggie Anderson, Harry Humes, Debra Bruce, Leslie Adrienne Miller, and translations of Karl Krolow by Stuart Friebert. As a sample the editor selected lines from "A Few Arguments With The Conspicuous," by Jeff Worley:

What if all the substantial

evidence is nothing but a trick
light plays, every sharp

penetrating image
really a marvelous blur?

The Pennsylvania Review announces that it publishes "the best contemporary prose and poetry twice yearly." It is a handsome magazine, 7×10", 80 pp. flat-spined, professionally printed on heavy stock with graphics, art, and ads, glossy card cover with b/w illustration on grey. Circulation is approximately 1,000 with 300 subscriptions, price per issue $5, subscription $10. **Sample: $5 postpaid. Pay is $5/page plus 2 copies. Submission deadlines are November 30 for Spring issue, April 1 for Fall issue. Submissions are not accepted between April 1 and September 1. Submissions are reported on in 8-10 weeks, and the magazine has no backlog at present. Writers should submit 3-6 poems, typewritten only, clear photocopies OK but no dot-matrix.**

‡PENSAR PRESS (V), Box 13235, Akron, OH 44313, founded 1987, editor Samuel Hinton, is a small independent press publishing poetry and fiction in chapbooks, paperbacks and hardcovers. **Currently not accepting poetry submissions.**

PENTAGRAM PRESS (II), 212 N. Second St., Minneapolis MN 55401, phone 612-340-9821, founded 1974, poetry editor Michael Tarachow, who is also printer and publisher. **Query with SASE before sending MSS."** Pentagram publishes broadsides, postcards and pamphlets in addition to books. They have recently published poetry by Philip Gallo, Theodore Enslin, and Robie Liscomb; a book by Clifford Burke is forthcoming. "Pentagram uses handset metal type to publish letterpress books of contemporary poetry. *Time* is the invisible factor: even a small project can take 300-500 hours. What would *you* sell that portion of your life for?" **Replies to queries next day. Payment variable. Catalog for 6x9 SASE.** "Poets hoping to be published by Pentagram—or any publisher—should be familiar with previous publications."

PEOPLENET (IV-Specialized, romance), P.O. Box 897, Levittown, NY 11756, phone 516-579-4043, founded 1987, editor/publisher Robert Mauro, is a newsletter **for disabled people focusing on dating, love, and relationships.** The editor wants **"any poetry on relationships, love and romance in any form. But the length should remain 10-20 lines. 3 or 4 poems at a time. We publish beginners, new poets."** As a sample the editor chose the first stanza of "How Many Times Have I Counted on Your Fingers" by Robert Mauro:

How many times have I
counted on your fingers

THE

Pennsylvania Review

VOLUME 4, NUMBER 1

ዓ!

This particular cover photo caught editor Deborah Pursifull's eye "because it suggests to me several themes at once: a sense of place; longing, belonging and not belonging; the passage of time; and the passing of people through time, among others. In particular, I appreciated the way the photo suggests themes of family, of generations, since a fair number of pieces in this issue deal with these themes to some degree." The picture is the product of Pittsburgh photographer Laura C. Miller, who describes her photography as, "a recording of the visual dialogue I have with the world."

> the ways of love
>   one finger at a time
> touching this one first
>   and that one in this place

Peoplenet appears quarterly, 12-15 pp., magazine-sized, offset, using graphics and ads, press run about 200, with that many subscriptions. Subscription $15. **Pays tearsheets only.** (Copies of the newsletter, which contains personal ads, go to subscribers only. Free brochure available.) **Poems should be double-spaced. No simultaneous submissions. Reports "immediately." Editor comments on rejected MSS. He says, "We want to publish poems that express the importance of love, acceptance, inner beauty, the need for love and relationship."**

PEQUOD: A JOURNAL OF CONTEMPORARY LITERATURE AND LITERARY CRITICISM (II, IV-Translations), Dept. of English, Room 200, New York University, 19 University Place, New York, NY 10003, contact poetry editor, is a semiannual literary review publishing **quality poetry, fiction, essays, and translations.** They have recently published poetry by Deborah Digges, Donald Revell, and Theodore Weiss. As a sample I selected the concluding lines of "At the Atlantic City Bus Station" by Stephen Dunn:

> ... A man
> with dredlocks
> is selling crack in the men's room.
>
> The tattooed man is making a muscle
>   and oh, the little heart
>   on his bicep has started to dance.

Subscription: $10 annually. **Sample: $5 postpaid.** It is a professionally-printed digest-sized 130 + pp., flat-spined magazine with glossy card cover. This magazine is sponsored by the National Poetry Foundation, listed under Organizations Useful to Poets.

PERCEPTIONS (IV-Women), 1945 S. 4th W., Missoula, MT 59801, founded 1982, poetry editor Temi Rose, is a "small prize-winning **women's poetry magazine for the promotion and development of women's consciousness of peace and hope and freedom to be ourselves."** They have recently published poetry by Doreen Cristo. As a sample the editor selected this haiku by Kitty Cutting:

> As silver birds soar
>   so my heart and whole being
>   ache to be with them.

Perceptions is digest-sized, 30 pp., photocopied from typescript, colored paper cover, and comes out three times a year. They publish about 250 of 1,000 poems received per year; their press run is 100 with 10 subscriptions of which 3 are libraries. Subscriptions: $10. **Sample: $3 postpaid. Guidelines available for SASE. Pays 1 copy. They consider simultaneous submissions and previously published poems and report in 1-3 months.**

PEREGRINE: THE JOURNAL OF AMHERST WRITERS & ARTISTS; AWA CHAPBOOK SERIES (II), Box 1076, Amherst, MA 01004, *Peregrine* founded 1983, Amherst Writers & Artists Press, Inc., 1987. **Open to all styles, forms, subjects but greeting-card verse.** They have recently published poetry by William Packard, Kathryn Machan Aal, A. D. Winans, and Carol Edelstein. As a sample the editors selected these lines by Nancy Dickinson:

> *The door is open*
> *to let in night like water.*
> *Sometimes planets, sometimes the moon*
> *flushing.*
> *But I can swim through, too,*
> *away from my bed . . .*

"We try to publish twice a year, but sometimes cannot because of finances. **We may hold poems for several months, and so we encourage simultaneous submissions."** *Peregrine* is digest-sized, 70 plus pp., flat-spined, professionally printed, with matte card cover. Their press run is 500. **Payment in contributors' copies. Sample: $4.50 postpaid.** The AWA Chapbook Series publishes handsome collections by AWA members on a cooperative basis—the poets paying 80% of the publishing costs and handling distribution.

PERIVALE PRESS; PERIVALE POETRY CHAPBOOKS; PERIVALE TRANSLATION SERIES (II, IV-Translations, anthology), 13830 Erwin St., Van Nuys, CA 91401, founded 1968, editor Lawrence P. Spingarn, publishes **Perivale Poetry Chapbooks, Perivale Translation Series**, anthologies. The collections by individuals are usually translations, but here are some lines from R. L. Barth from "Da Nang Nights: Liberty Song," in **Forced-Marching to the Styx:**

> *In sudden light we choose*
> *Lust by lust our bar:*
> *And whatever else we lose,*
> *We also lose the war.*

They publish an average of one 20 pp. saddle-stapled chapbook, one perfect-bound (20-70 pp.) collection, one anthology per year, all quality print jobs. Send SASE for catalog. Perivale publishes both on **straight royalty basis (10%, 10 author's copies) usually grant supported, and by subsidy, the author paying 100%, being repaid from profits, if any. "Payment for chapbooks accepted is 50 free copies of press run.** Authors should agree to promote books via readings, talk shows, orders and signings with local bookshops. **Contributors are encouraged to buy samples of chapbooks, etc., for clues to editor's tastes." Samples of previous poetry chapbooks: $5 postpaid.** (Barth title out of print.) Latest title: **Going Home** (chapbook) by Sheryl St. Germain. **To submit, query first, with sample of 6-10 poems, bio, previous books.** Spingarn, a well-known, widely published poet, offers criticism for a fee, the amount dependent on length of book.

PERMAFROST (II, IV-Regional), English Dept., University of Alaska, Fairbanks, AK 99775-0640, phone 907-474-5237, founded 1977. "Editors change annually." *Permafrost* is a biannual journal of poems, short stories, essays, reviews, b/w drawings and photographs. "We survive on both new and established writers, and hope and expect to see your best work (we are not the Siberia of mediocre poetry). **We publish any style of poetry provided it is conceived, written, revised with care; favor poems with strong, unusual images or poems with abstraction backed up by imagery; both must have universal applications. We discourage 'tourist poetry' which rarely works because of its hackneyed imagery and lack of universal theme; encourage poems about Alaska and by Alaskans, but they are works and writers at ease with their setting. We also encourage poems about anywhere and from anywhere. We are not a regional publication, but in order to support contemporary Alaskan literature, publish reviews only of work by Alaskan authors or publishers."** They have recently published poetry by Wendy Bishop, Jerah Chadwick, Leslie Leyland Fields, Linda Gregg, Patricia Monaghan, John Morgan, Peggy Shumaker, and Kim Stafford. The editors selected these sample lines from "Ancient Forests of the Near East" by Jerry Cable:

> *This year, no scavenging hip-deep*
> *in dead-white snow for twigs*
> *and scraps of lumber crusted*
> *with icy leaves.*

The digest-sized 100+ pp. journal is flat-spined, professionally printed, two-color paper cover with b/w graphics and photos, has a circulation of 500, 100 subscriptions of which 20 are libraries. Subscription: $7; per copy: $4. **Deadlines are December 1 and April 1. Return time is 1-3 months;**

"longer if work was submitted well before deadline and is under serious consideration." Do not accept submissions between April 1 and August 1. Sample: $4 postpaid. Submit no more than 5 poems, neatly typed or photocopied; considers simultaneous submissions but "expects to be told." Guidelines available for SASE, ("although most are listed here"). Pays 2 copies, reduced contributor rates on others. Editors comment only on manuscripts that have made the final round and then are rejected. Depth of comments vary.

‡PERMEABLE PRESS; HERMIT STREET REVIEW: YONI BLUESMAIL (II, IV-Form), 400 Duboce #217, San Francisco, CA 94117, phone 415-255-7939, founded 1984, as *Comet Halley Magazine*. "We have published 8 issues of a magazine, dozens of chapbooks and broadsides and commentary on the small press and the history of print. Currently publishing all of the above and moving into trade editions." *Hermit Street Review* (established 1990) appears irregularly, "but approx. 80 pp. per year." It is "to express the repressed." Sample: $2 postpaid. Send SASE for guidelines. Pays "copies, occasional honorarium." The press wants poetry that is "radical, investigative, critical; nothing cynical, naive." They have published poetry by Sue Luzzaro, Hugh Fox, Darin Peabody, Tony Moffit, Michael Hemmingson and Marilyn Berlin. Query regarding previously published poems and simultaneous submissions. Submit 3-5 samples, bio, publications. Pays 10% of press run for chapbooks and broadsides in the Yoni Bluesmail series. Editor comments on submissions "often."

‡THE PET GAZETTE (IV-Themes), 1309 N. Halifax, Daytona Beach, FL 32118, phone 904-255-6935, founded 1984, editor Faith A. Senior, a quarterly journal that wants "poems about animals, nature and/or ecology. Simple and easily understood, in behalf of animals overall, short poems preferred." She does not want "haiku, and ultra-contrived and/or highly intellectual." Poets frequently in *The Pet Gazette* are Vincent Hathaway, John Coulbourn, Rhoda Rainbow, Johnathan Russell, C. David Hay, and S. Mary Ann Henn. As a sample, she selected the following stanza from "The Crow" by Nellie S. Richardson:

> I asked a crow the other day
> "Why not sing soft and low?"
> He said, "I do the best I can,
> It's the only way I know,
> CAW! CAW!

Pet Gazette is magazine-sized, offset on 60 lb opaque paper, in many type styles with b/w photos and drawings, folded and saddle-stapled with b/w photos on cover, inserts from various pro-animal organizations. Circulation is 300, subscription $10 yearly. Sample copy available for $2 postpaid. Payment is in copies. Reporting time is "upon receipt," and time to publication is "sometimes a year, though usually much sooner."

PETERLOO POETS; POETRY MATTERS (II), 2 Kelly Gardens, Calstock, Cornwall PL18 9SA Great Britain, founded 1977, poetry editor Harry Chambers. *Poetry Matters* is an annual house journal to which you may not submit, but they publish collections of poetry under the Peterloo Poets imprint: flat-spined paperbacks, hardbacks, and poetry cassettes. Query with 10+ sample poems, bio, and list of publications. Considers simultaneous submissions and previously published poems if they have not been in book form. Pays 7.5%-10% royalties, $100 advance (for first volume, $200 for subsequent volumes), and 12 copies. Editor "normally, briefly" comments on rejections.

PHASE AND CYCLE; PHASE AND CYCLE PRESS (I, II), 3537 E. Prospect, Fort Collins, CO 80525, phone 303-482-7573, founded 1988, poetry editor Loy Banks. *Phase and Cycle* is a poetry magazine published semiannually. "We look for short-to-moderate-length poems of all kinds, especially those that set out 'the long perspectives open at each instance of our lives' (Larkin). We are looking for poetry that will pass technical inspection in the academic community. We are not regional or subservient to any 'school' of poetry. We prefer poems that are largely accessible rather than deliberately 'difficult.' " They have recently published poetry by William Kloefkorn, Mary Crow, Gilbert Allen, J.B. Goodenough, and R.R. Walter. The editor chose these lines from "Anomie" by Bruce Holland Rogers:

> The stars will not instruct us. Dumb
> As stones they blaze in unnamed
> Configurations and paralyze our tongues.
> What augury will you see, what fortune framed
> In your windows? How will you speak of it
> Now that the planetts wander another road?

The magazine is digest-sized, 48 pp., saddle-stapled. Sample: $2.50 postpaid. Guidelines available for SASE. Pays 1 copy. "A brief bio note may accompany poems." No simultaneous submissions or previously published poems. Reports in 5-10 weeks. Submissions are accepted throughout the year. Editor sometimes comments on rejections. Phase and Cycle Press has just published its first poetry chapbook, **Breathing In The World**, by Bruce Holland Rogers and Holly Arrow.

‡PHILOMEL (II); PHILOMATHEAN SOCIETY: PHILOMATHEAN BOOK AWARD (II, IV-Students), College Hall, University of Pennsylvania, Philadelphia, PA 19104, phone 215-898-8907, founded in the 1820s, re-established in 1950s, editor Yves-Emmanuel Morales. *Philomel* is a literary annual using **"any kind of poetry, no more than 300 words or 3 pp. per poem."** They also use stories, essays, and "witty recipes." They have recently published poetry by Juan David Acosta. As a sample, I selected these lines from "Daddy" by Linda Camba:

> *I remember being drawn up into your arms*
> *After a long day in the park,*
> *The wetness of sweat still mingling in your skin.*
> *I pretended to sleep as you climbed the stairs*
> *And rubbed my nose upon your polyester shirt.*

Philomel comes out each spring. It is flat-spined, 60 pp., 6 × 9, with matte card cover. Poems are selected by a committee of the Philomathean Society. Press run: 1,500 for 20 subscribers of which 3 are libraries, 1,400 distributed free to the university community. Price per issue: $3. **Sample, postpaid: $1.50. Pays 1 copy per poem.** The Philomathean Book Award, annual, is given only to University of Pennsylvania students, professors or university staff.

PHOEBE; THE GEORGE MASON REVIEW (II), 4400 University Dr., Fairfax, VA 22032, phone 703-323-3730, founded 1970, poetry editors Patricia Bertheaud and Naomi Thiers, is a literary quarterly which uses **"any contemporary poetry of superior quality."** They have recently published poetry by C. K. Williams, Peter Klappert and William Matthews. Circulation 3,500, with 30-35 pp. of poetry in each issue. Subscription: $13/year; $3.25/single issue, $6.50/double issue. *Phoebe* receives 2,500 submissions per year. **Submit up to 5 poems; submission should be accompanied by SASE and a short bio. No simultaneous submissions, no dot-matrix. Reports in 6-8 weeks. Pays in copies.**

PHOENIX BROADSHEETS; NEW BROOM PRIVATE PRESS (II), 78 Cambridge St., Leicester, England LE 3 0JP, founded 1968, poetry editor Toni Savage, publishes chapbooks, pamphlets and broadsheets on a small Adana Horizontal Hand Press. The editor wants poetry which is **"descriptive — not too modern, not erotica or concrete, up to 12 lines (for the sheets).** Also some personal background of the poet." He has recently published poems by Spike Milligan, Pamela Lewis,, Elizabeth Bewick, William Oxley, Tony Boyd, Roger McGough, and Arthur Caddick. Toni Savage selected these sample lines from "Amour" by John Cotton:

> *In matters of tristesse d'amour*
> *It is the young who suffer*
> *Those older endure.*

The broadsheets are letterpress printed on tinted paper (about 5 × 8″) with graphics. **Submit no more than 3 poems with cover letter giving "personal backgrounds and feelings." No pay. Poet receives 20-30 copies.** "My *Broadsheets* are *given* away in the streets. Edition is usually 200-300. They are given away to Folk Club, Jazz Club and theater audiences. The broadsheets started as a joke. Now much sought after and collected. This is my hobby and is strictly part-time. Each small booklet takes 1-3 months, so it is impossible to ascertain quantities of publications."

PHOENIX PRESS (V), 713 St. James, Pittsburgh, PA 15232, founded 1982, poetry editors Heywood Ostrow and Robert Julian, publishes 2-3 books a year **but accepts no unsolicited MSS.** They have recently published poetry by Robert Julian and Sebastian Barker. As a sample I selected these opening lines from **XII** by George Barker:

> *Ah most unreliable of all women of grace*
> *in the breathless hurry of your leave taking*
> *you forgot, you forgot for ever, our last embrace*

‡PIEDMONT LITERARY REVIEW; PIEDMONT LITERARY SOCIETY (I, II, IV-Form), Rt. 1, Box 512, Forest, VA 24551, founded 1976; poetry editor Gail White, Rt. 3, Box 243, Breaux Bridge, LA 70517 (and **poetry submissions should go to her address**). If you join the Piedmont Literary Society, $12 a year, you get the quarterly *Review* and a quarterly newsletter containing much market and contest information. Gail White says, **"I prefer all types of poems up to 32 lines. Each issue has a special section for oriental forms with an emphasis on haiku." Each also includes short fiction. She does *not* want: "smut, overly romantic, greeting-card verse."** She has recently taken poetry by Harold Witt, David Citino, Jane Greer, John Brugaletta, and Barbara Loots. As a sample she selected these lines by Martha Bosworth:

> *I know that woman puzzle-makers hide*
> *in outline drawings, flat and monochrome*
> *yet full of leafy features as a tree*
> *by running springs. Where branches subdivide*

cheekbones and chin emerge . . .
The quarterly is digest-sized, saddle-stapled, offset from typescript, matte card cover, using b/w graphics and photos, with 40-50 pp. of poetry in each issue, circulation 300 with 200 subscriptions of which 10 are libraries. **Sample: $3 postpaid. Send SASE for guidelines. Pays copies. Reports within 6 months. She "usually" comments on rejections.** They sponsor occasional contests; write to Forest, VA address for rules and dates. Gail White advises, "Be introspective while showing empathy for all mankind. Show some structure. No poems disguised as broken lines of prose."

PIG IRON (II, IV-Themes), Box 237, Youngstown, OH 44501, phone 216-783-1269, founded 1975, poetry editors Jim Villani and Nate Leslie, is a literary annual devoted to special themes. They want **poetry "up to 300 lines; free verse and experimental; write for current themes."** Forthcoming themes: Labor in the Post Industrial Age, Epistolary Fiction and the Letter as Artifact. They do *not* **want to see "traditional" poetry.** They have recently published poetry by César López, Dennis Brutus, Joseph Bruchac, Lowell Jaeger, Margaret Treitel, and Nancy Morejon. As a sample the editor selected the closing lines from Jim Daniels' poem "Called Back":

> *The quarters I drop*
> *into the coffee machine*
> *sing a song I have memorized*
> *— despite my lack of faith —*
> *like hymns from my childhood.*
> *I fold my hands around the cup*
> *thinking about how much I need*
> *this job: the first bitter sip.*

Pig Iron is magazine-sized, flat-spined, 96 pp., typeset on good stock with glossy card cover using b/w graphics and art, no ads, circulation 1,000. They have 200 subscriptions of which 50 are libraries. Price per issue: $8.95. Subscription: $8/1 year, $15/2 years. **Sample: $2.50 postpaid. Send SASE for guidelines. Pays $5 per poem plus 2 copies. Reports in 3 months, 12-18 months delay to publication. No simultaneous submissions. Dot-matrix, photocopies OK.**

THE PIKESTAFF FORUM; PIKESTAFF PUBLICATIONS, INC.; THE PIKESTAFF PRESS; PIKESTAFF POETRY CHAPBOOKS (II, IV-Children, teens), P.O. Box 127, Normal, IL 61761, phone 309-452-4831, founded 1977, poetry editors Robert D. Sutherland, James R. Scrimgeour and James McGowan, is "a not-for-profit literary press. Publishes a magazine of national distribution, *The Pikestaff Forum*; and a poetry chapbooks series." They want **"substantial, well-crafted poems; vivid, memorable, based in lived experience—*Not*: self-indulgent early drafts, 'private' poems, five finger exercises, warmed over workshop pieces, vague abstractions, philosophical woolgathering, 'journal entries,' inspirational uplift. The shorter the better, though long poems are no problem; we are eclectic; welcome traditional or experimental work. We won't publish pornography or racist/sexist material."** They have recently published poetry by Gayl Teller, J.W. Rivers, Lucia Cordell Getsi, Frannie Lindsay, and Fritz Hamilton. The editor selected these sample lines from Jeff Gundy's "C.W. Ponders the Pomes Even Now Winging Their Way Back to Him":

> *So, they come home. It's not their fault.*
> *They crook their heads and try to look*
> *on the bright side: they're back safe, still young.*
> *Maybe they'll grow.*

The Pikestaff Forum is an annual newsprint tabloid, 40 pp., "handsome, open layout. Trying to set a standard in tabloid design. Special features: poetry, fiction, commentary, reviews, young writers (7-17 in a special section), editors' profiles (other magazines), The Forum (space for anyone to speak out on matters of literary/publishing concern)." Circulation 1,200 with 200 subscriptions of which 5 are libraries. Price per copy: $2. Subscription: $10/6 issues. They receive 2,000-3,000 submissions per year, use 3%, have a year's backlog. **Sample: $2 postpaid. "Each poem should be on a separate sheet, with author's name and address. We prefer no simultaneous submissions—but if it is, we expect to be informed of it." No more than 6 poems per submission. Reports within 3 months. Pays 3 copies. Send SASE for guidelines. Query with samples and brief bio for chapbook submission. Replies to queries in 2 weeks, to submission (if invited) in 3 months. Photocopy OK, but "reluctantly" accepts dot-matrix. Pays 20% of press run for chapbooks. The editors "always" comment on rejections.** They advise, "For beginners: don't be in a hurry to publish; work toward becoming your own best editor and critic; when submitting, send only what you think is your very best work; avoid indulging yourself at the expense of your readers; have something to say that's worth your readers' time to read; before submitting, ask yourself, 'Why should *any* reader be asked to read this?'; regard publishing as conferring a responsibility."

PIKEVILLE REVIEW (II), Humanities Dept., Pikeville College, Pikeville, KY 41501, founded 1987, editor James Alan Riley, who says **"There's no editorial bias though we recognize and appreciate style and control in each piece. No emotional gushing."** *PR* appears once yearly, accepting about 10% of poetry received. Press run is 500. **Sample $3 including postage. Send SASE for guidelines. Pays in 5 copies. No simultaneous submissions or previously published poetry. Editor sometimes comments on rejections.** They also sponsor contests.

PINCHGUT PRESS (V), 6 Oaks Ave., Cremorne, Sydney, NSW 2090, Australia, founded 1948, publishes **Australian poetry. Not currently accepting poetry submissions. Send SASE for catalog to order samples.**

THE PIPE SMOKER'S EPHEMERIS (IV-Themes), 20-37 120th St., College Point, NY 11356, editor/publisher Tom Dunn, who says, "The *Ephemeris* is a limited edition, irregular quarterly **for pipe smokers and anyone else who is interested in its varied contents.** Publication costs are absorbed by the editor/publisher, assisted by any contributions—financial or otherwise—that readers might wish to make." There are 66 pages, offset from photoreduced typed copy, colored paper covers, with illustrations, stapled at the top left corner. The following lines are from "Coterie Fellowship" by R.W.:

> *There is no comparable moment*
> *When I light up my briar,*
> *To tamp that bowl of contentment,*
> *And to mix that gold with fire.*

Ephemeris seems to be supported by "members" rather than subscribers, but it gives no indication as to the cost of membership.

PIROGUE PUBLISHING (I, IV-Regional), Box 3640, Paradis, LA 70080, phone 504-758-1373, founded 1987, poetry editor Bill Roberts, publishes 3 flat-spined paperbacks a year. They want **poetry from their local region only, "poetry that is not riddled with obscure references to some antiquity, not overly stylish and lacking in substance."** They have recently published poetry by Everette Maddox and Julie Kane. **Query wtih 6 sample poems, bio, and publications. Reports on queries in 2 weeks, on MSS in 2 months. Pays 5-10% royalties plus 20 copies. Send $7 for sample postpaid. Editor sometimes comments on rejections. "If we are asked for criticism then a fee will be assessed based on length of MS.** As we are not a government-subsidized academic press, it is extremely difficult to justify publishing poetry. However, within the last two years we have done 3 poets because they are that good."

PITT POETRY SERIES; UNIVERSITY OF PITTSBURGH PRESS; AGNES LYNCH STARRETT POETRY PRIZE (II), 127 N. Bellefield Ave., Pittsburgh, PA 15260, founded 1968, poetry editor Ed Ochester, publishes **"poetry of the highest quality; otherwise, no restrictions—book MSS minimum of 48 pages."** Simultaneous submissions OK. They have published books of poetry by Etheridge Knight, Alicia Ostriker, Maggie Anderson, David Wojahn, Robley Wilson Jr., Liz Rosenberg, Larry Levis, Jane Flanders, and Leslie Ullman. **"Poets who have not previously published a book should send SASE for rules of the Starrett competition ($10 handling fee), the** *only* **vehicle through which we publish first books of poetry."** The Starrett Prize consists of cash award of $2,000 and book publication. Poets who have previously published books should query.

‡PIVOT (II), 250 Riverside Dr. #23, New York, NY 10025, phone 212-222-1408, founded 1951, editor Martin Mitchell, is a poetry annual that has published poetry by Philip Appleman, Arthur Gregor, William Matthews, Eugene McCarthy, Craig Raine and Robert Wrigley. As a sample I selected "Prescription" by David Ignatow:

> *What does he want of himself?*
> *How to write without reservation,*
> *yet without repugnance*
> *so that to value it,*
> *teeth, tongue and terror,*
> *he will accept the terror.*

It ia a handsome 6 × 9″ flat-spined, professionally printed magazine with glossy card cover, press run 1,200. Price per issue: $5. **Sample, postpaid: $3. Pays 2 copies. Reports in 3-5 weeks.**

A PLACE FOR POETS (I, IV-Subscribers), Box 3429 Manhattanville Station, New York, NY 10027, phone 212-549-4215, founded 1988, executive editor Alberto O. Cappas, is a quarterly newsletter for poets, 4 pp., professionally printed on glossy stock, open to beginners, **poems up to 31 lines.** They have recently published poetry by the editor and Annette B. Feldmann. As a sample the editor chose lines from his own "The Ruse":

> *. . . Stonewalls and Rockefeller, signs of things kept secret.*
> *You sing in the cold winter and all the politicians*

> will buy a ticket to your annual fundraiser.
> Be polite, do not wear polyester suits,
>   stay away from chuchifritos, drink martinis,
>   and speak English without broken-down clues.

Subscription: $20 "which inludes publication of two poems." Pays 2 copies; additional copies $2. (Regular price is $4/copy.)

PLAINS POETRY JOURNAL; STRONGHOLD PRESS (II, IV-Form), P.O. Box 2337, Bismarck, ND 58502, founded 1982, editor Jane Greer, publishes "**meticulously crafted, language-rich poetry which is demanding but not inaccessible. We love rhyme and meter and poetic conventions used in vigorous and interesting ways.** I do *not* want broken-prose 'free verse' or greeting card-type traditional verse. I want finely-crafted poetry which uses the best poetic conventions from the past in a way that doesn't sound as if it were *written* in the past. No specifications. I'm especially interested in compelling long poems and essays on poetry. Our credo is, 'no subject matter is taboo; treatment is everything.' "** They have recently published poetry by Gail White, Rhina P. Espaillat, Richard Moore, R.S. Gwynn, Paul Ramsey, R. L. Barth, Jack Flavin, and Edmund Conti. As a sample Jane Greer chose "A Theft of Time" by Kevin Wolfe:

> At the third stroke, I took my father's clock.
> It had run down for good, we thought, and he,
> The great works of his brain uncoiling in that shock,
> Would little need its round necessity.

Plains Poetry Journal is a quarterly, digest-sized, 44 pp. (of which about 40 are poetry), saddle-stapled, professionally printed on tinted paper with matte card cover, graphics, circulation 500, 400 subscriptions of which 50 are libraries. Subscription: $18. They receive 1,500-2,000 submissions per year, use about 200, seldom have more than 3 month backlog. **Sample: $4.50 postpaid. Submit "not less than 3 poems, not more than 10 at a time. Photocopy, hand-written, dot-matrix, simultaneous submissions, all OK." Reports usually same week. Pays copies. Send SASE for guidelines. Has ceased book publishing.** "Considering the rude and totally unnecessary slowness of most publishers, an author is *crazy* not to submit simultaneously." Jane Greer says **she comments on rejections "occasionally, especially if the MS is especially promising or if I think the poet is a child or teen** (it happens)." She comments, "Do enclose an SASE, and *don't* enclose an explanation of the poems. Above all understand that a poet never 'gets good,' he or she just keeps *working* at it. If you're willing to do this, I am, too."

PLAINSONG (II), Box 8245, Western Kentucky University, Bowling Green, KY 42101, phone 502-745-5708, founded 1979, poetry editors Frank Steele, Elizabeth Oakes and Peggy Steele, is an occasional poetry journal. "Our purpose is to print the best work we can get, from known and unknown writers. This means, of course, that we print what we like: poems about places, objects, people, moods, politics, experiences. **We like straightforward, conversational language, short poems in which the marriage of thinking and feeling doesn't break up because of spouse-abuse (the poem in which ideas wrestle feeling into the ground or in which feeling sings alone — and boringly — at the edge of a desert). Prefer poems under 20 lines in free verse. No limits on subject matter, though we like to think of ourselves as humane, interested in the environment, in peace (we're anti-nuclear), in the possibility that the human race may have a future.**" They have recently published poetry by William Matthews, Ted Kooser, William Stafford, Del Marie Rogers, Betty Adcock, Julia Ardery and Abby Niebauer. The editors selected these sample lines from "Dream of an Afternoon with a Woman I Did Not Know" by Robert Bly:

> Frost has made clouds out of the night weeds.
> In my dream we stopped for coffee, we sat alone
> Near a fireplace, near delicate cups.
> I loved that afternoon, and the rest of my life.

The magazine is 48-56 pp., 6 × 9", professionally printed, flat-spined, matte color card cover with photos and graphics, print run 600 with 250 subscriptions of which 65 are libraries. They use about 100 of the 2,000 submissions received each year. Subscription: $7; per copy: $3.50. **Sample: $3.50 postpaid. "We prefer poems typed, double-spaced. Simultaneous submissions can, of course, get people into trouble, at times." Reports "within a month, usually." Payment in copies. Send SASE for guidelines.**

PLAINSONGS (II), Dept. of English, Hastings College, Hastings, NE 68902, founded 1980, editor Dwight C. Marsh, a poetry magazine that **"accepts manuscripts from anyone, considering poems on any subject in any style."** Some recurrent contributors printed in the last year include Lyn Lifshin, Nancy Peters, Jonathan Russell, Mark Sanders, Roy Scheele, Don Welch, and Ross Winterowd. In the October 1989 issue, which included 37 poets, Peter Vandenberg's award poem "Meeting Youself on Vacation" begins:

> When the elevator doors open
> into the lobby of Fitzgerald's
> in Las Vegas, twenty rows of arms
> wait your grasp. Their only promise:
> to pull away when you let go.

Plainsongs is digest-sized, 40 pp., saddle-stapled, set on laser, printed on thin paper with b/w illustrations, one-color matte card cover with black logo. The magazine is financed by subscriptions, which cost $8 for three issues per year. **Sample copies are $3. Pay is two copies and a year's subscription, with three award poems in each issue receiving small monetary recognition. MS deadlines are August 15 for fall issue; November 15 for winter; March 15 for spring.**

PLAINSWOMAN (IV-Women, regional), P.O. Box 8027, Grand Forks, ND 58202, founded 1977, is a 16 pp. magazine-sized literary journal appearing 10 times a year, circulation 500, using some **poetry by and about women in the Great Plains. Guidelines available, include SASE. Pays two copies of issue in which poem appears. Sample: $2.**

PLANTAGENET PRODUCTIONS (V), Westridge, Highclere, Nr. Newbury, Royal Berkshire RG15 9PJ, England, founded 1964, director of productions Miss Dorothy Rose Gribble. Plantagenet issues cassette recordings of poetry, philosophy, and narrative (although they have issued nothing new since 1980). Miss Gribble says, "Our public likes classical work . . . We **have published a few living poets, but this is not very popular with our listeners, and we shall issue no more."** They have issued cassettes by Oscar Wilde, Chaucer, Pope, as well as Charles Graves, Elizabeth Jennings, Leonard Clark, and Alice V. Stuart. The recordings are issued privately and are obtainable only direct from Plantagenet Productions; write for list. Miss Gribble's advice to poets is: "If intended for a listening public, let the meaning be clear. If possible, let the music of the works sing."

‡THE PLASTIC TOWER (I,II), P.O. Box 702, Bowie, MD 20718, founded 1989, editors Carol Brown, and Roger Kyle-Keith, is a quarterly using **"everything from iamic pentameter to silly limericks, modern free verse, haiku, rhymed couplets — we like it all! Only restriction is length — under 40 lines preferred."** They have recently published poetry by Grace Cavalieri and Lyn Lifshin. As a sample, I selected the prose poem "1939" by Jennie VerSteeg:

> You pass your thumb so lightly over my mouth, as though I am a fading charcoal sketch
>   of a woman who could have loved you once — in France, in a dauguerrotype, with
>   absinthe, belly hair wet and curling in a bow.

It is digest-sized, 38-54 pp., saddle-stapled; "variety of typefaces and b/w graphics on cheap photocopy paper." Press run: 200. Subscription: $8/year. **Sample free for 65¢ SASE. Send SASE for guidelines. Pays 1-3 copies. Simultaneous submissions OK. Reports in 4-6 weeks. Editor comments on submissions "often."** Roger Kyle-Keith says, "Just *have fun*. Don't take rejection slips as personal indictments on your self worth, or acceptance slips a confirmation of your value to society. Writing should be enjoyable."

PLOUGHSHARES (III), Emerson College, 100 Beacon St., Boston, MA 02116, phone 617-926-9875, founded 1971, **The magazine is "a journal of new writing edited on a revolving basis by professional poets and writers to reflect different and contrasting points of view."** Recent editors have included Philip Levine, Maxine Kumin, Bill Knott and Derek Walcott. They have recently published poetry by Joseph Brodsky, Rita Dove, Garrett Kaoru Hongo, Carol Frost, and Marilyn Hacker. The quarterly is $5\frac{1}{2} \times 8\frac{1}{2}''$, 200 pp., circulation 3,800. Subscription: $15 domestic; $19 foreign. They receive approximately 3,000 poetry submissions per year. **Sample: $5 postpaid. "Due to revolving editorship, issue emphasis and submission dates will vary. We suggest you read a few issues and check editorial announcements in current issue." Reports in 3-5 months, pays $10 minimum per poem, $5/printed page per poem over 2 printed pages, up to $50 maximum per poet, plus contributor copies. Simultaneous submissions acceptable.**

THE PLOVER (CHIDORI) (IV-Form, bilingual), Box 122, Ginowan City, Okinawa, Japan 901-22, phone 1-011-81-098897-5042, founded 1989, co-editors Paul E. Truesdell, Jr. and Thomas Heffernan, is a biannual, bilingual (Japanese and English) journal using **haiku, senryu, and related forms in traditional, classical-traditional, or free-style. No "obviously 'desk-top', contrived, and extremely avant garde styles of haiku."** As a sample Thomas Heffernan selected one of his own haiku:

> The long drought . . .
> morning glories spill over
> the stones of the well

Winter and summer issues will be published, 24-48 pp. $6 \times 8\frac{1}{2}''$ flat-spined format, professionally printed with quality card cover. Their press run is to be 500 initially. Subscription: $16 or 2,000 yen (Japenese currency). **Sample: $7 postpaid. No pay. Reports in 2-4 weeks. Deadlines May 31** and November 30. Submit up to 20 haiku/senryu per submission; no more than 10 haiku per 8½ × 11 sheet, name and address upper lefthand corner. Simultaneous submissions acceptable provided editors are informed. The editor advises reading the books on haiku by Blyth and Henderson.

POCKET INSPIRATIONS (I, IV-Inspirational), P.O. Box 796, Weaverville CA 96093, founded 1989, editor Janey Mitchell, a "newsletter to uplift the heart and nourish the spirit. It has something for everyone, appearing quarterly, using **soul-stirring, all types of inspirational poetry.**" Open to reprints. Editor provides "kind and gentle comments/criticisms." They prefer short poems. "If you are not a subscriber or have not been previously published in *Pocket Inspirations*, there is a $1/poem reading fee." The editor says the magazine is approximately 24-28 pp., photocopied and stapled, and that "since each publication has a unique flavor of its own," she suggests you read an issue of the newsletter before submitting to them. Subscription: $12/year. **Sample: $3. Pays copies. Reports in 2-6 weeks.**

POEM; HUNTSVILLE LITERARY ASSOCIATION (II), English Dept., University of Alabama at Huntsville, Huntsville, AL 35899, founded 1967, poetry editor Nancy Frey Dillard, appears twice a year, a flat-spined 4½ × 7¾", 70 pp. journal, circulation 400 (all subscriptions, of which 90 are libraries), matte card cover, tinted paper, consisting entirely of poetry. "We are open to traditional as well as nontraditional forms, but we favor work with the expected compression and intensity of good lyric poetry and a high degree of verbal and dramatic tension. We welcome equally submissions from established poets as well as from less known and beginning poets. We do not accept translations or previously published works. We prefer to see a sample of 3-5 poems at a submission, with SASE. We generally respond within a month. We are a nonprofit organization and can pay only in copy to contributors. Sample copies are available at $5." They have recently published poetry by R. T. Smith, Norman Nathan, and Jane Hoogestraat. The editor selected as a sample the following lines from Robert Cooperman's "Lady Leicester Miscarries, 1776":

> My hairdo was the glory of my heart,
> my maid spending hours to make the curls
> and twists sprout like leaves
> in the bountiful elms of April.
> It towered a full two feet
> above my head. . . .

They receive about 2,000 submissions per year, use 210.

THE POEM FACTORY (II), Box 3655, Vancouver, BC V6B 3Y8 Canada, founded 1986, publisher Ed Varney. *The Poem Factory* appears three times a year. The committee of editors seeks **poetry that is "contemporary in style, innovative, arresting, challenging, intelligent, purposeful, playful, meaningful, avant-garde, modern, concrete, pattern, visual, phenomenological, Zen, academic, and excellent; poetry which aspires to excellence."** They do *not* want "long, redundant, imitative, classical, rhymed" poetry. The magazine is 32 pp., saddle-stapled, 4¼ × 7", professionally printed, with a b/w card cover. They accept about 25-30% of poetry received. Their press run is 500 with 80 subscriptions of which 20 are libraries. **Sample: $2 postpaid. Pays 2 or more copies. Simultaneous submissions OK. Reports in 3 months "at worst." Editor sometimes comments on rejections.** Ed Varney says, "Our plans include a series of nice broadsheets designed to become posters and post them around Vancouver. We invite correspondence with other publishers interested in expanding grass-roots interest in poetry thru new innovative 'marketing' plans."

POET AND CRITIC (II), 203 Ross Hall, Iowa State University, Ames, IA 50011, phone 515-294-2180, founded 1961, editor Neal Bowers, appears 3 times a year, 6x9", 48 pp. staple bound, professionally printed, matte card cover with color, circulation 400, 200 subscriptions of which 100 are libraries. Subscription: $16; per copy: $6. **Sample: $6 postpaid. Submit 3-5 poems. Reports in 2 weeks (often sooner). Pays 1 copy. Send SASE for guidelines.** The sample copy I examined focused on humorous poetry—10 poets, some represented by more than 1 poem. I selected as a sample the opening of "Kong Settles Down" by William Trowbridge:

> They've locked me in with this goddam lady gorilla,
> Russian bred, bulged up on steroids
> till she's damn near big as me. Shot-putter,
> they say. Couldn't pass the hormone test.

Neal Bowers advises beginning poets, "Read *Poet and Critic.*" I found I couldn't put this sample copy down!

POET INTERNATIONAL; WORLD POETRY SOCIETY; CPS ART-LETTRE (I, IV-Membership, translations), 208 W. Latimer Ave., Campbell, CA 95008, phone 408-379-8555, founded 1960, managing editor Bohumila Falkowski. *Poet International* is funded by the World Poetry Society, Intercontinental, to promote the translation and interchange of verse between diverse people of the world. Send SASE for brochure indicating special issues, anthologies and activities. **They accept for publication "all but 1%" of poetry submitted by members. Guidelines indicate exact format for submission. Sample $1, $1.50 for 2, includes postage. Pays 1 copy.** The editor says they want poetry "partial to form, free form, within length of 3 sonnets or 42 line/spaces. Not edited for style, subject or any purpose other than inherent zen." *Poet International* is a monthly, printed in India on newsprint, averaging 90 pp., digest-sized saddle-sewn, matte paper cover, circulation 1,000, over 700 subscriptions, of which 17% are libraries and gifts. Membership is $20 with 12 issues of *Poet* "carrying a minimum of 3 poems by subscriber annually. Discount for multiple-year payments. *CPS Art-Lettre* is a monthly mimeographed newsletter for members using some poetry."

POET LORE (II), The Writers Center, 7815 Old Georgetown Rd., Bethesda, MD 20814-2415, founded 1889, managing editor Sunil Freeman, editor Philip Jason, is dedicated "to the best in American and world poetry and objective and timely reviews and commentary. We look for **fresh uses of traditional form and devices, but any kind of excellence is welcome. The editors encourage narrative poetry and original translations of works by contemporary world poets.**" They have recently published poetry by Sharon Olds, John Balaban, William Heyen, Walter McDonald, Reginald Gibbons and Lloyd Van-Brunt. As a sample (though it is not representative) I chose the first stanza of "Hieroglyhics" by Amy Rothholz:

> September is lying on its side
> So blackberry brandy and professions of love
> Can swim down my throat.
> Put another quarter in the jukebox.
> Let the pretty lies fly.

The 6×9″, 64 pp. saddle-stapled, professionally printed quarterly, matte card cover, has a circulation to 600 subscriptions of which 200 are libraries. Subscription: $12; per copy: $4.50. They receive about 3,000 poems in freelance submissions per year, use about 100. **Sample: $4 postpaid. Submit typed author's name and address on each page. Photocopies OK. Reports in 3 months. Pays 2 copies.**

POET PAPERS; THE RECORD SUN (II, IV-Subscribers), P.O. Box 528, Topanga, CA 90290, founded 1969. *The Record Sun* is a 3-6 pp. quarterly tabloid which uses **quality poetry, mostly by its 7,000 subscribers. Sample: $2. Poet Papers publishes collections of poetry, mostly solicited. Always send SASE if you want a reply.**

POETIC JUSTICE (II), 8220 Rayford Dr., Los Angeles, CA 90045, founded 1982, poetry editor Alan C. Engebretsen, publishes "contemporary American poetry. **Quality poetry is what I want—no-nos are raw language and blue material.**" Poems about relationships and positive features of life are welcome. They have recently published Ella Cavis, Stan Proper, Kay Harvey, Michael Lenhart, Ida Fasel, Richard Haydon and Ruth F. Eisenberg. The editor selected these sample lines from "Twilight and Dawn" by Eleanor P. Liddell:

> I've known the gift of dawn, that first lifting
> Of the night, allowing eyes fused shut with tears
> To sense the promise of emerging day.

The magazine is digest-sized, 44 pp., professionally printed, tinted matte card cover, published irregularly, circulation 200 with 55 subscriptions of which 2 are libraries, **43 pp. of poetry per issue.** Subscription: $10, 4 issues; per copy: $3. They receive about 1,500 poems per year, use 160. No current backlog. **Sample: $3 postpaid. Prefer submissions of 4 poems at a time, typewritten. No query. Reports in 1-2 weeks. Pays contributor's copy. Send SASE for guidelines. No oversize envelopes. Use #10 legal size envelopes only. Editor comments on rejections "when I have something to say."**

‡**POETIC PAGE (I)**, P.O. Box 71192, Madison Heights, MI 48071-0192, phone 313-548-0865, founded 1989, editor Denise Martinson, appears bimonthly. **Each issue has a contest, $1/poem fee, prizes of $25, $15, and $10. All poetry published is that of contest winners. "All forms are used except explicit sex, violence, and crude. 20-24 lines.**" They have published poetry by Dan Gallik, Kay Weems, Alice McKenzie Swaim, Marion Ford Park, Denise Martinson and Pearl Bloch Segall. As a sample the editor selected these concluding lines from "At the Post Office" by Charles Corry:

> Big Chief chaws
> flavor awesome tales,
> dripping like quivering shaped notes
> past tobacco-curled grins
> as wrinkled WW-I vets
> enhance old glories.

Poetic Page is 24-32 pp., magazine-sized, photocopied from typescript on 20 lb. paper, press run 250, 10 are libraries. Subscription: $7.50. **Sample, postpaid: $1.50. Simultaneous submissions and previously published poems OK.** The editor says, "We want poets to say, 'now that's an excellent poem.' If I read a poem, submitted or read elsewhere, I'll climb the highest mountain, swim the deepest sea to obtain it for our readers. We illustrate the winners because we feel that poems are work and that work should be shown in the best possible way. We may not be expensive, but we publish a quality publication. We like to print the beginner's poem alongside the seasoned pro's. In other words, we love poetry."

‡**POETIC PURSUITS (I)**, Rt. 2, Box 73A, Independence, KS 67301, phone 316-331-7715, founded 1988, editor Barbara Bushnell, is a quarterly that wants **poetry with "focus on natural straight-from-the-heart feelings and reflective memories."** As a sample the editor selected these lines (poet unidentified):

> *There are always tears*
> *when I say goodbye —*
> *but I like to pretend*
> *the tears are drops of dew*
> *that sparkle in the sun.*

PP is 20 pp. digest-sized, saddle-stapled, photocopied from typescript with matte card cover. They give no indication of payment or circulation.

POETIC SPACE: POETRY & FICTION (I,IV-Social issues, political), P.O. Box 11157, Eugene, OR 97440, founded 1983, editor Don Hildenbrand, is a literary magazine with emphasis on contemporary poetry, fiction, reviews, interviews and market news. Accepts poetry and fiction that is **well-crafted and takes risks. We like poetry with guts.** Would like to see some poetry on social and political issues. **Erotic and experimental OK. No traditional, rhymed (unless of high-quality), sentimental, romantic.** "They have recently published John M. Bennett, Barbara Henning, Albert Huffstickler, Arthur Winfield Knight, Crawdad Nelson, Tyrone Williams, and Lawson Fusao Inada. The editors selected these sample lines from "Critic" by Sesshu Foster:

> *Just for the sake of peace and quiet I'd say*
> *go ahead and shoot all the poets*
> *but then the few would lie silenced*
> *bleeding with actual compassion like anyone*
> *else, while from the wounds of the rest*
> *would pour words words words words*

The magazine is 8½ × 11", saddle-stapled, 8-12 pp., offset from typescript and sometimes photo reduced. It is published 3-4 times a year. They use about 25% of the 200-300 poems received per year. Press run: 800-1,000 with 50 subscriptions of which 12 are libraries. Price per issue: "Free." Subscription: $15. **Sample: $2. Guidelines for SASE. Pays 1 copy, but more can be ordered by sending SASE and postage. MS should be typed, double-spaced, clean, name/address on each page. Reports in 2-4 months. No simultaneous submissions or previously published poems. Editor provides some critical comments.** Don Hildenbrand says, "We like poetry that takes chances, from the heart and guts. Originality, not mediocrity, is what we wish to see. Reputations are not considered."

‡**POETICAL HISTORIES (V,II)**, 27 Sturton St., Cambridge, CB1 2QG, U.K., founded 1985, editor Peter Riley, is a "small press publishing **poetry only."** Submissions temporarily suspended due to printing delays, and back-log of accepted texts. They publish poetry that is "British, modernist," not "concrete, experimental, amateur, translated, homely." They have recently published poetry by J.H. Prynne and Nicholas Moore. **They publish 3-4 chapbooks averaging 8 pp. per year.**

POETPOURRI; COMSTOCK WRITERS' GROUP INC.; SUMMER SIZZLER CONTEST (II), Box 3737, Taft Rd., Syracuse, NY 13220, founded 1987, phone 315-451-1406, published by the Comstock Writers' Group, Inc., and edited by their editorial board, biannually. **They use "work that is clear and understandable to a general readership, that deals with issues, ideas, feelings, and beliefs common to us all — well-written free and traditional verse. No obscene, obscure, patently religious, or greeting card verse."** They have recently published poems by Katharine Machan Aal, Robert Cooperman, Simon Perchik, Joseph Bruchac, Patrick Lawler, and Scott Sonders. The group selected these sample lines from "Rumor" by Kathleen Bryce Niles:

> *It was a sophisticated lie,*
> *Decked out in top hat and tails,*
> *It swept them off their feet*
> *And danced them around the floor*
> *In smooth measured steps.*

Poems may be submitted anytime for possible publication, 3-6 at a time, unpublished poems

only. Return time: about 6 weeks. Editors usually comment on returned submissions. They offer a yearly Summer Sizzler contest with over $400 in prizes, $2 per poem, 30 line limit, *Poetpourri* is 100 pp., digest-sized, professionally printed, perfect-bound raised cover. Circulation 500. Subscription $8. **Sample: $4 postpaid. Pays copies.** The Comstock Writers' Group also publishes a free newsletter periodically.

POETRY; THE MODERN POETRY ASSOCIATION; BESS HOKIN PRIZE; LEVINSON PRIZE; OSCAR BLUMENTHAL PRIZE; EUNICE TIETJENS MEMORIAL PRIZE; FREDERICK BOCK PRIZE; RUTH LILLY POETRY PRIZE, (III), 60 W. Walton St., Chicago, IL 60610, founded 1912, editor Joseph Parisi, "is the oldest and most distinguished magazine devoted entirely to verse," according to their literature, though *Poet Lore* is considerably older, as is *North American Review*, which publishes both prose and poetry. Nonetheless the historical role of *Poetry* in modern literature is incontrovertible: "Founded in Chicago in 1912, it immediately became the international showcase that it has remained ever since, publishing in its earliest years—and often for the first time—such giants as Ezra Pound, Robert Frost, T. S. Eliot, Marianne Moore and Wallace Stevens. *Poetry* has continued to print the major voices of our time and to discover new talent, establishing an unprecedented record. There is virtually no important contemporary poet in our language who has not at a crucial stage in his career depended on *Poetry* to find a public for him: John Ashbery, Dylan Thomas, Edna St. Vincent Millay, James Merrill, Anne Sexton, Sylvia Plath, James Dickey, Thom Gunn, David Wagoner—only a partial list to suggest how *Poetry* has represented, without affiliation with any movements or schools, what Stephen Spender has described as 'the best, and simply the best' poetry being written." Although its offices have always been in Chicago, *Poetry*'s influence and scope extend far beyond, throughout the U.S. and in over 45 countries around the world. Asked to select 4 lines of poetry "which represent the taste and quality you want in your publication" Joseph Parisi selected the opening lines of "The Love Song of J. Alfred Prufrock" by T. S. Eliot, which first appeared in *Poetry* in 1915:

> Let us go then, you and I,
> When the evening is spread out against the sky
> Like a patient etherized upon a table;
> Let us go, through certain half-deserted streets . . .

The elegantly printed flat-spined 5½ × 9" magazine appears monthly, circulation 7,000, 6,000 subscriptions of which 65% are libraries. Subscription: $25; $27 for institutions; per copy: $2.50. They receive over 70,000 submissions per year, use 300-350, have a 9 month backlog. **Sample: $3.50 postpaid. Submit no more than 6 poems. "Photocopy OK; no dot-matrix; letter-quality OK." Reports in 8-10 weeks. Pays $2 a line. Send SASE for guidelines. Five prizes (named in heading) ranging from $100 to $1,000 are awarded annually to poets whose work has appeared in the magazine that year. Only verse already published is eligible for consideration and no formal application is necessary.** *Poetry* also sponsors the Ruth Lilly Poetry Prize, an annual award of $25,000.

POETRY BREAK; BEING; LUCKY "7" POETRY CONTEST (I, IV-Spirituality/inspirational, psychic/ occult), P.O. Box 417, Oceanside, CA 92054, phone 619-722-8829, founded 1988, (*Poetry Break* formerly *The Creative Urge*, founded 1984), editor and publisher Marjorie Talarico. *Poetry Break* is a bimonthly magazine that publishes poetry only. All subjects and styles are welcome. *Being* is a bimonthly New Age, metaphysical and natural health journal. **For *PB* the editor wants rhyming, traditional, haiku, experimental poetry. No restriction in length. For *Being*, "poems/prose, articles, book reviews, short stories with emphasis on New Age, metaphysical, holistic health and healing, poetry to 100 lines." For both magazines, she does not want to see anything "pornographic/highly erotic, political. No death, child/animal/alcohol abuse, war. Upbeat, positive material only." Guidelines for both magazines are available for SASE.** She has recently published poetry by Jenny L. Kelly, Panos Christi, Jack Bernier, and Adele Veronica Shimp. As a sample she selected the following lines from "Women" by Paul Meyers:

> to touch you is to
> see the river spin
> silk into laughter,
> the sky bloom billows
> of cotton.

Poetry Break is digest-sized, 15-30 pp., sometimes illustrated with pen and ink drawings; it uses 80 to 100 poems bimonthly. Circulation is about 350. **Pays in copies only. "We accept photocopy, dot-matrix printed, handwritten (legible, please)." Reporting time is 6-12 weeks and time to publication is 2-6 months.** Subscription for *Poetry Break* is $10/year, $2 per issue. **Sample: $2 plus 7½ × 10½ SASE with 65¢ postage.** Subscription for *Being* is $12/year, $3 per single issue. **Sample: $3 plus 7½ × 10½ SASE with 65¢ postage. Please make checks/money orders for samples/subscriptions payable to Marjorie Talarico. Critiques for small fee.** *Being* recently published the work of: C. David Hay, Michael Wayne O'Neal, Carole O. Turner, and Genoa. The editor

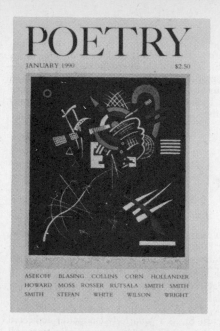

Founded in Chicago in 1912, Poetry has remained an international showcase by printing major voices of our time and discovering new talent, says editor Joseph Parisi. Poetry obtains art for covers from a number of sources, including individual artists, galleries and museums. This piece, "Small Worlds," was used courtesy of the Art Institute of Chicago.

selected these lines from "Song of Peace" by Merle Ray Beckwith:

> *Immortal visions rise*
> *That peace will reign on earth*
> *That each may know*
> *and each may show*
> *How much each soul is worth.*

"We are planning an Anthology of Horror to debut October 1992. Details for SASE." For details on *Poetry Break*'s Lucky "7" Poetry Contests, send SASE. The editor advises, "Don't be afraid to experiment with different styles. Keep your work circulating, and if a change is suggested, work with that editor. We care and are always willing to help."

THE POETRY CONNEXION (II, IV-Specialized), Wanda Coleman and Austin Straus, co-hosts, P.O. Box 29154, Los Angeles, CA 90029-0154, founded 1981, contact person Austin Straus. **"The Poetry Connexion"** is a radio program, usually live; poets coming to the LA area make contact several months in advance and send work with SASE just as though the program were a press. **"We are especially interested in poets who are planning to do readings in the Los Angeles area. Please notify us at least three months in advance for consideration as a guest on our program. Always include at least 6 poems and a vita in any submission."** The program is heard on the first, third, and fifth Saturdays of each month from 6:00 to 7:00 p.m. Its purpose is "to broaden the audience, reading and listening, for poetry in the Southern California area which is now experiencing a cultural 'boom' of sorts. **We are volunteer Pacifica Radio broadcasters and do not pay."** The co-hosts say, "We have a preference for the 'serious' poet who has published in recognized magazines. The poet may not necessarily have a book but must be on the verge of publishing, participating in workshops, readings, residencies, etc." Submissions are open, but they "prefer the accessible. We are also always most interested in poets whose lives are as committed and intense as their work."

POETRY DURHAM (II), English Dept., University of Durham, New Elvet, Durham, England DH1 3JT, edited by David Hartnett, Michael O'Neill, and Gareth Reeves, founded 1982, appears 3 times a year, 44 pp., digest-sized, professionally printed on good stock with glossy card cover, circulation 500, using **quality poetry and essays on modern poetry. Pays £12 per poem. All overseas subscriptions by international money order.** As a sample I selected the complete poem, "Deadly Nightshade," by Sally Carr:

> *Strange on the tongue*
> *those names that proffer ill—*
> *monkshood, hemlock and deadly nightshade.*
>
> *Offering the very sensation of death,*

> the moment of coming sleep
> in a room suffused with dark —
>
> they dare you to pick them.

POETRY EAST (II), Dept. of English, 802 West Belden Ave., De Paul University, Chicago, IL 60614, phone 312-341-8330, founded 1980, editor Richard Jones, "is a biannual international magazine publishing poetry, fiction, translations, and reviews. We suggest that authors look through back issues of the magazine before making submissions. **No constraints or specifications, although we prefer open form.**" They have published poetry by Tom Crawford, Thomas McGrath, Denise Levertov, Calway Kinnell, Sharon Olds, and Amiri Baraka. As a sample the editor chose "Cobalt" by David Ray:

> Cobalt wouldn't
> leap out to join
> the bomb, not
> the cobalt of
> this blue ming
> vase, not the cobalt
> of a bluejay's wing,
> not the cobalt of
> your eyes, my love.

The digest-sized flat-spined, 100+ pp., journal is professionally printed, glossy color card cover, circulation 1,200, 250 subscriptions of which 80 are libraries. They use 60-80 pp. of poetry in each issue. Subscription: $10; per copy: $7. They receive approximately 4,000 freelance submissions per year, use 10-20%, have a 9 week backlog. **Sample: $4.50 postpaid. Reports in 6-10 weeks. Pays copies. Editors sometimes comment on rejections.**

THE POETRY EXPLOSION NEWSLETTER (THE PEN) (I), Box 2648, Newport News, VA 23609-0648, phone 804-874-2428, founded 1984, editor Arthur C. Ford, Sr., is a "quarterly newsletter dedicated to the preservation of poetry." Arthur Ford wants **"poetry—40 lines maximum, no minimum. All forms and subject-matter with the use of good imagery, symbolism, and honesty. Rhyme and non-rhyme. No vulgarity."** He has recently published poetry by Ursula T. Gibon, Veona Thomas, and Virginia Goland. As a sample he chose his own poem, "Racism":

> Whether white as light
> Black, or still another,
> Only painters have the right
> To be, biased toward color.

The Pen is a newsletter containing 3-5 sheets of mimeographed on both sides of each sheet. He accepts about 40 of 125 poems received, press run 280, with 165 subscriptions of which 5 are libraries. Subscription: $12. **Send $3 for sample copy and more information. Pays 1 copy. Submit maximum of 5 poems. Simultaneous submissions and previously published poems OK. Editor comments on rejections "sometimes, but not obligated."** He holds poetry contests twice a year. He will criticize poetry for 15¢ a word. He comments: "Even though free verse is more popular today, we try to stay versatile."

POETRY FORUM (I), 5713 Larchmont Dr., Erie, PA 16509, phone 814-866-2543, poetry editor Gunvor Skogsholm, appears 3 times a year. **"We are open to any style and form. We believe new forms ought to develop from intuition. Length up to 50 lines accepted. Would like to encourage long themes. No porn or blasphemy, but open to all religious persuasions."** As a sample the editor selected these lines (poet unidentified):

> Is it anger I see in your eyes
> when they look at mine
> Because I see no smile or happiness
> there—merely a blank stare.

The magazine is 7 × 8½", 38 pp., saddle-stapled with card cover, photocopied from photoreduced typescript. "In the beginning months I accepted 80% of poetry received." **Sample: $1 postpaid. Send SASE for guidelines. They will consider simultaneous submissions and previously published poems.** They give awards of $50, $25, and $10 and 3 honorable mentions for the best poems in each issue. **Editor comments on poems "if asked, but respects the poetic freedom of the artist."** He says, "I believe today's poets should experiment more and not feel stuck in the forms that were in vogue 300 years ago."

POETRY HALIFAX DARTMOUTH; BS POETRY SOCIETY; NOVA SCOTIA POETRY AWARDS (I, II, IV-Regional), BS Poetry Society, 7074 North, Halifax, NS B3K 5J4 Canada, founded 1986, poetry editors Joe Blades and Eleonore Schönmaier, publishes the bimonthly literary magazine, *Poetry Halifax Dart-*

mouth with a calendar of literary activities, markets and announcements and the work of 5-12 writers in each issue, and articles relevant to writing. **"We're interested in quality writing with a broad span of interest. We are not specifically a regional magazine. Our contributors and readers are both national and international in range. We also publish short fiction, Canadian book reviews and b&w art. Encourage new writers. Rhymes rarely used. Will not accept material which is racist, sexist, homophobic or classist."** They have recently published poems by Susan Ioannou, Brian Burke, Robbie Newton Drummond, Liliane Welch and David Woods. As a sample the editor selected these lines from "Dying on the ice at 39 is hard" by John B. Lee:

> *His teammates gathered*
> *in a stunned huddle*
> *then breathed away from him*
> *on worried skates*
> *that day they tore their calendars*
> *like grieving widows.*

PHD is 24-36 pp., 7 × 8½", saddle-stapled, with matte card cover and b&w art and photos. They accept about 75 poets a year or ¼-⅓ of authors who submit. Press run is 250 for 75 subscriptions of which 12 are libraries. Subscription: $15. **Sample: $2 postpaid. Pays in 2 contributor's copies. Submit up to 6 poems with short bio. Reports in 2 months.** Send SASE for information on the annual Nova Scotia Poetry Awards, open to national and international entries. Entry fee.

POETRY IRELAND REVIEW (II, IV-Regional), 44 Upper Mount St., Dublin 2, Ireland, founded 1981, "provides an outlet for **Irish poets; submissions from abroad also considered. No specific style or subject matter is prescribed."** Occasionally publishes special issues—recently Latin American Poetry. The 6 × 8" quarterly uses 60 pp. of poetry in each issue, circulation 1,000, 450 subscriptions of which 50 are libraries. Subscription: $30; per copy: $8 (U.S.). They receive about 2,500 submissions per year, use 250, have a 3 month backlog. **Sample: $7 postpaid. Submit photocopies, no simultaneous submissions, no query. Reports in 3 months. Pays in copies.** The editors advise, "Keep submitting: good work will get through."

POETRY MAGIC (I, IV-Love/Romance, anthology), 1630 Lake Dr., Haslett, MI 48840, founded 1987, editor Lisa R. Church. Publishes an anthology and newsletter for writers, looking for **"no specific style. Open to all types, including haiku. Length should be no longer than one 8½ × 11" page but will consider longer poems. We want work from the writer/poet's heart and soul—not something that is 'forced.' No pornographic. Sexual themes are okay but will be left to the editor's decision."** They have published poetry by Scott Sonders, and Maria Bakkum. As a sample she selected these lines from "Gauntlets of Threadbare Silk" by Scott Sonders:

> *i begin again*
> *when mind and soul are through*
> *to start the walk long down the hall*
> *to lie alone and think of you*

The anthology is digest-sized, 170+ pages, flat-spined, 1-3 poems per page, with a matte cover with color art. $16.95 list price **No payment. Discount to authors.** Newsletter features articles, contest information, market listings and **poem relating to the art of writing.** Subscription: $12 for newsletter. **Sample, postpaid: $3. Pays 2 copies. Send SASE for guidelines. MS should be typed on one side of paper. "Will accept hand-written material only if it is legible—otherwise, it ends up in file 'trash.' "** Simultaneous submissions, previously published poems OK if stated as such. **Reports in 4-6 weeks. Editor comments "if time permits us to."** She says, "I have found those individuals who persistently work at their craft will receive the deserved recognition. I suggest that beginners circulate their poems and their name to many editors, which will allow the editors to become familiar with the name and the work. It is strongly suggested that at all times beginners present themselves in a professional manner. If SASE not enclosed, work will be discarded."

POETRY MOTEL; SUBURBAN WILDERNESS PRESS BROADSIDES & CHAPBOOKS; (I, II), 1619 Jefferson, Duluth MN 55812, phone 218-728-3728, founded 1984, poetry editors Andrea and Pat McKinnon and Bud Backen, aim **"to keep the rooms clean and available for these poor ragged poems to crash in once they are thru driving or committing adultery."** No specifications. They have recently published poetry by Jesse Glass, Robert Peters, Carolyn Stoloff, Kathy Brady and Albert Huffstickler.
Poetry Motel appears 1-2 times a year, 8½ × 7", digest, various covers, including wallpaper (issue 12) and chrome plated mylar (issue #10), circulation 500 (to 450 subscriptions), 50-60 pp. of poetry, prose, occassional essays and reviews. Sample: $4.95. They receive about 1,000 submissions per year, take 150, have 6-8 month backlog. **Submit 3-5 pp., informal cover letter, name and address on each page. Photocopy OK. Simultaneous submissions OK. Reports in 1-3 weeks. Pays in copies.** Editors are **"always glad to comment, on request."** They advise, "Poets should read as much poetry as they can

lay their hands on. And they should realize that although poetry is no fraternal club, today poets are responsible for its survival, both financially and emotionally. Join us out here—this is where the edge meets the vision."

‡POETRY NEW YORK: A JOURNAL OF POETRY AND TRANSLATION (II, IV-Translations), PhD Program in English, CUNY, 33 W. 42nd St., New York, NY 10036, phone 212-642-2206, founded 1985, editors Burt Kimmelman and Robert Thompson, is an annual. **"No specs. We favor translations of poetry."** I have not seen an issue, but the editor describes it as 4¼×5½" saddle-stapled, 80 pp., with glossy card cover. They accept about 20% of "blind submissions." Press run: 500 for 300 shelf sales. **Pays 2 copies. Reports in 3-4 months. Editor comments on submissions "at times."**

POETRY NIPPON PRESS; THE POETRY SOCIETY OF JAPAN; POETRY NIPPON; POETRY NIPPON NEWSLETTER (II, IV-Form, translations), 5-11-2, Nagaike-cho, Showa-ku, Nagoya, Japan 466, phone 052-833-5724, founded 1967, poetry editors Atsuo Nakagawa and Yorifumi Yaguchi (and guest editors). *Poetry Nippon,* a quarterly, uses **translations of Japanese poems into English, poems by Western and Japanese poets, tanka, haiku, one-line poems, essays on poetry and poets, poetry book reviews, poetry news, home and abroad. They want tanka, haiku, one-line poems and poems on contemporary themes and on Japan.** They have published poetry by Yorifumi Yaguchi and Mokuo Nagayama and Naoshi Koriyama. The editor selected these sample lines by James Kirkup:

> There is no other place
> like the room we were born in,
> The moment no one remembers
> is enshrined in it for ever.

Poetry Nippon has a circulation of 500 with 200 subscriptions of which 30 are libraries. Subscription: $29; per copy: $8. They use 25% of the 400 submissions they receive each year, have a 6-12 month backlog. **Sample free for 4 IRCs. Submit 2 poems, 5 tanka or 6 haiku, unpublished and not submitted elsewhere. "Deadline March 31 for nonmembers." Reports in 6 months for members. Payment is made in copies. Send SAE with 2 IRC's for guidelines.** Apparently you can join the Poetry Society of Japan, receive the *Newsletter* and *Poetry Nippon* and have other benefits. For example, **the editors provide criticism "on members' MSS only."** They sponsor contests for tanka and haiku and publish collections by individuals and anthologies.

POETRY NORTHWEST (II), 4045 Brooklyn NE, Seattle, WA 98105, phone 206-543-2992, founded 1959, poetry editor David Wagoner, is a quarterly which uses 48 pp. of poetry in each issue, circulation 2,000. Subscription: $10; per issue: $3. They receive 30,000 poems in freelance submissions per year, use 160, have a 6 month backlog. **Sample: $3 postpaid. Reports in 1 month maximum, pays 2 copies. They award prizes of $100, $50 and $50 yearly, judged by the editors. Occasionally editor comments on rejections.**

POETRY NOTTINGHAM; NOTTINGHAM POETRY SOCIETY; LAKE ASKE MEMORIAL OPEN POETRY COMPETITION; QUEENIE LEE COMPETITION (IV-Regional), Summer Cottage, West St., Shelford, Notts. NG12 1EJ England, phone 0602 334540, founded 1941, poetry editor Claire Piggott. Nottingham Poetry Society meets monthly for readings, talks, etc., and publishes quarterly its magazine, *Poetry Nottingham,* which is open to submissions from all-comers. **"We wish to see poetry that is intelligible to and enjoyable by the average reader. We do not want any party politics. Poems not more than 40 lines in length."** They have recently published poetry by Mary Jo Bang, Herbert Batt, Dan Hardner, and Hari Burrus from the USA and by Tony Cosier from Canada. The editor selected these sample lines by Henry Normal from "The House is Not the Same Since You Left":

> Nothing in the house will talk to me
> I think your armchair's dead
> The kettle tried to comfort me at first
> but you know what it's attention span is like
> I've not told the plants yet
> they think you're still on holiday.

There are 36 pp. of poetry in each issue of the 6×8", magazine, professional printing with b/w graphics, color matte card cover, circulation 325, for 200 subscriptions of which 20 are libraries. Subscriptions: £7 ($50 for 2 years USA); per copy: £1.50 ($6 USA). They receive about 1,500 submissions per year, use 120, usually have a 2-6 month backlog. **Sample: $6 or £1.50 postpaid. Submit at any time 3-5 poems, not more than 40 lines each, not handwritten, and previously unpublished. Send SAE and IRC for stamps. No need to query. Reports "within 3 months plus mailing time." Pays one copy. They publish collections by individual poets who were born, live or work in the East Midlands of England.** The Lake Aske Memorial Open Poetry Competition offers cash prizes and publication in *Poetry Nottingham.* Open to all. The Queenie Lee Competition is for members and subscribers only, offers a cash prize and publication. **Editor comments** "when I feel the poet is able to write something that I will accept." Her advice, especially for beginners, is "read the magazine before submitting anything; write the kind of poetry you believe in, which, if it is any good, will find a magazine to publish it." As a footnote, to help US poets understand some of the problems of editors in other countries, I'd like to quote Claire Piggott at length: "May I suggest that a general note about how to pay for small magazines from England that sell only a few copies in the USA, with a recommendation to send a draft for sterling, would be helpful to your readers. The price of our magazine is low (£7 annual subscription in the U.K.). If, however, I wish to exchange a draft from the USA, the bank charges me £3 commission (their commission being the same whether I am exchanging $10 or $10,000). Therefore, we are now asking that overseas subscribers who cannot arrange a draft for sterling should take out a two-year subscription for $50 to include all postage at increased rates. The advice about sterling drafts applies equally to sample copies; please allow £2.50 to include post."

POETRY ONLY; FORESTLAND PUBLICATIONS (I, IV-Themes), P.O. Box 213, Canterbury, CT 06331-0213, founded 1988, editor Geraldine Hempstead. *Poetry Only* is a magazine. **"No restrictions on form, length, or subject-matter. If it's a long poem, it better be exciting enough to keep me awake. No porn."** They have published poetry by Ray Mizer, Gary Scheinoha, Winnie Fitzpatrick, R. Allen Dodson, and Ken Stone. As a sample the editor quoted these lines by John Rautio:

> The world is nothing more you see
> than a Reflection of you and me
> the Rich are the ones in Poverty
> when they don't understand Life's simple poetry

Press run 100, with 15 subscribers, 75 distributed free. Subscription: $8.50. **Sample: $2 postpaid. All orders must be made payable to Geraldine Hilliard. Pays 1 copy. Send SASE for guidelines. They will consider simultaneous submissions and previously published poems.**

POETRY OF THE PEOPLE (I,IV-Anthology, humor, political, love/romance/erotica, nature, fantasy, themes), Box 13077, Gainesville FL 32604, founded 1986, poetry editor Paul Cohen. *Poetry of the People* appears once a month. **"We take all forms of poetry but we like humorous poetry, love poetry, nature poetry and fantasy. No racist or highly ethnocentric poetry will be accepted."** As an example the editor selected lines from a poem by Jenny L. Kelly.

> And then we two walk naked into the town
> Hand in hand among hordes of people
> Who stop and stare in utter disbelief
> Not at our nakedness
> But rather at our radiance

Poetry of the People has a circulation between 100 and 2,000. Copies are distributed to Gainesville residents for 25¢ each. **"I feel autobiographical information is important in understanding the poetry." Poems returned within two months. Editor comments on rejections often.** He advises, "be creative: there is a lot of competition out there." A dozen leaflets (8-16 pp., $4\frac{1}{2} \times 5\frac{1}{4}$, sometimes stapled on colored paper) of poetry are published each year, usually theme anthologies. **Pays 5 copies. Subscription: $8 per year. Sample $1.50. Make checks payable to Paul Cohen.**

THE POETRY PEDDLER; SNOWBOUND PRESS (I, II), P.O. Box 250, West Monroe, New York 13167, phone 315-676-2050, founded 1988, poetry editors J. J. Snow and A. M. Ryant. Snowbound Press publishes chapbooks by special arrangement. *PP* is a literary magazine of poetry, reviews, and essays on poetry appearing six times a year, using **"poems of clarity and intensity of feeling. We will consider rhymed poetry of a serious nature providing the rhyme doesn't overwhelm the message. Seldom does a rhymed poem meet this standard. Rhyme used to augment humor is welcome. No bigotry, pro-war, graphic violence, obscure poems."** Poetry recently published by Susan Manchester, Walt Phillips, Jack Karpan, Asha Eshe, and Chloe Morgan. As a sample J. J. Snow chose the last lines from his poem "Patty Patches":

> They found her last night
> perfect lips and all
> self-inflicted
> they said.

PP is 20 pp., magazine-sized, desktop publishing, with card covers, using some comptuer-generated graphics. **Send SASE for guidelines.** Subscription: $10. **Sample: $2. They will consider previously published poems (send complete publications information and statement that you now control rights) but no simultaneous submissions. "Handwritten OK if legible." Editor always comments on rejections.** Pays 1 copy. They sponsor one contest per year with entrance fees, cash awards and independent judging.

POETRY PLUS MAGAZINE; GERMAN PUBLICATIONS (I, IV-Subscribers), Route 1, Box 52, Pulaski, IL 62976, founded 1987, publisher/editor Helen D. German. *PPM* is a quarterly with articles about poetry, stories, and poems. **"We accept all styles. Length should be no more than 24 lines. Poets can write on any subject that offers a meaningful message. We want our poets to write poems that will make the reader really think about what has been said. Reader should not have to guess at what was said. We do *not* want any holiday poems, obscene poems, or sexual poems. Poems should not be indecent."** As a sample the editor selected the complete poem, "Poem" by C.K. Randall:

> golden
> dark
> rhythm
> in hands
> of silence
> dancing
> in
> weave

PPM is magazine-sized, 25-35 pp., photocopied from typescript, bound with tape, paper cover. Subscription: $12. **Sample: $3 postpaid. Send SASE for guidelines. Subscribers are paid up to $5 for outstanding poems; no payment to non-subscribers.** The editor says, "We stress the importance of obtaining and following the rules and standards of each publication you may be interested in. By following their guidelines you make it easier for the editor to accept your work. He/she knows you are a professional by your compliance to their requests. Never give up. Eventually your work will be published."

POETRY REVIEW; POETRY SOCIETY (II), 21 Earls Court Sq., London, SW5 9DE England, founded 1909, editor Peter Forbes. This quarterly publication is the journal of the Poetry Society. The only instructions as to type of poetry wanted are **"Intending contributors should study the magazine first."** They publish "all the leading UK poets, many American and European poets." Recent poets featured include Joseph Brodsky, Anthony Hecht, Derek Walcott, Tony Harrison, Craig Raine, Primo Levi, and Vikram Seth. As a sample, the editor chose four lines from David Sutton's "Geomancies":

> Like a careful Chinese geomancer
> I play the game: where shall I build my house?
> As if my days and money left more choice
> Than standard boxes, twenty to the acre.

Poetry Review is 6¾ × 9¾", 76 pp., offset on rough paper, with b/w graphics and photos. Stiff card cover, printed in two colors plus black on white, flat-spined. Circulation is 4,500, price per issue £3, subscription £15 ($32). All subscriptions, payable to *Poetry Review*, to: Central Books, 14 The Leathermarket, London SE1 3ER, England. **Sample available for £3.50 postpaid, guidelines for SASE. Pay is £10-15 poem, plus 1 copy. Reporting time is 10 weeks and time to publication varies.**

POETRY SOUTH (V, I, IV-Regional), 701 N. Monroe St., Clinton, MS 39056, founded 1988, editor Richard Garner, is a magazine appearing in April, August, and December, containing information for poets. **"All lengths and types of poems. Because of the huge amount of poetry received, we are forced to close our 'submissions doors' until further notice."** *Poetry South* is 20-30 pp. saddle-stapled, digest-sized, using sketches and bios with poems. In 1988 they accepted 40 of 50 submissions received. Subscription: $9. **Sample: $3 postpaid.**

‡POETRY TODAY (I), 3737 St. Johns Bluff Road S., #1001, Jacksonville, Fl 32216, founded 1989, editor Diane Chehab, appears monthly with poetry of **"any length or style, no restrictions. Looking for first-rate poetry, carefully-crafted and original. Very open to beginning poets. Use good taste, judgment. No smut."** As a sample the editor selected these lines from her own "Angel of Death":

> Empty halls
> Shadows
> Eclipse my tears
> Clutching at her shawl
> In the corner
> Full of fear
> A mourner—
> I stand near.

I have not seen an issue, but the editor describes it as digest-sized, 20-30 pp., saddle-stapled, color cover with b/w drawing. Subscription: $24. **Sample, postpaid: $3. Pays 2 copies. "Refrain from using dot matrix please."** They hope to have contests with monetary prizes in the future and to pay for poetry. They also encourage submissions of drawings for their covers. The editor says, "One must endeavor to read as much as possible, especially other poets. Study people for their reactions. Be the fly on the wall. Write as much as possible and save everything; don't throw anything away. You can use it later to gauge your progress and rewrite what you once thought belonged in the wastebasket."

POETRY USA; POETS FOR PEACE (I, II, IV-Themes, children), Ft. Mason Cultural Center, San Francisco, CA 94123, founded 1985, editor Herman Berlandt, who describes *Poetry: USA* as "a quarterly for **bold and compassionate poetry." Every issue has a thematic focus: for example, love and experience, four dozen ways of looking at the moon, in praise of other muses, etc. Send SASE for upcoming themes. The editor does not want "trite and phoney, 'elevated' stuff using contrived rhymes."** He has published poetry by Amy Gerstler, Mary Mackey, Diane di Prima, Neeli Chekovski, and Robert Bly. As a sample he selected these lines (poet unidentified):

> *When I called your name*
> *it was a question*
> *glimmering in the high air*
> *so beautiful*
> *it had no answer*

Poetry USA is a typeset unstapled tabloid, 16 pp., with photos, graphics and ads, circulation 10,000, distributed free "to reach 40,000 literati in the Bay Area" and available to others by subscription at $7.50/year. **Sample: $1.50 postpaid. "Big backlog, active file for a year. Suggest poems under 32 lines. No SASEs. Just send photocopies—if published, contributor will get copies." No other pay "as yet. Suggest that contributors subscribe to maintain good contact." One section of the tabloid is devoted to poetry by young poets.** They hold four annual contests, on the theme of each issue, with a $5 entry fee for a maximum of 4 entries. Four $25 prizes, plus publication (and awards for honorable mentions). Pays 2 copies. Contributors are encouraged to subscribe. Send SASE for guidelines. Previously published poems OK (if the editor knows).

POETRY WALES PRESS; POETRY WALES (II, IV-Ethnic), Andmar House, Trewsfield Ind. Estate, Tondu Rd., Bridgend, Mid-Glamorgan, CF31 4LJ Wales, founded 1965. *Poetry Wales*, a 72 pp. 253 × 185mm. quarterly, circulation 1,000, has a primary interest in **Welsh and Anglo-Welsh poets but also considers submissions internationally. Sample: £1.95. Pays.** The press publishes books of **primarily Welsh and Anglo Welsh poetry**, also biography, critical works and some fiction, distributed by Dufour Editions, Inc., Box 449, Chester Springs, PA 19425. I selected the first of 6 stanzas of "The Dark" by Richard Poole as a sample:

> *And now, it seems, you are fearful*
> *of the dark. You people black vacancies*
> *with monsters of your own imagining.*

POETRY WLU (I, II), Department of English, Wilfrid Laurier University, Waterloo, ON N2L 3C5 Canada, phone 519-884-1970, ext. 2308, founded 1979, editorial contact E. Jewinski, is an annual literary magazine "with emphasis on *all* poetry and *all* prose *under* 1,000 words. **20-30 lines are ideal; but all kinds and length considered."** As a sample I selected the complete poem "Elspeth" by Audrey P. Heutzenroeder:

> *Elspeth overturns elfin stones.*
> *Plays in the garden with toadie's bones.*
> *Recites tales dark and tragic.*
> *Dances with wizards and learns their magic.*

Poetry WLU is 6½ × 8″ saddle-stapled, typeset, with matte card cover using b/w art. They accept 15-20% of some 60-70 submissions received per year. Press run 300. **Sample: $3 postpaid. Pays 1 copy. Reports in 6-8 months. "When the editorial board has time, comments are made."** The magazine is published every March.

POETRY WORLD (IV, Translations), English Dept., University of Iowa, Iowa City, IA 52242, founded 1965, poetry editor Daniel Weissbort, appears twice annually, publishes "**translations into English of foreign poetry, articles on literary translation, reviews of translations. We want translations of contemporary or earlier poetry, preferably not the universally known figures, also oral poetry. We do *not* consider work written in English."** They have published poetry by Béalu, Reverdy, Rolf Jacobsen, Eskimo, Yugoslav folk poetry, etc. A durable little book. It has a circulation of 1,750, for 500 subscriptions of which 200 are libraries. The magazine is 160 pp., flat spine. **"Query advisable. 5-10 poems per individual poet. Format doesn't matter. Simultaneous submissions OK provided we are informed."** Reports in 3-6 months. Payment amount depends on funds available. Complimentary copies to contributors.

POETRY/LA, PEGGOR PRESS (IV-Regional), P.O. Box 84271, Los Angeles, CA 90073, phone 213-472-6171, founded 1980, editor Helen Friedland, assistant editor Barbara Strauss, "is a semi-annual anthology of **high quality poems by established and new poets living, working or attending school in the Los Angeles area. Otherwise, high literary quality is our only constraint.**" They have published poetry recently by Peter Levitt, Charles Bukowski, Carol Lem, Gerald Locklin, Amy Uyematsu, and Lee Chul Bum. As to selecting a sample, the editor says, "Since our orientation is eclectic, quoting one poem would draw too many submissions with that poem's traits." With that warning, I selected the opening lines of "Errant" by Ron Koertge, hoping his style is inimitable but does represent the quality of the magazine:

> *You wanted me to take care*
> *of that dragon who was bothering*
> *you, and I was glad to. He wasn't*
> *much bigger than a pig and had breath*
> *like a kitchen match.*

The flat-spined, digest-sized biannual, professionally printed, color matte card cover, circulation 500, 200 subscriptions of which 20 are libraries, uses about 120 pp. of poetry in each issue. Subscription: $8; per copy: $4.25. They receive 2,750 submissions per year, use 200. Almost all poems are published within 2-6 months from date of acceptance. **Sample: $3.50 postpaid. "We prefer about 4-6 pp., but will review all poems received. Clean photocopy is fine, simultaneous submissions are not. And, *please*, name and address on each poem (anonymous entries drive us crazy)."** They report in 1-6 months, pay copies only (one per printed page of the poet's work). **Send SASE for guidelines. Editor comments "in general, only if we believe the poem merits publication if certain difficulties can be resolved."**

POETS AT WORK; JESSEE POET MONTHLY/QUARTERLY CONTESTS (I, IV-Subscribers), RD 1, Portersville, PA 16051, founded 1985, Jessee Poet editor/publisher, **contributors are expected to subscribe.** Jessee Poet says, "I offer many contests, some of them are free with cash prizes. I am in contact with many of my readers and always answer the mail personally. **No poet who writes along the lines of good taste is ever turned away; all are published. I accept all forms of poetry, all styles and themes. Poetry is limited to 20 lines or fewer. *No exceptions.*** No porn; no profanity." He has recently published poetry by Charles Dickson, Ann Gasser, Ralph Hammond and Pat Anthony. As a sample Jessee selected his poem "Through the Night" as a sample:

> *I watched and waited holding your hand*
> *Aura of death filled the air;*
> *As dawn streaked the sky, I became aware*
> *That the Grim Reaper had taken command.*

Poets at Work is magazine-sized, 40-44 pp. saddle-stapled, photocopied from photoreduced typescript with colored paper cover. *PAW* appears every other month. In a year, he says, he has received "3,000 poems; all accepted but published at a rate of one or possibly two poems per poet per issue." (Prize-winning poems are printed.) Subscription is $16. **Sample: $3. Payment: nothing, not even a copy. Simultaneous submissions and previously published poems OK. Reports within 2 weeks. Contest prizes are "generally half of what I take in entry fees."** Fee varies from 2 poems/$1 to $1/poem and always one free contest. Send SASE for guidelines to the various contests Jessee Poet offers. He says, "I find that more and more poets are submitting poetry today than a year ago. The poets who are published in my magazine are instructed in only one thing from me: They may not criticize any other poet. This has worked beautifully, and my finest poets take their places side by side with my novices. Hopefully, none of us have yet written our finest poem, and all of us have room to grow. Beginning poets would do well to practice some of the established easier poetry forms before attempting the more complicated forms like the sonnet or free verse. Work with a dictionary nearby and check spelling. Use a thesaurus and rhyming dictionary." Chapbooks printed, reasonable prices. SASE for information.

POETS ON: (IV-Themes), 29 Loring Ave., Mill Valley, CA 94941, phone 415-283-2824, founded 1976, poetry editor Ruth Daigon, is a 48 pp. poetry semiannual, **each issue on an announced theme. "We want well-crafted, humanistic, accessible poetry. We don't want to see sentimental rhymed verse.**

ALWAYS submit MSS or queries with a stamped, self-addressed envelope (SASE) within your country or International Reply Coupons (IRCs) purchased from the post office for other countries.

Length preferably 40 lines or less, or at the very most 80 lines (2 page poems)." They have published poetry by Marge Piercy, Charles Edward Eaton, Joseph Bruchac, Sharon Olds, and Lyn Lifshin. As a sample the editor chose these lines from "Today" by William Stafford:

> *And it is already begun, the chord*
> *that will shiver glass, the song full of time*
> *bending above us. Outside, a sign:*
> *a bird intervenes; its wings tell the air,*
> *"Be warm." No one is out there, but a giant*
> *has passed through the town, widening streets touching*
> *the ground, shouldering away the stars.*

The digest-sized, professionally printed magazine, matte card cover with b/w graphics, has a circulation of 450, 350 subscriptions of which 125 are libraries. Subscription: $8; per copy: $4. They use about 5% of the 800 submissions they receive each year, have a 2-3 month backlog. **Sample: $4 postpaid. Query with SASE to find out the current theme. Submit 5-6 poems (40 lines or shorter). "We generally do not publish rhymed or overly-sentimental poems although we are open to experimentation. Again it's a good idea to read the magazine before submitting poetry." Submit between September 1-December 1 or February 1-May 1. Photocopy, dot-matrix OK. No handwritten MSS. Include short bio. Reports in 2-3 months. Pays 1 copy plus 2 year subscription. Editor sometimes comments on rejections.** Ruth Daigon advises, "The poet should make him/herself open to whatever is being done in the world of poetry, whether they like it or not, whether they agree with it or not, whether they understand it or not."

POETS. PAINTERS. COMPOSERS. (II), 10254 35th Ave. SW, Seattle, WA 98146, phone 206-937-8155, founded 1984, editor Joseph Keppler, who says *"Poets. Painters. Composers.* is an avant-garde arts journal which publishes poetry, drawings, scores, criticism, essays, reviews, photographs and original art. **If poetry, music, or art is submitted, the work should be exciting, knowledgeable, and ingenious."** The journal, which appears once or twice a year, has published such artists as Carla Bertola, Fernando Aguian, Ana Hatherly, and Sarenco, and such poets as Richard Kostelanetz, Carletta Wilson, D. Bauer, and Gregory Jerozal. As a sample the editor selected these lines from "Drawing a Candle" one of a series of poems about drawing by Carol Barrett:

> *Smell it first to make a good*
> *beginning. That will fix the next*
> *approach: the curve of a wine bottle*
> *spattered all night; the reach*
> *of a wedding stem, bud*
> *hidden in mantled pine . . .*

The very handsome, expensively printed journal is magazine-sized, 60 pp., most of it printed in black on white paper but with occasional inserts of colored paper, tissue, cutouts—one poem is even printed in its own little card folder. Mr. Keppler says, "each odd-numbered issue appears in an 8½×11" format; each even-numbered issue changes format: No. 2, for example, is published as posters; No. 4 appears on cassettes." Circulation is 300, no subscriptions. Each issue of the magazine carries an individual price tag, but "benefactors donating $300 receive every issue for life." **Sample of No. 2 available for $10.50 postpaid. Contributors receive 1 copy. "Contributors' poetry receives great care. All material is returned right away unless (a) it's being painstakingly examined for acceptance into the journal or (b) it's being considered as right for some other way of publishing it or (c) we died."** He expects to publish 3 chapbooks of poetry a year and will accept freelance submissions. **For chapbook publication poets should query first "if poet prefers," sending credits, 7 sample poems, bio, philosophy, and poetic aims. Pay for chapbooks will be in author's copies, number negotiable ("We're generous"); honorariums are given whenever possible.** Format of the chapbooks is expected to be "small, avant-garde, distinguished, exciting, experimental." Joseph Keppler says, "Poets' work is important work, and poetry is a most difficult art today. We maintain absolutely high standards, yet offer a hopeful critique . . . We want to develop the avant-garde here and everywhere. We expect to last well into the 21st Century and to change the way this culture understands literature. We intend to transform the role of poets in society. Advice for beginning poets? We're all beginning poets today."

POET'S REVIEW (IV-Subscribers), 806 Kings Row, London Village, Cohutta, GA 30710, phone 404-694-8441, founded 1988, publisher Bob Riemke, is a monthly booklet, digest-sized, 20 pp., photocopied from typescript with paper cover, using poetry by subscribers and making cash awards monthly and annually on basis of votes by subscribers. "Prefer rhyme. 44 lines or less. Any subject. No porn! No foreign languages." They have recently published poetry by J. Alvin Speers. As a sample the editor selected this staza from "The Captain and the Queen," a $500 winner in a 1988 issue, by Ashley C. Anders:

They had grown up together,
the Captain and his Queen;
She was a strong majestic ship . . .
He, a lad tall and lean.

Subscription: $36. **Sample: $4 postpaid. "Subscribers are sent a ballot along with their monthly booklet to vote for the poems they believe to be the best." Monthly prizes are $50, $25, and $10, plus 7 honorable mentions. "All $50 winners are presented to the subscribers again at the end of the year and compete for a $500, $250 and $100 prize."** 20-30 poems are printed each month along with the names of winners for the previous month.

POETS' ROUNDTABLE; POETS' STUDY CLUB OF TERRE HAUTE; POETS' STUDY CLUB INTERNA-TIONAL CONTEST (I, IV-Membership), 826 S. Center St., Terre Haute, IN 47807, phone 812-234-0819, founded in 1939, president/editor Esther Alman. Poets' Study Club is one of the oldest associations of amateur poets. It publishes every other month, *Poets' Roundtable*, a newsletter of market and contest information and news of the publications and activities of its members in a mimeographed, 10 pp. bulletin (magazine-sized, stapled at the corner, on colored paper), and circulation 2,000. They have also published an occasional chapbook-anthology of poetry by members "but do not often do so." **Dues: $6 a year, sample free for SASE. Uses short poems by members only. Simultaneous submissions and previously published poems OK.** They offer an annual Poets' Study Club International Contest, open to all, with no fees and cash prizes—a $25 and $15 award in 3 categories: traditional haiku, serious poetry, light verse, deadline February 1. Also contests for members only each two months. "We have scheduled criticism programs for members only."

‡POGMENT PRESS (V,IV-Regional), 11939 Escalante Ct., Reston, VA 22091, phone 703-758-0258, founded 1985, editor Jefferson D. Bates, an elderly man who writes, "I still have enough energy and enthusiasm to publish 3-4 chapbooks/year, but how long this will continue I have no idea. I publish area poets with whose work I am familiar. **I am not seeking mss from outside my immediate area of Washington, DC, Maryland, and Northern Virginia.** As long-time member of the Board of Director of the Writer's Center (now a member emeritus) I have an opportunity to meet (and hear readings by) many excellent poets. **I'm more concerned with the traditional forms and the niceties of rime and meter than are most publishers today. I love light, well-crafted verse** in the vein of Dorothy Parker, Ogden Nash, Samuel Hoffenstein, and others that I've admired from my youth. I love the 'Grooks' of Piet Hein, and look forward to Willard Espy's little masterpieces in the *Writer's Digest* each month." He has published books by Dean Blehert, Werner Low, and Marlene S. Veach, **10% royalties plus 10 copies.** "I do have a co-op arrangement somewhat similar to that of Northwoods Press. The author agrees to purchase a minimum of 200 copies at 50% off the list price." **He sometimes comments on rejections.**

POLYFIDELITOUS EDUCATION PRODUCTIONS, INC.; PEPTALK (I, IV-Themes, erotica), P.O. Box 5247, Eugene, OR 97405, founded 1984, editor Ryam Nearing. *Peptalk* "publishes articles, letters, poems, drawings related to **polyfidelity, group marriage, and multiple** *intimacy*." **They use "relatively short poems, though a quality piece of length would be considered but topic relevance is essential. Please no swinger or porno pieces."** Magazine-sized, 12 pp., few ads. Quarterly. Circulation 500. Subscription $10 a year. **Sample: $1.50 postpaid. Pays 1 copy. Responds "ASAP," delay to publication 2-6 months. MS should be "readable." Considers simultaneous submissions. Editor comments on rejections "sometimes—if requested."**

‡POLYPHONIES (III, IV-Translations), BP189, Paris 75665 CEDEX 14, France, founded 1985, editor Pascal Culerrier. Editorial committee: Laurence Breysse, Jean-Yves Masson, Alexis Pelletier, Patrick Piguet. Appears twice a year. **"Every case is a special one. We want to discover the new important voices of the world to open French literature to the major international productions. For example, we published Brodsky in French when he was not known in our country and had not yet the Nobel Prize. No vocal poetry, no typographic effects."** They have recently published poetry by Marie Luzi (Italy), Jeremy Reed (Great Britain), Octavio Paz (Mexico) and Claude Michel Cluny (France). I have not seen an issue, but the editor describes it as "16/24 cm." Press run: 1,000 for 300 + subscriptions. **Pays 2 copies. They use translations of previously published poems.** The editor says, "Our review is still at the beginning. We are in touch with many French editors. Our purpose is to publish together, side-by-side, poets of today and of yesterday."

PORTABLE WALL (I, IV-Humor), 215 Burlington, Billings, MT 59101, phone 406-256-3588, founded 1977, publisher Daniel Struckman. He wants **"humor, political, poetry as wisdom-friendship mind.** He has recently published poetry by Peter Koch, Michael Fiedler, and Anne Harris. As a sample he selected these lines by Wilbur Wood:

One step: snap twig.

> *Next step: crunch pinecone.*
> *Magpie, high in tree,*
> *Tilting head, eying me:*

PW is published twice a year and open to beginners, 40 pp., saddle-stapled, on heavy tinted stock with 2-color matte card cover, press run 200. **Sample: $5 postpaid. Pays 5 copies. Reports in 6 weeks, 6 months between acceptance and publication. Price per issue is $3, subscription $10 for 2 years.**

PORTLAND REVIEW (II), Box 751, Portland, OR 97207, phone 503-725-4468, founded 1954, editor Nancy Row, is a literary annual published by the Portland State University 3 times a year. **"Experimental poetry welcomed. No poems over 3 pages. No rhyming poetry."** The annual, which I have not seen, is magazine-sized, about 128 pp. They accept about 30 of 300 poems received each year. Press run is 500 for 100 subscriptions of which 10 are libraries. **Sample: $5. Send SASE for guidelines. Pays 1 copy. Simultaneous submissions OK.**

‡UNIVERSITY OF PORTLAND REVIEW (II), 5000 N. Willamette, Portland, OR 97203, phone 503-283-7144, appears twice a year—"a commentary on the contemporary scene intended for the college educated layman." As a sample of their poetry I selected the first stanza of "Un-Just Spring" by Mary Comstock:

> *Nothing is right this year.*
> *Rain is beating Spring back to the ground.*
> *Grass drowns about us.*
> *Buds never blossom,*

The 6x9" saddle-stapled, 44 pp. magazine uses about 10 pp. of poetry in each issue, has 200 subscribers of which 200 are libraries, sends out 600 complimentary copies. Subscription: $1; per copy: 50¢. They receive about a hundred submissions of poetry per year, use half, have a 1 year backlog. **Sample: 50¢ postpaid. Submit up to 4 poems any time. Reports within 6-12 months, pays 5 copies. The editors sometimes comment on rejections.**

POTATO EYES; NIGHTSHADE PRESS; SPUDWORKS (II, IV-Regional), P.O. Box 76, Troy, ME 04987, founded 1988, editors Roy Zarucchi and Carolyn Page, is a semiannual literary journal **"with a focus on writers who live along the Appalachian chain from southern Quebec to Alabama, though all U.S. and Canadian writers are welcome."** They have recently published poetry by Fred Chappell, Jim Wayne Miller, Robert Morgan, Pat Anthony, Shelby Stephenson, Karen Blomaine, and Barbara Crooker. As a sample the editors selected these lines from Glenn McKee's "Shutdown":

> *What's to become*
> *of my mental scrapbook*
> *once the power's gone?*
> *Who'll recollect sunlight*
> *caressing wheat shocks*
> *scythes lopping hogweeds*
> *at their hamstrings*
> *girls dancing jerseys*
> *barnward by milk time?*

Circulation is 800. *PE* is 6×9", 84+ pp. flat-spined, professionally printed, with wood block matte card cover. Subscription: $11 (Canadian $14). **Sample: $8 postpaid (back issue $5), or $7 Canadian. Reports in 2-8 weeks, and "those who submit receive a handwritten rejection/acceptance. We are open to any form other than rhymed, in batches of 3-5, but we tend to favor poetry with concrete visual imagery, solid intensity, and compression. We respect word courage and risk-taking, along with thoughtful lineation. We prefer rebellious to complacent poetry. We prefer a cover letter with brief bio along with SASE. Nightshade Press and Spudworks are the imprints under which they publish about 10 chapbooks/year, each 24 pp. "usually with hand-blocked open/ink covers, endsheets, and recycled 24 lb text, 65 lb. cover text. Nightshade Press chapbooks are published on a somewhat union arrangement based on poets' promotion with royalties paid to us. Spudworks assists those poets who seek a high-quality author-subsidized chapbook. We only publish poets with futures, poets whose work shows promise." For chapbook consideration query with bio and list of publications. "We prefer that poets appear first in our magazine. We like to feel that they are supportive enough to subscribe." Send SASE for catalog or $5 for sample chapbook. They advise, "Beginning poets should devour as much good poetry as possible in order to delineate their own style and voice. Look for a match between substance and sound.** We are particularly fond of poet-artists, but don't send originals of artwork."

POTES & POETS PRESS, INC.; ABACUS (II), 181 Edgemont Ave., Elmwood, CT 06110, phone 203-233-2023, press founded in 1981, magazine in 1984, editor Peter Ganick. The press publishes avant-garde poetry in magazine form under the *Abacus* imprint, one writer per 16-page issue. The P + Pinc books are perfect-bound and range from 80-120 pages in trade editions." **In addition to avant-garde, they want experimental or language-oriented poetry, not too much concrete poetry. No** *"New Yorker* **magazine,** *Ploughshares* **magazine, mainstream poetry."** They have published poems by Ron Silliman, Jackson Mac Low, Charles Bernstein, Cid Corman, and Theodore Enslin. The editors did not quote lines, and I have not seen samples. *Abacus* is magazine-sized, photocopied, no graphics, 12-18 pp.; it appears every 6 weeks. Circulation is 150, of which 40 are subscriptions and 10 go to libraries. Price per issue is $2.50, subscription $17/year. **Sample available for $2.50 postpaid. Pay is 12 copies. Simultaneous submissions are OK, as are photocopied or dot-matrix MSS. Reporting time is within 8 weeks and time to publication is 1 year. Freelance submissions are accepted for book publication. Writers should "just send the manuscript."** The press plans to publish 3 books of poetry per year with an average page count of 100, flat-spined paperbacks.

POULTRY, A MAGAZINE OF VOICE (IV-Humor), P.O. Box 4413, Springfield, MA 01101, founded 1979, editors Jack Flavin, Brendan Galvin and George Garrett, is a tabloid (2-3 times a year) of **"parody, satire, humor and wit, particularly of the modern literary scene." They do not want to see "serious" poetry.** They have recently published poetry by David R. Slavitt, Cecil J. Mullins, Bruce Bennett, Mindy Slater, Martha McFerren, Douglas A. Powell, the Apostle of Badism, and Richard Muegge. As a sample the editors selected these lines from "Oscar's English Dictionary," by Bruce T. Boehrer:

> *Oscar's English Dictionary suffers*
> *shitwits like you and me, forgives our errors,*
> *gathers them all together in one certain,*
> *vast absolution.*

The 11½×17" tabloid, 8 pp., unstapled, professionally printed on newsprint, uses b/w photos, graphics, drawings, press run 500, 250 subscribers of which 35 are libraries. Subscription: $5. **Sample: $2 postpaid. Pays 10 copies. Simultaneous submissions OK, "rarely" uses previously published poems.** Jack Flavin calls for "a little more humor and light, please, in the deadly serious (and oftentimes deadly) business of being a poet, a writer and getting published. Beginning poet? Get it down while it's hot, let it cool, and consider it with a cold eye a bit later. Learn to write by doing it, if you're lucky, under the watchful eye and with encouragement from a good critic."

‡PRACTICAL MYSTIC (IV-Spiritual, inspirational), Route 1 Box 14 Keoughs, Bishop, CA 93514, phone 619-873-4261, founded 1988, editor/publisher Eva Poole-Gilson, is **"a quarterly tabloid newspaper with an emphasis on spirituality and healing; a cross-roads where all beliefs may meet and become better acquainted"** using **"inspirational, mystical, transcendental"** poetry. They have recently published poetry by Will Inman, Perie Longo, and Karl Kempton. **Samples are free for 9 × 12 SASE (3 oz. postage). Simultaneous submissions and previously published poems OK. Reports in 3 months. Pays 2 copies. Editor sometimes comments on submissions.**

THE PRAIRIE JOURNAL (II); PRAIRIE JOURNAL PRESS (IV-Regional), Box 997, Station G, Calgary AB T3A 3G2 Canada, founded 1983, editor A. Burke, who wants to see **poetry of "any length, free verse, contemporary themes (feminist, nature, urban, non-political), aesthetic value, a poet's poetry." Does not want to see "most rhymed verse, sentimentality, egotistical ravings. No cowboys or sage brush."** They have published poetry by Mick Burrs, Lorna Crozier, Mary Melfi, Art Cuelho and John Hicks. As a sample I selected the opening lines of "In His Presence" by Ronald Kurt:

> *My father lifts*
> *me in his presence*
> *I am lowered in prayer*
> *in awe of bullet wounds*
> *and a will to live*

That is from a chapbook collection, **A Vision of Birds**, published by Prairie Journal Press, 7 × 8½" saddle-stapled, 36 pp., professionally printed on thin stock with Cadillac cover stock. Kurt is an Edmonton, Alberta, poet, his poetry having been published mostly in Canadian journals and by Canadian presses. *Prairie Journal*, is 7½x8½", 40-60 pp., offset with card cover, with b/w drawings, ads, appearing twice a year. They accept about 10% of the 200 or so poems they receive a year. Press run 500 per issue, 150 subscriptions of which 60% are libraries. Subscription: $6 for individuals, $12 for libraries. **Sample: $3 postpaid. Guidelines available for postage (but "no US stamps, please" — get IRCs from the Post Office). Pays 1 copy. Reports in 2 weeks. No simultaneous submission or previously published poems. For chapbook publication Canadian poets only (preferably from the region) should query with 5 samples, bio, publications. Responds to queries in 2 weeks, to MSS in 2 weeks. Pays $100.** "We also publish anthologies on themes when material is available. We receive very little poetry we can use." A. Burke advises, "Read recent poets! Experiment with line length, images, metaphors. Innovate."

THE PRAIRIE PUBLISHING COMPANY (III, IV-Regional), Box 2997, Winnipeg, MB R3C 4B5, Canada, phone 204-885-6496, founded 1963, publisher Ralph E. Watkins, is a "small-press catering to regional market, local history, fantasy, poetry and non-fiction," with flat-spined paperbacks. They want **"basically well-crafted poems of reasonable length"** and do not want to see **"the work of rank amateurs and tentative and time-consuming effort."** They have published collections of poetry by Brian Richardson and Brian MacKinnon. As a sample Nancy Watkins selected these lines by Brian Richardson:

> Tame grass grows in city parks
> Tarmac grows round windowless schools
> we're growing fast, we're getting big
> to make more room for bigger fools.

Their books I have seen are handsomely produced, $6 \times 9''$, using b/w photos and art along with the poems, glossy card covers. They publish about 1 a year, 68 pp. **Query with samples. Responds to queries in 6 weeks. Simultaneous submissions OK. Samples available at a 20% discount—send SASE or IRC for catalog.** Nancy Watkins notes, "Robert E. Pletta's point that most poets need to do more reading is well taken. We would endorse this suggestion."

PRAIRIE SCHOONER; STROUSSE—PRAIRIE SCHOONER PRIZE; SLOTE PRIZE; FAULKNER AWARD (II), 201 Andrews, University of Nebraska, Lincoln, NE 68588, phone 402-472-3191, founded 1927, editor Hilda Raz; "one of the oldest literary quarterlies in continuous publication; publishes poetry, fiction, personal essays, interviews and reviews." They want **"poems that fulfill the expectations they set up."** No specifications as to form, length, style, subject-matter or purpose. No simultaneous submissions. They have recently published poetry by Louise Erdrich, Howard Nemerov, Linda Pastan, Brigit Pegeen Kelly, Sydney Lea, Alicia Ostriker, Carole Oles, Brendan Galvin, and Rita Dove. The editors selected these sample lines by John Engman:

> Now there is no getting you back.
> Tom, who crashed. Lona, of cancer. John,
> of the heart. Thanks to each of you for my share
> of falling apart, if grieving is falling apart,
> if writing is grieving. I spent time at my desk
> But now that you are dead I will write a poem for you
> is a poor excuse only a poet would use, and poetry
> is words you can't forget, words said to friends,
> who forget them for you.

The magazine is $6 \times 9''$, flat-spined, 144 pp., circulation 2,000, and uses 70-80 pp. of poetry in each issue. Subscription: $15-one year; $4 per copy. They receive about 4,000 MSS (of all types) per year from which they choose 300 pp. of poetry. **Sample: $2 postpaid. "Clear copy appreciated." Reports in 2-3 months; "sooner if possible." Pays copies.** The $500 Strousse-Prairie Schooner Prize is awarded to the best poetry published in the magazine each year, the Slote Prize for beginning writers ($500) and six other *PS* prizes will also be awarded, and the Faulkner Award for Excellence in Writing is also offered ($1,000). Editors serve as judges. Hilda Raz comments, "*Prairie Schooner* receives a large number of poetry submissions; I expect we're not unusual. Our staff time doesn't allow criticial comments on MSS, but the magazine's reputation is evidence of our careful reading. We've been dedicated to the publication of good poems for a very long time and have for published work early in the career of many poets."

PRAKALPANA LITERATURE; KOBISENA (I, IV-Form), P-40 Nandana Park, Calcutta 700034, West Bengal, India, *Kobisena* founded 1972, *Prakalpana Literature* press founded 1974, magazine 1977, editor Vattacharja Chandan, who says, "We are small magazines which publish only *Prakalpana* (a mixed form of prose and poetry), Sarbangin (whole) poetry, essays on Prakalpana movement and Sarbangin poetry movement, letters, literary news and very few books on Prakalpana and Sarbangin literature. **Purpose and form: for advancement of poetry in the super-space age, the poetry must be really experimental and avant-garde using mathematical signs and symbols and visualizing the pictures inherent in the alphabet (within typography) with sonorous effect. That is Sarbangin poetry. Length: within 30 lines (up to 4 poems). Subject matter: society, nature, cosmos, humanity, love, peace, etc. Style: own. We do not want to see traditional, conventional, academic, religious and poetry of prevailing norms and forms."** They have recently published poetry by Dilip Gupta, Irving Weiss, John Byrum, and Geof Huth. As a sample the editor chose these lines from "Revolving Whirling Revolving" by Samir Kumar Rakshit:

> Downward
>
> | Rumbling | bubling | humming | buzzing |
> | racing | rushing | polishing | glossing |
> | running | all | turning | all |
> | hukka | hua | fukka | fua |

Prakalpana Literature, an annual, is 70 pp., digest-sized, saddle-stapled, printed on thin stock with matte card cover. *Kobisena*, which appears at least twice a year, is 16 pp., digest-sized, a newsletter format with no cover. Both are hand composed and printed by letterpress. Both use both English and Bengali. They use about 10% of some 400 poems received per year. The press run is 1,000 for each, and each has about 450 subscriptions of which 50 are libraries. **Samples: 6 rupees for *Prakalpana*, 2 rupees for *Kobisena*. Overseas: 4 IRCs and 2 IRCs respectively or exchange of avant-garde magazines. Send SAE with IRC for guidelines. Pays 1 copy. Simultaneous submissions OK. Previously published poetry OK. Reports in 6 months, publication within a year. After being published in the magazines poets may be included in future anthologies with translations into Bengali/English if and when necessary. "Joining with us is welcome but not a pre-condition." Editor comments on rejection "if wanted."** He says, "We believe that only through poetry, the deepest feelings of humanity as well as nature and the cosmos can be best expressed and conveyed to the peoples of the ages to come. And only poetry can fill up the gap in the peaceless hearts of dispirited peoples, resulted from the retreat of god and religion with the advancement of hi-tech. So, in an attempt, since the inception of Prakalpana Movement in 1969, to reach that goal in the avant-garde and experimental way we stand for Sarbangin poetry. And to poets and all concerned with poetry we wave the white handkerchief saying (in the words of Vattacharja Chandan) 'We want them who want us.'

THE PRESBYTERIAN RECORD (IV-Inspirational, religious), 50 Wynford Dr., Don, Mills, Ontario, Canada M3C 1J7, phone 416-441-1111, founded 1876, is "the national magazine that serves the membership of The Presbyterian Church in Canada (and many who are not Canadian Presbyterians). We seek to: stimulate, inform, inspire, to provide an 'apologetic' and a critique of our church and the world (not necessarily in that order!)." They want **poetry which is "inspirational, Christian, thoughtful, even satiric but *not* maudlin. No 'sympathy card' type verse a la Edgar Guest or Francis Gay. It would take a *very* exceptional poem of epic length for us to use it. Shorter poems 10-30 lines preferred. Blank verse OK (if it's not just rearranged prose). 'Found' poems. Subject matter should have some Christian import (however subtle)."** They have published poetry by Jean Larsen, Jeanne Davis, Joan Stortz, Marlow C. Dickson, Len Selle and J.R. Dickey. The magazine comes out 11 times a year, circulation 68,500. Subscription: $9.50. **Submit seasonal work 6 weeks before month of publication. Double-spaced, photocopy OK. "Dot-matrix semi-OK." Simultaneous submissions OK. Reports usually within a month. Pays $20-50 per poem.**

PRESCOTT STREET PRESS (IV-Regional), Box 40312, Portland, OR 97240-0312, founded 1974, poetry editor Vi Gale: **"Poetry and fine print from the Northwest."** Vi Gale says, "Our books and cards are the product of many hands from poet, artist, printer, designer, typesetter to bookstore and distributor. Somewhere along the line the editor/publisher [herself] arranges to pay one and all in the same way. Sometimes we have had grant help from the NEA and also from State and Metropolitan arts organizations. But most of our help has come from readers, friends and the poets and artists themselves. Everyone has worked very hard. And we are immodestly pleased with our labors! **We pay all of our poets. A modest sum, perhaps, but we pay everyone something. We are not a strictly regional press, although the poets I take on are connected with the Northwest in some way when we bring out the books."** Vi Gale publishes a series of postcards, notecards, paperback and hardback books of poetry in various artistic formats with illustrations by nationally known artists. Send SASE for catalog to order copies. I selected these sample lines by Rolf Aggestam from a postcard:

> *muttering. cold*
> > *hands split fresh kindling*
> > > *damn*
> *what a life. you are far away.*
> > *in the darkness we used to call*
> > *each other forth*
> > > *with fingers and a few small words.*
> *we created a little border*
> > *between darkness and darkness.*

Considers simultaneous submissions. "No UPS submissions, please."

THE PRESS OF MACDONALD & REINECKE (II), P.O. Box 840, Arroyo Grande, CA 93421-0840, phone 805-473-1947, founded 1974, poetry editor Lachlan P. MacDonald. "The press is a division of Padre Productions bringing together under one imprint drama, fiction, literary, nonfiction, and poetry. We publish poetry in broadsides, flat-spined paperbacks, chapbooks and hardcover. We are looking for **poetry of literary merit and also poetry suitable for travel and nature photo books. We are averse to tightly rhymed conventional poetry unless designed to appeal to the general humor market."** They recently published Terre Ouenhand's **Voices from the Well** and Steven Schmidt's **Avigation and Other Poems. Query with 5-6 samples, publication credits, bio.** The editor also wants to know "do they give readings or have marketing opportunities? Some authors distribute flyers to build up pre-publication orders sufficient to justify the print order." Replies to queries in 2-4 weeks, to submissions (if invited) in 2-6 months. Simultaneous submissions, photocopy, dot-matrix OK. MS should be double-spaced. Pays minimum of 4% royalties, 6 copies. The editor "frequently makes brief comments" on rejections. Send 6×9″ SASE for catalog. The editor advises, "Poets who have not published 10 or 20 poems in literary magazines are unlikely to have developed the craft we require. We also prefer books with a unifying theme rather than a sampling reflecting the author's virtuosity."

PRIMAVERA (II, IV-Women), 1448 E. 52nd St., Box 274, Chicago, IL 60615, phone 312-324-5920, founded 1975, co-editor Ruth Young, is "an irregularly published but approximately annual magazine of poetry, fiction and articles reflecting **the experiences of women. We look for strong, original voice and imagery, generally prefer free verse, fairly short length, related, even tangentially, to women's experience.**" They have recently published poetry by Chitra Divakaruni, Pamela Miller, Maxine Clair, and Martha Bergland. The editors selected these sample lines by Kathleen Patrick:

> *Fighting down the stallion in our throats,*
> *we all reach adulthood*
> *at precisely the same moment.*

The elegantly printed publication, flat-spined, generously illustrated with photos and graphics, uses 30-35 pp. of poetry in each issue, circulation 800. Price per issue: $6. They receive over 1,000 submissions of poetry per year, use 32. **Sample: $5 postpaid. Submit no more than 6 poems anytime, legible photocopy OK, no dot-matrix or queries. No simultaneous submissions. Reports in 1-2 months. Pays 2 copies. Send SASE for guidelines. Editors comment on rejections "when requested or inspired."**

PRIME TIMES (IV-Senior Citizen), National Association of Retired Credit Union People (NARCUP), 2802 International Lane, Suite 120, Madison, WI 53704, phone 608-241-1557, founded 1979, poetry editor Rod Clark, is a quarterly "**targeted to very active pre-retirees. Its purpose is to help its readers 'redefine' mid-life in creative ways. Needs in poetry: light-toned is fine, but heavier reflective themes are agreeable. Subject matter should be suitable for mature adults. Sexual/erotic themes** *fine.* **We prefer poetry that is gifted and genuinely poetic, but** *accessible.*" They do not often publish poetry and are often overstocked, but do consider excellent poetry. The editor chose this sample from "A List For Mornings" by Aurelia D. Wallace:

> *on my early morning walk into the sun*
> *I hunt fresh mementos of the dead*
> *washed up on shore by night tide*
>
> *half an angel wing (left side)*
> *one crab claw, sea urchin mummified*

The quarterly is magazine-sized, 40 pp., glossy paper and cover with many color illustrations, circulation 75,000. It is free to members of NARCUP, $10 per year to non-members. Per copy: $2.50. The editor reports receiving 50 submissions of freelance poetry per year and has published two. **Sample: $2.50 plus 5 stamps. Submit up to 3 pp. any time. Photocopy, dot-matrix, simultaneous submissions all OK. No queries, please. Reports in 8-12 weeks. Pays $50-250 per poem. Editor "sometimes" comments on rejections.**

PRINCETON UNIVERSITY PRESS; LOCKERT LIBRARY OF POETRY IN TRANSLATION (IV-Translations, bilingual); PRINCETON SERIES OF CONTEMPORARY POETS (V), 41 William St., Princeton, NJ 08540, phone 609-452-4900, literature editor Robert E. Brown. The Princeton Series of Contemporary Poets **is by invitation only.** "In the Lockert Library series, we publish simultaneous cloth and paperback (flat-spine) editions for each poet. Clothbound editions are on acid-free paper, and binding materials are chosen for strength and durability. Each book is given individual design treatment rather than stamped into a series mold. We have published a wide range of poets from other cultures, including well-known writers such as Hölderlin and Cavafy, and those who have not yet had their due in English translation, such as Ingeborg Bachmann and Faiz Ahmed Faiz. Manuscripts are judged with several criteria in mind: the ability of the translation to stand on its own as poetry in English; fidelity to the tone and spirit of the original, rather than literal accuracy; and the importance of the translated poet to the literature of his or her time and country. Originals are printed facing the translations." The editor says, "All our books in this series are heavily subsidized to break even. We have internal funds to cover deficits of publishing costs. We do not, however, publish books chosen and subsidized by other agencies, such as AWP. **Our series is an open competition, for which the 'award' is publication. We comment on semifinalists only.**" Send SASE for guidelines to submit. Send MSS only during respective reading periods stated in guidelines. Reports in 2-3 months. Simultaneous submissions OK if you tell them; photocopy, dot-matrix OK. Pays royalties (5% or more) on paperback and 12 author's copies.

PRISM INTERNATIONAL (II), Dept. of Creative Writing, University of British Columbia, Vancouver, British Columbia, Canada V6T 1W5, phone 604-228-2514, founded 1959, executive editors Blair Rosser and Heidi Neufeld Raine. "*Prism* is an international quarterly that publishes poetry, drama, short fiction, imaginative non-fiction, and translation into English in all genres. We have no thematic or stylistic allegiances: excellence is our main criterion for acceptance of MSS. **We want poetry that shows an awareness of the tradition while reiterating its themes in a fresh and distinctive way. We read everything.**" They have recently published poetry by Robert Bringhurst, Al Purdy, Diana Hartog, Charles Bukowski, P.K. Page, and Susan Muskgrave. As a sample the editor selected these lines by Michael Ondaatje:

> This is for people who disappear
> for those who descend into the code
> and make their room a fridge for Superman
> —who exhaust costume and bones that could perform flight
> who shave their moral so raw
> they can tear themselves through the eye of a needle

Prism is elegantly printed in a flat-spined 6×9″ format 80 pp., original color artwork on the glossy card cover, circulation to 1,000 subscribers of which 200 are libraries. Subscription: $12; single copy: $4. They receive 1,000 submissions per year, use 125, have 1-2 special issues per year, have a 1-3 month backlog. **Sample: $4 postpaid. Submit a maximum of 6 poems at a time, any print so long as it's typed. No query. Reports in 6-12 weeks** ("or we write to poets to tell them we're holding onto their work for a while"). **Pays $30 per printed page plus subscription. "We ask contributors to please buy copies." Send Canadian SASE or SAE with IRC's for guidelines. Editors often comment on rejections.** The editors say, "While we don't automatically discount any kind of poetry, we prefer to publish work that challenges the writer as much as it does the reader."

PRISONERS OF THE NIGHT; AMARANTH; MKASHEF ENTERPRISES; (IV-Science fiction, erotica), P.O. Box 368, Poway, CA 92064-0005, poetry editor Alayne Gelfand. *Prisoners of the Night*, founded 1987, **focusing on vampire erotica, uses poetry that is "erotic, unique, non-horror, non-pornographic, original visions of the vampire.** *Amaranth*, founded 1989, first issue is scheduled for early 1991, "erotic or not, visionary supernatural themes. *No* vampires, 'sword & sorcery' or devil worship." Poets who have appeared recently in *POTN* include John Carter, Wendy Rathbone, John Grey, Ann K. Schwader, and Della Van Hise. As a sample the editor selected the poem "Nightchild" by Cathy Buburuz:

> Weep not for the Nightchild
> for his is but a shallow grave
> and the passersby are many.

The intent of *POTN* is "to show the erotic, rather than the horrific aspects of the vampire." It is 150-200 pp., magazine-sized, perfect bound, with color cover, produced by high-speed photocopying with "full color cover art. All poems are illustrated." It appears annually, usually in May. Of over 400 poems received per year they use between 10 and 30. It has an initial print run of 3,000, but each issue is kept in print. **Sample (the per-issue price): $15 postpaid. Reading schedule for *POTN*: September-March annually. Send SASE for guidelines. Pays $2 per poem plus 1 copy. No more than 6 poems per submission. No simultaneous submissions or previously published poems. Reports "within 4 months." Editor sometimes comments on rejections.** *POTN* **wants unusual visions of the vampire as well as unusual poetic styles. We prefer non-rhyme and find humor too subjective to appeal to our readers. We really enjoy the unusual image, the surprise use of words." Same general guidelines for** *Amaranth***, SASE for specifics, same payment. Reading schedule: April-August annually.**

PROEM CANADA (I,IV-Youth, regional), P.O. Box 416, Peterborough, ON K9J 6Z3 Canada, phone 705-749-5686, founded 1986, editor Chris Magwood, appears in February and September each year, **publishing poetry and short fiction by Canadian writers between the ages of 16 and 26.** Regarding poetry, they have **"no length, style, or subject restrictions. However, the emphasis is on** *potential*. These are young writers, so technical flaws will be forgiven if the potential shows through. A well-finished but mediocre poem will receive less favor than an exciting but rough one." Each writer is paid $50 plus 1 copy. It is magazine-sized, 60-80 pp., printed on glossy stock with glossy cardboard cover. Subscription: $10 for 1 year, $17 for 2. **Sample: $5 postpaid. Send SAE and IRC for guidelines. They will consider simultaneous submissions but not previously published poems. Editors** *always* **comment on rejections.**

PROOF ROCK PRESS; PROOF ROCK (I, II, IV-Humor), Box 607, Halifax, VA 24558, founded 1982, poetry editors Serena Fusek and Don R. Conner. "We try to wake up a passive readership. We challenge our writers to search for something new under the sun; and improve on the old." The poetry they want is: **"adventure, contemporary, humor/satire, fantasy, experimental. Avoid overt sentimental-**

ity. **Poems up to 32 lines. All subjects considered if well done.**" As a sample I chose the opening lines of "The Hidden Reader" by Kurt J. Fickert:

> *They have forbidden me to read.*
> *Go bowling, they say; watch TV.*
> *Share a pizza with a friend.*
> *But I cheat: I plummet into a book,*

The digest-sized magazine appears 2-3 times per year, is offset from typescript copy, colored matte card cover, with 30-40 pp. in each issue, circulation 300, 100 subscriptions of which 8-10 are libraries. They receive 800-1,000 submissions per year, use 120-150, have a 3-6 month backlog. Subscription: $4; per copy: $2.50. **Sample: $2.50 postpaid. Submit no more than 6 pieces, year round. No query needed, though some issues are on announced themes. Photocopy, dot-matrix, simultaneous submissions OK. Reports "usually within 30 days." Pays 1 copy. Send SASE for guidelines.** Proof Rock Press publishes an occasional anthology and collections by individuals. **Query with 8-10 samples, bio and publishing credits. Reply to queries in 30 days, to submissions (if invited) in 1-3 months. Simultaneous submissions, photocopies, dot-matrix OK. Pays copies. Send $2.50 for a sample chapbook. Editor sometimes comments on rejections.** His advice is, "Be introspective. Accept the challenge of looking within and write from experience."

‡**PROPER TALES PRESS; MONDO HUNKAMOOGA; DWARF PUPPETS ON PARADE; COPS GOING FOR DOUGHNUTS EDITIONS; PROPER TALES POSTCARDS (II)**, Box 789, Sta. F, Toronto, Ontario, Canada M4Y 2N7, founded 1979, poetry editor Stuart Ross, who says, "I sell my titles out on the street. I find an empty corner or doorway, fling a sign around my neck, and sell my books. Sometimes I sell one or sometimes 20. Usually I sell about 10. And it's amazing who buys the books. People who have only read horoscopes and Harold Robbins are getting into my stuff, showing interest—not just other writers. I am interested in putting out books that wouldn't be published elsewhere. Proper Tales Press wants to inject excitement and quality into a publishing world inundated with the mundane and the repetitive. I want **surrealist poetry, bizarre, demento-primitivo. I** *don't* **want 'obscure to the point of inaccessibility,' religious, boring or confessional 'verse.'**" He has recently published poetry by Opal L. Nationo, John M. Bennett, Lillian Necakov, Randall Brock and Wain Ewing. As a sample he selected these lines from "Modern Times" by Stuart Ross:

> *This subway!*
> *It actually moves—*
> *and with me*
> *in it.*

Mondo Hunkamooga, a journal of small press reviews, does not use poetry. The other imprints are explained by Stuart Ross: *Dwarf Puppets on Parade* uses short poetry and fiction following specific rules. Details on request. Cops Going For Doughnuts Editions are one-pagers, and you know, if you need a quick read during your morning coffee, it's just the thing. They are all single prose pieces, because poetry and doughnuts just seem too much of a cliché." Proper Tales Press books are attractively printed, mostly inexpensive chapbooks in innovative formats. **Query with 10-30 samples, "short bio, a hello, some flattery,** *no* **philosophies, principles, etc. Who cares? Let's see** *poems.***" Reports in 1-90 days on submissions. No reading fee, "but we accept donations from Texan oilmen and wealthy widows." No simultaneous submissions. MS should be "legible; no ketchup stains." Photocopy, dot-matrix OK. Poets are paid: "negotiable, but usually" and get 10% of the press run. Send 6 × 9" SASE for catalog to order samples**—or send $2 or more: "the more $ the more books!" The editor "quite often" comments on rejections.

PROPHETIC VOICES (II); HERITAGE TRAILS PRESS (V), 94 Santa Maria Dr., Novato, CA 94947, founded 1982, poetry editors Ruth Wildes Schuler, Goldie L. Morales and Jeanne Leigh Schuler. "Our goal is to share thoughts on an international level. We see the poet's role as that of prophet, who points the way to a higher realm of existence." They publish *Prophetic Voices* twice a year and chapbooks. They want "**poetry of social commentary that deals with the important issues of our time. Poetry with beauty that has an international appeal. Do not want religious poetry or that with a limited scope. Open to any kind of excellent poetry, but publish mostly free verse. Limited number of long poems accepted due to lack of space.**" They have published Jack Brooks, Hazel F. Goddard, A. Manoussos, B. Z. Niditch, H. F. Noyes, Gloria H. Procsal, and Bo Yang. As a sample the editors selected these lines from "Illegitimate" by Mogg Williams:

> *My manuscripts were maladjusted words*
> *Which became a pregnancy in my head,*
> *An illegitimate thing with no abode. Hesitant, I cut*
> *the umbilical cord and gave the thing a home, and name.*
> *Its home was the asylum of my heart*
> *And its name was poetry.*

Prophetic Voices is digest-sized, 144 pp., perfect-bound, offset from typescript with matte card cover, colored stock with graphics. They have 100 pp. of poetry in each issue, circulation to 400 subscribers of which 10 are libraries. Subscription: $12; $14 to libraries; per copy: $6. They receive 4,000 submissions per year, use 800, have a 2 year backlog. **Sample: $5 postpaid. Photocopy OK. Submit 4 poems or less. Reports in 1-8 weeks. Pays 1 copy. Heritage Trails does not consider unsolicited MSS.** The editors advise, "Be aware of what is going on in the world around you. Even the personal poem should have universal appeal if it is to survive the test of time."

PROTEA POETRY JOURNAL (I), Box 876, Sutter Creek, CA 95685, phone 209-295-4539, founded 1987, poetry editor Carol Lynn Gunther. She says, "**I prefer avant-garde imagism; I dislike pretentious or slight poems. No limericks. Prefer free verse. No restrictions on subject matter or length. Thoroughly didactic poems are not welcome. Prefer Wallace Stevens to W. C. Williams.**" As a sample she chose these lines from Richard Cronshey's poem "The Genius of the Bells":

> *The scent of emptiness in airports*
> *in the august of her departure*
> *when I am furthest*

Protea is produced on off-set press, Ventura Desktop Publishing typesetting. Top-notch within small budget. She wants the magazine to be biannual—and **needs submissions. Send SASE for guidelines; $4 for sample copy. Pays 2 copies. No previously published poems, simultaneous submissions. Reports in 2-3 weeks. Comments on rejections "now and then, if they seem like serious poets."** Spring 1990 offered a $50 award for the best of issue and two $25 awards for honorable mention.

‡PROUT JOURNAL (II,IV-Nature/rural/ecology, political, social issues, spirtuality/inspirational), Box 2667, Santa Cruz, CA 95063, founded 1987, editors Roar Bjonnes and Michael Ellison, uses **"only poetry of high quality."** As a sample the editor selected these lines from "The Origin of the Praise of God" by Robert Bly:

> *As we walk we enter the magnetic fields of other bodies,*
> *and every smell we take in the communities of protozoa see,*
> *and a being inside leaps up toward it, as a horse rears at the*
> *starting gate. When we come near each other, we are drawn*
> *down into the sweetest pools of slowly circling energies, slowly circling smells . . . .*

PJ "general magazine format, 3-color glossy cover, newsprint inside, graphics, some ads." Press run: 10,000 for 1,000 subscriptions, 8,000 distributed free. Subscription: $8. **Sample, postpaid: $2. Pays 4 copies.**

PSYCH IT: THE SOPHISTICATED NEWSLETTER FOR EVERYONE(I, IV-themes, subscribers), 6507 Bimini Ct., Apollo Beach, FL 33572, founded 1986, editor Charlotte L. Babicky, is a quarterly newsletter using "any style, any psychologically-themed poetry. Any length. The purpose is to leave the reader with a message; one which will be remembered through images presented by the writer in the poetry. Well-thought-out, well-written poems." Poets recently published include Lenore Thomson, Mickey Huffstutler, Cecelia Marchand, Rochele H. Mehr, Helen B. Glass and Edna Shapiro. As a sample the editor selected these lines from "Fear" by Marian Ford:

> *The streets are darker and they smell of fear;*
> *When neon flashes unreal scenes appear.*
> *There is a desperation in the air;*
> *an inhalation of the raw despair*

It is a 10 pp. side-stapled, magazine-sized newsletter photocopied from typescript, with heavy grey/white parchment paper. Press run under 100. Subscription: $8. **Sample, postpaid: $2.50. Pays $1/poem. Guarantees to publish at least one of 3-5 poems submitted by subscribers. Nonsubscribers may enter contests but not submit. Send SASE for guidelines. Contest prizes vary, entry fee $1** for each poem.

PSYCHOPOETICA (II, IV-Themes), Dept. of Psychology, University of Hull, Hull HU6 7RX England, founded 1979, editor Dr. Geoff Lowe uses **"psychologically based poetry."** Judging by the examples I have read, that is not a very narrow category, though many of the poems in *Psychopoetica* are explicitly about psychology or psychological treatment. But most good poetry is in some sense "psychologically based," as the editor seems to recognize in these comments (from his guidelines): "**I prefer short, experimental, rhymed and unrhymed, light verse, haiku, etc., (and visual poems) I will read and consider any style, any length, providing it's within the arena of 'psychologically-based' poetry. I'm not too keen on self-indulgent therapeutic poetry (unless it's good and original), nor 'Patience Strong' type stuff. I like poetry that has some (or all!) of the following: humour, vivid imaginary, powerful feelings, guts and substance, originality, creative style, punch or twist, word-play, good craftsmanship, etc.**" Recently published poets include Sheila E. Murphy, Wes Magee, Andrew Gettler, and Ruth

Wildes Schuler. As a sample the editor selected this stanza from "The And Language" by Linda McFerrin:

> *Waking up from a dream*
> *I fell back,*
> *into the arms of language.*
> *Nursery rhymes ricocheted off the walls.*

The magazine appears 2-3 times a year, circulating to "several hundred and increasing." It is magazine-sized, loose-bound (pages held together by a plastic clasp), photocopied from typescript. **Sample: £1 ($2). Send SASE for guidelines. Pays 1 copy. Reports within 1 month. Considers simultaneous submissions. Editor "always" provides comments on rejections.** He says, "Too many potentially good submissions are still being spoilt by poor presentation: careful presentation of work is most important. But I continue to be impressed by the rich variety of submissions."

THE PTERODACTYL PRESS (III, IV-Regional), Main Street, Cumberland, IA 50843, phone 712-774-2244, founded 1970, poetry editor, owner/printer Floyd E. Pearce, publishes chapbooks, soft and hardcover books, sometimes broadsides and "special pieces." He has published poetry by W. D. Snodgrass, William Dickey, Adrianne Marcus, Mona Van Duyn, Howard Nemerov and Frederick Morgan — among our best poets. He will consider **"MS up to 60 pp.; form is open; any subject matter; any style; and I am not sure exactly what the purpose of poetry is! Look for strong techniques and unique voice. No religious, patriotic poetry."** Pays standard royalty, 10% plus about 6 copies. **"Encourage poet to take copies in place of royalties." Query with sample poems, credits, bio. Photocopies OK, no dot-matrix. Responds to queries in 2 weeks, to MSS in 6 months. Comment on rejections! "I try to. But I sometimes wonder if praise is the only thing that's wanted!** I'm publishing an Iowa Poets Series (for about 3 years to come). Phil Hey and I are co-editing the series. I'm not becoming a regional press, but do want to serve some of the best (and there are many good ones) Iowa poets." Floyd Pearce advises, "Find your voice and be true to it. Develop a strong technique. Read good poets. Don't avoid the obvious in either theme or subject matter. Let the magic happen."

THE PUCKERBRUSH PRESS· THE PUCKERBRUSH REVIEW (IV-Regional), 76 Main St., Orono, ME 04473, phone 207-581-3832, press founded 1971, *Review* founded 1978, poetry editor Constance Hunting, is a "small-press publisher of a literary, twice-a-year magazine focused on Maine and of flat-spined paperbacks of literary quality." The editor **does not want to see "confessional, dull, feminist, incompetent, derivative" poetry.** They have recently published poetry by James Laughlin, and the editor selected these sample lines from "The Emperor's Poet" by Sonya Dorman:

> *I was ordered to pray for fine weather*
> *yet I went to the west gate for a horse*
> *a gray mare with black moon nostrils.*
> *To feed her, I caught wind in a bucket.*

Submit with SASE. For book publication, query with 10 samples. Prefers no simultaneous submissions. Pays 10% royalties plus 10 copies. Editor comments on rejections. She offers criticism for a fee: $100 is usual.

PUDDING HOUSE PUBLICATIONS; PUDDING MAGAZINE; PUDDING WRITING COMPETITIONS; PUDDING HOUSE BED & BREAKFAST FOR WRITERS; OHIO POETRY THERAPY CENTER & LIBRARY (II, IV-Social issues), 60 N. Main St., Johnstown, OH 43031, phone 614-967-6060 (after 5 p.m.), founded 1979, poetry editor Jennifer Welch Bosveld, attempts to provide "a sociological looking glass through poems that provide 'felt experience' and share intense human situations. To collect good poems that speak for the difficulties and the solutions. To provide a forum for poems and articles by people who take poetry arts into the schools and the human services." They publish *Pudding* every five months, also chapbooks, anthologies, broadsides. They **"want experimental and contemporary poetry—what hasn't been said before. Speak the unspeakable. Don't want preachments or sentimentality. Don't want obvious traditional forms without fresh approach. Long poems are happily considered too, as long as they aren't windy."** They have recently published poetry by James Belcher, Lowell Jaeger, Rick Clewett, Alan Catlin, and Alfred Bruey. The editor selected these sample lines from "The Stroke" by Douglas M. Swisher:

> *The blister of his wristwatch burst:*
> *Time, a puddle to be sopped up.*

Pudding **is a literary journal with an emphasis on poetry arts in human service.** They use about 80 pp. of poetry in each issue — digest-sized, 80 pp., offset composed on IBM 1st Publisher,

Market categories: (I) Beginning; (II) General; (III) Prestige; (IV) Specialized; (V) Closed.

circulation 2,000, 1,800 subscriptions of which 50 are libraries. Subscription (3 issues): $12.75. Per copy: usually $4.75. **Sample: $4.75 postpaid. Submit 5-10 poems. No simultaneous submissions. Photocopies and previously published submissions OK. Send SASE for guidelines. Reports on same day (unless traveling). Pays 1 copy — to featured poet $10 and 4 copies. For chapbook publication, no query. $5 reading fee. Send complete MS with cover letter with publication credits and bio. Editor often comments, will critique on request for $3 per page of poetry or $25 an hour in person.** Jennifer Welch Bosveld shares, "Editors have pet peeves. Mine include: Postcards instead of SASE's (I won't respond); individually-folded rather than group-folded poems; cover letters that state the obvious." The Pudding Writing Competitions are for single poems (deadline September 30, fee $1/poem) and for chapbook publication ($9 entry fee). Pudding House Bed & Breakfast for Writers offers "luxurious rooms with desk, electric typewriter and all the paper you can use. Free breakfast, large comfortable home ½ block from post office. Location of the Ohio Poetry Therapy Center and Library. $40 single/night. Reservations recommended 3 months in advance. Send SASE for details.

PUERTO DEL SOL (II, IV-Translations, regional), New Mexico State University, Box 3E, Las Cruces, NM 88003, phone 505-646-3931, founded 1972 (in present format), poetry editor Joseph Somoza. "We publish a literary magazine twice per year. Interested in poems, fiction, essays, photos, translations from the Spanish. Also (generally solicited) reviews and dialogues between writers. **We want top quality poetry, any style, from anywhere. We are sympathetic to Southwestern work, but not stereotype (cactus and adobe). Anything that is interesting and/or moving. Poetry, of course, not verse (light or otherwise).**" They have recently published poetry by Bill Evans, Naton Leslie, Albino Carrillo, Connie Wanek, Jim Daniels, and Mary Ann Barnett. The 6 × 9″ flat-spined, professionally printed magazine, matte card cover with art, has a circulation of 650, 300 subscriptions of which 25-30 are libraries. 40-50 pp. are devoted to poetry in each 150 pp. issue, which also includes quite a lot of prose. Subscription $7.75; per copy: $5. They use about 60 of the 500 submissions (about 2,500 poems) received each year to fill up the 90 pp. of poetry two issues encompass. "Generally no backlog." **Sample: $3 postpaid. Submit 5-6 pp., 1 poem to a page. Simultaneous submissions not encouraged. Reports within 9 weeks. Pays copies. Editor comments "on every MS."** He advises: "Be true to yourself rather than worrying about current fashions — but *do* read as much of the best of contemporary poetry as you can find."

PURPLE PATCH; PROMOTION (I), 8 Beaconview House, Charlemont Farm, West Bromwich, England, founded 1975, editor Geoff Stevens, an "approximately quarterly" poetry and short prose magazine with reviews, comment, and illustrations. The editor says, **"prefer maximum of one page length (40 lines), but all good examples of poetry considered." He does not want "poor scanning verse, concrete poetry, non-contributing swear words and/or obscenities, hackneyed themes."** They have recently published poetry by J. Brander, H. Bartholemew, L. Kucharski, M. Kettner, and E.C. Lynskey. As a sample the editor chose these lines from "In Memory of Max Noiprox" by Sheila Jacob:

> With him
> I fingered jade,
> crossed the farago sea,
> saw the moon
> in a silver bowl

Purple Patch is magazine-sized, 14-20 pp. offset on plain paper, cover on the same stock with b/w drawing, side-stapled. Circulation "varies." Price is 3 issues for £2 in Great Britain; U.S. price is $5 per issue (submit dollars). **Contributors have to buy a copy to see their work in print. "All legible formats" are accepted. Reporting time is 1 month to Great Britain, longer to USA; time to publication is a maximum of 4 months.** The editor says, *Purple Patch* "is a founder-member of F.A.I.M. (Federation for Advancement of Independent Magazines) with 20 member magazines at present. All present member magazines publish poetry and beginners are welcome to submit to any of them." *Promotion* "published as demand requires, is a new idea to provide a platform of introduction of poets to editors, publishers, arts bodies, etc. **Five or six poets are included in each issue, with photograph, brief biography, a summary of their future aims, poems, and extracts of poems.** Copies are sent free of charge to publishers, editors, and others. **Included poets pay for inclusion.**" It is magazine-sized. 14-26 pp. offset on plain paper, cover of same stock with b&w drawing or photo. Circulation 50, not to general public but targeted recipients.

‡PYGMY FOREST PRESS (II), Box 591, Albion, CA 95410, phone 707-937-4929, founded 1987, editor/publisher Leonard Cirino, publishes flat-spined paperbacks. **Not considering new mss until spring 1991.** "Forms of any kind/length to 64 pp., subject matter open; especially ecology, prison, asylum, Third World, anarchist to far right. Prefer Stevens to Williams. I like Berryman, Roethke, Jorie-Graham; dislike most 'Beats.' Open to anything I consider 'good.' Open to traditional rhyme, meter, but must be modern in subject-matter." He has recently pubished **The Sixth Day** by James Doyle; **Fresh Water** by Crawdad Nelson; **For You/on stones** by L. Cirino; **The Elk Poems** by Kate Dougherty;

Close-up

Jennifer Bosveld
Editor
Pudding Magazine

no bodies here
not the one whose hard heels
echo on porch planks
not the one staring down
the shadowy path out the door
surprised
melancholy curtains move at the window
once
as though something
passed through
you
auditioned for this
it's your break the
chance you've been waiting for

Those lines, concluding "It's a Tennessee Williams Scenario ... " by Jennifer Bosveld, illustrate her use of poetry as a way of coping with life's difficulties. "It was not until the revising of the poem [which first appeared in *Amelia*] that I reached a catharsis regarding the real event. When I asked myself what would make the poem stronger, I wrote the last three lines and got on with my life." She has coined the term "applied poetry" for what is sometimes called "poetry therapy," and much of the great variety of activity described in the *Pudding* listing can best be described under that label.

She tells me, "I apply poetry writing skills to everything. I'm a better policy writer, administrator, advertising copywriter, teacher, editor, bed and breakfast operator, traveler, and publisher of poets because I am a poet first. And everything is interesting. Fireplace logs are little stanzas of poetic heat."

Jennifer attributes her interest in poetry from an early age to the influence of her mother, Maryanna Miller, "an English scholar and published writer herself." Her mother, she says, "read to me as she rocked me in the womb. It didn't matter if I understood everything she read to me; she knew how important it was for me to fall in love with the sounds of words, to develop a fascination with phraseology. I did. I wrote little flowery verses at age 7, published typically naive poems in my high school literary magazine, and filled frustrated little black journals with my 'deep' feelings. After all, this was before Poets-in-the-Schools."

She did not realize that she was suffering from undiagnosed dyslexia, which discouraged her from finishing college, but in a writing workshop at Ohio State University she "learned about this frustrating learning disability that is often found in extremely creative and intelligent people. Gee, me and Einstein!" As one of a nurturing group of writers around Columbus, she began giving readings at libraries, bookstores, bars, galleries, and writing conferences. "My mentors-by-example are David Citino (see the listing for *The Journal*) and William Stafford for the way they treat absolutely everyone with dignity.

"The only constant in my life has been poetry. Every aspect of my changing politics, loves, religion, and ethics can be discovered in my poetry and nowhere else." That is not because her poetry is usually "confessional" or autobiographical. "One of my most loved forms is the *persona* piece in which I might become the over-the-hill-hooker at 'Joe's Hole,' or take on some other alter-ego."

She is skeptical about poetry therapists who interpret too literally what a poet writes as self-description. "The place of poetry therapy (I prefer to call what I do 'applied poetry') is to empower each person to be her own poet/person/product whether in the design of her own words on the page and personal interpretation of other's works, or in her strut and life's work and play." In 1978 Jennifer and friends directed the Ohio Poetry Therapy Conference, a great success, and in 1979 started the Ohio Poetry Therapy Center and Library. That lead to *Pudding Magazine*. "I've added to my poetry library human services and social sciences materials that would marry these compartments in my brain called psychology, social work, poetry and literature." People come from all parts, including foreign countries, to use the resources in that library, which now is located at Pudding House Bed & Breakfast for Writers, where, she says, "Guests take **Poet's Market** to their luxurious rooms complete with typewriter, postage, and all the paper they can use. About 10 years ago when some poetry therapy peer group facilitator asked us to fantasize about where we would like to be 10 years from then, I wrote of a place like Pudding House—a large comfortable place where everything is at my fingertips, and I'm doing this, and this, and this, and this, and it's all relevant, and I'm inviting others to think and feel and play and heal here, too. It's 'Better living made possible through . . . poetry!' My license plate is P O E T, and the frame around it says, 'Poetry: A Basic Life Support System.' "

—Judson Jerome

Low-Tech In the Great Northwest by Gordon Black; **Obel** by Sheila Murphy; **Windows** by Philip Corwin. **Submit 10-15 poems with bio, publications. Simultaneous submissions, previously published material, photocopies OK (no dot-matrix). Reports on queries in 1-3 weeks, submissions in 2-4 weeks. Pays 10% of run—about 30-50 copies. He comments on "almost every" MS.** He holds a yearly contest with no awards (except publication). "Contestants are asked to buy a copy of the previous year's winner for $6 plus $1 postage. Can be waived if poor or institutionalized." Leonard Cirino says, "I am basically an anarchist. Belong to no 'school.' I fund myself. Receive no grants or private funding. Generally politically left, but no mainline Stalinist or Marxist. Plan to publish 3 books yearly."

‡THE PYRAMID (IV-Themes), The Inter-National Newsletter for the Inter-National Association for Widowed People, Inc., Box 3564, Springfield, IL 62708, a quarterly for I.A.W.P. members and subscribers, a publication for widowed people, and professional corporations, colleges, universities and people that service widowed people as well as interested community groups or organizations, circulation 34,000, uses **poetry on themes appropriate for widowed persons—nothing on married persons or couples. Buys 5 poems a year. Submit maximum of 2 poems, 100 lines maximum. Sample: $3. Pays $5-75.**

QUARRY MAGAZINE; QUARRY PRESS; POETRY CANADA (II, IV-Regional, teens), Box 1061, Kingston, Ontario, K7L 4Y5, Canada, Quarry Press founded 1952, *Poetry Canada* founded 1979, managing editor Linda Bussière, reviews editor Barry Depmster. "Quarry Press is designed to extend the range of material, poetry and prose, generally handled by *Quarry Magazine*—that is, to represent, as accurately as may be, the range of contemporary writing. We publish chapbooks, soft-bound books of stories and poetry—collections ranging from 60-150 pp., in addition to the quarterly *Quarry Magazine*. **We are interested in seeing any and all forms of contemporary verse.** *Quarry Magazine* **maintains a practical limit on length of submissions—that we cannot consider any single piece or series by one author that would print at more than 10 pages. Quarry Press considers MSS on an individual basis."** They have published poetry by Roo Borson, Kim Maltman, Roger Nash, Jane Munro, Fred Cogswell, and Don Bailey. The editor selected these sample lines from "I Met a Poem" by Dennis Cooley:

they say earth
shifts & glides
like a figure
skater double-axeling her way
across the screen

Quarry is a digest-sized, 130+ pp., flat-spined publication with an unusually attractive cover—textured matte ivory card with striking b/w drawing trimmed so the front is a half-inch short—professionally printed on egg-shell stock. There are 40-50 pp. of poetry in each issue, circulation 1,000, 600 subscriptions of which 140 are libraries. Subscription: $18 ($4 surcharge outside Canada); per copy: $5. They use about 70 of over a thousand submissions of freelance poetry received each year. "We are prompt. Very small backlog if any. 3-6 month lead time." **Sample: $5 postpaid. No limit on number or time of submissions; prefer typed (or WP) double-spaced; clear photocopies acceptable; query not necessary, though it will be answered. Reports in 6-8 weeks. Pays $10 per poem plus 1 year subscription. Send SASE for guidelines. For book consideration, query with 6-10 samples, publication credits, brief bio and current projects. "We give priority to Canadians because of our Arts Council funding and our own interest in promoting Canadian writing." Replies to queries in 30 days, to submissions (if invited) in 6-8 weeks. Photocopy, dotmatrix OK. Contract is for 10% royalties, 10 author's copies. Send 5 × 7" SASE for catalog to order samples. Editor "frequently" comments on rejections.** They conduct a High School Writers' Contest every second year" *Poetry Canada* is a quarterly magazine featuring interviews, essays, international criticism, and comprehensive reviews of every Canadian poetry book published. Each issue features a major Canadian poet on the cover and center spread (recent issues feature Marlene Nourbese Philip, Bronwen Wallace, and George Bowering). Circulation: 1,800 with 600 subscribers, 600 newsstand. Subscription: $15/year ($30/year institutions). **Sample: $4 postpaid. Submit average 10 poems with SAE, IRC. Reports within 4-8 weeks. Pays $20/poem.**

‡THE QUARTERLY (III), 201 E. 50th St., New York, NY10022, phone 212-572-2128 or 872-8231, founded 1987, editor Gordon Lish, is a literary quarterly publishing poetry, fiction, essays, and humor. They want **"poetry, period, meaning:** *not* **verse."** They have published poetry by Sharon Olds, Bruce Beasley, Jack Gilbert, and Thomas Lynch. It is 256 pp, digest-sized, flat-spined, with glossy card cover. Circulation: 15,000. Subscription: $36. **Sample, postpaid: $8.95. Pay: "rates vary but are modest" plus 2 copies. "Do not submit a batch of poems folded separately!"**

QUARTERLY REVIEW OF LITERATURE; QRL AWARDS (III, IV-Subscription, translation), 26 Haslet Ave., Princeton, NJ 08540, founded 1943, poetry editors T. Weiss and R. Weiss. After more than 35 years as one of the most distinguished literary journals in the country, *QRL* now appears as the *QRL Poetry Series*, in which 4-5 book length collections are combined in one annual volume, each of the 4-5 poets receiving a $1,000 Quarterly Review of Literature Award as a prize. The resulting 300-400 pp. volumes are printed in editions of 3,000-5,000, selling in paperback for $10, in hardback for $20. Subscription—2 paperback volumes containing 10 books: $20. **Manuscripts may be sent for reading during the months of November and May. The collection need not be a first book. It should be between 50-80 pp. if it is a group of connected poems, a selection of miscellaneous poems, a poetic play, a work of poetry translation, or it can be a single long poem of 30 pp. or more. Some of the poems may have had previous magazine publication. Also considers simultaneous submissions. SASE must be included for returned manuscripts. Manuscripts in English or translated into English are also invited from outside the U.S. Only one MS may be submitted per reading period and must include an SASE.** "Since poetry as a thriving art must depend partly upon the enthusiasm and willingness of those directly involved to join in its support, the editors require that **each MS be accompanied by a subscription to the series."**

QUEEN OF ALL HEARTS (IV-Religious), 26 S. Saxon Ave., Bay Shore, NY 11706, phone 516-665-0726, founded 1950, poetry editor Joseph Tusiani, a magazine-sized bimonthly, uses **poetry "dealing with Mary, the Mother of Jesus—inspirational poetry. Not too long."** They have published poetry by Fernando Sembiante and Alberta Schumacher. The editor selected these sample lines (poet unidentified):

> The toddler falters, Mary, catch him up
> (Gethsemane reveals the sombre cup.)
> Now the Passover Lamb dwells in the land
> (Amid wood shavings stands he fresh and tanned.

The 48 pp. professionally printed magazine, heavy stock, various colors of ink and paper, liberal use of graphics and photos, has 6,000 subscriptions at $12 per year. Per copy: $2.50. They receive 40-50 submissions of poetry per year, use 2 per issue. **Sample: $3 postpaid. Submit doublespaced MSS. Reports within 3-4 weeks. Pays 6 copies (sometimes more) and complimentary subscription. Sometimes editor comments on rejections.** His advice: "Try and try again! Inspiration is not automatic!"

QUEEN'S QUARTERLY: A CANADIAN REVIEW (II,IV-Regional), John Watson Hall, Queen's University, Kingston, Ontario, K7L 3N6, Canada, phone 613-545-2667, founded 1893, editors Martha J. Bailey and C. Thomson, is "a general interest intellectual review featuring articles on science, politics, humanities, arts and letters, extensive book reviews, some poetry and fiction. **We are especially interested in poetry by Canadian writers. Shorter poems preferred.**" They have recently published poetry by Darko R. Suvin, Kim Bridgford, and Raymond Souster. There are about 12 pp. of poetry in each issue, 6×9", 224 pp., circulation 1,500. Subscription: $18 Canadian, U.S. and foreign, $20 U.S. funds; per copy: $5 U.S. They receive about 400 submissions of poetry per year, use 40. **Sample: $5 U.S. postpaid. Submit no more than 6 poems at once. Photocopies OK but no simultaneous submissions. Reports in 12-16 weeks. Pays usually $25 (Canadian) per poem, plus 2 copies.**

QUICK BROWN FOX (II); MAD DOG PRESS (V), Box 47, Youngwood, PA 15697, founded 1987, editor K.K. Shields. **Mad Dog Press accepts no unsolicited MSS.** *Quick Brown Fox*, a 1-3 pp. broadsheet appearing "3-6 times a year" using "**informed contemporary poems; shorter poems (20 lines or less) have a better chance, although a solid longer poem will be considered. No pornography; erotica is OK; if you don't know the difference, don't submit. No political rants or raves (social issues OK if poem is solid). No mail art.**" They have recently published poems by Jon Forrest Glade, Blacky Hix, Michael Northrop, Lynne Savitt, Ken Sparling, and Richard Wilmarth. As a sample the editor selected these lines from "Take a Picture" by Bill Shields:

> I've left bayonets buried in the doors of women
> who loved me
> their warmth
> brushing the soul of a man
> crawling knee deep in the jungle grass

Press run is 300. **Sample: $1 cash and SASE. Pays 5 copies. The editor will consider simultaneous submissions and previously published poems. Editor sometimes comments on rejections.** She advises: "Look at a sample copy before submitting. Read poetry incessantly, from Catullus to Cummings, from Bukowski to Browning, and everything in between and beyond. Read, read, read. It's the only way to find you *own* style."

RACKHAM JOURNAL OF THE ARTS AND HUMANITIES (RAJAH) (I, IV-Students, themes), 411 Mason Hall, The University of Michigan, Ann Arbor, MI 48109, phone 313-763-2351, founded 1971, co-editors Thomas Mussio and Catharine Krieps, is "primarily a forum for the critical and **creative work of graduate students of the University of Michigan**" but each year they include two contributions by others. It is an annual journal with emphasis on criticism, fiction, poetry and translation. **Open to all varieties of poetry, but usually limited to 1-2 pp. in length. Nothing "pornographic or grotesque."** They have published poetry by Duchess Edmée de la Rochefoucauld and John Ditsky. The editor selected these sample lines by David L. Labiosa:

> The small dog makes me think
> of our island in Puerto Rico:
> confronted with the ponderous
> importer, person government . . .

RAJAH is 6×9", professionally printed, 120 pp. flat-spined, with b/w glossy card cover, using illustrations, photos, ads. Of 50 submissions from non-university graduate students they accept two. Press run is 400 for 200 subscriptions of which 150 are libraries. It sells for $3 to individuals, $5 to institutions. **Sample: $1.75 postpaid. Pays 2 copies. Include cover letter with submissions. No simultaneous submissions, but previously published poems OK. Reports in 4-6 months. Editor sometimes comments on rejections.**

‡RADCLIFFE QUARTERLY (IV-Specialized), 10 Garden St., Cambridge, MA 02138, phone 617-495-8608, editor Ruth Whitman, is an alumnae quarterly that **publishes alumnae and college-related poets.** They have recently published poetry by Patricia Filipowska and Rhea Kovar Sossen. As a sample the editor selected these lines (poet unidentified):

> Except to say it was brown, black
> or in between, you can't describe it
> nor any terror, guilt, fantasy . . .

Full-color cover, magazine-sized, with glossy paper cover. They accept 3 poems per issue, 12 per year, receive about 30 per year. Press run: 30,000 for 25,000 subscribers. **No pay. Samples free to alumnae.** The Dean's office sponsors a contest for poets, winners printed in the quarterly. Must be a Radcliffe student to enter.

RADIANCE: THE MAGAZINE FOR LARGE WOMEN (I, IV-Women), Box 31703, Oakland, CA 94604, phone 415-482-0680, founded 1984, publisher/editor Alice Ansfield, who **"wants to include poetry especially for large women. Need to have poetry reach women all over the country; hence not too political in language. It should be personal, empowering."** As a sample she quotes these lines by Canadian poet C.M. Donald:

> The fat woman in a crisis

> *loses a substantial amount*
> *of flesh.*
> *No one notices.*
> *She tells a few people. They*
> *say, 'Congratulations.'*
> *That which, in the thin*
> *is a measure of distress,*
> *cause for concern,*
> *is clearly*
> *—in the fat—*
> *praiseworthy.*

The quarterly is magazine-sized, professionally printed on glossy stock with full-color paper cover, 60 pp., saddle-stapled, using b/w graphics, photos and ads, circulation 20,000 to 4,000 subscriptions, 6,000 selling on newsstands or in bookstores, 2,000 sent as complimentary copies to media, clothing stores for large women, therapists, etc. Subscription: $12. **Sample: $2.50 postpaid. Send SASE for guidelines. Pays $10-40. Double-spaced, typed MS. Editor usually comments on rejections.**

RAG MAG; BLACK HAT PRESS (I), P.O. Box 12, Goodhue, MN 55027, phone 612-923-4590, founded 1982, poetry editor Beverly Voldseth accepts **poetry of "any length or style. No pornographic SM violent crap."** They have recently published poetry by Warren Lang, Syd Weedon, and Laurel Mills. As a sample the editor selected these lines from "Brain/Cow Poem" by Belinda Subraman:

> *I feed it*
> *as well as my father's cows*
> *stuff it full of classics*
> *and the best of modern*
> *literature philosophy psychology*
> *synthesize it into this*
> *smoother simplicity . . .*

Rag Mag, appearing twice a year, is 64 pp. flat-spined, digest-sized, professionally printed in dark type with tipped-in colored ads for books, with matte colored card cover. The editor says she accepts about 10% of poetry received. Press run is 200 for 50 subscriptions of which 4 are libraries. Subscription: $8. **Sample: $4.50 postpaid. "Send 6-8 of your best. Something that tells a story, creates images, speaks to the heart." Pays 1 copy.** They may publish chapbook or paperback collections of poetry under the imprint of *Black Hat Press*. Query first. **$25 reading fee for book or chapbook MS. Detailed comments provided. Submit 6-8 poems, bio, publications. Simultaneous submissions, previously printed material, photocopies OK. No dot-matrix. Reports in 6 weeks. Financial arrangements for book publication vary.** Recently published *Cherry Ferris Wheels* by Patrick McKinnon, 104 pp. of poetry.

‡RAINBOW CITY EXPRESS (I, IV-Spiritual, nature, women), Box 8447, Berkeley, CA 94707-8447, founded 1988, editor Helen B. Harvey, is a quarterly using **"excellent evocative material pertaining to individual spiritual insights and experiences, God-in-nature, women's issues. 30 lines maximum. No rhyming poems! No infantile beginners.** Please obtain and study at least one issue of *RCE* prior to submitting any manuscript." They have recently published poetry by James Dillet Freeman, and Coleman Barks. As a sample the editor offered these lines from one of her poems:

> *The sparkle on the spider's web,*
> *a dust mote on the air,*
> *the purple and white of columbines*
> *unseen, in dark, thick woods—*
> *Cloaked in this Seamless Garment,*
> *I am them All.*

They offer "sporadic contests with cash prizes and publication of winners." I have not seen an issue, but the editor describes it as 60-80 pp. magazine-sized, side-stapled, with "exquisite art and graphics, uplifting essays and poems, and ads." They accept about 25-45 poems per year. Press run 500-1,000 for 400-500 subscriptions, including several libraries. Subscription: $22. **Sample, postpaid: $6. Pays 1 copy.**

RAMBUNCTIOUS PRESS; RAMBUNCTIOUS REVIEW (II, IV-Regional), 1221 W. Pratt, Chicago, IL 60626, phone 312-338-2439, founded 1982, poetry editors Mary Dellutri, Richard Goldman, Beth Hausler, and Nancy Lennon. The *Review* appears once yearly in a handsomely printed, saddle-stapled, $7 \times 10''$ format, 48 pages. They want **"spirited, quality poetry, fiction, short drama, photos, and graphics. Some focus on local work, but all work is considered."** Recently they have published Richard Huttel, Julie Parson, Elizabeth Eddy, and offer these lines by Layle Silbert as a sample:

> *"Greeks dance*
> *on my ceiling*
> *to celebrate a wedding*
> *the chandelier has fallen*
> *& retsina drips*
> *through the hole*
> *into my glass*
> *I am a guest"*

They have a circulation of about 500 with 200 subscriptions, single copy $3 (**sample: $4 postpaid**). They receive 500-600 submissions a year and use 50-60, **reporting in 6 months. No special requirements for submission, will consider simultaneous submissions. No submissions accepted June 1 through August 31. No queries. Payment 2 copies. Occasional comments on MSS.** They run annual contests in poetry, fiction, and short drama.

RANGER INTERNATIONAL PRODUCTIONS; LION PUBLISHING; ROAR RECORDING (V), P.O. Box 71231, Milwaukee, WI 53211-7331, phone 414-332-7474 (formerly Albatross Press, then Lion Publishing), founded 1969, editor Martin Jack Rosenblum, publishes **"objectivist/projectivist poetry, primarily with action subjects by adventurers—such as the Harley poetry—**in flat-spined paper and hardcover chapbooks." They have recently published poetry by Karl Young, Howard McCord, Toby Olson, and Carl Rakosi. As a sample the editor selected his own poem "Late Fall on a Harley-Davidson" (in the book **The Holy Ranger**):

> *the leaves scatter into heaps still wet*
> *from night rain & the fog lifts valleys*
> *onto shaded helmet visor visions coming*
> *– – – –upon a road kill*
> *– – – –as though a ranger*
> *– –having followed the trail*
> *–that led to frigid air*
> *impossible to breath quick*
> *so head down right over the stench*

That book is 84 pp. flat-spined, digest-sized, with matte card cover, $14.95. They publish about 3 books a year. **Query regarding submissions. Payment "negotiable." Editor comments on submissions "always."** He says, "Poetry has been swept into an academic corner and dusted off of daily living spaces and this is what Ranger International Productions works against: we went to bring poetry out of academics and back into life's daily platform. Write hard, accept no public money and achieve honesty and integrity personally while studying the master poets in school or out. Control of the forms is essential. Control of the life is absolutely required."

RASHI (IV-Ethnic), Box 1198, Hamilton, New Zealand, founded 1985, editor Norman Simms, uses poetry on **"Jewish topics in English or any Jewish language such as Hebrew, Yiddish, Ladino, etc." They do not want poetry that is "pompous, self-indulgent nonsense."** They have recently published poems by Anne Ranasinghe and Simon Lichman. *Rashi*, a 6×8" 8 pp. newsletter, appears every 6-8 weeks. They accept about 25 of 40 poems received per year. Press run is 150 for 100 subscriptions of which 40 are libraries. Subscription: $15. **Sample $2 postpaid. Pays 1 copy. Subscription "recommended, but not necessary." Reports in 1 month. Editor comments on rejections for $5 per page.** He says, "This is a special part of our overall projects. We would like to see multi-lingualism develop, reinterpretation of ancient and medieval traditions."

‡READ ME (II), 1118 Hoyt Ave., Everett, WA 98201, phone 206-259-0804, founded 1988, editor Elizabeth Strong, is a "general interest quarterly of entertainment and ideas using **poetry that is less than 50 lines (preferred), no obscurity, open to form, quality of thought counts, nothing downbeat, self-indulgent.** They have recently published poetry by Denise Dumars, W. Gregory Stewart, Barbara Petoskey, and Don Croson. I have not seen an issue, but the editor describes it as tabloid size, 24 pp. newsprint, web offset, with line drawings, display ads and classified. Press run: 2,000 for 600+ subscribers of which 20 are libraries. They accept 50 or fewer poems of 500-750 received. Subscription: $5. **Sample, postpaid: $1.50. Pays $1-3 plus 2 copies.** There is a contest in each issue, a guest reader selecting the winner of a $50 U.S. bond.

REAL (RE ARTS & LETTERS) (II), Box 13007, Stephen F. Austin State University, Nacogdoches, TX 75962, phone 409-568-2101, founded 1968, editor Lee Schultz, is a scholarly, academic journal, which uses short fiction, drama, reviews, and interviews. Printed in the Spring and Fall, they hope to use **from 15 to 25 pages of poetry per issue. Sample $3.50 postpaid (1989 and earlier only). Writer's guidelines for SASE.** Circulation is about 400, more than half of which are major college libraries. Poetry submissions vary between 10 to 35 poems per week. **They acknowledge receipt of submissions**

and strive for a one-month decision. Submissions during summer semesters may take longer. Editors prefer a statement that the manuscript is not being simultaneously submitted; however, this fact is taken for granted when they receive a MS. "We presently do not receive enough formal or witty/ironic pieces. We need a better balance between open and generic forms. We're also interested in critical writings on poems or writing poetry. We will return poems rather than tie them up for more than a one-issue backlog (6 months)." The editor selected these sample lines from Jeffrey H. Collins' "Storm Mountain Climb":

> This fallen timber lies in designs
> As glaciers sheer in the slowest of motions.
> Here at a height even streams avoid,
> We are alive, we are alive . . .

Submit original and copy. Reports in 4-6 weeks, pays in copies.

‡RECOVERING POET'S REGISTRY AND EXCHANGE; BLACKBERRY PRESS (IV-Specialized), 2902 N. 21st Ave., Phoenix, AZ 85015, phone 602-340-0906, editor Susan Smith, is a small-press operation publishing chapbooks twice a year "with work of poets recovering from chemical, behavioral, and emotional addictions. Include bio with address and phone number for communication and poetry exchange with other recovering poets." They want "powerful recovery poetry, well-thought-out, edited. Any style. All subjects (life is a process of recovery). Limit poems to 1 page whenever possible. The purpose is to encourage and unite recovering poets who write poetry as therapy and healing. Nothing hyper-religious, my dog-&-me, preachy, self-righteous, promotion of Christianity or any organized religion." As a sample the editor selected these lines from her own poem, "Mother's Illusions":

> My mother's hands play deadly games
> caressing lies that led my life,
> abandoned in the frigid dark
> I watch my mother smile and cry.

Submit 3 samples and bio. Simultaneous submissions and previously published poems OK. You pay a one-time fee of $15 "includes one chapbook (with poetry and bio). An additional $10 for each publication thereafter with or without poet's contribution." The editor advises, "Ignore snobbish remarks about what makes 'good poetry.' Be totally honest and committed to communication. Write, edit, live with your creations and edit more whenever needed. Poetry can be therapeutic, but it doesn't have to be serious. It can be funny, cynical, sarcastic, morbid and bitter—as well as all the other poetic possibilities. Be yourself and capture moods, experiences, and feelings."

RED ALDER BOOKS; PAN-EROTIC REVIEW (II, IV-Erotica, feminist), P.O. Box 2992, Santa Cruz, CA 95063, phone 408-426-7082, founded 1971, poetry editor David Steinberg. "We specialize in publication of books on re-examination of traditional male roles, and creative, provocative erotica that is imaginative, top-quality, non-exploitative, especially if unconventional or explicitly sexual. It is our desire to demonstrate that erotica material can be evocative, sexy, powerful and energizing, without being cliché, exploitive of men's and women's frustrations, or male-dominant. Our work demands respect for the best of our erotic natures, for life, for love, and for our wonderful bodies." They have published poetry by Lyn Lifshin, James Broughton, Leslie Simon, Arthur Knight, and Cheryl Townsend. The editor chose a sample from a poem by Lenore Kandel:

> I look at you from the embrace of the tiger
> and our eyes meet in wonder
> little tongues, little hands, move faster
> and you cry out as you come
> spurting a fountain of flowers
> into the tiger's mouth.

Query with 5-10 sample poems. Replies to queries and/or submissions in 1-2 months. Simultaneous submissions, photocopies OK. Pays copies, occasional royalties. Sample book available for $9, postpaid. The editor advises, "Tell the truth; avoid playing the poet; pursue humility; be useful to someone beyond yourself; say something new, something unnoticed, about the life-force."

RED BASS (II, IV-Social issues, translations), 2425 Burgundy St., New Orleans, LA 70117, founded 1981, 8½ × 11" book format magazine *Red Bass*. Poetry editor Jay Murphy. "We want strong, innovative, committed verse. It helps to read the magazine to see the variety of styles employed before submitting." Recently published poets include Etel Adnan, Gerard Malanga, Joy Hargo, Ivan Arguelles, H.D. Moe, Gil Ott, and "Los Cinconegritos" of El Salvador. I selected this sample of lines from Jayne Cortez' "Blood Suckers":

> exploding way down in the dumps of Love Canal
> expanding themselves and vigorously sucking on

a medley of birth defects . . .

They have a circulation of about 3,000, over 400 subscriptions. It sells for $5 a copy and receives over 1,000 submissions per year. **"Submit poems that have not previously been published. We try to reply in 3-4 months, payment in copies. We comment on poems we feel are close to what we're looking for. We focus in more and more on translations and international poetics of an expressly committed nature,** but the poetry we have published, while varying in focus, tends to the experimental in form. Theme issues have ranged from Women's International Arts and For Palestine to Conspiracy Charges and What's Hot in Havana: A Look at the New Cuban Art. It may help to inquire about upcoming magazines and their topics."

THE RED CANDLE PRESS; CANDELABRUM (II, IV-Form), 9 Milner Rd., Wisbech PE13 2LR, England, founded 1970, editors Basil Wincote, B.A. and M. L. McCarthy, M.A., administrative editor Helen Gordon, B.A., was "founded to encourage poets working in **traditional-type verse, metrical unrhymed or metrical rhymed.** We're more interested in poems than poets: that is, we're interested in what sort of poems an author produces, not in his or her personality." They publish the yearly magazine, *Candelabrum,* occasional postcards, paperbound staple-spined chapbooks and occasional poetry leaflets. For all of these they want **"good-quality metrical verse, with rhymed verse specially wanted. Elegantly cadenced free verse is acceptable. No weak stuff (moons and Junes, loves and doves, etc.) No chopped-up prose pretending to be free verse. Any length up to about 50 lines for** *Candelabrum,* **any subject, including eroticism (but not porn) — satire, love poems, nature lyrics, philosophical — any subject, but nothing racist or sexist."** They have published poetry by Cory Wade, Andrew Moulton, Robert Sargent, Christine Michael, Webster Wheelock, and Freda Howell. The editors offer these lines by Robert Roberts as a sample:

> *I came across a dead snake on the bank;*
> *No subtle tempter, this, you'd take him for,*
> *Stark on the grass, the body's lustre rank;*
> *A lifeless literal fact, no less, no more.*

The digest-sized magazine, staple-spined, small type, exemplifies their intent to "pack in as much as possible, wasting no space, and try to keep a neat appearance with the minimum expense." They get in about 44 pp. (some 60 poems) in each issue. Circulation: 900 with 700 subscriptions, of which 22 are libraries. **Sample: $4 prepaid if payment is in bills. $10 prepaid if payment is by check. "We prefer bills."** They receive about 2,000 submissions per year, use approximately 5% of those, sometimes holding over poems for the next year or longer. **"Submit any time, IRC essential if return wished, and please check the weight — each poem on a separate sheet please, neat typescripts or neat** *legible* **manuscripts.** *Please* **no dark, oily photostats, no colored ink (only black or blue). Clear photocopies acceptable. Author's name and address on each sheet, please."** Reports in about 2 months. No simultaneous submissions. Pays one contributor's copy. The books published by **Red Candle Press "have been at our invitation to the poet, and at our expense. We pay the author a small royalty-advance, but he/she keeps the copyright."** The editors comment, "Traditional-type poetry is much more popular here in Britain, and we think also in the United States, now than it was in 1970, when we founded *Candelabrum* though some people are still rather scared of it. We **always welcome new poets, especially 'traditionalists,' and we like to hear from the U.S.A. as well as from here at home.** General tip: Study the various outlets at the library, or buy a sample, or borrow a copy from a subscriber, before you go to the expense of submitting your work."

RED CEDAR REVIEW (II), English Dept., Michigan State University, East Lansing, MI 48824, phone 517-355-7570, founded 1963, is a literary biannual (digest-sized, 80 pp., circulation 400, 200 subscriptions of which 100 are libraries) which uses poetry — **"any subject, form, length; the only requirement is originality and vision." The editors encourage work beyond animal poems, flora and fauna poems etc. No pornography.** They have published poetry by Michael J. Cesaro, Richard Todd Julius, and Sally McNall. The editor chose this sample by Susan Rawlins:

> *"I'll give you a dime to eat these raisins," she said.*
> *"Make it a quarter and you've got a deal."*
> *"A quarter? For a quarter I'll feed them to the dog."*
> *"Feed them to the dog."*
> *"Seriously. I'll give you a dime to eat these raisins."*

They receive about 400 submissions per year, use 30. Subscription $10. **Sample: $2 postpaid. Current issue $5. Submit only previously unpublished works. Reports in 2 months, sometimes longer. Pays 2 copies.** Editor sometimes comments on rejections.

RED RAMPAN' PRESS; RED RAMPAN' REVIEW; RED RAMPAN' BROADSIDE SERIES(V, IV-Form), 414 North Bentwood Dr., Midland, TX 79703-5350, phone 915-697-7689, founded 1981, poetry editor Larry D. Griffin. **"For 1991 we will consider long poems for Red Rampan' Boradside Series."** *RRR* is an "eclectic review quarterly." I have not seen a copy, but the editor says it is $6 \times 9''$, 48-60 pp., with a press run of 300, **"presently not accepting poetry."** The Press plans to publish flat-spined paperback collections.

THE REDNECK REVIEW OF LITERATURE (IV-Regional), P.O. Box 730, Twin Falls, ID 83301, phone 208-734-6653, editor Penelope Reedy, semiannual magazine publishing poetry, fiction, and essays **dealing with the contemporary West. The editor wants to see "any form, length, or style — not heavy on sex or politics. Want a sense of place — voices heard in the fields, at crossroads, hunting, etc." She does not want "porn; ethereal ditties about nothing; obscure."** She has published poetry by Tom Trusky, Thomas McClanahan, Gail-Marie Pahmeir, Bill Studebaker, Gerald Locklin, Rane Arroyo, and Mack Rozema. The magazine, which appears in the spring and fall each year, is $7 \times 10''$, offset, perfect bound, some advertising. Circulation is 300-500, of which 150 are subscriptions and 100-150 are newsstand sales. Price per issue is $7 postpaid. **Sample: $7 postpaid. Pay is 2 copies. Rejected MSS are reported on immediately, and no accepted MSS are held beyond 3 issues. Writers should submit "2-3 poems at a time, letter quality — don't like simultaneous submissions. Please send SASE with *enough* postage to return MSS." Criticism is sometimes given.** The editor says, "Take time — have something to say. Practice forms like sonnets, to learn how to pull images out of your head, to cover an idea completely. Read nursery rhymes to your kids, listen and observe."

REFLECT (IV-Themes), 3306 Argonne Ave., Norfolk, VA 23509, founded 1979, poetry editor W. S. Kennedy. They use **"spiral poetry: featuring an inner-directed concern with sound (euphony), mystical references or overtones, and objectivity — rather than personal and emotional poems. No love poems, pornography, far left propaganda; nothing overly emotional. (Don't write yourself into the poem.)** They have recently published poetry by Marikay Brown, B.Z. Niditch, Pearl Bloch Segall, and Stan Proper. As a sample the editor selected these lines by Ruth Wildes Schuler:

> *An oyster white Southern gypsy, you burst in a psychotic passion*
> *upon a sterile rigid world — Faulkner shades followed in*
> *mocking vermillion, haunting your tan golden footsteps and*
> *dropping seeds of corrupting decay from the Ritz Bar to the*
> *Riviera. They sought to lock you in the gilded cage of*
> *conformity, but you escaped them all, Zelda, by dancing a pale*
> *orchid waltz to madness.*

The quarterly is digest-sized, 48 pp., saddle-stapled, typescript. Subscription: $8. **Sample: $2 postpaid. Guidelines available for SASE. Reports within a month. No backlog. Pays 1 copy. Editor sometimes comments on rejections.**

REFLECTIONS (IV-Children/Teens), P.O. Box 368, Duncan Falls, OH 43734, phone 614-674-5209, founded 1980, is **"a poetry magazine by students from nursery school to high school"** — a project of the 7th and 8th grade journalism students from Franklin Local Schools, Duncan Falls Junior High School. Editor Dean Harper says it **"is a helpful magazine for students to learn how to submit their writing and to stimulate writing ideas."** *Reflections* also features excellent writing programs across the United States. They consider **all forms and lengths of poetry.** These are sample lines selected by the editor from "Victory" by Laura Salcius, age 14:

> *The determination shot through my body like lightening*
> *My teeth grit, my hands clenched*
> *And a fabulous strength spread through my soul.*
> *I was going to get her.*

Reflections comes out twice a year in an elegant magazine-sized format with a glossy, color photograph by a student on the front. Its 32 large pages are filled with poems (in rather small type), often with a b/w photograph of the student, and a few ads. It has a circulation of 1,000, with 700 subscriptions, of which 15 are libraries. **Sample $2, subscription $5. Reports within 10 days, 6 month backlog. Send SASE for guidelines. Pays in contributor's copy.** This is one of the few good places publishing poetry by children. They receive about 3,000 submissions a year, use about 200. **Considers simultaneous submissions.**

‡**REFLECTIONS; J&A MKTG. (I)**, 5522 W. Acoma Rd., Glendale, AZ 85306, phone 602-978-4740, founded 1989, editor A. Trotta. *Reflections* is a magazine appearing 2-3 times a year. J&A Mktg. is an imprint for publishing chapbooks. **"We aid in distribution of any chapbooks we publish."** The magazine uses **"any type (except haiku)/subject — no erotica. 15 line maximum. No racist, sexist, ageist, or antisemitic."** As a sample, I selected the complete poem "Poets" by Bailey:

> *Poets are all who love —*
> *who feel great truths —*
> *And tell them.*

It is 32 pp. digest-sized, saddle-stapled, photocopied from typescript with matte card cover. Press run: 200. **Sample copy $1.50. Send SASE for guidelines. Pays 1 copy. Simultaneous submissions and previously published poems OK. ("Name of publication where it appeared a must.") Reports in 2 weeks maximum. Editor comments on submissions "often if it merits it."** The editor says, "Write what you *feel*, not what you believe the editor wants to see and show you're a pro by sending that VIP-Self-Addressed-Stamped-Envelope with all correspondence. Don't *cram* envelope; 4-5 poems are sufficient.

RENDITIONS: A CHINESE-ENGLISH TRANSLATION MAGAZINE (IV-Translations), Research Center for Translation, CUHK, Shatin, NT, Hong Kong, editor Dr. Eva Hung, appears twice a year. **"Contents exclusively translations from Chinese, ancient and modern."** They also publish a paperback series of Chinese literature in English translation. They have recently published translations of the poetry of Gu Cheng, Shu Ting, Mang Ke, and Bei Dao. As a sample the editor selected a poem by Bing Xin, translated by John Cayley:

> The waves constantly press the cliff.
> The rocks are always silent, never answer,
> Yet this silence,
> has been pondered down the ages.

Renditions is magazine-sized, 180 pp., flat-spined, elegantly printed, often with side-by-side Chinese and English texts, using some b/w and color drawings and photos, with glossy card cover. **Sample: $9 postpaid. Pays "honorarium" plus 2 copies. Reports in two months. Use British spelling. They "will consider"** book MSS, for which they would like a query with sample poems. Books pay 10% royalties plus 10 copies. MSS usually not returned. Editor sometimes comments on rejections.

‡**RENEGADE (II)**, Box 314, Bloomfield Hills, MI 48303, phone 313-972-5580, founded 1988, editors Jeanine Pietrzak and Michael Nowicki, appears twice a year using stories, essays and poems. **"We are an eclectic publication. There is no preference for form or style; we simply wish to see polished work of good quality. Poems are generally of a length no more than 200 lines, no less than 10 lines. We try to avoid anything that is anarchistic, antifeminist, or of a derogatory nature to any group of persons or individuals."** They have recently published poetry by John Sinclair, M.L. Liebler, Linda Nemec Foster, and Laurence Pike. As a sample, I selected the first 2 of 5 stanzas of "Night Chain" by Murray Jackson:

> Extended hands with purple plums
> shine in the half light of night and
> reflect the glare of patent leather.
>
> The long sleeves of night reach
> to find nightmares to pour —
> we all stand in a circle and wait our turn.

Renegade is 32 pp. digest-sized, laser-printed, with matte card cover, b/w drawings and graphics. Ads welcome. They accept about 5% of 300 MS of 5 poems or less. Press run: 200 for 20 subscriptions, free to libraries and editors of other literary journals. 50 shelf sales. Subscription: $5.90. **Sample, postpaid: $2. Pays 1 copy, 2 on request. Reports in 3-6 months.** Editor comments on submissions "seldom."

THE RENOVATED LIGHTHOUSE MAGAZINE (IV-Subscribers), P.O. Box 21130, Columbus, OH 43221, founded 1986, editor R. Allen Dodson. *The Renovated Lighthouse Magazine* is a monthly "literary publication for interesting and insightful poetry and prose, also including fiction and artwork, using **poetry of any form, length, style, subject," requiring subscription of those poets it publishes.** As a sample the editor selected these lines (poet unidentified):

> And if there be flowers
> On some forgotten hill
> Pick the simplest of them for me
> For when we meet again
> Dearest to me both now and then
> I'll have a flower for you
> Of the deepest shade of blue.

It is 40 pp., digest-sized, card cover, saddle-stapled, photocopied from typescript. Press run 150. Subscription: $18/year ($21 foreign). **Sample: $1.50. Guidelines available. No simultaneous or previously published poems. Include cover letter. Reports in 1 week. Comments on rejections if asked.**

REPOSITORY PRESS (V, IV-Regional), RR. 7, Site 29, Comp. 8, Prince George BC V2N 2J5 Canada, founded 1972, publisher John Harris, publishes flat-spined paperbacks and chapbooks of **local poetry** and short stories. "I publish poetry by people I know. I advise poets to operate their own magazines and publishing companies."

RESPONSE (IV-Ethnic, students), 27 W. 20th St., 9th Floor, New York, NY 10011, phone 212-675-1168, FAX 212-929-3459, founded 1966, poetry editor Annette Harchik, is a "contemporary Jewish review publishing poetry, fiction and essays **by students and young adult authors." The only specification for poetry is that it be on a Jewish theme and have some significant Jewish content.** They have recently published poetry by Esty Schachter, Mark Zuss, Robert Paul Silverman, and Barbara Foster. As a sample the editor chose these lines by Estelle Gershgoren Novak:

> *Memory, like a stranger,*
> *speaks a foreign language*
> *understood only by those*
> *who have studied*
> *the strange grammar of the dead.*

They look for "creative, challenging and chutzapadik writing" from young writers. The quarterly is "between 96 and 120 pp.," flat-spined, $6 \times 9''$, professionally printed on heavy stock, with a glossy "varnished" cover with art work. Circulation 2,000 with 1,000 subscribers of which 30% are libraries. 1,000 distributed through bookstores and newsstands. Subscription: $16 ($8 for students); $20 for institutions. **Sample: $2 postpaid. Pays 5 copies. Reports in about 8 weeks. 6 months between acceptance and publication.**

RFD: A COUNTRY JOURNAL FOR GAY MEN EVERYWHERE (I, IV-Gay), Box 68, Liberty, TN 37095, founded 1974, poetry editor Steven Riel. *RFD* "is a quarterly for gay men with emphasis on lifestyles outside of the gay mainstream — poetry, politics, profiles, letters." They want **poetry with "personal, creative use of language and image, relevant to journal themes, political themes. We try to publish as many poets as we can so tend to publish shorter poems and avoid epics."** They have recently published poetry by Rudy Kikel, Ron Schreiber, Ian Young, and Assotto Saint. The issue I examined had 4 magazine-sized pp. of poetry, some dozen poems photoreduced from typescript arranged at various angles on the page, with b/w photos and drawings interspersed. As a sample the editor selected the opening lines of "Shadow" by L.E. Wilson:

> *I am a shadow among shadows*
> *a name whispered in a hurricane*
> *not immortal and nothing of the magic*
> *(but I remember magic) . . .*

RFD has a circulation of 2,000, 1,000 subscriptions — per year: $22 first class, $15 second class; per copy: $4.75. **Sample: $4.75 postpaid. Submit up to 5 poems at a time. Photocopies, simultaneous submissions OK. Reports in 2-6 months. Pays copies. Send SASE for guidelines. Editor sometimes comments on rejections.** "*RFD* looks for interesting thoughts, succinct use of language and imagery evocative of nature and gay men and love in natural settings."

THE RIALTO (II), 32 Grosvenor Rd., Norwich, Norfolk NR2 2PZ England, founded 1984, poetry editors John Wakeman and Michael Mackmin, wants **"poetry of intelligence, wit, compassion, skill, excellence, written by humans. Potential contributors are strongly advised to read *The Rialto* before submitting."** They have recently published poetry by Elizabeth Jennings, Carol Ann Duffy, and Peter Redgrove. As a sample the editors chose the last stanza of a new translation of Pablo Neruda's "Autumn Testament":

> *And now behind this page*
> *I will go without disappearing:*
> *I will leap into transparency*
> *like a swimmer of the sky,*
> *and then I will be so small*
> *that the wind will take me*
> *and will not know my name*
> *and I will not be when I awake:*
> *then I will sing in silence.*

The Rialto, which appears 3 times a year, is magazine-sized, 48 pp. saddle-stapled, beautifully printed on glossy stock with glossy b/w card cover, using b/w drawings. They accept subscriptions at $24. **Sample: $8.50 postpaid. Pays £5 per poem. No simultaneous submissions or previously printed poetry. Reports within 3 months. Editor "only rarely" comments on rejections.**

RIDGE REVIEW MAGAZINE; RIDGE TIMES PRESS (IV-Regional), Box 90, Mendocino, CA 95460, phone 707-964-8465, founded 1981, poetry editors Jim Tarbell, Judy Tarbell and Lucie Marshall, is a "bio-regional quarterly looking at economic, political and social phenomena of the area" which uses

only poets from Northern California. They have recently published poetry by Michael Sykes and Judith Tannenbaum. As a sample the editors chose these lines from "New Broom" by Kay Ryan:

> *New broom sweeps stiff,*
> *graceless thatch rakes,*
> *leaves tracks, but change*
> *comes unseen makes bristles*
> *sway that or this way*
> *turns tasks*
> *segue*

The 7×10" magazine, saddle-stapled, 50+ pp., matte card cover with art, photos and ads with text, circulation 3,500, 1,000 subscriptions, uses about 1 page of poetry per issue. Subscription: $7; per copy: $2. They use about 1 out of 20 poems submitted each year. **Considers simultaneous submissions. Sample: $3.85 postpaid. Photocopy, dot-matrix OK. Reports in about a week. Usually pays $10 per poem.**

RIO GRANDE PRESS; SE LA VIE WRITER'S JOURNAL (I, IV-Themes); EDITOR'S DIGEST (IV-Subscribers); P.O. Box 371371, El Paso, TX 79937, founded 1987, editor Rosalie Avara. *Se La Vie Writer's Journal* is a quarterly journal, digest-sized, with articles, cartoons, and humorous fillers about poetry and writing; and contests in poetry (monthly) and other genres. Prizes are $5-15 for poems, entry fee $5 for 3 poems. (Also special contests for subscribers.) Publishes 70% of MSS received per quarter, **"dedicated to encouraging novice writers, poets and artists; we are interested in original, unpublished MSS that reflect the 'life' theme (La Vie). Poems are judged on originality, clarity of thought and ability to evoke emotional response."** They have recently published poetry by Marian Ford Park, Alice Mackenzie Swaim, and Ana Pine. As a sample the editor selected some lines from a prize-winning poem, "The Flinders Ranges" by Keevil Brown:

> *The desert reduced*
> *to a heat wave of colours*
> *with tooth-proof rocks reflecting images*
> *as were mirrors reflecting*
> *each others' dreaming*
> *down infinite aisles of memories,*
> *and sand dunes crystallized*
> *from the thought waves of a god.*

SLVWJ is 60 pp., photocopied from typescript, with blue matte card cover, saddle-stapled. **Sample: $3.50 postpaid. Deadlines end of March, June, September, and December. Send SASE for guidelines. Pays 1 copy.** *Editor's Digest* is "for editors and by editors," quarterly, digest-sized, 50 pp., **dealing with issues concerning small press editors: "an opportunity for editors to express their side of writing and exchange view, with peers." Send SASE for details or $4 for sample. Uses some poetry from subscribers only.**

‡**RIVELIN GRAPHEME PRESS (II)**, The Annexe Kennet House, 19 High Street, Hungerford, Berkshire RG170NL England, founded 1984, poetry editor Snowdon Barnett, publishes **only poetry, hoping for 4 titles per year,** not less than 52-196 pp. each (flat-spined, digest-sized quality paperbacks with glossy covers), illustrated. These are obviously enthusiastic, ambitious publishers with an eye for quality. **Send book-length manuscript, typed, double-spaced, photocopy OK. Payment: 20 copies of first printing up to 2,000, then 5% royalties on subsequent printings. They prefer queries that contain biographical information, previous publications, and a photo, if possible.**

RIVER CITY; HOHENBERG AWARD (II), (formerly *Memphis State Review*), English Dept., Memphis State University, Memphis, TN 38152, phone 901-363-4438, founded 1980, editor Sharon Bryan. *River City* publishes fiction, poetry, interviews, and essays. Contributors have included Marvin Bell, Philip Levine, Maxine Kumin, Robert Penn Warren, W. D. Snodgrass, Mary Oliver, Fred Busch, Beth Bentley, Mona Van Duyn, and Peter Porter. The biannual is 6x9", perfect-bound, 100 pp., 40-50 pp. of poetry in each issue, professionally printed, two-color matte cover, circulation 1,000, subscription: $6. **Sample: $4 postpaid. Submit no more than 5 poems, none June-August. Photocopy OK. Reports in 2-12 weeks. Pays 2 copies (and cash when grant funds available).** $100 Hohenberg Award is given annually to best fiction or poetry selected by the staff.

RIVER RAT REVIEW (V), Box 24198, Lexington, KY 40524, founded 1987, editor Daryl Rogers, a little magazine publishing poetry as well as some short prose. **Currently not considering poetry submissions.**

RIVER STYX MAGAZINE; BIG RIVER ASSOCIATION (II), 14 S. Euclid, St. Louis, MO 63108, phone 314-361-0043, poetry editor Jennifer Atkinson, founded 1975, is "an international, multicultural journal publishing both award-winning and relatively undiscovered writers. We feature fine art, photography, poetry and short prose. They want "excellent poetry—thoughtful." They have published work by Adrienne Rich, Amy Clampitt, Toni Morrison, Amiri Baraka, Simon Ortiz, Milosz, and Margaret Atwood. As a sample the editors chose these lines by Derek Walcott:

> *What's missing from the Charles is the smell of salt*
> *though the thawed river, muscling toward its estuary,*
> *swims seaward with the Spring, then with strong shoulders*
> *heaves up the ice. The floes crack like rifle fire.*

River Styx appears 3 times a year. I have not seen it, but the editors describe it as 90 pp., digest-sized with b/w cover. They accept less than 10% of 500 MSS received a year. **Sample: $5 postpaid. Guidelines available for SASE. Pays $8 a page plus 2 copies. Submit "legible copies with name, address on each page. Submissions read in September and October only." Reports in 1 week to 2 months, publication within a year. Editor sometimes comments on rejections.**

RIVERRUN (I, II), Glen Oaks Community College, Centreville, MI 49032-9719, phone 616-467-9945, ext. 277, founded 1977, poetry editor Harvey Gordon, is a literary biannual, using **30-40 magazine-sized pp. of poetry in each issue—"no prejudices."** As a sample, the editor chose the complete poem, "Dining in Winter" by Philip Miller:

> *Almost forgotten,*
> *a red sun swims at dusk,*
> *catching the edge of his eye*
> *before he turns back to their meal*
> *and to the silence hung*
> *above the cool ring of silver.*

They have a print run of 500-550. **Sample: $3 postpaid. They receive 500-600 poems per year, use "as much as possible," have a 6-12 month backlog. Reports immediately, except from June 15- September 15. Pays 2 copies.**

RIVERWIND (II), General Studies, Hocking Technical College, Nelsonville, OH 45764, phone 614-753-3591 ext. 2375, founded 1982, poetry editor Cindy Dubielak, is a literary annual wanting **"work from serious writers. We are most open to work with serious content, though humor may be the vehicle. Do not want to see poetry from those who view it as a 'hobby.' We have not published limericks."** They have published poetry by Naton Leslie, Kate Hancock, Gloria Ruth, David Citino, Charles Semones, Walter McDonald, and Greg Anderson. As a sample the editor selected these lines (poet unidentified):

> *Sometimes I wake on the sofa, sleep on*
> *the sofa, or wake walking in the middle*
> *of a talk out of sense. Only while no one*
> *tears me out does it have sense for me.*

Riverwind is 6 × 9″ flat-spined, 80 pp., typeset, offset, with 2-color semiglossy card cover. Of 80-100 poems received they accept approximately 40. Press run is 1,000. Per issue: $3.50. **Sample back issue: $1 postpaid. Pays 2 copies. Submit batches of 3-5, no previously published poems, no simultaneous submissions. Reports in 2-8 weeks. Editor comments "particularly if we would like to see more of that person's work."** They hope to begin publishing chapbook collections.

ROAD/HOUSE; ROAD/HOUSE PRESS (V), 900 W. 9th St., Belvidere, IL 61008, phone 815-544-9581, founded 1975, editor Todd Moore, who says, **"I like poetry that goes off like a cherry bomb in the guts. I hate poetry that rhymes, whines, moans, snivels and preaches. Make the poem so good it feels like a bullet has gone through me."** He has recently published poetry by Ron Androla, Ann Menebroker, Tom House, Tony Moffeit, Pat McKinnon and Kurt Nimmo. As a sample he selected these lines from "Finding You" by Dennis Gulling:

> *I'm squeezing back the trigger*
> *laughing out loud while you beg*
> *on your knees for another chance . . .*
> *Bark like a dog, Baby . . .*

He **"rarely" accepts poetry for chapbook publication.** He publishes 2-4 a year, each 4-8 pp. in "cheap zerox." I have examined 8 samples. Typical is **the Intimacy** by Judson Crews, simply a folded piece of 8½ × 11″ paper with the title and a photograph on the front panel and an array of poems (in this case 15) in photoreduced typescript on the other 3 panels. **Query. Pays 25-50 copies.** Todd Moore says, **"I usually do not read nor invite MSS to be read unless I wish to publish them.** I have read an occasional MS for a friend. Read as much poetry as you can. Listen to the way people talk. Don't write for the critics. Don't write poems about poetry. Trust your instincts and go into yourself for your voice."

ROANOKE REVIEW (II), Roanoke College, Salem, VA 24153, phone 703-389-2351, ext. 367, founded 1968, poetry editor Robert R. Walter, is a semiannual literary review which uses **poetry that is "conventional; we have not used much experimental or highly abstract poetry."** They have published poetry by Peter Thomas, Norman Russell, Alan Seaburg, Mary Balazs, and Irene Dayton. I selected as a sample the second of two stanzas of "Of Shoes and Ships" by Ernest Kroll:

> *The shoes in snow divide a waveless sea*
> *Whose wake congeals as if it thought a trough*
> *Redress enough for snow's discourtesy,*
> *Redress enough — by fresh snow leveled off.*

RR is 6×9″, 52 pp., professionally printed with matte card cover with decorative typography, using 25-30 pp. of poetry in each issue, circulation 250-300, 150 subscriptions of which 50 are libraries. Subscription: $5.50; per copy: $3. They receive 400-500 freelance submissions of poetry per year, use 40-60, have a 3-6 month backlog. **Sample: $2.00 postpaid. Submit original typed MSS, no photocopies. Reports in 8-10 weeks. No pay.** The editor advises, "There is a lot of careless or sloppy writing going on. We suggest careful proofreading and study of punctuation rules."

‡**THE ROCKFORD REVIEW (II, IV-Membership, regional)**, P.O. Box 858, Rockford, IL 61105, founded 1971, is an annual publication of the Rockford Writers Guild, **publishing their poetry and prose, that of other writers in the Illinois-Wisconsin region, and contributors from elsewhere. "We are not averse to metered or rhymed verse, long narrative poems or dramatic monologues. We look for the magical power of the words themselves, a playfulness with language in the creation of images and fresh insights on old themes. The writer must have control of poetic line and stanzaic break — not interested in random words strewn on a page. A care for poetic space and pace is required.** They have recently published Todd Moore, Dwight E. Humphries, Rochelle Lynn Holt, and Christine Swanberg. Olivia Diamond, editor, selected these sample lines by Judy F. Ham.

> *I've paid the price of admission*
> *After life scalps me I am meant to*
> *Reverently, cradled in Hopalong's arms*
> *On the scorched desert floor, a mass,*
>
> *Of bloody injuns at my feet. Saved*
> *On celluloid in the final, grainy calm,*

Digest-sized, 92 pp., flat-spined, glossy cover with b/w photos. Circulation 750. Price per issue $6; subscription (2 year.) $8. **Reports in 6 weeks, 6-12 months between acceptance and publication. Considers simultaneous submissions. Pays 1copy.** Editors' Choice Prize of $50-100 (one each issue).

‡**ROCKY MOUNTAIN POETRY MAGAZINE (II); THE MONTANA POET (IV, Regional); GOLDEN STAR AWARD FOR POETRY (II)**, Box 269, Gallatin Gateway, MT 59730, founded 1987, editor Don "Cheese" Akerlow, *RMPM* is a quarterly publication using **"poems on any subject, any style. Interested in poetry from all walks of life."** Accepts haiku. They also use cartoons, philosophies, essays, and short stories up to 1,500 words. They have recently published poetry by Greg Keeler and Sandy Seaton. As a sample the editor selected these lines from his own poem "Want Ads":

> *I've been writin' poems for some 25 years*
> *Written cowboy poems about shootin', Ridin', and drinkin' beers*
> *Kickin' up my heels and once at the moon I did howl*
> *Guess that Chicken Factory is still with me cause my poems are still just plain foul.*

RMPM is magazine-sized, 20 pp, on slick coated paper. Their press run is 1,000. Subscription $10. **Sample: $3.95 postpaid. Guidelines available for SASE. Pays 1 copy. Considers simultaneous submissions or previously published poems. Reports in 4-6 weeks.** Each issue features a poet on the center page. The magazine annually sponsors a contest, entries accepted January 1-May 15, fees $2 for 1 poem, $1/each for any additional poems, prizes of $50, $25, $15, $10, and 6 honorable mentions. The Rocky Mountain Poetry Magazine Membership offers 4 issues plus The RMPM T-shirt (which sells for $10), plus 4 poems entered in the Golden Star competition, for $20. They also sponsor the Montana Poets' Hall of Fame, which annually places plaques to honor poets of Montana in the Beall Park Art Center in Bozeman, MT. The editor says, "I feel that poetry has too long been enjoyed by a select few. It is the purpose of *RMPM* to get more people involved in reading and enjoying poetry; to make reading poetry as commonplace as reading any other type of literature. Advice to beginning poet: Don't be discouraged. Believe in your work because, if it comes from within, you are pleasing at least one person, and keep sending your work to editors. I do not judge poetry on perfect grammar or structure but on feeling and that's what I look for when selecting poems for the magazine." The annual Golden Star contest has prizes of $50, $25, $15, $10 and 6 honorable mentions; fee: $2 for first poem, $1 for each additional.

Entries accepted Jan. 1-May 15. *The Montana Poet* (the former name of *RMPM*) is now a regional annual publication of Montana poetry. **The Montana Poet is an annual and accepts Montana poetry or poems about Montana only.**

‡ROCKY MOUNTAIN REVIEW OF LANGUAGE AND LITERATURE (IV-Membership, translations), Boise State University English Dept., Boise, ID 83725, phone 208-385-1246, founded 1947, poetry editor, **Doug Crowell, to whom poetry submissions should be sent, Department of English, Box 4530, Texas Tech University, Lubbock, TX 79409. Contributors to the literary quarterly must be members of Rocky Mountain Modern Language Association. Poetry should be "generally relatively short," but otherwise they will consider anything but "bad poetry."** The review has recently published poetry by Scott P. Sanders and translations of Antonio Cisneros and David Huerta. As a sample, the editor selected the following three lines (opening stanza) of "The Bathers" by Jerry Bradley:

> *In Cezanne's canvas the bathers are angels,*
> *Clean and without men, their clothes banked*
> *where earthwarm river, sky, and green field*
> *blend.*

The 6×9", 276 pp. flat-spined quarterly publishes work of interest to college and university teachers of literature and language; **poetry may be in English or other modern languages. Contributors are not paid and do not receive extra copies; subscription is part of RMMLA membership. Poets should submit two copies, *without author's name*. They report on submissions in 4-8 weeks and publish usually within 6 months but no more than 12 months after acceptance.** Circulation of the review is 1,100-1,200, all membership subscriptions. They accept a few ads from other journals and publishers.

ROHWEDDER: INTERNATIONAL JOURNAL OF LITERATURE & ART (II, IV-Translations), P.O. Box 29490, Los Angeles, CA 90029, founded 1986, editors Robert Dassanowsky-Harris, Nancy Locke, Nancy Antell, and Hans-Jurgen Schacht, who say their "international journal seeks the highest quality poetry and prose. It is **open to all styles and subject matter—foreign language with translation, multi-cultural also, experimental, open text and language-oriented poetry and prose.** We have published poetry from Lithuania, East and West Germany, Central America, Argentina, Portugal, Denmark, Poland, and the U.S." Writers recently published include Eugenio de Andrade, Halina Poswiatowska, Susana Thénon, Peter Schneider, and Simon Perchik. As a sample the editors selected lines from "6:00 a.m. in Tegucigalpa" by Zoe Anglesey:

> *Helicopters angle sideways roar on approach*
> *the gip gip of gibbit blades*
> *deploy zanates to secluded trees.*
> *Centrifugal gusts of wind*
> *scatter the vultures*
> *picking at fingers of unmatched hands*
> *and under their course the loosened leaves.*

Rohwedder (Rough Weather) is 8½×11", 50 pp., saddle-stapled, offset from typesetter with b/w art inside and on the glossy card cover. About half the issue is poetry. Press run: 1,000; subscription: $12. **Sample: $4.50 postpaid. Submit five poems. Pays in contributors' copies. No simultaneous submissions or previously published poems. Photocopy, dot-matrix OK. Cover letter with bio and credits. Reports in approximately 2 months.** Editor sometimes comments on rejections. Nancy Antell includes this quote for writers: "On the one hand, the correct political line is demanded of the poet; on the other, it is justifiable to expect his/her work to have quality." Walter Benjamin, "The Author as Producer" *Reflections* (1978).

ROLLING COULTER (II, IV-Religious), Messiah College, Grantham, PA 17027, phone 717-766-2511 (ext 7026), founded 1988, editor William Jolliff, appears twice a year. **"I look for poetry that is not necessarily religious but which shows some evidence of being informed by a religious world-view. I'm open to most forms, but work in traditional forms must be especially good to be printable. I don't want to see greeting card, calendar, or bulletin cover stuff."** They have recently published poetry by H. Arnett, Raeburn Miller, and Gene Doty. As a sample the editor selected these lines from "Leaving the Garden" by Bill Wood:

> *We do not know the full girth of expulsion.*
> *We know only command was disobeyed.*
> *What secrets could the crown vetch, dogwood,*
> *shaggy groundhog tell to shore up storms*
> *of why, and why, and why, and what . . .*

The Rolling Coulter is digest-sized, 40-60 pp., laser printed with 2-color cover. Their press run is 250 with 40 subscriptions. "We distribute to libraries at religious colleges, with or without charge." Subscription: $5/2 issues. **Sample: $2 postpaid. Pays 1 copy. Reports in 4-6 weeks.** Editor comments on rejections on request. "All work is read by the editor and at least one assistant. Read more poetry. There's a real difference between what students often read in their contemporary poetry anthologies and what is being published by the little magazines. A tremendous breadth is presented by the little magazines, but you need to read widely to find the magazines right for your work. If I think a little editorial help will make something publishable, I don't mind making suggestions (when time allows). Religious poetry currently has a rotten reputation; I want to help change that."

THE ROMANTIST (IV-Fantasy, Horror, Science Fiction), Saracinesca House, 3610 Meadowbrook Ave., Nashville, TN 37205, phone 615-226-1890, poetry editor Steve Eng, founded 1977, is a "literary magazine of non-fiction articles on fantasy, horror, and romantic literature, using **lyrical poetry — prefer fantasy and horror content. No homespun, gushy, trite verse with forced rhyme.**" They have published poetry by Donald Sidney-Fryer, Joey Froelich, Stephanie Stearns, and Richard L. Tierney. As a sample the editor selected these lines by John Gawsworth:

> *The worthy are not always just*
> *Nor are the noble always brave,*
> *And yet all mingle in the dust*
> *Of the one grave.*

The annual is magazine-sized, press run 300 numbered copies for 150 subscriptions of which 50 are libraries. **Sample: $10 postpaid. Contributors may purchase a copy for 50% of its price. They receive tear sheets. Submit no more than 3 poems at a time, double-spaced. Reports in 4 weeks. Editor sometimes comments on rejections.** He says, "Too much contemporary poetry is easy to write and hard to read. We resist the depressed, carefully jaded tone so often fashionable. We prefer lyric verse that reflects some knowledge of traditions of poetry, though we do not require the slavish adherence to any school."

‡ROOM MAGAZINE; ROOM PRESS (II), 29 Lynton Pl., White Plains, NY 10606-2818, phone 914-997-2798, founded 1985, editor John Perlman. *Room* appears twice a year, **"open to skillful innovation; no re-hash."** They have recently published poetry by Ray Di Palma, Craig Watson, Larry Eigner, and Karl Young. There are usually 2 poets in each issue. I have not seen an issue, but the editor describes it as varying in format, photocopied. **He usually solicits the material he uses.** Press run 150. **Pays copies. Reports "immediately." Query in regard to chapbook or book publication by Room Press. Pays copies.**

THE ROUND TABLE: A JOURNAL OF POETRY AND FICTION (II), 375 Oakdale Dr., Rochester, NY 14618, founded 1984, poetry editors Alan Lupack and Barbara Lupack. "We publish a journal of poetry and fiction. Currently, 1 issue a year. **Few restrictions on poetry — except high quality. We like forms if finely crafted. Very long poems must be exceptional.**" They have recently published poetry by Kathleene West, John Tagliabue, Wendy Mnookin, and Paul Scott. As a sample I chose the opening lines of "Homestead in Union" by David Memmot:

> *We live in a house we did not build*
> *and cannot revise overnight*
> *generations of unfinished dreams.*
> *These walls recall many weavers . . .*

The Round Table is digest-sized, 64 pp., perfect-bound, professionally printed (offset) with matte card cover. Circulation 125, for 75 subscriptions of which 3 are libraries. Subscription: $7.50. **Sample: $4 postpaid. "We like to see about 5 poems (but we read whatever is submitted but only from October 1-June 30)." Cover letter. Simultaneous submissions OK.** "But we expect to be **notified if a poem submitted to us is accepted elsewhere." Quality of poetry, not format, is most important thing. We try to report in 1 month, but — especially for poems under serious consideration — it may take longer. Pays copies.** In 1990 they published an issue of general poetry and fiction. They will alternate Arhturian and general issues.

ROWAN TREE PRESS (II), 124 Chestnut St., Boston, MA 02108, phone 617-523-7627, founded 1980, editors Nadya Aisenberg and Cornelia Veenendaal, a small general trade press publishing poetry, poetics, mysteries, fiction, anthologies and memoirs in flat-spined paperbacks. Recent authors include Berton Roueche, Robert Bly, Edwin Muir, and Robert Francis. **Reply to query within a month, to submission (if invited) in 3 months. Pays on royalty contract plus 10 copies. Write for brochure to order samples. Editor sometimes comments on rejections.** From the publisher's statement: "Low overhead, modest profit ambitions, and a firm desire to have our own mark on our books."

Use the General Index to find the page number of a specific publication or publisher.

THE RUGGING ROOM; RUGGING ROOM BULLETIN (IV-Themes), 10 Sawmill Dr., Westford, MA 01886, founded as a press in 1983, periodical in 1987, poetry editor Jeanne H. Fallier, publisher of "how-to books **related to traditional rug hooking and related subjects of interest to people in fibre crafts."** Verses of a philosophical theme, or concerning nature are acceptable if they refer to hand works, wool or fibers, the therapeutic value of hand-made fiber crafts, etc. She accepts "very short poems related to fibre arts (especially hooking) crafts—not more than ½ page." The *Rugging Room Bulletin*, is a newsletter, 8-16 pp., 8½ × 11" appearing 4 times a year printed on white stock, with b/w illustrations, ads and graphics. Circulation 300 but wide-spread, coast to coast. Subscription: $8. **Sample: $2.50 postpaid. Pays 3 copies plus 1 year subscription. Contributors are expected to buy 1 copy. Simultaneous submissions OK. Reports within about 2 weeks.**

‡THE RUNAWAY SPOON PRESS (IV-Form), Box 3621, Port Charlotte, FL 33949, phone 813-629-8045, founded 1987, editor Bob Grumman, is a "photocopy publisher of chapbooks of otherstream poetry & vizlation." He wants **"visual poetry, textual poetry mixed with visual images, verbo-visual collages, burning poodle poetry—or surprise me. No work in which politics is more important then esthetics."** *RASP* has recently published poetry by Karl Kempton, jwcurry, and Harry Polkinhorn. As a sample the editor selected this poem by G. Huth:

> ghohshthshs

The editor explains, "It's what I call an alphaconceptual poem—because its letters are *conceptually* important." The little books I have seen are about 4 × 5½", printed on good stock with matte card covers. He prints about 10 a year averaging 48 pp. **"Query is a good idea but not necessary. Simultaneous submissions and previously published poems OK. Pays 25% of first edition of 100. Sample books available for $3 apiece. Editor comments on submissions "always."** He advises, "Spread yourself outside your own work with critiques of others."

RURAL HERITAGE (I, IV-Rural), Box 516, Albia, IA 52531, phone 515-932-5084, founded 1975, editor Florence Holle and publisher D.H. Holle, **uses poetry related to rural living, Americana, is open as to length and form.** As a sample the editor selected these lines from "To Green Lea Trojan" by Brooks H. Rohde:

> Green Lea Trojan, you're for sale
> With ribbons in your mane and tail.
> Are you nervous thus not knowing
> Just to whom or where you're going?

RH is magazine-sized, quarterly, using b/w photos, graphics and ads, circulation 10,000 to 9,500 subscribers. Subscription: $12. Per issue: $3.50. **Sample: $4.50 postpaid. Guidelines available for SASE. Pays on publication 3-15¢ a word and 1 copy. Reports ASAP, 4-6 months between acceptance and publication.** Florence Holle says "submission must in some way be connected to celebrating our rich American rural heritage."

SACHEM PRESS (II, IV-Translations, bilingual), P.O. Box 9, Old Chatham, NY 12136, phone 518-794-8327, founded 1980, editor Louis Hammer, a small-press publisher of poetry and fiction, both hardcover and flat-spined paperbacks. **No new submissions, only statements of projects, until January 1991.** The editor wants to see "strong compelling, even visionary work, English-language or translations." He has recently published poetry by Cesar Vallejo, Yannis Ritsos, 24 leading poets of Spain, Miltos Sahtouris, and himself. As a sample, he selected the following lines from a poem by Felix Grande in the anthology, **Recent Poets of Spain**, translated by Louis Hammer and Sara Schyfter:

> I offend the way the cypresses offend. I'm
> the depressor. I'm the one who contaminates
> with his kisses a vomit of dark silences,
> a bleeding of shadows. I offend, love, I offend.

I have 5 sample publications by Sachem Press, all handsome flat-spined paperbacks with glossy two- or four-color covers; all are translations (from Greek or Spanish) except one by Louis Hammer. The small paperbacks average 120 pp. and the anthology of Spanish poetry contains 340 pp. Each poem is printed in both Spanish and English, and there are biographical notes about the authors. The small books cost $6.95 and the anthology $11.95. **Royalties are 10% maximum, after expenses are recovered, plus 50 author's copies.** Book catalog is free "when available," and poets can purchase books from Sachem "by writing to us, 33⅓% discount."

ST. ANDREW PRESS (IV-Religious), Box 329, Big Island, VA 24526, phone 804-299-5956, founded 1986, co-director Ray Buchanan, is a "small-press publisher of religious material (worship materials, lyrics and music, etc.), **specializing in meditations, lifestyle, church renewal, spirituality, hunger, peace and justice issues."** Any form or style up to 64 lines on subjects listed. "No profanity for shock value only; no sickeningly sweet idealism." As a sample the editor selected these lines from "Mary's Song" by Katherine Meyer which appeared in their newsletter:

> *I follow*
> *the seam of light*
> *stitched*
> *by my mothers,*
> *Eve's grief*
> *flows unbroken*
> *into Elizabeth's joy.*

They say they will publish 3 chapbooks and flat-spined paperbacks, averaging 64 pp., per year. **Submit 6 samples, bio, other publications. Simultaneous submissions, photocopies, dot-matrix, previously published poems OK. Reports in 2-4 weeks. Payment usually $10 minimum, averages more.** They will consider subsidy publishing. The editor says, "We are looking forward to doing more with poetry in the next couple of years. The amount we do will be largely determined by quality of submissions we receive."

SAINT ANDREWS REVIEW; SAINT ANDREWS PRESS (II), St. Andrews College, Laurinburg, NC 28352, founded 1970. The *Review* is a literary biannual, 6 × 9″, 120 pp., poetry editor E. Waverly Land, circulation 500-700, which **uses quality poetry. Sample: $7. Payment in copies.** Recently published poets in *St. Andrews Review* include Fred Chappell, Robert Morgan, James Laughlin, and A.R. Ammons. "We are dedicated to providing a vehicle for literature (poetry, fiction) of the highest quality from poets from all over the US and the world. We are interested in writers of established reputation and in new writers whose works show talent." **Send SASE with submissions; include name and address on every page submitted; no simultaneous submissions.** Obtain samples by writing Editor, St. Andrews Review.

ST. ANTHONY MESSENGER (IV-Religious), 1615 Republic St., Cincinnati, OH 45210, is a monthly magazine, circulation 380,000, 56 pp., for Catholic families, mostly with children in grade school, high school or college. In some issues, they have a **poetry page which uses poems appropriate for their readership. Their poetry needs are very limited but poetry submissions are always welcomed.** In the issue I examined there were 2 poems of 11 and 30 lines each. As a sample I selected "Mulching" by Rosemarie Canak Deisinger:

> *It was a dreary Autumn, not much color.*
> *The days hung limply, dull and brown, then fell . . .*
> *I think it was because life was so even*
>
> *It takes a sharp, cold threat withstood to color days —*
> *A grief averted, illness cured, marriage saved —*
> *To bring out saffron laughter, scarlet joy.*

Pays $2 a line on acceptance. Send SASE for guidelines and free sample.

ST. JOSEPH MESSENGER AND ADVOCATE OF THE BLIND (I, IV-Religious), 541 Pavonia Ave., P.O. Box 288, Jersey City, NJ 07303, phone 201-798-4141, founded 1898, poetry editor Sister Ursula Maphet, C.S.J.P., is a 30 pp. quarterly (16 pp., 8 × 11″), circulation 27,000, which wants "**brief but thought-filled poetry; do not want lengthy and issue-filled.**" Most of the poets they have used are previously unpublished. The editor selected a sample by Priscilla Snell:

> *While lo from heaven's all healing*
> *hands,*
> *gentle and soft and slow,*
> *falls cool upon earth's fevered brow*
> *God's sacrament of snow.*

There are about 2 pp. of poetry in each issue. Subscription: $5. They receive 400-500 submissions per year, use 50. **Send SASE for guidelines and free sample. Reports within 2 weeks. Pays $5-20 per poem. Editor sometimes comments on rejections.**

ST. LUKE'S PRESS; IRIS PRESS (V), Wimmer Trade Publishing Group, 4210 B.F. Goodrich Blvd., Memphis, TN 38118, phone 901-362-8900, executive editor Phyllis Tickle, founded 1975, publishes an occasional volume of poetry **by invitation only, on standard royalty contracts.** As a sample I selected the first stanza of "Snakes" by David Spicer:

> *They coiled like thick spaghetti,*
> *swallowed tails and rolled down the road*
> *barrel hoops with eyes, large circles*
> *of darkness spending behind my grandfather.*

That's from **Everybody Has a Story,** published in 1987 in a digest-sized 96 pp. flat-spined paperback, elegantly printed on quality stock with glossy b/w cover and full-cover slip jacket, $8.95.

SALMAGUNDI (III), Skidmore College, Saratoga Springs, NY 12866, founded 1965, edited by Peggy Boyers and Robert Boyers, has long been **one of the most distinguished quarterlies** of the sciences and humanities, publishing poets such as Robert Penn Warren, Louise Gluck, John Peck, Howard Nemerov and W. D. Snodgrass. These lines, for instance, are from "During Holy Week" by Seamus Heaney:

> *Dippings. Towellings. The water breathed on.*
> *The water mixed with chrism and with oil.*
> *Cruet tinkle. Formal incensation*
> *And the psalmist's outcry taken up with pride:*
> *Day and night my tears have been my bread.*

Each issue is handsomely printed, a thick, flat-spined book, priced at $5-10 (**sample: $4 postpaid.**). Subscriptions are $15 a year, $18 for two years. The magazine has a paid circulation of 5,400 with 3,800 subscriptions of which about 900 are libraries. **They use about 10-50 pages of poetry in each issue, receive 1,200 submissions per year and use about 20, have a year to 30 month backlog, and report in three months. Payment in copies only, no need to query, photocopies OK, with permission for sets of more than 5.**

SALMON PUBLISHING; THE SALMON INTERNATIONAL LITERARY MAGAZINE, (II, IV-Translations), Auburn, Upper Fairhill, Galway, Ireland, phone 62587, magazine founded 1981, Salmon Publishing in 1985, director/editor Jessie Lendennie, who says, **"It is hard to describe what good poetry is. I am open-minded as to style, subject matter, length, but prefer innovative work, and poetry of some social relevance. Translations from all languages welcome, and I am interested in seeing more contributions from women."** She doesn't like **"overtly sentimental, or doggerel verse, sloppily put-together work, obscure work."** She has recently published poetry by John Millett, Eithne Strong, Fritz Hamilton, Kathryn Machan, Knute Skinner, Nuala Archer, Beth Joselow, and James Liddy. As a sample she selected these lines from "Manchild" by Michael Heffernan:

> *. . . Whatever they said*
> *was there I took for granted, what was not*
> *was not, and what a man could do I did*
> *about the things I had some say about.*
> *Anything much else was in the mind of God,*
> *even the daybreak, what there was of it.*

The Salmon appears 3 times a year (autumn, spring, summer), 96 pp., flat-spined, 6 × 8½″, professionally printed on quality stock with two-color glossy card cover with b/w art. Its aim is "to present a quality journal with an international voice which also speaks intimately of Ireland." Jessie Lendennie says she accepts about 160 of 2,000 poems received. Press run is 900 for 150 subscriptions of which 20 are libraries, the rest of the copies going to shelf sales. Subscription: £6 (or $18 air mail, $10 surface for the U.S., including postage). **Sample: £2 (or $5) postpaid. Pays 1 copy. (Payment to contributors depends on Arts Council funding.) Submit no more than 5 at a time. No simultaneous submissions or poems previously published in Ireland. Reports in 6-12 weeks. Backlog. Salmon Publishing publishes 7-8 flat-spined collections of poetry per year. For book publication, query with 20 sample poems, bio and publishing credits. Reports on queries in 6 weeks. Pays 10% royalties. Editor sometimes comments on rejections.** She says, "Beginners must be open to the whole world of poetry, not just their little corner of it. That is, read contemporary poetry, think about what you're writing, be open to change."

SALT LICK; SALT LICK PRESS; SALT LICK SAMPLERS; LUCKY HEART BOOKS (II), 1804 E. 38½ St., Austin, TX 78722, founded 1969, poetry editor James Haining, publishes "new literature and graphic arts in their various forms." They have published poetry by Robert Creeley, Martha King, Susan Firer, Paul Shuttleworth, Wm. Hart, Robert Slater and Sheila Murphy. As a sample I selected this poem, "Stride Time" by the editor, James Haining:

> *her walking into the*
> *room from the rain*
> *what you would*
> *in the length say*
> *I hear so time*
> *for time*

The magazine-sized journal, 48 pp., saddle-stapled, matte cover, experimental graphics throughout, appears irregularly, print run of 1,500. They receive 400-600 poems per year, use 1-2%. **Sample: $5 postpaid. Reports in 1-6 weeks. Pays copies. To submit for book publication under the Lucky Heart Books imprint, send 20 samples, cover letter "open." Simultaneous submissions, photocopies, dot-matrix OK. Pays copies.**

SALTHOUSE (V), % English Dept., UW., Whitewater, 800 W. Main, Whitewater, WI 53190-1790, founded 1975, is a journal published every 3 years with a "very tailored perspective," according to its editor, DeWitt Clinton. He calls it **"A Journal of Geopoetics," and wants free verse which is "histori-cally, geographically, or anthropologically oriented."** Several poets he has published are Richard Shelton, Sybil Woods-Smith, Jeanne Larsen, Lynn Lifshin, Maggie Jaffe, Judith Roche, Jesse Glass, Jr., and Lynn Shoemaker. He selected these lines by Kirk Lumpkin as illustration :

> . . . *in the manzanita thicket,*
> *The sky is a silent blue shout,*
> *And from the heart of the hill*
> *comes a hymn.*

The magazine is 100 + pp., flat-spined, photocopied from typescript, with matte card cover, with a print run of about 300, circulation of 200, with 80 subscriptions of which 15 are libraries. **Sample: $6 postpaid.** He says that each issue uses 90 pages of material including poetry, and that he gets about 100 submissions per year, of which he uses less than one-tenth. **Reports in 3-5 months, no pay.** Instruction to writers: **"Please purchase a copy ($6) before submitting a manuscript."** Did not read MSS in 1990. **"Will announce reading period, and theme, in *Poets and Writers*."** Catalog available on request.

SAMISDAT (II), P.O. Box 129, Richford, VT 05476, founded 1973, is **one of the liveliest, least expensive publishing operations in the country,** edited by Merritt Clifton, author of the "Help!" column in *Small Press Review* and one of the most knowledgeable people I know about small presses and their history. He puts out a **semiannual magazine which is backlogged through 1990.** You can get a **sample copy of the magazine for $4.** For $20 you get the next 250 pages of magazines and chapbooks. Chapbooks done by special arrangement only. He says, "We want to see **direct, informed, memorable conscientious statement. We do not use patterned verse of any kind, shallow truisms, doggerel, or self-conscious artifice**," and he provides these lines as a sample of what he likes from a poem by Robert Underwood:

> *The first dollar,*
> *framed,*
> *hung like a crucifix.*

Be sure to **study a sample issue. He pays 2 complimentary copies; subscribers also receive a 1-issue subscription extension for each appearance.** Merritt Clifton adds, "We actively seek reprints, reviews, (etcetra) for our contributors in other publications—most items first published here do eventually reach a wider audience." **Don't be surprised by blunt or even indecent language on rejections**. Merritt Clifton speaks his mind plainly. But, as he says, "We are not really eager to take on a whole lot of new people. We're always open to people of **compatible outlook and literary competence,** but they're a rare breed. **I consider photocopied submissions obscenely rude.** Poets who expect individual consideration should extend the same." **Samisdat** is composed with a laser printer. Merritt Clifton's advice for would-be contributors is, "Remember that the object is to substantially contribute to a better world by informing, inspiring, questioning; the object of great poets is not merely getting published or getting famous."

SAN DIEGO POET'S PRESS; LA JOLLA POETS' PRESS (II), Box 8638, La Jolla, CA 92038, founded 1981, publisher Kathleen Iddings. **Query first with 6-10 pp. of your work and bio.** They have published poetry anthologies including such poets as Galway Kinnell, Allen Ginsberg, Robert Pinsky, Carolyn Kizer, Carolyn Forché, Tess Gallagher, Charles Bukowski, Diane O'Hehir, and John Balaban. As a sample of the type of poetry she's published, Kathleen Iddings selected these lines from "Yarrow Field" by Regina McBride, winner of the 1990 "American Book Series":

> *In our old yard the trees were temperate*
> *and sexual*
> *taller than parents*
> *with their eyes too far up.*
> *Their ancestors cut down,*
> *were made into our doorways and bedboards.*
> *These that stood were the sons and daughters*
> *of the carved frames and pedestals,*
> *the sons and daughters of our house.*

"One does not have to be a widely published poet, but this press is not for beginners." **Simultaneous submissions OK.** Watch *Poets and Writers* and *The Small Press Review* for announcements regarding anthology submissions or the "American Book Series," in which the winning poet receives $500 and the publishing of his/her *first* book of poetry. **Do not send manuscripts without seeing announcements.** LaJolla Poets' Press is another imprint for which Kathleen Iddings **prefers poets whose work has been published and is already accepted but "will not overlook excellence in an unpublished poet. Query with SASE, 6 of your best poems from your MS, and publishing bio."**

SAN FERNANDO POETRY JOURNAL; KENT PUBLICATIONS. INC.; CERULEAN PRESS (MINI AN-THOLOGY SERIES), (I, IV-Social issues, anthologies), 18301 Halsted St., Northridge, CA 91325, founded 1978, poetry editors Richard Cloke, Shirley Rodecker and Lori Smith (and, for the Mini Anthology Series, Blair H. Allen, 9651 Estacia Court, Cucamonga, CA 91730). The *San Fernando Poetry Journal* uses poetry of social protest. According to Richard Cloke, "Poetry, for us, should be *didactic* in the Brechtian sense. It must say something, must inform, in the tenor of our time. We follow Hart Crane's definition of poetry as architectural in essence, building upon the past but incorporating the newest of this age also, including science, machinery, sub-atomic and cosmic physical phenomena as well as the social convulsions wrenching the very roots of our present world." **Send SASE for guidelines which explain this more fully.** For example, I quote this passage from one of them for its general usefulness for poets: "In some, the end-line rhyming is too insistent, seeming *forced;* in others the words are not vibrant enough to give the content an arresting framework. Others do not have any beat (cadence) at all and some are simply not well thought out—often like first drafts, or seem like prose statements. Please try reworking again to get some energy in your statement. If your poetry is to succeed in impelling the reader to act, it must electrify, or at least command interest and attention." **They welcome new and unpublished poets.** As a sample the editor chose these lines by Jack Bernier:

> At the minimum wage scale
> I might get deeper in debt.
> What the hell, Henry, it beats
> collecting cans and taking them
> to a recycle machine that pays
> a penny which isn't worth a penny.

The flat-spined quarterly, photocopied from typescript, uses 100 pages of poetry in each issue, circulation 400, 350 subscriptions of which 45 are libraries. They use about 300 of the 1,000 submissions (the editor rightly prefers to call them "contributions") each year. **Sample: $2.50 postpaid. No specifications for MS form. Simultaneous submissions OK. Reports in 1 week, pays in copies.** The press, under its various imprints, also publishes a few collections by individuals. **Query with 5-6 pp. of samples. For the Mini Anthology Series, query Blair Allen at the address above.**

SAN JOSE STUDIES; CASEY MEMORIAL AWARD (II), San Jose State University, San Jose, CA 95192, phone 408-924-4476, founded 1975, poetry editor O. C. Williams. This "journal of general and scholarly interest, featuring critical, creative and informative writing in the arts, business, humanities, science and social sciences" uses poetry of "**excellent quality—no kinds excluded. Tend to like poems with something to say, however indirectly it may be communicated. Usually publish 7-12 pp. of verse in each issue. We like to publish several poems by one poet—better exposure for the poet, more interest for the reader.**" They have recently published poetry by David Citino, James Laughlin, William Burns and Walter McDonald. As a sample the editor chose these lines from "Sisyphus" by William Burns:

> Pride becomes me. My ache, to bone, will last
> Forever. But now it serves me, heavy with worth.
> Prevailing, I banish hell. I crave more weight.

SJS appears thrice yearly in a 6x9" flat-spined, 100+ pp. format, professionally printed, matte card cover, using b/w photos, circulation 450, 350 subscriptions of which 70-75 are libraries. Subscription: $12; per copy: $5. They receive about 120 submissions per year, use 8-10 authors, have a 1 year backlog. **Sample: $4 postpaid. No simultaneous submissions. Reports in 4-6 weeks. Pays 2 copies.** Annual award of a year's subscription for best poetry printed that year and a Casey Memorial Award of $100 for the best contribution in prose or poetry. O. C. Williams comments, "Poetry is both an art and a craft; we are not interested in submissions unless the writer has mastered the craft and is actually practicing the art."

SANDSCRIPT, CAPE COD WRITERS INC.; PROXADE DAVIS PRIZE (II), P.O. Box 333, Cummaquid, MA 02637, FAX: 508-771-1278, founded 1977, poetry editor Jean Lunn, appears twice a year. "**Any kind of poetry as long as it's good of its kind. (By poetry I do not mean greeting-card verse.) Subject matter of poems we have published ranges from the mythic to the personal; we have published poems in free verse (the bulk of our poetry), concrete poems, and strict forms including sonnet, sestina, canzone, villanelle, haiku, terza rima, ghazal, haibun, cinquain, etc. Send no poems that aren't finished.**" They have recently published poetry by Denise Levertov, Jared Carter, Ruth Whitman, Martin Robbins, Lyn Lifshin, Diana Der Hovanessian, Wendy Wilder Larsen, Simon Perchik, and David McCord. As a sample, the editor chose the first five lines of "The Python" by Bill Kemmett:

> I have not been fed for three weeks.
> Through a glass distance
>   I watch a baby, soft
>   flowing

in her silk altarpiece.
Sandscript is digest-sized, 46 pp., saddle-stapled, professionally printed with matte card cover. Their press run is 300-500 for about 50 subscriptions, 10% of which are libraries. 50% are sold at newsstands or bookstores. Subscription: $5 for 2 issues. **Sample: $2.50 postpaid. Guidelines are printed in each issue. Pays 2 copies. "No colored paper. Please do not send poems in large manila envelopes. They mess up our files.** When an issue has enough poems to warrant it, we give the Proxade Davis Prize of $25 for the best poem in an issue. The prize is usually, but not always, judged by a distinguished poet from outside the magazine." The editor says, "'Make it good and keep it clean' (E.B. White's advice about prose). Revise, revise, revise. Listen, listen, listen. Read. Go to workshops. Strict forms are coming back, thank God. Master them."

‡SANSKRIT (I), Cone Center, UNCC, Charlotte, NC 28223, phone 704-547-2326, founded 1965, editor Steven Sherril, is a literary-annual using **poetry "no restrictions as to form or genre, but we do look for maturity and sincerity in submissions. Nothing trite or sentimental. And no haiku."** They have recently published poetry by Anthony Abbott, Scott Owens and Christy Beatty. As a sample the editor selected these lines by Phyllis Gussler:

> *December broke your shins and blew*
> *pneumonia deep into your lungs.*
> *I drowned you in sour jokes until,*
> *like jetsam, your skeleton surfaced.*

Their purpose is "to encourage and promote beginning and established artists and writers." It is $9 \times 12''$, 60-65 pp. flat-spined, printed on quality matte paper with heavy matte card cover. "We received about 200 submissions in 1989 and accepted 20." Press run: 3,500 for about 100 subscriptions of which 2 are libraries. **Sample, postpaid $5.50. Pays 1 copy. Submit no more than 5 poems. Simultaneous submissions OK. Reports in 6-8 weeks. Editor comments on submissions "infrequently."**

SANTA MONICA REVIEW (V), 1900 Pico Blvd., Santa Monica, CA 90405, founded 1988, poetry editor Jim Krusoe, appears twice a year. **They are temporarily overstocked.**

‡SANTA SUSANA PRESS (V), CSU Libraries, 18111 Nordhoff St., Northridge, CA 91330, phone 818-885-2271, founded 1973, editor Norman Tanis, a small-press publisher of limited edition fine print books, history, literature and art, some poetry, all hardcover editions. **They do not accept freelance submissions of poetry. Poets should query first, and queries will be answered in 2 weeks. Honorariums paid depend on grant money.** The press has recently published books by George Elliott, Ward Ritchie, and Ray Bradbury, from whose "The Last Good Kiss" the editor selected the following lines as a sample:

> *What's past is past*
> *And the memory of mouths*
> *In a dry season, soon or late,*
> *Makes salivate the mind*

Book catalog is free on request; prices are high. For instance, **Reaching: Poems by George P. Elliott**, illustrated, is published in an edition of 350 numbered copies at $35 and 26 lettered copies at $60.

SATURDAY EVENING POST (IV-Humor), 1100 Waterway Blvd., Indianapolis, IN 46202, phone 317-636-8881, founded 1728 as the *Pennsylvania Gazette*, since 1821 as *The Saturday Evening Post*, Post Scripts editor Chuck Mason. *SEP* is a general interest, mass circulation monthly with emphasis on preventive medicine, using **"humorous light verse only. No more than 300 words per poem. Stay away from four-letter words and sexually graphic subject matter. No experimental verse (haikus, etc.) Morally, the *Post*** is an anachronism of the early 50s; most of its readers are elderly. Other than that, anything goes, as long as it's in good taste." As a sample the editor selected these lines (poet unidentified):

> *I find the witness box*
> *Is far too demanding.*
> *I can't stand lying.*
> *And I can't lie standing.*

Payment is $15/all rights. "Work for hire."

SATURDAY PRESS, INC.; EILEEN W. BARNES AWARD SERIES; INVITED POETS SERIES (II, IV-Women), Box 884, Upper Montclair, NJ 07043, phone 201-256-5053, founded 1975, poetry editor Charlotte Mandel with guest editors for contest which have included Maxine Kumin, Colette Inez, Sandra M. Gilbert, Maxine Silverman and Rachel Hadas. "Saturday Press, Inc., is a nonprofit literary organization. The Press has a **special—though not exclusive—commitment to women's poetry, and by**

sponsoring the Eileen W. Barnes Award Competition for first books by women over 40 seeks to offer opportunity for new poets who have delayed their writing careers. The MS is selected by means of open competition or, in alternate years, by editorial board decision. Query for current information. Not an annual event, the contest is widely posted when announced. The Invited Poets Series offers publication to established or less-known poets. We want **authoritative craft, strong, fresh imagery, sense of imagination and a good ear for syntax, sounds and rhythms. Language should lead the reader to experience a sense of discovery. Any form, content or style, but do not want polemic, jingles or conventional inspiration."** They have published books of poetry by Colette Inez, Janice Thaddeus, Jean Hollander, Anne Carpenter, Anneliese Wagner, Charlotte Mandel and Geraldine C. Little. As a sample the editor chose these lines from Geraldine C. Little's "Looking at a Pompiian Lady in an Exhibit":

> Everywhere, the spill
> of summer, air cracked
> by only birdbells, sails
> moving like old dances.

Do not send book MS without query. Enclose 1-3 samples and minimum summary of publications. Replies to queries in 2 weeks. If invited, book MS may be photocopied; simultaneous submission OK. No dot-matrix. "Prefer no binder, simple folder or paper clip." Pays 25-50 copies and possible honorarium ("depends on grants"). Send SASE for catalog to buy samples.

‡SCARP (II), School of Creative Arts, University of Wollongong, Box 1144, Wollongong, NSW, Australia 2500, phone 042-270985, founded 1982, editor Ron Pretty "is a small press publisher of poetry, prose fiction and new art. *Scarp* also contains articles and reviews. Both new and established writers are encouraged to contribute." It appears twice a year. **"Not restricted by genre or form or subject-matter or style or purpose, however we would prefer not to publish anything of an epic length."** They have published poetry by David P. Reiter, John Millet, Manfred Jurgenson and Debbie Westbury. As a sample the editor selected these lines by Steven Herrick:

> St. Mark's Bookstore, New York
> Hemingway's in the corner
> drinking his way through France
> & shooting up the bad guys in Spain

Scarp is 64-80 pp.digest-sized, flat-spined, with glossy card cover, b/w graphics, some (mainly local) ads. "*Scarp 15* received about 500 poems from 90 submitters. We published 15 poems from these." Press run: 1,000 for approximately 200 subscriptions of which 30 are libraries. Few shelf sales. Subscription: $20/4 issues. **Sample, postpaid: $5. Send SASE for guidelines. Pays $15 (Aust.) plus 1 copy. Subscription encouraged but not required. No more than 5 poems per submission. Poems previously unpublished in Australia OK. Submit during April and September.** Editor comments on submissions "rarely." He says, "Revise all poetry thoroughly. Well-presented work and a professional approach is essential for all poets who want to be taken seriously."

SCAVENGER'S NEWSLETTER; KILLER FROG CONTEST (IV-Science fiction/fantasy/horror), 519 Ellinwood, Osage City, KS 66523-1329, may seem an odd place to publish poems, but its editor, Janet Fox, uses 3-4 every month. The *Newsletter* is a **32-page booklet packed with news about science fiction and horror publications**, in tiny type (printed at an instaprint shop). **Janet prefers sf/fantasy/horror poetry, and will read anything that is off-beat or bizarre. Writing-oriented poetry is occasionally accepted but avoid "Oh poor pitiful me" themes. Poetry is used as filler so it must be 10 lines or under.** Recently published poets include: steve sneyd, Keith Allen Daniels, Walt Phillips and Marlys Bradley Huffman. As a sample she selected a short sample poem "One Small Step" by Ann K. Schwader:

> lunar dust footprint
>
> green wind breathes
> astronaut ashes.

Janet Fox says, "My interpretation of genre poetry isn't narrow; I've printed all sorts of great, strange stuff, but I don't care for light verse or anything that could be construed as 'cute'. She has around 760 subscribers. Subscription: $10/year. **Sample copy plus guidelines for $1.50, guidelines alone for SASE. Response: 1 month or less. "I like poems with sharp images and careful craftsmanship."At last report was "accepting about 1 out of 10 poems submitted."** You can use photocopy, dot-matrix, multiple submissions, simultaneous submissions (if informed) — even reprints if credit is given. No need to query. Payment: $2 on acceptance plus one copy. "I hold an annual 'Killer Frog Contest' for horror so bad or outrageous it becomes funny. There is a category for horror poetry. Has been opening April 1, closing July 1 of each year. Prizes $20 each in four categories: poetry, art, short stories and short short stories, plus the 'coveted' Froggie statuette." Entry free: $2 for each initial entry, $1 for additional entries. Every entrant receives a copy of the "Frog" anthology. The '89 anthology was **Rosemary's Tadpole** which is available for $2 postpaid.

SCIENCE FICTION POETRY ASSOCIATION; STARLINE; THE RHYSLING ANTHOLOGY (IV-Science fiction, anthology), 2012 Pyle Rd., Schenectady, NY 12303, for membership information. **For submissions: Robert Frazier, P.O. Box 1370, Nantucket, MA 02554. Founded 1978. The Association puts out two publications which use poetry: StarLine, a bimonthly magazine, and an annual, *The Rhysling Anthology*.** The magazine is the newsletter of the Association; the anthology is a yearly collection of final nominations from the membership "for the best SF/Fantasy long and short poetry of the preceding year." The Association also publishes a cassette tape anthology and a Science Fiction Poetry Handbook. The magazine has published poetry by Bruce Bosont, Thomas Easton, Andrew Joron, Steve Rasnic Tem, Nancy Springer, Joe Haldeman, and Diane Ackermann. Here are some sample lines from "Dactyl" by W. Gregory Stewart:

> *a wreck of pterodactyl*
> *lay across the yard this morning*
>
> *(I didn't know about it*
> *until Fred Mulvaney*
> *from across the street*
> *called up complaining.)*

They have 200 subscribers (1 library) paying $8 for the 6 issues per year (**sample: $1.50 postpaid**). The editor says he gets two or three hundred submissions per year and uses about 80 — mostly short (under 50 lines). He reports in a month, likes 2-3 poems per submission, typed, photocopy OK, dot-matrix "difficult but not refused," no simultaneous submissions, no queries, pays $1 for first 10 lines, 5¢/line thereafter. The digest-sized magazines and anthologies are saddle-stapled, inexpensively printed, with numerous illustrations and decorations. (You can order the anthology for $2.50.) They are "open to all forms — free verse, traditional forms, light verse — so long as your poetry shows skilled use of the language and makes a good use of science fiction, science, fantasy, or speculative motifs."

SCORE MAGAZINE; SCORE CHAPBOOKS AND BOOKLETS (IV-Form), 491 Mandana Blvd., #3, Oakland, CA 94610, poetry editors Craig Hill, Laurie Schneider, and Bill DiMichele, is a "small-press publisher of **visual poetry** in the magazine *Score*, booklets, postcards and broadsides. They want "**Poetry which melds language and the visual arts such as concrete poetry; experimental use of language, words and letters — forms. The appearance of the poem should have as much to say as the text. Poems on any subject; conceptual poetry; poems which use experimental, non-traditional methods to communicate their meanings.**" They don't want "traditional verse of any kind — be it free verse or rhymed." They have published poetry by Stephen-Paul Martin, Bruce Andrews, Karl Kempton, Kathy Ernst, and Bern Porter. They say that it is impossible to quote a sample because "some of our poems consist of only a single word — or in some cases no recognizable words." I strongly advise looking at a sample copy before submitting if you don't know what visual poetry is. *Score* is 18-30 pp., magazine-sized, offset, saddle-stapled, using b/w graphics, 2-color matte card cover, appearing 1 time a year in a press run of 200 for 25 subscriptions (6 of them libraries) and about 40 shelf sales. **Sample: $5 postpaid. Send SASE for guidelines. Pays 2 copies. Photocopies OK "as long as strong black." No simultaneous submissions. Previously published poems OK "if noted." For chapbook consideration send entire MS. No simultaneous submissions. Pay 8-16 copies of the chapbook. Almost always comments on rejections.** They subsidy publish "if author requests it."

SCRIVENER (II), 853 Sherbrooke St. W., Montreal, Quebec, Canada H3A 2T6, founded 1980, produced by students at McGill University, is a literary annual, magazine-sized, 64 pp., glossy paper with b/w art and photography, circulation 800, publishing "the best of new Canadian and American poetry," short fiction, essays, freelance reviews, freelance interviewers. which uses "**all types**" of poetry. They have published poetry by Lyn Lifshin and Leonard Cohen. As a sample the editor selected these lines from the beginning of "Girl In The White Wetsuit" by John R. Reed:

> *Moore's marble gazing*
> *On a glistening floor*
> *Leda arched against the swan*
> *A maple leaf, an open door*
> *Frost's ocean doing things*
> *It never did to land before.*

They use about 50 of 500 submissions received per year. **Sample: $3 postpaid. Submit early fall, 1 poem to a page. Photocopies, simultaneous submissions OK. All submissions must be accompanied by a covering letter with the name and address of the person submitting on each page of work. Reports in 8-12 weeks.** "Since the staff and publishing schedule are structured around the academic year, replies to submissions are not made during the summer months (i.e., mid-April to mid-September)." Editors often comment on rejections.

SEA FOG PRESS INC.; HARMONY: VOICES FOR A JUST FUTURE (I, IV-Themes), Box 210056, San Francisco, CA 94121-0056, phone 415-221-8527, press founded 1984, *Harmony* founded 1987, managing editor Rose Evans. "Press publishes **works that promote reverence for life—animal rights, peace, social justice, disabled rights, against war, death penalty, abortion, celebrate the aging, disabled. No anger or hostility.**" They have recently published poetry by Jean Blackwood. The editor selected these sample lines (poet unidentified):

> Blessed be the lord of old men
> sterile dry bones on park benches
> He loves them

Harmony: Voices for a Just Future (which I haven't seen) is published every other month on themes such as those listed above, and uses 2-3 poems per issue. Rose Evans says it is magazine-sized, 32 pp., offset, glossy, press run 2,000 for 450 subscriptions. Subscription $12. **Sample: $2** postpaid. Send SASE for guidelines. **Pays 2 copies. Simultaneous submissions OK and previously published poems "maybe." Reports in "2 months maximum." For chapbook consideration submit 2 sample poems. Pays 6 copies and 10% royalties. Sample chapbook: $4. Editor "sometimes"** comments on rejections. She advises, "Find out about the nature and goals of the press you are submitting to and send poetry appropriate for that press."

‡SEA TAILS (V, I, IV-Science Fiction/fantasy/horror), 6136 N. Hamilton, Peoria, IL 61614, phone 309-691-2231, founded 1987, editor Kurt Cagle, is a quarterly "small press **maritime fantasy magazine devoted primarily to the depiction of sea myths, legends, and environmental concerns** in writing, poetry, and song." He wants "rhymed or blank verse [unrhymed iambic pentameter]—with very few exceptions. To me unmetered poetry is not poetry. Up to 100 lines considered, though am looking usually for no more than 25-35 lines. Should be dedicated to merfolk or other sea legends, or should have some oceanic environmental impact. Nothing not pertinent to these themes." They have published poetry by Marge Simon (president of SPWAO), Cathy Burbunz, and John Grey. As a sample, the editor chose these lines from "In Reality" by John Grey:

> The old sea-farer
> grumbled and spat
> about how it weren't
> sharks you should fear
> in the deep swell of ocean
> but mermaids.

Sea Tails is 28-32 pp., magazine-sized, newsletter, side-stapled, desk-top publication, with artwork (primarily line art). "Often poetry is used to 'illustrate' the illustrations." Of 80-100 poems received he accepts 8-12 per issue. Press run 120 for 40 subscriptions. Subscription: $8. **Sample, postpaid: $2.50. Send SASE for guidelines. Pays 1 year subscription plus 1 copy. "Please include a cover letter with a brief bio and a phone number."** Simultaneous submissions and previously published poems OK. Editor sometimes comments on submissions. He says, "Too often the role of poet as storyteller becomes forgotten, particularly within the domain of academia. The poem as tale is the oldest expression of the imagination, and one of the duties of the poet, as of the artist, is to clarify and unearth the morass of concepts we call civilization. Poetry is a tool for expression, like the brush. And just as it's possible for a painter to be technically brilliant but uninspired, so can a poet make poems that are technical masterpieces, yet say nothing."

‡SEATTLE REVIEW (II, IV-Regional), Padelford Hall, GN-30, University of Washington, Seattle, WA 98195, phone 206-543-9865, founded 1978, poetry editor Nelson Bentley, appears twice a year using **"fiction, poetry, interviews (mainly with Northwest writers) and essays on the craft of writing (*not* literary criticism)."** They have published poetry by William Stafford, David Wagoner, Madeline DeFrees, Pattiann Rogers and Tess Gallagher. I have not seen a copy and the editor gives no information about format other than "110 pp." Press run 800-1,000. Subscription: $8. **Sample, postpaid: "half price, usually $2-3."** Pay "varies" plus 2 copies. Reports within 1-3 months. Editor comments on submissions "rarely."

SECOND AEON PUBLICATIONS (V), 19 Southminster Road, Roath, Cardiff, Wales, phone 0222-493093, founded 1966, poetry editor Peter Finch, is a "small press concerned in the main with **experimental literary works.**" He has recently published poetry by Bob Cobbing and himself. **Pays copies. Accepts no unsolicited MSS.**

RALPH W. SECORD PRESS; BIG TWO-HEARTED; MID-PENINSULA NEWS AND NOTES (I, II, IV-Humor, nature, themes), 424 Stephenson Ave., Iron Mountain, MI 49801, *News and Notes* founded 1964, Secord Press founded 1971, *Big Two-Hearted* founded 1985, director Gary Silver. Secord Press is a local, regional history publisher; *News and Notes* is a general library information newsletter which uses **light, library-oriented verse.** *Big Two-Hearted* is a three-times a year literary journal with emphasis on **"nature, out-of-doors, and individualism.** *open* — shorter, nature-oriented, 'northwoods' emphasis stands best chance. We will publish long poems if they are good. No profanity, morbidity or erotica. Also, our status as a public service organization (Mid-Peninsula Library Cooperative) necessitates that we maintain a taboo against traditional 'four-letter curse words.' These are immediate rejections."** They have published poetry by Donnell Hunter and Lyn Lifshin. The editor selected these sample lines by Rane Arroyo:

> *When I needed you the most*
> *You were in the forest*
> *Skinning Fall alive.*
> *There was no immediate danger.*

Their purpose is to publish "stories and poems to provide entertainment during long 20-degree-below winter. We publish for the fun of it." *Big Two-Hearted* is digest-sized, 60 + pp., saddle-stapled, offset, using bristol card covers, using original art work (especially of deer, geese, moose, etc.) No ads except for Secord Press. They receive about 400 poems a year, use about 90. Press run of 150, 12 subscriptions of which 2 are libraries. Subscription: $3. **Sample: $1 postpaid. Pays 1 copy. No simultaneous submissions or previously published poems. Reports in 90 days, up to 7 months between acceptance and appearance in the magazine.** Gary Silver advises, "Know the publication you're sending to. We reject most items not because of quality, but because material is inappropriate for our audience."

SEEMS (II), Box 359, Lakeland College, Sheboygan, WI 53082-0359, founded 1971, published irregularly (25 issues in 18 years). This is a handsomely printed, nearly square (7x8¼") magazine, saddle-stapled, generous with white space on heavy paper. Two of the issues are considered chapbooks, and the editor, Karl Elder, suggests that a way **to get acquainted would be to order** *Seems #14, What Is The Future Of Poetry?* **for $3,** consisting of essays by 22 contemporary poets, and "If you don't like it, return it, and we'll return your $3." There are usually about 15 pages of poetry per issue. Karl Elder says, **"For a clear idea of what I'm after by way of submissions, see my essay 'The Possiblites of Poetry'** in #19-20, a special double issue of poetry." He has recently used poetry by Philip Dacey, William Greenway, Hugh Ogden, Gregg Shapiro and Bayla Winters. He said it was "impossible" to select four illustrative lines, so I chose one of his own poems (in *Seems #16*):

> *"Crow's Feet (to Thomas James)"*
> *No sooner than vision*
> *began to ripen,*
> *the ravenous black dream*
> *straddled your eyes.*

The magazine has a print run of 350 for 150 subscriptions (40 libraries) and sells for $3 an issue (or $12 for a subscription — four issues). There is a **1-2 year backlog, reports in 1-8 weeks, pays copies.**

SEGUE FOUNDATION; ROOF BOOKS; SEGUE BOOKS (V); 303 E. 8th. St., New York, NY 10009, phone 212-473-0615, president James Sherry, is a small-press publisher of poetry, literary criticism, and film and performance texts. Most of their books are flat-spined paperback, some hard cover. They have published books by Jackson MacLow, Charles Bernstein, Ron Silliman and Diane Ward, but they **do not consider unsolicited MSS. Query first. Pays 10% of run.** The Foundation is also a distributor of a number of prestigious small-press magazines and books. Write for their catalog to buy samples.

SENECA REVIEW (II, IV-Translations), Hobart and William Smith Colleges, Geneva, NY 14456, phone 315-781-3349, founded 1970, editor Deborah Tall. They want **"serious poetry of any form, including translations. No light verse. Also essays on contemporary poetry."** Recently they have published poetry by Seamus Heaney, Rita Dove, Ray Carver, Stephen Dobyns, and Ellen Bryant Voigt. As a sample I chose the opening quatrain of "The Bells of Herrnau," one of the "Hellbrunn Sonnets" by Barbara Feyerabend:

> *Let the poem be cast like a bell, its great iron*
> *Mouth opened wide as an imagined*
> *Prehistoric bird's, producing sound*
> *Of a single, wondrous, dark exploding sun*

Seneca Review is 100 pp., 6×9" flat-spined, professionally printed on quality stock with matte card cover, appearing twice a year. Of 3,000-4,000 poems received they accept approximately 100. Press run is 600 for 250 subscriptions of which half are libraries. About 50 shelf sales. Subscription: $8/year, $15/2 years. **Sample: $5 postpaid. Pays 2 copies. Submit 3-5 poems. No simultaneous submissions or previously published poems. Reports in 3-10 weeks.**

‡SENIOR EDITION USA/COLORADO OLD TIMES (IV-Seniors, regional, themes), SEI Publishing Corporation, Suite 2240, 1660 Lincoln St., Denver, CO 80264, phone 303-837-9100, managing editor Rose Beetem, is a monthly tabloid "Colorado newspaper **for seniors (with national distribution)** emphasizing legislation, opinion and advice columns, local and national news, features and local calendar aimed at over-55 community." They want **"usually no haiku, religious/inspirational. Subject matter often to match** *Colorado Old Times*." Circ. 25,000. **Pays on publication. Publishes ms an average of 1-6 months after acceptance. Submit seasonal/holiday material 3 months in advance. Sample copy $1; writer's guidelines for SASE.** Senior Overlook column features **opinions of seniors about anything they feel strongly about: finances, grandkids, love, life, social problems, etc. (May be editorial, essay, prose or poetry). Buys 6-12 mss per year. Send complete MS. Length: 50-1,000 words. Pays $20, maximum.**

SENSATIONS; SENSATIONS BEST SONNET CONTEST (I,IV), 2 Radio Ave., A5, Secaucus, NJ 07094, founded 1987, founder David Messineo. **Subscription required before submission of material.**"*Sensations* is a literary magazine which **accepts material in English from beginning and established writers from around the world. Emphasis on poetry and short stories, with one cover story per issue, themes varied and controversial, yet aimed for an intelligent, open-minded audience. No limits on length, form. We'd like more writers from outside of the United States. We'd love material dealing with contemporary issues and current or historical events. No abstract material that only the writer can understand, no minimalist stories, and if it's a love poem, it should be remarkable and something others can appreciate."** As a sample, the founder selected these lines from "Breaking the Mirror" by J. Anthony Heck:

> Count the countless
> I.V. units.
> Count me as your son.
> Ask the question "why,"
> daddy,
> then disregard the pun . . .
> You spent the night
> with your 13 lovers:
> the color T.V. and 12 cold beers . . .

Sensations is magazine-sized, 60 pp., printed on LaserWriter. Third issue was first U.S. literary magazine to feature hologram on its cover. **For brochure and subscription, send a $12 check, made payable to "David Messineo,"** with *Sensations* in the memo section of the check, **along with an SASE,** to attention of David Messineo. **Do** *not* **send material until after subscribing and reading our brochure, which details our policies and deadlines. Simultaneous submissions OK if so indicated. Legible dot matrix accepted. Previously published poems used "on occasion." About 25% of submitted material is accepted. Reports in 4-6 weeks after deadline.** The founder says, "Material is chosen by a five member selection of literature staff; majority vote ensures publication. We can assist you in improving your craft, and encourage you to submit again if potential's there. We bring **unusual personal touches such as phone calls to writers on occasion and detailed feedback and thorough editing of rejected material.** All amounts raised go directly toward costs of publishing, marketing, and mailing; the debut issue was **sent to 23 countries across all 7 continents**. We've grown considerably in production quality since our debut issue; subscribe and see the improvement. Advice? A good writer can work as easily with meter or rhyme as with free verse. Beginning writers are advised to first work within the limitations of meter and rhyme, to help them improve their ability to choose the best words to say what they want to say in the best possible way. Read *any* magazine before sending material; throwing material into an envelope without reading the publication is a sure-fire way to waste your time and money." For *Sensations* Best Sonnet Contest, entries must be in standard Elizabethan, Shakespearean, or Petrarchan sonnet form, no more than one break in meter per sonnet. First prize: $50. Second prize: $25. Deadline for entries: January 1, 1991. Contest open to everyone. Entry fee: $5 (non-subscribers), $3 (active subscribers), plus SASE. Check must be made payable to "David Messineo." Up to three sonnets may be entered per person; fee is per person, not per sonnet. Top two winners shall be published in Summer 1991 issue of *Sensations*.Copyrights to material submitted are retained by writer; however, *Sensations* reserves the right to publish any submitted material at any future time. Send two copies of each entry, check, and SASE to David Messineo.

SEQUOIA (II), Storke Publications Building, Stanford, CA 94305, founded 1892, poetry editor Carlos Rodriguez, appears twice a year. "We are eclectic but would especially like to see **new kinds of beautiful language. Experimental formal/metrical work is welcome. Rhythm is important to us."** They have recently published poetry by Susan Howe, Seamus Heaney, Adrienne Rich, Rita Dove, James Merrill. As a sample the editor selected these lines by Ken Kesey:

> *She promised light to a secret land*
> *Took you gentle by the hand*
> *Picked your locks just like she planned*
> *and let the stranger in . . .*

Sequoia is 80-100 pp., 6 × 9", professionally printed, flat-spined, with a glossy card cover with art. Their press run is 800 with 400 subscriptions, of which half are libraries. They publish a small percentage of hundreds of unsolicited submissions. Subscription: $10. **Sample: $4 postpaid. Pays 2 copies. Reports in "2 months or more." They consider simultaneous submissions but not previously published poems.** The editor says, "*Sequoia* has a long tradition of encouraging 'formal' poetry. Nowadays it seems especially appropriate to remind poets that there is nothing inherently embarrassing about the craft of verse."

SERPENT & EAGLE PRESS (II), 273 Main St., Oneonta, NY 13820, phone 607-432-5604, founded 1981, poetry editor Jo Mish. "Our aim is to print fine limited letterpress editions of titles worth printing in all subject areas." In poetry they like "Imagist—Ezra Pound's not Amy Lowell's type." They have published poetry by Charlotte Mendez, Robert Bensen and Mike Newell. The chapbooks I have seen from this press are, indeed, elegantly designed and printed on handmade paper with hand-sewn wrappers. **For book consideration, query with 5 samples. No simultaneous submissions. Photocopy, dot-matrix OK. Pays 10 copies and $100 honorarium.**

SEVEN BUFFALOES PRESS; AZOREAN EXPRESS; BLACK JACK; VALLEY GRAPEVINE; HILL AND HOLLER ANTHOLOGY SERIES (IV-Rural, regional, anthologies), Box 249, Big Timber, MT 59011, founded 1973, editor Art Cuelho, who writes, "I've always thought that Rural and Working Class writers, poets and artists deserve the same tribute given to country singers." These publications all express that interest. For all of these publications Art Cuelho wants **poetry oriented toward rural and working people, "a poem that tells a story, preferably free verse, not longer than 50-60 lines, poems with strong lyric and metaphor, not gay, romantical, poetry of the head and not the heart, not poems written like grocery lists, or the first thing that comes from a poet's mind, no experimental or ivory tower, no women's lib (but half my contributors are women)."** He has published poetry by R.T. Smith, James Goode, Leo Connellan and Wendell Berry. As a sample he selected these lines by Jim Wayne Miller:

> *and black as a shrew in a snowy field of foxtracks,*
> *and move toward a setting winter sun*
> *red on the snow, musky—a sun*
> *that snaps small bones in a mouth of night.*

The Azorean Express, 5½ × 8½", 35 pp., side-stapled, appears twice a year, circulation 200. **Sample: $2.50 postpaid. Pays 1 copy. Reports in 1-2 weeks. Submit 4-8 poems. No simultaneous submissions.** *Black Jack* is an anthology series on Rural America that uses rural material from anywhere, especially the American West; *Valley Grapevine* is an anthology on central California, circulation 750 that uses rural material from central California. Sample: $4. Hill and Holler, Southern Appalachian Mountain series takes in rural mountain lifestyle and folkways. Sample copy: $4. Seven Buffaloes Press does not accept unsolicited MSS but publishes books solicited from writers who have appeared in the above magazines. Art Cuelho advises. Don't tell the editor how great you are. This one happens to be a poet and novelist who has been writing for 25 years. Your writing should not only be fused with what you know from the head, but also from what you know within your heart. Most of what we call life may be sor.e kind of gift of an unknown river within us. The secret to be learned is to live with ease the darkness. Because there are too many things of the night in this world, but the important clue to remember is that there are many worlds within us."

SEVENTEEN (IV-Teens), 850 3rd Ave., New York, NY 10022, phone 212-759-8100, founded 1944, poetry editor Robert Moritz, is a slick monthly, circulation 1,750,000, for teenage girls which is open to "**all styles of poetry up to 40 lines by writers 21 and under. We are looking for quality poetry by new young poets.**" Purchase sample ($1.75) at newsstands. Reports in 4-6 weeks. Pays $15. Send SASE for guidelines. They receive about 3,000 submissions per year, use 24-30, have a 12-18 month backlog.

SEWANEE REVIEW; AIKEN TAYLOR AWARD FOR MODERN POETRY (III), University of the South, Sewanee, TN 37375, founded 1892, thus being our nation's oldest continuously published literary quarterly, and one of the most awesome in reputation. George Core is editor, Audrey Reynolds, Business Manager. Each of the four issues per year is a hefty paperback of nearly 200 pages, conservatively bound in matte paper, always of the same typography. Fiction, criticism and poetry are invariably of the **highest establishment standards. Most of our major poets appear here from time to time.** Recent issues contain poetry by William Logan, Howard Nemerov, and Barry Spacks. The editor selected these lines from Neal Bowers's poem "Words for a Fireman's Funeral":

> *We who knew you stand before you now*
> *with all the alarm bells ringing,*
> *fighting our own consuming fire,*
> *each of us grasping this earth, this air.*

Circulation: 3,400. **Sample $5.75, pays 70¢/line, reports in 1-4 weeks.** The Aiken Taylor Award for Modern Poetry is awarded by *The Sewanee Review* and its publisher, the University of the South in Sewanee, TN, "for the work of a substantial and distinguished career."

THE SHAKESPEARE NEWSLETTER (IV-Themes), 1217 Ashland Ave., Chicago, Evanston, IL 60202, founded 1951, editor Louis Marder, is a 12-16 pp. quarterly of short scholarly articles, abstracts of articles and lectures, notes and reviews which also uses some **poetry related to and inspired by Shakespeare and/ or Shakespeare studies. Poetry which is inspired by Shakespeare's plays, characters, critics which give new insights are welcome. No parodies of the sonnets or of "To be, or not to be,"** etc. The editor chose a sample from "Fleance to James" by Patricia Connor Shroyer:

> *The fallen torch,*
> *A father's death before one's eyes . . .*
> *Two lights are out.*
> *Fear of mortality; no way but flight.*
> *Such is the end of childhood;*
> *And then . . . in ripened time,*
>   *The beginning of a new dynasty*

"I am not an anthologist but I print short pithy poems if **they are well expressed, incisive, insightful, clearly stated, comprehensible on first reading but growing in depth when reread. They should make a critical point which enlarges our appreciation of Shakespeare or his works."** 2,000 readers in 45 nations. **Payment in 3 copies. Sample copy $3 plus 60¢ postage first class.**

SHAMAL BOOKS (IV-Ethnic, anthologies), GPO Box 16, New York, NY 10116, phone 718-622-4426, founded 1976, editor Louis Reyes Rivera. Shamal Books is a small press whose purpose is **"to promote the literary efforts of African-American and Caribbean writers, particularly those who would not otherwise be able to establish their literary credentials as their concerns as artists are with the people."** The press publishes individual and "anthological" books and chapbooks, mostly flat-spined paper texts. Some poets recently published are SeKou Sundiata, Sandra Maria Esteves, Rashidah Ismaili, and the editor. As a sample, he selected the following lines by Zizwe Ngafua:

> *Tis the truth of cotton farms and*
>   *muddied bloodied Mississippi rivers and tamborine blues*

The editor wants to see **"poetry that clearly demonstrates an understanding of craft, content, and intent as the scriptural source of the word guiding and encouraging the intellect of the people."** He does not consider freelance submissions of individual MSS, but will look at work **only while anthologies are open. How many sample poems should you send? "two is cool."** The cover letter should include a **"leaning toward personal goals and poetic principles."** The editor will reply to queries within 2 months; **MSS of poetry should be "neat and single-spaced." Royalties for book authors are 15%. The editor says that he will subsidy publish "delicately – depends on resources and interest in work."** His future projects include "an international anthology; drama; prison anthology; books on language as a weapon; a collectivized publisher's catalog of Third World presses working out of NYC." His advice to poets is, "Certainly to study the craft more and to research more into the historical role that has been the hallmark of poetry across class and caste conscious lines that limit younger perspectives. Not to be as quick to publish as to be in serious study, then while looking to publish, looking as well into collective ventures with other poets for publication and distribution. Above all, *read!*"

‡SHARING THE VICTORY (IV-Themes), 8701 Leeds Road, Kansas City, MO 64129, phone 816-921-0909, founded 1959, assistant editor Dana J. King, managing editor Don Hilkemeier. The bi-monthly magazine (circulation 50,000) is published by the Fellowship of Christian Athletes and uses only 2-3 poems/year. **They want free verse on themes of interest to Christian athletes (high school and college, male and female). Pay is $30-50. Sample available for $1 with 8½x11" SASE (first class stamps for 3 oz.). Guidelines available free. Reporting time is 2 weeks and time to publication averages 3-4 months.**

HAROLD SHAW PUBLISHERS; WHEATON LITERARY SERIES (V), Box 567, Wheaton, IL 60189, phone 708-665-6700, founded 1967 Director of Editorial Services Ramona Cramer Tucker, is "small publisher of the Wheaton Literary Series and Northcote Books, **works of Christian and literary merit including** fiction, poetry, literary criticism and original prose" in flat-spined paperback and hardback books. They have recently published poetry by Madeleine L'Engle, John Leax, Sister Maura Eichner and Luci Shaw. **They publish on a 10/5% royalty basis plus 10 author's copies but prefer flat fee.** They publish a volume of poetry every 2 years. "Our work reflects **a Christian evangelical world-view,**

though this need not be explicit. In the future we may publish an anthology, rather than single poets."

SHAWNEE SILHOUETTE (I), Shawnee State University, 940 Second St., Portsmouth, OH 45662, phone 614-354-3205, founded 1985, editor Henry C. Mason, a literary quarterly that publishes poetry, prose, art work, and photography and occasionally sponsors a poetry contest. The editors want **"Any subject done in good taste; blank, and free verse conventional forms; no restriction on length or subject matter."** Recently published poets include Taylor Pierce, H.C. Mason, Harding Stedler, Lee Pennington, Louise Potter Logan, and Ken Stone. As a sample the editors chose the following lines by Abbra Grey:

> Your voice was cold
> like the plastic
> it traveled through
> never hinting
> it
> used to
> gently call my name.

Shawnee Silhouette is digest-sized, offset from MacIntosh Page Maker Program with Laser writer Plus, with b/w drawings and photographs, utilizing a variety of typestyles, 40 pp. saddle-stapled, matte card cover with b/w decoration. It is published 3 times/year (fall, winter, and spring). Single copy price is $2, subscriptions $5/year. **Pay is 1 copy. Send 3 poems per mailing; typed double-spaced, no simultaneous submissions. Reporting time is normally 3 months and time to publication is 6 months.** The editors say, "We are interested only in quality material and try to provide a diversity of styles and topics in each issue."

SHOE TREE: THE LITERARY MAGAZINE BY AND FOR YOUNG WRITERS; NATIONAL ASSOCIATION FOR YOUNG WRITERS (IV-Children), 215 Valle del Sol Drive, Santa Fe, NM 87501, phone 505-982-8596, founded 1985, editor-in-chief Sheila Cowing. **"We are open to submissions of poetry from young writers aged 6-14. The editor is particularly interested in fine poems. No haiku, cinquain or 'class-room assignments.'"** As a sample the editor chose thses lines by 7-year-old Hannah Gutstein:

> Skates turning backward kiss the ice
> Attack my heart
> Training it to yearn.

The professionally printed, flat-spined journal appears 3 times a year, 6×9", 64 pp., with cover art in color done by children. They accept 30 poems of approximately 3,500 received per year. Their press run is 1,500 with 1,000 subscriptions of which ⅓ are libraries. Subscription: $15 per year. **Sample: $5 postpaid. Guidelines and contest rules available for SASE. Pays 2 copies. Reports in 4-5 weeks.** They hold 3 contests in fiction, poetry and nonfiction in each issue with prizes of $25 and $10 and publication. Librarians and teachers may request sample copies. The editor says, "We urge young writers to write from the heart, draw from personal experience and shy away from trends."

SHOFAR (IV-Children, ethnic, religious), 43 Northcote Dr., Melville, NY 11747, founded 1984, publisher/editor Gerald H. Grayson, is a magazine **for American Jewish Children 9-13**, appearing monthly October through May (double issues Dec./Jan. and April/May). It is magazine-sized, 32 pp., professionally printed, with color paper cover. Their press run is 10,000 with 9,000 subscriptions of which 1,000 are libraries. Subscription: $14.95. **Sample: free for 90¢ postage and SASE. Send SASE for guidelines. Pays $25-50/poem. They will consider simultaneous submissions and "maybe" previously published poems. Reports in 6-8 weeks.**

SHOOTING STAR REVIEW (II, IV-Themes, ethnic), 7123 Race St., Pittsburgh, PA 15208, phone 412-731-7039, founded 1986, publisher Sandra Gould Ford, "our board of contributing editors includes Marita Golden, Reginald McKnight, Kristin Hunter and Woodie King, Jr. **"Each issue of *Shooting Star Review* explores a specific theme. Themes for 1991 include "Mothers and Daughters," deadline January 15; "Home and Community," deadline April 21; and "Star Child," deadline July 14, 1991. Free, comprehensive guidelines mailed with your SASE. This is an adult-oriented magazine dedicated to the African American Experience."** They have recently used poetry by Eloise Greenfield, Toi Derri-

ALWAYS submit MSS or queries with a stamped, self-addressed envelope (SASE) within your country or International Reply Coupons (IRCs) purchased from the post office for other countries.

cote and Chris Gilbert. As a sample Sandra Gould Ford selected these lines from "Theme for English B" by Langston Hughes:

> *The instructor said,*
> *"Go home and write a page tonight.*
> *And let that page come out of you*
> *Then it will be true."*

SSR is magazine-sized, 44 pp., offset with glossy cover and art, "illustrated with significant attention to design and graphics." It appears quarterly. **Sample: $3 postpaid. Bulk mail, shipped immediately with 9 × 12 envelope with $1 postage. Send SASE for guidelines. Payment: $8 per poem plus 2 complimentary copies. Reports in 12 weeks. Submit up to 6 poems.**

THE SIGNAL (II, IV-Translation), P.O. Box #67, Emmett, ID 83617, phone 208-365-5812, poetry editors Joan Silva and David Chorlton, "art, opinion, review, interview, exploratory short fiction, articles, essays. **Encourage scientific lit. speculation. Translations. Approach can be a little wild — but not tacky. As to poetry, no restrictions! We want an attitude that reveals caring what goes on in our world, planet caring, people caring, clear-minded, informed opinion, sharp, questioning outlook. Do not want to see poetry that is muddled, wishy-washy, impressed with image as opposed to substance, style as opposed to passion or personal conviction."** Recently published poets include Maurice Kenny, Nicolas Born, Trevor P. Edmands, Stephen Stepanchev, David Fisher, MaLay Roy Choudhury, Martin Robbins, and Robert Peters. As a sample Joan Silva selected these lines by Charlie Mehrhoff:

> *. . . blood rains down*
> *in the forest of your dreams*
>
> *blood rains down*
> *upon the walls of your life*
>
> *somewhere someone dancing*
> *somewhere someone dancing*
>
> *the pain of seeing*
> *oh the pain of seeing*

The Signal is magazine-sized, 64 pp. saddle-stapled, beautifully printed on heavy ruled stock with matte card cover, using b/w photography and art. It appears twice yearly. Subscriptions are $10 a year domestically, negotiable for foreign subscriptions. **Sample: $4 postpaid. Reporting time: 6-12 weeks. Pays in contributors' copies.** The editors announce a "Cup Award" in each issue for a "currently underappreciated" poet and feature work by that poet in the following issue. *"The Signal* has *no* grant, corporate, or academic funding. We depend 100% on reader support. Help keep us independent."

THE SIGNPOST PRESS; THE BELLINGHAM REVIEW; 49TH PARALLEL POETRY CONTEST (II), 1007 Queen St., Bellingham, WA 98226, phone 206-734-9781. Founded 1975, magazine editor Susan Hilton; book editor Knute Skinner. Publishes *The Bellingham Review* twice a year, runs an annual poetry competition, and publishes other books and chapbooks of poetry occasionally. **"We want well-crafted poetry but are open to all styles,"** no specifications as to form. Poets they have published recently include Sean Bentley, Biff Russ, Olga Broumas, Judith Skillman, Bruce Holland Rogers, John Bradley, B.A. St. Andrews and James Bertolino. As a sample, Susan Hilton selected these lines by Bruce Holland Rogers:

> *Milk pulses beneath her paper skin*
> *Her eyes are two holes of sky behind*
> *the veil of clouds where seabirds wheel*
> *light as foam*

Each issue of the *Review* has about 38 pp. of poetry. They have a circulation of 700 with 500 subscriptions. It's a digest-sized, saddle-stapled, typeset, with art and glossy cover. **Sample: four selected back issues $2 postpaid. Submit up to 6 pp. Photocopy, simultaneous submissions OK. Reports in 1-3 months, pays 1 copy plus a year's subscription.** Send SASE for rules for the next 49th Parallel Poetry Contest and query regarding book publication.

SILVER APPLES PRESS (V,II), Box 292, Hainesport, NJ 08036, phone 609-267-2758, founded 1982, poetry editor Geraldine Little. "We're a very small press with very limited funds. Published our first chapbook in 1988; open contest for same. We plan to publish randomly, as things turn us on and as funds permit — pamphlets, chapbooks, a set of postcards. **"We are over-committed at present. Not currently accepting poetry submissions."** They have published **Contrasts in Keening: Ireland** by Geraldine C. Little, and **Abandoned House** by Susan Fawcett and **The Verb to Love** by Barbara Horton from which these lines were selected:

The sky likes white best.
It stays far away so birds have to fly far
to reach it. It wants you to be lonely sometimes
unsure which way to go.
You have to stand still a long while.
Sometimes wind slows, stops.

SILVER WINGS (IV-Religious, spirituality, inspirational), Box 1000, Pearblossom, CA 93553-1000, phone 805-264-3726, founded 1983, and now published by Poetry on Wings, Inc., poetry editor Jackson Wilcox. "As a committed Christian service we produce and publish a quarterly poetry magazine. We want **poems with a Christian perspective, reflecting a vital personal faith and a love for God and man. Will consider poems from 3-20 lines. Quite open in regard to meter and rhyme.**" They have recently published poems by William T. Burke, Patricia Hock, C. David Hay, and Alice Mackenzie Swaim. The editor chose these sample lines from "Born Again" by Gladys O'Laughlin:
God Incarnate;
The sacrifice;
The awful cost;
— The Cross of Christ.
One perfect Life,
Born to be;
That mortal Gate
— To eternity.
The 32-36 pp. magazine is digest-sized, offset from typescript with hand-lettered titles on tinted paper with cartoon-like art, circulation 500 with 225 subscriptions. They receive 1,000 submissions per year, use 200. Another 300-400 come in as entries in contests sponsored by Silver Wings—send SASE for details. Subscription: $7. **Sample: $2 postpaid. Typed MSS, double-spaced. Reports in 3 weeks, providing SASE is supplied. Pays $9 in subscription and copy value. Rarely comments on rejections.** The editor says, "If a poet has had a faith experience, share it freely from the heart, using whatever words are warm and expressive. Thus the shared message becomes a powerful communication to bless others. We are glad to look at poetry that has an uplift to it. We are Christian by design and openly ecumenical in spirit..

SILVERFISH REVIEW; SILVERFISH REVIEW PRESS (II, IV-Translations), Box 3541, Eugene, OR 97403, phone 503-344-5060 founded 1979, poetry editor Rodger Moody, is an irregularly appearing digest-sized 48 pp. literary magazine, circulation 750. "The only criteria for selection is **quality. In future issues** *Silverfish Review* **wants to showcase translations of poetry from Europe and Latin America** as well as continue to print poetry and fiction of quality written in English." They have published poetry by Walter McDonald, Jon Davis, Dick Allen, Ivan Arguelles, D. M. Wallace, Walter Pavlich, Ralph Salisbury, Bob Austin, Christine Zawadiwsky, and Kathleen Spivack. As a sample the editor selected these lines by Floyd Skloot:
The thick-lipped bowl
spun slowly, its rim
stroked by her blade
scraping down the liver.
There are 36-48 pp. of poetry in each issue. The magazine is professionally printed in dark type on quality, stock, matte card cover with art. Subscription: for institution: $12; for individuals: $9; per issue: $3. They receive about 1,000 submissions of poetry per year, use 20, have a 6-12 month backlog. **Sample: $3, single copy orders should include $1 for postage and handling. Submit at least 5 poems to editor. Photocopies OK. No simultaneous submissions. Reports in 6 weeks. Pays 5 copies plus small honorarium when grant support permits. Silverfish Review Press will consider MSS for chapbook publication and conducts an annual chapbook competition with an award of $300 and 25 copies (with a press run of 750). Send SASE for rules.**

SING HEAVENLY MUSE! (IV-Feminist), Box 13299, Minneapolis, MN 55414, founded 1977, editor Sue Ann Martinson, fosters "the work of women poets, fiction writers, and artists. The magazine is **feminist in an open, generous sense: we encourage women to range freely, honestly, and imaginatively over all subjects, philosophies, and styles. We do not wish to confine women to women's subjects,** whether these are defined traditionally, in terms of femininity and domesticity, or modernly, from a sometimes narrow polemical perspective. We look for explorations, questions that do not come with ready-made answers, emotionally or intellectually. **We seek out new writers, many before unpublished.** The editors try to reduce to a minimum the common bureaucratic distance between a magazine and its readers and contributors. Although our staff is small, we encourage writers by discussing their work, and we solicit comments from our readers. This relationship makes *Sing Heavenly Muse!* a community where women with widely varying interests and ideas may meet and learn from one another." For poetry they have **"no limitations except women's writing."** They have published poetry by Ellen Bass, Celia Gilbert, Diane Glancy, and Patricia Hampl. The editor selected these sample lines by Linda Hogan:

> All bridges of flesh, all singing,
> all covering the wounded land,
> showing again, again
> that all boundaries are lies.

The magazine appears two times a year in a $6 \times 9''$ flat-spined, 125 pp. format, offset from typescript on heavy stock, b/w art, glossy card color cover, circulation 2,000, 275 subscriptions of which 50 are libraries. Subscription: $17 (3 issues); per copy: $6. They receive 1,500+ submissions per year, use 50-60, have a 5-6 month backlog. **Sample: $4 postpaid. Submit 3-10 pp., name and address on each page. Photocopy OK. No simultaneous submissions. Reports in 1-3 months, pays "usually $25 plus 2 copies." Generally accepts manuscripts for consideration in April and September. Inquire about special issues, contests. Send SASE for guidelines. Editors sometimes comment on rejections.**

‡**SINGLE TODAY (I, IV-Romance/love)**, 2500 Mt. Moriah #185, Memphis, TN 38115, phone 901-365-3988, founded 1986, president/owner P.M. Pederson, appears every other month, a small-press magazine for **singles, widowed, divorced, using "short free verse on love and romance, appealing to singles. Nothing vulgar, tasteless, rhyming."** As a sample the editor selected these lines by Kathleen S. McGown:

> But most of all
> You taught me
> How to love openly
> To search for the ends of the rainbow
> And to believe in the magic of one's dreams.

I have not seen an issue, but the editor describes it as magazine-sized. Press run 5,000 for 580 subscriptions. Subscription: $25. **Sample, postpaid: $4. Send SASE for guidelines. Pays 1 copy. Simultaneous submissions and previously published poems OK. Reports "same week." Editor sometimes comments on submissions.**

SINGLELIFE MAGAZINE (IV-Themes), 606 W. Wisconsin Ave., Milwaukee, WI 53203, fiction and poetry editor Leifa Butrick, is published every other month, circulation 24,000. *Singlelife* is a slick, 64-80 page magazine. **Sample: $3.50 postpaid. Buys 3-4 stories or poems "which are well-written and cast a new light on what being single means. No simple boy-meets-girl-at-the-laundromat." Reports within 2 weeks.** "Once a year, the magazine has a writers' contest (deadline January 1) in the fiction, poetry and essay categories with a $100 prize in each category." Following is an excerpt from the 1990 poem "The Lie" by Christina Zawadiwsky:

> you'll bring me back to life and place roses and violets
> in my hair and paint a picture of me in the sun
> with a black cat in my lap that's lazily licking
> a cup of ice cream. You'll return. I gave my life to you.

SINGULAR SPEECH PRESS (II, IV-Translations), 10 Hilltop Dr., Canton, CT 06019, phone 203-693-6059, founded 1976, editor Don D. Wilson. "We started in order to publish this editor's verse translations. Not a journal, we publish 24-64 page poetry mss—conventional or free, translated or not, not unduly subjective. They have published Wiliam Burns and Miljenko Kovacicek. The editor selected these sample lines from **Zoom** by Charles Fishman:

> Here, we exile bloodshed,
> ghosts of violence
> Hotel Peace is built again
> from the stones of shattered graves

For consideration, **query with 5-10 samples and bio. MS should be typed, double-spaced. Simultaneous submission, photocopies OK. Payment in copies (½ of printing). Editor sometimes comments on rejections. Reports within 2 weeks.**

SINISTER WISDOM (IV-Lesbian, feminist), P.O. Box 3252, Berkeley, CA 94703, founded 1976, editor and publisher Elana Dykewomon, a lesbian feminist journal. The editor says, **"We want poetry that reflects the diversity of women's experience—women of color, Third World, Jewish, old, young, working class, poor, disabled, fat, etc.—from a lesbian and/or feminist perspective. No heterosexual themes. We will not print anything that is oppressive or demeaning to women, or which perpetuates negative stereotypes."** The journal has recently published work by Adrienne Rich and Gloria Anzaldúa. The editor chose the following lines from Minnie Bruce Pratt's poem "#67 To Be Posted on 21st Street, Between Eye and Pennsylvania":

> *Like a movie, sudden threat*
> *Predictable. I get so tired of this disbelief.*
> *My tongue, faithful in my mouth, said: Yes, we are.*
> *the shout: Lesbians. Lesbians. Trying to curse*
> *us with our name. Me louder: That's what we are.*

The quarterly magazine is digest-sized, 128-144 pp. flat-spined, with photos and b/w graphics; I have not seen it. Circulation is 3,500 of which 1,000 are subscriptions and 100 go to libraries; newsstand sales and bookstores are 1,500. Price per issue is $5, subscription $17 US, $22 foreign. **Sample available for $6 postpaid. Pay is 2 copies. No simultaneous submissions. Reporting time is up to 9 months and time to publication 6 months-1 year.**

SISTERS TODAY (II, IV-Religious), The Liturgical Press, Collegeville, MN 56321, phone 612-363-2213, poetry editor Sister Audrey Synnott, 1437 Blossom Rd., Rochester, NY 14610, editor Sister Mary Anthony Wagner, has been published for about 60 years. Though it is a Roman Catholic magazine, **not all of the poetry it uses is on religious themes, and the editors do not want poetry that is "overly religious." They want "short (not over 25 lines) poems on any topic, using clean, fresh images and appeal to the reader's feelings and thoughts in a compelling way. They do not want poetry that depends "heavily on rhyme and on 'tricks' such as excessive Capitalization, manipulation of spacing, etc."** They have recently published poetry by Evelyn Mattern, Eileen Curteis, and Pat McKinnon. As a sample poetry editor Sister Audrey Synnott chose these lines from "Texas Ice Storm" by Sheryl Nelms:

> *sound gritches around*
> *like a hundred hands*
> *sqeezing*
> *cellophane*

ST, appearing 6 times a year beginning with January 1990, is 6 × 9" 64 pp., saddle-stapled, professionally printed with matte card cover, press run 9,000 for 8,500 subscribers. They receive about 100 poems per month, accept about 3. Subscription: $17. **Sample: $2 postpaid. Send SASE to poetry editor at Rochester, NY address (above) for guidelines. Pays $10 per poem and 2 copies. They like you to put your "complete legal name, address and social security number typed in the upper right corner." No simultaneous submissions. Previously published poems OK with publisher's release, but original poems much preferred. Reports within 1 month, 6-12 months until publication. Poetry Editor comments when a poem has come close to being accepted.**

‡SKYLARK (I), 2130 Charleroi, #8, Beauport, PQ G1E 3S1 Canada, founded 1989, editor Suzanne Fortin, appears every other month. **"The editor reads everything but generally accepts poetry that is traditional. Rhyme and free verse considered. Any subject matter. No Dadaist."** As a sample the editor selected these lines from "Praying for the Rapturous Bombs to Fall" by Brian Burke:

> *You pray for the rapturous bombs to fall*
> *your ears tuned to the apocalyptic blast*
> *convinced some nimble god*
> *will save those fevered few of you*

I have not seen an issue, but the editor describes it as digest-sized, 24-28 pp., photocopied with card cover. They accept 80% of submissions. Press run is "different each month." Subscription: $12. **Sample, postpaid: $2;** *all checks* **must be paid to Suzanne Fortin. Pays 1 copy. "Poems' titles to be listed on cover, name & address on each page. 100 lines per poem, maximum; 10 poems, maximum." Previously published poems OK. Reports in 2 months. Editor comments on submissions "infrequently."** She says to beginning poets, "Don't be trendy to be trendy. Don't give in to people who say 'this type of poetry is fashionable, not *your* kind.' or to groups or individuals who say there isn't an audience for your poetry."

SKYLARK (I, II, IV-themes), Purdue University Calumet, 2233 171st St., Hammond, IN 46323, phone 219-989-2262, founded 1972, editor Marcia Jaron, is "a literary annual, including **special theme.**" They are looking for **poems up to 60 lines. No horror, nothing extremely religious, no pornography.** They have recently published poetry by A. R. Ammons, Lyn Lifshin, B. Z. Niditch, Jonathan Russell and Charles Tinkham. As a sample the editor selected these lines from "for Barriss Mills" by Charles B. Tinkham:

> *but suddenly*
> *your words fell away*
> *forsythia and the brightness*
> *of magnolia*
> *climbed the trellis*
> *of the nearing dusk*
> *and distant sky*
> *and the day*

> *went out*
> *shining*
> *like a pure*
> *discovered smile*

Skylark is magazine-sized, saddle-stapled, 100+ pp., professionally printed, with matte card cover. Press run is 500-1,000 for 100 subscriptions of which 10 are libraries. Price: $5. **Sample: $2.50 postpaid. Pays 1 copy. "Will accept hand-printed submissions if legible, but prefer typed. Inquire as to annual theme for special section." They will consider simultaneous submissions. Reports in 3 months (longer in summer). Editor sometimes comments on rejections.**

SKYLINE MAGAZINE (IV-Themes), 857 Carroll St., Brooklyn, NY 11215, phone 212-807-5511, founded 1988, publisher William J. Lawrence, is a **"literary magazine on historical, cultural, social, demographic NYC, committed to a greater appreciation toward the city of New York" and uses poetry on those themes.** "Am not interested in poetry that could not be appreciated and understood by the layperson—i.e. non-poets." It appears quarterly, magazine-sized. Press run is 3,000-5,000 for 2,000 subscriptions, of which 20 are libraries. Price per issue: $2.95; subscription $15. **Payment "negotiated." They use 3-4 short poems per issue. Pays $25-100. Reports in 3-4 weeks.**

SLANT: A JOURNAL OF POETRY (II), Box 5063, University of Central Arkansas, Conway, AR 72032, founded 1986, is an annual using *only* poetry. They use **"traditional and 'modern' poetry, even experimental, moderate length, any subject on approval of Board of Readers; purpose is to publish a journal of fine poetry from all regions of the United States. No haiku, no translations."** They have recently used poetry by Marge Piercy, Andrea Budy and Gary Whitby. As a sample the editor selected this excerpt from "Sheltering the Enemy" by Suzanne Harvey:

> *I should evict you from this house*
> *You're no fit tenant for a landlord turned fifty*
> *You and this feeling that I'm twenty*
> *And ripe to launch my skiff on an uncertain sea*
> *Where the tide will never ebb or the wind subside*
> *Where the moon will wax out of season . . .*

Slant is professionally printed on quality stock, 145 pp. flat-spined, with matte card cover. They publish about 80-90 poems of the 2,500 received each year. Press run is 350 for 70-100 subscriptions. **Sample: $10 postpaid. Pays 1 copy. "Put name and address top of each page." Submit no more than five poems of moderate length. Allow 3-4 months from November 15 deadline for response. No multiple submissions or previously published poems. Editor comments on rejections "on occasion."**

SLATE & STYLE (IV-Specialized), 2704 Beach Dr., Merrick, NY 11566, phone 516-868-8718, editor Loraine Stayer, is a **quarterly for blind writers available on cassette, large print, and Braille,** "including articles of interest to blind writers, resources for blind writers. Membership/subscription $5 per year, $10 for Braille only (specify format). Division of the National Federation of the Blind." **Poems may be "5-30 lines. Prefer contributors to be blind writers, or at least writers by profession or inclination. No obscenities. Will consider all forms of poetry."** As a sample the editor selected "My name is helen" by Sister Lou Ella Hickman, I.W.B.S:

> *into the heart of fever*
> *i came*
> *whose breathing was the wild*
> *but wooden horse*
>
> *water*
> *into my hands*
> *was beauty . . .*

The print version is magazine-sized, 20-30 pp., unstapled, circulation 150 with 140 subscribers of which 4-5 are libraries. Subscription: $5 a year, Braille $10. Per issue: $1.25 except Braille. **Sample $2.50 postpaid. Send SASE for guidelines. Pays 1 copy. Reports in "2 weeks if I like it." No simultaneous submissions. Interested in new talent. Editor comments on rejections "if requested."** They sometimes offer contests, are considering adding a fiction and poetry section to the magazine. Loraine Stayer says, "What makes a line of words into poetry? . . . I'm not sure, I only know that when I read it, if it's poetry, I know it. And if it isn't I know that too."

SLIPSTREAM; SLIPSTREAM AUDIO CASSETTES (II, IV-Themes), Box 2071, New Market Station, Niagara Falls, NY 14301, phone 716-282-2616, founded 1980, poetry editors Dan Sicoli, Robert Borgatti, and Livio Farallo. *Slipstream* is a "small-press literary mag, uses about 70% poetry and 30% prose, also artwork. The editors like **new work with contemporary urban flavor. Writing must have a**

cutting edge to get our attention. Occasionally do theme issues. We like to keep an open forum, any length, subject, style. Best to see a sample to get a feel. Like city stuff as opposed to country. Like poetry that springs from the gut, screams from dark alleys, inspired by experience." They do not want to see "pastoral, religious, traditional, rhyming" poetry. They have recently published poetry by Alan Catlin, Lisa Harris, Gerald Locklin, M. Kettner, Charles Bukowski, Roger Cooperman, Ron Androla, Belinda Subraman, Kurt Nimmo and Elliot Richman. The editors selected these sample lines from "Paper Heroes" by Jeff Parsons:

> and leads him away,
> the tromp of the law's big, black boots
> only slightly muffled
> by the toilet tissue
> sticking to his heel

Slipstream appears 1-2 times a year, $7 \times 8\frac{1}{2}''$ format professionally printed, saddle-stapled, using b/w graphics, circulation 300, with 200 subscriptions of which 10 are libraries. About 60 of the 80+ pp. are devoted to poetry. They receive over 1,000 freelance submissions of poetry per year, use less than 10%. **Subscription: $7.50/2 issues. Sample: $3 postpaid. Reports in 2-8 weeks. Editor sometimes comments on rejections. Pays copies. Send SASE for guidelines. Some issues are on announced themes—e.g., a "working stiff" theme issue is planned for 1991. Also producing an audio cassette series. "Spoken word, songs, audio experiments, etc. are all welcome. Query for current needs."** Annual chapbook contest has December 1 deadline. Reading fee: $5. Submit up to 40 pp. of poetry, any style, previously published work OK with acknowledgments. Winner receives 50 copies. All entrants receive copy of winning chapbook. Dan Sicoli advises, "Most poetry mags publish for a specific audience, usually writers. Support the ones you like best. Funding is difficult and many mags live a very short life."

SLOUGH PRESS; SLOUGH PRESS CHAPBOOK POETRY CONTEST (II), Box 1385, Austin, TX 78767, editor Jim Cole, a small-press publisher of books of poetry, fiction, and non-fiction—chapbooks, flat-spined paperbacks, and hardcover books. **"Purpose—liberate the planet. New Age or alternative only. Bohemian, punks, hippies, political anarchists or marxists, Third World and 'minorities' encouraged—also renegade academics. If you've never read any of our books—out of a library or purchased from a bookstore or us—you don't know your market so don't bother to submit. We don't read manuscripts from tree wasters."** He has recently published books by Ricardo Sanchez, Chuck Taylor, and Janet McCann. He publishes 2 chapbooks, 2 paperbacks (with hardback copies) per year. **Submit 10 samples and "marketing ideas of the author. Simultaneous submissions, previously published material, photocopies OK. No dot-matrix. "I don't like random collections. I do like books of poetry or fiction that have an extrinsic interest beyond literature—political, ecological, historical, cultural, etc. I want books that will sell."** Financial arrangement "varies." The Slough Press Chapbook Poetry Contest, deadline December 1, offers the winner 20 copies of the chapbook. Entry fee: $8/MS. Each entry receives a previously published Slough Press book. Send SASE for rules.

SLOW DANCER; SLOW DANCER PRESS (II), Box 3010, RFD 1, Lubec, ME 04652, founded 1977, American editor Alan Brooks. *Slow Dancer* is a semi-annual magazine of British and American writing published by John Harvey in Nottingham, England (address: Flat 4, 1 Park Valley, The Park, Nottingham NG7 1BS); Slow Dancer Press publishes (very) occasional chapbooks of poetry and prose. The editor says, **"All types, lengths, subjects [of poetry] considered. We prefer to print multiple selections from contributors. We look for freshness of image and language, clarity and individuality, whatever the subject. We encourage submissions from previously unpublished poets and always judge the poem, not the 'name.' Prospective contributors should buy a sample copy if they want to learn our preferences. We will reject all poems which display knee-jerk alienation, cutesy formalism, or New Yorker-ese, as well as those which come with a cover letter explaining what they really mean."** He has recently published poems by Norman German, Verlena Orr, Li Min Hua, Grace Cavalier and Simon Armitage. As a sample, he selected the following lines from "Ted Hughes Is Elvis Presley" by Ian McMillan:

> At my poetry readings I sneer and rock my hips.
> I stride the moors
> in a white satin
> bloated as the full moon.

Most issues of *Slow Dancer* "feature a mix of British and North American writers, with a smattering of writers (in English) from all over." The magazine is digest-sized, offset from typed copy, on white stock, some line drawings and b/w photographs, short fiction, 48 pp., saddle-stitched with b/w glossy photo cover. Circulation is about 500, of which approximately 300 are subscriptions. Price per copy is $5. **Poems, previously unpublished, should be submitted one to a page, photocopy or dot-matrix OK if clear, simultaneous submissions OK. "The reading period is November 1-April 30: poems submitted outside this period will be returned unread."** Reporting time is 2 months. Slow Dancer Press publishes 1 or 2 chapbooks of poetry per year, 12-48 pp., format like that of the magazine, but **freelance submissions for chapbooks are not accepted. "We publish manuscripts by poets who have regular appearances in the magazine." Pay is in author's copies.** The editor says, "We are returning to an old *Slow Dancer* tradition: publishing fewer poets but more work by each contributor. If you like what you see in a sample issue, send a reasonable selection of your work. And please, do check your spelling."

SMALL POND MAGAZINE OF LITERATURE (II), Box 664, Stratford, CT 06497, phone 203-378-4066, founded 1964, poetry editor Napoleon St. Cyr, a literary tri-quarterly that features poetry . . . "and anything else the editor feels is original, important." Poetry can be **"any style, form, topic, so long as it is deemed good, except haiku, but limit of about 100 lines." Napoleon St. Cyr wants "nothing about cats, pets, flowers, butterflies, etc. Generally nothing under 8 lines."** Although he calls it name-dropping, he "reluctantly" provided the names of Heather Tosteson, Deborah Boe, Richard Kostela-netz, Fritz Hamilton, and Emilie Glen as poets recently published. He preferred not to supply sample lines, but I have, from a recent issue, selected the opening stanza of "Mother" by Vicky L. Bennett:

> *sits in splendid silence*
> *her dead fox collar*
> *wrapped high around her throat*

The magazine is digest-sized, offset from typescript on off-white paper, 40 pp. with matte card cover, saddle-stapled, art work both on cover and inside. Circulation is 300-325, of which about half go to libraries. Price per issue is $2.75; subscription $7 (for 3 issues). **Sample: $2.50 postpaid for a random selection, $3 current. Guidelines are available in each issue. Pay is two copies. The editor says he doesn't want 60 pages of anything; "dozen pages of poems max." He reports on submissions in 10-45 days (longer in summer), and publication is within 3-18 months.**

SMALL PRESS WRITERS & ARTISTS ORGANIZATION (SPWAO); SPWAO SHOWCASE; SPWAO NEWSLETTER (IV-Membership, Sci-fi/horror/fantasy), 5116 S. 143rd St., Omaha NE 68137; president Jeannette M. Hopper; newsletter editor John Rosenman. The organization publishes a tabloid newsletter, with an emphasis on aiding members, advice columns, short poetry, art, reviews, and they provide a poetry commentary service. Occasionally they publish chapbooks. **You must be a member to submit.** They don't want to see **"mainstream poetry, poetry obviously of a religious nature, highly sentimental, pornography, racial or political poetry (extremes, etc.)"** They have recently published poems by Bruce Boston, Wayne Allen Sallee, T. Winter-Damon, Denise Dumars, D.M. Vosk, and Keith Allen Daniels. As a sample Jeannette Hopper chose this complete poem, "Rottenous," by S.F. Willems:

> *Snifferous, Odoriferous!*
> *Little strips of flesherous . . .*
> *turned putrifacturous.*

Jeannette M. Hopper says, "If you want to publish poetry, learn to play with words the way a painter plays with paint, brushes, and other tools. Let your imagination rove free. And, just as a painter frames his works carefully, learn to present your poetry to editors in the most professional manner possible. Type clearly; submit one poem per page, and put your name and address on each page; be courteous and patient, but stand up for yourself as an artist. Never consider any market beneath you; one reader who appreciates your vision is better than no reader at all, which is what your poems will have if you leave them in a drawer."

GIBBS SMITH, PUBLISHER; PEREGRINE SMITH POETRY COMPETITION (II), Box 667, Layton, UT 84041, phone 801-544-9800, founded 1971; poetry series established 1988, contact Steve Chapman, publicist. **They want "serious, contemporary poetry of merit. No specs except book is only 64 pp."** They have recently published books of poetry by David Huddle and Carol Frost. Books are selected for publication through competition for the Peregrine Smith Poetry Prize of $500 plus publication. Entries are received in April only and require a $10 reading fee. All titles are printed in a uniform 5 × 9", 64 pp. paperback format on acid-free archival stock with covers featuring a facsimile design of early Victorian marbleized paper. A die-cut widow in the covers will reveal an original watercolor commissioned for each title. The first 1,500 copies of each edition will be personally signed by the author. The judge for the series and editor is Christopher Merrill, director of the Santa Fe Writers' Conference.

‡SMOKE SIGNALS (I), Meander Box 232, Flushing, NY 11385-0232, founded 1989, editor Joshua Meander, is a quarterly. **"No curse words in poems, little or no name-dropping, no naming of consumer products, no two-page poems, no humor, no bias writing, no poems untitled. 9-30 lines, poems with hope. Simple words, careful phrasing. Free verse, rhymed poems, sonnets, half page parables, myths and legends, song lyrics. Subjects wanted: love poems, protest poems, mystical poems, nature poems, poems of humanity, poems with solutions to world problems and inner conflict."** They have published poetry by Emilie Glen, Judson Crews, and Bob Barci. As a sample the editor selected these lines from "Donald" by Robert Bailey:

you said you had to leave this lonesome place
and find yourself another life somewhere
a land with values free of strife and care
I understood the anguish on your face.

I have not seen an issue, but the editor describes it as 5 pp., 2-3 poems per page, typeset. They receive 150 poems per year, use about 50. Press run 400, all distributed free. Subscription: $5. **Sample, postpaid: $1.25. Pays one copy. Reports in 6-8 weeks.** The editor says, "Stick to your guns; however, keep in mind that an editor may be able to correct a minor flaw in your poem. Accept only minor adjustments. Go to many open poetry readings. Respect the masters. Read and listen to other poets on the current scene. Make pen pals. Start your own poetry journal. Do it all out of pure love."

‡SNAKE NATION REVIEW (II), 2920 N. Oak, Valdosta, GA 31602, phone 912-242-1503, founded 1989, editor Roberta George, appears twice a year. **"Any form, length of 60 lines or less."** They have recently published poetry by Irene Willis and William Fuller. As a sample the editor selected these lines by David Kirby:

It need only sound,
not be right,
for all unhappy families
are not unhappy
in different ways.

The handsome 6 × 9″ flat-spined, 100 pp. magazine, matte card cover, has a press run of 1,000 for 200 subscriptions of which 11 are libraries. Subscription: $6. **Sample, postpaid: $5. Send SASE for guidelines. Pays 2 copies or prizes. Reports in 3 months. Editor comments on submissions sometimes.**

SNAKE RIVER REFLECTIONS (I, IV-Themes), (formerly *Writing Pursuits*), 1863 Bitterroot Drive, Twin Falls, ID 83301, phone 208-734-0746, appearing 10 times a year using **short (up to 20 lines) poems, "especially related to writing topics."** Pays 2 copies. Guidelines available for SASE. Sample: 25¢ postpaid. Subscription: $5. It is 3 pp., stapled at the corner, press run 100-200. They hold an annual contest, rules available in January.

SNOWY EGRET (II, IV-Nature), RR #1, Box 354, Poland IN 47868, founded 1922 by Humphrey A. Olsen, editor Karl Barnebey, poetry editor Alan Seaburg. **They want poetry that is "nature-oriented: poetry that celebrates the richness and beauty of nature or explores the interconnections between nature and the human psyche."** As a sample of poetry they have recently published they selected these lines from "The Diktaen Cave" by Conrad Hilberry:

The passage turns to perfect dark.
Candles cast
their shadows on the ledge where Zeus was born,

where goats and bees brought him their milk and honey.

Snowy Egret appears twice a year in a 56 pp. magazine-sized format, offset, saddle-stapled, with cover and original graphics. Of 500 poems received they accept about 20. Their press run is 800 for 500 subscribers of which 50 are libraries. **Sample: $8 postpaid. Pays $2/poem, $4/page plus 2 copies. Send 6 × 9 SASE for prospectus with examples of recently published works and writer's guidelines. Reports in 1 month; no backlog.**

SOCIAL ANARCHISM (IV-Political, social issues), 2743 Maryland Ave., Baltimore, MD 21218, phone 301-243-6987, founded (Vacant Lots Press) 1980, poetry editor Howard J. Ehrlich, is a digest-sized 96 pp. biannual, print run 1,200, using about 10 pp. of poetry in each issue which **"represents a political or social commentary that is congruent with a nonviolent anarchist and feminist perspective."** They have recently published poetry by Jacqueline Elizabeth Letalien, L.M. Harrod, Mark Colasurdo, Bridget Balthrop Morton, and Bert Hubinger. As a sample I selected the first stanza of "The Saga of Dick and Jane" by Bruce E. Hopkins:

My recollection is
That it was a college town
   a university town
Where people had degrees
And ate their chicken with knives and forks

Sample: $3 postpaid; $3.50 outside U.S. Submit up to 5 poems, "not in crayon." Considers simultaneous submissions. Reports in 4-6 weeks. Pays 5 copies.

SOCIAL JUSTICE: A JOURNAL OF CRIME, CONFLICT, WORLD ORDER (IV-Political, social issues), P.O. Box 40601, San Francisco, CA 94140, phone 415-550-1703, founded 1974, editor Gregory Shank, is a "quarterly journal addressing **violations of international law, human rights, and civil liberties;** the 'law and order' crime policies of the New Right, including the death penalty; crime and social justice under capitalism and socialism; community approaches to crime control and justice, using a **few poems, not in every issue.**" They want "**political poetry, reflecting personal experiences or expressing the aspirations of broader movements for social justice. Do not want anything unrelated to criminal justice themes or social movements.**" They have published poetry by Adrienne Rich, Jeremy Cronin and Luis Talamantes. As a sample I selected the closing lines from "A First Night in El Sing Sing" by Piri Thomas:

> *Hey—you're not a numba*
> *You got a name—*
> *They only got your body*
> *   not your brain—*

I have not seen it, but the editor describes it as 6×9″, laser printed, then photo offset, no graphics, 180-200 pp., flat-spined." They use 3-4 of 10-15 poems received. Press run is 2,000 for 1,700 subscriptions of which 700 are libraries, others distributed through bookstore sales. Subscription: $25; per issue: $7.50. **Sample: $9.50 postpaid. Pays 1 copy. No simultaneous submissions, previously published poems—"maybe." MS should be double-spaced, one inch margins, pica or elite, Courier if possible or on IBM compatible 5¼″ floppy. Reports in 1 week, time to publication 90 days. Editor sometimes comments on rejections.**

THE SOCIETY OF AMERICAN POETS (SOAP); UPPER ROOM PUBLISHING COMPANY; IN HIS STEPS RECORDS (I, IV-Religious, membership), 102 Demetree Rd., Warner Robins, GA 31093, phone 912-923-6687, founded 1984, editor Rev. Charles E. Cravey. *SOAP* is a literary quarterly of poetry and short stories. Upper Room publishes religious and other books. In His Steps publishes music for the commercial record market. "**Open to all styles of poetry and prose—both religious and secular. No gross or 'X-rated' poetry without taste or character.**" They have recently published poetry by Kenna Boniol, Shirley Beasley, Edward Hawkins, Louise Davis, and the editor. As a sample the editor selected these lines by Edward Bernstein:

> *Battered fortresses, hewn in time by men of warfare—*
> *Death, destruction, both weave their way through the myriads of time—*
> *Like a cancer growing deep within the soul.*

SOAP, the quarterly newspaper, uses **poetry by member/subscribers only.** (Membership: $15/ year.) **For book publication query. No pay. Editor "most certainly" comments on rejections.** The newspaper has poetry competitions in several categories with prize of $25-50. The editor says, "My future plan is to publish a nice 'slick' magazine for poets, religious articles, and short stories. Poets should be more careful in metering each line and in finding 'new' words to describe 'old' emotions, events, etc. Poetry should never 'bore' the reader, but serve to 'spark' the imagination and lead us on to higher realms of thought."

‡SOJOURNERS (IV-Religious, political), Box 29272, Washington, DC 20017, phone 202-636-3637, founded 1975, appears 10 times per year, "with approximately 46,000 subscribers. **We focus on faith, politics and culture from a radical Christian perspective. We use shorter poetry (not over 30 lines), which must be original. We are very open to various themes and seasonal poetry. We look for poetry related to the political and cultural issues covered by our magazine, but also publish poems which simply celebrate life. Poetry using noninclusive language (any racist, sexist, homophobic poetry) will not be accepted.**" As a sample the editor selected these lines (poet unidentified):

> *old ogala woman,*
> *i taste your hot salt tears*
> *burning slowly*
> *through a thousand wrinkles*
> *down a thousand years.*

I have not seen an issue, but the editor describes it as 52 pp., offset printing. It appears monthly except that there is one issue for August/September and February/March. Of 400 poems received per year they publish 8-10. Press run: 50,000 for 46,000 subscriptions of which 500 are libraries; 2,000 shelf sales. Subscription: $27. **Sample, postpaid: $2.75. Send SASE for guidelines. Pays $25/poem plus 5 copies. Submit no more than 3 at a time. Occasionally they use a previously published poem with reprint permission. Reports in 4-6 weeks. Editor comments on submissions "sometimes."**

‡SOLEIL PRESS (IV-Ethnic), Box 452, RFD 1, Lisbon Falls, ME 04252, phone 207-353-5454, founded 1988, contact Denis Ledoux, publishes and distributes **writing by and about Franco-Americans** in chapbooks and paperbacks. **Pays copies.**

SOLO FLYER; SPARE CHANGE POETRY PRESS (I), 2115 Clearview NE, Massillon, OH 44646, Spare Change Poetry Press founded 1979, editor David B. McCoy. **"Three 4-page flyers are published a year; each by an individual author. All styles of poetry using punctuation will be considered, but send only from May through Labor day."** Send up to 10 poems at a time. Payment: 20-25 copies. Free samples on request. Reports in 1-3 months. No submissions returned without SASE. As a sample I selected the closing lines of "The Tornado's Eye" by Margaret Alder Eaves:

> In the black windows of our house,
> my eyes are as empty as the one-armed doll's,
> washed as clear as the rain-swept streets
> in wake of the storm.

‡THE (SOMETHING) (IV-Form, themes), 1520 Bryn Mawr Ave., Racine, WI 53403, founded 1985, editor/publisher Mark M, is a bimonthly **"photocopied magazine of short, off-beat stuff for weirdos. No old-fashioned stuff."** Poets recently published include Dan Nielsen, Cryptomatic Lungworm and David Fujino. As a sample Mark M selected "The Brain" by Dan Nielsen:

> "man will never
> fully comprehend
> the mysteries
> of the brain."
>
> said the Brain.

I have not seen an issue, but the editor describes it as 12 pp., magazine-sized. They accept about 30 of 40 poems received. Press run 50 for 30 subscriptions. Subscription: $6. **Sample, postpaid: $1. Pays 1 copy. Reports in 2-3 weeks. Editor comments on submissions "sometimes."**

SONORA REVIEW (II), Dept. of English, University of Arizona, Tucson, AZ 85721, phone 602-621-8077, founded 1980, poetry editor Bill Marsh, a semi-annual literary journal that publishes "non-genre" fiction and poetry. **The editors want "quality poetry, literary concerns."** They have published poems by Olga Broumas, Jon Anderson, Jane Miller, and Charlie Smith. Some poems are published both in English and Spanish. As a sample, the editors chose the following lines by Linda Gregg:

> I love the places on your body where
> the patina is worn through to the bright metal
> by touching and kissing. Toe or knee.
> Nose or cheek or nipple. Your belly
> as you recline. Pity is where you are.

Sonora Review is a handsome magazine, 6×9", professionally printed on heavy off-white stock, 100 pp. flat-spined, with 2-color glossy card cover. Circulation is 500, of which 200 are subscriptions and 100 go to libraries. Price per copy is $4, subscription $6/year. **Back issue available for $4 postpaid. Pay is 2 copies. Poets should submit typed copy; dot-matrix, simultaneous submissions OK. Reporting time is 8 weeks and time to publication 6 months.** The magazine sponsors annual poetry awards with prizes of $100 and $50.

SOUNDINGS EAST (II), Salem State College, Salem, MA 01970, phone 508-741-6270, founded 1973, advisory editor Rod Kessler. "*SE* is published by Salem State College and is staffed by students. We accept short fiction (15 pp. max) and **contemporary poetry (5 pp. max)**. Purpose is to promote poetry and fiction in the college and beyond its environs. We **do not want graphic profanity**." They have recently published poetry by Martha Ramsey, Walter McDonald and Linda Portnay. The editor selected these sample lines from "Muscatine" by Debra Allbery:

> That night she dreams about California.
> The sun there is different — leisurely, decorative,
> shining like something you could never afford.
> Not like in the Midwest, where the sun is just
> one more day — laborer with a job to do. Traveling
> its rheumy eye over the fields in winter,
> burning too hard on summer weekends, desperate
> as anyone to have a good time. In her dream
> California is as seasonless as heaven.

SE appears twice a year, 64-68 pp. digest-sized, flat-spined, b/w drawings and photos, glossy card cover with b/w photo, circulation 2,000, 120 subscriptions of which 35 are libraries. They receive about 500 submissions per year, use 40-60. **Sample: $3 postpaid. Fall deadline November 15; Spring March 15. No manuscripts read over the summer. Photocopies, dot-matrix, simultaneous submissions OK. Reports within 1-4 months. Pays 2 copies.**

THE SOUNDS OF POETRY (I, IV-Bilingual/Foreign language), 8761 Avis, Detroit, MI 48209, phone 313-843-8478, founded 1983, publisher/senior editor Jacqueline Sanchez, associate editor Jousseline Mae. *The Sounds of Poetry* is typeset on a Macintosh Apple computer, printed on an AB Dick 360 Offset press. The newsletter is magazine-sized, 12 pp. saddle-stapled. "**We mainly publish lesser-known poets.**" They have recently published poetry by Rosamaria Munoz, Jose L. Garza, Ericka Sanchez, Jousseline Sanchez, Jessica Sanchez, Delfin Munoz, John Romero, John Baesl, Richard Lopez, Tony Moser and Daniel Nign III. The editor selected one of three stanzas of a poem by Curwin A. Dukes, "Magic Snowflake":

> *Magic snowflake of winter cold*
> *touch my heart and make it gold*
> *fall from heaven and melt away*
> *but you touch "art" here to stay*
> *If my heart I could only make*
> *stay forever like the magic snowflake.*

The majority of poems are in English, some in Spanish. Five issues a year ranging from 8-12 pages each. They have over 100 subscribers which include libraries and universities. Subscriptions: $5/year (4 issues). "**Sample: $1.50. Contributors receive 1 free copy in which their work appears. Submit poetry in batches of 5 with an SASE, cover letter and brief bio. Reports within 2-8 months.**" Their advice to new poets: "Keep writing, keep submitting, learn from mistakes. Each editor is different. Write with excitement, passion, paint a picture with words. Make us laugh, make us cry, make us care!"

SOUTH CAROLINA REVIEW (II), English Dept., Clemson, U., Clemson, SC 29634-1503, phone 803-656-3151, founded 1968, editor Richard J. Calhoun, is a biannual literary magazine "recognized by the *New York Quarterly* as one of the top 20 of this type." They will consider "**any kind of poetry as long as it's good. Format should be according to new MLA Stylesheet.**" They have recently published poems by F. C. Rosenburg, J. W. Rivers and Angela Walton. The editor selected these sample lines by John Lane:

> *Who is to say if bodies wrapped in a slow roll*
> *are mounted rock in a spreading floor,*
> *or if he did see a child grind off a bench*
> *like a loose glacier? I loved him with all his faults.*

It is a 6x9", 160+ pp., flat-spined, professionally printed magazine which uses about 8-10 pp. of poetry in each issue, has a circulation of 600, 400 subscriptions of which 200 are libraries. Subscription: $7. They receive about 1,000 freelance submissions of poetry per year of which they use 10, have a 2-year backlog. **Sample: $5 postpaid. Reports in 6-9 months, pays in copies.**

‡**SOUTH COAST POETRY JOURNAL (II)**, English Dept., California State University, Fullerton, CA 92634, founded 1986, editor John J. Brugaletta. The twice-yearly (January and June) magazine publishes poetry only. "**We'd like to see poems with strong imagery and a sense that the poem has found its best form, whether that form is traditional or innovative. We prefer poems under 40 lines, but we'll look at others. Any subject-matter or style.** We have recently published Denise Levertov, Mark Strand, X.J. Kennedy, and Robert Mezey." As a sample, the editor selected these lines from "The Last Defenders" by Tony Lucas:

> *We waited in our hole because*
> *we knew of nothing else to do,*
> *nowhere to go. We kept on hoping*
> *for the best. And when the worst*
> *caught up with us, we greeted it*
> *as something closer to relief.*
> *It was all over in a day.*

The journal is digest-sized, 60 pp., perfect-bound, offset, heavy paper cover, some line art. Print run is 500, 150 subscribers, 25 of which are libraries, 50 shelf sales. Subscription: $9, $5/issue. **Sample: $3.50 postpaid. Guidelines are available for SASE. Pay is 2 copies. No simultaneous submissions. Every submission is read by at least three editors. Submissions will be reported on in 4-6 weeks.** They conduct an annual poetry contest judged by eminent poets—most recently: Amy Clampitt. Entry fee is $3/poem.

‡The double dagger before a listing indicates that the listing is new in this edition. New markets are often the most receptive to submissions.

‡SOUTH DAKOTA REVIEW (II,IV-Regional, themes), University of South Dakota, Vermillion, SD 57069, phone 605-677-5220 or 677-5229, founded 1963, editor John R. Milton, is a "literary quarterly publishing poetry, fiction, criticism, essays. When material warrants, an emphasis on the American West; writers from the West; Western places or subjects; frequent issues with no geographical emphasis; periodic special issues on one theme, or one place or one writer. Looking for originality, some kind of sophistication, significance, craft—i.e., professional work. Nothing confessional, purely descriptive, too filled with self-importance." They use 6-10 poems/issue, "receive tons, it seems." Print run 650-900 for 450 subscriptions of which half are libraries. Subscription: $15/year, $25/2 years. **Sample, postpaid: $4. Pays 1 copy. Reports in 1-12 weeks. Editor comments on submissions "rarely."** He says, "Find universal meaning in the regional. Avoid constant 'I' personal experiences that are not of interest to anyone else. Learn to be less self-centered and more objective."

‡SOUTH END PRESS (V, I, IV-Social issues), 116 St. Botolph St., Boston, MA 02115, founded 1977, is "a **political press publishing books on various aspects of the movements for social change.**" They have published 2 books of poetry, but are **not currently reading poetry MSS.**

THE SOUTH FLORIDA POETRY REVIEW, (II), Box 5945, Ft. Lauderdale, FL 33310, *Review* founded 1983, poetry editor S.A. Stirnemann, uses **"previously unpublished free verse or traditional poetry, none that is religious without ingenuity. We try to attract a variety of poetic styles with a common denominator of quality. We take pride in finding 'new' talent, and admit to delight in publishing Florida poets who deserve the recognition, but we also publish nationally recognized poets."** They have published poetry by Siv Cedering, David Kirby, Lisel Mueller, Walter McDonald, Kathleen Spivack, William Stafford. The editors selected these sample lines from "At the Edge of the Hollow" by Edward Byrne:

> *A crane raises large rocks*
> *and spins slowly at the edge of the hollow.*
> *I watch it circle and admire the driver's skill,*
> *the way he seems to have a soft touch, able*
> *to balance the load fished from the bottom silt*

They have a new poetry review section and are looking for essay reviews of recently published books of poetry (published in the previous year) as well as interviews with established poets and essays on contemporary American poetry. The *Review* is perfect-bound, a magazine-sized triquarterly, 68 pp. (including tinted paper cover), circulation 500 with 400 subscriptions of which 20 are libraries. They receive about 2,000 submissions per year, use 130. **Sample: $3.50 postpaid; subscription: $7.50. "We read all year but less in the summer. Submit up to 6 poems, previously unpublished, with SASE and brief bio sketch." Reports within 3 months. Considers simultaneous submissions. Pays 2 copies.** "If we are attracted to a good MS we sometimes reject with suggestions. Submissions that are illegible or hand-corrected make a bad impression. We tend to like subtly strong images; poems, which have something new to say, with originality, even if the subject matter is old."

SOUTH HEAD PRESS; POETRY AUSTRALIA (II), Berrima NSW 2577, Australia, founded 1964, poetry editor John Millett. "We have published 122 issues of *Poetry Australia* (5-6 per year), minimum of 80 pp. per issue, and many books of poetry." 30-50 poets appear in each issue of *PA*. As a sample I selected the first two (of 8) stanzas of "Right Winger" by David Ray:

> *1*
> *On planes*
> *he always sat*
> *over the right wing.*
> *2*
> *When he went hunting*
> *he always shot*
> *the duck in the left wing.*

PA is professionally printed, 6×9¾" flat-spined, glossy card cover, $7.50 per copy. They invite **"unpublished verse in English from writers in Australia and abroad. MSS should be typed double-spaced on one side of paper with name and address on reverse side. Overseas contributors are advised that sufficient money for return postage should accompany poems. Stamps of one country are not legal tender in another. Rates for poems: $10 or 1 year's subscription. Overseas poets are paid in copies. South Head Press will consider submissions for book publication. Query with 3 samples. They pay advance and copies. Editor sometimes comments on rejections.** There is a list of books of poetry they have published in *Poetry Australia*, which serves as their catalog. The editor advises, "Read all you can of the best that has been published in the last 20 years. Include *PA, Hudson Review*, etc."

THE SOUTHERN CALIFORNIA ANTHOLOGY; ANN STANFORD POETRY PRIZES (III), c/o Master of Professional Writing Program, WPH 404, University of Southern California, Los Angeles, CA 90089-4034, phone 213-743-8255, founded 1983, is an "annual literary review of serious contemporary poetry and fiction. **Very open to all subject matters except pornography. Any form, style OK.**" They have recently published poetry by Robery Bly, John Updike, Denise Levertov, Peter Viereck, Donald Hall, James Merrill, and Yevgeny Yevtushenko. As a sample the editor selected these lines from "The Tent People of Beverly Hills" by James Ragan:

> *Faceless on the Boulevard of Mirrors,*
> *North along the flats of Rodeo's stripped*
> *baldhead mannequins*
> *they come treading on*

The anthology is digest-sized, 144 pp., paperback, with a semi-glossy color cover featuring one art piece. Circulation is 1,500, 50% going to subscribers of which 50% are libraries. 30% are for shelf sales. **Sample: $5.95 postpaid. Send SASE for guidelines. Pays 3 copies. Reports in 4 months. Submit 3-5 poems between September and January 3. All decisions made by mid-February. Legible photocopied submissions OK, computer printout submissions acceptable, no dot-matrix, no simultaneous submissions, no previously published poems.** The Ann Stanford Poetry Prizes ($750, $250, and $100) has a March 1 deadline, $10 fee (5 poem limit), for unpublished poems. Include cover sheet with name, address and titles and SASE for contest results. All entries are considered for publication.

SOUTHERN HUMANITIES REVIEW (II, IV-Translations), 9088 Haley Center, Auburn University, AL 36849, poetry editor R. T. Smith, co-editors T. L. Wright and D. R. Latimer, founded 1967, is a 100+ pp. 6×9" literary quarterly, circulation 800. **Interested in poems of any length, subject, genre. Space is limited, and brief poems are more likely to be accepted. "Several poems at a time recommended. Avoid sending faint computer printout. Pays 1 copy and $50 for the best poem published during the year. Translations welcome."** They have recently published poetry by Lars Gustaffson, Donald Hall, Paul Celan, Mary Ruefle, Robert Morgan, John Engels, and Denise Levertov. **Sample copy, $4,** subscription $12/year. The editors advise, "For beginners we'd recommend study and wide reading in English and classical literature, and, of course, American literature — the old works, not just the new. We also recommend study of or exposure to a foreign language and a foreign culture. Poets need the reactions of others to their work: criticism, suggestions, discussion. A good creative writing teacher would be desirable here, and perhaps some course work too. And then submission of work, attendance at workshops. And again, the reading: history, biography, verse, essays — all of it. We want to see poems that have gone beyond the language of slippage and easy attitudes."

SOUTHERN POETRY REVIEW; GUY OWEN POETRY PRIZE (II), English Dept., University of North Carolina, Charlotte, NC 28223, phone 704-547-4225, editor Robert Grey, founded 1958, a semi-annual literary magazine "with emphasis on effective poetry. **Not a regional magazine, but a natural outlet for new Southern talent.**" There are no restrictions on form, style, or content of poetry; length subject to limitations of space. **They do not want to see anything "cute, sweet, sentimental, arrogant or preachy."** They have recently published work by Linda Pastan, Judith Ortiz Cofer, David Ray, Stephen Sandy, Betty Adcock, and Walter McDonald. As a sample, I chose the first stanza from "Museum Piece" by Barbara Fritchie:

> *Past survival, he killed for*
> *trophies. His wife said dead things*
> *have no decorative value.*
> *She never understood*
> *the importance of a good mount.*

Southern Poetry Review is 6×9", handsomely printed on buff stock, 78 pp. flat-spined with textured, one-color matte card cover. Circulation is 1,000+, price per copy $3.50, subscription $6/year. **Sample available for $2 postpaid; no guidelines, but will answer queries with SASE. Pays 1 copy. Writers should submit no more than 3-5 poems. Reporting time is 4-6 weeks, and poems should be printed within a year of acceptance.** There is a yearly contest, the Guy Owen Poetry Prize of $500, to which the entry fee is a subscription; deadline is normally about May 1.

THE SOUTHERN REVIEW (II), 43 Allen Hall, Louisiana State University, Baton Rouge, LA 70803, phone 504-388-5108, founded 1935 (original series); 1965 (new series), poetry editors James Olney and Dave Smith, "is a literary quarterly which publishes fiction, poetry, critical essays, book reviews, with emphasis on contemporary literature in the US and abroad, and with special interest in Southern culture and history. Selections are made with careful attention to craftsmanship and technique and to the seriousness of the subject matter." By general agreement this is one of the most distinguished of literary journals. Joyce Carol Oates, for instance, says, "Over the years I have continued to be impressed with the consistent high quality of *SR*'s publications and its general 'aura,' which bespeaks careful editing, adventuresome tastes, and a sense of thematic unity. *SR* is characterized by a refreshing openness to new work, placed side by side with that of older, more established, and in many cases highly distinguished writers." The editors say they want **"No particular kinds of poetry. We are interested in any formal varieties, traditional or modern, that are well crafted, though we cannot normally accommodate excessively long poems (say 10 pp. and over)."** They have recently published poetry by David Baker, Susan Ludvigson, Frederick Turner, and W.D. Snodgrass. The editors selected these sample lines by Hayden Carruth:

> *Unquestionably*
> *we are crazy; if the doctors won't certify us, we*
> *can certify each other—we do it every day.*
> *We have become each other. We are the two-backed,*
> *two-faced, two-souled computerized contraption*
> *of the modern world, living in two houses. We are*
> *the best lovers in history. We truly are.*

The beautifully printed quarterly is massive: 6¾ × 10", 240+ pp., flat-spined, matte card cover, print-run 3,100 with 2,100 subscriptions of which 70% are libraries. Subscription: $15. They receive about 2,000 freelance submissions of poetry, use 10%. **Sample: $5 postpaid. Prefer 1-4 pp. submissions. Reports in 2 months. Pays $20/printed page plus 2 copies. Send SASE for guidelines.**

SOUTHERN ROSE REVIEW; TAPESTRY; NETHER WORLD; SOUTHERN ROSE PRODUCTIONS; SHAMROCK PRODUCTIONS (I, IV-Anthologies, horror), Rt. 3, Box 272-D, Ripley, MS 38663, founded 1988, editor Joan Cissom. These various imprints are for a variety of periodicals and chapbooks. *Southern Rose Review* (bimonthly) is for **"mainline" poetry;** *Tapestry* (monthly) and *Nether World* (quarterly) specialize in **horror.** All are newsletters photocopied from photoreduced typescript, samples $2.50 each. All sponsor regular contests with small prizes. **Send SASE for guidelines. They pay 2 copies.** As a sample the editor selected these lines from "Heartstones" by Dr. Emory D. Jones:

> *They hurt,*
> *shred the heart*
> *I heaving chest*
> *With sharp facets*
> *Next to lungs,*
> *Jeweled glint*
> *of cold glow—*
> *Hoarded pain.*

The editor says, "Our advice is first to learn the basics of poetry writing, then write regularly. Enter contests and earn credits from being published in small press publications. Then you may be ready to try for the big markets."

SOUTHWEST REVIEW; ELIZABETH MATCHETT STOVER MEMORIAL AWARD (II), 6410 Airline Rd., Southern Methodist University, Dallas, TX 75275, phone 214-373-7440, founded 1915, editor Willard Spiegelman. *Southwest Review* is a literary quarterly that publishes fiction, essays, poetry and interviews. "It is hard to describe our preference for poetry in a few words. We always suggest that potential contributors read several issues of the magazine to see for themselves what we like. But some things may be said: We demand **very high quality in our poems; we accept both traditional and experimental writing, but avoid unnecessary obscurity and private symbolism; we place no arbitrary limits on length but find shorter poems easier to fit into our format than longer ones. We have no specific limitations as to theme." No simultaneous submissions, no previously published work. Photocopies OK.** They have recently published poetry by Henri Cole, Rita Dove, Debora Greger, Frederick Turner, Edward Hirsch and John Koethe. As a sample I selected "The Fifteenth Summer" by James Merrill:

> *Why were we here?*
> *To flow. To bear. To be.*
> *Over the view his tree*
> *In slow, slow motion*
> *Held sway, the pointer of a scale so vast,*
>
> *Alive and variable, so inlaid*
> *As well with sticky, pungent gold,*
> *That many a year*
> *Would pass before it told*
> *Those mornings what they weighed.*

The 6 × 9" 144 pp. perfect-bound journal is professionally printed, matte text stock cover, circulation 1,500 with 1,200 subscriptions of which 600 are libraries. Subscription: $20. They receive about 700 freelance submissions of poetry per year, use 24. **Sample: $5 postpaid. Reports within** a month. **Pays cash plus copies. Send SASE for guidelines.** $100 annual Elizabeth Matchett Stover Memorial Prize for best poem, chosen by editors, published in preceding year.

SOU'WESTER (II), English Dept., Southern Illinois University, Edwardsville, IL 62026-1438, phone 618-692-2289, founded 1960, poetry editor Dickie Spurgeon, appears 3 times a year. **"No preferences" regarding kinds of poems. "We don't publish many that are shorter than 10 lines or so."** They have recently published poetry by Thomas Kretz and Roger Finch. The editor selected the last six lines of "Sonnet to Sombre Dawn" by William Meyer as a sample:

> *The truth of the traumatic*
> *morning light is the opening*
>
> *of the matrix of old moons,*
> *the sacrifice of the intellect*
> *to creation, the seedy complicity*
> *of the grey-green city.*

There are 25-30 pp. in each 6 × 9″ 80 pp. issue. The magazine is professionally printed, flat-spined, with textured matte card cover, circulation 300, 110 subscriptions of which 50 are libraries. Subscription: $10 (3 issues). They receive some 2,000 poems (from 600 poets) each year, use 36-40, have a 2 month backlog. **Sample: $5 postpaid. Simultaneous submission, photocopy and dot-matrix OK. Rejections usually within four weeks. Pays 2 copies. Editor comments on rejections** "usually, in the case of those that we almost accept. Read poetry past and present. Have something to say and say it in your own voice. Poetry is a very personal thing for many editors. When all else fails, we may rely on gut reactions, so take whatever hints you're given to improve your poetry, and keep submitting."

‡THE SOW'S EAR (II, IV-Regional, children), 245 McDowell St., Bristol, TN 37620, 615-764-1625, founded 1988, co-editors Errol Hess and Larry Richman, a quarterly. **"We are very open to form, style, length of poems. We see** *TSE* **as a three-ring circus—with a flair for the visual, which is very much lacking from most poetry journals. The inside ring is the central Appalachian community focused in the area where Tennessee, Kentucky, North Carolina, West Virginia and Virginia come close together. The middle ring is the broader Appalachian region; a culture where we believe a poetry renaissance is beginning. The outer ring is the largest possible community, wherever the English language is spoken and written in poetic form. We encourage submissions from school-age children and plan to feature occasionally a previously unpublished poet."** They have recently published poetry by Marge Piercy, David Huddle, Jim Wayne Miller, and Fred Chappell. As a sample the editor selected these lines from "Perfection" by Kerry Shawn Keys:

> *When the chips are down*
> *the axe should be in the air*
> *feet firmly planted on the ground*
> *the eyes foursquare and everywhere*
> *the grain of the wood*
> *parallel to the spine*
> *in line with earth and heaven.*

TSE is 32 pp. magazine-sized, saddle-stapled, with matte card cover, professionally printed. They accept about 150 of 2,000 poems submitted. Press run: 1,000 for 200 subscribers of which 15 are libraries. Shelf sales: 100-200. Subscription: $8. **Sample, postpaid: $3. Send SASE for guidelines. Pays 1 copy. Reports in 3-4 months. Simultaneous submissions OK if you tell them promptly when it is accepted elsewhere. Enclose brief bio. "We want to know if the poet has not yet been published or is a youth, as we have features for both. Editor comments on submissions "if poet specifically requests it."** Richman selects the kids' poems; others chosen by a 3-person board that meets quarterly. They offer an annual contest with fee of $2/poem, cash prizes. Larry Richman says, "We believe you can make an entire line of fantastic invisible accessories out of a mama pig's ear."

SPACE AND TIME (V, IV-Science fiction, fantasy), #4B, 138 W. 70th St., New York, NY 10023-4432, founded 1966, poetry editor Gordon Linzner, is a biannual "publishing **science fiction & fantasy material—particularly hard-to-market mixed genres and work by new writers. They are not accepting MSS at this time..**" They have published poetry by Steve Eng, Denise Dumars and Neal F. Wilgus. The editor selected these sample lines from "In Man's Image" by D.M. Vosk:

> *Gull and loon once left their print*
> *Within the oceans' reach*
> *Now a robot, stained with mint*
> *Is dancing on the beach*

The 120 pp. digest-sized journal, saddle-stapled, photo reduced from typescript with b/w drawings, has a circulation of 400-500 with 150 subscriptions of which 5 are libraries.

SPARROW PRESS; SPARROW POVERTY PAMPHLETS; VAGROM CHAPBOOKS (V, II), 103 Waldron St., West Lafayette, IN 47906, phone 317-743-1991, founded 1954, poetry editors Felix Stefanile and Selma Stefanile. This is one of the oldest and most highly respected small press publishers of poetry in the country. **"Sparrow Press has enough material in work to see it through 1991. We are not actively seeking manuscripts for this year. We are also in the planning stage for new ventures.** For those who want an idea of the kind of poetry we have been publishing for the past 37 years we maintain our offer of sample copies of our Sparrow Poverty Pamphlets at $2 a copy, and of our larger Vagrom Chap Books at $3 a copy. We also invite you to check out our ongoing discount sales catalogue; send 50¢." Following are some lines from their latest poet, Alice Monks Mears:

> *We gardeners: arbitrary weavers*
> *of living strands, of stems, spikes,*
> *hollow, fibrous, pliant, nettled.*
> *In their corruptible greens.*

SPECTACULAR DISEASES (II), 83B London Rd., Peterborough, Cambridgeshire PE2 9BS UK, founded 1974, Paul Green editor (various invited poetry editors). "The press presents **experimental writing with bias to the current French scene and to current, and past scenes, in the US, and Britain. Most poetry is solicited by the editors.** Long poems will be clearly accepted, if falling in the special categories." They have published poetry by Saúl Yurkievich, Jackson MacLow, and Bernard Noël. *Spectacular Diseases* is an annual digest-sized 40-60 pp." Sample of *SD* £1.75 postpaid. **Query before submitting as most material is invited. Pays in copies.** Under the Spectacular Diseases imprint a number of books and anthologies are printed. For book consideration, **query with about 16 samples; letter helpful but not essential. Pays 10% of run. Send postage for catalog to buy samples.**

SPECTRUM (II), Anna Maria College, Box 72-D, Paxton, MA 01612, phone 617-757-4586, founded 1985, poetry editor Joseph Wilson, is a "multidisciplinary national publication with liberal arts emphasis, presenting 6-8 poems in each 66 page issue: **poems of crisp images, precise language, which have something of value to say and say it in an authentic voice. Not the self-conscious, the 'workshop poem,' the cliché, the self-righteous.**" They have recently published poetry by William Stafford. *Spectrum* appears twice a year in a 6×9" flat-spined format, professionally printed on quality stock with 2-color matte card cover, using b/w photos and art. "We have had to solicit to get the poetry we want, but would rather not." Press run is 1,000 for 650 subscriptions (200 of them to libraries). Per copy: $4. Subscription: $7 for 1 year, $13 for 2 years. **Sample: $3. Pays $20 per poem plus 2 copies. No previously published poems or simultaneous submissions. Reports in 6 weeks.** Editor "occasionally" comments on rejections.

‡SPIDER EYES; TABOO TALES (I,IV-Horror, science-fiction, fantasy, erotic), (formerly Siamese Twin Magazine), 4262 El Carnal Way, Las Vegas, NV 89121, founded 1989, editor/publisher M. Shane Reynolds. *Spider Eyes* appears 3 times a year **"wide open to anything in horror, fantasy, sf, and erotic, all under 30 lines. Looking for creative freedom, bold and daring artistic expression. Submit up to 6 poems/time."** They have recently published poetry by John Grey, Janet Reedman, B.Z. Niditch, and Martha M. Vertreace. It is magazine-sized, 35-45 pp., photocopied from typescript, side-stapled, with matte card cover, using b&w fantasy drawings. They accept about 20% of submissions. Press run 100-150 for 32 subscribers. Subscription: $8.50. **Sample, postpaid: $3. Pays 1 copy. "The ordering of a sample before submitting is very, very much urged."** *Taboo Tales* is an annual, "just like *Spider Eyes*, will be erotic, controversial. Open to submissions the last 4 months of each year."

SPINDRIFT (II), Shoreline Community College, 16101 Greenwood Ave., Seattle, WA 98133, phone 546-4662, founded 1962, faculty advisor varies each year, currently Carol Orlock, is **open to all varieties of poetry except greeting-card style.** They have recently published poetry by Judith Barrington, Paula Jones, Sibyl James, Pesha Gertler, Tom Synder, and Richard West. *Spindrift*, an annual, is handsomely printed in an 8" square, flat-spined 125 pp. format, circulation 500. Price per issue: $6.50. **Sample: $5 postpaid. Send SASE for guidelines. Pays 1 copy. "Submit 2 copies of each poem, 6 maximum. Include cover letter with biographical information. We accept submissions until February 1—report back in March."** The editors advise, "Read what the major contemporary poets are writing. Read what local poets are writing. Be distinctive, love the language, avoid sentiment."

SPINSTERS INK; AUNT LUTE BOOKS (IV-Women), Box 410687, San Francisco, CA 94141, phone 415-558-9655, founded 1978, publisher Sherry Thomas, a small-press publisher of paperback books of fiction, non-fiction, some poetry—**by and for women. "Publishes 6-8 books a year."** As a sample, the publisher selected the following lines by Minnie Bruce Pratt:

> *getting to be a grown girl, I iron the cotton sheets*

> *into perfect blankness. No thump shakes Laura, dreaming in the straight-backed chair,*
> *upright, eyes closed, dark brown*
> *face crumpled in an hour's rest from generations of children*

That is from **We Say We Love Each Other,** a handsomely printed and designed flat-spined 6 × 9″ paperback, glossy card cover with two-tone photograph, 100 pp. with b/w photo of author on last page. The publisher **accepts freelance submissions but writers should query first. She reports on queries in 2 weeks, MS in 6 months. Photocopied MSS are OK, dot-matrix OK if double-strike. The cover letter should include credits and bio. Royalties are 8-12%.** The press publishes only one poetry title every two years.

THE SPIRIT THAT MOVES US; THE SPIRIT THAT MOVES US PRESS; EDITOR'S CHOICE (IV-Anthology), Box 820, Jackson Heights, NY 11372, phone 718-426-8788, founded 1974, poetry editor Morty Sklar. *"The Spirit That Moves Us* will be continuing its **Editor's Choice** series biennially, and publishing regular issues only occasionally. **Editor's Choice** consists of reprints from other literary magazines and small presses, where our selections are made from nominations made by the editors of those magazines and presses." 1987 (latest) **Editor's Choice,** $8 special (reg. $13 with postage); 1980 **Editor's Choice** (501 pages) $6 (reg. $11). The editor's advice: "Write what you would like to write, in a style (or styles) which is/are best for your own expression. Don't worry about acceptance, though you may be concerned about it. Don't just send work which you think editors would like to see, though take that into consideration. Think of the relationship between poem, poet and editor as personal. You may send good poems to editors who simply do not like them, whereas other editors might."

SPIRITUAL QUEST PUBLISHING (IV-Religious, anthologies, spirituality/inspirational), 505 St. Andrews Drive, Sarasota, FL 34243, founded 1988, editor Marla Bovinett, publishes two anthologies per year of **religious poetry, up to 26 lines, reports in 4 weeks.** They accept about 500 poems per year from 800 submissions. No information on payment. The editor selected this sample by C.F. Escue:

> *the leaves are changing now*
> *after an ending summer*
> *burning finally is a last*
> *visible display, like golden straw*
> *or the red brown stubble of a new mown field.*

Sample copy for $7.95 (includes postage). "For our coffee-table editions of a **A Joyful Noise,** we seek contemporary Christian poetry and inspirational verse to show how to cope with current issues. Recently published poetry by James Rooney, Robert Munro and Margaret Peacock. **Digest-size book, glossy color cover, perfect-bound.**

SPITBALL; CASEY AWARD (for best baseball book of the year) (IV-Sports), 6224 Collegevue Pl., Cincinnati, OH 45224, phone 513-541-4296, founded 1981, poetry editor Virgil Smith, is "a unique literary magazine devoted to poetry, fiction and book reviews *exclusively* **about baseball.** Newcomers are very welcome, but remember that you have to know the subject. We do and our readers do. Perhaps a good place to start for beginners is one's personal reactions to the game, *a* game, a player, etc. & take it from there." As a sample I selected the last stanza of "Curt Flood" by Tim Peeler:

> *you are a ghost at barterer's wing,*
> *your smoky gray eyes*
> *are two extra zeroes*
> *on every contract.*

The digest-sized 52 pp. quarterly, saddle-stapled, matte card cover, offset from typescript, has a circulation of 1,000, 750+ subscriptions of which 25 are libraries. Subscription: $12. They receive about 1,000 submissions per year, use 40—very small backlog. "Many times we are able to publish accepted work almost immediately." **Sample: $5 postpaid. "We are not very concerned with the technical details of submitting, but we do prefer a cover letter with some bio info. We also like batches of poems and prefer to use several of same poet in an issue rather than a single poem." Pays 2 copies.** "We encourage anyone interested to submit to *Spitball.* We are always looking for fresh talent. Those who have never written 'baseball poetry' before should read some first probably before submitting. Not necessarily ours. We sponsor the Casey Award (for best baseball book of the year) and the Casey Awards Banquet every January. Any chapbook of baseball poetry should be sent to us for consideration for the 'Casey' plaque that we award to the winner each year."

SPOON RIVER QUARTERLY (II,IV-Regional, translations), English Dept. Illinois State University, Normal, IL 61761, phone 309-438-3667, founded 1976, poetry editor Lucia Getsi, is a "poetry quarterly that features newer and well-known poets from around the country and world;" features **one Illinois poet per issue** at length for the *SRQ* Illinois Poet Series. The quarterly's last issue each year is a flat-spined anthology of the three Illinois poets of that volume year. (Spoon River Poetry Press, Box 1443,

The Spoon River Quarterly

VOLUME XIV   NUMBER 3

SUMMER 1989

Lucia Getsi, editor of **The Spoon River Quarterly,** *chooses cover photos that are "so alive they jump off the page at me." This photo of a run-down house in Tennessee is Getsi's mother's childhood home. She says, "There is a supernatural beauty here, the natural processes of decay as the house sags and begins to cave in, while the trees and shrubs, so carefully planted decades before, grow dense and wild, a lavish embrace of artifice back into the natural world." Getsi adds, "We want interesting and compelling poetry that operates beyond the ho-hum so-what level, in any form or style about anything." The photographer, Joe Beasley, owns a camera/ photography shop in McMinnville, Tennessee.*

Peoria, IL 61655, editor David Pichaske, is still in operation.) "We want interesting and compelling poetry that operates beyond the ho-hum, so-what level, in any form or style about anything; language that is fresh, energetic, committed, filled with some strong voice of authority that grabs the reader in the first line and never lets go. Do not want to see insipid, dull, boring poems, especially those that I cannot ascertain why they're in lines and not paragraphs; poetry which, if you were to put it into paragraphs, would become bad prose." They also use translations of poetry. They have recently published poetry by Linnea Johnson, Richard Jackson, Paulette Roeske, Bruce Guernsey, Diana Hume George, Jeff Gundy, and Kathariné Soniat. As a sample Lucia Getsi selected these lines by Helen Degen Cohen:

> *A darkness, a house*
> *we cannot come out of,*
> *cannot see out of.*
> *Nor even remember*

SRQ has a beautifully produced flat-spined 64 pp., digest-sized, laser set format with glossy card cover using photos, ads. They accept about 2½% of 200 MSS received per month. Press run is 500 for 300 subscriptions (75 of them libraries), and some shelf sales. Subscription: $10. **Sample: $3 postpaid. Pays 3 copies. Reports in 8 weeks. "No simultaneous submissions unless we are notified immediately if a submission is accepted elsewhere. We accept chapbook-length submissions of unpublished poems from poets who have an Illinois connection, by birth or current residence."** Editor comments on rejections "many times, if a poet is promising."

‡SQUEAKY WHEELS PRESS (IV-Anthology, specialized), 1720 Oregon St., Berkeley, CA 94703, phone 415-548-4121, founded 1987, editor Cheryl Marie Wade, managing editor Beverly Slapin, publishes an annual anthology of writing by disabled writers and artists. "We highly encourage submissions by people of color; lesbians and gay men; women and men with cancer, AIDS and other life-threatening disabilities; and people with hearing and/or visual impairments. No more than 6 poems. We welcome all styles and forms. We look for clear and powerful communication.' They have published poetry by editor Cheryl Marie Wade, Barbara Ruth, Neil Marcus, and S.Z. Spencer. As a sample the editor selected these lines from "I Am Not One of The" by Cheryl Marie Wade:

> *I am not one of the physically challenged—*
> *I'm a sock in the eye with gnarled fist*
> *I'm a French kiss with cleft tongue*
> *I'm orthopedic shoes sewn on a last of your fears*

Sample, postpaid: $10 for most recent anthology. Pays 1 copy, others at half-price. Simultaneous submissions and previously published poems OK. Editor comments on submissions "always." The 1989 anthology, **Close to the Truth,** is magazine-sized, comb bound (plastic spiral), professionally printed, 77 pp. with glossy card cover. "Our anthology is also a training project for disabled writers and poets who would like to learn other aspects of publishing, e.g., editing, choosing, ordering, layout, art, managing a publication. Be stalwart and courageous! Submit your work to as many sources as you can afford. Take rejections and criticism gracefully, and learn from them, even if you think the editor is full of crap. There's something to learn from every experience."

STAND MAGAZINE; NORTHERN HOUSE (II, IV-Translations), 19 Haldane Terrace, Newcastle on Tyne NE2 3AN, England. U.S. Editor: Prof. Jack Kingsbury, Box 1161, Florence, AL 35631-1161 (all U.S. contributions to U.S. editor please). *Stand*, founded by editor Jon Silkin in 1952, is a highly esteemed literary quarterly. Jon Silkin seeks more subscriptions from U. S. readers and also hopes "that the magazine **would be seriously treated as an alternative platform to American literary journals.**" He wants "**verse that tries to explore forms. No formulaic verse.**" They have recently published poems by such poets as Peter Redgrove, Elizabeth Jennings, Barry Spacks. I selected a sample from "The Meon Hill Picket" by Yann Lovelock:
> Something must be done about this.
> The beech leaves hiss on the hill's verge.
> From the little cars in the field below
> Hang-gliders climb the slope with their women.

Library Journal calls *Stand* "one of England's best, liveliest, and truly imaginative little magazines." Among better-known American poets whose work has appeared there are Robert Bly, William Stafford, David Ignatow, Philip Levine and Richard Eberhart. Poet Donald Hall says of it, "among essential magazines, there is Jon Silkin's *Stand*, politically left, with reviews, poems and much translation from continental literature." In its current format it is 6×8", flat-spined 80 pp., professionally printed in 2 columns, small type, on thin stock with glossy card cover, using ads. Circulation is 4,500 with 2,800 subscriptions of which 600 are libraries. Subscription: $16. **Sample: $4.50 postpaid. Pays £30 per poem (unless under 6 lines) and 1 copy (⅓ off additional copies).** Northern House "**publishes mostly small collections of poetry by new or established poets. The pamphlets often contain a group of poems written to one theme. Occasionally larger volumes are published**, such as the full length collection by Sorley Maclean, translated by Iain Crichton Smith." The sample I have seen is a handsomely printed chapbook, digest-sized: **The Constitution of Things** by Michael Blackburn, £1.25 or $2.50.

STAPLE (I, II), Derbyshire College of Higher Education, Mickleover, Derby, Derbyshire DE3 5GX United Kingdom Phone 0332-471811, FAX 294861, founded 1983, editorial contact D. C. Measham, business manager. This literary magazine appears 3 times a year. "**Nothing barred: Evidence of craft, but both traditional and modernist accepted; no totally esoteric or concrete poetry.**" They have published poetry by Jon Silkin, Philip Callow, Peter Cash, and David Craig. As a sample D. C. Measham selected these lines from "Two Spring Sonnets" by John Sewell:
> The husks split clean, an early butterfly
> swoons past, a new-lit dung fly plants his feet
> into my dung, his share of my beneficence.

Staple is professionally printed, flat-spined, $80+$ pp., with card cover. Of up to 2,000 poems received per year they accept about 10%. Their press run is 600 with 300 subscriptions of which 100 are libraries. Subscription: £5. **Sample: £1.50 postpaid. Guidelines available for SASE. Pays winners of open competitions, others 2 copies. They consider simultaneous submissions but previously published poems only under special circumstance. Reports in up to 2 months. Editor sometimes comments on rejections.** Send SASE (or SAE with IRC) for rules for their open biennial competitions (next competition: 1992).

STAR BOOKS, INC.; STARLIGHT MAGAZINE (I, IV-Spirituality/Inspirational), 408 Pearson St., Wilson, NC 27893, phone 919-237-1591, founded 1983, president Irene Burk Harrell, who says they are "**very enthusiastically open to beginners.** We have published nine volumes of poetry to date, four of which were written by persons who had no previous publication record. **All of our poetry must be specifically Christian, in line with the teachings of the Bible. We're looking for the fresh and the new. Can't use avant-garde and/or esoteric. For us the impact of the *thought* of a poem is paramount. Need more short poems, with short lines.**" They have published books of poetry by Marilyn Black Phemister, Jack McGuire, Maxine M. Roberson, Charlotte Carpenter, Maureen Arthur-Lynch, Dorothy Jones Clements, and Helena White. "Contributors to our *StarLight* magazine are largely previously unpublished." As a sample she selected these lines from Norma Woodbridge's "Priorities" in her **Meditations Of a Modern Pilgrim:**
> Lord,
> May I not dwell
> On peripheries,

> Busy about
> Inconsequential matters.

The book is 206 pp. flat-spined, typeset and printed in dark type on quality stock with glossy 2-color card cover, $7. *StarLight* is a quarterly, digest-sized, 60 pp., saddle-stapled, professionally printed, with matte card cover. Subscription: $15. **Guidelines available for SASE. Sample: $4 postpaid. Submit one poem per page, no cursive type, no erasable bond, no simultaneous submissions or previously published poems. Pays 3 copies of magazine; books pay 10% or more royalties. Submit 5-6 samples for book publication with cover letter including bio, publications, "something about yourself, especially about your relationship to God, and why you are writing. We are an exceedingly personal publishing house. Pray about whether to query or send full MS. In some cases one method is best, in some cases another. Either is acceptable." Reports in 1-4 weeks. They also publish approximately four chapbooks each year. Send SASE for guidelines.** They hold an annual Star Books Writers' Workshop in October. Irene Burk Harrell says, "Because God seems to be speaking to so many of His children today through poetry, and because established publishing houses are often closed to it on account of the demands of the bottom line, we are looking forward to publishing more and more anointed, God-given poetry of real excellence. Send us your best!"

‡**STAR ROUTE JOURNAL (I, IV-Regional)**, Box 1451, Redway, CA 95560, phone 707-923-3351, founded 1977, publisher/editor Mary Siler Anderson, is a newsprint tabloid publishing 10 issues per year, using poetry, fiction, essays and graphics. **"Not overly fond of rhyming. Length unimportant. Partial to Northern California poets. Nature and humanity. Some political poetry. Nothing cute or trite."** They have recently published poetry by William Everson, Dan Roberts, Edward Mycue, Crawdad Nelson, Nancy L. Clark and Walt Phillips. As a sample, I selected the whole poem, "Seeing" by Mary Messener:

> When I think of you
> it is gently
> a luminous green
> curve of light
> as pears passed one hand
> to another
> over a silent counter.

It is 16-28 tabloid pages. They use "a little more than half" of about 30 poems received per month. Press run: 1,000 for 250 subscriptions of which 3 are libraries, 300 shelf sales. Subscription: $10. Sample copy: $1. "Back issues not generally available." **Send SASE for guidelines. Pays subscription. "Please don't send your only copy; I'm very absent-minded." Include name and address on each poem submitted. Simultaneous submissions and previously published poems OK. Reports in 3 weeks. Editor comments on submissions.** "I can't seem to stop myself."

STARLIGHT PRESS (II, IV-Anthology, form), P.O. Box 3102, Long Island City, NY 11103, founded 1980, editor Ira Rosenstein, is a small press planning to publish an anthology of poetry, its second, within the next two years. This anthology will be dedicated to the sonnet form. **To submit for the anthology, send a maximum of 3 sonnets. While strictly metered, 14-line sonnets are welcome,** *Starlight* **is most open to expansions of the form: 16-line sonnets, sprung-metered sonnets, unmetered, half-rhymed, unrhymed, multi-stanza, use your creativity.** What matters is that all poems partake, however tenuous this description may seem, of 'sonnetness,' and, beyond that, that they constitute a vivid experience for the reader. As a sample the following lines are offered from "Why Bother?", by Ira Rosenstein:

> Utterly beautiful and penlessly so: she's never written a line
> Kind and friendly, leggy, imaginative lace, talkative and apt, compelling,
> Caring, illuminating, patient, passionate, interested, interesting;
> Here is a young woman to concede to: great, great fun, and very, very fine.

They will consider simultaneous submissions and previously published poems. Reports in 2 months. Pays 2 copies plus discount on additional Starlight publications.

STARMIST BOOKS (V), Box 12640, Rochester, NY 14612, founded 1986, president Beth Boyd, is a small-press publisher of poetry books, **"open to all forms except pornography. Responds with encouragement, comments. As of now, submissions by invitation only."** StarMist Books has recently published poetry by jani johe webster. Beth Boyd has selected as a sample these lines from her book, **Shadow and Rainbows:**

> We would think of Today as
>   a Treasure —
> all of these things we cannot
>   measure

> *The freshness of the*
>   *rain —*
> *The sting of the*
>   *wind —*
> *The twitter of a*
>   *bird —*

Payment is negotiable. Brochures available upon request. Editor sometimes comments on rejections. Advice: "To be aware with each moment of the poetry that surrounds us . . . to ever see it, hear it, taste it, smell it, feel it — write it."

STARSONG (I, IV-Science fiction/fantasy/horror), Rt. 2, Box 260B, St. Matthews, SC 29135, phone 803-655-5895, founded 1987, editor Larry D. Kirby, III, is a quarterly **"of sci-fi, fantasy, and horror,"** using poetry of "any form, any style, very open" none that is **"pretentious, where meaning is unclear."** He has published poetry by Ann K. Schwader, Cliff Burns, and Scott C. Virtes. As a sample he selected these lines from "Egor's Error" by Geri Eileen Davis:

> *Egor, you moron!*
> *I told you to evict them.*
> *Evict!*
> *Not eviscerate.*

Starsong is magazine-sized, 90-100 pp., photocopied with a heavy stock cover. He accepts about 20% of 400 poems received per year. Press run is over 400 for 50 subscriptions of which 5 are libraries. **Sample: $5 postpaid. Send SASE for guidelines. Pays 1 copy. No more than one poem per page, name and address on each page. Simultaneous submissions OK. Reports in 2 weeks — to be published in the next one or two issues. Editor usually comments on rejections.** He says, "Say what you mean in your work. Don't try to impress with obscured meanings. I hate that."

STATE STREET PRESS (II), Box 278, Brockport, NY 14420, phone 716-637-0023, founded 1981, poetry editor Judith Kitchen, **"publishes chapbooks of poetry (20-24 pp.) usually chosen in an anonymous competition.** State Street Press hopes to publish emerging writers with solid first collections and to offer a format for established writers who have a collection of poems that work together as a chapbook. We have also established a full-length publication — for those of our authors who are beginning to have a national reputation. We want **serious traditional and free verse. We are not usually interested in the language school of poets or what would be termed 'beat.' We are quite frankly middle-of-the-road. We ask only that the poems work as a collection, that the chapbook be more than an aggregate of poems — that they work together."** They have recently published poetry by Stephen Corey, Hannah Stein, Jerah Chadwick, Hilda Raz, and Sally Jo Sorensen. These sample lines are from "Once You Have a Name" by Peter Yovu:

> *There was no one to say a word.*
> *No one to say the sun lay in the sand*
> *like a hub of emptiness, like ambushed love,*
> *or three clouds nearly the same were black*
> *on top, glowing below. There were no tracks*
> *of tumbleweed or wind. There was a mound*
> *of sand in the shape of a turtle,*
> *a shadow coming home.*

The sample chapbook I have seen is beautifully designed and printed, 6 × 9", 30 pp., with textured matte wrapper with art. **Send SASE for guidelines and contest rules. There is a $5 entry fee, for which you receive one of the chapbooks already published. Simultaneous submissions encouraged. Photocopies OK. Dot-matrix OK "but we don't like it." Pays copies and small honorarium, and authors buy additional ones at cost, sell at readings and keep the profits.** Judith Kitchen comments, "State Street Press believes that the magazines are doing a good job of publishing beginning poets and we hope to present published and unpublished work in a more permanent format, so we do reflect the current market and tastes. We expect our writers to have published individual poems and to be considering a larger body of work that in some way forms a 'book.' We have been cited as a press that prints poetry that is accessible to the general reader."

‡STEREOPTICON PRESS (I), 534 Wahlmont Dr., Webster, NY 14580, founded 1981-2, editor/publisher Etta Ruth Weigl, is a **cooperative publisher (poet shares cost) of "short and well-crafted lyrics showing command of language and more than one level of meaning, but not needlessly obscure. No concrete, performance, 'shock' style, or avant-garde poems."** As a sample she chose these lines from "Winter Walk" by Eleanor A. McQuilkin:

> *The child was "going to a friend's house"*
> *And his voice spoke soft as crayon*
> *Drawing doorways on the land.*

MS should have no more than 1 poem per page. Submit query with 4-5 poems, bio, publications. Previously published material OK. Reports on queries in 6 weeks, MSS in 4 months. Pays 30 copies. "In order to maintain quality production, I reach cooperative agreement with the author, and both of us put money into the project. Arrangements vary, depending on author's needs and wishes. Editor must find MS of merit and marketable before discussion of terms can take place." She comments on rejections "only if MS comes very close to meeting my standards, but needs a bit more work."

THE STEVAN COMPANY; SOCIETY OF ETHICAL AND PROFESSIONAL PUBLISHERS OF LITERATURE; SEPPL NEWSLETTER (II, IV-Translations), 3010 Bee Cave Rd., Austin, TX 78746, founded 1980, editor Ann Botkin, publisher Kathryn McDonald. They want to see "no racist, religious bigotry, profanity, or sexist poetry. Thoughtful open verse, sestinas, sonnets, villanelles, haiku, tanka; current events OK. No violence or work extolling drugs. Anti-apartheid OK, feminist OK, environmental OK. Stay subtle, we even like romantic work, especially concerned with environment. No couplets, rhymes, limericks, don't like slang, confessional, new age, psychopomp. If you read *The New Yorker, The Atlantic*, and have read textbooks such as Voice Great Within Us, the major Mentor book of poems, e.e. cummings, R.H. Blyth, Li Po, William Blake, you're on track. Well-read poets usually write well. Our readers are very well read and read between 175-210 small press books per year. We prefer to work with experienced writers." They have recently published poetry by Jack Terahata (Japan), Nat Scammacca (Italy), and Dong Jiping (China). In addition to anthologies, they publish collections by individuals. Query with no more than 5 samples, bio, publication credits. "No lengthy cover letter, please do not inundate us with all 900 poems you have written. We prefer no previously published poems and usually not simultaneous submissions. No phone calls. Not necessary to subscribe or join SEPPL." Reading period June-August. They pay in copies. Reports in 6-8 weeks; publication within 1-2 years. Of 75-113 poems received in 30 MSS they accept 60 poems. Kathryn McDonald says, "We are not a vanity press, sometimes try to solicit grants, will accept money from foundations. The Society of Ethical Publishers agrees to maintain a code of ethics, can make legal referrals, sometimes offers mechanical advice to poets and publishers. This is a private club of like-minded publishers who wish to continue traditions and facilitate rapport between publisher and writer. Board members share mailing lists, copyright attorney and networking information. Members receive free samples, parties and share trade information (i.e., grants available, distributors, printers information, etc.) All members have excellent references, personal and professional. Many can translate and all are committed to their craft." The *SEPPL Newsletter* "contains feature stories, book release announcements, art reviews, general information, 12 pp., sporadically published, members may advertise; sample books received from non-members may or may not be reviewed. Published intermittently as material and funding permit. Stevan Company does organize readings for local writers, has workshops for writers, does video tapes of performance poetry for ACTV-TV, and generally treats our writers well by extending ourselves to prepare press releases and by referral to other publishers. We comment on rejections occasionally if requested. We publish poetry to provide voice to high ideals and emphasize the lyrical qualities of language. We will accept foreign language poems with English translation. We are not a political vehicle but are interested in current events."

‡STILL WATERS PRESS; STILL WATERS WRITING CENTER; WOMEN'S POETRY CHAPBOOK CONTEST; WINTER POETRY CHAPBOOK COMPETITION (II, IV-Women), 112 W. Duerer St., Galloway, NJ 08201, phone 609-652-1790, founded 1989, editor Shirley Warren, is a "small-press publisher of poetry chapbooks, short fiction chapbbooks, and poet's handbooks (contemporary craft). Especially interested in works by, for, and about women. We prefer poetry firmly planted in the real world, but equally mindful of poetry as art. The transformation from pain to perseverance, from ordinary to extraordinary, from defeat to triumph, pleases us. But we reject Pollyanna poetry immediately. Nothing sexist, in either direction. We don't want homosexual poetry. Most rhymed poetry doesn't work because it leads to strange manipulations of syntax to achieve rhyme. No patriarchal religious verse. Preferred length: 4 lines—2 pp. per poem. Form: no restrictions—we expect content to dictate the form." They have recently published poetry by Beverly Foss Stoughton and by Lynne H. deCourcy. As a sample the editor selected these closing lines from deCourcy's poem "Fire":

> the leaf arched and flamed and I leapt
> to stamp it out, as though I could
> stamp out the terror of anything
> I started in the world,
> as though I could
> stamp out the fires of hand and heart
> to come, love
> leaping from my fingertips and
> spreading out of control.

She publishes 4-8 books a year, including one or two flat-spined paperbacks and chapbooks averaging 16-28 pp. Query with 3 samples, bio, publications. Simultaneous submissions and previously published poems OK. Pays 10% of the press run. Editor comments on submissions "usually." Sample chapbooks: $4.95; pamphlets: $3. They hold 4 annual contests, each with $10 reading fee; send SASE for detailed guidelines. The editor says, "read other poets, both contemporary and traditional. Attend some workshops, establish rapport with your local peers, attend readings. Keep your best work in circulation. Someone out there is looking for you." The Still Waters Writing Center offers workshops, writing classes, and some readings.

THE STONE (II), % Greenpeace, 1112-B Ocean St., Santa Cruz, CA 95060, phone 408-426-9874 (home), founded 1967, editor Richard E. Jörgensen, is an irregularly published literary magazine using "mostly poetry, also some fiction and graphics, but these are usually solicited. **We're open to poetry submissions from anyone."** They want **"one-line and up (rarely publish epics or long poems). Concrete and naturalistic in style, grounded in experience, with imagery and implication as chief tools of expression. No confessional, generalization or statement-oriented, experimental and visual."** They have recently published poetry by David Kresh, Lyn Lifshin, Margot Trietel, Ruth Wildes Schuler and Janet Carncross Chandler. As a sample the editor selected these lines by Pamela Raphael:

> We drive in the dark to the airport
> Last night's loving a memory
> Already palm trees are in your mind
> Sea foam on your lips . . .

The Stone is flat-spined, 48-96 pp., digest-sized, photocopied from typescript, circulation 500 to 50 subscriptions of which 12 are libraries. Per issue: $5. **Sample: $1 postpaid. Pays 2 or more copies. Reports in 1-2 months, but it may be up to 2 years to publication. Submit 1-6 pp. of typed work. Editor "generally" comments on rejections. "Authors who submit must have patience."**

‡STONE CIRCLE PRESS (IV-Ethnic), P.O. Box 44, Oakland, CA 94604, founded 1987, editor Len Irving, publishes books **"of a Celtic nature. Backgrounded in Scotland, Ireland, Wales, Isle of Man, Cornwall, Brittany." We welcome Stonehenge rather than Acropolis material."** As a sample the editor selected these lines (poet unidentified):

> Shadows like horses
> Down palisades of night
> Bunched or racing in death-seeking gallop
> See the darkening cloud as their shadows
> Break the starting gate

They publish an average of 2 flat-spined paperbacks per year, averaging 100 pp. **Query with 6 samples. Responds to queries in 1 month. Pays 25 books.** "We are a nonprofit press associated with the Institute of Celtic Studies. We finance and publish the book. The author receives a stated number of books but no royalties." They also subsidy publish, providing "seed money and desk-top publication," seeking donations from all available sources.

STONE DRUM (II), Box 233, Valley View, TX 76272, editors Joseph Colin Murphey and Dwight Fullingim, "is published periodically on no fixed schedule, by Stone Drum Press, a private, non-profit organization." Vol. 2, No. 2 (Issue #8) published poetry by Cyd Adams, Charles Behlen, Jim Cody, Melvin Kenne, and Edmund Conti. As a sample the editor selected these lines from "A Hammock Made in Merida" by Jonathan London:

> . . . But these strings
> of cotton are woven
> of lives — in a prison
>
> in Merida, Yucatan. For a small
> price (a price
> too great?) we hang
>
> suspended, in our leisure
> between the dark
> backs of the Third
>
> World.

"Reading Periods will be September-November, annually. Please do not submit at other times." Pays copies. Poets wanting to submit material may write for sample copies of the magazine; single copies: $7, subscription: $12 for 2 issues. Editor will include a sheet of guidelines with sample copies. They publish "perhaps one" chapbook per year.

STONE PRESS (V), 1790 Grand River, Okemos, MI 48864, founded 1968, editor Albert Drake, publishes poetry postcards, posters, broadsides, chapbooks and books. **"Due to other publishing commitments, I'm unable to read poetry submissions during 1991."** He has published books by Earle Birney, Judith Goren, Lee Upton and James Kalmbach. Send for booklist to buy book samples.

STONE SOUP, THE MAGAZINE BY CHILDREN; THE CHILDREN'S ART FOUNDATION (IV-Children), P.O. Box 83, Santa Cruz, CA 95063, founded 1973, editor Ms. Gerry Mandel. *Stone Soup* publishes writing and art by children through age 13; they want to see free verse poetry but no rhyming poetry, haiku, or cinquain. The editor chose as a sample these four lines from "Cancun, A Paradise" by 9-year-old Lisa Osornio:

> *Dangling of the blue*
> *Drops of water splashed from the cool pool,*
> *orange ice drinks cool, going down into the water*
> *and swimming eight different ways.*

Stone Soup, published 5 times a year, is a handsome 6 × 8¾" magazine, professionally printed on heavy stock with 4 full-color art reproductions inside and a full-color illustration on the coated cover, saddle-stapled. A membership in the Children's Art Foundation at $22/year includes a subscription to the magazine, each issue of which contains an Activity Guide. There are 4 pp. of poetry in each issue. Circulation is 12,000, all by subscription; 2,000 go to libraries. **Sample: $4.50 postpaid. Submissions can be any number of pages, any format, but no simultaneous submissions. The editor receives 2,000 poetry submissions/year and uses only 20; she reports in 4 weeks. Guidelines are available for SASE. Pay is 2 copies plus discounts. Criticism will be given when requested.**

STORMLINE PRESS, INC. (V, IV-Rural), Box 593, Urbana, IL 61801, phone 217-328-2665, founded 1985, publisher Ray Bial, an independent press publishing fiction, poetry, and photography, **ordinarily only by invitation. Do not send unsolicited manuscripts.** "We prefer that you first study our publications, such as **A Turning**, by Greg Kuzma, to get an idea of the type of material we like to publish. **We publish both established and new poets, but in the latter case prefer to publish those poets who have been working some years to master their craft. We are presently committed through 1990."** May consider simultaneous submissions. Hard copy MSS are preferred, but photocopied or dot-matrix MSS are OK. Royalties will be 15% after production costs are covered, plus 25 author's copies. The press publishes 2-4 books of poetry each year with an average page count of 72. They are 6 × 9", some flat-spined paperbacks and some hardcover.

STORY LINE PRESS; NICHOLAS ROERICH POETRY PRIZE FOR FIRST BOOK OF POETRY (III, IV-Form), Three Oaks Farm, 27006 Gap Road, Brownsville, OR 97327-9718, phone 503-466-4352, **Story Line Press**, founded 1985, poetry editor Robert McDowell. Story Line Press publishes each year the winner of the Nicholas Roerich Poetry Prize for a First Book of Poetry ($1,000 plus publication and a paid reading at the Roerich Museum in New York City; a runner-up receives a full Story Line Press Scholarship to the Wesleyan Writers Conference in Middletown, Connecticut; $15 entry and handling fee). They have recently published poetry by Donald Hall, Colette Inez, Brenda Marie Osbey, Jane Reavill Ransom, and Beth Joselow.

STORYPOEMS (I, Form, subscribers), P.O. Box 293, Oak Ridge, NC 27310, founded 1989, editor J.R. McClintock, appears every 2 months. "Accepted poems *will tell definite stories and have definable beginning—middle—ends.* The story must be explicit, not merely implied. Poems may be of any style or form or length (within reason, 'space permitting'). Nothing purely lyric, reactive, no haiku, etc. An impression of a seascape would not be acceptable; the story of a seagoing experience would be. I prefer a definable though not necessarily 'conventional' pattern of rhythm." The editor describes it as 8 pp. typed/photocopied. Press run 100 for 20 subscribers. Subscription: $18. Single issue: $3.50. **Sample, postpaid: $10. Send SASE for guidelines. Pays "at least" $5/poem. "Only paid subscribers (single issue or full-year) are eligible to submit for possible publication."**

STRAIGHT; STANDARD PUBLISHING CO. (IV-Religious, teens), 8121 Hamilton Ave., Cincinnati, OH 45231, editor Carla J. Crane. Standard is a large religious publishing company. *Straight* is a weekly take-home publication (digest-sized, 12 pp., color newsprint) **for teens. Poetry is by teenagers, any style, religious or inspirational in nature. No adult-written poetry.** As a sample the editor selected the first stanza of "Turn to You" by Lonna Aleshire (19):

> *Whenever I'm lonely*
> *or feeling blue*
> *Please teach me to remember*
> *to turn to You.*

Guidelines available for SASE. Pays $5/poem plus 5 copies, reports in 4-6 weeks, publishes

acceptances in 9-12 months. Teen author must include birthdate. Photocopy, dot matrix, simultaneous submissions OK. "Many teenagers write poetry in their English classes at school. If you've written a poem on an inspirational topic, and your teacher's given you an 'A' on it, you've got a very good chance of having it published in *Straight*."

STRAIGHT AHEAD (I, IV-Subscription); SIARWOT PUBLISHING CO. (V), P.O. Box 2091, La Habra, CA 90632, founded 1987, editors Michael Walsh and Mark Walsh. *Straight Ahead* is published 2-4 times per year. Michael Walsh says, "We began in 1987 as a group of poets wishing to self-publish. We then began publishing others' poems and are desperately seeking new contributors. **New forms welcome. The unusual and original is praised here. Prefer poetry that relates to the human experience.** No visual poetry, haiku, porn, Satanist, long poems (over 1 page), or 'Bambi in the woods' types." They have recently published poetry by John Grey, Anita Poole, Bernard Hewitt, and Robert Johnson. As a sample I selected "Daggers" by Garrison L. Hillard:

> Trim and vicious was the day
> You went away
> The sky as blue as death
> And your final words
> Formed daggers
> From your breath

SA is 16-24 pp., digest-sized, photocopied on plain paper with paper cover, b/w cartoon art. Their press run is 400-450 with 50 subscriptions. Subscription: $8/year. **Sample: $1 postpaid. Pays 1 copy. Guidelines available for SASE. Reports in 4 weeks. "Subscribers are guaranteed one publication a year unless they send in pure trash." No comments unless requested.** They offer a "cover contest" (winner published on cover) with no entry fee for subscribers, $1/poem for nonsubscribers. The editor says, "We think too much ink is wasted on poetry that says nothing about our lives or the author's life. Avoid puns as though they were poison. Keep writing even if 90% is trash. The other 10% is worth the work." **Siarwot Publishing Co. also publishes chapbooks, but are not seeking submissions for chapbooks at this time.**

‡**THE STRAIN (II)**, Box 330507, Houston, TX 77233-0507, poetry editor Michael Bond, editor Norman C. Stewart, Jr. *The Strain* is a monthly magazine "concentrating on visual, verbal, and performance art to promote interaction between diverse art forms" using **"experimental or traditional poetry of very high quality. Guidelines with graphics $5 and 7 first-class stamps." Pays "no less that $5"** but generally no copies. Simultaneous submissions and previously published poems OK. I have not seen a copy. The editors' advice is to "read Judson Jerome."

STRUGGLE: A MAGAZINE OF PROLETARIAN REVOLUTIONARY LITERATURE (I, II, IV-Political, themes, workers' social issues, women, anti-racist), Box 13261, Harper Station, Detroit, MI 48213-0261, founded 1985, editor Tim Hall, is a "literary quarterly, content: the struggle of the working people against the rich. Issues such as: racism, war preparations, worker's struggle against concessions, the over-all struggle for genuine socialism." The **poetry they use is "generally short, any style, subject-matter must highlight the fight against the rule of the billionaires. No material unconnected to the fight to change society, but we welcome experimentation devoted to furthering such content."** They have recently published poetry by Robert Edwards, Charlie Mehrhoff, Nissa Annakindt, Alberto Aranda and Albert Chui Clark. As a sample the editor selected these lines from "If LA is Niggeragua, the Rich Created the Contrabands" by R. Nat Turner:

> Lights! Action! Ain't a glimmer of hope
> with only three shots — TV and dope
> or small-time crime, payin' the day
> Dyin' to survive the Amerikkkan Way
> in jungles of misery surrounded by greed —
> cubs hawkin' hubba — what caused the need?

Struggle is digest-sized, 24-36 pp., printed by photo offset or photocopy from typescript with typeset heads, using drawings, occasional photos of art work, and short stories, short plays and essays as well as poetry and songs (with their music). Subscription: $6 for 4 issues. **Sample: $1.50 postpaid. Pays 2 copies. Reports in 1-3 months. Accepted work usually appears in the next issue. Editor tries to provide criticism "with every submission."** Tim Hall says, "We want literature and art of discontent with the government and the social and economic system. Specific issues are fine. Show some passion and fire. Formal experiments, traditional forms both welcome. Especially favor works reflecting rebellion by the working people against the rich, against racism, sexism, militarism, imperialism. We support the revolutions and rebellions in Eastern Europe and the Soviet Union, having always considered these regimes state-capitalist and not at all socialist."

STUDENT LEADERSHIP JOURNAL, (IV-Students, religious), Box 1450, Downers Grove, IL 60515, phone 312-964-5700, editor Robert M. Kachur, is a "magazine for Christian student leaders on secular campuses. We accept a wide variety of poetry. Do not want to see trite poetry. Also, we accept little rhymed poetry; it must be very, very good." As a sample the editor selected the final lines of "Holy Saturday" by Kathleen T. Choi:

> *They left her to mourn in peace.*
> *Then something, smaller than hope,*
> *stirred in the shards of her soul,*
> *Like first movements in her womb.*

I have not seen *Student Leadership*, but Robert Kachur describes it as a quarterly, magazine-sized, 24 pp., 2-color inside, 2-color covers, with no advertising, 70% editorial, 30% graphics/art, 10,000 press run going to college students in the United States and Canada. Per issue: $2.95. Subscription: $12. Sample: $2.95 postpaid. Send SASE for guidelines. Pays $15-50 per poem plus 2 copies. "Would-be contributors should read us to be familiar with what we publish." No simultaneous submissions. Previously published poems OK. Reports in 2-3 months, 1-24 months to publication. Editor "occasionally" comments on rejections. He says, "Know your market— be familiar with a magazine's target audience and write to that audience."

STUDIO, A JOURNAL OF CHRISTIAN WRITING (II, IV-Religious), 727 Peel St., Albury 2640, New South Wales, Australia, founded 1980, publisher Paul Grover, a small-press literary quarterly "with contents focusing upon the Christian striving for excellence in poetry, prose and occasional articles relating Christian views of literary ideas." In poetry, the editors want "shorter pieces but with no specification as to form or length (necessarily less than 3-4 pages), subject matter, style or purpose. People who send material should be comfortable being published under this banner *Studio, A Journal of Christian Writing*. They have recently published poetry by John Foulcher and other Australian poets. As a sample, the editors selected the following lines by Les. A. Murray:

> *The poor man's anger is a prayer*
> *for equities Time cannot hold*
> *and steel grows from our mother's grace.*
> *Justice is the people's otherworld.*

Studio is digest-sized, professionally printed on high-quality colored stock, 32 pp., saddle-stapled, matte card cover, with graphics and line drawings. Circulation is 300, all subscriptions. Price per issue is $6 (Aus), subscription $37 (Aus) for overseas members. Sample available (air mail from U.S.) for $7 (Aus). Pay is 1 copy. Submissions may be "typed copy or dot-matrix or simultaneous." Reporting time is 2 months and time to publication is 6 months. The magazine conducts a bi-annual poetry and short story contest. The editor says, "Trend in Australia is for imagist poetry and poetry exploring the land and the self. Reading the magazine gives the best indication of style and standard, so send a few dollars for a sample copy before sending your poetry. Keep writing, and we look forward to hearing from you."

SUB-TERRAIN; ANVIL PRESS (II, IV-Social, themes, form/style), Box 1575, Stn. 'A', Vancouver, BC V6C 2P7, Canada, phone 604-876-8700, founded 1988, poetry editor Paul Pitre. Anvil Press is an "alternate small press publishing *Sub-Terrain* as a literary quarterly as well as broadsheets, chapbooks and the occasional monograph. Socially conscious literature dealing with themes related to oppression, injustice, and the state of the world in general." They want "work that has a point-of-view; work that has some passion behind it and is exploring issues that are of pressing importance; work that challenges conventional notions of what poetry is or should be; work with a social conscience. In short, what poetry should be: powerful, beautiful, important. No bland, flowery, uninventive poetry that says nothing in style or content." *Sub-Terrain* is 12-20 pp., $7 \times 10''$ offset with a press run of 500-750. Subscription: $8. Sample: $3 postpaid. Pays money only for solicited work; for other work, 3-5 copies ("depending on press run"). They will consider simultaneous submissions, but not previously published poems. Reports in 4-6 weeks. For chapbook or book publication submit 4 sample poems and bio, no simultaneous submissions. "We are willing to consider MSS. But I must stress that we are a co-op, depending on support from an interested audience. New titles will be undertaken with caution. We are not subsidized at this point and do not want to give authors false hopes—but if something is important and should be in print, we will do our best." Editor provides brief comment and more extensive comments for fees. He says, "Poetry, in our opinion, should be a distillation of emotion and experience that is being given back to the world. Pretty words and fancy syntax are just that. Where are the modern day writers who are willing to risk it all, put it all on the line? Young, new writers: show it all, bare your guts, write about what you fear! Believe in the power of life of the word. The last thing the world needs is soppy, sentimental fluff that gives nothing and says nothing."

‡**SULFUR MAGAZINE (II, IV-Translations)**, Dept. of English, Eastern Michigan University, Ypsilanti, MI 48197, phone 313-483-9787, founded 1981, poetry editor Clayton Eshleman, is a physically gorgeous and hefty (250+ pp. 6×7½", flat-spined, glossy card cover, elegant graphics and printing on quality stock) triquarterly that had earned a distinguished reputation. They have recently published poetry by John Ashbery, Ed Sanders, Gary Snyder, Jackson MacLow, Paul Blackburn and the editor (one of our better-known poets). I selected these sample lines from "Nan's Last Seance" by Peter Redgrove:

> The gold-searching ants rip up the knotty grains
> Of pure gold from the grassy sand, rip grains.
> They pile them in flahsing zigguarats.
> They are themselves gold-sheened as the summer flies are.

Publishes by EMU, *Sulfur* has a circulation of 2,000, using approximately 100 pp. of poetry in each issue. Subscription: $12. They use 5-10 of 150-200 submissions received per year. **Sample, postpaid: $6. "We urge would-be contributors to *read* the magazine and send us material only if it seems to be appropriate." Reports in "a few weeks." Pays $40 per contributor. Editor comments "sometimes, if the material is interesting."** Clayton Eshleman says, "Most unsolicited material is of the "I am sensitive and have practiced my sensitivity' school—with little attention to language as such, or incorporation of materials that lead the poem into more ample contexts than 'personal' experience. I fear too many young writers today spend more time on themselves, without deeply engaging their *selves*, in a serious psychological way—and too little time breaking their heads against the Blakes, Stevens, and Vallejos of the world. That is, writing has replaced reading. I believe that writing is a form of reading and vice versa. Of course, it is the quality and wildness of imagination that finally counts—but this 'quality' is a composit considerably dependent on assimilative reading (and translating, too)."

SUMMER STREAM PRESS (II, IV-Anthologies), Box 6056, Santa Barbara, CA 93160-6056, phone 805-965-4572, ext. 231, founded 1978, poetry editor David Duane Frost, publishes a series of books in hardcover and softcover, each presenting 6 poets, averaging 70 text pp. for each poet. "The mix of poets represents many parts of the country and many approaches to poetry. The poets in the initial two volumes have been published, but that is no requirement. We present 1-2 traditional poets in the mix and thus offer them a chance for publication in this world of free versers. The 6 poets share a **15% royalty. We require rights for our editions worldwide, and share 50-50 with authors for translation rights and for republication of our editions by another publisher. Otherwise all rights remain with the authors.** The first book features Martha Ellis Bosworth and poetry by Ruthann Robson, Clarke Dewey Wells, Robert K. Johnson, David Duane Frost and Ed Engle, Jr., from whose "Baking Catholic (Infallibility)" I selected these lines as a sample:

> The nun says the Catechism's true
> because the Pope's infallible.
> Gaylon passes me a note:
> God made his father that way, too.

To be considered for future volumes in this series, **query with about 12 samples, no cover letter. Replies to query in 30 days, to submission (if invited) in 6 months. Published poetry, simultaneous submissions, photocopy OK. Editor sometimes comments on rejections.**

THE SUN (II), 107 N. Roberson St., Chapel Hill, NC 27516, phone 919-942-5282, founded 1974, editor Sy Safransky, is "a monthly magazine of ideas" which uses "**all kinds of poetry.**" They have recently published poems by Wendell Berry, Ellen Carter, Cedar Koons, Louis Jenkins, and Edwin Rommond. *The Sun* is magazine-sized, 40 pp., printed on 50 lb. offset, saddle-stapled, with b/w photos, graphics and ads, circulation 15,000, 10,000 subscriptions of which 50 are libraries. Subscription: $28. They receive 1,000 submissions of freelance poetry per year, use 25, have a 1-3 month backlog. **Sample: $3 postpaid. Submit no more than 6 poems. Reports within 2 months. Pays $25 on publication and in copies and subscription. Send SASE for guidelines.**

SUN DOG: THE SOUTHEAST REVIEW (II), 406 Williams Bldg., English Department, Florida State University, Tallahassee, FL 32306, phone 904-644-4230, founded 1979, poetry editor Susan O'Dell Underwood. "The journal has a small student staff. We publish two flat-spined 100 pp. magazines per year of poetry, short fiction and essays. As a norm, we usually accept about 12 poems per issue. **We accept poetry of the highest caliber, looking for the most 'whole' works. A poet may submit any length, but because of space, poems over 2 pages are impractical. Excellent formal verse highly regarded.**" They have recently published poetry by David Bottoms, David Kirby, Peter Meinke, and Leon Stokesbury. As a sample the editor selected these lines by Tonya Robins:

> The ropes of my hair lengthen
> my fingernails celebrate seasons
> I harvest brittle white crops,
> fields of failed winter wheat,

> *tend casks of brilliant seed.*

SD is 6 × 9″ with a glossy card cover. Usually including half-tones, line drawings, and color art when budget allows. Press run of 1,250. Subscription: $8 for 2 issues. **Sample: $4 postpaid. Send SASE for guidelines. Pays 2 copies. Poems should be "typed single spaced, between 2-5 submissions at a time. If simultaneous submission say so. No previously published poems. Reports in 3 months. Editor will comment briefly on most poems, especially those which come close to being accepted.**

SUNSHINE MAGAZINE; GOOD READING MAGAZINE; THE SUNSHINE PRESS; HENRICHS PUBLICATIONS, INC. (I, IV-Inspirational, humor), P.O. Box 40, Litchfield, IL 62056, phone 217-324-3425, founded 1924, poetry editor Peggy Kuethe. *Sunshine Magazine* "is almost entirely a fiction magazine; *Good Reading* is made up of short, current interest factual articles." Both magazines use some poetry. "We do *not* publish free verse or abstract poetry, no haiku, no negative subjects, no violence, sex, alcohol. We use only uplifting, inspirational poetry that is of regular meter and that rhymes. Inspirational, seasonal, or humorous poetry preferred. Easy to read, pleasantly rhythmic. Maximum 16 lines — no exceptions." They have recently published poems by Loise Pinkerton Fritz, Catherine Hudson, Eunice Elmore Heizer, Dorothy Olston and Marion Schoeberlein. As a sample the editor selected these lines by Edith Summerfield:

> *Buds from their bonds unfurl;*
> *Trees shake out a crown of curls;*
> *The world becomes a living thing.*
> *Oh! Glories of eternal Spring.*

Both magazines are monthlies. *Sunshine* is 5¼ × 7¼″, saddle-stapled, 36 pp., of which 5 are poetry, circulation to 75,000 subscribers. Subscription: $10. They use about 7% of 2,500 submissions of poetry each year. **Sample: 50¢. Send SASE for guidelines. Absolutely no queries. Submit typewritten MS, 1 poem per page. Reports in 6-8 weeks. Pays 1 copy.** *Good Reading* uses about 4 poems per issue, circulation to 7,200 subscribers. Subscription: $9. **Sample: 50¢. Submission specifications like those for *Sunshine*. Pays 1 copy.** The editors comment, "We strongly suggest authors read our guidelines and obtain a sample copy of our magazines. Our format and policies are quite rigid and we make absolutely no exceptions. Many authors submit something entirely different from our format or from anything we've published before — that is an instant guarantee of rejection."

SUPERINTENDENT'S PROFILE & POCKET EQUIPMENT DIRECTORY (IV-Themes), 220 Central Ave., Box 43, Dunkirk, NY 14048, phone 716-366-4774, founded 1978, poetry editor Robert Dyment, is a "monthly magazine, circulation 2,500, for town, village, city, and county highway superintendents and DPW directors throughout New York State," and uses "**only poetry that pertains to highway superintendents and DPW directors and their activities." Submit no more than one page doublespaced.** Subscription: $10. They receive about 50 freelance submissions of poetry per year, use 20, have a 2 month backlog. **Sample: 80¢ postage. Reports within a month. Pays $5/poem.**

‡SWAMP ROOT (II), Rt. 2, Box 1098, Jacksboro, TN 37757, phone 615-562-7082, founded 1987, editor Al Masarik, is a poetry magazine appearing 3 times a year. "**All styles welcome, biased toward clarity, brevity, strong imagery.**" They have recently published poetry by Ted Kooser, Naomi Shihab Nye, Linda Hasselstrom, William Kloefkorn, and Diane Glancy. As a sample the editor selected these lines by Vivian Shipley:

> *Ocean was in early morning fog*
> *resting heavy on ridges in Harlan County*
> *and the frost, ribbed*
> *on the leaf of a blackberry bush.*

It is 6 × 9″ flat-spined on quality stock with matte card cover or glossy card cover, using b/w photos, drawings and collages interspersed with poetry. They receive about 20 submissions per week, use less than 1%. Press run: 1,000 for 63 subscriptions of which 12 are libraries, few shelf sales. Subscription: $12. **Sample, postpaid: $5. Pays 3 copies plus year's subscription. Simultaneous submissions and previously published poems used "sometimes." Reports in 1-4 weeks. Editor comments on submissions.**

‡SWORD OF SHAHRAZAD (I), P.O. Box 152844, Arlington, TX 76015-2844, founded 1988, editor Deb'y Gaj, appears 6 times per year, a "small press, workshop-in-a-magazine for fiction writers and poets. **There are no restrictions on form, subject-matter, style, or purpose — but try not to send us epics.**" They have recently published poetry by Howard Lakin (head writer for the TV series "Dallas"). As a sample the editor selected (from their Halloween issue) these lines from "Vampire Wine" by Thomas Zimmerman:

> *When your mind and eyes are dull*

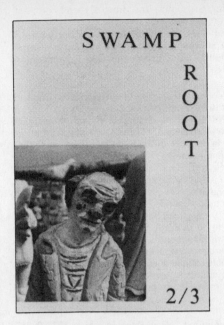

SWAMP

ROOT

2/3

In this issue of Swamp Root, featured poet Kent Taylor writes several pieces about his wife's death. Editor Al Masarik feels the photo of the sad clown seems to fit the theme and feelings anchored by Taylor. Jane Esmonde's photos make regular appearances in Swamp Root.

and slumber's dregs seal your lids,
I'll pierce your neck and madly gulp
the salty wine I find within.

It is 54 pp. digest-sized, saddle-stapled, typeset, laser printed. They publish "at least 20-25 poems per issue." Subscription: $16. **Sample, postpaid: $3. Send SASE for guidelines. Pays 1 copy. Simultaneous submissions and previously published poems OK. Editor comments on submissions "always.** We try to give individual criticisms of each poem we get. Our goal is to help writers—to give them feedback instead of just rejection or acceptance. My advice to poets is: read other poets, try all the different forms of poetry, and—most of all—*write!* Like everything else, poetry takes practice."

SYCAMORE REVIEW (II), Department of English, Purdue University, West Lafayette, IN 47907, phone 317-494-3783, founded 1988 (first issue May, 1989), editor Henry Hughes. "We accept personal essays (25 pp. max), short fiction (25 pp. max), and **quality poetry in any form (6 pp. max). There are no official restrictions as to subject-matter or style."** Recent contributors include Mary Oliver, John Updike, Simon Ortiz, Marge Piercy, Walter McDonald, and Maura Stanton. As a sample the editor selected the following lines by Diane Wakoski:

One curve of a cucumber stem, like a crochet hook,
protrudes from a row of peat pellets in my window hothouse.
How fast these seeds are showing
their green.

The magazine is semi-annual in a digest-sized format, 100 pp. flat-spined, professionally printed, with glossy, color cover. Their press run is 1,000 with 300 subscriptions of which 100 are libraries. Subscription: $7. **Sample: $4.50 postpaid. Pays 2 copies. Reports in 4 months. Cover letters not required but invited. Editor comments on about 20% of rejections.** Henry Hughes says, "The poet must read voraciously. Read poems published in *The New Yorker* and *Poetry* and read poems appearing in your community or university magazine. When you are ready to write (and you're always ready) begin not with an agenda or complete idea, but with an image, sensation or phrase—see where the poem takes you."

‡TABULA RASA (I), P.O. Box 1920, Station 'B', London, ON N6A 5J4 Canada, phone 519-654-2118, founded 1989, editors Paul Laxon, Gord Harrison, and John Kirnan, appears every other month using **"any type of poetry; no length or genre restrictions."** They have recently published poetry by Susan Lodnnou, John Grey, David Satherley, Richard Stevenson, B.Z. Niditch. As a sample the editors selected these lines from "Cities Sleeping" by Errol Miller:

Dweller, you are locked into tragic pretty zones

> *that the iceman avoids, his mouth dry, this planet*
> *lost or decaying wooden doorsteps,*
> *in a nameless sea of lights.*

It is 6 × 9″ flat-spined, 72 pp., professionally printed. Press run 500 for 50+ subscriptions of which several are libraries. Subscription: $20. **Sample, postpaid: $3.50. Send SASE for guidelines. Pays 2 copies. Simultaneous submissions and previously published poems OK. Reports in 4-8 weeks. Editors comment on submissions "if requested."**

TAK TAK TAK (II, IV-Translations, theme), P.O. Box 7, Bulwell, Nottingham NG6 OHW England, founded 1986, editors Andrew and Jim Brown, appears twice a year in print and on cassettes, and, in addition, publishes 1-2 collections of poetry per year. **"No restrictions on form or style. However, each issue of the magazine is on a theme, (i.e. 'Mother Country/Fatherland,' 'Travel') and *all* contributions must be relevant. If a contribution is long it is going to be more difficult to fit in than something shorter. Write for details of subject(s) etc. of forthcoming issue(s)."** They have published poetry by Thomas Hardy, Ted Milton, Georges Bataille, Zbigniew Herbert, Earl Blake, Andrei Codrescu, Li Min Mua, Nick Toczek, and Paul Buck. I have not seen it, but the editor describes it as "100 pp. A5, photolithographed, board cover, line drawings and photographs, plus cassette of poetry, music, collage. Of about 100 poems received in the past year we have used about 25." Press run 500. Subscription: £9 + £11.50 postpaid to U.S.A. (includes 2 issues with 10 cassettes). **Sample: £11.12 postpaid to U.S. Pays 1 copy. Submit "a selection of 5 or 6 with a bio of up to 30 words."** They consider simultaneous submissions and previously published poems. **Reports within 6 months. Editor sometimes comments on rejections.** They also publish 2 or 3 flat-spined paperbacks a year averaging between 40 and 130 pp. **For chapbook consideration send as many as possible sample poems, bio, publications. Reports in 2 months. Pays a negotiated number of copies.** The editors say, "Poetry is just one of the many creative forms our contributions take. We are equally interested in prose and in visual and sound media."

‡TAKAHE (II, IV-Translations), P.O. Box 13-335, Christchurch 1, New Zealand, phone (03)898567, founded 1989, poetry editor David Howard, is a literary quarterly. **"We have no preconceived specifications as to form, length, subject-matter, style, or purpose. We believe that poetry is, among other things, the art of significant silence. It demands an active reader whose trust in language matches that of the writer. No work that batters the reader about the head, that refuses to utilize silence and insists on spelling everything out — as if the reader was incapable of making connections."** They have recently published poetry by Michael Harlow, Elizabeth Smither, and Tony Beyer. As a sample the poetry editor selected these lines by Riemke Ensing:

> *A gesture*
> *of pink in several paper-hats. They alone*
> *are coming to the party.*

I have not seen an issue, but the poetry editor describes it as 56 pp. magazine-sized, desktop publishing with woodcut design on cover and some b/w graphics (including ads). They accept an average of 10% of 1,000 poems received a year. Press run: 200 for 119 subscriptions of which 21 are libraries, 81 shelf sales. Subscription: $20 NZ. **Sample, postpaid: $7.50 NZ. Pays 1 copy. Submit up to 7 poems. Simultaneous submissions and previously published poems OK (if not published in New Zealand). Reports in 1-2 months. Editor comments on submissions "as a matter of course (particularly if the poem is potentially publishable but needs further work)."** The editor says, "In poetry (as in prayer) the essential thing is the degree to which the silences between words are charged with significance. 'Less is more' — but only if the less is carefully weighed."

‡TALES OF THE OLD WEST; WESTERNER AWARDS (IV-Themes), PRG Publishing Co., Box 22866, Denver, CO 80222, phone 303-722-9966, publisher Keith Olsen, is a quarterly using **poetry, especially narrative, relevant to the old West.** They have recently published poetry by Ivan Kersner, Luke Warm, Arthur Winfield Knight, and Dorothy Stormer Hance. I have not seen an issue, but the editor describes it as 24 pp., digest-sized. They use 30-40 poems/year. **Sample, postpaid: $3. Pays copies. Simultaneous submissions and previously published poems OK.** The Westerner Awards are for an annual contest, deadline December 1, $25 prize, for narratives about the old West, free to subscribers ($5 for others).

TALISMAN: A JOURNAL OF CONTEMPORARY POETRY AND POETICS (II), Box 1117, Hoboken, NJ 07030, phone 201-798-9093, founded 1988, editor Edward Foster, appears twice a year. "Each issue centers on the poetry and poetics of a *major* contemporary poet and includes a selection of new work by other important contemporary writers. **We are particularly interested in poetry in alternative (*not* academic) traditions. We don't want traditional poetry."** They have recently published poetry by William Bronk, Robert Creeley, Ron Padgett, Anne Waldman, Hayden Carruth, and Rosmarie Waldrop. As a sample the editor selected a stanza of "The Section Called O" by Rachel Blau DuPlessis (in the Spring, 1990 Susan Howe issue):

> the wane and wax of
> other alphabets, primers
> of Adams and of Kings,
> their one word
> (Xantippe or Xenophon)
> for adequate narratives of X.

Talisman is digest-sized, flat-spined, 100+ pp. photocopied from typescript, with matte card cover. Their press run is 525 with "substantial" subscriptions of which many are libraries. "We are inundated with submissions and lost track of the number long ago." Subscription: $9 individual; $13 institution. **Sample: $5 postpaid. Pays 1 copy. Reports in 1 month.**

TALKIN' UNION (IV-Political, themes), Box 5349, Takoma Park, MD 20912, editor Saul Schniderman, is a twice yearly magazine featuring "songs, stories, poems, photos and cartoons home-made by America's greatest resource—its working people." **Poems must be related to work unions and the labor movement.** As a sample I selected the first of two stanzas of "My Union" by Marshall Dubin:

> Because I build it.
> Because I paid for it,
> Went to jail for it,
> Suffered for it,
> I love it.

The magazine also includes original union song lyrics with music. A labor history essay is featured in each issue. It is magazine-sized, 14 pp., saddle-stapled, photoreduced typescript, using b/w photos, art and cartoons, with a striking paper cover. Subscription: $7.50; $12 for institutions. **I have no information on submission, pay or circulation.**

‡TAMPA BAY REVIEW (II), 5458 N. Rivershore Dr., Tampa, FL 33603, founded 1989, managing editor Giunna Russo, is a literary journal appearing twice a year. "**We want poems (and short stories) which are innovative in language, rhythm, and subject matter. We tend toward free verse with strong metaphors and vibrant imagery. We are not interested in sentimental rhymed verse or inspirational poetry.**" They have recently published poetry by William Stafford, Silvia Curbelo, and Richard Mathews. As a sample the editor selected these lines from "Steal this Poem (If You Want To)" by Phyllis McEwen:

> Ride this poem
> like it has a big sleek back
> and a saddle of ice.
> Let it take you
> where you need to be

It is 50-60 pp. digest-sized, saddle-stapled, with matte card cover. Press run: 300 for 50 subscribers. "We accept about 20% of what we receive. Subscription: $7. **Sample, postpaid: $3** "if available. Our first issue has sold out!" **Send SASE for guidelines. Enclose up to 3 lines of biographical info with submission. Reports in 8-12 weeks. Payment is in contributor's copies. Editor comments on submissions "often." They "occasionally" use previously published poems. Send no more than 6-8 poems.** "We publish spring and fall. Poems are circulated once or twice to an editorial board, but final decisions are made by our poetry editor. *Tampa Bay Review* is published by Tampa Bay Poets, the area's long-established writers' group. Rights to published works revert to the author. Take risks in your writing. Your goals should be: first, to make your readers understand what you're expressing; and second, to make them sit up and say 'Ah ha!' "

TAMPA REVIEW (III, IV-Translations), P.O. Box 19F, University of Tampa, Tampa, FL 33606, phone 813-253-3333 ext. 621 or 424, founded 1964 as *UT Poetry* Review, became *Tampa Review* in 1988, poetry editors Kathryn Van Spanckeren and Donald Morrill, editor Richard Mathews, is an elegant annual of fiction, nonfiction and poetry (not limited to U.S. authors) wanting "**original and well-crafted poetry written with intelligence and spirit. No greeting card verse or inspirational verse.**" They have recently published poetry by Alberto Rios, Paul Mariani, Mark Halliday, Jordan Smith, and Susan Wood. As a sample the editors chose these lines by William Stafford:

> Clouds here have dawn before we do,
> but we keep the night and feed it dreams.

It is 96 pp., flat-spined, $7 \times 10''$ with a matte card color cover. They accept about 20 of 200 poems received a year. Their press run is 800 with 150 subscriptions of which 18 are libraries. **Sample: $7.50 postpaid. Pays $5-15 per poem plus 1 copy and 40% discount on additional copies. Unsolicited MSS are read only September-November. Reports in 4-6 weeks.**

TAPJOE: THE ANAPROCRUSTEAN POETRY JOURNAL OF ENUMCLAW (II, IV-Nature, social issues), P.O. Box 104, Grangeville, ID 83530, founded 1987, biannual plus occasional special issues/chapbooks. "We will **consider anything by anyone, however we have a definite preference for free verse poems 10-50 lines with a slant toward nature, social issues, the human environment, which is the environment as a whole. No sexism, racism, or unnecessary raw language.** They have recently published poetry by Mike Hiler, Walt Franklin, Anne-Marie Oomen, and Judith Barrington. These sample lines, selected by co-editor Noah Farnsworth, are from "Pawpaws" by Gary Cummisk:

> *When green leaves*
> *jaundice in the cold*
> *jade fruits ripen*
> *brown and weighty;*

The magazine is digest-sized, 24-35 pp., saddle-stapled, offset with matte card cover. Accepts 40-60 poems per year with 1,000+ submissions. Print run is 150-300. **Sample: $3 postpaid. Send SASE for guidelines. Pays 1 copy for each accepted poem. "Cover letters appreciated but not necessary. Prefer 4-5 poems per submission." No simultaneous submissions or previously published poems. Reports in 2-8 weeks "often longer.** Each submission is read by several people, which sometimes makes responses slow; however, we feel this is the only way to give each piece fair consideration." **No chapbook submissions at this time.** "We appreciate purchases of sample copies (and subscriptions) but nothing pleases us more than receiving a 'good' poem in the mail—do give us a try." Subscriptions are $10/4 issues. "If you haven't already, read Mary Oliver's *American Primitive*; it's the type of poetry we're looking for, and your education isn't complete without having read it."

‡TAPROOT; BURNING PRESS; KRAPP'S LAST TAPE (II), Box 18817, Cleveland Heights, OH 44118, founded 1980, editor Robert Drake, is a "micropress publisher of avant-garde and experimental literature and art. Also produces a weekly radio show (KLT) of music, noise, language-centered audio art and a series of audio cassettes." They want **"purposeful experiments with language in which form is the necessary outgrowth of content. No standard academic workshop slop."** I have not seen a copy of their quarterly, *TapRoot*, nor of any of their publications. The editor describes the magazine as "typically 50 pp. photocopied, handmade covers and binding." They accept less than 10% of 1,000-2,000 poems received per year. Press run is 250 typically for 50 subscriptions, 200 shelf sales. **Sample, postpaid: $2.50 when available. Pays 1 copy. "Contributors may buy more at cost." Submit "no more than a dozen at a time unless previously contacted. Simultaneous submissions OK, and previously published poems are sometimes used."** Burning Press published 8 chapbooks in 1989, averaging 50 pp. **For chapbook publication query with no more than 12 samples. Pays 20% press run. Author may buy more at cost.**

‡TAPROOT LITERARY REVIEW (I), 302 Park Rd., Ambridge, PA 15003, phone 412-266-8476, founded 1986, editor Tikvah Feinstein, is an annual contest publication, very open for beginners. There is a $5 entry fee for up to 10 poems, "preferably no longer than 25 lines each. All entrants receive a copy of *Taproot* if they also enclose a 6×9″ envelope and 85¢ postage. This is primarily a contest, though some out-of-state poets and fiction-writers are included as guest writers." They arrange readings for writers published in the magazine. Contest deadline December 31. SASE for details.

TAR RIVER POETRY (II), English Dept., East Carolina University, Greenville, NC 27834, phone 757-6041, founded 1960, editor Peter Makuck, associate editor Luke Whisnant. **"We are not interested in sentimental, flat-statement poetry. What we would like to see is skillful use of figurative language."** They have recently published poetry by William Matthews, Michael Mott, Betty Adcock, Robert Cording, James Applewhite, David Citino, Paula Rankin, Fred Chappell, and Patricia Goedicke. The editors selected these sample lines from "In Ireland I Remember The Foxes of Truro, Massachusetts" by Brendan Galvin:

> *I thought of how the foxes travel*
> *by synecdoche, the part-fox*
> *for the whole: the five-toed*
> *prints like thought-blossoms,*
> *four in a row across snowfall*

Tar River appears twice yearly, digest-sized 60 pp., professionally printed on salmon stock, some decorative line drawings, matte card cover with photo, circulation 900+ with 500 subscriptions of which 125 are libraries. Subscription: $8. They receive 6,000-8,000 submissions per year, use 150-200. **Sample: $4.50. "We do not consider simultaneous submissions. Double or single-spaced OK. We prefer not more than 6 pp. at one time. We do not consider MSS during summer months." Reports in 4-6 weeks. Pays copies. Send SASE for guidelines. Editors will comment "if slight revision will do the trick."** They advise, "Read, read, read. Saul Bellow says the writer is primarily a reader moved to emulation. Read the poetry column in *Writer's Digest*. Read the books recommended therein. Do your homework."

TATTOO ADVOCATE JOURNAL (IV-Themes), P.O. Box 8390, Haledon, NJ 07508, phone 201-790-0429, founded 1986, correspondence editor Pat Walsh, is a slick biannual magazine about tattooing using "**poetry that concerns itself with tattooing as a main theme or subtheme, politically left poetry about tolerance of lifestyles, on the theme of creativity. No sexually oriented or biker lifestyle.**" The magazine is flat-spined, 80 pp., magazine-sized, professionally printed on heavy, glossy stock, using full-color photographs inside and on cover. **Sample: $5.50 postpaid. Pays $25-100/poem.**

TEARS IN THE FENCE (II), 38 Hodview, Stourpaine, Nr. Blandford Forum, Dorset DT11 8TN, England, phone 0258-56803, founded 1984, general editor David Caddy, poetry editor Sarah Hopkins, a "**small press magazine of poetry, fiction, interviews, articles, reviews, and graphics. We are open to a wide variety of poetic styles. Work of a social, political, ecological and feminist awareness will be close to our purpose. However, we like to publish a balanced variety of work.**" The editors do not want to see "**didactic rhyming poems.**" They have recently published Paul Donnelly, Jesse Glass Jr., Astra, and Rochelle Lynn Holt. As a sample, they selected the following lines from "Colonial" by Chris Bendon:

> *As I stand in the middle of a sanded*
> *hockey pitch, my spaniel sketches circles,*
> *is rabbit, horse, golden lion. Enormous space*
> *enters my brain but it too shrinks.*

Tears in the Fence appears two times a year. It is magazine-sized, offset from typed copy on lightweight paper with b/w cover art and graphics, 60 pp., one-color matte card cover with black spiral binding. It has a print run of 600 copies, of which 129 go to subscribers and 155 are sold on newsstands. Price per issue is $4, **sample available for same price. Pay is 1 copy. Writers should submit 5 typed poems with IRC's. Reporting time is 3 months and time to publication 8-10 months "but can be much less."** The editor says, "I think it helps to subscribe to several magazines in order to study the market and develop an understanding of what type of poetry is published. Use the review sections and send off to magazines that are new to you."

‡THE TEITAN PRESS, INC., THELEMA PUBLICATIONS (V,IV-Psychic/occult), Suite 16B, 339 W. Barry, Chicago, IL 60657, phone 312-929-7892, founded 1985, president Franklin C. Winston, vice-president Martin P. Starr, is a "small-press publisher of **occultism with special emphasis on the works of Aleister Crowley (1875-1947)**, English poet and magician" in hardcover books. "**No outside submissions; we currently use only inhouse material.**"

TEJAS ART PRESS (IV-Ethnic), 207 Terrell Rd., San Antonio, TX 78209, phone 512-826-7803, founded 1978, poetry editor Robert Willson: "**only writers of North American Indian descent, chiefly poetry (also new drama) in original 'illustrated' art books. Subjects: open, but lean toward reservation life, or contacts between Indians and other civilizations.**" Each book should be a minimum of 100 pp., including illustrations; all books must be illustrated, either by the author, or by artists selected by the editors. Binding is softback. Copyright is in the name of the author. Usually 200 copies printed for a first book, but may be higher. **The author is given 25 copies free, for use to the media and friends, or for sale. The press also sends out another 25 copies for review and press. The author gets a commission on all books sold. Send at least 20 poems and a sample of illustrations available to the publisher (if any). Enclose a brief life story, list of previous books published, and photo.** They have recently published books by John H. Cornyn, Catherine E. Whitmar, and Luci Tapahonso. **Sample: $5 postpaid.**

‡TELSTAR; CAMELOT (I, II, IV-Themes), Box 208, Amelia OH 45102, founded 1989, editor Kathleen Lee Mendel, is a quarterly using **poetry on specified themes.** They sponsor 6 annual contests with fees $1-2, prizes up to $100. Send SASE for guidelines and forthcoming themes. "**Please don't submit fewer than 5 poems, 4-24 lines, any style. Pays $5/poem.** Annually selected subscriber is granted a $100 "Poet Laureate" award. The poem or article receiving the most votes from readers is awarded $25. They have recently published poetry by C. David Hay, Kay Weems, Wilfred Johnson, Byrdene Glenn, and Denise Martinson. As a sample the editor selected these lines by J.O. Schlucter:

> *They sit upon delicate ebony feet*
> *In a forgotten temple's jungle heat*
> *Guarding white-hot diamonds, emeralds, a ruby's glow*
> *Beneath yellow candles guttering low:*
> *It is The Hour of the Cat*

The quarterly is 40 pp., magazine-sized, flat-spined with matte card cover, photocopied from typescript. Press run: 200 for 100 subscribers of which 2 are libraries. Subscription: $16. **Sample, postpaid: $5. Pays $5 plus 1 copy. Simultaneous submissions and previously published poems**

OK. Reports in 6 weeks. No backlog. "Seldom is anything held for a future issue." Editor comments on submissions "always, if requested." They plan to publish one book per year until the year 2,000 on the theme of Camelot. They publish one book of children's poetry per year. *Lions, Lizards and Ladybugs* was published in 1989. **Reports in 48 hours on queries, 4 weeks on MSS.**

TENTH DECADE(III), 12 Stevenage Rd., London SW6 6ES, England, editors Robert Vas Dias, Tony Frazer, and Ian Robinson, founded 1983, it is published in conjunction with Oasis Books and Shearsman Books and comes out three times a year, about 60 pages, finely printed, saddle-stapled. Co-editor Robert Vas Dias says the magazine "**exists to publish postmodern, innovative writing, translations of contemporary French and other European writing, and critical articles on important but neglected poets.** Each issue contains the work of about 10 writers—of prose as well as of poetry. One of these is 'featured'—usually a British or American poet who has published significant work over a sustained period but who has received inadequate critical attention; 10-15 pages of his or her work appears, together with a specially commissioned review/essay. *Tenth Decade* tries to give a meaningful representation of the work, so that **at least 5 or 6 pages is devoted to each poet.** *Tenth Decade* is not a hobbyist's magazine so no competitions are run and no "theme" issues are dreamed up as a substitute for indifferent submissions. Potential contributors should definitely be familiar with the magazine before submitting." They have published Gilbert Sorrentino, Christopher Middleton, John Yau, Jon Silkin, Roy Fisher, Edwin Morgan, Jackson Mac Low, Bobbie-Louise Hawkins, Judith Kazantzis, August Kleinzahler, Toby Olson, René Char, and Gael Turnbull. Here are some lines from Eugène Guillevic's "Carnac" (translation by Robert Chandler):

> *You know how to bring*
> *Vagueness*
> *Into what's precise;*
> *And the sea colludes.*

About 40 pages of poetry in each issue, print run 500, 300 subscriptions, of which 50 are libraries. **Sample: $4 postpaid.** Annual subscription: $12. They receive about 1,000 submissions each year, use 3%. **Submissions should contain at least 6 pages of poetry, typed double-spaced. Photocopy OK, no dot-matrix, no simultaneous submissions. Do not send from June to August. Be sure to include sufficient postage or IRC's. If it's OK to dispose of the poetry, 2 IRC's are sufficient for airmail reply. Reports in 1-2 months. Payment is 2 copies.**

‡TESSERA (IV-Women, regional, translations), 350 Stong, York University, 4700 Keele St., North York, ON M3J 1P3 Canada, founded 1984, revived 1988, managing editor Barbara Godard, appears twice a year: "**feminist literary theory and experimental writing by women, preference to Canadians.**" It is digest-sized, 94 pp., professionally printed, digest-sized, with glossy card cover. Subscription: $18. **Sample, postpaid: $10. Pays nothing. Submit 4 copies. Simultaneous submissions and previously published ("sometimes") poems OK. Editor comments on submissions "sometimes."**

THE TEXAS REVIEW; THE TEXAS REVIEW CHAPBOOK AWARD (II), English Dept., Sam Houston State University, Huntsville, TX 77341, editor Paul Ruffin, founded 1976, is a biannual, 6×9″, 140+ pp., circulation 750-1,000, has recently published poetry by Donald Hall, Richard Wilbur, Richard Eberhart. I selected these sample lines from "When Insanity Comes a Knocking Throw Away the Door, The Log of the *Pequod 2*" by D. C. Berry:

> *The Japanese Magnolia is sheathed in amethyst.*
> *It's tighter than Dixie's hands at Vicksburg.*
> *It unknobs its bulge. It's a pure kamikaze fist*
> *socked into obtuse Mississippi.*

Sample: $2 postpaid. Submit 3-4 poems. No simultaneous or photocopied submissions. Reports in 4 weeks, pays 2 copies, one-year subscription.

TEXTILE BRIDGE PRESS; MOODY STREET IRREGULARS: A JACK KEROUAC NEWSLETTER (IV-Themes), Box 157, Clarence Center, NY 14032, founded 1978, poetry editor Joy Walsh. "**We publish material by and on the work of Jack Kerouac, American author prominent in the fifties. Our chapbooks reflect the spirit of Jack Kerouac. We use poetry in the spirit of Jack Kerouac, poetry of the working class, poetry about the everyday workaday life.** Notice how often the work people spend so much of their life doing is never mentioned in poetry or fiction. Why? **Poetry in any form.**" They have recently published poetry by Joseph Semenovich, Marion Perry, Bonnie Johnson, Boria Sax, Michael Basinski, Emanuel Fried, Mildred Crombie, Ted Joans, Michael Hopkins, Tom Clark, Jack Micheline, Carl Solomon, and ryki zuckerman. Joy Walsh selected these sample lines from "Indefinite Layoff" by Delores Rossi Script:

> *How desperately man*
> *needs to work.*

> *Society has shaped it so.*
> *Without it, it diminishes*
> *his existence.*

Moody Street Irregulars is a 28 pp. magazine-sized newsletter, biannual, circulation 700-1,000 (700 subscriptions of which 30 are libraries), using 3-4 pp. of poetry in each issue. Subscription: $7. They receive about 50 freelance submissions of poetry per year, use half of them. **Sample: $3.50 postpaid. Reports in 1 month. Pays copies.** Textile Bridge Press also publishes collections by individuals. For book publication, **query with 5 samples. "The work speaks to me better than a letter." Replies to query in 1 week, to submission (if invited) in 1 month. Simultaneous submission OK for "some things yes, others no." Photocopy, dot-matrix OK. Pays copies. Send SASE for catalog to buy samples. Editor comments on rejections "if they ask for it."**

‡**THALIA: STUDIES IN LITERARY HUMOR (I, IV-Subscribers, humor)**, Dept. of English, University of Ottawa, Ottawa, ON K1N 6N5 Canada, appears twice a year using **"humor (literary, mostly), preferably literary parodies."** I have not seen an issue, but the editor describes it as $7 \times 8\frac{1}{2}''$ flat-spined "with illustrated cover." Press run 500 for 475 subscriptions. Subscription: $13. **Sample, postpaid: $7.50. Contributors must subscribe. Simultaneous submissions and previously published poems OK. Editor comments on submissions.**

‡**THEMA (II, IV-Themes)**, Bothomos Enterprises, Box 74109, Metairie, LA 70033-4109, founded 1988, editor Virginia Howard, is a literary quarterly **using poetry related to specific themes. "Each issue is based on an unusual premise. Please, please send SASE for guidelines before submitting poetry to find out the upcoming themes. For example: 'the perfect imperfection' is the theme for Nov. 1, 1990; 'art from the canvas freed' is for Feb. 1, 1991. No scatologic language, alternate life-style, explicit love poetry."** They have recently published poetry by Kenneth Pobo, Reen Murphy, and Paul Humphrey. As a sample the editor selected these lines by Morgan Finn:

> *Bare feet drawn to hard earth,*
> *my eyes are new fruit*
> *watching mother down cellar on Mondays*
> *singsong memos to the washing machine*

Thema is digest-sized, 200 pp., professionally printed, with matte card cover. They accept about 25% of 120 poems received per year. Press run 500 for 150 subscriptions of which 15 are libraries. Subscription: $12. **Sample, postpaid: $5. Pays $10/poem plus 1 copy. Editor comments on submissions.**

THIRD LUNG REVIEW; THIRD LUNG PRESS; OXFAM POETRY CONTEST (II), Box 361, Conover, NC 28613, phone 704-465-1254, founded 1985, poetry editor Tim Peeler — "a small-press publisher of solicited poetry chapbooks and an annual poetry magazine. **We are wide open in terms of theme, subject matter, or style. We tend to give preference to poems dealing with social themes, but quality supercedes everything else. No self-indulgent, nostalgic, or forced rhyme."** They have recently published poetry by Hal J. Daniel III, Charles Bukowski, Judson Crews, and Peter Spiro. As a sample the editor selected these lines from "Madagascar" by Harry Calhoun:

> *Lambent forests aflame with blue-lipped mandrills.*
> *Noone here shoots his mother, cousin, uncle.*
> *Bananas feed us, herbal salves heal.*
> *The rococo soothing of loosely ornate liana.*
> *Booming, the spritz of animal staccato*
> *monkey thunder, the incumbency of green.*

Tim Peeler says he hopes to "provide a quality arena for energetic poetry and above-average graphics." *TLR* is 25 pp., magazine-sized, side-stapled, offset, using "mostly solicited" art. He accepts 20-25 of 100 poems submitted. Press run for the magazine 200. **Sample: $3 postpaid. Send SASE for guidelines. Pays 1 copy. Submit no more than 6 poems at a time. Simultaneous submissions and previously published poems OK. Reports in 2 weeks. No unsolicited submissions for chapbooks. Arrangements are made with individual authors, payment in copies.** The annual Oxfam Poetry Contest has a July 4 deadline, a $2 per poem required entry fee. Checks should be made payable to OXFAM. This year's cash prizes are $15, $10, $5 and publication.

THIRD WOMAN PRESS; THIRD WOMAN (IV-Women, ethnic), Chicano Studies, Dwinelle Hall 3412, University of California, Berkeley, CA 94720, phone 415-642-0240, founded 1981, poetry editors Norma Alarcon. **"Presently we are primarily interested in publishing the literary and artistic work of U.S. Latinas, Hispanic, Native American, and other US minority women in general. The journal as well as our publications are in Spanish or English. We prefer poetry that employs well-crafted images and metaphors and pays attention to musical rhythms. Any kind of form, length, and style, as long as it pertains to U.S. Latinas, Hispanic women, or Third World women."** They have recently published poetry by Sandra Cisneros and Luz Maria Umpierre. The editors selected these sample lines (poet unidentified):

> *Thin-printed lips still*
> *Lace your easter window*
> *Where once you told me*
> *Was your favorite place at dark*

Third Woman appears annually, digest-sized, flat-spined, 200 pp., professionally printed, glossy card cover with b/w art, circulation 2,000 for 500 subscriptions of which 105 are libraries, 70 shelf sales. They accept approximately 20% of 100 poems received for each issue. Subscription: $8.95 individuals, $15 institutions. **Send SASE for guidelines. Payment in copies, number "negotiable." No simultaneous submissions or previously published poems. Reports in 6-8 weeks. For book consideration query with bio and list of publications, no simultaneous submissions. Editor sometimes comments on rejections.** They sometimes sponsor contests. Occasionally they subsidy publish.

‡THIRD WORLD (I, IV-Regional), Rua da Gloria 122, sala 105, Rio de Janeiro, RJ Brazil 20241, phone 021-222-1370 or 242-1957, founded 1986, editor Bill Hinchberger, appears every other month, "a general interest publication presenting world affairs from a Third World perspective using poetry: **subject: the Third World, its people, cultures, hopes, aspirations, etc.; purpose: present a picture of the Third World devoid of stereotypes and Western biases. No work that paints a stereotypical picture of the Third World.** Our most recently published poetry was by anonymous Chinese writers reflecting on the recent pro-democracy protest." It is magazine-sized, glossy pages, professionally printed, with paper color cover. Print run 5,000 for 1,500 subscriptions, 2,000 shelf sales. Subscription: $9 (U.S.). **Sample, postpaid: $2 (U.S.). Pays free subscription "plus an agreed number of copies." Simultaneous submissions and previously published poems OK. Reports in 2 weeks, but "leave time for international mail: 1-4 months. We do not return MSS; do not send your only copy."** Editor comments on submissions "if requested, on a time-available basis." The editor says, "I would advise poets to join the National Writers Union."

‡13TH MOON (II, IV-Women), English Department, SUNY-Albany, 1400 Washington Ave., Albany, NY 12222, phone 518-442-4181, founded 1973, editor Judith Johnson, is a feminist literary magazine appearing twice a year in a 6×9¼" flat-spined, handsomely printed format with glossy card cover, using photographs and line arts, ads at $200/page. Press run 2,000 for 690 subscriptions of which 61 are libraries, 700 shelf sales. Subscription: $6.50. **Sample, postpaid: $6.50. Send SASE for guidelines. Pays 2 copies.**

THISTLEDOWN PRESS LTD. (V, IV-Regional), 668 East Place, Saskatoon, Saskatchewan, S7J 2Z5 Canada, phone 306-244-1722, founded 1975, Patrick O'Rourke, Editor-in-Chief, is "a literary press that specializes in **quality books of contemporary poetry by Canadian authors. Only the best of contemporary poetry that amply demonstrates an understanding of craft with a distinctive use of voice and language. Only interested in full-length poetry MSS with a 60-80 pp. minimum."** They have recently published books of poetry by Anne Campbell, Andrew Wreggitt, Robert Hilles, and Peter Christensen. **No unsolicitd MSS.** Canadian poets must **query first with letter, bio and publication credits. Poetry MS submission guidelines available upon request. Replies to queries in 2-3 days, to submissions (if invited) in 2-3 months. No authors outside Canada. No simultaneous submissions, unsolicited submissions, photocopies or dot-matrix. Contract is for 10% royalty plus 10 copies.** They comment, "Poets submitting MSS to Thistledown Press for possible publication should think in 'book' terms in every facet of the organization and presentation of the MSS: poets presenting MSS that *read* like good books of poetry will have greatly enhanced their possibilities of being published. We strongly suggest that poets familiarize themselves with some of our poetry books before submitting a query letter."

THORNTREE PRESS; GOODMAN AWARD; TROIKA (II), 547 Hawthorn Lane, Winnetka, IL 60093, founded 1986, contact Eloise Bradley Fink. This press publishes professionally printed digest-sized, flat-spined paperbacks, 96 pp. selected through competition for the Goodman Award in odd-numbered years. **Sample: $7.95 postpaid.** "Representative of our authors is Hilda Raz whose poems in **What Is Good** pack the eye with color and explore 'the explosion behind the forehead,' and occasionally seem to 'lick the undersides of rocks.' They link everyday and art. 'Everything stirs' and breaks apart in new ways, yet when Raz leaves us, it is with words to applique (us) while again." By spring of 1990, Thorntree Press will have published 11 books or 15 poets. "For the $400, $200, and $100 Goodman Awards we will be selecting three poets for **Troika III.**" Submit a stapled group of ten pages of original, unpublished poetry, single or double spaced, photocopied, with a $4 reader's fee. MSS will not be returned. (A SASE for winners' names may be included.) "The top fifteen finalists will be invited to submit a 30-page manuscript for possible publication in the **Troika.**"

THOUGHTS FOR ALL SEASONS: THE MAGAZINE OF EPIGRAMS (IV-Form, humor), % editor Prof. Michel Paul Richard, Sociology Dept., State University of New York, Geneseo, NY 14454, founded 1976, "is an irregular serial: **designed to preserve the epigram as a literary form; satirical.** All issues are commemorative, e.g., 1976, 1984, 1989, 1992." **Rhyming poetry will be considered although most modern epigrams are prose.** Prof. Richard has recently published poetry by David Kelly and offers this sample (poet unidentified):

> God created man in his own image—
> And lo! There stood Pithecanthropus.

TFAS is magazine-sized, offset from typescript on heavy buff stock with full-page cartoon-like drawings, card cover, 84 pp., saddle-stapled. Its press run is 500-1,000. The editor accepts about 20% of material submitted. There are several library subscriptions but most distribution is through direct mail or local bookstores and newsstand sales. Single copy: $3.75 plus $1.25 postpaid. **Send SASE for guidelines. Pays 1 copy. Simultaneous submissions OK, but not previously published epigrams "unless a thought is appended which alters it." Reports in 30 days. Editor comments on rejections.** The editor says, "This is the only magazine which is devoted to this literary form."

‡**THREE CONTINENTS PRESS INC. (IV-Ethnic, translations),** Suite 407, 1901 Pennsylvania Ave., N.W., Washington, DC 20006, phone 202-332-3886, founded 1973, poetry editor Donald Herdeck. "Published poets only welcomed, and only non-European and non-American poets ... We publish literature by creative writers from the non-western world (Africa, the Middle East, the Caribbean, and Asia/Pacific)—poetry *only* by non-western writers, or good translations of such poetry if original language is Arabic, French, African vernacular, etc." They have recently published poetry by Derek Walcott, Khalil Hawi, Mahmud Dawish, and Julia Fields. As a sample the editors selected "The Wind" from **Burden of Waves and Fruit** by the Indian poet Jayanta Mahapatra:

> My eyes are getting used to the dark.
> From time to time
> My old father comes at me
> with outstretched arms of judgement
> and I answer from no clear place I am in.

This collection is a digest-sized 98 pp., flat-spined, book professionally printed, glossy card cover with art. They also publish anthologies focused on relevant themes. **Query with 4-5 samples, bio, publication credits. Replies to queries in 5-10 weeks, to submissions (if invited) in 4-5 weeks. 10% royalty contract (5% for translator) with $100-200 advance plus 10 copies.** Send SASE for catalog to buy samples.

THE THREEPENNY REVIEW (II), P.O. Box 9131, Berkeley, CA 94709, phone 415-849-4545, founded 1980, poetry editor Wendy Lesser, "is a quarterly review of literature, performing and visual arts, and social articles aimed at the intelligent, well-read, but not necessarily academic reader. Nationwide circulation. **Want: formal, narrative, short poems (and others); do not want: confessional, no punctuation, no capital letters. Prefer under 50 lines but not necessary. No bias *against* formal poetry, in fact a slight bias in favor of it.**" They have recently published poetry by Thom Gunn, Frank Bidart, Robert Hass, Czeslaw Milosz, Brenda Hillman, Edgar Bowers, and Alan Shapiro. There are about 7-8 poems in each 36 pp. tabloid issue, circulation 7,500 with 6,000 subscriptions of which 300 are libraries. Subscription: $10. They receive about 4,500 submissions of freelance poetry per year, use 12. **Sample: $4 prepaid. Send 5 poems or fewer per submission. Reports in 2-8 weeks. Pays $50/poem.** Send SASE for guidelines.

‡**THRESHOLD BOOKS (IV-Religious, translations),** RD #4, Box 600, Dusty Ridge Rd., Putney, VT 05346, phone 802-254-8300, founded 1981, poetry editor Edmund Helminski, is "a small press dedicated to the publication of quality works in metaphysics, poetry in translation, and literature with some spiritual impact. **We would like to see poetry in translation of high literary merit with spiritual qualities, or original work by established authors.**" They will soon publish poetry by Rabia and Yunus Emre. The editor selected these sample lines by Jelaluddin Rumi, translated by John Moyne and Coleman Barks:

> We have this way of talking, and we have another.
> Apart from what we wish and what we fear may happen,
> We are alive with other life, as clear stones
> take form in the mountain.

That comes from a collection **Open Secret, Versions of Rumi**, published in a beautifully printed flat-spined, digest-sized paperback, glossy color card cover, 96 pp. Per copy: $7. **Query with 10 samples, bio, publication credits, and a SASE. Replies to queries in 1-2 months, to submissions (if invited) in 1-2 months. Simultaneous submissions, photocopies OK, or discs compatible with**

IBM, hard copy preferred. Publishes on 15% contract plus 10 copies (and 40% discount on additional copies). Send SASE for catalog to buy samples.

‡THUMBPRINTS, (I, IV-Themes, regional), 928 Gibbs, Caro, MI 48723, phone 517-673-5563, founded 1984, editor Janet Ihle, is the monthly 6 pp. Thumb Area Writers' Club newsletter that uses **poetry about writers and writing, nothing "vulgar." Maximum 20 lines.** As a sample, the editor selected the first of four stanzas from "That I Do Is Enough," by James P. Bonamy:

> *You see how easy it is to write?*
> *Yes, the ink sprays from the pen.*
> *Yes, the fingers twitch to make letters,*
> *Words, punctuation and, occasionally, sense.*

They sponsor seasonal contests for Michigan amateur writers. Press run: 40 for 26 subscriptions. Sample, postpaid: 75¢. **Send SASE for guidelines. Pays 1 copy. Simultaneous submissions and previously published poems OK. Reports in about 2 months. Editor comments on submissions "sometimes."**

TIDEPOOL; HAMILTON HAIKU PRESS (I, IV-Form), 4 E. 23rd St., Hamilton, ON L8V 2W6 Canada, phone 416-383-2857, founded 1984, publisher Herb Barrett who says, **"We charge $10 entry fee. Money returned if poetry not used." Send SASE for guidelines for details. He wants to see "haiku and contemporary short verse, any style or theme maximum 34 lines). No scatalogical vulgarity."** He has recently published poetry by Chris Faiers, Dorothy Cameron Smith, and Jeff Seffinga. As a sample I selected these lines by Dale Loucareas:

> *holding my heart-beat*
> *the burble of the creek*
> *now polluted*
>
> *where we played doctor*
> *& later skinny dipped*

Tidepool, published each October, is digest-sized, 80+ pp. saddle-stapled, professionally printed with matte card cover, circulation 400 with 150 subscribers of which 60-70 are libraries. Per issue: $5. **Sample: $5 postpaid. Pays 3-4 copies. Reports on submissions in 2-3 weeks. No dot-matrix. "Prefer unpublished material." Sometimes comments on rejections.** *Hamilton Haiku Press* **publishes chapbooks averaging 85 pp. For chapbook consideration submit 6 poems, bio, publications. Simultaneous submissions "seldom" accepted. No photocopies, dot matrix or previously published material. Pays 3 copies.**

TIDEWATER (II), 1230 S.E. Morrison #104, Portland, OR 97214, founded 1987, editor Scott Hartwich, is a literary quarterly "featuring a wide variety of writing from a wider variety of writers. **There are no specific guidelines for content or style, since we have not aimed our magazine toward any specific segment of society, or cause, or special-interest group. No hardcore erotica, no poems that preach."** They have recently published poetry by Meg Files, Kevin Griffith, and William Stafford. As a sample the editor selected these lines from "Crossing Through the Light" by Jacqueline Hartwich:

> *Dark descends like a hanging cradle, leafy and invisible*
> *and they can bear to make songs about the gone away place*
> *they name home now that they have settled in strange beds*
> *sah-tum sah-tum they hum and the flames leap hot leap high*
> *and after the last sah-tum the same huff of the leopards*
> *the same pad pad of the lepoards and the babies know to still*
> *their cries and watch fire tongues lick away the night.*

Tidewater is professionally printed, 8×7", saddle-stapled, 40-48 pp., with matte card cover using b/w art. Their press run is 1,000 with 300 subscriptions. Subscription: $10. **Sample: $3 postpaid. Guidelines available for SASE. Cover letter a "must." Pays 2-3 copies with a cash prize awarded to 1 poet every issue. Reports in 2 months (usually). Editor comments on rejections "only if requested in cover letter."** The *Tidewater* annual poetry contest is for poems 1-100 lines, theme: "three generations." Deadline: December 1. Entry fee: $1/poem, maximum $3 entry fee. Include SASE. First prize is $100 ("may increase"). He says, "Please take pride not only in your work, but in the presentation of your work. An adequate, well-worded cover letter, a cleanly typed manuscript and sufficient postage will show your respect for the editor. The poems, certainly, are my central concern, but there is nothing more frustrating than receiving a submission 'postage due.' "

TIFFANY AND SHORE PUBLISHERS; ANNUAL LEE SHORE POETRY AWARD (I), (formerly Lee Shore Publications), Suite 212, 1687 Washington Rd., Pittsburgh, PA 15228, phone 412-831-1731, founded 1988, owner Cynthia Semelsberger. **"Tiffany and Shore Publishers offers three types of publishing:**

co-op, straight publishing and subsidy publishing. We prefer to publish chapbooks of poetry, however we will consider children's manuscripts. We supply original artwork for each collection by artists such as Helen Kita and Sally Stormon. We try to publish 20 individual collections each year." **They accept MSS throughout the year.** The Annual Lee Shore Poetry Award closes December 15 and guidelines and category vary. Award is either publication or cash. They have a 67-acre farm that offers housing, workshops and seminars for poets, writers and artists. As a sample Cynthia Semelsberger selected these lines from John Murray's poem "Lady Luck" from his book **Visions of a Harp Player:**

> *She was born on parole*
> *nothin' would get in her way*
> *a first edition*
> *with no replacement price.*

They will consider simultaneous submissions and previously published poems. Poets must submit at least 25 poems to be considered. "We do encourage newer poets and we try to comment on rejections, although this may not always be possible." **Reports in 2-3 months.** Cynthia Semelsberger says, "Poets, be proud. You are the visionaries. Your interpretation of the world around you can shape the minds of men and women. So learn your craft. Develop your skills. Work on those metaphors. Don't be afraid of what you see. Support the work of your fellow poets ... someday you may need their help. Enjoy!"

‡TIGHTROPE (II); SWAMP PRESS (V), 323 Pelham Rd., Amherst, MA 01002, founded 1977, chief editor Ed Rayher. Swamp Press is a small-press publisher of "poetry, fiction and graphic art in limited edition, letterpress chapbooks. *Tightrope*, appearing 1-2 times a year, is a literary magazine of varying format, circulation 300, 150 subscriptions of which 25 are libraries. Subscription: $10 for 2 issues. The issue I have seen (January, 1987) is triangular in shape, folded 12" square sheets, elegantly printed on heavy eggshell stock, 44 pp., saddle-sewn, using art (some in colored ink) with colored matte card cover. It contains poems printed in various ways on the pages. As a sample I selected this complete poem (untitled) by Nancy Stewart Smith:

> *the sun*
> *slips down the golden bell's throat*
> *caught in a dewdrop*

Sample of *Tightrope*: **$6 postpaid. Send SASE for guidelines. Pays "sometimes" and provides 2 contributor's copies. Reports in 2 months, 6-12 months until publication. No simultaneous submissions.** Swamp Press has recently published books by Edward Kaplan, editor Ed Rayher, Alexis Rotella (a miniature 3×3" containing 6 haiku), Sandra Dutton (a 4 foot long poem), Frannie Lindsay (a 10×13" format containing 3 poems), Andrew Glaze, Tom Hazo, Carole Stone, and Steven Ruhl. Send SASE for catalog. **Not presently accepting freelance submissions for chapbook publication but when he publishes chapbooks he pays 5-10% of press run and, if there is grant money available, an honorarium (about $50). Sometimes comments on rejections.**

TIMBERLINE PRESS (V), Route 1, Box 162 I, Fulton, MO 65251, phone 314-642-5035, founded 1975, poetry editor Clarence Wolfshohl. "We do limited letterpress editions with the goal of blending strong poetry with well-crafted and designed printing. We lean toward **natural history or strongly imagistic nature poetry, but will look at any good work. Also, good humorous poetry. Currently, fully stocked with material.**" Recently published poets include Walter Bargen. **Payment policy: "50-50 split with author after** *Timberline Press* **has recovered its expenses." Reports in under 1 month.** Sample copies may be obtained by sending $4 requesting sample copy and noting you saw the listing in **Poet's Market.**

TIMBUKTU (II), P.O. Box 469, Charlottesville, VA 22902, phone 804-286-4521, founded 1987, editor Molly Turner, appears twice a year using **"poetry in all forms so long as it is original, intelligent and musical. Even Petrarchan sonnets can be experimental. We like experiments that work."** They have recently published poetry by Marin Sorescu, E.A. Gehman, and Michael Chitwood. As a sample the editor selected these lines by Robert Edwards:

> *A jaguar licks the alphabet, tasting the ancient salt*
> *of "A," lapping up the blood dripping from "Z."*
> *Yawning, he descends the hot steps of the pyramid*
> *in a green buzzing of flies to sleep by the fallen wheel*
> *of the calendar, his tail twitching with dream ...*

I have not seen *Timbuktu*, but the editor describes it as magazine-sized, 80 pp., flat-spined, using "lots of art, as well as fiction and essays, and a regular comic book. No ads. An independent magazine." Their press run is 600 with 250 subscriptions of which 10 are libraries. Subscription: $6. **Sample: $5 postpaid. Pays $5-50 plus 1 copy. Reports in 1-4 months.**

TIME OF SINGING, A MAGAZINE OF CHRISTIAN POETRY (I, IV-Religious, themes), P.O. Box 211, Cambridge Springs, PA 16403, founded 1958-1965, revived 1980, poetry editor Charles A. Waugaman. "The viewpoint is **unblushingly Christian—but in its widest and most inclusive meaning.** Moreover, it is believed that the vital message of Christian poems, as well as inspiring the general reader, will give pastors, teachers, and devotional leaders rich current sources of inspiring material to aid them in their ministries. We tend to have a Fall-Christmas issue, a Lent-Easter one, and a Summer one. But **we do have themes quite often. We tend to value content, rather than form. I hope we have variety."** They have recently published poetry by Benedict Auer, Thomas John Carlisle, John C. Cooper, Frances P. Reid, Tony Cosier, Mary Balazs, Edith Lovejoy Pierce, and Nancy Esther James. The editor selected these sample lines from "Patmos" by David Abrams:

> *John cries because a city has descended,*
> *Glinting and roaring with song as it comes.*
> *Behind John's eyelids, it touches down on Patmos*
> *And transforms each rock into a succulent flower.*

The triquarterly is digest-sized 40-44 pp., offset from typescript with decorative line-drawings scattered throughout, circulation 300+ with 150 subscriptions. Subscription: $9; per copy: $4. They receive over 500 submissions per year, use about 210, have a 4-month backlog. **Sample: $2.50. Prefer about 5 poems, double-spaced, no simultaneous submissions. Reports in 1-2 months. Pays 3 tearsheets of published poem. Send SASE for guidelines. Editor frequently comments with suggestions for improvement for publication. "We tend to be traditional. We like poems that are aware of grammar. Collections of uneven lines, series of phrases, preachy statements, unstructured 'prayers,' and trite sing-song rhymes usually get returned. We look for poems that 'show' rather than 'tell.' "** They also publish chapbooks of poets of the editor's selection and offer contests, "generally one for each issue on a given subject related to our theme."

TOAD HIWAY; STONE TALK (II), Box 44, Universal, IN 47884, phone 317-832-8918, founded 1988, poetry editors Doug Martin, Brian Beatty, John Colvin, and Kevin Anderson. *Toad Hiway* is a small magazine appearing irregularly using "all types of artwork, poetry, and fiction. **They want "alternative and poetry with a good sense of what's currently being published in mainstream American poetry, free verse, avant-garde. No greeting card, rhyme for rhyme's sake."** As a sample the editors selected these lines composed upon an electric stove, the burner being fed heat slowly by the steady hand of a psychic ex-lover in a kitchen very far from Istanbul, by Glen Armstrong:

> *I knew from the start that she wasn't*
> *A pollinaire's granddaughter, her recipes*
> *for swan were all southern fried, her Elvis*
> *dance was strange and angular nothing about*
> *her fit*

TH is a 20+ pp. pamphlet, saddle-stapled. Their press run is 250 with 2 subscriptions. "We accept about one in every 100 poems received." Subscription: $4. **Sample: $2. Pays 2 copies. Submit maximum of 5 poems, single-spaced. No simultaneous submissions, but they will consider previously published poems. Responds to submissions in 3 months maximum. Editor** "seldom" comments on rejections. *Stone Talk* is a cassette series, "produced irregularly, consisting of music, noise, poetry, altered-state conversations, and any other insane mutterings significant enough to be on tape." **Submit taped material to** *Toad Hiway*. **Sample** *ST*: **$3.** The editor says, "We would like to see more mainstream work in the styles of David Wojahn, Edward Hirsch, Cathy Song, etc. My advice to beginning poets is to live with the intensity of cutting the grass with one's teeth. Depression is essential at times for the poet. If you can weep while watching the Cosby Show, you have a good beginning."

TOLEDO POETS CENTER PRESS; 11×30; INMATE ARTS PRESS; GLASS WILL (V, IV-Regional, themes, anthologies, specialized), 32 Scott House, University of Toledo, Toledo, OH 43606, 419-473-0958, founded 1976, poetry editors Joel Lipman and Nick Muska, is a "small press **publisher of area writers, visual literature, and of inmate writing (from our writer's workshops at area jails)"** in broadsides, chapbooks, and flat-spined paperbacks. **"Submissions are not sought by Toledo Poets Center Press."** *11×30* is a "printerly publication of poetry, fiction, articles, literary news and gossip" and appears quarterly. Recent authors include Howard McCord, Michael Kasper, Bern Porter, Christy Sheffield-Sanford, (previously unpublished) Jack Kerouac. *Glass Will* "is a periodic anthology, more book-like (flat-spined) than magazine-like." 6×9¼", 266 pp. **It is a regional anthology of poetry appearing "infrequently" and publishing solicited work only. Pays a varied number of author's copies.** All publications are quality offset; samples of *11×30* for $1; sample of *Glass Will* for $5. Joel Lipman notes, **"our focus is on literary life in this region, on strong and provocative writing, and on composition and design that has beauty and permanence."**

TOUCH (IV-Religious, teens, themes), Box 7259, Grand Rapids, MI 49510, phone 616-241-5616, founded 1970, poetry editor Carol Smith: "Our magazine is a 24 pp. edition written **for girls 7-14 to show them how God is at work in their lives and in the world around them.** *Touch* **is theme-orientated.**

Brother George Klawitter, adviser for Viterbo College's Touchstone, says this cover art represents the theme of the publication because "our writers touch the joys of rural and small town Wisconsin—gardening, grandmothers, ponds, canoeing, etc." The artist is Paul G. Czerwonka, a Viterbo College graduate.

We like our poetry to fit the theme of each. We send out a theme update biannually to all our listed freelancers. We prefer short poems with a Christian emphasis that can show girls how God works in their lives." They have recently published poetry by Janet Shafer Boyanton and Iris Alderson. The editor selected these sample lines from Jacqueline Schiff's "Love Offering":

> It isn't easy, my parents say,
> To stick to the rules I must obey.
> Their rules are a gift of love to me—
> That's not always easy for me to see.

Touch is published 10 times a year, magazine-sized, circulation 15,600 with 15,000 subscriptions. Subscription: $8.50 US, $9.50 Canada, $10.50 foreign. They receive 150-200 freelance submissions of poetry per year, use 2 poems in each issue, have a 6 month backlog. **Sample and guidelines free with 8x10 SASE. Poems must not be longer than 20 lines—prefer much shorter. Simultaneous submissions OK. Query with SASE for theme update. Reports in 8 weeks. Pays $5-10 and copies.** "We have a rejection sheet that states the reason we have done so."

‡TOUCHSTONE (II), Viterbo College, La Crosse, WI 54601, phone 608-784-0268, founded 1950, moderator George Klawitter, is a literary quarterly using mostly poetry, short stories, and art work. "**Any form but no longer than 50 lines/poem. Nothing sentimental.**" As a sample the editor selected these lines (poet unidentified):

> It starts when you realize the language you use
> even in tense situations like teaching
> or calls to Mexico
> lacks anything to make it interesting

The magazine is digest-sized, 48 pp. saddle-stapled, with semi-glossy card cover. Press run 800 for 100 subscriptions of which 25 are libraries. Subscription: $5. **Sample, postpaid: $2.50. Send SASE for guidelines. Best poem gets $20. All get 1 copy. Submit 3-5. Reports in 2 months.** The editor says, "Write poetry that is rich in visual imagery. Strive to make your reader *see* what you are talking about. Do not philosophize. Do not moralize. Let the imagery carry the message."

TOUCHSTONE LITERARY JOURNAL; TOUCHSTONE PRESS (II, IV-Translations), Box 8308, Spring, TX 77387-8308, founded 1975, poetry editor William Laufer, is a semiannual using "**experimental or well-crafted traditional form, translations, no light verse or doggerel. In 1991 we will be particularly interested in looking at poetry about how land affects/influences/shapes people, i.e., plains poetry, island poetry, etc. Please include short bio including recent publications for our 'contributors' page.' No mail answered without SASE.**" They have recently published poetry by Walter Griffin, Sheila

Murphy, Michael L. Johnson, Walter McDonald, and Joyce Pounds Hardy. As a sample, I selected these lines from "Women" by Elena Andres:

> Encircling a motionless water
> a hundred arms of women
> curve themselves like arches
> they move in the wind
> like white serpents.

Touchstone, appearing twice a year, is digest-sized, flat-spined, 40 pp., professionally printed in small, dark type with glossy card cover. Subscription: $10. **Sample, postpaid: $3. Pays $3-5 plus 1 copy.**

‡TOWER POETRY SOCIETY; PINE TREE SERIES; TOWER (II), Dundas Public Library, 18 Ogilvie St., Dundas, Ontario, L9H 2S2, Canada, founded 1951, editor-in-chief Joanna Lawson. "The press is an outgrowth of Tower Poetry Society, started by a few members of McMaster University faculty to promote interest in poetry. We publish *Tower* twice a year and a few chapbooks. We want **rhymed or free verse, traditional or modern, but not prose chopped into short lines, maximum 35 lines in length, any subject, any comprehensible style.**" They have recently published poetry by Sparling Mills, John Ferns, Kenneth Samberg, and Catherine Bankier. The editor selected these sample lines by Tony Cosier:

> From forging brass he took to forging soul,
> gave up plowing soil to plow his skull,
> ripped open the eye that never closed again
> and took for tongue the howl of the beast in pain.

Tower is digest-sized, 40 pp., circulation 150, 60 subscriptions of which 8 are libraries. Subscription: $6 including postage. They receive about 400 freelance submissions of poetry per year, use 30, no backlog. **Sample: $2 postpaid. Limit submissions to 4 poems. Submit during February or August. Reports in 2 months. Pays 1 copy. "Comment if requested—no charge."** The editor advises, "Read a lot of poetry before you try to write it."

‡TOWNSHIPS SUN (IV-Rural, ecological, regional), 7 Conley St., P.O. Box 28, Lennoxville, Quebec J1M 1Z3 Canada, phone 819-566-7424, founded 1972, editor Patricia Ball, is a monthly newspaper in English "concerned with **history of townships, English community, agriculture, ecology, and using poetry on these themes.**" As a sample, I selected these opening lines from "A Poem for Bury (Quebec)" by Marjories Stokes Munroe:

> It's just a little village, where maples line the street,
> And graduates of years gone by, come back, their friends to greet.
> Three churches in our small town stand,
> Three schools, we think, the best ones in the land.

The tabloid has a press run of 2,500 for 2,000 subscribers of which 20 are libraries, and 500 shelf sales. Subscription: $12/year Canada, $17/year outside Canada. **Sample, postpaid: $1.50. Pays $10-30 plus 1 copy. "Will publish poems specifically about townships, townshippers, or of specific interest to townshippers."**

TRADESWOMEN MAGAZINE (IV-Women, themes), Box 40664, San Francisco, CA 94140, founded 1982, poetry editor Sue Doro, staff editors Molly Martin and Helen Dozenilek, is a national quarterly **"particular to women in non-traditional work"** and uses poetry **"pertaining to women in trades, tradeswomen as mothers, wives, male co-worker relationships."** Subscription: $35. **Sample: $2 postpaid. Guidelines available for SASE. They consider simultaneous submissions and previously published poems. Reports in 4 weeks. No backlog.**

TRADITION (IV-Themes), Box 438, Walnut, Council Bluffs, IA 51577, phone 712-366-1136, founded 1976, editor Robert Everhart, magazine, 6/year, that publishes **short poetry about traditional things—mostly music. The magazine covers "old-time music, folk-bluegrass-country, and lifestyles."** It is 7½ × 10½", newsprint (I have not seen a sample copy.) Circulation is 2,500, price per issue $1. **Sample: $1 postpaid, guidelines available for SASE, pays 10 copies. The editor reports on submissions in 6 months.** He says, "We have a poetry reading championship every Labor Day weekend in conjunction

ALWAYS submit MSS or queries with a stamped, self-addressed envelope (SASE) within your country or International Reply Coupons (IRCs) purchased from the post office for other countries.

with our annual old-time country music festival. Poets are encouraged to participate for judging, publication, and prizes."

TRAMP (II), P.O. Box 1386, Columbia, SC 29202, founded 1987 (first issue March, 1988), poetry editor Alan Howard. **"Prefer short poems in non-traditional forms. Special interest in themes of sensuality and spirituality. Wit is always welcome, from subtle to outrageous. Not interested in rhyming verse, unless it's a bit off-the-wall."** He has recently published poetry by David Chorlton, Gerald Locklin, Sheila Murphy, and Willie Smith. As a sample he selected these lines by Dan Raphael:

> *a tree allergic to its own needles,*
> *a tree standing on its head*
> *a digital tree, statistically significant,*
> *a patented tree, a moon-worshipping tree . . .*

Tramp, appearing 2-3 times a year (plus occasional supplements), is digest-sized, photocopied, saddle-stapled, using some graphics and artwork. Subscription: $10 for 4 issues. **Sample: $3 postpaid. Send SASE for guidelines. Pays 1 copy. Reports in 4-8 weeks. "Prefer batches of 3-6 poems. No simultaneous submissions please." Editor sometimes comments on rejections.**

TRANSNATIONAL PERSPECTIVES (III), CP161, 1211 Geneva 16 Switzerland, founded 1975, editor René Wadlow, is a "journal of world politics with some emphasis on culture that crosses frontiers." Uses 4-6 poems per issue, usually illustrated by drawing or photo. They want **"poems stressing harmony of nature, human potential, understanding of other cultures — relatively short. No humor, nationalistic themes, nothing 'overly' subjective."** They have recently published poems by Verona Bratesch and Janet Pehr. As a sample the editor selected these lines by Ondra Lysohorsky:

> *Out of all the colours, and shades of colour,*
> *Out of all shapes, from all perfumes*
> *A beauty arises I cannot view without pity;*
> *With all these senses the holiest Silence sings —*
> *While I know that this beauty so soon fades.*

TP appears 3 times a year; it "is oriented toward making policy suggestions in international organizations, especially in the United Nations." It is handsomely produced, magazine-sized, 48 pp., saddle-stapled with coated color paper cover. They receive about 100 poems per year, use 16. Press run is 5,000 for 4,000 subscriptions of which half are libraries. **Sample back issue free on request. Pays 5 copies, more if desired. Simultaneous submissions OK. No previously published poems. Reports in 1 month. Editor comments "rarely, on quality, only why not for *TP*."** René Wadlow says, "Poems in *TP* come from many countries, especially Eastern Europe, Scandinavia, and India, often translated into English, usually 'upbeat' since most of articles are on political and economic difficulties of the world."

TRESTLE CREEK REVIEW (II), 1000 West Garden, Coeur d'Alene, ID 83814, phone 208-769-3300, ext. 384, founded 1982-83, poetry editor Chad Klinger et al, is a "2 year college creative writing program production. Purposes: (1) expand the range of publishing/editing experience for our small band of writers; (2) expose them to editing experience; (3) create another outlet for serious, beginning writers. **We favor poetry strong on image and sound, the West and country vs. city; spare us the romantic, rhymed clichés. We can't publish much if it's long (more than 2 pp.)"** They have recently published poetry by Carol Jean Logue, Ron McFarland, and Timothy Pilgrim. Chad Klinger selected these lines by Lowell Jaeger:

> *Teenage and fond*
> *of tree limbs glazed like sweets, if she divines*
> *the odds she is belted snug,*
> *her knuckles white as the wheel binds,*
> *as her pulse slides nearer the invisible tug*
> *of eternal splash toward frozen light*
> *slipping off maples like chandeliers.*

TCR is a digest-sized 57 pp. annual, professionally printed on heavy buff stock, perfect-bound, matte cover with art, circulation 500, 6 subscriptions of which 4 are libraries. They receive freelance poetry submissions from about 100 persons per year, use 30. **Sample: $4. Submit before March 1 (for May publication) no more than 5 pp., no simultaneous submissions. Reports by March 30. Pays 2 copies.** The editor advises, "Be neat, be precise, don't romanticize or cry in your beer, strike the surprising, universal note. Know the names of things."

TRIQUARTERLY MAGAZINE (II), 2020 Ridge Ave., Evanston, IL 60208, phone 708-491-7614, founded 1964, editor Reginald Gibbons, is one of the most distinguished journals of contemporary literature. Some issues are published as books on specific themes. They have recently published poetry by C. K. Williams, Rita Dove, Alan Shapiro, Li-Young Lee, Lisel Mueller, W.S. DiPiero, Donald Davie, Bruce

Weigl, Thomas McGrath, and Sandra McPherson. The editor selected this sample poem "Second Footnote" by Margaret Randall:

> *They drag me away. I watch them*
> *walking off, hauling my thrashing body,*
> *watch as my starts of resistance*
> *diminish against their dull dragging gait.*
> *I have nothing left but my voice.*
> *With it*
> *I say Margaret Margaret Margaret Margaret*
> *until they drop me and run*
> *discarding me as they go.*
> *I laugh.*
> *I have myself back again. I am home.*

Triquarterly's three issues per year are 6×9″, 200+ pp., flat-spined, professionally printed with b/w photography, graphics, glossy card cover with b/w photo, circulation 4,500 with 2,000 subscriptions of which 35% are libraries, using about 40 pp. of poetry in each issue. Subscription: $18; per copy: $7.95. They receive about 3,000 freelance submissions of poetry per year, use 20, have about a 12 month backlog. **Sample: $4 postpaid. They do not read during the summer months. No dot-matrix or simultaneous submissions. Reports in 10-12 weeks. Payment varies. "We *suggest* prospective contributors examine sample copy before submitting."**

TROPOS (IV-Students, bilingual/foreign language), Dept. of Romance and Classical Languages, Wells Hall, MSU, East Lansing, MI 48824, phone 517-355-8350, founded 1977, is a "publication **of graduate students, for graduate students." They use poems that are "fairly short (1 page) in any romance language."** As a sample Catherine F. Danielou selected these lines by Anne-Marie Moscatelli:

> *Rousse, la lune douce*
> *Qui éclabousse*
> *Les cocotiers*

It is published once a year, using 6-10 poems in each issue. It is 92 pp., flat-spined, photocopied from word processed type with matte 2-color card cover, print run 200. **Sample: $7.50 postpaid. No simultaneous submissions. Reports in 3-5 months.**

TROUT CREEK PRESS; DOG RIVER REVIEW; DOG RIVER REVIEW POETRY SERIES; BACK POCKET POETS (II), 5976 Billings Rd., Parkdale, OR 97041, founded 1981, poetry editor Laurence F. Hawkins, Jr., prefers **"shorter poems (to 30 lines) but will consider longer, book or chapbook consideration. No restrictions on form or content. No pornography or religious verse."** They have recently published poetry by Judson Crews, Gerald Locklin, Arthur Winfield Knight, Connie Fox, Terence Hoagwood, and Joseph Semenovich. Laurence Hawkins selected these sample lines from "Measuring Time" by David Chorlton:

> *The eldest son marks a cross*
> *in the crust of a loaf, then cuts*
> *a first piece for his father.*
> *Supper is cheese again,*
> *and the same conversation as the day before . . .*

Dog River Review is a semiannual, digest-sized, 60 pp., saddle-stapled, offset from computer typescript with b/w graphics, circulation 300, 40 subscriptions of which 7 are libraries. Subscription: $6. They receive about 500 freelance submissions of poetry per year, use 40-50. **Sample: $2 postpaid.** Backpocket Poets is a series of 4×5¼″ chapbooks, professionally printed, 26 pp. saddle-stapled with matte card cover, selling for $2.50 each, a drawing or photo of the author on the back. The Dog River Review Poetry Series consists of digest-sized, professionally printed, saddle-stapled chapbooks with matte card covers. **Reports in 1 week-3 months. Payment in copies. Send SASE for guidelines. For book publication by Trout Creek Press, query with 4-6 samples. Replies to queries immediately, to submission (if invited) in 1-2 months. No simultaneous submissions. Photocopy, dot-matrix OK. No payment until** "material costs recovered. We also publish individual authors on cassette tape." Send SASE for catalog to buy samples. **Editor sometimes comments on rejections.**

TSUNAMI (II), Earthquake Press, P.O. Box 1442, Venice, CA 90294, editor-in-chief Lee Rossi, is a "small press publisher of **poets and poems that aren't afraid to take risks. We have no limitations as to style or subject matter, but we take eight or ten looks at any poem longer than two pages before we accept it. Our goal is to produce a book full of high-quality poems that tackle a variety of subjects. We enjoy narrative voice, concrete expressions of modern life, surrealism."** They have recently published poetry by James Krusoe, Clayton Eshleman, Ivan Argüelles, William Witherup and Robert Schuler.

As a sample they selected these lines from "Poolside, West L.A." by Eliot Schain:

> *The ice in my tumbler cracks*
> *apocalyptically*
> *as the sun beats down*
> *on these intense muscles.*

> *Intelligence will never save the world*

Tsunami appears twice a year—a digest-sized 60 pp., perfect bound, professionally printed, with glossy card cover and full-color art. **Submissions are read twice a year, in March and September. In their third year they received about 1,500 poems, used 100. Press run is 500 for 200 subscriptions, 300 shelf sales. Subscription: $10. Sample: $6 postpaid. Pays 1 copy. Simultaneous submissions and previously published work not accepted. Reports in "6-10 weeks." No comments on rejections.** The editors say, "We're polyglots—we accept many different voices, styles, tones. We feel that young poets should explore the possibilities of their voice and not stick with one tone or approach. We tap new voices nationwide."

TUCUMCARI LITERARY REVIEW (II), 3108 W. Bellevue Ave. Los Angeles, CA 90026, founded 1988, editor Troxey Kemper, assistant editor Neoma Reed, appears every other month. **"Prefer rhyming and established forms, 2-100 lines, but the primary goal is to publish good work. Nothing shaped like a Christmas tree, Easter egg, etc. No talking animals. No talking with God unless you tape His conversation and snap His photo. No haiku, senryu, renga, waka, tanka, choka, katauta, mondo, sedoka, somonka, or hokku. The quest here is for poetry that will be just as welcome many years later, as it is now. Preference is for readable, understandable writing of literary and lasting quality. Simple, sentimental rhymes and nostalgic recollections, yes, but not stilted, obscure snatches of jumbled words that require a dictionary at hand."** They have recently published poetry by Marian Ford Park, Patricia M. Johnson, Alice Mackenzie Swaim, Angie Monnens, Linda Hutton, Robert Cooperman, Betty M. Benoit, and Bettye K. Wray. As a sample the editor selected these lines from "The Fiddler's Prayer," a 34-line poem by Al Dial:

> *When I pick up this old fiddle and some old song of*
> *praise rings out,*
> *It just makes my day go lots better.*

The magazine is digest-sized, 48 pp., saddle-stapled, photocopied from typescript, with card cover. Their press run is 150-200. Subscription: $12; $20 for overseas. **Sample: $2 plus $2.64 for overseas. Send SASE for guidelines. Pay is 1 copy. No entry fees, no reading fees for contests. Considers simultaneous submissions and previously published poems. Reports within 1 month.** Acquires one-time rights. The editor advises, "Try to write a poem that 'says something,' expresses an idea or mood or *something*—not a jumble of prose words arranged in odd-shaped lines, trying to look like a poem and not saying anything. The established forms still stand as beacons for aspiring poets."

TURKEY PRESS (V), 6746 Sueno Rd., Isla Vista, CA 93117, founded 1974, poetry editor Harry Reese along with his wife, Sandra Reese, "is involved with publishing contemporary literature, producing traditional and experimental book art, one-of-a-kind commissioned projects and collaborations with various artists and writers. **We do not encourage solicitations of any kind to the press. We seek out and develop projects on our own."** They have published poetry by Thomas Merton, James Laughlin, Sam Hamill, Edwin Honig, Glenna Luschei, Tom Clark, Michael Hannon, Keith Waldrop, David Ossman, Peter Whigham, Jack Curtis, Kirk Robertson, and Anne E. Edge.

TURNSTONE PRESS (II, IV-Regional), 607-100 Arthur St., Winnipeg, MB R3B 1H3 Canada, phone 204-947-1555, founded 1975, is a "literary press publishing quality contemporary fiction, poetry, criticism" in flat-spined books (eight per year), having **a Canadian emphasis. They want "writing based on contemporary poetics, but otherwise wide-ranging. Welcome experimental, graphic, long poems, the unusual. Nothing overly concerned with traditional rhyme and meter."** They have recently published poetry by Di Brandt, David Arnason, and Kristjana Gunnars. As a sample they selected these lines by Robert Kroetsch:

> *This is a prairie road.*
> *This road is the shortest distance*
> *between nowhere and nowhere.*
> *This road is a poem.*

The sample book I have seen, **Waiting for Saskatchewan**, by Fred Wah (a Chinese-Canadian with several previous books of poetry to his credit), is handsomely printed, 98 pp. flat-spined, with glossy two-color card cover, $7.95. It was awarded the Governor General's Award for 1985. **Submit complete MS and bio. Photocopies, good dot-matrix OK, as are poems previously published in magazines. Reports in 2-3 months. Pays $100-200 advance, 10% royalties and 10**

Close-up

Lee Rossi
Editor-in-Chief
Tsunami

Desaparecidos
She calls them the "disappeareds,"
those places where she's lost the weight.
It's our little joke—
the stomach of a campesino,
the thighs of a union organizer,
the arms of a mamacita
ringing her husband's neck
as they drag him into the forest.

In addition to his job as editor-in-chief of *Tsunami*, Lee Rossi is a contributing editor of *Onthebus*, another Los Angeles literary magazine. "Although I've been publishing poems for about the last ten years, 90% of what's hit print has been in the last four. My first book of poetry, **Love It Be Me**, will be published this year by Bombshelter Press (Los Angeles)," says Rossi. His poetry also appears in the 1989 **New Poets of Los Angeles**, an anthology from Artifact Press, and in several other poetry magazines.

Rossi grew up in St. Louis. He has held a variety of jobs: he taught English and English as a second language (ESL) and sold computers for a large corporation. Currently he is a computer programmer/internal consultant in Los Angeles. He says he became interested in poetry in high school but "touched the live wire of the L.A. poetry scene" about four years ago. He also joined a poetry workshop run by Los Angeles poet Jack Grapes, a poet Rossi admires as a great teacher. Rossi stayed with the workshop for over a year and still goes back occasionally. He says that is where he hears some of the best work anywhere.

Tsunami was begun in 1986 as a cooperative venture among a group of Jack Grapes' students. Rossi joined the original editors several months later. Over time the various founding members of the staff have dropped out and Rossi is now busy running the magazine. "Tsunami," the name chosen by one of the original editors, means "a new wave, dynamism." Rossi says. "That's what I like about the name. We're rude, crude and socially unacceptable. At least I hope we are."

Rossi says he receives many submissions to *Tsunami*, about 250 to 300 poems a month, of which only five to ten are used. "Sifting the gold from the dross takes some doing, but I feel it's worth the effort because I get to be the first or second serious venue for young and relatively underpublished poets producing high-quality work."

He says he doesn't have any particular rules for submitting to *Tsunami* beyond the usual ones: don't submit a book; tell me who you are; buy a sample if you can afford to.

"In order for us to choose something, it has to have an edge, a real energy or emotion. Poetry is about emotion, not thought. The words are just ways of transcribing the emotional experience. If we don't feel that some genuine emotional moment is being communicated, then we're not interested. I'm really not interested in well-wrought poems, not per se. I look for poems that have a unique experience to relate or that speak with a unique voice. It's easy to get bored after reading 300 poems. Yet even after a poem's made the first cut,

TORY

he legendary magazine that once helped struggling writers
ke Truman Capote, J.D. Salinger, William Saroyan and
orman Mailer break into print has returned with captivat-
g stories by today's most promising new authors.

s a STORY subscriber, you'll count yourself among the first
enjoy the works of new writers destined for literary
claim. Each quarterly issue features more than 100 pages of brilliant
ort fiction printed on heavy premium paper. Use this postage-paid card
start your subscription today!

Please enter my one-year
subscription to STORY at the
low introductory rate of just
$17 for four quarterly issues.

I'm enclosing payment.
Please bill me.

NAME (please print)

ADDRESS   APT

CITY   STATE   ZIP

Outside U.S. add $4 and remit in U.S. funds. Watch for your first issue in 6-8 weeks!

Would you like to see your short stories in print?

Vriter's Digest School offers a home-study course in short story writing that can help you create
blishable manuscripts. You'll work one-on-one with a published short story author, learning
ep-by-step how to write stories that will interest editors. By the end of the course you'll have a
mplete manuscript ready to send to the publishers you selected with the help of your
structor.

you'd like free information on Writer's Digest School, just fill out and mail this
stage-paid card today.

me (Please Print)   Home Phone

ldress

ty   State   Zip

ail this card today. No postage needed.

Want to get your FREE information more quickly?
Just call our toll-free phone number 1-800-759-0963.

BUSINESS REPLY MAIL

FIST CLASS MAIL   PERMIT NO. 125   MT. MORRIS, IL

POSTAGE WILL BE PAID BY ADDRESSEE

STORY

PO BOX 396
MT MORRIS IL 61054-7909

BUSINESS REPLY MAIL

FIRST CLASS MAIL   PERMIT NO. 17   CINCINNATI, OH

POSTAGE WILL BE PAID BY ADDRESSEE

WRITER'S DIGEST SCHOOL
1507 DANA AVENUE
CINCINNATI OH 45207-9966

I look at it again for the quality of the language. Is it vivid? Is it fresh? Is it personal? So many of the poems I see are just not well written; they're full of clichés; they're vague; they're rehashes of the ideas or images of other poets. Why bother?" says Rossi.

"For me, one of the most important aspects of the whole literary enterprise, and one of the most neglected, is the literary community. I get my friends, my subscribers, most of my listeners, my critics and my emotional support from other poets. I think I'm particularly blessed to be living in Los Angeles. I've talked to other poets from other sections of the country and my impression is that there are very few places where the literary community is as large and energetic and where poets band together for mutual support and encouragement like they do in L.A. In short, *Tsunami* wouldn't exist without the support of the poets of Los Angeles. Yet wherever you are, as a writer you need the support of other writers," says Rossi.

He also advises poets to find a way to get their poetry published, even if it means publishing it themselves. "Poets should seize the power. They don't have to wait for somebody else to put a stamp of approval on their work. They should have faith in their work and get it out there."

Rossi says he has attended both classes and workshops and has had good and bad experiences with both. "I'd say if you're shopping for a workshop or a group, pick one where the main thing you get out of it is the encouragement to keep writing. Most poets I know are constantly fighting with their writer's block. Also try to find a group where the people are not hung up so much on the quality of individual pieces but understand that as an artist you have to take risks in order to meet the challenges of your experience," says Rossi. He believes it can be a great environment where poets can try new things without getting locked in a particular mode or stylistic straight jacket. "They mess up, they produce genuinely horrible stuff and *then* there's the magic. I've heard people produce completely wonderful poems that didn't sound a thing like their earlier work.

"One final word of advice. If at first you don't succeed, keep trying. It takes a while for an editor to get to know a writer. I generally try a particular market five or six times in a year before I give up. And then if I'd really like to publish there, I might try again a couple of years later, when I have a new body of publishable work. Patience and irony are necessary virtues not just for Bolsheviks but also for poets."

—Deborah Cinnamon

---

copies. Editor comments on rejections **"if we believe it has promise."** Send 9 × 12″ SASE (or, from the US, SAE with IRCs) for catalog to buy samples.

TWISTED (IV-Horror, fantasy), 22071 Pineview Dr., Antioch, IL 60002, phone 312-395-3085, founded 1985, editor/publisher Christine Hoard, an annual using **poetry of "horror/dark fantasy; humor OK. Form and style open. Not more than 1 page long."** They have recently published poetry by Denise Dumars, Janet Fox, Marge Simon, and Wayne Sallee. As a sample the editor selected these lines by poet Steve Sneyd:

> *under dank earth go*
> *white grubs seeking sockets to*
> *see through, souls to save*

I have not seen *Twisted,* but Christine Hoard describes it as "150 pp., magazine-sized, offset, vellum bristol cover, much art, some ads, 60 lb. matte paper. I receive a lot of poetry submissions, use 30-50 per issue." Press run is 300 for single-copy sales. **Sample: $6 postpaid, payable to Christine Hoard. Send SASE for guidelines. Pays 1 copy. "Don't submit more than four poems at a time. You should see a sample copy to get a 'feel' for what we publish."** No simultaneous **submissions, but previously published poems are sometimes accepted. Reports within 3 months. Editor often comments on rejections.** She says, "Poets of science fiction, horror, fantasy will be pleased to know there are *lots* of markets in the small press and some organizations are available to offer support and market information."

2 AM MAGAZINE; 2 AM PUBLICATIONS (IV-Science fiction/fantasy, horror), Box 6754, Rockford, IL 61125-1754, phone 815-397-5901, founded 1986, editor Gretta McCombs Anderson, wants **"fantasy, science fiction, heroic fantasy, horror, weird; any form, any style; preferred length is 1-2 pp. We want**

poetry that leaves an after-image in the mind of the reader." It has contained poetry by Mark Rich, G. N. Gabbard, and Leonard Carpenter, and the editor describes it as 68 pp., magazine-sized, offset on 60 lb. stock, cover printed on glossy stock, illustrations "by leading fantasy artists," uses ads, appears quarterly, circulation 1,000 with 250 subscriptions. Single copy: $4.95. Subscription: $19 a year. **Sample: $5.95 postpaid. Send SASE for guidelines. Pays 5¢ a line or $1 minimum plus 1 copy, 40% discount for more. Reports in 8 weeks, 6-12 months to publication. Submit no more than 5 poems at a time. "Prefer poems no more than 2 pages in length." Photocopies, simultaneous submissions OK. For chapbook consideration (32 pp. 4×5″, saddle-stapled) query with 5 sample poems, bio, aesthetic or poetic aims. "Poetry must have concrete images and patterned meter, evoke strong sense of mood, and express horror, fantasy or science fiction themes." Payment in royalties and copies. Editor "always" comments on rejections.** Gretta M. Anderson advises, "Read widely, be aware of what's already been done. Short poems stand a good chance with us. Looking for mood-generating poetry of a cosmic nature. Not interested in self-indulgent poetry."

TYRO MAGAZINE; TYRO WRITERS' GROUP (I, IV-Membership), 194 Carlbert St., Sault Ste. Marie, Ontario P6A 5E1, Canada, phone 705-253-6402, founded 1984, editor Stan Gordon, who says, "This bimonthly is a practice, learning and discussion medium for developing writers, publishing poetry, fiction and nonfiction submitted by members of Tyro Writers' Group. Widely published professionals provide advice, feedback on mail, and market opportunities." **Lifetime membership in the group costs $4, and you must be a member to submit. The magazine publishes "all types" of poetry, but does not want "anything that is morally offensive, legally dangerous, or wildly experimental."** Poets recently published include Audrey Fenton Roode, E. O. Schonmaier, Ruth Fenwick, Carole Ropeter, Elaine Tennyson, Michael M. Tomlin, Bret Campbell, Anne Fenton, and Joan G. Canfield. As a sample here is the last stanza of "Unemployed Frets" by Rodney Ross:

> *And yet*
> *there is another dawn*
> *And yet*
> *I am alive*
> *And sentient.*
> *And my dreams will not be still.*

The magazine is digest-sized, offset from typed copy with some b/w graphics, 80-120 pp. flat-spined, one-color matte card cover. Circulation is "about 500 and growing." Price per issue is $5, subscription $27/year. **Sample available for $5, guidelines for SASE. Contributors receive free copies. Simultaneous submissions considered. Submissions are reported on in 1 month. Time to publication is 6 weeks. Criticism is "always" provided on rejected MSS.** The editor says, "Writers develop skill through imitation, practice, exposure, and feedback. They learn to write by writing, become more published by getting published. We try to provide these experiences to writers with a wide range of skills, from frequently published to never-been-published."

‡U.C. REVIEW (II), % Office of the Registrar, U.C., University of Toronto, Toronto, ON M5S 1A1 Canada, is a literary magazine appearing twice a year using **"poetry, short prose and criticism, usually experimental in nature. We are open to all forms of literature but prefer challenging and innovative work. No specifications as to style or subject-matter. The work should be engaged to some extent, or at least aware of literary theory. It should be serious about the interaction between form and content, and about its place in the social sphere. No derivative or mainstream commodity poetry."** They have recently published poetry by Patricia Seaman and Yves Troendle. As a sample I selected the first stanza of the 15-line poem "Jocasta's Brooch (The Pasolini Version)" by Chris D'Iorio:

> *To weave backwards from the alleged torment,*
> *to forge sense from strange compulsions,*
> *I wrest vision from that eye, that fragment*

It is digest-sized. Press run 1,200 for 10 subscriptions of which 3 are libraries. Shelf sales in 3 Toronto bookstores. **Sample free. Send SASE for guidelines. Pays 4-6 copies. Reports "1 month after acceptance."** They send copies to small-press publications and some Toronto magazines for criticism. **Editor sometimes comments on rejections.**

ULTRAMARINE PUBLISHING CO., INC. (II), Box 303, Hastings-on-Hudson, NY 10706, founded 1974, editor C. P. Stephens, who says "We mostly distribute books for authors who had a title dropped by a major publisher—the author is usually able to purchase copies very cheaply. We use existing copies purchased by the author from the publisher when the title is being dropped." Ultramarine's recent list includes 250 titles, 90% of them cloth bound, one-third of them science fiction and 10% poetry. **The press pays 10% royalties. "Distributor terms are on a book by book basis, but is a rough split." Authors should query before making submissions; queries will be answered in 1 week. Simultaneous submissions are OK, as are photocopied or dot-matrix MSS, but no discs.**

UNDERPASS; UNDERPASS PRESS (I), #574-21, 10405 Jasper Ave., Edmonton, AB T5J 3S2 Canada, founded 1986, editors Barry Hammond and Brian Schulze. *Underpass* is a literary annual. The press publishes chapbooks and flat-spined paperbacks of poetry. They want **"contemporary, urban, avant-garde, concrete, or discursive prose-poems. Any length. No religious or nature poetry."** They have recently published poetry by Brian Burke, Sparling Mills and editor Barry Hammond. As a sample, Brian Schulze selected these lines from "Versailles" by James MacSwain:

> *Versailles is your reflection*
> *In the Hall of Mirrors.*
> *It states that when you are dead*
> *You will be put to other uses.*

Underpass is digest-sized. Their third issue was 60 pp., but they hope to increase size and continue the flat-spined format. It is offset printed with a laminated card cover using b/w and color graphics inside. "This year we received about eighty submissions and only used eighteen poets." Press run is 100-300. **Sample: $6.95 postpaid. Send SASE for guidelines. In 1989 paid $5/poem plus 2 copies. No simultaneous submissions or previously published poems. Editor sometimes comments on rejections. Deadline for each year is August 31st. Publication in late fall.**

UNDERWHICH EDITIONS (II, IV-Form, anthologies), Box 262, Adelaide St. Station, Toronto, Ontario, Canada M5C 2J4, phone 416-532-8134, founded 1978, poetry editors Richard Truhlar, Brian Dedora, Steven Smith, Beverley Daurio, Frank Davey, Paul Dutton, John Riddell, and j w curry are "dedicated to presenting in diverse and appealing physical formats, new works by contemporary creators, **focusing on formal invention and encompassing the expanded frontiers of musical and literary endeavor**" in chapbooks, pamphlets, flat-spined paperbacks, posters, cassettes, records and anthologies. They have recently published poetry by Gerry Shikatani, Keith Waldrop, Tristan Tzara and Richard Truhlar. The editors selected these sample lines from "The Sino-Korean Translations" by j w curry and Mark Laba:

> *disturb the*
> *the idea*
>
> *live in*
> *3 unities*

Query with 5-10 sample poems, cover letter and curriculum vitae. Reports in 1 year. Will not return large manuscripts. Photocopy, dot-matrix, discs compatible with Apple OK. No simultaneous submissions. Pays percent of run. Catalog available to buy samples.

UNITED METHODIST REPORTER; NATIONAL CHRISTIAN REPORTER; UNITED METHODIST REVIEW (IV-Religious), Box 660275, Dallas, TX 75266-0275, phone 214-630-6495, founded "about 1840." *UMR* is a weekly broadsheet newspaper, circulation 500,000+, "aimed at United Methodist primarily, ecumenical slant secondarily." They use at most one poem a week. **The poetry "must make a religious point — United Methodist or ecumenical theology; short and concise; concrete imagery; unobtrusive rhyme preferred; literary quality in freshness and imagery; not trite but easy to understand; short enough to fill 1-3 inch spaces. Do not want to see poems by 'my 13-year-old niece,' poems dominated by 'I' or rhyme; poems that are too long, too vague or too general; poems without religious slant or point."** As a sample the editor chose the whole poem, "The Good Neighbor" by Pollyanna Sedzoil:

> *She did her witnessing*
> *in such ordinary tones*
> *that only those few*
> *discerning ones*
> *who recognize each life*
> *as a unique poem*
> *were aware*
> *of the beautiful psalm*
> *alive in her daily faithfulness.*

Managing Editor John A. Lovelace says they use about 50 of 1,000 poems received per year. Poems may appear in all three publications. **Send SASE for guidelines. Pays $2 per poem and 1 copy. Send no more than 3-4 poems at a time. No simultaneous submissions or previously published poems. Time to publication can be up to a year. Editor comments on rejection "if it is promising."**

UNITY; DAILY WORD; WEE WISDOM (IV-Religious, children), Unity School of Christianity, Unity Village, MO 64065, founded 1893. "Unity periodicals are devoted to spreading the truth of practical Christianity, the everyday use of Christ's principles. The material used in them is constructive, friendly, and unbiased as regards creed or sect, and positive and inspirational in tone. We suggest that prospective contributors study carefully the various publications before submitting material. **Sample copies are sent on request. Complimentary copies are sent to writers on publication. MSS should be typewritten in double space. We accept MSS only with the understanding that they are original and previously unpublished. Unity School pays on acceptance 5¢ a word and up for prose and $1 a line for verse.**" *Unity Magazine* is a monthly journal that publishes **"articles and poems that give a clear message of Truth and provide practical, positive help in meeting human needs for healing, supply, and harmony. We pay a $20 minimum."** *Daily Word* is a "monthly manual of daily studies" which "buys a limited number of short devotional articles and poems." *Wee Wisdom* is a monthly magazine for boys and girls. **"Its purpose is character-building. Its goal is to help children develop their full potential. Short, lively nature and science stories and poems, readable by a third-grader. Character-building ideals should be emphasized without preaching."** As a sample I selected the last of three stanzas of "The Prayer of Faith" by Hannah More Kohaus:

> God is my health, I can't be sick;
> God is my strength, unfailing, quick;
> God is my all, I know no fear;
> Since God and love and Truth are here.

Many of the poems in the magazine are by children, submitted to the section called "Writers' Guild," edited by Judy Gehrlein. There is no payment for poems in this section except for complimentary copies and an award certificate and letter. Here is a sample, "I Love," by Wendy Strickland (Grade 4):

> I love the sand,
> I love the sea,
> I love the waves so high;
> But then I saw an airplane
> And wished that I could fly.

Wee Wisdom is 48 pp. saddle-stapled, digest-sized, with colorful art and graphics. **They also buy "rhymed prose for 'read alouds' " for which they pay $15 minimum.**

UNMUZZLED OX (IV-Themes, bilingual/foreign language), 105 Hudson St., New York, NY 10013, or Box 550, Kingston, Ontario K7L 4W5, Canada, founded 1971, poetry editor, Michael Andre, is a tabloid literary biannual. **Sample: free for 9x12″ SASE with 90¢ postage. Each edition is built around a theme or specific project.** The editor says, "The chances of an unsolicited poem being accepted are slight since I always have specific ideas in mind." He is currently assembling material for issues titled *Poems to the Tune*, "simply pomes to old tunes, a buncha contemporary *Beggar's Opera*. The other is tentatively called *The Unmuzzled OX Book of Erotic Verse*. **Only unpublished work will be considered, natch' but works may be in French as well as English."** The editor says, **"The last of my advisors has left me so I'm interested now especially in poetry that has an illustration, if not an obvious 'type' for its title." Subscription $20.**

THE UNSPEAKABLE VISIONS OF THE INDIVIDUAL (IV-Style), Box 439, California, PA 15419, phone 412-938-8956, founded 1971, poetry editors Arthur Knight and Kit Knight, is an "ongoing compendium of writings on, about and for the Beat Generation publishing anthologies, postcards, posters and annually, *the unspeakable visions of the individual*. **Poetry must be Beat-oriented, generally free verse, confessional."** They have published poetry recently by Allen Ginsberg, Gary Snyder, Gregory Corso, and Jack Kerouac. Each issue of *TUVOTI* uses 60-176 pp. of poetry, circulation 2,000. No subscriptions. **Sample: $3.50 postpaid. Submit maximum of 10 pp. Photocopy OK; no dot-matrix. Pays 2 copies and occasionally small cash payment, e.g. $10.** The editors advise, "Write honestly out of your own experience."

URBANUS (II), P.O. Box 3742, Silver Spring, MD 20918, founded 1987, editors Peter Drizhal and Cameron Bamberger, is a twice-yearly journal of poetry. **"Seeks *quality* contemporary and progressive poetry. Does not want to see anything self-indulgent, clichéd, rhymed."** They have recently published poetry by Arthur Knight, Martha Vertreace, Antler, Patrick McKinnon, John Tagliabue, and Karl Elder. As a sample I selected these lines from "harry was talking" by Todd Moore:

> . . . rain
> pounding thru the
> rolled down window
> stung my face the
> skid felt like a
> roller coaster ride
> thru lightning . . .

The digest-sized, 40 pp. saddle-stapled magazine uses roughly 3-5% of the submissions they receive. Their press run is 200. Subscription: $9. **Sample: $4.50 postpaid. Reports in 2-4 weeks, 6-9 months till publication. Pays 1 copy.**

‡**US1 WORKSHEETS; US1 POETS' COOPERATIVE (II)**, 21 Lake Drive, Roosevelt, NJ 08555, founded 1973, is a 20-25 pp. literary tabloid biannual in 11½×17", circulation 500, which uses **high quality poetry and fiction. Sample: $4.** "We use a rotating board of editors; it's wisest to query when we're next reading before submitting." Recently published poets include Alicia Ostreicher, Toi Derricotte, Elizabeth Anne Socolow, Jean Hollander, Pablo Medina, and David Keller. **"We read a lot but take very few. Prefer complex, well-written work. Write us for sample copies."**

UTAH HOLIDAY MAGAZINE (II, IV-Regional), Suite 2000, 807 E. South Temple, Salt Lake City, UT 84102, phone 801-532-3737, founded 1971, poetry editor Dorothy Solomon, is a "monthly magazine with a **strong regional focus that publishes a very limited amount of poetry as space permits."** Dorothy Solomon says that none of our category designations really applies. **The poetry they use is not necessarily regional, and "We are very open to beginners' submissions.** We don't care if somebody has been published elsewhere or not. We will offer criticism and suggestions to writers, and will also consider accepting something after revision, if we are happy with the revision. But **we do not have much space to run poetry, so writers should be advised there is a high likelihood we will either not accept their poems, or that they will have to wait a considerable amount of time before they see them in print. There are no particular specifications except that the poetry be quality work and that it hasn't been published previously. We are more apt to be able to publish shorter poems just because there is more likely to be space for them. Poems with a strong Utah regional focus would be more acceptable than those which refer to other regions. We like poetry with a unique way of looking at experience or the world."** They have, so far, published only regional writers. As a sample, I selected this haiku by Judith Lundin Lowe:

> *The blue heron . . .*
> *He spreads his wings over her;*
> *The stretched horizon.*

UHM is magazine-sized, 85-130 pages. "We look like any other regional magazine. We have b/w as well as 4-color pages, and regular slick magazine quality paper." Its press run is 19,000 for 14,000 subscriptions, 3,500 shelf sales. Subscriptions: $16.95. Single copy: $1.95. **Sample: $3, postpaid. Pays $25-50 "usually," plus 2-3 copies. They have "an extensive backlog." Simultaneous submissions OK. Reports "within 3 months." Editor sometimes comments on rejections.** She says, "We do not really consider ourselves a very viable market for poetry. We do encourage local people who have poetry, if it is good quality, to submit in hopes that we will have space for it. If people out of region have poems which relate to this region, we would especially encourage them, too."

UNIVERSITY OF UTAH PRESS (II), 101 University Service Bldg., Salt Lake City, UT 84112, phone 801-581-6771, publishes a poetry series under the editorship of the poet and critic Dave Smith. Each year a volume of original poetry is chosen from submitted MSS. **MSS are invited** *during the month of March only;* the volume selected for publication is announced the following September with other MSS returned during the summer. **Poetry collections should be at least 60 pp. in length and should be sent to Acquisitions Editor—Poetry, at the above address. They will accept MSS which are simultaneous submissions "provided we are notified that this is the case."**

VALLEY WOMEN'S VOICE (I, IV-Women), Student Union Bldg., University of Massachusetts, Amherst, MA 01003, founded 1979, collective editorial staff, is a "monthly women's newspaper run collectively with an open membership. Main purpose of paper is to **educate and empower women."** They want **"poems that are of different styles, preference given to work that deals with social change."** As a sample they selected these lines from "Halloween" by Frances Ford:

> *Let our Dark Ladies mourn me tonight.*
> *The spirits passed me by.*
> *Full moons away from my doorstep they skipped*
> *masked, hefting sweet baggage home . . .*
> *passing strange and sweet*

The 16 pp. newsprint tabloid is a monthly, circulation 5,000, 220 subscribers and exchanges. The centerfold is devoted to poetry, photos and graphics. **Pays in copies. Considers simultaneous submissions. Sample $1.** "As women's voices are so rarely heard, we reserve the voice solely for women's work. We want poems of variety and diversity, preference given to work that deals with lesbian existence and social change."

THE VANITAS PRESS (I, IV-Specialized, children), Platslagarevägen 4E1, 22230, Lund, Sweden, founded 1978, publisher (Mr.) March Laumer, who says, "The Press is the shoestringyest in existence. We publish to an extremely enthusiastic but equally extremely tiny market. **No royalties can be paid, as we distribute volumes at rock-bottom cost of production, mailing (even then subscribers must pay circa $15 a volume; we just can't ask for more to cover royalties).** But it is your chance to reach an audience of up to 2,000 readers. **Currently we issue only "latter-day novels" of the "Oz" saga.** Please read up the Oz books in your local public library, then send us short stories, outlines for novels, and/or Oz-oriented art; you're virtually certain to be published if material promising at all. A recently published verse insertion (in **A Fairy Queen in Oz**):

> *I saw a giraffe*
> *And I wanted to laugh,*
> *But I couldn't, you see.*
> *Something stuck in my throat when I tried*
> *And I very near cried*
> *As my feelings at once*
> *Ran amuck.*

VEGETARIAN JOURNAL; THE VEGETARIAN RESOURCE GROUP; JEWISH VEGETARIANS NEWSLETTER (I, IV-Themes, children/teens), Box 1463, Baltimore, MD 21203, founded 1982, poetry editor Debra Wasserman. *VJ* is bi-monthly, *JV* is quarterly, founded 1983. The Vegetarian Resource Group is a small-press publisher of non-fiction, sometimes incorporating poetry. **They want poetry on themes such as vegetarians, animal rights, and world hunger. "We appreciate humor and/or account of personal feelings about being vegetarian and a factual, scientific approach. Please, no graphic descriptions of animal abuse."** As samples, the editor selected these lines from a poem by Betty Jahn:

> *"But," comes the scientific outcry*
> *"Without this suffering of individuals, the species will die."*
> *I submit that our concern for the species is more a concern for ourselves,*
> *to palliate our loneliness and fear, as we empty the planet with our*
> *greed and ideas of the all-importance of the human species.*

JV is a 16 pp., magazine-sized newsletters, offset from typescript with typeset heads. *VJ* has a circulation of 4,000; *JV* of 800. **Pays copies. Simultaneous submissions and previously published poems OK. Editor makes short comments on rejections.** They offer an annual contest for ages 19 and under, $50 savings bond yearly for the best contribution on any aspect of vegetarianism. "Most entries are essay, but we would accept poetry with enthusiasm." Charles Stahler asks me to "note that *Vegetarian Journal* and *Jewish Vegetarians Newsletter* are published by two separate organizations, but are both edited from the same address." **Sample for *JV* is $1.50. Sample for *Vegetarian Journal* is $3.**

VEHICULE PRESS; SIGNAL EDITIONS (IV-Regional), Box 125 Station Place du Parc, Montreal, Quebec, H2W 2M9 Canada, phone 514-844-6073, poetry editor Michael Harris, publisher Simon Dardick, is a "literary press with poetry series, Signal Editions, **publishing the work of Canadian poets only."** They publish flat-spined paperbacks and hardbacks. Among the poets published are Louis Dudek, Marie-Claire Blais, Don Coles, David Solway, Susan Glickman, and Stephen Scobie. As a sample the publisher selected these lines by poetry editor Michael Harris:

> *Soon large in the parish will the thunder bunch*
> *its fists, the thunder roll its muscle*
> *and trees fall dead. Nothing rises, Jeffrey,*
> *as quietly as you. Not the wintering daisy*
> *at seed in the meadow, the grace of summer fields.*

They want Canadian poetry which is **"first-rate, original, content-conscious." Query with 10 poems ("a good proportion of which should already have been published in recognized literary periodicals") as sample, bio, publication credits, or poetic aims. Reports in 8 weeks. Photocopy, pays 10% royalties plus 8 author copies.**

VER POETS VOICES; POETRY POST; POETRY WORLD (IV-Members); VER POETS OPEN COMPETITION, Haycroft, 61/63 Chiswell Grn. Lane, St. Albans, County Herts. AL2 3AL, England, founded 1965, editor/organizer May Badman, a poetry group **"publishing members' work if it has reached a good standard.** We publish *Ver Poets Voices, Poetry Post*, and *Poetry World*, the last being an information sheet. **We aim at bringing members' work up to professional literary standards if it is not already there. All members receive our publications free and can buy further copies." Membership costs £8.50 overseas p.a.** They have recently published work by Beth Smith, Ruth Padel, Jane Wight, Geoffrey Holloway, and Edward Storey. As a sample, they selected the following lines from "To a Counsellor" by May Ivimy:

> *Your carpet bears the imprint*
> *Of my intricate defenses, and their ruin.*
> *Forgive me them.*
> *And if my pain has touched you,*
> *Pardon that, too.*
> *Regard not my discards, nor my false retreats,*

> *For Spring is always, and the fruit more shapely.*

Ver Poets Voices, which appears about twice a year, is digest-sized with a stapled card cover. It goes to the 250 members plus about 50 copies to shops, etc. *Poetry Post*, also a semi-annual, is magazine-sized with a card front cover. It reports on Ver Poets competitions and other matters concerning poetry. *Poetry World*, which appears 4 times/year, is a series of information sheets on national competitions and poetry events. The group organizes the Ver Poets Open Competition (an annual event), which has prizes of £500, £300, and £100 (two equal prizes—total £1,000.). They also organize six competitions per year for members only; winners are published in *Poetry Post*. **"All members are encouraged to send work for comment." Not more than 6 clearly typed or reproduced poems should be submitted at once. Reporting time is "by return of post" and time to publication is 6 months or less.** The editors say, "A lot of work is being done in England by small presses such as ourselves, and we provide continually the first few rungs of the ladder to success as poets. Members are offered free advice on their work and how to present it to editors. Also information on publishing opportunities."

VERSE (II), English Dept., College of William and Mary, Williamsburg, VA 23185, founded 1984, editors Henry Hart, Robert Crawford and David Kinloch, is "a poetry journal which also publishes interviews with poets, articles about poetry and book reviews." They **want "no specific kind; we only look for high quality poetry."** They have recently published poetry by A. R. Ammons, James Merrill, James Dickey, Galway Kinnell, Richard Kenney, John Hollander, Charles Wright, Robert Pinsky, Charles Simic, and Wendell Berry. As a sample they selected these lines from "Wolfe Tone" by Seamus Heaney:

> *Light as a skiff, manoeuvreable*
> *yet outmanoeuvred,*
>
> *I affected epaulettes and a cockade,*
> *wrote a style well-bred and impervious*
>
> *to the solidarity I angled for,*
> *and played the ancient Roman with a razor.*

Verse is published 3 times a year in a digest-sized, 90 pp., saddle-stapled format with card cover, using small type, professionally printed. They accept about 100 of 3,000 poems received. Press run: 700, to 300 subscribers of which 150 are libraries, 400 are sold on newsstands or in bookstores. Subscription: $12. **Sample: $3 postpaid. Pays 2 copies. Reports in 1 month, usually 4-5 months to publication. Simultaneous submissions OK.**

‡VERS-QUEBEC (IV-Foreign language, subscribers), Concours Vers-Québec, B.P. 503, Succ. K. Montréal H1N 3R2 Canada, is a quarterly newsletter, 6 stapled sheets, using **poetry in French by its subscribers**. 300 printed for 210 subscribers. Subscription: $6.

‡VERVE (II, IV-Themes), Box 3205, Simi Valley, CA 93093, founded 1989, editor Ron Reichick, is a quarterly **"open to any style — high literary free verse, traditional — as long as well crafted and fits the theme of issue. No sing-song rhyme, 4-letter words every 4th word."** They have recently published poetry by Jack Grapes, Gerald Locklin, Madeline Tiger, and Katharyn Machan Aal. As a sample the editor selected these lines from "When What We Have Done Cannot Be Undone" by Shirley Love:

> *Vision will return. We will see again*
> *with the eyes of prophets*
> *Bones over the blue mountains*
> *Shadow-fish across fields*

It is digest-sized, 40 pp., saddle-stitched, using bios of each contributor. Press run 300 for 60 subscriptions of which 3 are libraries. **Sample, postpaid: $3.50. Send SASE for guidelines and list of upcoming themes. Pays 1 copy. Submit up to 5 poems, 2 pages maximum per poem; "36 lines or less has best chance." Simultaneous submissions and previously published poems OK.** They sponsor 2 annual contests, each having prizes of $75, $50, and $25, entry fee $2. The editor advises, "Keep writing, keep submitting; listen to criticism but follow your instincts."

VESTAL PRESS, LTD. (IV-Themes, anthologies), 320 N. Jensen Rd., Box 97, Vestal, NY 13851-0097, founded 1961, contact Grace L. Houghton, is a "small-press publisher of **books on automatic music, carousels, antique phonographs, antique radios, early film history, postcard histories, many titles geared to hobbyists and collectors**" that has published a book of limericks on the history of the carousel such as this one:

> *The armor you see here is for*
> *those horses that go off to war.*
> *The nice shiny metal*
> *helps the knight prove his mettle*

and is intended to minimize gore.
The verses are by Harvey Roehl, and the charming b/w illustrations by Pat Hyman are suitable for coloring. They have also published an anthology on poetry of the cinema using poems by Vachel Lindsay, Ogden Nash, Gene Lockhart, Howard Moss, and about 75 other poets. **If you have a suggested project closely associated with one of the topics listed above, query. Replies to queries in 1-2 weeks. Pays 10% royalties.**

VICTIMOLOGY: AN INTERNATIONAL JOURNAL (IV-Themes), 2333 N. Vernon St., Arlington, VA 22207, phone 703-536-1750, is a quarterly "**specifically focusing on the victim, on the dynamics of victimization**, for social scientists, criminal justice professionals and practitioners, social workers and volunteer and professional groups engaged in prevention of victimization and in offering assistance to victims of rape, spouse abuse, child abuse, incest, abuse of the elderly, natural disasters, etc." **Sample: $5 postpaid. Send SASE for guidelines. Uses poetry relevant to the themes of the magazine up to 30 lines. Pays $10-25.**

VIGIL; AMMONITE; VIGIL PUBLICATIONS (II), Suite 5, Station Road, Gillingham, Dorset SP8 4QA England, founded 1979, poetry editor John Howard. *Vigil* was formerly *Period Piece and Paperback*. They want "**poetry with a high level of emotional force or intensity of observation. Poems should normally be no longer than 35 lines. Color, imagery and appeal to the senses should be important features. No whining self-indulgent, neurotic soul-baring poetry.**" They have recently published poetry by John Gonzalez, Roger Elkin, Brian Daldorph, and Richard Newman. As a sample the editor selected these lines by Malc Payne:

> he lived with a window
> full of trees
> marking his latest struggle
> to blown end

The digest-sized magazine is 40 pp., saddle-stapled, photoreduced typescript, with colored matte card cover. It appears 3 times a year, press run 200 for 80 subscriptions of which 6 are libraries. They accept about 60 of 200 submissions received. Subscription: £3.50. **Sample: £1.20 postpaid. Pays 2 copies. Editor sometimes comments on rejections. Submit no more than 6 poems at a time.** *Ammonite* appears twice a year with "**myth, image and word towards the secondary millenium . . . a seedbed of mythology for our future, potently embryonic.**" **Query regarding book publication by Vigil Publications.** The editor offers "appraisal" for £7.50 for a sample of a maximum of 12 poems.

THE VILLAGE IDIOT; MOTHER OF ASHES PRESS (II), Box 66, Harrison, ID 83833-0066, *The Village Idiot* founded 1970, Mother of Ashes Press founded 1980, editor Judith Shannon Paine. They want "**any poetry that breathes, pops, or moves. Purpose is to enrich and satisfy. Free verse preferred. No religious, juvenile, stream of consciousness (preachy) material.**" They have recently published poetry by Josephine D. Buffet and Rita Conroy. As a sample the editor selected these lines by Joyce Chandler:

> Are you a nutmeg from brazil finely ground
> a double spice for nose and tongue . . .

The Village Idiot appears irregularly in a 6 × 9" format, saddle-stapled, 56-60 pp., with matte card cover, using less than 10% of over 500 poems received a year. Their press run is 300 with 15 subscriptions of which 2 are libraries. Subscription: $15 for 5 issues. **Sample: $4 postpaid. Reports in 3 months, "often with suggestions. Time between acceptance and publication 6-12 months."** Pay is "nominal, with 2 copies on request." Editor sometimes comments on rejections. Mother of Ashes Press publishes books and chapbooks by invitation only. The editor says, "Poetry needs to breathe and age . . . Like fine wine. My advice to new poets is to get naked, go for the bones . . . without strong structuring, i.e. *Bones*, a poem is just so much mush. Take time. Be a proud word polisher. I only want to see the very very best a poet can manage. Free verse is not merely sentences set to look like poetry. All poetry should have discernable rhythm."

‡THE VILLAGER (II), 135 Midland Ave., Bronxville, NY 10708, phone 914-337-3252, founded 1928, editor Amy Murphy, poetry editor M. Josephine Colville, a publication of the Bronxville Women's Club for club members and families, professional people and advertisers, circulation 750, appears in 9 monthly issues, October-June. **Sample: $1.25 postpaid. They use one page or more of poetry per issue, prefer poems less than 20 lines, "in good taste only," seasonal (Thanksgiving, Christmas, Easter) 3 months in advance. They copyright material but will release it to author on request. Pays 2 copies. A SASE required.**

THE VINCENT BROTHERS REVIEW (II), 1459 Sanzon Dr., Fairborn, OH 45324, founded 1988, editor Kimberly A. Willardson, is a journal appearing three times a year. "**We look for well-crafted, thoughtful poems that shoot bolts of electricity into the reader's mind, stimulating a powerful response. We also**

welcome light verse and are thrilled by unusual, innovative themes/styles. We do not accept previously published poems or simultaneous submissions, sexist, racist, anti-Semitic poetry. Sloppy MSS containing typos and/or unintentional misspellings are automatically rejected." They have recently published poetry by Herbert Woodward Martin, Kim Carey and Denise Thomas. As a sample the editor selected these lines from "Still Life with Melancholy" by Todd A. Fry:

> the wind's blowing
> the parsley's dying
> 9:36
> I wonder where she's at
> how
>
> a car
> incense

TVBR is digest-sized, 56-64 pp., saddle-stapled, professionally printed, digest-sized with matte card cover. Their press run is 300. We have 80 subscribers, 4 of which are libraries. Subscription: $12. **Sample: $4.50 postpaid. Send SASE for guidelines. Pays 1 copy. Submit no more than 8 poems at a time, name and address on each page. Reports in 3-6 months (after readings by editor and 3 associate editors.) Editor "often" comments on rejections.** She advises, "Get involved in the poetry universe! Subscribe to poetry magazines and read them. Attend poetry readings and workshops."

VIOLETTA BOOKS (I, IV-Anthologies), Box 15151, Springfield, MA 01115, founded 1983, editor Kathleen Gilbert, runs an annual competition, entry fee $1 per poem up to 5, then unlimited for $5. First prize is $50 and copies of all Violetta books. Second prize is $35 and choice of 3 Violetta books. Third prize is $20 and choice of 2 Violetta books. A number of honorable mentions, all are published in an anthology, deadline May 30, 1990; anthology published in late September 1990. All winners receive a copy of the anthology. The editor looks for "clarity of meaning, fresh, vivid images, unordinary insights into daily life, mystical feeling rising from everyday experiences." She prefers "free verse. Prefer under 50 lines." **She does not want poetry that is "too personal, the overly sentimental, 'greeting card verse,' negativism, pollyannaism, or sing song rhyme." Submit 1 copy of each poem with poet's name and address on the back. Previously published poems OK** "as long as rights were returned to you following publication." Considers simultaneous submissions. All non-winning contestants get brief, constructive critique." She has recently published poetry by Laurie Lessen, Gilda Klausne and Phile Eisenberg. As a sample she selected these lines by June Owens from "Pebbles from the Aegean":

> taking us back to where we began,
> to some sea.
>
> to where oceans
> shine like second skies,

The anthology is digest-sized, 43 pp., offset from typescript, saddle-stapled, with matte card cover. Kathleen Gilbert says, "As a publisher of poetry and how-to books for writers, I hope to create an encouraging arena in which talented novices as well as more advanced poets can receive recognition for writing accessible and individualistic poetry." **Sample copy of anthology $3 postpaid, catalog for SASE.**

‡VIRGIN MEAT (IV-Horror), 2325 West Ave. K-15, Lancaster, CA 93536, phone 805-722-1758, founded 1986, editor Steve Blum, appears irregularly with fiction, poetry, and art. "Fiction is mildly erotic vampire and spooky happenings. **Poetry: very short, emotionally dark and depressing. No rhyming poetry.**" I have not seen an issue, but the editor describes it as "digest." Press run 300. **Sample: $2 postpaid. Send SASE for guidelines. Pays "1 copy for each 2 printed. Send no less than 4 at a time. Simultaneous submissions and previously published poems OK. All replies go out in the next day's mail."**

THE VIRGINIA QUARTERLY REVIEW; EMILY CLARK BALCH AWARDS (III), 1 West Range, Charlottesville, VA 22903, founded 1925, is one of the oldest and most distinguished literary journals in the country. It is digest-sized, 220+ pp., flat-spined, circulation 4,000. **They use about 15 pp. of poetry in each issue, pay $1/line, no length or subject restrictions.** The Emily Clark Balch awards offer annual prizes of $500 for the best poem published in the magazine during the year.

VIRTUE: THE CHRISTIAN MAGAZINE FOR WOMEN (IV-Religious), Box 850, Sisters, OR 97759, founded 1978, editor Becky Durost Fish, is a slick magazine, circulation 175,000, appearing 6 times a year, which **"encourages and integrates biblical truth with daily living." They want "well-written poetry with a Christian theme, easily accessible to popular audience, usually not longer than 20 lines"** and do not want **"verse/writing where the theme is explicit rather than implicit."** The editor selected these sample lines from "Enter In" by Cynthia Macdonald:

> *I think I would possess the land*
> *As Moses said.*
> *I would go in to it and live.*
> *But there what giants snarl and loom*
> *at me, what dangers lie ahead.*

Virtue is magazine-sized, 80 pp., saddle-stapled, with full-cover pages inside as well as on its paper cover. Subscription: $15.95. Price per issue: $2.95. **Sample: $3 postpaid. Send SASE for guidelines. Pays $20-40 per poem and 1 copy. Reports in 6-8 weeks, time to publication 3-9 months. Submit "no more than 3 poems, each on separate sheet, typewritten or dot-matrix; notify if simultaneous submission."**

VISION; TEAM (I, IV-Young Adults), Box 7259, Grand Rapids, MI 49510, phone 616-241-5616, editor Dale Dieleman. *Vision* founded 1977, is "a lifestyles magazine for young adults" appearing every other month. *Team* is a quarterly digest for volunteer youth workers. *Vision* is magazine-sized, 20 pp., professionally printed on good stock, using b/w photos and graphics, with a matte paper cover in 2 colors. As a sample the editor selected this haiku, "On Christmas," by George Ralph:

> *still in the pine trees*
> *sultry Florida night with*
> *Christmas cicadas*

They want **poetry "that reflects feelings and content to which young adults can relate in their personal lives and which will move them to a larger understanding of themselves and the world. We are looking for concise, fresh poetry, packed with images, contemporary in feel." Sample $1 with SAE plus 2 first class stamps. Guidelines for SASE. No rhymed or erotic poetry. Pays $10-25 per poem plus 1 copy. Specify "rights being offered." Simultaneous submissions and previously published poems OK. Reports in 1 month.**

VISION SEEKER & SHARER; RAINBOW PUBLICATIONS (IV-Themes), Trenwyth Higher Penpoll, St. Veep, NR. Lostwithiel, Cornwall PL22 0NG UK, founded 1987, editor David Allen Stringer, is a "libertarian New Age quarterly concerned with **human rights issues, especially Australian aborigines, Native American Indians, Gypsies, 'Hippies,' etc., animal rights and vegetarianism, alternative economics, ecology, visions of a future clean, harmonious and balanced world where humans are 'at one' with the rest of creation, using concerned poetry on social-ecological, etc. issues, 'spiritual' chants/poems/songs of religious or related nature, poems/songs from American Indians, love poems for the earth-mother and natural creation or 'the Great Spirit' in general. No 'purely' personal — like love poems to one person or 'what happened to me in the park yesterday' with no concern for anything beyond."** As a sample the editor selected these lines (poet unidentified):

> *We build "rainbow bridges" across the world,*
> *England to the Americas, England to India,*
> *Everywhere to everywhere from our spirit message centres*
> *Smoke signals in print or by telepathic powers*

It is magazine-sized, typescript, side-stapled with paper cover. Circulation 300 internationally. Subscription: £3 for 4, 75p each UK. $6 for 4, $1.50 each USA; postpaid. **No payment for poems. Editor sometimes comments on rejections.**

VOICES INTERNATIONAL (II), 1115 Gillette Dr., Little Rock, AR 72207, editor Clovita Rice, is a quarterly poetry journal, 32-40 pp., 6x9" saddle-stapled, professionally printed with b/w matte card cover. **Subscription: $10 per year. Sample: $2 postpaid (always a back issue). Prefers free verse but accepts high quality traditional. Limit submissions to batches of 5, double-spaced, 3-40 lines (will consider longer if good). Publishes an average of 18 months after acceptance. Pays copies.** "We look for poetry with a new focus, memorable detail and phrasing, and significant and haunting statement climax, all of which impel the reader to reread the poem and return to it for future pleasure and reference." The editor selected these sample lines from "Homesick" by Cecil J. Mullins:

> *The rain is a thin and naked sound*
> *And painful on the painted night*
> *Pinned wriggling on the unfirm ground*
> *By points of light.*

VOICES ISRAEL (I); MONTHLY POET'S VOICE (IV-Members), P.O. Box 5780, 46101 Herzlia, Israel, founded 1972, *Voices Israel* editor Mark Levinson, with an editorial board of 7, is an annual anthology of poetry in English coming from all over the world. **You have to buy a copy to see your work in print. Submit all kinds of poetry (up to 4 poems) each no longer than a sheet of typing paper.** They have recently published poetry by Yehuda Amichai, Eugene Pubnor, Alan Sillitoe, and Seymour Mayne. As a sample the editor selected these lines by John Evans:

> *The Glen, winnowed by wind and water,*
> *Is full of white and silence*
> *And an echo without a beginning.*

> *There beneath the snow lie all my shadows,*
> *Overgrown with wild roses, rooted in the rough,*
> *Attended by thorns, dripping with blood.*

The annual *Voices Israel* is 6¼x8″, offset from laser output on ordinary paper, approximately 121 pp. flat-spined with varying cover. Circulation 350, subscription $17. **Sample: $10 postpaid. Back copies: $10 postpaid; airmail extra. Contributor's copy: $15 airmail. Evaluation: $10 per poem. Deadline end of February each year; reports in fall.** *The Monthly Poet's Voice*, a broadside edited by Ezra Ben-Meir, **is open only to members of the Voices Group of Poets in English.** The editor advises, "Try to forget what you think you should feel, and write what you do feel."

VOL. NO. MAGAZINE (II, IV-Themes), 24721 Newhall Ave., Newhall, CA 91321, phone 805-254-0851, founded 1983, poetry editors Richard Weekley, Jerry Danielsen, Tina Landrum and Don McLeod. "*Vol. No.* publishes lively and concise works. Vivid connections. **Each issue has a theme. "Daily Bread," "Between a Poet and a Hard Spot" (humor), and "Third World" are pending. Send SASE for descriptions of these. No trivial, clichéd or unthoughtout work. Work that penetrates the ozone within. One-page poems have the best chance.**" They have recently published poetry by Octavio Paz, Anne Marple, William Stafford, Jane Hirshfield and Julian Pulley. The editors selected these sample lines by K. Dalton-El Saw:

> *At the top of the apple tree*
> *I curled, disinterested and*
> *snakelike into the cool grope of*
> *leaf and bark, the leaves winking*
> *against my cheek like eyelids*
> *closing in the darkness*

Vol. No. is a digest-sized, saddle-stapled, 32 pp. semiannual, circulation 300. Subscription: $5. They receive about 600 freelance submissions of poetry per year, use 60, have a 6 month backlog. **Sample: $3 postpaid. Submit limit of 6 poems. Photocopy and simultaneous submissions OK. Reports in 1-5 months. Pays 2 copies.**

W.I.M. PUBLICATIONS (WOMAN IN THE MOON) (I,IV-Gay, Women), 2215-R Market St., Box 137, Dept. PM, San Francisco, CA 94114, founded 1979, poetry editor SDiane Bogus, who says, "We are a small press with trade press ambitions. We publish poetry. We generally run 250-1,000 per press run and **give the author half or a percentage of the books. We pay royalties on our established authors. We prefer a query and a modest track record.**" She wants poetry by "**gay, black, women, prison poets, enlightened others — contemporary narrative or lyric work, free verse OK, but not too experimental for cognition. We prefer poems to be a page or less if not part of long narrative. No obviously self-indulgent exercises in the psychology of the poet. No sentimental forced rhymes or sonnets. No gross sexual references; no hate poems.**" Send SASE for guidelines. In addition to her own work, she has published poetry by Adele Sebastian. As a sample she selected these lines from "Versey Sketch of an Artful Dancer " by I. Lillian Randolph:

> *I write furiously*
> *in prose, in poetry*
> *with every new*
> *detail I catch*
> *in each new light*
> *of each new subject*

SDiane Bogus publishes 2-4 chapbooks and flat-spined paperbacks a year each averaging 40-100 pages. **Submit 6 sample poems and a statement of "vision and poetics, vision of the body (or selection) of the work; poetic mentors. Submit between April 1 and August 15 each year. We acknowledge submissions upon receipt. We report at end of reading season August 31-September 7. Simultaneous submissions, previously published poems, photocopies all OK. No dot-matrix.** Authors "**are asked to assist in promo and sales by providing list of prospective readers and promotional photos.**" To established authors we pay royalties 10-35%; others half press run in

Market categories: (I) Beginning; (II) General; (III) Prestige; (IV) Specialized; (V) Closed.

copies. "We may take advanced orders; no subsidy. We will accept subscriptions for a book in production at retail price. We produce the book, publish and give author ½ or percentage of books (authorial control). We then fill orders author has provided and others our promo has provided." Send 45¢ and SASE for catalog. Also, catalog gives sample of poets' work represented. *WIM* offers a criticism service for a fee. She says, "W.I.M. promotes readings for its poets, and encourages each poet who submits by way of a personal letter which discusses her or his strengths and weaknesses. Often we allow repeat submissions."

WAINWRIGHT (PHILADELPHIA) (II, IV-Themes), % Ostrics, Inc., P.O. Box 110207, West Park, OH 44111, founded 1985, poetry editor Margaret Hollis, who says, "Wainwright is a Philadelphia publisher (brainchild of C. E. Wainwright). **We are looking for unique poetic ideas/approaches, especially when they are also philosophico-metaphysical. No specifications as to form, length, style, etc. We do not want to see haiku, light verse, 'religious' verse, or that which is overwhelmed by rhyme and meter.**" They have recently published books of poetry by Matthew Klimczyk, Kate Melville, and Sy Leverty. As a sample she selected these "two pairs of 'anapoems' " from E. R. Cole's **Ding an sich:**

enter this something room where you will soon develop into dark
you enter into this dark room where something will soon develop.

the leaves sing to rafters and when I sleep she
and when she leaves I sing the rafters to sleep

Each of those two lines is a poem, occupying a single page, strung down the page with unusual spacing. The book is professionally printed on quality stock, a 72 pp. hardback with cloth cover and wrapper, $12.95. Wainwright publishes 3-4 books a year—chapbooks, flat-spined paperbacks, and hardbacks, averaging 50 pages. **Send entire MS, bio, list of publications. No simultaneous submissions. Previously published poems OK. Photocopy OK, no dot-matrix. Pays 12% minimum royalties, negotiable advance, and 5 copies.** Editor comments "occasionally, if MS is of merit."

‡WAKE FOREST UNIVERSITY PRESS (IV-Regional, ethnic), Box 7333, Winston-Salem, NC 27109, phone 919-759-5448, founded 1976, director and poetry editor Dillon Johnston. **"We publish only poetry from Ireland and bilingual editions of French poetry in translation. I am able to consider only poetry written by Irish poets or translations of contemporary French poetry. I must return, unread, poetry from American poets.**" They have recently published poetry by John Montague, Derek Mahon, Richard Murphy, Michael Longley, Paul Muldoon, Thomas Kinsella and Eilean N. Chuilleanain. **Query with 4-5 samples. Replies to queries in 1-2 weeks, to submissions (if invited) in 2-3 months. No simultaneous submissions. Photocopy OK. Publishes on 10% royalty contract with $500 advance, 6-8 author's copies.** Dillon Johnston comments, "because our press is so circumscribed, we get few direct submissions from Ireland. I would advise American poets to read your publication carefully so that they not misdirect to presses such as ours work that they, and I, value."

‡WALKING AND SINNING; ACCELERATOR PRESS (II), 1708 #4 M.L. King, Jr. Way, Berkeley, CA 94709, phone 415-549-2815, founded 1988 from *Legumes* (1982-86), poetry editor J.D. Buhl, is an annual **"of short poems, 9-10 per issue."** Wanting **"sparse, mysterious, humorous short pieces, not too much drama or technique, just pictures from the side, words that go together. Nothing long, overly political, self-conscious."** They have recently published poetry by Lisa Chang. It is 12 pp., digest-sized, saddle-stapled, with matte card cover. Press run 500. **Sample, postpaid: $1. Pays "unlimited" copies. Simultaneous submissions and previously published poems ("if solicited") OK.** Editor comments on submissions **"even on accepted pieces sometimes."** He says, *"Walking and Sinning* is a small, private publication, but not street level, slap-dash mimeo stuff. It looks simple and attractive, and I try to get it around. For each issue, I want a group of poems that sit well together, create a feel I can be proud of and that the writers can distribute. Send me child-like crazy thoughts and fears. Give it an edge, but don't throw the blade. Let it lie."

WASCANA REVIEW (II), University of Regina, Regina, Saskatchewan S4S 0A2 Canada, editor-in-chief Joan Givner, emphasizes literature and the arts for readers interested in serious poetry, fiction, and scholarship. Published poets include John V. Hicks, Lorna Crozier, Patrick Lane, Kristjana Gunnars, and Christopher Wiseman. Semiannual, circulation 300. **Sample, postpaid: $4 (Canadian). Photocopies OK. Buys 10-15 poems per issue, any form, 2-100 lines, pays $10/page.**

WASHINGTON REVIEW; FRIENDS OF THE WASHINGTON REVIEW OF THE ARTS, INC. (II, IV-Regional), Box 50132, Washington, DC 20004, phone 202-638-0515, founded 1974, literary editor Beth Joselow, is a bimonthly journal of arts and literature published by the Friends of the Washington Review of the Arts, Inc., a non-profit, tax-exempt educational organization. *WR* is tabloid-sized, using 2 of the large pp. per issue for poetry, saddle-stapled on high-quality newsprint, circulation 2,000 with

700 subscriptions of which 10 are libraries. **They publish primarily local Washington metropolitan area poets as well as poets from across the U.S. and abroad.** They have recently published poems by Paul Genega and Jerry Ratch. The editor selected these sample lines by Robert Kusch:

> *When you are old, your face is your hand*
> *and your hand is a root. With my own weight,*
> *I walk toward words I never started from.*

Sample: $2.50 postpaid. Pays 5 copies.

WASHINGTON WRITERS' PUBLISHING HOUSE (IV-Regional), P.O. Box 15271, Washington, DC 20003, phone 202-543-1905, founded 1975. An editorial board is elected annually from the collective. "We are a poetry publishing collective that publishes outstanding poetry collections in flat-spined paperbacks by **individual authors from the greater Washington, DC area (60 mile radius, excluding Baltimore) on the basis of competitions held once a year.**" They have recently published poetry by Myra Sklarew, Ann Darr, Barbara Lefcowitz, Maxine Clair, Ann Knox, Martin Galvin, and Sharon Negri. The editors chose this sample from "A Bracelet of Lies" by Jean Nordhaus:

> *The miner on the shady porch*
> *makes rain with his accordian. Your hands*
> *are two black spiders climbing up the spout*
> *Mother comes out carrying a pan of water.*

Submit 50-60 pp. MS with SASE only between July 1 and September 30. $5 reading fee. Poets become working members of the collective. "Interested poets may write for a brochure of published poets and sheet of guidelines."

THE WASHINGTONIAN MAGAZINE (IV-Regional), 1828 L St. NW, Suite 200, Washington, DC 20036, senior editor Margaret Cheney, who says, "We publish **very little poetry, except short poems by Washington poets or poetry with a Washington focus.**" Payment $35 on acceptance. The monthly has a circulation of 166,891. Sample copies are available from Back Issues department, **$3 postpaid.**

WATERFRONT PRESS (IV-Bilingual/foreign language), 52 Maple Ave., Maplewood, NJ 07040, founded 1982, president Kal Wagenheim, he has published poetry by Pedro Pietri, Lynne Alvarez, and Martin Espada (in English), and Manuel Ramos Otero (in Spanish). Waterfront specializes **in work by Puerto Rican and other Hispanic authors. No information given on submission or payment.**

WATERWAYS: POETRY IN THE MAINSTREAM; TEN PENNY PLAYERS; BARD PRESS (I, IV-Themes, children, anthologies), 393 St. Paul's Ave., Staten Island, NY 10304, founded 1977, poetry editors Barbara Fisher and Richard Spiegel, "publishes **poetry by adult and child poets in a magazine that is published 11 times a year. We do theme issues** and are trying to increase an audience for poetry and the printed and performed word. The project produces performance readings in public spaces and is in residence year round at our local library with workshops and readings. We publish the magazine, *Waterways,* anthologies of child poets; child poetry postcard series; chapbooks (adults and child poets). **We are not fond of haiku or rhyming poetry; never use material of an explicit sexual nature.** We are open to reading material from people we have never published, writing in traditional and experimental poetry forms. While we do 'themes' sometimes an idea for a future magazine is inspired by a submission so we try to remain open to poets' inspiration. Poets should be guided however by the fact that we are children's and animal rights advocates and are a NYC press." They have recently published poetry by Albert Huffstickler, Joanne Seltzer, Arthur Knight, and Kit Knight. As a sample, the editors chose these lines by Laurel Speer:

> *For a single individual at any moment in time, to die*
> *is the end. The ghettos live. The survivors remember.*
> *They write books. They ask us not to forget. They make*
> *us look at history. They say, "This is the way it was;*
> *this is the way it is. If you do not read at the very*
> *least, and think, you'll be fleeing, too. Never feel*
> *safe; never assume; keep vigilance; the ghetto lives.*

Waterways is published in a 40 pp. 4¼x7" wide format, saddle-stapled, Xerox and letter-press, from various type styles, using b/w drawings, matte card cover, circulation 150 with 58 subscriptions of which 12 are libraries. Subscription: $20. **Sample: $2.54 postpaid. They use 60% of freelance poems submitted. Submit less than 10 poems for first submission. No dot-matrix. Simultaneous submissions OK. Send SASE for guidelines for approaching themes.** "Since we've taken the time to be very specific in our response, writers should take seriously our comments and not waste their emotional energy and our time sending material that isn't within our area of interest. Sending for our theme sheet and for a sample issue and then objectively thinking about the writers's own work is practical and wise. Without meaning to sound 'precious' or unfriendly, the writer should understand that small press publishers doing limited editions and all production work in house are working from their personal artistic vision and know exactly what notes will harmonize, effectively counterpoint and meld. Many excellent poems are sent back to the writers by *Waterways* because they don't relate to what we are trying to create in a given month or months. Some poets get printed regularly in *Waterways*; others will probably never be published by us, not because the poet doesn't write well (although that too is sometimes the case) but only because we are artists with opinions and we exercise them in building each issue. **Reports in less than a month. Pays 1 copy. Editors sometimes comment on rejections.** They hold contests for children only. **Chapbooks published by Ten Penny Players are "by children only — and not by submission; they come through our workshops in the library and schools." Adult poets are published by us through our Bard Press imprint.** "Books evolve from the relationship we develop with writers who we publish in *Waterways* and whom we would like to give more exposure." No submissions. The editors advise, "We suggest that poets attend book fairs. It's a fast way to find out what we are all publishing."

‡**WAYNE REVIEW (I, II)**, Dept. of English, Wayne State University, 51 W. Warren, Detroit, MI 48202. Contact Mike Liebler. Appears twice a year using **any kind of poetry except that using footnotes.** They have recently published poetry by Ken Mikolowski, Bob Hershon, and Adam Cornford, It is magazine-sized and uses 20-30 pp./issue. It is distributed free. **Sample, postpaid: $2. Pays 1 copy and "eternal gratitude." Submit 3-10 poems, nothing handwritten. Simultaneous submissions and previously published poems OK. Reports in 1-2 months. Editor sometimes comments on submissions: "Ask nicely, we might."** The editor says, "Read a lot, talk a lot and respond to all things keeping in mind the idea that you are being heard. Start with that and do the work."

WEBSTER REVIEW (II, IV-Translations), Webster University, 470 E. Lockwood, Webster Groves, MO 63119, founded 1974, poetry editors Pamela Hadas and Jerred Metz, is a literary semiannual. They want **"no beginners. We are especially interested in translations of foreign contemporary poetry."** They have recently published poetry by Barbara F. Lefcowitz, Martin Robbins, Will Wells, Margherita Guidacci, and Chang Soo Ko. The editor selected these sample lines from "Wolf Watch," by Jim Barnes:

> Evil things, the stories go.
> I like them, cantankerous
> and fussy, murderous
> as old maids. Black
> as an ace of spades and crooked,
> they'll steal you blind
> if you get too friendly.

Webster Review is 104 pp. digest-sized, flat-spined, professionally printed with glossy card cover, circulation 1,000 with 500 subscriptions of which 200 are libraries. Subscription: $5; per copy: $2.50. They receive about 1,500 submissions of freelance poetry per year, use 120. **Sample free for SASE. Reports "within a month, usually." Pays $25-50, if funds permit. Contributors receive 2 copies. Editors comment on rejections "if time permits."**

WESLEYAN UNIVERSITY PRESS; WESLEYAN NEW POETS SERIES; WESLEYAN ESTABLISHED POET SERIES (II), 110 Mt. Vernon, Middletown, CT 06457, is one of the major publishers of poetry in the nation. **Send complete MS, samples cannot be reviewed, and SASE.** I selected as a sample from the Wesleyan New Poets Series ($15 submission fee), **White Dress**, by Brenda Hillman, these lines of "Coffee, 3 A.M.":

> You reject the dark but cannot quite
> Without a light from that blue window
> Make it go . . .
> How terror does become you, like a white dress.

Like other books in that series, this is a 6x8" flat-spined cloth and paperback, 64 pp., professionally printed with glossy jacket card cover. **Considers simultaneous submissions. No fee for the Wesleyan Established Poets Series, for poets who have already published one or more books. For translations, length of these two series 64-80.** Poetry publications from Wesleyan tend to get widely (and respectfully) reviewed.

WEST ANGLIA PUBLICATIONS; BEN-SEN PRESS (V), Box 2683, La Jolla, CA 92038, phone 619-453-0706, Ben-Sen founded 1978, West Anglia founded 1982, poetry editor Helynn Hoffa. "Ben-Sen is a working print shop and does books for a fee. West Anglia is a publishing company and assumes the cost of putting out the book and pays the author royalties or in books. In most cases publicity and distribution rests with the author." They publish anthologies, chapbooks, flat-spined paperbacks, and pamphlets. **"We look for authors who know the English language and how to use it correctly. Form, length, style is for the poet to decide. We do not want pornography, Marxist revolutionary, or how**

America oppresses the world." They have published books of poetry by Gary Morgan, Wilma Lusk, Kathleen Iddings, John Theobald, and Kenneth Morris. "Poets we wish we had printed: Sappho, Homer, John Keats, Marianne Moore, Alexander Pope, Elizabeth Barrett Browning, and Philip Larkin." And that takes JJ's prize for the most original and effective way of indicating the range of editorial taste that I have encountered. As a sample the editor chose lines from "Grandma Loves Me" by Geoffrey Mason:

> We cry out the names of our martyrs
> relatives, fathers, children,
> who once constituted hope
> I have no martyrs
> but the ink from my grandmother's arm
> runs in my blood.

Query with 5 sample poems. Cover letter "should include previous publication credits, awards." $10 reading fee with submissions. Editor supplies criticism at author's request for $15 per poem. She advises, "Keep writing. Learn the language. English is our most important tool: hone it, study it, use it properly."

WEST BRANCH (II), English Dept., Bucknell Hall, Bucknell University, Lewisburg, PA 17837, founded 1977, is a literary biannual. Recently published poems by D. Nurkse, Deborah Burnham, Jim Daniels, Anneliese Wagner, Betsy Sholl, David Citino, Barbara Crooker, and David Brooks. 100-120 pp., digest-sized, circulation 500, using **quality poetry. "We do not consider simultaneous submissions. Each poem is judged on its own merits, regardless of subject or form. We strive to publish the best work being written today." Reports in 6-8 weeks. Payment in contributors' copies and a subscription to the magazine.** One-year's subscription: $7. Two year (4 issues): $11. **Sample: $3.**

WEST COAST LINE; WEST COAST REVIEW BOOKS (II, IV-Regional), English Dept., Simon Fraser University, Burnaby, British Columbia, V5A 1S6 Canada, phone 604-291-4287, editor Roy Miki, founded 1965, *West Coast Line* (formerly *West Coast Review*) is published three times a year and **"favors work by both new and established Canadian writers, but it observes no borders in encouraging original creativity. Our focus is on contemporary poetry, short fiction, drama, criticism, and reviews of books.** The *Line* is *unique* in its continuing programme of publishing West Coast Review Books as part of the regular offering to subscribers." They have published poetry by Roo Borson, Erin Moure, Ron Silliman, and Anselm Hollo. The editor chose these sample lines from "A Little Reality" by P.K. Page:

> Gwendolyn,
> your garden of square roots
> grows in this circle:
> from my pots and pans—
> a silver chaparral of leaves and flowers . . .

The magazine is handsomely printed on glossy paper, 6×9", flat-spined 80 pp. They accept about 20 of the 500-600 poetry MSS received per year. Approximately 26 pages of poetry per issue. Press run 800 for 500 subscriptions of which 350 are libraries, 150 shelf sales. Subscriptions $15. Single copies: $8. **Send SASE for guidelines. Pays approximately $10 (Canadian) per printed page plus a one-year subscription. Reports on submissions in 6-8 weeks, 2-8 months till publication. No simultaneous submissions or previously published poetry. MSS returned only if accompanied by sufficient Canadian postage or IRC.**

WEST OF BOSTON (II), Box 2, Cochituate Station, Wayland, MA 01778, phone 508-653-7241, founded 1983, poetry editor Norman Andrew Kirk, wants to see **"Poetry of power, compassion, originality, and wit—and talent, too."** As a sample of poetry he likes he selected these lines (poet unidentified):

> Come to my museum of poetry.
> The masterpieces of my mind
> are cast about like the misplaced
> children of a mad whore.

For book or chapbook submission query with 5-10 sample poems, credits, and bio. Simultaneous submissions, photocopies, dot-matrix, previously published poems all OK. Pays 10% of press run. Editor "sometimes" comments on rejected MSS.

WEST WIND REVIEW (II, IV-Anthology), English Department, Southern Oregon State College, Ashland, OR 97520, phone 503-482-6181, founded 1982, poetry editor Geri Couchman, is an annual **"looking for sensitive but strong verse that delights and impresses with its humanistic insights and style. We are seeking rich poetry that celebrates all aspects of men's and women's experiences, both exalted and tragic. We are looking to print material that reflects ethnic and social diversity."** The *West Wind Review* has grown in size and scope since its beginning in 1982. The editor offers, as a poetry example, these lines by Pete Beckwith:

for this fire, this wood.
the moment caught, the fire
inevitable, the joys of solid
returning.

WWR is handsomely printed, flat-spined, 200 pp., digest-sized, appearing each spring. They receive about 600-700 submissions each year, publish 40-50 poems. Their press run is 500. **Sample: $7 postpaid. Guidelines available for SASE. Pays 1 copy. "Limit of 5 poems not exceeding 50 lines" per submission. They will consider simultaneous submissions but not previously published poems. Reports in 8-12 weeks after December 1 deadline. There is a $50 award for the best poem in an annual contest, $2/poem entry fee.**

‡**WESTERLY (II)**, Dept. of English, University of Western Australia, Nedlands 6009, Australia, phone (09) 380-2101, founded 1956, editors Dennis Haskell, Peter Cowan, and Bruce Bennett. *Westerly* is a literary quarterly publishing quality short fiction, poetry, literary critical, and socio-historical articles, and book reviews. "No restrictions on creative material. Our only criterion [for poetry] is literary quality. We don't dictate to writers on rhyme, style, experimentation, or anything else. We are willing to publish short or long poems. We do assume a reasonably well read, intelligent audience. Past issues of *Westerly* provide the best guides. Not consciously an academic magazine." They have recently published work by Ee Tiang Hong, Bruce Dawe, Diane Fahey, Dimitris Tsaloumas, Nicholas Hasluck, and Chris Wallace-Crabbe. The quarterly magazine is 7×10″, "electronically printed," 96 pp. with some photos and graphics. Circulation is 1,000. Price per copy is $6 (Aus.) plus overseas postage via surface mail, subscription $20 (Aus.)/year. **Sample available for $6 (Aus.) surface mail, $7 (Aus.) airmail. Pay for poetry is $40 plus 1 copy. "Please do not send simultaneous submissions." Reporting time is 1-2 months and time to publication approximately 6-12 weeks, sometimes longer.** The advice of the editors is: "Be sensible. Write what matters for you but think about the reader. Don't be swayed by literary fashion. Read magazines if possible before sending submissions. Read. Read. Read poetry of all kinds and periods."

WESTERN PRODUCER PUBLICATIONS; WESTERN PEOPLE (IV-Regional), Box 2500, Saskatoon, Saskatchewan, S7K 2C4 Canada, phone 306-665-3500, founded 1923, managing editor Liz Delahey. *Western People* is a magazine supplement to *The Western Producer*, a weekly newspaper, circulation 135,000, which uses "**poetry about the people, interests, and environment of rural Western Canada.**" The editor offers this sample from "Whose Mother" by Ilien Coffey:

She wheels herself along the gleaming corridors
Past rooms whose occupants have seen a better day
her every need is met...Kind strangers see to that;
she's warm, well fed and yet she yearns for yesterday.

The magazine-sized supplement is 16 pp., newsprint, saddle-stapled, with color and b/w photography and graphics. They receive about 800 submissions of freelance poetry per year, use 40-50. **Sample free for postage (2 oz.)—and ask for guidelines. One poem per page, maximum of 3 poems per submission. No dot-matrix. Name, address, telephone number upper left corner of each page. Reports within 4 weeks. Pays $15-40 per poem.** The editor comments, "It is difficult for someone from outside Western Canada to catch the flavor of this region; almost all the poems we purchase are written by Western Canadians." They also publish books.

‡**WESTVIEW: A JOURNAL OF WESTERN OKLAHOMA (IV-Regional)**, 100 Campus Drive, SOSU, Weatherford, OK 73096, phone 405-774-3077, founded 1981, editor Leroy Thomas, Ph.D., is a quarterly using **poetry related to Western Oklahoma. "Our preference is free verse up to 60 lines. No rhymed poetry, poetry of a risqué nature, no poetry containing four-letter words."** They have recently published poetry by Sheryl Nelms, Maggie Culver Fry, Ernestine Gravley, Lynn Riggs, and Sandra Soli. As a sample, I selected these lines beginning "A Special Night" by Pat Kourt:

The midway at the fair unwraps memories of . . .
strings of flickering, flashing lights promising risky surprises.
a kaleidoscope of reeling rides and mechanical merry-go-round music.

Westview is magazine-sized, saddle-stapled 44 pp., with glossy card cover in full-color. They use about 25% of 100 poems received a year. Press run: 1,000 for 500 subscribers of which about 25 are libraries, 150 shelf sales. **Subscription: $8. Sample, postpaid: $4. Send SASE for guidelines.** "MSS are circulated to an editorial board; we usually respond within a month." Payment in contributor's copies. Editor comments on submissions "always." He says, "It's still possible to be decent and clean and be published."

WEYFARERS; GUILDFORD POETS PRESS; SURREY POETRY CENTER (II), 9, White Rose Lane, Woking, Surrey, U.K. GU22 7JA, founded 1972, administrative editor Margaret Pain, poetry editors John Emuss, Margaret Pain, Susan James, and Martin Jones. They say, "We publish *Weyfarers* magazine three times a year. All our editors are themselves poets and give their spare time free to help other poets." They describe their needs as "**all types of poetry, serious and humorous, free verse and rhymed/ metered, but mostly 'mainstream' modern. Excellence is the main consideration. NO hard porn, graphics, way-out experimental. Any subject publishable, from religious to satire. Not more than 40 lines preferred, though longer poems considered if excellent.**" They have recently published poetry by David Schaal, Paul Groves, Lisa Kucharski, Prescott Foster and Fritz Hamilton. As an example the editors chose lines from Jeffrey Wheatley's "His Hands":

> *Anonymous organ music crawled along a tape as*
> *bearers, with a slow professional grace,*
> *shouldered his casket to the apse.*

> *The silent engineering of the place*
> *would have impressed him as an ex-mechanic.*
> *He'd have called the flowers a waste . . .*

The digest-sized saddle-stapled format contains about 28 pp. of poetry (of a total of 32 pp.) The magazine has a circulation of "about 285," including about 175 subscriptions of which 4 are libraries. They use about 125 of 1,200-1,500 submissions received each year. **Sample current issue: $4 in cash USA (or £1-40 UK) postpaid. Submit no more than 6 poems, one poem per sheet. No previously published or simultaneous submissions. Payment 1 copy.** "We are associated with Surrey Poetry Center, who have an annual Open Poetry Competition. The prize-winners are published in *Weyfarers*." They sometimes **comment briefly, if requested,** on rejections. And their advice to poets is, "Always read a magazine before submitting. And read plenty of modern poetry."

WHEAT FORDER'S PRESS; PRIMERS FOR THE AGE OF INNER SPACE (IV-Themes), Box 6317, Washington, DC 20015-0317, founded 1974, poetry editor Renée K. Boyle. This is a 100% subsidy press, asking for camera-ready copy. "We publish for embassies on topics of interest to 3rd world countries. We have a series called Primers for the Age of Inner Space. **We seek poetry and book-length essays for this which reflects ideas in sciences, psychology, metahistory reflecting modern thought** *at its leading edges."* **Considers simultaneous submissions.** As a sample the editor selected these lines from "Graffiti on the Wall of Time":

> *That man himself is dead, who being yet in life*
> *reports that God no longer lives, because in him*
> *the image of that God*
> *no longer rises.*

Query with 5-10 samples and cover letter giving "publication record, precise aim in writing poetry (as fanciful as you wish), express modern thought. Skip modern vulgarities, sex, pot, and all that jazz—it's going nowhere." Terms for cooperative publishing, author paying all costs, worked out individually.

WHETSTONE (I, II), Department of English, University of Lethbridge, 4401 University Drive, Lethbridge, Alberta, T1K 3M4 Canada, editors are Mary Jan Tallon and David Cooper, appears twice a year with writing by beginners and published authors. "**Open to any kind of poetry, as long as it's of good quality.**" They have recently published poems by Susan Musgrave and Rhonda McAdam. As a sample the editor selected lines from "The Technology of Arrogance Which Enters the Mind Unasked and Poisons it with Visions of Paradise" by Kim Maltman:

> *. . . the use of wood becomes like*
> *faith, or love, or sorrows,*
> *that once-removed shadow world in which objects*
> *are inseparable from our desires . . .*

Whetstone is digest-sized, 80+ pp. saddle-stapled, professionally printed in bold face type with two-color matte card cover, circulation 500 with 200 subscriptions of which 25 are libraries, $4 (Can.)/copy, subscription $7. **Sample: $4 postpaid. Guidelines available for SASE. Pays $10 and 1 copy. Any length of poetry. Photocopy, dot-matrix OK. Editor sometimes comments on rejections.** They have competitions with $100 for best poem, $10 entry fee (which includes subscription) for up to 4 poems.

THE WHITE LIGHT (IV-Occult), Box 93124, Pasadena, CA 91109, phone 818-794-6013, founded 1973, editor Rev. White, is a **quarterly magazine** of "Ceremonial magick and occultism. There is a poetry section which uses fairly short—page or so—poems on magick. No free form, avant-garde, and similar **rubbish. If it's about magick or closely related areas, forget it.**" As a sample I selected the opening stanza of "Isis Lives Again" by Gerina Dunwich:

> *Desert winds howl, sandstorms bite*
> *the hounds of hell rip apart the night*

> *with silver fangs*
> *serpent sharp*
> *and glistening.*

The issue I have seen is digest-sized with 8 blue pages and 4 yellow ones, photocopy from typescript with cartoons and ads, saddle-stapled with card cover. It comes out quarterly. Rev. White says he receives 30 or so pages of poetry per issue and actually prints 1-2. Press run 200 with 100 subscribers of which 2 are libraries. Subscription: $5. **Sample: $1.25 postpaid. Pays 5 copies. Simultaneous submissions and previously published poetry OK. Reports in 1 week. Usually 4 months to publication.** The editor advises, "Keep trying, don't quit. As far as writing poetry about magick, it helps to know something about the subject."

WHITE PINE PRESS (V, IV-Translations), 76 Center St., Fredonia, NY 14063, phone 716-672-5743, founded 1973, poetry editors Dennis Maloney and Elaine LaMattina. White Pine Press publishes poetry, fiction, literature in translation, essays—perfect-bound paperbacks. "At present we are **not accepting unsolicited MSS. Inquire first.**" They have published poetry by William Kloefkorn, Marjorie Agosin, Migel Hernandez, Peter Blue Cloud, Basho, Pablo Neruda, Maurice Kenny, and James Wright. As a sample I chose this stanza of "Poems at the Edge of Day" by John Brandi:

> *Poems are acts of death*
> *burning clean*
> *at the edge of day*
> *to renew life.*

Query with 4-5 samples, brief cover letter with bio and publication credits. Reply to queries in 2-4 weeks, to submissions (if invited) in 4 weeks. Simultaneous submissions, photocopy, dot-matrix OK. Pays 5-10% of run. Send $1 for catalog to buy samples.

JAMES WHITE REVIEW: A GAY MEN'S LITERARY QUARTERLY (IV-Gay), Box 3356 Traffic Station, Minneapolis, MN 55403, phone 612-291-2913, founded 1983, poetry editor Greg Baysans **uses all kinds of poetry by gay men.** They have published poetry by Tom Young, James Broughton, and Robert Peters. The magazine has a circulation of 2,500 with 600 subscriptions of which 25 are libraries. They receive about 1,400 submissions per year, use 100, have a 6 week backlog. **Sample: $2 postpaid. Submit a limit of 8 poems or 250 lines. A poem can exceed 250 lines, but it "better be very good." They report in 4 months. Paying currently with 3 contributor's copies. Send SASE for guidelines. Subscriptions $10/year (US).**

‡THE WHITE ROSE LITERARY MAGAZINE; KIM WHYBROW MEMORIAM (I, IV-Specialized), 14 Browning Rd., Temple Hill, Dartford, Kent DA1 5ET England, editor Mrs. Nancy Whybrow. The magazine, a quarterly, was first published in January, 1986; I have not seen a copy. The editor asks for **contributions of poems, short stories, anecdotes relating to local history; she includes a section of entries by disabled people. Poems could be of any length, form, or subject.** The Kim Whybrow Memoriam, an annual contest in memory of her son, has a first prize of £50 plus an engraved trophy, 2nd prize of £25, and 3rd and 4th prizes of £12.50 each. Entry fee: £1/poem. Proceeds (less prize money) are donated to National Childrens Charity. Enter between April 30 and December 20, 1990. Maximum length 40 lines. No names on entries (which are not returned). Enclose sealed envelope with name of poem on the outside and your name and address on the inside. Price of the magazine is £1.50.

TAHANA WHITECROW FOUNDATION; CIRCLE OF REFLECTIONS (IV-Anthologies), Box 18181, Salem, OR 97305, phone 503-585-0564, founded 1987, executive director Melanie Smith. The Whitecrow Foundation conducts **one spring/summer poetry contest on Native American themes in poems up to 30 lines in length. Deadline for submissions May 31. No haiku, Seiku, erotic, or porno poems. Fees are $2.75 for a single poem, $10 for 4; prizes are $125, $75, $40, and 4 honorable mentions at $10 each.** Winners, honorable mentions, and selected other entries are published in a periodic anthology, **Circle of Reflections.** Winners do not receive free copies but are encouraged to purchase it for $4.95 plus $1 handling in order to "help ensure the continuity of our contests." As a sample Melanie Smith selected these lines:

> *how civilized we've become*
> *when we abuse these people*
> > *with no*
> *pangs of conscience . . .*

> *do elders teachings fall*
> *— as dying leaves . . .*
> > > ©Tahana

Melanie Smith adds, "We seek unpublished Native writers. Poetic expressions of full-bloods, mixed bloods, and empathetic non-Indians need to be heard. Future goals include chapbooks and native theme art. Advice to new writers—keep writing, honing, and sharpening your material; don't give up—keep submitting."

‡**WHOLE NOTES; DAEDALUS PRESS (I, II, IV-Children)**, P.O. Box 1374, Las Cruces, NM 88004, phone 505-382-7446, *WN* founded 1984; Daedalus Press founded 1988, editor Nancy Peters Hastings. *WN* appears twice a year. Daedalus Press publishes one chapbook per year by a single poet. **"All forms will be considered."** They have recently published poetry by Bill Kloefkorn, Carol Oles, Keith Wilson, Greg Kuzma, Ted Kooser, and Harold Witt. As a sample the editor selected these lines from "Resurrection" by Elizabeth Banset:

> *Some legacies the earth refuses to inherit,*
> *unless we force them far enough*
> *below the frostline,*
> *like memories or unwilled passions . . .*

WN is 16-20 pp., digest-sized, "nicely printed," staple bound, with a "linen 'fine arts' cover." Press run 400 for 100 subscriptions of which 10 are libraries. They accept about 10% of some 300-400 submissions per year. Subscription: $6. **Sample, postpaid: $3. Pays 2 copies. They prefer submissions of 3-7 poems at a time. Some previously published poems used. Reports in 2-3 weeks. For 20 pp. chapbook consideration, submit 3-15 samples with bio and list of other publications. Pays 50 copies of chapbook. Editor sometimes comments on rejections.** The editor says, "In the fall of each even-numbered year I edit a special issue of *WN* that features writing by young people (under 18)."

THE WICAZO SA REVIEW (IV), MS25-188, Indian Studies, Eastern Washington University, Cheney, WA 99004, phone 509-359-2871, founded 1985, poetry editor Elizabeth Cook-Lynn, is a "scholarly magazine appearing twice a year devoted to the developing of Native American Studies as an academic discipline, using **poetry of exceptional quality."** They have recently used poetry by Simon Ortiz, Joy Harjo, Gray Cohoe, and Earle Thompson. As a sample the editor chose these lines by Ray Young Bear:

> *With the Community's great "registered" Cottonwood*
> *Smoldering under an overcast sky*
> *no one will believe we are here*
> *in the middle & deepest part*
> *of the flood*

TWSR is magazine-sized, 40-46 pp., saddle-stapled, professionally printed on heavy glossy stock with b/w glossy card cover, press run 500, using only 3-4 poems per issue. Once in a while they "feature" an exceptional poet. **Pays 3 copies. Back issue price: $7.50.**

WIDE OPEN MAGAZINE (I), 116 Lincoln St., Santa Rosa, CA 95401, phone 707-545-3821, founded 1984, poetry editors Clif Simms and Lynn L. Simms. **"We want to publish as many poets as possible with a minimum of 100 each issue. We want to give exposure to as many poets as we can. We want poetry in all forms, styles and contents, maximum of 16 lines per poem. We like concrete images, wit, irony, humor, paradox, and satire."** They have recently published poetry by Patricia A. Lawrence, Marian Ford Park, and Arnold Lipkind. The editors selected these sample lines from "Vigil" by Christine Christian:

> *Along the bluff you come, a grin*
> *Slowly forming. We'll share*
> *An apple warm from my pocket,*
> *A life warm from love.*

Wide Open is a quarterly, magazine-sized, 96 pp. saddle-stapled, offset from photo reduced typescript, many poems to a page, card cover with graphics, circulation 1,000, subscriptions including 5 libraries. Subscription: $24; per issue: $10. They use 90% of the 2,000 submissions received per year, have a 3 month maximum backlog. **Sample: $7 postpaid. Submit 3 poems at a time, maximum 16 lines per poem, one per page, name and address on each page. Simultaneous submissions, photocopy, dot-matrix, neat handwriting all OK. Reports usually within 3 months. No pay. Contributors may buy copy at 30% discount (i.e., $7 instead of $10).** There is a quarterly poetry contest, $150 in prizes, no fee. Contributors automatically entered. This magazine obviously offers beginners an easy way to get into print, though $6 seems an excessive charge for a 48 pp. magazine. The editors advise, "Submit, submit, submit. Use concrete images. Avoid Latinate diction."

WILDERNESS (II, IV-Nature/ecology), 2006 NE 24th Ave., Portland, OR 97212, (poetry submissions should be sent to this address), founded 1935, poetry editor John Daniel, is a slick quarterly magazine of "The Wilderness Society, one of the oldest and largest American conservation organizations." Requests for sample and subscriptions should go to *Wilderness*, 1400 Eye St. NW, Washington, DC

20005. They want **"poetry related to the natural world. Shorter poems stand a better chance than longer, but all will be read. Poetry in any form or style is welcome."** They have recently published poetry by Wendell Berry, Reginald Gibbons, Mary Oliver, Naomi Shihab Nye, and William Stafford. The magazine is published on slick stock, full-color, professionally printed, with full-color paper cover, saddle-stapled, 76 pp. Their press run is 340,000 with 300,000 subscriptions. Subscription: $15. **Sample: $3.50 postpaid. Pays $100 plus 2 copies on publication. Responds in six weeks. No simultaneous submissions or previously published material. Editor comments on rejections** "occasionally. **No rejection form; all submissions are answered with a personal note."**

‡**WILDFLOWER (I, II, IV-Nature),** Box 4757, Albuquerque, NM 87196-4757, founded 1981, editor/ publisher Jeanne Shannon, is a leaflet appearing 6-8/year in a 1-page format (either as broadside or folded to digest-size), publishing **poetry, preferably "in which nature plays a role. Generally do not like rhymed poetry unless the rhyme is skillfully done and unobtrusive. Not interested in trite, singsong, sentimental 'bad greeting-card verse.' Poems on spiritual themes are welcome, but overtly 'religious' poetry is not."** They have recently published poetry by Ed Orr, Katharyn Machan Aal, Carl Mayfield, and Gene Frumkin. As a sample the editor selected these lines from "Wintering" by Karen McKinnon:

> *Winter giving way to the tight*
> *red buds of tulip urgent to uncurl*
> *as desert willow forces up*
> *the banks of arroyos . . .*

Subscription: $5. **Sample, postpaid: $1. Pays 5 copies. Simultaneous submissions and previously published poems OK. Editor comments on submissions "often."** She advises, "Read! Especially read the poets you particularly like."

WILDWOOD JOURNAL; THE WILDWOOD PRIZE IN POETRY (II, IV-Students), N.S. Wallace, Arts 213 3300 Cameron St. Road, Harrisburg, PA 17110-2999. *Wildwood Journal,* an annual, is **open only to students, alumni, and faculty of Harrisburg Area Community College,** but the Wildwood Prize is open to any poet, $500 annually, $5 reading fee. Final selection for the prize is made by a distinguished poet (in 1990 Harry Humes) who remains anonymous until the winner is announced. Poems are accepted between September 1 and November 15. Rules available for SASE.

THE WILLIAM AND MARY REVIEW (II), Campus Center, College of William and Mary, Williamsburg, VA 23185, phone 804-221-3290, founded 1962, editor William Clark, a 112 pp. annual, **"is dedicated to publishing new work by established poets as well as work by new and vital voices."** They have published poetry by Dana Gioia, Cornelius Eady, Amy Clampitt, Henri Cole, Julie Agoos, Diane Ackerman, and Phyllis Janowitz. They accept 15-20 of about 5,000 poems submitted per year. Press run is 5,500. They have 250 library subscriptions, about 500 shelf sales. **Sample: $4.50 postpaid. Pays 4 copies. Submit 1 poem per page, batches of no more than 6 poems. Reports in approximately 2 months.**

WILLOW SPRINGS (II, IV-Translations), Box 1063, Eastern Washington University, Cheney, WA 99004, phone 509-458-6429, founded 1977. They have published poetry by Denise Levertov, Carolyn Kizer, Michael Burkard, Russell Edson, Dara Wier, Thomas Lux, Madeline DeFrees, Hayden Carruth, Al Young, Odysseas Elytis, W.S. Merwin, Olga Broumas, Kay Boyle and Lisel Mueller. *Willow Springs* is a semiannual, 6x9", 90 pp., flat-spined, professionally printed, with glossy 2-color card cover with art, circulation 800, 230 subscriptions of which 30% are libraries. They use 1-2% of some 4,000 freelance poems received each year. **Sample: $4 postpaid. Submit September through May. "We do not read in the summer months." Include name on every page, address on first page of each poem. Brief cover letter saying how many poems on how many pages. No simultaneous submissions. Reports in 1-3 months. Pays 2 copies, others at half price, and pays cash when funds available. Send SASE for guidelines. "We are especially interested in translations from any language or period. We publish** quality poetry and fiction that is imaginative, intelligent, and has a concern and care for language."

WIND MAGAZINE (I, II), Box 809K, RFD #1, Pikeville, KY 41501, phone 606-631-1129, founded 1971, poetry editor Quentin R. Howard. *"Wind* since 1971 has published hundreds of poets for the first time and today there are at least 125 who are publishing widely in many magazines and have books to their credit. I have also published about 15 people who had stopped writing and submitting to 'little' magazines because many young editors were not acquainted with much of their work. There's nothing unique about *Wind;* like all 'little' magazines it is **friendly (too friendly at times) toward beginning writers who have something to say and do so effectively and interestingly. I have no taboos. I invent my own taboos on reading each MS. But plain old raw vulgarity for shock effect is out. Save your postage! I don't want simple broken prose, neither greeting card-type verse; nor please no love verse and soothing graveyard poetry; none please enamoured of death; believe me it's still being**

written. I'm not picky about form, style, subject matter nor purpose; but length (pages and pages) makes me frown no matter how much I love it. 'Little' magazines are a squeamish group when it comes to space." They have recently published poetry by Peter Brett, Jacqueline Marcus, Harold Witt, Katharine Privett, Hale Chatfield, Michael Johnson, Real Faucher, and Jonathan London. The editor selected these sample lines by Charles Semones:

> Summer is the bad word in our yearly grammar.
> It fits no sensible sentence. No one can write the syntax
> of summer right. Our shared radio clears its throat nightly:
> static the thickness of phlegm drowns out Beethoven and conmen peddling Jesus.

Wind appears irregularly, digest-sized, averaging 86 pp. per issue of which 60 are poetry, saddle-stapled, professionally printed with matte card cover, circulation 455, subscriptions 412 of which 21 are libraries. Subscription: $7 for 3 consecutive issues. They use about 200 of 3,600 freelance submissions of poetry per year, sometimes have as much as a year backlog. **Sample: $2.50 postpaid. Submit at least 3-6 poems. "Photocopies and simultaneous submissions scare me." Shorter poems have a better chance here. Reports in 2-4 weeks. Pays contributor's copies. Editor comments on rejections, "Now and then when time permits. There's many pitfalls about this."** Quentin Howard advises, "Presentation is all-important in deciding on poems."

WINDFALL; WINDFALL PROPHETS CHAPBOOK SERIES; FRIENDS OF POETRY (II), English Dept. University of Wisconsin at Whitewater, Whitewater, WI 53190, phone 414-472-1036, founded 1979, poetry editor Ron Ellis. *Windfall* is a "semi-annual magazine of intense, highly crafted work with occasional longer poems. Both mag and chapbook series sponsored by non-profit Friends of Poetry and UW-Whitewater English Department. **We want a fusion of craft and imagination, controlled daring. Don't want generalized 'wisdom,' workshop poetry, contrived excitement. Dislike imitative but enjoy syncretic styles. Any subject or purpose: the inevitable and inimitable expression of the subject."** They have recently published poetry by Douglas A. Powell, Ralph J. Mills Jr., Christine Swanberg, Gay Davidson, Jean Tobin, and Edward Mycue. The editor selected these sample lines from "Snout" by Skip Renker:

> To be something like
> an aardvark. To have
> a black sniffer, moist, the in-
> sides of the broad nostrils
> lined with veins that wind
> like crimson snakes far back
> into the brain. . . .

Windfall is 40-50 pp., digest-sized, circulation 200, 50 subscriptions, using 40-45 pp. of poetry in each issue. Subscription: $5. They receive about 700 submissions of freelance poetry per year, use 70. **Reports in 3-8 weeks. Sample: $2 postpaid for current issue; $1 for back issue. Submit 4-6 poems before March for mid-year issue, before October for year-end issue. Pays 1 copy.** Windfall Prophets Press publishes chapbooks for which **poet must pay $200 toward production costs ("more or less, subject to negotiation"). Query with 2-3 samples. $10 reading fee for submission (if invited). Simultaneous submissions, crisp, clear photocopy or dot-matrix OK, or discs compatible with MS-DOS. Poet receives all copies except 20, is responsible for promotion and distribution of the chapbook under Windfall Prophets logos. Editor comments on rejections "when MS shows sufficient excellence."**

THE WINDLESS ORCHARD; THE WINDLESS ORCHARD CHAPBOOKS (II), English Dept., Indiana University, Fort Wayne, IN 46805, phone 219-481-6841, founded 1970, poetry editor Robert Novak, a "shoestring labor of love—chapbooks only from frequent contributors to magazine. Sometimes publish calendars." They say they want "**heuristic, excited, valid non-xian religious exercises. Our muse is interested only in the beautiful, the erotic, and the sacred,**" but I could find nothing erotic or sacred in the sample issue sent me, and the kinds of beauty seemed about like those in most literary journals, as these lines by Wayne Kvam, selected by the editors as a sample, indicate:

> Wolfgang, the waiter comes over
> red shirt bulging
> like an apple
> says "crisp oak, birch, and lime"
> into this thin air.

The Windless Orchard appears 3-4 times a year, 50+ pp., digest-sized, offset from typescript, saddle-stapled, with matte card cover with b/w photos. The editors say they have 100 subscriptions of which 25 are libraries, a print run of 300, total circulation: 280. There are about 35 pp. of poetry in each issue. Subscription: $8. They receive about 3,000 freelance submissions of poetry per year, use 200, have a 6 month backlog. **Considers simultaneous submission. Sample: $3 postpaid. Submit 3-7 pp. Reports in 1 day-4 months. Pays 2 copies. Chapbook submissions** by invitation only to contributors to the magazine. Poets pay costs for 300 copies, of which The Windless Orchard Chapbook Series receives 100 for its expenses. Sample: $3. Editors sometimes comment on rejections. They advise, "Memorize a poem a day, do translations for the education."

WINEBERRY PRESS (V, IV-Regional), 3207 Macomb St. NW, Washington, DC 20008, phone 202-363-8036, founded 1983, founder and president Elisavietta Ritchie, publishes anthologies and chapbooks of poems by **Washington area poets but accepts no unsolicited MS because of a large backlog.** She has recently published poetry by Judith McComb, Elizabeth Follin-Jones. As a sample Elisavietta Ritchie selected these lines from "Looking Forward" by Maxine Combs, included in **Swimming Out Of The Collective Unconscious:**

> *Nothing is promised*
> *Like land crabs scuttling*
> *across a road, unexpected,*
> *sightings are gifts.*

WINSTON-DEREK PUBLISHERS, INC.; SCYTHE BOOKS; MAGGPIE PUBLICATIONS; HOMESPUN ANTHOLOGY SERIES (IV-Religious, anthologies), P.O. Box 90883, Nashville, TN 37209, phone 615-321-0535, founded 1977, senior editor Robert Earl, "is a religious and traditional trade publishing house. Our publications are for a general, intellectual, and church audience. Even our mystery series is slanted for a Christian. We accept no MSS that are vulgar (in the common sense of the term), use cheap language or are derogative of other cultures, races and/ or ethnic origins. We have accounts with more than 5,000 Christian bookstores in America and abroad. We want to see **poetry that's inspirational, religious, family life, academic and/ or scholarly. We do not accept poetry of the avant-garde type, sensuous or erotic.**" They have recently published poetry by Grandma Marie Moon, Manohar S. Kelkar, Susan Glovsky, Marvis and Carmelo Garnello, and Betty H. Hall.The editors selected these sample lines from "Little Princess" by Leonard A. Slade, Jr.:

> *She is nine now.*
> *Breast imprint her blouse,*
> *tears drip from her eyes.*
> *She is growth, pain, a question.*

Submit complete book MS. "A good cover letter is always in order. Reply to query in 4 weeks, to submission in 4-6 weeks. MS should be "preferably typed, double-spaced. No simultaneous submissions. Photocopy, dot-matrix OK. Pays 10-15% royalties plus 20 copies. Send 9x12" SASE and $1 for catalog to order samples." They offer a "best poetry MS of the year award — a poetry workshop scholarship. Judges: Robert Earl and Marjorie Staton." Publishes 3 chapbooks per year, program is essentially for the artistic poet whose works are of sublime quality, yet lack the quantity to compile a volume." The editor advises, "Write poetry that is literate. Stay with a definite style. Poetry is more than prose writing, one either has to be gifted or well trained or both."

THE WIRE; PROGRESSIVE PRESS (I, IV-Form), 7320 Colonial, Dearborn Heights, MI 48127, phone 517-394-3736, founded 1981, editor Sharon Wysocki. *The Wire* is an "alternative arts" publication that appears 2-3 times a year. It publishes **"language and experimental poetry" but no sonnets. "We are also looking for short form erotic poems. Regarding all submissions, the poet has a much better chance for publication in *The Wire* if the poem is in short form.** Poets recently published include Ivan Argüelles, Paul Weinman, and Joseph Raffa. As a sample, the editor selected "Kerosene Madonna" by Lyn Lifshin:

> *gets you*
> *hot is*
> *cheap sucks*
> *your air*

The Wire is photocopied on 8½x11" offset paper, 9 pp., with graphics, stapled at the top left corner. Price per issue is $1 and a subscription is $3.75 (checks should be made out to Progressive Press). **Guidelines are available for SASE. Contributors receive 1 copy. Photocopied and simultaneous submissions are OK, but print must be dark enough for photocopying. Submissions are reported in 6 months and time to publication is the same. Criticism of rejected MSS is provided.**

WISCONSIN ACADEMY REVIEW (IV-Regional), 1922 University Ave., Madison, WI 53705, phone 608-263-1692, founded 1954, poetry editor Faith B. Miracle, "distributes information on scientific and cultural life of Wisconsin and provides a forum for **Wisconsin (or Wisconsin background) artists and authors. They want good lyric poetry; traditional meters acceptable if content is fresh. No poem over 65 lines.**" They have published poetry by Credo Enriquez, David Martin, Felix Pollak, Ron Wallace and John Bennett. *Wisconsin Academy Review* is a magazine-sized 48 pp. quarterly, professionally printed on glossy stock, glossy card cover with b/w photo, circulation 1,800, with 1,500 subscriptions of which 109 are libraries. They use 4-12 pp. of poetry per issue. Of over 100 freelance submissions of poetry per year they use about 15, have a 6-12 month backlog. **Sample: $3 postpaid. Submit 5 pp. maximum, double-spaced. Photocopy, dot-matrix OK. Must include Wisconsin connection if not Wisconsin return address. Reports in 4-6 weeks. Pays 5 copies. Editor sometimes comments on rejections.**

UNIVERSITY OF WISCONSIN PRESS; BRITTINGHAM PRIZE IN POETRY (II), 114 N. Murray St., Madison, WI 53715, phone 608-262-4922, Brittingham Prize inaugurated in 1985, poetry editor Ronald Wallace. The University of Wisconsin Press publishes primarily scholarly works, but they offer the annual **Brittingham Prize of $500 plus publication. The contest is the only way in which this press publishes poetry. Send SASE for rules. Submit between September 1 and October 1, unbound MS volume 50-80 pp., name, address, and telephone number on title page. Poems must be previously unpublished in book form. Poems published in journals, chapbooks, and anthologies may be included but must be acknowledged. There is a non-refundable $10 reading fee which must accompany the MS.** (Checks to University of Wisconsin Press.) **Enclose self-addressed postcard for acknowledgment and a 10x13" unpadded, self-addressed stamped envelope—whether you want your MS back or not.** Qualified readers will screen all MSS. Winner will be selected by "a distinguished poet who will remain anonymous until the winner is announced in mid-February." Past judges include C.K. Williams, Maxine Kumin, Mona Van Duyn, Charles Wright, Gerald Stern, and Mary Oliver. **No translations.** Recent winners are Jim Daniels, Patricia Dobler, David Kirby, Lisa Zeidner, Stefanie Marlis, and Judith Vollmer.

THE WISCONSIN RESTAURATEUR (IV-Themes), 125 W. Doty, Madison, WI 53703, phone 608-251-3663, founded 1933, poetry editor Jan LaRue, is a "trade association monthly (except November-December combined), circulation 4,200, for the promotion, protection, and improvement of the Wisconsin foodservice industry." They use "**all types of poetry, but must have food service as subject. Nothing lengthy or off-color (length 10-50 lines).**" **Reports in 1-2 months. They buy 6-12 per year, pay $2.50-7.50/poem. Sample: $1.75 plus postage. Send SASE for guidelines.** Editor sometimes comments on rejections. She advises, "Study many copies of the mag."

THE WISE WOMAN (I, IV-Feminist), 2441 Cordova St., Oakland, CA 94602, founded 1980, editor and publisher Ann Forfreedom, is a quarterly journal "**focusing on feminist issues, feminist spirituality, Goddess lore, and feminist witchcraft.**" They want "**mostly shorter poetry—by both women and men—dealing with these themes. No Christian-oriented poetry.**" They have recently published poetry by Lisa Yount. As a sample the editor selected these lines from"A Universe Beginning," by Kendra Usack:

> *From her blood*
> *comes the first surge,*
> *the hot explosion,*
> *then nebulas unfold . . .*

TWW is magazine-sized, approximately 32 pp., offset. "At least 20 poems received per year; accept about 50% of appropriate poems." Subscription: $15. **Sample: $4 postpaid. Pays 1 copy. MS should be typed, double-spaced with writer's name and address on each page. They will consider previously published poems.** Ann Forfreedom says, "I prefer poems that are active, come from the writer's deep experiences or feelings, are brief, and are applicable to many kinds of people. A focus on Goddess culture, nature, or feminist issues is helpful. Good spelling is deeply appreciated."

‡**THE WISHING WELL (IV-Membership, women)**, P.O. Box G, Santee, CA 92071-0167, founded 1974, editor/publisher Laddie Hosler, is a "contact magazine for **gay and bi-sexual women** the world over; members' descriptions, photos, some letters, and poetry published with their permission only, resources, etc., listed. I publish writings only for and by members so membership is required." 1-2 pp. in each issue are devoted to poetry, "**which can be 6" to full page—depending upon acceptance by editor, 3" width column.**" As a sample I selected this stanza from "Inner Voice" (poet identified only by membership #):

> *The passion I feel for you is warm*
> *Like the color of fall leaves*
> *Hold me; and smell the drifting wood smoke;*
> *as the shadows of the night fall on us.*

The copy I have seen is 7x8" offset press from photoreduced typescript (mostly italics), with soft matte card cover. It appears bimonthly and goes to 800 members. **A sample is available for $5. Membership in *Wishing Well* is $55 for 4-7 months. Membership includes the right to publish poetry, a self description (exactly as you write it), and to have responses forwarded to you, and** other privileges, including publishing classified ads for 50¢ a word.

WITHOUT HALOS; OCEAN COUNTY POETS COLLECTIVE (II), Box 1342, Point Pleasant Beach, NJ 08742, founded 1983, editor-in-chief Frank Finale, an annual publication of the Ocean County Poets Collective; it prints "good contemporary poetry." The magazine **"accepts all genres, though no obscenity. Prefers poetry no longer than 2 pages. Wants to see strong, lucid images ground in experience." They do not want "religious verse, or greeting card lyrics."** Some poets published recently are Sallie Bingham, Emilie Glen, Geraldine C. Little, Judi Kiefer Miles, Hal Sirowitz, and Rich Youmans. As a sample, the editor selected lines from the following poem, "Dead Armadillos," by Gail White:

> *I give you the armadillo:*
> *not quite a nuisance, not yet a treasure.*
> *Just give us time. Let enough*
> *of them try to cross the road.*
> *When we're down to the last half dozen,*
> *we'll see them with the eyes of God.*

Without Halos is digest-sized, handsomely printed with b/w artwork inside and on the cover, 56 pp. flat-spined with glossy card cover. Circulation is 1,000, of which 100 are subscriptions and 100 are sold on newsstands; other distribution is at cultural events, readings, workshops, etc. Price per issue is $4. **Sample available for $4 postpaid, guidelines for SASE. Pay is 1 copy. The editors "prefer letter-quality printing, double-spaced, no more than 5 poems. Name and address should appear in top left-hand corner. Sloppiness tossed back."** Reporting time is 2-4 months and all acceptances are printed in the next annual issue, which appears in the winter. **Submit between January 1 and June 30 only.**

‡WITNESS (II), Suite 200, 13000 Northwestern Hwy., Farmington Hills, MI 48018, phone 313-626-1110, founded 1987, editor Peter Stine, is a literary quarterly **"highlighting role of writer as witness to his or her times. Emphasis on matters of conscience."** Using poetry in **"any form, serious, illuminating contemporary life, and moral/political issues, not children's poetry or solipsistic stuff."** They have recently published poetry by Donald Hall, Louis Simpson, and Russell Edson. As a sample, I selected the first stanza of "Unnatural Act" by Tom Lynch:

> *Taking the blue barrel between her lips*
> *she thinks of all the ones who'd ever promised her*
> *passion or romance or companionship—*
> *a place she could call home, or a little safety.*
> *Safety would have been enough. But they never,*
> *after all she'd done for them, they never stayed.*

It is flat-spined, professionally printed, 100 pp., with glossy card cover. They accept fewer than 10% of 600 submissions received per year. Press run 3,000 for 500 subscriptions of which 50 are libraries, 900 shelf sales. Subscription: $16. **Sample, postpaid: $5. Send SASE for guidelines. Pays $10/page plus 2 copies.**

WITWATERSRAND UNIVERSITY PRESS (IV-Foreign languages), University of the Witwatersrand, Johannesburg, WITS 2050 South Africa, phone 011-716-2023, **publishes poetry in African languages only.** In their Black Writers Series for instance, they have published poems in Zulu, Xhosa, and Southern Sotho. Send SAE with IRCs for catalog to buy samples.

WOLSAK AND WYNN PUBLISHERS LTD. (II), Box 316, Don Mills Post Office, Don Mills, ON M3C 2X9 Canada, phone 416-222-4690 or 944-1623, founded 1982, poetry editors Heather Cadsby and Maria Jacobs, publishes 4-6 flat-spined literary paperbacks per year (56-100 pp.). They have recently published collections of poetry by Douglas Burnet Smith. Here is a sample of "Cultural Differences" from **The Word for Sand** by Heather Spears:

> *They have a soft way of touching their genitals*
> *When they are standing and thinking of something else*
> *not furtively*
> *as the men in my culture might*
> *(even in private furtively)*
> *but a light touch, simple and unimportant—*
> *the way a man might touch his pocket for cigarettes,*
> *or his mouth, as he considers the right word—*
> *without awkwardness, without arrogance,*
> *without shame,*
> *without any emphasis at all.*

The books are handsomely printed. **Sample: $8 U.S. or $10 Canadian. Send samples with query, bio, publications. No simultaneous submissions, no dot-matrix. Reports on queries in 2-4**

months. Pays 10% royalties or 10% of press run. Maria Jacobs says "W&W prefers not to prescribe. We are open to *good* writing of any kind."

WOMAN OF POWER, A MAGAZINE OF FEMINISM, SPIRITUALITY AND POLITICS (IV-Feminist, themes), Box 827, Cambridge, MA 02238-0827, founded 1983. "The purpose of *Woman of Power* is to give women a voice, and we accept submissions from women only. We honor the collective and individual voices of women, and **encourage women from all nations, backgrounds, classes, religions, races, and spiritual paths to submit work.** We read everything that is submitted and try to respond personally to each submission. We are a quarterly publication and **each issue has a theme. Interested poets are encouraged to write (with SASE) for the upcoming themes, for our selection of works greatly depends on how well the poem fits the theme of each issue.** We will not print poetry which serves to further separate us from each other, work that could be seen as racist, classist or homophobic. We encourage work that is sensitive, imaginative, sensual, erotic, clear and that speaks of a woman's experience in the world. It can be all or any one of these, and can be of any length, 120 line maximum. We ask that each poet only submit 5 poems per issue. We have no style specifications. Subject matter should relate to the theme, but it is in each woman's interpretation that we build the diversity of work. The purpose should be to entertain, enlighten, make the reader laugh or cry, transform or point out something she has discovered that she wishes to share. We are not interested in work that is anti-male, but rather pro-female." They have published poetry by Adrienne Rich, Kalioaka, Yoko Ono, and Veronica Verlyn Culver. As a sample the editors selected these lines by Marge Piercy:

> *Nothing living moves in straight lines*
> *but in arcs, in epicycles, in spirals, in gyres.*
> *Nothing living grows in cubes or cones or rhomboids*
> *but we take a little here and give a little here*
> *and we change*

The quarterly is magazine-sized, 88 pp., saddle-stapled, professionally printed in 2 columns, b/w graphics, photos and ads, glossy cover with photos, circulation 15,000 with 4,500 subscriptions of which 300 are libraries. Subscriptions: $26 (4 issues). They use 10-12 of 300 submissions of freelance poetry per year. **Sample: $7 US, $8 Canada. "Send for deadlines and themes. Thematic quality very important. Photocopy OK. Send only 5 poems, any length. Simultaneous submissions OK, but we must know in the cover letter." Reports within 1 month of deadline. Pays 2 copies and 1 year subscription. Send SASE for guidelines. Editor comments on rejections.**

WOMENWISE (IV-Women, feminist), 38 South Main St., Concord, NH 03301, phone 603-225-2739, founded 1978, Editorial Committee, "a quarterly newspaper that deals specifically with issues relating to women's health—research, education, and politics." They want "**poetry reflecting status of women in society, relating specifically to women's health issues.**" They do not want "poetry that doesn't include women or is written by men; poetry that degrades women or is anti-choice." They have recently published poems by Marge Piercy. *WomenWise* is a tabloid newspaper, 12 pp. on quality stock with b/w art and graphics. Its circulation is 3,000+. Price per copy is $2, subscription $7/year. **Sample available for $2 postpaid. Pay is a 1-year subscription. Submissions should be typed double-spaced. Reporting time and time to publication varies. Send for a sample issue.**

‡WOODLEY MEMORIAL PRESS; THE ROBERT GROSS MEMORIAL PRIZE FOR POETRY (IV-Regional), English Department, Washburn University, Topeka, KS 66621, phone 913-295-6448, founded 1980, editor Robert Lawson, publishes 1-2 flat-spined paperbacks a year, **collections of poets from Kansas or with Kansas connections, "terms individually arranged with author on acceptance of MS."** Send SASE for guidelines for Robert Gross Memorial Poetry and Fiction Prize ($100 and publication). **"We charge $5 reading fee for unsolicited MSS." Reports on queries in 2 weeks, on MSS in 2 months, published 1 year after acceptance. Samples may be individually ordered from the press for $5.** As a sample the editor selected these lines from "Taiitsu's White Heron" by Michael L. Johnson:

> *Here Taiitsu sees*
> *himself: small fish are enough*
> *for this lazy bird*
> *brushed with just a few thin strokes —*

THE WORCESTER REVIEW; WORCESTER COUNTY POETRY ASSOCIATION, INC. (II,IV-Regional), 6 Chatham St., Worcester, MA 01609, phone 508-797-4770, founded 1973, managing editor Rodger Martin. *TWR* appears twice a year with emphasis on poetry. **New England writers are encouraged to**

Use the General Index to find the page number of a specific publication or publisher.

submit, though work by other poets is used also. They want "work that is crafted, intuitively honest, and empathetic, not work that shows the poet little respects his work or his readers." They have used poetry by Richard Eberhart, William Stafford, and Walter McDonald. As a sample I chose the opening of Louise Monfredo's "I Hold Truth":

> that two-faced
> child of mine, over
> sideways in the tub
> to wash its hair
>
> while it screams murder
> soap in the eyes
> you're killing me

TWR is 6 × 9″ flat-spined, 64 + pp., professionally printed in dark type on quality stock with glossy card cover, press run of 1,000 for 300 subscriptions (50 of them libraries) and 200 shelf sales. **Subscriptions $10. Sample $4 postpaid. Send SASE for guidelines. Pays $10 per poem, depending upon grants, plus 2 copies. Submit maximum of 5 pages. "I recommend 3 or less for most favorable readings." Simultaneous submissions OK "if indicated." Previously published poems "only on special occasions." Reports in 12-15 weeks. Editor comments on rejections "if MS warrants a response."** They have an annual contest for poets who live, work, or in some way (past/present) have a Worcester County connection. The editor advises, "Read some. Listen a lot."

WORD & IMAGE: THE ILLUSTRATED JOURNAL; WORD & IMAGE PRESS (I), 3811 Priest Lake Drive, Nashville, TN 37217, phone 615-361-4733, founded 1986, editor and publisher Joanna O. Long, appears twice a year. **"Material should be strongly visual. Poems limited to 40-50 lines. We are open to all forms if images are vivid, but traditional, well-crafted forms are preferred.** We often use b/w photos/artwork to enhance the poem." Recently published poets include Marguerite B. Palmer, William Hobby, C. David Hay, and Loleta Ramsay. " 'At Winter's End' by Jack Hart exemplifies the kind of nature imagery we like":

> All beauty now is from the roots—
> Redbuds, or willow's greening shoots;
> Who sees worn shades of cream and peach,
> The rolled, and lightfilled leaves of beech.

Vivid images, universal themes, and attention to form will help you place your poems in *Word & Image.*" Joanna Long describes her magazine as "general interest, high quality journal of the arts. *WAT* is 7 × 8½″, with b/w illustrations. She accepted about half of all MSS submitted in 1989. Press run is 500-1,000 for 250 subscriptions, with shelf sales in local stores. Subscription: $7 per year. **Sample: $3 postpaid. Pays 1 copy. Contributors are encouraged to subscribe, to study. Limit of 5 poems per submission. No simultaneous submissions, but previously published poems OK if credit line given. Reports in 3-5 weeks. Editor sometimes comments on rejections.** "Special issues (5½ × 8½″) are occasionally published. Themes: Seasonal, holidays, collections of poems."

THE WORD WORKS; THE WASHINGTON PRIZE (II), Box 42164, Washington, DC 20015, founded 1974, poetry editors Karren Alenier, J. H. Beall, Barbara Goldberg, and Robert Sargent, "is a nonprofit literary organization publishing contemporary poetry in single author editions usually in collaboration with a visual artist. We sponsor an ongoing poetry reading series as well as educational programs and the Washington Prize—an award of $1,000 for a book length manuscript by a living American poet." Submission open to any American writer except those connected with Word Works. Send SASE for rules. Entries accepted between February 1 and March 1. Deadline is March 1 postmark. They publish perfect bound paperbacks and occasional anthologies and want **"well-crafted poetry, open to most forms and styles (though not political themes particularly). Experimentation welcomed."** The editors chose these sample lines by John Bradley from "So Many Stars":

> In winter, Katharina, the heart
> contracts. The night expands.
> . . . Last night, on
> the edge of the plateau, I heard
> one of the unborn, calling out
> from an ungathered potato
> to a roaming farm dog: Leave me
> alone.

"We want more than a collection of poetry. We care about the individual poems—the craft, the emotional content, and the risks taken—but we want manuscripts where one poem leads to the next. We strongly recommend you read the books that have already won the Washington Prize.

Buy them, if you can, or ask for your libraries to purchase them. (Not a prerequisite.) **Currently we are only reading unsolicited manuscripts for the Washington Prize." Simultaneous submissions OK if so stated. Photocopy OK, no dot-matrix. Payment is 15% of run (usually of 500). Send SASE for catalog to buy samples. Occasionally comments on rejections.** The editors advise, "get community support for your work, know your audience, and support contemporary literature by buying and reading small press."

WORDWRIGHTS CANADA (IV-Theme), P.O. Box 456, Station O, Toronto, Ontario, M4A 2P1 Canada, director Susan Ioannou, is a "small press with an interest in **poetry on a single theme** and books on poetics in layman's, not academic, terms. Susan Ioannou selected these sample lines from Denis Stokes' "Pine Hills Running" in **Scarborough Poems**:

> *Running, I return to these rows, a green hilled place,*
> *each species of trees I did not know*
> *then, as a kid amid grassfires, graves*
> *—names I still keep learning*

She wants to see **book-length manuscripts on a single theme to be published as 64 pp. paperback, saddle-stapled chapbooks. Send complete MS and cover letter giving credits, philosophy, asethetic or poetic aims. Responds in 6 weeks. Photocopy, dot-matrix OK. Pays $50 advance, 10% royalties, and 5% of press run in copies. Editor rarely comments on rejections, but Wordwrights** offers a separate "Manuscript Reading Service." Request order form to buy samples. The editor comments, "We have no interest in narcissistic poetry of despair. Instead of mirrors of the brooding self, we seek windows on the wider world of shared human experience. We want poetry founded in courage and insight. Also, small books on the aesthetics of writing poetry—both craft and reflection—such as our latest title, **Writing Reader-friendly Poems: Over 50 Rules of Thumb for Clearer Communication**, to supplement our Canadian writer's market directories: **Literary Market Directory** and **Literary Markets That Pay**."

WORLDWIDE POETS' CIRCLE; POETRY BY THE SEAS (IV-Membership), (formerly *North County Poets' Circle*), P.O. Box 74, Oceanside, CA 92054-0010. Commenced publishing in 1985, Jan Renfrow, editor publisher and co-founder. **"We are a membership society. Only members of** *WWPC* **may submit material to our small monthly magazine,** *Poetry By The Seas*. **Always include an SASE. We get too many queries and submissions without any return envelopes or postage.** Members are entitled to a variety of benefits and privileges, including participation, either in person or in absentia, in our six-month taping programs, and in any and all scheduled readings. We offer critiquing upon request, and we welcome poets of all ages in all occupations and at all levels of experience and proficiency. You need not be pre-published to join us." Annual membership fee is $15 domestic (including Canada); $20 overseas. Senior citizens and full-time students may join for $13 domestic; $18 abroad. Membership includes a year's subscription to *Poetry By The Seas*. Sample copies of *Poetry By The Seas*, are available for $2 domestic; $4 overseas. "We strongly believe in the therapeutic healing power of the creative arts."

WORMWOOD REVIEW PRESS; THE WORMWOOD REVIEW; THE WORMWOOD AWARD (II), P.O. Box 8840, Stockton, CA 95208-0840, phone 209-466-8231, founded 1959, poetry editor Marvin Malone. This is one of the oldest and most distinguished literary journals in the country. "The philosophy behind *Wormwood:* (i) avoid publishing oneself and personal friends, (ii) avoid being a 'local' magazine and strive for a national and international audience, (iii) seek unknown talents rather than establishment or fashionable authors, (iv) encourage originality by working with and promoting authors capable of extending the existing patterns of Amerenglish literature, (v) avoid all cults and allegiances and the you-scratch-my-back-and-I-will-scratch-yours approach to publishing, (vi) accept the fact that magazine content is more important than format in the long run, (vii) presume a literate audience and try to make the mag readable from the first page to the last, (viii) restrict the number of pages to no more than 40 per issue since only the insensitive and the masochistic can handle more pages at one sitting, (ix) pay bills on time and don't expect special favors in honor of the muse, and lastly and most importantly (x) don't become too serious and righteous." Marvin Malone wants "**poetry and prose poetry that communicate the temper and range of human experience in contemporary society; don't want religious poetry and work that descends into bathos; don't want imitative sweet verse. Will not consider simultaneous submissions. Must be original; any style or school from traditional to ultra experimental, but** *must* **communicate; 3-600 lines.**" He has recently published poetry by Ron Koertge, Gerald Locklin, Charles Bukowski, Edward Field, and Lyn Lifshin. As a sample he offers these lines by Phil Weidman:

> *I feel sorry*
> *for our dobie.*
> *She doesn't*
> *have hands.*

She does her
loving with a
soft pink tongue
backed by a
set of shark
white teeth.

The digest-sized quarterly, offset from photo reduced typescript, saddle-stapled, has a usual print run of 700 with 500 subscriptions of which about 210 are libraries. Subscription: $8. Yellow pages in the center of each issue feature "one poet or one idea"—in the issue I examined, 8 pp. devoted to Jennifer Stone's "Notes from the Back of Beyond," passages from her diary. **Sample: $4 postpaid. Submit 2-10 poems on as many pages. No dot-matrix. Reports in 2-8 weeks, pays 2-10 copies of the magazine or cash equivalent ($6-30). Send SASE for guidelines. For chapbook publication, no query; send 40-60 poems. "Covering letter not necessary—decisions are made solely on merit of submitted work." Reports in 4-8 weeks. Pays 35 copies or cash equivalent ($105).** Send $4 for samples or check libraries. They offer the Wormwood Award to the Most Overlooked Book of Worth (poetry or prose) for a calendar year, judged by Marvin Malone. He comments on rejections if the work has merit. He advises, "Have something to say. Read the past and modern 'master' poets. Absorb what they've done, but then write as effectively as you can in your own style. If you can say it in 40 words, do *not* use 400 or 4,000 words."

WRIT (II,IV-Translations), 2 Sussex Ave., Toronto, Ontario, M5S 1J5 Canada, phone 416-978-4871, founded 1970, editor Roger Greenwald, associate editor Richard Lush, is a "literary annual publishing new fiction, poetry, and translation of high quality; has room for unestablished writers." **No limitations on kind of poetry sought; new forms welcome. "Must show conscious and disciplined use of language." They do not want to see "haiku, purely formal exercises, and poetry by people who don't bother reading."** They have published poems by Rolf Jacobsen, Goran Sonnevi, Adelia Prado, Pia Tafdrup, Gunnar Harding, Richard Lush, Charles Douglas, Anne Michaels, Robert Kenter, and Joel Oppenheimer. As a sample the editor selected these lines from "Moby Dick" by Joel Sloman:

My companions' storms no longer move me from my austere stand.
What's a little inconsequential babble when we know
Our plans are made with the help of vast turbulent forces,
That the incomplete and unfulfilled
Plunge in the stream, contributing factors.

The magazine is 6 × 9″, 96 pp. flat-spined and sewn, professionally printed on heavy stock, matte card cover with color art, circulation 700, 125 subscriptions of which 75 are libraries, about 125 store and direct sales, $6/copy. **Sample: $6 postpaid. Pays 2 copies and discount on bulk purchases. Reports in 8-12 weeks. Does not consider submissions between May-July. Acceptances appear in the next issue published. Poems must be typed and easily legible, printouts as close to letter quality as possible with new ribbon. Photocopies OK. No simultaneous submissions. Editor "sometimes comments on rejections."** The editor advises, "Read a copy of the magazine you're submitting to. Let this give you an idea of the quality we're looking for. But in the case of *WRIT*, don't assume we favor only the styles of the pieces we've already published (we can only print what we get and are open to all styles). Enclose phone number and SASE with Canadian stamps or international reply coupons."

‡WRITE NOW!, (IV-Themes), P.O. Box 1014, Huntington, IN 46750, founded 1989, editor Emily Jean Carroll. *Write Now!* **uses a limited amount of poetry up to 36 lines. Payment is 1 copy.** As a sample the editor selected, "Authorship" by Rhoda Rainbow:

All the happiness
I seek,
Is time to write
A book a week.

Write Now! is bimonthly, digest-sized, 28-32 pages. Subscription $12 ($15 Canada). **Sample $1.50.** "On Assignment" features themed poetry contests each issue with awards of $5 plus copy for first place, $3 plus copy, second place, and 2 copies, third place. Poets should send SASE for schedule.

THE WRITER; POET TO POET (I, II), 120 Boylston St., Boston, MA 02116, founded 1887, "Poet to Poet" column by Denise Dumars. This monthly magazine for writers has an instructional column to which poets may submit work for possible publication and comment by Denise Dumars. **There is no pay, and MSS are not acknowledged or returned. Submit no more than 3 poems, no longer than 30 lines each, not on onion skin or erasable bond, name and address on each page, one poem to a page.** Readers may find suggestions in the column for possible themes or types of poems. As a sample I chose the first stanza of "Refective Wall" by William R. Stoddart:

> The autumn sunset is there
> hanging on my parents' wall
> like The Last Supper,
> or a black velvet Elvis
> in a five and dime.

Subscription: $24.75 (introductory offer: 6 issues for $10). Single copy: $3 (available in bookstores and on newsstands).

WRITER'S DIGEST (IV-Themes/writing, humor); WRITER'S DIGEST WRITING COMPETITION (II), 1507 Dana Ave, Cincinnati, Ohio 45207, phone 513-531-2222, founded 1921. *Writer's Digest,* senior editor Thomas Clark, is a monthly magazine for freelance writers—fiction, nonfiction, poetry and drama. "All editorial copy is aimed at helping writers to write better and become more successful. **Poetry is part of 'The Writing Life' section of *Writer's Digest* only. These poems should be generally light verse concerning 'the writing life'—the foibles, frenzies, delights and distractions inherent in being a writer. No poetry unrelated to writing. Some 'literary' work is used, but must be related to writing. Preferred length: 4-20 lines."** They have recently published poems by Charles Ghigna, Willard R. Espy and Michael Bugeja. As a sample, Tom Clark chose this poem, "Octopus Outreach" by Sue Walker:

> A writer and an octopus
> share more than you may think.
> Their grasp sometimes exceeds their reach
> and they use a lot of ink.

They use 2 short poems per issue, about 25 per year of the 1,000 submitted. *Writer's Digest* has a circulation of 225,000. Subscription: $21. **Sample: $2.75 postpaid. Do not submit to Judson Jerome. Submit to Bill Strickland, Submissions Editor, each poem on a separate page, no more than 4 per submission. Dot-matrix is discouraged, photocopy OK. Previously published, simultaneous submissions OK if acknowledged in covering letter. Reports in 3 months. Pays $20-50 per poem. Send SASE for guidelines. Editor comments on rejections "when we want to encourage or explain decision."** Poetry up to 16 lines on any theme is eligible for the annual Writer's Digest Writing Competition—poetry judge for 1990, Bob Wallace. Watch magazine for rules and deadlines, or write for a copy of the contest's rules.

THE WRITER'S EXCHANGE; R.S.V.P. PRESS (I, IV-Themes/writing, anthologies), Box 394, Society Hill, SC 29593, phone 803-378-4556, founded 1983, editor Gene Boone, is a digest-sized newsletter for writers and poets with a special emphasis on beginners. Gene Boone also publishes an annual poetry anthology. He wants **"poems 3-16 lines on writing, but I will consider other subjects as well."** He has recently published poetry by Linda Hutton, Dale Loucareas, Vic Chapman, and himself. As a sample he selected these sample lines (poet unidentified):

> A hurried world, spinning too fast
> Modern technology replaces dreams
> With skyscraper nightmares
> God watches as we dance at Satan's feet.

TWE is 6-8 pp., size varies issue-to-issue, saddle-stitched, with a colored paper cover. It is published quarterly. He accepts about half or more of the poetry received. Press run is 75. Subscription: $5 a year. **Sample: $1 postpaid. Send SASE for guidelines. Pays 1 copy. "I prefer typed MSS, one poem per page, readable. Poets should always proofread MSS before sending them out. Errors can cause rejection." No simultaneous submissions. Previously published poetry OK. Responds in 2-4 weeks, usually 4 months until publication.** He offers cash awards for quarterly contests sponsored through the magazine. Send SASE for current rules. He says he comments on rejections, "If I feel it will benefit the poet in the long run, never anything too harsh or overly discouraging."

WRITERS FORUM (II, IV-Regional), University of Colorado, Colorado Springs, CO 80933-7150, *Writer's Forum* founded 1974, Victoria McCabe is poetry editor. *Writer's Forum*, an annual, publishes both beginning and well-known writers, giving **"some emphasis to contemporary Western literature,** that is, to representation of living experience west of the 100th meridian in relation to place and culture. We collaborate with authors in the process of revision, reconsider and frequently publish revised work. We are open to **solidly crafted imaginative work that is verbally interesting and reveals authentic voice. We do not seek MSS slanted for popular appeal, the sentimental, or gentle, pornographic or polemical, and work primarily intended for special audiences such as children, joggers, gays, and so on is not for us. Send 3-5 poems."** They have recently published poems by William Stafford, David Ray, Kenneth Fields, Harold Witt, and Judson Crews. As a sample the editor chose the closing lines from "Make Believe; Ukraine 1932-33" by Rawdon Tomlinson:

> In the last act the body eats itself;

> *Tissue and albumen consumed by breathing,*
> *The skin colors dust-gray and the hands swell;*
> *You can't imagine the energy of eating—*

The annual is digest-sized, 225+ pp., flat-spined, professionally printed with matte card cover, using 40-50 pp. of poetry in each issue, circulation 800 with 100 subscriptions of which 25 are libraries. **The list price is $8.95 but they offer it at $5.95 to readers of *Writer's Digest.*** They use about 25 of 500 freelance submissions of poetry per year. **Pays 1 copy. Reports in 3-6 weeks. Simultaneous submissions OK if acknowledged. Photocopy, dot-matrix OK.**

‡WRITERS FORUM; AND; KROKLOK (IV-Form), 89A Petherton Rd., London N5 2QT England, founded 1963, editor Bob Cobbing, is a "small press publisher of experimental work with occasional issues of magazines dealing with sound and visual poetry in cards, leaflets, chapbooks, occasional paperbacks, and magazines. **"Explorations of 'the limits of poetry' including 'graphic' displays, notations for sound and performance, as well as semantic and syntactic developments, not to mention fun. Current interest in computer poetry—visual and verbal."** They have recently published poetry by Maggie O'Sullivan, Bruce Andrews, Geraldine Monk, Adrian Clarke, and Bill Griffiths. As a sample the editor selected these lines (poet unidentified):

> *a glimpse leaps extraneous poise Mid*
> *career specifics mister Or did you*
> *want issues? Fetishised like this negotiate*
> *Howdo Hunan Hoedown*

The magazines are published "very irregularly" and use "very little unsolicited poetry; practically none." Press run "varies." **Payment "by arrangement." Many poems should be submitted camera-ready.** Under the imprint Writers Forum they publish 12-18 books a year averaging 24 pp. **Samples and listing: $5. For book publication, query with 6 samples, bio, publications. Pays "by arrangement with author."** The editor says, "We publish only that which surprises and excites us; poets who have a very individual voice and style."

WRITERS' HAVEN JOURNAL (I, IV-Humor), 3341 Adams Ave., San Diego, CA 92116, phone 619-282-3363, founded 1983, poetry editor Hal "b" Alexander, is a "literary monthly publishing articles on the art and craft of writing, all types of poetry, short fiction, cartoons and illustrations. **Open to all types of poetry: traditional, experimental, shape poems, etc. I like poets who have something meaningful to say, not just hearts and flowers poetry. Humor OK, too. Love poetry that has vivid imagery and unique twists."** As a sample, the editor selected the poem "Ablaze!" by Diane Marie Perrine:

> *I*
> *never realized*
> *how devastating*
> *a housefire was*
> *until*
> *I followed*
> *those sirens*
> *home.*

WHJ is published by the Writers' Bookstore & Haven, 28 pp., 7×8", circulation 350, including 260 subscriptions. They receive about 500 poems a year, **should be typed, as it should appear, one poem on each sheet, 1-3 poems at a time, 25 lines or less. Pays $5-15 plus one copy. No simultaneous submissions or previously published poems. Responds within 3 to 6 weeks, 1-2 months until publication. Sample: $1.95.**

WRITERS' JOURNAL; MINNESOTA INK, (I, II, IV-Teen/young adult), Box 9148, N. St. Paul, MN 55109, phone 612-433-3626, *Writer's Journal* founded 1980, poetry editor Esther M. Leiper, is a bimonthly magazine "for writers and poets that offers advice and guidance, motivation, inspiration, to the more serious and published writers and poets. Esther Leiper has a regular column in which she analyzes and discusses poems sent in by readers. **"We'd like to see a variety of poetry, but no erotica, vulgar, religious, or badly written." Prefers shorter to longer (25 lines maximum).** Some of the more recent poets they have published are: Linda Moore Spencer, Florence Crouse, James Bobrick, Sandy Macebuh, John Stidham, Edward Velie, Mildred Nelson, John Brillhart, Barbara Shirk Parish, Jean Liebenthal, West Schultz, Jack Hart, and Esther Leiper. As a sample the opening four lines of a poem that won First Prize in the 1989 Spring Poetry Contest were selected as a sample (poet unidentified):

> *I grow orange, oxidized by four o'clock*
> *windshield reflections. Cows drip sun, flick the*
> *excess from their tails. Plump milkweed ash scatters*
> *before it is touched. Tribal leaves gather,*

The *Writers' Journal* is magazine-sized, professionally printed, 36 pp. (including paper cover), using 4-8 pp. of poetry in each issue, including column. Circulation 35,000. They receive about

400 submissions per year of which they use 30-40 (including those used in Esther's column). **Sample copy: $3 postpaid. Photocopy OK, no query. Reports in 1-2 months. Pays 25¢/line.** *Minnesota Ink* founded 1987, poetry editor Anthoney Stomski, is "a national publication for writers and readers of fiction, nonfiction, and poetry. **We are open to style prefer light-hearted pieces and of good taste.**" The opening lines from a poem written by Jessie Stomski, a fourth grader were selected as a sample:

> *Time goes fast and lonely.*
> *For everything I gaze at*
> *seems beautiful to me*
> *Secrets deep in my heart never*
> *seem to swim shallow.*

Minnesota Ink is a magazine-sized, professionally printed, 24 pp. (including paper cover), using 2-3 pp. of poetry in each issue. Circulation: 20,000. They receive about 300 submissions per year of which they use 50-60. **No simultaneous submissions or previously published poems. Submit one typed poem per page. Sample: $3 postpaid. Photocopy OK, no query. Reports in 3-4 weeks, payment varies.** *Writers' Journal* has Spring and Fall poetry contests for previously unpublished poetry. Deadlines: April 15 and November 30. Reading fee: $2 first poem, $1 each poem thereafter. Contact Esther Leiper. *Minnesota Ink* has Winter and Summer poetry contests for previously unpublished poetry. Deadlines: February 28 and August 15. Reading fee: $2 first poem, $1 each poem thereafter. Contact Anthoney Stomski.

WRITER'S LIFELINE (I), Box 1641, Cornwall, ON K6H 5V6, Canada, phone 613-932-2135, founded 1974, published 3 times in 1990, containing articles and information useful to writers and **poetry fillers.** "**We avoid sex.**" As a sample I selected this complete poem, "Greatest Peace," by Merle Ray Beckwith:

> *The greatest peace*
> *Upon this earth*
> *Lies in our souls.*
> *God knows its worth.*

WL is digest-sized, 36-40 pp., saddle-stitched with paper 2-color cover, professionally printed in small type, poems sometimes in bold or italics. Circulation is 1,500. Subscriptions: $18. **Sample: $3 postpaid. Send SASE for guidelines. Pays 3 copies. Responds in 4 weeks, usually 4 months until publication.**

WRITER'S NEWSLETTER (I); THE ACORN (I, IV-Children), 1530 7th St., Rock Island, IL 61201, phone 309-788-3980, founded 1970, poetry editor Betty Mowery. *Writer's Newsletter* is a "newsletter for writers with short articles, poetry, fiction (no more than 500 words), and writers conferences." They want poetry "**no more than 20 lines. No restrictions as to types and style but no pornography.**" Only one page is devoted to poems. *WN* appears 6 times a year. They take more than half of about a hundred poems received each year. Press run is 380 for 375 subscriptions of which 10 are libraries. Subscription: $5. **Sample: $1. Pays 1 copy. Simultaneous submissions and previously published poems OK. Reports in 1 week.** *The Acorn* is a "newsletter for young authors and teachers or anyone else interested in our young authors. **Take only MSS from kids K-12th grades. Poetry no more than 20 lines.** It also takes articles and fiction, no more than 500 words." It appears 6/year and "**we take well over half of submitted MSS.**" Press run 100, 6 going to libraries. Subscription: $6. **Sample, postpaid: $1. Pays 1 copy. Simultaneous submissions and previously published poems OK. Reports in 1 week.**" Editor Betty Mowery advises, "Beginning poets should submit again as quickly as possible if rejected. Study the market: don't submit blind. Always include a SASE or rejected manuscripts will not be returned."

WRITERS' OWN MAGAZINE (I, IV-Subscribers), 121 Highbury Grove, Clapham, Bedford, Bedfordshire MK41 6DU England, phone 0234-65982, founded 1982, editor Eileen M. Pickering, uses **poetry in "any form up to 32 lines. Definitely *no* pornography or blasphemy. Preference given to nature, animals, wholesome deep emotion.**" She has recently published poetry by Marjorie G. Harvey and Margaret Munro Gibson. As a sample she selected these lines from "Profligate Spring" by Wendy Parker:

> *Such a profligate Spring! Breathless with beauty*
> *heaped upon beauty and blossoming from*
> *All Hallows through to May; a cherry tree*
> *thrust breat-bright flowers lush pinkly eve,*

WOM is digest-sized, 48 pp. including paper cover, offset from typescript, saddle-stapled. Subscription: $20 per year (or £1 sterling money order). **You have to subscribe to submit and receive no extra free copies if published. Submit up to 6. May be handwritten (very legibly) or typed. Considers simultaneous submissions. Reports within 1 week, time to publication up to 1 year.** *Writer's Own* also publishes 24 pp. chapbooks on a subsidy basis (unless poet is very well-known.) The magazine holds quarterly poetry competitions with small cash and booklet prizes, open to subscribers only. Eileen M. Pickering advises, "Subscribe to as many poetry mags as you can afford and let your name become well-known within the small mag presses."

WRITERS' RENDEZVOUS (I, IV-Themes/writing, form), #8, 3954 Mississippi St., San Diego, CA 92104, phone 619-296-2758, poetry editor Karen Campbell, is a newsletter for freelance writers. **"Poetry should rhyme or be haiku (but not mandatory). We prefer writer-oriented poetry, only e.g., 'Ode to Walt Whitman' and 'Writer's Problem.' No avant-garde."** As a sample I selected the first of two stanzas of "Writer's Problem," poet unidentified:

> *Here I sit,*
> *I'll have a fit*
> *My poem needs a theme.*
> *I think I'll scream.*

WR is photocopied on ordinary paper, both sides—24 pages, stapled in the upper left-hand corner. It comes out quarterly. They take about 80 of 200 poems submitted. **Sample: $3 postpaid. Send SASE for guidelines. Pays 1 copy. Simultaneous submissions and previously published poems OK. Reports in about 4 weeks, about 4 months until publication. Editor "sometimes" provides comments on rejected MSS.** She says, "Many poetry submissions reveal that the writer has not studied our preferences in style and topic. (Poetry not on topic is automatically rejected.) Please be sure you are familiar with the market before wasting your time—and the editor's—with inappropriate submissions."

WRITER'S RESCUE; KEITH PUBLICATIONS; WRITE TO FAME; CONTESTS & CONTACTS (I,IV-Subscription, children), Box 248, Youngtown, AZ 85363-0248, founded 1985, editor Mary L. Keith, who says *"Write to Fame*, a monthly newsletter, was created out of my desires and needs as a writer." It conducts writing contests and contains news of current contests and markets and articles about writing for writers under eighteen, beginners of all ages, and more experiences writers and uses **poetry written by subscribers. Payment for poems is "up to $1."** I have selected the following sample stanza by Sharon Lynn Drake:

> *Thunder in the distance,*
> *The landscape is hazy,*
> *Ninety degress and humid—*
> *Enough to make one lazy*

Subscription: $20. **Sample, postpaid: $2.50.** Keith Publications publishes chapbooks selected through contests. Send SASE for contest rules.

‡WRITING (V), Box 69609, Station K, Vancouver BC V5K 4W7, Canada, phone 604-688-6001, founded 1980, editor Jeff Derksen, is a literary magazine appearing 3 times per year using **"socially committed, innovative writing."** I have not seen a copy, but the editor describes it as 96 pp., 6×9″, with "colour cover." They accept about 10% of submissions received. Press run 700 for 300 subscriptions of which 20% are libraries, 200 shelf sales. Subscription: $18. **Sample, postpaid: $6. Pays subscription. Currently accepts no unsolicited poetry.**

WYOMING, THE HUB OF THE WHEEL . . . A JOURNEY FOR UNIVERSAL SPOKESMEN; THE WILLOW BEE PUBLISHING HOUSE (I, II, IV-Themes, humor), Box 9, Saratoga, WY 82331, phone 307-326-5214, founded 1985, managing editor Dawn Senior, who says "We publish a semi-annual literary-art magazine devoted to themes of Peace, The Human Race, Positive Relationships, and the Human Spirit and all its Possibilities. We have a general audience interested in peace, humanism, the environment, society, and universal messages." The editor's instructions are: **"Poetry should be real. We look for a haunting quality in the work which makes the reader want to read each piece again, and again. Usually accept work which is personal and creates emotion in the reader (yet *says* something) rather than works which are purely intellectual, factual. We're especially open to high quality work from minority writers from the U.S. or anywhere in the world."** Her negatives are: **"Don't list emotions. Don't 'sum up' what it is you are saying. Leave some mystery. Strong images, natural rhythms, use of metaphor are necessary; without them, it's merely verse or an editorial."** She has published poetry by Jung-Ja Choi, Gary David, Rochelle Lynn Holt, Graciany Miranda-Archilla, and Asher Torren. As a sample, she chose the following lines by Yearn Hong Choi:

> *the woods belong to the trees.*
> *the woods belong to the saint.*
> *the saint is hiding all the beautiful*
> *things with the green leaves*
> *from modern man*
> *who is passing by*
> *the woods*
> *65 mph.*

Wyoming, The Hub of the Wheel is a 6×9″ paperback, flat-spined, 80-100 pp., offset with b/w artwork, glossy card cover with b/w illustration. It appears semi-annually. Circulation about 500, of which 40% will be subscriptions. Price per issue is $6, subscription $10. **Sample $5 postpaid, guidelines available for SASE. Pay is 1 copy. Writers should submit up to 5 poems, maximum of 80 lines per poem. Photocopies, dot-matrix, and simultaneous submissions are OK. "Prefer unpublished poems." Send submissions from September 1 to December 15 only. Submissions are reported on in 4-16 weeks, and time to publication is 6-18 months.** The editor says, "About 10% of our publication is open to new and/or previously unpublished writers. Our editorial biases preclude our accepting material which lauds alcohol or drugs, or which contains sexually explicit passages of a coarse nature. We would reject outright any material which in subject, thought, or language is contrary to our themes. No religious material. Humor is welcome if it is poetry and not verse. If you like our approach, send us something and see what happens."

‡X-CALIBRE; CARMINA PUBLISHING (II), One, 33 Knowle Rd., Bristol, Great Britain BS4 2EB, phone 44-272-715144, founded 1986, editor Ken Taylor, has recently published poetry by John Gonzalez, Sylvia Kantaris, John Light, Falcastron, and Ann Keith. As a sample he selected his own "The Alchaemical Wedding":

> *We are gathered here this evening*
> *to celebrate the tryst of*
> *space and time . . .*
>
> *Let us all confess forever*
> *we're guests in Life's wide world*
> *and hosts to Love.*

X-Calibre is an annual publishing **previously unpublished poetry** with "copious b/w drawings/ illustrations," 104 pp., paperback, with glossy lithographed cover. They accept about 20% of 1,000 poems received/year. Press run 500 for 200 shelf sales. **Sample, postpaid: £3. Send SAE, IRC for guidelines. Pay is "nominal" with discount on copies. Reports in 1 month. For paperback publication by Carmina Publishing, query with samples, brief bio, list of publications. Responds to queries in 1 month, to MSS in 2 months. Pays £50 advance, 10% royalties, and 10 copies.** The editor advises, "Experiment!"

YALE UNIVERSITY PRESS; THE YALE SERIES OF YOUNGER POETS; THE YALE REVIEW (III), 92A Yale Station, New Haven CT 06520, phone 203-432-0900, founded 1908, poetry editor (Yale University Press) Charles Grench. First I would like to report on *The Yale Review*, one of our most important intellectual quarterlies. Penelope Laurans, Associate Editor, responds in a way that will help many readers understand why so many of our major markets are "drying up" because of inappropriate submissions by too many poets. She writes, "Our experience with listings in books like **Poet's Market** is so unhappy—literally hundreds of submissions which we do not have the staff to handle—that I feel at the moment we should decline your offer. I am sorry about this because it certainly seems that you are making an admirable effort to publish a responsible, accurate book—but our recent experiences with floods of mail have frightened us." Good poets will continue to place some of their best work with **YR**, and they will continue to publish some of the most outstanding poetry in the country. But **I join Penelope Laurans in begging most of you to stop pestering these high-prestige publications until you have good, objective reason to believe that your work measures up to the quality of the poetry published there. Otherwise you make it difficult for yourself and all of us.** Similar warnings should probably apply to the Yale Series of Younger Poets, which is one of the most prestigious means available to launch a book publishing career. It is **open to poets under 40 who have not had a book previously published—a book MS of 48-64 pp. Entry fee: $5. Submit February 1-28 each year. Send SASE for rules and guidelines.** Poets are not disqualified by previous publication of limited editions of no more than 300 copies or previously published poems in newspapers and periodicals, which may be used in the book MS if so identified. Recent winners have been Richard Kenney, Julie Agoos, Pamela Alexander and George Bradley. Publication of the winning volume each year is on a standard royalty contract plus 10 authors' copies, and the reputation of the contest guarantees more than the usual number of reviews."

YANKEE MAGAZINE; YANKEE ANNUAL POETRY CONTEST (II), Main St., Dublin, NH 03444, phone 603-563-8222, founded in 1935, poetry editor Jean Burden since 1955, is one of the first places where my own poetry was published—30 years ago—and is still going strong, still with the same poetry editor! Though it has a New England emphasis, the poetry is not necessarily about New England or by New Englanders, and it has a national distribution to more than a million subscribers. They want to see **"high quality contemporary poems in either free verse or traditional form. Does not have to be regional in theme. Any subject acceptable, provided it is in good taste. We look for originality in thought, imagery, insight—as well as technical control."** They do not want poetry that is "cliché-ridden, banal verse." They have recently published poetry by William Stafford, Liz Rosenberg, Josephine Jacobsen, Nancy Willard, Linda Pastan, Paul Zimmer, and Hayden Carruth. As a sample I selected these lines from "After a Brubeck Concert" by Miller Williams:

> *But I will be also, when six hundred years have passed,*
> *one of seventeen million who made love*
> *aiming without aiming to at one*
> *hardly imaginable, who may then be doing*
> *something no one I know has ever done*
> *or thought of doing, on some distant world*
> *we did not know about when we were here.*

The monthly is $6 \times 9''$ 170+ pp., saddle-stapled, professionally printed, using full-color and b/w ads and illustrations, with full-color glossy paper cover. They receive over 30,000 submissions a year, accept about 50-60 poems per year. Subscription $19.95. **Submit poems up to 32 lines, free verse or traditional. Uses 4-5 poems/monthly issue. Pays $50/poem, all rights; $35, first magazine rights. Reports in 2-3 weeks. Approximately 18 month backlog. No simultaneous submissions or previously published poems. Submissions without SASE "are tossed." Editor comments on rejections "only if poem has so many good qualities it only needs minor revisions."** Annual poetry contest judged by a prominent New England poet and published in the January issue, with awards of $150, $100, and $50 for the best 3 poems in the preceding year. Jean Burden advises, "Study previous issues of *Yankee* to determine the kind of poetry we want. Get involved in poetry workshops at home."

YELLOW MOON PRESS (II, IV-Themes/specialized, form, anthologies), Box 1316, Cambridge, MA 02238, phone 617-628-7894, founded 1978, poetry editor Robert B. Smyth, assistant editor Mica K. Knapp, is a **"publisher of works relating to the oral tradition, or spoken word, as it pertains to poetry, storytelling, and music."** They publish chapbooks and flat-spined paperbacks and are looking for **"male writers whose work explores men and masculinity. Imagery should be solidly based in the natural world. No epics."** They have published poetry by Robert Bly and offer these lines (poet unidentified) as a sample:

> *apple orchards laden with*
> *the low hushed angle of the afternoon sun*
> *in autumn*

They publish 1-2 collections per year averaging 24-48 pp. For example, **The Shelter of the Roar**, by Connie Martin (her first book), is digest-sized, 32 pp., saddle-stapled, professionally printed on buff stock with matte card cover, $3. **Query with 5-10 samples, letter, bio, and credits. Simultaneous submissions, photocopies, dot-matrix, previously published individual poems all OK. Responds to queries in 2-4 weeks, to MSS in 4-8 weeks. Pays 10% royalties.**

YOUNG AMERICAN: AMERICA'S NEWSPAPER FOR KIDS (I, IV-Children, humor), Box 12409, Portland, OR 97212, phone 503-230-1895, founded 1983, editor Kristina T. Linden, is a 16-32 pp. tabloid newsprint supplement every other week to suburban newspapers, circulation 4.6 million, which features news, science, entertainment, fiction, and **"light verse for the sophisticated youth of today (ages 5-15). Nothing depressing, religious, sexy, or juvenile."** The sample is from "Return of the princess and the pea" by Myrna Topol:

> *There once was a princess,*
> *A dainty girl, she*
> *You've all heard the story,*
> *The one with the pea.*
>
> *Propped up on a mattress,*
> *Pam turned black and blue.*
> *The pea was the problem,*
> *What's a princess to do?*

They accept about 10% of some 500 poems received per year. **Sample: $1.50 postpaid. Pays 7¢ a word plus 2 copies. No simultaneous submissions or previously published poems. Reports within 4 months, up to a year until publication. SASE or no return of MS. IRCs not appreciated.** Kristina Linden says, "Our circulation and frequency is increasing."

YOUNG AUTHOR'S MAGAZINE (IV-Children), 3015 Woodsdale Blvd., Lincoln, NE 68502, phone 402-421-3712, editor Jane Austin, is a quarterly literary magazine focusing on **creative writing by students in grades K-12.** Circulation 12,891. **Sample: $5.95 postpaid. Send SASE for guidelines. Buys 600-700 poems per year, no maximum limit on number submitted.**

‡**THE YOUNG CRUSADER (IV-Children, themes)**, National Woman's Christian Temperance Union, 1730 Chicago Ave., Evanston, IL 60201, is a monthly publication for members of the Loyal Temperance Legion and young friends of their age—**about 6-12 years**. The digest-sized leaflet, 12 pp., uses **"short poems appropriate for the temperance and high moral value and nature themes and their young audience."** I selected as a sample the first of 5 stanzas of "Leprechaun's Gold" by Dianne W. Shauer:

> On the 17th day of March, two
> days past the ides, look for wee,
> little old men, who, when they see
> you, will hide.

They pay 10¢/line for poetry.

‡**THE YOUNG SOLDIER (IV-Religious, children)**, The Salvation Army, 799 Bloomfield Ave., Verona, NJ 07044. Editor: Robert R. Hostetler. Monthly **Christian/religious magazine for children, ages 8-12.** **"Only material with clear Christian or Biblical emphasis is accepted."** The following sample is the closing stanza of "Caretaker" by Beth M. Applegate:

> For God takes care
> Of such wonderful things
> As nights and days and winters and springs.
> He built the mountains
> And made the sea
> And keeps watch over a child like me.

Circulation 48,000. **Free verse, light verse, traditional. Buys 6-18 poems/year. Length: 4-20 lines. Submit seasonal/holiday material 6 months in advance. Photocopied and previously published submissions OK. Computer printout submissions OK; prefers letter-quality. Reports in 1 month. Sample copy for 8 × 11 SAE with 3 first class stamps. Writer's guidelines for 10 SASE. Pays 3-5¢/word ($5 minimum) on acceptance.**

YOUNG VOICES MAGAZINE (IV-Children, Regional), P.O. Box 2321, Olympia, WA 98507, phone 206-357-4683, founded 1988, publisher/editor Steve Charak, is "a magazine of **creative work of elementary and middle school-age children. The age limit is rigid."** It appears every other month, press-run 1,000 for 500 subscribers of which 30 are libraries. Subscription: $15 for 1 year, $28 for 2. **Sample: $3 postpaid. Send SASE for guidelines. Pays $3/poem plus 1 copy (5 copies if you are a subscriber). Editor comments "definitely, on every piece of writing."** He says, "Forget the necessity to rhyme. Make each word count with feeling. Feeling determines whether I accept a poem or a story."

Z MISCELLANEOUS (II), Box 20041, Cherokee Station, New York, NY 10028, founded 1987, poetry editor Esther M. Leiper (see listing for *Writer's Journal*), editor Charles Fabrizio, appears quarterly. Esther Leiper notes, "As a child I liked to view the world through colored cellophane and bits of sea-worn glass. I stared into prism depths for hours turning ceiling into floor and causing straight white walls to be multi-hued and curving. Most of all, on storm nights, I loved studying landscape in the tense, illumining instant of lightning. How brief, but overwhelming! **These days I seek poems that provide the same sort of wonder as the shivery feel of a storm flash; the stark, altered reality and the danger smell of ozone. I think of the 'Z' in *Z Miscellaneous* as being the zap and zig-zag of lightning. Write a poem that changes my mindscape and I'll take it plus ask to see more."** They have published poetry by Katharyn Machan Aal, Aisha Eshe, J. Kates, Eugenia Moore, and Charles Webb. As a sample Esther Leiper selected these lines by William James Kovanda:

> the crunch of hundreds of small mollusks
> under my boots
> and i too am negligent of the beauty
> that surrounds me
> in injury.

ZM averages 90+ pp., magazine-sized, bound with a side clip, offset from typescript with glossy card cover with b/w art. "Several thousand poems arrive; we accept about two hundred plus per year." Press run is 350 for 150+ subscriptions and 3 libraries. Subscription: $12/year. **Sample: $4 postpaid; $7 Canada; $10 foreign. Send SASE for guidelines. Pays $5 per poem plus tearsheets. Uses poems up to 30 lines. "Please, no exceptions! We try to comment on rejections, time permitting."** Esther Leiper says, "Wait till you have read your first hundred books of poetry and written your first hundred poems before submitting anything anywhere. OK—maybe I exaggerate ... but it is still good advice. Beginners have to know the heritage of poetry and explore their own capabilities before they can present themselves with a claim to the title poet."

ZEPHYR PRESS (II, IV-Translations), 13 Robinson St., Somerville, MA 02145, founded 1980, editors Ed Hogan, Hugh Abernethy, Leora Zeitlin, **charges a $15 reading fee for unsolicited MS and provides an editorial critique if the MS is rejected.** Poetry editor Hugh Abernethy says, "We publish an occasional poetry chapbook of 18-25 poems. We accept about 2% or less of the MSS we receive. **We are in principle open to all forms and subjects. However, we tend not to be interested in haiku or traditional rhymed forms. We are interested in translations of high literary quality.** Our most recent publication is **The Complete Poems of Anna Akhmatova**, translations by Judith Hemschemeyer. In general, we do not tend to publish "name" poets, but we are very selective. Their catalog lists books of poetry by Sue Standing, Anne Valley Fox and Miriam Sagan, from whose "Autumn Equinox" these sample lines were selected:

> *Up on the roof in the wind*
> *Hair in my face, fog rolling in,*
> *Freeway streaming, laundry flapping.*
> *The wheel turns and we*
> *Are on the wheel.*

That is from *Aegean Doorway*, a flat-spined paperback, 43 pp., 6×9″, set in 12 point Aldine Roman, printed on acid free paper, sewn binding, glossy card cover, printed in an edition of 1,000 — $3.95. **Query with 5 sample poems. Simultaneous submissions, photocopies OK. Responds to queries in 3 weeks, to MS in 4-10 weeks. Pays 10% of print run. Sample: $3.95 plus 75¢ postage and handling.** The poetry editor says, "Given the small number of poetry titles we do, we are not a good bet for publication; we're a better bet, alas, for a useful critique of the work our poetry editor sees."

‡ZERO HOUR (IV-Themes), Box 766, Seattle, WA 98111, phone 206-621-8829, founded 1987, editor Jim Jones, **is "a thinking person's tabloid. Each issue is devoted to a theme (cults, addiction, pornography, etc.) in which some poetry is printed."** They have recently published poetry by Jesse Bernstein. I have not seen an issue, but the editor describes it as having 40 pp. It appears 3 times a year. Of 20 pieces of poetry received per year they take about 3. Press run: 3,000 for 2,000 shelf sales. **Sample, postpaid: $4. Pays 5 copies. Simultaneous submissions and previously published poems OK.**

ZERO ONE; DANCING PATCH MAGAZINE(V), 39 Minford Gardens, West Kensington, London W14 OAP England, phone 01602-9142, poetry editor and publisher Arthur Moyse. He describes *Dancing Patch Magazine* (which I have not seen) as a "literary quarterly, anarchist oriented, egotistical, clichés. **To avoid disappointments we do not seek submissions for we operate on the 'old pals act' style."** He has recently published poems by Cunliffe, Woods, and Gould. As a sample he selected these lines by Charles Crute:

> *I rolled Old Laughter on our bed of tears*
> *with tender coppers bought the rose*
> *and found within her vein'd arms*
> *a moments ease, a nights repose*

DPM appears 3-4 times a year. The editor describes it as magazine-sized. He says he receives "too much poetry, takes hardly any." His press run is "secret" as is his number of subscriptions and most other information about it (such as how to buy a sample). He advises, "Just write it and send it off off off. Give up waiting for editorial acceptance or rejection. Just write and post."

‡ZOLAND BOOKS INC. (III), 384 Huron Ave., Cambridge, MA 02138, phone 617-864-6252, founded 1987, publisher Roland Pease, is a "literary press: fiction, poetry, photography, gift books, books of literary interest" using **"high-quality" poetry, not sentimental.** They have recently published poetry by William Corbett, Marguerite Bouvard, and Marge Piercy. They publish 5-8 books a year, flat-spined, averaging 96 pp. **Query with 15 sample poems, bio, publications. No simultaneous submissions. Reports on queries in 4 weeks. Pays 5-10% royalties plus 5 copies.** Editor comments on submissions "occasionally."

ALWAYS submit MSS or queries with a stamped, self-addressed envelope (SASE) within your country or International Reply Coupons (IRCs) purchased from the post office for other countries.

ZONE 3; THE RAINMAKER AWARDS (II), Center for the Creative Arts, Box 4565, Austin Peay State University, Clarksville, TN 37044, phone 615-648-7031 or 648-7891, founded 1986, editors Malcolm Glass and David Till, is a poetry journal appearing 3 times a year. "We will 'evolve,' we think, to include stories, essays, reviews, photographs; but emphasis will remain on poetry. **We want poems that match form and function; poems deeply rooted in place, mind, heart, experience, rage, imagination, laughter, and so clearly rooted** *in contemporary language* **that they establish an enduring value. No restrictions on subject-matter, length, etc. No sentimentality, of either the 'left' or 'right.' No poems written primarily because the poet wants to publish poems.**" They have published poetry by Greg Kuzma, Dave Etter, Albert Goldbarth, Philip Dacey, Donald Finkel, Laurel Speer, Lynn Luria-Sukenick, and Neal Bowers. As a sample David Till selected these lines from Lynn Luria-Sukenick's prose poem "Atlantic Salmon":

> *Maybe the fresher water will seem thick to me,*
> *maybe the river remembering will be heavy with*
> *stories. But they tell me I'm going upriver*
> *to get a story, going to become the alphabet*
> *that will let a million salmon say, "Once upon a time."*

Zone 3 is flat-spined, with a poem on the matte card cover, professionally printed, circulation 500. **Sample: $3 current issue, $4-5 back issues, postpaid. Pays 5 copies and small honoraria when available. Reports in 3-4 months after current deadline. Submit typed MS double-spaced, 2-7 poems. No simultaneous submissions. Subscription: $8 for 3 issues.** The Rainmaker Awards in Poetry, offered by Austin Peay State University, are $500, $300 and $100 and publication in *Zone 3*, spring issue. Fee: 1 year's subscription. Deadline December 31.

‡ZYMERGY (II), P.O. Box 1746 Place du Parc, Montréal, PQ H2W 2R7 Canada, founded 1987, editor Sonja A. Skarstedt, is a "literary biannual with emphasis on poetry, short fiction, essays." They want poetry "**imaginative, well-crafted, clear, powerful, concise, experimental, fresh. No greeting-card poetry, pornography, violence, ranting, i-smile introspection, haiku or one-line puffs, patriarchal or religious, 'prose' shaped like a poem.**" They have recently published poetry by Ralph Gustafson, Phyllis Webb, Shulamis Yelin, and Louis Dudek. As a sample the editor selected these lines from "Words" by Allen Feider:

> *Who would have predicted that explosions of stars*
> *Would have written these words, that thermonuclear*
> *Furnaces burning hydrogen would collapse in*
> *Iron to lead to fusion in this hand?*

The magazine is digest-sized, 165 pp. flat-spined, with laminated card cover, professionally printed in 11-point Bodoni type. Press run: 1,000. 10% of subscriptions are from libraries. Subscription: $12 US. **Sample, postpaid: $6 US. Pays 2 copies. Send "selection of 5-10 photocopied or originals. We rarely use just one poem; prefer a selection by each poet. Reports in 2-4 weeks. Editor comments on submissions "when the poetry shows promise or when there are small problems with certain poems."** The editor says, "Read as much as you can. Write as much as you can. As is true of any other occupation: those who work hard and persist will eventually reach their goals (talent helps). Do not expect to make a living out of poetry. Write because you like to write, not because there's 'nothing else' you're good at."

Other Poetry Publishers

Each year we contact all publishers currently listed in **Poet's Market** requesting they give us updated information for our next edition. We also mail listing questionnaires to new and established publishers who have not been included in past editions. The following magazine and book publishers either did not respond to our request to update their listings for 1991 (if they indicated a reason, it is noted in parentheses after their name), or they are publishers who did not return our questionnaire for a new listing (designated by the words "declined listing" after their names).

The reason some of these publishers are not included in the directory are temporary (e.g., overstocked, temporarily suspending publication, etc.), but *before submitting to any of the following I suggest you write a brief letter (enclosing SASE) inquiring whether they are now interested in receiving submissions.* (Also see question three in What Poets Want to Know for further discussion on submitting to publishers not listed in the Publishers of Poetry section.)

Acheron Press
Ailanthus Poetry Magazine
  (temporarily suspended)
Akwekon Literary Journal
The Albany Review (no
  unsolicited poetry)
All In Wall Stickers
The Altadena Review (ceasing
  publication)
Ambit
Ambrosia Poetry Magazine
Ampersand
Anemone Press Inc.
Angeltread
Another Chicago Press
Another Place to Publish
  (ceased publication)
Antaeus/Ecco Press (declined
  listing)
The Apple Blossom
  Connection (no longer
  publishing)
Aquarius
Association for Authors
Atlantic Monthly Press
  (declined listing)
The Asymptotical World
The Atavist
Audio/Visual Poetry
  Foundation
Bad Haircut Quarterly
Balance Beam Press (no longer
  publishing)
Bedlam Press
Bennington Review (not
  currently publishing)
Best Cellar Press
Big Cigars
Blizzard Publishing Ltd. (not
  publishing poetry)
Blue Begonia Press
Bold Print (overstocked)
Branch Redd Books
Branden Publishing Co.
  (requested deletion)
George Braziller, Inc. (declined
  listing)
Brilliant Star
The Broken Stone
Bronte Street (suspended
  publication)
C.L.A.S.S. Magazine
California Quarterly (declined
  listing)
Cardinal Press
Carn
Carnegie-Mellon University
  Press
Cencrastus
The Centennial Review
  (currently not accepting
  mss)
Central Park (declined listing)
Changing Men
Changing Woman Magazine
The Charioteer
Children's Album
Children's Magic Window
  Magazine
The Christian Way
Close Cover Before Striking
Compass (declined listing)

Connecticut River Review
The Connecticut Writer
Conspiracy of Silence
Corpus Journal
Cotton Boll/Atlanta Review
Country Roads Quarterly
Crazyhorse (declined listing)
Cross-Canada Writers'
  Magazine (no longer
  published)
Crowdancing (suspended
  indefinitely)
Current
Daughters of Sarah
  (overstocked)
The DeKalb Literary Arts
  Journal (no longer
  published)
Detroit Black Writers Guild
Dimension: Contemporary
  German Arts and Letters
Diplomacy World
The Disciple
Doc(k)s
Doors Into and Out of Dorset
Dragon's Teeth Press
The Dream Shop
Dust (from the Ego Trip)
E.P. Dutton (no poetry)
The Echo Room
Edges
El Espiritu Del Valle (The
  Spirit of the Valley)
Emotions
Empo Magazine
Empty Mirrors
The Ensign (asked to be
  deleted)
Equivalencias
Erespin Press
Euroeditor
European Judaism
Fat Tuesday
The Fessenden Review (out of
  business)
The First East Coast Theater
  and Publishing Co., Inc.
Foist Magazine (out of print)
Forum (Ball State University)
  (no longer published)
Foundation of Light and
  Metaphysical Education
  (no longer publishing)
Frugal Chariot
Glory
Golden Quill Press
Granta (no poetry)
Great Plains Canal and Avalon
  Dispatch
The Green Book (did not
  respond)
Grove Press, Inc. (delined
  listing)
The Hampden-Sydney Poetry
  Review
Handshake Editions
Harvest Magazine (requested
  deletion)
Herring Cove Press
Hobo Stew Review
Hodder and Stoughton
  Educational

Home Planet News
Horses West
Ice River (suspended
  publication)
Imagine
Immobius (defunct)
Implosion
The Inside from the Outside
  (discontinued temporarily)
International Poetry Review
International Poets Academy
Intimacy/Black Romance (no
  longer publishing poetry)
Iolaire Arts Association
Ion Books
Italian Times
Jabberwocky (requested no
  listing this year)
Jackson's Arm
Just Buffalo Literary Center
Kairos
Kana
Kangaroo Court Publishing
Kavitha
Kawabata Press
The Keepsake Press (ceased
  operations)
La Kancerkliniko
Label Magazine
Lake Street Press
L'Apache
Last Issue (no longer
  publishing)
Librado Press (temporarily
  suspended)
Light and Life Magazine
Lightworks
Linwood Publishers
Lips
Littlewood Press
The Lockhart Press
The Loft Press (no longer
  publishing)
Longhouse (declined listing)
Luna Ventures
Lyra
Macmillan Publishing Co.
  (requested deletion)
Mainichi Daily News
Manna (requested deletion)
Mariscat Press
Maryland Poetry Review
McCall's (no longer using
  poetry)
Melquiades (out of business)
Mendocino Commentary
Merging Media
Meridian (ceased publication)
Methuen, Inc. (declined listing)
Metro Muse
Michaels on Etiquette
University of Missouri Press
Modern Images (declined
  listing)
Mother Duck Press (invitation
  only)
Mothers Today
Moving Out
Music of the Spheres
National Forum
Natural Heritage (requested
  deletion)

New Blood (overstocked)
The New Press
New Yarn
Newest Review
Nnidnid
No Name Newsletter for Poets
Noovo Masheen (ceasing publication)
North Atlantic Review (declined listing)
Ocean View Books
Ommation Press
Open Magazine
Oread
Other Poetry (ceased publication)
Outrigger Publishers Ltd. (suspending publication)
Owl Creek Press
Oxalis
Oxford Magazine
Pangloss Papers (suspended publication)
Panorama of Czech Literature (ceased publication)
Pantheon Books (declined listing)
Paris/Atlantic International Magazine of Poetry
Passages North
Pennywhistle Press
Petronium Press
Pig Paper (no longer publishing)
Pig Press
Pinchpenny (ceased publication)
The Plowman (unresolved complaints)
Poetic Liberty (temporarily suspended)
Poetry & Audience
Poetry Jacksonville, Inc.
Poetry Kanto
Poetry Quarterly
Poetry Toronto (ceased publication)
Poet's Parliament (ceased publication)
Point Riders Press
Ports O' Call
The Pottersfield Portfolio
The Press of the Third Mind
Pressed Curtains
Printed Matter
Prospice
Ptolemy/The Browns Mills Review (declined listing)
Pueblo Poetry Project
Purple Heather
G.P. Putnam's (declined listing)
Quarry West
Quill Books (unresolved complaints)
The Raddle Moon (declined listing)
Ragweed Press (deletion requested)
Rarach Press
Raw Dog Press
Reconstructionist
Recovery Life
Religious Humanism
Relix Magazine (deletion requested)
Renaissance Woman
Rhino
Rhododendron
The Rideau Review Press
Right Here (ceased publication)
Ripples
River City
Room of One's Own (declined listing)
Ruddy Duck Press
Sackbut Press
St. Martin's Press (declined listing)
Scrap Paper Review (ceased publication)
Scripsi
Second Coming Press (suspended publication)
Seeds of Light (deletion requested)
Self and Society
SF3, Inc
Shameless Hussy Press (publisher retiring)
Sheba Review (discontinued publishing)
The Sheep Meadow Press (declined listing)
Shenandoah (deletion requested)
Shirim (declined listing)
Sidewinder (suspended indefinitely)
Simon & Schuster (declined listing)
Smoke
Soaptown (ceased publication)
Solutions
Sono Nis Press (deletion requested)
Sore Dove Publishers (out of business)
Sphinx-Women's International Literary/Art Review (declined listing)
Spokes
Sports & Fitness
Street Press/Street Magazine (declined listing)
Stride Magazine
Sub Rosa Press
Summerfield Journal (no longer published)
Sunrust Magazine
Swift Kick
Tandava
Tara's Literary Arts Journal (out of business)
Theopoiesis
Tidewater Patriot
Tikkun Magazine (deletion requested)
Tin Wreath
Toronto Life (no unsolicited mss)
Tray Full of Lab Mice Publications (temporarily suspended)
Treetop Panorama (no longer publishing)
Triglav Press
Trouvere Company (unresolved complaints)
Unfinished Monument Press
Unicorn Press (declined listing)
Unique Graphics (very overstocked)
The Unknowns (ceased publication)
Vanguard Press, Inc.
Verlag Golem
Viaztlan: A Journal of Arts & Letters (declined listing)
Viking Penguin, Inc. (declined listing)
Vintage '45 (publication discontinued)
Voices in the Wilderness (deletion requested)
Warthog Press
The Wayside
Westwords
What
Whimsy (no longer published)
Whiskey Island Magazine
White Ewe Press (declined listing)
The White Rock Review (declined listing)
Whole Earth Review (deletion requested)
Widener Review
The Windhorse Review
Wisconsin Review
Women-In-Literature, Inc.
Women's Quarterly Review (no longer publishing)
Women's Studies Quarterly
Wood Thrush Books (currently not publishing poetry)
The Wooster Review (out of business)
Working Classics
The Write Age (magazine discontinued)
Writer's Guidelines (no longer publishing)
Writing (England)
Xanadu (declined listing)
Yak Magazine (deletion requested)
Yellow Press
Yellow Silk (declined listing)
Yesterday's Magazette
Z Magazine
Zelo Magazine (no longer published)

_____ *Contests and Awards*

Included in this section are *only* the contests and awards *not* associated with specific organizations or publishers listed elsewhere. Use the General Index first in order to locate a specific contest or award.

But you will find listed here everything from prestigious honors such as the Pulitzer Prizes and Guggenheim Fellowships to contests with entry fees and small prizes sponsored by local poetry societies and little magazines. Many of the most important are coded **V:** Don't call us, we'll call you. But there's a place for everyone. Some of the smaller contests seem to be almost family affairs. Subscribers to little magazines apparently enjoy competing with one another and seeing winning poems by names they recognize, if not by themselves, appear in print.

Such recognition may be gratifying, though it means little in regard to establishing a literary reputation. Most of the poets I know rarely, if ever, enter contests, and when they do, they stick to those which confer some prestige among their peers—those sponsored, for instance, by the Poetry Society of America (see listing in Organizations Useful to Poets). But the tastes of judges, even those with a record of publication, are so unpredictable that a contest is very much like a lottery. Winning doesn't mean your poem would be regarded as good by a different judge, and losing doesn't mean another judge might not have given it a prize.

I have tried to weed out those contests that seem to me exploitative of poets, though, for the most part, you have to rely on your own judgment as to whether a contest is a scam. If it costs you $3 a poem to enter and all the prizes are, say $15, $10 and $5, you can figure that it takes only 10 entries to fill the kitty. Sometimes judges are paid fees, and sometimes there are publicity and other costs. But contests with fees are often money-makers. They may be as innocent as a cake sale as a way to raise money for a small press or organization, but you shouldn't be deluded about your chances of collecting money. Other contests have no fees but are inducements to get you to buy something—for example, an anthology containing your poem. Beware of advertisements in magazines for contests. If you see one saying, in effect, "Poems Wanted," you can be sure that what is wanted is in your wallet.

In general, a beginning poet would be well-advised to put more effort into submitting work for publication than into entering contests unless he enjoys the social aspects of participating in a harmless hobby. But there are many excellent opportunities listed here, especially for poets who have already achieved a substantial publishing record.

In addition to the listings, notice at the end of the section the long list of "Additional Contests and Awards" which cross-refers the many magazines, presses, and organizations offering contests and awards in their listings. If a highly-reputed literary magazine such as *Negative Capability* or *Poetry* or an organization such as the Academy of American Poets conducts a contest or confers an award, it is likely to be one that is respected in the literary world.

The rules and dates for all contests, not to mention their judges or contest chairpeople, change annually. In each case do not enter until you have found out (usually by sending an SASE) the most current rules and deadlines and, where applicable, have obtained appropriate entry forms.

AAA ANNUAL NATIONAL LITERARY CONTEST; ARIZONA LITERARY MAGAZINE (I), Suite 117-PM, 3509 Shea Blvd., Phoenix, AZ 85028-3339, sponsoring organization Arizona Authors' Association, award director Velma Cooper. 42 lines maximum, $4 entry fee, submit between January 1 and July 29. Prizes are $125, $75, $40, 3 honorable mentions $10 each. Include SASE with entry for contest results; no material will be returned. Winners are announced and prizes awarded in October. Winning entries are published in a special edition of *Arizona Literary Magazine*. Entries must be typed, double-spaced on 8½×11″ paper. Write for more information and entry rules, enclose SASE.

MILTON ACORN POETRY AWARD; PRINCE EDWARD ISLAND LITERARY AWARDS (IV-Regional), The Prince Edward Island Council of the Arts, P.O. Box 2234, Charlottetown, P.E.I. C1A 8B9 Canada. Awards are given annually for short stories, poetry, children's literature, novels or historical works, creative writing and playwriting. Writers must have been resident at least 6 of the 12 months before the contest. Submit September 27-February 15. For the Milton Acorn Poetry Award, participants may submit as many entries as they wish, each of no more than 5 pp. Prizes for '89-90: A trip for 2 via Air Nova to Ottawa, Montreal or Quebec City, first prize; $200 and $100, second and third prizes.

‡**ACTS INSTITUTE, INC. (II)**, Box 10153, Kansas City MO 64111, beginning in 1991 this foundation will be offering money grants to those individuals/teams/groups accepted by artists/writers colonies who need financial assistance to be able to attend. Send SASE for 1991 application materials.

‡**ALBERTA CULTURE AND MULTICULTURALISM POETRY AWARD (IV-Regional)**, Alberta Culture and Multiculturalism, 12th Fl., CN Tower, 10004-104 Ave., Edmonton, AB T5J OK5 Canada, is $1,000 for a book of poetry by an Alberta author. Please contact the Film and Literary Arts Branch at the above address for competition deadlines and regulations.

AMERICAN LITERARY TRANSLATORS ASSOCIATION; RICHARD WILBUR PRIZE FOR POETRY; UNIVERSITY OF MISSOURI PRESS (IV-Translations), Box 830688 University of Texas at Dallas, Richardson, TX 75083-0688, executive secretary Sheryl St. Germain. The Richard Wilbur Prize for Poetry is offered in even numbered years (alternating with the Gregory Rabassa Prize for Fiction), offering book publication by the University of Missouri Press of a translation of any book of poems into English, December 15 deadline. **Do not contact the University of Missouri Press regarding this award. All information should be requested from ALTA.**

AMERICAN POETRY ASSOCIATION POETRY CONTESTS (I), Dept. PM-91, P.O. Box 1803, Santa Cruz, CA 95061-1803. Though the primary business of the American Poetry Association is publishing anthologies which poets have to buy to be included—at the cost of $40—their quarterly contests are a genuine opportunity for poets to win substantial cash awards. I will go into the matter at length, because these contests resemble a number of similar plans offered by other companies, not listed in this book, operating for profit, though their names sound like those of nonprofit organizations. The APA's quarterly contests (deadlines March 31, June 30, September 30, and December 31) have no entry fees, and most of their invitational contests (held 2-3 times per year, all entrants of the quarterly contests are invited to enter) require no entry fee. The APA says that winners need not purchase books to win and "the considerable majority of winners have not bought anything at all. All winners, in both the quarterly and invitational contests are published without any need to buy a book." The judges make photocopies of promising poems; the originals are returned for proofreading by those who want to pay to be published. Contest entry is simple and automatic. Every submission that follows the APA guidelines of one original poem, no more than 20 lines long, is entered when it first arrives. What need to know is that they will be tempted to buy to get published, and many poets find the temptation irresistible. The stakes are high. According to the APA, "over $165,000 in prizes have been awarded to thousands of winning poets since 1981." Winners are published in the **American Poetry Anthology** and receive a copy free. Each entrant to the quarterly contests is sent a copy of **The Poet's Guide to Getting Published**, a four-page leaflet with some practical tips about such things as public readings and other ways of becoming published and known.

AMERICAN-SCANDINAVIAN FOUNDATION TRANSLATION PRIZE; SCANDINAVIAN REVIEW (IV-Translation), 127 E. 73rd St., New York, NY 10021, for the best translation into English of a work (which may be poetry) of a Scandinavian author born after 1889, $1,000, publication in the *Scandinavian Review*, and a bronze medallion. To enter, first request rules.

ARKANSAS POETRY DAY CONTEST; POETS' ROUNDTABLE OF ARKANSAS (I), over 30 categories, many open to all poets, deadline September 18. Bulletins mailed out in July. For copy send SASE to Opal Jane O'Neal, 421 Dell, Hot Springs, AR 71901.

ARTIST TRUST; ARTIST TRUST GAP GRANTS; ARTIST TRUST FELLOWSHIPS (IV-Regional), 512 Jones Bldg., 1331 Third Ave., Seattle, WA 98101, phone 206-467-8734. **Artist Trust** is a nonprofit arts organization that provides grants to artists (including poets) who are residents of the state. AT also publishes a 16-page quarterly tabloid of news about arts opportunities and cultural issues.

ARVON INTERNATIONAL POETRY COMPETITION (III), Kilnhurst, Kilnhurst Rd., Todmorden, Lancashire OL14 6AX, England, phone 070-681-6582, jointly sponsored by Duncan Lawrie Limited and *The Observer*. Poems (which may be of any length and previously unpublished) must be in English. First prize is £5,000 ($8,425), and other cash prizes. Distinguished poets serve as judges.

BARNARD NEW WOMEN POETS PRIZE; WOMEN POETS AT BARNARD; BARNARD NEW WOMEN POETS SERIES; BEACON PRESS (IV-Women), Barnard College of Columbia University, 3009 Broadway, New York, NY 10027-6598. Women Poets at Barnard holds open competition for readers in an annual series. Three finalists are selected from the applicants for readings, and manuscripts from these are judged for an award of $1,500 and publication in the Barnard New Women Poets Series, Beacon Press. The competition is open to any woman poet with a book-length MS of 50-100 pages who has not yet published a book (exclusive of chapbooks). Deadline September 1. Submit two copies of MS with SASE, postcard for acknowledgement or receipt.

BAVARIAN ACADEMY OF FINE ARTS LITERATURE PRIZE (V), Max Josephplatz 3, 8 Munich 22, West Germany, is an award of DM 30,000 awarded annually to an author in the German language to honor a distinguished literary career—by nomination only.

GEORGE BENNETT FELLOWSHIP (II), Phillips Exeter Academy, Exeter, NH 03833 provides a $5,000 fellowship plus room and board to a writer with a MS in progress. The Fellow's only official duties are to be in residence while the Academy is in session and to be available to students interested in writing. The committee favors writers who have not yet published a book-length work with a major publisher. Send SASE for application materials. Deadline December 1.

‡BERLIN ARTISTS' PROGRAM (III), German Academic Exchange Service, (Deutscher Akademischer Austauschdienst), Bureau Berlin Box 12640, Steinplatz 2, 1000 Berlin 12, West Germany, director Dr. Joachim Sartorius, enables 15-20 internationally known and recommended composers, filmmakers and writers to spend a year taking an active part in the cultural life of Berlin. Screening committee meets in March or April.

BOLLINGEN PRIZE (V), Yale University Library, New Haven, CT 06520, $10,000 to an American poet for the best poetry collection published during the previous two years, or for a body of poetry written over several years. **By nomination only.** Judges change biennially. Announcements in January of odd-numbered years.

BRANDEIS UNIVERSITY CREATIVE ARTS AWARDS (V), Brandeis University, Kutz Hall 211, Waltham, MA 02254, contact Mary Anderson. Medals, citations and split honorarium of $2,500 recognizing high achievement in literature, music, dance, theater, film, by nomination only.

BREAD LOAF WRITERS' CONFERENCE (III), Middlebury College, Middlebury, VT 05753, phone 802-388-3711, fellowships and scholarships. Candidates for fellowships must have book published. Candidates for scholarships must have published in major literary periodicals or newspapers. One letter of nomination required by March 15; applications and supporting materials due by April 15. Awards are announced in June for the conference in August.

BUCKNELL SEMINAR FOR YOUNGER POETS; STADLER SEMESTER FOR YOUNGER POETS (IV-Students), Bucknell University, Lewisburg, PA 17837, 717-524-1853, director John Wheatcroft. In the spring of 1991, the Stadler Semester for Younger Poets will be added to the Seminar for Younger Poets and the Poet-in-Residence Series. The Stadler Sememster is distinctive in allowing undergraduate poets almost four months of concentrated work centered in poetry. Guided by practicing poets, the apprentice will write and read poetry and will receive critical response. The two Fellows selected will work with Bucknell's writing faculty. The visiting Poet-in-Residence also will participate in the program. Fellows will earn a semester of academic credit by taking four units of study: a tutorial or individual project with a mentor poet, a poetry-writing workshop, a literature course, and an elective. Undergraduates from four-year colleges with at least one course in poetry writing are eligible to apply; most applicants will be second-semester juniors. Send a 12-15 page portfolio and a letter of self-presentation (a brief autobiography that expresses commitment to writing poetry, cites relevant courses, and lists any publications). Also include a transcript, two recommendations (at least one from a poetry-writing instructor), and a letter from the academic dean granting permission for the student to attend Bucknell for a semester. The Bucknell Seminar For Younger Poets is not a contest for poems but for 10 fellowships to the Bucknell Seminar, held for 4 weeks in June every year. Seniors and juniors from American colleges are eligible to compete for the ten fellowships, which consist of tuition, room, board, and spaces for writing. Application deadline for each year's seminar is March 1 of the previous year. Students chosen for fellowships will be notified on April 1.

THE MARY INGRAHAM BUNTING FELLOWSHIP PROGRAM (IV-Women), Radcliffe College, 34 Concord Ave., Cambridge, MA 02138, supports women who want to pursue independent study in the creative arts (among other things). The stipend is $20,500 for a fellowship fulltime July 1-June 30, requiring residence in the Boston area. Applicants in creative arts who do not have doctorates should be at the equivalent stage in their careers as women who have received doctorates two years before applying. Deadline October 2.

BUSH ARTIST FELLOWSHIPS (IV-Regional), E-900 First National Bank Bldg., 332 Minnesota St., St. Paul, MN 55101, are for South and North Dakota, Western Wisconsin and Minnesota residents over 25 years of age to help published writers (poetry, fiction, literary nonfiction and playwriting), visual artists, choreographers and composers set aside time for work-in-progress or exploration of new directions. Maximum of 15 awards of a maximum of $26,000 (and up to $7,000 additional for production and traveling expenses) are awarded each year for 6-18 month fellowships. Deadline October 31.

CALIFORNIA WRITERS' ROUNDTABLE POETRY CONTEST (I), under the auspices of the Los Angeles Chapter, Women's National Book Association, Lou Carter Keay, chairman, Suite 807, 11684 Ventura Blvd., Studio City, CA 91614-2652. An annual contest with $50, $25 and $10 cash prizes for unpublished poems on any subject, in various forms, not more than 42 lines in length. WNBA members may submit free; nonmembers pay $3 per poem entry fee. Deadline is September 30. Send SASE for guidelines.

CANADIAN AUTHORS ASSOCIATION LITERARY AWARDS; THE AIR CANADA AWARD; CANADIAN AUTHORS ASSOCIATION (IV-Regional), 121 Avenue Rd., Toronto, ON M5R 2G3 Canada, $5,000 in each of 4 categories (fiction, poetry, non-fiction, drama) to Canadian writers, for a published book in the year of publication (or, in the case of drama, first produced), deadline December 31. Nominations may be made by authors, publishers, agents, or others. The Air Canada Award is an annual award of two tickets to any Air Canada destination, to a Canadian author, published or unpublished, under 30 who shows the most promise. Nominations are made before April 30 by CAA Branches, or other writers' organizations and the award is given at the CAA banquet in June.

CAPRICORN BOOK AWARD; WRITER'S VOICE (II, III), Writer's Voice, 5 W. 63rd St., New York, NY 10023, $500 and publication of a book of poems of at least 48 pp. by an author over 40. MS should be double-spaced. $10 entry fee. December 31 deadline.

CINTAS FELLOWSHIP PROGRAM (IV-Regional), Institute of International Education, 809 United Nations Plaza, New York, NY 10017, makes awards of $10,000 to young professional Cuban writers and artists living outside of Cuba. Deadline for applications March 1.

CITY OF REGINA WRITING AWARD (IV-Regional), Saskatchewan Writers Guild, Box 3986, Regina, SK S4P 3R9 Canada, is $3,300 awarded annually to a writer living in Regina as of January 1 to work for 3 months on a specific project. Deadline March 16.

CLARK COLLEGE POETRY CONTEST (I), % Arlene Paul, 4312 NE 40th St., Vancouver, WA 98661, jointly sponsored by Clark College, Oregon State Poetry Association, and Washington Poetry Association, deadline February 9, $3 per poem entry fee (checks payable to Clark College Foundation), prizes of $50, $75 and $100, for poems up to 25 lines, unpublished, not having won another contest. Entries in duplicate, name and address on one copy only.

INA COOLBRITH CIRCLE ANNUAL POETRY CONTEST (IV-Regional), %Tom Berry, Treasurer, 761 Sequoia Woods Place, Concord, CA, 94518, has prizes of $10-50 in each of several categories for California residents only. Poems submitted in 3 copies, no names on copies. Enclose a 3x5" card with name, address, phone number, category, title, first line of poem and status as member or non-member. Members of the Ina Coolbrith Circle pay no fee; others pay $5 for 3 poems (limit 3). Deadline in August. For further information contact Tom Berry.

‡ABBIE M. COPPS POETRY COMPETITION; GARFIELD LAKE REVIEW (I,II), contest chairperson Linda Jo Scott, Dept. of Humanities, Olivet College, Olivet, MI 49076, phone 616-749-7000, annual, $150 prize and publication in the *Garfield Lake Review*, $2/poem entry fee for unpublished poem up to 100 lines. Deadline fixed each year. Submit unsigned, typed poem, entrance fee, and name, address, and phone number in a sealed envelope with the first line of the poem on the outside. 1991 judge to be announced.

COUNCIL FOR WISCONSIN WRITERS, INC.; PAULETTE CHANDLER AWARD (IV-Regional), Box 55322, Madison, WI 53705. The Paulette Chandler Award, $1,500, is given annually to a poet (1990 and even years) or short story writer (1991 and odd years). Wisconsin residents only. Submit letter of application and 5 poems, published or unpublished, by January 16. "Award is based on ability and need." Send SASE for rules. The Council also offers annual awards of $300 or more for a book of poetry by a Wisconsin resident, published within the awards year (preceding the January 16 deadline). Entry form and entry fee ($10 for members of the Council, $15 for others) required.

‡CREATIVE ARTIST PROGRAM (IV-Regional), Cultural Arts Council of Houston, 1964 West Gray, Suite 224, Houston, TX 77019-4808, phone 713-527-9330, offers annual awards of at least $4,000 to individual Houston artists. Unless funding prohibits, writers are included in the competition. Deadline for entry October 15.

DALY CITY POETRY CONTEST (I), Daly City History, Arts & Science Commission, Serramonte Library, 40 Wembley Dr., Daly City, CA 94015, held annually, prizes of $25, $10, and $5 in various categories, entry fee of $1/poem, published or unpublished, January 4 deadline. Send SASE for rules.

‡DEAR MAGNOLIA (I), 612-22 Ave. South, Birmingham, AL 35205, editors Bettye K. Wray and Frank Theodore Kanelos, offers an annual contest for poems up to 42 lines, $3/poem fee (make checks payable to K-Wray Publications), prizes of $75 plus an engraved silver bowl; $50 and an engraved plaque; and 5 "Azalea High Merit Awards" of $10 each and a certificate. Annual deadline July 15. Winners announced September 15. Submit 2 copies, name and address on only one. All poems will be destroyed after the judging.

DEEP SOUTH WRITERS CONFERENCE; JOHN Z. BENNETT AWARD (I); BERNARD MEREDITH AWARD (IV-Nature), USL Drawer 44691, University of Southwestern Louisiana, Lafayette, LA 70504-4691; Bennett Award, any form, is $200 first prize, $100 second prize; Meredith Award, nature poem, is $50; entry fee is $5 for up to five submissions in each category; no manuscripts are returned; selected pieces are published in *The Chapbook*, the DSWC annual; authors are paid in copies and retain publication rights; July 15 deadline; winners are notified prior to the annual September Conference meeting; send SASE for contest rules.

BILLEE MURRAY DENNY POETRY AWARD (II), % Janet Overton, Lincoln College, Lincoln, IL 62656, awarded annually, prizes of $1,000, $500 and $250. Open to poets who have not previously published a book of poetry with a commercial or university press (except for chapbooks with a circulation of less than 250). Enter up to 3 poems, 100 lines/poem or less at $2/poem. Poems may be on any subject, using any style, but may not contain "any vulgar, obscene, suggestive or offensive word or phrase. Entry form and fees, payable to Poetry Contest, Lincoln College, must be postmarked no later than May 31." Winning poems are published in **The Denny Poems**, a biennial anthology, available for $4 from Lincoln College. Send SASE for entry form.

‡MAURICE ENGLISH POETRY AWARD (III), 2222 Rittenhouse Square, Philadelphia, PA 19103, is presented annually to an author in his or her sixth (or beyond) decade of life for a distinguished book of poems published during the preceding calendar year—$1,000 award and a request for a public reading in Philadelphia at Philadelphia Art Alliance during October. The family of Maurice English gives the award as a tribute to him, a poet whose work did not appear in book form until his 55th year.

THE NORMA EPSTEIN AWARD FOR CREATIVE WRITING (IV-Students, Regional), Registrar, University College, University of Toronto, Toronto, ON M5S 1A1, Canada, phone 416-978-3171, $1,000 every other year to undergraduate or graduate student enrolled in a Canadian university. Deadline May 15 of odd-numbered years. Send SASE for rules.

ERGO!; BUMBERSHOOT (II), Box 9750-0750, Seattle, WA 98109, phone, 206-622-5123, founded 1973, producing director, Louise DiLenge, an annual publication *ERGO!* is issued in conjunction with *Bumbershoot* a multi-arts festival at the Seattle Center on Labor Day weekend. "Fifteen hundred will be published for distribution prior to and at the Festival. Included will be selected works by the Writers-in-Performance invitational participants and winners of the Written Works Competitions in addition to the official literary arts program schedule." Six honoraria will be awarded for written works. Poets and writers must submit a book, chapbook or typewritten manuscript. Considers simultaneous submissions. Deadline for application is mid-February. For application forms and further details write *Bumbershoot* at the address above. *ERGO!* **sample available for $5 postpaid. Competition guidelines available with a SASE.**

EUROPEAN POETRY LIBRARY; EUROPEAN POETRY TRANSLATION PRIZE; EUROPEAN COMPETITION FOR COMPOSITION IN MUSIC AND POETRY (IV-Translation, Form, Regional), European Poetry Library, Blijde Inkomststraat 9, B-3000, Louvain, Belgium. Every third year the European Poetry Translation Prize of 5,000 ecus is awarded to a published book of translated poetry (second prize will be in 1991). Also every third year (next in 1992), there are prizes in several categories (40,000-50,000 BF) awarded to composers in the 12 member states of the European Community for setting to music published or unpublished poems in the language of one of those states. Both projects are supported by the European commission of the European communities.

FEDERATION INTERNATIONALE DES TRADUCTEURS; CARL-BERTIL NATHHORST TRANSLATION PRIZE; ASTRID LINDGREN TRANSLATION PRIZE (IV-Translation), Heiveldstraat 245, B-9110 Ghent, Belgium, or, for American applicants: American Translators Association, 109 Croton Ave., Ossining, NY 10562, attn: Rosemary Malia. The Carl-Bertil Nathhorst prize is awarded once every 3 years for "promoting translation, improving the quality thereof and drawing attention to the role of the translator in bringing the people of the world together." The Astrid Lindgren Prize is awarded every 3 years for "promoting the translation of works written for children."

‡FLORIDA STATE WRITING COMPETITION; FLORIDA FREELANCE WRITERS' ASSOCIATION (I), P.O. Box 9844, Fort Lauderdale FL 33310, is an annual contest with categories in free verse and traditional, prizes up to $100 in each category, fees $2/poem for members of the FFWA, $2.50 for others. March 15 deadline.

FOSTER CITY ANNUAL WRITERS' CONTEST (II), F.C. Committee for the Arts, 650 Shell Blvd., Foster City, CA 94404, chairman Ted Lance.Yearly competition in fiction, poetry, children's stories and humor. $5 entry fee, $300 prize in each category. April 1 - August 31. Send SASE for instructions.

FRIENDS OF LITERATURE; ROBERT AND HAZEL FERGUSON MEMORIAL AWARD (IV-Regional), %Mabel Munger, 300 N. State St., Chicago IL 60610, phone 312-321-1459, is a $200 annual award for a book of poetry published by a recognized trade publisher by poets who have some connection with Chicago. Submit 2 copies of books by January 15.

LEWIS GALANTIERE PRIZE (IV-Translation), American Translators Association, 109 Croton Ave., Ossining, NY 10562, $500 awarded in even-numbered years for promising works in literary translation by new translators. Deadline: June 1, 1991.

GEORGIA STATE POETRY SOCIETY, INC.; BYRON HERBERT REECE NATIONAL AWARDS; THE REACH OF SONG; GEORGIA STATE POETRY SOCIETY NEWSLETTER (I,IV-Anthologies, form), Box 120, Epworth, GA 30541. The society sponsors a number of contests open to all poets, described in their quarterly *Newsletter* (membership $15/year) and sponsors an annual anthology, **The Reach of Song**. The Byron Herbert Reece International Awards have prizes of $250, $100, $50, $25, $15, and $10. Entry fee: $5, first poem, $1 each additional. Deadline, January 15. SASE for guidelines. Sample newsletter $2; **Reach of Song**, $7.50.

GOETHE PRIZE OF THE CITY OF FRANKFURT (V), %Amt Für Wissensehaft und Kunst Brückenstrabe 3-7, 6,000 Frankfurt am Main 70, West Germany, an award of DM 50,000 every three years to a writer whose creative work has shown a continuation of Goethe's ideas and thoughts, by nomination only.

GREAT LAKES COLLEGES ASSOCIATION NEW WRITERS' AWARDS (III), %Paul Loukides, Director, English Dept., Albion, MI 49224, one in fiction and one in poetry, are given each year to a writer whose first book has been published in the previous year. The author is committed to visiting several of the 12 GLCA colleges, receiving transportation costs and living costs and an honorarium of at least $200 from each, giving a public reading and participating in promotional activities. Applications are by publishers, each of whom may submit four copies of only one book for each award. Past winners include Clark Blaise, Louise Erdrich, Andrew Hudgins, Collette Inez, Charles Dickinson, Charlie Smith, and Gabrielle Burton.

GROLIER POETRY PRIZE; GROLIER POETRY PEACE PRIZE; ELLEN LA FORGE MEMORIAL POETRY FOUNDATION, INC. (II, IV-Themes), 6 Plympton St., Cambridge MA 02138. The Grolier Poetry Prize is open to all poets who have not published either a vanity, small press, trade, or chapbook of poetry. Two poets receive an honorarium of $150 each. Four poems by each winner and two by each of four runners-up are chosen for publication in the *Grolier Poetry Prize Annual*. Submit 7-10 poems, not more than 15 double-spaced pages. Opens January 1st of each year; deadline March 15. The Grolier Peace Prize of $500 is for "the poem [published or unpublished] that best raises the consciousness and understanding of the danger of nuclear weapons and the importance of international arms control," opens April 20, awarded in September. MS not to exceed 5 pages. For both contests: submit one MS in duplicate, without name of poet. On a separate sheet give name, address, phone, and titles of poems. $5 entry fee for either contest, checks payable to the Ellen La Forge Memorial Poetry Foundation, Inc. Enclose self-address stamped postcard if acknowledgement of receipt is required.

GUGGENHEIM FELLOWSHIPS (III), John Simon Guggenheim Foundation, 90 Park Ave., New York, NY 10016. Approximately 170 Guggenheims are awarded each year to persons who have already demonstrated unusual capacity for productive scholarship or unusual creative ability in the arts. The amounts of the grants vary. The average grant is about $26,500. Application deadline October 1.

HACKNEY LITERARY AWARDS; BIRMINGHAM-SOUTHERN WRITER'S CONFERENCE (II), Birmingham-Southern College, Box A-3, Birmingham, AL 35254. This competition, sponsored by the Cecil Hackney family since 1969, offers $2,000 in prizes for poetry and short stories as part of the annual Birmingham-Southern Writer's Conference. Poems with a maximum of 50 lines must be postmarked by December 31; only original, unpublished manuscripts may be entered. Winners are announced at the conference, which is held in March.

W.H. HEINEMANN PRIZE; THE ROYAL SOCIETY OF LITERATURE (III), 1 Hyde Park Gardens, London W2 2LT England, is given each year to a book published in English (and not a translation). "The purpose of the bequest is the encouragement of genuine contributions to literature. The Testator, however, wished the Committee to give preference to those publications which are less likely to command big sales—e.g., poetry, biography, criticism, philosophy, history—though novels, if of sufficient distinction, will not be overlooked." They are especially interested in the work of younger authors who are not yet widely recognized. Publishers should submit books by October 31.

HIGH TIDE POETRY CONTEST (I), 5 Broad St., Milford, CT 06460. SASE for details.

CLARENCE L. HOLTE LITERARY PRIZE (IV-Ethnic), Schomburg Center for Research in Black Culture, The New York Public Library, The Phelps Stoke Fund, 515 Malcolm X Blvd., New York, NY 10037, $7,500 awarded every other year to a living writer "for an original published work linking the cultural heritage of African peoples with the African diaspora in the new world." The award is made by a jury of scholars of international reputation. The next award is to be given November 1990. For further information call (212)862-4141.

HENRY HOYNS FELLOWSHIPS (II), Dept. of English, University of Virginia, Charlottesville, VA 22903, are 6 fellowships (3 poetry, 3 fiction) with stipends of $9,600 each for candidates for the M.F.A. in creative writing. Deadline February 15. Sample poems/prose required with application.

IMAGE (IV-Regional), Seattle Arts Commission, 305 Harrison St., Seattle, WA 98109, contact Linda Knudsen for *Image* and Individual Arts Program. SAC "is accepting previously unpublished poetry, short fiction and essays by professional Northwest writers for inclusion in *Image*, SAC's annual literary supplement to its monthly newsletter, **Seattle Arts**, circulated to more than 8,500 readers and made available at various distribution points around Seattle. A 4-member selection panel will review the applications, including writing samples and resumes. Each selected writer will receive $100 for the first publication rights to the work and will retain copyright. The written works published in *Image* will be highlighted by original graphic designs." Submit maximum of 5 poems, each no more than 100 lines, in 4 copies without author's name—name, address, and title of each work on separate sheet.

INTERNATIONAL READING ASSOCIATION CHILDREN'S BOOK AWARDS (IV-Children), % Walter Barbe, 823 Church St., Honesdale, PA 18431, $1,000 given annually to two authors whose 1st or 2nd book published during the calendar year shows unusual promise for a career in children's literature. Two categories: Younger readers (ages 4-10), and older readers (ages 10-16+). Send 10 copies to Walter Barbe.

IOWA ARTS COUNCIL LITERARY AWARDS (IV-Regional), State Capitol Complex, Des Moines, IA 50319, of $1,000 and $500, for an unpublished poem or group of poems, of 50-150 lines by a legal resident of Iowa. January 15 deadline.

IRISH-AMERICAN CULTURAL INSTITUTE LITERARY AWARDS (IV-Ethnic/foreign language), Box 5026, 2115 Summit Ave., St. Paul, MN 55105, for Irish writers who write in Irish or English, **resident in Ireland,** with published work. A total of $10,000 in prizes awarded every other year.

ITALIAN CULTURAL CENTRE SOCIETY; F.G. BRESSANI LITERARY PRIZE (IV-Ethnic), 3075 Slocan St., Vancouver, BC V5M 3E4 Canada, phone 604-430-3337. The F. G. Bressani Prize, offered every other year, $500 in two categories (poetry and fiction) to the "best books written from a viewpoint of any of Canada's ethnic minority groups; written in English or French; and authored by a Canadian citizen or landed immigrant." The Society also offers other awards.

JOHANN-HEINRICH-VOSS PRIZE FOR TRANSLATION (V), German Academy for Language and Literature, Alexandraweg 23, D-6100 Darmstadt, West Germany, is an annual award of DM 15,000 for outstanding lifetime achievement for translating into German, by nomination only.

THE CHESTER H. JONES FOUNDATION NATIONAL POETRY COMPETITION (II), Box 498, Chardon, OH 44024, an annual competition for persons in the USA, Canadian and American citizens living abroad. Prizes: $1,000, $500, $250, and $50 honorable mentions. Winning poems plus others called "commendations" are published in a chapbook available for $3.50 from the foundation. Entry fee $1/ poem, no more than 10 entries, no more than 32 lines each. Deadline March 31. Distinguished poets serve as judges.

KENTUCKY STATE POETRY SOCIETY (I), % R. Franklin Pate, 5018 Wabash Pl., Louisville, KY 40214, offers an annual contest with 40 categories and over $1,500 in prizes. Deadline July 10. Various forms and subjects; 32 line limit. Open to all. $1 fee in most categories. Prizes from $5 to $75, 1st prize winners published in *Pegasus*. "Do not submit without sending a SASE for contest sheet. We do *not* return MS."

LOUISA KERN AWARD (II, IV-Regional), Creative Writing Office, GN-30, University of Washington, Seattle, WA 98195, $1,900 (may be shared by two writers) to assist a literary endeavor. Preference is given to writers from or living in the Pacific Northwest. Submit up to 25 pp., typed, single-spaced, by April 1.

D. H. LAWRENCE FELLOWSHIP (III), University of New Mexico, Albuquerque, NM 87131, chair, Scott P. Sanders, offers a creative writer a 3 month summer residence on the Lawrence Ranch near Taos, NM, and a $1,250 stipend. Application fee: $10. Deadline: January 31 annually.

THE STEPHEN LEACOCK MEDAL FOR HUMOUR (IV-Humor, regional), Mrs. Jean Bradley Dickson, Award Chairman, Stephen Leacock Associates, Box 854, Orillia, ON L3V 3P4 Canada, phone 705-325-6546, for a book of humour (can be verse) by a Canadian citizen. Submit 10 copies of book, 8x10 b/w photo, bio, and $25 entry fee. Deadline for entry December 31 each year.

THE LEAGUE OF MINNESOTA POETS CONTEST (I, IV-Members, students), % Susan S. Chambers, RR #2, Box 86, Good Thunder, MN 56037, offers 14 different contests in a variety of categories and prizes of $5-75 for poems up to 60 lines, fees of $2 to enter all categories for members and $1 per category for non-members. There is one category for students, grades 6 through 12. July 31 deadline. Winners are not published. Write for details.

‡**LEEK ARTS FESTIVAL INTERNATIONAL POETRY COMPETITION (I, II)**, 44 Rudyard Rd., Biddulph Moor, Stoke-on-Trent ST8 7JN U.K., annual, with prizes of £1,000, £500, 5 of £100 and 5 annual subscriptions to *Prospice* (see publisher's listing), fees £2 per poem (or $5 U.S.). Deadline April 30. No longer than 40 lines. Submit anonymously, name and address on cover sheet. Make checks payable to Leek Arts Festival. IRCs for prize winners.

THE LOFT-MCKNIGHT WRITERS' AWARDS (IV-Regional), 2301 E. Franklin Ave., Minneapolis, MN 55406, will distribute $80,000 in grants to Minnesota poets and creative writers. Applicants must be state residents for at least 1 year prior to applying. Writers who have received grants in literature totaling $12,000 or more over the 2 years prior to applying are not eligible. Writers should send SASE for guidelines.

MACARTHUR FELLOWS (V), John D.and Catherine T. MacArthur Foundation, Suite 700, 140 S. Dearborn St., Chicago, IL 60603. An anonymous committee selects individuals to whom the foundation awards large grants.

MAPLECON SF; FANTASY WRITING COMPETITION (IV-Themes, science fiction/fantasy), %Madona Skaff, Literary Coordinator, 2105 Thistle Crescent, Ottawa, ON K1H 5P4 Canada, no fee. "Total length (1 or more poems) 12-200 lines. Open to anyone regardless of status as a writer. Entry must be based on a science, science fiction or fantasy theme. Please, no resubmissions from previous years." Deadline is in June. Awards (certificates and varying prizes) are made at Maplecon, the Ottawa Regional Science Fiction/Fantasy Convention in July (or mailed to those not present). Please include SASE with all correspondence.

MASSACHUSETTS ARTISTS FELLOWSHIP PROGRAM (IV-Regional), The Artists Foundation, Inc., 8 Park Plaza, Boston, MA 02116, fellowships of $10,000 to poets and other artists who are residents of Massachusetts over 18, not students.

MASSACHUSETTS STATE POETRY SOCIETY NATIONAL POETRY DAY CONTEST (I), %Jeanette C. Maes, 64 Harrison Ave., Lynn, MA 09105, offers prizes of $5-25 in 8 categories. Fee: $3 covers entries in as many of 9 categories as poet wishes to enter. Send SASE for rules. Deadline September 1.

MID-SOUTH POETRY FESTIVAL (I, IV-Regional), P.O. Box 11188, Memphis, TN 38111, holds an annual poetry festival first weekend in October. Contests deadline in September. There are 24 to 30 categories with cash prizes, and other awards totaling approximately $1,500. Eligibility may vary; however, many contests for all poets anywhere; many for Mid-South area poets. Entry fees may vary. Poetry Society of Tennessee is Festival Sponsor with co-sponsorship by other Mid-South poetry societies. Send SASE for contest rules and information. Brochure will be sent in June or July.

‡MILFORD FINE ARTS COUNCIL NATIONAL POETRY CONTEST (I,II), 5 Broad St., Milford CT 06460. SASE for details.

MONTANA INSTITUTE OF THE ARTS WRITERS CONTESTS; MARY BRENNEN CLAPP MEMORIAL AWARD (IV-Regional, membership), P.O. Box 1872, Bozeman MT 59771, holds two annual contests with a March 31st deadline. One is for all Montana poets, for unpublished poems up to 100 lines, in a group of three, no fee, for the Mary Brennen Clapp Memorial Award of $50 and prizes of $40, $30, and $20. Must submit 3 poems. The other is for members of the institute with categories in traditional, modern, haiku, doggeral/cowboy, and limerick, with awards of $25, $10, and $5 in each category, fee $1 per poem. March 31 deadline. Send SASE for guidelines.

JENNY MCKEAN MOORE FUND FOR WRITERS, (III), Dept. of English, George Washington University, Washington, D.C. 20052, provides for a Visiting Lecturer in creative writing for about $31,000 for 2 semesters. Apply by November 1 with 3 letters of recommendation, resume, and writing sample of 25 pp. or less.

NASHVILLE NEWSLETTER POETRY CONTEST (I), P.O. Box 60535, Nashville, TN 37206-0535, Roger Dale Miller, Editor/Publisher. Founded 1977. Reporting time 6-10 weeks. Published quarterly. Sample copy $3. Any style or subject up to 40 lines. One unpublished poem to a page with name, address in upper left corner. Entry fee of $5 for up to 3 poems. Must be sent all at once. Prizes of $50, $25, and $10 with at least 50 Certificates of Merit.

NATIONAL ENDOWMENT FOR THE ARTS; FELLOWSHIPS FOR CREATIVE ARTISTS; FELLOWSHIPS FOR TRANSLATORS (III), Literature Program, 1100 Pennsylvania Ave. NW, Washington, DC 20506. The Fellowships for Creative Artists comprise the largest program for individual grants available for American poets (and other writers and artists). Dozens of awards of $20,000 are made each year to poets who have published a book or at least 20 poems in magazines in the last 10 years. Decisions are made solely on the quality of the submitted material by a panel of distinguished writers. Guidelines available September of each year. They also offer grants of up to $10,000 to nonprofit organizations to support residencies for published writers of poetry, Fellowships for Translators ($10,000 or $20,000), and other programs to assist publishers and promoters of poetry. Write for complete guidelines.

‡NATIONAL LEAGUE OF AMERICAN PENWOMEN (ALEXANDRIA BRANCH) POETRY CONTEST (I), Box 398, Annandale, VA 22003, annually, offering $100 worth of prizes in each of 6 categories for unpublished poems, 40-line limit. Submit 2 copies. Fee: $1 per poem. Deadline August 1.

NATIONAL LIBRARY OF POETRY (I, IV-Anthology), 5-E Gwynns Mill Ct., Box 704-Z, Owings Mills, MD 21117, twice a year offers a contest with a total of $3,000 in prizes ($1,000 grand prize) and publication in an anthology for poems of up to 20 lines. See the write-up for American Poetry Association for an explanation of this type of contest/anthology. NLP's advertising states, "There are no entry fees, no subsidy payments, and no purchase of any kind required," but you probably have to buy a copy of the anthology if you want to own one with your poem in it. Deadlines June 30 and December 30.

NATIONAL POETRY SERIES ANNUAL OPEN COMPETITION (II, III), 26 W. 17th St., New York, NY 10011, between January 1 and February 15 considers book-length (approximately 48-64 pp.) MSS, entry fee $15. Manuscripts will not be returned. The five winners are published by participating small press, university press, and trade publishers. Send SASE for complete submissions procedures.

NATIONAL WRITERS CLUB ANNUAL POETRY CONTEST (I), Suite 620, 1450 S. Havana, Aurora, CO 80012, award director James L. Young, an annual contest with prizes of $100, $50, $25 and $10 plus honorable mentions. Entry fee $6/poem; additional fee charged if poem is longer than 40 lines. Deadline June 8. All subjects and forms are acceptable.

WOULD YOU USE THE SAME CALENDAR YEAR AFTER YEAR?

Of course not! If you scheduled your appointments using last year's calendar, you'd risk missing important meetings and deadlines, so you keep up-to-date with a new calendar each year. Just like your calendar, *Poet's Market*® changes every year, too. Many of the publishers move, contact names change, and even the publishers' needs change from the previous year. You can't afford to use an out-of-date book to plan your marketing efforts!

So save yourself the frustration of getting submissions returned in the mail, stamped MOVED: ADDRESS UNKNOWN. And of NOT submitting your work to new listings because you don't know they exist. **Make sure you have the most current marketing information by ordering *1992 Poet's Market* today.** All you have to do is complete the attached post card and return it with your payment or charge card information. Order now, and there's one thing that won't change from your *1991 Poet's Market* — the price! That's right, we'll send you the 1992 edition for just $19.95. *1992 Poet's Market* will be published and ready for shipment in September 1991.

Let an old acquaintance be forgot, and toast the new edition of *Poet's Market*. Order today!

(See other side for more books by Judson Jerome)

- -

To order, drop this postpaid card in the mail.

❏ **YES!** I want the most current edition of *Poet's Market*.® Please send me the 1992 edition at the 1991 price — $19.95.* (NOTE: *1992 Poet's Market* will be ready for shipment in September 1991.) #10208
Also send me:
_____ (1836) The Poet's Handbook, $10.95* (available NOW)
_____ (10123) On Being A Writer, $19.95* (available NOW)
Plus postage & handling: $3.00 for one book, $1.00 for each additional book. Ohio residents add 5½% sales tax.
❏ Payment enclosed (Slip this card and your payment into an envelope)
❏ Please charge my: ☐ Visa   ☐ MasterCard

Account # _____ Exp. Date _____

Signature _____

Name _____

Address _____

City _____ State _____ Zip _____

(This offer expires August 1, 1992.)

1507 Dana Avenue
Cincinnati, OH 45207

5776

MORE BOOKS FOR POETS

The Poet's Handbook
by Judson Jerome
Here's expert instruction on how to use figurative language, symbols, and concrete images; how to tune your ear to sound relationships; the requirements for lyric, narrative, dramatic, didactic, and satirical poetry. 244 pages/$10.95, paperback

On Being a Writer
edited by Bill Strickland
Conversational, inspirational, and thought-provoking, this book is a wonderful collection of dialogue, essays and advice from 31 of the greatest writers of our time. Nikki Giovanni and others share tidbits of information and solid technical advice on writing, plus a compelling "inside" look at their writing preferences and passions.
224 pages/32 b&w illus./$19.95

Use coupon on other side to order today!

‡NATIONAL WRITERS' UNION ANNUAL NATIONAL POETRY COMPETITION (II), Box 2409, Aptos, CA 95001, phone 408-427-2950 or 659-4536. See National Writers' Union listing under organizations. The Santa Cruz/Monterey Local 7 chapter at this address sponsors an annual competition with entry fee: $3 per poem; prizes of $150, $100, and $50, with prominent poets as judges. Send SASE for rules beginning in February.

NEUSTADT INTERNATIONAL PRIZE FOR LITERATURE; WORLD LITERATURE TODAY (V), University of Oklahoma, Room 110, 630 Parrington Oval, Norman, OK 73019, $25,000 given every other year in recognition of life achievement or to a writer whose work is still in progress, nominations from an international jury only.

NEVADA POETRY SOCIETY ANNUAL CONTEST (I), P.O. Box 5741, Reno, NV 89513, award director Lorraine Caraway. This contest offers cash awards in several categories. Please send a SASE for exact details. Entries must be received by September 1. Winning poems are read at the October meeting of the Nevada Poetry Society.

NEW ENGLAND POETRY CLUB; DANIEL VAROUJAN AWARD; FIRMAN HOUGHTON AWARD; NORMA FARBER AWARD; BARBARA BRADLEY AWARD; ROSALIE BOYLE PRIZE; ERIKA MUMFORD PRIZE (I), 2 Farrar St., Cambridge, MA 02138. The contests sponsored by New England Poetry Club have a $2/poem fee for non-members (free to members), all with a June 30th deadline, all "judged by well-known poets." The Varoujan Award of $500 is for a poem "worthy of Daniel Varoujan, an Armenian poet killed by the Turks in 1915." The Firman Houghton Award is $250 (named for a former NEPC president); the Norma Farber Award is $100 for a sonnet or sonnet series; the Rosalie Boyle Prize of $100 is for a poem over 30 lines; the Erika Mumford Prize for a poem of exotic or faraway setting is $250; and the Barbara Bradley Award of $200 for a lyric poem under 21 lines written by a woman. Poems should be sent in duplicate with name of writer on one to Lois Ames, NEPC Contests, 285 Marlboro Road, Sudbury MA 01776, before June 30th annually.

NEW YORK FOUNDATION FOR THE ARTS (IV-Regional), 5 Beekman St., New York, NY 10038, annually offers a fellowship of $7,000 for poets who are at least 18 and have resided in New York State for the 2 years prior to application. Submit up to 15 pages of poetry (at least 2 poems), 3 copies of a one-page resume, and support material by September 4. No SASE.

NORDMANNS-FORBUNDET (NORSEMEN'S FEDERATION) (IV-Translation), Radhusgt. 23b, N-0158 Oslo 1, Norway, phone 02/42 75 14 or 02/42 23 76, FAX 02/33 32 26, information officer Mrs. Dina Tolfsby. The Nordmanns-Forbundet, in its desire to make Norwegian culture known abroad, awards an annual grant (maximum 15,000 Norwegian crowns) to one or more publishing houses introducing Norwegian fiction or poetry in translation (preferably contemporary). Application deadline is March 1 of each calendar year with winners announced later in the spring. Payment is made at the time of publication.

NORTH CAROLINA HAIKU SOCIETY INTERNATIONAL CONTEST (IV-Form), Rebecca Rust contest manager, 326 Golf Course Dr., Raleigh, NC 27610. Haiku in English. Maximum of 5 haiku; $1 entry fee for each haiku. Prizes: $50, $25, $15, $10, and $10. Deadline in hand is December 31. Entrants should send a SASE for copy of rules.

‡THE NORTH CAROLINA POETRY SOCIETY, ZOE KINCAID BROCKMAN MEMORIAL BOOK AWARD CONTEST (IV-Regional), %Leon Hinton, 4618 N. NC 62, Burlington, NC 27217, is an annual contest for a book of poetry (over 20 pages) by a North Carolina poet (native-born or current resident for three years). Send SASE for details. $200 cash prize and Revere-style bowl awarded in 1990.

‡OHIOANA BOOK AWARDS; OHIOANA KROUT MEMORIAL AWARD FOR POETRY (IV-Regional), Ohioana Library Association, 65 S. Front St., Rm. 1105, Columbus, OH 43215. Ohioana Book Awards given yearly to outstanding books published each year. Up to 6 awards may be given for books (including books of poetry) by authors born in Ohio or who have lived in Ohio for at least 5 years, and the Ohioana Poetry Award (with the same residence requirements), made possible by a bequest of Helen Krout, of $1,000 is given yearly "to an individual whose body of work has made, and continues to make, a significant contribution to the poetry of Ohio, and through whose work as a writer, teacher, administrator, or in community service, interest in poetry has been developed." Nominations to be received by December 31.

OREGON INDIVIDUAL ARTISTS FELLOWSHIPS (IV-Regional), Oregon Arts Commission, 835 Summer St. NE, Salem, OR 97301, are $3,000 awards granted in even years (e.g., 1990, 1992) to a resident of Oregon. "Emphasis is on the poet's body of work and potential as a professional writer. It is not a poetry contest." Submit up to 30 pp. with application form and documentation between March and September 1, 1992 (or in subsequent even years).

NATALIE ORNISH POETRY AWARD; TEXAS INSTITUTE OF LETTERS (IV-Regional), % James Hoggard, Dept. of English, Midwestern State University, Wichita Falls, TX 76308-2099. The Texas Institute of Letters gives annual awards for books by Texas authors in 8 categories, including a $1,000 award for best volume of poetry. Books must have been first published in the year in question, and entries may be made by authors or by their publishers; deadline January 4 of the following year. One copy of each entry must be mailed to each of three judges, with "information showing an author's Texas association . . . if [it] is not otherwise obvious." Poets must have been in Texas, have spent formative years there, or currently reside in the state. Write for complete instructions.

‡OTTAWA-CARLETON BOOK AWARD (IV-Regional), Carol Sage, Arts Advisory Board, Regional Municipality of Ottawa-Carleton, 222 Queen St., 14th Floor, Ottawa, ON KIP 5Z3 Canada, awarded annually to residents of the Ottawa-Carleton Region, deadline January 15.

P.A.L.S. CLUB NEWSLETTER CONTESTS; POEM AND LETTER SOCIETY OF AMERICA (I, IV-Membership), P.O. Box 60535, Nashville, TN 37206-0535, founded 1988, offers 2-4 poetry contests per year, with $5 fee for non-members for up to 3 poems, prizes of at least $50, $25, and $10 and at least 50 Certificates of Merit. Membership is $20 a year. Members pay no entry fees for contests and receive the newsletter free.

PENNSYLVANIA POETRY SOCIETY ANNUAL CONTEST; WINE AND ROSES POETRY CONTEST; PEGASUS CONTEST FOR STUDENTS; THE ANIMAL KINGDOM CONTEST; SAMUEL FREIBERG MEMORIAL AWARD; LOTTIE KENT RUHL MEMORIAL AWARD (I, IV-Members), 623 N. 4th St., Reading, PA 19601, award director Dr. Dorman John Grace. The deadline for the society's annual contest, which has 11 categories open to nonmembers and 4 to members only, is January 15. Grand prize in category 1 (open) will be $100 in 1991; prizes in other categories range from $10-25, plus publication. Entry fees are $1.50/poem for nonmembers except for the grand prize, which requires an entry fee of $2/poem for everybody. For information regarding the Pennsylvania Poetry Society Contest contact Dr. Dorman John Grace (same address as above). The Wine and Roses poetry contest, sponsored by the Wallace Stevens Chapter for unpublished poems in serious and light verse, has prizes of $50, $25, and $15 plus publication and telecast; entry fee $1/poem; deadline June 1; write to Dr. Dorman John Grace. For information about the Pegasus Contest for Students, write to Anne Pierre Spangler, Contest Chairman, 1685 Christian Dr., R.D. #2, Lebanon, PA 17042. For information about the Animal Kingdom Contest, the Samuel Freiberg Memorial Award, and the Lottie Kent Ruhl Memorial Award, write to Kay M. Freiberg, Contest Chairman, 40 Meadowbrook Rd., Carlisle, PA 17013. Deadline, December 31. In each category are awards of $20, $15, and $10, fee $1 per poem.

‡POETIC PERSPECTIVE, INC. (I), 110 Onieda St., Waxahachie, TX, 75165, founded in 1989 by Pat Haley, editor. Several poetry contests each year with $3 per poem entry fee, prizes of $50, $25, and $10. Up to 35 lines, maximum of 60 characters and spaces per line. SASE for themes and guidelines.

‡POETRY ARTS PROJECT (IV-Political, social), United Resource Press, 4521 Campus Dr., #388, Irvine, CA 92715, holds an annual contest, March 31 deadline, for poems on political and social issues, with prizes of "possible publication and definite prizes in U.S. Savings Bonds of various denominations," $3 per poem jury fee. "Absolutely must send SASE to receive entry form. Poetry will not be returned if it is a winner."

POETRY OF HOPE AWARD (II, IV-Themes, Youth), P.O. Box 21077, Piedmont, CA 94620, awarded annually, $200 first prize ($100 for junior division), December 30 deadline, is for a poem up to 100 lines expressing "the spirit of hope" using inspirational themes. Themes should speak to the "healing" of social problems (i.e. war/peace, human rights, the homeless, the earth/ecology, etc., within the human condition). Hope for all that is possible—for the highest good, for all of humankind, and for all of creation. Application needed. No fee. Send SASE.

POETRY SOCIETY OF MICHIGAN ANNUAL COMPETITIONS; THE PSM OPEN; PSM POETRY CONTEST FOR YOUNG PEOPLE; THE KENNETH HEAFIELD CONTEST FOR YOUNG ADULTS (I, IV-Children), 401 Cottage St., Olivet MI 49076; awards director Gwendolyn Niles, 1218 State St., St. Joseph MI 49085. The Annual Competition (11 categories) has awards of up to $35 plus publication, fee for non-members $1/entry; for members, $1 for all 11 categories. The PSM Past Presidents Award category permits previously published poems. Deadline: November 15. The PSM Open has awards of $100, $30, and $20, and permits previously published poems, fee $2/poem for all entrants. Deadline: November 15. The PSM Poetry Contest for Young People has awards in 3 categories of $10 and 2 of $5, plus publication, no entry fee, deadline November 15. The Heafield Prize is $50, no fee, deadline November 15. Send SASE for guidelines. Sample copies of *Peninsula Poets*: $4; include SASE for society information.

‡POETRY SOCIETY OF TEXAS (I, IV-Membership), Corresponding Secretary Faye Carr Adams, 4244 Skillman, Dallas, TX 75206, offers 90 contests, prizes $25-350, some open to non-members for a fee of $2 per poem, awards at an annual Awards Dinner. Send SASE (business size envelope) for rules booklet.

POETS AND PATRONS, INC.; ANNUAL CHICAGOLAND CONTESTS; INTERNATIONAL NARRATIVE CONTEST (II, IV-Regional, form), The Annual Chicagoland Contests, Carol Spelius, Chairman, 373 Ramsay Road, Deerfield IL 60015 are open to all poets residing within 60 miles of Chicago. Send SASE for rules after March 1. One $3 registration fee for 20 contests in various categories with prizes of $25 and $10 in each, prizes of $75 and $25 for 2 poems judged best of 1st Prize winners and $25 and $15 to 2 judged best of the 2nd Prize winners. Deadline August 1. The International Narrative contest (Chairman Constance Vogel, 1206 Hutchings Avenue, Glenview, IL 60025) is open to all. Send SASE after March 1 for rules, deadline Sept. 1 (postmark), no entry fee, prizes of $75 and $25.

POETS CLUB OF CHICAGO INTERNATIONAL SHAKESPEAREAN SONNET CONTEST (II, IV-Form), Chairman June Shipley, 2930 Franklin St., Highland, IN 46322. Contest has a deadline of September 1st (postmark). Write for rules, include SASE, not earlier than March. No entry fee. Prizes of $50, $35, and $15.

POETS' DINNER CONTEST (IV-Regional), 2214 Derby St., Berkeley, CA 94705. Since 1926 there has been an annual awards banquet sponsored by the ad hoc Poets' Dinner Committee; usually at Spenger's Fish Grotto (a Berkeley Landmark). Three typed copies of poems in not more than three of the eight categories are submitted anonymously without fee (January 15 deadline), and the winning poems (grand prize, 1st, 2nd, 3rd, and honorable mentions in 8 categories) are read at the banquet. **Contestant must be present to win.** Prizes awarded cash; honorable mention, books. The event is nonprofit.

POETS OF THE VINEYARD CONTEST (I), %Winnie E. Fitzpatrick, P.O. Box 77, Kenwood, CA 95452, an annual contest sponsored by the Sonoma County Chapter (PofV) of the California Federation of Chaparral Poets with entries in 7 categories: A) traditional forms, (32 line maximum); B) free verse, 16 lines or less; C) free verse, 17-32 lines; D) light or humorous (32 line maximum); E) short verse (maximum of 12 lines); F) haiku/senryu and tanka; G) theme poem on grapes, vineyards, wine, viticulture (32 line maximum). Submit 2 copies, 1 with identification; category in upper right-hand corner. Prizes in each category are $20, $15, and $10, with a grand prize chosen from category winners ($50). Deadline February 1, entry fee $2/poem. Prize winning poems will be published in the annual **Winners Anthology**.

POETS RENDEZVOUS CONTEST; INDIANA STATE FEDERATION OF POETRY CLUBS (I), % Paula Fehn, 3302 Bellemeade Avenue, Evansville, IN 47715, The Poets Rendezvous Contest offers $715 in prizes for poems in 17 categories, $5 fee covers 17 categories in different forms and subjects, September 1 deadline. The Indiana State Federation of Poetry Clubs also has contest with January 15 and July 15 deadlines for poems no longer than 1 page, $1/poem fee, prizes of $25, 15, and 10 with 10 honorable mentions.

‡THE E.J. PRATT GOLD MEDAL AND PRIZE FOR POETRY (IV-Student), Office of Student Awards, University of Toronto, Toronto, ON M5T 2Z9 Canada, to a full- or part-time graduate or undergraduate student for a poem or suite of poems of approximately 100 lines. Entries are submitted under a pseudonym with information on the poet's identity in a separate envelope. Deadline in March.

PRESIDIO LA BAHIA AWARD; SUMMERFIELD G. ROBERTS AWARD (IV-Regional), Sons of the Republic of Texas, 5942 Abrams Rd., Suite 222, Dallas, TX 75231. Both may be awarded for poetry. The Presidio La Bahia Award is an annual award or awards (depending upon the number and quality of entries) for writing that promotes research into and preservation of the Spanish Colonial influence on Texas culture. $2,000 is available, with a minimum first prize of $1,200. Entries must be in quadruplicate and will not be returned. Deadline September 30. The Summerfield G. Roberts Award, available to U.S. citizens, is an annual award of $2,500 for a book or manuscript depicting or representing the Republic of Texas (1836-46), written or published during the calendar year for which the award is given. Entries must be submitted in quintuplicate and will not be returned. Deadline January 15.

PULITZER PRIZE IN LETTERS (III), % Secretary of the Pulitzer Prize Board, 702 Journalism, Columbia University, New York, NY 10027, offers 5 prizes of $3,000 each year, including one in poetry, for books published in the calendar year preceding the award. Submit 4 copies of published books (or galley proofs if book is being published after November), photo, bio, entry form and $20 entry fee. July 1 deadline for books published between January 1 and June 30; November 1 deadline for books published between July 1 and December 30.

REDWOOD ACRES FAIR POETRY CONTEST (I), Box 6576, Eureka, CA 95502, offers an annual contest with various categories for both juniors and seniors with entry fee of 50¢ per poem for the junior contests and $1 per poem for the senior contests, May 30 deadline.

MARY ROBERTS RINEHART FOUNDATION AWARD (III), %Roger Lathbury, Mary Roberts Rinehart Fund, English Dept., George Mason University, 4400 University Dr., Fairfax, VA 22030. Two grants are made annually to writers who need financial assistance "to complete work definitely projected." The amount of the award depends upon income the fund generates; the 1989 amount will be around $950 in each category. Grants in fiction and poetry are given in even-numbered years, those in drama and nonfiction in odd numbered years. A writer's work must be nominated by an established author or editor; no written recommendations are necessary. Nominations must be accompanied by a sample of the nominee's work, up to 25 pp. of poetry and 30 pp. of fiction. Deadline: November 30.

THE ROBERTS FOUNDATION WRITING AWARDS (II, IV-Anthologies), Box 1868, Pittsburg, KS 66762, an annual competition, deadline September 1, for poetry, short fiction, and essays. The poetry prizes are $500, $200, and $100, fee $5 for up to 5 poems, $1 for each additional poem. Winners appear in an annual anthology that you may purchase for $3. Send SASE for guidelines and entry form.

ANNA DAVIDSON ROSENBERG AWARD (IV-Ethnic), Judah L. Magnes Museum, 2911 Russell St., Berkeley, CA 94705, offers prizes of $100, $50, and $25 (honorable mention) for up to 12 pp. of 1-5 poems on the Jewish Experience in English. There is a Youth Commendation along with the prize if a winner is under 19. Deadline August 31 each year. **Do not send poems without entry form; write between April 15 and July 15 for entry form and guidelines (enclose SASE).**

SAN FRANCISCO FOUNDATION; JOSEPH HENRY JACKSON AWARD; JAMES D. PHELAN AWARD (IV-Regional), 685 Market St., Suite 910, San Francisco, CA 94105. The Jackson Award ($2,000), will be made to the author of an unpublished work-in-progress in the form of fiction (novel or short stories), non-fictional prose, or poetry. Applicants must be residents of northern California or Nevada for three consecutive years immediately prior to the deadline date of January 15th, and must be between the ages of 20 through 35 as of the deadline. The Phelan Award ($2,000) will be made to the author of an unpublished work-in-progress in the form of fiction (novel or short stories), non-fictional prose, poetry or drama. Applicants must be California-born (although they may now reside outside of the state), and must be between the ages of 20 through 35 as of the January 15th deadline. MSS for both awards must be accompanied by an application form, which may be obtained by sending a SASE to the above address. Entries are accepted between November, 15 and January 15.

SAN MATEO COUNTY FAIR FINE ARTS COMPETITION (I), Box 1027, San Mateo, CA 94403-0627, phone 415-574-3873, for unpublished poetry. Adult and youth divisions. Write or call for entry form and additional information. Adult Division awards of $100, $50, and $25; fee $6 for 1 poem or $10 for 2. Youth Division awards of $50, $25 and $15; fee $3 for 1 poem or $5 for 2. Limit 2 entries per division. July 6th deadline for poems.

CARL SANDBURG AWARDS (IV-Regional), sponsored by Friends of the Chicago Public Library, 78 E. Washington St., Chicago, IL 60602. Given annually to Chicago-area writers for new books in 4 categories, including poetry. Each author receives $1,000. Publisher or authors should submit two copies of books published between June 1 of one year and May 31 of the next. Deadline: September 1.

SASKATCHEWAN WRITERS GUILD ANNUAL LITERARY AWARDS (IV-Regional), SWG Literary Awards Convenor, Box 3986, Regina, SK S4P 3R9 Canada, offers 3 prizes of $1,000 for long MS (every fourth year for poetry) and 3 prizes of $100 and $50 honorable mentions for 1 poem up to 100 lines. $15 entry fee for long MSS, $4 for single poems. Deadline February 28.

SCHOLASTIC WRITING AWARDS (IV-Teens), Scholastic Inc., 730 Broadway, New York, NY 10003, provide college-bound high school seniors with $100-1,000 grants. Write for rules book between August and December 15.

DELMORE SCHWARTZ MEMORIAL AWARD IN POETRY (V), New York University, College of Arts and Sciences, Washington Square, New York, NY 10003, is offered every 1-3 years to an outstanding young poet, ordinarily one who has published no more than one book or to an older poet whose work has been neglected. Nominations are not accepted. The judges, Theodore Weiss and M. L. Rosenthal, make their choices on the basis of their knowledge of the poetic situation and consultation with one another. The awards given to date have been for $1,000 each. Not to be applied for individually.

‡SCOTTISH INTERNATIONAL OPEN POETRY COMPETITION; THE AYRSHIRE WRITERS' & ARTISTS' SOCIETY, 108 Overtoun Rd., Springside, Irvine, Ayrshire, Scotland, KA11 3BW. Open to all poets, Inaugurated in 1972 it is the longest running poetry competition in the U.K. Entries are free, restricted to two per person and should be accompanied by International Reply Coupons and S.A.E. December deadline. Special award ceremony March. First prize, U.K. Section, MacDiarmid Trophy and $100. First prize, International Section, The International Trophy. Scots Section, The Clement Wilson Cup. Diplomas are awarded to runners up. Competition opens September each year.

SOUTH DAKOTA POETRY SOCIETY CONTESTS (I), Present Chairman of S.D. State Poetry Society Contests Audrae Visser, 710 Elk, Elkton, SD 57026, 10 categories, August 31 deadline.

‡SPARROWGRASS POETRY FORUM (I), Dept. PM, 203 Diamond St., Box 193, Sistersville, WV 26175, offers six annual free contests, each of which has $1,000 in prizes, including a $500 grand prize. Entrants are solicited to buy an anthology. See the listing for American Poetry Association for a discussion of this kind of contest. I list it because the prizes are substantial. You do not have to buy the anthology to win. Contest deadlines are the last day of every other month. Send 1 original poem, no longer than 20 lines. Name and address at the top of the page. Any style, any subject.

WALLACE E. STEGNER FELLOWSHIPS (IV-Young adults), Creative Writing Program, Stanford University, Stanford, CA 94305, 4 in poetry, $9,000 plus tuition of $3,500, for promising young writers who can benefit from 2 years instruction and criticism at the Writing Center. Previous publication not required, though it can strengthen one's application. Deadline January 1.

SYRACUSE UNIVERSITY FELLOWSHIPS IN CREATIVE WRITING; THE CORNELIA WARD FELLOWSHIP (II), Graduate School Admissions, 206 Steele Hall, Syracuse, NY 13244. The Cornelia Ward Fellowship in creative writing carries a stipend of $8,775; three others carry stipends of $6,240; all pay tuition for one year. University Fellowhips are available with stipends of $8,775 and graduate teaching assistantships with stipends of $7,957 to $8,500 and scholarships. All applicants must be candidates for the M.A. degree in Creative Writing. Deadline January 1.

‡THERAFIELDS FOUNDATION CHAPBOOK AWARD (IV-Regional), Therafields Foundation, 316 Dupont St., Toronto, ON M5R 1V9 Canada, $1,000 (Canadian) prize for the best poetry chapbook (10-48 pp.) in English published in Canada in the preceding year. Submit 3 copies by March 31.

TOWSON STATE UNIVERSITY PRIZE FOR LITERATURE; ALICE & FRANKLIN COOLEY ENDOWMENT (IV-Regional), Towson State University, Towson, MD 21204, $1,000 for a book or book MS by a Maryland writer under 40. If published, the book must have appeared within 3 years of application. Award is on the basis of aesthetic excellence. Deadline May 1. Contact for guidelines.

THE TRANSLATORS ASSOCIATION; JOHN FLORIO PRIZE; SCHLEGEL-TIECK PRIZE, SCOTT-MONCRIEFF PRIZE (IV-Translation), 84 Drayton Gardens, London SW 10 9SB, England. These three prizes are all for translation of 20th century literature in books published in the U.K. The John Florio Prize of £900 is for the best translation from Italian, awarded every other year. The annual Schlegel-Tieck Prize of £2,000 is for translation from German. The annual Scott-Moncrieff Prize of £1,500 is for translation from French. Publishers only should submit books before December 31.

LAURA BOWER VAN NUYS CREATIVE WRITING CONTEST (V,I,II), Black Hills Writers Group, 3902 W. Chicago, Rapid City, SD 57702. **"We will be holding the contest in even-numbered years only."** Categories: professional and non-professional. $15, $12, and $10 in each category plus a subscription to *The Writer* for the Best of Show award. Fee: $2 per poem. March deadline.

VIRGINIA PRIZE (IV-Regional), sponsor Virginia Commission for the Arts, administered by Virginia Center for the Creative Arts, Mt. San Angelo, Sweet Briar, VA 24595, award administrator Craig Pleasants. Three annual awards ($10,000, $5,000, and $2,500) for previously unpublished collections of poems, no less than 40 pages, open to Virginia residents only. April 1, postmark deadline. No special format for entry, no entry fees; write for rules.

VOICES OF THE SOUTH CONTEST; SOUTHERN POETRY ASSOCIATION (I), Box 524, Pass Christian, MS 39571. The Southern Poetry Association founded 1986, poetry editor Mildred Klyce. SPA offers networking, publishing, critique service, personal communication, and assistance in publication of SPA members chapbooks. $10 annual membership fee includes newsletter. The association sponsors a number of contests, some for members only, some, such as the Voices of the South Contest, open to all. Prizes total $200. $2 entry fee/poem (not over 24 lines). June 9 deadline. High scoring poems are published in an anthology (which the poet is not required to purchase).

THE W. D. WEATHERFORD AWARD (IV-Regional), Berea College, CPO 2336, Berea, KY 40404, for the published work (including poetry) which "best illuminates the problems, personalities, and unique qualities of the Appalachian South." The award is for $500 and sometimes there are special awards of $200 each.

‡WESTERN HERITAGE AWARDS (IV-Themes), National Cowboy Hall of Fame and Western Heritage Center, 1700 Northeast 63rd St., Oklahoma City, OK 73111, began in 1960 offering trophies, bronze replicas of a Charles M. Russell sculpture, in various areas of western literature, music, film and television, each March in the Founders Hall at the National Cowboy Hall of Fame. Wranglers trophies are awarded to producing organizations and leading creators or those who have made an outstanding contribution to our western heritage. The 1990 Award for poetry went to Walter McDonald for his book *Rafting the Brazos*, published by University of North Texas Press. Write for information about submitting entries.

WESTERN STATES BOOK AWARDS; WESTERN STATES ARTS FEDERATION (IV-Regional), 236 Montezuma Ave., Santa Fe, NM 87501, presents biennial book awards to outstanding authors and small publishers of fiction, creative nonfiction, and poetry. The awards include cash prizes of $2,500 for winning authors, $5,000 for their respective publishers and other benefits, including the opportunity for the publishers to work with, and learn from, a committee of book industry leaders. MSS must be written by an author living in Alaska, Arizona, California, Colorado, Hawaii, Idaho, Montana, Nevada, New Mexico, Oregon, Utah, Washington, or Wyoming. Work must already have been accepted for publication by a publisher in one of these states. Work must be submitted by the publisher, submitted in MS form (not previously published in book form) with a minimum length of 48 pages. Publisher must have published at least 3 books (excluding magazines and chapbooks), since January 1989 and be able to print a first edition of at least 2,000 books. Write for more information.

WFNB ANNUAL LITERARY CONTEST; THE ALFRED G. BAILEY AWARD; WRITERS' FEDERATION OF NEW BRUNSWICK (IV-Regional), P.O. Box 37, Station A, Fredericton, NB E3B 4Y2 Canada, for poets who are residents of New Brunswick, offers prizes of $200, $100, $30, for unpublished poems of up to 100 lines (typed, double-spaced), $14 Canadian entry fee. Deadline February 14. Send SASE for guidelines. The Alfred G. Bailey Award is given annually for poetry MSS of 48 pp. or more.

WHITING WRITERS' AWARDS; MRS. GILES WHITING FOUNDATION (V), Room 3500, 30 Rockefeller Plaza, New York NY 10112, director Gerald Freund. In each of the program's first five years, the Foundation made awards of $25,000 to ten candidates chosen by a Selection Committee drawn from a list of recognized writers, literary scholars, and editors. Recipients of the award were selected from nominations made by writers, educators, and editors from communities across the country whose experience and vocations bring them in contact with individuals of unusual talent. The nominators and selectors are appointed by the Foundation and serve anonymously. Beginning in 1990, the award amount will be set at $30,000. **Direct applications and informal nominations are not accepted by the Foundation.**

OSCAR WILLIAMS & GENE DERWOOD AWARD (V), Community Funds, Inc., 415 Madison Ave., New York, NY 10017, is an award given annually to nominees of the selection committee "to help needy or worthy artists or poets." Selection Committee for the award does not accept nominations. Amount varies from year to year.

‡WOODNOTES; ANNUAL HAIKU COMPETITION-INTERNATIONAL; HAIKU POETS OF NORTHERN CALIFORNIA (IV-Form), 478 A Second Ave., San Francisco, CA 94118, award director Vincent Tripi, annual, prizes of $100, 2 categories, $75 second, $50 third. Fee: $1/haiku, entries on $3 \times 5''$ cards, on issues pertaining to both sexes and nature, no more than 17 syllables. Deadline October 31. Winning poems published in *Woodnotes*, journal of the HPNC.

WORLD ORDER OF NARRATIVE AND FORMALIST POETS (II, IV-Form), P.O. Box 174, Station A, Flushing, NY 11358, contest chairman Dr. Alfred Dorn. This organization sponsors contests in at least fifteen categories of traditional and contemporary poetic forms, including the sonnet, blank verse, ballade, villanelle, triolet, limerick, free verse, and new contrapuntal forms created by Alfred Dorn. Prizes total at least $4,000 and range from $20 to $200. Only subscribers to *The Formalist* will be eligible for the competition, as explained in the complete guidelines available from the contest chairman. "We look for originality of thought, phrase and image, combined with masterful craftsmanship. Trite, trivial or technically inept work stands no chance." Postmark deadline for entries: November 15.

WRITERS' FEDERATION OF NOVA SCOTIA ANNUAL WRITING COMPETITION (IV-Regional), Dawn Rae Downton, Executive Director, Writers' Federation of Nova Scotia, Suite 203, 5516 Spring Garden Road, Halifax, Nova Scotia, B3J 1G6 Canada, for up to 15 poems. Deadline January 31. Please write for rules and a mandatory entry form.

WRITERS' GUILD OF ALBERTA BOOK AWARD (IV-Regional), Writer's Guild, 10523 100th Ave., Edmonton, AB T5J 0A8 Canada, 403-426-5892, awarded in six categories, including poetry. Eligible books will have been published anywhere in the world between January 1 and December 31. Their authors will have been resident in Alberta for at least twelve of the eighteen months prior to December 31. Contact either the WGA head office, or the Alberta Playwrights' Network for registry forms. Unpublished manuscripts are not eligible. Except in the drama category, anthologies are not eligible. Four copies of each book to be considered must be mailed to the WGA office no later than December 31. Submissions postmarked after this date will not be accepted. Three copies will go to the three judges in that category; one will remain in the WGA library. Works may be submitted by authors, publishers, or any interested parties.

WRITERS UNLIMITED (I), %Voncile Ros, 3020 Frederic St., Pascagoula, MS 39567, offers an annual literary competition, deadline September 20. There are up to 20 categories with cash prizes up to $50 and book prizes. Do not use the same poem for more than one category. $5 entry fee covers entries in all categories up to 20. Send SASE for contest rules.

Additional Contests and Awards

The following listings also contain information on Contests and Awards. Read the listings and/or send SASEs for more details about their offerings. (See the General Index for page numbers.)

Adroit Expression, The
Advocate, The
Albatross
Alms House Press
Amaranth Review, The
Amelia
America
American Academy & Institute
   of Arts & Letters, The
American Poetry Center
American Poetry Review
American Tolkien Society
Americas Review
Analecta
And Review, The
Anhinga Press
Apropos
Archer, The
Arte Publico Press
Associated Writing Programs
Atlanta Writing Resource
   Center
Bay Area Poets Coalition
   (BAPC)
Bell's Letters Poet
Bitterroot
Black Bear Publications
Black Horse
Black River Review
Black Warrior Review, The
Blue Unicorn
Breakthrough!

Brussels Sprout
California State Poetry
   Quarterly (CQ)
Canada Council, The
Canadian Author & Bookman
Cape Rock, The
Caravan Press
Ceilidh
Celtic Dawn
Chakra
Chelsea
Chiron Review
Cincinnati Poetry Review
Cleveland State University
   Poetry Series
Cochran's Corner
Columbia
Concho River Review
Council of Literary Magazines
   and Presses
Country Woman
Coydog Review
Crazyquilt Quarterly
Creative With Words
   Publications (C.W.W.)
Cricket
Crystal Rainbow
Cutbank
Delhi-London Poetry
   Quarterly
Devil's Millhopper Press, The
Eighth Mountain Press, The

Eleventh Muse, The
Emerald City Comix & Stories
Epoch
Fairbanks Arts Association
Federation of British Columbia
   Writers
Feelings (FL)
Felicity
First Time
Flume Press
Folio: A Literary Journal
Footwork
For Poets Only
Formalist, The
Free Focus
Frogmore Papers
Frogpond: Quarterly Haiku
   Journal
Galaxy of Verse Literary
   Foundation, A
Golden Isis Magazine
Grain
Great Lakes Poetry Press
Greensboro Review, The
Haiku Canada
Haiku Journal
Haiku Quarterly
Half Tones to Jubilee
Heartland Journal: By Older
   Writers for Readers of All
   Ages
Heaven Bone Press

Helter Skelter
Hippopotamus Press
Hob-Nob
Hoosier Challenger
Housewife-Writer's Forum
Hudson Review, The
Hummingbird
Hutton Publications
Independent Review, The
International Black Writers
Iowa Woman
James Books, Alice
Just Between Us
Kansas Quarterly
Korone
Lane Literary Guild, The
League of Canadian Poets, The
Lip Service
Literature and Belief
Loft, The
Louisiana Literature
Lucidity
Lyric, The
MacGuffin, The
Madison Review, The
Magnetic North
Malahat Review, The
Mayberry Gazette, The
Mid-American Review
Midwest Poetry Review
Mind's Eye Fiction & Poetry
     Quarterly
Minotaur Press
Mr. Cogito Press
Modern Haiku
Muse
Music City Song Festival
My Restless Soul
Nation, The
National Federation of State
     Poetry Societies, Inc.
Nebraska Review, The
Negative Capability
NER/BLQ (New England
     Review/Bread Loaf
     Quarterly)
New Delta Review
New Horizons Poetry Club
New Letters
New Poetry Review
Nimrod International Journal
     of Contemporary Poetry
     and Fiction
North Carolina Writers'
     Network
North, The
Northeastern University Press
Nostalgia: A Sentimental State
     of Mind
Ohio State University Press/
     The Journal Award in
     Poetry
Orbis
Oregon State Poetry
     Association, The
Overtone Press
Palanquin Press
Panhandler, The

Paris Review, The
Parnassus Literary Journal
Pasque Petals
Pearl
Pen American Center
Philomel
Piedmont Literary Review
Pikeville Review
Pitt Poetry Series
Plainsongs
Poetic Page
Poetpourri
Poetry
Poetry Break
Poetry Center of the 92nd
     Street Y, The
Poetry Committee of the
     Greater Washington Area,
     The
Poetry Explosion Newsletter,
     The
Poetry Forum
Poetry Halifax Dartmouth
Poetry Magic
Poetry Nippon Press
Poetry Northwest
Poetry Nottingham
Poetry Only
Poetry Peddler, The
Poetry Society of America
Poetry USA
Poets at Work
Poets House
Poet's Review
Poets' Roundtable
Prairie Schooner
Princeton University Press
Protea Poetry Journal
Psych It: The Sophisticated
     Newsletter for Everyone
Pudding House Publications
Pygmy Forest Press
Quarry Magazine
Quarterly Review of Literature
Radcliffe Quarterly
Rainbow City Express
Read Me
Renovated Lighthouse
     Magazine, The
Rio Grande Press
River City
Rockford Review, The
Rocky Mountain Poetry
     Magazine
San Diego Poet's Press
San Jose Studies
Sandscript
Saturday Press, Inc.
Scavenger's Newsletter
Sensations
Sewanee Review
Shawnee Silhouette
Shoe Tree
Signpost Press, The
Silver Apples Press
Silver Wings
Silverfish Review
Sing Heavenly Muse!

Singlelife Magazine
Slate & Style
Slipstream
Slough Press
Smith Publisher, Gibbs
Snake River Reflections
Society of American Poets, The
Sonora Review
South Coast Poetry Journal
Southern California Anthology
Southern Humanities Review
Southern Poetry Review
Southern Rose Review
Southwest Review
Sow's Ear, The
Spitball
Staple
State Street Press
Still Waters Press
Story Line Press
Straight Ahead
Studio
Tales of the Old West
Taproot Literary Review
Telstar
Texas Review, The
Third Lung Review
Third Woman Press
Thorntree Press
Thumbprints
Tidewater
Tiffany and Shore Publishers
Time of Singing
Tradition
University of Arkansas Press,
     The
University of Iowa Press
University of Massachusetts
     Press, The
University of Utah Press
University of Wisconsin Press
Vegetarian Journal
Ver Poets Voices
Verve
Violetta Books
Virginia Quarterly Review, The
West Wind Review
Weyfarers
Whetstone
White Rose Literary Magazine,
     The
Whitecrow Foundation
Wide Open Magazine
Wildwood Journal
Winston-Derek Publishers, Inc.
Woodley Memorial Press
Worcester Review
Word Works, The
Wormwood Review Press
Write Now!
Writer's Digest
Writer's Exchange
Writers' Journal
Writers' Own Magazine
Writer's Rescue
Yale University Press
Yankee Magazine
Zone 3

Greeting Cards

You will find many publishers saying, when describing in their listings what they *don't* want to see, "no greeting card verse." For them, and for many others, literary poetry and the messages on greeting cards are antithetical. On the other hand, I know of people who regard themselves as poets and who have literally made millions of dollars on what I would regard as greeting card verse, so the distinction is not hard and fast. If the kind of sentiments you express in your writing are those that large portions of the population might identify with, you may not do well by submitting to literary magazines, but you may succeed in the greeting card market.

There are no jobs for poets as poets, but the people who are most regularly paid for writing verse, write greeting cards. It takes a knack, and maybe you have it. One afternoon I sat at my word processor and hammered out some 75 greeting card messages (both verse and prose) that I sent to a major greeting card company. They bought more than 40 of them, and my check was for just under a thousand dollars. Many an afternoon after that I tried to repeat my success, but I haven't sold a single message since. I had the knack one afternoon.

Some, though, have it on a regular basis. A young woman at a writers' workshop recently gave me a whole booklet of her verses for evaluation. I thought it was dreadful as poetry, but I could tell that the poet had a gift for writing greeting cards. I put her in touch with a representative of a greeting card company who was on the workshop staff, and before the workshop was over, the two of them were seriously discussing the possibility of the young woman taking a fulltime job writing greeting cards. Such companies go to a great deal of effort to recruit writers. I visited the corporate headquarters of one where I was shown a floor of mostly empty cubicles. They wanted my help in finding young writers who would consider a greeting card career.

The stereotypes that people who scorn greeting cards carry in their heads are likely to be outdated. Most greeting card verses have moved far beyond the sentimental rhymes of bygone times, though there is still a market for them. One humorist I met at a greeting card company had previously been a writer for an advertising agency. "I write Frisbees," he said. He also writes copy for mugs, T-shirts, stuffed animals, and other products. He showed me the computer bank where the company stored the card ideas and messages they had bought for future use. You summoned up examples by categories. For instance, you wouldn't want the whole file of Father's Day cards; there would be thousands. So you choose a sub-category. He chose "threatening." "Let's see whether there are any threatening Father's Day cards," he said. Sure enough, there was one. On the front panel was to be a fierce looking gorilla with its arm raised and the message, "You'd better enjoy your Father's Day . . . " Not everyone can dream up ideas like that.

The best way to learn about greeting cards is by spending hours reading them in the stores. But many companies that buy freelance work offer "tipsheets" for potential contributors. If you're interested in illustrating greeting cards, see **The Art and Craft of Greeting Cards**, North Light Books. (See Other Books of Interest list at the back of this book.)

Here are listings of greeting card companies interested in freelance submissions. Study their products in a greeting card store, write for their tipsheets and try your hand.

AMBERLEY GREETING CARD CO., 11510 Goldcoast Dr., Cincinnati, OH 45249-1695, founded 1966, editor Ned Stern, uses 80% freelance material for cards in these categories: **humor for birthdays, anniversaries, get well, and thinking-of-you. Send SASE for tipsheet (updated annually). Submit on**

3x5″ cards. "Need very short and to the point humor." No long poems, big words. "We're selling to the masses, not the classes." Pays $40. No comments on rejections.

AMCAL, 1050 Shary Ct., Concord, CA 94518, phone 415-689-9930, founded 1975, started publishing greeting cards in 1984, markets to "upper market gift and stationery stores. Large number of traditional shops and country stores. Few urban trendy retailers. **80% of their texts come from freelancers. Send SASE for tipsheets. All traditional categories considered. Submit on typing paper, with date, name, address.** "Simple verses that hit the target in one or two lines. Inspirational or more complex verses for new lines. We are always loking for new lines, so the right collection of verses may be the basis of our next series of greeting cards." **Pays "flat fee only. Negotiable before submitting work. After receiving samples of their work, if they fit our project, we send complete information." Always comments on rejections.** President David Walbolt advises, "Don't be discouraged if your work isn't accepted right away. We have had pros who strike out on some subject yet come back and do very well on something else. You have to understand that you may not always be 'right' for every project. Find out what you are best at and exploit that niche."

ARGUS COMMUNICATIONS, One DLM Park, Allen, TX 75002, phone 214-248-6300, founded as Argus Press in the '20s and has been publishing greeting cards for 6 years. Product manager Susan M. Smith. The company has 9 different product lines in cards, posters and postcards. **90% of their texts come from freelancers. Send SASE for Market Letter and "general request for greeting card or poster information. Freelancers with whom we develop a strong relationship receive specific request letters as copy is needed."** They use seasonal cards, Christmas. **"Please type copy, with inside and outside copy on same side of index card. Do not clutter with extra information, like art ideas. It really detracts from the editorial, which should be able to stand on its own. See our Market Letter for characteristics of copy. Only use prose copy at this time. Do not want to see dated jokes, blue humor, ideas lifted from product already on the market."** As a sample I selected a card with a photograph of a pair of puppies and the line, "It's not nice/ When you feel sick . . . " on the outside. Inside is: . . . So please get well—/And make it quick!" A sample poster has a photo of a mountain climber hanging by a rope on a cliff face, silhouetted against a deep red sunset with the caption: "I can let things happen . . . /or I can make them happen." The editors advise, "a) Write to your market. Know what the company wants and send appropriate material; b) be neat and correct; c) edit your own work first; send out only your best, not everything you think of; and d) keep trying; like anything else, writing gets better with practice."

BLUE MOUNTAIN ARTS, INC., Dept. PM, Box 1007, Boulder, CO 80306, founded 1971, publishes "notecards and seasonal cards which feature **sincere and sensitive poetry and prose on love, friendship, family, philosophies, and other aspects of life.** In addition, we also publish calendars and gift books. Our products appeal to both men and women, and to people of all ages." **Send SASE for tipsheet, updated annually. "We prefer that submissions be typewritten; both cards and typing paper are OK. Always include phone number, and keep us advised of address changes.**" If freelancers are curious about the type of material we publish, we suggest that they visit a card or book store and get a feel for the material there. **We're looking for** *original* **writings about real emotions and feelings, written from real experience. We suggest that the freelancer have someone in mind (a friend, family member, etc.) as they write. We publish unrhymed poetry. Length does not matter.** We do not accept artwork or photography, novels, short stories, or narrative poems. **For worldwide, exclusive rights we pay $200 per poem selected; for one-time permission to include a poem in an anthology we pay $25."**

BRILLIANT ENTERPRISES, 117 W. Valerio St., Santa Barbara, CA 93101, founded 1967, editor Ashleigh Brilliant, publishes "illustrated **epigrams of universal appeal**" on postcards, often buying from freelancers. **Send $2 for catalog and samples, in lieu of tipsheet.** There is **"no limit" on the categories of texts they buy. Submit on 3½x5″ cards with camera-ready art. Pays $40. Editor "sometimes" comments on rejections.** They sent sample postcards, but they say, "our line is so extensive, varied, and unusual that **no submissions should be made before careful study of our catalog.**" One sample is a pink card with a wreath of flowers and, inside it, the text: "All I want is a warm bed and a kind word and unlimited power." Another, in orange, shows a file of thousands of people crowding toward an open door, with the text: "APPRECIATE ME NOW/and avoid the rush." (Messages are copyrighted: ©Ashleigh Brilliant 1970, 1982).

THE CALLIGRAPHY COLLECTION, INC., 2604 N.W. 74th Pl., Gainesville, FL 32606, founded 1983, contact artist Katy Fischer, publishes framed prints of watercolors with calligraphy "sold in middle to upper end gift shops throughout the country. They appeal to women 20-50. **The prints are such as the end user will keep for years. The sayings need to have lasting appeal and have a personal 'me to you' flavor. No poetry that rhymes. Form of submission does not matter, but include phone with name and address. If what you submit has potential we will gladly go further with you. We would like to see 1-2**

Close-up

Susan Polis Schutz
Poet/Co-founder
Blue Mountain Arts, Inc.

You Deserve the Best
This life is yours
Take the power
to choose what you want to do
and do it well
Take the power
to love what you want in life
and love it honestly
Take the power
to walk in the forest
and be a part of nature
Take the power
to control your own life
No one else can do it for you
Nothing is too good for you
You deserve the best
   Take the power
   to make your life
   healthy
   exciting
   worthwhile
   and very happy

Photo by Jared

As a teenager, Susan Polis Schutz began writing poetry as a means of venting feelings. Today, almost 30 years later, she still expresses her emotions on paper, but she's not the only one who reads them. Susan is one of the best-selling poets in the United States, and Blue Mountain Arts, Inc., which she co-founded with her husband, Stephen, is the largest publisher of poetry in the world.

Probably one reason her poetry is so popular is it is written in order to communicate her feelings to others. Like literary poets, she focuses on the deeper meanings of life as they relate to family, love, friendship and nature. The difference is her work has not a hint of obscurity and can be taken at face value. Literary purists may scoff, but the mainstream reader appreciates and supports the simple words she uses to describe not-so-simple sensibilities.

Susan began writing at age seven by designating herself a juvenile journalist in her hometown of Peekskill, New York. It was there she put together a neighborhood newspaper for her friends. In her teens she started writing poetry. "I found it hard to express my feelings verbally, so I wrote them in a free-flowing poetic form. Not only was I able to communicate my feelings to the people I was writing to, but I was also able to understand my feelings a lot better."

Susan and Stephen moved to Colorado shortly after their 1969 marriage so he could accept a position as a physicist. But they soon found they were not content with just lunching together every day and made plans to spend all their time together. Stephen, a talented artist "responsible for the beautiful look of the Blue Mountain cards and books," left the scientific world for a professional partnership with his wife. Together they supported themselves by combining her poetry and his illustrations.

At first they made posters. They traveled the country in a pick-up truck while bartering their handmade silkscreen prints for food, lodging or gas. For the trip, they took along enough posters to last a year, they thought. To their surprise, the posters sold out in two months. Before long, the exposure of their work resulted in an overwhelming demand for a collection of Susan's poems—hence the birth of the Blue Mountain Press.

In 1972, Blue Mountain Press published **Come Into the Mountains, Dear Friend**, a collection of Susan's poems expressing sentiments of unconditional love for Stephen. The book was deemed "the most beautiful book in print" at the time and made publishing history by selling over 500,000 copies. Several other books have followed since that first one, all of them best-sellers. **Love Love Love**, the most recent book, was on the B. Dalton bestseller list.

Today Susan still lives in Colorado and continues to collaborate with her husband in nourishing the life of Blue Mountain Arts. In addition to books, the company also produces prints, calendars and greeting cards. Blue Mountain offers several lines of greeting cards, including Airebrush Feelings™, Watercolor Feelings™, the Susan Polis Schutz and Stephen Schutz Collection™, and the newest line, Occasion Gallery™.

Altogether, more than 10 million books and 150 million notecards containing Susan's poems have been sold. Despite the volume, though, her poems continue to carry an essence denoting quaint, non-egregious placidity. She says "I can only be creative when I am inspired; therefore, whenever I am inspired, I will immediately sit down and write regardless of where I am or what I am doing."

Susan says submissions of poetry to the editors of Blue Mountain Arts are definitely invited, but adds that the odds for publication can be slim, since the staff receives many thousands of poems a year. However, "I encourage all poets to continue writing, not only for publication purposes, but as a way of releasing their emotions and for a better understanding of their feelings. The most important thing, however, is even if they are rejected, they should always feel very lucky to be able to express their emotions in writing."

—*Lisa Carpenter*

---

examples of creations you like best and not be deluged." Pays $50-100. "If you submit work we are interested in we can go from there on an individual basis." No comments on rejections.

‡COMSTOCK CARDS, Suite 18, 600 South Rock Blvd., Reno, NV 89502, phone 702-333-9400, FAX 702-333-9406, founded 1986, general manager Patti P. Wolf, art director David Delacroix, produces cards, notepads, and invitations for "sophisticated adults." Twenty-five percent freelance writers. **Tipsheets updated quarterly, available for SASE. Buys 50 freelance ideas/samples per year. Submit seasonal/holiday material 1 year in advance. Reports in 5 weeks. Buys all rights. Submit on 3×5" cards indicating message for outside and inside. "No hearts, flowers or anything cutesy. We want outrageous humor, rude, sexy, etc."** A sample card pictures a grinning man's face peering through a urinal surrounded by a Christmas wreath, with "URINAL" on the outside and "My Christmas Dreams!" on the inside. Needs **humorous, informal, invitations and "puns, put-downs, put-ons. No conventional, soft line or sensitivity." Prefers to receive 25 cards per batch. Pays $50-75 per card idea.** "Always keep holiday occasions in mind and personal me-to-you expressions that relate to today's occurrences. Ideas must be simple and concisely delivered. A combination of strong image and strong gag line makes a successful greeting card. Consumers relate to themes of work, sex and friendship combined with current social, political and economic issues."

‡CREATE-A-CRAFT, Box 330008, Fort Worth TX 76163-0008, 817-929-1855, editor Mitchell Lee. **Buys 2 freelance ideas/samples per year; receives 300 submissions annually. Submit seasonal/holiday material 1 year in advance. Submissions not returned even if accompanied by SASE.** "Not enough staff to

take time to package up returns." Buys all rights. Sample greeting cards are available for $2.50 and a #10 SASE. Needs announcements, conventional, humorous, juvenile and studio. "Payment depends upon the assignment, amount of work involved, and production costs involved in project." No unsolicited material. "Send letter of inquiry describing education, experience, or resume with one sample first. We will screen applicants and request samples from those who interest us."

‡ELDERCARDS, INC., Box 202, Piermont, NY 10968, phone 914-359-7137, editors Steve Epstein and Lenore Bernowitz. 10 percent of material is freelance written. **Receives 20 submissions annually.** Submit seasonal/holiday material 3 months in advance. Reports in 1 month. Pays royalties. Needs announcements, conventional, humorous, informal, invitations, sensitivity and studio. Prefers unrhymed verse. Submit 24 ideas/batch. Pays $50. Other product lines: Calendars ($10-200), post cards ($50) and posters ($10-200). "Market is contemporary, upbeat, humorous, for 20-50 years old. Writers should be mindful of current trends and emotional issues."

EPHEMERA, INC., 275 Capp St., San Francisco, CA 94110, phone 415-552-4199, founded 1978, editor Ed Polish: "We publish novelty pin-back buttons with **irreverent, provocative and outrageously funny slogans on them. We encourage writers to be as weird, rude and/or shocking as they like!**" They buy 98% of their material from freelancers, pay $25/each. Payments due upon production; approximately January 1, May 1 and September 1. Send SASE for guidelines. Samples: "Are you an artist, or did you just get dressed in the dark"; "I have no idea what I'm doing out of bed"; "Give me a quarter or I'll touch you"; "Hi. How are you? Get out of my way." **Obscenities OK.** Retail catalog available for two 25¢ stamps.

FREEDOM GREETING CARD COMPANY, INC., 1619 Hanford St., Levittown, PA 19057, phone 215-945-3300, FAX 215-547-0248, founded 1969, president Jerome Wolk. "**We produce standard everyday greeting cards, all holidays, Black greeting cards, Spanish cards, specialties such as inspirational, alternative modern young people style, clever quips, and sentimental family relationships.**" They buy 100% of their material from freelancers." Submit on 3x5 cards with phone number and the types of text that you are used to doing. "We use good two-liners, four-liners, eight-liners and, on inspirational cards, as much as 16-20 lines." Payment "depends on the quality of the work and the originality of the concept." Editor "always" comments on rejections.

GALLANT GREETINGS CORP., 2654 W. Medill Ave., Chicago, IL 60647-9976, phone 312-489-2000; 800-621-4279. "We welcome fresh new writers with open arms, but we ask that they do their homework! I advise them to visit every available card shop, study the different styles, then creatively develop a style of their own. At Gallant, we are flexible and an assortment in styles is the goal we seek. We hope that writers have fun and enjoy what they do, because it does show up in the work they do." **90% of their material is bought from freelancers.** Send SASE for tipsheets, updated 1-2 times a year. Submit on 3x5 cards, text on front, information on back. Editor sometimes comments on rejections. Pays $50/card, response time 2-3 weeks. "We try to look at seasonal ideas 9-12 months before the actual holiday to give us the lead time we need." Submit to Alex H. Cohen, Creative Director.

LOVE GREETING CARDS, INC., 663 N. Biscayne River Dr., Miami, FL 33169, phone 305-685-LOVE, founded 1984, editor Norman Drittel, publishes cards for "**35-60 yr. range women**" and buys about **40% of their material from freelancers.** Write for samples. Seasonal, humor, anniversaries and birthdays, get well, thank-you, thinking-of-you. As a sample I selected a glossy card with a photo of a rose on the outside and, inside: "When a Sister is as thoughtful/ And as wonderful as you,/ It's natural to think of her/ With love the whole year through./ And when your birthday comes along,/ A card like this can't start/ To tell you all the wishes/ That it brings you from the heart."

‡MAINE LINE CO., Box 947, Rockland ME 04841, phone 207-594-9418, founded 1979, editor Perri Ardman. Buys 100-300 freelance ideas/samples per year. Receives approximately 2,500 submissions per year. Submit photocopies (1 idea per page) or index cards. Please send SASE for return of samples. Reports in 2 months. Material copyrighted. Buys card and related-product rights. Pays on acceptance. Writer's guidelines for #10 SAE and 2 first class stamps. Market list is regularly revised. "No seasonal. We use non-humorous, as well as humorous material. We are expanding into 'sensitive language,' and 'inspirational' greeting cards and 'light, cute' greeting cards. Still, we do not want cliches or corny sap. Messages, whether 'light' or 'sensitive', must be real and reflect attitudes and feelings of real people in today's world. Unrhymed material is preferred. Cope, encouragement, support." Other Product Lines: Wacky, outrageous humor needed for buttons, mugs, key chains, magnets, tee-shirts, plaques and other novelty items. "We prefer copy that stands on its own humor rather than relies on four-letter words or grossly suggestive material. Material that is mildly suggestive is OK. 'Inspirational' material for the above items also requested. Please send for our guidelines. Copy should speak to universal truths that most people will recognize. Writers need not submit any visuals with copy but

may suggest visuals. Lack of drawing ability does not decrease chances of having your work accepted; however, we also seek people who can both write and illustrate. Writers who are also illustrators or graphic artists are invited to send samples or tearsheets. Be sure to send an SASE with appropriate postage for return of your material if you want to get it back."

MERLYN GRAPHICS, P.O. Box 9087, Canoga Park, CA 91309, founded 1988, editor B. Galling, publishes "humorous, photographic greeting cards **appealing mainly to women's interest. Trendy and fun." They buy 50% of their material from freelancers.** Christmas, Valentine's, humor, anniversaries and birthdays, get-well, thank-you, thinking-of-you, apologies. **Submit on 3x5 or other cards. "Very brief, one-liners, very funny, not too smutty, but sexy is OK." Pays $50/submission published. Send SASE for guidelines.** Find samples in stores.

OUTREACH PUBLICATIONS, Box 1010, Siloam Springs, AR 72761, phone 501-524-9381, founded 1971, Editor Joan Aycock looks for **"a relational, inspirational message for our line of greeting cards that ministers love, encouragement and comfort to the receiver"** for all major seasonal lines (example: Mother's Day, Easter, Graduation, etc.), all everyday occasions (example: get well, birthday, anniversary, baby congratulations, friendship, etc.) and special occasion cards (example: Confirmation, missionary, ordination, etc.). **Send SASE for guidelines. Submit on 3x5 cards with name, address, phone number and social security number. Pays from $30. Review time usually 4-6 weeks.**

PAPEL, 7355 Lankershim Blvd., North Hollywood, CA 91609, founded 1956, director of product development Arlene Slater, sometimes uses freelance submissions (30%) for messages on mugs, underpants, caps, trivets and other products. These are **"impulse social expressions, positive, meaningful messages that range from very short hilarious one-liners to 30-40 word messages of love, friendship, or philosophy."** They use material in these categories: seasonal, humor, anniversaries and birthdays, get well, thinking-of-you, love, friendship, inspirational, midlife crisis, sports humor, office humor. **Submit on 3x5″ cards. "Must be professional freelancers who have written for major greeting card companies such as Hallmark. Do not want to see unexperienced work." Pay "variable depending on size of job. I do not want any requests for samples."** They have a catalog which illustrates the messages on their products. Products are too varied to illustrate by samples, but for instance an office mug has "Tell Me It's Just PMS—And I'll Staple Your Head to the Floor." A "midlife crisis" mug has the message "Tease Me About My Age, and I'll Beat You With My Cane."

PARAMOUNT CARDS, INC., Box 6546, Providence, RI 02940-6546, founded 1906, write Attn: Freelance Coordinator. **Buys about 10% of material from freelancers. Send SASE for guidelines, updated yearly.** Seasonal, all holidays, humor, anniversaries and birthdays, get-well, thank-you, thinking-of-you, religious-inspirational. **Submit on 3x5 cards. Rates vary. No comments on rejections.**

PLUM GRAPHICS, INC., Box 136 Prince Station, New York, NY 10012, contact Kirsten Coyne, publishes "die-cut greeting cards, modern fun, colorful, for children to adults. Most of the copy is for birthday cards. **Send SASE for guidelines. "We call for copy submissions 2-3 times/year. Submit on 3x5 cards."** As samples, they sent a card cut in the shape of a pig, inside message (on 2 lines): "Somebody squealed/ It's your birthday." Another in the shape of a cocktail drink: "Sip-a-de-do-dah/ What a wonderful day. Happy Birthday." **"No traditional poetry. Copy should be short, concise, understandable, not esoteric, not flowery." Pays $40-50 for copy.**

RUSS BERRIE AND COMPANY, INC., 111 Bauer Dr., Oakland, NJ 07436, phone 201-337-9000 ext. 332, founded 1963, editorial manager Terri Evens. "Although we do have greeting cards, we are primarily a giftware manufacturer. We occasionally buy copy for giftware items—mugs, plaques, figurines, frames, pads, buttons, stuffed animals, caps, t-shirts, etc. **All of our products are aimed at a mainstream audience—nothing too risque or avant-garde.** They keep freelancers on file and phone them with specific assignments. "I sometimes write a tipsheet when we have a particular need and send it to freelancers in my files." All holidays, especially Christmas and Valentine's, humor, anniversaries and birthdays, thinking-of-you, love, friendship. **Submit on 3x5 cards, with phone number.** As samples the editor sent "Love Notes" cards, one with the message (front panel): "When you're lonely/ call me/ When you're sad/ tell me/ When you're happy/ share it with me/ When you're angry . . . / I still care." Humor: "It's not stress—just a bad perm." Verse: "Friends can be forever/ I know this is true/ Because I'm sure I have/ A forever friend in you." "I reached out and you were there/ To love, to comfort and to care." Terri Evens says, "Our requirements vary widely from item to item. This is why I prefer to deal with writers on a specific project basis, rather than having them send in large amounts of copy for no particular reason. When this happens, I generally hang onto the ones I like until I have some place to put them, but I can't pay until the copy is used. **I like to see polished work. Too often, prose that is submitted to me is formless and rambling, and poems have sloppy rhymes and meter. Take your prose ideas and boil them down to their most concise form; we're more likely to**

take something short than a large block of copy. Make sure that rhymes are not forced, contrived or overly cute. Please note that we don't accept poetry without a specific, upbeat social expression message. We are not a literary journal, nor are we interested in seeing purely literary work."

‡MARCEL SCHURMAN CO., INC., 2500 N. Watney Way, Fairfield, CA 94533, founded 1950, creative editor Marshall Berman, publishes "greeting cards for everyday and seasonal markets. Many styles include fine artwork and very traditional text. In general, we do not publish rhymed verse outside of our juvenile card line." Buy 20 percent of texts from freelancers. Tipsheets available for SASE. Submit text and "conceptual images (if possible)" on 3 × 5″ cards. The editor advises, "Research pays off. Learn the characteristics of the market you're trying to reach. Keep those characteristics in mind throughout your creative process. Brainstorm with yourself. Write everything down. There's always time to massage and hone the copy at a later date. This is a tight market. Persistence is often the key. Read lots of signs and billboards . . . they can be an inspiration for given themes."

SONMARK, INC., 184 Quigley Blvd., New Castle, DE 19720, phone 302-322-9909, founded 1985. Director of product development Gladys King, publisher of seasonal, holiday, humor, anniversary and birthday, get well, thank-you, and thinking-of-you cards. **Not accepting any material at this time.**

‡SUNRISE PUBLICATIONS, INC., Box 2699, Bloomington IN 47402, phone 812-336-9900. Contact: product manager. 75 percent freelance written. Bought 200 freelance ideas/samples last year; receives an estimated 2,000 submissions annually. Reports in 2 months. Acquires greeting card rights only. Pays on acceptance. Free writer's guidelines. Market list is regularly revised. Needs conventional, humorous, informal. No "off-color humor or lengthy poetry." Prefers unrhymed verses/ideas. "We like short one- to four-line captions, sincere or clever. Our customers prefer this to lengthy rhymed verse. Submit ideas for birthday, get well, friendship, wedding, baby congrats, sympathy, thinking of you, anniversary, belated birthday, thank yous, fun and love." Payment varies. "Think always of the sending situation and both the person buying the card and its intended recipient. Most card purchasers are aged between 18 and 45 years, and are female."

WARNER PRESS INC.; SUNSHINE LINE; REGENT, Box 2499, Anderson, IN 46018, founded in 1880 as Gospel Trumpet, product editor Cindy Maddox, who says "We are a religious company, **so most of what we purchase is religious in nature. Majority of purchases are for boxed greeting card verses. Request guidelines for details.** We purchase some longer inspirational poems for our Bulletin service." They use 65% work from freelancers. They use cards in these categories: **holidays, especially Christmas, a few Easter, anniversaries and birthdays, get well, thank-you, thinking-of-you, and inspirational. Submit on numbered 3 × 5″ cards. "Want: original concepts, consistent rhythm if rhyming poem, unique free verse. Don't want: to specific person, typical rhyme schemes, multiple submissions (50) of same type." They pay approximately $15, more for longer verses or exceptional quality.** As samples the editor chose these two: "The best way to show/someone special we care/ Is to lift them to God/ with the gift of prayer" by B.J. Hoff, and "May the promise of/ eternal life through Christ/ bring hope and comfort/ in the midst of tears."

‡WESTERN GREETINGS, INC., P.O. Box 81056, Las Vegas, NV 89180. Editor: Barbara Jean Sullivan. **100 percent of material is freelance written. Buys 15 freelance samples per year. Reports in 1 month. Buys all rights. Pays on acceptance. Writer's guidelines/nondisclosure form for #10 SAE. Market list sent when available. Needs: Humorous, sensitivity, soft line for everyday and Christmas, Western and Indian themes. Accepts rhymed and unrhymed verse.** "All art is pre-selected. We ask our writers to write verse based only on the descriptions we send you. **Western cards include the cowboy, mountain man, Indian, cowgirl, western stilllife and landscape.** Our cards are reproduced from Western and Southwest art. Target audiences are people who love the West, the outdoors and history of the West or who want to send a card home from the West. Most card buyers are women. **We don't use vulgar verse. We like warm, compassionate, thoughtful, caring verse. Humorous/upbeat is also used."** Include phone number on submissions. **"We pay $25/submission, up to $60 for an 8-line poem. Send $2 for 8 pp. color catalog and sample card."**

WILLIAMHOUSE-REGENCY INC., 28 West 23 St., New York, NY 10010, art director Nancy Boecker, is "looking for sentiments for wedding invitations and Christmas cards." They accept a very small percentage of text from freelancers. Send SASE for tipsheet.

WIZWORKS, P.O. Box 240, Masonville, CO 80541-0240, founded 1988. Address Director, Creative Recruitment. They distribute greeting cards through supermarkets using a vending machine that prints cards on site using a high resolution color printer. Consumers will preview cards on a color CRT. **"We are seeking very specific prose/poetry directed to non-occasion and holiday needs.** We are planning an initial line of 2,500 cards per machine with monthly revisions. We expect to rely almost exclusively on freelance submissions." **Send $1 for guidelines.** Seasonal, all holidays, humor, anniversaries and birthdays, get-well, thank-you, thinking-of-you, apologies, life crisis/transition. **"Our need is for very specific text/poetry. Specific age, sex, life event, crisis, etc. We are less interested in generalized themes." Submit on 3x5 cards. Pays 1% royalties quarterly. They use primarily short verse (4 lines). "Honest, realistic clever, personal, very specific to age, sex, relationship, life event, etc. Not interested in generalized flowery traditional poetry." Editor always comments on rejections.** Individuals who have the ability to provide complete card concepts are preferred.

Resources

Writing Colonies

Are you sitting there trying to concentrate on this book, or on your computer or typewriter, while children are screaming, the phone is ringing off the wall, dinner is boiling over on the stove, or your secretary seems to have a finger stuck on the intercom call button? Maybe you need to get away from it all.

Much fine poetry has been produced at some of the prestigious colonies listed below. Above all, writing colonies are the setting for many new friendships and associations among writers and artists. It is an honor to be accepted by some—and one may go to those as to a temple, awed by the spiritual presence of great poets who have been there over the years.

Writers' colonies are best for those who have a project underway, something definite to work on. Have some alternative plans in mind, in case your project dries up on you. Take with you the reference books and other resources you will need.

I would guess that most of our major poets have spent some time in one or another of these colonies, and it can be an experience that awakens and deepens your sense of what it means to participate in the long fellowship of our art. We may all be grateful that benefactors have provided these "resorts" to foster creativity in the arts—and should learn to use them respectfully and well.

‡THE EDWARD F. ALBEE FOUNDATION, INC.; THE WILLIAM FLANAGAN MEMORIAL CREATIVE PERSONS CENTER ("THE BARN"), 14 Harrison St., New York, NY 10013, phone 212-226-2020, for information and application forms; the Center is at South Fairview Ave., Montauk, NY 11954, phone 516-668-5435. The Albee Foundation maintains the Center (better known as "The Barn") in Montauk, on Long Island, offering 1-month residencies for writers, painters, sculptors, and composers, open June 1-October 1, accommodating 6 persons at a time. Applications accepted at the Harrison Street address by regular mail only January 1-April 1. Fellowship announcements by May 15. "Located approximately 2 miles from the center of Montauk and the Atlantic Ocean, 'The Barn' rests in a secluded knoll that offers privacy and a peaceful atmosphere. The Foundation expects all those accepted for residence to work seriously and to conduct themselves in such a manner as to aid fellow residents in their endeavors. The environment is simple and communal. Residents are expected to do their share in maintaining the condition of 'The Barn' as well as its peaceful environment."

ATLANTIC CENTER FOR THE ARTS, 1414 Art Center Ave., New Smyrna Beach, FL 32168, phone 904-427-6975. The Center was founded in 1979 by a sculptor and painter, Doris Leeper, who secured a seed grant from The Rockefeller Foundation. That same year the Center was chartered by the state of Florida and building began on a 10-acre site. The Center was officially opened in 1982. Since 1982, 35 Master Artists-in-Residence sessions have been held. At each of the 3-week sessions internationally known artists from different disciplines conduct interdisciplinary workshops, lecture, critique work in progress. They also give readings and recitals, exhibit their work, and develop projects with their "associates"—mid-career artists who come from all over the U.S. to work with the Masters. The Center is run by an advisory council which chooses Masters for residencies, helps set policies, and guides the Center in its growth. The process of becoming an associate is different for each master artist. Recent poets in residence at the center include Howard Nemerov (January 1988), James Dickey (June 1987), Fred Chappell (April 1989), Henry Taylor (June 1989) and Ron Padgett (March-April 1990).

BELLAGIO STUDY AND CONFERENCE CENTER, The Rockefeller Foundation, 1133 Avenue of the Americas, New York, NY 10036, Susan Garfield, Manager, offers five-week residencies in the Italian Alps from January 20-December 20 for artists and scholars. Room available for spouses. Residents must pay their own travel cost.

BLUE MOUNTAIN CENTER, Blue Mountain Lake, NY 12812, provides free room and board for published poets (and other writers) for 4-week periods 4 times a year June-October. Apply before March 1 with samples, project description, and the period you want to stay. Spouses apply individually.

CENTRUM, % Sarah Muirhead, coordinator, Residency Program, Box 1158, Port Townsend, WA 98368, offers 1-month residencies, September through May. Centrum provides individual cottages, a stipend of $75/week, and solitude. Families welcome. Located in Fort Worden State Park on the Strait of Juan de Fuca. Also sponsors the annual Port Townsend Writers' Conference held in July, and other workshops and seminars.

THE CLEARING, Box 65, Ellison Bay, WI 54210, phone 414-854-4088, resident managers Donald and Louise Buchholz, "is first a school, then a place of self-discovery." Made up of cabins and lodges in a rustic setting overlooking Green Bay, it offers a variety of courses, including courses in writing and poetry, May-October. Fees include tuition, room (dormitory or twin-bedded room), and board.

CUMMINGTON COMMUNITY OF THE ARTS, RR #1, Box 145, Cummington, MA 01026, 413-634-2172, offers residencies to artists in all disciplines from 1-3 months. Living/studio spaces are in individual cabins or two main houses, on 100 acres in the Berkshires. Work exchange available. During July and August, artists with children from age 5-12 are encouraged to apply. Cummington sponsors the Summer Children's Program which offers supervised activity for the children of artists in residence. Application deadlines: January 1 for residences during April and May; March 1 for residences during June, July, and August; June 1 for residences during September, October, November.

DOBIE-PAISANO PROJECT, The University of Texas, Main Building 101, Attn: Audrey N. Slate, Austin, TX 78712, offers two annual fellowships of $7,200 and 6-month residency at Frank Dobie's ranch, Paisano, for Texans, Texas residents, or writers whose work has been substantially identified with the state. Apply by January 22. Write for application and guidelines.

DORLAND MOUNTAIN ARTS COLONY, P.O. Box 6, Temecula, CA 92390, established 1979, is a 300 acre Nature Conservancy preserve which offers 1-2 month residences for writers, visual artists and composers in a rustic environment with no elecricity, propane appliances (refrigerator, water heater, cooking stove). Residents provide their own meals. A donation of $150/month is requested. Write for application form. Deadlines the first of September and March.

DORSET COLONY HOUSE RESIDENCIES; AMERICAN THEATRE WORKS, INC.; DORSET THEATRE FESTIVAL; Box 519, Dorset, VT, available to writers September-May for periods of 1 week-2 months for intensive work. Requested fee of $75 per week, but ability to pay is not a criterion in awarding residencies. Connected with Dorset Theatre Festival, a production company with an interest in new scripts.

FINE ARTS WORK CENTER IN PROVINCETOWN, Box 565, 24 Pearl St., Provincetown, MA 02657, provides monthly stipends of $375 and studio/living quarters for 7 uninterrupted months for 20 young artists and writers (10 of each) who have completed their formal training and are capable of working independently. The Center has a staff of writers and artists who offer manuscript consultations, arrange readings and slide presentations and visits from other distinguished writers and artists. Several established writers are invited each year for extended residencies. Each year they publish *Shankpainter*, a magazine of prose and poetry by the writing fellows. Sessions run from October 1-May 1. Applications, accompanied by a $20 processing fee, must be received by February 1.

GREEN RIVER WRITERS RETREAT, Western Kentucky University, Bowling Green, KY, contact Deborah Spears, 403 S. Sixth St., Ironton, OH 45638, phone 614-533-1081, July 20-August 5, provides rooms in a conference center for $8 per night stayed, registration fee is $15. Applicants furnish a résumé and samples of work along with a statement of goals. Beginning writers will be accepted and furnished with sponsors of whom they can ask assistance with their writing.

HAMBIDGE CENTER FOR CREATIVE ARTS AND SCIENCES, Box 339, Rabun Gap, GA 30568, phone 404-746-5718. The Center is located on six hundred acres of unspoiled wooded slopes, mountain meadows and streams, near Dillard, GA. It is listed on the National Register of Historic Places. Resident Fellowships of 2 weeks-2 months are awarded to individuals engaged in the artistic, scientific, humanistic and educational professions for the purpose of solitude and the pursuit of creative excellence. Those accepted are given a private cottage equipped with a kitchen, sleeping and bathing facilities and a work area. Center is open from May-October. There is also a work-study internship for younger individuals approaching the end of their formal study (requiring 20 hours of work per week). For more information and application forms send SASE (2oz.). Allow approximately 2 months for processing. Applications are reviewed year round.

HAWK, I'M YOUR SISTER, WOMEN'S WILDERNESS CANOE TRIPS, WRITING RETREATS, Beverly Antaeus, P.O. Box 9109, Santa Fe, NM 87504. This organization offers wilderness retreats for women, many of them with writing themes including the Voice That is Great Within Us: A Writing Retreat with Linda Trichter Metcalf; Between the Earth & Silence: A Writing Retreat with W.S. Merwin (coed); and The River as Metaphor: A Writing Retreat with Sharon Olds. The canoe trips are held all over the United States and typically last 8-10 days with fees $800-1,250. Write for annual listing of specific trips.

THE MACDOWELL COLONY, 100 High St., Peterborough, NH 03458, founded 1907, offers residencies to established writers, composers, visual artists, and filmmakers. Over 3,000 artists have stayed there, many of them producing major works. Apply 8 months before desired residency. Private studio, room and meals provided. Accepted artists are asked to contribute toward residency costs. Current application form is necessary; write address above or call 603-924-3886 or 212-966-4860. Average residency is 5-6 weeks. Professional work samples required with application.

THE MILLAY COLONY FOR THE ARTS, INC., Steepletop, P.O. Box 3, Austerlitz, NY 12017-0003, founded in 1974, assistant director Gail Giles, provides work space, meals and sleeping accommodations at no cost for a period of one month. Apply with samples of your work before February 1 for June-September; before May 1 for October-January; before September 1 for February-May.

MONTALVO CENTER FOR THE ARTS; MONTALVO BIENNIAL POETRY COMPETITION, Box 158, Saratoga, CA 95071, presents theatre, musical events and other artistic activities. (I once was on the panel of a poetry workshop there.) They have an Artist-in-Residence program which has 6 apartments available for artists (including poets) for maximum 3-month periods. ($100 single, $115 for a couple. No children or pets.) Limited financial assistance available. They offer a biennial poetry competition open to residents of Oregon, Nebraska, Washington and California, with a prominent judge (Lucille Clifton in 1990), with a first prize of $1,000 (and 3-month residency), other prizes of $500, $300, and 8 honorable mentions. Submit 3 poems in duplicate, entry fee $5, October 10 deadline. Send SASE for rules.

THE NORTHWOOD INSTITUTE ALDEN B. DOW CREATIVITY CENTER, Midland, MI 48640-2398, phone 517-832-4478, founded 1979, director Carol Coppage, offers fellowships for 10-week summer residencies at the Northwood Institute Campus. Travel and all expenses are paid. Applicants can be undergraduates, graduates, or those without any academic or institutional affiliation, including citizens of other countries (if they can communicate in English). Projects may be in any field, but must be new and innovative. Write for application. Annual deadline December 31 for following summer.

PALENVILLE INTERARTS COLONY, 2 Bond St., New York, NY 10012, offers 1-8 week residencies in Palenville, New York, for seclusion or for interaction among artists of various disciplines in a relaxed and creative atmosphere. Fee (negotiable): $175 per week. Open June 1 to September 30. Application deadline is April 1st.

RAGDALE FOUNDATION, 1260 N. Green Bay Road, Lake Forest, IL 60045, founded 1976, director Michael Wilkerson, provides a peaceful place and uninterrupted time for 12 writers, scholars, composers and artists. Meals, linen and laundry facilities are provided. Each resident is assigned private work space and sleeping accommodations. Couples are accepted if each qualifies independently. Residents may come for 2 weeks to 2 months. The fee is $70 per week. Some financial assistance available. The Foundation also sponsors poetry readings, concerts, workshops and seminars in writing. Ragdale is open year-round except for June 15-30 and December 15-January 1. Apply four months in advance of anticipated residency.

MILDRED I. REID WRITERS COLONY IN NEW HAMPSHIRE, Penacook Road, Contoocook, NH 03229, phone 603-746-3625. Winter address Apt. 5, 917 Bucida Road, Delray Beach, FL 33483, phone 407-278-3607. The Mildred Reid Writers Colony is run as a private enterprise; there are weekly sessions from July 8 to August 19. The sessions are held at a chalet in the country, 10 miles west of Concord, NH. Cost of a week at the Colony ranges from $130 for a single room and shared bath to $220 double rate for a log cabin in the pines. Fees include room, breakfast, two private conferences and two class sessions weekly. Kitchen facilities are available, and a village with restaurants within walking distance. Ms. Reid gives private consultations at $5/half hour.

SPLIT ROCK ARTS PROGRAM, 306 Wesbrook Hall, 77 Pleasant St., SE, University of Minnesota, Minneapolis, MN 55455, is a summer series of week-long residential workshops in the visual and literary arts and in the nature and applications of creativity, on the Duluth campus of UM "in the green hills near the city's summit." 1990 writing faculty included Paulette Alden, Christina Baldwin, Alan Burns, Arlene Cardozo, Carolyn Forche, Kate Green, Linda Hogan, Phebe Hanson, Jane Howard, Valerie Miner, Gary Paulsen, Jerry Vizenor. Tuition ranges from $211-266 for workshops taken for credit and $210-256 for workshops taken for no credit. Housing is $80 for a double, $115 for a single, in two-bedroom suites. Meals are in UMD's cafeteria, cooked by participants in their apartments or in a Duluth restaurant. Other housing options are also available; they range from $75-150 per week.

UCROSS FOUNDATION RESIDENCY PROGRAM, 2836 US Hwy. 14-16, Clearmont, WY 82835, phone 307-737-2291, Program Director Elizabeth Guheen. There are four concurrent positions open in various disciplines, including poetry, each extending from 2 weeks to 4 months. No charge for room, board or studio space, and they do not expect services or products from guests. Send SASE for information form, which must be accompanied by a work sample and general description of the work you plan to do at Ucross. Residents are selected from a rotating panel of professionals in the arts and humanities in October and March for, respectively, the Spring and Fall residencies. Semi-annual application deadlines are March 1 and October 1.

‡VERMONT STUDIO SCHOOL & COLONY; VISUAL ARTISTS AND WRITERS RESIDENCIES, P.O. Box 613, Johnson, VT 05656, phone 802-635-2727, founded 1984, offers 4 and 8-week residencies for painters, sculptors and writers in November and January through April. Applications accepted all year, reviewed monthly. They can accommodate 16 painters, 4 sculptors, and 4-6 writers at a time, "who, together with the year-round VSC staff artists, form a dynamic working community" in the Green Mountains. "This environment creates the opportunity for as much solitude and retreat or interchange and support as each fellow wishes. Fellowships available covering most costs. Writers' work spaces as well as housing for all Fellows are provided in individual accommodations in colony residences in the village of Johnson, all within walking distance of each other as well as the Red Mill complex that contains the dining hall, lounge, offices, gallery. Johnson State College is also within walking distance."

VIRGINIA CENTER FOR THE CREATIVE ARTS, Mt. San Angelo, Sweet Briar, VA 24595, director William Smart, provides residencies for 13 writers (and 9 visual artists and 3 composers) for 1-3 months at the 450 acre Mt. San Angelo estate. The normal fee is $20 per day. Financial assistance is available.

‡WOMEN'S STUDIO WORKSHOP, Box 489, Rosendale, NY 12472, phone 914-658-9133, founded 1979, offers grants to artists to use "extensive studios located in the foothills of the Shawangunk Mountains 100 miles north of New York City." It is a printmaking, papermaking, and book arts center. Grants are for 1-3 months September 1-June 30, providing housing and a $2,000 per month stipend. Send SASE for application form, requiring bio, 3 writing samples, cover letter describing the proposed project, and preferred time of residency. December 15 deadline. "Public Service is an integral component of all WSW's activities, which may range from conducting a lecture/demonstration to teaching a class in curating an exhibit."

THE WRITERS COMMUNITY, West Side YMCA Center for the Arts, New York NY 10023, phone 212-787-6557, offers an advanced 3-month master writing program in poetry, October-December, March-May (application deadline mid-September, mid-February), working with a writer-in-residence. All members are asked to contribute $85 to the program, but there are no other fees. Submit biographical information, a minimum of 10 pp. of poetry, which may be published material. All material should be typed or printed and copies should be retained. MSS cannot be returned. Call for application deadlines.

THE HELENE WURLITZER FOUNDATION OF NEW MEXICO, Box 545, Taos, NM 87571, offers residencies to creative, *not* interpretive, artists in all media, rent free and utilities free, for varying periods of time, usually 3 months, from April 1 to September 30, annually. Residents are responsible for their food. No families. No deadlines on application.

YADDO, Box 395, Saratoga Springs, NY 12866-0395, founded 1926, c/o President Myra Sklarew, offers residencies to authors, visual artists and composers who have already achieved some recognition in their field and have new work under way. During the summer 35 guests can be accommodated, 12 during the winter. Some guests live in rooms in the mansion during the summer, or in other residences and in cottages around the estate; in the winter the mansion is closed, but guests live and work in West House, Pine Garde, and East House and outside studios. The hours 9-4 are a quiet period reserved for work. There is no fixed charge for a guest stay, but voluntary contributions of up to $20/day to help defray costs of the program are accepted. Application deadlines are January 15 and August 1. A $20 application fee is required.

Additional Writing Colonies

The following also offer facilities for writers. Read their listings for details. See the General Index for page numbers.

Pudding House Publications
Tiffany and Shore Publishers

ALWAYS submit MSS or queries with a stamped, self-addressed envelope (SASE) within your country or International Reply Coupons (IRCs) purchased from the post office for other countries.

Organizations
Useful to Poets

An organization of poets may sound like a contradiction in terms, but the truth is, our breed is fairly well organized. You may need support (emotional or financial) and be able to find it if you know how to get in touch with people like yourself nationally or in your local area. For instance, most states have arts councils and many of these offer grants for individual writers. Check your state's listings in your local phone directory. The arts council's number will be given or there will be a general phone number to call for such specific information. Check out, too, the National Federation of State Poetry Societies (see their listing in this section) to see whether your state or city has a chapter you might join. Consider joining the Poetry Society of America or the Academy of American Poets (both listed in this section) to receive their publications and to become eligible for their awards. Keep an eye on *Poets & Writers* (see Publications Useful to Poets) for ads and announcements from a wide range of organizations available to you, some of them offering grants and awards for which you may apply.

Though writing is, in general, a lonely occupation, it is sometimes surprising to look up and discover that we are, in fact, surrounded by a vast support system of groups which have been formed to share, encourage and foster our work. There is probably a writers' group or club in your area. If not, it is easy to form one. Just put up notices on public bulletin boards, or take out an ad in your local paper, suggesting that interested writers get together at some specific time and place. Often public libraries have rooms available for such purposes if you don't want to use your home. There are many more closet poets (and other writers) around the country than you might believe.

I have listed here some of the major organizations which offer support of various kinds to poets, and some representative samples of smaller groups.

ACADEMY OF AMERICAN POETS; FELLOWSHIP OF THE ACADEMY OF AMERICAN POETS; WALT WHITMAN AWARD; THE LAMONT POETRY SELECTION; HAROLD MORTON LANDON TRANSLATION AWARD; PETER I.B. LAVAN YOUNGER POETS AWARD, 177 E. 87th St., New York, NY 10128, founded 1934, by Marie Bullock. I quote Robert Penn Warren, from the *Introduction to Fifty Years of American Poetry*, an anthology published in 1984 containing one poem from each of the 126 Chancellors, Fellows and Award Winners of the Academy: "What does the Academy do? According to its certificate of incorporation, its purpose is 'To encourage, stimulate, and foster the production of American poetry. . . .' The responsibility for its activities lies with the Board of Directors and the Board of 12 Chancellors, which has included, over the years, such figures as Louise Bogan, W. H. Auden, Witter Bynner, Randall Jarrell, Robert Lowell, Robinson Jeffers, Marianne Moore, James Merrill, Robert Fitzgerald, F. O. Matthiessen, and Archibald MacLeish—certainly not members of the same poetic church." They award fellowships, currently of $20,000 each, to distinguished American poets (no applications taken)—50 to date—and other annual awards. The Walt Whitman Award pays $1,000 plus publication of a poet's first book by a major publisher (Doubleday in 1990). MSS of 50-100 pp. must be submitted between September 15 and November 15 with a $10 entry fee. The Lamont Poetry Selection, for a poet's second book, is again a prize of $1,000 and publication. The Academy distributes 2,000 copies to its members. Submissions must be made by a publisher, in MSS form, prior to publication. Poets entering either contest must be American citizens. The Harold Morton Landon Translation Award is for translation of a book-length poem, a collection of poems, or a verse-drama translated into English from any language. One award of $1,000 each year to a U.S. citizen. Only publishers may submit the book. Write for guidelines. The Peter I.B. Lavan Younger Poets Awards of $1,000 each are given annually to three younger poets selected by Academy Chancellors (no applications taken). *Poetry Pilot* is an informative periodical sent to those who contribute $20 or more per year or who are members. Membership: $45 per year.

THE AMERICAN ACADEMY & INSTITUTE OF ARTS & LETTERS; THE ARTS AND LETTERS AWARDS; MICHAEL BRAUDE AWARD FOR LIGHT VERSE; THE GOLD MEDAL OF THE ACADEMY; WITTER BYNNER FOUNDATION POETRY PRIZE; FELLOWSHIP TO THE AMERICAN ACADEMY IN ROME; JEAN STEIN AWARD; MORTON DAUWEN ZABEL PRIZE (V), 633 W. 155th St., New York, NY 10032, offers annual awards in the arts, several of which are given to poets—by nomination only. **No applications for these awards are accepted.** These are: The Arts & Letters Awards of $5,000 each, given to 8 writers annually, some poets; the Michael Braude Award for Light Verse of $5,000, given biennially for light verse in the English language; The Gold Medal of the American Academy and Institute of Arts and Letters, given to a poet every 6 years; Award of Merit of $5,000 for an outstanding artist in one field of the arts, given to a poet once every 6 years; the Witter Bynner Foundation Poetry Prize of $1,500; a fellowship to the American Academy in Rome, including lodging and a stipend to a poet or fiction writer; the Jean Stein Award of $5,000 given every 3rd year to a poet whose work takes risks in expressing its commitment to the author's values and vision; the Morton Dauwen Zabel Prize of $5,000 given every 3rd year to a poet of "progressive, original and experimental tendencies rather than of academic and conservative tendencies." The 7 members of the jury are all Academy-Institute members appointed for a 3-year term. **Candidates (only published writers are considered) must be nominated by a member of the academy-institute.**

‡AMERICAN POETRY CENTER; ALL MUSE: PENNSYLVANIA'S LITERARY NETWORK NEWSLETTER; YOUNG VOICES OF PENNSYLVANIA POETRY CONTEST, 1204 Walnut St., Philadelphia, PA 19107, phone 215-546-1510, 800-ALL-MUSE (in Pennsylvania), program director Christopher Jones, sponsors Poetry Week, Pennsylvania's statewide literary festival in March, which kicks-off the Center's year-round activities that include: Young Voices, a statewide poetry contest for students aged 5-18, the winners of which are published and give readings of their work at libraries during APC's Poetry Week festival; a Residency Program to bring poets and theater artists to work with students at schools throughout the Philadelphia area, arranging day-, week-, or month-long residencies for poets-in-residence by experienced Philadelphia-based poets, with a similar program for theater artists; also arranges for residence poets to help teachers learn how to use poetry as a learning tool in the classroom; and *All Muse*, their free, professionally printed, magazine-sized, saddle-stapled, 30 pp. newsprint publication, which appears in January and September, 20,000 copies distributed free, giving regional events, publications, workshops, profiles, and other news. Their All-Muse hotline provides recorded messages about upcoming literary events in the area.

ASSOCIATED WRITING PROGRAMS; AWP CHRONICLE; THE AWP AWARD SERIES, Old Dominion University, Norfolk, VA 23529-0079, founded 1967, offers a variety of services to the writing community, including information, job placement assistance, publishing opportunities, literary arts advocacy and forums. Annual individual membership is $40; placement service extra. For $15 you can subscribe to the *AWP Chronicle* (published six times a year), containing information about grants and awards, publishing opportunities, fellowships, and writing programs. They have a catalog of over 250 college and university writing programs. The AWP Award Series selects a volume of poetry each year to be published ($10 entry fee). Send SASE for submission guidelines. Query after September. Their placement service helps writers find jobs in teaching, editing and other related fields.

ATLANTA WRITING RESOURCE CENTER, INC., Room 105, The Arts Exchange, 750 Kalb St., Atlanta, GA 30312, "is for everyone with an interest in writing, whether for print or electronic media or simply for personal satisfaction. The Center will provide reference materials, guidelines information samples, standard writing formats, and other resources for effective writing and marketing." There is a bi-monthly critique group for poets and short story writers, and a monthly open reading and open house called "Writers' Brawl" on the fourth Thursday of each month. The Center has regular open hours (staffed by executive director and volunteers) with personal work space including typewriters, computers, reference books, and other resources. They publish a quarterly newsletter highlighting Center activities and Atlanta's literary events, and they provide news of contests, writers' conferences, etc. They also sponsor an annual contest for previously unpublished original poems. Small cash prizes and honorable mentions. Winners published in *The Chattahoochee Review*. Write for current guidelines. Literary magazines and journals as well as their writers' guidelines are available at the Center. They also hold workshopw aimed at improving literary and marketing skills.

AUTHORS LEAGUE FUND, 234 W. 44th St., New York, NY 10036, makes interest-free loans to published authors in need of temporary help because of illness or an emergency. No grants.

BEYOND BAROQUE LITERARY/ARTS CENTER, Box 2727, 681 Venice Blvd., Venice, CA 90291, phone 213-822-3006, director D.B. Finnegan, a foundation established in 1968 that has been funded by the NEA, state and city arts councils, and corporate donations. Foundation members get a calendar of events, discounts on regularly scheduled programs, and borrowing privileges in the small-press library of 3,000 volumes of poetry, fiction, and reference materials, including audio tapes of Beyond Baroque readings. Beyond Baroque contains a bookstore open 5 days a week, including Friday evenings to coincide with regular weekly readings and performances. About 130 writers are invited to read each year; there are also open readings.

BLACK CULTURAL CENTRE FOR NOVA SCOTIA, Box 2128 East Dartmouth, NS B2W 3Y2 Canada, phone 902-434-6223, founded 1977 "to create among members of the Black communities an awareness of their past, their heritage and their identity; to provide programs and activities for the general public to explore, learn about, understand and appreciate black history, black achievements and black experiences in the broad context of Canadian life. The Centre houses a museum, reference library, archival area, small auditorium and studio workshops."

BURNABY WRITERS' SOCIETY, 6450 Deer Lake Ave., Burnaby, BC, V5G 2J3, Canada, contact person Eileen Kernaghan. Corresponding membership in the society, including a newsletter subscription, is open to anyone, anywhere. Yearly dues are $20. Sample newsletter in return for SASE with Canadian stamp. The Society holds monthly meetings at The Burnaby Arts Centre (address above), with a business meeting at 7:30 followed by a writing workshop or speaker. Members of the society stage regular public readings of their own work.

THE WITTER BYNNER FOUNDATION FOR POETRY, INC., P.O. Box 2188, Santa Fe, NM 87504, phone 505-988-3251, president Douglas W. Schwartz. The Foundation awards grants exclusively to nonprofit organizations for the support of poetry-related projects in the area of: 1) support of individual poets through existing nonprofit institutions; 2) developing the poetry audience; 3) poetry translation and the process of poetry translation; and 4) uses of poetry. The Foundation "may consider the support of other creative and innovative projects in poetry." Grant applications must be received by February 1 each year; requests for application forms should be submitted to Steven Schwartz, Administrator, at the address above.

THE CANADA COUNCIL; GOVERNOR GENERAL'S LITERARY AWARDS; INTERNATIONAL LITERARY PRIZES, 99 Metcalfe St., Box 1047, Ottawa, ON K1P 5V8, phone 613-237-3400, established by Parliament in 1957, "provides a wide range of grants and services to professional Canadian artists and art organizations in dance, music, theatre, writing and publishing, visual arts, and media arts." The Governor General's Literary Awards, valued at $10,000 (Canadian) each, are given annually for the best English-language and best French-language work in each of six categories, including poetry. A jury reviews all books by Canadian authors, illustrators and translators published in Canada or abroad during the previous year (December 1-November 30). **Applications are not accepted.** There are four International Literary Prizes (Canada-Australia, Canada-French Community of Belgium, Canada-Japan, and Canada-Switzerland) of $2,500-3,000 each, selected by juries. Except for the Canada-Japan Prize, applications are not accepted.

CANADIAN CONFERENCE ON THE ARTS, 126 York St., Suite 400, Ottawa, ON K1N 5T5 Canada, phone 613-238-3561, was created for "the encouragement of the federal, provincial, and municipal governments, as well as the corporate and private sector, to develop policies which will ensure the continued growth of the arts and the cultural industries in Canada." It supplies members with information on political issues affecting the daily lives of artists and writers. Members receive *Arts Bulletin*, a quarterly new magazine of the organization; *Arts News* and other information on cultural issues of the day; counseling, general representation, and active support. They sponsor conferences such as taxation and the artist, and offer other services. Membership for individuals is $10 for students and senior citizens, $25 for others, or organizational members on a sliding scale (depending on the organization's budget) of $60-900.

CANADIAN SOCIETY OF CHILDREN'S AUTHORS, ILLUSTRATORS & PERFORMERS, Box 260, Station L, Toronto, ON M6E 4Z2 Canada, phone 416-654-0903, president Priscilla Galloway, is a "Society of Professionals in the field of children's culture. Puts people into contact with publishers, offers advice to beginners, and generally provides a visible profile for members; 250 professional members and over 800 associates which are termed 'friends.' An annual conference in Toronto the last week of October provides workshops to people interested in writing, illustrating, and performing for children." Membership is $50 per year, which includes a subscription to the quarterly *Canscaip News* and a free copy of the Membership Directory.

COSMEP, THE INTERNATIONAL ASSOCIATION OF INDEPENDENT PUBLISHERS; COSMEP NEWSLETTER, Box 703, San Francisco, CA 94101. If you are starting a small press or magazine or are embarking on self-publication, you should know about the advantages of membership in COSMEP. Send SASE for brochure. They are the largest trade association for small press in the U.S. Included among membership benefits is the monthly *COSMEP Newsletter*, which prints news and commentary for small publishers.

COUNCIL OF LITERARY MAGAZINES AND PRESSES, DIRECTORY OF LITERARY MAGAZINES; CLMP NEWS; CLMP GENERAL ELECTRIC FOUNDATION AWARDS FOR YOUNGER WRITERS, 666 Broadway, New York, NY 10012 provides annual grants to various literary magazines and publishes an annual directory useful to writers: The *Directory of Literary Magazines*, which has detailed descriptions of over 425 literary magazines which are supported by CLMP, as well as the tri-quarterly *CLMP News*. They also administer the General Electric Foundation Awards for Younger Writers, designed to recognize excellence in younger and less established creative writers and to support the literary magazines that publish their work. Nominations are accepted before April 30 from editors of noncommercial literary magazines published in the US and its territories.

‡COWBOY POETRY GATHERING; RODEO COWBOY POETRY GATHERING; WESTERN FOLKLIFE CENTER, P.O. Box 888, Elko, NV 89801, phone 702-738-7508, FAX 702-738-8771. The Rodeo Cowboy Gathering can be contacted at the same address, though it is held at Cashman Theater, Las Vegas. Both of these gatherings are sponsored by Western Folklife Center, Box 81105, Salt Lake City, UT 84158, phone 801-533-5391, FAX 801-533-4233, executive director Hal Cannon. There is an annual 4-day January gathering of cowboy poets in Elko, and a one-day gathering during the National Finals Rodeo in Las Vegas in December. The Western Folklife Center publishes and distributes books and tapes of cowboy poetry and songs as well as other cowboy memorabilia. The well-established tradition of cowboy poetry is enjoying a renaissance, and thousands of cowboy poets participate in these activities. Membership in the Western Folklife Center is $20/individual, $50/family. Poetry submissions for consideration must be submitted by October 15 with proven ranching experience and no more than three poems performed on a cassette tape. This is not a contest.

FAIRBANKS ARTS ASSOCIATION; ENVOY; TANANA VALLEY FAIR CREATIVE WRITING CONTEST, Box 72786, Fairbanks, AK 99707. FAA publishes the newsletter, *Envoy*, eight times/year, providing news and market tips especially for Alaskan writers, subscription $10/year. FAA also conducts the Creative Writing Divison for the Tanana Valley Fair, and sponsors a Community Reading Series, for Alaskan and visiting writers.

FEDERATION OF BRITISH COLUMBIA WRITERS, M.P.O. Box 2206, Vancouver, BC V6B 3WC Canada, Executive Director Lynne Melcombe, "is a non-profit organization of professional and aspiring writers in all genres." They publish a newsletter of markets, political reports, awards and Federation news, act as "a network centre for various other provincial writer's organizations; host, promote and organize workshops, public readings, literary competitions and social activities, publish directories which are distributed to schools, businesses, and organizations which may request the services of writers; and represent writers' interests on the BC Book Prizes Committee, the BC Book Promotion Council, and other professionally related organizations."

FESTIVAL OF POETS AND POETRY AT ST. MARY'S; EBENEZER COOKE POETRY FESTIVAL, St. Mary's College of Maryland, St. Mary's City, MD 20686, phone 301-862-0239, is an annual event held during the last two weekends in May of each year. Approximately 18 guest poets and artists participate in and lead workshops, seminars and readings. Concurrent with the Festival, St. Mary's College offers an intensive 14-day poetry writing workshop. The Ebenezer Cooke Poetry Festival is now a bi-annual event in August of even numbered years, held in the name of the first Poet Laureate of Maryland. Poets from Maryland and the surrouding areas are invited to give 5-minute readings, enjoy a crab feast and otherwise celebrate together.

GREAT SWAMP POETRY SERIES; DISTINGUISHED AMERICAN POETS SERIES; THE FIRST AMERICAN POETRY DISC, County College of Morris, Randolph, NJ 07869, phone 201-328-5471 or 328-5460, DAPS founded 1974, GSPS founded 1986, director Sander Zulauf. Outstanding New Jersey poets and poets who write about New Jersey (such as Maria Gillan, Hal Sirowitz, Jean Hollander, James Richardson, Thomas Reiter, and Laura Boss) are invited to read for GSPS for modest honoraria. "America's best poets" — e.g., they have had readings by James Wright, Elizabeth Bishop, Philip Levine, Howard Nemerov, William Stafford, Lyn Lifshin, Paul Zimmer, and Gwendolyn Brooks — are invited to read in the DAPS for respectable honoraria (at least 2 readings per year). They have produced TFAPD, a laser disk anthology of poetry readings taken from the college archives in 3 volumes: **I. An Introduction to Poetry; II. Contemporary American Poetry; III. James Wright.** All programs are approximately one hour each and are available in laser, Beta and VHS formats.

‡HAIKU INTERNATIONAL ASSOCIATION, Box 257, Tokyo 100-91 Japan, founded 1989, "would like to encourage understanding of the rich diversity of haiku by introducing to each other the works of haiku poets, in their original languages or their translations, through publications of the Association."

They publish a bulletin and sponsor events and activities. Membership: $30 U.S. or equivalent for individuals, $300 for sponsoring groups, $500 for corporations.

ILLINOIS WRITERS, INC., P.O. Box 1087, Champaign, IL 61820, founded 1975, editor Kevin Stein, associate editor Jim Elledge. The *Review* publishes essays, reviews, and commentary. While reviews and essays often focus on Illinois authors, presses, and journals, the *Review* also publishes work devoted to books and authors of national prominence. Commentary addresses larger issues or movements in contemporary writing. For example, the emergence of language poetry and the present state of the creative writing workshop. We welcome sample books and chapbooks for review. The *Review* is journal-sized (8½x5½) with cover photos or graphic art, appearing semi-annually. Its circulation is about 400. A subscription is included with the $15 per year membership fee, as well as six issues of a newsletter which offers manuscript submission information, conference notices, and brief articles of interest to writers, publishers, and libraries. Price per issue is $4. Payment presently in copies but reinstituting payment of $25 per article. Reporting time varies from 6-8 weeks.

INTERNATIONAL WOMEN'S WRITING GUILD, Box 810, Gracie Station, New York, NY 10028, phone 212-737-7536, founded 1976, "an alliance of women who value creativity and mutual support"; the women can write either for publication or for personal growth. The Guild publishes a bimonthly 24 page newsletter which includes member's needs, achievements, contests, and publishing information. A manuscript referral service introduces members to literary agents. Other activities are writing conferences and retreats; "regional clusters" (independent regional groups); job referrals; round robin manuscript exchanges; sponsor of the "Artist of Life" award; group health and life insurance; legal aid at group rates. Membership in the nonprofit Guild costs $35/year in the US and $45/year foreign.

‡**INTERSECTION FOR THE ARTS,** 446 Valencia St., San Francisco, CA 94103, phone 415-626-2787. Blue Chip Reading Series.

THE LANE LITERARY GUILD, Lane Regional Arts Council, 411 High St., Eugene, OR 97401, is "a volunteer organization dedicated to encouraging and supporting poets and writers in Lane County, Oregon. We hold monthly readings featuring new and established poets and writers. Our readers are drawn from talent locally as well as from other cities and parts of the country. We also hold workshops, symposia, and literary contests. Our funding comes from membership fees, donations at readings, and from grant support by the Cultural Services Division of the City of Eugene, by the Oregon Arts Commission, and by the National Endowment for the Arts. We are interested in hearing from poets and writers from around the country who will be in our neighborhood and might be interested in being one of our readers."

THE LEAGUE OF CANADIAN POETS; WHEN IS A POEM; WHO'S WHO IN THE LEAGUE OF CANADIAN POETS; HERE IS A POEM; POETRY MARKET FOR CANADIANS; NATIONAL POETRY CONTEST; F.R. SCOTT TRANSLATION AWARD; GERALD LAMPERT MEMORIAL AWARD; PAT LOWTHER MEMORIAL AWARD, 24 Ryerson Ave., Toronto, ON M5T 2P3, Canada, phone 416-363-5047, founded 1966, executive director Angela Rebeiro. The League's aims are the advancement of poetry in Canada and promotion of the interests of professional, committed Canadian poets. Information on full and associate membership can be obtained by writing for the brochure, League of Canadian Poets: Services and Membership. The League publishes a biannual **Museletter** (magazine-sized, 30 pp.) plus eight 4-page issues: **When is a Poem,** on teaching poetry to children; a directory volume called **Who's Who in The League of Canadian Poets** that contains one page of information, including a picture, bio, publications, and "what critics say" about each of the members; **Here is a Poem,** a companion anthology to **When Is a Poem,** featuring the work of Canadian poets, and **Poetry Markets for Canadians** which covers contracts, markets, agents and more. The League's members go on reading tours, and the League encourages them to speak on any facet of Canadian literature at schools and universities, libraries, or organizations. The League has arranged "thousands of readings in every part of Canada"; they are now arranging exchange visits featuring the leading poets of such countries as Great Britain, Germany, and the U.S. The League sponsors a National Poetry Contest with prizes of $1,000, $750 and $500; the best 50 poems published in a book. Deadline January 31. Entry fee $5 per poem. Poems should be unpublished, under 75 lines and typed. Names and addresses should *not* appear on poems but on a separate covering sheet. Please send SASE for complete rules, info on judges, etc. Open to Canadian citizens or landed immigrants only. The F.R. Scott Translation Award of $500 is for a published book of translation submitted (4 copies) by a professional publisher, January 30 deadline. The Gerald Lampert Memorial Award of $500 is for a first book of poetry written by a Canadian, published professionally. The Pat Lowther Memorial Award of $500 is for a book of poetry written by a Canadian woman and published professionally. Write for entry forms. It is also the address of Writers Union of Canada which provides services and information to members, including a writer's guide to Canadian publishers ($3) and a variety of other publications to assist writers.

THE LITERARY CENTER, Box 85116, Seattle, WA 98145-1116, phone 206-547-2503, maintains a resource library and small press collection. Sponsors workshops in poetry and fiction, 2 readings a month, a quarterly magazine (16-24 pages) featuring writers and publishers from the Northwest. Subscriptions $15 a year. **Sample copy $1. Query for book reviews, articles, or interviews.**

THE LOFT, 2301 E. Franklin Ave., Minneapolis, MN 55406, phone 612-341-2211, founded 1974, executive director Susan Broadhead. The Loft was begun by a group of poets looking for a place to give readings and conduct workshops and evolved into a sophisticated hub of activity for creative writing in all genres managed by an 19-member board of directors, and staff of 10. This past year 1,900 members contributed $30/year to the Loft; it was further supported by $46,000 from individuals, plus government, foundation and corporate grants. The Loft offers over 75 eight-week courses each year, in addition to 30 workshops and panels. Its publication readings and emerging voices readings are meant for Minnesota writers whereas the Mentor Series and Creative Non-fiction residency feature nationally known writers. The Loft publishes a monthly newsletter called *A View from the Loft*. The Loft's present quarters are in an old church, which has offices and classrooms in the basement and performance areas on the main floor. See also The Loft-McKnight Writers Awards under Contests and Awards.

‡**MAINE WRITERS & PUBLISHERS ALLIANCE; MAINE IN PRINT; MAINE WRITERS CENTER**, 19 Mason St., Brunswick, ME 04011, phone 207-729-6333, founded 1975, according to membership coordinator Paul Doiron, is "a nonprofit organization dedicated to promoting all aspects of writing, publishing, and the book arts. Our membership currently includes over 1,300 writers, publishers, librarians, teachers, booksellers, and readers from across Maine and the nation. For an individual contribution of $20 per year members receive a range of benefits including *Maine in Print*, a monthly compilation of calendar events, updated markets, book reviews, grant information, interviews with Maine authors and publishers, articles about writing, and more. The Alliance distributes selected books about Maine and by Maine authors and publishers, and it maintains a bookstore, reference library, performance space, and word processing station at the Maine Writers Center in Brunswick. MWPA regularly invites writers to read from their works and to conduct Saturday workshops."

NATIONAL FEDERATION OF STATE POETRY SOCIETIES, INC., Membership Chairman: Barbara Stevens, 900 E. 34th St., Sioux Falls, SD 57105; Contest chairperson: Amy Jo Zook, 3520 State Rt. 56, Mechanicsburg, OH 43044. "NFSPS is a nonprofit organization exclusively educational and literary. Its purpose is to recognize the importance of poetry with respect to national cultural heritage. It is dedicated solely to the furtherance of poetry on the national level and serves to unite poets in the bonds of fellowship and understanding." Any poetry group located in a state not already affiliated but interested in affiliating with NFSPS may contact the membership chairman. Canadian groups may also apply. "In a state where no valid group exists, help may also be obtained by individuals interested in organizing a poetry group for affiliation." Most reputable state poetry societies are members of the National Federation and advertise their various poetry contests through their quarterly bulletin, *Strophes*, available for SASE and $1, editor Kay Kinnaman, Route 3, Box 348, Alexandria, IN 46001. Beware of organizations calling themselves state poetry societies (however named) that are not members of NFSPS, as such labels are sometimes used by vanity schemes trying to sound respectable. Others, such as the Oregon State Poetry Association and the Virginia State Poetry Societies, are quite reputable, but they don't belong to NFSPS. NFSPS holds an annual meeting in a different city each year with a large awards banquet, addressed by an honorary chairman. They sponsor 50 national contests in various categories each year, including the NFSPS Prize of $1,000 for first place; $400, second; $200, third; with entry fees ($3 for the entire contest for members, $5 for NFSPS Award; $1/poem for non-members and $5 for NFSPS award up to 4 poems per entry). All poems winning over $10 are published in an anthology. Rules for all contests are given in a brochure available from Kay Kinnaman at *Strophes* or Amy Jo Zook at the address above; you can also write for the address of your state poetry society.

THE NATIONAL POETRY FOUNDATION; SAGETRIEB; PAIDEUMA, University of Maine at Orono, ME 04469, Marie M. Alpert, Publications Coordinator. "The NPF is a non-profit organization concerned with publishing scholarship on the work of 20th century poets, particularly Ezra Pound and those in the Imagist/Objectivist tradition. We publish *Paideuma*, a journal devoted to Ezra Pound scholarship, and *Sagetrieb*, a journal devoted to poets in the imagist/objectivist tradition, as well as two other journals of contemporary poetry and comment — *The New York Quarterly*, and *Pequod*. [See separate listings for *New York Quarterly* and *Pequod*.] NPF conducts a conference each summer and celebrates the centennial of an individual 20th century poet. Marianne Moore's centennial was celebrated in June of 1987, and T. S. Eliot's 100th year was celebrated in August of 1988." Sample copies: $8.95 for *Paideuma* or *Sagetrieb*; $5.00 for *New York Quarterly* or *Pequod*.

NATIONAL WRITERS UNION, 13 Astor Place, Seventh Floor, New York NY 10003, offer members such services as contract bargaining, a grievance committee, contract guidelines, health insurance, press credentials, computer discounts, car-rental discounts, and caucuses and trade groups for exchange of information about special markets. Members receive *The American Writer,* the organization's newsletter. Membership is $55 for those earning less than $5,000 per year; $95 for those earning $5,000-$25,000; and $135 for those earning more than $25,000.

NORTH CAROLINA WRITERS' NETWORK: THE NETWORK NEWS; NORTH CAROLINA POETRY CHAPBOOK COMPETITION; THE RANDALL JARRELL POETRY PRIZE, P.O. Box 954, Carrboro, NC 27510, established 1985, supports the work of writers, writers' organizations and literary programming statewide. A $25 donation annually brings members the bimonthly *The Network News* newsletter containing organizational news, national market information and other material of interst to writers, and access to the Resource Center, Writers' Exchange, Workshops, Literary Brokerage and Press Service. 1,300 members nationwide. Also sponsors competitions in short fiction, one-act plays and nonfiction essays for North Carolinians.

THE OREGON STATE POETRY ASSOCIATION, % Mary Scheirman, 950 Spalding Road, Coos Bay, OR 97420, phone 503-267-7236, newsletter editor Lindsay Thompson, founded 1956 for "the promotion and creation of poetry," has over 400 members, $10 dues, publishes a quarterly *OSPA Newsletter,* and sponsors contests twice yearly, October and April, with total cash prizes of $300 each (no entry fee to members, $2 per poem for non-members; out of state entries welcome). Themes and categories vary. For details write to Leona Ward, 1645 S.E. Spokane St., Portland, OR 97202 after August 1 and February 15 each year. The association sponsors workshops, readings, and seminars around the state.

PEN AMERICAN CENTER; PEN WRITERS FUND; PEN TRANSLATION PRIZE: RENATO POGGIOLI AWARD; GRANTS AND AWARDS, 568 Broadway, New York, NY 10012, phone 212-334-1660, "is the largest of more than 80 centers which comprise International PEN, founded in London in 1921 by John Galsworthy to foster understanding among men and women of letters in all countries. Members of PEN work for freedom of expression wherever it has been endangered, and International PEN is the only worldwide organization of writers and the chief voice of the literary community." Its total membership on all continents is approximately 10,000. "The 2,500 members of the American Center include poets, playwrights, essayists, editors, novelists (for the original letters in the acronym PEN), as well as translators and those editors and agents who have made a substantial contribution to the literary community. Membership in American PEN includes reciprocal privileges in foreign centers for those traveling abroad. Branch offices are located in Cambridge, Houston, Chicago, and San Francisco. Among PEN's various activities are public events and symposia, literary awards, assistance to writers in prison and to American writers in need (grants and loans up to $1,000 from PEN Writers Fund). Medical insurance for writers is available to members. The quarterly *PEN Newsletter* is sent to all members, and is available to nonmembers by subscription. The PEN Translation prize, sponsored by the Book-of-the-Month Club, 1 each year of $3,000 for works published in the current calendar year. The Renato Poggioli Award, $3,000 annually, to encourage a promising translator from the Italian who has not yet been widely recognized. Candidates with a project in literary translation planning a journey to Italy will be favored. Submit resume, sample translation and description of project before February 1. They publish **Grants and Awards** biennially, containing guidelines, deadlines, eligibility requirements and other information about hundreds of grants, awards, and competitions for poets and other writers: $7.50 postpaid. Send SASE for booklet describing their activities and listing their publications, some of them available free.

PERSONAL POETS UNITED, 860 Armand Ct. NE, Atlanta, GA 30324, % Jean Hesse, who started a business in 1980 writing poems for individuals for a fee (for greetings, special occasions, etc). Others started similar businesses, after she began instructing them in the process, especially through a cassette tape training program and other training materials. She then organized a support group of poets around the country writing poetry-to-order, Personal Poets United, hoping to have local chapters in key areas and a national conference. Send SASE for free brochure.

PITTSBURGH POETRY EXCHANGE, 159 S. 16th St., Pittsburgh, PA 15203, phone 412-488-8840, founded 1974 as a community-based organization for local poets. It functions as a service organization and information exchange, conducting ongoing workshops, readings, forums, and other special events. No dues or fees. "At our open workshop we each drop a dollar into the basket which we turn over to City Books as 'rent' for use of the space. Any other monetary contributions are voluntary, often from outside sources. We've managed not to let our reach exceed our grasp." Contact Michael Wurster at the above address or phone number.

Close-up

Allan Lefcowitz
Chairman
Bethesda Writer's Center

Death
The dark, morbid,
macabre, cavern of my soul
looks to you for sustenance,
for warm, hopeful, encouraging,
words,
like a blood-sucking leech
waiting, forever, eternally forever,
on the silent axis of Time.

To call these lines deathless would be an act of supreme pessimism. But when the staff at the Bethesda Writer's Center dreamed them up over beers at a local tavern, they weren't aiming for literary immortality. They were producing the worst possible poems for submission to the plethora of vanity contests and anthologies. Al Lefcowitz, the chairman of the board of the Center, reprinted some telling responses from these "publishers" in *Carousel*, the Center newsletter. "Death" and similar poems would be called "vivid and profound." Then the acceptance letter would suggest the poet buy an expensive anthology to have the privilege of seeing the published work.

"The various publishing scams work," Lefcowitz says, "by exploiting people's ignorance of how real publishing operates. We try to get accurate information out to our members through *Carousel*, the workshops, anyone who calls up to ask about an offer, whatever."

Publishing *Carousel* is just one of the Center's functions. It offers a small press book and magazine gallery, workshops, computer access and typesetting facilities. It now publishes the long-lived magazine *Poet Lore*, whose circulation has doubled since the Center took it over. From nine people around Al Lefcowitz's dining room table during the planning stages in the mid-1970s, the organization has grown to 2,000 members, with a mailing list of 6,000 and a $325,000 annual budget. About 85 percent of that money is income earned from memberships, book sales and workshop fees. The remainder comes from government grants.

Originally, the National Endowment for the Arts (N.E.A.) had no guidelines for "literary centers," which meant that the Board had to apply for grant money under several different categories. So Lefcowitz and the others wrote a set of standards that has become the N.E.A.'s model for such organizations, including: physical space, a fulltime paid staff, writer services (e.g. computers, fax, typesetting, reference) and an educational program. People wanting to start similar organizations in their own areas have come from all over the country, and even from Senegal, to tour the Bethesda facility.

Lefcowitz's advice to such people includes stressing the importance of sufficient affordable space. "Aim to have a paid staff down the line," he says. "When using volunteers always assume that their energy and enthusiasm could flag unexpectedly, and be prepared to do without them. Let in everybody—poets, novelists, journalists, trade writers." He says that a Writer's Center predecessor in Maryland failed because they restricted their membership. "Listen to your community. If you don't have a lot of small press in the area you don't need to invest in typesetting. You don't need a big computer room if all the local writers have machines already. But you may want to run a bulletin board." Above all, he credits the Center's success to its mix of services. "People come to a reading, they buy a book. Someone comes to a workshop and learns that we have readings. Somebody comes in to buy a book and sees the typesetting facilities."

For the founders of such an organization, the group itself is likely to become their creative art for a good long time. Before helping found the Writer's Center, Lefcowitz had several plays produced by local theaters and won a Maryland State Arts Council prize for his drama. The time pressures of chairing the Center Board and teaching at the Naval Academy have consumed all of his creative energy until just this year. Now, following a bypass operation, he plans to step down from the Board to allow a new generation to move into the organization leadership. He just recently submitted two new plays to contests.

His contribution to the Writer's Center is likely to endure even what he sees as the inevitable decline in general literacy. A fan of science fiction, he speculates, without rancor, about a future in which fewer people read as fewer people need to. "How many significant cultures in history were generally literate?" he asks. "Indeed, there will likely be cultures on Earth that will never attain general literacy as they develop. They'll skip that stage. Maybe one of the reaons for the success of the Writer's Center is that it provides a meeting place for some of those who still cherish the written word."

—Jim Henley

THE POETRY CENTER OF THE 92ND STREET Y; DISCOVERY/THE NATION POETRY CONTEST, 1395 Lexington Ave., New York, NY 10128, phone 212-415-5760, offers annual series of readings by major literary figures (34 readings September-May), writing workshops, and lectures. You may join the center to participate in and be informed of these activities. Also co-sponsors the Discovery/The Nation Poetry Contest. Deadline mid-February. Send SASE for information.

THE POETRY COMMITTEE OF THE GREATER WASHINGTON AREA, The Folger Shakespeare Library, 201 E. Capitol St. SE, Washington, DC 20003, phone 202-544-7077, president and chairman of the board Karren L. Alenier, formed in the mid-70s at the invitation of the poetry coordinator of the Folger Library, meets informally 5 times a year "to talk about the poetry scene, promote poetry in whatever ways we can (mostly letter writing, some projects also) and to support a DC archival project at the George Washington University." The membership (by invitation) consists of about 60 people who represent major and minor poetry organizations in the metropolitan area (a few from Baltimore also). Annual sponsors of Celebration of Washington Poetry, a reading and book sale highlighting area poets and presses and the Poetry Committee Book Award for best book of poetry by Washington area poet within the past calendar year.

THE POETRY PROJECT AT ST. MARK'S CHURCH IN THE BOWERY, 10th St. and 2nd Ave., New York, NY 10003, phone 212-674-0910, was established in 1966 by the US Dept. of H.E.W. in an effort to help wayward youths in the East Village. It is now funded by a variety of government and private sources. Artistic Director: Ed Friedman. Program Coordinator: Kimberly Lyons. From October through May the project offers workshops, talks, staged readings, performance poetry, lectures and an annual 4-day symposium, and a series of featured writers who bring their books to sell at the readings. If the reading is a publication party, the publisher handles the sales.

POETRY RESOURCE CENTER OF MICHIGAN, 111 E. Kirby, Detroit MI 48202, phone 313-972-5580, "is a nonprofit organization which exists through the generosity of poets, writers, teachers, publishers, printers, librarians, and others dedicated to the reading and enjoyment of poetry in Michigan. The *PRC Newsletter* and *Calendar* is available by mail [monthly] for an annual membership donation of $20 or more, and is distributed free of charge at locations throughout the state. To obtain copies for distribution at poetry functions, contact the editor or any member of the PRC Board of Trustees.

POETRY SOCIETY OF AMERICA; POETRY SOCIETY OF AMERICA AWARDS, 15 Gramercy Park, New York, NY 10003, phone 212-254-9628, is a nonprofit cultural organization in support of poetry and of poets, member and nonmember, young and established, which sponsors readings, lectures, and workshops both in New York City and around the country. Their peer group workshop is open to all members and meets on a weekly basis. They publish a newsletter of their activities. And they sponsor a wide range of contests. The following are open to members only: Gordon Barber Award ($200); Gertrude B. Claytor Award ($250); Gustav Davidson Award ($500); Mary Carolyn Davies Award ($250); Alice Fay Di Castegnola Award ($2,000); Emily Dickinson Award ($100); Consuelo Ford Award ($250); Cecil Hemley Memorial Award ($300); Lucille Medwick Memorial Award ($500). Nonmembers may enter as many of the following contests as they wish, no more than 1 entry for each, for a $5 fee: Ruth Lake Award (III), $100 for a poem of retrospection any length; Elias Lieberman Student Poetry Award, $100 for students in grades 9-12; John Masefield Memorial Award (II) for a narrative poem in English up to 300 lines, $500, translations ineligible; Celia B. Wagner Award (II), $250 any form or length; Robert H. Winner Memorial Award (II), $800 for a poem "characterized by delight in language and the possibilities of discovery in ordinary life," line limit 150. (All have a deadline of December 31; awards are made at a ceremony and banquet in late spring. The Society also has 3 book contests open to nonmembers, but publishers only may enter books; they must obtain an entry form, and there is a $5 fee for each book entered. Book awards are: Melville Cane Award (II), $500 in even-numbered years awarded to a book of poems, in odd years to prose work on poetry; Norma Farber Award (III), $1,000 for a first book; William Carlos Williams Award (III), $1,250 for a book of poetry published by a small press, nonprofit or university press, by a permanent resident of the U.S.—translations not eligible. The Shelley Memorial Award of $2,000 is by nomination of a jury of 3 poets. For necessary rules and guidelines for their various contests send SASE after September 1. Membership: $35.

POETS & WRITERS, INC., See **Poets & Writers** under Publications Useful to Poets.

POETS' CORNER, THE CATHEDRAL CHURCH OF ST. JOHN THE DIVINE, Cathedral Heights, 1047 Amsterdam Ave. at 112 St., New York, NY 10025, initiated in 1984 with memorials for Emily Dickinson, Walt Whitman, Washington Irving, Robert Frost, Herman Melville, Nathanial Hawthorne, Edgar Allen Poe, Henry James, Henry David Thoreau, Mark Twain, Ralph Waldo Emerson, William Faulkner, and Wallace Stevens. It is similar in concept to the English Poets' Corner in Westminster Abbey, and was established and dedicated to memorialize this country's greatest writers.

POETS HOUSE; THE REED FOUNDATION LIBRARY; POETRY TEACHER OF THE YEAR AWARD; TRANSLATION FUND, 351 W. 18th St., New York, NY 10011, phone 212-627-4035, founded 1985, Lee Ellen Briccetti, executive director, "is a library, resource center and meeting place for poets and poetry readers from all parts of the aesthetic spectrum. Programs and events are designed to serve as platforms for discussion and emphasize cross-cultural and inter-disciplinary exchange. The Reed Foundation Library is an open-access poetry collection comprised of 20,000 volumes, including books, journals, small press publications and other fugitive poetry materials. Donations to the library are welcomed." Poets House sponsors several annual events: a NY/NJ Teachers Conference; a conference for the chairpeople of English Departments; the Poetry Teacher of the Year Award, which divides a prize of $1,000 between a teacher and her/his school library for the purchase of poetry materials; and in alternate years the Translation Fund Selection, which awards a publishing contract and a monetary prize to a manuscript chosen on the literary merit of the translation.

POETS IN PUBLIC SERVICE, INC., One Union Square, Suite 612, New York, NY 10003, sends professional, practicing writers trained as creative writing teachers into schools and community agencies to conduct writing workshops with youngsters. Poets, playwrights and fiction writers in the New York metropolitan area are invited to apply for training in the conduct of school programs. Work subsequent to successful training varies during the school year. Writers of all ethnic backgrounds are encouraged to apply. Since its founding in 1973 as New York State Poets-in-the-Schools, *PIPS* has utilized the services of over 240 writers to serve more than 3,200 schools and 15 community agencies reaching a total of 350,000 young people. A *PIPS* writer can expect to work an average of 1-4 days per week during the school year."

POETS-IN-THE-SCHOOLS, Most states have PITS programs that send published poets into classrooms to teach students poetry writing. If you have published poetry widely and have a proven commitment to children, contact your state arts council, Arts-in-Education Dept., to see whether you qualify. Three of the biggest are Poets in Public Service (formerly NYSPITS), 1 Union Square, Suite 612, New York, NY 10003, phone 212-206-9000; California Poets-in-the-Schools, 2845 24th St., San Francisco, CA 94110, phone 415-695-7988; and COMPAS, Landmark Center, #308, 75 West 5th St., St. Paul, MN 55102.

THE SOCIETY OF AUTHORS; THE AUTHOR, 84 Drayton Gardens, London SW10 9SB, England, advises members on business matters, takes up their complaints and institutes legal proceedings, sends them a quarterly journal, *The Author*, publishes guides regarding agents, copyright, income tax, contracts, etc., offers them retirement and medical insurance programs, administers trust funds for their benefit, organizes special interest groups (e.g., broadcasters, children's writers, etc.), and pursues campaigns on behalf of the profession (e.g., for legislative changes).

SONGWRITER'S AND POET'S CRITIQUE, 11599 Coontz Road, Orient OH 43146, phone 614-877-1727, a nonprofit association whose purpose is to serve songwriters, poets and musicians in their area. The president of the organization says, "We provide information on songwriting, how to copyright your work, and contact publishers. We critique songs and poems of our members and guests to improve our craft, and we network songwriters, musicians and lyricists who wish to collaborate. We have a four-track recorder and a library of books and tapes that we circulate among members. We are a talented and diverse group. Some members are published and recorded writers. Dues are $12/year and we invite all songwriters, musicians and poets in the Columbus area to visit and share their creativity. Please call or write for more information."

‡UNITED AMATEUR PRESS, % Velma Lamoreaux, 8 South 5th St., Marshalltown, IA 50158, a group (approximately 260 members) requiring a membership fee of $7 plus a "credential," which can be a poem, essay, or story written by the applicant, or any item edited, published, or printed by the applicant. The mailer accepts and "bundles" — "an envelope of papers with writings authored by members," and then circulates these bundles to all other members. There is a publication called *The United Amateur*, which appears monthly and publishes winners of "Laureate Awards" in 8 categories including both serious and humorous poetry.

WELFARE STATE INTERNATIONAL, The Ellers, Ulverston, Cumbria LA12 0AA England, phone 0229-581127/57146, FAX 0229 581232, founded 1968, artistic director John Fox, is a "celebratory arts company of national and international status creating functional poetry both visual and verbal, for ceremonial occasions. Commissions range from small-scale domestic celebrations to city-scale spectaculars." They publish poster poems in limited editions, dramatic songs and interludes for performance works, and poetic masques.

WOODLAND PATTERN, Box 92081, 720 E. Locust St., Milwaukee, WI 53202, phone 414-263-5001, executive director Anne Kingsbury, who calls it "a semi-glamorous literary and arts center." Ms. Kingsbury regards the Center as a neighborhood organization; it includes a bookstore that concentrates on contemporary literature, much of it small press, much of it poetry. It also incorporates a multi purpose gallery/performance/reading space, where exhibitions, readings, a lecture series, musical programs, and a writers' support group are held. The *Woodland Pattern Newsletter*, mailed free to 1,500 people, contains an annotated calendar, book announcements, and pieces about visiting writers.

THE WRITER'S CENTER; CAROUSEL; POET LORE, 7815 Old Georgetown Rd., Bethesda, MD 20814, phone 301-654-8664, founder and chairman of the board Allan Lefcowitz, director Jane Fox. This is an outstanding resource for writers not only in Washington DC but in the wider area ranging from southern Pennsylvania to North Carolina and West Virginia. The Center offers 150 multi-meeting workshops each year in writing, typesetting, word processing, and graphic arts, and provides a research library. It is open 7 days a week, 10 hours a day. Some 2,200 members support the Center with $25 annual donations, which allows for 5 paid staff members. There is a book gallery at which publications of small presses are displayed and sold. The Center's publication, *The Carousel*, is an 8-page tabloid that comes out 6 times a year. They also sponsor 40 annual performance events, which include presentations in poetry, fiction, and theater. The Center is now publisher of *Poet Lore* — 100 years old in 1989 (see listing under publishers).

THE WRITERS ROOM, 153 Waverly Pl., 5th Floor, New York NY 10014, phone 212-807-9519, provides a "home away from home" for any writer "with a serious commitment to writing," who needs a place to work. It is open 24 hours a days, 7 days a week, offering desks, storage space, and "an alternative to isolation" for up to 135 writers. Space is allotted on a quarterly basis (which may be extended indefinitely) and costs $150 per quarter. The Room is supported by the National Endowment for the Arts, the New York State Council on the Arts, and other public and private sources, and it encourages applications. "The Writers Room also offers monthly readings and workshops for its residents, and has occasional exhibits on 'writerly' subjects, such as revision."

Additional Organizations Useful to Poets

Also read the following listings for information on other organizations for poets. See the General Index for page numbers.

Aesthetic Rapture
American Association of
  Haikuists Newsletter
Bay Area Poets Coalition
  (BAPC)
Berkeley Poets Cooperative
  (Workshop & Press)
Canadian Author & Bookman
Cleaning Business Magazine
Detroit Black Writers' Guild
Eleventh Muse
Frogpond: Quarterly Haiku
  Journal
Greenfield Review Press, The
Groundswell
Haiku Canada
Helter Skelter
Illinois Writers, Inc.
International Poets of the
  Heart
Kwibidi Publisher
Matilda Publications
  Productions

Memory Plus Enterprises Press
Midwest Villages & Voices
New Horizons Poetry Club
New York Quarterly
Nightsun
Onionhead
Pasque Petals
Peregrine
Philomel
Piedmont Literary Review
Poem
Poet International
Poetpourri
Poetry
Poetry Halifax Dartmouth
Poetry Nippon Press
Poetry Nottingham
Poetry Review
Poetry World
Poets' Roundtable
Poets-in-the-Schools
Pudding House Publications
Rockford Review, The

Shoe Tree
Small Press Writers & Artists
  Organization (SPWAO)
Society of American Poets, The
Stevan Company, The
Still Waters Press
Talisman
Tyro Magazine
Ver Poets Voices
Washington Review
Washington Writers'
  Publishing House
Weyfarers
Whitecrow Foundation
Windfall
Without Halos
Worcester Review
Word Works, The

Market conditions are constantly changing! If you're still using this book and it is 1992 or later, buy the newest edition of Poet's Market at your favorite bookstore or order directly from Writer's Digest Books.

Publications Useful to Poets

You are holding in your hands one of the most useful publications for poets that I know of, but there are many more. Even an occupation as haphazard as ours has its quota of professional journals and guides. First you write poetry. Then it occurs to you that you are a *poet*. What does that mean? One thing it is likely to mean is that you have an interest in such publications as are listed in this section.

Sometimes I'm invited to give a talk. Occasionally I get an invitation to give a poetry reading. But usually people want to hear from me about writing. They usually don't even ask to hear about how to write poetry, or how to write better. They want to know how they can *market* their writing. Well, *market*, as you know by now, is a rather ironic term when applied to poetry. Mostly we poets are in the business of giving our work away—and finding even that is not easy. So we're always looking for tips—and finding them in such publications as are listed here.

Only in America (and to some extent in other English-speaking countries) do you find so many books and magazines about writing, along with writing workshops and courses in creative writing in schools and colleges. We seem to be a people desperate to get into print. I think that is a reflection of something important about our democratic spirit. "I could write a book!" is one of our favorite expressions. Each individual believes his life is significant; experience and wisdom and even feelings and thoughts should be recorded. Diaries are insufficient (though many of us keep those, too). We want to be pros—in verse or prose. We want to live in the public eye. And we like to read about other writers, about books and magazines we may never see, about our craft and our business. Below is just a sampling of the many publications responding to that interest.

Also, many take up writing, especially poetry, more for social than artistic reasons. They like to participate in a fellowship, a kind of club-by-mail, in which they can become acquainted with work by a lot of other people like themselves. Some publications cater to that interest; they provide a forum in which beginners can discover and address one another. Often these publications are labors of love by editors/publishers who know firsthand the frustrations of getting started in writing and want to provide a service for beginning writers. Whatever your poetic interests or needs are, you will find useful publications in this section.

Since publications in this list are those that do not, in general, publish poetry, they provide only a sampling of magazines pertinent to our field. Many of our literary magazines are to some degree professional journals and so are useful to us as writers as well as open to us as markets. Those especially focusing on writing are cross-referred at the end of this section, under "Additional Publications Useful to Poets."

AD-LIB PUBLICATIONS, 51 N. Fifth St., Fairfield, IA 52556-1102, phone 515-472-6617, 800-669-0773, publisher John Kremer, publishes how-to books about book publishing and self-publishing, such as **1001 Ways to Market Your Books, Independent Publisher's Bookshelf, and Directory of Book, Catalog, and Magazine Printers**, and **Book Publishing Resource Guide** (also available on IBM PC or MacIntosh disk as a database). Send SASE for catalog.

THE BOTTOM LINE PUBLICATION, Star Route Box 21AA, Artemas, PA 17211, phone 814-458-3102, founded 1988, editor-publisher Kay Weems (see *Felicity* under publishers), is a monthly newsletter listing over 100 publications and contests for writers each month and reproducing guidelines of still others. Information is presented in chronological order by deadline date, and then in alphabetical order. Circulation: 50-100. Subscription: $25. Sample: $2.50.

CANADIAN POETRY, English Dept., University of Western Ontario, London, Ontario, Canada N6A 3K7, phone 519-661-3403, founded 1977, editor Prof. D.M.R. Bentley, is a biannual journal of critical articles, reviews, historical documents (such as interviews), and an annual bibliography of the year's work in Canadian poetry studies. It is a professionally printed, scholarly edited, flat-spined 100+ pp. journal which pays contributors in copies. Subscription: $10. Sample: $5. **Note that they publish no poetry except as quotations in articles.**

DUSTBOOKS; INTERNATIONAL DIRECTORY OF LITTLE MAGAZINES AND SMALL PRESSES; SMALL PRESS REVIEW, Box 100, Paradise, CA 95967. Dustbooks publishes a number of books useful to writers. Send SASE for catalog. Among their regular publications, **International Directory** is an annual directory of all small presses and literary magazines, about 5,000 entries, a third being magazines, half being book publishers, and the rest being both. There is very detailed information about what these presses and magazines report to be their policies in regard to payment, copyright, format and publishing schedules. *Small Press Review* is a monthly magazine, newsprint, carrying current updating of listings in **ID**, small press needs, news, announcements and reviews—a valuable way to stay abreast of the literary marketplace. I have a regular column in this magazine carrying information on poetry markets.

FACTSHEET FIVE, 6 Arizona Ave., Rensselaer, NY 12144-4502, phone 518-479-3707, founded 1982, editor Mike Gunderloy, is a "small press reviewer of other small press publications, with 1,000+ reviews per issue. We review poetry magazines, chapbooks, and books. **We do not print any poetry.**" The editor describes it as magazine-sized, typeset, 128 pp., web offset on newsprint with b/w and color graphics and ads, press run 7,000+ for 3,500 subscribers of which 20 are libraries. Per issue: $3; subscription $15/6 issues.

THE LETTER EXCHANGE, published by The Readers' League, % Stephen Sikora, Box 6218, Albany, CA 94706. Published 3 times each year, *The Letter Exchange* is a digest-sized magazine, 36 pp., that publishes four types of listings: regular (which are rather like personal classifieds); ghost letters, which contain lines like "Send news of the Entwives!"; amateur magazines, which publicizes readers' own publishing ventures; and sketch ads, in which readers who would rather draw than write can communicate in their chosen mode. All ads are coded, and readers respond through the code numbers. Subscription to *The Letter Exchange* is $16/year, and sample copies are $6 postpaid for current issue. Poets who are so inclined often exchange poems and criticism with each other through this medium.

LITERARY MAGAZINE REVIEW, %The English Dept., Denison Hall, Kansas State University, Manhattan, KS 66506, founded 1981, editor G.W. Clift, a quarterly magazine (digest-sized, perfect-bound, about 80 pp.) that publishes critiques, 2-5 pp. long, of various literary magazines, plus shorter "reviews" (about ½ page), directories of literary magazines (such as British publications), and descriptive listings of new journals during a particular year. Single copies are available for $4 or subscriptions for $12.50 year.

OHIO WRITER, Box 770464, Cleveland, OH 44107, is a newsletter for Ohio writers or those connected with Ohio, a bimonthly, 8-16 pp. professionally printed in colored ink on off-white stock, containing news and reviews of Ohio events and publications: $12 a year.

PARA PUBLISHING, Box 4232-880, Santa Barbara, CA 93140-4232, phone 805-968-7277, Orders: 800-PARAPUB, FAX: 805-968-1379. Author-publisher Dan Poynter publishes how-to books on book publishing and self-publishing. **Is There a Book Inside You?** shows you how to get your book out. **The Self-Publishing Manual, How to Write, Print and Sell Your Own Book** is all about book promotion. **Publishing Short-Run Books** shows you how to typeset and lay out your own book. Poynter also publishes **Publishing Contracts on Disk, Book Fairs** and fifteen Special Reports on various aspects of book production, promotion, marketing and distribution. *Free* book publishing information kit; send 45¢ SASE.

THE POETRY CONNECTION, 301 E. 64th St. #6K (PM), New York, NY 10021, 212-249-5494, Editor/ Publisher: Sylvia Shichman, is a new "poetry contest information grapevine service whereby poetry contest flyers are distributed to poets and writers, provides information on poetry information books, and mailings of poetry contests for poetry publications and literary organizations, and other information about activities pertaining to poetry." Mini-sample: $3 plus 2 SASEs. Subscription: $25 (1 year/6 issues), $15 (6 months/3 issues).

POETS' AUDIO CENTER, THE WATERSHED FOUNDATION, Box 50145, Washington, DC 20004. This is an international clearinghouse for ordering any poetry recording available, from both commercial and noncommercial producers. Catalog available free ("an introduction to our collection"); they stock over 500 titles. **Not accepting applications at this time.**

POETS & WRITERS, INC.; A DIRECTORY OF AMERICAN POETS AND FICTION WRITERS; WRITER'S GUIDE TO COPYRIGHT; AUTHOR AND AUDIENCE; LITERARY AGENTS; POETS & WRITERS MAGA-ZINE, 72 Spring St., New York, NY 10012, phone 212-226-3586 or 800-666-2268 (California only), is our major support organization. Their many helpful publications include *Poets and Writers Magazine* (formerly *Coda*), which appears 6 times a year ($18 or $3 for a single copy), magazine-sized, 64 pp., offset, has been called *The Wall Street Journal* of our profession, and it is there that one most readily finds out about resources such as I am listing here, current needs of magazines and presses, contests, awards, jobs and retreats for writers, and discussions of business, legal and other issues affecting writers. *P&W* also publishes a number of valuable directories such as their biennial **A Directory of American Poets and Fiction Writers ($19.95 paperback),** which editors, publishers, agents and sponsors of readings and workshops use to locate over 6,600 active writers in the country. (You may qualify for a listing if you have a number of publications.) They also publish **A Writer's Guide to Copyright; Author And Audience** a list of over 600 organizations which sponsor readings and workshops involving poets and fiction writers, including a section on how to organize and present a reading or workshop; **Literary Agents: A Writer's Guide;** and many reprints of articles from *Coda* and *Poets & Writers Magazine* which are useful to writers, such as "How to Give an Unsolicited Manuscript the Best Chance"; "22 Heavens for Writers (information on writers' colonies)."

BERN PORTER INTERNATIONAL, 22 Salmond Rd., Belfast, ME 04915, founded 1911, is a monthly journal that reviews books of poetry. Also provides sleeping bag space for poets and writers May 1 thru November 1 for the cost or free will contribution. No smoking. No drugs. No telephone.

‡PROSETRY; HORSEPOEM COMPETITION, The Write Place, P.O. Box 117727, Burlingame CA 94011, phone 415-347-7613, P.D. Steele, editor. A monthly newsletter written for and about writers. "We feature new and newly published poets and prose writers with a 'guest writer' column each month. We include new markets, contests, seminars and workshops as well as general poetry potpourri gleaned from our subscribers." 50% freelance written. Also sponsors annual Horsepoem Competition with an equine theme for traditional poetry, haiku and short short stories. Prizes $50, $25, $15; certificates to all winners. Top winners appear in December issue of *Prosetry*. Reading fee: $2/poem, $2 for each 4 haiku or less. Make checks out to The Write Place.

REVERSE, 221 NE 104th St., Miami FL 33138, founded 1988, poetry editors Jan McLaughlin and Bruce Weber, appears twice a year with prose and accompanying poems on themes planned usually a year in advance. Winter/Spring 1990 discusses the work of unknown poets who deserve recognition. We are open to unsolicited MSS, but prospective contributors should query first to obtain upcoming themes. We will, on occasion, publish a poem if it concerns a theme, but the poem should include an introduction on the theme by the poet. Poems alone are not usually accepted." Prose should be double-spaced, poetry submitted as the poet wishes it to appear in print. Reports in 2-6 weeks. Submissions should be from 1-10 pp.

THE WASHINGTON INTERNATIONAL ARTS LETTER, Box 12010, Des Moines, IA 50312; appears 6 times per year, 10 pp. newsletter on grants and other forms of assistance to the arts and humanities — mostly ads for directories to various programs of support in the arts. Subscription: $40 for individuals; $57.60 for organizations.

WRITER'S DIGEST BOOKS; WRITER'S YEARBOOK; WRITER'S DIGEST; WRITER'S MARKET; ON BEING A POET; THE POET'S HANDBOOK, 1507 Dana Ave., Cincinnati, OH 45207, phone 800-543-4644 outside Ohio, or 513-531-2222. Writer's Digest Books publishes and distributes a remarkable array of books useful to writers, such as **Writer's Market,** a general guide to about 750 book publishers, of which about 450 publish fiction and/or poetry. *Writer's Digest* is a monthly magazine about writing with frequent articles and much market news about poetry, in addition to my monthly column and Poetry Notes. See entry in Publishers of Poetry section. *Writer's Yearbook* is a newsstand annual for freelance writers, journalists and teachers of creative writing, with articles regarding poetry. WDB publishes my books about writing poetry: **On Being a Poet** and **The Poet's Handbook,** and the book you are now using.

THE WRITER'S NOOK NEWS, Suite 181, 38114 Third St., Willoughby, OH 44094, editor Eugene Ortiz, is a quarterly publishing articles on the craft and business of writing with columns on marketing, contests and awards, conferences, tax legislation, books, prose and poetry, and other topics. It is offset from laser typesetting on 20 lb stock. Sample: $4. Subscription: $14.40 for one year, $33.60 for three, $204 for Lifetime Subscription. "We also publish **The Nook News Conferences & Klatches Bulletin**, a quarterly with the latest information on national and international writers' meetings and **The Nook News Market Bulletin**, a quarterly compiled with the latest market information. Our latest publication, **The Nook News Contests & Awards Bulletin**, features up-to-date listings of competitions for writers, poets, playwrights, etc. Rates are the same for all four publications."

WRITER'S N.W.; WRITERS NORTHWEST HANDBOOK; MEDIA WEAVERS, Rt. 3, Box 376, Hillsboro, OR 97124, phone 503-621-3911, is a professionally published tabloid quarterly giving market news, reviews of books of Northwest authors or presses, software reviews, literary activity, interviews, articles and other pertinent information for writers in the Northwest. **Writers NW Handbook** is like a **Writer's Market** (see listing in this section) for the Northwest (including Canada): $14.95 + $2 p&h ($3 to AK, HI, and Canada).

THE WRITER'S YELLOW PAGES, Steve Davis Publishing, Box 190831, Dallas, TX 75219, hardbound, 456 pp., 24,000 entries, a directory of agents, associations, bibliographers, book clubs, book producers, book publishers, book reviewers, book stores, distributors, software publishers, conferences, workshops, contests, awards, data bases, electronic mail systems, editors, proofreaders, grammar hotlines, greeting card publishers, magazines, manuscript analysts, newspapers, printers, publicists, TV and radio networks, typesetters, typists and other things. The price is $19.95 plus $2 shipping and handling.

Additional Publications Useful to Poets

Also read the following listings for other publications useful to poets. See the General Index for page numbers.

Academy of American Poets
American Poetry Center
Associated Writing Programs
Black Buzzard Press
Borealis Press
Byline Magazine
Canadian Conference on the Arts
COSMEP
Council of Literary Magazines and Presses
Earthwise Publications/ Productions
Fairbanks Arts Association
Federation of British Columbia Writers
Frank: An International Journal of Contemporary Writing and Art
Greenfield Review Press, The
Guidelines Magazine
Haiku International Association
Hutton Publications
Illinois Writers, Inc.
International Poets of the Heart

International Women's Writing Guild
Intro
League of Canadian Poets, The
Literary Center, The
Literary Markets
Lone Star Publications of Humor
Maine Writers & Publishers Alliance
Muse
National Federation of State Poetry Societies, Inc.
National Writers Union
New Horizons Poetry Club
North Carolina Writers' Network
Oregon State Poetry Association, The
Parnassus
Pen American Center
Pequod
Poetry Halifax Dartmouth
Poetry Plus Magazine
Poetry Resource Center of Michigan
Poetry South

Poets' Roundtable
Proper Tales Press
Rio Grande Press
Second Aeon Publications
Seneca Review
Shoe Tree
Small Press Writers & Artists Organization (SPWAO)
Snake River Reflections
Society of Authors, The
Stevan Company, The
Thumbprints
Ver Poets Voices
Wordwrights Canada
Writer, The
Writer's Digest
Writer's Exchange
Writers Forum
Writers' Haven Journal
Writers' Journal
Writer's Lifeline
Writer's Newsletter
Writers' Own Magazine
Writers' Rendezvous
Writer's Rescue

U.S. and Canadian Postal Codes

United States

AL	Alabama	MI	Michigan	UT	Utah		
AK	Alaska	MN	Minnesota	VT	Vermont		
AZ	Arizona	MS	Mississippi	VI	Virgin Islands		
AR	Arkansas	MO	Missouri	VA	Virginia		
CA	California	MT	Montana	WA	Washington		
CO	Colorado	NE	Nebraska	WV	West Virginia		
CT	Connecticut	NV	Nevada	WI	Wisconsin		
DE	Delaware	NH	New Hampshire	WY	Wyoming		
DC	District of Columbia	NJ	New Jersey				
FL	Florida	NM	New Mexico				
GA	Georgia	NY	New York				

AL Alabama
AK Alaska
AZ Arizona
AR Arkansas
CA California
CO Colorado
CT Connecticut
DE Delaware
DC District of Columbia
FL Florida
GA Georgia
GU Guam
HI Hawaii
ID Idaho
IL Illinois
IN Indiana
IA Iowa
KS Kansas
KY Kentucky
LA Louisiana
ME Maine
MD Maryland
MA Massachusetts

MI Michigan
MN Minnesota
MS Mississippi
MO Missouri
MT Montana
NE Nebraska
NV Nevada
NH New Hampshire
NJ New Jersey
NM New Mexico
NY New York
NC North Carolina
ND North Dakota
OH Ohio
OK Oklahoma
OR Oregon
PA Pennsylvania
PR Puerto Rico
RI Rhode Island
SC South Carolina
SD South Dakota
TN Tennessee
TX Texas

UT Utah
VT Vermont
VI Virgin Islands
VA Virginia
WA Washington
WV West Virginia
WI Wisconsin
WY Wyoming

Canada

AB Alberta
BC British Columbia
LB Labrador
MB Manitoba
NB New Brunswick
NF Newfoundland
NT Northwest Territories
NS Nova Scotia
ON Ontario
PEI Prince Edward Island
PQ Quebec
SK Sasketchewan
YT Yukon

Bio. Some publishers ask you to send a short biographical paragraph with your submission; it is commonly called a "bio." They may also ask for your important previous publications, or "credits."

Cover letter. Letter accompanying a submission giving brief account of publishing credits and biographical information. See the advice and sample letter in the What Poets Want to Know article.

Digest-sized. Approximately 5½ × 8½″, the size of a folded sheet of conventional typing paper.

Flat-spined. What many publishers call "perfect-bound," glued with a flat edge (usually permitting readable type on the spine).

IRC. International Reply Coupon, postage for return of submissions from another country. One IRC is sufficient for one ounce by *surface mail*. If you want an air mail return, you need one IRC for each half-ounce. Do not send checks or cash for postage to foreign countries: The exchange rates are so high it is not worthwhile for editors to bother with. (Exception: Many Canadian editors do not object to US dollars; use IRCs the first time and inquire.) When I am submitting to foreign countries—or submitting heavy manuscripts within the US—I am likely to instruct the editor to throw the manuscript away if it is rejected, and to notify me by air mail, for which I provide postage. It is cheaper to make another print-out or photocopy than to pay postage for such manuscripts.

Magazine-sized. Approximately 8½ × 11″, the size of conventional typing paper unfolded.

MS, MSS. Manuscript, manuscripts.

Multiple submission. Submission of more than one poem at a time; most publishers of poetry *prefer* multiple submissions and many specify how many should be in a packet.

P. Abbreviation for pence.

p., pp. Page, pages.

Perfect-bound. See Flat-spined.

Query letter. Letter written to a publisher to elicit interest in a manuscript or to determine if submissions are acceptable. Also see advice and sample book query letter in the What Poets Want to Know article.

Saddle-stapled. What many publishers call "saddle-stitched," folded and stapled along the fold.

SAE. Self-addressed envelope.

SASE. Self-addressed, stamped envelope. *Every* publisher requires, with any submission, query, request for catalog, or sample, a self-addressed, stamped envelope. This information is so basic I exclude it from the individual listings but repeat it in bold type at the bottom of many pages throughout this book. The return-envelope (usually folded for inclusion) should be large enough to hold the material submitted or requested, and the postage provided—stamps if the submission is within your own country, IRCs if it is to another country—should be sufficient for its return.

Simultaneous submission. Submission of the same manuscript to more than one publisher at a time. Most magazine editors *refuse to accept* simultaneous submissions. Some book and chapbook publishers do not object to simultaneous submissions. In all cases, notify them that the manuscript is being simultaneously submitted elsewhere if that is what you are doing.

Subsidy Press. See Vanity press.

Tabloid-sized. 11 × 15″ or larger, the size of an ordinary newspaper folded and turned sideways.

Vanity press. A slang term for a publisher that requires the writer to pay publishing costs, especially one that flatters an author in order to generate business. These presses use the term "subsidy" to describe themselves. Some quite respectable presses cannot operate without financial support from their authors and so require subsidies, so it is difficult to tell the difference, but flattery can serve as a warning.

Indexes

Chapbook Publishers Index

Chapbook means simply "cheap book." Most chapbooks are pamphlets of 30 pages or less, and an increasing number of publishers are bringing them out—sometimes as awards for the winners of competitions. When a poet has 30-40 poems published in good magazines, he is likely to think in terms of chapbook publication. It is good to have a mini-collection in a relatively inexpensive format—one that is easy (and inexpensive) to mail—to share with friends and family and to sell at readings. Chapbooks are rarely reviewed, rarely sold in bookstores, but they are a common intermediate step between magazine and book publication. And they usually don't disqualify you for first-book competitions.

As is true of most contests sponsored by publishers, chapbook competitions are likely to be thinly disguised money-raisers. But their fees are rarely as high as $10; they rarely get a thousand entrants (I recently judged one that had only 13); and a copy of the winning chapbook to all entrants is reasonably generous—and good for the winning poet who is unlikely to have any other way of distributing the book to an interested audience. Moreover, most small press publishers would be unable to afford bringing out chapbooks on any other basis—unless the poet contributed to the cost of publication, a "cooperative" practice that is not uncommon.

But you should not kid yourself about chapbook publication. If you win a competition, you may get a little publicity for it. There may be a cash award, but you may be paid only in copies—for example, a percentage of the press run. Most sales will be those you make yourself and there is unlikely to be much press attention.

Here are the publishers listed in *Poet's Market* that offer chapbook publication:

Abbattoir Editions
Abbey
Adastra
Agog
Albatross
Alchemy Press
Allegheny Press
Alms House Press
Alta Napa Press
Amaranth Review, The
Amelia
American Tolkien Society
And Review, The
Androgyne Books
Anhinga Press
Ansuda Publications
Applezaba Press
Arjuna Library Press
Atticus Review/Press

Awede Press
Axe Factory Review
Baby Connection News
    Journal, The
Baker Street Publications
Beat Scene Magazine
Bellevue Press, The
Beloit Poetry Journal, The
Berkeley Poets Cooperative (Workshop &
    Press)
Bits Press
Black Bear Publications
Black Buzzard Press
Black Warrior Review, The
Box Dog Press
Breakthrough!
Callaloo Poetry Series
Canoe Press
Carpenter Press

Spoon River Quarterly
Stand Magazine
Star Books, Inc.
State Street Press
Stereopticon Press
Still Waters Press
Stone Circle Press
Stone Drum
Stone Press
Stormline Press, Inc.
Sub-Terrain
Tak Tak Tak
Tapjoe
Taproot
Texas Review, The
Textile Bridge Press
Third Lung Review
Tidepool
Tiffany and Shore Publishers
Tightrope
Timberline Press
Time of Singing
Toledo Poets Center Press
Tower Poetry Society

Trout Creek Press
Two AM Magazine
Underpass
Underwhich Editions
Village Idiot
W.I.M. Publications (Woman in the Moon)
Wainwright
Washington Writers' Publishing House
Waterways
West Anglia Publications
West of Boston
Whole Notes
Windfall
Windless Orchard, The
Wineberry Press
Winston-Derek Publishers, Inc.
Wordwrights Canada
Wormwood Review Press
Writers Forum
Writers' Own Magazine
Writer's Rescue
Yellow Moon Press
Zephyr Press

Subject Index

The following index is a general guide to help save you time in your search for the proper market for your poem(s).

The categories are listed alphabetically and contain the magazines, publishers and contests and awards that buy or accept special categories of poetry, most of which are coded IV in their listings.

Check through the index first to see what subjects are represented. Then, if you are seeking a magazine or contest for your poem on fantasy, for example, look at the section under Science Fiction/Fantasy/Horror. After you have selected a possible market, refer to the General Index for the correct page number. Then find the listing and read the requirements *carefully*.

In the section *Themes*, there are publishers and magazines which publish a particular theme or subject or publications directed to a special audience. The poetry these markets accept would therefore be subject-related. The *Regional* section lists those outlets which publish poetry about a special geographic area or poetry by poets from the region; and the category *Form/Style* contains those magazines and presses that prefer a specific poetic style or form: haiku, sonnets, epic, narrative, etc.

We do not recommend that you use this index exclusively in your search for a market. Most of the magazines, publishers and contests are very general in their specifications, and they don't choose to be listed by category. Also, many specialize in one subject area but are open to other subjects as well. Reading *all* the listings is still your best marketing tool.

Anthology
Anthology of Magazine Verse & Yearbook of American Poetry
Ashland Poetry Press, The
Blind Beggar Press
C.A.L., Conservatory of American Letters
Charnel House
Delaware Valley Poets, Inc.
Envoi
Georgia State Poetry Society, Inc.
Great Lakes Poetry Press
Haiku Journal
Hens Teeth
Herbooks
Insight Press
Judi-isms
Kitchen Table: Women of Color Press
Lake Shore Publishing
Lodestar Books
M.A.F. Press
Mud Creek
My Restless Soul
Nada Press
National Library of Poetry
New Directions Publishing Corporation
New Poets Series, Inc.
Night Roses
Papier-Maché Press
Perivale Press
Poetry Magic
Poetry of the People
Roberts Foundation Writing Awards, The

San Fernando Poetry Journal
Science Fiction Poetry Association
Seven Buffaloes Press
Shamal Books
Southern Rose Review
Spirit That Moves Us, The
Spiritual Quest Publishing
Squeaky Wheels Press
Starlight Press
Summer Stream Press
Three Continents Press Inc.
Toledo Poets Center Press
Underwhich Editions
Vestal Press, Ltd.
Violetta Books
Voices Israel
Waterways
West Anglia Publications
West Wind Review
Whitecrow Foundation
Wineberry Press
Winston-Derek Publishers, Inc.
Word Works, The
Writer's Exchange
Yellow Moon Press

Bilingual/Foreign Language
Atalantik
Bilingual Review Press
Cross-Cultural Communications
Ediciones Universal
El Gato Tuerto

Ellipse
Feh! A Journal of Odious Poetry
Five Fingers Review
Footwork
Free Venice Beachhead
Gairm
Garm Lu: A Canadian Celtic Arts Journal
Gávea-Brown Publications
La Nuez
Language Bridges Quarterly
Maroverlag
Nada Press
New Renaissance, The
Notebook/Cuaderno: A Literary Journal
Osiris
Plover, The
Princeton University Press
Sachem Press
Sounds of Poetry, The
Tropos
Unmuzzled Ox
Vers-Quebec
Waterfront Press
Witwatersrand University Press

Children/Teen/Young Adult

Advocacy Press
alive now!
Bellflower Press
Blind Beggar Press
Broken Streets
Cat Fancy
Chalk Talk
Children's Better Health Institute
Clubhouse
Clyde Press, The
Communications Publishing Group
Coteau Books
Council for Indian Education
Creative With Words Publications (C.W.W.)
Cricket
Dolphin Log
Evangel
Feelings (FL)
Gospel Publishing House
Hanging Loose Press
Harcourt Brace Jovanovich, Publishers
Hartland Poetry Quarterly, The
Highlights for Children
Holiday House, Inc.
Houghton Mifflin Canada Ltd.
Housewife-Writer's Forum
International Reading Association Children's
    Book Awards
Kwibidi Publisher
Lighthouse
Lodestar Books
Lothrop, Lee & Shepard Books
Louisville Review
Mennonite Publishing House
Merlyn's Pen: The National Magazine of Student Writing, Grades 7-10
Nazarene International Headquarters
Pandora
Peacemaking for Children
Pelican Publishing Company
Pikestaff Forum
Poetry of Hope Award

Poetry Society of Michigan Annual Competitions
Poetry USA
Proem Canada
Quarry Magazine
Reflections
Scholastic Writing Awards
Seventeen
Shoe Tree
Shofar
Sow's Ear, The
Stegner Fellowships, Wallace E.
Stone Soup
Straight
Touch
Unity
Vanitas Press, The
Vegetarian Journal
Vision
Waterways
Whole Notes
Writers' Journal
Writer's Newsletter
Young American
Young Author's Magazine
Young Crusader, The
Young Soldier, The
Young Voices Magazine

Ethnic/Nationality

Adrift (Irish)
Africa World Press (African, African American, Carribean, Latin America)
Afro-Hispanic Review
Agada (Jewish)
American Dane
Arte Publico Press (U.S. Hispanic)
Atalantik (Bengalese)
Bear Tribe Publishing (Native American)
Bilingual Review Press (Hispanic)
Black American Literature Forum
Black Scholar, The
Blind Beggar Press (Black, Third World)
Callaloo Poetry Series (North, South, Central, Latin America; Carribean, Europe, Africa)
Carolina Wren Press (minorities)
Chapman (Scottish)
Clyde Press, The (folk tales)
Communications Publishing Group (Black, Hispanic, Asian-American, Native American)
Council for Indian Education (American Indian)
Detroit Black Writers' Guild
Eagle Wing Press (American Indian)
Ediciones Universal (Spanish/Cuban)
El Barrio (Latino/Detroit)
El Gato Tuerto (Spanish, Latin American, Carribean)
El Tecolote (U.S. Latino, Latin American)
Essence (Black women)
Gairm (Scottish Gaelic)
Garm Lu: A Canadian Celtic Arts Journal
Gávea-Brown Publications (Portuguese-American)
Holte Literary Prize, Clarence L. (African)
International Black Writers

Form/Style

Gay/Lesbian

Bay Windows
Black Horse
Calyx
Clothespin Fever Press
Conditions
Fag Rag
Firebrand Books
First Hand
Gay Men's Press, The
Herbooks
Manroot Books
Northwest Gay and Lesbian Reader, The
Renovated Lighthouse Magazine, The
RFD
Sinister Wisdom
W.I.M. Publications (Woman in the Moon)
White Review, James

Humor

Above the Bridge Magazine
Agog Publications
Ag-Pilot International Magazine
Big Mouse, The
Bits Press
Cacanadadada
Capper's
Collages & Bricolages
Columbus Single Scene
Country Woman
Feather Books
Feh! A Journal of Odious Poetry
Golf Digest
Good Housekeeping
Hoosier Challenger
Housewife-Writer's Forum
Howling Dog
Hutton Publications
Journal of New Jersey Poets
Krax
Ladies' Home Journal
Lake Effect
Latest Jokes Newsletter
Latter Day Woman
Leacock Medal for Humour, The Stephen
Libido
Lone Star Publications of Humor
Mayberry Gazette, The
National Enquirer
New Yorker, The
Paris Review, The
Parnassus Literary Journal
Poetry of the People
Portable Wall
Poultry, A Magazine of Voice
Proof Rock Press
Saturday Evening Post
Sunshine Magazine
Thalia
Thoughts for All Seasons
Writer's Digest
Writers' Haven Journal
Wyoming
Young American

Love/Romance/Erotica

Baker Street Publications
Cosmic Trend

Crescent Moon
Eidos Magazine: Erotic Entertainment for Women
Expedition Press
Explorer Magazine
Hawaii Review
Implosion Press
Libido
Modern Bride
Peoplenet
Poetry Magic
Poetry of the People
Prisoners of the Night
Red Alder Books
Secord Press, Ralph W.
Single Today
Spider Eyes
Taproot

Membership/Subscription

Apropos
Bell's Letters Poet
Breakthrough!
Bucknell Seminar for Younger Poets
Channels
Cochran's Corner
Delaware Valley Poets, Inc.
Dialogue, The Magazine for the Visually Impaired
Emshock Letter
Epstein Award for Creative Writing, The Norma
Feelings (PA)
First Hand
Galaxy of Verse Literary Foundation, A
Gotta Write Network
Haiku Canada
Haiku Journal
Harvard Advocate, The
High/Coo Press
Honeybrook Press
Illuminations Press
International Poets of the Heart
Interstate Religious Writers Association Newsletter and Workshop
Intro
Kwibidi Publisher
Latin American Literary Review Press
League of Minnesota Poets Contest
Living Streams
Lynx
Lyric, The
Memorable Moments
Midwest Poetry Review
Midwest Villages & Voices
Mirrors
Montana Institute of the Arts Writers Contests
New Horizons Poetry Club
P.A.L.S. Club Newsletter Contests
Pasque Petals
Pennsylvania Poetry Society Annual Contest
Place for Poets, A
Poet International
Poet Papers
Poetry Society of Texas
Poets at Work
Poet's Review
Poets' Roundtable

Guernica Editions Inc. (Canada)
High Plains Press (WY, The West)
Honest Ulsterman (Northern Ireland)
Image (Northwest)
Iowa Arts Council Literary Awards
James Books, Alice (New England)
Journal of New Jersey Poets
Kansas Quarterly
Katuah: Bioregional Journal of the Southern Appalachians
Kau Kau Kitchen Newsletter, The (Hawaii)
Kennebec: A Portfolio of Maine Writing
Kern Award, Louisa (Pacific Northwest)
Lake Effect (upstate NY)
Landfall (New Zealand)
Laughing Dog Press (Pacific Northwest)
Leacock Medal for Humour, The Stephen (Canada)
Little River Press (New England)
Loft-McKnight Writers' Awards, The (MN)
Loonfeather (MN)
Louisiana Literature
Magnetic North (Northern New England)
Massachusetts Artists Fellowship Program
Matrix (Canada)
Mayapple Press (Great Lakes region)
Middle East Report
Mid-South Poetry Festival
Midwest Villages & Voices
Montana Institute of the Arts Writers Contests
Mosaic Press (Canada)
New Mexico Humanities Review
New Quarterly, The (Canada)
New Rivers Press (MN)
New Welsh Review
New York Foundation for the Arts
Next Exit (Ontario, eastern North America)
Night Tree Press (Adirondacks, North Country NY)
Northeast Journal (RI)
Northern New England Review
Northwest Magazine (Pacific Northwest)
Now and Then (Appalachia)
Ohioana Book Awards
Onthebus (Los Angeles)
Oregon East
Oregon Individual Artists Fellowships
Ornish Poetry Award, Natalie (TX)
Ottawa-Carleton Book Award
Out Loud (Los Angeles)
Pasque Petals (SD)
Permafrost (AK)
Pinchgut Press (Australia)
Pirogue Publishing (LA)
Poetry Halifax Dartmouth (Canada)
Poetry Ireland Review
Poetry Nottingham (England)
Poetry South
Poetry/LA, Peggor Press (Los Angeles)
Poets and Patrons, Inc. (Chicago area)
Poets' Dinner Contest (CA)
Pogment Press (DC, MD, northern VA)
Potato Eyes (Appalachian chain/Quebec-Alabama)
Prairie Publishing Company, The (Manitoba, Canada)
Prescott Street Press (Northwest)
Presidio La Bahia Award (TX)

Proem Canada
Pterodactyl Press, The (IA)
Puckerbrush Press, The (ME)
Puerto Del Sol (southwestern US)
Quarry Magazine (Canada)
Queen's Quarterly (Canada)
Rambunctious Press (Chicago)
Redneck Review of Literature, The (western US)
Repository Press (British Columbia, Canada)
Ridge Review Magazine (northern CA)
Rockford Review, The (IL-WI)
Rocky Mountain Poetry Magazine
San Francisco Foundation
Sandburg Awards, Carl (Chicago area)
Saskatchewan Writers Guild Annual Literary Awards
Seattle Review (Northwest)
Senior Edition USA/Colorado Old Times
Seven Buffaloes Press (rural America, American West, central CA, southern Appalachia)
South Dakota Review
Sow's Ear, The (central Appalachia)
Spoon River Quarterly (IL)
Star Route Journal (northern CA)
Tessera (Canada)
Therafields Foundation Chapbook Award (Canada)
Third World
Thistledown Press Ltd. (Canada)
Thumbprints (MI)
Toledo Poets Center Press
Townships Sun (Quebec, Canada)
Towson State University Prize for Literature (MD)
Turnstone Press (Canada)
University of North Texas Press (TX)
Utah Holiday Magazine
Vehicule Press (Canada)
Virginia Prize
Wake Forest University Press (Ireland)
Washington Review (DC)
Washington Writers' Publishing House (DC)
Washingtonian Magazine, The (DC)
Weatherford Award, The W.D. (Appalachian South)
West Coast Line (Canada)
Western Producer Publications (western Canada)
Western States Book Awards
Westview (western OK)
WFNB Annual Literary Contest (New Brunswick, Canada)
Wineberry Press (DC)
Wisconsin Academy Review
Woodley Memorial Press (KS)
Worcester Review (New England)
Writers' Federation of Nova Scotia Annual Writing Competition
Writers Forum (The West)
Writers' Guild of Alberta Book Award

Religious
alive now!
Archae: A Palaeo-Review of the Arts
Baptist Sunday School Board
Broken Streets
Channels

Your Guide to Getting Published

Learn to write publishable material and discover the best-paying markets for your work. Subscribe to *Writer's Digest*, the magazine that has instructed, informed and inspired writers since 1920. Every month you'll get:

- Fresh markets for your writing, including the names and addresses of editors, what type of writing they're currently buying, how much they pay, and how to get in touch with them.
- Insights, advice, and how-to information from professional writers and editors.
- In-depth profiles of today's foremost authors and the secrets of their success.
- Monthly expert columns about the writing and selling of fiction, nonfiction, poetry and scripts.

Plus, a $12.00 discount. Subscribe today through this special introductory offer, and receive a full year (12 issues) of *Writer's Digest* for only $18.00—that's a $12.00 savings off the $30 newsstand rate. Enclose payment with your order, and we will add an extra issue to your subscription, absolutely **free**.

Detach postage-free coupon and mail today!

Subscription Savings Certificate
Save $12.00

Yes, I want pr ofessional advice on how to write publishable material and sell it to the best-paying markets. Send me 12 issues of *Writer's Digest* for just $18...a $12 discount off the newsstand price. (Outside U.S. add $4 and remit in U.S. funds.)

☐ Payment enclosed (Send me an extra issue free— 13 in all)

☐ Please bill me

Writer's ®
DIGEST

Guarantee: If you are not satisfied with your subscription at any time, you may cancel it and receive a full refund for all unmailed issues due you.

Name (please print)

Address   Apt.

City

State   Zip

Basic rate, $24.   VEPM9

Writer's®

DIGEST

How would you like to get:

- up-to-the-minute reports on new markets for your writing
- professional advice from editors and writers about what to write and how to write it to maximize your opportunities for getting published
- in-depth interviews with leading authors who reveal their secrets of success
- expert opinion about writing and selling fiction, nonfiction, poetry and scripts
- ...all at a $12.00 discount?

Prout Journal
Pudding House Publications
Red Bass
St. Joseph Messenger and Advocate of the Blind
San Fernando Poetry Journal
Social Anarchism
Social Justice: a Journal of Crime, Conflict,
    World Order
South End Press
Struggle
Sub-Terrain
Tapjoe

Specialized
Axis (men)
Carnegie Mellon Magazine (alumni)
Harvard Advocate, The (university affiliation)
New Methods: The Journal of Animal Health
    Technology (animals)
Peoplenet (disabled)
Poetry Connexion, The (Los Angeles radio)
Radcliffe Quarterly (alumni)
Recovering Poet's Registry and Exchange (ad-
    diction recovery)
Slate & Style (blind writers)
Squeaky Wheels Press (disability)
Vanitas Press, The ("Oz" saga)
White Rose Literary Magazine, The (disabled
    persons)
Yellow Moon Press (men)

Spirituality/Inspirational
Alchemy Press
Axis
Belladonna, The
Capper's
Chakra
Converging Paths
Crescent Moon
Emshock Letter
Fish Drum
Insight Press
Integrity International
Oblates
Pocket Inspirations
Poetry Break
Practical Mystic, The
Presbyterian Record, The
Prout Journal
Rainbow City Express
Renovated Lighthouse Magazine, The
St. Joseph Messenger and Advocate of the Blind
Silver Wings
Spiritual Quest Publishing
Star Books, Inc.
Sunshine Magazine
Tramp

Sports
Aethlon: The Journal of Sport Literature
Eldritch Tales Magazine in the Weird Tales Tra-
    dition
Golf Digest
Peoplenet
Spitball

Students
Allegheny Review
Analecta
Fiddlehead, The
Lyric, The
Merlyn's Pen: The National Magazine of Stu-
    dent Writing, Grades 7-10
Modern Haiku
Philomel
Rackham Journal of the Arts and Humanities
Student Leadership Journal
Wildwood Journal

Themes
Aesthetic Rapture (philosophy)
American Atheist Press
American Squaredance Magazine
American Studies Press, Inc. (women)
American Tolkien Society
And (computer-related)
Androgyne Books (alchemy, erotic fantasy, auto/
    biographical, surrealism/dada)
Apalachee Quarterly (changes annually)
Ashland Poetry Press, The (as announced)
Axis (male/ecological/religious)
Bear Tribe Publishing (earth awareness, self-
    sufficiency, sacred places, native people)
Bellflower Press (supportive)
Bishop Publishing Co. (American folk)
Black Mountain Review
Byline Magazine (writers, writing)
Calli's Tales (animals)
Caring Connection (caregiving, handicapped)
Cat Fancy
Cats Magazine
Chelsea
Christmas, The Annual of Christmas Literature
    and Art
Classical Outlook, The (classical)
Cleaning Business Magazine
Climbing Art (mountains, moutaineering)
Columbus Single Scene (single living)
Communications Publishing Group (college
    preparation, career planning, life skills)
Converging Paths (Pagan)
Cool Traveler Newsletter, The (artistic refer-
    ences)
Cosmic Trend (New Age)
Delhi-London Poetry Quarterly (contemporary)
Dickinson Studies (Emily Dickinson)
Dolphin Log (marine environment, ecology, nat-
    ural history, water-related)
Dramatika (theater, mail art)
Dream International Quarterly (dreams)
Equlibrium
Event (as announced)
Expecting (expectant mothers)
Feather Books (religion, nature)
Feh! A Journal of Odious Poetry
Felicity
Fighting Woman News (women in martial arts,
    self-defense, combative sports)
Friends Journal (Quakerism)
Futurific Magazine (humanity, human achieve-
    ments)
Galactic Discourse ("Star Trek")
Gandhabba

Translations

Celtic Dawn
Chelsea
Chinese Literature
Classical Outlook, The
Collages & Bricolages
Colorado Review
Columbia University Translation Center
Coop Antigruppo Siciliano
Crab Creek Review
Cross-Cultural Communications
Cumberland Poetry Review
El Gato Tuerto
Ellipse
European Library of Poetry
Federation Internationale Des Traducteurs
Field
Frank: An International Journal of Contemporary Writing and Art
Frogpond: Quarterly Haiku Journal
G. W. Review
Galatiere Prize, Lewis
Graham House Review
Guernica Editions Inc.
Hawaii Review
Intertext
Iris
Italica Press
Jacaranda Review
Kalliope
Lactuca
Lang Publishing, Inc., Peter
Latin American Literary Review Press
Liftouts Magazine
Manhattan Review, The
Mid-American Review
New Directions Publishing Corporation
New Laurel Review, The
New Orleans Review
New Renaissance, The
New Rivers Press
New Yorker, The
Nordmanns-Forbundet (Norsemen's Federation)
Notus: New Writing
Orbis
Osiris
Panjandrum Books
Parnassus
Partisan Review
Pequod
Perivale Press
Poet International
Poetry Nippon Press
Poetry World
Princeton University Press
Puerto Del Sol
Quarterly Review of Literature
Red Bass
Renditions
Rocky Mountain Review of Language and Literature
Rohwedder
Sachem Press
Salmon Publishing
Seneca Review
Signal, The
Silverfish Review
Singular Speech Press

Southern Humanities Review
Spoon River Quarterly
Stand Magazine
Stevan Company, The
Sulfur Magazine
Tak Tak Tak
Takahe
Tampa Review
Tessera
Three Continents Press Inc.
Threshold Books
Touchstone Press
Translators Association, The
Webster Review
White Pine Press
Willow Springs
Writ
Zephyr Press

Women/Feminism

Aireings
American Studies Press, Inc.
Anima: The Journal of Human Experience
Arizona Women's Voice
Barnard New Women Poets Prize
Bunting Fellowship Program, The Mary Ingraham
Calyx
Carolina Wren Press
Collages & Bricolages
Colorado Review
Conditions
Cosmopolitan
Country Woman
Detroit Black Writers' Guild
Earth's Daughters: A Feminist Arts Periodical
Eidos Magazine: Erotic Entertainment for Women
Eighth Mountain Press
Essence
Feminist Studies
Firebrand Books
Fireweed: A Feminist Quarterly
Five Fingers Review
Free Focus
Frontiers: A Journal of Women Studies
Good Housekeeping
Harvard Advocate, The
Herbooks
Heresies
Herspectives
How(Ever)
Hurricane Alice
Implosion Press
Iowa Woman
Iris
James Books, Alice
Kalliope
Kitchen Table: Women of Color Press
Korone
Latter Day Woman
Laughing Dog Press
Lilith Magazine
Mayapple Press
Midland Review
Miriam Press
Off Our Backs

Geographical Index

Use this Geographical Index especially to locate small presses and magazines in your region. Much of the poetry being published today reflects regional interests; also publishers often favor poets (and their work) from their own regions.

The listings in this index are arranged alphabetically within the geographical sections; refer to the General Index for specific page numbers. Also check your neighboring states for other regional opportunities.

The last three sections, Canada, United Kingdom and Foreign listings, all require a SAE with IRC's for return of your poetry.

Alabama
Abscond
Alabama Literary Review
Aura Literary/Arts Magazine
Birmingham Poetry Review
Black Warrior Review, The
Caesura
College English
Dreams and Nightmares
Druid Press
Negative Capability
Poem
Southern Humanities Review

Alaska
Alaska Quarterly Review
Explorations
Fairbanks Arts Association
Intertext
Permafrost

Arizona
Amaranth Review, The
Arizona Women's Voice
Bilingual Review Press
Fennel Stalk
Haiku Quarterly
Hayden's Ferry Review
Newsletter Inago
Recovering Poet's Registry and Exchange
Reflections
Sonora Review
Writer's Rescue

Arkansas
Nebo: A Literary Journal
Slant
University of Arkansas Press, The
Voices International

California
Advocacy Press
Aesthetic Rapture
Agada
Alta Napa Press
Amelia
Americas Review
Androgyne Books

Anthology of Magazine Verse & Yearbook of
    American Poetry
Applezaba Press
Arete: Forum for Thought
Ars Poetica Press Newsletter
Arundel Press
Asylum
Atticus Review/Press
Aurora Poetry Letter
Bay Area Poets Coalition (BAPC)
Berkeley Poetry Review
Berkeley Poets Cooperative (Workshop &
    Press)
Berkeley Review of Books, The
Beyond Baroque Literary/Arts Center
Bishop Publishing Co.
Black Scholar, The
Black Sparrow Press
Blue Unicorn, A Triquarterly of Poetry
Bottomfish
Cadmus Editions
California State Poetry Quarterly (CQ)
Camellia
Caravan Press
Cat Fancy
CCR Publications
Ceilidh: An Informal Gathering for Story &
    Song
City Light Books
Clothespin Fever Press
Conditioned Response Press
COSMEP
Coydog Review
Crazyquilt Quarterly
Creative With Words Publications (C.W.W.)
Creativity Unlimited Press
Daniel and Company, Publisher, John
Dark Nerve
Dolphin Log
Dream International Quarterly
El Gato Tuerto
El Tecolote
Famous Last Words
Five Fingers Review
Flume Press
Free Lunch
Free Venice Beachhead
Galactic Discourse

Frontiers: A Journal of Women Studies
Heart
High Plains Literary Review
Integrity International
Just Between Us
Laughing Bear Press
Phase and Cycle
Senior Edition USA/Colorado Old Times
Tales of the Old West
Writers Forum

Connecticut
Broken Streets
Chicory Blue Press
Connecticut Poetry Review, The
Eagle Wing Press
Embers
Golf Digest
Hobo Jungle: A Quarterly Journal of New Writing
Poetry Only
Potes & Poets Press, Inc.
Singular Speech Press
Small Pond Magazine of Literature
Wesleyan University Press
Yale University Press

Delaware
Delaware Valley Poets, Inc.
En Passant Poetry

District Of Columbia
Aerial
American Scholar, The
Folio: A Literary Journal
G. W. Review
Lip Service
Middle East Report
New Republic, The
Off Our Backs
Poetry Committee of the Greater Washington Area, The
Sojourners
Three Continents Press Inc.
Washington Review
Washington Writers' Publishing House
Washingtonian Magazine, The
Wheat Forder's Press
Wineberry Press
Word Works, The

Florida
Ajax Poetry Letter
Albatross
American Studies Press, Inc.
Anhinga Press
Apalachee Quarterly
Calli's Tales
Cathartic, The
Cats Magazine
Crystal Rainbow
Dramatika
Earthwise Publications/Productions
Ediciones Universal
Feelings
Florida Review, The
Gulf Stream Magazine
Half Tones to Jubilee

Human Quest, The
Kalliope
Key West Review
Middle Eastern Dancer
National Enquirer
New Collage Magazine
Onionhead
Panhandler, The
Pet Gazette, The
Poetry Today
Psych It: The Sophisticated Newsletter for Everyone
Runaway Spoon Press, The
Small Press Writers & Artists Organization (SPWAO)
South Florida Poetry Review, The
Spiritual Quest Publishing
Sun Dog
Tampa Bay Review
Tampa Review
University of Central Florida Contemporary Poetry Series

Georgia
Adara
Atlanta Writing Resource Center
Chattahoochee Review, The
Classical Outlook, The
Dickey Newsletter, James
Georgia Journal
Georgia Review, The
Mots Et Images: Press-Work Project
Old Red Kimono
Parnassus Literary Journal
Personal Poets United
Poet's Review
Snake Nation Review
Society of American Poets, The
University of Georgia Press

Hawaii
Aloha, The Magazine of Hawaii and the Pacific
Hawaii Review
Kau Kau Kitchen Newsletter, The

Idaho
Ahsahta Press
Cold-Drill Books
Confluence Press
Emshock Letter
Honeybrook Press
Hutton Publications
Limberlost Press
Redneck Review of Literature, The
Rocky Mountain Review of Language and Literature
Signal, The
Snake River Reflections
Tapjoe
Trestle Creek Review
Village Idiot

Illinois
Aim Magazine
Algilmore
Alternative Fiction & Poetry
Chicago Review
Christian Century, The

Maine
Beloit Poetry Journal, The
Black Fly Review
C.A.L., Conservatory of American Letters
Kennebec: A Portfolio of Maine Writing
Maine Writers & Publishers Alliance
Memorable Moments
National Poetry Foundation, The
Potato Eyes
Puckerbrush Press, The
Slow Dancer
Soleil Press

Maryland
Abbey
Antietam Review
Blind Alleys
Callaloo Poetry Series
Cochran's Corner
Dickinson Studies
Dolphin-Moon Press
Feminist Studies
Festival of Poets and Poetry at St. Mary's
Galileo Press, The
Hanson's: A Magazine of Literary and Social Interest
Johns Hopkins University Press, The
Monocacy Valley Review
New Poets Series, Inc.
Nightsun
Passager
Plastic Tower, The
Poet Lore
Social Anarchism
Talkin' Union
Urbanus
Vegetarian Journal
Writer's Center, The

Massachusetts
Aborignal SF
Adastra Press
Agni
Ark, The
Arts End Books
Atlantic, The
Bay Windows
Boston Literary Review (BLUR)
Boston Review
Christian Science Monitor, The
Christopher Publishing House, The
Eidos Magazine: Erotic Entertainment for Women
Faber and Faber, Inc.
Fag Rag
Figures, The
Godine, Publisher, David R.
Golden Isis Magazine
Harvard Advocate, The
Houghton Mifflin Co.
Jam To-Day
James Books, Alice
Little River Press
Loom Press
Massachusetts Review, The
New Renaissance, The
Northeastern University Press
Oak Square

O-Blek
On the Edge
Osiris
Partisan Review
Peregrine
Ploughshares
Poultry, A Magazine of Voice
Radcliffe Quarterly
Rowan Tree Press
Rugging Room, The
Sandscript
Science Fiction Poetry Association
Soundings East
South End Press
Spectrum
Tightrope
University of Massachusetts Press, The
Valley Women's Voice
Violetta Books
West of Boston
Woman of Power
Worcester Review
Writer, The
Yellow Moon Press
Zephyr Press
Zoland Books Inc.

Michigan
Above the Bridge Magazine
American Tolkien Society
Bennett & Kitchel
Bridge, The
Canoe Press
Clubhouse
Detroit Black Writers' Guild
El Barrio
Expedition Press
Frog Gone Review
Hartland Poetry Quarterly, The
Howling Dog
Japanophile
Lotus Press Inc.
MacGuffin, The
Michigan Quarterly Review
Mobius
Nada Press
Nomos Press Inc.
Notus: New Writing
Pandora
Poetic Page
Poetry Magic
Poetry Resource Center of Michigan
Rackham Journal of the Arts and Humanities
Red Cedar Review
Renegade
Riverrun
Secord Press, Ralph W.
Sounds of Poetry, The
Stone Press
Struggle
Sulfur Magazine
Thumbprints
Touch
Tropos
Vision
Wayne Review
Wire, The
Witness

Nimrod International Journal of Contemporary
   Poetry and Fiction
Westview

Oregon
Archer, The
Arrowood Books, Inc.
Breitenbush Books, Inc.
Calyx
Eighth Mountain Press
Lane Literary Guild, The
Metamorphous Press
Mr. Cogito Press
Mud Creek
Northwest Magazine
Northwest Review
NRG
Oregon East
Poetic Space
Polyfidelitous Education Productions, Inc.
Portland Review
Prescott Street Press
Silverfish Review
Tidewater
Trout Creek Press
University of Portland Review
Virtue
West Wind Review
Whitecrow Foundation
Wilderness
Young American

Pennsylvania
Adroit Expression, The
Allegheny Press
Allegheny Review
Alternative Press Magazine
American Poetry Center
American Poetry Review
And
Anima: The Journal of Human Experience
Apropos
Axe
Bassettown Review, The
Black Bear Publications
Boulevard
Carnegie Mellon Magazine
Collages & Bricolages
Cool Traveler Newsletter, The
Country Journal
Creeping Bent
Feelings (PA)
Felicity
Friends Journal
Gettysburg Review, The
Green World Press
Grit
Hellas: A Journal of Poetry and the Humanities
Highlights for Children
Hob-Nob
Latin American Literary Review Press
Mennonite Publishing House
Miraculous Medal, The
Northern Pleasure
Overtone Press
Painted Bride Quarterly
Paper Air Magazine
Pennsylvania English

Pennsylvania Review
Philomel
Pitt Poetry Series
Pittsburgh Poetry Exchange
Poetry Forum
Poets at Work
Quick Brown Fox
Rolling Coulter
Shooting Star Review
Taproot Literary Review
Tiffany and Shore Publishers
Time of Singing
Unspeakable Visions of the Individual, The
West Branch
Wildwood Journal

Rhode Island
Copper Beech Press
Deviance
Gávea-Brown Publications
Haunts
Merlyn's Pen: The National Magazine of Student Writing, Grades 7-10
Northeast Journal

South Carolina
Belladonna, The
Devil's Millhopper Press, The
Nostalgia: A Sentimental State of Mind
South Carolina Review
Starsong
Tramp
Writer's Exchange

South Dakota
Hens Teeth
National Federation of State Poetry Societies, Inc.
Pasque Petals
South Dakota Review

Tennessee
Aethlon: The Journal of Sport Literature
alive now!
American Association of Haikuists Newsletter
Baptist Sunday School Board
Co-Laborer
Cumberland Poetry Review
Depot Press
Mature Years
Music City Song Festival
Now and Then
Old Hickory Review
RFD
River City
Romantist, The
St. Luke's Press
Sewanee Review
Single Today
Sow's Ear, The
Swamp Root
Winston-Derek Publishers, Inc.
Word & Image
Zone 3

Texas
Aileron Press
American Atheist Press

Juniper Press
Madison Review, The
Magazine of Speculative Poetry, The
Mid Coaster
Modern Haiku
Northern Review, The
Peacemaking for Children
Prime Times
Ranger International Productions
Salthouse
Seems
Singlelife Magazine
Something, The
Touchstone
University of Wisconsin Press
Windfall
Wisconsin Academy Review
Wisconsin Restaurateur, The
Woodland Pattern

Wyoming
High Plains Press
Wyoming

U.S. Virgin Islands
Caribbean Writer, The
Eastern Caribbean Institute

Canada
Acta Victoriana
Alchemist, The
Alpha Beat Soup
Anerca
Anjou
Antigonish Review, The
Ariel, A Review of International English Literature
Black Cultural Centre for Nova Scotia
Borealis Press
Breakthrough!
Burnaby Writers' Society
Caitlin Press, The
Canadian Author & Bookman
Canadian Conference on the Arts
Canadian Dimension: A Socialist News Magazine
Canadian Literature
Canadian Society of Children's Authors, Illustrators & Performers
Capilano Review, The
Carousel Literary Arts Magazine
Chalk Talk
Charnel House
Chastity and Holiness Magazine
Coach House Press
Cosmic Trend
Coteau Books
Dalhousie Review, The
Daybreak
Descant
Egorag
Ellipse
Event
Existere
Federation of British Columbia Writers
Feh! A Journal of Odious Poetry
Fiddlehead, The
Fireweed: A Feminist Quarterly

Garm Lu: A Canadian Celtic Arts Journal
Goose Lane Editions
Grain
Green's Magazine
Guernica Editions Inc.
Haiku Canada
Herspectives
Houghton Mifflin Canada Ltd.
Inkstone: A Quarterly of Haiku
K
Kola
League of Canadian Poets, The
Legend
Literary Markets
Macmillan of Canada
Malahat Review, The
Matrix
Mosaic Press
Music Works
New Quarterly, The
Next Exit
Our Family
Ouroboros
Out Magazine
Poem Factory, The
Poetry Halifax Dartmouth
Poetry WLU
Prairie Journal
Prairie Publishing Company, The
Presbyterian Record, The
Proem Canada
Proper Tales Press
Quarry Magazine
Queen's Quarterly
Repository Press
Scrivener
Skylark
Sub-Terrain
Tabula Rasa
Tessera
Thalia
Thistledown Press Ltd.
Tidepool
Tower Poetry Society
Turnstone Press
Tyro Magazine
U.C. Review
Underpass
Underwhich Editions
Unmuzzled Ox
Vehicule Press
Vers-Quebec
Wascana Review
West Coast Line
Western Producer Publications
Whetstone
Wolsak and Wynn Publishers Ltd.
Wordwrights Canada
Writ
Writer's Lifeline
Writing
Zymergy

United Kingdom
Acumen Magazine
Agenda Editions
Agog Publications
Aireings

General Index

Can't find a poetry publisher's listing? Check pages 415-417 at the end of the Publishers of Poetry section for Other Poetry Publishers.

Can't find a poetry publisher's listing? Check pages 415-417 at the end of the Publishers of Poetry section for Other Poetry Publishers.

Can't find a poetry publisher's listing? Check pages 415-417 at the end of the Publishers of Poetry section for Other Poetry Publishers.

Can't find a poetry publisher's listing? Check pages 415-417 at the end of the Publishers of Poetry section for Other Poetry Publishers.

Can't find a poetry publisher's listing? Check pages 415-417 at the end of the Publishers of Poetry section for Other Poetry Publishers.

Can't find a poetry publisher's listing? Check pages 415-417 at the end of the Publishers of Poetry section for Other Poetry Publishers.

Can't find a poetry publisher's listing? Check pages 415-417 at the end of the Publishers of Poetry section for Other Poetry Publishers.

Can't find a poetry publisher's listing? Check pages 415-417 at the end of the Publishers of Poetry section for Other Poetry Publishers.

Can't find a poetry publisher's listing? Check pages 415-417 at the end of the Publishers of Poetry section for Other Poetry Publishers.

Can't find a poetry publisher's listing? Check pages 415-417 at the end of the Publishers of Poetry section for Other Poetry Publishers.

Can't find a poetry publisher's listing? Check pages 415-417 at the end of the Publishers of Poetry section for Other Poetry Publishers.

Can't find a poetry publisher's listing? Check pages 415-417 at the end of the Publishers of Poetry section for Other Poetry Publishers.

Can't find a poetry publisher's listing? Check pages 415-417 at the end of the Publishers of Poetry section for Other Poetry Publishers.

Other Books of Interest

Annual Market Books

Artist's Market, edited by Lauri Miller $21.95
Children's Writer's & Illustrator's Market, edited by Connie Eidenier (paper) $15.95
Humor & Cartoon Markets, edited by Bob Staake (paper) $15.95
Novel & Short Story Writer's Market, edited by Robin Gee (paper) $18.95
Photographer's Market, edited by Sam Marshall $21.95
Poet's Market, by Judson Jerome $19.95
Songwriter's Market, edited by Mark Garvey $19.95
Writer's Market, edited by Glenda Neff $24.95

General Writing Books

Annable's Treasury of Literary Teasers, by H.D. Annable (paper) $10.95
Beginning Writer's Answer Book, edited by Kirk Polking (paper) $13.95
Discovering the Writer Within, by Bruce Ballenger & Barry Lane $16.95
Getting the Words Right: How to Rewrite, Edit and Revise, by Theodore A. Rees Cheney (paper) $12.95
How to Write a Book Proposal, by Michael Larsen (paper) $10.95
Just Open a Vein, edited by William Brohaugh $15.95
Knowing Where to Look: The Ultimate Guide to Research, by Lois Horowitz (paper) $15.95
Make Your Words Work, by Gary Provost $17.95
On Being a Writer, edited by Bill Strickland $19.95
The Story Behind the Word, by Morton S. Freeman (paper) $9.95
12 Keys to Writing Books that Sell, by Kathleen Krull (paper) $12.95
The 29 Most Common Writing Mistakes & How to Avoid Them, by Judy Delton $9.95
The Wordwatcher's Guide to Good Writing & Grammar, by Morton S. Freeman (paper) $15.95
Word Processing Secrets for Writers, by Michael A. Banks & Ansen Dibell (paper) $14.95
Writer's Block & How to Use It, by Victoria Nelson $14.95
The Writer's Digest Guide to Manuscript Formats, by Buchman & Groves $17.95

Nonfiction Writing

Basic Magazine Writing, by Barbara Kevles $16.95
The Complete Guide to Writing Biographies, by Ted Schwarz $19.95
Creative Conversations: The Writer's Guide to Conducting Interviews, by Michael Schumacher $16.95
How to Sell Every Magazine Article You Write, by Lisa Collier Cool (paper) $11.95
How to Write Irresistible Query Letters, by Lisa Collier Cool (paper) $10.95
The Writer's Digest Handbook of Magazine Article Writing, edited by Jean M. Fredette (paper) $11.95
Writing Creative Nonfiction, by Theodore A. Rees Cheney $15.95

Fiction Writing

The Art & Craft of Novel Writing, by Oakley Hall $17.95
Best Stories from New Writers, edited by Linda Sanders $16.95
Characters & Viewpoint, by Orson Scott Card $13.95
The Complete Guide to Writing Fiction, by Barnaby Conrad $17.95
Cosmic Critiques: How & Why 10 Science Fiction Stories Work, edited by Asimov & Greenberg (paper) $12.95
Creating Characters: How To Build Story People, by Dwight V. Swain $16.95
Creating Short Fiction, by Damon Knight (paper) $9.95
Dare to Be a Great Writer: 329 Keys to Powerful Fiction, by Leonard Bishop $16.95
Dialogue, by Lewis Turco $13.95
Fiction Is Folks: How to Create Unforgettable Characters, by Robert Newton Peck (paper) $8.95
Handbook of Short Story Writing: Vol. I, by Dickson and Smythe (paper) $9.95
Handbook of Short Story Writing: Vol. II, edited by Jean M. Fredette $15.95
How to Write & Sell Your First Novel, by Collier & Leighton (paper) $12.95
One Great Way to Write Short Stories, by Ben Nyberg $14.95
Manuscript Submission, by Scott Edelstein $13.95
Plot, by Ansen Dibell $13.95
Revision, by Kit Reed $13.95
Spider Spin Me a Web: Lawrence Block on Writing Fiction, by Lawrence Block $16.95
Storycrafting, by Paul Darcy Boles (paper) $10.95
Theme & Strategy, by Ronald B. Tobias $13.95
Writing the Novel: From Plot to Print, by Lawrence Block (paper) $10.95

Special Interest Writing Books

Armed & Dangerous: A Writer's Guide to Weapons, by Michael Newton (paper) $14.95
The Art & Craft of Greeting Cards, by Susan Evarts (paper) $15.95
The Children's Picture Book: How to Write It, How to Sell It, by Ellen E.M. Roberts (paper) $18.95
Comedy Writing Secrets, by Melvin Helitzer $18.95
The Complete Book of Scriptwriting, by J. Michael Straczynski (paper) $11.95
The Craft of Lyric Writing, by Sheila Davis $19.95
Deadly Doses: A Writer's Guide to Poisons, by Serita Deborah Stevens with Anne Klarner (paper) $16.95
Editing Your Newsletter, by Mark Beach (paper) $18.50
Families Writing, by Peter Stillman $15.95
How to Write a Play, by Raymond Hull (paper) $12.95
How to Write Action/Adventure Novels, by Michael Newton $13.95
How to Write & Sell A Column, by Raskin & Males $10.95
How to Write and Sell Your Personal Experiences, by Lois Duncan (paper) $10.95
How to Write Mysteries, by Shannon OCork $13.95
How to Write Romances, by Phyllis Taylor Pianka $13.95
How To Write Science Fiction & Fantasy, by Orson Scott Card $13.95
How to Write Tales of Horror, Fantasy & Science Fiction, edited by J.N. Williamson $15.95
How to Write the Story of Your Life, by Frank P. Thomas (paper) $11.95
How to Write Western Novels, by Matt Braun $13.95
Mystery Writer's Handbook, by The Mystery Writers of America (paper) $11.95
The Poet's Handbook, by Judson Jerome (paper) $10.95
Successful Lyric Writing (workbook), by Sheila Davis (paper) $18.95
Successful Scriptwriting, by Jurgen Wolff & Kerry Cox $18.95
Travel Writer's Handbook, by Louise Zobel (paper) $11.95
TV Scriptwriter's Handbook, by Alfred Brenner (paper) $10.95
The Writer's Complete Crime Reference Book, by Martin Roth $19.95
Writing for Children & Teenagers, 3rd Edition, by Lee Wyndham & Arnold Madison (paper) $12.95
Writing the Modern Mystery, by Barbara Norville $15.95
Writing to Inspire, edited by William Gentz (paper) $14.95

The Writing Business

A Beginner's Guide to Getting Published, edited by Kirk Polking (paper) $11.95
The Complete Guide to Self-Publishing, by Tom & Marilyn Ross (paper) $16.95
How to Sell & Re-Sell Your Writing, by Duane Newcomb $11.95
How to Write with a Collaborator, by Hal Bennett with Michael Larsen $11.95
How You Can Make $25,000 a Year Writing, by Nancy Edmonds Hanson (paper) $12.95
Is There a Speech Inside You?, by Don Aslett (paper) $9.95
Literary Agents: How to Get & Work with the Right One for You, by Michael Larsen $9.95
Professional Etiquette for Writers, by William Brohaugh $9.95
Time Management for Writers, by Ted Schwarz $10.95
The Writer's Friendly Legal Guide, edited by Kirk Polking $16.95
Writer's Guide to Self-Promotion & Publicity, by Elane Feldman $16.95
A Writer's Guide to Contract Negotiations, by Richard Balkin (paper) $11.95
Writing A to Z, edited by Kirk Polking $19.95

To order directly from the publisher, include $3.00 postage and handling for 1 book and $1.00 for each additional book. Allow 30 days for delivery.

Writer's Digest Books
1507 Dana Avenue, Cincinnati, Ohio 45207
Credit card orders call TOLL-FREE
1-800-289-0963
Prices subject to change without notice.

Write to this same address for information on *Writer's Digest* magazine, Writer's Digest Book Club, Writer's Digest School, and Writer's Digest Criticism Service.

Career Steps to Literary Recognition

1. Read widely in poetry of the past and present.
2. Study poetic techniques and elements of poetry.
3. Learn the mechanics of submission and professional conduct (see The Business of Poetry).
4. Familiarize yourself with the range of markets in Poet's Market. Buy sample copies of publications and study them.
5. Begin submitting your work. Choose those markets in the (I) category and (IV) categories that reflect your tastes and special interests. Often it is best to start with publications in your area (see Geographical Index).
6. Attend poetry readings; acquaint yourself with resources such as libraries, clubs and organizations.
7. Attend writers' workshops and conferences; build relationships with poets and editors.
8. Enter contests and competitions judiciously, but concentrate on magazine publication. Avoid vanity scams.
9. As you begin getting acceptances from magazines, try the (II) category markets that seem to share your tastes.